NATIONAL UND

a division of ALM Media, LLC

2020 TAX FACTS ON INSURANCE & EMPLOYEE BENEFITS

Robert Bloink, J.D., LL.M., William H. Byrnes, Esq., LL.M, CWM®

2020Tax Facts on Insurance & Employee Benefits is your complete source for tax information as it relates to these two critical business and financial planning areas. With thousands of easy-to-use Q&As that cover the most critical topics, Tax Facts helps advisers of all kinds understand the tax implications of the recommendations that they make for their clients.

Insurance and employee benefits are complicated tools that each carry their own set of tax issues, and advisers cannot possibly make the thorough and complete assessments that clients depend on without understanding this ever-changing area. These two volumes provide guidance on:

- Annuities and life insurance products
- ERISA regulations for employee benefit plans
- Health insurance, including Healthcare Reform
- Long-term care insurance
- Disclosure and recordkeeping requirements
- Qualified and nonqualified compensation plans
- Defined contribution and defined benefit deferred compensation plans
- Funded and unfunded plans
- PBGC requirements
- Estate and gift tax planning and consequences
- Traditional IRAs and Roth IRAs
- And more!

This 2020 edition has been completely updated, featuring:

- Answers to questions covering the new Individual Coverage HRAs (ICHRAs)
- New rules on reporting requirements for insurance policy sales under the 2017 Tax Act

- Updated coverage of deductibility premium payments paid pursuant to divorce and separation agreements
- Expanded coverage of trust-owned life insurance policies
- Updated rules for determining compensation for nondiscrimination testing
- New content on documentation requirements for pre- and post-mortem distributions from qualified plans
- The effect of HRAs and QSEHRAs
- Updated deductible values, cost-sharing limits, wellness program information, and Federal Poverty Guidelines
- Changes in the employer mandate to offer coverage and the penalty for not meeting affordability requirements
- The effect of the individual mandate repeal
- A 2020 update on related taxes, such as tanning bed tax, the additional Medicare tax, medical device tax, and Medicare tax on investment income of 3.8%, and the continuing delay in implementation of the Cadillac Tax
- Updated inflation numbers

Related titles also available:

- Tax Facts on Investments
- Tax Facts on Individuals & Small Business
- Field Guide: Estate & Retirement Planning, Business Planning & Employee Benefits
- Social Security & Medicare Facts
- Healthcare Reform Facts
- The Tools & Techniques of Employee Benefit and Retirement Planning

For customer service questions or to place additional orders, please call 1-800-543-0874 or email CustomerService@nuco.com.

VOLUME 1

2020 TAX FACTS

ON INSURANCE & EMPLOYEE BENEFITS

• Annuities • Cafeteria Plans • Compensation
• Disclosure Requirements • HRAs • MEPs
• Estate and Gift Taxation • Health Insurance
• Healthcare Reform • International Tax
• Life Insurance • Long-Term Care Insurance
• Pensions and Profit Sharing • Structured Settlements
• Taxation of Individuals

Robert Bloink, Esq., LL.M.
William H. Byrnes, Esq., LL.M., CWM®

2020 Edition

Tax Facts on Insurance and Employee Benefits (formerly *Tax Facts 1*) is published annually by the Professional Publishing Division of The National Underwriter Company. This edition reflects selected pertinent legislation, regulations, rulings and court decisions as of October 15, 2019.

ISBN 978-1-949506-80-8
ISSN 0496-9685

The National Underwriter Company
4157 Olympic Blvd., Suite 225
Erlanger, KY 41018

Printed in U.S.A.

TABLE OF CONTENTS

TAX FACTS ON INSURANCE & EMPLOYEE BENEFITS – VOLUME 1

TAX FACTS ON INSURANCE & EMPLOYEE BENEFITS – VOLUME 2

APPENDICES AND TABLES

TAX FACTS ON INVESTMENTS

APPENDICES AND TABLES

TAX FACTS ON INDIVIDUALS & SMALL BUSINESS

APPENDICES AND TABLES

ABOUT THE NATIONAL UNDERWRITER COMPANY

a division of ALM Media, LLC

For over 110 years, The National Underwriter Company, *a division of ALM Media, LLC* has been the first in line with the targeted tax, insurance, and financial planning information you need to make critical business decisions. Boasting nearly a century of expert experience, our reputable Editors are dedicated to putting accurate and relevant information right at your fingertips. With *Tax Facts*, *Tools & Techniques*, *Field Guide*, *FC&S®, FC&S Legal* and other resources available in print, eBook, and online, you can be assured that as the industry evolves National Underwriter will be at the forefront with the thorough and easy-to-use resources you rely on for success.

Update Service Notification

This National Underwriter Company publication is regularly updated to include coverage of developments and changes that affect the content. If you did not purchase this publication directly from The National Underwriter Company, *a division of ALM Media, LLC* and you want to receive these important updates sent on a 30-day review basis and billed separately, please contact us at (800) 543-0874. Or you can mail your request with your name, company, address, and the title of the book to:

The National Underwriter Company
a division of ALM Media, LLC
4157 Olympic Boulevard
Suite 225
Erlanger, KY 41018

If you purchased this publication from The National Underwriter Company, *a division of ALM Media, LLC,* directly, you have already been registered for the update service.

Contact Information

To order any National Underwriter Company title, please

- call 1-800-543-0874, 8-6 ET Monday – Thursday and 8 to 5 ET Friday
- online bookstore at www.nationalunderwriter.com, or
- mail to Orders Department, The National Underwriter Company, *a division of ALM Media, LLC*, 4157 Olympic Blvd., Ste. 225, Erlanger, KY 41018

INTRODUCTION TO 2020 TAX FACTS ON INSURANCE & EMPLOYEE BENEFITS

Welcome to the 2020 edition of *Tax Facts on Insurance & Employee Benefits*. This year's *Tax Facts* features both new and enhanced content designed to help you provide clients with the most relevant tax planning advice possible. We have continued our comprehensive coverage of the 2017 tax reform legislation in this year's edition, explaining both the changes that have been made and how the newly revamped tax code, regulations and administrative guidance diverge from previously existing law. As the IRS continues to release guidance implementing the changes, we continue to keep you up-to-date on how those developments might impact your clients.

Throughout this year's edition of *Tax Facts*, we have provided more than a bare bones discussion of the tax code changes. This year's materials also discuss the planning implications brought about by the new rules that might impact your clients. We continue to add to our detailed discussion of the proposed regulations interpreting the newly created Section 199A deduction for qualified business income of certain pass-through entities, and we have also updated our materials to include coverage of the still-emerging regulations interpreting the new bonus depreciation rules.

We are pleased to introduce new content on the final rules governing individual coverage health reimbursement arrangements (known as ICHRAs). These materials go beyond the basic qualification requirements to explain how using an ICHRA can impact an employer's obligations under the Affordable Care Act and how the ICHRA may impact the employee right to claim a premium tax credit.

Tax Facts has also been expanded to include materials on the changes to qualified retirement plan rules introduced by the Bipartisan Budget Act of 2018. While some of these changes become effective as of January 1, 2019, many of the rules governing hardship distributions only became effective beginning in 2020. In response to our subscribers' requests, we have added to our existing coverage of retirement accounts in *Tax Facts on Insurance and Employee Benefits* to include an analysis of the newly expanded availability of multiple employer plans (MEPs), which can allow employers to join together in order to offer valuable retirement benefits to employees.

Throughout *Tax Facts*, you will find an expansion of our "planning points," each offering a piece of practical advice written by a practitioner who is an expert in the field, which will assist you in providing your clients with the most knowledgeable guidance possible. Many of these planning points in our 2020 edition continue to focus on tax reform, both with respect to planning opportunities that have been created and questions that remain. We have also continued to reorganize many of our more complicated questions, splitting questions into discrete subparts that make these questions simpler and easier to understand. When combined with our updated IRS code-based index, we believe this will streamline your research process and save you time and effort.

This year's edition also includes annual inflation-adjusted numbers for 2020, both throughout the text and in our easy-to access appendices.

Additional changes throughout the year—including revenue rulings, case law decisions, and legislative and regulatory activity—are available through subscription to our online tax service. We continue to produce *Tax Facts Intelligence Weekly*, a weekly electronic newsletter that delivers updates every week to your email on recent rulings, regulations and cases affecting *Tax Facts* content—including analysis of tax reform issues that could most strongly impact your clients and business. This publication is automatically sent to you as part of your Tax Facts subscription.

This edition of *Tax Facts* was developed with the assistance of authors Professor William H. Byrnes and Professor Robert Bloink. Prof. Byrnes serves as an Associate Dean and Professor of Law at the Texas A&M School of Law and has been the author of numerous books, treatises and scholarly articles. Prof. Bloink is an insurance industry expert whose practice incorporates sophisticated wealth transfer techniques, as well as counseling institutions in the context of their insurance portfolios. He is also a professor of tax at Texas A&M Law School.

ABOUT THE EDITORS

ABOUT THE AUTHORS

Robert Bloink, Esq., LL.M.

Robert Bloink worked to put in force in excess of $2B of longevity pegged portfolios for the insurance industry's producers in the past five years. His insurance practice incorporates sophisticated wealth transfer techniques, as well as counseling institutions in the context of their insurance portfolios and other mortality based exposures. Professor Bloink is working with William Byrnes, Associate Dean of Special Projects of Texas A&M School of Law, on development of executive programs for insurance underwriters, wealth managers and financial planners.

Previously, Mr. Bloink served as Senior Attorney in the IRS Office of Chief Counsel, Large and Mid-Sized Business Division, where he litigated many cases in the U.S. Tax Court, served as Liaison Counsel for the Offshore Compliance Technical Assistance Program, coordinated examination programs audit teams on the development of issues for large corporate taxpayers, and taught continuing education seminars to Senior Revenue Agents involved in Large Case Exams. In his governmental capacity, Mr. Bloink became recognized as an expert in the taxation of financial structured products and was responsible for the IRS' first FSA addressing variable forward contracts. Mr. Bloink's core competencies led to his involvement in prosecuting some of the biggest corporate tax shelters in the history of our country

William H. Byrnes, Esq., LL.M.

William Byrnes is the leader of National Underwriter's Financial Advisory Publications, having been appointed in 2010. He is a professor and an associate dean of Texas A&M University School of Law. He is one of the leading authors and best-selling authors in the professional markets with 30 books that have sold in excess of 100,000 copies in print and online, with thousands of online database subscribers. His National Underwriter publications include Tax Facts, Advanced Markets, and Sales Essentials.

Mr. Byrnes held senior positions of international tax for Coopers & Lybrand and has been commissioned and consulted by a number of governments on their tax and fiscal policy. He has served as an operational board member for companies in several industries including fashion, durable medical equipment, office furniture and technology.

He pioneered online legal education in 1994. In 1998 he developed the first online program to achieve American Bar Association acquiescence. His Master, LL.M. and doctoral programs are leveraged by wealth managers, financial planners and life insurance underwriters.

LEAD CONTRIBUTING EDITOR

Alexis Long, J.D.

Alexis Long formerly practiced corporate law as an associate with the business transactions group at Schulte Roth & Zabel in New York City. She was a corporate, securities and finance editor for the Practical Law Company before moving to Thomas Jefferson School of Law as publications director. Alexis is currently publications director at the Texas A&M School of Law. She holds a J.D. from the University of Michigan Law School.

THE TAX FACTS EDITORIAL ADVISORY BOARD

Kevin W. Blanton, J.D.

Kevin W. Blanton, J.D., is Assistant Vice President and Associate Counsel, Advanced Markets, for the U.S. Individual Life operations of John Hancock Financial, a Manulife company. In his current position Mr. Blanton provides advanced marketing support to John Hancock's home office employees, field personnel, and producers. In addition, he is responsible for the development of innovative advanced marketing materials, programs, and strategies. Mr. Blanton is also a recurring host on John Hancock's weekly JHAM Radio program and a regular speaker at industry meetings around the country.

Prior to joining Manulife Financial in 1999, Mr. Blanton practiced law in the private sector for many years in the Boston area, concentrating on estate planning, probate, business succession planning, corporate benefits, and charitable planning for high net worth individuals and companies. Mr. Blanton also provided tax compliance advice for several large national mutual fund companies as part of the

Tax Department of Coopers & Lybrand in Boston and served as bond counsel for more than 100 New England municipalities and state agencies.

Mr. Blanton received his Bachelor of Arts degree in economics from The University of Michigan, Ann Arbor, Michigan, and his Juris Doctor degree *cum laude* from Boston University School of Law. Mr. Blanton is licensed to practice law in the Commonwealth of Massachusetts, the State of New York, and the State of Texas, and is a member of the American Bar Association, the Massachusetts Bar Association, the New York State Bar Association, the Texas State Bar Association, and the Boston Bar Association.

Caroline Brooks, J.D., CFP®

Caroline (Carly) Brooks is Associate Counsel with the Advanced Markets Group for the U.S. Individual Life operations of John Hancock. In her role as an Advanced Markets attorney, she provides life insurance, tax, estate planning, and business planning expertise to home office employees, field personnel, and producers. She serves as a lead author and editor of technical advanced marketing materials and is a frequent speaker at industry events across the country.

Carly received her Bachelor of Arts degree, *magna cum laude*, in Criminal Justice and Political Science from the University at Albany, SUNY, in Albany, New York. Carly received her Juris Doctor with a concentration in Estate Planning and her Master of Business Administration from Western New England University School of Law, Springfield, Massachusetts. Carly is licensed to practice law in the Commonwealth of Massachusetts and holds the Certified Financial Planner (CFP®) designation. She currently serves on the Editorial Advisory Board for Tax Facts, a publication of The National Underwriter Company, is a co-author of the 19th Edition of the Tools and Techniques of Estate Planning, a Leimberg Library publication, and has been published in Broker World.

Carly lives in Boston, Massachusetts, where she is very active in the greater Boston trusts and estates and legal community. She is the current President of the Boston Trusts and Estates Consortium, serves on the Member Involvement Committee for the Boston Estate Planning Council, and is active in the Massachusetts Women's Bar Association.

Martin J. Burke, III, Esq.

Martin Burke is a principal owner of the Matthews Benefit Group, Inc., a third party administration firm in St. Petersburg Florida. In addition to ensuring the firm's continued compliance with all applicable regulations, he is involved in the development of custom-tailored retirement plans designed to meet specific goals for business owners.

Mr. Burke is a graduate of Lycoming College, Pennsylvania, and the University of Maryland School of Law. Mr. Burke is licensed to practice law in Maryland and Florida.

He is coauthor of the *403(b) Answer Book Forms & Worksheets for Aspen Publishers* as well as a regular contributing editor for the *401(k) Advisor.*

Anne Berre Downing, J.D.

Anne Berre Downing, J.D. has a Bachelors of Arts in English and Political Science from Agnes Scott College, and received her Doctor of Law degree from Emory University School of Law. She has practiced labor, employment, and commercial law, and served as adjunct faculty for twenty-four years before transitioning to academe full time. She speaks and writes internationally on issues involving law, leadership, conflict resolution and academic employment. She has served as a Professor of Business Law and Dispute Resolution at Western Carolina University and has directed other universities' pre-law, dispute resolution, and Moot Court programs. She is an accomplished mediator, author and editor and is currently a Fellow at the Israeli Center for Peace.

Jonathan H. Ellis, J.D., LL.M. (Taxation)

Mr. Ellis is currently a Shareholder in the law firm of Plotnick & Ellis, P.C., where his practice focuses primarily on estate planning, estate administration, elder law, and the representation of closely held businesses.

He has a B.S. in Accounting from Pennsylvania State University, J.D. from Widener University, and LL.M. (Taxation) from Temple University. In addition, Mr. Ellis is Executive Editor and Co-author, and along with Stephen Leimberg, et.al., of *Tools and Techniques of Estate Planning*, 16th Edition, The National Underwriter Company, as well as a Co-Author of the 15th Edition. Also, Mr. Ellis is the author of the book "Drafting Wills and Trusts in Pennsylvania", 2010 Edition for PBI Press. Mr. Ellis is also a member of the Editorial Advisory Board for Tax Facts 2012 through 2015, The National Underwriter Company. In addition, he is the author of 30 articles for Pennsylvania Tax Service Insights (LexisNexis Matthew Bender). Finally, he is a former member of the Adjunct Faculty at Villanova Law School where he taught Family Wealth Planning.

Mr. Ellis frequently speaks to a variety of groups, including attorneys, accountants and financial planners throughout Pennsylvania, New Jersey, Delaware and Maryland. Mr. Ellis is also the Course Planner for the PBI Courses "Drafting Wills and Trusts in Pennsylvania", "Wills v. Trusts: A Primer on the Right Tool for Your Clients", "Use of Trusts", and "Post-Mortem Estate Planning", and a participant in a variety of additional courses for PBI. He is also an annual participant in the Villanova University's annual tax conference, cosponsored with the Internal Revenue Service.

He is a member of the Pennsylvania, New Jersey and Florida Bars; the Montgomery County Bar Association; and the Philadelphia Estate Planning Council. Mr. Ellis is also a Fellow of the American College of Trust and Estate Counsel.

Stephen D. Forman, CLTC

Stephen Forman is senior vice president and co-founder of Long Term Care Associates, Inc. (LTCA), a national marketing firm focused exclusively on long-term care solutions. LTCA helped pioneer this field, with roots stretching back to 1972, pre-dating the LTC entry of many of today's carriers.

Mr. Forman has authored more than 50 articles on the topics of long-term care insurance, sales, marketing and regulation, and was chosen by National Underwriter to revise the latest edition of its popular franchise, "The Advisor's Guide to Long-Term Care." He has advised several major carriers in the design phase of their products, helped re-design Washington State's LTC Training requirement, and speaks frequently with the media, including Kiplinger's and Consumer Reports. His columns have been honored as as one of "7 Health Insurance Blogs You Should Know About," and he was recently named one of the "Top 20 Most Creative People in the Insurance Industry."

Mr. Forman graduated magna cum laude from UCLA and has been an active member of American MENSA since 2012.

Randy Gardner J.D., LL.M., MBA, CPA, CFP®

Randy Gardner is a Professor of Tax and Financial Planning and former Director of the Certificate in Financial Planning Program at the University of Missouri – Kansas City. He is an estate planning attorney with over 30 years of experience and one of the founders of onlineestateplanning.com. He is coauthor of *101 Tax Saving Ideas* and *Tools and Techniques of Income Tax Planning* and is a highly rated discussion leader who has been recognized as an Outstanding Educator by the Missouri Society of CPAs. Mr. Gardner brings his teaching experience and tax planning expertise to Garrett Members as the Network Tax, Estate & Financial Planning Coach.

In addition to teaching, Mr. Gardner is a member of WealthCounsel, LLC, serves on the Editorial Board of The Journal of Financial Planning, and is former member of the Council on Examinations of the Certified Financial Planner Board of Standards. He is a member of the AICPA, the Missouri Society of CPAs, and the Kansas Bar Association. He has also written many articles for publications such as the Journal of Financial Planning, Taxation for Accountants, Practical Tax Strategies, and Tax Adviser.

Johni Hays, J.D.

Johni Hays is Vice-President of Thompson and Associates. With almost 20 years' experience as a practicing attorney in charitable and estate planning, Johni Hays is a recognized expert on the subject of charitable gift planning. Johni is the author of the book, *Essentials of Annuities* and co-author of the book, *The Tools and Techniques of Charitable Planning.* Johni serves on the Editorial Advisory Board for the books *Tax Facts on Investments* and *Tax Facts on Insurance and Employee Benefits*. She serves as a charitable planning author of Steve Leimberg's electronic newsletter service, LISI, found at www.leimbergservices.com. Johni has been quoted in the Wall Street Journal and has published charitable planning articles in Estate Planning Magazine, Planned Giving Today, Fundraising Success, Life Insurance Selling and the National Underwriter magazines.

Johni is in demand as a national lecturer on estate and charitable planning, probate, living wills, annuities, life insurance, retirement planning and IRAs, as well as income, estate and gift taxation. Johni has been engaged in the practice of law with an emphasis in charitable and estate planning since 1993.

Prior to joining Thompson & Associates, Johni served as the Senior Gift Planning Consultant for The Stelter Company. Prior to that Johni was the Executive Director of the Greater Des Moines Community Foundation Planned Giving Institute. In addition, Johni practiced estate planning with Myers Krause and Stevens, Chartered law firm in Naples Florida, where she specialized in estate planning.

Johni graduated cum laude with a Juris Doctor degree from Drake University in Des Moines, Iowa, in 1993. She also holds a Bachelor of Science degree in Business Administration from Drake University and graduated magna cum laude in 1988.

Johni is the president of the Charitable Estate Planning Institute and she also serves on the national board of the Partnership for Philanthropic Planning (PPP) formerly the National Committee on Planned Giving. Johni serves on the Technical Advisory Board for the Stelter Company and is a charter member of PPP's Leadership Institute. She is also a member of the Mid-Iowa Planned Giving Council and the Mid-Iowa Estate and Financial Planners Council (president 2007-2008). Johni has been a member of both the Iowa Bar and the Florida Bar since 1993. She resides in Johnston, Iowa, with her husband, Dave Schlindwein.

Chuck Hodges, J.D., LL.M.

Chuck Hodges is the Chair of the Domestic & International Tax Team of the law firm of Kilpatrick Townsend & Stockton. Mr. Hodges focuses his practice on civil and criminal federal tax controversies and complex tax planning. He has been involved in more than 100 cases against the IRS and state revenue agencies, involving all areas of tax law. Mr. Hodges handles approximately fifteen cases against the IRS per year, recovering more than

$1 million for his clients from the IRS in reimbursement of attorneys' fees at the conclusion of their trial victory. As a tax litigator, he has handled all stages of tax controversies, including all administrative and judicial levels from examination through court proceedings.

Mr. Hodges has represented a broad range of taxpayers, including individuals, estates, closely held businesses, tax-exempt organizations, and publicly traded corporations. A substantial number of these engagements have involved the defense of TEFRA partnerships and limited liability companies. He has represented taxpayers in many different federal courts, including the U.S. Tax Court, the U.S. District Court for the Northern District of Georgia, the U.S. District Courts for the Middle District and Southern District of Florida, the U.S. District Court for the Southern District of Mississippi, the U.S. District Court for the District of Arizona, the U.S. District Court for the District of South Carolina, the U.S. Court of Federal Claims, and the U.S. Court of Appeals for the Fifth, Ninth and Eleventh Circuits.

Mr. Hodges has been a key litigator in various cases earning him honors and recognition. He has been listed as a "Leader in the Field" for Taxation by Chambers USA: *America's Leading Lawyers for Business* each year since 2005. He was recognized by his peers in the 2015 edition of *The Best Lawyers in America*®, and each of the five years immediately preceding, for the area of Tax Law. In 2014 and each of the five years immediately preceding, Mr. Hodges was named a Georgia "Super Lawyer" and previously a Georgia "Rising Star" by *SuperLawyers* magazine. Throughout his career, Mr. Hodges has provided insight as an industry leader for some of the nation's top news outlets including the *Wall Street Journal, Bloomberg, BusinessWeek, Forbes and Law 360*. He is AV® rated by Martindale-Hubbell.*

Paul Hood, Jr., J.D., LL.M.

L. Paul Hood L, Jr. received his J.D. from Louisiana State University Law Center in 1986 and Master of Laws in Taxation from Georgetown University Law Center in 1988. Paul is a frequent speaker, is widely quoted and his articles have appeared in a number of publications, including BNA Tax Management Memorandum, BNA Estates, Gifts & Trusts Journal, CCH Journal of Practical Estate Planning, Estate Planning, Valuation Strategies, Digest of Federal Tax Articles, Loyola Law Review, Louisiana Bar Journal, Tax Ideas, The Value Examiner and Charitable Gift Planning News. He has spoken at programs sponsored by a number of law schools, including Duke University, Georgetown University, New York University, Tulane University, Loyola (N.O.) University, and Louisiana State University, as well as many other professional organizations, including AICPA and NACVA. From 1996-2004, Paul served on the Louisiana Board of Tax Appeals, a three member board that has jurisdiction over all State of Louisiana tax matters.

A self-described "recovering tax lawyer," Paul is the author or co-author of four other books, and is the proud father of two boys who are the apples of his eye, Paul III and Evan. Happily married to Carol A. Sobczak, Paul lives with Carol in Toledo OH, where he serves as the Director of Planned Giving for The University of Toledo Foundation.

Erik M. Jensen

Erik Jensen is the Burke Professor of Law at Case Western Reserve University in Cleveland, Ohio, where he has been on the faculty for over thirty years. Professor Jensen has also taught at the Cornell Law School, from which he earned his law degree in 1979. His work has been recognized through election as a fellow of the American College of Tax Counsel and as a member of the American Law Institute.

Professor Jensen's professional activities have been extensive. Before entering teaching, Professor Jensen was a tax associate with the New York City law firm of Sullivan & Cromwell.

He has spoken widely on tax matters and is author of *The Taxing Power* (Praeger 2005) and of several dozen articles on taxation and other subjects. He is also Editor of the *Journal of Taxation of Investments*. He serves as Vice-Chair for Law Development of the Sales, Exchanges, and Basis Committee of the American Bar Association Section of Taxation.

Jay Katz, J.D., LL.M.

Jay Katz is a tax attorney in Delaware with more than a decade of experience in private practice litigating tax cases and handling audits, collection matters, and offers in compromise for corporate and individual clients. He has earned LLMs in taxation from both the NYU and University of Florida graduate tax programs. During twelve years as a professor at Widener University Law School and Beasley School of Law at Temple University, Jay has taught virtually every tax and estate planning course on the curriculum and was the director of the Widener tax clinic.

In addition to being a coauthor of the 4th Edition of *The Tools & Techniques of Income Tax Planning*, Jay has penned seven published tax articles, including "An Offer in Compromise You Can't Confuse: It is not the Opening Bid of a Delinquent Taxpayer to Play Let's Make a Tax Deal with the Internal Revenue Service," 81 *Miss. L. J.* 1673 (2012) (lead article); "The William O. Douglas Tax Factor: Where Did the Spin Stop and Who Was He Looking Out For?" 3 *Charlotte Law Review* 133 (2012) (lead article); and "The Untold Story of Crane v. Commissioner Reveals an Inconvenient Tax Truth: Useless Depreciation Deductions Cause Global Basis Erosion to Bait A Hazardous Tax Trap For Unwitting Taxpayers," 30 *Va. Tax Rev.* 559 (2011).

Robert S. Keebler, CPA, MST, AEP (Distinguished)

Robert Keebler is a partner with Keebler & Associates, LLP. He is a 2007 recipient of the prestigious Distinguished Estate Planners award from the National Association of Estate Planning Counsels. Mr. Keebler has several times been named by *CPA Magazine* as one of the top 100 most influential practitioners in the United States. His practice includes family wealth transfer and preservation planning, charitable giving, retirement distribution planning, and estate administration.

Mr. Keebler frequently represents clients before the IRS National Office in the private letter ruling process and in estate, gift, and income tax examinations and appeals, and he has received more than 150 favorable private letter rulings including several key rulings of first impression. He is the author of over 100 articles and columns and is the editor, author, or coauthor of many books and treatises on wealth transfer and taxation.

Sonya King, J.D., LL.M.

Sonya King has been involved with tax issues affecting estate, retirement, business, and charitable planning for fifteen years. Prior to joining New York Life's Advanced Planning Group in 2010, Ms. King worked at the National Underwriter Company where she was an editor of *Tax Facts* and the *Tools & Techniques* series. She authored numerous articles on life insurance, annuities, retirement, income tax, health and welfare plans, and charitable and estate planning. Sonya is a coauthor of the *Tools & Techniques of Income Tax Planning*.

Before that, Ms. King served as a judicial law clerk to the Honorable Donald R. Ford at the Eleventh District Court of Appeals in Warren, Ohio, and also as a trust officer with Key Bank. Prior to attending law school, she was a registered principal (Series 24) and licensed insurance agent for a major life insurance company.

Ms. King graduated from Duke University where she received her Bachelor of Arts degree. She earned her law degree (J.D.) from the University of Akron and her tax law degree (LL.M.) from Case Western Reserve University. She is a member in good standing of the Ohio State Bar Association.

Alson R. Martin, J.D., LL.M.

Alson R. Martin is a Partner of Lathrop & Gage LLP in Overland Park, Kansas. The firm also has offices in Los Angeles, California; Denver & Boulder, Colorado; Washington, D.C.; Chicago, Illinois; Kansas City, St. Louis, Jefferson City, Springfield & Columbia, Missouri; Boston, Massachusetts; and New York, New York.

Al is a Fellow of the American College of Tax Counsel and American College of Employee Benefits Counsel, as well as a charter Life Member of the American Tax Policy Institute. Mr. Martin is listed in the book The Best Lawyers in America (from inception in three categories), Outstanding Lawyers of America, Missouri-Kansas Super Lawyers, Ingram's Best Lawyers in Kansas City (three categories), American Lawyer Media & Martindale-Hubbell™ Top Rated Lawyers in Health Care, and Guide to Leading U.S. Tax Lawyers. He was selected by Best Lawyers as the 2010 Kansas City, KS Corporate Lawyer of the Year and 2013 Tax Lawyer of the Year.

Al is the author of *Healthcare Reform Facts* (2015), *Limited Liability Companies and Partnerships* (3rd edition, 2011) and coauthor of *Kansas Corporation Law & Practice (Including Tax Aspects)* (5th edition, 2011), and has written many articles in various publications. He was also Technical Editor of Panel Publication's monthly newsletter *The 401k Advisor* from 1990- 2012. He has published numerous articles and made hundreds of speeches. Mr. Martin was for many years Co-Chair and speaker at the Annual Advanced Course of Study Professional Service Organizations, a faculty member for the ALI-ABA Courses Estate Planning for the Family Business Owner and Sophisticated Estate Planning Techniques, as well as speaker at many national meetings of the American Bar Association Tax Section, the ESOP Association Annual Convention, Mountain States Pension Conference, Southern Federal Tax Conference, Notre Dame Estate Planning Symposium and the Ohio Pension Conference, as well as the Alabama, Georgia Federal, Kansas, Missouri, and Tennessee Tax conferences.

He is President and Director of the Small Business Council of America, and he was a delegate to the 1995 White House Conference on Small Business and the 2006 Savers' Summit, Washington, D.C. Mr. Martin has testified in Congress.

Al graduated with Highest Distinction from Kansas University and was a Phi Beta Kappa, Summerfield Scholar, Student Body President. He received his J.D., *cum laude*, and LL.M. in taxation from New York University School of Law, where he was a Root-Tilden Scholar and Note & Comment Editor, *New York University Law Review*.

Gregory E. Matthews, CPA

Gregory Matthews is a principal and CEO and senior benefit and compliance consultant with Matthews Benefit Group, Inc., in St. Petersburg, Florida. He is the creator and author of the monthly employee benefits newsletter *401(k) Advisor*, author of the *Payroll Answer Book*, and coauthor of the *403(b) Answer Book Forms & Worksheets* for Aspen Publishers. He is a frequent speaker at regional and national benefit programs. Mr. Matthews also authored and taught Course 6 of the American Institute of CPAs' "Compensation and Benefits" in the Tax Certificate Program.

Mr. Matthews is the past chair of the IRS Gulf Coast EP/EO Liaison Council and has participated as a speaker in national AICPA, ASPPA, ABA, and ALI-ABA tax/benefits programs.

Gregory is a graduate of the University of Tampa (mathematics) and completed his accounting and mathematical studies at Strayer University and American University, Washington, D.C.

Mr. Matthews is a member of the Florida Institute of Certified Public Accountants, the American Institute of Certified Public Accountants, the ESOP Association, the Profit Sharing Council of America, and the American Society of Pension Professionals & Actuaries.

Caroline B. McKay, J.D.

Caroline B. McKay is an Associate Counsel of the Advanced Markets department for John Hancock Insurance (USA). In her current position, Caroline provides estate and business planning support to home office employees, field personnel, and producers. Caroline is also a recurring host on John Hancock's weekly JHAM Radio program and a regular speaker at industry meetings around the country.

Caroline is a contributing author of the 16th edition of The Tools & Techniques of Estate Planning by Stephan Leimberg and previously has been published on Wealth Management.com.

Prior to joining John Hancock, Caroline was in private practice in the Boston area where she concentrated her practice on estate planning, probate, business succession planning, and charitable planning for moderate and high net worth individuals and companies.

Caroline received her Bachelor of Arts degree, *magna cum laude*, in History from Colby College in Waterville, Maine, and her Juris Doctor degree *cum laude* from Suffolk University Law School, Boston, Massachusetts. While at Suffolk Law, she was a member of the Law Review and was published in the Suffolk University Law Review. Upon receiving her J.D., Caroline spent one year clerking for the Honorable Chief Justice Paul Suttell of the Rhode Island Supreme Court.

Jonathan Neal

Jonathan Neal has more than thirty years of experience in the retirement planning industry dealing directly with seniors. He writes both public and industry related articles on retirement planning issues and products that are primarily focused on the senior marketplace. In April 2009 his book "Reverse Mortgages – What Every Financial Advisor Should Know" was released. This book tackles the complexities of reverse mortgages and the various perceptions that seniors, financial and insurance advisors, and mortgage brokers are presently dealing with.

Over the years his articles have introduced some unique ideas and tools designed to help seniors better understand different insurance and investing concepts, such as The LTC Calculator, which is a tool that helps LTCi representatives and seniors work together to find a realistic daily LTCi coverage needs. Another example is the premium versus cost formula he developed in order to provide advisors with an functional mathematical formula to provide seniors with realistic quantified numbers based on their individual situation to help them understand not only what it would take to fund a LTCi policy, but also identify where those funds can be found in their present portfolio.

In addition to his articles, he has written twenty-five continuing education courses that have been approved by various state insurance departments, which include but are not limited to the following: Basic Long-Term Care, Long-Term Care, The History of Long-Term Care in the United States, Service Providers for Long-Term Care Patients, The Stats, Facts & Myths of Long-Term Care Planning, Funding Long-Term Care Annuities, Long-Term Care Annuities, Life Long-Term Care,

Fixed Annuities, Immediate Annuities, Basic Variable Annuities, The Fundamentals of Long-Term Care Polices, Professional Ethics, Retirement Planning, IRA Fundamentals, Stretch IRA Concepts, Retirement Plans, and Reverse Mortgages.

John L. Olsen, CLU, ChFC, AEP

John Olsen is a financial and estate planner practicing in St. Louis County, Missouri. He has been active in the financial services industry for more than forty years. John is a past President of the St. Louis chapter of the National Association of Insurance and Financial Advisors, a current Board member of the St. Louis chapter of the Society of Financial Service Professionals, and the current Vice President of the St. Louis Estate Planning Council.

Mr. Olsen is coauthor, with Michael Kitces, CLU, ChFC, CFP, MSFS, of *The Advisor's Guide to Annuities* (National Underwriter Co. 4th ed., 2014), with Jack Marrion, D.M, of *Index Annuities: A Suitable Approach* (www.indexannuitybook.com) and author of *Taxation and Suitability of Annuities for the Professional Advisor"* (2nd expanded Kindle edition to be released in Fall, 2014) and numerous articles on annuities, insurance, and financial planning. He offers consulting services on annuities to other advisors and expert witness services in litigation involving annuities or life insurance.

David Pratt

David Pratt was born in England and received a law degree from Oxford University. He worked for law firms in London and Cleveland before moving to Albany, New York. In Albany, he practiced with a law firm and two accounting firms before joining the faculty of Albany Law School in 1994. He continues to advise clients and serves as an expert witness on employee benefits issues.

He has written numerous articles on employee compensation and benefits topics, and is a Senior Editor of the *Journal of Pension Benefits* and a fellow of the American College of Employee Benefits Counsel. He is the author of *The Social Security and Medicare Answer Book* and the coauthor of *Pension and Employee Benefit Law, 5th edition* (with John Langbein and Susan Stabile), *Taxation of Distributions from Qualified Plans* (with Dianne Bennett and others) and *ERISA and Employee Benefit Law: the Essentials* (with Sharon Reese, ABA Publications).

Louis R. Richey, J.D.

Lou Richey is recognized as an experienced executive and employee benefits attorney and consultant, with special expertise on 409A nonqualified deferred compensation plans and other retirement plans. He has over 30 years of experience in executive and employee benefits compensation consulting, planning and insurance for Fortune 1000 public companies as well as closely-held and tax-exempt organizations and their employees. He is also the founder of the Retirement Plans Nexus, an organization that designs and implements retirement & benefit plans for companies.

Currently Mr. Richey serves as Senior Vice- President with Infosys McCamish Systems LLC, located in Atlanta, Georgia. Infosys McCamish Systems is one of the nation's leading providers of outsourced administrative and other back-office support services for life insurance carriers, and other major financial services organizations. Mr. Richey helps lead the McCamish *Retirement Services Group* and is the legal & *content expert* for all of Infosys McCamish's executive, employee and qualified and nonqualified pension benefit web-based marketing, design and plan administration platforms.

At earlier points in his career, Mr. Richey served as a senior marketing officer, or technical compensation & senior consultant with employers like American Express Company, the General American Life Insurance Company, William M. Mercer, Magner Network & several offices of the Management Compensation Group (MCG) and M Group.

Lou is a graduate of Wabash College in Indiana, a cum laude graduate of the Indiana University Law School and is a member of the Indiana & Georgia Bars as well as the Federal Bar. He is currently a member of the BNA & The National Underwriter Editorial Advisory Boards and has served on the editorial advisory boards of several other major industry publications. He is also a retired Chairman of the Board of Visitors of the Indiana University Law School, Indianapolis. He has been named a Kentucky Colonel and an Arkansas Traveler in recognition of his professional contributions to the legal profession.

Mr. Richey lectures widely on the impact and implications of 409A, executive and employee benefit topics, retirement planning, financial services marketing, insurance, and financial planning, including major conferences and institutes such as the New York University Federal Tax Institute , the Southwest Federal Tax Conference, the Notre Dame Estate Planning Institute , the American Society of Actuaries Annual Conference, the LIMRA Advance Marketing Conference, the NACD and a host of other professional services conferences and local meetings.

Mr. Richey's comments have appeared in Business Week, The Wall Street Journal, Forbe's Magazine, and Investor's Daily, and he has appeared on the Financial News Network for National Public Radio. He has authored or co-authored a number of books, and BNA portfolios, plus more than 300 articles, audios and videos on compensation and tax topics.

Mr. Richey can be reached at LouRichey@aol.com.

Jeff Sadler

Jeff Sadler began his career as an underwriter in the disability income brokerage division of the Paul Revere Life Insurance Company following his graduation from the University of Vermont in 1975. Disability income and long-term care insurance have been the primary focus of his career, leading to the founding of Sadler Disability Services, Inc. with his father, Raymond Sadler, in 1989.

Over the last several years, Mr. Sadler has authored a number of insurance books, including *The Long Term Care Handbook* (1996, 1998 and 2003),

How To Sell Long Term Care Insurance (2001 and 2006), *Disability Income: The Sale, The Product, The Market* (1991 and 1995), *How To Sell Disability Income* (2005), and *The Managed Care and Group Health Handbook* (1997), all published by the National Underwriter Company. Other books by Mr. Sadler include *Business Disability Income* (1993) and *Understanding LTC Insurance* (1992).

He has been very active in the industry, currently serving as the Chair of the National Association of Health Underwriters' Long-Term Care Advisory Group. He is a past president of the Central Florida Association of Health Underwriters, the Gulf Coast Health Underwriters, the Florida Association of Health Underwriters, and the Central Florida General Agents and Managers Association. He is a past winner of the Stanley Greenspun Health Insurance Person of the Year Award and the NAHU Distinguished Service Award.

Jamie Scott, J.D.

Jamie Scott serves as Chair of Cincinnati law firm Graydon Head's Employee Benefits and Executive Compensation Practice Group. He has worked with clients of all sizes to design and implement qualified retirement plans (including ESOPs), nonqualified deferred compensation plans, incentive compensation plans, and welfare benefit plans.

He also has significant experience in working with the Internal Revenue Service and Department of Labor on compliance issues. Mr. Scott has extensive estate planning experience, which enables him to advise clients on estate planning issues that arise when a large part of a client's estate consists of retirement plan assets. In 2010, he was named an "Ohio Super Lawyer" by Super Lawyers Magazine for his work in Employee Benefits/ERISA. Based on the grading and comments of his peers, Jamie is recognized with an AV Rating, the highest rating given to lawyers by Martindale-Hubbell.

Mr. Scott received his J.D. from Brigham Young University in 1983 and a B.B.A in Accounting from the University of Cincinnati in 1978. He is admitted to practice law in Ohio and Texas. He is member and former chair of the Cincinnati Bar Association, Employee Benefits Committee; Warren County Bar Association; ASPPA Benefits Council of Greater Cincinnati; Warren County MRDD Board Member; and member of the Lebanon City Schools Citizens Audit Advisory Committee.

Lou Shuntich, J.D., LL.M.

Lou Shuntich has a wealth of knowledge and expert advice to offer in the Advanced Planning arena. He earned his B.S. Cum Laude from Rider University, his J.D. from The College of William and Mary, and his LL.M. (in Taxation) from New York University. He is a Certified Retirement Counselor and is licensed for life, health, variable annuities, and Series 6 and 63.

He is the Associate Editor of the *Journal of Financial Service Professionals.* He previously served in the Law Department of Prudential-Financial as

Vice President and Corporate Counsel specializing in business insurance, estate planning, and compensation planning. He also served as Senior Vice President, Advanced Planning for Lincoln Benefit Life Company.

He is a member of the Association for Advanced Life Underwriting Business Insurance and Estate Planning and Nonqualified Plans Broad Committees. He is past chairman of the American Council of Life Insurance Split Dollar Task Force and has served on the Life Underwriter Training Council's Content and Techniques Committee.

In addition, he is a member of the Speakers Bureau of the Society of Financial Service Professionals and the Speakers Bureau of the National Association of Estate Planners and Councils. He has appeared on the CNBC Power Lunch and Health and Lifestyles programs answering questions about retirement and estate planning. He has five published books on advanced marketing subjects, including *The Estate Planning Today Handbook*, *The Complete Guide to Compensation Planning With Life Insurance*, and *The Life Insurance Handbook*, all published by Marketplace, as well as *Key Life Insurance Model Agreements* and *The Next Step, Successfully Graduating To Life Insurance Advanced Markets*, both published by the National Underwriter Company.

He has also published multiple articles including those in the *Journal of Financial Service Professionals*, *AALU Quarterly Magazine*, *Brokers World Magazine* and *Life Insurance Selling*.

Bruce A. Tannahill, J.D., CPA/PFS, CLU, ChFC, AEP

Bruce Tannahill is an experienced tax, estate and business planning attorney and CPA with expertise in estate and business planning, qualified plans, IRAs, life insurance, and annuities. In his role as Director, Estate and Business Planning for Massachusetts Mutual Life Insurance Company, he assists MassMutual agents in serving their clients on estate planning, business planning, Social Security, and personal planning matters.

Bruce is a nationally recognized author on the topics of retirement planning and trust and estate issues. He is a co-author of three books. His articles have been published in various industry and professional publications, including *Trusts & Estates*, *Estate Planning*, *Probate & Property*, and the *Journal of Financial Service Professionals*. He was the Qualified Plans & Retirement Counseling columnist for the *Journal of Financial Service Professionals* from 2012 through May 2015.

He serves as CLE Committee vice Chair for the ABA Real Property, Trust & Estate Law Section and is a former Director of the Society of Financial Service Professionals. He also served as Chair of the Synergy Summit, an organization of leading financial service professional organizations.

He received his Juris Doctor, with distinction, from the University of Missouri at Kansas City, Kansas City, MO and his BSBA in Accounting, Summa Cum Laude, from University of Dayton. He is admitted to practice before the U.S. Tax Court and the Supreme Courts of Kansas, Missouri, and Ohio.

In his spare time, he enjoys volunteering for the FIRST Robotics Competition, reading, and watching baseball.

Robert Toth, J.D., ACEBC

Bob Toth is the Principal of the Law Office of Robert J. Toth, Jr., LLC, and has been practicing employee benefits law since 1983. His practice focuses on the design, administration, and distribution of financial products and services for retirement plans, particularly on complex fiduciary and prohibited transaction issues, annuities in deferred compensation plans, and 403(b) plans. Mr. Toth is a Fellow of American College of Employee Benefits Counsel and is on the faculty of ALI-ABA Advance Law of Pensions. In addition, he managed the legal affairs of Lincoln Financial Group's retirement plan business. Mr. Toth is also an Adjunct Professor at John Marshall Law School where he teaches 403(b) and 457 plan courses.

Mr. Toth coauthored Thompson Publishing's *403(b) and 457 Technical Requirements Handbook* and is a contributing author to Aspen Publishing's *403(b) Answer Book*. He is also Chair of ASPPA's IRS Governmental Affairs Sub-Committee and writes on current employee benefits issues at the *businessofbenefits.com*, where more on his background, publications, and presentations can be found.

William J. Wagner, J.D., LL.M., CLU

William J. Wagner is a Senior Editor with Forefield, Inc., a provider of Web-based applications that facilitate the communication of financial planning knowledge and advice between financial institutions, their advisors, and their customers.

Mr. Wagner is the author of the *Ultimate IRA Resource* (including the IRA Calculator) and the *Ultimate Trust Resource* (including the Trust Calculator). Previously, he was a Senior Associate Editor of *Tax Facts on Insurance & Employee Benefits*, *Tax Facts on Investments*, and *Tax Facts News*, all published by The National Underwriter Company.

Jayne Elizabeth Zanglein

Jayne Elizabeth Zanglein is a prolific writer on employee benefits. She contributes regularly to journals such as the *ABA Supreme Court Preview*, the *Journal of Taxation of Employee Benefits*, and the *NYU Review of Employee Benefits and Executive Compensation*. Her treatise, *ERISA Litigation*, was published in 2003 and is now in its fourth edition. She serves as an employee benefits expert and neutral in class action cases.

She is the cochair of the Fiduciary Duties Committee of the ABA Section on Labor and Employment Law's subcommittee on Employee Benefits. She has served on various task forces including Governor Cuomo's Task Force on Pension Fund Investments. She has worked on pension fund reform in Ontario and South Africa. She currently teaches law and dispute resolution at Western Carolina University.

Randy L. Zipse, J.D., AEP (Distinguished)

Randy Zipse serves as Vice President, Advanced Markets, at Prudential. In this position, Mr. Zipse provides advanced sales support across the company, assisting distribution channels and working with sales vice presidents, independent producers, and financial institutions to develop business opportunities and enhanced advanced marketing solutions for clients.

Mr. Zipse has written numerous articles on trust taxation, estate planning, and business succession planning, which have appeared in the Journal of *Financial Service Professionals, BrokerWorld, Estate Planning, Life Insurance Selling, LAN*, and the National Underwriter news magazines. He is coauthor with Stephan R. Leimberg of *Tools and Techniques of Charitable Planning.* He has also been a frequent lecturer at industry meetings, including AALU, International Forum, Million Dollar Round Table, New York University Tax Institute, University of Miami Heckerling Tax Institute, and the Hawaii Tax Institute.

Mr. Zipse also serves as author of National Underwriter's popular *Field Guide on Estate Planning, Business Planning, & Employee Benefits* publication.

Prior to joining Prudential, Mr. Zipse was Senior Vice President at Highland Capital where he was responsible for the Advanced Markets group, which provided estate and business planning support to home office employees, field personnel, and producers.

Mr. Zipse was Senior Counsel and VP of the Manulife Financial Advanced Markets team. Before that he worked as an attorney in private practice. An honors graduate of the University of Northern Iowa, Mr. Zipse subsequently received his J.D. from Drake University College of Law (Order of the Coif, class rank number one), and is a member of the Iowa, Texas, and Missouri Bars.

OTHER CONTRIBUTORS

William H. Alley, CLU, ChFC, RHU, LUTCF, MSFS, AEP, CLTC, is Principal and CEO of Alley Financial Group, LLC in Lexington, Kentucky. Bill entered the life insurance business in 1960, having graduated from Columbia Military Academy and attended the University of Kentucky. Bill has developed a successful practice in the areas of retirement and succession planning, estate analysis, financial planning, and business insurance. Bill is a past president of the Lexington and Kentucky Life Underwriters Association, past president of the Lexington Chapter of the Society of Financial Service Professionals, a past trustee of the National Association of Insurance and Financial Advisors and a twenty-five year member of the Million Dollar Round Table. He is also a past National Director for the Society of Financial Service Professionals. Bill is a frequent speaker on insurance and financial planning as well as the author of numerous articles on insurance and financial matters.

Ward B. Anderson, CLU, ChFC, is president of Compensation Planning & Administration Systems, Inc., an employee benefit consulting firm involved in the design, installation and funding of tax qualified retirement plans, selective executive benefit plans and group life, health and disability plans. Ward is immediate past president of the Society of Financial Service Professionals. He has been a frequent speaker to legal, accounting and financial planning groups on the topics of estate planning, uses of life insurance, employee benefit planning, taxation of employee benefit plans and planning for retirement plan distributions. Ward attended the University of Kansas and the University of Kansas School of Law.

Marcela S. Aroca is a litigator based in Windsor, Ontario practicing exclusively in tax and civil litigation. During her eighteen year career, Marcela has developed into an expert in the field and has appeared at all trial and appellate Courts in Ontario, the Federal Court, the Federal Court of Appeal and has appeared in writing to the Supreme Court of Canada. When Marcela is not working at her practice, she teaches Income Tax Law, Advanced Tax Law, Civil Procedure, and Contract Law at the University of Windsor, Faculty of Law.

Gregory W. Baker, J.D., CFP®, CAP, is Senior Vice President of Legal Services for Renaissance, the nation's leading third-party administrator of charitable gifts. For the past eighteen years, he has provided trust, tax and philanthropic financial planning advice to over 4,000 attorneys and 7,000 financial planners in all 50 states regarding more than 14,000 charitable remainder trusts, more than 800 charitable lead trusts, and numerous foundations, charitable gift annuities and donor-advised funds. Baker's advice has helped advisors close cases for their high net worth clients in the areas of charitable, investment, retirement, gift, estate and tax planning. Baker is currently an Advisory Board Member of the Chartered Advisor in Philanthropy designation at the American College, member of the Financial Planning Association, National Committee on Planned Giving and the Indiana Bar. Baker was previously VP, Charitable Fiduciary Risk Manager for the Merrill Lynch Center for Philanthropy & Nonprofit Management in Princeton, NJ. Baker speaks at national and local conferences for professional advisors, high net worth clients and charities regarding charitable gift planning, asset-allocation, investment modeling and tax issues.

Ted R. Batson, Jr., MBA, CPA, is Senior Vice President of Professional Services for Renaissance, the nation's leading third-party administrator of charitable gifts. Since his employment in 1993, Batson has developed a wealth of practical, hands-on experience in dealing with complex issues related to the creative use of unmarketable and unusual assets to fund charitable gifts. He routinely consults with the more than 2,000 attorneys, CPAs and financial service professionals who look to Renaissance for case assistance. Batson has spoken to numerous groups regarding charitable planning and has been published in several professional publications. Batson is a member of the American Institute of Certified Public Accountants (AICPA) and the Indiana CPA Society. He is a graduate of Asbury College (BA in computer science) and Indiana University (MBA in accounting).

Lawrence Brody, J.D., LL.M, is a partner in Bryan Cave LLP, a national and international law firm, and a member of the firm's Private Client Group. He is an adjunct professor at Washington University School of Law and a visiting adjunct professor at the University of Miami School of Law. Mr. Brody focuses his practice on estate planning for high net worth individuals and the use of life insurance in estate and nonqualified deferred compensation planning, He is the author of two BNA Tax Management Portfolios and two books for the National Underwriter

Company, and is a frequent lecturer at national conferences on estate and insurance planning. Mr. Brody received the designation of Accredited Estate Planner by the National Association of Estate Planners and Councils, and was awarded its Distinguished Accredited Estate Planner designation in 2004.

Fred Burkey, CLU, APA, is a retired Advanced Sales Consultant with Ameritas Life Insurance Corporation (previously Union Central Life Insurance Corporation). He joined Union Central in 1981 after nine years of insurance sales in the greater Cincinnati area. He served in agent support departments including pension sales, agency development, and individual annuity sales. Fred is a member of the National Association for Variable Annuities, the Society of Financial Service Professionals, and the National Institute of Pension Administrators.

Donald F. Cady, J.D., LL.M., CLU, is the author of *Field Guide to Estate, Employee, & Business Planning* and *Field Guide to Financial Planning*. He is a graduate of St. Lawrence University with a B.A. in Economics, where he received the Wall Street Journal Award for excellence in that subject. He received his J.D. degree from Columbia University School of Law, holds the degree of LL.M. (Taxation) from Emory University School of Law, and is a member of the New York Bar. For twenty years, Don was with the Aetna Life Insurance & Annuity Company in various advanced underwriting positions. Don is a frequent speaker on the subjects of estate planning, business planning and employee benefits for business and professional organizations.

Natalie B. Choate, Esq., is an estate planning attorney with the firm of Nutter, McClennen, and Fish, LLP. A Regent of the American College of Trust & Estate Counsel, she is the author of two books, *Life and Death Planning for Retirement Benefits* and *The QPRT Manual*, and is a frequent lecturer on estate planning topics. She is listed in *The Best Lawyers in America*.

Stephan R. Leimberg is CEO of LISI, Leimberg Information Services, Inc., a provider of email/internet news and commentary for professionals on recent cases, rulings, and legislation. He is also CEO of Leimberg & LeClair, Inc., an estate and financial planning software company, and President of Leimberg Associates, Inc., a publishing and software company in Bryn Mawr, Pennsylvania. Leimberg is the author of the acclaimed *Tools and Techniques* series, with titles on estate planning, employee benefits, financial planning, charitable planning, life insurance planning, income tax planning, investment planning, and practice management. Mr. Leimberg is a nationally known speaker and an award-winning author.

Martin A. Silfen, Esq., is an attorney and author with twenty-five years of practice in the areas of retirement planning and estate planning. Mr. Silfen was senior partner in the law firm of Silfen, Segal, Fryer & Shuster, P.C. in Atlanta. He is currently Senior Vice President of Brown Brothers Harriman Trust Company, New York, New York. Mr. Silfen is a nationally recognized expert in retirement tax planning, having authored *The Retirement Plan Distribution Advisor* and served as Retirement Planning columnist for *Personal Financial Planning*. He has also authored several articles for *Estate Planning*.

Editor

Jason Gilbert, J.D., M.A., is a senior editor with the Practical Insights Division of The National Underwriter Company, a division of ALM Media, LLC. He edits and develops publications related to tax and insurance products, including titles in the *Advisor's Guide* and the *Tools & Techniques* series of investment and planning products. He also develops content for National Underwriter's other financial services publications and online products. He has worked on insurance and tax publications for more than nine years.

Jason has been a practicing attorney for more than a dozen years in the areas of criminal defense, products liability, and regulatory enforcement actions. Prior to joining National Underwriter, his experience in the insurance and tax fields has included work as a Westlaw contributor for Thomson Reuters and a tax advisor and social media contributor for Intuit. He is an honors graduate from Wright State University and holds a J.D. from the University of Cincinnati College of Law as well as a master's degree in Economics from Miami University in Ohio.

Editorial Services

Connie L. Jump, Sr. Manager, Editorial Operations

Patti O'Leary, Sr. Editorial Assistant

Emily Brunner, Editorial Assistant

ABBREVIATIONS

Acq. (Nonacq.)	Commissioner's acquiescence (nonacquiescence) in decision
AFTR	American Federal Tax Reports (Research Institute of America, early decisions)
AFTR2d	American Federal Tax Reports (Research Institute of America, second series)
AJCA 2004	American Jobs Creation Act of 2004
ARRA 2009	American Recovery and Reinvestment Act of 2009
ATRA 2012	American Taxpayer Relief Act of 2012
BTA	Board of Tax Appeals decisions (now Tax Court)
BTA Memo	Board of Tax Appeals memorandum decisions
CA or -- Cir.	United States Court of Appeals
CB	Cumulative Bulletin of Internal Revenue Service
CCA	Chief Counsel Advice
Cl. Ct.	U.S. Claims Court (designated U.S. Court of Federal Claims in 1992)
CLASS Act	Community Living Assistance Services and Support Act
COBRA	Consolidated Omnibus Budget Reconciliation Act of 1985
CRTRA 2000	Community Renewal Tax Relief Act of 2000
Ct. Cl.	Court of Claims (designated U.S. Claims Court in 1982)
DOL Adv. Op.	Department of Labor Advisory Opinion
EGTRRA 2001	Economic Growth and Tax Relief Reconciliation Act of 2001
EIEA 2008	Energy Improvement and Extension Act of 2008
ERISA	Employee Retirement Income Security Act of 1974
ERTA	Economic Recovery Tax Act of 1981
Fed.	Federal Reporter (early decisions)
Fed. Cl.	U.S. Court of Federal Claims
Fed. Reg.	Federal Register
F.2d	Federal Reporter, second series (later decisions of U.S. Court of Appeals to Mid-1993)
F.3rd	Federal Reporter, third series (decisions of U.S. Court of Appeals since Mid-1993)
F. Supp.	Federal Supplement (decisions of U.S. District Courts)
FSA	Field Service Advice
FSA	Flexible spending account
FTE	Full-time equivalent employee
GCM	General Counsel Memorandum (IRS)
HCE	Highly compensated employee
HIPAA '96	Health Insurance Portability and Accountability Act
HHS	The Department of Health and Human Services
HRA	Health Reimbursement Account
HSA	Health Savings Account
IR	Internal Revenue News Release
HIREA (2010)	Hiring Incentives to Restore Employment Act
IRB	Internal Revenue Bulletin of Internal Revenue Service
IRC	Internal Revenue Code
IRS	Internal Revenue Service
IRSRRA '98	IRS Restructuring and Reform Act of 1998
IT	Income Tax Ruling Series (IRS)
ITCA	Installment Tax Correction Act of 2000
JCWAA	Job Creation and Worker Assistance Act of 2002
JGTRRA 2003	Jobs and Growth Tax Relief Reconciliation Act of 2003

KETRA 2005	Katrina Emergency Tax Relief Act of 2005
Let. Rul.	Letter Ruling (issued by IRS)
MERP	Medical Expense Reimbursement Plan
MFDRA 2007	Mortgage Forgiveness Debt Relief Act of 2007
MHPAEA	Mental Health Parity and Addiction Equity Act
MSA	Archer medical savings account
NHCE	Non highly compensated employee
NMHPA	Newborns' and Mothers' Health Protection Act
OBRA	Omnibus Budget Reconciliation Act of (year of enactment)
P.L.	Public Law
PLR	Private Letter Ruling
P&PS Rept.	Pension and Profit Sharing Report (Prentice-Hall)
PBGC	Pension Benefit Guaranty Corporation
PFEA 2004	Pension Funding Equity Act of 2004
PHSA	Public Health Service Act
PPA 2006	Pension Protection Act of 2006
PPACA	Patient Protection and Affordable Care Act
Prop. Reg.	Proposed Regulation
PTE	Prohibited Transaction Exemption
REA '84	Retirement Equity Act of 1984
Rev. Proc.	Revenue Procedure (issued by IRS)
Rev. Rul.	Revenue Ruling (issued by IRS)
SBJPA '96	Small Business Job Protection Act of 1996
SBWOTA 2007	Small Business and Work Opportunity Tax Act of 2007
SCA	IRS Service Center Advice
TAM	Technical Advice Memorandum (IRS)
TAMRA '88	Technical and Miscellaneous Revenue Act of 1988
TC	Tax Court (official reports)
TC Memo	Tax Court memorandum decisions (official reports)
TC Summary Opinion	Tax Court Summary Opinion
TD	Treasury Decision
TEAMTRA 2008	Tax Extenders and Alternative Minimum Tax Relief Act of 2008
TEFRA	Tax Equity and Fiscal Responsibility Act of 1982
Temp. Reg.	Temporary Regulation
TIPA 2007	Tax Increase Prevention Act of 2007
TIPRA 2005	Tax Increase Prevention and Reconciliation Act of 2005
TIR	Technical Information Release (from the IRS)
TRA	Tax Reform Act of (year of enactment)
TRA '97	Taxpayer Relief Act of 1997
TRA 2010	Tax Relief Act of 2010
TRHCA 2006	Tax Relief and Health Care Act of 2006
TTCA 2007	Tax Technical Corrections Act of 2007
URAA '94	Uruguay Round Agreements Act of 1994
US	United States Supreme Court decisions
USERRA '94	Uniformed Services Employment and Reemployment Rights Act of 1994
USTC	United States Tax Cases (Commerce Clearing House)
VTTRA 2001	Victims of Terrorism Tax Relief Act of 2001
WFTRA 2004	Working Families Tax Relief Act of 2004
WHBAA 2009	Worker, Homeownership, and Business Assistance Act of 2009
WHCRA	Women's Health and Cancer Rights Act
WRERA 2008	Worker, Retiree, and Employer Recovery Act of 2008

COMPLETE LIST OF QUESTIONS

2020 TAX FACTS ON INSURANCE & EMPLOYEE BENEFITS, VOLUME 1

PART I: LIFE INSURANCE

In General

1. What is life insurance?

2. Are premiums paid on personal life insurance deductible for income tax purposes?

3. Can a taxpayer deduct interest paid on a loan to purchase or carry a life insurance, endowment, or annuity contract?

4. Are there any exceptions to the rule that disallows a deduction for interest paid on a loan to purchase or carry a life insurance, endowment or annuity contract?

5. How is a systematic plan of borrowing to buy life insurance treated?

6. Can the rules that disallow a deduction for interest paid on a loan to purchase or carry a life insurance, endowment or annuity contract be avoided by having one spouse use funds borrowed by the other spouse?

7. Is the interest increment earned on prepaid life insurance premiums taxable income?

8. Are annual increases in the cash surrender value of a life insurance policy taxable income to the policyholder?

9. Is the owner of a limited-pay life insurance policy liable for any tax when the policy becomes paid-up?

Living Proceeds

10. What are the rules for taxing living proceeds received under life insurance policies and endowment contracts?

11. How are cash distributions received as a result of changes in the benefits of a life insurance contract taxed?

12. How are policy loans under life insurance policies and endowment contracts treated?

13. For tax purposes, what is a life insurance policy that is classified as a modified endowment contract (MEC)?

14. What is the "seven pay test" and how does it apply to a modified endowment contract (MEC)?

Dividends

Policy Loans

33. Are there any exceptions to the general rule of nondeductibility of policy loan interest for unborrowed policy cash values?

34. What are the general interest deduction rules?

35. If the beneficiary of life insurance pays the interest on a policy loan, is this a gift to the insured?

Disposition: Sale or Purchase of a Contract

36. What are the income tax consequences when the owner of a life insurance or endowment contract sells the contract?

37. How is gain on the surrender of a cash value life insurance policy calculated after 2008?

38. How is gain on the sale of a cash value life insurance policy calculated after 2008? How did the 2017 Tax Act change the rules governing gain on the sale of a life insurance policy?

39. How is gain on the sale of a term life insurance policy calculated after 2008? How did the 2017 Tax Act change the rules governing gain on the sale of a life insurance policy?

40. How is gain on the sale or surrender of a life insurance policy before 2009 calculated?

41. Will the owner of a life insurance policy recognize a loss when the policy is sold for its cash surrender value?

42. What are the tax results if a life insurance policy is sold subject to a nonrecourse loan?

43. How is the purchaser of a life insurance or endowment contract taxed?

Disposition: Policy Exchanges

44. Does tax liability arise when a policyholder exchanges one life insurance contract for another?

45. Is there any tax liability when a policyholder exchanges a life insurance policy insuring one life for a policy insuring two lives?

46. Is there any tax liability when a joint and last survivor policy is exchanged for a single life policy on the surviving insured?

47. Is there any tax liability when a whole life policy subject to indebtedness is exchanged for a new policy subject to the same indebtedness?

48. Is there any tax liability when two individual policies are exchanged for two interests in a group universal life policy?

49. Is the exchange of life insurance policies for annuities a tax-free exchange?

50. Does the substitution of one insured for another qualify as a tax-free exchange?

Disposition: Surrender, Redemption, or Maturity

51. What are the income tax consequences when the owner of a life insurance or endowment contract takes the lifetime maturity proceeds or cash surrender value in a one lump sum cash payment?

52. If a life insurance policyholder elects to receive endowment maturity proceeds or cash surrender values under a life income or installment option, is the gain on the policy taxable to the policyholder in the year of maturity or in the year of surrender?

53. Can tax on the gain at maturity of an endowment contract be postponed?

Accelerated Death Benefit

54. What is the income tax treatment of an accelerated death benefit payment from a life insurance contract?

55. Are there any special rules that apply to chronically ill insureds?

56. Are there any exceptions to the general rule of non-includability for accelerated death benefits?

57. What is the income tax treatment of an amount received from a viatical settlement provider?

58. Are there special rules regarding the income tax treatment of an amount received by a chronically ill insured from a viatical settlement provider?

59. Are there any exceptions to the general rule that viatical settlements are not included as taxable income?

60. What are the new reporting requirements that the 2017 tax reform legislation imposed on taxpayers involved in reportable policy sales?

61. Are amounts received as living proceeds of life insurance and endowment contracts subject to withholding?

62. Does the surrender or sale of a life insurance or endowment contract ever result in a deductible loss?

Death Proceeds

63. Are life insurance proceeds payable by reason of the insured's death taxable income to the beneficiary?

64. Is the death benefit under the double indemnity clause of a life insurance policy subject to federal income tax?

65. What is a "life insurance contract" for purposes of the death benefit exclusion for contracts issued after December 31, 1984?

66. How is the cash value accumulation test met?

67. How is the guideline premium and cash value corridor test met?

68. What is a "life insurance contract" for purposes of the death benefit exclusion for policies issued before January 1, 1985?

69. How are proceeds taxed if a life insurance policy is owned by someone other than the insured?

70. If life insurance death proceeds are left on deposit with the insurance company under an interest-only option, is the interest taxable income to the beneficiary?

Life Income and Installment Options

71. If excludable death proceeds are held by an insurer and are paid under a life income or installment option, how are the payments treated for income tax purposes?

72. If excludable death proceeds are held by an insurer and are paid under a life income or installment option, how are the payments treated for income tax purposes if the installments are payable based on the life of the beneficiary?

73. If excludable death proceeds are held by an insurer and are paid under a life income or installment option, how are the payments treated for income tax purposes if the installments are payable based on a fixed period?

74. If excludable death proceeds are held by an insurer and are paid under a life income or installment option, how are the payments treated for income tax purposes if the installments are payable based on a fixed amount?

75. Is a surviving spouse entitled to an additional exclusion for interest on death proceeds paid out via a life income or installment option upon the spouse's death?

76. What are the tax consequences of changing the method of receiving the proceeds of a life insurance policy?

77. Are death proceeds wholly tax-exempt if an existing life insurance policy is sold or otherwise transferred for valuable consideration?

78. Are death proceeds of life insurance wholly tax-exempt if the policy has been transferred as a gift?

79. Will the transfer of a life insurance policy between spouses result in loss of the tax exemption for the death proceeds?

Estate Tax Issues

80. What benefits payable at death are included in the term "life insurance" for estate tax purposes?

81. When are death proceeds of life insurance includable in an insured's gross estate?

82. If life insurance proceeds are payable to an insured's estate, is the value of the proceeds includable in the insured's estate?

83. When are life insurance proceeds includable in an insured's gross estate even though the insured has no incident of ownership in the policy and the proceeds are not payable to the insured's estate?

84. Are the proceeds from life insurance taken out to pay an insured's death taxes includable in the insured's estate?

85. When are life insurance proceeds payable to a beneficiary other than the insured's estate includable in the insured's estate?

86. What are the incidents of ownership that will cause life insurance proceeds to be includable in the insured's estate?

87. What are the incidents of ownership of employer-paid death benefits that would cause life insurance proceeds to be includable in the insured's estate?

88. If an insured holds incidents of ownership at death as a fiduciary or by reason of a retained right to remove a trustee and appoint another, will the life insurance proceeds be includable in the insured's estate?

89. If an insured possesses incidents of ownership at death as a fiduciary or by reason of a retained right to remove a trustee and appoint another, are there any situations in which the life insurance proceeds will not be includable in the insured's estate?

90. Are life insurance proceeds includable in the insured's estate if someone other than the insured took out the policy and owns it at the insured's death?

91. Can an insured remove existing life insurance from the insured's gross estate by an absolute assignment of the policy?

92. Can an insured remove existing life insurance from the insured's gross estate by an absolute assignment of the policy but retain a reversionary interest?

93. Are the general rules for including life insurance proceeds in the insured's gross estate applicable to proceeds payable under a qualified pension or profit-sharing plan?

94. May a life insurance beneficiary be required to pay estate tax attributable to death proceeds?

95. May a life insurance beneficiary make a qualified disclaimer of an amount equal to the beneficiary's proportionate share of death taxes when the decedent directed that death taxes be paid entirely out of the probate estate?

96. When are death proceeds of life insurance given away by an insured within three years of the insured's death includable in the insured's gross estate?

97. Is life insurance owned by a corporation on its majority shareholder included in the shareholder's estate when the shareholder divested an interest in the corporation within three years of death?

98. Are there any situations in which death proceeds of life insurance that were given away by an insured within three years of the insured's death are not included in the insured's gross estate?

99. If a donor dies within three years of making a gift of a life insurance policy on the life of another, is the value of the policy includable in the donor's gross estate?

100. If an employer provides, under a nonqualified agreement or plan, an income benefit only for certain survivors designated by family or marital relationship to the employee, how is the benefit treated for estate tax purposes in the employee's estate?

101. Is the value of a survivor benefit payable by an employer under a nonqualified salary continuation or deferred compensation agreement includable in the employee's gross estate?

102. When is the value of a survivor benefit payable by an employer under a nonqualified salary continuation or deferred compensation agreement excludable from the employee's gross estate?

103. Can arrangements for payment of the proceeds of life insurance and annuity contracts attract the generation-skipping transfer tax?

104. Can the transfer to an irrevocable life insurance trust of an amount used to make premium payments qualify for the generation-skipping transfer tax annual exclusion?

105. How can the generation-skipping transfer (GST) tax exemption be leveraged using an irrevocable life insurance trust?

106. What are the income tax results when an individual transfers an existing life insurance policy to or purchases a policy for the individual's former spouse in connection with a divorce settlement?

107. What is the tax treatment of other transfers of an existing life insurance policy in connection with a divorce settlement to which the nonrecognition rules do not apply?

108. What is the tax treatment when an existing life insurance policy is owned and maintained by a former spouse?

109. If an individual is required by a court decree or separation agreement to pay premiums on a life insurance policy for a former spouse, are the premiums taxable income to the recipient spouse? Are they deductible by the payor spouse?

110. If life insurance proceeds are required under the terms of a property settlement agreement or a divorce decree to be paid to certain beneficiaries, are the proceeds includable in the insured's estate?

111. When life insurance proceeds are required under the terms of a property settlement agreement or a divorce decree to be paid to certain beneficiaries, is an offsetting deduction allowable?

112. Is the deduction under IRC Section 2053(a)(3) considered a claim against the insured's estate?

113. Is a deduction under IRC Section 2053(a)(4) considered a debt against the insured's estate?

Gifts and Charitable Gifts

114. If a taxpayer gives a spouse a life insurance policy, is the taxpayer entitled to a gift tax marital deduction?

115. If a primary beneficiary of life insurance proceeds payable under a settlement option has the power to withdraw part of the proceeds, does the beneficiary's failure to exercise the power constitute a taxable gift to contingent beneficiaries?

116. How are split-dollar life insurance arrangements treated for gift tax purposes?

117. What is the advantage of the "split-gift" law where one spouse gives a life insurance, endowment, or annuity contract to a third person?

118. Does an employee covered under a survivor income benefit plan make a gift of the survivor benefit for federal gift tax purposes?

119. How are life insurance policies and endowment contracts valued for gift tax purposes?

120. May a charitable contribution deduction be taken for the gift of a life insurance policy or premium? May a charitable contribution deduction be taken for the gift of a maturing annuity or endowment contract?

121. May a charitable contribution deduction be taken for a gift of an interest in a split-dollar arrangement?

122. Are there any exceptions to the disallowance rule for transfers of charitable gift annuity contracts?

123. Are there any penalties that can be imposed upon a charitable institution in connection with a gift of life insurance where a deduction is not allowable?

124. May a charitable contribution deduction be taken for a gift of a life insurance policy if the donor retains a right, shared with the donee charity, to change charitable beneficiaries?

125. May a charitable contribution deduction be taken for a gift of the annuity portion of a split-life contract?

126. If life insurance proceeds are payable to a religious, charitable, or educational organization, is their value taxable in the insured's gross estate?

127. Are gifts of life insurance to charitable organizations subject to gift tax?

128. How are single premium life insurance policies, including single premium variable life insurance policies, taxed?

Creditor Insurance

129. If a debtor pays premiums on a life insurance policy on his or her life in favor of his or her creditor, may the debtor take an income tax deduction for these premium payments?

130. Can a creditor deduct premiums paid on life insurance purchased on the life of the creditor's debtor?

131. If a creditor pays premiums on a life insurance policy held as collateral for a business debt, can the creditor claim an income tax deduction for the premium payments?

132. If a creditor pays premiums on a life insurance policy securing a non-business debt, can the creditor deduct the premium payments?

133. If a stockholder's personal life insurance is used as collateral security for the corporation's debt, are the premiums deductible?

134. May a creditor take a bad debt deduction for a worthless debt even though the creditor holds an insurance policy on the life of the debtor as collateral?

135. Are proceeds received by a creditor from insurance purchased on the life of the creditor's debtor exempt from income tax as life insurance proceeds?

136. Are life insurance proceeds received by a creditor as collateral assignee or beneficiary "as interest appears" exempt from income tax?

137. If an insured assigns a life insurance policy as collateral for a loan, are the proceeds includable in the insured's gross estate?

138. If an insured assigns a life insurance policy in which a spouse is the named beneficiary, will the full amount of the proceeds qualify for the marital deduction?

139. Are proceeds of government life insurance exempt from income tax?

140. If a qualified plan trust distributes a life insurance policy to an employee, is the value of the contract taxable to the employee in the year of distribution?

141. Can the federal government reach the cash value of a taxpayer's life insurance for collection of back income taxes?

142. Can the federal government collect an insured's delinquent income taxes from a beneficiary who receives life insurance death proceeds?

143. Does the income taxation of a life insurance policy that insures more than one life differ from the taxation of a policy that insures a single life?

144. How is the value of a life insurance policy determined for income tax purposes?

145. What is the tax treatment when shares of stock received in a demutualization are sold?

Life Insurance Trusts

146. Can a life insurance trust result in income tax savings for the grantor?

147. If income of an irrevocable funded life insurance trust is used to pay premiums on a policy insuring the grantor's life, is the income that is used taxable to the grantor?

148. Can a grantor create an irrevocable funded life insurance trust, carrying insurance on the grantor's spouse, without being taxed on trust income used for premium payments?

149. When is life insurance trust income taxable to some person other than the trust, grantor, or income beneficiary?

150. What income is taxable to a life insurance trust?

151. What income is taxable to the beneficiaries of a life insurance trust?

152. May the grantor of a life insurance trust take a deduction for interest paid by the trust on a policy loan when the policy is held by the trust?

153. Are death proceeds of life insurance taxable income if they are payable to a trust?

154. Is there a gift for gift tax purposes when a grantor transfers a life insurance policy to an irrevocable trust in which the grantor has no interest?

155. If income-producing property is transferred to an irrevocable life insurance trust to fund premium payments, does the value of the property constitute a gift?

156. How is the gift tax value of a "reversionary interest trust" measured?

157. Does the transfer of a life insurance policy to an irrevocable trust for the benefit of the grantor's spouse qualify for the gift tax marital deduction?

158. If a grantor creates a revocable trust with a life insurance policy on the life of another person and names third parties as trust beneficiaries, is a gift made when the insured dies and the trust becomes irrevocable?

159. Does the gift of a life insurance policy in trust (or a gift of subsequent premiums) qualify for the gift tax annual exclusion?

160. Is the annual gift tax exclusion available when a life insurance policy is placed in an irrevocable trust for a minor beneficiary?

161. Do transfers to a trustee of an irrevocable life insurance trust of amounts to be used by the trustee to pay premiums qualify for the gift tax annual exclusion?

162. If the beneficiary of a Crummey trust allows the right to withdraw a contribution to the trust to go unexercised, when will the beneficiary be deemed to have made a transfer subject to gift or estate tax?

163. May dividends paid on a life insurance policy in trust be gifts of a present interest even though the policy itself was a gift of a future interest?

164. When can a beneficiary of life insurance proceeds be held liable for payment of federal estate tax falling on the insured's estate?

165. How are proceeds of community property life insurance treated in the insured's estate?

166. How are proceeds of community property life insurance treated in the insured's estate in Louisiana?

167. When life insurance on the life of a spouse is bought with community funds and one of the spouses is designated the policy owner, is the policy community property or is it the separate property of the spouse designated as the owner?

168. What are the estate tax results in the insured's estate when life insurance premiums have been paid with both community and separate funds?

169. When can death proceeds of community property life insurance payable to someone other than the surviving spouse be includable in the surviving spouse's gross estate?

170. How is community property life insurance taxed when the spouse who is not the insured dies first?

171. How are life insurance paid-up additions purchased with dividends treated for estate tax purposes?

172. What rules are applicable to including life insurance accumulated and post-mortem dividends in an insured's estate?

173. Are life insurance proceeds paid under a double-indemnity clause includable in an insured's gross estate?

174. Are proceeds of life insurance issued under U.S. government programs includable in the insured's estate?

175. Are the proceeds of group term life insurance from an employer includable in an insured's estate?

176. If an employee assigns his or her incidents of ownership in group term life insurance, are the proceeds includable in the employee's estate?

177. Is an assignment of group term life insurance within three years before the death of an employee includable in the employee's gross estate?

178. If a grantor creates a revocable life insurance trust with a policy on the grantor's life, will the proceeds be includable in his or her estate?

179. If policies on an insured's life are placed in an irrevocable life insurance trust, are the proceeds includable in the estate?

180. When are death proceeds includable in the estate of a life income beneficiary of a life insurance trust?

181. If an income beneficiary has the power to invade the corpus of a trust, will the value of the trust assets over which the income beneficiary has the power be includable in the income beneficiary's gross estate upon the income beneficiary's death?

182. Are life insurance proceeds includable in an insured's estate if they are payable to an irrevocable trust and the trustee has the power to use them for payment of the insured's estate debts and death taxes?

183. If a grantor funds his or her life insurance trust by transferring income-producing property to the trustee, is the value of the funding property includable in the grantor's gross estate?

184. If a grandparent creates a funded irrevocable life insurance trust with policies on the life of his or her child for the benefit of grandchildren, is anything includable in the grantor's gross estate?

185. How is a "reversionary interest trust" taxed under the estate tax law?

186. What is the reciprocal trust doctrine, and how does it affect life insurance trusts?

187. Is a life insurance policy loan deductible as a claim against the estate?

Marital Deduction

188. May a trust intended to qualify for the marital deduction as a "power of appointment trust" authorize the trustee to retain or acquire life insurance policies?

189. May a trust intended to qualify for the marital deduction as qualified terminable interest property (QTIP) authorize the trustee to retain or acquire life insurance policies?

190. If a decedent directs his or her executor or a trustee to buy a nonrefundable life annuity for the decedent's surviving spouse, will the annuity qualify for the marital deduction?

191. When will life insurance or annuity proceeds payable to the surviving spouse qualify for the marital deduction?

192. Will life insurance or annuity proceeds qualify for the marital deduction if payable to a surviving spouse under a settlement option with a surviving spouse's estate designated as contingent beneficiary? What if they are payable to a surviving spouse as a straight life annuity?

193. Can life insurance settlements naming the spouse as primary beneficiary and other persons as contingent beneficiaries be arranged so that the proceeds qualify for the marital deduction?

194. What is a general power to appoint the proceeds of a life insurance policy for purposes of the marital deduction?

195. Does the use of a "delay clause" disqualify life insurance proceeds for the marital deduction?

196. Does a common disaster clause disqualify life insurance proceeds for the marital deduction?

197. Can operation of the Uniform Simultaneous Death Act result in loss of the marital deduction?

198. Can proceeds of community property life insurance passing to the surviving spouse qualify for the marital deduction?

199. Does estate taxation of a life insurance policy that insures more than one life differ from taxation of a policy that insures a single life?

200. If a policy owner who is not the insured dies before the insured, is the value of the unmatured life insurance policy included in the policy owner's gross estate?

201. If the insured elects a settlement option for the insured's primary beneficiary and names contingent beneficiaries, will the value of any unpaid life insurance proceeds be includable in the primary beneficiary's estate?

202. If the surviving income beneficiary dies possessing the power during his or her lifetime to appoint the life insurance proceeds only to his or her children, are the proceeds includable in the surviving income beneficiary's estate?

203. If life insurance proceeds are payable to the surviving spouse's estate, but remain unpaid at the primary beneficiary's death, is the money includable in the primary beneficiary's gross estate?

204. If an insured elects a settlement option naming contingent beneficiaries, but still gives the primary beneficiary power to withdraw proceeds, are life insurance proceeds remaining unpaid at the primary beneficiary's death includable in the primary beneficiary's estate?

205. Can an insured give a primary beneficiary limited, noncumulative withdrawal rights without causing any remaining unpaid life insurance proceeds to be includable in the primary beneficiary's estate?

206. If the primary beneficiary is given the power to revoke contingent beneficiaries and appoint to his or her estate under a settlement option, are life insurance proceeds remaining unpaid at the primary beneficiary's death includable in his or her estate?

207. If a beneficiary elects the settlement option, are life insurance proceeds remaining unpaid at the beneficiary's death includable in his or her estate?

208. How are life insurance proceeds valued for an insured's estate tax return?

209. If the amount of life insurance proceeds collectible from the insurer is not determinable when the estate tax return is filed, what amount is reportable on the return?

210. Can gift tax be collected from the donee of a life insurance policy or proceeds?

211. Does gift taxation of a life insurance policy that insures more than one life differ from taxation of a policy that insures a single life?

212. Do premiums gratuitously paid on life insurance owned by and payable to another constitute gifts?

213. Do premiums paid by one of several beneficiaries of an irrevocable life insurance trust constitute gifts to the other beneficiaries?

214. If a life insurance policy is owned by someone other than the insured, is there a gift when the insured dies and the proceeds are paid to the owner's designated beneficiary?

215. Does a taxable gift occur when a donor spouse assigns community property life insurance to a donee spouse?

216. If one spouse uses community property to purchase life insurance on either spouse's life and names a child as beneficiary, does the death of the insured spouse give rise to a taxable gift from the noninsured spouse?

217. Are death-benefit-only (DBO) plans subject to gift tax?

Gift Tax Annual Exclusion

218. May the annual exclusion of $15,000 for gifts to each donee be applied against gifts of life insurance policies and premiums?

219. When is the gift of a life insurance policy considered the gift of a future interest that deprives the donor of the gift tax annual exclusion?

220. Is the annual exclusion available when an insured transfers ownership of a life insurance policy to two or more donees jointly?

221. Will the gift of a life insurance policy fail to qualify for the annual exclusion merely because the policy has no cash value?

222. Does the outright gift of a life insurance policy qualify for the gift tax annual exclusion, even if the gift is to a minor?

223. When a life insurance policy has been given away, are premiums subsequently paid by the donor gifts of a present interest qualifying for the annual exclusion or are they a future interest?

224. If an insured, within three years of his or her death, makes a gift of life insurance on which the insured pays a gift tax, is the gift also subject to estate tax?

Disability Provisions Under Life Policies

225. Are premiums paid for disability provisions under a life insurance policy deductible as medical expenses?

226. Is disability income payable under the provisions of a personal life insurance policy included in gross income?

227. Are life insurance premiums that have been waived because of the insured's disability taxable income to the insured?

228. If a corporation attaches a disability income rider to a key person life insurance policy, what are the tax consequences to the corporation and to the key person?

Irrevocable Life Insurance Trusts (ILITs)

229. What type of trust is an irrevocable life insurance trust (ILIT)?

230. Who are the parties to an irrevocable life insurance trust (ILIT)?

231. How does an irrevocable life insurance trust work?

232. Are life insurance proceeds from an irrevocable trust taxable? How can an ILIT be used as an estate planning tool?

233. What are some of the advantages of using an irrevocable life insurance trust?

234. Who should serve as trustee of an ILIT and what role does the trustee play?

235. What are the types of life insurance policies that can be used to fund an ILIT?

236. What are the gift tax implications of making a gift to an ILIT in the form of premiums paid on the life insurance policy?

237. What are some of the differences between a funded and unfunded irrevocable life insurance trust (ILIT)?

238. How can an irrevocable life insurance trust (ILIT) be terminated?

PART II: GROUP TERM LIFE INSURANCE

239. How does the Department of Labor fiduciary standard impact advisors who sell life insurance or disability insurance?

240. What are the tax benefits of employer provided group term life insurance?

241. What is group term life insurance?

242. Who is an employee for purposes of determining whether group term life insurance benefits are excludable?

243. Is supplemental life insurance coverage treated as group term life insurance?

244. Is term insurance provided to a group of fewer than ten employees "group" term insurance?

245. Are premiums paid for group term life insurance deductible business expenses?

246. Is the cost of group term life insurance coverage provided by an employer taxable income to an insured employee?

247. Is group term life insurance coverage on the lives of an employee's spouse and dependents taxable income to the employee?

248. Are there any exceptions to the general rule that limits the annual exclusion for term life insurance to $50,000 per employee?

249. Must group term life insurance provide nondiscriminatory benefits? How is group term life insurance taxed if a plan is discriminatory?

250. How is it determined whether a group term life insurance plan is discriminatory?

251. Is the cost of employer-provided group term life insurance subject to Social Security tax?

252. What information returns must an employer that maintains a group term life insurance plan file with respect to the plan?

253. If an employer provides life insurance under a group term life insurance policy, what are the advantages of a group carve-out plan to employees and to the employer?

254. May any part of a benefit under a policy be treated as group term life insurance if the policy also provides permanent benefits? If so, what part?

255. What are the tax consequences of dividends paid to an employee under a policy that provides both permanent benefits and group term life insurance?

256. What is a retired lives reserve? Is an employee taxed on employer contributions to such a reserve? May an employer deduct contributions to a reserve?

257. Is the cost of group permanent life insurance paid by an employer taxable income to an insured employee?

258. Are premiums that an employer pays on group permanent life insurance for its employees deductible by the employer?

259. Are death proceeds payable under group life insurance exempt from income tax?

260. What is group survivor income benefit insurance?

PART III: BUSINESS LIFE INSURANCE

In General

261. What is business life insurance?

262. Are premiums paid on business life insurance deductible as business expenses?

263. Are premiums paid on business life insurance taxable income to an insured?

264. Can a corporation deduct premiums it pays on a policy insuring the life of an employee or stockholder?

265. If a stockholder pays premiums on insurance on the life of one of the corporation's officers and the corporation is beneficiary of the proceeds, may the stockholder deduct the premium payments as business expenses?

266. If a stockholder purchases insurance on the life of another stockholder to fund obligations under a cross purchase plan, can the stockholder deduct the premiums paid on the policy?

267. Where a key person life insurance policy is owned by and payable to an employer corporation, are premiums paid by the corporation taxable to the key person?

268. Are premiums paid by a corporation on life insurance to fund a stock redemption agreement taxable to an insured stockholder?

269. Are life insurance premiums paid by a corporate employer taxable income to an insured employee if proceeds are payable to the employee's estate or personal beneficiary and the policy is owned by the employee?

270. Are life insurance premiums paid by a corporate employer taxable income to an insured employee if proceeds are payable to the employee's estate or personal beneficiary and the policy is owned by the corporation?

271. If a corporation pays life insurance premiums on policies owned by stockholders and the policies are used to fund a cross-purchase agreement, are premium payments taxable income to stockholders?

272. What is a Section 162 bonus plan and what are the income tax consequences to an employee and employer?

273. What are the tax consequences when an S corporation pays a premium on a life insurance policy insuring a shareholder or employee?

274. Are premiums deductible when paid by a partnership or by a partner for insurance on the life of a copartner?

275. How is a corporation taxed on payments under an annuity contract or on living proceeds from an endowment or life insurance contract?

276. Are death proceeds of business life insurance exempt from income tax?

277. What special requirements must be satisfied by employer-owned life insurance contracts issued after August 17, 2006, in order for death proceeds to be received income tax-free?

278. What reporting requirements apply to employer-owned life insurance?

Proceeds Taxable Because of Transfer for Value

279. Will a sale or other transfer for value of an existing life insurance policy or any interest in a policy cause loss of an income tax exemption for death proceeds?

280. What is a transfer for value of a life insurance policy or an interest in a policy?

281. Is the transfer of a life insurance policy subject to a nonrecourse loan a transfer for value that could cause the loss of income tax exemption for death proceeds?

282. Can an existing life insurance policy be sold to the insured without loss of the income tax exemption for death proceeds?

283. Can an existing life insurance policy be transferred between two trusts, both of which were established by the insured, without loss of the income tax exemption for death proceeds?

284. If an employer or an employer's qualified plan sells or distributes a policy on an employee's life to an insured's spouse or to another member of an insured's family, will the transfer cause loss of the tax exemption for the death proceeds?

285. Will a policyholder's sale of life insurance policy to a corporation result in a loss of the tax exemption for the death proceeds?

286. If a corporation sells or distributes a life insurance policy to a stockholder who is not the insured, will the transfer cause a loss of the tax exemption for the death proceeds?

287. Does a transfer for value problem arise when an insurance-funded stock redemption plan is changed to a cross-purchase plan, or vice versa?

288. Will a transfer of a life insurance policy by one stockholder to another, or by a stockholder's estate to a surviving stockholder, cause loss of the tax exemption for the proceeds?

289. Is there a loss of the income tax exemption for death proceeds following a transfer of life insurance policies between partners or to a partnership in which the insured is a partner?

307. What are the income tax consequences of funding a stock redemption agreement with life insurance?

308. Will the accumulated earnings tax be imposed where corporate earnings are used to purchase business life insurance?

309. How is gain realized by an S corporation on sale, surrender, or redemption of a life insurance or endowment policy taxed?

310. If an S corporation redeems a shareholder's stock, how are redemption payments taxed?

311. What are the income tax consequences when a deceased partner's interest is liquidated under a business purchase agreement?

312. How is "goodwill" treated when a deceased partner's interest is liquidated under a business purchase agreement?

313. What are the income tax consequences when a deceased partner's interest is sold under a business purchase agreement?

314. What are the income tax results of a partnership income continuation plan?

315. What is the tax treatment of life insurance purchased to fund a partnership business purchase agreement?

316. How was corporate-owned life insurance treated for purposes of the corporate alternative minimum tax prior to 2018?

317. How was corporate-owned life insurance treated for purposes of the corporate alternative minimum tax prior to 2018 when policies have divided ownership?

Insurance on Key Persons, Partners, Stockholders

318. If a partnership purchases and owns life insurance on the life of a partner, are policy proceeds includable in the insured partner's estate?

319. If a corporation purchases life insurance on the life of a key person to indemnify it against loss on account of the key person's death, are proceeds includable in the insured's estate?

320. If partners or stockholders enter into a buy-sell agreement and each purchases life insurance on each other's lives to fund the agreement, are proceeds includable in an insured's gross estate?

321. If life insurance is owned by and payable to a partnership or corporation to fund purchase of an owner's business interest, are proceeds includable in the insured owner's estate?

322. How is a closely held business interest valued for federal estate tax purposes where there is a purchase agreement?

PART IV: HEALTH INSURANCE

Employer-Provided Health Insurance

COBRA Continuation Coverage Requirements

359. What are the tax implications of any premium reductions under the COBRA temporary premium assistance rules?

360. Are all employers subject to COBRA continuation coverage requirements?

361. What is a qualifying event for purposes of COBRA continuation coverage requirements?

362. Under what circumstances do employees serving in the military receive COBRA-like health insurance coverage continuation?

363. What is gross misconduct for the purposes of disqualifying an employee and the employee's beneficiaries from COBRA health insurance continuation requirements?

364. For how long must COBRA continuation coverage generally be provided?

365. What is the maximum required period of COBRA continuation coverage? Are there any exceptions to this required maximum period?

366. Who is a qualified beneficiary for purposes of COBRA continuation coverage requirements?

367. Who is a covered employee for purposes of the COBRA continuation coverage requirements? Who is a similarly situated non-COBRA beneficiary?

368. Who must pay the cost of COBRA continuation coverage and how is the cost calculated?

369. What is the Health Coverage Tax Credit?

370. How does an individual claim the additional 7.5 percent retroactive health coverage tax credit?

371. When must an election to receive COBRA continuation coverage be made?

372. What notice of COBRA continuation coverage is required?

373. Which entity is responsible for providing COBRA continuation coverage following a business reorganization?

374. What are the results for COBRA purposes if an employer stops making contributions to a multiemployer health plan?

375. What are the consequences of breaching COBRA continuation coverage requirements?

Disability Income Coverage

376. What are the tax consequences when a corporation buys disability insurance on a key person under which benefits are paid to the corporation?

377. Are premiums paid for business overhead expense disability insurance deductible as a business expense?

Health Savings Accounts

The Health Care Reform Law

441. What are the rules regarding reimbursement of non-prescription medicines?

442. What changes does the ACA mandate that affect health FSAs?

443. Can participation in a health FSA impact an individual's ability to contribute to an HSA?

444. Is an employer permitted to sponsor health FSAs if it does not otherwise offer health coverage to employees?

445. Under the ACA, can a health reimbursement arrangement (HRA) be integrated with health insurance coverage without violating the prohibition on annual dollar limits on benefits?

446. What new rules will apply in determining whether a health reimbursement arrangement (HRA) can be used to provide reimbursement for individual health insurance premiums without violating the prohibition on plans that place annual dollar limits on available benefits beginning in 2020?

447. What are the permissible classes of employees that employers can use to determine whether to offer individual coverage HRA benefits to a certain group?

448. How does the use of an individual coverage HRA impact the employee's ability to claim the premium tax credit?

449. How does the use of an individual coverage HRA impact the employer's potential liability under the ACA employer mandate?

450. Can an individual coverage HRA be used where a participant is covered under one type of health coverage and his dependents are covered under another (i.e., Medicare)?

451. What is the new "excepted benefit HRA" that employers may offer beginning in 2020?

452. What notice requirements apply with respect to individual coverage HRAs?

453. Under the ACA, can an employer reimburse an employee for the cost of individual health insurance coverage without violating the prohibition on plans that place annual dollar limits on available benefits?

454. What are the consequences if an employer reimburses its employees for the cost of individual health insurance premiums?

455. How does the ACA affect HSAs and Archer MSAs?

456. How does the ACA affect the use of debit cards to pay for medical care expenses?

457. What is the required W-2 reporting for health insurance expenses?

458. What is the new simple cafeteria plan that is available beginning in 2011?

459. What are the requirements for the new simple cafeteria plan?

PART V: LONG-TERM CARE INSURANCE

PART VI: ANNUITIES

In General

Amounts Not Received as an Annuity

518. What basic tax rules govern dividends, cash withdrawals, loans and partial surrender amounts received under annuity contracts before the annuity starting date?

519. What basic tax rules govern other amounts received under annuity contracts (that are not dividends, cash withdrawals, loans or partial surrenders) before the annuity starting date?

520. What is the effect of a tax-free exchange on the tax treatment of amounts received under annuity contracts before the annuity starting date?

521. Is an individual who transfers an annuity contract without adequate consideration treated as receiving amounts "as an annuity"?

522. Are multiple annuity contracts aggregated for purposes of determining the amount of a distribution that is includable in income?

523. What is a guaranteed lifetime withdrawal benefit rider?

524. What is a lifetime income benefit rider (LIBR)?

525. What penalties apply to premature distributions under annuity contracts?

526. What special rules apply to premature annuity payments that are exempt from the 10 percent penalty by reason of the "substantially equal periodic payment" (SEPP) rule if the SEPP is later modified?

527. Are dividends payable on an annuity contract taxable income?

528. What is the tax treatment of dividends where annuity values are paid in installments or as a life income?

Amounts Received as an Annuity

529. How are annuity payments taxed?

530. How are annuity payments taxed to a beneficiary if an annuitant under a life annuity payout with a refund feature dies and there is value remaining in the refund feature?

531. What are the tax consequences for a taxpayer who wishes to annuitize only a portion of an annuity contract?

532. What is a market value adjusted annuity?

533. How can the investment in the contract be determined for purposes of the annuity rules?

534. Does the presence of a long-term care rider to an annuity contract impact the calculation of investment in the contract for purposes of the annuity rules?

Amounts Received as an Annuity

552. How are payments under a variable immediate annuity taxed?

553. How is the value of a refund or period-certain guarantee determined under a variable annuity contract?

554. If payments from an immediate variable annuity drop below the excludable amount for any year, is the balance of the exclusion lost?

555. What is a wraparound or investment annuity? How is the owner taxed prior to the annuity starting date?

556. What is a private placement variable annuity (PPVA)?

557. What is the difference between a longevity annuity and a deferred annuity?

558. What is a qualified longevity annuity contract (QLAC)? What steps has the IRS taken to encourage the purchase of QLACs?

559. What types of retirement accounts can hold a qualified longevity annuity contract (QLAC)?

560. Can a taxpayer purchase both QLACs and non-QLAC DIAs within an IRA and remain eligible to exclude the QLAC value when calculating RMDs? How is the non-QLAC DIA treated in such a case?

561. May an individual purchase a QLAC after the required beginning date (RBD)?

562. Are the death benefits under a deferred annuity triggered upon the death of the owner of the annuity, or upon the death of the annuitant?

563. What are the rules that allow 401(k) plan sponsors to include deferred annuities in target date funds (TDFs)?

564. Can a taxpayer combine a deferred income annuity ("longevity annuity") with a traditional deferred annuity product?

565. Can a grantor trust own a deferred annuity contract? How is a deferred annuity owned by a grantor trust taxed?

566. If a grantor trust owns a deferred annuity and the grantor is not the annuitant, whose death triggers the annuity payout?

567. Does the surrender of a deferred annuity contract ever result in a deductible loss?

568. Is a deductible loss sustained under a straight life annuity if the annuitant dies before payments received by the annuitant equal the annuitant's cost?

Disposition of an Annuity Contract

569. What are the income tax consequences to the owner of an annuity contract if the owner sells the contract?

570. How is the purchaser of an existing immediate annuity contract taxed?

571. When is a policy owner deemed to have exchanged one annuity contract for another?

572. What is the tax treatment of a partial 1035 exchange of an annuity contract?

573. When is the exchange of one annuity contract for another a nontaxable exchange?

574. Is the exchange of one annuity contract for another permissible if the owner-beneficiary inherited the annuity from a deceased original owner?

575. Are there special rules for exchanging one annuity contract for another where the insurer issuing the contract is under rehabilitation?

576. When is a policy owner required to recognize gain on the exchange of one annuity contract for another?

577. When is the exchange of one annuity contract for another a taxable transaction?

578. What is the tax treatment for an annuity with a long-term care rider?

579. What constitutes a gift of an annuity contract? What constitutes a gift of a premium?

580. Can the owner of an annuity contract avoid income and penalty taxes by assigning the right to receive the payments to another individual while retaining ownership of the contract?

581. What are the income tax consequences when a deferred annuity contract is transferred as a gift?

582. What are the income tax consequences when a deferred annuity is transferred to a trust?

583. Does the purchase of a joint and survivor annuity result in a taxable gift?

584. Is the naming of an irrevocable beneficiary under a refund annuity a gift?

585. When does the gift of an annuity between spouses qualify for the gift tax marital deduction?

586. What is the gift tax value of an annuity contract or of a donee's interest in a joint and survivor annuity?

587. Can the purchase of a private annuity result in a taxable gift?

588. What are the income tax consequences when the owner of an annuity contract takes the lifetime maturity proceeds or cash surrender value in a lump sum cash payment?

589. If a policyholder elects to receive endowment maturity death benefit proceeds, or cash surrender values under a life income or installment option, is the gain on the policy taxable to the policyholder in the year of maturity/death/surrender or as payments are received?

590. Is the full gain on a deferred annuity or retirement income contract taxable in the year the contract matures?

591. Are there any considerations that a taxpayer should be made aware of when deciding whether to surrender an annuity or accept a buyback offer?

592. If an annuitant dies before a deferred annuity matures or is annuitized, is the amount payable at the annuitant's death subject to income tax?

593. How long does the beneficiary of an annuity have in which to elect to take death proceeds as an annuity, rather than as a lump sum, and thus avoid being in constructive receipt of all contract gain?

594. What distributions are required when the owner of an annuity contract dies before the entire interest in the contract has been distributed?

595. Are there any exceptions to the rule that the entire interest in an inherited deferred annuity contract must be distributed within five years of the original owner's death?

596. What does the term "designated beneficiary" mean in the context of an inherited deferred annuity? Can the designated beneficiary be a trust?

597. If an individual purchases an annuity contract to meet alimony payments, how are payments taxed to the recipient? What are the tax results to the purchaser?

598. May a charitable contribution deduction be taken for the gift of a maturing annuity or endowment contract?

599. Is there a taxable gift when an individual covered under a qualified plan, a tax sheltered annuity, or an individual retirement plan irrevocably designates a beneficiary to receive a survivor benefit payable under the plan?

600. Is there a taxable gift when a nonparticipant spouse waives the right to receive a qualified joint and survivor annuity or a qualified preretirement survivor annuity?

601. What are the gift tax consequences to the spouse of an individual who designates a third party beneficiary to receive a survivor benefit payable under a qualified plan, a tax sheltered annuity, or an individual retirement plan if community property law applies?

602. If a person who is covered under an individual retirement plan contributes to a similar plan covering his or her non-employed spouse, are such contributions considered gifts?

603. Are amounts received under commercial annuity contracts subject to withholding?

Private Annuity

604. What is a private annuity?

605. How are payments received under a private annuity issued after October 18, 2006 taxed?

606. How are payments taxed that are received under a private annuity issued before October 19, 2006?

607. What are the tax consequences to the obligor in a private annuity transaction?

Charitable Gift Annuity

608. What is a charitable gift annuity?

609. How are payments received under a charitable gift annuity agreement taxed?

610. What are the tax consequences to the obligor in a charitable annuity transaction?

611. How is a corporation taxed on payments under an annuity contract or on living proceeds from an endowment or life insurance contract?

612. How are damage payments taxed if an annuity is used to fund a judgment or settle a claim for damages on account of personal injuries or sickness?

613. If a qualified plan trust distributes an annuity contract to an employee, is the value of the contract taxable to the employee in the year of distribution?

614. How is an employee taxed on periodic retirement benefits under a qualified pension, annuity, or profit sharing plan if the annuity starting date is after December 31, 1997?

615. How is an employee taxed on periodic retirement benefits under a qualified pension, annuity, or profit sharing plan if the annuity starting date is after November 18, 1996 and before January 1, 1998?

616. How is an employee taxed on periodic retirement benefits under a qualified pension, annuity, or profit sharing plan if the annuity starting date is after July 1, 1986 and before November 19, 1996?

617. How is an employee taxed on periodic retirement benefits under a qualified pension, annuity, or profit sharing plan if the annuity starting date is on or before July 1, 1986?

618. What is the simplified safe harbor method that can be used to determine the tax treatment of periodic retirement benefits under an annuity with a starting date before November 19, 1996?

619. How are variable annuity benefits taxed to an employee that are payable under a qualified pension or profit sharing plan?

620. Does the interest of a donee spouse in a joint and survivor annuity qualify for the marital deduction?

Annuities and the Estate

621. What are the estate tax results when a decedent has been receiving payments under an annuity contract?

622. How can an annuity be used by an individual as an estate planning tool?

623. What are the estate tax results when a decedent has been receiving payments under an optional settlement of endowment maturity proceeds or life insurance cash surrender value?

624. If an individual purchases a deferred or retirement annuity and dies before the contract matures, is the death value of the contract includable in his or her estate?

625. In the case of a joint and survivor annuity, what value is includable in the gross estate of the annuitant who dies first?

626. What is the estate tax value of a survivor's annuity under a joint and survivor annuity contract?

627. In the case of a refund or period-certain annuity, is the balance of the guaranteed amount, payable after annuitant's death, includable in the annuitant's gross estate?

628. Are death proceeds payable under a single premium annuity and life insurance combination includable in an annuitant's gross estate?

629. If a decedent purchased an annuity on the life of another person, will the value of the contract be includable in his or her gross estate?

630. If a person makes a gift of an immediate annuity, will the value of any refund be includable in the donee-annuitant's estate?

631. If a decedent has been receiving payments under a private annuity, what is includable in the decedent's estate?

632. What is a Medicaid compliant annuity? How can Medicaid compliant annuities be used in an individual's planning?

633. Is the value of a death benefit payable under a nonqualified employee annuity includable in an employee's gross estate?

634. Is a death or survivor benefit under a tax sheltered annuity includable in an employee's gross estate if the decedent died after 1984?

635. Is a death or survivor benefit under a tax sheltered annuity includable in an employee's gross estate if the decedent died after 1953 and before 1985?

636. What is a secondary market annuity?

Structured Settlements

637. What is a structured settlement?

638. Why might the parties to a judgment prefer to use a structured settlement rather than a lump sum payment?

PART VII: FEDERAL INCOME TAXATION

General Rules

Gross Income

701. How is a loss realized on a sale between related persons treated for income tax purposes?

702. How is an individual taxed on capital gains and losses?

703. What is the "netting" process used to determine whether a taxpayer has a capital loss for the year? Can capital losses be carried into other tax years?

704. How have the capital gain rates for individuals changed between 2003 and the present?

705. What lower rates apply for qualified dividend income?

706. What is qualified dividend income?

707. What are the reporting requirements under JGTRRA 2003?

708. How are gains and losses treated for "traders in securities"?

709. How are gains and losses calculated for "traders in securities" when securities are sold subject to nonrecourse liabilities and the mark-to-market rules apply?

710. What is a "like-kind" exchange? How is it taxed?

711. How is the tax treatment of a like-kind exchange altered if, in addition to like-kind property, the taxpayer also receives cash or nonlike-kind property in the exchange?

712. How is the tax treatment of a like-kind exchange altered if one or more parties assumes a liability of the other party or receives property subject to a liability in the exchange?

713. What is the tax basis of property received in a tax-free (or partially tax-free) like-kind exchange?

714. How is a like-kind exchange between related parties taxed?

Adjusted Gross Income

715. How is adjusted gross income determined?

716. What is the deduction for depreciation?

717. How is depreciation on property placed in service after 1986 calculated?

718. How do the bonus depreciation rules apply to used property under the 2017 Tax Act?

719. Are there any situations where a taxpayer can now claim bonus depreciation with respect to used property in which the taxpayer previously held an interest? How do the bonus depreciation rules apply to leased property?

720. Is bonus depreciation available in situations involving a partnership buyout?

721. What is the alternative depreciation system that may be used to calculate depreciation on property placed in service after 1986?

Deductions

Standard Deduction

Credits

763. What is the residential energy efficient property credit that may be taken against the tax?

764. What is the alternative motor vehicle credit that may be taken against the tax?

765. What tax credits are available for plug-in electric vehicles?

766. What is the new tax credit for employers that provide paid family and medical leave to employees?

Alternative Minimum Tax

767. How is the alternative minimum tax calculated?

768. What is Alternative Minimum Taxable Income (AMTI) for purposes of calculating the alternative minimum tax?

769. What is the alternative minimum tax exemption?

770. What adjustments are made to taxable income in computing alternative minimum taxable income (AMTI)?

771. What items of tax preference must be added to alternative minimum taxable income (AMTI)?

772. What credit against regular tax liability is allowed for a taxpayer who is subject to the alternative minimum tax in subsequent years?

Social Security Taxes

773. What are the Social Security tax rates?

774. Who must pay the self-employment tax?

Community Property

775. How can community property law affect the federal income tax treatment of investment income?

776. How is community income reported if spouses live apart?

777. How does community property law affect the federal income tax treatment of dividends received from corporate stock?

778. If spouses move from a community property state to a common law state, will their community property rights in the property they take with them be recognized and protected by the law of their new domicile?

Divorce

779. Do transfers of property between spouses, or between former spouses incident to a divorce, result in taxable gains and losses?

780. What are the tax results of corporate stock redemptions where a spouse or former spouse is treated as receiving or constructively receiving the proceeds, or where the redemption is incident to divorce?

781. Are alimony payments included in the gross income of the recipient? May the payor spouse take a deduction for these payments?

782. What is alimony? What types of payments between former spouses do not qualify as alimony payments?

783. What are the recapture rules that apply with respect to alimony payments made during the first three years of divorce?

784. Is child support taxed in the same manner as alimony payments?

Trusts and Estates

785. How is the federal income tax computed for trusts and estates?

786. Are trusts and estates required to pay estimated tax?

787. What is a grantor trust? How is a grantor trust taxed?

Corporations and Other Business Entities

788. How is a corporation taxed?

789. How is a corporation taxed on capital gains?

790. How was a corporation's alternative minimum tax calculated prior to repeal by the 2017 Tax Act?

791. How was the alternative minimum tax calculated for certain small corporations prior to repeal by the 2017 Tax Act?

792. What is the accumulated earnings tax?

793. What is the personal holding company tax?

794. How are corporations that are classified as professional corporations and associations taxed?

795. What is an S corporation? How is an S corporation taxed?

796. How are S corporations taxed under the 2017 tax reform legislation?

797. How is an S corporation's deduction for qualified business income determined?

798. What is a QSSS? Can an S corporation own a QSSS?

799. Under what circumstances may an S corporation be taxed at the corporate level?

Choice of Entity

PART VIII: FEDERAL ESTATE TAX, GIFT TAX, GENERATION-SKIPPING TRANSFER TAX, AND VALUATION

Estate Tax

817. When are gifts made within three years of death includable in a decedent's gross estate under IRC Section 2035?

818. When are gifts with a life interest retained by the donor includable in the donor's gross estate under IRC Section 2036?

819. When are gifts taking effect at death includable in a decedent's gross estate under IRC Section 2037?

820. When are gifts includable in the decedent's gross estate under IRC Section 2038 where a decedent retains a power to revoke or amend?

821. When are annuities or annuity payments includable in a decedent's gross estate under IRC Section 2039?

822. Are joint interests includable in a decedent's gross estate under IRC Section 2040?

823. What is a qualified joint interest? When is a qualified joint interest included in a decedent's gross estate?

824. When are powers of appointment includable in a decedent's gross estate under IRC Section 2041?

825. What is a general power of appointment?

826. What non-cumulative annual withdrawal rights may the grantor give beneficiaries without subjecting the power to estate and gift taxes?

827. When are life insurance proceeds includable in a decedent's gross estate under IRC Section 2042?

828. Are transfers made for insufficient consideration includable in a decedent's gross estate under IRC Section 2043?

829. When is marital deduction property in which a decedent had an income interest includable in the gross estate under IRC Section 2044?

830. When are disclaimers includable in a decedent's gross estate under IRC Section 2046?

831. What additional amounts may be includable in a decedent's gross estate?

832. In whose estate is property held in custodianship under the Uniform Gifts to Minors Act or the Uniform Transfers to Minors Act includable for federal estate tax purposes?

833. Is an education savings account includable in an individual's gross estate?

834. Is a qualified tuition program includable in an individual's gross estate?

835. Is the value of a life insurance agent's renewal commissions includable in the gross estate?

836. What estate tax exclusion is available for a qualified conservation easement?

837. What deductions are allowed from the gross estate in arriving at the taxable estate for federal estate tax purposes?

838. What deductions for expenses, indebtedness and taxes are allowed from the gross estate in arriving at the taxable estate for federal estate tax purposes?

839. If an estate sells a large block of stock through an underwriter, are the underwriting fees deductible from the gross estate?

840. What deductions for casualty and theft losses may be taken from the gross estate?

841. What deductions for charitable bequests are allowed from the gross estate in arriving at the taxable estate for federal estate tax purposes?

842. Can a trust that does not otherwise qualify for the estate tax charitable deduction be reformed in order to qualify?

843. What is the estate tax marital deduction?

844. What is qualified terminable interest property (QTIP)?

845. Can a QTIP election be voided after it is made if it is unnecessary for transfer tax purposes?

846. When will a terminable interest in property cause that property to fail to qualify for the estate tax marital deduction?

847. When will property held in trust qualify for the marital deduction?

848. How is the availability of the estate tax marital deduction affected when the surviving spouse is not a United States citizen? What is a QDOT?

849. What estate tax deduction was available for qualified family-owned business interests before 2005?

850. What estate tax deduction is allowed for death taxes paid at the state level?

851. What credits are allowed against the federal estate tax?

852. What is the Section 2010 "unified credit" that is allowed against the federal estate tax?

853. What is the Section 2011 credit for state death taxes which can be taken against the federal estate tax?

854. What is the Section 2012 credit for gift tax that can be taken against the federal estate tax?

855. What is the Section 2013 credit for estate tax on prior transfers that can be taken against the federal estate tax?

856. What is the Section 2014 foreign death tax credit that can be taken against the federal estate tax?

857. What are the requirements for filing a federal estate tax return and paying the tax?

858. What are the minimum return requirements for determining whether an estate tax return must be filed?

859. Can the time for paying the estate tax be extended?

860. Can the time for paying the estate tax be extended if the estate includes a closely held business interest?

861. What is an interest in a closely held business for purposes of the IRC Section 6166 estate tax deferral?

862. Are there any circumstances that would cause the termination of the estate tax deferral for estates including a closely held business interest?

863. Can the time for paying the estate tax be extended if the estate includes a reversionary or remainder interest?

Generation-Skipping Transfer Tax

864. What is the federal generation-skipping transfer tax?

865. What is a generation-skipping transfer (GST) on which a generation-skipping transfer tax is imposed?

866. How is the amount of tax on a GST determined?

867. What is the GST exemption and how is it applied in determining the GST tax?

868. What is a GST trust?

869. What is the inclusion ratio and how is it used for purposes of the GST tax?

870. How is property valued for purposes of the GST tax?

871. Are charitable lead annuity trusts treated differently than other types of trusts for GST tax purposes?

872. What is the estate tax inclusion period (ETIP) for GST tax purposes?

873. When are portions of a severed trust treated as separate trusts for GST tax purposes?

874. How is the GST tax applied to nontaxable gifts?

875. What is a reverse QTIP election and how is it made for GST tax purposes?

Gift Tax

897. When will a gift of a donor's interest in real estate qualify for the gift tax annual exclusion?

898. When will a gift of property to a minor qualify for the gift tax annual exclusion?

899. When will a gift of property to a corporation qualify for the gift tax annual exclusion?

900. How does the splitting of gifts between spouses affect the gift tax annual exclusion?

901. What gift tax exclusion applies, if any, for gifts made for education or medical expenses?

902. What is the gift tax marital deduction?

903. Is a gift tax deduction allowed for gifts to charity?

904. What is the gift tax unified credit?

905. What are the requirements for filing the gift tax return and paying the tax?

Valuation

906. How is investment property valued for federal transfer tax purposes?

907. How does the executor's election of the alternate valuation method affect the valuation of property for federal estate tax purposes?

908. What property is "included property" for purposes of the alternative valuation method for determining federal estate tax? What property is excluded?

909. How are stocks and bonds listed on an exchange or in an over-the-counter market valued for federal transfer tax purposes?

910. What effect does it have on valuation of shares of stock for federal transfer tax purposes if they are pledged as security?

911. How are notes, mortgages, and mortgage participation certificates valued for federal transfer tax purposes?

912. How are life estates, remainders, and private annuities valued for federal transfer tax purposes?

913. How are Series E/EE and H/HH United States Savings Bonds valued for federal transfer tax purposes?

914. How is a non-negotiable savings certificate issued without discount by a Federal Reserve member bank valued for federal estate tax purposes when death occurs between interest periods?

915. How are mutual fund shares valued for federal transfer tax purposes?

916. How are United States silver coins valued for federal estate tax purposes?

917. How are interests in a closely-held business valued for federal transfer tax purposes?

936. How did the 2017 tax reform legislation impact the viability of the family limited partnership (FLP) as an estate planning strategy?

937. How did the 2017 tax reform legislation impact the advisability of using trust structures such as spousal lifetime access trusts (SLATs) in estate planning strategies?

938. What do taxpayers need to be aware of with respect to the impact of the 2017 tax reform legislation on using portability in their estate planning?

939. Is it still advisable for taxpayers to attempt to leverage potential valuation discounts post-tax reform?

940. Did tax reform make any changes that impact inherited IRAs? What should taxpayers consider when designating a beneficiary to inherit an IRA post-reform

PART IX: INTERNATIONAL TAX

941. What is the difference between a resident alien and a nonresident alien?

942. When does a foreign individual become a U.S. taxpayer who is required to file a U.S. tax return?

943. What rules apply when a U.S. citizen or resident alien is married to a nonresident alien and the couple wishes to file a joint U.S. tax return?

944. When a U.S. citizen is a resident of a foreign country and earns income in that foreign country, is that income included in the taxpayer's gross income for U.S. tax purposes?

945. What is the foreign earned income exclusion?

946. What are the bona fide residence and physical presence tests that can allow a U.S. individual to qualify for the foreign earned income exclusion?

947. What is the foreign housing exclusion (or deduction)?

948. Can U.S. individuals employed in a foreign country receive U.S. Social Security credit?

949. What are some of the considerations that a U.S. citizen or resident should be aware of when participating in a retirement plan while residing in a foreign country?

950. Are employer contributions to a foreign retirement account on behalf of a U.S. individual exempt from U.S. reporting requirements?

951. What assets of a foreign individual (nonresident alien) are subject to U.S. estate tax?

952. How does the estate of a foreign individual (nonresident alien) calculate the amount of U.S. estate tax owed?

953. Is the estate of a foreign individual entitled to the same deductions as a U.S. individual?

954. May a nonresident alien's estate claim an estate tax exemption upon the death of the nonresident alien?

955. Can a life insurance policy or annuity contract issued to a U.S. person by a foreign life insurance company qualify for the tax benefits traditionally afforded to U.S. life insurance policies?

956. What considerations should a U.S. citizen or resident alien be aware of when disposing of real property that is located in a foreign country?

U.S. Individuals and Taxation in Mexico

957. Can U.S. individuals purchase land in Mexico for investment purposes?

958. What is a restricted zone purchase for purposes of real property transactions taking place in Mexico?

959. What are the tax and reporting obligations of U.S. purchasers of real property in Mexico?

960. How should Mexican clients seeking to open investment accounts in the U.S. structure their investment holdings in a tax efficient manner?

U.S. Individuals and Taxation in Canada

961. Why is residency significant in Canadian taxation, and how is Canadian residency determined for tax purposes?

962. When is an individual considered a "resident" of Canada for tax purposes?

963. What is a part-year resident of Canada for tax purposes?

964. When is an individual considered to be a non-resident of Canada for tax purposes?

965. When does a U.S. individual establish permanent residency in Canada?

966. What are the general filing requirements for U.S. citizens living in Canada on a full-time basis?

967. Can U.S. citizens living in Canada be subject to double taxation?

968. Are U.S. citizens that receive income from property situated in Canada, such as dividends or interest, subject to tax in Canada, and if so, are there withholding requirements?

969. Are U.S. citizens employed or carrying on business in Canada subject to tax in Canada, and if so, are there withholding requirements?

970. What is FATCA, and does a U.S. citizen living in Canada need to be concerned with it?

971. What is FBAR, and does a U.S. citizen living in Canada need to be concerned with FBAR requirements?

972. What is the effect of a disposition of Canadian real property in respect of a U.S. citizen that is a Canadian resident for tax purposes?

973. What is the effect of a disposition of Canadian real property in respect of a U.S. individual that is not a Canadian resident for tax purposes?

974. Does Canada have estate taxes?

975. Does a Canadian citizen need to be concerned if the Canadian citizen's spouse is a U.S. citizen?

976. What considerations apply to U.S. citizens who participate in Canadian retirement plans (such as RRSPs) while residing in Canada?

977. Is renouncing U.S. citizenship a viable option to citizens permanently living in Canada?

978. Does a U.S. citizen living in Canada need to be concerned with the net investment income tax (NIIT), or "Medicare Tax," and if so, is there tax relief available?

PART I: LIFE INSURANCE

In General

1. What is life insurance?

Life insurance is a contract under which, in exchange for premium payments, an insurance company agrees to pay a death benefit if the person whose life is insured dies while the contract is in force. There are two general categories of life insurance: term coverage and permanent coverage. Term coverage is for a specific period of time, which can last for as little as one year or possibly as long as thirty years. Permanent insurance is intended to cover an insured for the rest of the insured's life. Permanent life insurance can be financed with a single premium, a fixed number of premiums over several years, or premiums paid over the remainder of the insured's life.

2. Are premiums paid on personal life insurance deductible for income tax purposes?

No. Premiums paid on personal life insurance are a personal expense and are not deductible.[1] Internal Revenue Service (IRS) regulations specifically provide that "[p]premiums paid for life insurance by the insured are not deductible."[2] It is immaterial whether the premiums are paid by the insured or by some other person. For example, premiums paid by an individual for insurance on the life of his or her spouse are nondeductible personal expenses of the individual. Premiums are not deductible regardless of whether the insurance is government life insurance or regular commercial life insurance.[3] Although personal life insurance premiums, as such, are not deductible, they may be deductible as the payment of alimony (prior to 2018, see Q 109), as charitable contributions (Q 120 to Q 127), or as ordinary and necessary business expenses (Q 269).

3. Can a taxpayer deduct interest paid on a loan to purchase or carry a life insurance, endowment, or annuity contract?

Single Premium Contract

Interest paid or accrued on indebtedness incurred to purchase or continue in effect a single premium life insurance, endowment, or annuity contract purchased after March 1, 1954, is not deductible.[4] For this purpose, a single premium contract is defined as one on which substantially all the premiums are paid within four years from the date of purchase, or on which an amount is deposited with the insurer for payment of a substantial number of future premiums.[5] One court has held that payment in the first four years of 73 percent of total annual premiums for a limited-pay policy did not constitute payment of "substantially all" of the premiums.[6] Another

1. IRC Secs. 262(a) and 264.
2. Treas. Reg. §1.262-1(b)(1).
3. *Kutz v. Comm.*, 5 BTA 239 (1926).
4. IRC Sec. 264(a)(2).
5. IRC Sec. 264(c).
6. *Dudderar v. Comm.*, 44 TC 632 (1965), acq. 1966-2 CB 4.

court has ruled that payment of eight annual premiums in the first four years on a whole life policy was neither "substantially all" nor a "substantial number" of the premiums.[1]

When a single premium annuity is used as collateral to either obtain or continue a mortgage, the IRS has found that IRC Section 264(a)(2) disallows the allocable amount of mortgage interest to the extent that the mortgage is collateralized by the annuity. However, this result does not hold when a taxpayer's use of available cash to purchase an annuity results in a larger home mortgage or when a taxpayer does not surrender an annuity even though cash obtained from the surrender would make it possible to reduce the amount of the mortgage.[2] A general counsel memorandum has concluded that borrowing against the cash value of a single premium life insurance policy is equivalent to using the policy as collateral.[3]

In restating the rule concerning single premium contracts, the conference committee report accompanying the Tax Reform Act of 1986 (TRA '86) states that "no inference is intended that universal life insurance policies are always treated as single premium contracts."[4] It is still unclear whether the four exceptions applicable to contracts other than single premium contracts, discussed in Q 4, can be used in the case of universal life contracts.

Other than Single Premium Contract

A deduction is denied under IRC Section 264(a)(3) for interest on indebtedness incurred or continued to purchase or carry a life insurance, endowment, or annuity contract, that is not a single premium contract, if it is purchased pursuant to a plan of purchase that contemplates the systematic direct or indirect borrowing of part or all of the increases in the cash value of such contract (either from the insurer or otherwise).

4. Are there any exceptions to the rule that disallows a deduction for interest paid on a loan to purchase or carry a life insurance, endowment or annuity contract?

There are four exceptions to this disallowance rule.[5] However, with respect to interest paid or accrued on policies or contracts covering an individual who is a "key person," the deduction may be limited as explained in Q 30, or denied entirely, even if one of the four exceptions to this disallowance rule is met.

The four exceptions are:

(1) *The seven-year exception*. The deduction will not be disallowed under this rule when no part of four of the annual premiums due during the seven-year period, beginning with the date of payment for the first premium on the contract, is paid by means of indebtedness. If there is a substantial increase in the premiums, a new

1. *Campbell v. Cen-Tex, Inc.*, 377 F. 2d 688 (5th Cir. 1967).
2. Rev. Rul. 95-53, 1995-2 CB 30 (clarifying and superseding Rev. Rul. 79-41, 1979-1 C.B. 124).
3. GCM 39534 (7-17-86).
4. H.R. Conf. Rep. No. 99-841 (TRA '86) *reprinted in* 1986-3 CB 341. See also General Explanation of the Tax Reform Act of 1986 at pp. 579, 580.
5. IRC Sec. 264(d).

seven-year period for the contract commences on the date the first increased premium is paid. However, a new seven-year period does not begin upon transfer of the policy, whether for value or by gift.[1] A new seven-year period does not commence if modification of a life insurance policy after December 31, 1990, becomes necessary because of the insurer's financial insolvency.[2] The addition to a policy of a provision that interest on policy loans is payable in arrears rather than in advance will not cause a new seven-year period to begin.[3] A systematic plan of purchase will be presumed when there is borrowing in connection with more than three of the annual premiums due during the seven-year period, but will not be presumed earlier.[4]

Once a taxpayer has used borrowed funds to pay four of the first seven annual premiums, the taxpayer cannot undo the effect of this action by repaying the policy loan.[5] If in any year during the seven-year period, the taxpayer, in connection with any premium, borrows more than an amount necessary to pay one annual premium, the excess will be treated as though he or she borrowed to pay premiums that were paid in prior years with non-borrowed funds (beginning with the first prior year and working backwards).[6]

Example. Taxpayer, in Year 1, purchased a $100,000 policy and the annual premium was $2,200. The taxpayer paid the first four premiums without borrowing. In Year 5, the taxpayer borrowed $10,000 with respect to the policy. The borrowing will be attributed first to paying the premium for Year 5 and then attributable to paying the premium for Years 4, 3, 2, and 1 (in part).

If borrowing in connection with any premium in any year exceeds the premium for that year *plus* premiums paid in prior years without borrowing, the excess will be attributed to premiums (if any) paid in advance for future years. However, once the seven-year exception has been satisfied, and the seven-year period has expired, there would appear to be no limit under this exception to the amount that might be borrowed (from the policy or otherwise) to pay premiums on the policy. (But if a substantial number of premiums are *prepaid*, the policy might be considered a single-premium policy – see Q 3.)

Thus, three of the first seven annual premiums may be borrowed, and the interest deduction would not be disallowed by reason of this rule, provided the balance of premiums during the seven-year period is paid with non-borrowed funds. But if the seven-year exception is not met, and the taxpayer cannot rebut the presumption of a systematic plan of borrowing, the interest deduction will be disallowed under this rule for all future years and for all prior years not closed by the statute of limitations. This assumes, of course, that none of the other exceptions to this rule applies.[7]

(2) *$100-a-year exception*. Regardless of whether there is a systematic plan of borrowing, the interest deduction will not be disallowed under this rule for any taxable year in which the interest (in connection with such plans) does not exceed $100.

1. Rev. Rul. 71-309, 1971-2 CB 168.
2. Rev. Proc. 92-57, 1992-2 CB 410; Let. Rul. 9239026.
3. Let. Rul. 9737007.
4. Treas. Reg. §1.264-4(c).
5. Rev. Rul. 72-609, 1972-2 CB 199.
6. See Treas. Reg. §1.264-4(c)(ii).
7. Treas. Reg. §1.264-4(d)(1).

But when such interest exceeds $100, the entire amount of interest (not just the amount in excess of $100) is nondeductible under IRC Section 264(a)(3).[1]

(3) *Unforeseen event exception.* If indebtedness is incurred because of an unforeseen substantial loss of income or unforeseen substantial increase in the taxpayer's financial obligations, the deduction will not be disallowed under this rule even though the loan is used to pay premiums on the contract. An event is not "unforeseen," however, if at the time the contract was purchased it could have been foreseen.[2]

(4) *Trade or business exception.* If indebtedness is incurred in connection with the taxpayer's trade or business, the interest deduction will not be denied under IRC Section 264(a)(3) (but see Q 732 to Q 735 for a discussion of the limits that apply in deducting trade or business interest after 2017). Thus, if an insurance policy is pledged as part of the collateral for a loan, the interest deductions will come within this exception if the taxpayer can show that the amounts borrowed actually were used to finance the expansion of inventory or other similar business needs.[3] The IRS has ruled privately that a company that borrowed against key-person life insurance policies to take advantage of the policies' lower interest rate and generally to improve its financial position by reducing its overall debt was considered to have incurred the policy loan interest in connection with its trade or business.[4] But borrowing to finance business life insurance (such as key person, split dollar, or stock purchase plans) is not considered to be incurred in connection with the borrower's trade or business.[5] Systematic borrowing to finance a life insurance policy is not debt incurred in connection with an employer's trade or business even when the net death proceeds and the amounts borrowed in excess of premiums are used to fund employee retirement benefits.[6]

The interest deduction will not be disallowed under IRC Section 264(a)(3) if any one of these exceptions applies. For example, even though the purchase of business life insurance does not come within the trade or business exception, the interest deduction may be allowed if the borrowing comes within the four-out-of-seven exception, provided no other IRC section operates to disallow or limit the interest deduction (Q 30).

5. How is a systematic plan of borrowing to buy life insurance treated?

In one revenue ruling, the IRS found systematic borrowing in a plan that contemplated purchase of mutual fund shares and a policy of whole life insurance, together with the insured's use of the shares as security for notes executed each year in the amount of the cumulative premium and accrued interest.[7] When there is a systematic plan of borrowing, the borrowing

1. Treas. Reg. §1.264-4(d)(2).
2. Treas. Reg. §1.264-4(d)(3).
3. See Treas. Reg. §1.264-4(d)(4).
4. Let. Rul. 9138049.
5. *American Body & Equipment Co. v. U.S.*, 511 F.2d 647 (5th Cir. 1975).
6. Rev. Rul. 81-255, 1981-2 CB 79.
7. Rev. Rul. 74-500, 1974-2 CB 91.

will be treated as a plan for borrowing the increases in cash value of the policy, regardless of whether the borrowing is direct or indirect (that is, regardless of whether the borrowing is from the insurer, a bank, or some other person). Moreover, such a plan need not involve a pledge of the contract, but may contemplate unsecured borrowing or the use of other property.[1] When there is a systematic plan, and none of the exceptions applies, a deduction will be disallowed for interest on the entire amount borrowed, not just for interest on the borrowing equal to the increases in the cash value.[2]

Historically, the general disallowance rule applies only with respect to life insurance contracts purchased after August 6, 1963. However, IRS regulations state that this date relates to the date of purchase by the taxpayer, whether the purchase is from the insurer or from a previous policyowner. When a policy issued in 1959 was to be exchanged, the purchase date of the new policy was considered the date upon which the exchange was made, with the taxpayer losing the benefit of a policy issued prior to August 6, 1963.[3]

6. Can the rules that disallow a deduction for interest paid on a loan to purchase or carry a life insurance, endowment or annuity contract be avoided by having one spouse use funds borrowed by the other spouse?

These disallowance rules cannot be avoided by having one spouse use funds borrowed by the other. When a husband borrowed money and transferred it to his wife, who used it to buy tax-exempt securities, the interest deduction was denied on the basis that the transfer of the borrowed funds was without economic substance because the purpose of the husband's borrowing was to enable the wife to buy tax-exempt securities.[4]

7. Is the interest increment earned on prepaid life insurance premiums taxable income?

Yes. Any increment in the value of prepaid life insurance or annuity premiums or premium deposit funds constitutes taxable income in the year it is applied to the payment of a premium or is made available for withdrawal, whichever occurs first.[5] The interest treated as taxable income, however, will be included in the cost basis of the contract. Thus, for purposes of IRC Section 72, the cost of the contract would be the amount of premiums paid other than by discount, plus the amount of discounted funds and any increments on such funds that were subject to income taxation. The rule taxing interest increments has no applicability, however, to single premium policies. A later ruling explains in detail how the interest will be taxed.[6]

1. Treas. Reg. §1.264-4(c)(2).
2. Treas. Reg. §1.264-4(b).
3. GCM 39728 (4-29-88). However, see also PLR 200804010 (acquisition as part of merger not a purchase for purposes of IRC Section 264(a)(3)).
4. Rev. Rul. 79-272, 1979-2 CB 124 (citing *Drybrough v. Comm.*, 42 TC 1029 (1964)).
5. Rev. Rul. 65-199, 1965-2 CB 20.
6. Rev. Rul. 66-120, 1966-1 CB 14.

8. Are annual increases in the cash surrender value of a life insurance policy taxable income to the policyholder?

The Internal Revenue Code does not explicitly provide for the tax treatment of increases in the cash surrender value of a life insurance policy unless those values are accessed, directly or indirectly. In a case involving a cash basis taxpayer, the Tax Court held that the cash values were not constructively received by the taxpayer where the taxpayer could not reach them without surrendering the policy. The necessity of surrendering the policy constituted a substantial "limitation or restriction" on their receipt.[1] Likewise, the Tax Court has held that the cash surrender values of paid-up additions are not constructively received by the policyholder.[2] Similarly, it would appear that the same "limitation or restriction" would prevent accrual for an accrual basis taxpayer, because income does not accrue until "all the events have occurred" that fix the right to receive the income.[3] The same rule applies whether the policy is a single premium policy or a periodic premium policy.

Tax on the "inside buildup" of cash surrender values generally is not deferred in the case of contracts issued after December 31, 1984 that do not meet the statutory definition of a "life insurance contract" (Q 65).[4] In such cases, the *excess* of the sum of (1) the increase in net surrender value (cash surrender value less any surrender charges) during the taxable year and (2) the cost of life insurance protection for the year *over* premiums paid under the contract during the year is taxable to the policyholder as ordinary income.[5] "Premiums paid" generally means those paid under the contract less amounts received but excludable from income under IRC Section 72(e) (e.g., dividends).[6] The cost of life insurance protection is the lesser of the cost of individual insurance on the life of the insured determined on the basis of uniform premiums or the mortality charge, if any, stated in the contract.[7] If the contract originally meets the statutory definition and then ceases to do so, income on the contract for all prior years is included in gross income in the year it ceases to meet the definition.[8] See Q 36 and Q 37 for a discussion of the new rules for determining basis under the 2017 Tax Act.

If a variable insurance contract is an insurance contract under applicable state law and would otherwise meet the definitional requirements of IRC Section 7702, the annual increases in cash surrender value may nevertheless be taxed under the rules in the above paragraph if the underlying segregated asset account is not adequately diversified (Q 555).

If a policy does not meet the IRC Section 7702(a) definition of a life insurance contract, the income on the contract for the year is considered a nonperiodic distribution and is subject to certain reporting and withholding requirements. The same is true for a variable life

1. *Cohen v. Comm.*, 39 TC 1055 (1963), *acq.* 1964-1 CB 4.
2. *Nesbitt v. Comm.*, 43 TC 629 (1965).
3. Treas. Reg. §1.446-1(c)(1)(ii).
4. IRC Sec. 7702(g).
5. IRC Sec. 7702(g)(1)(B).
6. IRC Sec. 7702(f)(1).
7. IRC Sec. 7702(g)(1)(D).
8. IRC Sec. 7702(g)(1)(C).

insurance contract that does not meet the diversification requirements of regulations under IRC Section 817(h).[1]

The "inside buildup" of cash surrender values of corporate-owned life insurance is generally included in the calculation of the alternative minimum tax (Q 316). (Note that the corporate AMT was repealed for tax years beginning after 2017).

On December 7, 2015, the U.S. Congressional Joint Committee on Taxation issued a report containing a change of its procedure:

> "Historically, the Joint Committee staff has included in its report on tax expenditures some items for which no provision of the Federal tax law specifically allows an exclusion, but which are nonetheless excluded from income. Among these are the exclusion of all Medicare benefits from taxation, *the exclusion of investment income on life insurance and annuity contracts*, and the exclusion of cash public assistance. This report no longer includes tax expenditure estimates for these items." [Emphasis added.]

By no longer listing the exclusion of inside buildup of life insurance and annuities as a "tax expenditure, the Committee appears to join the broadly held and long-standing view that despite specific provisions of the Internal Revenue Code exempting (or deducting) such buildup, the proper taxation of life insurance and annuities does not include such amounts.

9. Is the owner of a limited-pay life insurance policy liable for any tax when the policy becomes paid-up?

No. Taxable income is not realized unless the policy is sold or surrendered.

Living Proceeds

10. What are the rules for taxing living proceeds received under life insurance policies and endowment contracts?

Generally speaking, living proceeds are proceeds received during an insured's lifetime. The rules in IRC Section 72 govern the income taxation of amounts received as *living proceeds* from life insurance policies and endowment contracts. IRC Section 72 also covers the tax treatment of policy dividends and forms of premium returns.

Payments to which IRC Section 72 applies are of three classes: (1) "amounts not received as an annuity," (2) payments of interest only, and (3) "amounts received as annuities."

When living proceeds are held by an insurer under an agreement to pay interest, the interest payments are taxable in full (Q 21).[2] Periodic payments on a principal amount that will be returned intact on demand are interest payments.[3]

1. Rev. Rul. 91-17 1991-1 CB 190, as amplified by Rev. Proc. 2008-41, 2008-2 CB 155.
2. IRC Sec. 72(j); Treas. Reg. §1.72-14(a).
3. Rev. Rul. 75-255, 1975-2 CB 22.

All amounts taxable under IRC Section 72 other than annuities and payments of interest are classed as *amounts not received as an annuity*. These include policy dividends, lump-sum cash settlements of cash surrender values and endowment maturity proceeds, and cash withdrawals and amounts received on partial surrender.[1]

The income tax treatment of life insurance *death proceeds* is governed by IRC Section 101, not by IRC Section 72. Consequently, the annuity rules in IRC Section 72 do not apply to life income or other installment payments under optional settlements of death proceeds. However, the rules for taxing such payments are similar to IRC Section 72 annuity rules (Q 63 to Q 79).

Living proceeds received under life insurance contracts and endowment policies are taxed according to the same rules, whether they are single premium or periodic premium policies. Except for interest and annuity settlements, they are taxed under the "cost recovery rule" no matter when the contract was entered into or when premiums were paid. In other words, such amounts are included in gross income only to the extent they exceed the investment in the contract (as reduced by any prior excludable distributions under the contract). Living proceeds or distributions received from a life insurance policy that has failed the seven pay test of IRC Section 7702A(b) and, therefore, is classified as a modified endowment contract are taxed under different rules (Q 124).

Planning Point: Assuming no policy loans, dividends, or prior cash value surrenders, a life insurance contract can be surrendered with no taxable gain, provided the aggregate premiums are equal to or exceed the cash values (Q 51). Assume after fifteen years the aggregate premiums of a universal life policy are equal to the cash values, the policy is surrendered, and nothing is included in gross income. Over the life of this contract *untaxed* interest earnings have been used to pay the mortality charges (i.e., the amount-at-risk element of the contract). In contrast, if term insurance had been originally purchased, premiums would have come from after-tax income. *Donald F. Cady, J.D., LL.M, CLU.*

11. How are cash distributions received as a result of changes in the benefits of a life insurance contract taxed?

Cash distributions received as a result of certain changes in the benefits of a contract may not be taxed under the cost recovery rule, but are taxed under the "interest-first" rule. Any change in the benefits under a life insurance contract or in other terms of the contract (other than automatic increases such as change due to the growth of the cash surrender value, payment of guideline premiums, or changes initiated by the company) that was not reflected in any earlier determination or adjustment will require a redetermination as to whether the definitional guidelines of IRC Section 7702 are still satisfied (Q 65).[2] (A modification made to a life insurance contract after December 31, 1990, that is necessitated by the insurer's financial insolvency, however, will not cause retesting under IRC Sections 7702(f)(7)(B)-(E).)[3] If such a change occurs during the fifteen-year period beginning on the issue date of the policy *and* reduces the benefits under the contract, then any cash distribution made to the policyholder as a result of such change will be

1. Treas. Reg. §1.72-11.
2. IRC Sec. 7702(f)(7)(A).
3. Rev. Proc. 92-57, 1992-2 CB 410; Let. Rul. 9239026.

taxed as ordinary income to the extent there is income on the contract; however, the amount to be included will be limited to the applicable recapture ceiling.[1]

If the change occurs during the five-year period beginning on the issue date of a traditional life policy (that is, a policy that originally qualified under IRC Section 7702 by satisfying the cash value accumulation test), the recapture ceiling is the *excess of* the cash surrender value of the contract immediately before the reduction *over* the net single premium immediately after the reduction. If the change occurs during the five-year period beginning on the issue date of a universal life policy (that is, a policy that originally qualified under IRC Section 7702 by satisfying the guideline premium/cash value corridor tests), the recapture ceiling is the greater of (1) the *excess of* the aggregate premiums paid under the contract immediately before the reduction *over* the guideline premium limitation for the contract, taking into account the proper adjustment for the change in benefits, or (2) the *excess of* the cash surrender value of the contract immediately before the reduction *over* the cash value corridor immediately after the reduction.[2]

If the change occurs after the five-year period and during the fifteen-year period beginning on the date of issue of the policy, the recapture ceiling is the *excess of* the cash surrender value of the contract immediately before the reduction *over* the cash value corridor immediately after the reduction.[3]

Distributions made in anticipation of a reduction in benefits under the contract will be treated as resulting from a change in the contract. Any distribution that reduces the cash surrender value of a contract and that is made within two years before a reduction in benefits under such contract will be treated as made in anticipation of a reduction.[4]

The IRS has provided examples of how these rules work.[5]

12. How are policy loans under life insurance policies and endowment contracts treated?

Policy loans under life insurance policies and endowment contracts are not treated as distributions (Q 29). However, the treatment differs for loans made from life insurance policies classified as modified endowment contracts (Q 13).[6]

If a loan is still outstanding when a policy is surrendered or allowed to lapse, the borrowed amount becomes taxable at that time to the extent the cash value exceeds the owner's basis in the contract, as if the borrowed amount was actually received at the time of surrender or lapse and used to pay off the loan. (If a policy loan is outstanding at the time of an IRC Section 1035 tax-free exchange, the amount of the *net* reduction, if any, in the taxpayer's outstanding loan will be considered "boot" (Q 44) and taxable as ordinary income at that time to the extent there is income on the contract, without regard to basis.) If a loan is outstanding at the time of death, the

1. IRC Sec. 7702(f)(7)(B).
2. IRC Sec. 7702(f)(7)(C).
3. IRC Sec. 7702(f)(7)(D).
4. IRC Sec. 7702(f)(7)(E).
5. Rev. Rul. 2003-95, 2003-33 IRB 358.
6. IRC Secs. 72(e)(5)(A)(i), 7702(f)(7)(B)(iii).

distribution of the face amount of the policy will be reduced by the amount of the outstanding loan. Proceeds received on account of the death of the insured are generally tax-free (Q 63). The benefit of tax-free death proceeds in excess of cost may be lost, however, in the case of a policy transferred for value (Q 279 to Q 290).

13. For tax purposes, what is a life insurance policy that is classified as a modified endowment contract (MEC)?

A modified endowment contract (MEC) is one that meets the requirements of IRC Section 7702 (Q 65), was entered into on or after June 21, 1988, and fails to meet the seven pay test (Q 14). A contract that is received in exchange for a contract meeting this definition is also an MEC.[1] Distributions from MECs are subject to taxation rules that differ from the rules governing the taxation of distributions from life insurance policies that are not MECs (Q 15).

14. What is the "seven pay test" and how does it apply to a modified endowment contract (MEC)?

A life insurance contract will fail the seven pay test if the accumulated amount paid under the contract at any time during the first seven contract years exceeds the sum of the net level premiums that would have been paid on or before such time if the contract provided for paid-up future benefits after the payment of the seven level annual payments.[2] Generally, the "amount paid" under the contract is defined as the premiums paid less distributions, not including amounts includable in gross income.[3] An amount received as a loan or the repayment of a loan does not affect the amount paid under the contract.[4] Additionally, amounts paid as premiums during the contract year but returned to the policyholder with interest within sixty days after the end of the contract year will reduce the sum of the premiums paid during the contract year. The interest paid on the premiums returned must be included in gross income.[5]

When a whole life insurance policy is coupled with an increasing whole life rider plus a term insurance rider, and the amount of coverage provided under the term rider increases or decreases solely in relation to the amount of coverage provided by the base policy and whole life rider, the IRS has ruled privately that the policy's "future benefits" for purposes of IRC Section 7702A(b) are equal to the aggregate amount of insurance coverage provided under the base policy, the whole life rider, and the term insurance rider at the time the policy is issued.[6] When a variable whole life policy is coupled with a twenty-year decreasing term rider, the future benefits for purposes of IRC Section 7702A(b) are equal to the coverage under the base policy plus the lowest amount of coverage under the term rider at any time during the first seven contract years.[7]

The seven level premiums are determined when the contact is issued, and the first contract year death benefit is deemed to be provided to the contract's maturity, disregarding any scheduled

1. IRC Sec. 7702A(a).
2. IRC Sec. 7702A(b).
3. IRC Sec. 7702A(e)(1).
4. H. R. Conf. Rep. No. 100-1104 (TAMRA '88) *reprinted in* 1988-3 CB 593.
5. IRC Sec. 7702A(e)(1).
6. Let. Rul. 9519023.
7. Let. Rul. 9513015.

death benefit decrease after the first seven years.[1] In one private letter ruling, the death benefit for purposes of applying IRC Section 7702A(c)(1)(B) was the policy's "target death benefit," defined as the sum of the base policy death benefit and a rider death benefit.[2]

If there is a reduction in benefits under the contract within the first seven contract years, the seven pay test is applied as if the contract had originally been issued at the reduced benefit level. Any reduction in benefits due to the nonpayment of premiums is not taken into account, however, if the benefits are reinstated within ninety days after the reduction.[3]

In the case of a contract that pays a death benefit only on the death of one insured that follows or occurs at the same time as the death of another insured, if the death benefit is reduced below the lowest level of death benefit provided during the contract's first seven years, the MEC rules must be applied as if the contract had originally been issued at that lower benefit level. This rule is effective for contracts entered into on or after September 14, 1989.[4]

15. How are distributions from modified endowment contracts (MECs) taxed?

Generally, distributions from MECs are taxed differently than distributions from policies that meet the seven pay test (Q 10). Distributions, including loans, from an MEC are taxable as income at the time received to the extent that the cash value of the contract immediately before the payment exceeds the investment in the contract.[5] Basically, this means that distributions from MECs are taxed as income first and recovery of basis second. The investment in the contract is increased to the extent that a distribution was includable in the taxpayer's income. A loan that is retained by the insurance company to pay policy premiums is considered an amount received under the contract.[6]

Distributions made during the contract year and any subsequent contract year in which the contract fails the seven pay test are taxed as discussed above. In addition, under IRS regulations, distributions in anticipation of a failure of the seven pay test also are taxed as above. A distribution made within two years prior to the failure of the seven pay test is a distribution made in anticipation of a failure.[7]

This manner of taxation for distributions does not apply to the assignment or pledge of an MEC to pay burial or prearranged funeral expenses if the contract's maximum death benefit does not exceed $25,000.[8]

For the purpose of determining the amount includable in gross income, all MECs issued by the same company to the same policyholder within any calendar year are treated as one

1. IRC Sec. 7702A(c)(1).
2. Let. Rul. 9741046.
3. IRC Sec. 7702A(c)(2).
4. IRC Sec. 7702A(c)(6).
5. IRC Sec. 72(e)(10).
6. H. R. Conf. Rep. No. 100-1104 (TAMRA '88) *reprinted in* 1988-3 CB 592.
7. IRC Sec. 7702A(d).
8. IRC Sec. 72(e)(10)(B).

MEC. This rule does not apply generally to contracts purchased by a trust described in IRC Section 401(a) that is exempt from tax under IRC Section 501(a), purchased as part of an IRC Section 403(a) plan, or described in IRC Section 403(b), or to an individual retirement annuity or an individual retirement account.[1]

Penalty Tax

A 10 percent penalty tax is imposed on any amount received by a taxpayer under an MEC that is includable in gross income unless the distribution is made after the taxpayer becomes disabled, attains age 59½, or the distribution is part of a series of substantially equal periodic payments made for the taxpayer's life or life expectancy or the joint lives or joint life expectancies of the taxpayer and the taxpayer's beneficiary.[2]

16. Which life insurance contracts are subject to the seven pay test?

Subject to the following exceptions, life insurance contracts entered into after June 20, 1988, are subject to the seven pay test.[3] Contracts entered into prior to this date are "grandfathered" for purposes of the seven pay test.

If the death benefit under a grandfathered contract increases by more than $150,000 over the death benefit in effect as of October 20, 1988, the contract becomes subject to the material change rules (Q 17) and may lose its grandfathered status. This rule does not apply if the contract required at least seven annual premiums as of June 21, 1988, and the policyholder continued to make at least seven annual premium payments.[4] In determining whether a material change has occurred, the death benefit payable as of June 20, 1988, rather than the lowest death benefit payable during the first seven years, is applicable.[5]

A policy entered into before June 21, 1988, may lose its grandfathered status and, therefore, may be treated as if it were entered into after this date, if (1) the policy death benefit is increased or an additional qualified benefit is purchased after June 20, 1988, and (2) prior to June 21, 1988, the contract owner did not have the right to obtain such an increase or addition without providing additional evidence of insurability. If a term life insurance contract is converted after June 20, 1988, to a policy that is not term insurance, without regard to the right of the owner to such a conversion, the policy will lose its grandfathered status.[6] A policy entered into before June 21, 1988, did not lose its grandfathered status when the insurer changed the policy loan provision to make interest payable in arrears rather than in advance.[7] The IRS has stated that modification of a life insurance contract after December 31, 1990, that is made necessary by the insurer's insolvency will not affect the date on which the contract was issued, entered into, or purchased for purposes of IRC Section 7702.[8]

1. IRC Sec. 72(e)(12).
2. IRC Sec. 72(v).
3. TAMRA '88 Sec. 5012(e)(1).
4. TAMRA '88 Sec. 5012(e)(2), as amended by OBRA '89 Sec. 7815(a)(2).
5. H.R. Conf. Rep. No. 100-1104, (TAMRA '88) *reprinted in* 1988-3 CB 595-596.
6. TAMRA '88 Sec. 5012(e)(3).
7. Let. Ruls. 9714029, 9412023, 9117011.
8. Rev. Proc. 92-57, 1992-2 CB 410.

17. How will material changes in the benefits or terms of a life insurance contract be treated for purposes of the seven pay test?

If there is a material change in the benefits or terms, the contract will be treated as a new contract entered into on the day the material change was effective and the seven pay test, with appropriate adjustments to reflect the cash surrender value of the contract, must be met again.[1] Modification of a life insurance contract after December 31, 1990, that is made necessary by the insurer's financial insolvency, however, will not cause commencement of a new seven year period for purposes of the seven pay test.[2]

For a contract that has been materially changed, the seven pay premium for each of the seven years following the change is reduced by the cash surrender value of the contract as of the effective date of the material change multiplied by a fraction, the numerator of which is the seven pay premium for future benefits under the contract and the denominator of which is the net single premium for future benefits under the contract.[3]

A material change is defined as any increase in the death benefit under the contract or any increase in, or addition of, a qualified additional benefit under the contract. However, any increase due to the payment of premiums necessary to fund the lowest level of the death benefit and qualified additional benefits payable in the first seven contract years or to the crediting of interest or other earnings, including dividends, is not considered a material change. Additionally, to the extent provided in IRS regulations, any cost-of-living increase funded over the period during which premiums are required to be paid under the contract and that are based on a broad-based index is not considered a material change.[4]

For purposes of IRC Sections 101(f), 7702, and 7702A, a material change to a contract does not occur when a rider that is treated as a qualified long-term care insurance contract under IRC Section 7702B is issued or when any provision required to conform any other long-term care rider to these requirements is added (Q 475).[5]

18. Are MEC dividends "amounts received under the contract"?

Any dividend of an MEC that is retained by the insurer to pay either principal or interest on a policy loan is an amount received under the contract. Any dividend that is retained by the insurer for purposes of purchasing paid-up insurance is not an amount received under the contract.[6]

19. Is the exchange of a life insurance policy under IRC Section 1035 subject to the seven pay test?

The effect of an IRC Section 1035 exchange on the grandfathered status of a policy issued prior to June 21, 1988, and thus not subject to the seven pay test of IRC Section 7702A, is not

1. IRC Sec. 7702A(c)(3)(A).
2. Rev. Proc. 92-57, 1992-2 CB 410.
3. H.R. Conf. Rep. No. 100-1104, (TAMRA '88) *reprinted in* 1988-3 CB 595.
4. IRC Sec. 7702A(c)(3)(B).
5. HIPAA '96, Sec. 321(f)(4).
6. See 72(e); see also H.R. Conf. Rep. No. 100-1104, (TAMRA '88) *reprinted in* 1988-3 CB 592.

entirely clear.[1] In a private ruling, the IRS has taken the position that a life insurance contract received in an IRC Section 1035 exchange for a life insurance contract issued before June 21, 1988, will be considered as issued and entered into on the date that it is received in exchange for the previous contract and, thus, apparently will be subject to the seven pay test.[2]

If an MEC requiring the payment of at least seven annual premiums was entered into after June 20, 1988, but before November 10, 1988, and was then exchanged within the three months following November 10, 1988, for a contract that meets the requirements of the seven pay test, the new contract is not treated as an MEC if the taxpayer recognized gain, if any, on the exchange.[3]

20. How can life insurance companies correct failures to comply with the modified endowment contract (MEC) rules?

Life insurance companies may correct "inadvertent non-egregious" failures to comply with the MEC rules by submitting a request for relief to the IRS. The request must meet certain requirements and give detailed information about the MECs at issue. To obtain relief, a life insurance company must pay an amount calculated individually for each policy and bring the policies into compliance with IRC Section 7702A by, generally, increasing the policy's death benefit or refunding excess premiums and earnings. Not all life insurance policies are eligible for correction under this procedure.[4]

21. What are the tax consequences of leaving life insurance cash surrender values or endowment maturity proceeds with the insurer under the interest-only option?

The interest is fully taxable to the payee as it is received or credited.[5]

Under some circumstances, election of the interest option will postpone tax on the proceeds. If the option is elected before maturity or surrender without reservation of the right to withdraw the proceeds, the proceeds are not constructively received in the year of maturity or surrender.[6] But if the right of withdrawal is retained, the IRS apparently considers the proceeds as constructively received when they first become withdrawable.[7] (It can be argued, however, that the proceeds are not constructively received when the policyholder has a contractual right to change to another option.) If the option is elected on or after the maturity or surrender date, the proceeds are constructively received in the year of maturity or surrender. The sixty-day extension rule, applicable to the election of a life income or installment option, does not apply to an election of the interest option (see Q 52 and Q 589 for exclusion of exception).

If the proceeds are constructively received, the entire gain on the contract (if any) is taxable in the year of constructive receipt as if the proceeds had been actually received in a one sum

1. See H.R. Conf. Rep. No. 100-1104, (TAMRA '88) *reprinted in* 1988-3 CB 596.
2. Let. Rul. 9044022.
3. TAMRA '88 Sec. 5012(e)(4).
4. Rev. Proc. 2008-39, 2008-29 IRB 143, *superseding*, Rev. Proc. 2007-19, 2007-7 IRB 515, and Rev. Proc. 2001-42, 2001-2 CB 212.
5. IRC Sec. 72(j); Treas. Reg. §1.72-14(a).
6. *Frackelton v. Comm.*, 46 BTA 883 (1942), acq.; see *Fleming v. Comm.*, 241 F.2d 78 (5th Cir. 1957).
7. See Treas. Reg. §1.451-2; *Blum v. Higgins*, 150 F.2d 471 (2d Cir. 1945).

settlement (Q 51). If the proceeds are not constructively received, the gain will be taxable to the person who ultimately receives the proceeds.[1]

Dividends

22. Are dividends payable on a participating life insurance policy taxable income?

As a general rule, all dividends paid or credited before the maturity or surrender of a contract are tax-exempt as return of investment until an amount equal to the policyholder's basis has been recovered. More specifically, when aggregate dividends plus all other amounts that have been received tax-free under the contract exceed aggregate gross premiums, the excess is taxable income (see, however, Q 13).[2]

It is immaterial whether dividends are taken in cash, applied against current premiums, used to purchase paid-up additions, or left with the insurance company to accumulate interest. Thus, accumulated dividends are not taxable either currently or when withdrawn (but the *interest* on accumulated dividends is taxable (Q 23)) until aggregate dividends plus all other amounts that have been received tax-free under the contract exceed aggregate gross premiums. At that point, the excess is taxable income.[3] It is immaterial whether the policy is premium-paying or paid-up. However, dividends paid on life insurance policies that are classified as modified endowment contracts under IRC Section 7702A may be taxed differently (Q 13).

Dividends are considered to be a partial return of basis; hence they reduce the cost basis of the contract. This reduction in cost must be taken into account in computing gain or loss upon the sale, surrender, exchange, or lifetime maturity of a contract (Q 533).

23. Is interest earned on life insurance dividend accumulations currently taxable to the policyholder?

Yes. The interest must be included in the policyholder's gross income for the first taxable year during which it can be withdrawn, whether it actually is withdrawn or not.[4] If the interest is credited annually and is subject to withdrawal annually, it constitutes gross income to the policyholder each year as it is credited to the policyholder's account. But if the interest is withdrawable only on the anniversary date of the policy (or on some other specified date), it is gross income to the policyholder for the taxable year in which the anniversary date (or other specified date) falls.[5] The Tax Court has held that the interest can be included in the policyholder's gross income only for the first taxable year in which the taxpayer either actually or constructively receives it (the first year it is withdrawable); thus, the IRS cannot include the interest in the policyholder's gross income for a later year, even though the interest was not reported in the year it was constructively received. To tax the interest, IRS must reopen the policyholder's return for the prior year.[6]

1. IRC Secs. 61(a), 691(a).
2. IRC Sec. 72(e)(5); Treas. Reg. §1.72-11(b)(1).
3. IRC Sec. 72(e)(5).
4. Treas. Reg. §1.451-2.
5. Treas. Reg. §1.61-7.
6. *Cohen v. Comm.*, 39 TC 1055 (1963), acq. 1964-1 CB 4.

24. What is the tax treatment of life insurance dividends when endowment maturity values or cash surrender values are paid in installments or as life income?

In the case of life insurance cash surrender values and endowment maturity values, total excludable dividends paid or credited before the payments begin are subtracted from gross premiums to determine the net premium cost of the contract.[1] It is this net premium cost that is used in computing the portion of the payment that may be excluded from gross income (the *investment in the contract*). The treatment of dividends that are used to purchase paid-up additions is discussed in Q 25.

25. What are the tax results when life insurance or endowment dividends are used to purchase paid-up insurance additions?

Normally, no tax liability will arise at any time when life insurance or endowment dividends are used to purchase paid-up insurance additions. Dividends not in excess of investment in the contract are not taxable income (see, however, Q 13 with regard to modified endowment contracts), the annual increase in the cash values of the paid-up additions is not taxed to the policyholder (see Q 8), and death proceeds are tax-free.[2] In effect, dividends reduce the cost basis of the original amount of insurance and constitute the cost of the paid-up additions. Consequently, upon maturity, sale, or surrender during an insured's lifetime, gross premiums, including the cost of paid-up additions, are used as the cost of the insurance in computing gain upon the entire amount of proceeds, including proceeds from the additions. See Q 36 to Q39 for a discussion of the new rules for determining basis under the 2017 Tax Act.

The treatment of cash value increases and the death benefit of a contract subject to the definitional requirements of IRC Section 7702 will be different if the contract fails to meet certain requirements (Q 65).

26. Are dividends that are credited to a paid-up life insurance or endowment policy taxable income?

Regardless of whether a policy is premium paying or paid-up, dividends credited to an unmatured life insurance or endowment contract are taxed as discussed in Q 22.

27. If accumulated or post-mortem life insurance dividends are received by a deceased insured's beneficiary, are they taxable income to the beneficiary?

No, such dividends are not taxable income to the beneficiary. Accumulated dividends are exempt as property received by inheritance.[3] Terminal and post-mortem dividends are exempt as amounts received under a life insurance contract and paid by reason of the death of the insured.[4] Moreover, it appears that accumulated interest, if constructively

1. IRC Sec. 72(c)(1).
2. IRC Sec. 72(e)(5); *Nesbitt v. Comm.*, 43 TC 629 (1965); IRC Sec. 101(a).
3. IRC Sec. 102.
4. IRC Sec. 101(a)(1).

received by a policyholder in a prior year, is not taxable to a beneficiary even though the policyholder neglected to report the interest (Q 78).[1]

28. When life insurance death proceeds are held under a settlement option, are excess interest dividends taxable to the beneficiary?

Yes,[2] unless the proceeds are payable under a life income or installment option and the beneficiary is the surviving spouse of an insured who died before October 23, 1986. A surviving spouse of an insured who died before October 23, 1986, may exclude up to $1,000 annually of the interest (guaranteed and excess) received under an installment or life income option (Q 71).

Policy Loans

29. Are life insurance policy loans taxable?

A loan taken from a life insurance policy that *is not* classified as a modified endowment contract under IRC Section 7702A is not includable in income because it is not treated as a distribution under IRC Section 72.[3]

By contrast, a loan taken from a life insurance policy that *is* classified as a modified endowment contract is treated as a distribution under IRC Section 72 and is includable in income at the time received to the extent that the cash value of the contract immediately before the distribution exceeds the investment in the contract (Q 13).[4] Unless the loan is made under certain specific circumstances (Q 13), a 10 percent penalty tax is imposed on the amount of the loan that is includable in gross income.[5]

If a loan is still outstanding when a policy is surrendered or allowed to lapse, the borrowed amount becomes taxable at that time to the extent the cash value exceeds the owner's basis in the contract, as if the borrowed amount was actually received at the time of surrender or lapse and used to pay off the loan.[6] If a loan is outstanding at the time of death, the distribution of the face amount of the policy usually is reduced by the amount of the outstanding loan.

Planning Point: Because withdrawals from life insurance policies not classified as modified endowment contracts are ordinarily not subject to income tax up to the amount of cost basis in the contract, it is typical to first take withdrawals until basis is exhausted and then take policy loans. By taking withdrawals up to basis and then by taking loans after that, amounts received from the policy during lifetime can be maximized and income taxes minimized. However, it is important that a program of withdrawals and loans be carefully monitored so as not to result in a policy lapse which could cause adverse income tax consequences as well as loss of the policy death benefit.

---

1. *Cohen v. Comm.*, 39 TC 1055 (1963), acq.
2. IRC Secs. 101(c) and (d)(1).
3. IRC Sec. 72(e)(5).
4. IRC Sec. 72(e).
5. IRC Sec. 72(v).
6. See *Atwood v. Comm.*, TC Memo 1999-61.

30. Can a life insurance policy owner take an income tax deduction for the interest paid on a policy loan?

To be deductible, interest paid by a policy owner on a policy loan must meet the rules discussed below and, if applicable, the rules discussed in Q 4. However, even if the interest is deductible under those rules, the amount of the deduction may be limited depending on whether the interest is classified as personal interest, trade or business interest, investment interest, or interest taken into account in computing income or loss from passive activities. Generally, the determination is made by tracing the use to which the loan proceeds are put.[1] Thus, interest on a loan used to pay premiums on personal life insurance may come within an exception explained in Q 4, but the deduction may not be available because personal interest is not deductible. There is little guidance as to whether interest on a loan used to buy life insurance can be considered investment interest (Q 732). Borrowing to finance business life insurance generally has not been considered incurred in connection with the borrower's trade or business (Q 4).

General Rule of Nondeductibility for Policy Loan Interest (Contracts Issued After June 8, 1997)

Generally, no deduction is allowed for any interest paid or accrued on any indebtedness with respect to life insurance policies owned by a taxpayer covering the life of any individual, or any endowment or annuity contracts owned by the taxpayer covering any individual.[2] This provision generally is effective for contracts issued after June 8, 1997, in taxable years ending after this date. For purposes of this effective date, any material increase in the death benefit or other material change in the contract will be treated as a new contract. However, in the case of a master contract, the addition of covered lives is treated as a new contract only with respect to the additional covered lives.[3]

The IRS has ruled that disallowed interest under IRC Section 264(a)(4) reduces earnings and profits for the taxable year in which the interest would have been allowable as a deduction but for its disallowance under that section. It does not further reduce earnings and profits when the death benefit is received under a life insurance contract.[4]

General Rule of Nondeductibility for Policy Loan Interest (Contracts Issued Prior to June 9, 1997)

For contracts issued prior to June 9, 1997, the general rule under IRC Section 264(a)(4) states that no deduction is allowed for any interest paid or accrued on any indebtedness with respect to life insurance policies owned by a taxpayer that covered the life of any individual who is an officer or employee of, or who is financially interested in, any trade or business carried on by the taxpayer. The same rule applies to any endowment or annuity contracts owned by a taxpayer that cover any individual.[5]

1. See Temp. Treas. Reg. §1.163-8T.
2. IRC Sec. 264(a)(4).
3. See IRC Sec. 264(f)(4)(E) for the definition of "master contract." TRA '97 Sec. 1084(d), as amended by IRSRRA '98 Sec. 6010(o)(3)(B).
4. Rev. Rul. 2009-25, 2009-38 IRB 365.
5. IRC Sec. 264(a)(4), prior to amendment by TRA '97 Sec. 1084(b)(1).

Prior to legislation enacted in 1996, there was an exception to this general rule for policies with less than $50,000 of indebtedness. However, effective for interest paid or accrued after October 13, 1995, the ability to deduct policy loan interest paid on company-owned life insurance policies with loans of less than $50,000 was eliminated.[1]

31. Are there any exceptions to the rule that interest paid on a policy loan is nondeductible for key-person policies?

Yes. The general nondeductibility rule does not apply to any interest paid or accrued on any indebtedness with respect to policies or contracts covering an individual who is a "key person" to the extent that the aggregate amount of the indebtedness with respect to policies and contracts covering the individual does not exceed $50,000.[2]

A "key person" is an officer or 20 percent owner of the taxpayer. The number of persons who may be treated as key persons is limited to the greater of: (1) five individuals, or (2) the lesser of 5 percent of the total officers and employees of the taxpayer or 20 individuals. If the taxpayer is a corporation, a 20 percent owner is defined as any person who directly owns (1) 20 percent or more of the outstanding stock of the corporation or (2) stock possessing 20 percent or more of the total combined voting power of all of the corporation's stock. If the taxpayer is not a corporation, a 20 percent owner is any person who owns 20 percent or more of the capital or profits interest in the taxpayer.[3]

Generally, all members of a controlled group are treated as a single taxpayer for purposes of determining a 20 percent owner of a corporation and for applying the $50,000 limitation. This limitation is allocated among the members of a controlled group in the manner prescribed by the IRS.[4]

Interest in excess of the amount that would have been determined had the "applicable rate of interest" been used cannot be deducted. The applicable rate of interest for any month is the interest rate described as "Moody's Corporate Bond Yield Average – Monthly Average Corporates" as published by Moody's Investors Service (the Moody's Rate).[5]

The IRC also specifies the manner in which to determine the applicable rate of interest for pre-1986 contracts. For a contract purchased on or before June 20, 1986 with a fixed interest rate, the applicable rate of interest for any month is the Moody's Rate for the month in which the contract was purchased. If a contract with a variable interest rate was purchased on or before June 20, 1986, the applicable rate of interest for any month in an applicable period is the Moody's Rate for the third month preceding the first month in such period. "Applicable period" is the twelve-month period beginning on the date the policy is issued, unless the taxpayer elects a number of months (not greater than twelve) other than such twelve-month period to be its

1. IRC Sec. 264(a)(4), as amended by HIPAA '96 Sec. 501(a) but before amendment by TRA '97 Sec. 1084.
2. IRC Sec. 264(e)(1).
3. IRC Sec. 264(e)(3).
4. IRC Sec. 264(e)(5)(A).
5. IRC Sec. 264(e)(2).

applicable period. Such an election, if made, applies to the taxpayer's first taxable year ending on or after October 13, 1995, and all subsequent taxable years.[1]

If any amount was received from a life insurance policy, or endowment or annuity contract subject to IRC Section 264(a)(4), upon the complete surrender, redemption, or maturity of the policy or contract during calendar years 1996, 1997, or 1998 or in full discharge during these years of the obligation under the policy or contract that was in the nature of a refund of the consideration paid for the policy or contract, then the amount is includable in gross income ratably over the four-taxable-year period beginning with the taxable year the amount would have been included in income but for this provision.[2]

32. How is interest expense allocated to life insurance policy cash values?

No deduction is allowed for the portion of the taxpayer's interest expense that is allocable to unborrowed policy cash values. The portion that is allocable to unborrowed policy cash values is an amount that bears the same ratio to the interest expense as the taxpayer's average unborrowed policy cash values of life insurance policies and annuity and endowment contracts issued after June 8, 1997, bear to the sum of: (1) the average unborrowed policy cash values, in the case of the taxpayer's assets that are life insurance policies or annuity or endowment contracts, and (2) the average adjusted bases of such assets in the case of the taxpayer's assets that do not fall into this category.[3]

"Unborrowed policy cash value" is defined as the excess of the cash surrender value of a policy or contract (determined without regard to surrender charges) over the amount of any loan with respect to the policy or contract. For purposes of this provision, if the cash surrender value of a policy determined without reference to any surrender charge does not reasonably approximate its actual value, the amount taken into account is the greater of the amount of the insurance company liability or the insurance company reserve for the policy.[4]

33. Are there any exceptions to the general rule of nondeductibility of policy loan interest for unborrowed policy cash values?

There is an exception to the general rule of nondeductibility of policy loan interest expense that is allocable to unborrowed policy cash values. The exception applies to any policy or contract owned by an entity engaged in a trade or business if the policy or contract covers only one individual who, at the time first covered by the policy or contract, is: (1) a 20 percent owner of the entity, or (2) an individual who is not a 20 percent owner but who is an officer, director, or employee of the trade or business. (A 20 percent owner is defined in IRC Section 264(e)(4)). A policy or contract covering a 20 percent owner will not fail to come within this exception simply because it covers both the owner and the owner's spouse. Apparently, however, the policy will not qualify for this exception if spouses of officers, directors, or employees who are not also 20 percent owners are covered. For purposes of this rule, if coverage for each insured under a

1. IRC Sec. 264(e)(2)(B)(ii).
2. HIPAA '96, Sec. 501(d)(1).
3. IRC Sec. 264(f).
4. IRC Sec. 264(f)(3).

master contract (that is not a group life insurance contract) is treated as a separate contract for certain purposes, the coverage for each insured is treated as a separate contract.[1]

The exception is effective generally for contracts issued after June 8, 1997, in taxable years ending after this date. For purposes of this effective date, any material increase in the death benefit or other material change in the contract will be treated as a new contract. However, in the case of a master contract, the addition of covered lives is treated as a new contract only with respect to the additional covered lives.[2]

34. What are the general interest deduction rules?

As a general tax principle, interest is deductible by a cash basis taxpayer only to the extent the taxpayer actually pays it in cash or cash equivalent in the tax year.[3] Thus, if the interest due on a policy loan is not paid but is merely deducted [withdrawn] by the insurer from principal at the time of making the loan or merely added to loan principal, it is not currently deductible by a cash basis taxpayer.[4] Likewise, a cash basis taxpayer cannot deduct interest owing on a policy loan that is deducted by the insurer from the proceeds of a new loan with the balance being remitted to the policyholder.[5] But if interest that has been deducted from or added to the principal amount of the policy loan is later paid, it is deductible by the cash basis taxpayer when paid.[6] If the interest has been added to the loan principal, a deduction is allowable when, on maturity or surrender of the policy or on the death of the insured, the insurer deducts the accumulated interest from the proceeds.[7]

Cash basis taxpayers deduct prepaid interest over the period to which it relates, not in the year it is prepaid.[8] An accrual basis taxpayer can deduct interest in the year it accrues, regardless of whether the interest is actually paid in that year.[9]

Only the person who owns a policy when the interest accrues is entitled to the deduction. A policy owner who takes out a policy loan and later makes an absolute assignment of the policy subject to the loan is not entitled to deduct interest that accrues after the assignment. For example, if a father continues to pay interest on policy loans after giving the policy to his children, he cannot deduct payments of interest accruing after the transfer.[10] Nor can a husband deduct on a separate return the interest he pays on a policy loan when the policy is owned by his spouse.[11] Similarly, a person to whom the policy has been assigned cannot pay and deduct interest that has accrued before the assignment.[12]

1. IRC Sec. 264(f)(4)(E).
2. TRA '97 Sec. 1084(d), as amended by IRSRRA '98 Sec. 6010(o)(3)(B). See IRC Sec. 264(f)(4)(E) for the definition of "master contract."
3. IRC Sec. 163; Treas. Reg. §1.163-1.
4. Rev. Rul. 73-482, 1973-2 CB 44.
5. *Keith v. Comm.*, 139 F.2d 596 (2d Cir. 1944).
6. Rev. Rul. 73-482, above.
7. *Est. of Hooks v. Comm.*, 22 TC 502 (1954), acq. 1955-1 CB 5.
8. IRC Sec. 461(g).
9. *Corlett v. Comm.*, 5 TCM (CCH) 94; IRC Sec. 461(h).
10. *Dean v. Comm.*, 35 TC 1083 (1961), nonacq. 1973 AOD LEXIS 238 (1973).
11. *Colston v. Burnet*, 59 F.2d 867 (DC Cir. 1932); see *Sherman v. Comm.*, 18 TC 746 (1952), nonacq. 1964-2 CB 9.
12. *Fox v. Comm.*, 43 BTA 895 (1941); see also *Orange Securities Corp. v. Comm.*, 45 BTA 24 (1941).

When a policyholder makes unspecified installment payments covering both premiums and interest, payments will be applied first toward premiums, and only the balance will be considered deductible interest.[1] Payments specified and applied as interest, however, will be treated as such.[2]

IRC Section 265(a)(2) forbids the deduction of interest on loans to purchase or carry tax-exempt investments. Borrowing to enable an insured to buy a key person policy on the insured from the insured's employer was held sufficiently unrelated to the insured's investment in tax-exempt bonds so that interest on the loan was deductible to the extent that the tax-exempt bonds were not used as collateral for the loan.[3]

Several cases have disallowed the deduction of interest on loans that were considered "sham" transactions – that is, transactions that offered the taxpayer nothing of economic substance other than a hoped-for deduction.[4]

Annual loans against cash value to pay current premiums were not considered "sham" in *Coors v. U.S.*,[5] *Lee v. U.S.*,[6] and *Golsen v. U.S.*[7] The important factors in these cases were the following:

- There was no prepayment of interest or premiums;
- The owner needed liquidity to meet premium payments;
- Death benefits were at all times substantial;
- Policies were standard policies; and
- The loans were straightforward, ordinary, and available to any policyholder.[8]

The deduction of interest on a policy loan in each of the first three policy years and the subsequent surrender of the policy in the fourth year was not considered a sham when a change in the tax law eliminated the insured's need for the policy death benefit.[9]

In a case involving corporate owned life insurance policies, the Tax Court held that payments from the corporation to the insurance companies were not "interest" paid on policy loans but were, in fact, constructive dividends to the insured shareholders. The court noted that payment of these amounts by the corporation conferred an economic benefit on the shareholders by increasing both the policy cash values and the death benefits.[10]

1. *Evans v. Comm.*, 5 TCM (CCH) 438 (1946).
2. *Kay v. Comm.*, 44 TC 660 (1965).
3. *Levitt v. U.S.*, 517 F.2d 1339 (8th Cir. 1975).
4. *Winn-Dixie Stores, Inc. v. Comm.*, 254 F. 3d 1313, 2001-2 USTC ¶50,495 (11th Cir. 2001); *IRS v. CM Holdings, Inc.*, 2002-2 USTC ¶50,596 (3rd Cir. 2002); *American Elect. Power Co. v. U.S.*, 2003-1 USTC ¶50,416 (6th Cir. 2003).
5. 215 Ct. Cl. 840 (1978).
6. 215 Ct. Cl. 831 (1978).
7. 80-2 USTC 9741.
8. See *Coors v. U.S.*, above.
9. *Shirar v. Comm.*, TC Memo 1987-492, *rev'd*, 916 F.2d 1414 (9th Cir. 1990).
10. *Young v. Comm.*, TC Memo 1995-379.

Deduction of interest paid on a policy loan by a grantor trust is discussed in Q 152; the deductibility of interest on a loan under a tax-sheltered annuity is discussed in Q 4059.

35. If the beneficiary of life insurance pays the interest on a policy loan, is this a gift to the insured?

No, there is no gift to the insured, unless the insured owns the policy.[1]

Disposition: Sale or Purchase of a Contract

36. What are the income tax consequences when the owner of a life insurance or endowment contract sells the contract?

Editor's Note: The 2017 Tax Act reversed the IRS position in Revenue Ruling 2009-13, and instead now provides that in determining basis, no adjustment is made for mortality, expense or other reasonable charges incurred under the contract (the "cost of insurance") in the case of a policy sale. Therefore, on sale of a cash value insurance policy, the insured's basis is no longer reduced by the cost of insurance.[2] This new rule for determining basis is effective retroactively, to transactions entered into after August 25, 2009.[3]

Until 2009, the question of whether the cost of insurance protection should be subtracted or not from the premiums paid was unsettled. A commonly held view was that the cost of insurance protection should *not* be subtracted from the premiums paid (thus decreasing the amount of taxable gain), and this view was supported by case law, and was codified by the 2017 tax reform legislation.[4] Conversely, in 2005 guidance, the IRS had indicated that on a sale of a life insurance policy, it would consider the basis of the contract to be the premiums paid *minus* the cost of insurance protection – thus, increasing the amount of taxable gain.[5]

In 2009, the IRS issued Revenue Ruling 2009-13 (discussed in Q 37, Q 38 and Q 39), which aimed to provide definitive guidance to policyholders who surrender or sell their life insurance contracts in life settlement transactions.[6] Essentially, according to the revenue ruling, the basis is *not* adjusted for the cost of insurance protection when a policy is surrendered (Situation 1), but the cost of insurance protection *is* subtracted from the premiums paid when the policy is sold (Situations 2 and 3). The 2017 Tax Act explicitly reverses this IRS position retroactively, for transactions entered into after August 25, 2009, and provides that basis will not be adjusted in the case of a policy sale.

See Q 60 for the new reporting requirements that apply when a life insurance contract is sold in a life settlement transaction.

1. *Seligmann v. Comm.*, 9 TC 191 (1947).
2. IRC Sec. 7702(c)(3)(B)
3. IRC Sec. 1016(a)(1)(A).
4. See Q 40.
5. ILM 200504001.
6. Rev. Rul. 2009-13, 2009-21 IRB 1029, as superseded in part by Pub. Law No. 115-97 (the 2017 Tax Act)..

37. How is gain on the surrender of a cash value life insurance policy calculated after 2008?

Editor's Note: The 2017 Tax Act reversed the IRS position in Revenue Ruling 2009-13, and instead now provides that in determining basis, no adjustment is made for mortality, expense or other reasonable charges incurred under the contract (the "cost of insurance") in the case of a policy sale. Therefore, on sale of a cash value insurance policy, the insured's basis is no longer reduced by the cost of insurance.[1] This new rule for determining basis is effective retroactively, to transactions entered into after August 25, 2009.[2]

Revenue Ruling 2009-13 explains how to calculate the amount and character of gain upon the surrender or sale of a life insurance policy by the insured.[3] The example below illustrates the results upon surrender of a cash value policy (Situation 1). For examples illustrating the treatment of the sale of a cash value life insurance policy and the sale of a term life insurance policy, see Q 38 and Q 39.

Revenue Ruling 2009-13: Situation 1

Facts: On January 1, 2001, John Smith bought a cash value life insurance policy on his life. The named beneficiary was a member of John's family. John had the right to change the beneficiary, take out a policy loan, or surrender the policy for its cash surrender value. John surrendered the policy on June 15, 2008, for its $78,000 cash surrender value, including a $10,000 reduction for the cost of insurance protection provided by the insurer (for the period ending on or before June 15, 2008). Through that date, John paid policy premiums totaling $64,000, and did not receive any distributions from or loans against the policy's cash surrender value. John was not terminally or chronically ill on the surrender date.

Amount of income recognized. The IRS determined that the "cost recovery" exception (to the "income first" rule) applied to the non-annuity amount received by John.[4] Under that exception, a non-annuity amount received under a life insurance contract (other than a modified endowment contract) is includable in gross income to the extent it exceeds the "investment in the contract." For this purpose, "investment in the contract" means the aggregate premiums (or other consideration paid for the contract before that date) *minus* the aggregate amount received under the contract before that date that was excludable from gross income. The IRS ruled that John must recognize $14,000 of income: $78,000 (which included a $10,000 reduction for cost of insurance) *minus* $64,000 (premiums paid).

Character of income recognized: The IRS concluded that the $14,000 was ordinary income, not capital gain. The IRS determined that the life insurance contract was a "capital asset" described in IRC Section 1221(a). However, relying on earlier guidance, the IRS reiterated that the surrender of a life insurance contract does *not* produce a capital gain,[5] and further determined that

1. IRC Sec. 7702(c)(3)(B)
2. IRC Sec. 1016(a)(1)(A).
3. Rev. Rul. 2009-13, 2009-21 IRB 1029, as superseded in part by Pub. Law No. 115-97 (the 2017 Tax Act).
4. IRC Sec. 72(e)(5).
5. Rev. Rul. 64-51, 1964-1 CB 322.

IRC Section 1234A (which applies to gains from certain terminations of capital assets) does not change this result.

See Q 60 for the new reporting requirements that apply when a life insurance contract is sold in a life settlement transaction.

38. How is gain on the sale of a cash value life insurance policy calculated after 2008? How did the 2017 Tax Act change the rules governing gain on the sale of a life insurance policy?

Editor's Note: The 2017 Tax Act reversed the IRS position in Revenue Ruling 2009-13, and instead now provides that in determining basis, no adjustment is made for mortality, expense or other reasonable charges incurred under the contract (the "cost of insurance") in the case of a policy sale. Therefore, on sale of a cash value insurance policy, the insured's basis is no longer reduced by the cost of insurance.[1] This new rule for determining basis is effective retroactively, to transactions entered into after August 25, 2009.[2]

Revenue Ruling 2009-13 explained how to calculate the amount and character of gain upon the surrender or sale of a life insurance policy by the insured.[3] The example below illustrates the results upon the sale of a cash value life insurance policy (Situation 2) prior to the clarification that reversed this position in the 2017 Tax Act. For examples illustrating the results upon the surrender of a cash value policy (Situation 1) and the sale of a term life insurance policy (Situation 3), see Q 37 and Q 39.

Revenue Ruling 2009-13: Situation 2

In Situation 2, the IRS took the position that the cost of insurance protection must be *subtracted* from the premiums paid when determining the adjusted basis in the contract. The 2017 Tax Act explicitly reverses this IRS position retroactively, for transactions entered into after August 25, 2009.

Facts: On January 1, 2001, John Smith bought a cash value life insurance policy on his life. The named beneficiary was a member of John's family. John had the right to change the beneficiary, take out a policy loan, or surrender the policy for its cash surrender value. John sold the policy on June 15, 2008, for $80,000 to a B, a person unrelated to John and who would suffer no economic loss upon John's death. Through that date, John paid policy premiums totaling $64,000, and did not receive any distributions from or loans against the policy's cash surrender value, which, at the time, was $78,000, including a $10,000 reduction for the cost of insurance protection provided by the insurer (for the period ending on or before June 15, 2008). John was not terminally or chronically ill on the sale date.

Amount of income recognized. The IRS first stated the general rule that gain realized from the sale or other disposition of property is the excess of the amount realized over the adjusted basis

1. IRC Sec. 7702(c)(3)(B)
2. IRC Sec. 1016(a)(1)(A).
3. Rev. Rul. 2009-13, 2009-21 IRB 1029, as superseded in part by Pub. Law No. 115-97 (the 2017 Tax Act).

for determining gain.[1] The IRS determined that the amount John realized from the sale of the life insurance policy was $80,000.[2]

The adjusted basis for determining gain or loss is generally the cost of the property minus expenditures, receipts, losses, or other items properly chargeable to the capital account.[3] The IRS specifically pointed out that Section 72, which involves the taxation of certain proceeds of life insurance contracts, has no bearing on the determination of the basis of a life insurance policy that is sold because that section applies only to amounts received *under* the policy, which was not the case in this situation.

Next, the IRS noted that both the IRC and the courts acknowledge that a life insurance policy – while only a single asset – may have both investment and insurance characteristics.[4] The IRS then stated that to measure a taxpayer's gain on the sale of a life insurance policy, the basis must be *reduced* by the portion of the premium paid for the policy that has been expended for the provision of insurance before the sale.[5]

Against that backdrop, the IRS determined that John had paid premiums totaling $64,000 through the date of sale, and that $10,000 would have to be subtracted from the policy's cash surrender value as cost of insurance charges. Thus, John's adjusted basis in the policy as of the date of sale was $54,000 ($64,000 premiums paid - $10,000 expended as the cost of insurance). Accordingly, the IRS ruled that John would have to recognize $26,000 of income upon the sale of the life insurance policy, which is the excess of the amount realized on the sale ($80,000) over John's adjusted basis in the contract ($54,000).

Character of income recognized. The "substitute for ordinary income" doctrine (which essentially holds that ordinary income that has been earned but not recognized by a taxpayer cannot be converted into capital gain by a sale or exchange) was held by the IRS to be applicable in this situation. The IRS stated, however, that the doctrine is limited to the amount of income that would be recognized if a policy were *surrendered* (i.e., to the inside build-up under the policy). Thus, if the income recognized on a *sale* (or exchange) of a policy exceeds the "inside build-up" under the policy, the excess may qualify as gain from the sale or exchange of a capital asset.[6]

In Situation 2, because the "inside build-up" in John's life insurance policy was $14,000 ($78,000 cash surrender value - $64,000 aggregate premiums paid), the IRS concluded that that amount would constitute ordinary income under the doctrine. Because the policy was a capital asset (under Section 1221) and had been held by John for more than one year, the remaining $12,000 of income represented long-term capital gain.[7]

---

1. IRC Secs. 1001(a), 1011.
2. IRC Sec. 1001(b).
3. IRC Secs. 1011, 1012, 1016.
4. See IRC Sec. 7702; *London Shoe Co. v. Comm.*, 80 F.2d 230 (2nd Cir. 1935); *Century Wood Preserving Co. v. Comm.*, 69 F.2d 967 (3rd Cir. 1934).
5. *London Shoe Co. v. Comm.*, 80 F.2d 230 (2nd Cir. 1935); *Century Wood Preserving Co. v. Comm.*, 69 F.2d 967 (3rd Cir. 1934); *Keystone Consolidated Publishing Co. v. Comm.*, 26 BTA 1210, 12 (1932). See also Treas. Reg. §1.1016-2(a). But compare Rev. Rul. 2009-14, 2009-21 IRB 1031, Q 51.
6. See, e.g., *Comm. v. Phillips*, 275 F.2d 33, 36, n.3 (4th Cir 1960).
7. IRC Sec. 1222(3).

Effective date: The IRS has declared that the holding in Situation 2 will not be applied adversely to sales occurring before August 26, 2009.[1]

Planning Point: Prior to the 2017 Tax Act, a life settlement, or seemingly any transfer for value to a party lacking insurable interest, constituted a transaction possibly subject to income taxation. Revenue Ruling 2009-13 concluded that the policy basis is first reduced by the "cost of insurance" (COI) charges (a proposition which is no longer valid). The amount received in excess of basis is ordinary income up to the policy cash surrender value. Amounts in excess of cash surrender value are capital gain.

See Q 60 for the new reporting requirements that apply when a life insurance contract is sold in a life settlement transaction.

39. How is gain on the sale of a term life insurance policy calculated after 2008? How did the 2017 Tax Act change the rules governing gain on the sale of a life insurance policy?

Editor's Note: The 2017 Tax Act reversed the IRS position in Revenue Ruling 2009-13, and instead now provides that in determining basis, no adjustment is made for mortality, expense or other reasonable charges incurred under the contract (the "cost of insurance") in the case of a policy sale. Therefore, on sale of a term life insurance policy, the insured's basis is no longer reduced by the cost of insurance.[2] This new rule for determining basis is effective retroactively, to transactions entered into after August 25, 2009.[3]

Revenue Ruling 2009-13 explained how to calculate the amount and character of gain upon the surrender or sale of a life insurance policy by the insured.[4] The example below illustrates the results upon the sale of a term life insurance policy (Situation 3), as previously enforced by the IRS. However, as noted in the editor's note above, the IRS position has explicitly been superseded by statute. For examples illustrating the results upon surrender of a cash value policy or the sale of a cash value policy, see Q 37 and Q 38.

Revenue Ruling 2009-13: Situation 3

In Situation 3, the IRS took the position that the cost of insurance protection must be *subtracted* from the premiums paid. This position is no longer valid, and the cost of insurance may *not* be subtracted.

Facts: On January 1, 2001, John Smith bought a fifteen year level premium term life insurance policy on his life. The policy had a $500 monthly premium. The named beneficiary was a member of John's family. John had the right to change the beneficiary, take out a policy loan, or surrender the policy for its cash surrender value. John paid $45,000 total premiums through June 15, 2008, at which point he sold the policy for $20,000 to a B, a person unrelated to John

1. Rev. Rul. 2009-13, 2009-21 IRB 1029, as superseded in part by Pub. Law No. 115-97 (the 2017 Tax Act).
2. IRC Sec. 7702(c)(3)(B)
3. IRC Sec. 1016(a)(1)(A).
4. Rev. Rul. 2009-13, 2009-21 IRB 1029, as superseded in part by Pub. Law No. 115-97 (the 2017 Tax Act).

and who would suffer no economic loss upon John's death. John was not terminally or chronically ill on the sale date.

Amount and character of income recognized: The IRS stated that absent other proof, the cost of the insurance provided to John each month was presumed to equal the monthly premium under the policy ($500). Consequently, the cost of insurance protection provided to John during the 89.5-month period was $44,750 ($500 monthly premium times 89.5 months). Thus, John's adjusted basis in the policy on the date of sale to B was $250 ($45,000 total premiums paid - $44,750 cost of insurance protection). The IRS concluded that John was required to recognize $19,750 long-term capital gain upon the sale of the term life policy ($20,000 amount realized - $250 adjusted basis).[1]

Effective date: Pre-reform, the IRS has declared that the holding in Situation 3 will not be applied adversely to sales occurring before August 26, 2009.[2]

Planning Point: Under the 2017 Tax Act, the otherwise available exceptions to the transfer for value rule generally do not apply if the sale was a reportable policy sale (i.e., most commercial transfers) for tax years beginning after 2017.

See Q 60 for the new reporting requirements that apply when a life insurance contract is sold in a life settlement transaction.

40. How is gain on the sale or surrender of a life insurance policy before 2009 calculated?

Gain up to the amount of the contract's cash surrender value should be taxed to the seller as ordinary income. According to the decided cases, the amount of taxable gain is determined in the same way as upon surrender of a contract (Q 51). In other words, gain is determined by subtracting the net premium cost (i.e., gross premiums less dividends to the extent excludable from income) from the sale price.[3] Therefore, under applicable case law, the cost of insurance protection is *not* deducted from the premiums paid. While later guidance indicated that on a sale of a life insurance policy, the IRS considered the basis of the contract to be the premiums paid *minus* the cost of insurance protection, the 2017 Tax Act superseded this position by statute in providing that the cost of insurance protection cannot be subtracted from basis (effective with respect to transfers entered into after August 25, 2009).[4]

Before Revenue Ruling 2009-13 (see Q 37 to Q 39), the issue of whether gain in excess of the contract's cash surrender value (such as in a life settlement) is ordinary income or capital gain was unsettled. Some argued that the entire gain should be ordinary income. But others contended that gain in excess of the contract's cash surrender value should receive capital gain treatment. In support of the argument that a portion of a life settlement should be treated as a capital gain, proponents pointed to a footnote in the *Phillips* case in which the IRS conceded that

1. IRC Sec. 1222(3).
2. Rev. Rul. 2009-13, 2009-21 IRB 1029, as superseded in part by Pub. Law No. 115-97 (the 2017 Tax Act).
3. *Gallun v. Comm.*, 327 F.2d 809 (7th Cir. 1964); *Comm. v. Phillips*, 275 F.2d 33 (4th Cir. 1960); *Est. of Crocker v. Comm.*, 37 TC 605 (1962); *Neese v. Comm.*, TC Memo 1964-288; see also *Cohen v. Comm.*, 39 TC 1055 (1963).
4. ILM 200504001, Pub. Law No. 115-97 (the 2017 Tax Act), amending IRC Sec. 1016(a)(1)(A).

in certain situations the sale of a life insurance contract might result in capital gain treatment.[1] However, in a technical advice memorandum, the IRS pointed out that even if a life insurance contract is treated as a capital asset, the entire gain from the sale of a contract should be treated as ordinary income.[2]

In another case, the Tax Court held that settlement proceeds ($500,000) received by the taxpayer (a former corporate executive) with respect to a life insurance policy represented an extinguishment of the taxpayer's claim to ownership of the policy, as opposed to a sale or exchange of a capital asset. Accordingly, the proceeds were taxable as ordinary income.[3]

41. Will the owner of a life insurance policy recognize a loss when the policy is sold for its cash surrender value?

Normally there will be no loss when a life insurance policy is sold for its cash surrender value (Q 62).

For the treatment of amounts received from a viatical settlement provider, see Q 57.

42. What are the tax results if a life insurance policy is sold subject to a nonrecourse loan?

If a contract sold is subject to a nonrecourse loan, the transferor's obligation under the loan is discharged and the amount of the loan is considered an amount received on the transfer.[4]

For the treatment of amounts received from a viatical settlement provider, see Q 57.

Planning Point: A life insurance policy may be exchanged for an annuity tax-free under IRC Section 1035, after which the resulting annuity must have the same basis as the original life insurance policy. See Q 44 and Q 49. The rules for recognizing a loss on the surrender of an annuity in a loss position are more liberal than those governing life insurance. See Q 567.

---

43. How is the purchaser of a life insurance or endowment contract taxed?

Editor's Note: The 2017 Tax Act reversed the IRS position in Revenue Ruling 2009-13, and instead now provides that in determining basis, no adjustment is made for mortality, expense or other reasonable charges incurred under the contract (the "cost of insurance") in the case of a policy sale. See Q 36 to Q 39.

If a purchaser receives lifetime proceeds under a life insurance or endowment contract, the purchaser is generally taxed in the same way as an original owner would be taxed, but with the following differences. The purchaser's cost basis is the consideration the purchaser paid for the contract, plus any premiums the purchaser paid after the purchase, less any excludable dividends and unrepaid excludable loans received by the purchaser after the purchase.[5] It also should be

1. *Comm. v. Phillips*, 275 F.2d 33, fn.3 (4th Cir. 1960).
2. TAM 200452033.
3. *Eckersley v. Comm.*, TC Memo 2007-282.
4. Rev. Rul. 2009-13, 2009-21 IRB 1029.
5. Treas. Reg. §1.72-10(a).

noted that the purchase of a life insurance policy will, under some circumstances, result in loss of the income tax exemption for the death proceeds, under IRC Section 101(a)(2), the so-called "transfer-for-value" rule (see Q 279 through Q 290).

Revenue Ruling 2009-14

In 2009, the IRS released guidance regarding the different tax consequences for an investor (B) upon the receipt of either (1) death benefits or (2) sale proceeds with regard to a term life insurance policy that the investor purchased for profit.[1]

Situation 1 – Receipt of Death Benefits by Third Party Who Purchases Term Life Policy from Insured: John Smith is a U.S. citizen residing in the United States. B (a U.S. "person" within the meaning of Section 7701(a)(30)) purchased a fifteen-year level premium term life insurance policy on John's life for $20,000 on June 15, 2008, when the remaining term of the policy was seven years, six months, and fifteen days. B named himself beneficiary of John's policy immediately after acquiring it. B purchased the policy with a view to profit, and the likelihood that B would allow the policy to lapse was remote. B was unrelated to John, had no insurable interest in John's life, and would not suffer economic loss upon John's death. B paid monthly premiums totaling $9,000. Upon John's death (December 31, 2009), the insurance company paid $100,000 to B.

The IRS determined that the purchase of the policy by B was a transfer for value that did not qualify for any of the potential exceptions to the rule. Accordingly, the amount received because of John's death was excludable from gross income under IRC Section 101(a)(1), although under IRC Section 101(a)(2) the exclusion would be limited to the sum of the actual value of the consideration paid for the transfer ($20,000) and other amounts paid by B ($9,000), or $29,000. Therefore, the IRS ruled that B was required to recognize $71,000 of gross income, which is the difference between the total death benefit received ($100,000) and the amount excluded under IRC Section 101 ($29,000). With respect to the character of the gain, the IRS determined that neither the surrender of a life insurance or annuity contract, nor the receipt of a death benefit from the issuer under the terms of the contract, produces a capital gain. Accordingly, the IRS ruled that the $71,000 of income recognized by B upon the receipt of the death benefits under the contract was ordinary income.

Situation 2 – Resale of Policy by Third Party Who Bought Term Life Policy from Insured: The facts here are the same as immediately stated above, except that: (a) John did not die; and (b) on December 31, 2009, B sold the policy to C (unrelated to John or B) for $30,000. The IRS found that in this situation, unlike Situation 2 of Revenue Ruling 2009-13 (Q 38), no reduction to basis for the cost of insurance charges was necessary because unlike John, B did not purchase the policy for protection against economic loss. The IRS therefore distinguished this situation from Revenue Ruling 2009-13 (which has now been overruled in part by the 2017 Tax Act) because B acquired and held the policy solely with a view to profit. Accordingly, the IRS required B to recognize only $1,000 on the sale of the life insurance policy ($30,000 – [$20,000 + $9,000]). Because the term life insurance policy was not property excluded from capital gain treatment

1. Rev. Rul. 2009-14, 2009-21 IRB 1031.

under IRC Sections 1221(a)(1) through 1221(a)(8), and because it had been held for more than one year, the IRS characterized the $1,000 of gain recognized by B under IRC Section 1001 as long-term capital gain (citing Revenue Ruling 2009-13). In addition, because the policy was a term policy without any cash value, the substitute for ordinary income doctrine (under *United States v. Midland-Ross Corp.*[1]) did not apply.

Disposition: Policy Exchanges

44. Does tax liability arise when a policyholder exchanges one life insurance contract for another?

The IRC provides that the following are *nontaxable* exchanges: (1) the exchange of a life insurance policy for another life insurance policy, for an endowment or annuity contract, or for a qualified long-term care insurance contract, (2) the exchange of an endowment contract for an annuity contract, for an endowment contract under which payments will begin no later than payments would have begun under the contract exchanged, or for a qualified long-term care insurance contract, (3) the exchange of an annuity contract for another annuity contract or for a qualified long-term care insurance contract, and (4) the exchange of a qualified long-term care insurance contract for another qualified long-term care insurance contract.[2] These rules do not apply to any exchange having the effect of transferring property to any non-U.S. person.[3]

If an exchange involves life insurance policies, the policies must be on the life of the same insured. Otherwise, the exchange does not qualify as a tax-free exchange under IRC Section 1035(a).[4]

Planning Point: If a policy loan is outstanding at the time of an IRC Section 1035 tax-free exchange, the amount of the *net* reduction, if any, in the taxpayer's outstanding loan will be considered "boot" and taxable as ordinary income at that time to the extent there is income on the contract, without regard to basis.

45. Is there any tax liability when a policyholder exchanges a life insurance policy insuring one life for a policy insuring two lives?

In a private ruling, the IRS concluded that exchanges of policies insuring a single life for a policy insuring two lives do not qualify for nonrecognition treatment under IRC Section 1035. The IRS reached this outcome in all of the following situations:

(1) Spouse A exchanges a policy insuring only Spouse A's life for a policy that insures the lives of both Spouse A and Spouse B;

(2) Spouse A exchanges two life insurance policies, one of which insures Spouse A and the other of which insures Spouse B, for a single second-to-die policy insuring the lives of both Spouse A and Spouse B;

1. 381 U.S. 54, 57 (1965).
2. IRC Sec. 1035(a).
3. IRC Sec. 1035(c).
4. Treas. Reg. §1.1035-1.

(3) Spouse A and Spouse B jointly exchange separate policies each of which insures the life of one spouse for a single jointly-owned second-to-die policy that insures the lives of both Spouse A and Spouse B;

(4) A trust owns and exchanges a policy insuring the life of Spouse A for a policy that insures the lives of both Spouse A and Spouse B; and

(5) A trust owns and exchanges two life insurance policies, one of which insures Spouse A and the other of which insures Spouse B, for a single second-to-die policy insuring the lives of both Spouse A and Spouse B.[1]

46. Is there any tax liability when a joint and last survivor policy is exchanged for a single life policy on the surviving insured?

In a private ruling, the IRS has sanctioned IRC Section 1035 treatment for the exchange of a joint and last survivor life insurance policy, following the death of one of the insured persons, for a universal variable life insurance policy that insures the survivor. The IRS noted that at the time of the exchange, both policies were insuring the same single life and that the new policy would better suit the policy owner's needs because it was less costly.[2] The IRS reached the same conclusion in another private ruling in which a second-to-die policy was exchanged after the death of one insured for a policy insuring only the survivor.[3]

47. Is there any tax liability when a whole life policy subject to indebtedness is exchanged for a new policy subject to the same indebtedness?

When a whole life policy with an outstanding loan was exchanged for another whole life policy subject to the same indebtedness, the exchange was treated as an entirely tax-free exchange.[4] The IRS reached the same conclusion when one policy was exchanged for another subject to the same indebtedness and the taxpayer contemplated making withdrawals or partial surrenders from the policy to reduce the indebtedness.[5] The cost basis of the new contract will be the cost basis of the old, plus the amount of gain recognized, minus the amount of cash or other property received (with proper adjustments for premiums paid and dividends received after the exchange).[6]

Planning Point: Applying a step-transaction doctrine approach, life insurance companies typically treat loans repaid from policy values within six months (or a year) before or after the exchange as having been extinguished at the time of the exchange and will generally report such an extinguishment as taxable gain (to the extent of gain in the policy). It is important to know the reporting policy of the company issuing the new policy if a quick repayment of a carry-over loan is contemplated. But, even if not reported, extinguishment of the carry-over loan from policy values shortly before or after issue could be regarded by the IRS as extinguished at issue – possibly creating taxable income.

1. Let. Rul. 9542037.
2. Let. Rul. 9248013.
3. Let. Rul. 9330040.
4. Let. Ruls. 8806058, 8604033.
5. Let. Rul. 8816015.
6. IRC Sec. 1031(d); Treas. Reg. §1.1031(d)-1.

48. Is there any tax liability when two individual policies are exchanged for two interests in a group universal life policy?

The IRS has ruled privately that the exchange of two individual life insurance policies for two participating interests in a group universal life insurance policy qualifies as a valid IRC Section 1035(a) transfer.[1] Thus, there is no tax liability.

49. Is the exchange of life insurance policies for annuities a tax-free exchange?

The IRS has concluded that the exchange of two nonparticipating flexible premium life insurance policies, each issued by a different life insurance company, for a single nonparticipating flexible premium variable annuity contract, issued by a third life insurance company, is a proper IRC Section 1035 exchange. The IRS agreed that the annuity could be initially issued in the amount of the proceeds received from the first policy and then increased in value when the proceeds of the remaining policy arrived.[2]

When a life insurance policy was exchanged for an annuity plus an additional cash payment, the IRS concluded that the exchange qualified for IRC Section 1035 treatment. The additional cash payment into the newly-issued annuity was needed to meet the annuity's minimum premium requirement. Further, noting that administrative delays should not convert a tax-free exchange to a taxable one, the IRS concluded that if the two amounts were not received at the same time, the insurance company could issue the annuity in an amount equal to the cash payment and then later increase the value of the annuity when the funds from the life insurance policy were received.[3]

50. Does the substitution of one insured for another qualify as a tax-free exchange?

The substitution of one insured for another under an exchange-of-insureds option on a corporate-owned key person policy is treated by the IRS as a sale or other disposition under IRC Section 1001 and not as a tax-free exchange under IRC Section 1035(a).[4] The IRS determined that an insurance company's exchange of old corporate-owned life insurance contracts (modified endowment contracts (MECs) issued after June 8, 1997) for new corporate-owned contracts qualified as a tax-free exchange under IRC Section 1035 when each new contract would insure the life of the same individual who was insured under the old contract.[5] The IRS also has ruled that if a taxpayer (employer) that owns MECs issued by the same insurance company in the same calendar year exchanges some of those MECs for new MECs issued by a second insurance company, the new contracts are *not* required to be aggregated with the remaining original contracts under IRC Section 72(e)(12).[6]

1. Let. Rul. 9017062.
2. Let. Rul. 9708016.
3. Let. Rul. 9820018.
4. Rev. Rul. 90-109, 1990-2 CB 191.
5. Let. Rul. 200711014. See also Let. Rul. 200801001.
6. Rev. Rul. 2007-38, 2007-25 IRB 1420.

The IRS has ruled that if a taxpayer receives a check from a life insurance company under a nonqualified annuity contract, the endorsement of the check to a second company, as consideration for a second annuity contract, does *not* qualify as a tax-free exchange under IRC Section 1035(a)(3). Instead, the amount received by the taxpayer is taxed on an income-first basis under IRC Section 72(e).[1]

See Q 19 for a discussion of the effect of an IRC Section 1035 exchange on the grandfathered status of a policy issued prior to June 21, 1988, and thus not subject to the seven pay test of IRC Section 7702A.

Disposition: Surrender, Redemption, or Maturity

51. What are the income tax consequences when the owner of a life insurance or endowment contract takes the lifetime maturity proceeds or cash surrender value in a one lump sum cash payment?

Amounts received on complete surrender, redemption, or maturity of a life insurance or endowment contract are taxed under the cost recovery rule (Q 10). If the maturity proceeds or cash surrender value exceeds the cost of the contract, the excess is taxable income in the year of maturity or surrender, even if the proceeds are not received until a later tax year.[2] (For computation of "cost," see Q 533.) The gain is ordinary income, not capital gain.[3]

The IRC provides that aggregate premiums are the investment in the contract, which is used for computing *gain* upon the lifetime maturity or surrender of a life insurance or endowment contract (Q 533).[4] Consequently, although the portion of the premiums paid for current life insurance protection is generally a nondeductible personal expense, that portion nevertheless may be included in the investment in the contract for the purpose of computing gain upon the surrender or lifetime maturity of the policy.

> *Example.* Mr. Green purchases a whole life policy in the face amount of $100,000. He uses dividends to purchase paid-up additions. Over a twenty-year period, gross premiums amount to $47,180. Of this amount, $13,018 represents the net protection portion of the premiums, and $34,162 the investment portion. At the end of the twenty-year period, Mr. Green surrenders his policy for its cash surrender value of $48,258 (cash value of the original $100,000 policy plus cash value of insurance additions). His investment in the contract is $47,180 (not $47,180 less $13,018). Thus, his taxable gain is $1,078 ($48,258 - $47,180), not $14,096 ($48,258 - $34,162).

In a 2009 Revenue Ruling, the IRS reiterated the above conclusion, ruling that a policy owner who surrenders a policy in a life settlement transaction is not required to subtract the cost of insurance charge from the policy owner's investment in the contract. In the revenue ruling, the cash surrender value of the subject policy was $78,000 (the IRS assumed that the cash surrender value already reflected the subtraction of the cost of insurance protection ($10,000)). The amount of premiums paid was $64,000. According to the IRS, the taxpayer's recognized

1. Rev. Rul. 2007-24, 2007-21 IRB 1282.
2. See *Kappel v. U.S.*, 369 F. Supp. 267 (W.D. Pa. 1974).
3. IRC Sec. 72(e); Treas. Reg. §1.72-11(d).
4. IRC Sec. 72(e)(6).

gain was only $14,000 ($78,000 surrender proceeds – $64,000 investment in the contract), all of which was declared ordinary income by the IRS.[1] (For a more detailed analysis, see Situation 1, "Surrender of Cash Value Policy," in Q 37.)

The 2017 Tax Act has changed this result with respect to sales of life insurance policies, however. Under the 2017 law, the cost of insurance protection is not subtracted when determining the policy's basis.[2]

Prior to this clarification, with respect to a viatical settlement, the IRS ruled privately that at the time of the assignment to a viatical settlement company, the *basis* of a whole life policy was equal to premiums paid *less* the sum of the cost of insurance protection provided up to the assignment date and any amounts, such as dividends, that were received under the contract but were not included in gross income. The cost of insurance protection in the private letter ruling was found to equal the aggregate premiums paid less the cash value of the policy. This ruling implies that, at least according to the IRS, the terms "basis" and "investment in the contract" do not mean the same thing.[3] This result would no longer be viable under the new law.

Planning Point: Under the 2017 Tax Act, the otherwise available exceptions to the transfer for value rule generally do not apply if the sale was a reportable policy sale (i.e., most commercial transfers) for tax years beginning after 2017.

For a discussion of the exception to the general rule that gain on endowment maturities and cash surrenders is taxable income, see Q 139 on government life insurance.

52. If a life insurance policyholder elects to receive endowment maturity proceeds or cash surrender values under a life income or installment option, is the gain on the policy taxable to the policyholder in the year of maturity or in the year of surrender?

Ordinarily, a cash basis taxpayer is treated as having *constructively received* an amount of cash when it first becomes available to the taxpayer without substantial limitations or restrictions. The taxpayer must report this amount as taxable income even though the taxpayer has not actually received it.[4] When an endowment contract matures, or any type of contract is surrendered, a lump-sum payment generally becomes available to the policyholder unless, *before* the maturity or surrender date, the taxpayer has elected to postpone receipt of the proceeds under a settlement option. For an exception to this general rule, see Q 589.

53. Can tax on the gain at maturity of an endowment contract be postponed?

Yes.

With an election to have proceeds paid under an installment or life income option, the gain can be spread over a fixed period of years or over the payee's lifetime (Q 52). Tax on the

1. Rev. Rul. 2009-13, 2009-21 IRB 1029, as superseded in part by Pub. Law No. 115-97 (the 2017 Tax Act).
2. IRC Sec. 1016(a)(1)(A).
3. Let. Rul. 9443020.
4. Treas. Reg. §1.451-2.

gain also may be postponed by electing the interest-only option before maturity and retaining no withdrawal rights (Q 21).

Another method to postpone the gain appears to be a situation in which the endowment is exchanged before maturity for a deferred annuity (Q 44, Q 571). The IRS has ruled that the exchange of an endowment for an annuity is a tax-free exchange.[1]

Some contracts provide that the owner may elect to continue the contract in force to an optional maturity date. If the contract so provides, and the election is made before the original maturity date, the owner should not be in constructive receipt of the gain under the policy before the optional maturity date. There are no specific rulings on this, however.

See also Q 65 with respect to contracts subject to the definitional rules of IRC Section 7702.

Accelerated Death Benefit

54. What is the income tax treatment of an accelerated death benefit payment from a life insurance contract?

Generally, any amount received under a life insurance contract on the life of a terminally ill insured or a chronically ill insured will be treated as an amount paid by reason of the death of the insured.[2] Amounts received under a life insurance contract by reason of the death of the insured are not includable in gross income.[3] See Q 63. Thus, an accelerated death benefit meeting these requirements will generally be received free of income tax.

However, amounts paid to a chronically ill individual are subject to the same limitations that apply to long-term care benefits. Generally, this is a limitation of the amount of benefits per day ($370 in 2019 and $360 in 2017 and 2018).[4] See Q 489. More specifically, if the total periodic long-term care payments received from all policies and any periodic payments received that are treated as paid by reason of the death of the insured (under IRC Section 101(g)) exceed a per-diem limitation, the excess must be included in income (without regard to IRC Section 72). (If the insured is terminally ill when a payment treated under IRC Section 101(g) is received, the payment is not taken into account for this purpose.)[5]

The per-diem limitation is equal to the greater of (1) a $370 per day limitation in 2019 ($360 in 2017 and 2018) or (2) the actual costs incurred for qualified long-term care services provided for the insured less any payments received as *reimbursement* for qualified long-term care services for the insured.[6] This figure is adjusted for inflation annually.[7] Accelerated death benefits paid to terminally ill individuals are not subject to this limit.

1. Rev. Rul. 72-358, 1972-2 CB 473; Rev. Rul. 68-235, 1968-1 CB 360.
2. IRC Sec. 101(g)(1).
3. IRC Sec. 101(a).
4. IRC Secs. 101(g)(3)(D), 7702B(d).
5. IRC Sec. 7702B(d)(1).
6. IRC Sec. 7702B(d)(2); Rev. Proc. 2009-50, 2008-45 IRB 617, as modified by Rev. Proc. 2010-47, 2010-2 CB 827; Rev. Proc. 2016-55; Rev. Proc. 2017-58; Rev. Proc. 2018-57.
7. IRC Secs. 7702B(d)(4), 7702B(d)(5).

Example. In 2019, Mr. Heller received qualified long-term care services for thirty days at a total cost of $7,500. A qualified long-term care insurance contract paid him a benefit of $370 per day, $11,100 total. In addition, $500 of the cost of the qualified long-term care services was reimbursed by another source. Thus, $500 of the $11,100 benefit is includable in income by Mr. Heller.

A terminally ill individual is a person who has been certified by a physician as having an illness or physical condition that can reasonably be expected to result in death within twenty-four months following the certification.[1]

A chronically ill individual is a person who is not terminally ill and who has been certified by a licensed health care practitioner as unable to perform, without substantial assistance, at least two activities of daily living (ADLs) for at least ninety days or a person with a similar level of disability. Further, a person may be considered chronically ill if he requires substantial supervision to protect himself from threats to his health and safety due to a severe cognitive impairment and this condition has been certified by a healthcare practitioner within the previous twelve months.[2] See Q 475. The ADLs are: (1) eating; (2) toileting; (3) transferring; (4) bathing; (5) dressing; and (6) continence.[3]

55. Are there any special rules that apply to chronically ill insureds?

There are several special rules that apply to chronically ill insureds. Generally, the tax treatment outlined in Q 54 will not apply to any payment received for any period unless the payment is for costs incurred by the payee (who has not been compensated by insurance or otherwise) for qualified long-term care services provided to the insured for the period. Additionally, the terms of the contract under which the payments are made must comply with: (1) the requirements of IRC Section 7702B(b)(1)(B); (2) the requirements of IRC Sections 7702B(g) and 4980C that the Secretary specifies as applying to such a purchase, assignment, or other arrangement; (3) standards adopted by the National Association of Insurance Commissioners (NAIC) that apply specifically to chronically ill insureds (if such standards are adopted, similar standards under number (2) above cease to apply); and (4) standards adopted by the state in which the policyholder resides (if such standards are adopted, the analogous requirements under number (2) and, subject to IRC Section 4980C(f), standards under number (3) above cease to apply).[4]

"Qualified long-term care services" are defined as "... necessary diagnostic, preventive, therapeutic, curing, treating, mitigating, and rehabilitative services, and maintenance or personal care services, which..." are required by a chronically ill individual and are provided under a plan of care set forth by a licensed healthcare practitioner.[5]

1. IRC Sec. 101(g)(4)(A).
2. IRC Secs. 101(g)(4)(B), 7702B(c)(2)(A).
3. IRC Sec. 7702B(c)(2)(B).
4. IRC Sec. 101(g)(3)(B).
5. IRC Sec. 101(g)(4)(C); IRC Sec. 7702B(c)(1).

56. Are there any exceptions to the general rule of non-includability for accelerated death benefits?

There is one exception to this general rule of non-includability for accelerated death benefits. Accelerated death benefits paid to (1) any taxpayer other than the insured if (2) the taxpayer has an insurable interest in the life of the insured because the insured is a director, officer, or employee of the taxpayer or if the insured is financially interested in any trade or business of the taxpayer, are exceptions from the special treatment afforded to payment of certain accelerated death benefits (see Q 54 and Q 55).[1]

57. What is the income tax treatment of an amount received from a viatical settlement provider?

A viatical settlement provider is "any person regularly engaged in the trade or business of purchasing, or taking assignments of, life insurance contracts on the lives of insureds" who are terminally or chronically ill, provided that certain licensing and other requirements are met.[2] To be considered a viatical settlement provider a person must be licensed for such purposes in the state in which the insured resides. The IRS has provided guidance on when viatical settlement providers will be considered licensed.[3]

If any portion of a death benefit under a life insurance contract on the life of a terminally or chronically ill insured is sold or assigned to a viatical settlement provider, the amount paid for the sale or assignment will be treated as an amount paid under the life insurance contract by reason of the insured's death.[4] In other words, such an amount will not be includable in income (Q 63).[5]

A terminally ill individual is a person who has been certified by a physician as having an illness or physical condition that can reasonably be expected to result in death within twenty-four months following the certification.[6]

A chronically ill individual is a person who is not terminally ill and who has been certified by a licensed healthcare practitioner as being unable to perform, without substantial assistance, at least two activities of daily living (ADLs) for at least ninety days or a person with a similar level of disability. Further, a person may be considered chronically ill if the person requires substantial supervision to protect himself or herself from threats to his or her health and safety due to severe cognitive impairment and this condition has been certified by a healthcare practitioner within the previous twelve months.[7] See Q 475. The activities of daily living are:

(1) eating;

(2) toileting;

1. IRC Sec. 101(g)(5).
2. IRC Sec. 101(g)(2)(B)(i).
3. Rev. Rul. 2002-82, 2002-2 CB 978.
4. IRC Sec. 101(g)(2)(A).
5. See IRC Sec. 101(a).
6. IRC Sec. 101(g)(4)(A).
7. IRC Secs. 101(g)(4)(B), 7702B(c)(2)(A).

(3) transferring (moving oneself from a bed to a chair, to another chair, *etc.*);

(4) bathing;

(5) dressing; and

(6) continence.[1]

If an insured resides in a state that does not require licensing of viatical settlement providers, the insured must meet the standards for either a terminally ill individual or a chronically ill individual.[2] The requirements applicable to an insured who is a terminally ill individual are met if the person: (1) meets the requirements of Sections 8 and 9 of the Viatical Settlements Model Act of the NAIC, and (2) meets the requirements of the Model Regulations of the NAIC in determining amounts paid by such person in connection with such purchases or assignments.[3] The requirements applicable to an insured who is a chronically ill individual are met if the person: (1) meets requirements similar to the requirements of Sections 8 and 9 of the Viatical Settlements Model Act of the NAIC, and (2) meets the standards of the NAIC for evaluating the reasonableness of amounts paid by such person in connection with such purchases or assignments with respect to chronically ill individuals.[4]

Planning Point: The term "viatical settlement" is technical in its definition that viatical settlements refer to only those cases where the insured under the policy is terminally ill. Where the insured is not terminally ill, the terminology of "high net worth transactions" or "senior settlements" may be more appropriate. Transactions involving senior settlements, rather than "viatical settlements" are not necessarily taxed in the same manner.

58. Are there special rules regarding the income tax treatment of an amount received by a chronically ill insured from a viatical settlement provider?

There are several special rules that apply to chronically ill insureds. Generally, the tax treatment outlined above will not apply to any payment received for any period unless such payment is for costs incurred by the payee (who has not been compensated by insurance or otherwise) for qualified long-term care services provided to the insured for the period. Additionally, the terms of the contract under which such payments are made must comply with:

(1) the requirements of IRC Section 7702B(b)(1)(B) (defining "long-term care contract");

(2) the requirements of IRC Sections 7702B(g) and 4980C (Q 475) that the IRS specifies as applying to such a purchase, assignment, or other arrangement (relating to consumer protection provisions);

(3) standards adopted by the NAIC that apply specifically to chronically ill insureds (if such standards are adopted, similar standards under number (2) above cease to apply); and

1. IRC Sec. 7702B(c)(2)(B).
2. IRC Sec. 101(g)(2)(B).
3. IRC Sec. 101(g)(2)(B)(ii).
4. IRC Sec. 101(g)(2)(B)(iii).

(4) standards adopted by the state in which the policyholder resides (if such standards are adopted, the analogous requirements under number (2) and, subject to IRC Section 4980C(f), standards under number (3) above cease to apply).[1]

59. Are there any exceptions to the general rule that viatical settlements are not included as taxable income?

There is one exception to this general rule of non-includability for viatical settlements. The rules outlined above do not apply to any amount paid to any taxpayer other than the insured if the taxpayer has an insurable interest in the life of the insured because the insured is a director, officer or employee of the taxpayer or if the insured is financially interested in any trade or business of the taxpayer.[2]

60. What are the new reporting requirements that the 2017 tax reform legislation imposed on taxpayers involved in reportable policy sales?

The 2017 Tax Act imposes certain reporting requirements when an existing life insurance policy has been sold in a "reportable policy sale". The requirements apply to anyone who acquires a life insurance contract (or an interest in a life insurance contract) in a reportable policy sale (see below). These requirements are effective for reportable policy sales made after December 31, 2017 and reportable death benefits paid after December 31, 2017.

Planning Point: The IRS has released proposed regulations with respect to those reporting requirements, which will not be enforceable (i.e., no reporting is currently required) until final regulations are released. Forms 1099-LS and 1099-SB now contain instructions regarding these reporting requirements under the proposed regulations, which may change when final rules are released.[3]

Planning Point: The proposed regulations would exclude from certain aspects of the new rules situations where an individual or entity acquires a C corporation that owns life insurance contracts, so long as the life insurance contracts do not represent more than 50 percent of the corporation's assets. Generally, the new rule created by tax reform would make cause certain life insurance contracts to lose their tax-preferred status if transferred in a reportable policy sale (and most business combinations would qualify as such). Under the proposed regulations, however, the pre-tax reform exceptions to the transfer for value rule could apply when a C corporation is acquired.[4]

The buyer must report information to the IRS, the seller and the insurance company that issued the policy, including:

(1) His or her name, address and TIN,

(2) The name, address and TIN of whoever received payment for the interest in the policy,

(3) The date of the sale,

1. IRC Sec. 101(g)(3)(B).
2. IRC Sec. 101(g)(5).
3. Notice 2018-41, REG-103083-18.
4. See Prop. Treas. Reg. §1.101-1(e)(3)(ii).

(4) The name of the policy issuer, and

(5) The amount of the payment.[1]

When the insurance company receives this notice, it must report the following information to the IRS and the seller:

(1) The name, address and TIN of the seller,

(2) The basis of the insurance contract, and

(3) The policy number.[2]

A "reportable policy sale" means a sale where the acquirer has no substantial family, business or financial relationship with the insured (apart from the interest in the life insurance contract). The rules also apply with respect to indirect acquisitions made by way of purchasing an interest in a partnership, trust or other entity that holds an interest in the life insurance contract.[3]

When a reportable death benefit (a death benefit paid after a reportable policy sale) has been paid, the life insurance company is required to report certain information to the IRS and to the payee, including:

(1) The name, address and TIN of the person making the payment,

(2) The name, address and TIN of each recipient of payment,

(3) The date of each payment,

(4) The gross amount of the payment, and

(5) The payor's estimate of the buyer's basis in the contract.[4]

61. Are amounts received as living proceeds of life insurance and endowment contracts subject to withholding?

Yes.

A payee, however, generally may elect not to have anything withheld. Only the amount that it is reasonable to believe is includable in income is subject to withholding. Amounts are to be withheld from periodic payments at the same rate as wages. Payments are periodic, even if they are variable, if they are payable over a period of more than a year. If payments are not periodic, 10 percent of the includable amount is withheld. Payments to a beneficiary of a deceased payee are subject to withholding under the same rules.[5] An election out of withholding will be ineffective, generally, if a payee does not furnish his or her taxpayer identification number (TIN,

1. IRC Sec. 6050Y(a)(1).
2. IRC Sec. 6050Y(b).
3. IRC Sec. 6050Y(d)(2).
4. IRC Sec. 6050Y(c).
5. IRC Sec. 3405; Temp. Treas. Reg. §35.3405-1T (A-9, A-10, A-12, A-17, F-19 through 24).

usually the payee's Social Security number) to the payor, or furnishes an incorrect TIN to the payor and the payor is so notified by the IRS.[1]

62. Does the surrender or sale of a life insurance or endowment contract ever result in a deductible loss?

A loss deduction can be claimed only if the loss is incurred in connection with the taxpayer's trade or business or in a transaction entered into for profit.[2] If the surrendered contract is a life insurance policy, ordinarily there will be no deductible loss, even though the cash surrender value is less than the net premium cost. The IRC expressly provides that a taxpayer's investment in the contract is the "aggregate premiums paid," but this may be different than the contract's "basis" (Q 37, Q 51). The IRC, however, is silent with respect to cost basis for computing loss. Several courts have held that the portion of the premiums paid for life insurance protection cannot be included in the cost basis. They reason that this portion is not a recoverable investment, but a nondeductible expense.[3] There can be no loss, therefore, if the cash surrender value equals the policy reserve. But if the contract is surrendered in a policy year in which the reserve exceeds the cash surrender value, the difference *may* be allowable as a loss, provided the policy was purchased in connection with the taxpayer's trade or business or in a transaction entered into for profit.[4] Apparently the Tax Court considers the purchase of a personal cash value policy as a transaction entered into for profit to the extent of the policy's investment feature.[5] A Texas district court, however, does not consider it a transaction for profit even to this extent.[6]

A different situation exists where, because of the insurance company's insolvency, the policy owner receives less than the stated cash surrender value. In this case, the difference between the amount received and the stated cash surrender value is a deductible loss.[7]

Death Proceeds

63. Are life insurance proceeds payable by reason of the insured's death taxable income to the beneficiary?

Generally, no. As a general rule, death proceeds are excludable from the beneficiary's gross income.[8] Death proceeds from single premium, periodic premium, or flexible premium policies are received income tax-free by the beneficiary regardless of whether the beneficiary is an individual, a corporation, a partnership, a trustee, or the insured's estate.[9] With some exceptions (as noted below), the exclusion generally applies regardless of who paid the premiums or who owned the policy.

1. IRC Sec. 3405(e)(12).
2. IRC Sec. 165.
3. *London Shoe Co., Inc. v. Comm.*, 80 F.2d 230 (2nd Cir. 1935); *Century Wood Preserving Co. v. Comm.*, 69 F.2d 967 (3rd Cir. 1934); *Keystone Consol. Publishing Co. v. Comm.*, 26 BTA 1210 (1932).
4. See *London Shoe Co., Inc.*, supra.
5. *Cohen v. Comm.*, 44 BTA 709 (1941); *Fleming v. Comm.*, 4 TCM (CCH) 316 (1945).
6. *Arnold v. U.S.*, 180 F. Supp. 746 (N.D. Texas 1959).
7. *Cohen*, supra; *Fleming*, supra.
8. IRC Sec. 101(a)(1).
9. Treas. Reg. §1.101-1(a)(1).

Note that death proceeds from certain employer-owned life insurance contracts received by the employer as beneficiary will not be excluded from the employer's taxable income unless certain requirements are met (Q 276).[1]

Planning Point: When presenting a key person proposal it is important to ask the prospect, "How much additional gross sales would it take to equal the income-tax-free benefits of life insurance?" Also point out that the sales revenue will be needed at a time when the business has lost a person critical to the creation of that revenue. *William H. Alley, CLU, ChFC, MSFS, LUTCF, Alley Financial Group, LLC.*

Proceeds from group life insurance can qualify for the exclusion as well as proceeds from individual policies. Under certain conditions, accelerated death benefits paid prior to the death of a chronically or terminally ill insured may qualify for this exclusion (Q 54). On the other hand, death benefits under annuity contracts do not qualify for the exclusion because they are not proceeds of life insurance within the meaning of IRC Section 101(a)(1).

In order to come within the exclusion, the proceeds must be paid "by reason of the death of the insured." In other words, the exclusion applies only to proceeds that are payable because the insured's death has matured the policy. When the policy has matured during the insured's lifetime, amounts payable to the beneficiary, even though payable at the insured's death, are not "death proceeds." Proceeds paid on a policy covering a missing-in-action member of the uniformed services were excludable, even though no official finding of death had been made by the Defense Department.[2]

If death proceeds are paid under a life insurance contract (as defined in IRC Section 7702 and discussed in Q 65), the exclusion extends to the full amount of the policy proceeds. For example, if an insured dies after having paid $6,000 in premiums on a $100,000 policy, the full face amount of $100,000 is excludable from the beneficiary's gross income (not just the $6,000 that represents a return of premiums). The face amount of paid-up additional insurance and the lump sum payable under a double indemnity provision also are excludable under IRC Section 101(a)(1). When the death proceeds are received in a one sum cash payment, the entire amount is received income tax-free. However, the exclusion does not extend to interest earned on the proceeds after the insured's death. Thus, if the proceeds are held by the insurer at interest, the interest is taxable (Q 70). If the proceeds are held by the insurer under a life income or other installment option, the tax-exempt proceeds are prorated over the payment period, and the balance of each payment is taxable income (Q 71).

Generally, in the case of a contract issued after 1984 that is a life insurance contract under applicable law but that does not meet the definitional requirements explained in Q 65, only the excess of the death benefit over the net surrender value (cash surrender value less any surrender charges) will be excludable from the income of the beneficiary as a death benefit.[3] Generally, the exclusion is similarly limited to the amount of the death benefit in excess of the net surrender value in the case of a flexible premium contract that is subject to, but fails to meet, the

1. IRC Sec. 101(j).
2. Rev. Rul. 78-372, 1978-2 CB 93.
3. IRC Sec. 7702(g)(2).

guidelines of IRC Section 101(f) (Q 65). Nevertheless, in either case, a part of the cash surrender value also will be excludable as a recovery of basis to the extent the basis has not been previously recovered; presumably, when a contract subject to the definition of a life insurance contract in IRC Section 7702 fails to meet that definition, or when a variable contract is not adequately diversified, unrecovered cash value increases previously includable in income will be recoverable tax-free as a part of basis.

In addition, all or part of the proceeds may be taxable income in the following circumstances:

- In some instances, the policy or an interest in the policy has been transferred for valuable consideration (Q 77, Q 279);
- The proceeds are received under a qualified pension or profit-sharing plan (Q 3960);
- The proceeds are received under a tax-sheltered annuity for an employee of a tax-exempt organization or public school (Q 4042);
- The proceeds are received under an individual retirement endowment contract (Q 3672);
- The proceeds are received by a creditor with no other insurable interest from insurance on the life of the debtor (Q 135, Q 136);
- There is no insurable interest in the life of the insured (Q 292);
- The proceeds are received as corporate dividends or compensation (Q 291);
- The proceeds are received as alimony by a divorced spouse (Q 106);
- The proceeds are received as restitution of embezzled funds (Q 293); and
- Proceeds received by a corporation may be subject to an alternative minimum tax (Q 316) (but note that the corporate AMT was repealed for tax years beginning after 2017).

64. Is the death benefit under the double indemnity clause of a life insurance policy subject to federal income tax?

No. The death benefit is generally tax-exempt as proceeds payable by reason of an insured's death.[1] If the proceeds are held under a settlement option, the regular rules apply (Q 70, Q 71).

65. What is a "life insurance contract" for purposes of the death benefit exclusion for contracts issued after December 31, 1984?

Under IRC Section 7702, for death proceeds of a life insurance contract (including an endowment contract) issued after December 31, 1984, to be fully excludable from the beneficiary's gross income, the contract generally must be a life insurance contract under applicable

1. IRC Sec. 101(a); Treas. Reg. §1.101-1(a)(1).

state (or applicable local foreign) law *and* must meet one of two alternative tests: the cash value accumulation test (Q 66) or the guideline premium and corridor test (Q 67).[1] Any plan or arrangement provided by a church or a convention or association of churches to its employees or their beneficiaries that provides for the payment of a death benefit is not required to meet the requirement that the arrangement constitute a life insurance contract under applicable law.[2]

The IRS may waive an insurer's failure to satisfy the requirements of IRC Section 7702(a) if the errors were reasonable and reasonable steps to remedy the errors have been taken.[3] For example, when six life insurance policies were temporarily out of compliance with the guideline premium test requirements due to the inadvertence of the insurer's employees during a change in computer systems, the IRS granted such a waiver after the insurer increased the policy death benefits.[4] When a combination of clerical errors (including lost records, missed testing dates, and the failure to make scheduled premium adjustments) and the conversion of the insurance company's policy administration system from a manual procedure to a fully computerized one caused policies to be out of compliance, the IRS granted a waiver, but required that the policies be brought into compliance within ninety days.[5] When a clerk failed to realize that a certificate holder had paid in additional premiums that put a group universal life certificate out of compliance, the IRS granted a waiver provided that the company refund the excess premiums, with interest, or increase the policy death benefit from the time of noncompliance.[6] The IRS refused to waive an insurer's failure to satisfy these requirements, however, when several policies were discovered to be out of compliance due to the company's use of a software program that contained an "inherent structural flaw."[7]

Modification of a life insurance contract after December 31, 1990, that is necessitated by the insurer's insolvency will not affect the date on which the contract was issued, entered into, or purchased for purposes of IRC Section 7702.[8]

66. How is the cash value accumulation test met?

To satisfy the cash value accumulation test, the cash surrender value of a contract, according to its terms, must not at any time exceed the net single premium that would be necessary at such time to fund future benefits (death benefits, endowment benefits, and charges for certain additional benefits, such as a disability waiver) under the contract.[9] The *cash surrender value* of a contract is its cash value, disregarding any surrender charges, policy loans, or reasonable termination benefits. The *net single premium* is determined by using (1) an annual effective interest rate of 4 percent or the interest rate(s) guaranteed in the contract, whichever is greater, (2) the mortality charges specified in the contract or if none are specified, the charges used in figuring the statutory reserves for the contract, and (3) any other charges specified in the contract.

1. IRC Sec. 7702(a).
2. IRC Sec. 7702(j).
3. IRC Sec. 7702(f)(8).
4. Let. Rul. 9042039. See also Let. Ruls. 9801042, 9727025, 9621016.
5. Let. Rul. 9416017. See also Let. Ruls. 200006030, 199924028, 9834020, 9838014.
6. Let. Rul. 9623068. See also Let. Ruls. 200027030, 9805010, 9601039, 9517042, 9322023, 9146016, 9146011.
7. Let. Rul. 9202008.
8. Rev. Proc. 92-57, 1992-2 CB 410; Let. Rul. 9239026. See also Let. Rul. 9305013.
9. IRC Sec. 7702(b).

For contracts issued on or after October 21, 1988, the mortality charges used must be reasonable charges that meet the requirements, if any, identified in the applicable regulations and that do not exceed the mortality charges specified in the "prevailing commissioners' standard tables" at the time the contract is issued.[1] The 2017 Tax Act modified the definition of the prevailing commissioners' standard tables, see footnote 2 below. The exercise of an option to change a policy's death benefit after October 21, 1988, added to the policy by endorsement prior to this date, did not cause the policy to become subject to the reasonable mortality requirements of IRC Section 7702(c)(3)(B)(i), as amended by Technical and Miscellaneous Revenue Act (TAMRA).[2]

Proposed regulations provide three safe harbors for meeting the reasonable mortality charge requirement in contracts that insure only one life and that are entered into on or after October 21, 1988.[3] A contract issued before October 21, 1988 will meet the reasonable mortality charge requirements if it has mortality charges that do not differ materially from the charges actually expected to be made.[4] Any other reasonable charges taken into account for purposes of determining the net single premium must be reasonably expected to actually be paid and must be actually specified in the contract.[5]

67. How is the guideline premium and cash value corridor test met?

To meet the guideline premium and cash corridor test, the contract must first meet certain guideline premium requirements and, second, the contract must fall within the *cash value corridor*.

For the contract to meet the *guideline premium requirement*, the sum of the premiums paid under the contract must not at any time exceed *the greater of* (1) the guideline single premium as of such time, or (2) the sum of the guideline level premiums to such date.[6]

Premiums paid for purposes of this section means those paid under the contract less excludable amounts that are not received as an annuity under IRC Section 72(e) (e.g., dividends).[7]

The *guideline single premium* is the premium necessary to fund future benefits under the contract, determined at the time the contract is issued using the same factors as for the net single premium (Q 66), except that the annual effective rate of interest is 6 percent instead of 4 percent.[8]

The *guideline level premium* is the level annual amount payable over a period not ending before the insured reaches age ninety-five, computed in the same manner as the single guideline

1. IRC Sec. 7702(c)(3)(B)(i). The prevailing commissioners' standard tables are defined in IRC Section 807(d)(5). See, also, 2001 CSO Table. The 2017 Tax Act (Pub. Law No. 115-97) modified the definition of "prevailing commissioners' standard tables" to include the most recent NAIC tables used for computing reserves under the laws of at least 26 states' insurance laws when the contract was issued. If there is any change in these tables from one year to the next, the issuer may use the prevailing commissioners' standard tables as of the beginning of the preceding calendar year with respect to any contract issued after the change and before the close of the 3-year period beginning on the first day of the year of change.
2. Let. Rul. 9853033.
3. Prop. Treas. Reg. §1.7702-1.
4. TAMRA '88 Sec. 5011(c).
5. IRC Sec. 7702(c)(3)(B)(ii).
6. IRC Sec. 7702(c).
7. IRC Sec. 7702(f)(1).
8. IRC Sec. 7702(c)(3).

premium, except the annual effective rate remains at the greater of 4 percent or the rate guaranteed in the contract.[1] The IRC sets forth certain rules for computing the guideline premiums and benefits and provides special rules that, in limited circumstances, make exceptions for failing to meet the guideline premium requirements or allow premiums paid to be returned at the end of the year to correct such failures.[2]

A contract falls within the *cash value corridor* if the death benefit payable under the contract at any time is at least equal to an applicable percentage of the cash surrender value (see table below).

TABLE

In the case of an insured with an attained age as of the beginning of the contract year of:		The applicable percentage decreases by a ratable portion for each full year:	
More than	**But not more than**	**From**	**To**
0	40	250	250
40	45	250	215
45	50	215	185
50	55	185	150
55	60	150	130
60	65	130	120
65	70	120	115
70	75	115	105
75	90	105	105
90	95	105	100

The determination of whether a variable life insurance contract meets either the cash value accumulation test (Q 66) or the guideline premium cash corridor test must be made whenever the death benefit under the contract changes, but at least once during each twelve-month period.[3]

Planning Point: Generally, use of the guideline premium test will provide higher policy cash values than the cash value corridor test when cash accumulation is the primary purpose of the policy. However, it is advisable to run the product illustration using both tests to optimize the product design.

A variable life insurance contract will not be treated as a life insurance contract, and taxed accordingly, for any period that the underlying investments of the segregated asset account are not "adequately diversified" (Q 554).[4]

The IRS has ruled that sub-accounts within variable life policies that were invested in hedge funds available to the general public would be considered owned by the policy owners, and thus currently taxed on the income.[5] Sub-accounts within a variable life contract may invest in

1. IRC Sec. 7702(c).
2. IRC Sec. 7702(f)(1)(B).
3. IRC Sec. 7702(h)(9).
4. IRC Sec. 817(h).
5. Rev. Rul. 2003-92, 2003-33 IRB 350.

mutual funds that are available to the general public.[1] The IRS has clarified what is meant by the phrase "general public."[2]

In Revenue Procedure 2010-28, the IRS provides a safe harbor addressing the application of IRC Sections 7702 and 7702A to life insurance contracts that mature after the insured individual reaches age 100. The Revenue Procedure also addresses the treatment of amounts received under a life insurance contract after it has matured. Under the safe harbor, the IRS will not challenge the qualification of a contract as a life insurance contract under IRC Section 7702, or assert that a contract is a modified endowment contract under IRC Section 7702A (Q 13), provided that the contract satisfies the requirements of those provisions using all of the Age 100 Testing Methodologies in Section 3.02 of Revenue Procedure 2010-28.[3]

Contracts issued after June 30, 1984, that provide an increasing death benefit and have premium funding more rapid than ten-year level premium payments must satisfy the definition generally applicable to contracts issued after 1984, with certain exceptions.[4]

68. What is a "life insurance contract" for purposes of the death benefit exclusion for policies issued before January 1, 1985?

A policy issued before January 1, 1985, that is exchanged for one issued after December 31, 1984, will be treated as a contract issued after 1984 and subject to the definitional requirements of IRC Section 7702 discussed in Q 65, according to the General Explanation of the Deficit Reduction Act of 1984 (the General Explanation). The General Explanation states that a change in policy terms after December 31, 1984, could be considered an exchange that would bring the policy under the IRC Section 7702 definitional requirements. Examples of "changes in terms" are changes in "amount or pattern of death benefit, the premium pattern, the rate or rates guaranteed on issuance of the contract, or mortality and expense charges."[5] A change in minor administrative provisions or a loan rate change generally would not be considered to result in an exchange, the General Explanation adds. Modification of a life insurance contract after December 31, 1990, that is made necessary by the insurer's insolvency will not affect the date on which the contract was issued, entered into, or purchased for purposes of IRC Section 101(f).[6]

Otherwise, universal life insurance and any other flexible premium contract, issued before January 1, 1985, qualify for the death proceeds exclusion only if (1) the sum of the premiums does not exceed at any time a guideline premium (see below) *and* the death benefit is not less than a certain percentage of the cash value (140 percent until the start of the policy year the insured attains age forty, thereafter reducing 1 percent for each year over forty, but not below 105 percent) *or* (2) the contract provides that the cash value may not at any time exceed the net single premium for the death benefit at that time.

1. Let. Rul. 200420017.
2. Rev. Rul. 2007-7, 2007-7 IRB 468.
3. Rev. Proc. 2010-28; 2010-2 C.B. 270.
4. DEFRA Sec. 221(d)(2).
5. General Explanation of the Deficit Reduction Act of 1984 at p. 656.
6. Rev. Proc. 92-57, 1992-2 CB 410; Let. Rul. 9239026.

The guideline premium is the greater of (1) the single premium necessary to fund future benefits under the contract based on the maximum mortality rates and other charges fixed in the contract and the minimum interest rate guaranteed in the contract at issue, but at least 6 percent, or (2) the aggregate level annual amounts payable over the life of the contract (at least twenty years but not extending beyond age ninety-five, if earlier) computed in the same manner as the single premium guideline (using an annual effective rate of 4 percent instead of 6 percent). The IRS can allow excessive premiums paid in error to be returned (with interest) within sixty days after the end of the policy year; in such case, the policy will still qualify as life insurance.[1]

The death benefit of a flexible premium contract entered into before January 1, 1983, will be excludable if the contract met the requirements on September 3, 1983. In determining if the level annual premium guideline is met by such a contract, an annual effective interest rate of 3 percent may be substituted for 4 percent.[2]

For life insurance contracts (other than flexible premium contracts) issued before January 1, 1985, there is no clear definition of "life insurance" for purposes of the tax-free death benefit. Despite this, the death proceeds are not considered proceeds of life insurance unless the contract under which they are paid provided protection against the risk of early death. The IRS has taken the position that, for income tax purposes, a contract is a life insurance contract if it contained an element of life insurance risk at any time.[3] Thus, the IRS apparently has not attempted to tax the proceeds of a retirement income contract, even when the insured's death has occurred after the cash value has exceeded the face amount but before the maturity of the contract. This ruling involved a contract purchased by a qualified retirement plan and the IRS could attempt to limit its position to such contracts.[4] On the other hand, the Tax Court has held that a retirement income contract is an annuity contract once the element of risk has disappeared.[5] The IRS also has ruled that the exclusion applies to variable life insurance death benefits that may increase or decrease, but not below a guaranteed minimum amount, on each policy anniversary depending on the investment experience of the separate account of the prior year's net premium.[6] Regulations provide that death benefits having the characteristics of life insurance proceeds payable by death under contracts such as workers compensation and accident and health contracts are excludable under IRC Section 101(a).[7]

69. How are proceeds taxed if a life insurance policy is owned by someone other than the insured?

The proceeds are taxed in the same manner as if the insured owned the policy. When a person retains all the incidents of ownership in an endowment or annuity contract but designates another to receive the maturity proceeds, the proceeds will be taxed to the owner rather than to

1. IRC Sec. 101(f).
2. TEFRA Sec. 266(c).
3. See Rev. Rul. 66-322, 1966-2 CB 123.
4. See GCM 38934 (12-8-82); GCM 39022 (8-12-83).
5. *Evans v. Comm.*, 56 TC 1142 (1971).
6. Rev. Rul. 79-87, 1979-1 CB 73.
7. Treas. Reg. §1.101-1(a)(1).

the payee (Q 580). For possible gift tax consequences when a policy is owned by one individual but insures another, see Q 214.

70. If life insurance death proceeds are left on deposit with the insurance company under an interest-only option, is the interest taxable income to the beneficiary?

Yes. All amounts paid or credited to a beneficiary as interest (excess and guaranteed) must be included in the beneficiary's gross income regardless of whether the insured or the beneficiary elected the option.[1] The interest is taxable in the first year that it can be withdrawn. If the beneficiary elects an option under which there is no right to withdraw either principal or interest for a specified number of years, the entire amount of accumulated interest is taxable in the year during which it first becomes withdrawable.[2] But if the beneficiary has a right to withdraw principal, the interest is taxable when credited even though the agreement stipulates that the interest cannot be withdrawn.[3]

The principal amount held by the insurer, representing the value of the proceeds at the insured's death, is income tax-free to the recipient when withdrawn (Q 63).

For a discussion of the tax treatment when proceeds are held for a period under the interest option and subsequently paid under a life income or installment settlement, see Q 71.

Life Income and Installment Options

71. If excludable death proceeds are held by an insurer and are paid under a life income or installment option, how are the payments treated for income tax purposes?

The "amount held by the insurer" (usually the one-sum proceeds payable at the insured's death) is prorated over the payment period. (If the settlement arrangement involves a life income with a guaranteed refund, or a guaranteed number of payments, the value of the guarantee must be subtracted from the one-sum proceeds before making the proration.) These prorated amounts determine the portion of each payment that may be treated as a return of principal. Consequently, the beneficiary may exclude this portion of each payment from gross income.[4] All amounts received in excess of these prorated amounts are treated as interest, and are taxable as ordinary income to any beneficiary other than the surviving spouse of an insured who died before October 23, 1986. Such a surviving spouse is entitled to exclude up to $1,000 of such interest annually in addition to the prorated amount of principal.[5]

See Q 72 for a discussion of the treatment of a life income option, Q 73 for a discussion of the treatment of a fixed period option and Q 74 for a discussion of the treatment of death proceeds payable in installments based on a fixed amount.

1. IRC Sec. 101(c); Treas. Reg. §1.101-3(a).
2. Treas. Reg. §1.101-4 (g), Ex. 1.
3. *Strauss v. Comm.*, 21 TC 104 (1953); see also Rev. Rul. 68-586, 1968-2 CB 195.
4. IRC Sec. 101(d)(1); Treas. Reg. §1.101-4(a)(1)(i).
5. IRC Sec. 101(d)(1)(B), prior to repeal by TRA '86 Sec. 1001(a); Treas. Reg. §1.101-4(a)(1)(ii).

72. If excludable death proceeds are held by an insurer and are paid under a life income or installment option, how are the payments treated for income tax purposes if the installments are payable based on the life of the beneficiary?

If the installments are payable for the lifetime of the beneficiary (a life income option), the "amount held by the insurer" is divided by the beneficiary's life expectancy to determine the amount that may be excluded from gross income each year as a return of principal. In the case of amounts paid with respect to deaths occurring after October 22, 1986, the beneficiary's life expectancy must be determined using IRS annuity tables V and VI.[1] In the case of amounts paid with respect to deaths occurring before October 23, 1986, the beneficiary's life expectancy is taken from the mortality table that the insurer uses in determining the amount of the installments (not from the IRS annuity tables).[2] If there is a refund or period-certain guarantee, the amount held by the insurer must be reduced by the present value of the guarantee before prorating for the exclusion.[3] The present value of the guarantee is determined by using the insurer's interest rate and the applicable mortality table. The excludable amount, once determined, remains the same even though the beneficiary outlives his or her life expectancy. The balance of the payments is taxable income to any beneficiary other than the surviving spouse of an insured who died before October 23, 1986. The spouse of such an insured may exclude up to $1,000 of interest each year in addition to excluding the prorated amount of principal. If the beneficiary dies before receiving all guaranteed amounts, the secondary beneficiary receives the balance of the guaranteed refund, or guaranteed payments, tax-free.[4] Excess interest allowed by the company in addition to the guaranteed refund would be taxable income to the secondary beneficiary, however.[5]

> *Example.* Insured husband died after October 22, 1986. Insured's widow elects to receive $75,000 of death proceeds under a refund life income option. The company guarantees her payments of $4,000 a year. According to Table V and the interest rate used by the insurer, her life expectancy is twenty-five years and the present value of the refund guarantee is $13,500. The $75,000 must first be reduced by the value of the refund guarantee ($75,000 – $13,500 = $61,500). This reduced amount, $61,500, is then divided by her life expectancy to find the amount that she may exclude from gross income each year as return of principal. This amount is $2,460 ($61,500 ÷ 25). Her taxable income from the guaranteed payment is $1,540 a year ($4,000 – $2,460). If the widow dies before receiving the full $75,000, the balance of the guaranteed amount will be received tax-free by the secondary beneficiary.

If a joint-and-survivor option is elected, the "amount held by the insurer" is divided by the life expectancy of the beneficiaries as a group to determine the annual exclusion of principal (see above for the appropriate mortality table to be used). The same amount of principal is excludable during the joint lives and the lifetime of the survivor.[6]

1. IRC Sec. 101(d)(2)(B)(ii); Treas. Reg. §1.101-7.
2. Treas. Reg. §1.101-4(c).
3. Treas. Reg. §1.101-4(e).
4. Treas. Reg. §1.101-4(d)(3).
5. Treas. Reg. §1.101-4(d)(3) and (g), Ex. 7.
6. Treas. Reg. §1.101-4(d)(2) and (g), Ex. 5.

73. If excludable death proceeds are held by an insurer and are paid under a life income or installment option, how are the payments treated for income tax purposes if the installments are payable based on a fixed period?

The "amount held by the insurer" is divided by the number of installment payments to be made in the fixed period. The quotient is the portion of each payment that is excludable from the beneficiary's gross income as a return of principal. The balance of each guaranteed payment generally must be included in the beneficiary's gross income. In addition to the prorated amount of principal, the surviving spouse of an insured who died before October 23, 1986, may exclude up to $1,000 of interest each year (guaranteed and excess).[1] If the primary beneficiary dies before the end of the fixed period, the secondary beneficiary may exclude the same amount of prorated principal from gross income, but all interest (guaranteed and excess) is includable.[2]

> *Example.* Insured spouse died after October 22, 1986. Insured's widow elects to receive $50,000 of proceeds in ten annual installments of $5,500 each. As a second payment, she receives $5,950 (guaranteed payment plus $450 excess interest). She may exclude $5,000 of the payment as a return of principal ($50,000 ÷ 10). Consequently, she must include in income the balance of the payment ($950).

74. If excludable death proceeds are held by an insurer and are paid under a life income or installment option, how are the payments treated for income tax purposes if the installments are payable based on a fixed amount?

The "amount held by the insurer" is divided by the number of payments required to exhaust principal and guaranteed interest. The quotient is the portion of each payment that is excludable from the beneficiary's gross income as a return of principal. The balance of each guaranteed payment generally must be included in the beneficiary's gross income.[3] The surviving spouse of an insured who died before October 23, 1986, may exclude up to $1,000 of interest each year in addition to the prorated amount of principal. Payments extending beyond the guaranteed period (payments comprised entirely of excess interest) are fully taxable. (There is a difference of opinion as to whether the surviving spouse's $1,000 annual interest exclusion, even if otherwise available, can be applied to these additional excess interest payments.) If the primary beneficiary dies before the end of the guaranteed payment period, the secondary beneficiary may exclude the same amount of prorated principal from gross income.

75. Is a surviving spouse entitled to an additional exclusion for interest on death proceeds paid out via a life income or installment option upon the spouse's death?

In addition to the prorated exclusion of principal (see Q 71 to Q 74), the surviving spouse of an insured *who died prior to October 23, 1986,* is entitled to exclude from gross income up to $1,000 of interest (guaranteed and excess) in each taxable year. (The surviving spouse's $1,000 annual

1. Treas. Reg. §1.101-4(a)(2), Ex. 1 and 2.
2. Treas. Reg. §1.101-4(a)(2), Ex. 3.
3. Treas. Reg. §1.101-4(g), Ex. 2.

exclusion was repealed for surviving spouses of insureds who die after October 22, 1986.) No more than $1,000 of interest may be excluded annually with respect to one insured, regardless of the number of policies. But if the beneficiary is the surviving spouse of more than one insured, the beneficiary is entitled to a $1,000 annual interest exclusion with respect to policies on the life of each insured.[1] To qualify for this additional exclusion, the surviving spouse must have been married to the insured when the insured died. An absolute divorce disqualifies the beneficiary, although a legal separation or an interlocutory decree does not.[2] The surviving spouse's remarriage does not affect his or her qualification.[3] This $1,000 annual exclusion is available only with respect to the interest element in life income or installment payments; it is not available with respect to interest payments under an interest-only option. In other words, the settlement must provide for a substantial diminution of principal during the period the interest is received.[4] It would appear that because payments of proceeds (including interest) from National Service Life Insurance (NSLI) otherwise are exempted from taxation, the receipt of NSLI proceeds under an installment settlement will not reduce the $1,000 annual exclusion (Q 139).

76. What are the tax consequences of changing the method of receiving the proceeds of a life insurance policy?

The surviving spouse of an insured who died before October 23, 1986, is not precluded from obtaining the benefits of the $1,000 annual interest exclusion at a later date simply because the surviving spouse originally elected to leave the proceeds with the insurer under the interest-only option. A new election to take the proceeds under a life income or other installment option will entitle the surviving spouse to the annual interest exclusion.[5] During the time the proceeds are held under the interest-only option, the interest will be fully taxable to him or her as received (Q 70). Payments under the life income or installment option will be treated as explained in Q 71 to Q 74.

Insured Died Before August 17, 1954

In tax years beginning before January 1, 1977, the full installment or life income payment was tax-free to the beneficiary except excess interest, provided the option was elected under a contract right.[6] Effective for tax years beginning on or after January 1, 1977, IRC Section 101(f) was repealed.[7] As a result, these payments fall within the general rules (above) applicable where the insured died after August 16, 1954.

77. Are death proceeds wholly tax-exempt if an existing life insurance policy is sold or otherwise transferred for valuable consideration?

Editor's Note: The 2017 Tax Act added a new exception to the transfer for value rule for commercial transfers (i.e., life settlement transactions, also known as viatical settlements).

---

1. IRC Sec. 101(d)(1)(B), prior to repeal by TRA '86 Sec. 1001(a); Treas. Reg. §1.101-4(a)(2), Ex. 2.
2. Treas. Reg. §1.101-4(a)(1)(ii); see *Eccles v. Comm.*, 19 TC 1049 (1953), *aff'd* 208 F.2d 796 (4th Cir. 1953).
3. Rev. Rul. 72-164, 1972-1 CB 28.
4. Treas. Reg. §1.101-3(a).
5. Rev. Rul. 65-284, 1965-2 CB 28.
6. IRC Sec. 101(f) as in effect prior to January 1, 1977.
7. TRA '76 Sec. 1901(a)(16).

As a general rule, death benefit proceeds received by the beneficiary of the policy are wholly exempt from income tax (Q 63, Q 65). An exception to this rule, however, is that the proceeds are not wholly exempt if the policy, or any interest in the policy, has been transferred, by assignment or otherwise, for valuable consideration.[1] This exception is known as the "transfer for value rule." Under this rule, the proceeds will be subject to income tax to the extent that they exceed the consideration paid (and premiums subsequently paid) by the person to whom the policy is transferred. Also, for contracts issued after June 8, 1997 (in taxable years ending after this date), any interest paid or accrued by the transferee on indebtedness with respect to the policy is added to the amount exempt from tax after the transfer if the interest is not deductible under IRC Section 264(a)(4).[2]

This unfavorable result is avoided if the transfer for value is "to the insured, to a partner of the insured, or to a partnership in which the insured is a partner, or to a corporation in which the insured is a shareholder or officer, or if the basis of the policy in the hands of the transferee must be determined (at least in part) by reference to the transferor's basis (e.g., carryover basis). For tax years beginning after 2017, these exceptions will not apply if the policy was transferred in a reportable policy sale (see Q 279)."[3] (For application of the transfer for value rule to business insurance, see Q 279 to Q 290.)

Planning Point: If a transfer is contemplated and no exception is available, it is generally accepted that creation of a partnership between the insured and the transferee at or near the time of transfer can avoid the application of the transfer for value rule. This newly created partnership, however, should have a valid purpose (other than tax avoidance) so as to not be disregarded by the IRS. Likewise, a transfer for less than adequate consideration may be considered part gift/part sale such that it qualifies as an exception under the so-called "basis exception." Please note that the exceptions above do NOT include a transfer to a fellow shareholder of a corporation in which the insured is a shareholder. It is often (wrongly) assumed that a transfer to a fellow shareholder or officer is an exception since the transfer to a fellow partner is an exception.

The unfavorable result, however, is not avoided merely because the person to whom the policy is transferred has an insurable interest in the insured. For example, often an insured will transfer his or her policy to a son or daughter. If the transfer is a gift, the named beneficiary will receive the proceeds wholly free of income tax. But if the insured receives valuable consideration for the transfer, the proceeds will be taxable income to the beneficiary (to the extent they exceed the consideration, premiums, and other amounts subsequently paid).[4] The fact that no money was exchanged for the policy does not necessarily mean that the transfer was a gift and therefore was not subject to the transfer for value rule. For example, when two insured individuals assign policies on their own lives to each other at about the same time, it could be argued that neither transfer was a gift. The transfer of a policy subject to a nonrecourse loan may be a transfer for value (Q 280).

1. IRC Sec. 101(a)(2).
2. IRC Sec. 101(a)(2).
3. IRC Secs. 101(a)(2), 101(a)(3).
4. Treas. Reg. §1.101-1(b); *Bean v. Comm.*, TC Memo 1955-195.

However, when a policy is owned by someone other than the insured, a transfer for value to the insured will not cause loss of tax exemption for the proceeds. Moreover, in the case of successive transfers, the proceeds will be wholly tax-exempt if the final transfer, or the last transfer for value, is to the insured or to his or her partner, a partnership in which the insured is a partner, or a corporation in which the insured is a shareholder or officer (see Q 279).[1] See Q 79 for a transfer to a spouse (or former spouse, if incident to a divorce).

78. Are death proceeds of life insurance wholly tax-exempt if the policy has been transferred as a gift?

Generally, the donee steps into the shoes of the donor. Thus, the entire proceeds are exempt if they would have been exempt had the policy been retained by the donor. If the donor purchases the policy from another owner and no exceptions to the transfer for value rule (Q 77) apply, however, then only the consideration paid by the donor, plus net premiums (and certain other amounts) subsequently paid by the donor and donee, is exempt.

As an exception to this general rule, however, the proceeds will be wholly tax-exempt – despite any previous transfer for value – if the final transfer is made to the insured, a partner of the insured, a partnership in which the insured is a partner, or a corporation in which the insured is an officer or shareholder. For tax years beginning after 2017, these exceptions will not apply if the policy was transferred in a reportable policy sale.[2] The IRS has ruled that when a life insurance policy subject to a policy loan is transferred, there is a transfer for value; if the transfer is partly a gift, it may come within one of the exceptions to the transfer for value rule (Q 279, #3).[3]

79. Will the transfer of a life insurance policy between spouses result in loss of the tax exemption for the death proceeds?

The transfer of a life insurance policy between spouses (or former spouses if incident to a divorce, Q 106) generally will not result in the loss of exemption for the death proceeds if the transfer occurs after July 18, 1984, (unless the transfer is pursuant to an instrument in effect on or before such date), or after December 31, 1983, and both spouses (or former spouses if incident to a divorce) elect to have the nonrecognition rules of IRC Section 1041 apply.

The transferee is treated as having acquired the policy by gift and the transferor's basis is carried over to the transferee.[4] IRC Section 101(a)(2)(A) provides that the transfer for value rule does not apply if the basis of the contract for determining gain or loss in the hands of the transferee is determined by reference to the basis of the contract in the hands of the transferor. If a life insurance policy with a loan is transferred in trust and gain is recognized by the transferor (Q 106), the basis in the transferee's hands is adjusted to reflect the gain, but the transfer may nonetheless come within an exception to the transfer for value rule (Q 279 #3).

1. IRC Sec. 101(a)(2)(B); Treas. Reg. §1.101-1(b).
2. Treas. Reg. §1.101-1(b); *Hacker v. Comm.*, 36 BTA 659 (1937).
3. Rev. Rul. 69-187, 1969-1 CB 45; Let. Rul. 8951056.
4. IRC Sec. 1041.

If the transfer occurs either prior to July 19, 1984, or after July 18, 1984, but pursuant to an instrument in effect before such date *and* no election to have the nonrecognition rules of IRC Section 1041 apply has been made, then the nature of the transfer determines whether the transfer for value rule applies. If the transfer was made pursuant to a property settlement agreement incident to a divorce, then the policy may be considered to have been transferred for value (e.g., in exchange for the release of marital rights). If the transfer between spouses was in the nature of a gift, then no loss of the exemption would result.

Estate Tax Issues

80. What benefits payable at death are included in the term "life insurance" for estate tax purposes?

IRC Section 2042 deals with the estate taxation of proceeds from insurance on the life of a decedent. According to regulations, the term "insurance," as used in IRC Section 2042, means life insurance of every description, including death benefits paid by fraternal societies operating under the lodge system.[1] In the case of a retirement income endowment, the death proceeds are treated as insurance proceeds under IRC Section 2042 if the insured dies before the terminal reserve value equals or exceeds the face value. If the insured dies after that time, the proceeds are treated as death proceeds of an annuity contract (Q 621, Q 624).[2]

With respect to the proceeds of "no-fault" automobile liability insurance, the IRS has ruled on three categories of benefits:

(1) *Survivors' loss benefits*. These are benefits payable only to certain named dependent survivors of the insured. If the insured dies leaving no such eligible dependents, no benefits are paid. The value of any such benefit is not includable in the insured's gross estate under IRC Section 2033 or under IRC Section 2042(2) because if the proceeds are life insurance (an issue the ruling did not decide) the insured would not have owned any incidents of ownership (Q 86) at his or her death.[3]

(2) *Basic economic loss benefit*. This benefit covers the insured's medical expenses and loss of income arising from the insured's injury while operating an automobile. The value of this benefit is includable in the insured's gross estate under IRC Section 2033, but not under IRC Section 2042(1) (life insurance proceeds payable to or for the insured's estate).[4]

(3) *Death benefit*. This is a benefit payable unconditionally to the estate of the insured and to the estate of any passenger in the insured's car killed in a covered accident. The value of this benefit is includable under IRC Section 2042(1) in the estate of each insured receiving the benefit.[5]

1. Treas. Reg. §20.2042-1(a).
2. Treas. Reg. §20.2039-1(d).
3. Rev. Rul. 82-5, 1982-1 CB 131.
4. Rev. Rul. 83-44, 1983-1 CB 228.
5. Rev. Rul. 83-44, above.

81. When are death proceeds of life insurance includable in an insured's gross estate?

They are includable in the following four situations:

(1) The proceeds are payable to the insured's estate, or are receivable for the benefit of the insured's estate (Q 82 to Q 84);[1]

(2) The proceeds are payable to a beneficiary other than the insured's estate but the insured possessed one or more incidents of ownership in the policy at the time of the insured's death, whether exercisable by the insured alone or only in conjunction with another person (Q 85 to Q 92);[2]

(3) The insured has made a gift of the policy on the insured's life within three years before his or her death (Q 96);[3] or

(4) The insured has transferred the policy for less than an adequate consideration (i.e., the transaction was not a bona fide sale) and the transfer falls within one of the rules for includability contained in IRC Sections 2035, 2036, 2037, 2038, or 2041. Under these circumstances, the value of the proceeds in excess of the value of the consideration received is includable in an insured's estate.[4] A grantor may retain the power to substitute property of an equivalent value. Such a power, in and of itself, generally does not cause the trust corpus to be includable under IRC Section 2036 or 2038.[5]

82. If life insurance proceeds are payable to an insured's estate, is the value of the proceeds includable in the insured's estate?

Yes. The entire value of the proceeds must be included in the insured's gross estate even if the insured possessed no incident of ownership in the policy, and paid none of the premiums.[6] But see Q 167 and Q 168 for the rule in community property states. Proceeds payable to an executor in the executor's individual capacity rather than as executor for the insured's estate were not treated as payable to the insured's estate by the Tax Court.[7]

83. When are life insurance proceeds includable in an insured's gross estate even though the insured has no incident of ownership in the policy and the proceeds are not payable to the insured's estate?

Proceeds are includable in an insured's gross estate if they are receivable by or *for the benefit of* the insured's estate. Thus, if the beneficiary is under a legally binding obligation to pay debts or taxes of the insured's estate, the amount of proceeds required to discharge these debts and

1. IRC Sec. 2042(1).
2. IRC Sec. 2042(2).
3. IRC Sec. 2035.
4. IRC Sec. 2043.
5. Rev. Rul. 2008-22, 2008-16 IRB 797.
6. IRC Sec. 2042(1); *Est. of Bromley v. Comm.*, 16 BTA 1322 (1929).
7. *Est. of Friedberg v. Comm.*, TC Memo 1992-310.

taxes (to the extent of the beneficiary's obligation) is includable in the insured's gross estate. This is so even though the insured possessed no incidents of ownership in the policy at the insured's death.[1] State law generally requires a life insurance beneficiary to forfeit the proceeds if the beneficiary is convicted of feloniously killing the insured. Where state law further provides that in such case proceeds will be distributed to beneficiaries of the insured's estate (other than to the felon), it has been held that the proceeds are treated for federal estate tax purposes as payable to the insured's estate.[2] (With respect to insurance assigned as collateral, see Q 137; for discretionary powers that may be granted to a trustee, see Q 182.)

84. Are the proceeds from life insurance taken out to pay an insured's death taxes includable in the insured's estate?

Yes.

The proceeds are includable in the insured's gross estate if the beneficiary has a legally binding obligation to use them to pay the insured's death taxes.[3] For powers that may be given to a trustee, see Q 182.

Planning Point: Proceeds should not be includable in the gross estate merely because the beneficiary lends the proceeds to the estate, or uses the proceeds to buy assets from the estate. Liquidity can be provided to an estate in this manner.

85. When are life insurance proceeds payable to a beneficiary other than the insured's estate includable in the insured's estate?

Proceeds are includable in an insured's gross estate if the insured *legally possessed* and could *legally exercise* any incidents of ownership at the time of the insured's death. It does not matter that the insured did not have possession of the policy and therefore was unable to exercise ownership rights at the time of death,[4] or that the insured was unable as a practical matter to effect any change in the policy because the policy was collaterally assigned.[5]

The proceeds are includable even if the insured cannot exercise his or her ownership rights alone, but only in conjunction with another person.[6] It has been held that an insured did not possess incidents of ownership where the insured had paid no premiums, did not regard the policy as the insured's own, and had made an irrevocable designation of beneficiary and mode of payment of proceeds.[7] (For what constitutes an incident of ownership, see Q 86.) But even if the proceeds are payable to a beneficiary other than the insured's estate, and the insured possesses no incidents of ownership in the policy, the proceeds are nevertheless includable in the insured's gross estate if they are receivable for the benefit of the insured's estate (Q 83). Even though the

1. Treas. Reg. §20.2042-1(b)(1); *Hooper v. Comm.*, 41 BTA 114 (1940), nonacq. 1940-1 CB 3 (1940); *Est. of Rohnert v. Comm.*, 40 BTA 1319 (1939); *Pacific Nat'l Bank of Seattle (Morgan) v. Comm.*, 40 BTA 128 (1939); *Davidson's Est. (Fourth Nat'l Bank in Wichita) v. Comm.*, 158 F.2d 239 (10th Cir. 1946).
2. *Est. of Draper v. Comm.*, 536 F.2d 944 (1st Cir. 1976); *First Kentucky Trust Co. v. U.S.*, 84-2 USTC ¶13,581 (6th Cir. 1984); Let. Rul. 7909056.
3. Treas. Reg. §20.2042-1(b)(1).
4. *Comm. v. Est. of Noel*, 380 U.S. 678 (1965).
5. *Est. of Goodwyn v. Comm.*, TC Memo 1973-153.
6. IRC Sec. 2042(2); *Goldstein's Est. v. U.S.*, 122 F. Supp. 677 (Ct. Cl. 1954).
7. *Morton v. U.S.*, 457 F.2d 750, 29 AFTR 2d 72-1531 (4th Cir. 1972).

insured retains no incidents of ownership in the policy, the proceeds may be includable in the insured's estate if the insured has transferred the policy within three years before the insured's death (Q 96; see also Q 179).

86. What are the incidents of ownership that will cause life insurance proceeds to be includable in the insured's estate?

Proceeds are includable in an insured's gross estate if the insured possesses any incidents of ownership at death including, but not limited to, the following:

- the right to change the beneficiary;
- the right to surrender or cancel the policy;
- the right to assign the policy;
- the right to revoke an assignment;
- the right to pledge the policy for a loan; or
- the right to obtain a policy loan.[1]

The reservation of a right to make premium loans has been held to be an incident of ownership.[2] A right to change contingent beneficiaries, who are to receive benefits after the primary beneficiary's death, also is an incident of ownership.[3]

The mere right to change the time or manner of payment of proceeds to the beneficiary, as by electing, changing, or revoking settlement options, has been held an incident of ownership,[4] but the Tax Court and the U.S. Court of Appeals for the Third Circuit have held to the contrary.[5] (In 1981, the IRS reiterated its opposition to the Third Circuit's holding in *Connelly*, and indicated its intent to continue to oppose that result in all circuits except the Third (Pa., Del., N.J., Virgin Islands).[6]

According to a technical advice memorandum, trust provisions that changed the beneficial interest from a decedent's spouse to the decedent's children if the decedent and the decedent's spouse became divorced were not the equivalent to a retained incident of ownership that would bring the life insurance proceeds into the decedent's estate.[7] The memorandum implies that the result would have been different if the trust had provided that the beneficial interest would revert to the decedent upon divorce.

---

1. Treas. Reg. §20.2042-1(c)(2); *Chase Nat'l Bank v. U.S.*, 278 U.S. 327 (1929); *Est. of DeVos v. Comm.*, TC Memo 1975-216; *Est. of Riefberg v. Comm.*, TC Memo 1982-70; *Allentown Nat'l Bank v. Comm.*, 37 BTA 750 (1938).
2. *Est. of McCoy v. Comm.*, TC Memo 1961-40.
3. *Broderick v. Keefe*, 112 F.2d 293 (1st Cir. 1940); *Est. of Newbold v. Comm.*, 4 TCM (CCH) 568 (1945).
4. *Est. of Lumpkin v. Comm.*, 474 F.2d 1092 (5th Cir. 1973).
5. *Lumpkin v. Comm.*, 56 TC 815 (1971), rev'd by 5th Cir. (above); *Billings v. Comm.*, 35 BTA 1147 (1937), acq. withdrawn 1972-1 CB 3; *Est. of Connelly v. U.S.*, 551 F.2d 545 (3rd Cir. 1977).
6. Rev. Rul. 81-128, 1981-1 CB 469.
7. TAM 8819001.

The right to receive disability income is an incident of ownership if payment of disability benefits would reduce the face amount payable at death.[1] But where an employer corporation owned the policy and the insured employee was entitled to benefits under a disability income rider, the IRS did not claim that the right to the disability income was an incident of ownership that would cause the proceeds to be includable in insured's gross estate.[2]

A more than 5 percent reversionary interest in the proceeds is an incident of ownership (Q 84).[3] When a wife, who owned insurance on her husband's life and who was the primary beneficiary, changed the contingent beneficiary from her estate to whomever the insured named in his will, the IRS ruled that the insured did not possess at his death an incident of ownership (Q 90).[4]

87. What are the incidents of ownership of employer-paid death benefits that would cause life insurance proceeds to be includable in the insured's estate?

An employee insured's right to designate the beneficiary of an employer-paid death benefit is not treated as an incident of ownership in the insurance funding the benefit if the employer is sole owner of the policy and sole beneficiary for its exclusive use.[5] (However, see Q 3636 through Q 3638 for potential income tax implications.) The IRS has taken the position that if the insured under a corporation-owned policy has an agreement with the corporation giving the insured the first right to purchase the policy for its cash surrender value if the corporation decides to discontinue the coverage, the purchase option is an incident of ownership.[6] The Tax Court has held, however, that the insured's contingent purchase option as described in Revenue Ruling 79-46 is not an incident of ownership within the meaning of IRC Section 2042(2).[7]

The IRS also has ruled that where, under an insured stock redemption agreement, a stockholder had the right to purchase the policies the corporation owned on the insured's life if the insured ceased being a stockholder, such contingent purchase option was not an incident of ownership in the insurance.[8] An insured who held the right to purchase a policy upon termination of a buy-sell agreement did not possess incidents of ownership so long as the contingency had not occurred, but would possess incidents once the agreement was terminated.[9]

Also, a shareholder was not treated as holding incidents of ownership in a life insurance policy where the shareholder could purchase a corporate-owned policy upon disability, or upon a cross-purchase of the shareholder's stock if the shareholder dissented to sale of the corporation to a third party or a public offering.[10] However, an insured was treated as holding incidents of

1. *Old Point Nat'l Bank v. Comm.*, 39 BTA 343 (1939).
2. *Est. of Morrow v. Comm.*, 19 TC 1068 (1953), acq. 1954-1 CB 5, nonacq. 1979-2 CB 2; *Est. of Dorson v. Comm.*, 4 TC 463 (1944).
3. IRC Sec. 2042(2).
4. Rev. Rul. 79-117, 1979-1 CB 305.
5. *Est. of Morrow*, above in Q 86.
6. Rev. Rul. 79-46, 1979-1 CB 303.
7. *Est. of Smith v. Comm.*, 73 TC 307 (1979), acq. in result, 1981-1 CB 2.
8. Let. Rul. 8049002.
9. TAM 9127007.
10. Let. Rul. 9233006.

ownership in a policy held in a trusteed buy-sell arrangement where the insured was considered to have transferred the policy to the trust and retained the right to purchase the policy for its cash surrender value.[1]

The right to receive dividends has been held *not* to be an incident of ownership in the policy.[2] It has been held that if the insured has the power to terminate the interest of the primary beneficiary with only the consent of the secondary beneficiary, the insured has an incident of ownership.[3] However, a sole shareholder would not be treated as holding incidents of ownership in a life insurance policy on the shareholder's own life where a collateral consequence of a termination of an employee's employment would be a termination of the employee's option agreement to purchase the shareholder's stock with a corresponding change in beneficiary of the insurance proceeds held in an irrevocable life insurance trust created by the employee.[4]

The assignment of a life insurance policy by a third-party owner as an accommodation to the insured to cover the insured's debts does not in itself create in the insured an incident of ownership.[5] But if a policy owner collaterally assigns a policy as security for a loan and then makes a gift of the policy subject to the assignment, the donor will be deemed to have retained an incident of ownership.[6]

Where an insurance funded buy-sell agreement prohibited each partner from borrowing against, surrendering, or changing the beneficiary on the policy each owned on the life of the other partner without the insured's consent, the Tax Court held that the decedent-insured did not possess an incident of ownership in the policy insuring the decedent-insured's life.[7] However, it has been reported that the IRS, citing an internal ruling dated January 7, 1971, has declined to follow the decision.[8]

An insured was treated as holding incidents of ownership in a policy held in a trusteed buy-sell arrangement where the trust could only act as directed by the shareholders through the buy-sell agreement and the insured could thus withhold consent to the exercise of policy rights.[9]

Where an insured absolutely assigned a policy that required the insured's consent before the policy could be assigned, or the beneficiary changed, to someone who had no insurable interest in the insured's life, the IRS ruled that the insured had retained an incident of ownership.[10]

Similarly, the Tax Court has held that an employee's right to consent to a change of beneficiary on a split dollar policy owned by the employee's employer on the employee's life is an

1. TAM 9349002.
2. *Est. of Bowers v. Comm.*, 23 TC 911 (1955), acq; *Old Point Nat'l Bank*, supra.
3. *Est. of Goodwyn v. Comm.*, TC Memo 1973-153.
4. TAM 9421037.
5. *Est. of Goodwyn*, supra.
6. *Est. of Krischer v. Comm.*, TC Memo 1973-172.
7. *Est. of Infante v. Comm.*, TC Memo 1970-206 (appeal dismissed), nonacq. 1971 AOD LEXIS 310 (1971).
8. 55 *Taxes* (CCH) 146 (Feb. 1977).
9. TAM 9349002 (cf. Let. Ruls. 9511009 and 9622036, in which no estate inclusion was required for life insurance held in a trust to fund a corporate buy-sell agreement).
10. Rev. Rul. 75-70, 1975-1 CB 301.

incident of ownership.[1] The Tax Court also has held that where the insured assigned policies, retaining the right to consent to the assignee's designating as beneficiary, or assigning the policies to, anyone who did not have an insurable interest in the insured's life, the assignee's act of designating an irrevocable beneficiary did not eliminate the insured's retained incidents of ownership. The Third Circuit reversed the Tax Court in this case, however, taking the position that because under the facts presented the insured could not have enjoyed any economic benefit from exercising the insured's veto power over the designation of beneficiaries or assignees, the insured's retained power did not amount to an incident of ownership.[2] The insured's right to purchase the policy from an assignee was treated as equivalent to the right to revoke an assignment, which is an incident of ownership.[3]

88. If an insured holds incidents of ownership at death as a fiduciary or by reason of a retained right to remove a trustee and appoint another, will the life insurance proceeds be includable in the insured's estate?

Revenue Ruling 84-179[4] provides that incidents of ownership held by the insured in a fiduciary capacity will cause the proceeds to be included in the insured's estate only if (1) the incidents are exercisable for the insured's personal benefit, *or* (2) the insured transferred the policy or at least some of the consideration for purchasing or maintaining the policy to the trust from personal assets *and* the incidents of ownership devolved upon the insured as part of a prearranged plan involving the participation of the insured. The IRS states that this position is consistent with *Skifter*, *Fruehauf*, and *Hunter*, courts of appeals decisions discussed below.

The regulations say that a decedent is considered to have an "incident of ownership" in an insurance policy on the decedent's life held in trust if, under the terms of the policy, the decedent (either alone or in conjunction with another person or persons) has the power (as trustee or otherwise) to change the beneficial ownership in the policy or its proceeds, or the time or manner of enjoyment thereof, even though the decedent has no beneficial interest in the trust.[5] The IRS says it will read this regulation in accordance with its position adopted in Revenue Ruling 84-179, above. The courts have taken three different views of the regulation:

First, the U.S. Court of Appeals for the Sixth Circuit has held that the possession by the insured of incidents of ownership in a fiduciary capacity is not enough to bring the proceeds into the insured's estate under IRC Section 2042(2) unless the insured had the power at death to benefit the insured or the insured's estate by exercising any of the incidents.[6] This also appears to be the view of the Tax Court.[7] See, also, *Est. of Jordahl v. Comm.*,[8] where the Tax Court held that the decedent's right, as trustee of a funded life insurance trust of which the decedent was grantor and in which the decedent had an income interest, to borrow against the policies to keep them in effect if trust income was insufficient, was not an incident of ownership because

1. *Schwager v. Comm.*, 64 TC 781 (1975).
2. *Est. of Rockwell v. Comm.*, 57 AFTR 2d 1491, 779 F.2d 931 (3rd Cir. 1985), rev'g TC Memo 1984-654.
3. TAM 9128008.
4. 1984-2 CB 195, revoking Rev. Rul. 76-261, 1976-2 CB 276.
5. Treas. Reg. §20.2042-1(c)(4).
6. *Est. of Fruehauf v. Comm.*, 427 F.2d 80 (6th Cir. 1970).
7. *Est. of Skifter v. Comm.*, 56 TC 1190 (1971), *rev'd* 468 F.2d 699, *nonacq.* 1978-1 CB 3 (see text below).
8. 65 TC 92 (1975), *acq.* 1977-1 CB 1.

in fact the income never was insufficient. The court, in *Jordahl*, also ruled that the decedent's reservation of the right, as grantor, to substitute "other policies of equal value" for those held in trust at any time was not an incident of ownership.

Second, the U.S. Court of Appeals for the Second Circuit has limited the application of the foregoing regulation as follows: If an insured at death possesses incidents of ownership in the insurance only as a consequence of having received them by transfer from a third-party policy owner long after the insured had been divested of all interest in the insurance (if the insured ever had any interest), then the proceeds are not includable in the insured's estate under Section 2042(2) unless the insured possessed the power to benefit the insured or the insured's estate by exercising any of the incidents the insured possessed. If an insured is also the policy owner and is the transferor of the insurance to a trust, then any incidents of ownership the insured possesses at death, as trustee or otherwise, will cause includability of the proceeds in the insured's estate, even if the insured cannot benefit economically by exercising those incidents.[1]

Third, the U.S. Court of Appeals for the Fifth Circuit takes the view that the insured's mere possession at death of an incident of ownership (even the limited right, as trustee, to alter the time or manner of payment of death proceeds to the beneficiary), regardless of whether the insured or the insured's estate could have benefited by exercising the incident and regardless of how the insured came into possession of such incident, is sufficient to cause the proceeds to be included in the insured's estate under IRC Section 2042(2).[2]

The Fifth Circuit seems to stand alone in its broad view of IRC Section 2042(2). Courts outside the Fifth Circuit (in addition to the Tax Court and Second and Sixth Circuits) generally have taken the view that an insured who receives fiduciary powers over policies of insurance on the insured's life from a third-party policy owner does not (merely by reason of possessing those powers) possess incidents of ownership in such policies unless it is possible for the insured or the insured's estate to benefit economically by exercising any of those powers.[3] Where the decedent-insured as executor was given the power to surrender policies for cash to pay death taxes and settlement costs, because such costs were paid with nonprobate assets, it was held that the decedent did not possess incidents of ownership but only a power over a contingency that never arose.[4] It has been held, however, that if the insured has the power to benefit by exercising a fiduciary power, it does not matter that the insured can exercise the power only with the consent of co-trustees whose interests in the trust are adverse to the insured's own interests.[5] If an insurance trust gives the trustee-insured the power to deal with the insurance policies held by the trust as if the trustee-insured were the absolute owner and without the necessity to account to anyone for the trustee-insured's dealings, the trustee-insured still has fiduciary powers that must be exercised only for the exclusive benefit of the trust beneficiaries. If the trustee-insured violates his or her fiduciary duty by, say, pledging the policies to secure a personal loan, the

1. *Est. of Skifter v. Comm.*, 468 F.2d 699 (2nd Cir. 1972).
2. *Rose v. U.S.*, 511 F.2d 259 (5th Cir. 1975); *Terriberry v. U.S.*, 517 F.2d 286 (5th Cir. 1975), cert. denied 424 U.S. 977. In Rev. Rul. 84-179, above, IRS revoked Rev. Rul. 76-261, which supported the Fifth Circuit's position.
3. *Gesner v. U.S.*, 220 Ct. Cl. 433, 600 F2d 1349 (Ct. Cl. 1979); *Hunter v. U.S.*, 624 F.2d 833 (8th Cir. 1980). See also *Est. of Connelly v. U.S.*, 551 F.2d 545 (3rd Cir. 1977).
4. *Hunter*, above.
5. *Gesner*, above.

trustee-insured's wrongful act does not convert these powers into incidents of ownership for purposes of IRC Section 2042.[1]

89. If an insured possesses incidents of ownership at death as a fiduciary or by reason of a retained right to remove a trustee and appoint another, are there any situations in which the life insurance proceeds will not be includable in the insured's estate?

A technical advice memorandum advised that if a trustee possessed incidents of ownership in a life insurance policy held for the trust and the insured/grantor retained the right to remove trustees and appoint anyone other than the insured/grantor as trustee, the insured/grantor retained incidents of ownership in the policy that would cause the insurance proceeds to be included in the insured/grantor's estate under IRC Section 2042(2).[2] However, for purposes of IRC Sections 2036 or 2038, the IRS will no longer include trust property in a decedent grantor's estate when the grantor retains the right to replace the trustee but can replace the trustee only with an independent corporate trustee.[3] (One wonders whether the IRS will extend its policy with regard to trustee removal under IRC Sections 2036 and 2038 to IRC Section 2042.) A later letter ruling determined that the right to replace a trustee *for cause* with someone other than the insured/grantor was not an incident of ownership.[4]

The issue of incidents of ownership in a trust generally can be avoided by providing that an insured cannot exercise any incident of ownership in a policy on the insured's life (even as a trustee).[5] In private letter ruling 9748020, the IRS concluded that where a spouse resigned as trustee of a credit shelter bypass trust (in which the decedent had given the spouse an income interest) prior to purchase of life insurance by the trust on the spouse's life, proceeds of the life insurance would not be includable in the other spouse's estate provided that:

(1) the spouse has not transferred any assets to the trust;

(2) the premiums for the policy are paid from the trust corpus;

(3) the spouse does not maintain the policy with personal assets;

(4) the spouse is not reinstated as trustee.

90. Are life insurance proceeds includable in the insured's estate if someone other than the insured took out the policy and owns it at the insured's death?

Proceeds ordinarily are not includable in the insured's gross estate if the insured has never owned the policy and the proceeds are not payable to or for the benefit of his estate.[6] (But see

1. *Est. of Bloch v. Comm.*, 78 TC 850 (1982).
2. TAM 8922003.
3. Rev. Rul. 95-58, 1995-2 CB 191; Est. of *Wall v. Comm.*, 101 TC 300 (1993).
4. Let. Rul. 9832039.
5. See Let. Rul. 9348028.
6. IRC Sec. 2042.

Q 83.) If the terms of the policy give the insured any legal incidents of ownership, however, the proceeds may be included in the insured's gross estate even though a third party purchased the policy and always has retained physical possession of it.[1]

Even though a policy says clearly that incidents of ownership belong to the insured, if it also is clear from facts outside the policy that it was the intention and belief of the parties involved in purchasing the insurance that these ownership rights were to be, and were, placed in another, courts may allow the "intent facts" to override the "policy facts." That is, they may find that the insured did not actually possess the incidents of ownership the policy said were exercisable by the insured.[2]

On the other hand, even though the policy does not give the insured any incidents of ownership, an incident of ownership may be given to the insured by an outside document, such as a corporate resolution, a trust indenture, or another agreement between the insured and the third party.[3] The fact that the insured has had no opportunity to exercise the legal incidents of ownership is immaterial.[4] Also, if the insured causes insurance to be bought on the insured's life by another with funds supplied by the insured and then dies within three years of the purchase, the proceeds may be includable in the insured's estate (Q 96). In *Est. of Margrave v. Comm.*,[5] the U.S. Court of Appeals for the Eighth Circuit affirmed a 9-7 decision of the Tax Court holding that the proceeds of a wife-owned policy, payable revocably to the trustee of a revocable trust created by the insured husband, were not includable in the insured's estate under either IRC Section 2042 (incidents of ownership test – see Q 86) or IRC Section 2041 (general power of appointment). The IRS has agreed to follow the holding in *Margrave*.[6]

91. Can an insured remove existing life insurance from the insured's gross estate by an absolute assignment of the policy?

Yes, assuming the insured lives for at least three years after the assignment (Q 96), the insured assigns *all* incidents of ownership, and the assignee is not legally obligated to use the proceeds for the benefit of the insured's estate.[7]

If the form of the assignment reserves any incidents of ownership to the insured, the proceeds may be included in the insured's gross estate despite the insured's clear intention to transfer all ownership rights.[8] It has been held that where the insured had paid no premiums and had never treated the policy as the insured's own, the insured's irrevocable designation of beneficiaries and mode of payment of proceeds was an effective assignment of all of the insured's incidents of ownership in the policy.[9] The amount of any *premiums* paid on the assigned policy by the insured

1. *U.S. v. Rhode Island Hosp. Trust Co.*, 355 F.2d 7 (1st Cir. 1966).
2. *National Metropolitan Bank v. U.S.*, 87 F. Supp. 773 (Ct. Cl. 1950); *Schongalla v. Hickey*, 149 F.2d 687 (2d Cir. 1945), cert. denied 326 U.S. 736; *Watson v. Comm.*, TC Memo 1977-268; *First Nat'l Bank of Birmingham v. U.S.*, 358 F.2d 625 (5th Cir. 1966); Let. Rul. 8610068.
3. *Est. of Thompson v. Comm.*, TC Memo 1981-200; *St. Louis Union Trust Co. (Orthwein) v. U.S.*, 262 F. Supp. 27 (E.D. Mo. 1966); *Est. of Tomerlin v. Comm.*, TC Memo 1986-147.
4. *Comm. v. Est. of Noel*, 380 U.S. 678 (1965).
5. 71 TC 13 (1978), aff'd 45 AFTR 2d ¶148,393 (8th Cir. 1980).
6. Rev. Rul. 81-166, 1981-1 CB 477.
7. Treas. Reg. §§20.2042-1(b)(1), 20.2042-1(c)(1); *Lamade v. Brownell*, 245 F. Supp. 691 (M.D. Pa. 1965).
8. *Est. of Piggott v. Comm.*, 340 F.2d 829 (6th Cir. 1965).
9. *Morton v. U.S.*, 457 F.2d 750, 29 AFTR 2d 72- 1531 (4th Cir. 1972).

may be included to the extent they are paid within three years of death (Q 96). (For indirect possession of incidents of ownership, see Q 86, Q 179, and Q 319. See Q 175 for information on the assignment of group term insurance coverage.)

92. Can an insured remove existing life insurance from the insured's gross estate by an absolute assignment of the policy but retain a reversionary interest?

A reversionary interest in a policy is an incident of ownership if, immediately before the insured's death, the value of the reversionary interest is worth more than 5 percent of the value of the policy.[1] The insured will have no such reversionary interest, however, if the policy is purchased and owned by another person, or if the policy is absolutely assigned to another person by the insured. Regulations state that the term "reversionary interest" does not include the possibility that a person might receive a policy or its proceeds by inheritance from another person's estate, by exercising a surviving spouse's statutory right of election, or under some similar right. They also state that, in valuing a reversionary interest, interests held by others that would affect the value must be taken into consideration. For example, a decedent would not have a reversionary interest in a policy worth more than 5 percent of the policy's value, if, immediately before the decedent's death, some other person had the unrestricted power to obtain the cash surrender value of the policy; the value of the reversionary interest would be zero.[2]

An insured was treated as holding a reversionary interest in a policy held in a trusteed buy-sell arrangement where the insured was considered to have transferred the policy to the trust and retained the right to purchase the policy for its cash surrender value upon termination of the buy-sell agreement.[3] However, a policy held in a trusteed buy-sell arrangement would not be includable in an insured's estate under IRC Section 2042 where (1) proceeds would be received by a partner's estate only in exchange for purchase of the partner's stock, and (2) all incidents of ownership would be held by the trustee of the irrevocable life insurance trust.[4]

93. Are the general rules for including life insurance proceeds in the insured's gross estate applicable to proceeds payable under a qualified pension or profit-sharing plan?

Yes, generally, for estates of decedents dying after 1984; but see Q 3974 for details.

94. May a life insurance beneficiary be required to pay estate tax attributable to death proceeds?

Yes, under either of two circumstances:

(1) The decedent/insured has directed in his or her will that the life insurance beneficiary pay the share of death taxes attributable to the proceeds.

1. IRC Sec. 2042(2).
2. Treas. Reg. §20.2042-1(c)(3).
3. TAM 9349002.
4. Let. Rul. 9511009.

(2) The state of the decedent's domicile has a statute that apportions the burden of death taxes among probate and nonprobate beneficiaries in the absence of any direction from the decedent regarding where the burden of death taxes should fall.

Most states have statutes that apportion death taxes (federal, state, or both) among the beneficiaries of an estate, probate and nonprobate, under circumstances in which the decedent has not directed otherwise. A few states place the death tax burden on the probate estate (technically, the residuary estate).

A federal apportionment statute provides in pertinent part as follows: "Unless the decedent directs otherwise in his will, if any part of the gross estate on which tax has been paid consists of proceeds of policies of insurance on the life of the decedent receivable by a beneficiary other than the executor, the executor shall be entitled to recover from such beneficiary such portion of the total tax paid as the proceeds of such policies bear to the taxable estate."[1]

In *McAleer v. Jernigan*,[2] the decedent's former wife was the beneficiary of insurance on the decedent's life. The decedent, who died domiciled in Alabama, did not direct in his will where the burden of death taxes should fall. The Alabama statute said that unless the decedent directed otherwise, the executor was to pay death taxes out of estate property (i.e., from the residuary estate). The statute also said that the executor was under no duty to recover any pro rata portion of such taxes from the beneficiary of any nonprobate property. In a suit by the executor to recover from the life insurance beneficiary a pro rata share of the estate tax due (the insurance proceeds having been found includable in the gross estate for federal estate tax purposes), the U.S. Court of Appeals for the Eleventh Circuit held that the federal statute, IRC Section 2206, prevailed over the state statute and allowed the executor to recover.

95. May a life insurance beneficiary make a qualified disclaimer of an amount equal to the beneficiary's proportionate share of death taxes when the decedent directed that death taxes be paid entirely out of the probate estate?

Yes.

In *Est. of Boyd v. Comm.*,[3] in an unusual factual situation, the decedent's son was left the decedent's entire probate estate, $153,000, under decedent's will plus $389,000 of life insurance proceeds as the policy beneficiary. The decedent's second wife (the son's step-mother) received nothing. The decedent's will directed his executor to pay out of the probate estate the tax (an estimated $78,000) allocable to the life insurance proceeds. The son disclaimed the entire probate estate *and* any right to have the probate estate pay any death tax attributable to the life insurance proceeds. The IRS refused to give effect to the second disclaimer, which had the effect of reducing the amount of marital deduction the estate claimed. The disclaimer statute says that a qualified disclaimer means an irrevocable and unqualified refusal to accept an *interest*

1. IRC Sec. 2206.
2. 804 F.2d 1231, 86-2 USTC ¶13,705 (11th Cir. 1986), rev'g and remanding 86-2 USTC ¶13,704 (S.D. Ala. 1986).
3. 819 F.2d 170, 87-1 USTC ¶13,720 (7th Cir. 1987), *rev'g* 85 TC 1056 (1985).

in property. The court recognized the subject of the second disclaimer as an interest in property for purposes of the statute and allowed the claimed marital deduction.

Planning Point: Remember that under IRC Section 2518 and many state statutes, a disclaimer is qualified only if (among several other requirements) no portion of the disclaimed interest passes to the disclaiming party as a result of the disclaimer. It is important to consider where the disclaimed interest passes after the disclaimer is made.

96. When are death proceeds of life insurance given away by an insured within three years of the insured's death includable in the insured's gross estate?

Proceeds are automatically includable in the insured's gross estate without regard to the insured's motives in making the gift.[1] Also includable is the amount of any gift tax paid by the decedent or the decedent's estate on the transfer.[2] The exception provision from gifts as to which the decedent was not required to file a gift tax return does not apply to a "transfer with respect to a life insurance policy."[3] The quoted language, part of the amendment of IRC Section 2035 made by the Revenue Act of 1978, seems broad enough to include gifts of both policies and premium payments. (However, committee reports explaining the provision indicate that it was not the intention to treat as a "transfer with respect to a life insurance policy" any gifts of premium payments made more than three years after the donor has made a gift of the policy. See Congressional committee explanation of Section 702(f) of the Revenue Act of 1978.) (See Q 175 for special rules applicable to group insurance.)

When the insured makes a gift of the policy within three years of death, the value of any premiums the insured pays gratuitously after making the gift is not added to the proceeds includable in the insured's estate.[4] Courts had held under earlier versions of IRC Section 2035 that if any premiums paid after the transfer are paid by the donee rather than by the insured, only proceeds in the ratio of premiums paid by the donor to total premiums paid are includable in the donor's estate.[5] The proportional proceeds rule where the donee pays premiums after the transfer also has been applied to deaths occurring after 1981 even though payment of premiums no longer determines includability of proceeds under the transfers within the three years of death rule.[6] If premiums are paid from property owned jointly by the decedent and donee, the burden is on the donee to prove the extent to which the premiums were paid out of property originally owned by the donee.[7]

For the bringback rule of Section 2035 to apply when (1) a policy is purchased on the initiative of the insured with funds provided by the insured, (2) a third party is designated owner

1. IRC Sec. 2035.
2. IRC Sec. 2035(b).
3. IRC Sec. 2035(c)(3).
4. *Peters v. U.S.*, 572 F.2d 851, 78-1 USTC ¶13,239 (Ct. Cl. 1978).
5. *Liebmann v. Hassett*, 148 F.2d 247 (1st Cir. 1945); *Est. of Silverman v. Comm.*, 61 TC 338 (1973), *aff'd* 521 F.2d 574 (2nd Cir. 1975); Treas. Reg. §20.2035-1(e).
6. *Est. of Friedberg v. Comm.*, TC Memo 1992-310; TAM 9128008.
7. *Peters v. U.S.*, above.

of the policy, and (3) the insured dies within three years of the purchase, there would have to be a transfer for purposes of IRC Sections 2036, 2037, 2038, or 2042.

Courts have determined that insurance proceeds are not included in an insured's estate, even though death occurred within three years of the policy purchase, if (1) the policy is owned by a third party, (2) the policy is not made payable to the insured's estate, and (3) the insured held no incidents of ownership in the policy under IRC Section 2042.[1] Indeed, attorney fees were awarded to the taxpayers in the *Perry* case because the position of the United States was not substantially justified.[2] Due to the adverse court decisions, the IRS has announced that it will no longer litigate its position (although it still believes that substance should prevail over form and that the "beamed transfer" theory should be applied to such "indirect transfers" of life insurance within three years of death).[3]

In TAM 9323002, life insurance proceeds were not included in an insured's estate where:

(1) the insured applied for the policy,

(2) the insured then had the policy split into two policies and named her two sons as owners and beneficiaries prior to paying any premiums,

(3) the insured's sons paid all premiums, and

(4) the insured died within three years of purchase of the policy.

The memorandum determined that under the terms of the contract and state law, no contract existed before the first premium was paid and the life insurance contract was issued and delivered. The memorandum also concluded that although it appeared that the decedent passed something of value to her two sons (i.e., although the insurance company's premium rates had increased between the first and second step, the earlier lower premium rates were obtained by the sons), it was unlikely that such transfer constituted a transfer of incidents of ownership.

An exchange of policies by an irrevocable trust was not treated as a transfer within three years of death where the original transfer of the policy had occurred more than three years before death, the decedent had no interest in the policy at the time of the exchange, and the decedent's signature was not essential to the exchange.[4] The decedent-insured did not transfer the policy within three years of death, even though the policy was amended within three years of death to provide that a trust, rather than the decedent, was the owner, where the intent of the parties clearly indicated through extrinsic evidence that the decedent had ceased being the owner of the policy more than three years before death.[5]

1. *Est. of Leder v. Comm.*, 893 F.2d 237, 90-1 USTC ¶60,001 (10th Cir. 1989); *Est. of Headrick v. Comm.*, 918 F.2d 1263, 90-2 USTC ¶60,049 (6th Cir. 1990); *Est. of Perry v. Comm.*, 927 F.2d 209, 91-1 USTC ¶60,064 (5th Cir. 1991).
2. *Est. of Perry v. Comm.*, 91-1 USTC ¶60,073 (5th Cir. 1991).
3. AOD 1991-012.
4. TAM 8819001.
5. Let. Rul. 9651004.

97. Is life insurance owned by a corporation on its majority shareholder included in the shareholder's estate when the shareholder divested an interest in the corporation within three years of death?

Life insurance owned by a corporation on its majority shareholder was not included in the shareholder's estate where the shareholder sold her interest in the corporation within three years of death. The corporation had always owned the policy, paid the premiums, and been beneficiary of the proceeds.[1] However, where a majority shareholder reduced his interest in a corporation to 40 percent within three years of death and proceeds of life insurance owned by the corporation on such shareholder were payable to the shareholder's daughter, proceeds were included in the shareholder's estate.[2] Also, where a corporation transferred a life insurance policy to the beneficiary within three years of the controlling shareholder's death, proceeds were included in the controlling shareholder's estate even though the shareholder transferred his interest in the corporation to his son after the corporation's transfer of the life insurance policy and prior to his death.[3] (See also Q 319.) Where a non-majority shareholder held the right to purchase a policy on his life from a corporation upon termination of a buy-sell agreement and the shareholder caused the corporation to transfer the policy to an irrevocable trust within three years of the shareholder's death, the proceeds were included in the shareholder's estate.[4]

98. Are there any situations in which death proceeds of life insurance that were given away by an insured within three years of the insured's death are not included in the insured's gross estate?

An exception is provided to the transfers within three years of death rules for any bona fide sale for adequate and full consideration.[5] It is unclear whether consideration equal to the interpolated terminal reserve of a policy plus any unexpired premiums is adequate to avoid the transfers within three years of death rule. TAM 8806004 interpreted full consideration as requiring that the consideration must be adequate relative to what would be included in the estate (i.e., the proceeds), not relative to what is transferred (i.e., the policy). See *Est. of Pritchard v. Comm.*,[6] where consideration equal to the cash surrender value was inadequate. However, TAM 9413045 accepted the interpolated terminal reserve plus any unexpired premiums as adequate consideration.

99. If a donor dies within three years of making a gift of a life insurance policy on the life of another, is the value of the policy includable in the donor's gross estate?

No. IRC Section 2035 brings back into a decedent's estate certain gifts made within three years of death. The bring-back rule of Section 2035 applies to a transfer of an interest in property

1. Let. Rul. 8906002.
2. Rev. Rul. 90-21, 1990-1 CB 172, situation 2.
3. Rev. Rul. 90-21, 1990-1 CB 172, situation 1.
4. TAM 9127007.
5. IRC Sec. 2035(d).
6. 4 TC 204 (1944).

that is included in the value of the gross estate under IRC Sections 2036, 2037, 2038, or 2042, or would have been included under any of these sections if such interest had been retained by the decedent. IRC Section 2042 has to do with proceeds of insurance *on the life of the decedent*.

IRC Section 2033 (which includes property in which a decedent had any interest at all) governs whether the value of a policy owned by the decedent on the life of *another* is includable in the decedent's estate. A transfer of an interest in property included in the value of the gross estate under Section 2033, or that would have been included under Section 2033 if the interest had been retained by the decedent, is not among the enumerated sections under the bring-back rule of Section 2035. Thus, the value of a policy owned by a decedent on the life of another and transferred by the decedent within three years of the decedent's death (occurring after 1981) will not normally be brought back into the decedent's estate under Section 2035.

100. If an employer provides, under a nonqualified agreement or plan, an income benefit only for certain survivors designated by family or marital relationship to the employee, how is the benefit treated for estate tax purposes in the employee's estate?

The threshold issue is whether the survivor income benefit plan is treated as insurance or as an annuity (see Q 260 for background).

If it is treated as life insurance, includability of the value of the survivor benefit in the employee's estate is determined under the rules applicable to death proceeds of insurance. The controlling statute in this case is usually IRC Section 2042, although IRC Section 2035 also comes into play if the decedent-insured has transferred or relinquished any rights in the benefit within three years of death (Q 81, Q 174). If the plan is treated as an annuity, includability is usually determined under IRC Section 2039(a), but not under IRC Section 2042 (see Q 101 and Q 102, particularly the discussion of death-benefit-only plans in Q 102).

Case law and IRS rulings dealing with the estate taxation of survivor income benefits tend to support the view of the U.S. Court of Appeals for the Second Circuit. In *All v. McCobb*,[1] the Second Circuit held that a survivor income benefit plan that was uninsured and unfunded lacked the necessary insurance elements of risk-shifting and risk-distribution to be treated as insurance. (See also the cases cited at Q 260.) *Est. of Lumpkin v. Comm.*,[2] *Est. of Connelly v. U.S.*,[3] and *Est. of Smead v. Comm.*[4]all involve insured plans that the courts treated as group insurance.

In Letter Ruling 8046110, a plan funded by group life insurance was treated as insurance. Following Revenue Ruling 69-54 (Q 176), the IRS ruled that because the decedent insured died possessing the right to convert his group life insurance into individual insurance, an incident of ownership, the sum used by the insurance company in determining the amount of the

1. 321 F.2d 633 (2nd Cir. 1963).
2. 474 F.2d 1092 (5th Cir. 1973).
3. 551 F.2d 545 (3rd Cir. 1977).
4. 78 TC 43 (1982), acq. in result, 1984-2 CB 2.

survivor annuity payable was includable in the decedent's estate.[1] Revenue Ruling 77-183,[2] *Est. of Schelberg v. Comm.*,[3] and *Est. of Van Wye v. U.S.*,[4] all involved uninsured and unfunded plans that the courts treated as annuities.

No estate tax cases or rulings have been found that deal with *uninsured funded* plans (but see Q 260).

101. Is the value of a survivor benefit payable by an employer under a nonqualified salary continuation or deferred compensation agreement includable in the employee's gross estate?

Yes, it is includable under IRC Section 2039(a) if (1) it is provided for "under any form of contract or agreement," and (2) the decedent had a right to receive the payments for life, for any period not ascertainable without reference to the decedent's death, or for any period that does not in fact end before the decedent's death.

The statute applies where the decedent was receiving payments and had a nonforfeitable right to future payments at the time of death. Regulations make it equally clear, however, that the IRS will consider the statute applicable whether the decedent had a right to present or future payments at the time of death and whether the rights were forfeitable or nonforfeitable.

The regulations provide: "The term 'contract or agreement' includes any arrangement, understanding or plan, or any combination of arrangements, understandings or plans arising by reason of the decedent's employment."[5] Although the Tax Court has stated that an enforceable contract is a prerequisite to the application of IRC Section 2039,[6] later case law has led to a less rigid rule. When there is no legally enforceable contract, other circumstances may exist that would cause an annuity to be considered as having been paid under a contract or agreement for purposes of the statute. Thus, if the survivor annuitant has a controlling interest in the company, if consideration for the annuity is found, or if the company has in the past consistently paid annuities pursuant to an unenforceable plan, the annuity may be considered as having been paid under a contract or agreement; if no such circumstances are found, a legally enforceable contract must exist.[7]

It has been argued that payments under a deferred compensation contract have no estate tax value if they were forfeitable to the executive during his or her lifetime. This argument is based on the theory that the estate tax value is to be determined as of the moment prior to death. However, it is now rather firmly established that the value is to be determined as of the moment after death when the contingencies have ceased to have an operative effect.[8] In *Silberman v. U.S.*,[9]

1. See Treas. Reg. §20.2042-1(a)(3).
2. 1977-1 CB 274.
3. 70 TC 690 (1978), rev'd on other grounds, 79-2 USTC ¶13,321 (2nd Cir. 1979).
4. 686 F.2d 425, 82-2 USTC ¶13,485 (6th Cir. 1982).
5. Treas. Reg. §20.2039-1(b).
6. *Est. of Barr v. Comm.*, 40 TC 227 (1963), acq. in result only, 1978-1 CB 1.
7. *Neely v. U.S.*, 613 F.2d 802 (Ct. Cl. 1980); *Courtney v. U.S.*, 54 AFTR 2d 84-6492 (N.D. Ohio, 1984). See also Let. Rul. 8005011.
8. *Goodman v. Granger*, 243 F.2d 264 (3rd Cir. 1957).
9. 28 AFTR 2d 6282 (W.D. Pa. 1971).

the commuted value of the widow's benefit was includable in the employee's estate even though the employee had to render consulting services to get retirement benefits.

The estate tax cannot be avoided by providing for the retirement pay and death benefit under separate contracts; IRS regulations interpret the statutory term "contract or agreement" to include "any combination of arrangements, understandings or plans arising by reason of the decedent's employment."[1]

The death benefit is includable in the gross estate whether it is payable in a lump sum or in periodic payments, and whether it is forfeitable or nonforfeitable to the survivor. Forfeitability will be taken into account in connection with the valuation of the benefit in the employee's estate.[2] For example, where the employer has a right to recover remaining unpaid benefits upon the death or remarriage of the employee's surviving spouse, the value of the death benefit in the employee's estate will not include the value of this refund feature.[3] (Such a forfeiture provision, however, would make the benefit ineligible for the marital deduction.) When the death benefit is payable as an annuity, the commuted value of the payments is the proper estate tax value.[4] The commuted value of annuity payments is determined by use of the Estate and Gift Tax Valuation Tables.

Thus, a widow's benefit under a typical deferred compensation agreement is includable in the gross estate by reason of IRC Section 2039(a). Even if it were not includable under IRC Section 2039(a), however, it probably would be includable under one of the other estate tax sections.[5]

102. When is the value of a survivor benefit payable by an employer under a nonqualified salary continuation or deferred compensation agreement excludable from the employee's gross estate?

Under certain circumstances, an unfunded deferred compensation agreement that provides death benefits only may escape inclusion in the employee's gross income. If the employee has no right to any post-employment retirement or disability benefits, other than benefits under a qualified pension or profit-sharing plan (that is, only a pure survivor benefit is provided), the benefit is not subject to estate tax under IRC Section 2039(a).[6] In determining whether the deceased employee had any post-employment benefits, all rights and benefits accruing to the employee and others by reason of the employee's employment (except those under a qualified pension or profit-sharing plan) will be treated as one contract or plan under IRC Section 2039(a).[7]

The section cannot be avoided, for instance, by providing lifetime benefits under one agreement, and the death benefit under another.[8] However, courts have held that the mere fact that

1. Treas. Reg. §20.2039-1(b).
2. Treas. Reg. §20.2039-1(b)(2)(Ex. 2).
3. *Allen v. Comm.*, 39 TC 817 (1963), acq. 1964-1 CB 4.
4. *Est. of Beal v. Comm.*, 47 TC 269 (1966), acq. 1967-2 CB 1.
5. See *Goodman v. Granger*, 243 F.2d 264; *Est. of Leoni v. Comm.*, 7 TCM (CCH) 759 (1948); *Est. of Davis v. Comm.*, 11 TCM (CCH) 814 (1952); Rev. Rul. 260, 1953-2 CB 262.
6. *Est. of Fusz v. Comm.*, 46 TC 214 (1966), acq. 1967-2 CB 2; Rev. Rul. 76-380, 1976-2 CB 270.
7. Treas. Reg. §20.2039-1(b).
8. Treas. Reg. §20.2039-1(b)(2)(Ex. 6); *Est. of Beal v. Comm.*, supra; *Gray v. U.S.*, 410 F.2d 1094 (3rd Cir. 1969).

at death the employee was covered under a plan that, had the employee lived and been found totally and permanently disabled sometime in the future, would have paid the employee benefits, was not sufficient to bring the value of the survivor benefit under a death-benefit-only ("DBO") plan into the employee's estate under IRC Section 2039(a).[1] The IRS has announced that it will follow this decision in all circuits.[2] If the agreement provides for payments to the employee after the employee becomes too incapacitated to perform services, or requires only nominal services after a certain age, payments will be treated as postretirement benefits of the employee.[3] On the other hand, if substantial services are necessary to receive the payments, the payments have been held to be salary rather than retirement or disability benefits.[4] Similarly, a plan paying a wage-related benefit and designed to provide for disability resulting in only a temporary absence from work is considered to pay benefits in the nature of salary, not a post-employment benefit.[5]

A pure survivor benefit is not includable in a decedent's gross estate under IRC Section 2033 because no interest is held by the decedent at death.[6] Nonetheless, under certain circumstances the value of a pure survivor benefit may be included in a decedent's gross estate under other estate tax provisions.

Courts have ruled that by giving consideration (e.g., agreeing to continue in the company's employ) for the survivorship benefit, a decedent makes a transfer of the benefit to the survivor.[7] If the decedent holds a reversionary interest of more than 5 percent of the value of the benefit, its value is includable under IRC Section 2037.[8] If the decedent retains the power to alter, amend, revoke, or terminate the agreement or to change the beneficiary, either alone or with the consent of the employer or someone else, the value could be included under IRC Sections 2036 and 2038.[9] Generally, the mere possibility that an employee could (i) negotiate a new agreement with his or her employer, (ii) exert influence as an officer, shareholder, or director to secure desired changes, or (iii) terminate the plan by terminating employment, has not been held a retention of such powers.[10]

In TAM 8701003, which concerned a DBO plan between a corporation and its controlling stockholder, the IRS agreed with the reasoning in the *Kramer*, *Hinze*, and *Harris* cases cited above and concluded that the stockholder-employee's voting power did not give the stockholder-employee rights that would make the value of the death benefit includable in his estate under

1. *Est. of Schelberg v. Comm.*, 612 F.2d 25, 79-2 USTC ¶13,321 (2nd Cir. 1979), rev'g 70 TC 690 (1978); *Est. of Van Wye v. U.S.*, 686 F.2d 425, 82-2 USTC ¶13,485 (6th Cir. 1982).
2. *Looney v. U.S.*, Docket No. 83-8709 (11th Cir., motion filed 1-26-84).
3. *Silberman v. U.S.*, 333 F. Supp. 1120 (W.D. Pa. 1971); *Gaffney v. U.S.*, 200 Ct. Cl. 744 (1972); *Hetson v. U.S.*, 75-2 USTC 13,098 (Ct. Cl. 1975).
4. *Kramer v. U.S.*, 406 F.2d 1363 (Ct. Cl. 1969).
5. Rev. Rul. 77-183, 1977-1 CB 274; *Est. of Siegel v. Comm.*, 74 TC 613 (1980); see also *Est. of Schelberg* and *Est. of Van Wye*, above.
6. *Kramer v. U.S.*, 406 F.2d 1363 (Ct. Cl. 1969); *Est. of Porter v. Comm.*, 442 F.2d 915 (1st Cir. 1971); *Hinze v. U.S.*, 29 AFTR 2d 1553 (C.D. Cal. 1972); *Harris v. U.S.*, 29 AFTR 2d 1558 (C.D. Cal. 1972); see also *Worthen v. U.S.*, 192 F. Supp. 727 (D. Mass. 1961).
7. *Est. of Fried v. Comm.*, 445 F.2d 979 (2nd Cir. 1971); *Est. of Porter v. Comm.*, supra; *Est. of Bogley v. U.S.*, 206 Ct. Cl. 695 (1975); see also *Worthen v. U.S.*, supra and *Molter v. U.S.*, 146 F. Supp. 497 (E.D. N.Y. 1956); however, for a contrary view, see *Hinze v. U.S.*, supra, and *Harris v. U.S.*, supra.
8. *Est. of Fried v. Comm.*, supra; *Est. of Bogley v. U.S.*, supra; Rev. Rul. 78-15, 1978-1 CB 289; Let. Rul. 7802002.
9. Rev. Rul. 76-304, 1976-2 CB 269; *Est. of Siegel v. Comm.*, 74 TC 613 (1980); Let. Rul. 8943082.
10. *Kramer v. U.S.*, supra; *Est. of Whitworth v. Comm.*, TC Memo 1963-41; *Hinze v. U.S.*, supra; *Harris v. U.S.*, supra; Let. Rul. 7827010.

IRC Sections 2036 or 2038. However, in *Est. of Levin v. Comm.*,[1] an annuity payable under a DBO plan was included in the estate of the deceased controlling shareholder and chair of the board under IRC Section 2038 because the decedent was considered to have held until his death the right to amend or revoke an annuity payable by the corporation to his wife if he should die while still in the employ of the controlled corporation and if certain eligibility requirements (tailor-made for the decedent) were met.

For the gift tax implications of DBO plans, see Q 217.

Voluntary Payments

If the payment is not made under a contract or plan, but is purely voluntary on the part of the employer, it is not subject to tax in the employee's estate.[2]

103. Can arrangements for payment of the proceeds of life insurance and annuity contracts attract the generation-skipping transfer tax?

Yes. Regardless of what form an arrangement may take (whether, for example, the arrangement is a life insurance trust, an agreement with the insurer for payment of proceeds under settlement options, or an outright payment to a beneficiary), if an insured (or annuitant) transfers benefits to a "skip person," generally, the insured has made a generation-skipping transfer.

For purposes of the generation-skipping transfer (GST) tax, the term "trust" includes any arrangement (such as life estates, estates for years, and insurance and annuity contracts) other than an estate that, although not a trust, has substantially the same effect as a trust.[3] In the case of an arrangement that is not a trust but that is treated as a trust, the term "trustee" means the person in actual or constructive possession of the property subject to such arrangement.

The IRS has been given authority to issue regulations that may modify the generation-skipping rules when applied to trust equivalents, such as life estates and remainders, estates for years, and insurance and annuity contracts.[4] The committee report states that such authority, for example, might be used to provide that the beneficiary of an annuity or insurance contract be required to pay any GST tax.

Regulations provide that the executor is responsible for filing and paying the GST tax if (1) a direct skip occurs at death, (2) the property is held in a trust arrangement, which includes arrangements having the same effect as an explicit trust, and (3) the total value of property subject to the direct skip is less than $250,000. The executor is entitled to recover the GST tax attributable to the transfer from the trustee (if the property continues to be held in trust) or from the recipient of the trust property (if transferred from the trust arrangement).

1. 90 TC 723 (1988).
2. *Est. of Barr v. Comm.*, 40 TC 227 (1963), acq. in result only, 1978-1 CB 1; *Est. of Albright v. Comm.*, 42 TC 643 (1964); *Est. of Morrow v. Comm.*, 19 TC 1068 (1953), acq. 1954-1 CB 5, nonacq. 1979-2 CB 2; *Garber v. Comm.*, TC Memo 1958-121; *Worthen v. U.S.*, supra; *Est. of Bogley v. U.S.*, supra.
3. IRC Sec. 2652(b).
4. IRC Sec. 2663(3).

Regulations provide a number of examples that treat insurance proceeds as a trust arrangement. Where insurance proceeds held by an insurance company are to be paid to skip persons in a direct skip at death (a direct skip can occur whether proceeds are paid in a lump sum or over a period of time) and the aggregate value of such proceeds held by the insurer is less than $250,000, the executor is responsible for filing and paying the GST tax. Consequently, the insurance company can pay out the proceeds without regard to the GST tax (apparently, the insurance company could not do so if the executor attempts to recover the GST tax while the company still holds proceeds). When the value of the proceeds in the aggregate equals or exceeds $250,000, however, the insurance company is responsible for filing and paying the GST tax.[1]

104. Can the transfer to an irrevocable life insurance trust of an amount used to make premium payments qualify for the generation-skipping transfer tax annual exclusion?

Yes.

If certain requirements are met, a transfer to an irrevocable life insurance trust can qualify for the annual exclusion (and thus avoid the generation-skipping transfer (GST) tax). A nontaxable gift, which is a direct skip, has an inclusion ratio of zero (i.e., it is not subject to GST tax). Nontaxable gifts are defined as gifts eligible for the annual exclusion (see Appendix D for amounts) (doubled if gifts are split between spouses), as well as certain transfers for educational or medical expenses. However, with respect to transfers after March 31, 1988, the nontaxable gift that is a direct skip to a trust for the benefit of an individual has an inclusion ratio of zero only if (1) during the life of such individual no portion of the trust corpus or income may be distributed to or for the benefit of any other person, and (2) the trust would be included in such individual's estate if the trust did not terminate before such individual died.[2] Thus, separate shares or separate trusts, as described in the preceding sentence, must be created for each such individual if premium payments are to be covered by the annual exclusion for GST tax purposes.

Planning Point: Because of the separate share requirement, the annual exclusion is generally not used for generation-skipping life insurance trusts. Instead, the trust is usually protected by allocating the GST exemption to all transfers to the trust.

105. How can the generation-skipping transfer (GST) tax exemption be leveraged using an irrevocable life insurance trust?

Leveraging of the GST tax exemption (see Appendix D) can be accomplished by allocating the exemption against the discounted dollars that the premiums represent when compared with the ultimate value of the insurance proceeds. However, in the case of inter vivos transfers in trust, allocation of the GST exemption is postponed until the end of an estate tax inclusion period (ETIP).[3] In general, an ETIP would not end until the termination of the last interest held by either the transferor or the spouse of the transferor during the period in which the property being transferred would have been included in either spouse's estate if that spouse died.

1. Treas. Reg. §26.2662-1(c)(2).
2. IRC Sec. 2642(c).
3. IRC Sec. 2642(f).

Of course, the transferor should be given no interest that would cause the trust property to be included in the transferor's estate. Furthermore, the transferor's spouse should be given no interest that would cause the trust property to be included in the transferor spouse's estate if the transferor spouse were to die.

The property is not considered as includable in the estate of the spouse of the transferor by reason of a withdrawal power limited to the greater of $5,000 or 5 percent of the trust corpus if the withdrawal power terminates no later than sixty days after the transfer to the trust.[1] Also, the property is not considered as includable in the estate of the transferor or the spouse of the transferor if the possibility of inclusion is so remote as to be negligible (i.e., less than a 5 percent actuarial probability).[2] Furthermore, the ETIP rules do not apply if a reverse qualified terminable interest property (QTIP) election is made.[3] Otherwise, if proceeds are received during the ETIP, the allocation of the GST exemption must be made against proceeds rather than premiums and the advantage of leveraging is lost.

Example 1. [Twenty years in this example only is based upon the $1 million GST exemption prior to any inflation or other adjustment after 1998.] G creates a trust for the benefit of his children and grandchildren. Each year he transfers to the trust $50,000 (to be used to make premium payments on a $2 million insurance policy on his life) and allocates $50,000 of his GST exemption to each transfer. Assuming G makes no other allocations of his GST exemption, the trust will have a zero inclusion ratio (i.e., it is not subject to GST tax) during its first twenty years. At the end of twenty years, G will have used up his GST exemption and the trust's inclusion ratio will increase slowly with each additional transfer of $50,000 to the trust. If G died during the twenty-year period, the insurance proceeds of $2 million would not be subject to GST tax. Part of the $2 million proceeds may be subject to GST tax if G died in a later year. To ensure that the trust has a zero inclusion ratio, use of a policy that becomes paid-up before the transfers to trust exceed the GST exemption may be indicated.

Example 2. Same facts as in Example 1, except that the trust is created for G's spouse, S, during her lifetime, and then, to benefit children and grandchildren. If the trust is intended to qualify for the marital deduction (apparently, other than if a reverse QTIP election is used), the valuation of property for purpose of the ETIP rule is generally delayed until G or S dies because the property would have been included in S's estate if she died during the ETIP. Consequently, if the $2 million insurance proceeds are received during the spouse's lifetime, the GST exemption is allocated against the $2 million proceeds, and a substantial amount of GST tax may be due upon subsequent taxable distributions and taxable terminations from the trust. Because allocation of the exemption must be made against the proceeds if they are received during the ETIP, the advantage of leveraging enjoyed in Example 1 is lost.

NOTE: The 2011 $5 million GST tax lifetime exemption was inflation-adjusted to $5.12 million in 2012, $5.25 million in 2013, $5.34 million in 2014, $5.43 million in 2015, $5.45 million in 2016, $5.49 million in 2017, $11.18 million in 2018, $11.4 million in 2019, and $11.58 million in 2020. The 2010 Tax Relief Act also unified the lifetime gift exemption with the estate tax exemption.[4] The American Taxpayer Relief Act of 2012 (ATRA 2012) made this unification permanent, so that the $5 million lifetime exemption will continue to be indexed annually for inflation, and the 2017 Tax Act doubled the $5 million base to $10 million.

1. Treas. Reg. §26.2632-1(c)(2)(ii)(B).
2. Treas. Reg. §26.2632-1(c)(2)(ii)(A).
3. Treas. Reg. §26.2632-1(c)(2)(ii)(C).
4. Tax Relief, Unemployment Insurance Reauthorization, and Job Creation Act of 2010, Section 302(b)(1), Pub. Law 111-312 (2010), amending 26 U.S.C. §2505(a). See also, The American Taxpayer Relief Act of 2012, Public Law 112-240, Rev. Proc. 2013-15, Rev. Proc. 2014-61, Rev. Proc. 2015-53, Rev. Proc. 2016-55, The 2017 Tax Act, Pub. Law No. 115-97, Rev. Proc. 2018-18, Rev. Proc. 2018-57, Rev. Proc. 2019-44.

This increased exemption will provide transferors with flexibility in funding life insurance premiums through irrevocable life insurance trusts as it allows the transferor to front-pay premium payments with the unused portion of the $10 million exemption ($20 million for married couples), as indexed. In addition, ATRA 2012 made the portability of unused exemptions between spouses permanent, so that any unused exemption of a spouse who dies in a tax year beginning after 2010 may be used by the surviving spouse.[1] (See Q 851.)

106. What are the income tax results when an individual transfers an existing life insurance policy to or purchases a policy for the individual's former spouse in connection with a divorce settlement?

No gain generally is recognized by the transferor if an existing policy is transferred to a spouse, or former spouse incident to a divorce, after July 18, 1984, unless the transfer is pursuant to an instrument in effect on or before such date or the transfer is, under certain circumstances, in trust.

When no gain is recognized, the transferee will be treated as having acquired the policy by gift and the transferor's cost basis for the policy (net premiums paid) is carried over to the transferee.[2] As a result, any such transfer of an existing policy will not cause the death benefit proceeds to be includable in the income of the transferee under the transfer for value rule (Q 79) due to the "basis exception." A transfer is incident to a divorce if the transfer occurs within one year after the date the marriage ceases or is related to the cessation of the marriage.[3] Thus, a transfer of property occurring not more than one year after the date on which the marriage ceased need not be related to the cessation of the marriage to qualify for Section 1041 treatment. A transfer of a policy is treated as related to the cessation of the marriage if the transfer is pursuant to a divorce or separation instrument and the transfer occurs not more than six years after the date on which the marriage ceases.[4]

If property is transferred in trust for the benefit of the spouse or former spouse, however, gain will be recognized by the transferor to the extent that the sum of the liabilities assumed plus the amount of liabilities to which the property is subject exceed the total of the adjusted basis of all property transferred. Therefore, when a policy with a loan is transferred in trust, gain will be recognized to the extent the total liabilities of all property transferred to the trust exceed the total basis of all items of property transferred. When gain is recognized on a transfer in trust, the transferee's basis is adjusted to reflect the amount of gain recognized by the transferor. Payments from an insurance trust to which the property is transferred for the benefit of a spouse or former spouse will be taxed to the spouse or former spouse as a beneficiary and not taxed as alimony.[5]

1. Tax Relief, Unemployment Insurance Reauthorization, and Job Creation Act of 2010, Section 303(b)(1), Pub. Law 111-312 (2010), amending 26 U.S.C. §2010(c)(4). See also, The American Taxpayer Relief Act of 2012, Public Law 112-240, Rev. Proc. 2013-15, Rev. Proc. 2014-61, Rev. Proc. 2015-53, Rev. Proc. 2016-55, The 2017 Tax Act, Pub. Law No. 115-97, Rev. Proc. 2018-18, Rev. Proc. 2018-57.
2. IRC Sec. 1041.
3. Temp. Treas. Reg. §1.1041-1T, A-6.
4. Temp. Treas. Reg. §1.1041-1T, A-7. See also *Joseph R. Belot v. Commissioner*, TC Memo 2016-113, June 13, 2016 (Tax Court expansively interpreted the "pursuant to a divorce or separation agreement" requirement to find transfer incident to a divorce).
5. General Explanation of the Revenue Provisions of the Deficit Reduction Act of 1984, at p. 711.

Both spouses or both former spouses may elect to have these rules apply to all transfers after 1983 and also may elect to have these rules apply to transfers after July 18, 1984, under divorce or separation instruments in effect before July 19, 1984.

107. What is the tax treatment of other transfers of an existing life insurance policy in connection with a divorce settlement to which the nonrecognition rules do not apply?

If an existing policy was transferred before July 19, 1984, or after July 18, 1984 pursuant to an instrument in effect prior to such date (and no election is made to have the IRC Section 1041 nonrecognition rules apply), then the following rules apply.

If the fair market value of the policy at the time of transfer exceeds the transferor's cost basis for the policy (net premiums paid), the transferor may have some taxable gain. (For fair market value, see Q 144.) In *Comm. v. Davis*,[1] the U.S. Supreme Court held that a transfer of property by a husband in exchange for his wife's relinquishment of her marital rights is a taxable exchange, and the value of the marital rights exchanged is equal to the fair market value of the property at time of transfer. The *Davis* rule apparently would apply to such a transfer involving a life insurance policy.

The value of the policy transferred would not be taxable to the transferee and would not be deductible by the transferor.[2] The same results would follow if a spouse purchased a single premium policy for the spouse's former spouse pursuant to the divorce settlement.[3] Pre-2019, these values were not taxable to the recipient and deductible by the payor because they represented single sum payments rather than periodic payments of alimony. For tax years beginning after 2018, alimony is no longer deductible by the payor.

Transfer of an existing policy can result in adverse tax consequences to the former spouse. If the policy is assigned to the former spouse, the proceeds are received as life insurance proceeds and not as alimony income. However, it would seem that the former spouse is a purchaser for value and, consequently, the proceeds would be subject to the transfer for value rule (Q 77, Q 79).[4] Hence, the profit (the excess of the proceeds over the value of the contract on the date of transfer plus all premiums and certain other amounts paid thereafter) would be taxable to the former spouse as ordinary income.[5]

108. What is the tax treatment when an existing life insurance policy is owned and maintained by a former spouse?

Editor's Note: The 2017 Tax Act eliminated the previously existing above-the-line deduction for alimony for tax years beginning after 2018, and provides that alimony and separate maintenance payments are no longer included in the income of the recipient.

1. 370 U.S. 65 (1962).
2. *Ashcraft v. Comm.*, 252 F.2d 200 (7th Cir. 1958), aff'g 28 TC 356 (1957).
3. *Morrison v. Comm.*, TC Memo 1956-146.
4. See *Comm. v. Davis*, supra.
5. IRC Sec. 101(a)(2).

If the policy is not transferred but the former spouse is required, under the divorce decree or agreement, to own and maintain a policy as security for post-death payments, installment payments of the proceeds would be taxable as alimony. Pre-2019, payments from an insurance trust established to discharge post-death obligations were fully taxable to the recipient spouse.[1]

109. If an individual is required by a court decree or separation agreement to pay premiums on a life insurance policy for a former spouse, are the premiums taxable income to the recipient spouse? Are they deductible by the payor spouse?

Editor's Note: The 2017 Tax Act eliminated the previously existing above-the-line deduction for alimony for tax years beginning after 2018, and provides that alimony and separate maintenance payments are no longer included in the income of the recipient.

Premiums Paid Pursuant to Instruments Executed After 1984

Assuming that all the other alimony requirements are met, premiums paid by the payor spouse for term or permanent life insurance on the payor spouse's life pursuant to a divorce or separation instrument executed after December 31, 1984, qualify as alimony payments on behalf of the recipient spouse to the extent that the recipient spouse is the owner of the policy.[2] Pre-2019, premium payments that qualified as alimony payments generally were deductible by the payor spouse.[3] Note that the new rules governing alimony payments only apply for divorce agreements entered into on or after January 1, 2019, unless taxpayers divorcing in 2018 specifically agreed to apply the new rules.

Premiums Paid Pursuant to Instruments Executed Before 1985

If an existing policy is absolutely assigned to a recipient spouse, or a new policy that gives full ownership rights is purchased for the recipient spouse, the premiums are includable in the recipient spouse's gross income and are deductible by the spouse who assigned or purchased the policy.[4] This is the result even though, under the terms of the decree or agreement, (1) the payor's obligation to pay premiums will cease upon the remarriage of the recipient spouse,[5] (2) the recipient spouse's rights in the insurance terminate if the recipient spouse does not survive the payor spouse, or (3) the recipient spouse's exercise of ownership rights is subject to the approval of the divorce court.[6]

If the payor spouse retains ownership rights in the policy, or if the recipient spouse's interest is contingent (as where the policy itself or the right to name the beneficiary will revert to the payor upon the recipient spouse's death or remarriage), the premiums are not taxable to the recipient spouse and are not deductible by the payor.[7]

1. IRC Sec. 71 (prior to repeal by Pub. Law No. 115-97); IRC Sec. 682; Treas. Reg. §§1.71-1(c)(2), 1.101-5.
2. Temp. Treas. Reg. §1.71-1T, A-6.
3. See IRC Sec. 215, prior to repeal by Pub. Law No. 115-97.
4. See, e.g. *Carmichael v. Comm.*, 14 TC 1356 (1950); Rev. Rul. 70-218, 1970-1 CB 19.
5. *Hyde v. Comm.*, 301 F.2d 279 (2nd Cir. 1962).
6. *Stevens v. Comm.*, 439 F.2d 69 (2nd Cir. 1971).
7. See e.g. *Kiesling v. Comm.*, 349 F.2d 110 (3rd Cir. 1965); *Sperling v. Comm.*, TC Memo 1982-681.

It is not sufficient that the decree or agreement requires that the recipient spouse is to remain primary beneficiary; the payor spouse must give up all ownership and control.[1] A voluntary assignment not required by the decree or agreement is also not sufficient.[2] Payments are not deductible alimony taxable to a recipient spouse where a policy is assigned to a trust that confers only a lifetime interest and the children are remaindermen.[3] When the policy is placed in escrow merely as security for the payor's obligation to pay alimony, it is clear, under the foregoing rules, that the premiums are neither taxable to the recipient nor deductible by the payor.[4]

The Tax Court has held that even though a policy is assigned absolutely to the recipient spouse and the payor spouse is required to pay premiums, if the policy is *term* insurance, the premiums are neither includable in the recipient's income nor deductible by the payor.[5] The result is the same even when the term policy has a conversion privilege, if the recipient would have to pay the additional premium on conversion.[6]

Similarly, a payor spouse's policy loan repayments required by a separation agreement are not taxable to the recipient spouse, nor deductible by the payor, when the payor retains ownership of the policy and the recipient is the irrevocable beneficiary only until death or remarriage.[7]

The payor spouse's deduction, provided by IRC Section 215, is based on the inclusion of the same item in the recipient's gross income under IRC Section 71.[8]

110. If life insurance proceeds are required under the terms of a property settlement agreement or a divorce decree to be paid to certain beneficiaries, are the proceeds includable in the insured's estate?

Includability of Proceeds or Premiums

The IRS has ruled that where a divorced wife had an absolute right, under terms of a property settlement agreement incorporated by reference in a divorce decree, to annuity payments after the death of her former husband, and such payments were to be provided by insurance on his life maintained by him for that purpose, the former husband possessed no incidents of ownership in the insurance at his death. As a result, no part of the insurance proceeds was includable in his estate.[9] (See Q 81 for the general rules of includability.) Also, the Tax Court has held that where a divorced husband was required under a property settlement agreement to maintain insurance on his life payable to his former wife, if living, but otherwise to their surviving descendants or to his former wife's estate if there were no surviving descendants, the insured possessed no incidents of ownership in the insurance. The insurance, in other words, was not merely security

1. Rev. Rul. 57-125, 1957-1 CB 27; *Greenway v. Comm.*, TC Memo 1980-97.
2. *Cole v. U.S.*, 76-1 USTC ¶9256 (E.D. Ill. 1975).
3. *Kinney v. Comm.*, TC Memo 1958-209.
4. *Blumenthal v. Comm.*, 183 F.2d 15 (3rd Cir. 1950).
5. *Brodersen v. Comm.*, 57 TC 412 (1971).
6. *Wright v. Comm.*, 62 TC 377 (1974), aff'd 76-2 USTC ¶9736 (7th Cir. 1976).
7. *Auerbach v. Comm.*, TC Memo 1975-219.
8. *Mandel v. Comm.*, 229 F.2d 382 (7th Cir. 1956).
9. Rev. Rul. 54-29, 1954-1 CB 186.

for other obligations.[1] In another case, the Tax Court held that where an insured was subject to a court order requiring the insured to maintain insurance on his life payable to his minor children, such court order, operating in conjunction with other applicable state law, effectively nullified incidents of ownership the insured would otherwise possess by policy terms.[2]

When, on the other hand, the divorced husband was merely required to maintain a stated sum of insurance on his life payable to his former wife so long as she lived and remained unmarried, the insured was held to have retained a reversionary interest sufficient in value to make the proceeds includable in his estate (Q 86).[3] It also has been held that where, pursuant to a divorce decree, the proceeds of insurance maintained by a divorced husband on his own life to secure alimony payments are paid following the insured's death directly to the former wife, the proceeds are includable in the insured's estate. The Board of Tax Appeals reasoned that because the proceeds satisfy a debt of the decedent or his estate, the result is the same as if the proceeds are received by the decedent's executor (Q 81).[4]

111. When life insurance proceeds are required under the terms of a property settlement agreement or a divorce decree to be paid to certain beneficiaries, is an offsetting deduction allowable?

Where insurance proceeds payable to a divorced spouse are required to be included in the insured's estate, it is sometimes possible to secure an offsetting deduction either (1) on the basis that the beneficiary's right to the proceeds amounts to a claim against the estate representing a personal obligation of the decedent existing at the time of death[5] or (2) on the basis that the beneficiary's interest in the proceeds amounts to an indebtedness against the proceeds included in the estate.[6]

A deduction is not allowed on either basis, however, if the claim or indebtedness is founded on an agreement between the spouses in the nature of a property settlement agreement not supported by "adequate and full consideration in money or money's worth."[7] Where (i) property is transferred from a decedent or from a decedent's estate to a former spouse of the decedent pursuant to a property settlement agreement, (ii) divorce occurred within a three-year period measured from the date one year before the agreement was entered into, and (iii) the property is includable in the decedent's gross estate, the transfer is considered to be made for an adequate and full consideration in money or money's worth.[8] A relinquishment or promised relinquishment of marital rights in property is not consideration in money or money's worth.[9] Although one court held that a wife's right to support is a "marital right in property,"[10] the IRS

1. *Est. of Bowers v. Comm.*, 23 TC 911 (1955), acq. 1955-2 CB 4.
2. *Est. of Beauregard v. Comm.*, 74 TC 603 (1980), acq. 1981-1 CB 1.
3. Rev. Rul. 76-113, 1976-1 CB 276.
4. *Est. of Mason v. Comm.*, 43 BTA 813 (1941), nonacq. 1941-1 CB 17 (1941).
5. IRC Sec. 2053(a)(3).
6. IRC Sec. 2053(a)(4).
7. IRC Sec. 2053(c)(1)(A).
8. IRC Sec. 2043(b)(2).
9. IRC Secs. 2053(e), 2043(b).
10. *Meyer's Est. v. Helvering*, 110 F.2d 367 (2nd Cir. 1940), cert. den. 310 U.S. 651.

has declined to follow the decision[1] and declares instead that a release of support rights by a spouse constitutes consideration in money or money's worth.[2] The Tax Court has consistently agreed that a spouse's relinquishment or promised relinquishment in a separation agreement of support rights is consideration in money or money's worth.[3]

Even though it is found that the relinquishment or promised relinquishment of support rights is consideration in money or money's worth, it also must be found that the claim or indebtedness against property was "contracted bona fide and for an adequate and full consideration in money or money's worth."[4] It must be found, in other words, that that which is sought to be deducted from the estate was bargained for in exchange for support rights. Thus, the executor of the estate must be prepared to show, according to applicable local law, the value of the support rights at the time the separation agreement was entered into. If the executor is unable to establish a dollar value by any reasonable approach, such as taking into account the value of the marital assets and the former spouses' incomes and their expenses, the deduction sought will be denied.[5] If a dollar value of the support rights is established, the deduction allowed cannot exceed that amount or, if less, the amount of the claim.

If insurance proceeds are payable to a former spouse pursuant to the terms of a property settlement agreement (but not pursuant to a court decree), the insured's estate may be permitted an offsetting deduction to the extent of the value of any support rights relinquished by the former spouse under the agreement.[6] But to the extent the proceeds exceed the value of such support rights, no deduction is allowable if the only other consideration given by the former spouse was relinquishment or promised relinquishment of inheritance rights in the decedent's property. For information on how to value support rights, see Revenue Ruling 71-67[7] and *Est. of Fenton v. Comm.*[8]

When a property settlement agreement is incorporated in a divorce decree, and when the divorce court is free to ignore the allowances made in the agreement and to set different allowances in its own discretion instead, the obligations of the parties are not "founded upon a promise or agreement" but upon the divorce decree. In this case, a deduction of a proper claim or indebtedness under IRC Section 2053 is allowable without regard to the nature of the consideration given by the former spouse.[9] Even if both the agreement and the court decree provide that the covenants in the agreement shall survive any decree of divorce that may be entered, the obligations of the parties are still founded on the court decree, not on a promise or agreement.[10]

1. Rev. Rul. 68-379, 1968-2 CB 414.
2. Rev. Rul. 71-67, 1971-1 CB 271; Rev. Rul. 75-395, 1975-2 CB 370.
3. *McKeon v. Comm.*, 25 TC 697 (1956); *Est. of Glen v. Comm.*, 45 TC 323 (1966); *Est. of Iverson v. Comm.*, 65 TC 391 (1975), rev'd and remanded on another issue, 552 F.2d 977 (3rd Cir. 1977); *Est. of Satz v. Comm.*, 78 TC 1172 (1982). See also *Bowes v. U.S.*, 77-2 USTC ¶13,212 (N.D. Ill. 1977).
4. IRC Sec. 2053(c)(1)(A).
5. *Est. of Iverson*, *Est. of Satz*, both cited above.
6. *Gray v. U.S.*, 78-1 USTC ¶13,244 (C.D. Cal. 1978), on remand; *Est. of Fenton v. Comm.*, 70 TC 263 (1978).
7. 1971-1 CB 271.
8. 70 TC 263 (1978).
9. *Comm. v. Maresi*, 156 F.2d 929 (2nd Cir. 1946); *Comm. v. Est. of Watson*, 216 F.2d 941 (2nd Cir. 1954), acq. 1958-1 CB 6; *Young v. Comm.*, 39 BTA 230 (1939); *Est. of Mason v. Comm.*, 43 BTA 813 (1941).
10. *Harris v. Comm.*, 340 U.S. 106 (1950); *Est. of Robinson v. Comm.*, 63 TC 717 (1975).

On the other hand, where a property settlement agreement is incorporated in a divorce decree, but under applicable state law the divorce court is not free to disregard the provisions of a valid property settlement agreement, the obligations of the parties are held to be founded upon a promise or agreement and not upon the divorce decree. In such case, the availability of the offsetting estate tax deduction is limited as previously explained.[1]

Also, the IRS has ruled that where life insurance proceeds were payable to an insured husband's minor children pursuant to a divorce decree, the deduction was not allowable because (1) the decree exceeded the support obligation imposed by state law in requiring the spouse to maintain insurance on his life payable to his children, and (2) the maintenance of the insurance was not contracted for a full and adequate consideration.[2]

112. Is the deduction under IRC Section 2053(a)(3) considered a claim against the insured's estate?

The IRS has held that the availability of the deduction under IRC Section 2053(a)(3) depends upon the nature of the insured's legal obligation under the divorce decree. If the insured's obligation was simply to keep the policy in full force and effect with all premiums paid as long as the former spouse lived and remained unmarried, and the insured did that, then no obligation survived the insured's death and the insured's estate would not be entitled to a deduction. If, on the other hand, the divorce decree provided for the payment to the decedent's former spouse of a specific sum of money upon the decedent's death, and the decedent provided the funds by the purchase of life insurance, then the payment of the required amount would be a personal obligation of the decedent, so it would be payable from the decedent's estate if the insurer was unable to meet its obligation. Under these circumstances, any proceeds payable to the former spouse to discharge the decedent's obligation would be deductible under IRC Section 2053(a)(3).[3]

113. Is a deduction under IRC Section 2053(a)(4) considered a debt against the insured's estate?

The Tax Court has allowed an offsetting deduction under IRC Section 2053(a)(4) where a divorced husband was required under the terms of a property settlement agreement incorporated in a divorce decree to maintain a certain amount of insurance on his life payable to his former spouse, and where the proceeds were paid upon his death directly from the insurer to the former spouse as beneficiary. The court held that the proceeds were property included in the estate and subject to an indebtedness even though, because the proceeds were paid directly to the former spouse, it was not necessary for her to file a claim against the estate.[4] The Tax Court also has allowed a deduction under IRC Section 2053(a)(4) where the decedent had been ordered through a divorce decree to assign two policies to the decedent's former spouse.[5]

1. *Est. of Bowers v. Comm.*, 23 TC 911 (1955), acq. 1955-2 CB 4; *Est. of Barrett v. Comm.*, 56 TC 1312 (1971); *Gray v. U.S.*, 541 F.2d 228 (9th Cir. 1976), reversing and remanding 391 F. Supp. 693; *Est. of Satz v. Comm.*, 78 TC 1172 (1982); Rev. Rul. 60-160, 1960-1 CB 374; Rev. Rul. 75-395, 1975-2 CB 370.
2. Rev. Rul. 78-379, 1978-2 CB 238.
3. Rev. Rul. 76-113, 1976-1 CB 276.
4. *Est. of Robinson v. Comm.*, 63 TC 717 (1975), acq. 1976-2 CB 2.
5. *Est. of DeVos v. Comm.*, TC Memo 1975-216.

The position of the IRS now is that when a divorced spouse is required by the terms of a divorce decree to maintain insurance on his or her life payable to his or her former spouse, the estate is allowed an offsetting deduction under IRC Section 2053(a)(4) until the beneficiary spouse dies or remarries.[1] (On these facts, the deduction would not be allowed under IRC Section 2053(a)(3) – see above.) The IRS has ruled similarly when, in a paternity action adjudicating custody and support rights, the insured was required by court decree to maintain insurance on the insured's life for the benefit of the insured's child.[2]

Gifts and Charitable Gifts

114. If a taxpayer gives a spouse a life insurance policy, is the taxpayer entitled to a gift tax marital deduction?

Yes.

An outright gift of a life insurance policy to the donor's spouse qualifies for the gift tax marital deduction on the same basis as the gift of a bond or any other similar property.[3] The same should hold for subsequent premiums paid on the policy by the donor. An annual exclusion may be allowed instead of the marital deduction if the donee spouse is not a U.S. citizen. See Q 157 for gift of policy in trust.

115. If a primary beneficiary of life insurance proceeds payable under a settlement option has the power to withdraw part of the proceeds, does the beneficiary's failure to exercise the power constitute a taxable gift to contingent beneficiaries?

Where the primary beneficiary has an annual, limited, noncumulative right of withdrawal, the beneficiary has made a gift to contingent beneficiaries when the beneficiary fails to exercise the right. A lapse of the right is subject to gift tax only to the extent that the right to withdraw exceeded the greater of $5,000 or 5 percent of the value of the proceeds at the time of lapse (Q 205).[4]

116. How are split-dollar life insurance arrangements treated for gift tax purposes?

Gifts may arise in a split-dollar arrangement when a donor provides a benefit to a donee. For example, an employee or shareholder who irrevocably assigns his or her interest in a compensatory or shareholder split-dollar arrangement (Q 4008) to a third party (such as a family member) may make gifts to such third party (including annual gifts of the amount the employee or shareholder is required to include in income). Also, a donor may make gifts to an irrevocable life insurance trust under a private split-dollar arrangement.

1. Rev. Rul. 76-113, 1976-1 CB 276.
2. Let. Rul. 8128005.
3. *Kidd v. Patterson*, 230 F. Supp. 769 (N.D. Ala. 1964).
4. IRC Sec. 2514(e).

The treatment of split-dollar arrangements may differ depending on whether the arrangement was entered into or modified after September 17, 2003.

Post-September 17, 2003, Arrangements

Regulations generally provide that the treatment of a split-dollar arrangement depends on whether the donor is the owner of the life insurance contract.[1] Even if the donee is named as the policy owner, the donor may be treated as the owner if the only economic benefit provided to the donee is the value of current life insurance protection.

If a life insurance trust is the owner of the policy, the donor makes premium payments, and the donor is entitled to recover an amount equal to the premiums, the donor is treated as making a loan to the trust in the amount of the premium payment. If the loan is repayable on the death of the donor, the term of the loan is equal to the donor's life expectancy on the date of the payment (under Treasury Regulation Section 1.72-9 (see Table V in Appendix A)). The value of the gift equals the premium payment less the present value (determined under IRC Section 7282) of the donor's right to receive repayment. If there is no right to repayment, the value of the gift equals the premium payment.

If the donor is treated as the owner of the policy, the donor is treated as making a gift to the trust. The value of the gift equals the economic benefits provided to the trust, less the amount of premium paid by the trustee. If the donor's estate is entitled to receive the greater of (1) the aggregate premiums paid by the donor or (2) the cash surrender value, the gift is equal to the cost of life insurance protection less premiums paid by the trustee. If the donor's estate is entitled to receive the lesser of (1) the aggregate premiums paid by the donor or (2) the cash surrender value, the gift is equal to the cost of life insurance protection, plus the amount of cash surrender value to which the trust has current access (except to the extent taken into account in an earlier year) and any other economic benefit provided to the trust (except to the extent taken into account in an earlier year), less premiums paid by the trustee. If the donor is treated as the owner of the policy, amounts received by the life insurance trust under the contract (e.g., dividends or policy loan) are treated as gifts from the donor to the trust.

No matter who is treated as the owner of the life insurance policy, there may be a gift upon transfer of an interest in a policy to a third party. See Revenue Ruling 81-198, below.

Pre-September 18, 2003, Arrangements

In a 1978 ruling, a wife owned a policy on the split-dollar plan on the life of her husband. The husband's employer paid the portion of the premiums equal to annual cash value increases and was entitled to reimbursement from death proceeds. The IRS ruled that the value of the life insurance protection provided by the employer, which the IRS also ruled was included in the husband's income (Q 4008), was deemed to be a gift from the husband to the wife, subject to the gift tax.[2]

1. TD 9092, 2003-46 IRB 1055; Treas. Reg. §§1.61-22, 1.7872-15.
2. Rev. Rul. 78-420, 1978-2 CB 67, revoked by Rev. Rul. 2003-105, 2003-40 IRB 696, for split-dollar arrangements entered into or modified after September 17, 2003.

In Revenue Ruling 81-198,[1] an employee made a gift of his rights under a basic plan of split-dollar insurance (as described in Q 4008) in which the insurance was premium paying and was in force for some time. The IRS ruled that three elements are valued. First, the value of the insured's rights in the policy at the date of the gift is the interpolated terminal reserve plus the proportionate part of the last premium paid before the date of the gift covering the period beyond that date, reduced by the total of premiums paid by the employer. Second, the premiums paid by the insured following the date of the gift are gifts on the date paid. Third, the value of the life insurance protection provided by the employer, included in the employee's gross income, is deemed to be a gift by the employee.

In a letter ruling dated December 4, 1972, the IRS found that a gift of the amount at risk under a split-dollar plan is valued as the greater of (1) the value of the insurance protection as computed for income tax purposes (Q 4009) or (2) the difference between the premium payment and the increase in the cash surrender value of the policy. A later technical advice memorandum stated that, with respect to a split-dollar plan, a gift may be made of (1) the value of the insurance protection and (2) increases in cash surrender values in excess of premiums paid by, and returnable to, the corporation.[2]

117. What is the advantage of the "split-gift" law where one spouse gives a life insurance, endowment, or annuity contract to a third person?

If the gift qualifies as a present interest gift (Q 218), each spouse's annual exclusion ($14,000 in 2013-2017, increasing to $15,000 in 2018-2019 and 2020, see Appendix D) can be applied to reduce or eliminate the gift tax. Thus, $30,000 (in 2020, 2 × $15,000) can be subtracted from the value of the contract given and from premiums paid by the donor as gifts in subsequent years (so long as the spouse consents each year) in computing taxable gifts for years in which the gifts are made. The consenting spouse's unified credit also can be applied against any gift tax imposed on the spouse's gift where the gift is in excess of the allowable exclusion or is a future interest gift. (See also Q 214.)

118. Does an employee covered under a survivor income benefit plan make a gift of the survivor benefit for federal gift tax purposes?

No.

Under a survivor income benefit plan, an employer provides an income benefit for certain survivors designated by family or marital relationship to the employee. An employee does not make a gift of the survivor benefit at the time of death.[3] Note that neither Revenue Ruling 81-31 nor *Est. of DiMarco v. Comm.* addressed whether an employee should be treated each year as (1) receiving compensation equal to the value of providing a death benefit or survivor income benefit to an eligible survivor if the employee died during the year, and (2) transferring such

1. 1981-2 CB 188.
2. TAM 9604001.
3. Rev. Rul. 92-68, 1992-2 CB 257, revoking Rev. Rul. 81-31, 1981-1 CB 475 (in which the Service treated an employee as making a gift of the benefit from a death-benefit-only plan in the year of the employee's death); *Est. of DiMarco v. Comm.*, 87 TC 653 (1986), acq. in result, 1990-2 CB 1.

value to the eligible survivor. The use of the annual exclusion and the marital deduction might protect such a gift from any gift tax. (See Q 100 for estate tax aspects and Q 260 for income tax aspects.)

119. How are life insurance policies and endowment contracts valued for gift tax purposes?

Generally, the value of a gift of life insurance is established through the sale by the company of comparable contracts.[1]

If a new policy is purchased for another, or is transferred as a gift immediately after purchase, its gift value is the gross premium paid by the donor to the insurance company.[2]

If a person makes a gift of a previously purchased policy, and the policy is single-premium or paid-up, its gift value is the single premium that the company would charge currently for a comparable contract of equal face value on the life of a person who is the insured's age at the time of the gift.[3] A 1978 ruling concerned a single premium life policy in force for 20 years where the replacement cost of a single premium life policy of the same face value on the same insured was substantially less than the cash surrender value of the existing policy. The IRS ruled that the replacement contract would not be "comparable" and that in the absence of information pertaining to a "comparable contract" the value of the policy would be determined by reference to the interpolated terminal reserve value (see below).[4]

If the gift is of a policy on which further premiums are payable, the value is established by adding the "interpolated terminal reserve" (the reserve adjusted to the date of the gift) and the value of the unearned portion of the last premium.[5]

Example. A gift is made four months after the last premium due date of an ordinary life insurance policy issued nine years and four months before the gift was made by the insured, who was thirty-five years of age at date of issue. The gross annual premium is $2,811. The computation is as follows:

Terminal reserve at end of tenth year	$14,601.00
Terminal reserve at end of ninth year	$12,965.00
Increase	$1,636.00
One-third of such increase (the gift having been made four months following the last preceding premium due date) is	$545.33
Terminal reserve at end of ninth year	$12,965.00
Interpolated terminal reserve at date of gift	$13,510.33
Two-thirds of gross premium ($2,811)	$1,874.00
Value of gift	$15,384.33

1. Treas. Reg. §25.2512-6.
2. Treas. Reg. §25.2512-6(a), Example 1.
3. Treas. Reg. §25.2512-6(a), Example 3.
4. Rev. Rul. 78-137, 1978-1 CB 280.
5. Treas. Reg. §25.2512-6(a), Example 4.

The amount of a policy loan outstanding at the time of the gift would be subtracted.[1]

The effect of the circumstance that the insured is uninsurable at the time of the gift is uncertain; there is no case directly on point.[2]

See Q 116 regarding gifts with respect to split-dollar arrangements.

If the gift of the policy or contract is conditioned upon payment of the gift tax by the donee, the value of the gift is reduced by the amount of the gift tax paid by the donee.[3]

A group term life policy assigned by an employee to an irrevocable trust on the day before a monthly premium was due was held to have no ascertainable value for gift tax purposes, but it was also held that after the assignment the employee would be deemed to have made a gift to the assignee whenever the employer paid a premium.[4] A 1984 revenue ruling valued the gift as follows: If the plan of group term insurance is nondiscriminatory or the employee is not a key employee, the Table I rates may be used. If the employee chooses not to use Table I, or if the plan is discriminatory and the employee is a key employee, the employee should use the actual cost allocable to the employee's insurance by obtaining the necessary information from the employer. The rates apply to the full face amount of the insurance.[5] Projecting the holding of the 1984 ruling to the nondiscrimination rules applicable to taxable years ending after October 22, 1986 (Q 249), it would seem that if the plan of group term insurance is discriminatory with respect to the employee, the employee must use the higher of Table I rates or actual cost.

120. May a charitable contribution deduction be taken for the gift of a life insurance policy or premium? May a charitable contribution deduction be taken for the gift of a maturing annuity or endowment contract?

Yes, subject to the limits on deductions for gifts to charities.

The amount of any charitable contribution must be reduced by the amount of gain that would have represented ordinary income to the donor had the donor sold the property at its fair market value.[6] Gain realized from the sale of a life insurance contract is taxed to the seller as ordinary income (Q 36). Therefore, the deduction for a gift of a life insurance policy to a charity is restricted to the donor's cost basis in the contract when the value of the contract exceeds the premium payments. Thus, if a policy owner assigns the policy itself to a qualified charity, or to a trustee with a charity as irrevocable beneficiary, the amount deductible as a charitable contribution is either the value of the policy or the policy owner's cost basis, whichever is less (Q 144).[7] It is not necessary, however, to reduce the amount of the contribution when, by reason of the transfer, ordinary income is recognized by the donor in the same taxable year in which

1. IRS Form 712, Part II.
2. See *U.S. v. Ryerson*, 312 U.S. 260 (1941); 54 Harvard L. Rev. 895 (1941); *Est. of Pritchard v. Comm.*, 4 TC 204 (1944); Treas. Reg. §25.2512-1.
3. Rev. Rul. 75-72, 1975-1 CB 310. See also Rev. Rul. 76-104, 76-1 CB 301; Rev. Rul. 76-105, 76-1 CB 304.
4. Rev. Rul. 76-490, 1976-2 CB 300.
5. Rev. Rul. 84-147, 1984-2 CB 201.
6. IRC Sec. 170(e)(1)(A).
7. See *Behrend v. Comm.*, 23 BTA 1037 (1931), *acq.* X-2 CB 5; *Tuttle v. U.S.*, 305 F. Supp. 484 (1969).

the contribution is made.[1] Letter Ruling 9110016, in which the IRS denied a charitable deduction when a policy was assigned to a charity that had no insurable interest under state law, was revoked after the taxpayer decided not to proceed with the transaction.[2]

Premium payments also are deductible charitable contributions if a charitable organization or a trustee of an irrevocable charitable trust owns the policy.[3] It is not settled whether premium payments made by the donor to the *insurer* to maintain a policy given to the charity, instead of making cash payments directly to the *charity* in the amount of the premiums, are gifts *to* the charity or merely gifts *for the use* of the charity. The difference is important when the donor wishes to take a charitable deduction of more than 30 percent of the donor's adjusted gross income. When the policy is merely assigned to a charitable organization as security for a note, the premiums are not deductible even though the note is equal to the face value of the policy and is payable from the proceeds at either the insured's death or the maturity of the policy. The reason is that the note could be paid off and the policy recovered after the insured has obtained charitable deductions for the premium payments. A corporation, as well as an individual, can take a charitable contribution deduction for payment of premiums on a policy that has been assigned to a charitable organization.[4]

Planning Point: For a number of reasons, including concerns over the rules limiting a tax deduction to the lesser of fair market value or basis and because of the uncertainty regarding tax consequences of premium payments made by the donor directly to the insurance company on a policy owned by a charity, it is generally preferable for a donor to make cash gifts to a charity and allow the charity to pay premiums on policies owned by the charity. It is important, however, not to require that the cash gifts be used for premium payments.

121. May a charitable contribution deduction be taken for a gift of an interest in a split-dollar arrangement?

No deduction is allowed for a transfer to a charitable organization made after February 8, 1999, if in connection with the transfer the charitable organization directly or indirectly pays, or has previously paid, any premium on any "personal benefit contract" with respect to the transferor. Further, no deduction is allowed if there is an understanding or expectation that any person will directly or indirectly pay any premium on a personal benefit contract with respect to the transferor.[5] A personal benefit contract is any life insurance, annuity, or endowment contract if a direct or indirect beneficiary under the contract is the transferor, a member of the transferor's family, or any other person (other than certain charitable organizations) designated by the transferor.[6]

In a case decided under rules in effect before 1999, a charitable deduction was not allowed where the charity provided a receipt stating that the donors received no benefit from their

1. Treas. Reg. §1.170A-4(a).
2. Let. Rul. 9147040.
3. *Hunton v. Comm.*, 1 TC 821 (1943); *Behrend v. Comm.*, 23 BTA 1037 (1931); Let. Ruls. 8708083, 8304068.
4. Rev. Rul. 58-372, 1958-2 CB 99.
5. IRC Sec. 170(f)(10)(A).
6. IRC Sec. 170(f)(10)(B).

charitable contribution. The court held that in fact the donors were receiving a benefit under the charitable split-dollar arrangement.[1]

In a ruling involving a paid-up policy, the IRS took the position that no deduction will be allowed for gifts made after July 31, 1969, involving a split-dollar plan in which the donor gives a charity the cash surrender value and gives a noncharitable beneficiary the balance. A gift of the cash surrender value is considered a gift of less than an entire interest in the property whether the donor retains the right to designate the beneficiary of the risk portion or irrevocably designates the beneficiary prior to making the gift.[2] Two 1969 revenue rulings, which allow a deduction, apply only to gifts made on or before July 31, 1969.[3]

122. Are there any exceptions to the disallowance rule for transfers of charitable gift annuity contracts?

There are exceptions to the disallowance rule for certain transfers involving charitable gift annuity contracts (Q 608) and charitable remainder trusts.[4]

123. Are there any penalties that can be imposed upon a charitable institution in connection with a gift of life insurance where a deduction is not allowable?

A charitable organization that pays premiums after December 17, 1999, on a life insurance, annuity, or endowment contract in connection with a transfer for which a charitable deduction was not allowable is subject to a penalty tax equal to the amount of premiums paid.[5] The IRS has indicated that other penalties may be imposed on charitable organizations involved in charitable split-dollar plans.[6]

124. May a charitable contribution deduction be taken for a gift of a life insurance policy if the donor retains a right, shared with the donee charity, to change charitable beneficiaries?

While the IRC generally disallows a charitable deduction for gifts of less than the donor's entire interest in property, it does permit limited exceptions to this rule. One of these is a gift of an "undivided interest" in property. This means that the donor may give less than his entire interest and still take a charitable gift deduction if he gives "a fraction or percentage of each and every substantial interest or right" he owns in the property.[7]

In a letter ruling, the IRS took the position that a gift of a life insurance policy to a charity was deductible even though the donor retained the right, exercisable in conjunction with the donee charity, to change the charitable beneficiaries. The IRS reasoned that by sharing the right to

1. *Addis v. Comm.*, 2004-2 USTC ¶50,291 (9th Cir. 2004).
2. Rev. Rul. 76-143, 1976-1 CB 63.
3. Rev. Rul. 69-79, 1969-1 CB 63; Rev. Rul. 69-215, 1969-1 CB 63.
4. IRC Secs. 170(f)(10)(D), 170(f)(10)(E).
5. IRC Sec. 170(f)(10)(F).
6. Notice 99-36, 1999-2 CB 1284.
7. IRC Sec. 170(f)(3)(B)(ii); Treas. Reg. §1.170A-7(b)(1)(i).

change charitable beneficiaries, the donor had given an undivided interest in the right he retained and thus the gift came within the exception to the rule against deducting partial interest gifts.[1]

125. May a charitable contribution deduction be taken for a gift of the annuity portion of a split-life contract?

The IRS has ruled that a gift to charity of the annuity portion of a split-life contract is not deductible because it is a gift of less than the donor's entire interest in property.[2] The IRS reasoned that the donor, prior to making the gift, exercised the right to purchase the annual term insurance and, thus, the donor had retained a right in the property. Furthermore, the donor's subsequent annual cash contributions equal to the annuity premiums were treated by the IRS as given in exchange for the charity's continued election to allow the donor to renew the term life insurance. Thus, the donor continued to retain the right to purchase the annual term insurance. Because the donor retained a right, the donor's gift of the annuity portion was of less than the donor's entire interest in the property.[3] The ruling did not clearly deal with the deduction of the annual cash contributions and some commentators believe they might be deductible. However, the reasoning of the IRS – that the annual contributions were in exchange for the continued right to renew the term insurance – suggests that the donor's entire interest in the cash contributions was not given.

126. If life insurance proceeds are payable to a religious, charitable, or educational organization, is their value taxable in the insured's gross estate?

Generally, no. If the insured has any incident of ownership in the policy at the time of death, the proceeds are includable in the insured's gross estate, but a charitable deduction is allowable for their full value.[4]

If, however, the law in the state of the donor's domicile does not recognize that a charity has an insurable interest in the life of the donor, complications may arise. In some states, a charity may not have an insurable interest with respect to a newly issued insurance policy given to the charity or for a policy applied for and issued to the charity as owner and beneficiary. If the charity does not have an insurable interest and the insurer or the insured's estate raises the question of lack of an insurable interest, the insured's estate may be able to recover the proceeds (or the premiums paid). The proceeds are includable in the insured's estate to the extent that the proceeds could be received by the insured's estate. No charitable deduction may be allowed if the executor recovers the proceeds for the estate or if the executor were to fail to recover the proceeds and the proceeds passed to charity.[5]

1. Let. Rul. 8030043.
2. See IRC Sec. 170(f)(3).
3. Rev. Rul. 76-1, 1976-1 CB 57.
4. IRC Secs. 2042(2), 2055; *McKelvy v. Comm.*, 82 F.2d 395 (3rd Cir. 1936); *Comm. v. Pupin*, 107 F.2d 745 (2nd Cir. 1939).
5. See Let. Rul. 9110016 (revoked by Let. Rul. 9147040 when state law was amended to permit an insured to immediately transfer a newly purchased life insurance policy to charity).

127. Are gifts of life insurance to charitable organizations subject to gift tax?

Generally, no. An individual may take a gift tax deduction for the full value of gifts to qualified charities of life insurance and annuity contracts, and of premiums or consideration paid for such contracts owned by qualified charities.[1] Such a deduction is not allowed where an insured assigns (even irrevocably) to a charity the cash surrender value of a life insurance policy (either paid-up or premium paying), including a right to death proceeds equal to the cash surrender value immediately before death, if the donor retains the right to name or change the beneficiary of proceeds in excess of the cash surrender value and to assign the balance of the policy subject to the charity's right to the cash surrender value. According to the IRS, such a gift is neither one of the donor's entire interest in the property nor one of an undivided portion of the donor's entire interest in the property (Q 121), and so the deduction is disallowed under IRC Section 2522(c).[2]

If the law in the state of the donor's domicile does not recognize that a charity has an insurable interest in the life of the donor, a charitable deduction may not be allowed for a gift of a newly issued insurance policy (or premiums paid on the policy) or for gifts of premium payments on a policy applied for and issued to the charity as owner and beneficiary.[3]

128. How are single premium life insurance policies, including single premium variable life insurance policies, taxed?

A single premium life insurance policy generally is treated in the same manner as a multiple-premium life insurance policy for income tax purposes. For all life insurance policies that meet the definition of life insurance (Q 65), cash surrender value increases generally are not taxed until received (Q 8) and death proceeds generally are received income tax-free (Q 63).

The tax treatment of policy loans depends on whether the policy is treated as a modified endowment contract (MEC). Most single premium policies are considered MECs; policies entered into on or after June 21, 1988, that do not meet the seven pay test of IRC Section 7702A(b) are classified as MECs. Loans from MECs are taxable as income at the time received to the extent that the cash value of the contract immediately before the payment exceeds the investment in the contract.[4] These distributions also may be subject to a penalty tax of 10 percent (Q 13).[5]

Life insurance policies, including single premium policies, issued prior to June 21, 1988, generally are grandfathered and are not subject to the seven pay test. Loans from these policies will not be treated as taxable income. Loans from policies that are not grandfathered but that meet the requirements of the seven pay test also are not treated as taxable income. Any outstanding loan becomes taxable income at the time of policy surrender or lapse, however, to the extent that the loan exceeds the owner's basis in the contract (Q 10). If policy death proceeds are tax-free, the amount of the loan is not taxed but is treated as part of the tax-free

1. IRC Sec. 2522.
2. Rev. Rul. 76-200, 76-1 CB 308.
3. See Let. Rul. 9110016 (revoked by Let. Rul. 9147040 when state law was amended to permit an insured to immediately transfer a newly purchased life insurance policy to charity).
4. IRC Sec. 72(e).
5. IRC Sec. 72(v).

death proceeds (Q 65). Note that a grandfathered policy may lose its grandfathered status if it undergoes a material change in its terms or benefits or is exchanged for another life insurance policy under IRC Section 1035 (Q 13).

Creditor Insurance

129. If a debtor pays premiums on a life insurance policy on his or her life in favor of his or her creditor, may the debtor take an income tax deduction for these premium payments?

No.

The answer is the same regardless of whether the debtor takes out a new policy for the benefit of the creditor or assigns an existing policy to the creditor. The deduction will be denied even though the debtor was required to take out the policy to obtain the loan. If the debt is personal, the premiums are nondeductible personal expenses.[1] If the debt is a business debt, the deduction is denied under IRC Section 264(a)(1), which provides that no deduction is allowed for premiums on any life insurance policy, endowment, or annuity contract if the taxpayer is directly or indirectly a beneficiary under the policy or contract. For this purpose, the insured debtor is at least indirectly a beneficiary under the policy because the proceeds may be used to satisfy the insured's debt.[2]

IRC Section 264(a)(1) also acts as a bar to a nonbusiness deduction. Thus, the deduction was denied for premiums the taxpayer paid on insurance used as collateral for a bank loan to a company in which the taxpayer was a major stockholder; the premiums were paid to protect the taxpayer's personal securities, which were also part of the collateral for the loan.[3]

The deduction is disallowed even when the person who pays the premiums is merely a guarantor and therefore only secondarily liable for the debt.[4]

130. Can a creditor deduct premiums paid on life insurance purchased on the life of the creditor's debtor?

Based on the reasoning of the cases cited in Q 132, it appears unlikely that the creditor can secure a nonbusiness expense deduction. Moreover, when proceeds are receivable as tax-exempt life insurance proceeds, it would appear that IRC Section 265(a)(1) prohibits that deduction of premiums (Q 335).

If the debtor is directly or indirectly a beneficiary under the policy, IRC Section 264(a)(1) prohibits the deduction (Q 262). The IRS has allowed a business expense deduction for premiums paid by a taxpayer in the business of selling property for one-year term insurance purchased on the lives of installment purchasers where no separate charge was made for the insurance and

1. IRC Sec. 262.
2. *Glassner v. Comm., cert. denied,* 385 U.S. 819 (1966); *O'Donohue v. Comm.,* 33 TC 698 (1960); *Hanson v. Comm.,* TC Memo 1970-15; Rev. Rul. 68-5, 1968-1 CB 99.
3. *Carbine v. Comm.,* 85-2 USTC ¶9854 (11th Cir. 1985).
4. *D'Angelo Assoc., Inc. v. Comm.,* 70 TC 121 (1978), acq. in result, 1979-1 CB 1.

where the death proceeds (payable to the seller) were in the amount of the unpaid balance of the purchase price. Proceeds receivable by the seller were treated as collections on the purchase price, *not* as life insurance proceeds excludable under IRC Section 101(a).[1]

131. If a creditor pays premiums on a life insurance policy held as collateral for a business debt, can the creditor claim an income tax deduction for the premium payments?

The IRS takes the position that the creditor cannot claim a deduction unless the creditor shows that the creditor's right to reimbursement for the premium payment was worthless in the year of payment. Thus, if the creditor has a right to proceed against the debtor for reimbursement, the debtor must be insolvent or the claim must be otherwise uncollectible. If the creditor has a right, express or implied, to reimbursement from the policy, the cash surrender value must be insufficient to cover the balance of the unpaid debt and the premium payment. If the creditor has both rights, both must be worthless.[2] Premiums that are not deductible are treated as additional advances that increase the debt.

Courts, however, have allowed the deduction without regard to the taxpayer's ability to recover the premium out of the cash surrender value of the policies.[3]

The IRS would disallow a deduction for the premium payment if the creditor has taken a bad debt deduction for the debt and the cash surrender value of the policy is sufficient to provide reimbursement for the premium payment. In *Charleston Nat'l Bank*, however, the court held that the premium payment was deductible even though the creditor had taken a bad debt deduction for the debt and the cash surrender value exceeded the current premium and premium payments not deducted in prior years.

The deduction is allowable not as a bad debt but as an ordinary and necessary business expense, incident to the protection of the collateral.[4]

If premiums that have been deducted are later recovered from the proceeds, the recovery must be reported as taxable income. If the premiums have not been deducted, however, the recovery will be tax-free.[5]

1. Rev. Rul. 70-254, 1970-1 CB 31.
2. Rev. Rul. 75-46, 1975-1 CB 55.
3. *Comm. v. Charleston Nat'l Bank*, 20 TC 253 (1953) *aff'd*, 213 F.2d 45 (4th Cir. 1954); *First Nat'l Bank & Trust Co. v. Jones*, 143 F.2d 652 (10th Cir. 1944).
4. *First Nat'l Bank & Trust Co. v. Jones*, supra; *Blumenthal v. Comm.*, TC Memo 1963-269, *aff'd*, 14 AFTR 2d 5094 (4th Cir. 1964). See also Rev. Rul. 75-46, above.
5. *St. Louis Refrigerating & Cold Storage Co. v. U.S.*, 162 F.2d 394 (8th Cir. 1947).

132. If a creditor pays premiums on a life insurance policy securing a non-business debt, can the creditor deduct the premium payments?

The deduction has been denied on the ground that the premium payments are a capital investment rather than expenses incurred "for the production or collection of income, or for the management, conservation and maintenance of property held for the production of income."[1]

133. If a stockholder's personal life insurance is used as collateral security for the corporation's debt, are the premiums deductible?

If the insured stockholder pays the premiums, the stockholder is denied a deduction on the ground that the premium payments are not an ordinary and necessary expense of carrying on the stockholder's business.[2] If the corporation pays the premiums, they are nondeductible under IRC Section 264(a)(1) because the corporation is indirectly a beneficiary under the policy.[3]

134. May a creditor take a bad debt deduction for a worthless debt even though the creditor holds an insurance policy on the life of the debtor as collateral?

Yes, provided the cash surrender value of the policy is less than the debt. The creditor may deduct the difference between the cash surrender value and the debt or, if the policy has no cash surrender value, the creditor may deduct the full amount of the worthless debt. The creditor may take the deduction even though the creditor continues to hold the policy and the face of the policy exceeds the debt. Collateral need not be liquidated to establish the worthless portion of the debt.[4] If a deduction was not previously taken, a deduction for the uncollectible balance may be taken in the year the creditor surrenders the policy.[5] No bad debt deduction will be allowed at any time, however, for advances that were made when prior loans exceeded the face of the policy and the debtor was insolvent.[6]

135. Are proceeds received by a creditor from insurance purchased on the life of the creditor's debtor exempt from income tax as life insurance proceeds?

If a creditor has an insurable interest other than as creditor (e.g., the debtor also is a key person) and has the unconditional right to retain proceeds unaffected by the size of the debt, the proceeds are received tax-free.[7]

In some states, a creditor's insurable interest in the creditor's debtor is limited to indemnification of the amount of the debt (plus premiums the creditor has paid) as of the insured's death. The creditor must hold any excess for the debtor's estate. Where this is so it would appear, based

1. *U.S. v. Mellinger*, 228 F.2d 688 (5th Cir. 1956); *Home News Publishing Co. v. Comm.*, TC Memo 1969-167; see also *Blumenthal v. Comm.*, TC Memo 1963-269, *aff'd*, 14 AFTR 2d 5094 (4th Cir. 1964).
2. *Morison v. Comm.*, TC Memo 1960-243.
3. See Rev. Rul. 68-5, 1968-1 CB 99.
4. *Hatboro Nat'l Bank v. Comm.*, 24 TC 786 (1955).
5. *Mattlage v. Comm.*, 3 BTA 242 (1925).
6. *Blumenthal v. Comm.*, TC Memo 1963-269, *aff'd*, 14 AFTR 2d 5094 (4th Cir. 1964).
7. *Thomsen & Sons, Inc. v. U.S.*, 73-2 USTC ¶9637 (7th Cir. 1973); *Harrison v. Comm.*, 59 TC 578 (1973), acq. 1973-2 CB 2.

on the reasoning of Revenue Ruling 70-254 and the *Landfield* case (Q 136), that the proceeds would not be considered to have been paid by reason of the insured's death, and therefore would not be exempt as life insurance proceeds under IRC Section 101(a).

Courts in other states, however, have held that where (i) the creditor initiates the purchase of insurance and pays the premiums, (ii) the amount of the insurance is reasonably proportionate to the amount of the debt, and (iii) the debtor consents to the insurance, the creditor's insurable interest, or right of recovery, goes to the full proceeds, not just to the amount of debt, expenses, and interest. Thus, even if the debtor has paid the debt before his or her death, the creditor is entitled to the full proceeds. Under this view, it would appear that the proceeds would be received "by reason of the death of the insured" and therefore should be entitled to the exemption of IRC Section 101(a). If the proceeds are receivable as tax-exempt life insurance proceeds, it would appear that deduction of the premiums would be denied by reason of IRC Section 265(a)(1), which provides that expenses incurred for acquiring tax-exempt income are not deductible.

136. Are life insurance proceeds received by a creditor as collateral assignee or beneficiary "as interest appears" exempt from income tax?

If a creditor is collateral assignee, the creditor receives the proceeds as a recovery on the collateral and not as life insurance proceeds.[1] Consequently, if the creditor has not taken a bad debt deduction, the proceeds are received tax-free as a return of capital. They are tax-free, that is, to the extent of the unpaid debt and any premiums the creditor has paid but not deducted (Q 132, Q 133). If the creditor, however, has received the tax benefit of a bad debt deduction, the proceeds must be reported as taxable income (except to the extent they represent a recovery of premium payments for which no deduction has been taken). If a portion of the proceeds represents interest on the debt, that portion is taxed as ordinary income to the creditor.[2]

If the creditor is named beneficiary as the creditor's "interest might appear" on a policy owned by the debtor, the creditor receives the proceeds as payment of the debt and not as life insurance proceeds. Because the creditor must prove the debt to collect the proceeds, the proceeds are received because of the insured's indebtedness rather than "by reason of the death of the insured," and hence are not exempt under IRC Section 101(a). The proceeds, therefore, constitute taxable income to the creditor to the same extent that direct repayment of the loan would have resulted in income. This is so regardless of whether the debtor or the creditor has paid the premiums.[3]

A different situation arises if the creditor takes title to the insurance policy and releases the debtor from further obligation. Under these circumstances, the proceeds are received as life insurance proceeds, but a transfer for value has taken place (Q 279). As a result, the proceeds are taxable income to the creditor to the extent that they exceed the value of the policy at the

1. Treas. Reg. §1.101-1(b)(4).
2. *St. Louis Refrigerating & Cold Storage Co. v. U.S.*, 162 F.2d 394 (8th Cir. 1947); *First Nat'l Bank v. Comm.*, TC Memo 1943.
3. *McCamant v. Comm.*, 32 TC 824 (1959); Rev. Rul. 70-254, 1970-1 CB 31.

time of transfer and premiums and certain other amounts (Q 279) paid after the transfer.[1] There should be no tax liability under the transfer for value rule, however, if the creditor is a partner of the insured, a partnership in which the insured is a partner, or a corporation in which the insured is an officer or stockholder, unless the transaction qualified as a reportable policy sale (for tax years beginning after 2017).[2]

137. If an insured assigns a life insurance policy as collateral for a loan, are the proceeds includable in the insured's gross estate?

Yes.

This is true regardless of policy ownership or beneficiary designation. To the extent that the creditor has a right to collect the debt from the proceeds, the proceeds are considered to be receivable for the benefit of the estate (Q 81).[3] It is immaterial whether the debt is actually paid from estate assets or that the beneficiary has a right to recover from the estate the amount of proceeds paid to the creditor.[4] The amount of the debt outstanding at the date of the insured's death, with interest accrued to that date, is deductible in determining the taxable estate even though the debt is paid from the proceeds.[5] (For a policy loan, see Q 187.)

138. If an insured assigns a life insurance policy in which a spouse is the named beneficiary, will the full amount of the proceeds qualify for the marital deduction?

As a general rule, if a property interest passing to a surviving spouse is subject to an encumbrance, only the value of the property interest in excess of the amount of the encumbrance qualifies for the marital deduction.[6] If the debt that is secured by the policy is actually paid from estate assets, or if the spouse-beneficiary has a right of subrogation against the estate and the estate is solvent, the full amount of the proceeds qualifies for the marital deduction despite the collateral assignment.[7] (For a policy loan, see Q 187.)

139. Are proceeds of government life insurance exempt from income tax?

Yes.

The entire amount of the death proceeds is exempt, including the interest element in installment settlements. Likewise, any gain realized on lifetime proceeds from matured endowments or surrender of policies is exempt from income tax. Dividends also are exempt from income

1. *Federal Nat'l Bank v. Comm.*, 16 TC 54 (1951), nonacq. 1951-2 CB 5 (1951).
2. IRC Sec. 101(a)(2)(B).
3. IRC Sec. 2042(1); Treas. Reg. §20.2042-1(b); *Fidelity Trust Co. (Matthews) v. Comm.*, 3 TC 525 (1944); *Est. of Hofferbert v. Comm.*, 46 BTA 1101 (1942); *Morton v. Comm.*, 23 BTA 236 (1931); cf. *Prichard v. U.S.*, 397 F.2d 60 (5th Cir. 1968) and *Bintliff v. U.S.*, 462 F.2d 403 (5th Cir. 1972).
4. *Est. of Gwinn v. Comm.*, 25 TC 31 (1955); *Hornstein (Reinhold) v. Comm.*, 3 TCM (CCH) 285.
5. Treas. Reg. §§20.2042-1(b)(1), 20.2053-4.
6. IRC Sec. 2056(b)(4)(B).
7. *Est. of Gwinn v. Comm.*, 25 TC 31 (1955), acq. 1956-1 CB 4; *Wachovia Bank & Trust Co. v. U.S.*, 163 F. Supp. 832 (Ct. Cl. 1958); Treas. Reg. §20.2056(b)-4(b).

tax.[1] The interest on accumulated dividends is not taxable.[2] Accumulated dividends applied to the purchase of additional National Service Life Insurance and the additional paid-up insurance acquired are not subject to federal income tax.[3]

140. If a qualified plan trust distributes a life insurance policy to an employee, is the value of the contract taxable to the employee in the year of distribution?

If the contract is a life insurance, retirement income, endowment, or other contract providing life insurance protection, the *fair market value* of the contract at the time of distribution must be included in the distributee's income to the extent that it exceeds the distributee's basis (Q 3940, Q 3960).[4] Inclusion of the contract's fair market value in the distributee's income is not required at the time of distribution, however, to the extent that within sixty days after it is distributed (1) all or any portion of the contract is irrevocably converted to an annuity with no life insurance element, or (2) the contract is treated as a rollover contribution under IRC Section 402(c) (Q 3982).[5]

The fair market value standard also applies if the contract is sold by the plan to a participant or beneficiary. If the fair market value of the contract exceeds the value of the consideration, then such excess (i.e., the "bargain element") is treated as a distribution to the distributee under the plan for all purposes under the IRC. This treatment of the "bargain element" as a distribution applies for transfers occurring after August 28, 2005. For transfers occurring before August 29, 2005, the "bargain element" is includable in the distributee's gross income, but is not treated as a distribution for qualification purposes.[6]

The fair market value standard is effective for distributions or sales occurring after February 12, 2004.[7] Fair market value includes the policy cash value and all other rights under the contract (including any supplemental agreements thereto, whether or not guaranteed).[8] The IRS has issued safe harbor guidance for determining the fair market value of life insurance contracts.[9] Under the safe harbor, fair market value may be the greater of (1) the interpolated terminal reserve and any unearned premiums, plus a pro rata portion of a reasonable estimate of dividends expected to be paid for that policy year, and (2) the product of the "PERC amount" (PERC stands for premiums, earnings, and reasonable charges) and the applicable "Average Surrender Factor." For details on these calculations, see Q 144.

Conversion to annuity contract. If a policy is converted, it then will be subject to the rules for annuity contracts (provided the annuity is nontransferable; see above). The IRS has taken the position that the mere elimination of the element of risk in a retirement income contract when

1. 38 U.S.C. §5301(a); Rev. Rul. 71-306, 1971-2 CB 76.
2. Rev. Rul. 91-14, 1991-1 CB 18.
3. Rev. Rul. 72-604, 1972-2 CB 35.
4. Treas. Reg. §1.402(a)-1(a)(1)(iii).
5. Treas. Reg. §1.402(a)-1(a)(2).
6. See Treas. Reg. §1.402(a)-1(a)(1)(iii).
7. See Rev. Proc. 2005-25, 2005-17 IRB 962.
8. Treas. Reg. §1.402(a)-1(a)(2)(iii).
9. See Rev. Proc. 2005-25, 2005-17 IRB 962.

the reserve exceeds the face amount does not convert the insurance contract into an annuity contract. According to the IRS, the insured must act to convert the contract into an annuity contract that has at no time contained an element of life insurance protection.[1] If the policy is distributed in a lump sum distribution, the taxable amount is eligible for favorable capital gains and special averaging treatment to the extent that such rules are still applicable (Q 3958).

Death benefit. When a life insurance contract matures by reason of the insured's death *after* the policy has been distributed from the plan, the proceeds are wholly tax-exempt to the beneficiary.[2]

141. Can the federal government reach the cash value of a taxpayer's life insurance for collection of back income taxes?

Yes.

The law is well settled that state exemption laws cannot immunize the cash values of a taxpayer's life insurance from federal tax collection. Moreover, the government can enforce its tax lien despite a gratuitous assignment of the policy with intent to avoid tax collection.[3]

Under a summary levy procedure, the IRS may reach the loan value of a policy subject to a tax lien, but the policy may be kept in force.[4] The insurance company pays over the present loan value of the policy or, if less, the balance of the tax liability. The company also must pay the IRS the amount of any policy loans (other than automatic premium loans) made after the company had notice of the lien. The company is not liable, however, for policy loans made before it had notice of the lien, or for automatic premium loans made after it had notice if the automatic premium loan agreement was entered into before it had notice.[5]

The IRC says the tax levy is satisfied if the insurer pays over "the amount which the person against whom the tax is assessed could have had advanced" to that person by the insurer on the date prescribed by law for the satisfaction of the levy (plus any amounts advanced by the insurer after knowledge of the lien other than under a preexisting automatic premium loan provision in the policy).[6]

The IRS can reach funds in an annuity contract under the same summary levy procedure mentioned above.[7] Further, the IRS also can reach insurance commission payments with a tax lien. For example, where several life insurance agents assigned their commissions to another agent and that agent, in turn, assigned the funds to an irrevocable trust, the IRS was able to reach the commissions to satisfy a tax lien against several of the agents.[8]

1. Rev. Rul. 66-322, 1966-2 CB 123.
2. Rev. Rul. 63-76, 1963-1 CB 23.
3. *Knox v. Great West Life Assurance Co.*, 212 F.2d 784 (6th Cir. 1954); *U.S. v. Heffron*, 158 F.2d 657 (9th Cir. 1947).
4. IRC Sec. 6321.
5. IRC Sec. 6323(b)(9).
6. IRC Sec. 6332(b).
7. IRC Sec. 6321; see *Prudential Ins. Co. v. Allen*, 98-1 USTC ¶50365 (S.D. Ind. 1998).
8. *American Trust v. American Community Mut. Ins. Co.*, 98-1 USTC ¶50369 (6th Cir. 1998).

142. Can the federal government collect an insured's delinquent income taxes from a beneficiary who receives life insurance death proceeds?

A government tax lien survives an insured's death. Consequently, if a tax lien has attached to the cash surrender value during the insured's life, the taxes can be collected from the proceeds to the extent of the cash surrender value at death. If life insurance proceeds are exempt from the claims of the insured's creditors under applicable *state* law, however, the insured's unpaid taxes cannot be collected from that portion of the proceeds that exceeds the cash surrender value.[1] If the tax assessment was not made until after the insured's death, the beneficiary is not liable for any of the insured's back taxes provided the proceeds are exempt from claims of the insured's creditors under state law.[2]

A different situation exists where the beneficiary is a surviving spouse who has filed joint returns with the insured. When joint returns have been filed, the surviving spouse generally is liable for the back taxes in his or her own right.[3] Thus, the entire proceeds received by a surviving spouse may be subject to a lien for the unpaid taxes.

In one case, in which a wife who was the beneficiary of a policy insuring her husband's life had been indicted but not yet convicted of his murder at the time the IRS served a levy on the policy proceeds, the court found that, under applicable state law, the wife had a property interest in the proceeds and thus the insurance company acted properly in paying the proceeds to the IRS in response to the levy.[4]

In another case, a surviving spouse used the proceeds of a policy insuring the deceased spouse to purchase annuities for the benefit of their children. The court ruled that the IRS was able to reach the funds, in payment of the couple's delinquent income taxes, after the annuity purchase.[5]

In another case, a wife received two death benefit checks from policies insuring her husband's life, placed the checks in a safe deposit box, and then attempted to renounce her interest in the death proceeds under state law after the IRS seized the checks for payment of taxes. A federal district court granted the government's motion for summary judgment, ruling that the wife had accepted the proceeds, and that they were subject to the IRS lien.[6]

143. Does the income taxation of a life insurance policy that insures more than one life differ from the taxation of a policy that insures a single life?

Basically, no.

Multiple-life policies may insure two or more lives. Typically, a "first-to-die" or "joint life" policy pays a death benefit at the death of the first insured person to die while a "second-to-die" or

1. *U.S. v. Bess*, 357 U.S. 51 (1958).
2. *Comm. v. Stern*, 357 U.S. 39 (1958).
3. IRC Sec. 6013(d)(3).
4. *State Farm v. Howell*, 96-1 USTC ¶50092 (8th Cir. 1996).
5. *Flake v. U.S.*, 95-2 USTC ¶50588 (D. Ariz. 1995).
6. *Federated Life Ins. Co. v. Simmons*, 97-2 USTC ¶50490 (N.D. Ga. 1997).

"survivorship" policy does not pay a death benefit until the death of the survivor. Estate planning and business continuation planning are two of the more common uses for these types of policies.

Generally, multiple-life policies are subject to the same definition of life insurance applicable to policies insuring a single life. One exception is that for purposes of calculating the net single premium under IRC Section 7702, multiple-life policies may not take advantage of the three safe harbor tests set forth in proposed regulations for meeting the reasonable mortality charge requirement (Q 65).[1]

For multiple-life policies that meet the definition of life insurance, cash surrender value increases generally are not taxed until received (Q 8) and death proceeds generally are received income tax-free (Q 63). Multiple-life policies are subject to the seven pay test of IRC Section 7702A(b) (Q 13) in the same manner as single life policies. Distributions from life insurance policies entered into before June 21, 1988, or from policies entered into on or after this date that meet the seven pay test, are included in gross income only to the extent they exceed the investment in the contract (Q 10). Policies entered into on or after June 21, 1988 that do not meet the seven pay test become classified as modified endowment contracts. Distributions, including loans, from modified endowment contracts are subject to taxation rules that generally are less favorable than the rules governing the taxation of distributions from life insurance policies that are not modified endowment contracts (Q 13).

In a private letter ruling, the IRS concluded that exchanges involving policies insuring a single life for a policy insuring two lives did not qualify for nonrecognition treatment under IRC Section 1035. The IRS reached this outcome in five similar fact patterns (Q 44).[2]

In another private ruling, however, the IRS approved IRC Section 1035 treatment of the exchange of a joint and last survivor life insurance policy, following the death of one of the insured persons, for a universal variable life insurance policy that insured the survivor (Q 44).[3]

There has been no formal guidance from the IRS as to which rates should be used to measure economic benefit when a multiple-life policy is used in an arrangement that requires the insured or insureds to include the economic benefit of the coverage in income. The most frequently used rates have been those derived from U.S. Life Table 38, which also is used to derive the P.S. 58 rates. P.S. 58 rates generally may not be used in arrangements entered into after January 27, 2002; however, in those situations, Table 2001 may be used. According to the IRS, taxpayers should make appropriate adjustments to the Table 2001 rates if the life insurance protection covers more than one life.[4] When the policy death benefit is payable at the second death, it generally is believed that following the first death, the Table 2001 rates (or P.S. 58 rates, if appropriate) for single lives should be used to measure the survivor's economic benefit. See volume 2, Appendix G for P.S. 58 and Table 2001 rates.

1. Prop. Treas. Reg. §1.7702-1(c).
2. Let. Rul. 9542037.
3. Let. Rul. 9248013; see also Let. Rul. 9330040.
4. Notice 2002-8, 2002-1 CB 398.

For estate taxation of policies insuring more than one life, see Q 199. For gift taxation of these policies, see Q 211.

144. How is the value of a life insurance policy determined for income tax purposes?

Transfers of property after June 30, 1969 in connection with the performance of services are governed by IRC Section 83. For transfers before February 13, 2004, Treasury Regulation Section 1.83-3(e) provided that, "In the case of a transfer of a life insurance contract, retirement income contract, endowment contract, or other contract providing life insurance protection, only the cash surrender value of the contract is considered to be property."

For transfers after February 12, 2004, the Treasury Regulations generally treat the policy's fair market value (specifically the policy cash value and all other rights under the contract, including any supplemental agreements to the contract, whether or not they are guaranteed, other than current life insurance protection) as property. For transfers of life insurance contracts that are part of split-dollar arrangements that are *not* subject to the split-dollar regulations (Q 4013), however, only the cash surrender value of the contract is considered property.[1]

The IRS has provided a safe harbor on how to determine the fair market value of a life insurance contract.[2] The fair market value of a life insurance contract may be the greater of either: (1) the interpolated terminal reserve and any unearned premiums, plus a pro rata portion of a reasonable estimate of dividends expected to be paid for that policy year, or (2) the product of the "PERC amount" (PERC stands for premiums, earnings, and reasonable charges) and the applicable "Average Surrender Factor."

The PERC amount for a life insurance contract that is not a variable contract is the aggregate of:

(1) the premiums paid on the policy without a reduction for dividends that offset the premiums, plus

(2) dividends that are applied to purchase paid-up insurance, plus

(3) any other amounts credited or otherwise made available to the policyholder, including interest and similar income items, but not including dividends used to offset premiums and dividends used to purchase paid up insurance, minus

(4) reasonable mortality charges and other reasonable charges, but only if those charges are actually charged and those charges are not expected to be refunded, rebated, or otherwise reversed, minus

(5) any distributions (including dividends and dividends held on account), withdrawals, or partial surrenders taken prior to the valuation date.

1. Treas. Reg. §1.83-3(e).
2. Rev. Proc. 2005-25, 2005-17 IRB 962.

The PERC amount for a variable life contract is the aggregate of:

(1) the premiums paid on the policy without a reduction for dividends that offset the premiums, plus

(2) dividends that are applied to increase the value of the contract, including dividends used to purchase paid-up insurance, plus or minus

(3) all adjustments that reflect the investment return and the market value of the contract's segregated asset accounts, minus

(4) reasonable mortality charges and other reasonable charges, but only if those charges are actually charged on or before the valuation date and those charges are not expected to be refunded, rebated, or otherwise reversed, minus

(5) any distributions (including dividends and dividends held on account), withdrawals, or partial surrenders taken prior to the valuation date.

The Average Surrender Factor is 1.0 when valuing life insurance contracts for purposes of the rules regarding group term life (Section 79), property transferred in connection with the performance of services (Section 83), and certain transfers involving deferred compensation arrangements (Section 402(b)). This is because under these rules no adjustment for potential surrender charges is allowed.

The IRS pointed out that the formulas in its safe harbor rules must be interpreted in a reasonable manner, consistent with the purpose of determining the contract's fair market value. Specifically, the rules are not allowed to be interpreted in such a way as to understate a contract's fair market value.

For transfers of property before July 1, 1969, the IRS ruled that the value of an unmatured policy is determined for income tax purposes in the same manner as for gift tax purposes (see Q 119).[1] In one case, the court accepted the value stipulated by the parties in an arm's length agreement.[2]

145. What is the tax treatment when shares of stock received in a demutualization are sold?

A "demutualization" occurs when a mutually-owned life insurance company (i.e., a company owned by its policyholders, or "members") converts into a publicly-owned company (i.e., a company owned by its shareholders). Essentially, the members exchange their rights in the mutual life insurance company (i.e., voting and dividend rights) for shares of stock in the "demutualized" company.

In one case, a taxpayer (a trust) was a former policyholder in a mutual life insurance company and received shares of stock when that company "demutualized." The taxpayer sold its

1. Rev. Rul. 59-195, 1959-1 CB 18.
2. *Gravois Planing Mill v. Comm.*, 9 AFTR 2d 733 (8th Cir. 1962).

shares and then reported gain, based on the then-prevalent belief that the "basis" of such stock was zero. The U.S. Court of Federal Claims held that the taxpayer was entitled to a refund of tax paid. The court analyzed the application of the "open transaction doctrine" to the transaction, and then determined that because the amount received by the trustee was less than the trust's cost basis in the policy as a whole, the taxpayer, in fact, did not realize any income on the sale of the shares.[1]

However, in two more recent published opinions, courts reached what appear to be inconsistent decisions on the issue of basis in demutualization stock making the law in this area very unclear. In *Reuben v. US*,[2] the court found that no portion of premiums paid prior to demutualization created basis; therefore the taxpayer had no basis at all in stock received in a demutualization. As a result, all of the proceeds from sale of demutualization stock represented capital gain. This decision appears to be totally inconsistent with the holding in *Fisher*. While in *Dorrance v. U.S.*,[3] the lower court allowed "equitable apportionment" of premiums to determine basis in the demutualization stock, the Ninth Circuit reversed, finding that the taxpayers had zero basis in the mutual rights that were eliminated in the demutualization. The Ninth Circuit rejected the district court finding that the taxpayers had basis in the stock, finding instead that they had not shown that they had paid for the stock (after demutualization, the taxpayers retained their life insurance contracts and continued to pay premiums). The distribution of stock occurred because of the requirement that the insurance company fairly allocate its surplus upon demutualization, not based on premiums that the taxpayers had paid in the past. Because of the uncertainty in this area, a taxpayer considering sale of stock received in a demutualization should consult his or her tax advisor before completing the sale.

Life Insurance Trusts

146. Can a life insurance trust result in income tax savings for the grantor?

Income tax savings can be achieved by the creation of an unfunded life insurance trust. Additionally, a life insurance policy creates no currently taxable income regardless of whether it is placed in trust. Income tax savings can result only when income-producing property is placed in trust to fund the premium payments, and only if tax liability is shifted from the grantor to a lower bracket taxpayer – that is, to the trust or to a trust beneficiary.

A funded revocable trust will not result in income tax savings. If the trust is revocable, the income from the funding property will be taxed to the grantor. Even if the trust is irrevocable, however, there are other conditions that will cause the trust income to be taxed to the grantor.

Generally speaking, trust income is taxable to the grantor if the:

(1) grantor or trustee, or both, can revoke the trust without the beneficiary's consent;

1. *Fisher. v. U.S.*, 2008-2 USTC ¶50,481 (Ct. Cl. 2008), *aff'd per curiam*, No. 2009-5001 (Fed. Cir. 2009).
2. 111 AFTR 2d 620 (2013).
3. 877 F. Supp 2d 827, 110 AFTR 2d 2012- 5176 (2012); 807 F.3d 1210 (2015).

(2) trust income is, or in the discretion of the grantor or a non-adverse party, or both, may be (a) distributed to the grantor or the grantor's spouse, (b) accumulated for future distribution to the grantor or the grantor's spouse (Q 148), or (c) applied to pay premiums on insurance on the life of the grantor or the grantor's spouse (Q 147);

(3) income is or may be used for the support of the grantor's spouse or is actually used for the support of a person whom the grantor is legally obligated to support, or is or may be applied in discharge of any other obligation of the grantor;

(4) grantor retains certain administrative powers or the power to control beneficial enjoyment of trust principal or income; or

(5) value of a reversionary interest, at the inception of the trust, exceeds 5 percent of the value of the trust.[1]

If the income of the trust is payable to a lineal descendant of the grantor and the trust provides that the grantor's reversionary interest takes effect only on the death of the beneficiary before the beneficiary attains age twenty-one, the income of the trust will not be taxed to the grantor even though the value of the grantor's reversionary interest exceeds 5 percent of the value of the trust.[2]

Planning Point: One of the more common planning strategies involves the "so-called" sale of life insurance to an "intentionally defective trust" or "IDIT." The sale to the IDIT can be a very effective estate planning technique, but it should be remembered that income tax earned by the IDIT will remain taxable to the grantor of the trust. While this may not seem problematic at the time the IDIT is created, in some instances, with good planning and successful investment within the IDIT, situations sometimes arise where the income tax attributable from the IDIT to the grantor can become burdensome. It may be advisable to consider making the IDIT such that the grantor trust power (i.e., the retained power causing grantor trust status for income taxes) can be "turned off" at a future point if it no longer makes sense that the grantor pay the trust's income taxes. Creating an IDIT should only be done with the assistance of a competent tax advisor.

---

147. If income of an irrevocable funded life insurance trust is used to pay premiums on a policy insuring the grantor's life, is the income that is used taxable to the grantor?

Yes, unless the policy is irrevocably payable to a charity.[3] It is immaterial whether the insurance is taken out by the grantor before the trust is created or by the trustee after it is created.[4] The rule applies to income used to pay the investment portion of the premium as well as to income used for pure insurance protection.[5] It also applies to income used for policies dedicated to business uses as well as to those for personal estate planning purposes.[6]

1. IRC Secs. 671-677; Rev. Rul. 75-257, 1975-2 CB 251.
2. IRC Sec. 673(b).
3. IRC Sec. 677(a)(3); *Burnet v. Wells*, 289 U.S. 670 (1933).
4. *Stockstrom v. Comm.*, 3 TC 664 (1944).
5. *Heffelfinger v. Comm.*, 87 F.2d 991 (8th Cir. 1937), *cert. denied*, 302 U.S. 690 (1937).
6. *Vreeland v. Comm.*, 16 TC 1041 (1951).

Moreover, trust income is taxable to the grantor if, without the approval or consent of an adverse party, it *may* be used for the payment of premiums on insurance on the grantor's life, even though it is not actually used for this purpose. Thus, where policies on the grantor's life are placed in the trust, trust income is taxable to the grantor to the extent that the trustee has discretionary power to use it for premium payments.[1]

If the policies are owned by the grantor or by someone other than the trust, however, the trust income is taxable to the grantor only if it actually is used to pay premiums, or if the trustee is specifically authorized to use it for this purpose.[2]

When the trustee is empowered to purchase insurance on the grantor's life, but does not do so, the grantor is not taxed merely because of the trustee's power; there must be policies existing in the tax year during which it would have been possible for the trustee to pay premiums.[3] When a trust beneficiary has voluntarily used income received from the trust to pay premiums on insurance on the grantor's life, the income has not been taxed to the grantor.[4]

Because the law states that the trust income will be taxed to the grantor if it is used to pay the premiums "without the approval or consent of any adverse party,"[5] some have suggested that it may be possible, in some cases, to use trust income for such premium payments. If a beneficiary uses the trust income to pay premiums subject to the grantor's direction or pursuant to an understanding with the grantor, however, the income will be taxable to the grantor.[6] Thus, where the income of a trust for the benefit of the grantor's children is to be used for premium payments on insurance on the grantor's life, the income will be taxable to the grantor even though each beneficiary is to consent in writing (revocable at will) to have his or her share of the income applied to the payment of premiums.[7]

148. Can a grantor create an irrevocable funded life insurance trust, carrying insurance on the grantor's spouse, without being taxed on trust income used for premium payments?

No.

The grantor is taxed on trust income used for the payment of insurance premiums on the life of the grantor or the *grantor's spouse*. If the insurance is on the life of someone other than the grantor or the grantor's spouse, however, this provision does not apply. Thus, a grandmother can fund a trust carrying insurance on the life of her son in favor of her grandchildren without being taxed on the trust income under IRC Section 677(a)(3).

1. *Rieck v. Comm.*, 118 F.2d 110 (3rd Cir. 1941).
2. *Iverson v. Comm.*, 3 TC 756 (1944); *Weil v. Comm.*, 3 TC 579 (1944), acq.
3. *Rand v. Comm.*, 116 F.2d 929 (8th Cir. 1941) *cert. denied*, 313 U.S. 594 (1941); *Corning v. Comm.*, 104 F.2d 329 (6th Cir. 1939).
4. *Booth v. Comm.*, 3 TC 605 (1944), acq.
5. IRC Sec. 677(a).
6. *Foster v. Comm.*, 8 TC 197 (1947), acq.
7. Rev. Rul. 66-313, 1966-2 CB 245.

149. When is life insurance trust income taxable to some person other than the trust, grantor, or income beneficiary?

A person who has exclusive power to vest the corpus (principal) or income of a trust in the grantor (even though the power cannot be exercised in the case of a minor because no guardian has been appointed), or who has released such a power but retained controls similar to those that would subject the grantor to tax, is taxed on the income of the trust (Q 146).[1] If the grantor is taxable on the trust income, however, the other person will not be taxed under this rule, at least with respect to a power to vest income. When a grantor transfers a business interest to a trust, the trust, under certain circumstances, may be viewed by the IRS as a business organization itself.[2]

150. What income is taxable to a life insurance trust?

Generally, a life insurance trust is taxed on: (1) income that, under the terms of the trust, is accumulated for future distribution to someone other than the grantor, and (2) income that the trustee has discretion to accumulate or distribute, but that is not paid or credited to a beneficiary in the taxable year.[3]

151. What income is taxable to the beneficiaries of a life insurance trust?

Trust beneficiaries are liable for tax stemming from income that is distributed to them, or should have been distributed to them, in the taxable year, to the extent that the income does not exceed the trust's "distributable net income" for the year.[4]

Prior to 2018, to deter taxpayers from shifting tax liability to a lower bracket beneficiary, trust income taxable to a beneficiary under eighteen years of age could be taxed at the marginal tax rate of the beneficiary's parents. For tax years beginning after 2017 and before 2026, the unearned income of minors is taxed at the income tax rate that applies to trusts and estates.

152. May the grantor of a life insurance trust take a deduction for interest paid by the trust on a policy loan when the policy is held by the trust?

If the grantor is taxed as the owner of the trust, the grantor apparently is allowed an interest deduction, in the rare instances when a deduction is allowable, to the same extent as any other owner of the policy (Q 3, Q 30). The IRC provides that when the grantor (or any other person) is treated as the owner of any part of a trust, the trust's deductions, as well as income and credits against tax, attributable to that part of the trust will be taken into account in computing that person's taxable income.[5] Trusts that are treated as owned by the grantor are sometimes referred to as "defective" because, as a general rule, the pass-through of trust income is undesirable. A "defective" trust may be useful, however, if a deduction can be passed through to the grantor. (Where favorable estate tax results are sought, attention also should be given to the matters discussed in Q 178 to Q 186.)

1. IRC Sec. 678; Rev. Rul. 81-6, 1981-1 CB 385.
2. See Rev. Rul. 75-258, 1975-2 CB 503.
3. IRC Sec. 641; Treas. Reg. §1.641(a)-2.
4. IRC Secs. 652, 662.
5. IRC Sec. 671.

The IRS has ruled privately that where nonadverse trustees had authority to use trust income to pay premiums on policies on the grantor's life (not irrevocably payable for a charitable purpose), or had discretion to pay trust income or principal to the grantor's spouse, the grantor would be taxed as owner of the trust and could take the trust's deductions.[1]

153. Are death proceeds of life insurance taxable income if they are payable to a trust?

No, such proceeds generally are tax-exempt income to the trustee and to the beneficiary when distributed (Q 63, Q 65).

When proceeds are retained by the trust, earnings on the proceeds are taxed in the same manner as other trust income.[2] The $1,000 annual interest exclusion, available where insurance proceeds are payable to a surviving spouse of an insured who died before October 23, 1986, under a life income or installment option, is not available if the proceeds are payable to a trust (Q 71). Under some circumstances, proceeds of a policy transferred for value to a trust may not be wholly tax-exempt (Q 279, Q 282).

154. Is there a gift for gift tax purposes when a grantor transfers a life insurance policy to an irrevocable trust in which the grantor has no interest?

Yes.[3] The value of the gift will be the fair market value of the policy as of the date of the transfer (Q 119). There is no gift if the trust is revocable.[4] An employee's assignment of a group life policy to an irrevocable trust was held not to be a taxable gift because the policy had no ascertainable value (Q 119, Q 159, Q 212).[5]

155. If income-producing property is transferred to an irrevocable life insurance trust to fund premium payments, does the value of the property constitute a gift?

Generally, the full value of the property, in addition to the value of the policy, constitutes a gift. (But see Q 156, relating to reversionary interest trusts.) Subsequent premium payments by the trustee from trust income will not constitute additional gifts from the grantor. This is true even though the insurance is on the life of the grantor and the grantor remains personally liable for the income tax on the trust income, which may be used to pay premiums.[6]

156. How is the gift tax value of a "reversionary interest trust" measured?

A reversionary interest trust is a trust whose property will, on specified circumstances, revert to the grantor.

1. Let. Ruls. 8118051, 8007080, 7909031.
2. IRC Sec. 101; Treas. Reg. §1.101-1.
3. Treas. Reg. §25.2511-1(h)(8).
4. Treas. Reg. §25.2511-2(c).
5. Rev. Rul. 76-490, 1976-2 CB 300.
6. *Comm. v. Est. of Beck*, 129 F.2d 243 (2d Cir. 1942); *Lockard v. Comm.*, 166 F.2d 409 (1st Cir. 1948).

In a reversionary interest trust, the gift is the right to receive *trust income* during the trust term. The value of this right is determined and taxed in the year the trust is established. The value of the gift generally is the value of the property transferred less the value of the grantor's retained interest.[1] The value of these income and reversionary (or remainder) interests are determined using the estate and gift tax valuation tables. For example, assuming a valuation table interest rate of 7 percent and a trust term of forty-five years, the value of the gift of income is 0.952387 times the value of the property (1 - 0.047613) (see Appendix C). However, if the reversionary interest is not a qualified interest, the value of the gift is generally the full value of the property transferred to the trust.

Planning Point: To avoid the above result, an annuity or unitrust interest generally should be given to the trust rather than an income interest.

157. Does the transfer of a life insurance policy to an irrevocable trust for the benefit of the grantor's spouse qualify for the gift tax marital deduction?

The gift tax marital deduction generally is not available for a gift in trust unless the donee spouse has at least the right to all the income from the property and a general power of appointment over the principal, or unless the donee spouse's income interest is a "qualifying income interest for life" in the property transferred, in which case the donee spouse does not usually have to have a general power of appointment over the principal. Because a life insurance policy ordinarily does not produce income before maturity, the requirement that the donee spouse receive all the income for life will not be met unless the donee spouse has the power to compel the trustee to convert the policy to income-producing property, or the power to terminate the trust and demand the policy.[2] An annual exclusion may be allowed instead of the marital deduction if the donee spouse is not a U.S. citizen.

158. If a grantor creates a revocable trust with a life insurance policy on the life of another person and names third parties as trust beneficiaries, is a gift made when the insured dies and the trust becomes irrevocable?

Yes. In one case, a wife placed a policy on her husband's life in a revocable trust for their children. It was held that a gift from the wife to the children was made when the insured died and the trust became irrevocable. The value of the gift was the full amount of the death proceeds.[3] If the trust had been irrevocable, the annual premiums paid by the wife, instead of the proceeds, would have constituted gifts.[4]

159. Does the gift of a life insurance policy in trust (or a gift of subsequent premiums) qualify for the gift tax annual exclusion?

In the usual case, no annual exclusions are allowable either on the creation of the trust or on the payment of premiums (Q 219, Q 223).[5]

1. Treas. Reg. §25.2512-9(a)(1)(i).
2. Treas. Reg. §§25.2523(e)-1(f)(4), 25.2523(e)-1(f)(6).
3. *Goodman v. Comm.*, 156 F.2d 218 (2d Cir. 1946).
4. *Watkins v. Comm.*, 2 TCM (CCH) 252(1943).
5. Treas. Reg. §25.2503-2; *Comm. v. Boeing*, 123 F.2d 86 (9th Cir. 1941).

Example. C transfers certain insurance policies on C's own life to a trust created for the benefit of D. Upon C's death the proceeds of the policies are to be invested, and the net income paid to D during D's lifetime. Because the income payments to D will not begin until after C's death, the transfer in trust represents a gift of a future interest in property against which no exclusion is available.[1]

If the beneficiary were given the power to demand trust principal, apparently the annual exclusion would be available.[2] Such a power, however, would cause the trust principal to be includable in the beneficiary's gross estate.

Where an employee assigned his group life insurance policy to an irrevocable trust, the IRS ruled that subsequent premiums paid by the employer qualified for the annual exclusion as gifts of a present interest by the *employee*. Under the terms of the trust, the beneficiary or the beneficiary's estate was to receive the full proceeds of the policy immediately on the insured's death.[3] In a later ruling, the facts essentially were the same, except that the trust terms directed the trustee to retain the insurance proceeds, paying income to the insured's children for life, with the remainder to the grandchildren; the employer's premium payments following the assignment were held to be gifts of a future interest in property, therefore not qualifying for the annual exclusion.[4] (See also Q 80, Q 168.)

The IRS also has allowed the gift tax annual exclusion when a grantor created a trust with an initial contribution of a $50,000 group term policy on the grantor's life and $1,000 in cash. The trust gave the grantor's spouse a $3,000 annual noncumulative withdrawal right and provided that any asset in the trust, including the insurance policy, could be used to satisfy the demand. In this private letter ruling, the IRS held that the grantor's initial contribution, as well as the grantor's employer's subsequent premium payments on the group term insurance, would qualify for the exclusion.[5]

For a discussion of the special provision with respect to gifts in trust to minors, see Q 160. For a discussion of Crummey withdrawal rights, see Q 161.

160. Is the annual gift tax exclusion available when a life insurance policy is placed in an irrevocable trust for a minor beneficiary?

IRC Section 2503(c) provides that there is a gift of a present interest if the property that constitutes the gift and all income from the property (1) *may* be expended for the benefit of the minor, and (2) *will*, to the extent not so expended, pass to the minor when the minor is age twenty-one, or, if the minor dies before reaching age twenty-one, be payable to the minor's estate or as the minor may appoint under a general power of appointment.[6] The fact that under local law a minor is legally unable to exercise a power or to execute a will does not cause the

1. Treas. Reg. §25.2503-3(c)(Ex. 2).
2. *Halsted v. Comm.*, 28 TC 1069 (1957), acq. 1958-2 CB 5.
3. Rev. Rul. 76-490, 1976-2 CB 300.
4. Rev. Rul. 79-47, 1979-1 CB 312.
5. Let. Rul. 8006109.
6. IRC Sec. 2503(c).

transfer to fail to satisfy the conditions.[1] Any premiums paid on the policy by the grantor should qualify as gifts of a present interest (Q 223).

161. Do transfers to a trustee of an irrevocable life insurance trust of amounts to be used by the trustee to pay premiums qualify for the gift tax annual exclusion?

Although such transfers would ordinarily be future interest gifts, it has been held that they will be treated as present interest gifts, qualifying for the exclusion, to the extent the trust beneficiaries are given immediate withdrawal rights with respect to the amounts transferred.[2] Such trusts are known as *Crummey* trusts, after the case of *Crummey v. Commissioner.*[3]

> *Example.* G creates an irrevocable insurance trust for each of his four children, transferring amounts (additions) from year to year to fund the trusts. Two of the children are minors when the trusts are created and for several years thereafter, but neither has a court-appointed guardian. The trusts provide that with respect to the additions, each child may demand in writing at any time (up to the end of the calendar year in which an addition is made) the sum of $5,000 or the amount of the addition, whichever is less, payable immediately in cash. If a child is a minor when an addition is made, the child's guardian may make such demand on the child's behalf and hold the amount received for the benefit and use of the child. To the extent demands for payment are not made by the beneficiaries, the trustee is directed to use the additions to pay insurance premiums as needed and to purchase additional insurance and investments for the trust. G transfers to each trust $5,000 each year the trusts are in existence. Each trust provides that it is irrevocable for the lifetime of the beneficiary and that the trust assets will revert to the grantor only if the beneficiary dies before age twenty-one. All children survive past age twenty-one. By the rule of the *Crummey* case, G is entitled under present law to $20,000 in gift tax annual exclusions each year ($5,000 for each child). It does not matter that the minor children never had guardians appointed. Had the trusts given the beneficiaries immediate payment rights of no more than $2,000 each with respect to the additions, G's exclusions would be limited to $8,000 per year (assuming he made no other present-interest gifts to his children during the year).

The IRS has ruled that when the beneficiary of a discretionary trust was a competent adult, contributions to the trust did not qualify for the annual exclusion because the beneficiary did not receive timely notice or have actual knowledge of the right to demand immediate distribution of contributions.[4]

Another ruling allowed the annual exclusion where the trust provided for timely written notice to the beneficiaries of their withdrawal rights, and where the beneficiaries were given a thirty-day period within which to exercise their withdrawal rights.[5]

Yet another ruling allowed the exclusion where the trust required the trustee to notify the beneficiaries within seven days of receipt of additional contributions and further required that the beneficiaries be given thirty days after receipt of notice within which to exercise their withdrawal rights.[6] If the beneficiary is given reasonable notice of the right to withdraw and a

1. Treas. Reg. §25.2503-4.
2. *Crummey v. Comm.*, 397 F.2d 82 (9th Cir. 1968); Rev. Rul. 73-405, 1973-2 CB 321; Let. Ruls. 7826050, 7902007, 7909031, 7947066, 8007080, 8118051, 8445004, 8712014, 9625031.
3. *Crummey v. Comm.*, 397 F.2d 82 (9th Cir. 1968).
4. Rev. Rul. 81-7, 1981-1 CB 474; Let. Rul. 7946007.
5. Let. Rul. 8003033. See also Let. Ruls. 8517052, 8813019.
6. Let. Rul. 8004172.

reasonable time within which to exercise the right, the fact that a calendar year ends between the date of the transfer and the date the beneficiary received notice does not transform a present interest gift into a future interest gift.[1]

The annual exclusion was not allowed, however, when the beneficiaries waived their right to receive notice of contributions to the trust with respect to which their withdrawal rights could be exercised. Furthermore, the annual exclusion was not allowed because the grantor set up a trust that provided that notice was to be given to the trustee as to whether a beneficiary could exercise a withdrawal power with respect to a transfer to the trust and the grantor never notified the trustee that the withdrawal powers could be exercised with respect to any of the transfers to the trust. Thus, the gifts were not transfers of a present interest under the meaning of IRC Section 2503(b).[2]

The value of a withdrawal right may be reduced, even to zero, if the trustee has discretion to invade the trust corpus for the benefit of non-*Crummey* beneficiaries.[3] The exclusion is allowed only to the extent there is cash, or assets reducible to cash, in the trust to satisfy any beneficiary demand rights, or to the extent the trustee is required to maintain sufficient liquidity to meet immediate withdrawal demands.[4]

Where appointment of a legal guardian would be necessary to enable a beneficiary to exercise the withdrawal right, sufficient time (at least thirty days) should be allowed to make the appointment before the right to withdraw terminates.[5] "If there is no impediment under the trust or local law to the appointment of a guardian and the minor donee has a right to demand distribution, the transfer is a gift of a present interest that qualifies for the annual exclusion allowable under Section 2503(b) of the Code."[6]

Reciprocal *Crummey* trusts have been unsuccessfully tried in an attempt to increase each donor's annual exclusion. In Revenue Ruling 85-24,[7] A, B, and C, partners in the X partnership, each created a *Crummey* trust for their children. Each contributed $20,000 to the trust initially. A's trust gave his child, F, a power to withdraw $10,000 of the contribution within sixty days, and gave B and C each the power to withdraw $5,000 on the same terms. B's trust gave his child, G, the power to withdraw $10,000, and gave A and C each the power to withdraw $5,000. C's trust gave his child, H, the power to withdraw $10,000, and gave A and B each the power to withdraw $5,000. A, B, and C each claimed a $20,000 gift tax exclusion for the year in which the trusts were created. The IRS ruled that A, B, and C were entitled to only a $10,000 exclusion for the gifts to their children. No gift tax exclusions were allowable with respect to the *Crummey* powers the partners gave one another. These transfers, according to the IRS, were not gifts because they were based on adequate consideration, namely, the consideration for the

1. Rev. Rul. 83-108, 1983-2 CB 167.
2. TAM 9532001.
3. Let. Ruls. 8107009, 8213074.
4. Let. Ruls. 8126047, 8134135. But see also Let. Ruls. 7909031, 8007080, 8006109, 8021058, which allowed the exclusion where liquidity requirements were not clearly stated.
5. Let. Ruls. 8022048, 8134135, 8326074, 8517052, 8610028, 8616027.
6. Rev. Rul. 73-405, 1973-2 CB 321. See also Let. Ruls. 8326074, 8335050, 8517052, 8610028, 8616027, 8701007. But see also *Naumoff v. Comm.*, TC Memo 1983-435, and Let. Rul. 8229097.
7. 1985-1 CB 329.

reciprocal transfers among the partners was each partner's forgoing the exercise of the right of withdrawal in consideration of the other partners' similar forbearance. The IRS said further that upon the lapse of a partner's withdrawal power, the child's gift (from his parent) was increased by $5,000, but the failure of the partner to exercise the power was not considered a lapse of a general power of appointment (i.e., not a gift) because the transfer to the partner was not a gift.

Since August 24, 1981, the IRS has had the following types of *Crummey* insurance trusts under extensive study and has stated that it will not issue rulings or determination letters on the allowability of the gift tax annual exclusion for transfers of property to such trusts until it resolves the issues through publication of a revenue ruling, revenue procedure, or regulation:

(1) The trust corpus consists or will consist substantially of insurance policies on the life of the grantor or the grantor's spouse;

(2) The trustee or any other person has a power to apply the trust's income or corpus to the payment of premiums on policies of insurance on the life of the grantor or the grantor's spouse;

(3) The trustee or any other person has a power to use the trust's assets to make loans to the grantor's estate or to purchase assets from the grantor's estate;

(4) The trust beneficiaries have the power to withdraw, on demand, any additional transfers made to the trust; and

(5) There is a right or power in any person that would cause the grantor to be treated as the owner of all or a portion of the trust under IRC Sections 673 to 677.[1]

The IRS has ruled with respect to *Crummey* trusts that the annual exclusion could not be applied to trust contributions on behalf of trust beneficiaries who had withdrawal rights as to the contributions (except to the extent they exercised their withdrawal rights) but who had either no other interest in the trust (a naked power) or only remote contingent interests in the remainder.[2] The Tax Court, however, has rejected the IRS's argument that a power holder must hold rights other than the withdrawal right to obtain the annual exclusion. The withdrawal right (assuming there is no agreement to not exercise the right) is sufficient to obtain the annual exclusion.[3] (Language in *Cristofani* appears to support use of naked powers although the case did not involve naked powers.) The IRS has stated that, applying the substance over form doctrine, the annual exclusions should not be allowed where the withdrawal rights are not in substance what they purport to be in form. If the facts and circumstances show an understanding that the power is not meant to be exercised or that exercise would result in undesirable consequences, then creation of the withdrawal right is not a bona fide gift of a present interest and an annual exclusion should not be allowed.[4]

1. Rev. Proc. 2009-3, Sec. 4.46, 2009-1 IRB 107.
2. TAMs 9141008, 9045002, 8727003.
3. *Est. of Cristofani v. Comm.*, 97 TC 74 (1991), acq. in result, 1996-2 CB 1.
4. Action on Decision 1996-010.

In TAM 9628004, annual exclusions were not allowed where transfers to the trust were made so late in the first year that *Crummey* withdrawal power holders had no opportunity to exercise their rights, most power holders had either no other interest in the trust or discretionary income or remote contingent remainder interests, and withdrawal powers were never exercised in any year. However, annual exclusions were allowed where the IRS was unable to prove that there was an understanding between the donor and the beneficiaries that the withdrawal rights should not be exercised.[1] In TAM 97310004, annual exclusions were denied where eight trusts were created for eight primary beneficiaries, but *Crummey* withdrawal powers were given to sixteen persons who never exercised their powers; most power holders held either a remote contingent interest or no interest other than the withdrawal power in the trusts in which the power holder was not the primary beneficiary.

Substance over form analysis may be applied to deny annual exclusions when indirect transfers are used in an attempt to obtain inappropriate annual exclusions for gifts to intermediate recipients.[2] For example, suppose that in 2018, A transfers to B, C, and D $15,000 each. By arrangement, B, C, and D each immediately transfer $15,000 to E. The annual exclusion for A's indirect transfers to E is limited to $15,000 and A has made taxable gifts of $30,000 to E. Under the appropriate circumstances, the substance over form analysis might even be used to deny annual exclusions for *Crummey* powers.

162. If the beneficiary of a Crummey trust allows the right to withdraw a contribution to the trust to go unexercised, when will the beneficiary be deemed to have made a transfer subject to gift or estate tax?

The withdrawal power held by a *Crummey* trust beneficiary is a general power of appointment. If a *Crummey* trust provides for a contingent beneficiary to succeed to the interest of the primary beneficiary in the event of the primary beneficiary's death before the trust terminates, the primary beneficiary's failure to exercise the withdrawal right acts as a transfer to the contingent beneficiary, either at the time of the lapse of the withdrawal right or at the time of the primary beneficiary's death. The amount thus transferred is subject to federal gift or estate tax to the extent it exceeds the greater of $5,000 or 5 percent of the aggregate value of the assets out of which, or the proceeds of which, the exercise of the withdrawal right could be satisfied.[3]

A spouse who is given a withdrawal power would be treated as making gifts to remainder persons each time the spouse allows a withdrawal power to lapse to the extent that the lapsed power exceeds the greater of $5,000 or 5 percent of the trust principal. Furthermore, the value of the gift would not be reduced by the spouse's retained income interest or the spouse's interest in principal subject to an ascertainable standard because such interests are not qualified retained interests under IRC Section 2702.[4]

1. *Est. of Kohlsaat*, TC Memo 1997-212; *Est. of Holland v. Comm.*, TC Memo 1997-302.
2. *Heyen v. U.S.*, 945 F.2d 359, 91-2 USTC ¶60,085 (10th Cir. 1991).
3. IRC Sec. 2514(e).
4. Let. Rul. 9804047.

In those cases, then, in which (1) the primary beneficiary's gift or estate tax liability is to be avoided, and (2) the trust value is less than $300,000 in the case of a $15,000 withdrawal right, or less than $600,000 in the case of a $30,000 withdrawal right (two spouses, as grantors, splitting the gift), the "5 or 5" limitation must be dealt with.

Planning Point: A hanging power is one method that has been used in an attempt to manage the "5 or 5" limitation. A hanging power is designed to lapse in any year only to the extent that the power does not exceed the $5,000 or 5 percent ("5 or 5" limitation). Any excess is carried over to succeeding years and lapses only to the extent that the power does not exceed the "5 or 5" limitation in such years.

Example. Beginning in 2002, parents transfer an amount equal to eight (2 donors × 4 donees) times the annual exclusion to a trust each year. Four children are each given a right to withdraw an amount equal to two (2 donors) times the annual exclusion annually. Upon non-exercise of the power to withdraw, the power lapses in any year to the extent of the greater of $5,000 or 5 percent of corpus. To the extent that a power does not lapse in a year, it is carried over and added to any power arising in the succeeding year. The hanging power is eliminated in the tenth year (i.e., when carryover equals zero).

YEAR	CORPUS ($)	POWER ($)	LAPSE ($)	CARRYOVER ($)
2002	80,000	20,000	5,000	15,000
2003	168,000	37,000	8,400	28,600
2004	256,000	50,600	12,800	37,800
2005	344,000	59,800	17,200	42,600
2006	432,000	64,600	21,600	43,000
2007	528,000	67,000	26,400	40,600
2008	624,000	64,600	31,200	33,400
2009	720,000	57,400	36,000	21,400
2010	824,000	47,400	41,200	6,200
2011	928,000	32,200	32,200	0

In Letter Ruling 8901004, a hanging *Crummey* withdrawal power written in the form of a tax savings clause was ruled invalid. Many commentators believe that a hanging power that lapses only to the extent that the power does not exceed the "5 or 5" limitation (rather than by reference to whether there would be a taxable gift) would be valid.

A power holder is not treated as making a gift upon the lapse of a general power if the power holder is, in effect, still the owner of the property after the lapse. Consequently, other methods used in an attempt to manage the "5 or 5" limitation include giving the power holder a testamentary limited power to appoint the property to other than the power holder or the power holder's estate, and vesting the property in the power holder.

Under each of these methods for managing the "5 or 5" limitation for gift tax purposes, estate tax inclusion could result (Q 181, Q 205).

Since August 24, 1981, the IRS has had the following types of *Crummey* insurance trust under extensive study and has stated that it will not issue rulings or determination letters on the applicability of IRC Section 2514(e) to a beneficiary's lapse of a withdrawal power when:

(1) The trust corpus consists or will consist substantially of insurance policies on the life of the grantor or the grantor's spouse;

(2) The trustee or any other person has a power to apply the trust's income or corpus to the payment of premiums on policies of insurance on the life of the grantor or the grantor's spouse;

(3) The trustee or any other person has a power to use the trust's assets to make loans to the grantor's estate or to purchase assets from the grantor's estate;

(4) The trust beneficiaries have the power to withdraw, on demand, any additional transfers made to the trust; and

(5) There is a right or power in any person that would cause the grantor to be treated as the owner of all or a portion of the trust under IRC Sections 673 to 677.[1]

163. May dividends paid on a life insurance policy in trust be gifts of a present interest even though the policy itself was a gift of a future interest?

Yes. If the trustee is directed to pay the dividends to the trust beneficiary, the value of probable dividends will be considered a gift of a present interest.[2]

164. When can a beneficiary of life insurance proceeds be held liable for payment of federal estate tax falling on the insured's estate?

The executor has primary liability for paying federal estate tax and is expected to pay it from the probate estate before distribution.[3] Under IRC Section 2206, unless the decedent has directed otherwise, the executor ordinarily may recover from a named beneficiary such portion of the total tax paid as the proceeds included in the gross estate and received by the beneficiary bear to the taxable estate. In the case of insurance proceeds receivable by the surviving spouse and qualifying for the marital deduction, IRC Section 2206 applies, if at all, only to proceeds in excess of the aggregate amount of the marital deduction allowed the estate. Most states also have apportionment laws under which life insurance beneficiaries share the estate tax burden with estate beneficiaries. It is not entirely clear whether IRC Section 2206 imposes a duty on the executor to seek apportionment, or only gives the executor the power to do so. When the executor is unable to recover a pro-rata share of the estate tax from the beneficiary of the life insurance proceeds, the estate cannot claim a deduction under IRC Section 2054; it is a bad debt and as such is not deductible under IRC Section 2054. A legatee whose share of the estate bears the burden of tax attributable to the proceeds, however, is entitled to a bad debt deduction.[4]

1. Rev. Proc. 2009-3, Sec. 4.46, 2009-1 IRB 107.
2. *Tidemann v. Comm.*, 1 TC 968 (1943).
3. IRC Secs. 2002, 2205.
4. Rev. Rul. 69-411, 1969-2 CB 177.

If the government is unable to collect the estate tax from the insured's estate, the tax can be collected from the beneficiary of the life insurance proceeds up to the full amount of the proceeds if the value of the proceeds was includable in the gross estate. Any person who receives property includable in a decedent's gross estate under IRC Sections 2034 to 2042 is liable for the tax.[1] It is immaterial that the insured's will directed payment from the insured's general estate.[2] An insurance company holding the proceeds under a settlement option is not liable for the tax.[3] There is a split of authority as to whether transferee liability for interest on any unpaid tax is limited to the amount of proceeds received from the decedent's estate.[4]

165. How are proceeds of community property life insurance treated in the insured's estate?

Generally speaking, community property is recognized for federal tax purposes as belonging one-half to each spouse. Consequently, if life insurance proceeds are community property, when the insured spouse dies first, only one-half of the proceeds are includable in that spouse's gross estate regardless of whether they are payable to that spouse's estate, the surviving spouse, or some other beneficiary.[5] Where community proceeds are payable to the insured's estate, only one-half is considered receivable by or for the benefit of the decedent's estate; the other half is received on behalf of the insured's spouse. Where community proceeds are payable to a beneficiary other than the insured's estate, the fact that under local community property law the insured had management powers over the insurance is not construed to mean that the insured possessed incidents of ownership (Q 86) in the insured's spouse's community half.[6] Local community property law determines the nature and extent of ownership of policy proceeds and policy rights. (With respect to life insurance issued under U.S. government programs, see Q 174. See Q 169 for estate tax results where deaths of insured and spouse occur simultaneously.)

166. How are proceeds of community property life insurance treated in the insured's estate in Louisiana?

By way of contrast with the law in other community property states, it has been held under Louisiana law that the presumption of community generally applicable to property acquired with community funds during marriage does not apply to life insurance acquired by a spouse on the spouse's own life payable to the other spouse irrevocably, or on the spouse's life where the spouse has named himself or herself policy owner and revocable beneficiary. In these cases, the policies were held to be the separate property of the noninsured spouse.[7]

---

1. IRC Secs. 6324(a), 6901; Treas. Reg. §20.2205-1; *U.S. v. Melman*, 398 F. Supp. 87 (E.D. Mo. 1975), aff'd 530 F.2d 790 (8th Cir. 1976).
2. *Lansburgh v. Comm.*, 35 BTA 928 (1937), acq. 143 CB 14; *Matthews v. Comm.*, 9 TCM 397.
3. *John Hancock Mut. Life Ins. Co. v. Comm.*, 128 F.2d 745 (D.C. Cir. 1942).
4. *Baptiste v. Comm.*, 29 F.3d 1533, 94-2 USTC ¶60,178 (11th Cir. 1994), aff'g in part 100 TC 252 (1993); *Baptiste v. Comm.*, 29 F.3d 439, 94-2 USTC ¶60,173 (8th Cir. 1994), cert. den., rev'g in part 100 TC 252 (1993).
5. Treas. Reg. §20.2042-1(b)(2); *DeLappe v. Comm.* (La.) 113 F.2d 48 (5th Cir. 1940); *Howard v. U.S.* (La.) 125 F.2d 986 (5th Cir. 1942); *Est. of Moody v. Comm.* (Tex.) 42 BTA 987 (1940); *Lang v. Comm.* (Wash.) 304 U.S. 264 (1938); *Est. of Levy v. Comm.* (Cal.) 42 BTA 991 (1940); *McCoy v. Comm.* (Cal.) 29 BTA 822 (1934), nonacq. 1934-1 CB 24; *Nance v. U.S.* (Ariz.) 430 F.2d 662 (9th Cir. 1970).
6. Treas. Reg. §20.2042-1(c)(5).
7. *Catalano v. U.S.*, 429 F.2d 1058 (5th Cir. 1969); *Est. of Saia v. Comm.*, 61 TC 515 (1974), nonacq. 1978-2 CB 4; *Bergman v. Comm.*, 66 TC 887 (1976), acq. in result, 1976-2 CB 1.

Under Louisiana law, life insurance proceeds were excluded entirely from an insured decedent's estate where the policy was treated as the separate property of the decedent's spouse and the proceeds were not payable to decedent's estate.[1] In Louisiana, the proceeds of life insurance, if payable to a named beneficiary other than the insured's estate, are not treated as part of the insured's estate and are not subject to community claims.[2] Under Louisiana law, the presumption of community where the policy is purchased with community property applies if one spouse is both the insured and the named owner.[3] Therefore, if a Louisiana decedent purchases a life insurance policy during marriage, names the decedent as owner, and does not transfer ownership of the policy, the proceeds are presumed to be community property and one-half the proceeds are includable in the decedent's estate.[4]

167. When life insurance on the life of a spouse is bought with community funds and one of the spouses is designated the policy owner, is the policy community property or is it the separate property of the spouse designated as the owner?

Life insurance acquired after marriage, with community funds, generally is presumed to be community property, notwithstanding that only one of the spouses is designated the policy owner. The mere act of designating the noninsured spouse as policy owner, say for the purpose of achieving certain tax results, will not of itself rebut the presumption; there must also be clear and convincing evidence that the policy was intended by the spouses to be the separate property of the spouse designated as owner and under his or her sole control. In several cases, and in a revenue ruling, the presumption was *not* rebutted.[5] In several others, the presumption *was* rebutted.[6] In Louisiana, the general presumption that property acquired with community funds during marriage is community property does not apply to life insurance acquired by one spouse under some circumstances (Q 166).

In a 1986 case involving Nevada residents, the Tax Court came to the conclusion that although the decedent/husband/insured and his wife had succeeded in making the insurance policy the separate property of the wife, one-half the death proceeds payable to the wife as beneficiary was nonetheless included in the decedent's estate. Two circumstances accounted for this unusual result: First, the premiums were paid entirely with community property, and second, the insured died in 1978 and within three years of the date the policy was purchased. Following the reasoning in the line of cases represented by *Bel*, *Detroit Bank & Trust Co.*, and *First Nat'l Bank of Oregon*, the Tax Court held that the payment of the premium with community

1. Rev. Rul. 94-69, 1994-2 CB 241.
2. *T.L. James & Co., Inc. v. Montgomery*, 332 So. 2d 834 (1976).
3. *Est. of Burris v. Comm.*, TC Memo 2001-210.
4. Rev. Rul. 2003-40, 2003-17 IRB 813.
5. *Comm. v. Fleming*, 155 F.2d 204 (5th Cir. 1946); *Freedman v. U.S.*, 382 F.2d 742 (5th Cir. 1967); *First Nat'l Bank of Midland, Texas (Mathers) v. U.S.*, 69-1 USTC ¶12,574 (1968), rev'd on other grounds 423 F.2d 1286 (5th Cir. 1970); *Lutich v. U.S.*, 29 AFTR2d 1583 (N.D. Cal. 1972); *Est. of Meyer v. Comm.*, 66 TC 41 (1976); *Est. of Madsen v. Comm.*, TC Memo 1979-289, 659 F.2d 897 (9th Cir. 1981); 82-2 USTC ¶13,495 (S.C. Wash. 1982); 82-2 USTC ¶13,500 (9th Cir. 1982), aff'g TC Memo 1979-289; *Daubert v. U.S.*, 533 F. Supp. 66 (W.D. Tex. 1981); Rev. Rul. 67-228, 1967-2 CB 331.
6. *Parson v. U.S.*, 460 F.2d 228 (5th Cir. 1972); *Waite v. U.S.*, 32 AFTR2d 6238 (N.D. Tex. 1973); *Est. of McKee v. Comm.*, TC Memo 1978-108, appeals dismissed; *Kern v. U.S.*, 491 F.2d 436 (9th Cir. 1974); *Est. of Wilmot v. Comm.*, TC Memo 1970-240; *Kroloff v. U.S.*, 487 F.2d 334 (9th Cir. 1973); *Est. of Crane v. Comm.*, TC Memo 1982-174; *Miner v. U.S.*, 50 AFTR2d ¶6,137 (S.D. Tex. 1982), gov't will not appeal; *Est. of Hutnik v. U.S.*, 83-2 USTC ¶13,539 (S.D. Tex. 1983).

funds amounted to a transfer by the decedent to his wife of his community half of the funds so used, and therefore also amounted to a transfer of the policy itself within three years of death for purposes of IRC Section 2035.[1]

168. What are the estate tax results in the insured's estate when life insurance premiums have been paid with both community and separate funds?

Where premiums have been paid partly with the insured's separate funds and partly with community funds, one of two basic approaches is taken, depending on local law. Under California and Washington law, a "premium tracing rule" is applied, which says that the proceeds are part separate and part community in the proportion that the premiums were paid with separate and community funds. Accordingly, in estate tax cases involving California and Washington residents in which this issue is presented, the insured's estate includes the proportion of proceeds considered paid for with the insured's separate property and one-half the proportion of proceeds considered paid for with community property.[2]

Louisiana, Texas, and probably New Mexico (and possibly also Arizona) apply the "inception of title" doctrine in determining whether such proceeds are separate or community: proceeds of life insurance bought initially as separate property remain separate property, although the community is entitled to be reimbursed for premiums paid from community funds. Conversely, proceeds of insurance bought initially as community property remain community property, although the separate estate is entitled to be reimbursed for premiums paid from separate funds.

In the case of a Texas decedent who purchased life insurance as separate property, the amount includable in the gross estate as life insurance proceeds under IRC Section 2042 (Q 80) was the face amount of policy proceeds less the amount of premiums paid with community funds. In addition, one-half the premiums paid with community funds was separately includable in the gross estate under IRC Section 2033 as the decedent's interest in community property.[3]

Apparently, in the case of Louisiana decedents, if the proceeds are community property and payable to the insured's estate, none of the proceeds are includable in the decedent's gross estate under IRC Section 2042(2). If the proceeds are community property and payable to a named beneficiary other than the surviving spouse, the surviving spouse is deemed to have made a gift of the proceeds to that third-party beneficiary on the decedent's death under IRC Section 2511.[4] When the beneficiary is the surviving spouse, however, the treatment will be the same as in the case of a Texas decedent.[5] Nothing is included in the insured's estate if the policy is treated as the separate property of the noninsured spouse and the proceeds are not payable to the insured's estate (Q 165).[6]

1. *Est. of Hass v. Comm.*, TC Memo 1986-63.
2. *Lang v. Comm.*, 304 U.S. 264 (1938).
3. Rev. Rul. 80-242, 1980-2 CB 276, modifying Rev. Rul. 54-272, 1954-2 CB 298; *Est. of Wildenthal v. Comm.*, TC Memo 1970-119.
4. Rev. Rul. 94-69, 1994-2 CB 241.
5. Rev. Rul. 80-242.
6. Rev. Rul. 94-69, 1994-2 CB 241.

There are no rulings or cases on this issue concerning New Mexico or Arizona decedents.

If a resident of a community property state whose law provides that the income from a spouse's separate property is community property makes a gift of property (e.g., life insurance or premium dollars) to his or her spouse, the donor spouse does not, by operation of that law, retain an interest that will cause any portion of the transferred property to be included in the donor's gross estate under IRC Section 2036.[1]

169. When can death proceeds of community property life insurance payable to someone other than the surviving spouse be includable in the surviving spouse's gross estate?

If the insured elects to have death proceeds held under an interest or installment option for the insured's surviving spouse with proceeds remaining at the surviving spouse's death payable to another, a portion of such remaining proceeds may be includable in the surviving spouse's gross estate under IRC Section 2036 as a transfer by the surviving spouse of his or her community property interest with life income retained. Such a transfer will be imputed to the surviving spouse if under state law the insured's death makes the transfer absolute (Q 216). The amount includable is the value of the surviving spouse's community half of the remaining proceeds going to the beneficiary of the remainder interest, less the value (at the insured's death) of the surviving spouse's income interest in the *insured's* community half of the proceeds.[2] In states where the noninsured spouse has a vested interest in the proceeds of community property life insurance (e.g., California and Washington), a gift of the surviving spouse's community property interest should not be imputed to the surviving spouse unless the surviving spouse has consented to or has acquiesced in the insured's disposition of the proceeds.[3] But see, *Est. of Bothun v. Comm.*,[4] decided under California law, where an IRC Section 2036 transfer was imputed to the surviving spouse-primary beneficiary when, because the surviving spouse failed to survive a fifteen-day delayed payment clause, proceeds were paid to the contingent beneficiary. The opinion contained no suggestion of any evidence that the noninsured spouse had consented to the delayed payment clause.

The IRS has ruled that where community property life insurance is payable to a named beneficiary other than the noninsured spouse, if deaths of the insured and the insured's spouse occur simultaneously when both possess the power to change the beneficiary in conjunction with the other, one-half of the proceeds is includable in each spouse's estate without regard to whether local law provides a presumption as to survivorship.[5]

1. *Est. of Wyly v. Comm.*, 610 F.2d 1282 (5th Cir. 1980).
2. *U.S. v. Gordon*, 406 F.2d 332 (5th Cir. 1969).
3. See *Whiteley v. U.S.*, 214 F. Supp. 489 (W.D. Wash. 1963).
4. TC Memo 1976-230.
5. Rev. Rul. 79-303, 1979-2 CB 332.

170. How is community property life insurance taxed when the spouse who is not the insured dies first?

One-half of the value of the unmatured policy is includable in the non-insured spouse's gross estate.[1] The value of the policy is determined under Treasury Regulation Section 20.2031-8 (Q 200).[2] The amount includable in the estate of the surviving insured spouse upon his or her subsequent death is determined by applying state law to the facts presented to ascertain the extent to which the proceeds are treated as community property or as separate property of the insured.[3]

171. How are life insurance paid-up additions purchased with dividends treated for estate tax purposes?

They are treated in the same manner as other insurance. Proceeds are includable in the insured's estate if the proceeds are payable to or for the benefit of the insured's estate, or if the insured has any incidents of ownership in the policy at the time of his or her death (Q 81).[4]

172. What rules are applicable to including life insurance accumulated and post-mortem dividends in an insured's estate?

Accumulated dividends (including interest thereon) and post-mortem dividends are reported together with the face amount of the policy on Schedule D of the insured's estate tax return.[5]

173. Are life insurance proceeds paid under a double-indemnity clause includable in an insured's gross estate?

Yes. They are subject to the same rules as other life insurance proceeds and may be included in the insured's gross estate (Q 81, Q 175).[6]

174. Are proceeds of life insurance issued under U.S. government programs includable in the insured's estate?

Yes.

Such proceeds are includable despite a federal law that provides that no tax can be levied on government life insurance. The estate tax is not a tax *on* property itself, but a tax on the right to transfer property at death. Hence, the exemption from taxes does not apply to the estate tax. Proceeds of a policy owned by the insured at the time of his or her death are includable in the insured's estate (government life insurance is nonassignable).[7]

---

1. *U.S. v. Stewart* (Cal.) 270 F.2d 894 (9th Cir. 1959); *California Trust Co. v. Riddell* 136 F. Supp. 7 (S.D. Cal. 1955); Rev. Rul. 74-284, 1974-1 CB 276 (N.M.).
2. Rev. Rul. 75-100, 75-1 CB 303.
3. See *Scott v. Comm.* (Cal.) 374 F.2d 154 (9th Cir. 1967); *Est. of Cavenaugh v. Comm.* (Tex.), 51 F.3d 597, 95-1 USTC ¶60,195 (5th Cir. 1995), rev'g in part 100 TC 407 (1993); *Est. of Cervin v. Comm.*, 111 F.3d 1252, 97-1 USTC ¶60,274 (5th Cir. 1997), rev'g TC Memo 1994-550; Rev. Rul. 75-100, above (Tex.).
4. IRC Sec. 2042.
5. *See* http://www.irs.gov/pub/irs-pdf/f706.pdf and http://www.irs.gov/pub/irs-pdf/f712.pdf (last accessed January 14, 2019).
6. *Est. of Ackerman v. Comm.*, 15 BTA 635 (1929); *Est. of Wright v. Comm.*, 8 TC 531 (1947); see *Comm. v. Est. of Noel*, 380 U.S. 678 (1965).
7. IRC Sec. 2042; *U.S. Trust Co. of N.Y. v. Helvering*, 307 U.S. 57 (1939); Rev. Rul. 55-622, 1955-2 CB 385.

The U.S. Supreme Court has held that community property laws cannot interfere with the right of an insured to name his or her own beneficiary of his or her National Service Life Insurance (NSLI).[1] Consequently, it has been held that even though an insured and the insured's spouse are residents of a community property state and all premiums have been paid with community funds, the entire proceeds of government life insurance issued to service members and veterans are includable in the insured's gross estate for federal estate tax purposes as if they were the insured's separate property.[2] The Supreme Court of California has held that this ruling is not authority with respect to Federal Employees Group Life Insurance, and that community property rights can be asserted in the proceeds of such insurance notwithstanding the insured's beneficiary designation.[3] If the California decision is followed in the federal courts, then the proceeds from the Federal Employees' Group Life Insurance Program (EGLI) and probably Servicemen's Group Life Insurance as well are includable in the insured's estate on the same basis as the proceeds of regular group life insurance (Q 167 to Q 168). In the case of EGLI, the master policy previously specifically prohibited assignment, but assignment is now permissible (generally, effective October 3, 1994).

Life insurance proceeds were includable in a federal judge's estate where the judge attempted to assign an EGLI policy that was not assignable at the time of the attempted assignment. The judge also attempted to assign the policy after a limited 1984 change in the EGLI law permitted some assignments. However, such attempts were made within three years of the judge's death and were caught by the gifts within three years of death rule (Q 96). The assignments made after the 1984 change in EGLI law were not permitted to relate back to the pre-1984 attempted assignment because assignments were not permissible before 1984.[4]

The IRS has held that in community property states that determine whether life insurance is separate or community property according to the "inception of title" doctrine (Q 168), the proceeds from the NSLI purchased initially as the insured's separate property are separate property even though later premiums were paid with community funds.[5]

175. Are the proceeds of group term life insurance from an employer includable in an insured's estate?

The general rules for including life insurance proceeds in the gross estate apply (Q 81). Accordingly, the proceeds are includable if they are payable to or for the benefit of the insured's estate, or if the insured possesses any incident of ownership in the policy at the time of his or her death. There is no question, for example, that if at the employee's death the employee possessed the right to designate or change the beneficiary of his or her group life insurance, the employee possessed an incident of ownership within the meaning of IRC Section 2042(2).[6] In addition to the general rules concerning incidents of ownership, in group life insurance, the insured's right

1. *Wissner v. Wissner*, 338 U.S. 655 (1949).
2. *Est. of Hutson v. Comm.*, 49 TC 495 (1968) (NSLI); *Hunt's Estate v. U.S.*, 4 AFTR 2d 5069 (E.D. Tex. 1959) (USGLI); Rev. Rul. 56-603, 1956-2 CB 601 (USGLI, NSLI, and policies issued under the Servicemen's Indemnity Act of 1951).
3. *Carlson v. Carlson*, 11 Cal. 3d 474, 521 P.2d 1114 (1974).
4. *Hays v. U.S.*, 95-2 USTC ¶60,203 (S.D. Ill. 1995).
5. Rev. Rul. 74-312, 1974-2 CB 320.
6. *Chase Nat'l Bank v. U.S.*, 278 U.S. 327 (1929); *Est. of Henry v. Comm.*, TC Memo 1987-119.

to convert to an individual policy on termination of employment is *not* an incident of ownership.[1] Moreover, the power of an employee to effect cancellation of his or her coverage by terminating his or her employment is *not* an incident of ownership.[2]

Estate tax regulations that attribute corporate-held incidents of ownership to an insured who is a stockholder-employee under certain circumstances (Q 319) provide (as amended in 1979) that in the case of group term life insurance, as defined in the regulations under Section 79, the power to surrender or cancel a policy held by a corporation "shall not be attributed to any decedent" through his or her stock ownership.[3] (See Q 241 for the definition of group term life insurance.)

Drawing somewhat of a parallel to the controlling stockholder regulations, the IRS has held that a partnership's power to surrender or cancel its group term life insurance policy is not attributable to any of the partners. According to the IRS, it does not matter that partners do not qualify for the income exclusion provided in IRC Section 79 (Q 246) because they are not employees. Under the facts of the ruling, the insured partner was one of thirty-five partners.[4] The IRS has ruled privately in a case involving optional contributory plans of group life insurance that provide that if an employee opts not to participate on his or her own, certain specified relatives of the employee could, with the employee's consent, apply and pay for the insurance on the employee's life and own all incidents of ownership. The plan also provided that should the third-party applicant-owner cease to qualify as such, the insurance would terminate, in which event the employee would be eligible again to apply for coverage on his or her own. The IRS held that the employee did not possess an incident of ownership within the meaning of IRC Section 2042.[5]

The Tax Court has held that the death proceeds of a combination group term life and disability income policy are taxable for estate tax purposes under IRC Section 2042 as proceeds of life insurance.[6]

176. If an employee assigns his or her incidents of ownership in group term life insurance, are the proceeds includable in the employee's estate?

It is possible for an employee to assign all of his or her incidents of ownership in group term life insurance so long as both the policy and state law permit an absolute assignment of all the insured's interest in the insurance, including the conversion privilege, if any. If the employee completes such an assignment during his or her lifetime, the employee will be deemed not to have retained an incident of ownership in the insurance under IRC Section 2042(2).[7] In a

1. *Est. of Smead v. Comm.*, 78 TC 43 (1982), acq. in result, 1984-2 CB 2; Rev. Rul. 84-130, 1984-2 CB 194, modifying Rev. Rul. 69-54, Situation 2, 1969-1 CB 221; GCM 39272 (8-16-84); AOD 1984-056.
2. Rev. Rul. 72-307, 1972-1 CB 221; *Landorf v. U.S.*, 408 F.2d 461 (Ct. Cl. 1969); *Est. of Lumpkin v. Comm.*, 56 TC 815 (1971), rev'd on other grounds, 474 F.2d 1092 (5th Cir. 1973).
3. Treas. Reg. §20.2042-1(c)(6).
4. .Rev. Rul. 83-148, 1983-2 CB 157; GCM 39034 (9-21-83).
5. Rev. Rul. 76-421, 1976-2 CB 280.
6. *Est. of Perl v. Comm.*, 76 TC 861 (1981).
7. Rev. Rul. 69-54, 1969-1 CB 221, as modified by Rev. Rul. 72-307, 1972-1 CB 307, and Rev. Rul. 84-130, 1984-2 CB 194.

contributory plan, there is apparently the additional requirement that the assignment must give the assignee the right to continue to pay the insured's share of the premiums.

Almost all states have enacted laws that specifically permit the assignment of a group policy, including assignment of the conversion privilege. An assignment (including the conversion privilege) of a group policy was held to be effective even though state law neither expressly permitted nor prohibited the assignment.[1] In another case, an assignment was upheld where the master contract permitted the assignment but the individual certificates contained provisions against assignment.[2] An attempted assignment will fail where the terms of the master contract specifically prohibit assignment.[3] In the absence of express statutory permission, establishment of the law may require case-by-case litigation.

177. Is an assignment of group term life insurance within three years before the death of an employee includable in the employee's gross estate?

An assignment of group term life insurance made within three years before the death of the insured will cause the proceeds to be included in the insured's gross estate under IRC Section 2035 (Q 96).[4] It has been held that where a prospective insured applied for group coverage and had ownership of the certificate placed in another, the prospective insured made a transfer of the insurance within the meaning of IRC Section 2035.[5]

Similarly, in *Levine v. U.S.*,[6] where the decedent/insured's controlled corporation procured the insurance and where the insured had his wife sign as the applicant and the beneficiary (the insured died in 1978, within three years of the insurance purchase), the proceeds of the life insurance were includable in the decedent/insured's estate.

The IRS has ruled that an annual renewal of group term insurance by mere payment of the renewal premium does not create a new agreement but merely continues the old agreement, and that, therefore, as to an employee who has assigned his or her coverage, renewal is not a new transfer of insurance coverage for purposes of IRC Section 2035. Therefore, if the insured has transferred the insured's coverage under such a plan more than three years before death, the death proceeds will not be brought back into the insured's estate under IRC Section 2035.[7]

The IRS has also ruled that although (1) an employee cannot, by agreement with an assignee of the employee's life coverage, effectively assign life coverage that the employee may receive in the future furnished by a new insurance carrier, and (2) a change of insurance carrier necessitates a new assignment of an employee's coverage to the same assignee "and the new arrangement is identical in all relevant aspects to the previous arrangement" with the old carrier, the new assignment will not cause the proceeds to be includable in the employee's estate under IRC

1. *Landorf v. U.S.*, 408 F.2d 461 (1969).
2. *Est. of Gorby v. Comm.*, 53 TC 80 (1969), acq. 1970-1 CB xvi.
3. *Est. of Bartlett v. Comm.*, 54 TC 1590 (1970).
4. Let. Rul. 8022025.
5. *Kahn v. U.S.*, 349 F. Supp. 806 (N.D. Ga. 1972).
6. 10 Cl. Ct. 135, 86-1 USTC ¶13,667 (Cl. Ct. 1986).
7. Rev. Rul. 82-13, 1982-1 CB 132.

Section 2035 if the employee dies within three years after the new assignment, but more than three years after the first assignment.[1]

A later private ruling dealt with the assignment of the insured's rights in a group life policy that was later replaced by a policy virtually identical in all material respects with the prior policy, but issued by a different carrier. The new policy provided that an employee's irrevocable assignment of the employee's rights in the old policy would be effective to vest in the assignee the insured's rights under the new policy. No new assignment was made after issuance of the new policy. The IRS stated that if applicable local law would not recognize the provision in the new policy as constituting a valid assignment of rights in the new policy, the insured would be treated as the owner of the policy at the insured's death.[2] The U.S. Court of Appeals for the Seventh Circuit held that the proceeds of a group life policy were includable in the decedent's gross estate where the insured died within three years of the issuance of a policy offered by the employer in exchange for an earlier group life insurance policy. In this case, the insured was required to execute a new assignment when the second policy was issued.[3]

Where the issuance of a life insurance policy to a trust created by the insured's children was treated as an exercise of the conversion rights under a group policy in which the insured had held incidents of ownership that the insured had not previously assigned and the insured died within three years of the conversion, the insured was considered to have transferred incidents of ownership in the policy within three years of death, and the proceeds were included in the insured's estate.[4]

178. If a grantor creates a revocable life insurance trust with a policy on the grantor's life, will the proceeds be includable in his or her estate?

Yes. The entire value of the proceeds is includable in the grantor's gross estate. If the grantor has funded the trust, the funding property is also includable.[5]

179. If policies on an insured's life are placed in an irrevocable life insurance trust, are the proceeds includable in the estate?

Ordinarily, they are not.[6] The proceeds will be included in the insured's gross estate, however, if the insured retains any incident of ownership in the policy at the time of death, whether the ownership right is exercisable by the insured alone or only in conjunction with another person (Q 81).[7] Even though the insured has assigned the policy to the trustee, the proceeds will be included in the insured's gross estate if, under the terms of the trust instrument, the insured has a right to the cash surrender values.[8] The mere right to give investment advice, in the case of a

1. Rev. Rul. 80-289, 1980-2 CB 270, revoking Rev. Rul. 79-231.
2. Let. Rul. 8230038.
3. *American Nat'l. Bank v. U.S.*, 832 F.2d 1032, 87-2 USTC ¶13,738 (7th Cir. 1987).
4. Let. Rul. 9141007.
5. IRC Sec. 2038(a); Treas. Reg. §20.2042-1(c)(4).
6. *Est. of Crosley v. Comm.*, 47 TC 310 (1966), acq. 1967-2 CB 2.
7. Treas. Reg. §20.2042-1(c)(4); *Farwell v. U.S.*, 243 F.2d 373 (7th Cir. 1957); *In re Rhodes' Est.*, 174 F.2d 584 (3rd Cir. 1949); *Est. of Seward v. Comm.*, 164 F.2d 434 (4th Cir. 1947).
8. *St. Louis Union Trust Co. (Orthwein) v. U.S.*, 262 F. Supp. 27 (E.D. Mo. 1966).

funded trust, is not considered an incident of ownership in the policy.[1] See Q 96 for tax results where the trust was established within three years of death, or the insured paid premiums within three years of death. For a discussion of whether the right to control payment of the proceeds when such right is held by the insured as trustee is an incident of ownership, see Q 88.

180. When are death proceeds includable in the estate of a life income beneficiary of a life insurance trust?

If a life income beneficiary is the owner of insurance policies payable to a life insurance trust at the time of the insured's death and the life income beneficiary is still the beneficiary at the time of death, an amount equal to the death proceeds will be includable in the life beneficiary's estate under IRC Section 2036(a)(1) as a transfer of the proceeds with a life income interest retained.[2]

In one case, an insured husband created a nonfunded revocable life insurance trust under which his wife was the life income beneficiary and the wife paid premiums out of her own funds. The court held that on the death of the wife, who died after the husband, the premium payments were not considered transfers, and the proceeds therefore were not includable in her estate under IRC Section 2036(a)(1).[3] However, when a trust is irrevocable, there is a possibility that payment of premiums by the income beneficiary may cause the income beneficiary to be considered a co-grantor of the trust. Thus, the income beneficiary may be considered to have made a transfer with a retained income interest. This would cause the portion of the proceeds attributable to such premiums to be includable in the income beneficiary's estate upon the income beneficiary's subsequent death.[4] Trust beneficiaries would not hold incidents of ownership in life insurance under IRC Section 2042 where (1) a beneficiary could not make contributions to a trust that might hold life insurance on the beneficiary's life and (2) a beneficiary's limited power of appointment could not be exercised if the trust held life insurance on the beneficiary's life.[5]

181. If an income beneficiary has the power to invade the corpus of a trust, will the value of the trust assets over which the income beneficiary has the power be includable in the income beneficiary's gross estate upon the income beneficiary's death?

If the income beneficiary, as the insured's surviving spouse, is given a "qualifying income interest for life" in the trust, the trust corpus (or the specific portion thereof in which the income beneficiary has the income interest) will be includable in the income beneficiary's estate if the marital deduction election is made, whether or not the income beneficiary is given a power to invade the corpus of the trust.[6] If the income beneficiary's interest is not a "qualifying income interest for life" in the trust, if the power is deemed a general power of appointment within the meaning of IRC Section 2041, and if the income beneficiary either (1) possessed the power at death or (2) exercised or released the power during life by a disposition of such a nature that

1. *Est. of Mudge v. Comm.*, 27 TC 188 (1956).
2. Rev. Rul. 81-166, 1981-1 CB 477.
3. *Goodnow v. U.S.*, 302 F.2d 516, 157 Ct. Cl. 526 (1962).
4. IRC Sec. 2036(a)(1).
5. Let. Rul. 9602010.
6. IRC Sec. 2044.

if it were a transfer of property, the property would be includable in the income beneficiary's estate under any of IRC Sections 2035-2038, the value of the trust assets will be includable in the income beneficiary's gross estate.

In the case of a power created on or before October 21, 1942, property subject to the power would be includable in the income beneficiary's estate under IRC Section 2041 only if the income beneficiary exercised the power by will or as in (2) above.[1] The lapse of a power during the power holder's lifetime is considered a release of such power (as in (2) above), but only to the extent that property that could have been appointed by exercise of the powers that lapsed in any calendar year exceeded in value at the time of the lapse the greater of (a) $5,000, or (b) 5 percent of the value of the assets over which the lapsed powers existed (Q 205).[2]

Subject to the exceptions noted below, the income beneficiary would be deemed to hold a general power of appointment if the income beneficiary had the power to invade the trust corpus for his or her benefit or for the benefit of his or her estate, creditors, or estate creditors. The following powers would *not* be deemed general powers of appointment for purposes of IRC Section 2041 if possessed by the income beneficiary:

1. A power to invade the corpus for the income beneficiary's benefit if the power is limited by an "ascertainable standard" relating to the income beneficiary's "health, education, support, or maintenance."

2. A power of appointment created on or before October 21, 1942, which is exercisable by the income beneficiary only in conjunction with another person.

3. A power of appointment created after October 21, 1942, which is exercisable by the income beneficiary only in conjunction with the creator of the power or with a person having a substantial interest in the property subject to the power adverse to exercise of the power in favor of the income beneficiary.[3]

Five percent of a family trust (as well as 100 percent of a marital trust) was includable in the surviving spouse's estate where the surviving spouse held a power of withdrawal over all of the marital trust and a contingent power to withdraw 5 percent annually from the family trust if the marital trust was exhausted.[4]

In the past, through a number of letter rulings, the IRS determined that a beneficiary who has the power to remove a trustee will be treated as holding any powers held by the trustee for purposes of determining whether the beneficiary holds a general power of appointment.[5] However, for purposes of IRC Sections 2036 or 2038, the IRS no longer includes trust property in a decedent grantor's estate where the grantor retains the right to replace the trustee but can replace

1. IRC Sec. 2041(a).
2. IRC Sec. 2041(b)(2).
3. IRC Sec. 2041(b)(1).
4. *Est. of Kurz v. Comm.*, 95-2 USTC ¶60, 215 (7th Cir. 1995).
5. Let. Ruls. 8916032, 9113026 (does not apply to transfers in trust before October 29, 1979, if trust was irrevocable on October 28, 1979).

the trustee with only an independent corporate trustee.[1] More recently, the power to remove a trustee and replace the trustee with an independent corporate trustee was not treated as the retention of powers held by the trustee for purposes of IRC Section 2041.[2] This may represent an extension by the IRS of its policy with regard to trustee removal under IRC Sections 2036 and 2038 to IRC Section 2041. Similarly, a beneficiary's right to veto a replacement trustee and to petition a court for appointment of an independent replacement trustee was not treated as a general power of appointment.[3]

See Q 186 regarding the reciprocal trust doctrine.

182. Are life insurance proceeds includable in an insured's estate if they are payable to an irrevocable trust and the trustee has the power to use them for payment of the insured's estate debts and death taxes?

Yes.

Life insurance proceeds are includable in the insured's estate if the trustee is *required* to use the proceeds to discharge estate obligations. The amount of proceeds required for payment of such debts and taxes is includable in the insured's gross estate, whether the proceeds actually are used for such purposes or not.[4] If the trustee's power is merely discretionary, however, and the trust is for the benefit of named individuals, the proceeds are includable in the insured's estate to the extent they are actually used for such purposes.[5] (See also Q 83.)

Planning Point: Liquidity for an insured's estate can be aided by authorizing the trustee to lend proceeds to the estate or to use them to buy assets from the estate; such powers, if only discretionary, should not subject the proceeds to inclusion in the insured's estate.

183. If a grantor funds his or her life insurance trust by transferring income-producing property to the trustee, is the value of the funding property includable in the grantor's gross estate?

It should not be includable in the grantor's estate if, generally, (1) the trust is irrevocable and the grantor has retained no power to alter or amend, (2) the grantor has retained no interest or control over enjoyment of the property or income, and (3) the grantor does not have a reversionary interest in excess of 5 percent.[6] If the grantor retains power to withdraw and surrender policies placed in the trust, the funding property may be includable in the grantor's gross estate.[7]

1. Rev. Rul. 95-58, 1995-2 CB 191; *Est. of Wall v. Comm.*, 101 TC 300 (1993).
2. Let. Rul. 9607008.
3. Let. Rul. 9741009.
4. Treas. Reg. §20.2042-1(b)(1); *Hooper v. Comm.*, 41 BTA 114 (1940), nonacq. in part at 1941-1 CB 7 (1940) ; *Pacific Nat'l Bank of Seattle (Morgan Will) v. Comm.*, 40 BTA 128 (1939); *Est. of Rohnert v. Comm.*, 40 BTA 1319 (1939); *Est. of Logan v. Comm.*, 23 BTA 236 (1931).
5. *Est. of Wade v. Comm.*, 47 BTA 21 (1942); *Old Colony Trust Co. (Flye's Est.) v. Comm.*, 39 BTA 871 (1939), acq. 1939-2 CB 27.
6. IRC Secs. 2036, 2037, 2038; *First Nat'l Bank of Birmingham (Est. of Sanson) v. Comm.*, 36 BTA 651 (1937), acq. 1937-2 CB 24; *Est. of Carlton v. Comm.*, 34 TC 988 (1960), nonacq. 1964-1 CB 9; Rev. Rul. 81-164, 1981-1 CB 458.
7. Treas. Reg. §20.2042-1(c)(4); *Est. of Resch v. Comm.*, 20 TC 171 (1953), acq. 1953-2 CB 6.

184. If a grandparent creates a funded irrevocable life insurance trust with policies on the life of his or her child for the benefit of grandchildren, is anything includable in the grantor's gross estate?

Perhaps. If the grandparent retains any interest in or control over the insurance or the funding property, the value of the trust assets at the grantor's death (or at an alternate valuation date), including the insurance policies or proceeds held in trust, could be includable in the grandparent's gross estate under one or more of the following IRC Sections: 2036, 2037, 2038, or 2041.[1] The incidents of ownership test of IRC Section 2042 (Q 86) is inapplicable because the grantor is not the insured.

185. How is a "reversionary interest trust" taxed under the estate tax law?

If the trust instrument provides that the trust will end on the grantor's death, the entire value of the property is includable in the grantor's gross estate. Otherwise, the grantor's reversionary interest is includable in the estate. The longer the trust term, the less will be the value of the reversion in the grantor's estate. This value is determined by use of the Estate and Gift Tax Valuation Tables found in Appendix C. If the gift of the income interest was a taxable gift, the amount of the gift, if not included in the gross estate, will be added to the taxable estate for purposes of computing the tentative estate tax. Nothing will be includable in the *beneficiary's* estate if the trust instrument provides for termination on the beneficiary's death. Otherwise, the value of the right to income will be includable. This value decreases as the trust term draws to a close.[2]

186. What is the reciprocal trust doctrine, and how does it affect life insurance trusts?

Assume there are two insureds, A and B, each of whom wishes to create funded life insurance trusts for the same beneficiaries, with each retaining certain life interests in the property transferred. Each realizes that the retention of such interests will cause the value of the property each transfers to be included in his or her gross estate (Q 182, Q 183). They reason that if they give these interests to the *other*, there should be no basis for includability of the trust assets in their own estates, assuming the trusts are irrevocable.

The reciprocal trust doctrine, developed by the courts, prevents this estate tax result. If the parties were to go ahead with their plan, the doctrine would be applied so as to "uncross" the trusts. For estate tax purposes, A would be treated as grantor of the trusts in form created by B, and vice versa. The doctrine is applied when trusts are interrelated and the arrangement, to the extent of mutual value, leaves the grantors in approximately the same economic position in which they would have been had each retained life interests in the trusts the grantor in form created. There is no need to find that the trusts were exchanged in "payment" for each other, nor that there was a specific "tax avoidance" motive involved in their creation.[3] The U.S. Court of Appeals for the Sixth Circuit and the Tax Court, in split decisions, have held that application of the reciprocal trust doctrine does not require that the grantors have crossed *economic* interests in

1. *Comm. v. Est. of Arents*, 297 F.2d 894 (2nd Cir. 1962), cert. denied 369 U.S. 848.
2. Treas. Reg. §20.2031-7(d)(2)(ii).
3. *U.S. v. Grace*, 395 U.S. 316 (1969). See also *Est. of Moreno v. Comm.*, 260 F.2d 389 (8th Cir. 1958).

the trusts they have created.[1] The U.S. Court of Appeals for the Federal Circuit appears to concur with the Tax Court in this view (see case cited below). The reciprocal trust doctrine also has been applied to uncross transfers of assets in custodianship under the Uniform Gifts to Minors Act.[2]

A letter ruling uncrossed reciprocal discretionary distribution rights given to trustees where each trustee was given a discretionary power to make distributions to the other trustee. Consequently, the decedent in this letter ruling was treated as holding a general power to appoint trust corpus to himself and the corpus was included in his estate.[3]

187. Is a life insurance policy loan deductible as a claim against the estate?

No. A policy loan is considered an advancement of part of the policy proceeds, not an enforceable claim against the estate.[4] Only the excess of the proceeds over the amount of the policy loan is includable in the gross estate.

Marital Deduction

188. May a trust intended to qualify for the marital deduction as a "power of appointment trust" authorize the trustee to retain or acquire life insurance policies?

Under a "power of appointment trust," the surviving spouse must be entitled for life to all of the income. This condition contemplates a trust holding income-producing property. Thus, if the trustee is empowered to retain or acquire non-income-producing property (such as life insurance), the condition probably will not be satisfied unless the trustee is required to make payments to the surviving spouse out of other trust assets to replace the lost income, or unless the trust gives the surviving spouse the power to compel the trustee to convert the non-income-producing property to income-producing property.[5]

189. May a trust intended to qualify for the marital deduction as qualified terminable interest property (QTIP) authorize the trustee to retain or acquire life insurance policies?

Under a qualified terminable interest property (QTIP) trust, the surviving spouse must be entitled for life to all the income. This condition contemplates a trust holding income-producing property. Thus, if the trustee is empowered to retain or acquire non-income-producing property (such as life insurance), the condition probably will not be satisfied unless the trust gives the surviving spouse the power to compel the trustee to convert the non-income-producing property to income-producing property, or unless the trustee is restrained under a state law "prudent person" rule to treat the surviving spouse fairly by protecting the spouse's income interest.[6]

---

1. *Est. of Green v. U.S.*, 68 F. 3d 151, 95-2 USTC ¶60,216 (6th Cir. 1995); *Est. of Bischoff v. Comm.*, 69 TC 32 (1977).
2. *Exchange Bank & Trust Co. of Fla. v. U.S.*, 694 F. 2d 1261, 82-2 USTC ¶13,505 (Fed. Cir. 1982).
3. Let. Rul. 9235025.
4. Treas. Reg. §§20.2042-1(a)(3), 20.2053-4; *Kennedy v. Comm.*, 4 BTA 330 (1926).
5. Treas. Reg. §§20.2056(b)-5(f)(4), 20.2056(b)-5(f)(5); Rev. Rul. 75-440, 1975-2 CB 372; *Est. of Robinson v. U.S.*, 1980 US Dist. LEXIS 14673 (E.D. Tenn. 1980).
6. TAM 8745003.

190. If a decedent directs his or her executor or a trustee to buy a nonrefundable life annuity for the decedent's surviving spouse, will the annuity qualify for the marital deduction?

No. The surviving spouse's interest in the annuity is considered a non-deductible terminable interest even though no interest in the annuity has passed from the decedent to any other person.[1] Such an annuity will not fail to qualify, however, if it is bought under a general investment power authorizing investments in both terminable interests and other property.[2]

191. When will life insurance or annuity proceeds payable to the surviving spouse qualify for the marital deduction?

There are five basic arrangements for the payment of proceeds to the surviving spouse that will qualify for the marital deduction:

(1) proceeds payable in a lump sum to the surviving spouse (regardless of whether contingent beneficiaries are named or whether the surviving spouse actually elects to receive the proceeds under a settlement option);[3]

(2) proceeds payable solely to the surviving spouse or to the surviving spouse's estate (Q 192);

(3) proceeds payable to the surviving spouse under a settlement option with contingent beneficiaries named, provided the surviving spouse is given a general power of appointment over the proceeds (Q 193, Q 194);

(4) proceeds of a survivor annuity where only the surviving spouse has the right to receive payments during such spouse's lifetime, unless otherwise elected by the decedent spouse's executor;[4] and

(5) proceeds held under the interest option for the surviving spouse for the surviving spouse's lifetime, when interest is payable to the surviving spouse at least annually, and there is no power in any person to appoint any of the proceeds to anyone other than the spouse during the surviving spouse's lifetime – if the executor elects to have proceeds qualify.

Arrangements (4) and (5) make the proceeds qualified terminable interest property; however, to the extent provided in the regulations, an *annuity* interest is to be treated in a manner similar to an income interest in property (regardless of whether the property from which the annuity is payable can be separately identified).[5] A specific portion must be determined on a fractional or percentage basis.[6] The proceeds likewise will qualify for the marital deduction if they are payable

1. Treas. Reg. §20.2056(b)-1(c)(2)(i).
2. IRC Sec. 2056(b)(1)(C); Treas. Reg. §20.2056(b)-1(f).
3. Treas. Reg. §20.2056(c)-2(b)(3)(ii).
4. IRC Sec. 2056(b)(7)(C).
5. IRC Sec. 2056(b)(7)(B)(ii).
6. IRC Sec. 2056(b)(10).

outright to the surviving spouse under the insured's or the annuitant's will or intestate laws, or to a trust that qualifies for the marital deduction. The marital deduction is not available unless the insured or annuitant is actually survived by his or her spouse, or is legally presumed to have been survived by his or her spouse (Q 197). Thus, a provision in the disposing instrument that the proceeds are payable to the spouse on the sole condition that the spouse survive the insured or annuitant will not disqualify the proceeds (Q 195, Q 196).

A marital deduction generally is not allowable when the surviving spouse is not a U.S. citizen unless the transfer is to a qualified domestic trust.

192. Will life insurance or annuity proceeds qualify for the marital deduction if payable to a surviving spouse under a settlement option with a surviving spouse's estate designated as contingent beneficiary? What if they are payable to a surviving spouse as a straight life annuity?

If the proceeds are payable only to the surviving spouse or to his or her estate, they will qualify.[1] For example, the following settlement would qualify: life income to a widow with a twenty-year certain period, and should she die within the twenty-year period, the balance of the guaranteed payments to be commuted and paid to her estate. The following settlement also would qualify: interest to widow for life, and principal to her estate at her death. Likewise, the proceeds will qualify if they are payable to the surviving spouse under a straight life annuity settlement with no refund or period-certain guarantee (no portion of the proceeds would be payable to any other person after her death).[2]

If proceeds are payable under a no-refund life annuity to the surviving spouse, qualification is not affected by the fact that an annuity also is payable to another, so long as the respective rights to their annuities are not tied together in any way.[3] When only the surviving spouse has the right to receive payments from a survivor annuity during such spouse's lifetime, such proceeds are treated as qualified terminable interest property unless otherwise elected by the decedent spouse's executor.[4]

193. Can life insurance settlements naming the spouse as primary beneficiary and other persons as contingent beneficiaries be arranged so that the proceeds qualify for the marital deduction?

Yes.

When there is a possibility that one or more persons may receive some unpaid proceeds after the spouse's death, the spouse receives only a *terminable interest* in the proceeds. As a rule, terminable interests do not qualify for the marital deduction. As an exception to the general rule, however, a settlement naming contingent beneficiaries will qualify if the spouse is given a general power of appointment over the proceeds and certain other requirements are met.

1. IRC Sec. 2056(a); Treas. Reg. §20.2056(c)-2(b)(3).
2. Treas. Reg. §20.2056(b)-1(g), Example (3).
3. Rev. Rul. 77-130, 1977-1 CB 289.
4. IRC Sec. 2056(b)(7)(C).

Specifically, an insured may elect an interest-only, life income, or installment option for his or her spouse, naming contingent beneficiaries to receive the proceeds after the spouse's death, and the proceeds will qualify, provided the settlement meets the following conditions:

(1) The interest or installments must be payable annually or more frequently, and the first payment must be payable no later than thirteen months after the insured's death;

(2) All amounts payable during the spouse's life must be payable only to the spouse;

(3) The spouse must have a *general power of appointment* over the proceeds (a power to appoint the proceeds to himself or herself or to his or her estate – see Q 194);

(4) The spouse's power to appoint must be exercisable by the spouse alone and in all events, whether exercisable by will or during life; and

(5) The proceeds must not be subject to a power in any other person to appoint against the spouse.[1]

An alternative settlement naming contingent beneficiaries does not require that the spouse be given any power over the proceeds so long as the spouse has a "qualifying income interest for life" in the proceeds, and so long as the executor elects to have such proceeds qualify for the marital deduction. The surviving spouse has a "qualifying income interest for life" if he or she is entitled to all the income from the proceeds, payable annually or more frequently, and no person has a power to appoint any part of the proceeds to any person other than the surviving spouse. The insured or anyone else, including the surviving spouse, can designate beneficiaries to receive proceeds remaining at the spouse's death, and the spouse may be (but need not be) given the right to withdraw proceeds during his or her lifetime (Q 191).

It is not necessary that the entire proceeds qualify. If a specific portion of the proceeds meets the conditions outlined above, that specific portion will qualify for the deduction.[2]

The specific portion, however, must be determined on a fractional or percentage basis.[3]

194. What is a general power to appoint the proceeds of a life insurance policy for purposes of the marital deduction?

For purposes of the marital deduction, the donee of a general power of appointment must have the power to appoint the property to himself or herself or to his or her estate.[4] Thus, if the surviving spouse-beneficiary has the power to revoke contingent beneficiaries and name his or her estate instead, the surviving spouse-beneficiary is deemed to have a general power to appoint to his or her estate. Or, if the surviving spouse-beneficiary can withdraw the principal

1. IRC Sec. 2056(b)(6); Treas. Reg. §20.2056(b)-6; *Est. of White v. Comm.*, 22 TC 641 (1954); *Est. of Zeman v. Comm.*, TC Memo 1958-68; *Est. of Fiedler v. Comm.*, 67 TC 239 (1976), acq. 1977-1 CB 1; Rev. Rul. 76-404, 1976-2 CB 294.
2. IRC Secs. 2056(b)(6), 2056(b)(7); Treas. Reg. §20.2056(b)-6(b).
3. IRC Sec. 2056(b)(10).
4. IRC Sec. 2056(b)(6).

sum for his or her own use, the surviving spouse-beneficiary is deemed to have a general power to appoint to himself or to herself or to his or her estate.[1] The surviving spouse-beneficiary need not possess both powers; either will suffice. The term "power to appoint" need not be used in the insurance policy. Thus, even where the surviving spouse is not given the power to revoke contingent beneficiaries, the proceeds will qualify if the surviving spouse is given the power to withdraw the proceeds during his or her life and the power is exercisable *in all events*. Insurance companies normally impose some administrative restrictions on the exercise of withdrawal rights. Regulations state, however, that limitations of a formal nature – such as requirements that reasonable intervals must elapse between partial exercise – will not cause disqualification.[2]

195. Does the use of a "delay clause" disqualify life insurance proceeds for the marital deduction?

A "delay clause" is a provision that may be inserted into life insurance contracts providing that a surviving spouse will only be paid if alive at the end of a certain period of time after the death of the first spouse. The "delay clause" will not disqualify the proceeds unless the delay period specified is for more than six months. For example, the beneficiary arrangement may provide that payment will be made to the insured's spouse if the spouse is living at the end of sixty days after the insured's death, otherwise payment is to contingent beneficiaries.

Under the general rules, a delay clause would create a terminable interest and, accordingly, disqualify the proceeds. The reason is that such a clause creates a possibility that the surviving spouse's interest will end (if the surviving spouse dies within the delay period) and the contingent beneficiaries will receive the proceeds. Under a specific exception, however, such a clause will not disqualify the proceeds if: (1) the delay period does not exceed six months, and (2) the surviving spouse actually survives the delay period. However, any clause that creates the possibility that the surviving spouse may have to survive longer than six months to receive the proceeds ordinarily will disqualify the proceeds for the marital deduction – even though the spouse survives the period and actually receives the proceeds.[3]

Planning Point: Although – because of the special exception – a delay clause does not always result in loss of the marital deduction, the clause should not be used when it is important to secure the marital deduction with respect to the proceeds for the insured's estate or else a lose-lose situation will be created. If the spouse survives the delay period, the clause will have served no purpose. If the surviving spouse does not live through the full delay period, the clause will result in loss of the marital deduction.

196. Does a common disaster clause disqualify life insurance proceeds for the marital deduction?

Where a true common disaster clause is used, the beneficiary-spouse will not receive the proceeds if he or she dies of injuries sustained in the same accident (or other disaster) that causes

1. Treas. Reg. §20.2056(b)-6(e)(4); Rev. Rul. 55-277, 1955-1 CB 456.
2. Treas. Reg. §20.2056(b)-5(g)(4). See also *Est. of Cornwell v. Comm.*, 37 TC 688 (1962), acq. *Est. of Jennings v. Comm.*, 39 TC 417 (1962), acq.
3. IRC Sec. 2056(b)(3); Treas. Reg. §20.2056(b)-3(b); Rev. Rul. 54-121, 1954-1 CB 196; TAM 8747003; but see *Eggleston v. Dudley*, 257 F.2d 398 (3rd Cir.). See also Rev. Rul. 70-400, 1970-2 CB 196.

the death of the insured, regardless of how long that spouse actually survives the insured. A common disaster clause creates a terminable interest. But as a special exception to the terminable interest rule, a clause will not disqualify the proceeds unless the death of the insured and that of the spouse actually are caused by the same disaster.[1] A true common disaster clause is seldom used in an insurance policy.

197. Can operation of the Uniform Simultaneous Death Act result in loss of the marital deduction?

Yes.

If the insured and spouse-beneficiary die under circumstances that make it impossible to determine the order of death (usually when both are killed in the same accident), the Uniform Simultaneous Death Act creates a presumption that the *beneficiary* died first. Because it is presumed that the spouse-beneficiary did *not* survive, the act would result in loss of the marital deduction. It is possible to reverse the statutory presumption, however, by inserting a so-called "reverse simultaneous death clause" in the policy. This clause provides that, if the order of death cannot be determined, it will be presumed that the insured died first. This would save the marital deduction.[2] It cannot save the marital deduction, however, if there is evidence that the beneficiary actually died first.

198. Can proceeds of community property life insurance passing to the surviving spouse qualify for the marital deduction?

Yes, and without limit as to amount.[3]

199. Does estate taxation of a life insurance policy that insures more than one life differ from taxation of a policy that insures a single life?

Basically, no. Application of the rules, however, generally depends on when proceeds are payable. With a "first-to-die" or "joint life" policy, proceeds are payable at the death of the first insured to die. With a "second-to-die," "survivorship," or "joint and survivor" policy, proceeds are payable at the death of the last survivor.

In general, proceeds of a first-to-die policy will be included in the insured's estate if the proceeds are payable to or for the benefit of the insured's estate, or if the insured held incidents of ownership in the policy at death or within three years of death (Q 81). Also, the value of a first-to-die policy will be included in the estate of a policy owner who is not the insured (Q 200).

The value of a second-to-die policy will be included in the estate of a policy owner who is not the insured (Q 200). For the same reasons, at the first death, the value of a second-to-die policy will be included in the estate of the decedent/insured if the decedent/insured is a policy owner. At the second death, proceeds of a second-to-die policy will be included in the insured's

1. IRC Sec. 2056(b)(3).
2. Treas. Reg. §20.2056(c)-2(e).
3. IRC Sec. 2056.

estate if (1) the proceeds are payable to or for the benefit of the insured's estate, or (2) the insured held incidents of ownership in the policy at death or within three years of death (Q 81).

Planning Point: Second-to-die policies frequently are used to provide for deferral of estate taxes through use of the marital deduction until the surviving spouse's death. First-to-die policies frequently are used to provide funds for a buy-sell agreement or to provide some funds at the death of the first spouse to die.

For income taxation of multiple-life life insurance, see Q 143. For gift taxation of multiple-life life insurance, see Q 211.

200. If a policy owner who is not the insured dies before the insured, is the value of the unmatured life insurance policy included in the policy owner's gross estate?

Yes.[1] The value of the policy is determined in the same manner as for gift tax purposes, substituting the date of death for the date of the gift (Q 119).[2]

A revenue ruling involved the estate tax valuation of a third-party-owned policy on a split-dollar plan (Q 4008). The policy had been in force for some time and premiums remained to be paid after the decedent-policy owner's death. Premiums and proceeds were split between the decedent and the insured's employer, to whom the policy had been collaterally assigned. It was ruled that the amount includable in the decedent's estate was the interpolated terminal reserve plus the proportionate part of the gross premium paid before the date of the decedent's death that covered the period extending beyond that date, less the amount of the employer's interest in the policy.[3]

Where the executor elects to value assets six months after death (alternate valuation), any increase in policy value due to payment of premiums or accrual of interest during the six months following death is excluded in determining the estate tax value of the policy.[4] But if the executor elects to value the estate by the alternative valuation method, and the insured dies before the optional valuation date (six months after the policy owner's death), the entire value of the proceeds is includable in the policy owner's gross estate.[5]

Where the owner-beneficiary of a life insurance policy and the insured die simultaneously (to all appearances), and where policy proceeds are distributed as if the owner-beneficiary predeceased the insured (as provided in the Uniform Simultaneous Death Act, except where the policy or other controlling instrument provides otherwise), the value of the policy (valued as described above) is likewise included in the owner-beneficiary's estate under IRC Section 2033.[6]

1. IRC Sec. 2033.
2. Treas. Reg. §20.2031-8; *DuPont Est. v. Comm.*, 233 F.2d 210 (3rd Cir. 1956); *Est. of Donaldson v. Comm.*, 31 TC 729 (1959).
3. Rev. Rul. 79-429, 1979-2 CB 321.
4. Rev. Rul. 55-379, 1955-1 CB 449.
5. Rev. Rul. 63-52, 1963-1 CB 173.
6. *Chown v. Comm.*, 428 F.2d 1395 (9th Cir. 1970); *Old Kent Bank & Trust Co. v. U.S.*, 430 F.2d 392 (6th Cir. 1970); *Meltzer v. Comm.*, 439 F.2d 798 (4th Cir. 1971); *Wien v. Comm.*, 441 F.2d 32 (5th Cir. 1971); Rev. Rul. 77-181, 1977-1 CB 272; *Est. of Goldstone v. Comm.*, 78 TC 1143 (1982).

In Revenue Ruling 77-181, A and B each owned policies on the other's life with proceeds payable to the owner or the owner's estate. A and B died under circumstances in which the Uniform Simultaneous Death Act provisions applied, so that the proceeds of the policies on A's life were paid to B's estate and the proceeds of policies on B's life were paid to A's estate. The IRS ruled that the amount to be included in the gross estate of each was the sum of the date-of-death interpolated terminal reserve value of the policies each decedent owned at death and the proportionate part of the gross premium last paid covering the post-death period. Where, in the instrument controlling disposition of policy proceeds, the presumed order of the deaths is reversed from that provided in the uniform act, simultaneous deaths of the policy owner-beneficiary and the insured will cause the death proceeds to be includable in the policy owner's estate.[1] (See also Q 214.)

201. If the insured elects a settlement option for the insured's primary beneficiary and names contingent beneficiaries, will the value of any unpaid life insurance proceeds be includable in the primary beneficiary's estate?

As a general rule, proceeds are not includable in the primary beneficiary's estate unless the primary beneficiary has a general power of appointment over the proceeds (Q 194, Q 202) or was the insured's surviving spouse and has a "qualifying income interest for life" in proceeds as to which the marital deduction was allowed (Q 193).[2] The transfer to contingent beneficiaries is from the insured, not from the primary beneficiary. (For a limited, noncumulative power to withdraw, see Q 205.) With respect to community property insurance, however, one-half of the proceeds belongs to the noninsured spouse (assuming policy premiums were paid with community property funds). Consequently, when the noninsured spouse is the primary beneficiary, one-half of the proceeds will be includable in the insured spouse's estate, and one-half of the value of the proceeds remaining at the noninsured spouse's death will be includable in the noninsured spouse's estate.[3]

202. If the surviving income beneficiary dies possessing the power during his or her lifetime to appoint the life insurance proceeds only to his or her children, are the proceeds includable in the surviving income beneficiary's estate?

If the surviving spouse has a "qualifying income interest for life" in the proceeds, the proceeds will be includable in the surviving spouse's estate if the marital deduction election was made regardless of whether the surviving spouse has any power to appoint the proceeds (Q 193).[4] If the surviving spouse does not have a "qualifying income interest for life" in the proceeds, according to a 1979 revenue ruling, the answer depends on whether the income beneficiary at the surviving spouse's death could have discharged his or her legal duty to support the children, in whole or in part, by exercising the power to appoint the proceeds. To the extent the surviving spouse could have appointed the proceeds, the power would be treated

1. Rev. Rul. 77-48, 1977-1 CB 292.
2. IRC Secs. 2041, 2044.
3. IRC Sec. 2036. *Whiteley v. U.S.*, 214 F. Supp. 489 (W.D. Wash. 1963). See *Tyre v. Aetna Life Ins. Co.*, 353 P. 2d 725 (Cal. 1960).
4. IRC Sec. 2044.

as a general power of appointment and the proceeds would be includable. Under the facts of the ruling, it was held that no part of the proceeds was includable because all of the income beneficiary's children were adults at the time of the surviving spouse's death and the surviving spouse was not obligated under local law to provide for their support.[1] See Q 186 regarding the reciprocal trust doctrine.

203. If life insurance proceeds are payable to the surviving spouse's estate, but remain unpaid at the primary beneficiary's death, is the money includable in the primary beneficiary's gross estate?

Yes. Because the beneficiary can dispose of the remaining proceeds as desired through a will, the beneficiary is deemed to have a general power of appointment over the proceeds (Q 194).[2]

204. If an insured elects a settlement option naming contingent beneficiaries, but still gives the primary beneficiary power to withdraw proceeds, are life insurance proceeds remaining unpaid at the primary beneficiary's death includable in the primary beneficiary's estate?

If the primary beneficiary has a "qualifying income interest for life" in the proceeds, the proceeds will be includable in the primary beneficiary's estate if the marital deduction election was made, whether the primary beneficiary has a power to withdraw any of the proceeds or not (Q 193).[3] Otherwise, a full power of withdrawal constitutes a *general power of appointment* (Q 194).[4] Whether the possession of such a power by the primary beneficiary will cause the remaining proceeds to be taxable in the primary beneficiary's estate depends upon when the power was created. If the primary beneficiary has an unrestricted power to withdraw the proceeds, and the power was created after October 21, 1942, the value of any proceeds remaining unpaid at the primary beneficiary's death will be included in the primary beneficiary's gross estate.[5] (For a limited, noncumulative withdrawal right, see Q 205.) If the primary beneficiary's power of withdrawal was created before October 22, 1942, the value of the unpaid proceeds is not includable in the primary beneficiary's gross estate merely because the primary beneficiary possessed the power.[6] A power of appointment is created when the insured executes the supplementary contract electing the settlement option. This is the date the power is created even though the insured retains the right to surrender the policy and to change the beneficiary.[7]

1. Rev. Rul. 79-154, 1979-1 CB 301.
2. IRC Sec. 2041(a); Rev. Rul. 55-277, 1955-1 CB 456; *Keeter v. U.S.*, 461 F. 2d 714, 29 AFTR 2d 72-1540 (5th Cir. 1972). Contra, *Second Nat'l Bank of Danville, Ill. v. Dallman*, 209 F.2d 321 (7th Cir. 1954).
3. IRC Sec. 2044.
4. Treas. Reg. §20.2056(b)-6(e)(4).
5. IRC Sec. 2041(a)(2).
6. IRC Sec. 2041(a)(1).
7. Treas. Reg. §20.2041-1.

205. Can an insured give a primary beneficiary limited, noncumulative withdrawal rights without causing any remaining unpaid life insurance proceeds to be includable in the primary beneficiary's estate?

If the insured gives a primary beneficiary (e.g., a spouse) a "qualifying income interest for life" in the proceeds, the proceeds will be includable in the primary beneficiary's estate if the marital deduction election was made, regardless of whether the primary beneficiary has a power to withdraw any of the proceeds (Q 193).[1] If the primary beneficiary does not have such an interest in the proceeds, the insured can give a beneficiary a noncumulative right to withdraw each year up to $5,000 or 5 percent of the balance of the proceeds, whichever is greater. If the beneficiary's annual withdrawal right does not exceed these limits, the amounts the primary beneficiary could have withdrawn but did not withdraw are not includable in the primary beneficiary's gross estate (except the unwithdrawn amount that the primary beneficiary could have withdrawn in the year of his or her death).[2]

> *Example*. The proceeds of a $100,000 life insurance policy are left with the insurer under the interest-only option for the insured's daughter. The daughter is given a noncumulative right to withdraw $5,000 a year. She does not have a power to appoint the proceeds to her estate. The daughter dies seven years later, having withdrawn none of the proceeds. Only $5,000, the amount she could have withdrawn in the year of death, is includable in her gross estate.[3]

If the beneficiary's noncumulative withdrawal right exceeds the $5,000/5 percent limits, the aggregate withdrawable amounts in excess of these limits that the beneficiary did not withdraw will be includable in the beneficiary's gross estate (but not in excess of the full proceeds). Thus, if the daughter in the example above had a power to withdraw $6,000 annually, and she did not withdraw the excess amount, then the amount includable in her gross estate would be $12,000 [6 × $1,000 (amount in excess of $5,000 for six years) + $6,000 (year of death)].

206. If the primary beneficiary is given the power to revoke contingent beneficiaries and appoint to his or her estate under a settlement option, are life insurance proceeds remaining unpaid at the primary beneficiary's death includable in his or her estate?

If a beneficiary has the power to appoint to his or her estate, then the beneficiary has a general power of appointment over the proceeds.[4] Generally, such a power, given to a surviving spouse-beneficiary, will qualify the proceeds for the marital deduction in the insured's estate (Q 193), but will cause remaining unpaid proceeds to be includable in the beneficiary's estate. However, includability in the beneficiary's estate will depend on when the power was created. If the power was created *after* October 21, 1942, the proceeds remaining unpaid at the primary beneficiary's death are includable in his or her estate.[5] If the power was created *before* October 22, 1942, the proceeds remaining unpaid at the beneficiary's death are includable in

1. IRC Sec. 2044.
2. IRC Sec. 2041(b)(2).
3. Rev. Rul. 79-373, 1979-2 CB 331.
4. Treas. Reg. §20.2056(b)-6(e)(4).
5. IRC Sec. 2041(a)(2).

his or her estate only if the beneficiary exercised the power. (See Q 204 with respect to when a power is created.)

207. If a beneficiary elects the settlement option, are life insurance proceeds remaining unpaid at the beneficiary's death includable in his or her estate?

Yes. If proceeds are payable to a beneficiary in a lump sum and, after the insured's death, the beneficiary elects a settlement option as primary beneficiary, the proceeds are includable in his or her estate.[1] Likewise, if the beneficiary as *policy owner* elects a settlement for himself or herself and contingent beneficiaries, the remaining proceeds are includable in the beneficiary's gross estate.[2]

208. How are life insurance proceeds valued for an insured's estate tax return?

The full face amount plus paid-up additions, accumulated dividends (with interest thereon), and post-mortem dividends, less policy loans, should be included in Schedule D of the estate tax return.[3] The date-of-death value is used, regardless of whether the executor elects the optional alternative valuation date.[4]

209. If the amount of life insurance proceeds collectible from the insurer is not determinable when the estate tax return is filed, what amount is reportable on the return?

The unsatisfactory answer appears to be that a determination of the fair market value of the insurance claim or claims at the date of death or at the alternate valuation date must be made from the facts and circumstances of the particular case.[5] This problem is most likely to be encountered when an insured's death occurs during the policy's contestable period and there is a question whether the insured made material misrepresentations in applying for the insurance or whether the insured's death resulted from suicide.

210. Can gift tax be collected from the donee of a life insurance policy or proceeds?

Yes. If the gift tax is not collected from the donor, the donee is liable for the tax. The government can collect the gift tax from the donee-beneficiary, and the latter's liability is not limited to the policy's cash value.[6]

1. IRC Sec. 2036; *Est. of Tuohy v. Comm.*, 14 TC 245 (1950); *Rundle v. Welch*, 184 F. Supp. 777 (S.D. Ohio 1960); Let. Rul. 8051019.
2. *Est. of Pyle v. Comm.*, 313 F.2d 328 (3rd Cir. 1963).
3. See Estate Tax Form 706, Schedule D, and Form 712. Treas. Reg. §20.2042-1(a)(3).
4. Rev. Rul. 58-576, 1958-2 CB 625.
5. *American Nat'l Bank & Trust Co. v. U.S.*, 594 F.2d 1141 (7th Cir. 1979); Let. Rul. 8308001.
6. IRC Sec. 6324(b); *Comm. v. Chase Manhattan Bank*, 259 F.2d 231 (5th Cir. 1958).

211. Does gift taxation of a life insurance policy that insures more than one life differ from taxation of a policy that insures a single life?

Basically, no. However, application of the rules may depend on when proceeds are payable. With a "first-to-die" or "joint life" policy, proceeds are payable at the death of the first insured to die. With a "second-to-die," "survivorship," or "joint-and-survivor" policy, proceeds are payable at the death of the last survivor.

Thus, with a "first-to-die" policy, a policy owner who is not the insured may be treated as making a gift to beneficiaries when an insured dies. Also, with a "second-to-die" policy, at the second death, a policy owner who is not the insured may be treated as making a gift to beneficiaries (Q 214).

Planning Point: Second-to-die policies generally are viewed as providing low-cost premiums for gift tax purposes; conversely, first-to-die premiums generally appear high compared to premiums to insure one life.

For income taxation of multiple-life life insurance, see Q 143. For estate taxation of multiple-life life insurance, see Q 199.

212. Do premiums gratuitously paid on life insurance owned by and payable to another constitute gifts?

Generally, yes. If an individual pays a premium on a life insurance policy in which he or she has no ownership rights, the individual has made a gift of the premium.[1] Where, for example, a wife paid premiums on a policy owned by her husband and payable to his estate, she was held to have made a gift to her husband even though she had a contingent interest in the policy as a beneficiary of his estate. Under present law, however, such a gift would qualify for the unlimited marital deduction (Q 114).[2] A gift of premiums may qualify for the gift tax annual exclusion (Q 218).

Ordinarily the premium payer will be considered the donor. However, where an employee assigned his group life insurance policy to an irrevocable trust he had created for his beneficiary, the IRS ruled that premiums subsequently paid by the employer were gifts from the *employee* to the trust.[3] (See also Q 154, Q 159.)

213. Do premiums paid by one of several beneficiaries of an irrevocable life insurance trust constitute gifts to the other beneficiaries?

Yes. Premiums paid in excess of the amount necessary to protect one beneficiary's actuarially determined interest constitute gifts to the other beneficiaries.[4]

---

1. *Comm. v. Boeing*, 123 F.2d 86 (9th Cir. 1941).
2. *Harris v. Comm.*, 10 TC 741 (1948), nonacq. 1948-2 CB 5.
3. Rev. Rul. 76-490, 1976-2 CB 300; Rev. Rul. 79-47, 1979-1 CB 312.
4. *Comm. v. Berger*, 201 F.2d 171 (2nd Cir. 1953).

214. If a life insurance policy is owned by someone other than the insured, is there a gift when the insured dies and the proceeds are paid to the owner's designated beneficiary?

Yes. For example, if a wife owns a policy on the life of her spouse and their children are named beneficiaries, subject to the wife's right to change beneficiaries, there is a gift from the wife to the children when her spouse (the insured) dies. The value of the gift would be the value of the entire proceeds.[1] Under such circumstances, the gift of the proceeds will *not* be considered a split gift between the wife and her late spouse-insured under IRC Section 2513 (Q 117), even if the executor signs a "consent of spouse" and files a gift tax return on behalf of the deceased spouse.[2]

In another example: A bought insurance on the life of B, revocably designating Y as beneficiary; Y is trustee of a trust established by A. The trust provided that trust income was payable to B for life, then to A for life, then trust corpus to the children of A and B. The trust also provided that for purposes of the trust agreement, if A and B died simultaneously, A would be presumed to have survived B. A and B died simultaneously. It was held that there was a taxable gift of the proceeds from A to the children of A and B.[3] (See also Q 200.)

In addition, in another example: D created an unfunded revocable insurance trust under which life income was payable to B for life and the remainder to E and F. B purchased a life insurance policy on D's life designating the trust as beneficiary and paying all the premiums. While B was alive, D died and the insurance proceeds were paid to the trust. B, until the death of D, possessed all the incidents of ownership in the policy, including the right to change the beneficiary. It was held that B made a completed gift for gift tax purposes to E and F on D's death; the value of the gift was the amount of the policy proceeds less the present value of B's life estate determined by use of the Estate and Gift Tax Valuation Table at Appendix C.[4]

215. Does a taxable gift occur when a donor spouse assigns community property life insurance to a donee spouse?

Generally, no. The assignment qualifies for the unlimited marital gift tax deduction applicable to interspousal gifts, even though the policy is community property.[5] (The assignment is actually of the donor spouse's one-half community property interest, because the donee spouse already owns the other one-half.) An annual exclusion may be allowed instead of the marital deduction if the donee spouse is a non-U.S. citizen.

1. See *Goodman v. Comm.*, 156 F.2d 218 (2d Cir. 1946).
2. Rev. Rul. 73-207, 1973-1 CB 409.
3. Rev. Rul. 77-48, 1977-1 CB 292; *Est. of Goldstone v. Comm.*, 78 TC 1143 (1982).
4. Rev. Rul. 81-166, 1981-1 CB 477.
5. IRC Sec. 2523.

216. If one spouse uses community property to purchase life insurance on either spouse's life and names a child as beneficiary, does the death of the insured spouse give rise to a taxable gift from the noninsured spouse?

Perhaps. If under state law the insured spouse's death makes the transfer of the non-insured spouse's community interest absolute, a gift will be imputed to the noninsured spouse of half the amount of the proceeds of such insurance payable to the child (the result would be the same for any third party).[1] This result has been followed under Texas and Louisiana law.[2]

In Louisiana, life insurance owned by one spouse either may be separate or community property even if community property is used to purchase the policy. As a result, a noninsured spouse could be treated as making a gift of all or one-half of the proceeds when the insured spouse dies and proceeds are paid to the child.[3] When the noninsured spouse, as beneficiary, receives his or her community share or more, no gift is imputed to the noninsured spouse of amounts also payable to a third-party beneficiary unless there is evidence of donative intent.[4]

217. Are death-benefit-only (DBO) plans subject to gift tax?

No, at least not at the time of death. Revenue Ruling 92-68[5] revoked Revenue Ruling 81-31,[6] in which the IRS treated an employee as making a gift of the benefit from a DBO plan in the year of the employee's death.[7] Note that neither Revenue Ruling 81-31 nor *Est. of DiMarco v. Comm.* addressed whether an employee should be treated each year as (1) receiving compensation equal to the value of providing a death benefit or survivor income benefit to an eligible survivor if the employee died during the year, and (2) transferring such value to the eligible survivor. The use of the annual exclusion and the marital deduction might protect such a gift from any gift tax. (See Q 101 for estate tax aspects.)

Gift Tax Annual Exclusion

218. May the annual exclusion of $15,000 for gifts to each donee be applied against gifts of life insurance policies and premiums?

Yes, if the gifts are made in such manner that they are gifts of present interests.

The annual exclusion of $15,000 (up from $14,000 in 2013-2017[8], see Appendix D) is not available for gifts of future interests (Q 219). If the gift of the policy is a gift of a present interest, premiums subsequently paid by the donor also will qualify for the exclusion (Q 223). The annual exclusion is effectively $30,000 in 2020 (2 × $15,000, see Appendix D) if the donor

1. Treas. Reg. §25.2511-1(h)(9).
2. Rev. Rul. 48, 1953-1 CB 392 (La.); Rev. Rul. 232, 1953-2 CB 268 (Texas); *Comm. v. Chase Manhattan Bank*, 259 F.2d 231 (5th Cir. 1958).
3. See Rev. Rul. 94-69, 1994-2 CB 241, revoking Rev. Rul. 48, above; Rev. Rul. 232, above; Rev. Rul. 2003-40, 2003-17 IRB 813.
4. *Kaufman v. U.S.*, 462 F.2d 439 (5th Cir. 1972).
5. Rev. Rul. 92-68, 1992-2 CB 257, revoking Rev. Rul. 81-31, below.
6. Rev. Rul. 81-31, 1981-1 CB 475.
7. *Est. of DiMarco v. Comm.*, 87 TC 653 (1986), acq. in result, 1990-2 CB 1.
8. Rev. Proc. 2017-58, Rev. Proc. 2018-57.

makes a gift to a third party with the consent of his or her spouse (Q 117). For gifts from one spouse to another, see Q 114.[1]

> *Example.* Donor, a widower, assigns a policy on his life to his son in 2020. The policy's value is $15,000. The gift tax annual exclusion of $15,000 (in 2020, see Appendix D) can be applied against the gift of the policy. The donor may continue to pay the annual premium of $1,500 in subsequent years and need not report the premium payments for gift tax purposes so long as they fall within the gift tax annual exclusion for such subsequent year (unless he gives his son other gifts in any one year that together with the premium payments exceed the annual exclusion for such year).

When the value of a policy exceeds the annual exclusion, the insurance company may consent to split it into two or more smaller policies. By giving the donee one policy in each of several succeeding years, the entire value can fall within the annual exclusions. In some instances, however, such a split would result in a higher premium.

219. When is the gift of a life insurance policy considered the gift of a future interest that deprives the donor of the gift tax annual exclusion?

A future interest is created when restrictions are placed upon the donee's right to receive benefits or to exercise ownership rights under the policy. The gift of a policy is not considered a gift of a future interest merely because the obligations under the contract are payable at some time in the future. However, a future interest in these contractual obligations can be created by limitations contained in a trust or other instrument of transfer used in effecting a gift (Q 159).[2] (But see Q 160 for gifts in trust to minors.) A gift of a policy to a corporation is a gift of a future interest to its shareholders.[3] In one case, gifts made to individual partnership capital accounts were treated as gifts of a present interest that qualified for the gift tax annual exclusion because the partners were free to make immediate withdrawals of the gifts from their capital accounts.[4]

220. Is the annual exclusion available when an insured transfers ownership of a life insurance policy to two or more donees jointly?

No. If joint action is required to exercise ownership rights in the policy, it is a gift of a future interest.[5]

Planning Point: If gifts of premiums are subsequently made by the donor they should be made separately to each donee and the donees may then pay the premiums to the insurance company. That way the gifts of premiums will qualify for the annual gift tax exclusion.

---

221. Will the gift of a life insurance policy fail to qualify for the annual exclusion merely because the policy has no cash value?

No.[6]

---

1. IRC Sec. 2503(b), Treas. Reg. §§25.2503-3(a), 25.2503-3(c)(Ex. 6).
2. Treas. Reg. §25.2503-3.
3. Rev. Rul. 71-443, 1971-2 CB 337.
4. *Wooley v. U.S.*, 90-1 USTC ¶60,013 (S.D. Ind. 1990).
5. *Skouras v. Comm.*, 188 F.2d 831 (2nd Cir. 1951).
6. Rev. Rul. 55-408, 1955-1 CB 113.

222. Does the outright gift of a life insurance policy qualify for the gift tax annual exclusion, even if the gift is to a minor?

Yes.

The exclusion can be applied against the value of the policy at the time of the gift and to subsequent premium payments.[1] An outright gift of a policy to a minor qualifies for the exclusion even though a guardian is not appointed.[2] A gift of life insurance under a Uniform Gifts to Minors Act or a Uniform Transfers to Minors Act generally qualifies for the gift tax annual exclusion. All but a few states have modified the Uniform Act to include gifts of life insurance. Any transfer of property to a minor under statutes patterned after either the model act or the uniform act constitutes a complete gift for federal gift tax purposes to the extent of the full fair market value of the property transferred. Such a gift generally qualifies for the gift tax annual exclusion authorized by IRC Section 2503(b).[3] If the subject of the gift is life insurance, its "full fair market value" would presumably be established by the same rules applicable to gifts of life insurance generally (Q 119).

223. When a life insurance policy has been given away, are premiums subsequently paid by the donor gifts of a present interest qualifying for the annual exclusion or are they a future interest?

The payment of premiums is a gift of a present interest if the gift of the policy was a present interest gift. Likewise, the premium is a future interest gift if the gift of the policy was a future interest gift (Q 212).[4]

224. If an insured, within three years of his or her death, makes a gift of life insurance on which the insured pays a gift tax, is the gift also subject to estate tax?

Both the insurance proceeds and the gift tax paid will be included in the gross estate.[5]

Disability Provisions Under Life Policies

225. Are premiums paid for disability provisions under a life insurance policy deductible as medical expenses?

No.[6]

1. IRC Sec. 2503(b); Treas. Reg. §§25.2503-3(c)(Ex. 6), 25.2511-1(a), 25.2511-1(g).
2. *Baer v. Comm.*, 2 TCM (CCH) 285 (1943), aff'd 149 F.2d 637 (8th Cir. 1945); Rev. Rul. 54-400, 1954-2 CB 319; see *Daniels v. Comm.*, 10 TCM (CCH) 147 (1951).
3. Rev. Rul. 56-86, 1956-1 CB 449; Rev. Rul. 59-357, 1959-2 CB 212; Rev. Rul. 73-287, 1973-2 CB 321.
4. *Baer v. Comm.*, ¶43,294 P-H TC Memo (1943), aff'd 149 F.2d 637 (8th Cir. 1945); *Roberts v. Comm.*, 2 TC 679 (1943); *Comm. v. Boeing*, 123 F.2d 86 (9th Cir. 1941); *Bolton v. Comm.*, 1 TC 717 (1943).
5. IRC Sec. 2035.
6. IRC Sec. 213(d)(1).

226. Is disability income payable under the provisions of a personal life insurance policy included in gross income?

No. Benefits received under a disability rider are tax-exempt as "amounts received through accident or health insurance ... for personal injuries or sickness." There is no limit on the amount of disability income that can be received tax-free.[1] Benefits are exempt whether received by the insured, or by a person or corporation having an insurable interest in the insured.[2]

227. Are life insurance premiums that have been waived because of the insured's disability taxable income to the insured?

No. When waived, the premiums are exempt as "amounts received through accident or health insurance ... for personal injuries or sickness."[3] However, the Tax Court seems to have indicated that they are not constructively received by the insured. Although not directly addressed in the case, apparently the waived premiums would also not be taxable to the insured since they were not constructively received by the insured.[4]

Note that because premiums paid for a supplementary benefit such as a waiver of a premium must be excluded from premium cost (Q 533), a policy on which premiums have been waived for a period of years would have a lower cost basis than a similar policy where the taxpayer paid the premiums.

228. If a corporation attaches a disability income rider to a key person life insurance policy, what are the tax consequences to the corporation and to the key person?

Where the employee is a designated payee of the disability income, the tax consequences are uncertain. However, it would seem that the disability rider should be treated as accident and health insurance, separable from the life insurance, and that the results would be as follows: the corporation could deduct, as a business expense, the premiums paid for the disability income coverage;[5] the premiums would not be taxable to the key person;[6] and the disability income would be taxable to the key person.[7] A tax credit may be available to the key person.

If the disability income is payable to the corporation, the corporation cannot deduct the premium payments,[8] but the disability income is tax-exempt to the corporation.[9] If the corporation uses the disability income to make disability retirement payments to the key person, it would

---

1. IRC Sec. 104(a)(3).
2. *Castner Garage, Ltd. v. Comm.*, 43 BTA 1 (1940), acq.
3. IRC Sec. 104(a)(3).
4. *Est. of Wong Wing Non v. Comm.*, 18 TC 205 (1952).
5. IRC Sec. 162(a).
6. IRC Sec. 106(a).
7. IRC Sec. 104(a)(3).
8. IRC Sec. 265(a)(1).
9. IRC Sec. 104(a)(3); *Castner Garage, Ltd. v. Comm.*, 43 BTA 1 (1940), acq.; *Rugby Prod. Ltd. v. Comm.*, 100 TC 531 (1993); Rev. Rul. 66-262, 1966-2 CB 105.

seem that the corporation could deduct the payments as a compensation expense. The payments would be taxable to the key person,[1] but the key person might be eligible for a tax credit.

Irrevocable Life Insurance Trusts (ILITs)

229. What type of trust is an irrevocable life insurance trust (ILIT)?

An irrevocable life insurance trust (ILIT) is a trust funded primarily by life insurance which cannot be modified, amended or revoked without the permission of the beneficiary. It is mechanism used in estate planning in which a grantor effectively removes all of his rights of ownership to the assets of the trust.[2]

230. Who are the parties to an irrevocable life insurance trust (ILIT)?

Typical parties to an irrevocable life insurance trust include a grantor, trustees and beneficiaries. The grantor typically creates and establishes the funding mechanism for the trust. In the case of an ILIT, the funding source would be a life insurance policy.

Gifts or transfers made to the ILIT are permanent, and the grantor relinquishes control over transferred assets to the trustee. The trustee manages the ILIT and is the individual holding the property in trust. Beneficiaries are those entitled to receive the benefits of the trust.[3]

231. How does an irrevocable life insurance trust work?

The irrevocable life insurance trust is created during the grantor's life. The trustee purchases a policy on the life of the grantor. The trust should be the owner and premium payor of the policy and the grantor/ insured should have no ownership interests in the life insurance policy. The beneficiaries of the trust are often family members of the grantor—a spouse, children, grandchildren, and spouses of children and grandchildren.

Because the trust is funded with a life insurance policy on the grantor's life, funding may be accomplished using an existing policy that the grantor gifts to the trust. Unless the insurance policy is paid up, the trustee will have to pay the annual premiums. The grantor usually makes annual transfers of cash to the trust so that the trustee can pay the premiums.[4] These annual transfers are gifts, meaning that the gift tax annual exclusion may be available to shelter the annual cash transfers from the federal gift tax up to the annual exclusion amount ($15,000 for 2018-2020).[5]

Planning Point: The grantor can also make a gift of an existing life insurance policy to the trust, but the insured must survive for at least three years in order to keep the policy out of his or her taxable estate. This provision is known as the "three year rule" or the "bringback rule," as it "brings back" assets transferred within three years of a decedent's death into his or her gross estate. *Desiree Day, J.D.*

---

1. IRC Sec. 104(a)(3).
2. https://www.irs.gov/tax-professionals/tax-code-regulations-and-official-guidance.
3. Restatement (Second) of Trusts §3 (1959).
4. IRC Sec. 677.
5. https://www.irs.gov/businesses/small-businesses-self-employed/frequently-asked-questions-on-gift-taxes.

232. Are life insurance proceeds from an irrevocable trust taxable? How can an ILIT be used as an estate planning tool?

While life insurance proceeds are an income tax-free benefit,[1] they are includable in the insured's estate for estate tax purposes if the proceeds are payable: (1) to the estate, either directly or indirectly; or (2) to named beneficiaries, if the insured possessed any incidents of ownership in the policy at the time of death.[2]

For individuals with a large estate tax liability, using insurance proceeds can worsen this tax burden by inflating the insured's gross estate for federal estate tax purposes.[3] Using an ILIT can allow death proceeds from the life insurance to pass into the trust, where funds can be distributed income tax-free to the trust beneficiaries as directed by the trust documents. By avoiding the insured's estate, insurance proceeds in an ILIT do not increase the estate of the decedent, thus avoiding additional estate tax.

233. What are some of the advantages of using an irrevocable life insurance trust?

An ILIT can present many advantages to individuals who possess significant amounts of life insurance. One of the primary benefits is that the ILIT strategy can help reduce estate tax liability, as discussed in Q 232, as it removes life insurance from the decedent's gross estate. Further, the ILIT strategy may reduce the amount of insurance coverage needed by the insured, since his or her estate tax bill will be lowered due to funding through an ILIT.

Planning Point: As an example, assume that an individual dies and leaves a $12.18 million estate. $1 million of that amount is life insurance and there is an $11.18 million estate tax exemption. The estate would then be responsible for estate taxes on $1 million of the total gross estate. Assuming the estate tax is 40 percent, this estate tax liability translates to $400,000. Having an ILIT would remove the $1 million life insurance proceeds from the taxable estate. Therefore, the $400,000 tax liability that would otherwise be assumed is eliminated. *Desiree Day, J.D.*

Creating an ILIT also helps the insured protect the cash value of the life insurance policy from creditors. In an ILIT, the grantor no longer legally owns the assets or controls the trust. Due to this loss of ownership and control, a future creditor cannot satisfy a judgement against assets held in an ILIT.

Planning Point: It is critical to understand that the extent of creditor protection in an ILIT is largely based on state creditor regulations. Clients should be sure to consult their local laws. *Desiree Day, J.D.*

Another advantage of an ILIT is that it can allow the grantor to control when, how and why the beneficiaries receive the proceeds of the life insurance policy. This is set out in the trust documents. Upon the insured's death, the life insurance proceeds will pay to the trust. The trust documents will then detail the disbursement of the funds.

1. IRC Sec. 101(a)(1).
2. IRC Sec. 2042.
3. IRC Sec. 2206.

An ILIT will also help protect the benefits of a beneficiary who is receiving government aid, and prevents the court from controlling insurance proceeds if beneficiary is incapacitated. This can be accomplished by naming the trust as the beneficiary of the insurance policy. Most insurance companies will not knowingly pay to an incompetent or disabled person, but if the trust is the beneficiary, the trustee can use the funds to provide for that individual without court interference.

234. Who should serve as trustee of an ILIT and what role does the trustee play?

The role of a trustee is extremely critical in an ILIT if the tax advantages of the structure are to be realized. The integrity of the individual or the institution must be a primary priority because of their role as fiduciary and controller of the trust. The trustee can be the trust creator or family members, unrelated person(s), an institutional or corporate trustee such as a trust department of a banking institution or any combination of the these options. When choosing a trustee, it is important to consider the experience, knowledge and expertise of the trustee.

The trustee should be one with the experience and capacity to handle the types of investments contained in the trust, and must have the necessary skills to sufficiently administer the trust for the benefit of the trust beneficiaries.

Choosing the appropriate trustee also dictates whether the income from the trust will be treated as taxable income to the grantor. This can occur because the trustee has a relationship with the grantor that is prohibited by statute or because the trustee administers the trust in a way designed to circumvent tax regulation and benefit the grantor.[1] This problem will occur if the trustee is considered to be related or a subordinate party to the grantor.[2] However, this problem will not occur if the related or subordinate party is also considered to be an adverse party. An adverse party is one that has a beneficial interest in the trust, one who has the power of appointment over trust assets or one whose interest would be adversely affected by the exercise or the non-exercise of a power held by the non-adverse party.[3]

235. What are the types of life insurance policies that can be used to fund an ILIT?

When funding an ILIT, various forms of life insurance can be used that will minimize both income taxation and estate taxation at death. The first type of life insurance is known as term life insurance. This can be in the form of annual renewable term, decreasing term or level premium term, but the primary distinguishing feature of term life insurance is that it will only last for a designated amount of time. It is rare to fund an ILIT with this type of insurance because of the short duration of the policies, which makes it possible that the grantor will outlive the funding mechanism of the trust.

1. IRC Sec. 671(a), Rev. Rul. 2004-64, 2004-2 CB 7.
2. IRC Sec. 674(c).
3. IRC Sec. 672(a-b).

Another type of life insurance that is more commonly used to fund an ILIT is whole life insurance. Whole life insurance can be in the form of single premium whole life insurance (in which a lump sum payment is paid upfront) or a policy on which premiums are paid on a permanent basis until the policy is "paid up." There is a buildup of cash value in the policy which varies by insurance carrier and by year. Depending upon the chosen policy, universal life insurance and indexed universal life insurance have a unique feature which allows the premiums to be paid on a level (equal) basis, or the premiums can be adjustable. This type of policy always carries a cash value that is built up within the account, and this cash value is typically linked to a particular fixed rate or index option(s).

Variable life insurance is another type of insurance that can be used to fund an ILIT. Variable life insurance premium structures are similar to the universal and indexed universal life policies, but variable life insurance policies are distinguished by the cash build-up, which is dependent upon the performance of the investment portfolio of the insurance company.[1]

Planning Point: It is important to be thoroughly aware of the variation of insurance products that can be provided and the insurance carrier to be used. Various ratings companies such as AM Best or Standard & Poor's are vital resources to be used in determining the financial strength of various carriers. *Desiree Day, J.D.*

236. What are the gift tax implications of making a gift to an ILIT in the form of premiums paid on the life insurance policy?

Gifts made to an ILIT typically come in the form of the grantor paying premiums on the life insurance policy, and must be made correctly in order to avoid creating gift tax liability. If the amount of the premiums is directly transferred to the trustee in cash, gift tax liability can arise. A grantor can make annual tax-free gifts up to annual gift tax exclusion amount ($15,000 in 2018-2020, or $30,000 for spouses that consent to gift splitting)[2] to each beneficiary of the trust.

For the premium payments to qualify for the annual gift tax exclusion amount, rather than the grantor making a gift directly to each beneficiary to pay the premiums, the funds are given to the trustee for the benefit of each beneficiary.[3] The trustee then notifies each beneficiary that a gift has been received on their behalf and the trustee pays the premium on the insurance policy. To avoid gift tax liability, it also is crucial that the trustee, using what is known as a "*Crummey*" letter,[4] notify the beneficiaries of the trust of their right to withdraw a share of the contributions within a thirty-day period. After thirty days have expired, the trustee can then use the contributions to pay the insurance policy premium. The *Crummey* letter qualifies the transfer for the annual gift tax exclusion by making the gift a present interest gift (rather than future interest gift) thus avoiding the need in most cases to file a gift tax return.[5]

1. IRC Sec. 7702.
2. See IRS FAQ, available at https://www.irs.gov/businesses/small-businesses-self-employed/frequently-asked-questions-on-gift-taxes.
3. Let. Rul. 9809032.
4. *Crummey v. Commissioner*, 397 F.2d 82, 68-2 U.S. Tax Cas. (CCH) ¶12541, 22 A.F.T.R.2d (P-H) ¶6023 (9th Cir. 1968).
5. Treas. Reg. §25.2512-6(a).

237. What are some of the differences between a funded and unfunded irrevocable life insurance trust (ILIT)?

An ILIT may be either "funded" or "unfunded." In a funded trust, the trust owns income-producing assets, such as securities, in addition to the life insurance policy. Income generated by these underlying investment assets may be used to pay the insurance premiums. The grantor not only transfers the life insurance policy to the trust, but also transfers other property to the trust from which the premium payments may be made. The major drawback of the funded life insurance trust is that the trust income may be taxed to the grantor if it can be used to pay premiums on a policy on the life of the grantor or his or her spouse.

In an unfunded trust, the only asset owned by the trust is the life insurance policy. The trustee has no other property in the trust with which to pay premiums, and is dependent on annual cash gifts from the grantor. This results in the need to transfer funds into the trust to be used to pay the premiums on the policy. Gifts of premium dollars to the trust by the grantor may be sheltered from gift tax using the annual gift tax exclusion. Gifts to an unfunded trust, however, will be considered present interest gifts, qualifying for the annual gift tax exclusion only to the extent that the trust beneficiaries are given immediate withdrawal rights with respect to the amounts transferred to the trust (see Q 237 on gifting as a method for funding an ILIT).

238. How can an irrevocable life insurance trust (ILIT) be terminated?

In most situations, termination procedures are predicated upon the trust language coupled with any applicable specific state regulations, but there are some general guidelines that can be followed when a grantor wishes to terminate an ILIT. There are many reasons to terminate an ILIT, such as when the life insurance policy has become too expensive to maintain or the policy has lapsed. The grantor may also wish to terminate if he or she is no longer satisfied with the terms of the trust, or if the federal estate tax exemption has increased substantially since the trust was created (or the grantors estate has decreased) and as a result, no estate tax issues exist to warrant continuation of the ILIT.

A grantor can ensure that his or her ILIT can be terminated by including terms in the governing trust document to terminate it. To allow for flexibility in terminating the trust, the governing instrument may contain a provision enabling the trustee or a "special" trustee to terminate it for specified reasons. This type of provision should be coupled with trust language outlining the provisions of termination. Even with this language, there is no guarantee that a court would agree that the ILIT should be terminated if the termination was challenged.

There are also tax considerations to be weighed when terminating an ILIT. Generally, the proceeds of a life insurance policy that are received due to the death of the insured are not taxable. But if the policy is sold during the insured's lifetime, tax liability may arise under the transfer for value rule unless one of the exceptions to the rule can be satisfied (see Q 279 for more information on the transfer for value rule).[1]

1. IRC Sec. 101.

PART II: GROUP TERM LIFE INSURANCE

239. How does the Department of Labor fiduciary standard impact advisors who sell life insurance or disability insurance?

Editor's Note: The applicability date of the fiduciary rule was repeatedly delayed, finally being vacated entirely by the 5th Circuit. As of the date of this publication, the DOL has yet to release a replacement rule.

While advisors who provide advice relating to health savings accounts will be covered by the Department of Labor's heightened fiduciary standard, certain related products, such as disability and term life insurance policies, are expressly excluded from the definition of investment property and are thus not subject to the fiduciary standard. This is the case to the extent that these products do not contain an investment component. As a result, presumably, permanent life insurance policies that do contain an investment component will be subject to the DOL fiduciary rule.[1]

240. What are the tax benefits of employer provided group term life insurance?

An employer may provide employees with up to $50,000 of group term life insurance protection each year without cost to employees. The taxable value of group term insurance in excess of the exclusion amount generally is determined under a table (Table I) provided by the IRS (Q 246). The exclusion generally is not available unless the insurance provided under the plan satisfies the definition of group term life insurance (Q 241, Q 244). If insurance provided does not meet the definition of group term life insurance, an employer's premium cost is includable in employee income.

If a plan provides group term life insurance that is discriminatory, the exclusion is not available to key employees (Q 249). The taxable cost to a key employee of the entire amount of insurance under a discriminatory plan is the higher of the actual cost or the cost under Table I.

A premium paid by an employer is deductible. Group term life insurance may be provided under term policies or under policies providing a permanent benefit (Q 254). An employer also may provide permanent life insurance to employees on a group basis (Q 257, Q 258).

A death benefit of group life insurance, whether term or permanent, generally is excludable from a beneficiary's income (Q 259).

241. What is group term life insurance?

For group term life insurance to qualify for special tax exclusion by employees, the life insurance must meet the following four conditions:

1. 29 CFR 2510.3-21(g)(4).

General Death Benefit

First, it must provide a general death benefit that is excludable from gross income under IRC Section 101(a). Under the regulations, travel insurance and accident and health insurance including amounts payable under a double indemnity clause rider do not provide a general death benefit.[1] Employer contributions for these benefits are contributions to a health plan under IRC Section 106 instead of Section 79 (Q 332).

Group of Employees

Second, it must be provided to a group of employees as compensation for personal services performed as employees. A group of employees are all of the employees of an employer, or fewer than all if membership in the group is determined solely on the basis of age, marital status, or factors related to employment including membership in a union, duties performed, compensation received, and length of service. See Q 242 for a detailed discussion of the group requirement.

Employer Provided Policy

Third, the insurance must be provided under a policy carried directly or indirectly by an employer. A policy meets this requirement if an employer pays any part of the cost, directly or through another person, or arranges for payment by employees and charges at least one employee less than his or her Table I cost and at least one other employee more than his or her Table I cost. The policy can be a master policy or a group of individual policies.

Regulations define the term policy as including all obligations of an insurer that are offered or that are available to a group of employees because of the employment relationship, even if they are in separate documents.[2] An employer may elect to treat obligations not providing permanent benefits as separate policies if the premiums are properly allocated. An employer also may elect to treat an obligation providing permanent insurance as a separate policy if:

(1) the employee buys the policy directly from the insurer and pays the full cost;

(2) the employer's part in the sale is limited to selection of the insurer, the type of coverage, and certain sales assistance, such as providing employee lists to the insurer, permitting use of the employer's premises for solicitation, and collecting premiums through payroll deduction;

(3) the obligation is sold on the same terms and in substantial amounts to individuals who do not purchase, and whose employers do not purchase, any other obligations from the insurer; and

(4) no employer-provided benefit is conditioned on purchase of the obligation.[3]

1. Treas. Reg. §1.79-1(f)(3).
2. Treas. Reg. §1.79-0.
3. Treas. Reg. §1.79-0.

Computed under a Formula

Fourth, the amount of insurance provided each employee must be computed under a formula that precludes individual selection of such amounts. The formula must be based on factors such as age, years of service, compensation, or position. This requirement may be satisfied even if the amount of insurance provided is determined under alternate schedules based on the amount each employee elects to contribute. The amount of insurance under each schedule must be computed under a formula that precludes individual selection.

Where one factor, percentage of compensation, of a two factor formula covered all employees but one, and the other factor, position, applied to only one position held by only one individual, the president, the Tax Court held that the formula did not preclude individual selection of jumbo coverage for the president.[1]

On the other hand, a formula based on positions that included several individuals in each category was held to preclude individual selection.[2]

Where the amount of an employee's insurance protection under a group program is reduced by the amount of the employee's death benefit under the employer's pension plan, the group protection is not group term life insurance because the formula for determining the amount is based on a factor other than, and not comparable to, age, years of service, compensation, or position.[3]

A provision in a group term life insurance plan that offered employees the option to reduce their coverage by certain amounts, but not below $50,000, was found not to preclude individual selection of the insurance amounts.[4]

Instead of a lump sum settlement of death benefits, an employer may select payment of equal installments over a fixed period of time without affecting the plan's status as group term life insurance.[5]

Federal group term life insurance covering federal civilian employees qualifies as group term life insurance.[6]

Term life insurance to be provided after retirement that is offered by certain educational institutions under a cafeteria plan is treated as group term life insurance (Q 3501).[7]

If employer-provided term life insurance does not qualify as group term insurance, the premium paid by the employer is includable in the employee's income.[8]

1. *Towne v. Comm.*, 78 TC 791 (1982). See also *Whitcomb v. Comm.*, 84-1 USTC ¶9472 (1st Cir. 1984).
2. *N.W.D. Investment Co. v. Comm.*, TC Memo 1982-564.
3. Let. Rul. 8342008.
4. Let. Ruls. 9701027, 9319026.
5. Rev. Rul. 77-163, 1977-1 CB 18.
6. Rev. Rul. 55-357, 1955-1 CB 13.
7. IRC Sec. 125(d)(2)(C).
8. Treas. Reg. §1.61-2(d)(2)(ii)(A); Let. Rul. 8636018.

If an insurer providing group term life insurance also makes available a permanent benefit to members of the group because of the employment relationship, see Q 254.

242. Who is an employee for purposes of determining whether group term life insurance benefits are excludable?

In order to qualify as group term life insurance, the benefits must be provided to a group of employees as compensation for personal services performed as employees. A group of employees are all of the employees of an employer, or fewer than all if membership in the group is determined solely on the basis of age, marital status, or factors related to employment including membership in a union, duties performed, compensation received, and length of service.

The purchase of something other than group term life insurance generally is not a factor related to employment. For example, credit life insurance provided to all employees who purchase automobiles is not provided to a group within the definition, because membership is not determined solely on the basis of age, marital status, or factors related to employment.

Participation in an employer's pension, profit sharing, or accident and health plan is considered a factor related to employment, even if employee contributions are required. Ownership of stock in an employer corporation is not a factor related to employment. Participation in an employer's stock bonus plan, however, may be a factor related to employment. A group of employees may include stockholder-employees, other than more-than-2 percent shareholders in an S corporation.[1] If a group of employees consists of fewer than ten employees, see Q 244.

A person is an employee if his or her relationship to the person for whom services are performed is that of employer-employee, or if he or she formerly performed services as an employee, except to the extent the person currently performs services as an independent contractor.[2] Insurance on the life of a self-employed person, whether he or she is the employer or someone who performs services for the employer as an independent contractor, is not excludable. Thus, insurance for a partner or sole proprietor is not excludable even though he or she is included in the coverage for employees.

S corporation employees who own more than 2 percent of the outstanding stock or more than 2 percent of the total voting power of the S corporation are treated as partners; therefore, insurance is not excludable to the extent it covers such stockholders.[3] Other S corporation employees may take the exclusion.

Insurance provided for an individual in his or her capacity as a corporate owner or as a director does not qualify for the exclusion.[4]

Insurance for a commission salesperson is not excludable unless an employer-employee relationship exists between the salesperson and the company that pays the premiums.[5] Full-time

1. Treas. Reg. §1.79-0.
2. Treas. Reg. §1.79-0.
3. IRC Sec. 1372.
4. *Whipple Chrysler-Plymouth v. Comm.*, TC Memo 1972-55; *Enright v. Comm.*, 56 TC 1261 (1971).
5. Rev. Rul. 56-400, 1956-2 CB 116; see also IRC Sec. 3508.

life insurance salespersons who are classified as employees for Social Security purposes are considered employees for group term.[1]

243. Is supplemental life insurance coverage treated as group term life insurance?

Supplemental group term life insurance paid for entirely by employees was not considered group term life insurance under IRC Section 79 where the supplemental policy and the basic group term life insurance paid for by the employer were not considered the same policy because they were provided by unrelated insurers.[2]

Where employee-paid supplemental group term life insurance was purchased from the same insurer providing basic employer-paid group term life insurance, the supplemental and basic coverages were treated as one policy under IRC Section 79. Because premiums were allocated properly, the employer could elect to treat the coverage as three separate policies (basic coverage, supplemental smoker coverage, and supplemental nonsmoker coverage) for purposes of deciding whether the policies were carried directly or indirectly by the employer. Thus, the employees had no imputed income from the supplemental coverage.[3]

In another private ruling, supplemental life insurance coverage offered by a VEBA was considered part of an employer's policy issued by the same insurer, but the employer could elect to treat it as a separate policy because there were no permanent benefits and the premiums were properly allocated between the VEBA's supplementary coverage and the employer's coverage. The coverage under the VEBA's policy was not provided directly or indirectly by the employer because the employer was not paying any part of the coverage and because all rates charged the participants were less than the Table I rates.[4]

In a similar situation, a supplemental employee group term life insurance program provided through a VEBA was not treated as a policy carried directly or indirectly by an employer. Thus, assuming that the employer elected to treat its basic life insurance program and its supplemental group term insurance as separate policies, no income was imputed to employees under IRC Section 79(a) who purchased supplemental coverage.[5]

244. Is term insurance provided to a group of fewer than ten employees "group" term insurance?

Yes.

As a general rule, life insurance provided to a group cannot qualify as group term life insurance for income tax purposes unless, at some time during the calendar year, it is provided to at least ten full-time employees who are members of the group of employees of the employer.

1. IRC Sec. 7701(a)(20); Treas. Reg. §1.79-0.
2. Let. Rul. 8518037. See also Let. Rul. 8820022.
3. Let. Ruls. 9227019, 9149033. See also Let. Rul. 200033011.
4. Let. Rul. 8906023.
5. Let. Ruls. 9611058, 9549029, 201350032.

Insurance for fewer than ten employees, however, may qualify as group term life insurance if:

(1) it is provided for all full-time employees; and

(2) the amount of protection is computed either as a uniform percentage of compensation or on the basis of coverage brackets established by an insurer under which no bracket exceeds 2½ times the next lower bracket and the lowest bracket is at least 10 percent of the highest bracket. Eligibility and amount of coverage may be based on evidence of insurability but determined solely on the basis of a medical questionnaire completed by the employee and not requiring a physical examination.[1] Additional voluntary medical information may not be made the basis of a premium rate determination.[2]

For the purposes of determining how many are included in a group, and if all of them are eligible, employees who elect not to receive insurance are considered included even if they would have to contribute toward the cost of term insurance. If an employee must contribute to the cost of benefits other than term insurance, such as permanent benefits, to get term insurance, the employee is not counted in determining if term life insurance is provided to ten or more employees if the employee declined the term insurance.[3]

Although bona fide brackets that are temporarily empty probably do not disqualify a plan, a bracket not used since a plan's inception the previous year was disregarded in one case with the result that protection provided in the bracket immediately above was more than 2½ times that provided in the bracket immediately below.[4]

If evidence of insurability is not a factor, then insurance not meeting the above requirements, which provides protection for fewer than ten full-time employees, may nevertheless qualify if: (1) it is provided under a common plan to employees of two or more unrelated employers, and (2) insurance is restricted to, but mandatory for, all employees of an employer who belong to or are represented by a particular organization, such as a union, that carries on substantial activities other than obtaining insurance.

Insurance for fewer than ten full-time employees will not be disqualified merely because, under the terms of a policy, no insurance is provided for those employed less than six months or who are part-time employees, that is, whose customary employment is not more than twenty hours per week or five months in any calendar year, or those who are age sixty-five or older.[5]

For purposes of determining how many employees are provided insurance, all life insurance provided under policies carried by an employer is taken into account even if the policies are with different insurers.[6] This gives support to the concept that supplemental coverage for

1. Treas. Reg. §1.79-1(c).
2. Rev. Rul. 75-528, 1975-2 CB 35.
3. Treas. Reg. §1.79-1(c)(5).
4. Rev. Rul. 80-220, 1980-2 CB 35.
5. Treas. Reg. §1.79-1(c)(4).
6. Treas. Reg. §1.79-1(c).

fewer than ten may be superimposed on an existing group term life insurance program covering more than ten employees without taking into consideration the special requirements for groups of fewer than ten.[1]

245. Are premiums paid for group term life insurance deductible business expenses?

Yes.

Premiums paid by an employer for group term insurance on the lives of employees are deductible.[2] This is so even if a plan discriminates in favor of key employees (Q 249).

A corporation may deduct premiums it pays for coverage on the lives of commission salespersons irrespective of whether an employer-employee relationship exists between the salesperson and the corporation.[3]

No deduction will be allowed for the cost of coverage on the life of an employee if an employer is directly or indirectly a beneficiary under a policy.[4]

If group term proceeds are to be used to fund a buy-sell agreement between stockholders of a corporation, the IRS may deny the corporation a business expense deduction for its premium payments (Q 299).

Contributions will not be deductible unless, when considered with all an employee's other compensation, they are reasonable (Q 3519).

Current deduction of contributions to a welfare benefit fund (Q 4081) to provide group life insurance to employees is strictly limited. Contributions to a welfare benefit fund to provide life insurance benefits to employees are subject to certain requirements (Q 4083).

246. Is the cost of group term life insurance coverage provided by an employer taxable income to an insured employee?

The cost of up to $50,000 of group term life insurance coverage generally is tax-exempt. The cost of coverage in excess of $50,000 is taxable to employees. An employee who is working for more than one employer must combine all group term coverage and is entitled to exclude the cost for no more than $50,000. If an employee contributes toward the cost of the insurance, all of the employee's contribution for coverage up to $50,000 and for excess coverage is allocable to coverage in excess of $50,000. In other words, the employee may subtract his or her full contribution from the amount that would otherwise be taxable to the employee.[5] The employee cannot carry over from year to year any unused portion of his or her contributions.

1. See also Rev. Rul. 70-162, 1970-1 CB 21.
2. IRC Sec. 162(a); Rev. Rul. 56-400, 1956-2 CB 116.
3. Rev. Rul. 56-400, supra.
4. IRC Sec. 264(a).
5. IRC Sec. 79(a).

The cost of coverage in excess of $50,000, which is the amount that is taxable to an employee, is to be calculated on a monthly basis. The steps are as follows:

(1) Find the total amount of group term life insurance coverage for the employee in each calendar month of the employee's taxable year, and if a change occurs during any month, take the average at the beginning and end of the month;

(2) subtract $50,000 from each month's coverage;

(3) to the balance, if any, for each month, apply the appropriate rate from the tables of monthly premium rates (below);

(4) from the sum of the monthly costs, subtract total employee contributions for the year, if any.[1]

The cost is determined on the basis of the life insurance protection provided to an employee during the employee's tax year, without regard to when the premiums are paid by an employer.

To compute the cost of excess group term life insurance coverage, the rates in the table immediately below should be used.[2]

*Uniform Premiums for $1,000 of Group Term Life Insurance Protection**

Rates Applicable to Cost of Group-Term Life Insurance Provided After June 30, 1999

5-Year Age Bracket	Cost per $1,000 of Protection for One-Month Period
Under 25	$0.05
25 to 29	.06
30 to 34	.08
35 to 39	.09
40 to 44	.10
45 to 49	.15
50 to 54	.23
55 to 59	.43
60 to 64	.66
65 to 69	1.27
70 and above	2.06

* In using the above table, the age of the employee is the employee's attained age on the last day of the employee's taxable year.

1. Treas. Reg. §1.79-3.
2. Treas. Reg. §1.79-3(d)(2).

The exemption of the cost of up to $50,000 of group term life is not available with respect to group term insurance purchased under a qualified employees' trust or annuity plan. The provisions of IRC Section 72(m)(3) and Treasury Regulation Section 1.72-16 apply to the cost of the protection purchased under qualified plans and no part of the cost is excludable from an employee's gross income (Q 3933).[1]

Premiums for supplemental insurance in excess of $50,000 provided by an employer under a group term insurance plan are not taxable to an insured employee when paid by a family member to whom the employee has assigned the insurance.[2] If the cost of the coverage in excess of $50,000 is shared by an employer and assignee, the employer's portion of the cost is includable in the insured employee's gross income.[3]

The exemption for the first $50,000 is not available to key employees if a plan discriminates in their favor (Q 249).

247. Is group term life insurance coverage on the lives of an employee's spouse and dependents taxable income to the employee?

Group term coverage on the lives of an employee's spouse and dependents is not included in the otherwise applicable $50,000 exemption (see Q 246). The cost of this coverage will be income-tax free, however, if the face amount does not exceed $2,000.[4] In determining whether coverage in excess of $2,000 is excludable from income as a de minimis fringe benefit, only the excess of the cost over the amount paid by the employee on an after tax basis for the coverage is taken into consideration.

In one case where dependent group term life insurance was available to employees through a voluntary employees' beneficiary association ("VEBA") and the employer's only role in the arrangement was to provide administrative services as an independent contractor, the life insurance coverage was not a fringe benefit subject to taxation under Treasury Regulation Sections 1.61-21 or 1.61-2(d)(2)(ii)(b). No amount was therefore includable in employees' income.[5]

Where an employer's group term life insurance plan permits employees to extend group life benefits to domestic partners and their dependents, the cost of this group term coverage is not excludable from income under either IRC Section 79 or IRC Section 132(a)(4). Rather, the Table I cost of the coverage is includable in an employee's gross income under IRC Section 61.[6]

248. Are there any exceptions to the general rule that limits the annual exclusion for term life insurance to $50,000 per employee?

There are certain exceptions to the $50,000 ceiling on tax-exempt coverage discussed in Q 246. The cost of group term life insurance, even for amounts over $50,000, is tax-exempt:

1. IRC Sec. 79(b)(3); Treas. Reg. §1.79-2(d).
2. Rev. Rul. 71-587, 1971-2 CB 89.
3. Rev. Rul. 73-174, 1973-1 CB 43.
4. Notice 89-110, 1989-2 CB 447.
5. Let. Ruls. 9549029, 9151033.
6. Let. Rul. 9717018.

(1) to a former employee who (x) has terminated his or her employment as an employee with the employer and has become permanently disabled, (y) has terminated his or her employment on or before January 1, 1984, and was covered by the plan or by a predecessor plan when he or she retired if the plan was in existence on January 1, 1984, or the plan is a comparable successor to such a plan, or (z) who has terminated his or her employment as an employee after January 1, 1984, having attained age fifty-five on or before January 1, 1984, and having been employed by the employer at any time during 1983 if the plan was in existence on January 1, 1984, or the plan is a comparable successor to such a plan, unless the individual retires under the plan after 1986 and the plan is discriminatory after that date not taking into account insurance provided to employees who retired before January 1, 1987;

(2) if a charitable organization is designated as beneficiary, where this designation may be made with respect to all or any portion of the proceeds, but no charitable contributions deduction is allowable for such a designation; or

(3) if an employer is beneficiary, unless the employer is required to pay proceeds over to an employee's estate or beneficiary.[1]

Any contribution toward group term life insurance, but not toward permanent benefits, made by an employee during a taxable year generally reduces, dollar for dollar, the amount that otherwise would be included in the employee's gross income for term insurance. No reduction is permitted, however, for a prepayment made by an employee for coverage after retirement or for payments allocable to insurance where the cost is not taxed because of one of the foregoing exceptions.[2]

249. Must group term life insurance provide nondiscriminatory benefits? How is group term life insurance taxed if a plan is discriminatory?

If a plan covers any key employees and the plan discriminates in favor of them either as to eligibility to participate or with respect to the kind or amount of benefits, the key employees may not exclude the cost of the first $50,000 of coverage. A key employee in a discriminatory plan must include the higher of the actual cost or the specified uniform premium Table I cost (Q 246). Employees who are not key employees may exclude the cost of $50,000 of coverage even if a plan is discriminatory.[3] For a discussion of when a group term life insurance plan will be found to be discriminatory, see Q 250.

A key employee essentially is the same as a key employee in a top heavy plan (Q 3919). A key employee is an employee who, at any time during the employer's tax year was:

1. IRC Sec. 79(b); Treas. Reg. §1.79-2; TRA '84 Sec. 223(d), as amended by TRA '86, Sec. 1827(b)(1); Temp. Treas. Reg. §1.79-4T, A-1. See also Let. Rul. 9149010.
2. Treas. Reg. §§1.79-2(a)(2), 1.79-3(g)(2).
3. IRC Sec. 79(d).

(1) an officer of an employer having annual compensation greater than $185,000[1] (in 2020, up from $180,000 in 2019). Not more than the greater of three individuals or 10 percent of the employees need be considered officers, but in any event no more than fifty individuals may be considered officers;

(2) a more-than-5 percent owner of an employer; or

(3) a more-than-1 percent owner, determined without considering those employees who are not counted in testing for discriminatory eligibility, having an annual compensation from an employer of more than $150,000.[2]

A key employee also is any former employee who was a key employee when he or she retired or separated from service.[3]

For purposes of determining corporate ownership, the attribution rules of IRC Section 318 apply. Rules similar to the attribution rules apply to determine non-corporate ownership as well in calculating attribution, although a 5 percent ownership test will apply rather than a 50 percent test.

In determining the percentages of ownership, only the particular employer is considered; other members of a controlled group of corporations or businesses under common control and other members of an affiliated service group are not aggregated. They are aggregated, however, for purposes of determining the employee's compensation and in testing for discrimination.[4]

Exemption for Church Plans

Church plans for church employees are exempt from nondiscrimination requirements. A church plan generally is one established by a church or convention or association of churches that is tax-exempt under IRC Section 501(c)(3). A church employee includes a minister, or an employee of an organization that is tax-exempt under IRC Section 501(c)(3), but does not include an employee of an educational organization above the secondary level, other than a school for religious training, or an employee of certain hospital or medical research organizations.[5]

250. How is it determined whether a group term life insurance plan is discriminatory?

A plan is considered discriminatory in favor of key employees with respect to eligibility to participate unless:

(1) it benefits at least 70 percent of all employees;

(2) at least 85 percent of participants are not key employees;

1. Notice 2018-83, Notice 2019-59.
2. IRC Sec. 416(i)(1)(A).
3. IRC Sec. 79(d)(6).
4. IRC Sec. 414(t); Temp. Treas. Reg. §1.79-4T, A-5.
5. IRC Sec. 79(d)(7).

(3) the plan benefits a class of employees found by the IRS not to be discriminatory; or

(4) if the plan is part of a cafeteria plan, the requirements for cafeteria plans are met (Q 3501).[1]

Individuals who do not need to be counted include:

(1) employees with fewer than three years of service;

(2) part-time and seasonal employees;

(3) employees excluded from a plan who are covered by a collective bargaining agreement if group term life insurance was the subject of good faith bargaining, and

(4) certain nonresident aliens.[2]

Benefits are discriminatory unless all benefits available to key employee participants are available to all other participants.[3] Benefits are not discriminatory, however, merely because the amount of insurance bears a uniform relationship to the total compensation of employees, or to their basic or regular rate of compensation.[4]

All policies providing group term life insurance to a key employee or key employees carried directly or indirectly by an employer will be considered a single plan for purposes of determining whether an employer's group term insurance plan is discriminatory. An employer may treat two or more policies that do not provide group term life insurance to a common key employee as constituting a single plan.[5]

251. Is the cost of employer-provided group term life insurance subject to Social Security tax?

Yes. The cost of group term life insurance that is includable in the gross income of the employee is considered wages subject to Social Security tax.[6]

The general rule is that an employee may exclude the cost of the first $50,000 of employer-provided group term life insurance from income (Q 246). Therefore, only the cost of coverage in excess of $50,000 generally will be subject to the Social Security tax.

An employer is required to report amounts includable in the wages of current employees for purposes of the Social Security tax on employees' W-2 forms. An employer generally may treat wages as though paid on any basis so long as they are treated as paid at least once each year.[7]

1. IRC Sec. 79(d)(3)(A).
2. IRC Sec. 79(d)(3)(B).
3. IRC Sec. 79(d)(4).
4. IRC Sec. 79(d)(5).
5. Temp. Treas. Reg. §1.79-4T, A-5.
6. IRC Sec. 3121(a)(2).
7. Notice 88-82, 1988-2 CB 398.

Social Security tax must be paid by an employee if a payment for group term life insurance is considered wages and is for periods during which there is no longer an employment relationship between the employer and the employee. An employer is required to separately state the portion of an employee's wages that consist of payments for group term life insurance and the amount of Social Security tax.[1]

252. What information returns must an employer that maintains a group term life insurance plan file with respect to the plan?

The cost of excess group term life insurance is not subject to withholding, but an employer that provides excess coverage must file an information return for each calendar year and must provide statements to employees receiving the excess coverage. Each employer reports as if it were the only employer carrying group term insurance on an employee.[2]

An employer that maintains a group term life insurance plan is required to file an information return with the IRS indicating the number of its employees, the number of employees eligible to participate in the plan, the number of employees participating in the plan, the cost of the plan, the taxpayer identification number of the employer and the type of business in which it is engaged. The employer also must report on the return the number of its highly compensated employees, the number of highly compensated employees eligible to participate in the plan, and the number of highly compensated employees actually participating in the plan.[3] For plan years beginning prior to the issuance of further guidance from the IRS, group term life insurance plans are not required to meet the reporting requirements of IRC Section 6039D.[4]

253. If an employer provides life insurance under a group term life insurance policy, what are the advantages of a group carve-out plan to employees and to the employer?

Under a group carve-out plan, an employer removes or carves-out one or more highly-compensated employees from the life insurance coverage provided by a group term life insurance policy under IRC Section 79. The carved-out employees are provided life insurance coverage through individual policies. Low term insurance rates on individual policies and lower minimum premiums on permanent policies contribute to the popularity of this type of plan. The portability of the individual policies also makes this arrangement attractive to highly-compensated executives who typically are selected to participate.

Early in the development of the group carve-out plan, employees were provided coverage with individual policies that still were a part of the group insurance plan (Q 241). Currently, the purchase and ownership of individual life insurance policies often is structured in one of several ways, including a split dollar arrangement (Q 4008), an IRC Section 162 bonus plan (see Q 272), or a death benefit only arrangement (Q 101).

1. IRC Sec. 3102(d).
2. IRC Sec. 6052(a).
3. IRC Sec. 6039D.
4. Notice 90-24 1990-1 CB 335, as modified by Notice 2002-24, 2002-1 CB 785.

Under a group carve-out plan, the income tax consequences to both employer and carved-out employees are the same as if the alternative method of providing life insurance coverage existed independently of the group term plan. In a possible exception to this general rule, however, the IRS concluded in a technical advice memorandum released in 2000 that a split dollar arrangement entered into as part of a group carve-out plan should be taxed as group term life insurance. Thus, the economic benefit taxed to an employee was measured by Table I rates (Q 246) rather than the insurer's substitute rates that were used with the split dollar arrangement (Q 4009).[1] Despite this, it seems almost universally accepted by practitioners that a group carve out plan structured as split dollar should be taxed as a split dollar plan and not as group term under the Table I rates.

In deciding whether to adopt a carve-out arrangement, the fact that individual policy arrangements mentioned above generally do not afford an employer a deduction for policy premiums must be considered. The premiums for group term life insurance generally are deductible to an employer (Q 245).

254. May any part of a benefit under a policy be treated as group term life insurance if the policy also provides permanent benefits? If so, what part?

Yes. A policy that provides a permanent benefit may be treated in part as group term life insurance if (1) the policy or the employer designates in writing the part of the death benefit that is group term life insurance, and (2) the part of the death benefit designated as group term for any policy year is at least the difference between the total death benefit under the policy and the employee's deemed death benefit (defined below) at the end of the policy year.[2]

A permanent benefit is an economic value extending beyond one policy year that is provided under a life insurance policy.[3] For example, paid-up or cash surrender values are permanent benefits. The following features are not permanent benefits:

(1) a right to convert or continue life insurance after group life insurance coverage terminates;

(2) any other feature that provides no economic benefit to an employee other than current insurance protection; and

(3) a feature providing term life insurance at a level premium for a period of five years or less.

To determine whether a policy provides a permanent benefit, it is necessary to determine what a policy is. Under the broad definition of "policy" provided in the regulations (Q 241), if permanent benefits are provided (by reason of the employment relationship) under unrelated plans to members of a group provided group term life insurance is issued by the same insurer

1. TAM 200002047.
2. Treas. Reg. §1.79-1(b)(1).
3. Treas. Reg. §1.79-0.

or an affiliate, they would appear to be permanent benefits under the same policy that provides group term life insurance.

If a policy providing group life insurance provides permanent benefits, the cost of the permanent benefits, reduced by amounts paid for them by an employee, but not by amounts paid for group term life insurance, is included in the employee's income according to a formula. The formula for determining the annual cost of the permanent benefit is: X(DDB2 – DDB1). DDB2 is the employee's deemed death benefit at the end of the policy year; DDB1 is the employee's deemed death benefit at the end of the preceding policy year; and X is the premium for one dollar of paid-up whole life insurance at the employee's attained age at the beginning of the policy year.[1]

The deemed death benefit at the end of a policy year is equal to R/Y where R is the net level premium reserve at the end of that policy year for all benefits provided to an employee by the policy, or if greater, the cash value at the end of the policy year; and Y is the premium for one dollar of paid-up whole life insurance at the employee's age at the end of the policy year.[2]

The net level premium reserve (R) and the net single premiums (X or Y) in the formulas must be based on the 1958 CSO Mortality Table and 4 percent interest.[3]

If a policy year and an employee's tax year are not the same, the cost of the permanent benefits is allocated between an employee's tax years. The cost allocated to the tax year in which the policy year begins is determined by multiplying the cost of the permanent benefit for the policy year, using the formula for determining cost, by the fraction of the annual premium paid during an employee's tax year. The balance of the cost, if any, is allocated to the next employee tax year. Each tax year the employee totals the costs of permanent benefits allocated to that year.

255. What are the tax consequences of dividends paid to an employee under a policy that provides both permanent benefits and group term life insurance?

If an employee pays nothing toward the cost of permanent benefits, all dividends under a policy that actually are received or that are constructively received by an employee are includable in the employee's income.[4]

If an employee pays a part or all of the cost of the permanent benefits, the amount of dividends includable by the employee is determined under this formula: (D + C) – (PI + DI + AP), where D equals the total dividends received by the employee in the employee's current and all preceding taxable years; C equals the total cost of permanent benefits for the employee's current and all preceding tax years, using the formula in Q 254; PI equals the total premium included in the employee's income under the formula in Q 189 for the employee's current and all preceding tax years; DI equals the total amount of dividends included in the employee's income under the formula in this answer for all preceding tax years of the employee; and AP equals the total

1. Treas. Reg. §1.79-1(d)(2).
2. Treas. Reg. §1.79-1(d)(3).
3. Treas. Reg. §1.79-1(d)(4).
4. Treas. Reg. §1.79-1(d)(5).

amount paid for the permanent benefits by the employee in the current and all preceding tax years of the employee.[1] It appears that an employee who pays no more than allocated cost will be taxed under the formula on the amount of dividends the employee receives.

256. What is a retired lives reserve? Is an employee taxed on employer contributions to such a reserve? May an employer deduct contributions to a reserve?

A retired lives reserve is a fund for continuing group term life insurance on retired employees. Employer contributions to a reserve should not be taxable to a current employee if he or she has no present interest in the fund, which means that the employee is not in actual or constructive receipt of any part of the fund or of a current economic benefit.

When an employee retires, the present value of any future group term life insurance coverage that may become non-forfeitable on retirement, or the value of the amount set aside by an employer to fund such coverage, will not be taxed to the employee immediately on retirement. The cost of group term insurance will be included in the income of a retired employee under IRC Section 79 in the year in which the coverage is received, regardless of whether the coverage vests upon retirement.[2]

Contributions to a retired lives reserve to fund postretirement life insurance benefits over the working lives of covered employees may be subject to limits on deduction of contributions to welfare benefit funds (Q 4083). Temporary regulations provide that certain retired lives reserves maintained by an insurance company are "funds" (Q 4081)[3] and contributions to a fund to provide postretirement life insurance for a key employee must be accounted for separately (Q 4089).

The conclusion reached in one letter ruling was that there was no income to an employer arising out of:

(1) an employer's assignment to an IRC Section 501(c)(9) trust, a voluntary employees' beneficiary association, of all its rights in an insurance policy under which the insurer maintained a retired lives reserve;

(2) an agreement by a trustee with an insurance company that amounts credited to a reserve would be invested under the general direction of the trustee in a separate account of the insurer or used to purchase annuity contracts; and

(3) payments to a trustee under annuity contracts to be used to provide group term life insurance for retired employees.

The conclusion reached in the ruling was based on the fact that at the time of the transfer the employer had no right to recover the reserve as long as any active or retired employee

1. Treas. Reg. §1.79-1(d)(5).
2. IRC Sec. 83(e)(5).
3. Temp. Treas. Reg. §1.419-1T, A-3(c); Ann. 86-45, 1986-15 IRB 52.

remained alive and the possibility of reversion was unrealistic because of the large number of employees (Q 4091).[1]

If a plan provides life insurance benefits exclusively for retirees, legislative history indicates that the plan will be considered to be a deferred compensation plan.[2] An employer's deduction would be limited under IRC Section 404(a)(5) to the amount includable in an employee's income, and allowed only if separate accounts are maintained for each covered employee.

257. Is the cost of group permanent life insurance paid by an employer taxable income to an insured employee?

Yes. Where a group life insurance policy provides permanent benefits but does not meet the requirements necessary for any part of the benefit to be treated as group term life insurance (Q 254), an insured employee will be taxed as follows: premiums paid by an employer for insurance on the life of an employee generally will be includable in the insured employee's gross income if the proceeds of the insurance are payable to the beneficiary of the employee.[3] For the tax treatment of the cost of group permanent insurance under a qualified plan, see Q 3936.

258. Are premiums that an employer pays on group permanent life insurance for its employees deductible by the employer?

Yes, if each employee's right to the insurance on his or her life is non-forfeitable when the premiums are paid.

If an employee has only a forfeitable right to the insurance, an employer cannot deduct premium payments.

If an employee's rights change from forfeitable to non-forfeitable, an employer may deduct the fair market value of the policy in the employer's taxable year in which or with which ends the employee's tax year in which the employee's rights become non-forfeitable, and the fair market value (Q 144) of the policy is includable in the employee's gross income.[4]

An employee generally will be deemed to have properly included the amount as compensation in gross income if the employer satisfies the reporting requirements of IRC Section 6041 or IRC Section 6041A.[5] Premiums paid after the employee's rights become non-forfeitable are deductible when paid.

259. Are death proceeds payable under group life insurance exempt from income tax?

Yes.

---

1. Let. Rul. 8741021. See also Let. Rul. 9542022.
2. H.R. Conf. Rep. No. 98-861 (TRA '84) reprinted in 1984-3 CB 411.
3. Treas. Reg. §1.61-2(d)(2)(ii).
4. IRC Sec. 83(h); Treas. Reg. §1.83-6(a)(1).
5. Treas. Reg. §1.83-6(a)(2).

Death proceeds received by individuals are wholly tax-exempt whether received from group permanent or group term insurance.[1] Where group term life insurance coverage is provided to domestic partners of employees by an employer, death proceeds paid on the death of a domestic partner are excluded from income under IRC Section 101.[2] The same rules as are applicable to proceeds under individual policies generally apply (Q 63 to Q 71). Special rules apply if insurance is payable under a qualified pension or profit sharing plan (Q 3961, Q 3962).

260. What is group survivor income benefit insurance?

A group term product that provides for a death benefit only if there is a survivor who qualifies for benefits under the plan (a lump sum payment of the commuted value of benefits is not available) may be called a reversionary annuity or life insurance. Regardless of the name, a plan that shifts the risk of loss resulting from premature death from an individual or family to a large group is an essential ingredient of insurance.[3]

An individual survivorship annuity was characterized as life insurance in *Cowles v. U.S.*[4] Benefits under a self-insured state program were held to be life insurance proceeds in *Ross v. Odom*.[5]

On the other hand, another self-insured state program was held not to be insurance because of the lack of actuarial soundness and the lack of a definite death benefit payable on death, as there was no death benefit if there was no surviving spouse. The court reasoned that absent a definite benefit payable in any event on the employee's death, there was no risk-shifting.[6]

Following the reasoning of this case, the IRS concluded that a program that paid a monthly benefit only to certain survivors on an employee's death did not exhibit the risk-shifting characteristic of life insurance. Thus, the death benefit was not eligible for tax-free treatment under IRC Section 101(a), and was taxed as an employee death benefit.[7]

Policies issued after December 31, 1984, generally are life insurance contracts if they meet the definition discussed in Q 65. If these products are held to be life insurance, they are taxed as group term life insurance if they meet the requirements in Q 241.

If they are annuities, the tax consequences are explained in Q 3530 to Q 3537 and Q 101.

1. IRC Sec. 101(a); Treas. Reg. §1.101-1.
2. Let. Rul. 9717018.
3. *Helvering v. LeGierse*, 312 U.S. 531 (1941).
4. *Cowles v. U.S.*, 59 F. Supp. 633 (S.D.N.Y. 1945), rev'd, 152 F.2d 212 (2nd Cir. 1945).
5. *Ross v. Odom*, 401 F. Supp. 464, 22 AFTR 2d 5624 (5th Cir. 1968).
6. *Davis v. U.S.*, 323 F. Supp 858, 27 AFTR 2d 71-844 (S.D. W. Va. 1971). See also *Barnes v. U.S.*, 801 F. 2d 984, 86-2 USTC ¶9692 (7th Cir. 1986), cert. denied, 480 U.S. 945 (1987).
7. TAM 9117005.

PART III: BUSINESS LIFE INSURANCE

In General

261. What is business life insurance?

Business life insurance is life insurance owned by a business, regardless of whether the business is a sole proprietorship, partnership, or corporation. The insurance can have a number of different purposes. For example, the insurance can be used to insure the life of a key employee, whose death could have a considerable negative impact on the business. The insurance could be purchased as part of a buy-sell agreement where the business is obligated to purchase the ownership interest of an owner who dies. The insurance also could be used to fund a non-qualified retirement package for a single employee or a number of employees.

262. Are premiums paid on business life insurance deductible as business expenses?

Life insurance premiums generally are not deductible if the payer of the premium has any interest in the policy or proceeds.

IRC Section 264(a)(1) expressly provides that no deduction shall be allowed for premiums paid on any life insurance policy, or endowment or annuity contract, if a taxpayer is directly or indirectly a beneficiary under the policy or contract. Where Section 264(a)(1) applies, the premiums are not deductible even though they otherwise would be deductible as ordinary and necessary business expenses.[1] The rule under Section 264(a)(1) is an all or nothing rule. Even though the payer of a premium has a right to receive only a portion of the proceeds, the entire premium is nondeductible. The deduction cannot be divided but must either be allowed or disallowed in total.[2] The rule under Section 264(a)(1) applies regardless of the form of insurance, so it makes no difference whether premiums are paid on term, ordinary life, or endowment policies.

Deduction of a premium clearly is prohibited under Section 264(a)(1) where a taxpayer who is the payer of the premium is designated as the beneficiary in the policy. For example, premiums paid on key person insurance, where an employer normally is both owner and beneficiary of a policy, clearly are nondeductible by reason of IRC Section 264(a)(1). A deduction likewise is denied under Section 264(a)(1) where a premium payer is only indirectly a beneficiary under a policy. Thus, a deduction is denied where a taxpayer, even though not a named beneficiary, has some beneficial interest in a policy, such as the right to change the beneficiary, to make loans, to surrender the policy for cash, or to draw against proceeds held in trust for the insured's spouse.[3]

1. Treas. Reg. §1.264-1(a).
2. Rev. Rul. 66-203, 1966-2 CB 104.
3. Rev. Rul. 70-148, 1970-1 CB 60; Rev. Rul. 66-203, supra.

An employer is permitted to deduct premiums paid on insurance covering the life of an employee, however, if the employer is not directly or indirectly a beneficiary under the policy and the premiums represent additional reasonable compensation for services rendered by an employee. Thus, if an employer has no ownership rights or beneficial interest in a policy and proceeds are payable to an employee's estate or personal beneficiary, premiums ordinarily are deductible by the employer as additional compensation to the employee.[1] The deduction will not be denied merely because an employer may derive some benefit indirectly from the increased efficiency of an employee.[2]

263. Are premiums paid on business life insurance taxable income to an insured?

Premiums generally are not taxable to an insured if the insurance is purchased for the benefit of the business and the insured has no interest in the policy. Thus, premiums paid on key person life insurance, where an employer is both owner and beneficiary of the policy, are not taxable to the insured employee.[3]

If life insurance premiums are paid by an employer on a policy insuring the life of an employee and the proceeds are payable to a beneficiary of the employee, there generally is some taxable income to the employee (Q 269, Q 271). There are exceptions to this general rule in the case of group life insurance (Q 246) and qualified pension and profit sharing plans (Q 3936).

264. Can a corporation deduct premiums it pays on a policy insuring the life of an employee or stockholder?

It may not do so under IRC Section 264(a)(1) if the corporation either is directly or indirectly a beneficiary under the policy (Q 262). This is true even if a corporation has only a partial beneficial interest in a policy.[4]

A corporation cannot deduct premiums it pays on key person insurance or on a policy insuring the life of a stockholder purchased to fund the corporation's redemption of the insured's stock. Normally, in these instances, the corporation is both owner and beneficiary of a policy, so a deduction is not allowed by reason of IRC Section 264(a)(1). Even though a corporation may have no right to the cash value of a policy, and no right to name or change the beneficiary, the corporation cannot deduct the premiums if the policy proceeds are to be used in payment for stock that is to be surrendered to the corporation. In this case, the deduction is not allowed because the premium payments are not ordinary and necessary business expenses but are capital expenditures, as payments for the acquisition of a corporate asset: treasury stock.[5]

1. IRC Sec. 162(a); Treas. Reg. §1.162-7.
2. Treas. Reg. §1.264-1(b).
3. *Casale v. Comm.*, 247 F.2d 440 (2d Cir. 1957); *U.S. v. Leuschner*, 14 AFTR 2d 5599, 336 F. 2d 246 (9th Cir 1964) *Lacey v. Comm.*, 41 TC 329 (1963), *acq.* 1964-2 CB 6; Rev. Rul. 59-184, 1959-1 CB 65.
4. *National Indus. Investors, Inc. v. Comm.*, TC Memo 1996-151.
5. Rev. Rul. 70-117, 1970-1 CB 30; Rev. Rul. 74-503, 1974-2 CB 117.

On the other hand, if a corporation purchases life insurance for an employee and the corporation has no ownership rights or beneficial interest in the policy, premiums are ordinarily deductible as additional compensation for the employee's services.[1]

To be deductible, however, premium payments must constitute reasonable compensation.[2] The question of whether compensation is reasonable can arise in the case of a stockholder-employee of a close corporation. If the total amount paid to and on behalf of a stockholder-employee is an unreasonable return for his or her services, the IRS may treat the premium payments as a distribution of profits or dividends rather than as compensation. This also may be the result where there is no evidence, such as board of directors' minutes, to show that premium payments were intended as compensation.[3]

The deduction certainly will be disallowed where surrounding circumstances affirmatively show that premiums were not paid as compensation. In *Atlas Heating & Ventilating Co. v. Comm.*,[4] for example, evidence showed that premiums actually were paid to fund a stock purchase agreement between individual stockholders; consequently, they were not compensation, but dividends. The policies were owned by the stockholder-employees and proceeds were payable to their personal beneficiaries. The insureds had agreed that, on each of their deaths, an amount of stock equal to the proceeds received by the deceased insured's beneficiaries would be turned in to the corporation and then distributed pro rata to the surviving stockholders.

Planning Point: Despite *Atlas*, it isn't uncommon to use individually-owned life insurance to fund a buy-sell agreement. However, it is important to structure the agreement in a manner that does not set the purchase price as the amount of the insurance.

In the case of an S corporation, see Q 273.

265. If a stockholder pays premiums on insurance on the life of one of the corporation's officers and the corporation is beneficiary of the proceeds, may the stockholder deduct the premium payments as business expenses?

No.

The premium payments are not related to the taxpayer's trade or business. The business of the corporation is not the stockholder's business.[5]

1. IRC Sec. 162(a).
2. Treas. Reg. §1.162-7.
3. *Boecking v. Comm.*, TC Memo 1993-497; *Est. of Worster v. Comm.*, TC Memo 1984-123; *Champion Trophy Mfg. Corp. v. Comm.*, TC Memo 1972-250.
4. *Atlas Heating and Ventilating Co. v. Comm.*, 18 BTA 389 (1929).
5. *Cappon v. Comm.*, 28 BTA 357 (1933).

266. If a stockholder purchases insurance on the life of another stockholder to fund obligations under a cross purchase plan, can the stockholder deduct the premiums paid on the policy?

No.

The premium payments are in the nature of capital expenditures. That is, they are amounts paid to acquire a capital asset.[1] Furthermore, IRC Section 264 denies a deduction for the payment of premiums on a life insurance policy if the taxpayer is directly or indirectly a beneficiary under the life insurance policy, whether or not the death benefit is used to fund a buy/sell obligation.

267. Where a key person life insurance policy is owned by and payable to an employer corporation, are premiums paid by the corporation taxable to the key person?

No.[2]

In *Casale*, the insured was president of the corporation and owned 98 percent of its stock. The corporation was both owner and beneficiary of a retirement income contract on the president's life, which the corporation had purchased to hedge its obligation to the insured under a deferred compensation agreement. The Tax Court held that premiums paid by the corporation were taxable income to the insured. The Second Circuit reversed, however, on the grounds that the corporation's separate entity could not be ignored and that the insured had received no current economic benefit that would constitute taxable income. The IRS has agreed to follow the Second Circuit's decision as precedent in dealing with similar cases.[3]

However, see *Goldsmith v. U.S.* (Q 3561).[4]

268. Are premiums paid by a corporation on life insurance to fund a stock redemption agreement taxable to an insured stockholder?

No.

The premiums are not income to a stockholder even though the stockholder has the right to designate the beneficiary, provided the beneficiary's right to receive the proceeds is conditioned on the transfer of stock to the corporation.[5]

Likewise, premiums are not taxable income to an insured stockholder when a trustee is named beneficiary, provided the trustee is obligated to use the proceeds to purchase the insured's stock for the corporation.[6]

---

1. Rev. Rul. 70-117, 1970-1 CB 30; *Whitaker v. Comm.*, 34 TC 106 (1960).
2. *Casale v. Comm.*, 247 F.2d 440 (2d Cir. 1957); Rev. Rul. 59-184, 1959-1 CB 65.
3. Rev. Rul. 59-184, supra. See also: *Lacey v. Comm.*, 41 TC 329 (1963), *acq.*, 1964-2 CB 6.
4. *Goldsmith v U.S.*, 78-1 USTC ¶9312 (Ct. Cl. 1978).
5. *Sanders v. Fox*, 253 F.2d 855 (10th Cir. 1958); *Prunier v. Comm.*, 248 F.2d 818 (1st Cir. 1957); Rev. Rul. 59-184, 1959-1 CB 65.
6. Rev. Rul. 70-117, 1970-1 CB 30.

269. Are life insurance premiums paid by a corporate employer taxable income to an insured employee if proceeds are payable to the employee's estate or personal beneficiary and the policy is owned by the employee?

Yes.[1] If dividends are applied to reduce current premiums, only the net premium is taxable income to the employee.[2]

As a rule, the premium payments are considered additional compensation to the employee and therefore deductible by the employer. If an employer is a close corporation and the employee a stockholder, the IRS may contend they are dividends taxable to the insured but not deductible by the corporation (Q 264; in the case of an S corporation, see Q 273).

Even where an insured employee and owner of the corporation was not the owner of the policy, but the employee's son or spouse was owner and beneficiary, the payment of premiums on the insurance was considered an economic benefit to the employee and as such includable in the employee's gross income.[3]

Where a stockholder-employee contends that premiums paid by the corporation on the employee's personal insurance were merely loans, the premiums will be taxed to the employee as dividends unless the employee can produce evidence to show that the employee intended to reimburse the corporation for its outlays.[4]

270. Are life insurance premiums paid by a corporate employer taxable income to an insured employee if proceeds are payable to the employee's estate or personal beneficiary and the policy is owned by the corporation?

Any arrangement between a life insurance contract "owner" and a "non-owner" is treated as a split-dollar life insurance arrangement – even if it does not strictly meet the statutory definition of a "split-dollar life insurance arrangement" – if it is a compensatory arrangement. Final regulations on split dollar state that such arrangements should be classified as economic split-dollar.[5]

An arrangement is a compensatory arrangement if:[6]

(1) It is entered into in connection with the performance of services; [7]

(2) The employer or service recipient pays, directly or indirectly, all or any portion of the premiums; and[8]

1. Treas. Reg. §1.61-2(d)(2)(ii)(A); *Canaday v. Guitteau*, 86 F.2d 303 (6th Cir. 1936); *Yuengling v. Comm.*, 69 F.2d 971 (3rd Cir. 1934).
2. *Weeks v. Comm.*, 16 TC 248 (1951); *Sturgis v. Comm.*, 10 TCM (CCH) 136.
3. *Brock v. Comm.*, TC Memo 1982-335; *Champion Trophy Mfg. Corp. v. Comm.*, TC Memo 1972-250; see IRC Sec. 301(c).
4. *Schwartz v. Comm.*, TC Memo 1963-340.
5. Treas. Reg. §1.61-22 (b)(2)(ii).
6. Treas. Reg. §1.61-22 (b)(2)(ii).
7. Treas. Reg. §1.61-22(b)(2)(ii)(A).
8. Treas. Reg. §1.61-22 (b)(2)(ii)(B).

(3) Either[1]

(a) the beneficiary of all or any portion of the death benefit is designated by the employee or service provider, or is any person whom the employee or service provider would reasonably be expected to designate as the beneficiary,: or

(b) the employee or service provider has any interest in the policy cash value of the insurance contract.[2]

In one case, where an employee's beneficiary was named irrevocably, the full premiums were taxed to the employee even though the corporation owned the policy.[3]

Where a corporation owned a policy designating an insured employee's family as beneficiary and could change the beneficiary, premium payments were not income to the employee.[4] The Tax Court suggested that the P.S. 58 costs might be taxable to the employee each year the employee's family is beneficiary. After 2001, P.S. 58 rates generally may not be used, but Table 2001 may be used (Q 4013).

Planning Point: To avoid confusion on the tax results when premiums are paid by a business but the policy beneficiary is someone other than the business, it is important to properly document the transaction. If the transaction is intended to be a loan it is important to have signed loan documents and to either pay or account for the accrued interest on an ongoing basis. If the arrangement is economic benefit split dollar, then a split dollar agreement should be executed and payment of economic benefit costs should be made annually.

271. If a corporation pays life insurance premiums on policies owned by stockholders and the policies are used to fund a cross-purchase agreement, are premium payments taxable income to stockholders?

Yes.

They are considered distributions of dividends to the stockholders who own the policies.[5]

Planning Point: Depending on the situation, treatment as ordinary income rather than as a dividend may be preferred. If ordinary income treatment is preferred, the corporation (assuming that the stockholders provide services to the corporation and that the total compensation for such services remains reasonable) could increase compensation to the stockholders who could pay the premiums themselves. Ordinary income would be taxable to the stockholder and deductible by the corporation.

In the case of an S corporation, see Q 273.

1. Treas. Reg. §1.61-22 (b)(2)(ii)(C).
2. Treas. Reg. §1.61-22 (b)(2)(ii)(C)(1).
3. *Comm. v. Bonwit*, 87 F.2d 764 (2nd Cir. 1937).
4. *Rodebaugh v. Comm.*, TC Memo 1974-36, *aff'd*, 518 F. 2d 173, 75-2 USTC ¶9526 (6th Cir. 1975), but this point was not appealed.
5. *Doran v. Comm.*, 246 F.2d 934 (9th Cir. 1957); Rev. Rul. 59-184, 1959-1 CB 65.

272. What is a Section 162 bonus plan and what are the income tax consequences to an employee and employer?

An IRC Section 162 bonus plan or an executive bonus plan is a nonqualified employee benefit arrangement in which an employer pays a compensation bonus to a selected employee who then uses the bonus payment to pay premiums on a life insurance policy insuring his or her life. (Often, as a convenience, the employer will pay the bonus directly to the insurer on behalf of the employee. See Q 269.) The policy is owned personally by the employee.

A compensation bonus generally is deductible to a corporate employer if an employee's total compensation is a reasonable amount.[1] Whether used to pay policy premiums or not (Q 269), a compensation bonus is includable in gross income to an employee.[2] At death, policy death proceeds are received by an employee's beneficiary income tax-free (Q 63).[3] Any policy withdrawals, surrenders, or loans made by an employee are taxed as they would be if the employee had purchased the policy without the benefit of the bonus arrangement (Q 10, Q 13, Q 30).

273. What are the tax consequences when an S corporation pays a premium on a life insurance policy insuring a shareholder or employee?

An S corporation generally does not pay taxes; instead, items of income, deduction, loss, and credit are passed through to shareholders who report their pro rata shares on their individual returns. Payment of premiums by an S corporation should be characterized as a nondeductible expense, as deductible compensation, or as a nondeductible distribution of profits under the same general rules applicable to regular (C) corporations (Q 264 to Q 271). The resulting tax treatment of the shareholders would differ in some instances.

Where the payment is a nondeductible expense, as it would be if a corporation was both owner and beneficiary of a key person policy, each shareholder reduces his or her basis in his or her shares by his or her proportionate part of the nondeductible expense.[4]

If particular premium payments are considered compensation as in the example where an employee owns a policy or has a beneficial interest in it (Q 269 to Q 271), the amount of compensation would be deductible in determining the corporation's income or loss that is reported pro rata by each shareholder. The amount of compensation then would be included in income by the insured employee.[5]

If a premium payment is considered a distribution with respect to stock to an individual shareholder (Q 269, Q 271), the tax treatment would depend on whether or not a corporation has accumulated earnings and profits. If a corporation has no accumulated earnings and profits,

1. IRC Sec. 162(a)(1), Treas. Reg. §1.162-9.
2. IRC Sec. 61(a).
3. IRC Sec. 101(a)(1).
4. IRC Sec. 1367(a)(2)(D).
5. IRC Secs. 1363, 1366.

the payment is treated first as a return of investment and then as capital gain. If a corporation has accumulated earnings and profits, part of the distribution might be treated as a dividend.[1] An S corporation may have accumulated earnings and profits from years when it was a C corporation or as the result of a corporate acquisition.

Planning Point: An S corporation cannot have more than one class of stock. In order to avoid an inadvertent termination of the S election, care must be taken to avoid treating shareholders differently. In Private Letter Ruling 9735006, the Treasury ruled that a split dollar agreement between a single shareholder and the S corporation did not create a second class of stock because the split dollar arrangement required reimbursement for premiums paid. Arrangements not involving reimbursement, however, could be problematic. Before an S corporation pays insurance premiums, a qualified tax advisor should be consulted.

In a revenue ruling issued in 2008, the IRS outlined the effects of premiums paid by an S corporation on an employer-owned life insurance ("EOLI") contract and the benefits received by reason of death of the insured on its accumulated adjustments account ("AAA") under IRC Section 1368. The IRS ruled that premiums paid by an S corporation on an EOLI contract, of which the S corporation is directly or indirectly a beneficiary, do not reduce the S corporation's AAA, and benefits received by reason of the death of the insured from an EOLI contract that meets an exception under IRC Section 101(j)(2) do not increase the S corporation's AAA.[2]

274. Are premiums deductible when paid by a partnership or by a partner for insurance on the life of a copartner?

No.

This is true regardless of who is named beneficiary. Premiums paid for any life insurance, or endowment or annuity contract, are not deductible if a taxpayer is directly or indirectly a beneficiary under the policy or contract.[3] Whether insurance is purchased as a key person policy or to finance the purchase of an insured's partnership interest, the premium paying partner will benefit from the policy.[4] For insurance purchased by a partnership on the life of an employee who is not a partner, see Q 262 and Q 263.

275. How is a corporation taxed on payments under an annuity contract or on living proceeds from an endowment or life insurance contract?

With respect to the tax consequences to a corporation under an annuity or on living proceeds from endowment and life insurance contracts, the same rules that are applicable to personal insurance and endowment contracts (Q 10 to Q 62) apply.[5] The same rules that

---

1. IRC Sec. 1368.
2. Rev. Rul. 2008-42, 2008-30 IRB 175.
3. IRC Sec. 264(a)(1).
4. Treas. Reg. §1.264-1.
5. See IRC Sec. 11(a).

apply to increases in the cash value of policies for personal insurance (Q 8) also apply to business-owned insurance.

To the extent that contributions are made after February 28, 1986 to a deferred annuity contract held by a corporation or other entity that is not a natural person, the contract is not treated for tax purposes as an annuity contract. Income on the contract is treated as ordinary income received or accrued by the owner during the taxable year.[1] Thus, if payments received in a year plus amounts received in prior years plus the net surrender value at the end of the year, if any, exceed premiums paid in the year and in prior years plus amounts included in income in prior years, the excess amount is includable in income. The rule and exceptions are discussed in Q 511.

To the extent an annuity contract is not subject to this rule, payments received under the contract will be subject to the rules applicable to personal annuity contracts.

276. Are death proceeds of business life insurance exempt from income tax?

Under rules applicable to life insurance contracts generally, the entire lump sum payable at an insured's death is ordinarily exempt from regularly calculated income tax whether the beneficiary is an individual, a corporation, a partnership, a trust, or the insured's estate (Q 64, Q 65).[2]

See Q 277 for special requirements applicable to employer-owned life insurance contracts entered into after August 17, 2006.

If proceeds are paid out under a life income or other installment option, the amount payable at death may be prorated and recovered from the payments in equal tax-free amounts over the payment period, but the interest element is taxable (Q 71). Proceeds received by a partnership or by an S corporation retain their tax-exempt character when passed on to individual partners or shareholders. Proceeds received tax-free by a regular (C) corporation are, when paid out, usually taxable to the recipients as compensation or dividends (Q 273, Q 291).

Death proceeds are not always wholly tax-exempt. For example, the IRC expressly provides that proceeds are taxable, under some circumstances, where a policy has previously been sold or otherwise transferred for a valuable consideration (Q 279 to Q 290).

The IRC also provides a special rule for proceeds payable under a qualified pension or profit sharing plan. There, only the amount in excess of the cash surrender value is tax-exempt under IRC Section 101(a) (Q 3961 to Q 3963).

The same rule applies to proceeds received under a tax sheltered annuity (Q 4076) and proceeds received under individual retirement endowment contracts (Q 3672).

1. IRC Sec. 72(u).
2. IRC Sec. 101(a); Treas. Reg. §1.101-1(a).

There are other instances, too, where the exemption is not available because proceeds are not considered to be received as life insurance proceeds. These include proceeds that are taxable as dividends or compensation (Q 291), proceeds taxable because of lack of insurable interest (Q 292), proceeds taxable as a return of embezzled funds (Q 293), and proceeds of creditor insurance (Q 136, Q 139).

Even though proceeds are tax-exempt, it has been ruled they can reduce an otherwise deductible capital loss. Where liquidation of a business after a partner's death resulted in a loss, but life insurance on that partner had been purchased by the other partner for the express purpose of protecting his capital investment in the business, the court ruled that because the loss was compensated for by insurance, it was not deductible. IRC Section 165(a) provides that "[t]here shall be allowed as a deduction any loss sustained during the taxable year and not compensated for by insurance or otherwise."[1]

For the treatment of proceeds under the alternative minimum tax, see Q 316.

277. What special requirements must be satisfied by employer-owned life insurance contracts issued after August 17, 2006, in order for death proceeds to be received income tax-free?

An employer-owned life insurance contract is defined as a life insurance contract (1) owned by a person or entity engaged in a trade or business where (2) that person or entity, or certain related persons, is a beneficiary under the contract, and (3) the contract covers the life of an insured who is an employee when the contract is issued.[2]

For life insurance contracts entered into after August 17, 2006, certain requirements must be met for death proceeds of an employer-owned life insurance contract to be received income tax-free.

One set of requirements is that before an employer-owned life insurance contract is issued, an employer must meet certain notice and consent requirements. An insured employee must be notified in writing that the employer intends to insure the employee's life and the maximum face amount the employee's life could be insured for at the time the contract is issued. The notice also must state that the policy owner will be the beneficiary of the death proceeds of the policy. The insured also must give written consent to be the insured under the contract and consent to coverage continuing after the insured terminates employment.[3] Note that there is no cure provision under IRC Section 101(j) if the notice requirements are not satisfied before the policy is issued. However, in very fact-specific circumstances, the IRS has recognized that the documentation secured by an employer in the course of applying for a life insurance policy on the life of an employee has inadvertently constituted "notice and consent" under the statute.[4]

1. *Johnson v. Comm.*, 66 TC 897 (1976), *aff'd*, 78-1 USTC ¶9367 (4th Cir. 1978).
2. IRC Sec. 101(j)(3)(A).
3. IRC Sec. 101(j)(4).
4. Let. Rul. 201417017

Another set of requirements relates to an insured's status with an employer. The insured must have been an employee at any time during the twelve month period before death or a director or highly compensated employee at the time the contract was issued. A highly compensated employee is an employee classified as highly compensated under the qualified plan rules of IRC Section 414(q), except for the election regarding the top paid group (Q 3920), or under rules regarding self-insured medical expense reimbursement plans of IRC Section 105(h) (Q 341), except that the highest paid 35 percent instead of 25 percent will be considered highly compensated.[1]

Alternatively, death proceeds of employer-owned life insurance will not be included in an employer's income, assuming the notice and consent requirements are met, if the amount is paid to:

(1) a member of an insured's family, defined as a sibling, spouse, ancestor, or lineal descendent;

(2) any individual who is the designated beneficiary of the insured under the contract (other than the policy owner);

(3) a trust that benefits a member of the family or designated beneficiary; or

(4) the estate of the insured.

If death proceeds are used to purchase an equity interest from a family member, beneficiary, trust, or estate, the proceeds will not be included in an employer's income.[2]

278. What reporting requirements apply to employer-owned life insurance?

The Pension Protection Act of 2006 ("PPA 2006") imposes new reporting requirements on all employers owning one or more employer-owned life insurance contracts. Final reporting regulations were issued in November 2008.[3] In addition, the IRS released Notice 2009-48 on certain issues that may arise when dealing with employer-owned life insurance contracts with respect to the IRC Section 101(j) notice and consent requirements and IRC Section 6039I's information reporting requirements, both of which were enacted under PPA 2006. The guidance, which conveniently is presented in a question-and-answer format, is effective June 15, 2009, but the IRS has announced that it will not challenge a taxpayer who made a good faith effort to comply with IRC Section 101(j) based on a reasonable interpretation of the provision before that date.[4]

1. IRC Sec. 101(j)(2)(A).
2. IRC Sec. 101(j)(2)(B).
3. IRC Sec. 6039I; T.D. 9431, 73 Fed. Reg. 65981 (11-6-2008).
4. Notice 2009-48, 2009-24 IRB 1085.

Proceeds Taxable Because of Transfer for Value

279. Will a sale or other transfer for value of an existing life insurance policy or any interest in a policy cause loss of an income tax exemption for death proceeds?

Yes, as a general rule.

IRC Section 101(a)(2) provides that if a policy or any interest in a policy is transferred for a valuable consideration, death proceeds generally will be exempt only to the extent of the consideration paid by the transferee and net premiums, if any, paid by the transferee after the transfer. Any interest paid or accrued by the transferee on indebtedness with respect to the policy is added to the exempt amount if the interest is not deductible under IRC Section 264(a)(4).[1] This provision regarding interest paid or accrued applies to contracts issued after June 8, 1997, in taxable years ending after this date. Further, for purposes of this provision, any material increase in a death benefit or other material change in a contract shall be treated as a new contract with certain limited exceptions.[2]

The balance of death proceeds is taxable as ordinary income. This is the so-called transfer for value rule. If a sale or other transfer for value comes within any of the following exceptions to the transfer for value rule, the exemption is available despite the sale or other transfer for value:

(1) the sale or other transfer for value is to the insured (Q 282);[3]

(2) the sale or other transfer for value is to a partner of the insured, to a partnership in which the insured is a partner, or to a corporation in which the insured is an officer or shareholder (Q 285 to Q 290).[4] Members of a limited liability company ("LLC") taxed as a partnership are considered to be partners for this purpose; or[5]

(3) the basis for determining gain or loss in the hands of the transferee is determined in whole or in part by reference to the basis of the transferor. This occurs, for example, where a policy is transferred from one corporation to another in a tax–free reorganization (Q 290), where a policy is transferred between spouses (Q 106), or where a policy is acquired in part by gift (Q 79).[6]

The exceptions to the transfer for value rule do not apply if the transfer occurred in a reportable policy sale. A reportable policy sale means the acquisition of a life insurance contract (directly or indirectly) if the acquirer has no substantial family, business or financial relationship with the insured individual apart from the interest in the life insurance contract. This includes acquiring an interest in a partnership, trust or other entity that

1. IRC Sec. 101(a)(2).
2. TRA '97, Sec. 1084(d).
3. IRC Sec. 101(a)(2)(B).
4. IRC Sec. 101(a)(2)(B).
5. Let. Rul. 9625013.
6. IRC Sec. 101(a)(2)(A); Rev. Rul. 69-187, 1969-1 CB 45; Let. Rul. 8951056.

holds an interest in the life insurance contract.[1] This new rule is effective for transfers occurring after December 31, 2017.

Planning Point: Notice that the exceptions include transfers to a partner of the insured or a partnership in which the insured is a partner. But, notice that the exception only includes a transfer to a corporation in which the insured is an officer or shareholder; it does not include a transfer to another officer or shareholder.

Planning Point: Under IRC Section 1041, no gain or loss is recognized upon the transfer of property between married taxpayers. As a result, the basis in the hands of the transferor in such a transfer is equal to the basis in the hands of the transferee, *i.e.*, carry-over basis. For this reason, a sale between such spouses or between trusts of which each spouse is a grantor, may qualify for an exception to the transfer-for-value rule under the basis exception of IRC Section 101(a)(2)(A), all other things being equal.

280. What is a transfer for value of a life insurance policy or an interest in a policy?

Any transfer for a valuable consideration of a right to receive all or part of the proceeds of a life insurance policy is a transfer for value. The transfer for value rule extends far beyond outright sales of policies. The naming of a beneficiary in exchange for any kind of valuable consideration would constitute a transfer for value of an interest in the policy. Even the creation by a separate contract of a right to receive all or part of the proceeds would constitute a transfer for value.

On the other hand, a mere pledging or assignment of a policy as collateral security is not a transfer for value.[2] A transfer of a policy by a corporation to a stockholder as a distribution in liquidation is a transfer for value.[3] A transfer for value can occur even though the policy transferred has no cash surrender value.[4] A transfer will be considered a transfer for value even though no purchase price is paid for the policy or interest in the policy, provided the transferor receives some other valuable consideration.[5]

In one case, two policies were purchased on the life of an officer-stockholder, one by the insured and the other by the corporation. Subsequently, the insured entered into an agreement with two employees for the purchase of his stock at his death. The policies were transferred to a trustee for use in partially financing the agreement and the employees took over the payment of premiums. On the insured's death, the proceeds were applied to the purchase of his stock. The court held that the employees were transferees for value even though they had paid no purchase price for the policies. Their agreement to make premium payments and to purchase the stock constituted a valuable consideration. Consequently, the employees were taxed on the difference between the premiums they had paid and the proceeds applied toward their purchase of the insured's stock.[6]

1. IRC Sec. 101(a)(3).
2. Treas. Reg. §1.101-1(b)(4).
3. *Lambeth v. Comm.*, 38 BTA 351 (1938).
4. *James F. Waters, Inc. v. Comm.*, 160 F.2d 596 (9th Cir. 1947).
5. *Monroe v. Patterson*, 197 F. Supp. 146 (N.D. Ala. 1961).
6. *Monroe v. Patterson*, supra.

There was a transfer for value where two shareholders assigned to each other existing policies that had no cash values on their own lives to fund a cross-purchase agreement.[1]

Similarly, where a partnership named two partners as cross-beneficiaries on policies owned by the partnership, a transfer for value had taken place.[2]

If a transferor receives no valuable consideration whatsoever, there is no transfer for value.[3]

The transfer of a policy to a grantor trust treated as owned by the transferor was not a transfer for value where the insureds, terms, conditions, benefits, and beneficial interests other than naming the trustee as beneficiary and nominal owner did not change.[4]

The transfer of a life insurance policy from one grantor trust to another grantor trust, where both trusts are treated as owned by the same taxpayer, will not be treated as a transfer for value.[5] See Q 283 for a more detailed discussion of the application of the transfer for value rule in a situation involving multiple grantor trusts.

The replacement of a jointly owned policy with two separately owned policies was also not a transfer for value.[6]

Other rules govern transfer to a grantor trust owned by an insured (Q 282 and Q 283) and transfers of policies to a qualified retirement plan (Q 3961).

281. Is the transfer of a life insurance policy subject to a nonrecourse loan a transfer for value that could cause the loss of income tax exemption for death proceeds?

Since a transfer of a policy subject to a nonrecourse loan discharges the transferor of obligations under the loan, the transferor is treated as receiving an amount equal to the discharged obligations.[7] Thus, there may be a transfer for value when a life insurance contract is transferred that is subject to a policy loan. Nonetheless, where the value of a policy exceeded the outstanding loan, a transfer was ruled in part a gift and within one of the exceptions to the transfer for value rule because the basis of the policy in the hands of the transferee was determinable in part by reference to the basis of the policy in the hands of the transferor (Q 279).[8]

In Letter Ruling 8951056, the IRS found that the gratuitous transfer of a policy subject to a nonrecourse loan was held part gift, part sale. Because the transferor's basis was greater than the amount of the loan, the basis of the policy in the hands of the transferee was the basis in the hands of the transferor at the time of transfer and thus the transfer fell within the same exception to the transfer for value rule.[9]

1. Let. Rul. 7734048.
2. Let. Rul. 9012063.
3. *Haverty Realty & Investment Co. v. Comm.*, 3 TC 161 (1944).
4. Let. Rul. 9041052.
5. Rev. Rul. 2007-13, 2007-11 IRB 684.
6. Let. Rul. 9852041.
7. Treas. Reg. §1.1001-2(a).
8. Rev. Rul. 69-187, 1969-1 CB 45.
9. But see Let. Rul. 8628007.

282. Can an existing life insurance policy be sold to the insured without loss of the income tax exemption for death proceeds?

Yes.

Sale to the insured is an exception to the transfer for value rule (Q 279).[1] For example, if a corporation purchases a policy insuring a key person and later sells it to the insured, the proceeds will be received wholly tax-exempt by the beneficiary despite the sale to the insured.[2] Moreover, a transfer to a trust that is treated as owned wholly or in part by the insured (such as a grantor trust) comes within the exception as a transfer to the insured to the extent the insured is treated as owner.[3] An individual is treated as owner of a trust where the individual retains control over property the individual has transferred to the trust so that the income on that property is taxable to the individual under IRC Sections 671-679.

Where a policy is transferred more than once but the last transfer, or the last transfer for value, is to the insured, the proceeds will be wholly tax-exempt regardless of any previous sale or other transfer for value.[4] If the insured transfers the policy for a valuable consideration, and the transfer does not come within any of the exceptions to the transfer for value rule, the proceeds again will lose their tax-exempt status.

283. Can an existing life insurance policy be transferred between two trusts, both of which were established by the insured, without loss of the income tax exemption for death proceeds?

A sale to the insured is an exception to the transfer for value rule (Q 279).[5] The IRS has ruled privately that a transfer between two trusts, one of which benefitted the taxpayer directly (Trust A) and the second of which was a grantor trust established by the taxpayer (as grantor) for the benefit of his children and grandchildren (Trust B), would not violate the transfer for value rule because the transaction fell within the exception permitting sale of a policy to the insured himself.[6]

While both trusts were irrevocable, the taxpayer retained the power to reacquire assets he had placed within Trust B by substituting assets of equal value. The independent trustee responsible for overseeing Trust B was required to ensure that any substituted assets were of equal value to the assets the taxpayer chose to reacquire.

Trust A owned a life insurance policy on the taxpayer's life, which the taxpayer wished to transfer into Trust B using his power of substitution. Because the taxpayer was both grantor of Trust B *and* the insured individual under the policy, the transaction was considered a transfer of the policy to the insured himself (the grantor and the grantor trust are treated as a single entity for tax purposes).

1. IRC Sec. 101(a)(2)(B).
2. See Let. Rul. 8906034.
3. *Swanson v. Comm.*, 518 F.2d 59 (8th Cir. 1975); Rev. Rul. 2007-13.
4. Treas. Reg. §1.101-1(b)(3)(ii).
5. IRC Sec. 101(a)(2)(B).
6. Let. Rul. 201235006.

Therefore, even though the transfer was technically a transfer of the policy from one trust to another, it was considered to fall within the exception to the transfer for value rule permitting transfers to the insured himself.

Further, the value of the policy would not be included in the taxpayer's gross estate for estate tax purposes even though the taxpayer retained the right to move the policy between two irrevocable trusts. Typically, this type of power over an asset could cause the courts to find that a taxpayer retained incidents of ownership in an asset sufficient to warrant the asset's inclusion in the estate.

In this case, however, the taxpayer could never reduce the value of the assets in Trust B because he was required to substitute assets of equal value—and an independent trustee was present to verify equivalence. Additionally, the taxpayer could not increase his own net worth through a transfer because, again, the values of the substituted assets were required to be equal.

Likewise, the IRS found that the transfer of a survivorship policy insuring the joint lives of husband and wife between trusts both of which the husband insured was the grantor, where the husband and wife were also partners in a partnership unrelated to either trusts.[1]

284. If an employer or an employer's qualified plan sells or distributes a policy on an employee's life to an insured's spouse or to another member of an insured's family, will the transfer cause loss of the tax exemption for the death proceeds?

Yes, generally, unless the transferee is a partner of the insured. This transfer does not come within any of the exceptions to the transfer for value rule (Q 279). If a sale is involved, death proceeds will be taxable to the extent that they exceed the consideration paid by the purchaser plus net premiums, if any, paid after the sale. Any interest paid or accrued by the transferee on policy indebtedness may be added to the exempt amount under certain circumstances (Q 279).

A transfer to an insured, followed by a gift from the insured to the insured's spouse or family member (Q 280) or a sale to the insured's spouse after July 18, 1984, (Q 106) would avoid taxation of proceeds under the transfer for value rule. A federal appeals court refused to treat a direct transfer by an employer to the wife of an insured employee for a consideration as two transfers merged into one: a transfer to the insured employee and then a gift from him to his wife.[2]

285. Will a policyholder's sale of life insurance policy to a corporation result in a loss of the tax exemption for the death proceeds?

Generally, yes, but not if the insured is an officer or shareholder of the corporation. IRC Section 101(a)(2)(B) provides that the transfer for value rule does not apply if the transfer is to a corporation in which the insured is a shareholder or officer (Q 279). Moreover, where a policy is transferred more than once, but the last transfer is to a corporation in which the insured is an

1. Let. Rul. 201332001.
2. *Est. of Rath v. U.S.*, 608 F.2d 254 (6th Cir. 1979).

officer or shareholder, the proceeds will be wholly tax-exempt regardless of any previous sale or other transfer for value.[1]

Proceeds will lose their income tax-exempt status by sale to a corporation if an insured is merely a non-stockholder, non-officer employee, or director because this kind of sale does not come within the exceptions to the transfer for value rule (Q 279).

It also is doubtful whether a person who is only nominally an officer, with no real executive authority or duties, would be considered an officer.[2] Regulations do not define the term officer for this purpose.

It should be noted that the important relationship is that between an insured and a corporation. In other words, even though a policyholder is not an insured, the exception will apply provided the insured is an officer or shareholder in the corporation to which the policy is transferred.

Where an employer purchases a policy from an employee for contribution to a qualified plan, see Q 3961. See Q 279 for a discussion of the impact of the 2017 tax reform legislation.

286. If a corporation sells or distributes a life insurance policy to a stockholder who is not the insured, will the transfer cause a loss of the tax exemption for the death proceeds?

Yes. This would be a transfer for value without an exception.

The transfer of a policy to a corporation in which the insured is a shareholder can be made without loss of the tax exemption, even where the transferor is not the insured (Q 285).[3] The exception does not apply to a transfer in the reverse direction (Q 287). Of course, if an independent exception enumerated under IRC Section 101(a)(2) applied, then the transfer would not affect the tax-free nature of the death benefit. For example, if the corporation transferred the policy to a stockholder who is a partner of the insured or that is a partnership in which the insured is a partner, the death benefit would still be received by that party income-tax free.

287. Does a transfer for value problem arise when an insurance-funded stock redemption plan is changed to a cross-purchase plan, or vice versa?

Yes. If a corporation sells a policy on stockholder A's life to stockholder B, proceeds will lose their tax-exempt status (Q 286). Even if the corporation does not sell a policy, but merely distributes it to stockholders, there will be a transfer for value. Valuable consideration may be found, for example, in relieving the corporation of its obligation to continue premium payments and its obligation to redeem the stock or in satisfying the corporation's dividend obligation to its stockholders.[4] The danger cannot be averted by a transfer to the insured and a subsequent transfer by the insured to another stockholder (Q 288).

1. Treas. Reg. §1.101-1(b)(3)(ii).
2. See Rev. Rul. 80-314, 1980-2 CB 152.
3. IRC Sec. 101(a)(2)(B).
4. See *Lambeth v. Comm.*, 38 BTA 351 (1938); *Monroe v. Patterson*, 197 F. Supp 146 (N.D. Ala. 1961).

A transfer by a corporation to a shareholder was ruled to fall within an exception where stockholders also were partners in a bona fide, although unrelated, partnership.[1]

Similarly, a transfer of a reverse split dollar policy from a corporation to two shareholders who also were partners of the insured for the purpose of funding a cross-purchase agreement fell within the partner exception to the transfer for value rule.[2]

Further, a transfer of policies insuring shareholders/partners from a corporation to a partnership established specifically to receive and manage the policies was considered within the partnership exception to the transfer for value rule.[3] However, had the transfer been to a trust for purposes of funding a similar arrangement – the policies would probably have been subject to the transfer for value rule without an exception.

On the other hand, a change from a cross-purchase plan between individual stockholders to a stock redemption plan can be accomplished without violating the transfer for value rule. In each instance, a stockholder will be transferring a policy he or she owns on another stockholder's life to a corporation in which the insured is a shareholder. This kind of transfer qualifies as one of the exceptions to the transfer for value rule (Q 285).[4]

288. Will a transfer of a life insurance policy by one stockholder to another, or by a stockholder's estate to a surviving stockholder, cause loss of the tax exemption for the proceeds?

Yes, unless the person to whom the policy is transferred is the insured (Q 282) or unless the stockholders are also partners in a bona fide partnership (Q 289).

The exceptions to the transfer for value rule do not include transfers between individual stockholders (Q 286).[5] This is important to note in connection with an insurance funded buy-sell agreement on the cross-purchase plan where the plan involves more than two stockholders. After the first death, a survivor may wish to purchase a policy on the life of another survivor from the deceased's estate. This purchase would disqualify the death proceeds for income tax exemption.

Moreover, suppose parties to a stock redemption plan wish to change to a cross-purchase plan and the corporation sells or distributes the policies to the insureds themselves. If the insureds then sell the policies to each other or exchange policies, the proceeds will lose their tax-exempt status. Even if no money is involved in the transaction, a valuable consideration can be found in the reciprocal transfers (Q 280).

Planning Point: To avoid transfer for value problems, some planners recommend that a policy owned by a shareholder on his or her own life be transferred to the corporation of which he or she is a shareholder. Then, subsequent to the transfer, the corporation enters into an endorsement split dollar agreement with an employee who desires to purchase the shares on the shareholder's death.

1. Let. Rul. 9347016, Let. Rul. 9045004.
2. Let. Rul. 9701026.
3. Let. Rul. 9309021.
4. IRC Sec. 101(a)(2)(B).
5. IRC Sec. 101(a)(2).

289. Is there a loss of the income tax exemption for death proceeds following a transfer of life insurance policies between partners or to a partnership in which the insured is a partner?

No.

The transfer for value rule does not apply where a policy is transferred to a partner of the insured or to a partnership in which the insured is a partner.[1] The partnership actually must operate as a partnership, however, and not exist in form only.[2] A partner can sell a policy on the partner's life to the partnership or to another partner. A retiring partner can sell to an incoming partner the policy the partner owns on another partner's life. A partnership can sell a policy to an insured partner or to a copartner of the insured. Where a partnership owns a key person policy on the life of a non-partner, there is no transfer for value when a new partner enters or an existing partner leaves the partnership, provided the partnership is not terminated by that action.[3]

Sale of a policy to a member of an insured's family who is not a partner would disqualify the proceeds for exemption. Where there is an insurance-funded buy-sell agreement between more than two partners and a partner dies, a surviving partner may buy policies on the lives of other surviving partners from the deceased's estate without loss of tax exemption for the death proceeds.[4]

The IRS has ruled in a private letter ruling that members of a limited liability company ("LLC"), which was classified as a partnership for federal tax purposes, would be considered partners for purposes of the transfer for value rule.[5]

A transfer for value by a corporation to a partnership in which an insured shareholder is a partner comes within the exception.[6] Similarly, a transfer to shareholders who are partners, even though in an unrelated partnership, falls within the exception.[7] Further, the IRS has ruled privately that a transfer of policies insuring shareholders/partners from a corporation to a partnership established specifically to receive and manage the policies comes within the exception.[8]

A sale of policies by an insured's grantor trust to a limited partnership where the insured was a limited partner was ruled to fall within the exemption.[9]

The IRS has indicated, however, that it will not issue rulings concerning whether or not the exception applies to a transfer of a life insurance policy to an unincorporated organization where substantially all of the organization's assets consist or will consist of life insurance policies on the lives of its members.[10]

1. IRC Sec. 101(a)(2)(B).
2. *Swanson v. Comm.*, 518 F.2d 59 (8th Cir. 1975), *aff'g* TC Memo 1974-61. But see Let. Rul. 9309021.
3. Let. Rul. 9410039.
4. See Let. Rul. 9727024.
5. Let. Rul. 9625013.
6. Let. Rul. 9042023.
7. Let. Rul. 9347016, Let. Rul. 9045004.
8. Let. Rul. 9309021.
9. Let. Rul. 9843024.
10. Rev. Proc. 2006-3, 2006-1 IRB 122; Rev. Proc. 2017-3, 2017-1 IRB 130.

If a policy is transferred more than once and the last transfer, or the last transfer for value, is to a partner of the insured or to a partnership in which the insured is a partner, proceeds will be entirely tax-exempt regardless of any previous transfer for value.[1]

290. Is there a loss of the tax exemption for death proceeds after a life insurance policy is transferred to a corporation in a tax-free organization or reorganization?

No, if the insured is an officer or shareholder in the corporation to which the policy is transferred (Q 285).

Moreover, even where an insured is not an officer or shareholder of a transferee corporation, proceeds will not lose their tax-exempt status if a policy is transferred as part of a general tax-free transfer. For example, a transfer of property in organizing a corporation is tax-free if immediately after the transfer the persons who exchanged property for stock own at least 80 percent of the voting stock and 80 percent of all other classes of stock in the corporation. This kind of transfer usually takes place, for example, when an unincorporated business is incorporated.

Other examples of tax-free transfers include tax-free reorganizations, which include statutory mergers, consolidations and the transfers of substantially all the property of one corporation solely in exchange for the voting stock of another corporation.[2] Where an asset changes hands in a tax-free transfer, the tax basis of the asset does not change.[3] Consequently, such a transfer comes within the exception to the transfer for value rule set forth in IRC Section 101(a)(2)(A) (Q 279).

If proceeds would not have been exempt had a policy been retained by a transferor, the tax-free transfer will not cause them to become tax-exempt unless the insured is an officer or shareholder of the transferee corporation.[4]

If a corporation purchases the assets of another corporation in a transaction that is not a tax-free reorganization and those assets include a life insurance policy, the sale will cause a loss of exemption for the proceeds unless the insured is an officer or shareholder of the purchasing corporation (Q 285).[5]

291. When are death proceeds of life insurance taxable as dividends or compensation?

Proceeds that have been received tax-free by a C corporation lose their tax-exempt character as life insurance proceeds on distribution to employees or shareholders. Consequently, where a corporation is both owner and beneficiary of a policy, the proceeds generally will be tax-free to the corporation (but see Q 276). If the corporation distributes the proceeds to its shareholders, however, the shareholders will be treated as having received a taxable dividend.[6]

1. Treas. Reg. §1.101-1(b)(3)(ii).
2. IRC Sec. 368.
3. IRC Sec. 358.
4. Treas. Reg. §1.101-1(b)(3).
5. IRC Sec. 101(a)(2)(B); *Spokane Dry Goods Co. v. Comm.*, 1 TCM (CCH) 921 (1943).
6. Rev. Rul. 71-79, 1971-1 CB 112.

If an insured is an employee and proceeds are received by a corporation and then paid to the employee's widow or other personal beneficiary under the terms of an employment contract, they may be treated as taxable compensation for the employee's past services.[1]

On the other hand, if a corporation has no ownership rights in a policy and is not the beneficiary, proceeds should be received tax–free by the beneficiary as life insurance proceeds (Q 63, Q 65).[2] Where a corporation paid the premiums on a policy that was held by a trustee for the benefit of certain shareholders and the corporation had no ownership rights in the policy, the court held the proceeds received by the shareholders were tax-exempt life insurance proceeds.[3] The IRS has indicated, however, that the premiums when paid by a corporation may, in some circumstances, be taxed to shareholders as dividends (Q 269).[4]

Where a corporation owns a policy and is not the beneficiary, it appears that the proceeds are taxable as dividends and possibly as compensation. Where the proceeds of a policy were payable to a trustee for the benefit of shareholders but the corporation had substantial ownership rights in the policy, the court conceded that the proceeds were life insurance proceeds but said that they also were in the nature of dividends and under such circumstances, the dividend provisions of the tax law would prevail.[5]

The U.S. Court of Appeals for the Sixth Circuit reached an opposite conclusion in the *Ducros* case. There, a policy was owned by a corporation and individual stockholders were named as revocable beneficiaries in the policy. The court held that the proceeds received by shareholders directly from the insurance company were life insurance proceeds and, therefore, tax-exempt.[6]

The IRS has announced its refusal to follow *Ducros* as precedent in disposing of similar cases.[7] Revenue Ruling 61-134 states that it is the position of the IRS "that life insurance proceeds paid to stockholders of a corporation are taxable as dividends in cases where the corporation uses its earnings to pay the insurance premiums and has all incidents of ownership including the right to name itself beneficiary, even though the corporation does not name itself beneficiary and, therefore, is not entitled to and does not in fact receive the proceeds."

The same principle should apply if proceeds of a corporate owned policy are payable directly to an insured employee's beneficiary, although the proceeds ordinarily would be taxable compensation rather than dividends. Nonetheless, a Technical Advice Memorandum has held that proceeds of a corporate owned and paid for life insurance policy naming as revocable beneficiary the wife of the insured-stockholder were not dividends because she was not a stockholder and the estate-stockholder was not a beneficiary. The proceeds were not income in respect of a decedent, but rather were life insurance death proceeds received tax-free under IRC Section 101(a).[8]

1. *Essenfeld v. Comm.*, 311 F.2d 208 (2d Cir. 1962).
2. IRC Sec. 101(a).
3. *Doran v. Comm.*, 246 F.2d 934 (9th Cir. 1957).
4. Rev. Rul. 59-184, 1959-1 CB 65.
5. *Golden v. Comm.*, 113 F.2d 590 (3rd Cir. 1940).
6. *Ducros v. Comm.*, 272 F.2d 49 (6th Cir. 1959).
7. Rev. Rul. 61-134, 1961-2 CB 250.
8. TAM 8144001.

Assuming, but not deciding on, the validity of Treasury Regulation Section 20.2042-1(c)(6) (Q 319), the Tax Court has held that where a corporation owned insurance on the life of a controlling stockholder and where the beneficiary named by the corporation was the insured's wife, who owned stock in the corporation, death proceeds were not taxable to the beneficiary as a dividend but were excludable from her income as proceeds of life insurance under IRC Section 101(a)(1).[1]

In the case of an S corporation, each shareholder increases basis in the stock by the share of the death proceeds received by the corporation, whether taxable or not. In the event a closing of the books election is made under IRC Section 1377(a)(2) for a cash basis S corporation, the basis increase will be allocated to the surviving shareholders rather than apportioning some of the basis increase to the decedent's shares.[2] Thereafter, any distribution of proceeds should be determined to be compensation or a distribution with respect to stock as if it were a regular C corporation (Q 294).

Where insurance is used to fund a stock redemption agreement, see Q 307.

292. If a corporation takes out a life insurance policy on a person in whose life the corporation has no insurable interest, will death proceeds be exempt from income tax?

Under the 2017 Tax Act, the exceptions to the transfer for value rule do not apply if the policy was transferred in a transaction that qualifies as a reportable policy sale. See Q 279 for details.

There is danger that proceeds may be considered taxable income from a wagering contract instead of tax-exempt life insurance proceeds.[3] If there is an insurable interest when a policy is taken out, the contract will not be considered a wagering contract, even if an insurable interest is not present at death.[4] Insurable interest is determined by the laws of the various states. Consequently, if there is an insurable interest under applicable state law, death proceeds should qualify as life insurance proceeds under IRC Section 101(a).

293. Where a life insurance policy is assigned to an employer in restitution of funds embezzled by an insured, are proceeds tax-exempt to the employer?

No.

The employer does not receive the proceeds as life insurance payable by reason of the insured's death but as a restitution of embezzled funds. Consequently, the income tax exclusion under IRC Section 101(a) does not apply. If the employer has claimed a loss deduction, the employer must report the proceeds as a recovery of a previously deducted embezzlement loss.[5]

---

1. *Est. of Horne v. Comm.*, 64 TC 1020 (1975), acq. in result, 1980-1 CB 1.
2. But see Let. Rul. 200409010.
3. *Atlantic Oil Co. v. Patterson*, 331 F.2d 516 (5th Cir. 1964).
4. *Ducros v. Comm.*, 272 F.2d 49 (6th Cir. 1959).
5. *Tennessee Foundry & Mach. Co. v. Comm.*, 399 F.2d 156 (6th Cir. 1968).

294. What are the tax consequences for death proceeds of a life insurance policy purchased by an S corporation?

Where an S corporation is beneficiary of a policy and death proceeds are received as tax-exempt income, each stockholder's pro rata share of the proceeds is tax-exempt to him or her and the basis of each stockholder's stock is increased by his or her share of the tax-exempt proceeds.[1] An S corporation's delay in receiving death proceeds that will be used to purchase a deceased shareholder's shares will result in an increase in the basis of each shareholder's shares, not just the shares of the surviving shareholders.[2]

Planning Point: There are special notice, consent, and reporting requirements applicable to employer owned policies entered into after August 17, 2006 (Q 276). If these requirements are not met, a portion of the death benefit becomes taxable income.

If a corporation is neither owner nor beneficiary, proceeds of a policy paid for by the corporation should be tax-free to the beneficiary as life insurance proceeds (Q 63 to Q 79). The transfer for value rule has an impact on the taxation of death proceeds (Q 279). If a corporation owns a policy but is not the beneficiary, the characterization of the proceeds is not entirely clear (Q 291). If they are treated as a distribution of profits, that is, as dividends in the case of a regular C corporation, they would be taxed as a return of basis, capital gain, or dividends. If proceeds paid to a beneficiary of a policy owned by a corporation are treated as corporate distributions, they also should be treated as tax-free proceeds to the corporation that increase each shareholder's basis pro rata.

295. If an employer owns a policy on the life of an employee and sells the policy to the employee for its cash surrender value, can the sale result in taxable income to the employee or to the employer?

Transfers of property after June 30, 1969, in connection with the performance of services are governed by IRC Section 83. Effective for transfers after February 12, 2004, regulations under IRC Section 83 provide that, "In the case of a transfer of a life insurance contract, retirement income contract, endowment contract, or other contract providing life insurance protection, or any undivided interest therein, the policy cash value and all other rights under such contract (including any supplemental agreements thereto and whether or not guaranteed), other than current life insurance protection, are treated as property."

In other words, the cash surrender value may not fully reflect the value of the property transferred. Although it isn't clear, the policy's "interpolated terminal reserve" (for a whole life policy) or "tax reserve" (for a universal life policy) may more accurately reflect the value of a life insurance policy. For guaranteed policies, especially universal life policies with a lifetime guaranty, the policy may have a value well in excess of policy cash surrender value. Before selling a policy to the insured, it may be advisable to attain a professional independent valuation.

1. IRC Secs. 1366(a)(1)(A), 1367(a)(1)(A).
2. Let. Rul. 200409010.

For a policy which is part of a split dollar arrangement entered into on or before September 17, 2003, and which is not materially modified after that date, only the cash surrender value is considered "property."[1] Therefore, if a policy's actual value was more than the cash surrender value, then a sale may result in taxable income to an employee.

Under prior regulations where only the cash surrender value was considered property, the IRS concluded that where full ownership of a life insurance policy was transferred from an employer corporation to a key person, IRC Section 83 required that the employee include as income a policy's cash surrender value, less any payments the employee made for the policy.[2]

If a policy is sold by an employer for its cash surrender value, which is less than the total premiums paid, the employer can exclude from gross income the amount received from the sale of the insurance policy to the employee.[3] No loss deduction is allowable, however, when total premiums paid exceed the sale price (Q 62).

If a policy is sold by an employer for the cash surrender value, which exceeds the employer's basis in the contract, the amount realized by the employer in excess of basis is taxable income to the employer.

296. If an employee or stockholder sells a life insurance policy to the corporation for its cash surrender value, does the employee or stockholder realize a taxable gain?

Yes, if the cash surrender value is greater than the employee or stockholder's net premium cost. The gain is ordinary income, not capital gain.[4] Normally, there is no deductible loss where a policy is sold for adequate consideration (Q 62). If the policy sold is subject to a nonrecourse loan, the amount realized on the sale includes the amount of the loan (Q 280).[5]

297. What are the income tax consequences when a corporation transfers a life insurance policy to an employee or stockholder without consideration?

When a corporation transfers a life insurance policy to an employee or stockholder without consideration, the entire value of the policy is taxable to the employee or stockholder as compensation or as a dividend. For the value of a policy that has not yet matured, see Q 144.

Where a transferee is a stockholder-employee, the circumstances of a distribution will determine whether it is compensation or dividend. In *Thornley v. Comm.*,[6] the Tax Court ruled on a case involving insurance on the lives of two stockholders that was purchased by a corporation to fund a stock redemption agreement. The agreement provided that on the first death, policies on the survivor's life were to be distributed to the survivor without cost. The Tax Court held

1. Treas. Reg. §1.83-3(e).
2. Let. Rul. 8905010.
3. Rev. Rul. 70-38, 1970-1 CB 11.
4. *Gallun v. Comm.*, 327 F.2d 809 (7th Cir. 1964).
5. Treas. Reg. §1.1001-2(a).
6. 41 TC 145 (1963).

that the value of the unmatured policies was taxable as a dividend to the survivor in the year the other stockholder died.

In another Tax Court case, the value of a life insurance policy constituted long-term capital gain to an officer-stockholder who received the policy in exchange for his stock in the corporation.[1]

In a similar case, however, capital gains treatment was denied where there was no proof that a policy was received as part of the redemption price of stock.[2]

If an employee's rights are subject to a substantial risk of forfeiture (Q 3536), the full value of the policy is not taxable until the employee's rights become substantially vested. The net premium cost of life insurance protection is taxable to the employee during the period the contract remains substantially non-vested.[3]

If an employee takes a policy subject to a nonrecourse loan, the employee has given consideration to the extent of the loan amount (Q 280).

To the extent there is gain in a policy, an employer's transfer of the policy to an employee or a stockholder triggers taxable income to the employer, similar to the sale of the policy (Q 295).

If a transfer is to someone other than an insured, the transfer for value rule should be considered.

298. Will sale of a deceased's stock under a cross-purchase insurance-funded buy-sell agreement result in income tax liability to the deceased's estate?

Normally, no taxable gain will result to a deceased's estate if stock is sold to surviving individual shareholders at its full market value under a standard buy-sell agreement. At the stockholder's death, the stockholder's estate receives a new tax basis in the stockholder's stock equal to its fair market value at the time of death or an alternate valuation date.[4] Because the sale price under a properly designed buy-sell agreement usually is accepted as the fair market value of the stock, the basis and sale price normally will be the same (Q 322). Consequently, there should be no capital gain. Since individuals, rather than the corporation, purchase the stock, the payment cannot be regarded as a dividend (Q 300). However, if the parties to the buy-sell agreement are related, additional caution should be taken to determine that the sale price under the buy-sell agreement is reasonable.

1. *Parsons v. Comm.*, 54 TC 54 (1970).
2. *Wilkin v. Comm.*, TC Memo 1969-130.
3. Treas. Reg. §1.83-1(a)(2).
4. See IRC Sec. 1014.

299. What are the income tax consequences of funding a stock purchase agreement with life insurance?

Premiums

Regardless of whether a stockholder pays premiums on a policy on the life of another stockholder or on a policy on the stockholder's own life to fund an agreement, the stockholder cannot deduct premium payments (Q 266).[1]

If stockholders attempt to use company-paid group term life insurance to fund their buy-sell agreement, the company may be denied a deduction for its premium payments. The IRS has held, in a private ruling, that premium payments under these circumstances are not related to a corporation's trade or business.[2] Moreover, if stockholders reciprocally name each other as beneficiaries of their insurance or reciprocally agree to apply proceeds to the purchase of their stock, the proceeds may be taxable under the transfer for value rule unless an exception to the rule exists (Q 280).

Premiums paid by an insured's associate stockholders are not taxable income to the insured. If a corporation pays premiums on insurance to fund a buy-sell agreement between individual stockholders, premium payments will be taxable dividends to those stockholders (Q 271).[3] If an S corporation pays premiums, see Q 273.

Death Proceeds

Provided the parties have not violated the transfer for value rule, death proceeds are received free of income tax by surviving stockholders (Q 276).[4] Each survivor applies the tax-free proceeds received to purchase stock from a deceased's estate.

Cost Basis

The amount a survivor pays an estate for stock becomes the survivor's cost basis in the stock. This cost basis will be used to calculate the survivor's gain or loss should the survivor dispose of the stock during the survivor's lifetime. If a survivor holds stock until death, the estate will receive a stepped-up basis in the stock. An exception existed for decedents dying in 2010 under a modified carryover basis system that was put into place for that year only.

A cross-purchase agreement commonly gives each survivor a right to purchase from the deceased's estate the unmatured policy on the survivor's own life. If an agreement calls for transfer of a policy without cost to an insured, it would seem that the insured's cost basis for the stock should be reduced by the value of the policy. The Sixth Circuit Court of Appeals has held otherwise.[5]

After the first death, continued use of policies to fund a buy-sell agreement between survivors **could** bring adverse tax results under the transfer for value rule (Q 279 and Q 288).

1. IRC Secs. 262, 264(a)(1).
2. Let. Rul. 6206295970A.
3. *Doran v. Comm.*, 246 F.2d 934 (9th Cir. 1957); *Paramount-Richards Theatres, Inc. v. Comm.*, 153 F.2d 602 (5th Cir. 1946); see also Rev. Rul. 59-184, 1959-1 CB 65.
4. IRC Sec. 101(a).
5. *Storey v. U.S.*, 305 F.2d 733 (6th Cir. 1962).

Planning Point: Compared to a stock redemption agreement, use of a cross-purchase agreement between stockholders provides flexibility to convert to a stock redemption agreement using the same life insurance policies, which (Q 287) provides the surviving stockholders with an increased cost basis (Q 298), avoids increasing the estate tax value of the decedent's estate (Q 299), avoids application of family attribution rules (Q 300), and does not expose death benefits to the alternative minimum tax (Q 316).

300. If a corporation redeems all of its stock owned by a deceased stockholder's estate, will the amount paid by the corporation be taxed as a dividend distribution to the estate?

As a general rule, any payment by a corporation other than an S corporation to a shareholder will be treated as a dividend rather than a capital transaction even if the payment is made to redeem stock.[1]

If a payment is treated as a dividend, the entire amount paid to an individual generally will be taxed at the generally applicable capital gains rate, with no deduction for basis, and earnings and profits of the corporation will be reduced by the amount of money or other property distributed by the corporation.[2] Under the American Taxpayer Relief Act of 2012 ("ATRA"), the maximum dividend rate was increased to 20 percent for taxpayers who fall within the 39.6 percent income tax bracket (i.e., individual taxpayers earning over $400,000 annually and married taxpayers filing jointly who earn over $450,000 annually, as adjusted for inflation. The amounts for 2016 are $415,050 and $466,950, increasing to $418,400 and $470,700 in 2017).[3]

Under the 2017 Tax Act, in 2018, the 20 percent rate will apply to joint filers who earn more than $479,000 (half that amount for married taxpayers filing separately), heads of households who earn more than $452,400, single filers who earn more than $425,800, and trusts and estates with more than $12,700 in income. In 2019, the 20 percent rate will apply to joint filers who earn more than $488,850 (half that amount for married taxpayers filing separately), heads of households who earn more than $461,700, single filers who earn more than $434,550, and trusts and estates with more than $12,950 in income. In 2020, the 20 percent rate will apply to joint filers who earn more than $496,600 (half that amount for married taxpayers filing separately), heads of households who earn more than $469,050, single filers who earn more than $441,450, and trusts and estates with more than $13,150 in income.[4]

There are several exceptions, discussed below, to the general rule that allow a payment to be treated as a sale or exchange. If a payment is characterized as a sale or exchange, it will be taxed as a capital gain.

In the context of closely held corporations, the characterization of a stock redemption is important for at least two additional reasons.

1. IRC Sec. 301(a); Rev. Rul. 55-515, 1955-2 CB 222.
2. IRC Secs. 312(a), 316(a).
3. American Taxpayer Relief Act of 2012, Pub. Law No. 112-240, Sec. 102, IR-2015-119 (October 22, 2015), Rev. Proc. 2016-55, Pub. Law No. 115-97.
4. IRC Sec. 1(j)(5), Rev. Proc. 2018-57, Rev. Proc. 2019-44.

First, if a redemption is treated as a sale or exchange, the basis of the shares retained by the seller, if any, is unaffected by the transaction. If a redemption is treated as a dividend, the basis of the shares redeemed is added to the basis of the shares retained.[1]

Second, if a redemption is treated as a sale or exchange, the part of the distribution properly chargeable to earnings and profits is an amount not in excess of the ratable share of earnings and profits of the corporation attributable to the redeemed stock.[2] If a redemption is treated as a dividend, earnings and profits of the corporation are reduced by the amount of money or other property distributed by the corporation.[3]

One of the exceptions to dividend treatment mentioned above is contained in IRC Section 302(b)(3). IRC Section 302(b)(3) provides that if a corporation redeems all of a shareholder's remaining shares so that a shareholder's interest in the corporation is terminated, the amount paid by the corporation will be treated as a payment in exchange for the stock, not as a dividend. In other words, the redemption will be treated as a capital transaction (Q 305).[4]

There will be no taxable dividend, then, if a corporation redeems all of its stock owned by an estate. In determining what stock is owned by an estate, the constructive ownership or attribution-of-ownership rules contained in IRC Section 318 must be applied.

Consequently, to achieve non-dividend treatment under IRC Section 302(b)(3), a corporation must redeem not only all of its shares actually owned by an estate, but also all of its shares constructively owned by the estate.

One of these constructive ownership rules provides that shares owned by a beneficiary of an estate are considered owned by the estate. For example, assume that a decedent owned 250 shares of Corporation X's stock, so that the decedent's estate now actually owns 250 shares. Assume further that a beneficiary of the decedent's estate owns 50 shares. Because the estate constructively owns the beneficiary's 50 shares, the estate is deemed to own a total of 300 shares. Redemption of the 250 shares actually owned, therefore, will not affect a redemption of all the stock owned by the estate.

Furthermore, stock owned by a close family member of a beneficiary of an estate may be attributed to an estate beneficiary, because of the family constructive ownership rules, and through the estate beneficiary to the estate. An estate beneficiary would be considered to own, by way of family attribution rules, shares owned by the decedent's spouse, children, grandchildren, and parents.[5]

It has been held that where, because of hostility among family members, a redeeming shareholder is prevented from exercising control over stock that the individual would be deemed

1. Treas. Reg. §1.302-2(c).
2. IRC Sec. 312(n)(7).
3. IRC Secs. 312(a), 316(a).
4. Rev. Rul. 77-455, 1977-2 CB 93.
5. IRC Sec. 318(a).

to own constructively under attribution rules, the attribution rules will not be applied to the individual.[1]

On the other hand, the IRS has indicated it will not follow that decision and has ruled that the existence of family hostility will not affect its application of attribution rules.

If certain conditions are met, however, the IRS will not apply the ruling to taxpayers who have acted in reliance on the IRS's previously announced position on this issue.[2] The Fifth Circuit also has taken the position that the existence of family hostility does not prevent application of attribution rules, thus creating disagreement between the two circuit courts that have ruled on the question.[3] The Tax Court consistently has held that hostility within a family does not affect application of attribution rules.[4]

Planning Point: Constructive ownership rules are complicated and their application requires expert legal advice. It generally may be said that a danger of dividend tax treatment exists in every case involving a family-owned corporation engaging in a stock redemption. There are, however, means available in some cases to avoid the harsh operation of the rules (Q 301, Q 302). A partial redemption may be able to escape dividend tax treatment even in a family-owned corporation (Q 303).

---

301. How can attribution of stock ownership among family members be avoided?

In attempting to qualify under the complete redemption rules (Q 300), the adverse effect of family attribution rules, that is, the rules that attribute stock ownership between family members as distinct from other attribution rules that attribute stock ownership from or to estates, trusts, or business entities, ordinarily may be overcome if a shareholder from whom stock is redeemed:

(1) retains no interest in the corporation except as a creditor immediately after redemption;

(2) does not acquire any such interest other than stock acquired by bequest or inheritance within ten years after the date of the redemption; and

(3) files an agreement, called a waiver agreement, to notify the IRS of a redeeming shareholder's acquisition of a forbidden interest within the ten year period.[5]

With respect to distributions after August 31, 1982, an entity such as a trust or estate that terminates its interest may waive family attribution rules as long as the related party, that is, a beneficiary, stockholder, or partner through whom ownership of stock is attributed to the entity, joins in the waiver. The language of the IRC prohibits waiver of entity attribution.[6]

---

1. *Robin Haft Trust v. Comm.*, 510 F.2d 43(1st Cir. 1975).
2. Rev. Rul. 80-26, 1980-1 CB 66; IRC Sec. 7805(b).
3. *David Metzger Trust v. Comm.*, 693 F.2d 459 (5th Cir. 1982), *cert. den.*, 463 U.S. 1207 (1983).
4. See *Cerone v. Comm.*, 87 TC 1 (1986).
5. IRC Sec. 302(c)(2)(A). As for what constitutes a forbidden retained interest, see *Lynch v. Comm.*, 801 F.2d 1176 (9th Cir. 1986); *Cerone v. Comm.*, 87 TC 1 (1986); *Seda v. Comm.*, 82 TC 484 (1984); *Est. of Lennard*, 61 TC 554 (1974), *acq. in result*, 1974-2 CB 3; Rev. Rul. 70-104, 1970-1 CB 66; Rev. Rul. 71-426, 1971-2 CB 173; Rev. Rul. 71-562, 1971-2 CB 173; Rev. Rul. 84-135, 1984-2 CB 80.
6. IRC Sec. 302(c)(2)(C).

Family attribution rules will not be waived (1) if any portion of redeemed stock was acquired, directly or indirectly, by a redeeming shareholder within ten years before redemption from any member of the shareholder's family named in the family attribution rules, or (2) if any member of a redeeming shareholder's family named in the family attribution rules owns stock in the corporation at the time of the redemption and the person acquired any stock in the corporation from the redeeming shareholder within ten years before the redemption, unless the acquired stock is redeemed in the same transaction.

The foregoing limit does not apply if an acquisition (as in (1)) or a disposition (as in (2)) by a redeeming shareholder did not have as one of its principal purposes avoidance of federal income tax.[1]

One ruling illustrates the application of this limit on the limitation. A son and his father's estate owned all the outstanding stock of X corporation. The son's mother was the sole beneficiary of the estate. The son was active in the business; his mother was not. After the executor distributed the stock to the mother, X corporation redeemed all the mother's stock so that the son could have complete ownership of X corporation. The mother's waiver agreement was effective to prevent the attribution to her of her son's stock, even though she had acquired the redeemed stock indirectly from her husband within ten years of the redemption, because her acquisition of the stock did not have as one of its principal purposes the avoidance of federal income tax.[2]

302. Can an executor avoid attribution of stock ownership from an estate beneficiary to the estate by distributing the beneficiary's legacy before the redemption of the estate-held stock?

As a relief provision, regulations state that, "A person shall no longer be considered a beneficiary of an estate when all the property to which he is entitled has been received by him, when he no longer has a claim against the estate arising out of having been a beneficiary, and when there is only a remote possibility that it will be necessary for the estate to seek the return of property or to seek payment from him by contribution or otherwise to satisfy claims against the estate or expenses of administration."[3]

Thus, estate-beneficiary constructive ownership rules can be avoided, in some instances, by distributing a beneficiary-shareholder's legacy to the beneficiary-shareholder before redemption takes place. Many states have apportionment laws calling for allocation of estate taxes among estate beneficiaries in all cases where a decedent did not direct otherwise by will.

If distribution of a legacy to a beneficiary-shareholder in one of those states occurs before payment of estate taxes or without deduction for a beneficiary's share of the taxes, the shareholder still will be considered a beneficiary of the estate within the meaning of the regulation even after the distribution.[4]

1. IRC Sec. 302(c)(2)(B).
2. Rev. Rul. 79-67, 1979-1 CB 128.
3. Treas. Reg. §1.318-3(a).
4. *Est. of Webber v. U.S.*,404 F.2d 411, 22 AFTR 2d 5911 (6th Cir. 1968).

Moreover, even if a shareholder's legacy has been distributed to the shareholder and he or she no longer has any claim against the estate, or the estate against the shareholder, if a member of the shareholder's family remains a beneficiary of the estate, the shareholder's shares may be attributed to the estate through the family member.[1]

The relief provision under Treasury Regulation Section 1.318-3(a) is not available if a residuary legatee of an estate owns stock, because a residuary legatee's interest in the estate does not cease until the estate is closed.[2]

Moreover, if a trust is a beneficiary of an estate and a surviving shareholder is a beneficiary of the trust, the surviving shareholder's stock will be attributed to the trust and through the trust to the estate.[3]

303. What is a Section 303 stock redemption?

Estates of decedents comprised largely of close corporation stock commonly have a liquidity problem. Congress enacted IRC Section 303 expressly to aid these estates in solving this problem and to protect small businesses from forced liquidations or mergers due to the heavy impact of death taxes. Within the limits of IRC Section 303, surplus can be withdrawn from the corporation free of income tax.

In certain instances, stock of a public corporation also may be redeemed under IRC Section 303.

Any payments by a corporation to a shareholder generally are treated as dividends (Q 300). IRC Section 303 provides that, under stipulated conditions (see Q 304), a corporation can redeem part of a deceased stockholder's shares without the redemption being treated as a dividend. Instead, the redemption price will be treated as payment in exchange for the stock as a capital transaction (Q 305). An IRC Section 303 redemption can safely be used in connection with the stock of a family-owned corporation because constructive ownership rules are not applied in an IRC Section 303 redemption (Q 300).[4]

The stock of any corporation, including an S corporation, may qualify for an IRC Section 303 redemption. Moreover, any class of stock may be redeemed under IRC Section 303. Thus, a nonvoting stock, common or preferred, issued as a stock dividend or issued in a lifetime or post-death recapitalization can qualify for the redemption.[5]

Where a corporation issued nonvoting shares immediately prior to and as a part of the same transaction as the redemption, a valid IRC Section 303 redemption was made.[6]

1. IRC Sec. 318(a)(5)(A).
2. Rev. Rul. 60-18, 1960-1 CB 145.
3. Rev. Rul. 67-24, 1967-1 CB 75; Rev. Rul. 71-261, 1971-1 CB 108.
4. IRC Secs. 318(a) and 318(b).
5. Treas. Reg. §1.303-2(d).
6. Rev. Rul. 87-132, 1987-2 CB 82.

IRC Section 306 stock is preferred stock distributed to shareholders as a stock dividend, the sale or redemption of which may subject the proceeds to income tax treatment as dividend income because of special rules contained in IRC Section 306. A distribution in redemption of IRC Section 306 stock will qualify under IRC Section 303 to the extent the conditions of IRC Section 303 are met.[1]

304. What conditions must be met for a stock redemption to qualify as a Section 303 stock redemption and thus obtain non-dividend treatment?

The following conditions must be met if a stock redemption is to qualify under IRC Section 303 for non-dividend treatment:

(1) The stock that is to be redeemed must be includable in the decedent's gross estate for federal estate tax purposes.

(2) The value for federal estate tax purposes of all stock of a redeeming corporation that is includable in a decedent's gross estate must comprise more than 35 percent of the value of the decedent's adjusted gross estate.[2] The "adjusted gross estate" for this purpose is the gross estate less deductions for estate expenses, indebtedness and taxes[3] and for unreimbursed casualty and theft losses.[4] The total value of all classes of stock includable in a gross estate is taken into account to determine whether this 35 percent test is met, regardless of which class of stock is to be redeemed.[5]

IRC Section 303(b) provides that a corporate distribution in redemption of stock will qualify as an IRC Section 303 redemption if all the stock of the corporation that is included in determining the value of a gross estate exceeds 35 percent of the adjusted gross estate. Although most gifts made by a donor within three years of the donor's death are not brought back into the donor's gross estate under IRC Section 2035, certain kinds of gifts are brought back. These are described in Q 817 in the "first kind of exception" gifts. Gifts of corporation stock that fall within this classification are part of a gross estate for purposes of computing the 35 percent requirement (or the 20 percent requirement discussed below) and a corporation's redemption of this stock will qualify as a sale or exchange if all other requirements of IRC Section 303 are satisfied. IRC Section 2035(c)(1)(A) states generally that the three year rule will apply for the purposes of IRC Section 303(b). The Treasury and the IRS interpret the foregoing as follows: If a decedent makes a gift of any kind of property within three years of his or her death, the value of the property given will be included in the decedent's gross estate for purposes of determining whether the value of the corporation stock in question exceeds 35 percent of the value of the gross estate, but a distribution in redemption of that stock will not

1. Treas. Reg. §1.303-2(d).
2. IRC Sec. 303(b)(2)(A).
3. IRC Sec. 2053.
4. IRC Sec. 2054.
5. Treas. Reg. §1.303-2(c)(1).

qualify as an IRC Section 303 redemption unless the stock redeemed actually is a part of the decedent's gross estate.[1]

The stock of two or more corporations will be treated as that of a single corporation, provided that 20 percent or more of the value of all of the outstanding stock of each corporation is includable in a decedent's gross estate.[2] Only stock directly owned is taken into account in determining whether the 20 percent test has been met; constructive ownership rules do not apply even when they would benefit a taxpayer.[3] Stock that, at a decedent's death, represents the surviving spouse's interest in property held by the decedent and the surviving spouse as community property or as joint tenants, tenants by the entirety, or tenants in common is considered to be includable in a decedent's gross estate for the purpose of meeting the 20 percent requirement.[4] The 20 percent test is not an elective provision; that is, if a distribution in redemption of stock qualifies under IRC Section 303 only by reason of the application of the 20 percent test and also qualifies for sale treatment under another section of the IRC, the executor may not elect to have only the latter section of the IRC apply and thus retain undiminished the IRC Section 303 limits for later use. All distributions that qualify under IRC Section 303 are treated as IRC Section 303 redemptions in the order they are made.[5]

(3) The dollar amount that can be paid out by a corporation under protection of IRC Section 303 is limited to an amount equal to the sum of (x) all estate taxes, including the generation-skipping transfer tax imposed by reason of the decedent's death, and federal and state inheritance taxes attributable to a decedent's death, plus interest, if any, collected on these taxes, and (y) funeral and administration expenses allowable as estate deductions under IRC Section 2053.[6]

(4) The stock must be redeemed not later than (x) three years and ninety days after the estate tax return is filed, which return must be filed within nine months after a decedent's death, (y) sixty days after a Tax Court decision on an estate tax deficiency becomes final, or (z) if an extension of time for payment of tax is elected under IRC Section 6166, the time determined under the applicable section for payment of the installments. For any redemption made more than four years after a decedent's death, however, capital gains treatment is available only for a distribution in an amount that is the lesser of (a) the amount of the qualifying death taxes and funeral and administration expenses that are unpaid immediately before the distribution, or (b) the aggregate of these amounts that are paid within one year after the distribution.[7]

1. Rev. Rul. 84-76, 1984-1 CB 91.
2. IRC Sec. 303(b)(2)(B).
3. *Est. of Byrd v. Comm.*, 388 F.2d 223, 21 AFTR 2d 313 (5th Cir. 1967).
4. IRC Sec. 303(b)(2)(B).
5. Treas. Reg. §1.303-2(g); Rev. Rul. 79-401, 1979-2 CB 128.
6. IRC Secs. 303(a), 303(d).
7. IRC Secs. 303(b)(1), 303(b)(4).

(5) The shareholder from whom stock is redeemed must be one whose interest is reduced directly, or through a binding obligation to contribute, by payment of qualifying death taxes and funeral and administration expenses, and the redemption will qualify for capital gains treatment only to the extent of that reduction.[1] That is, "the party whose shares are redeemed [must actually have] a liability for estate taxes, state death taxes, or funeral and administration expenses in an amount at least equal to the amount of the redemption."[2]

305. Does redemption under an insurance-funded stock redemption agreement result in capital gain to a deceased stockholder's estate?

No. An estate typically realizes no capital gain as a result of a redemption. Where a redemption is a capital transaction (Q 300 to Q 303), an estate has no tax liability unless the price paid by the corporation exceeds the new tax basis of the stock redeemed.

When a stockholder dies, his or her stock receives a new basis equal to its fair market value at date of death or at an alternate valuation date.[3]

As sale price under a proper stock redemption agreement generally is accepted as the fair market value of shares (Q 322), the sale price should equal the estate's basis and no gain or loss should be realized by an estate.

For decedents dying in 2010, modified carryover basis rules in IRC Section 1022 may apply, so stock may not receive a full basis step-up.

306. If a close corporation redeems stock from a decedent's estate, is the amount paid for the stock taxable as a constructive dividend to the surviving stockholder or stockholders?

No.

A surviving stockholder will not be treated as having received a constructive dividend merely because the percentage of interest in a corporation is increased by a redemption.[4] A redemption may result in a constructive dividend to a survivor if the survivor had an obligation to purchase the stock, for example, under a cross-purchase agreement, and redemption by the corporation satisfies that personal obligation.[5]

A survivor does not realize taxable income from a redemption unless his or her obligation to purchase stock was primary and unconditional. Thus, there is no constructive dividend if a survivor has assigned his or her obligation to the corporation before conditions for performance of

1. IRC Sec. 303(b)(3).
2. H.R. Rep. No. 94-1380 at 35 (Estate and Gift Tax Reform Act of 1976), *reprinted in* 1976-3 CB (Vol. 3) 735 at 769.
3. IRC Secs. 1014(a)(1), 1014(a)(2).
4. *Holsey v. Comm.*, 258 F.2d 865 (3rd Cir. 1958); Rev. Rul. 58-614, 1958-2 CB 920; Rev. Rul. 59-286, 1959-2 CB 103.
5. *Smith v. Comm.*, 70 TC 651 (1978).

the contract arose, if the buyout contract contained a provision permitting the stockholder to call on the corporation to buy the stock, or if the survivor could have elected not to buy the stock.[1]

307. What are the income tax consequences of funding a stock redemption agreement with life insurance?

Premiums

The IRS does not consider premiums paid by a corporation under a stock redemption agreement to be ordinary and necessary business expenses. Furthermore, regardless of whether a corporation, trust, or insured's spouse or estate is named beneficiary in a policy, the corporation either directly or indirectly is a beneficiary under the policy because the proceeds will be used to discharge its obligation to redeem the stock. Consequently, the corporation cannot deduct the premium payments (Q 264).[2]

Moreover, regardless of who is named beneficiary, premium payments are not taxable income to stockholders if a corporation owns the policy and the right of a beneficiary to receive proceeds is conditioned on the transfer of stock to the corporation (Q 268).

Death Proceeds

Death proceeds ordinarily are received tax-free.[3] Prior to 2018, death proceeds may have been subject to tax under the corporate alternative minimum tax (Q 316), which was repealed by the 2017 Tax Act.[4] In addition, death proceeds are taxable unless a status exception exists and notice and consent requirements for employer-owned life insurance are met (Q 276).

Cost Basis

Because proceeds become part of a corporation's general assets, the value of stock owned by each surviving stockholder will be increased by a share, proportionate to his or her stock interest, of the difference between the death proceeds and the cash surrender value prior to death. The cost basis of a survivor's stock will not be increased. Consequently, the increase in value due to the insurance may result in some additional gain if a survivor sells the stock during the survivor's lifetime. If a survivor holds the stock until death, the stock will receive a new tax basis equal to its fair market value at the time of the survivor's death, thus eliminating this effect. Decedents who died in 2010, however, may not receive a full step up in basis.[5]

For the result under a stock purchase plan, see Q 299.

In the case of an S corporation, each shareholder's basis is increased by the shareholder's share of the death proceeds, whether taxable or not, when they are received by the corporation.[6]

1. *Pulliam v. Comm.*, TC Memo 1984-470; Rev. Rul. 69-608, 1969-2 CB 42.
2. IRC Secs. 162(a), 264(a)(1); Rev. Rul. 70-117, 1970-1 CB 30.
3. IRC Sec. 101(a).
4. IRC Sec. 56.
5. IRC Sec.1022.
6. See IRC Sec. 1366(a) and 1367.

A corporation has no income tax basis problem; even if redeemed stock is carried as treasury stock and subsequently is resold, the corporation realizes no gain regardless of basis.[1]

Effect on Corporate Earnings and Profits

Revenue Ruling 54-230[2] states that earnings and profits will be increased by the excess of insurance proceeds over aggregate premiums paid, apparently on the assumption that no part of premiums have been deducted from earnings and profits. For taxable years beginning after July 18, 1984, if a corporation distributes amounts in a redemption under IRC Sections 302(a) or 303, the part of the distribution properly chargeable to earnings and profits is an amount not in excess of the ratable share of the earnings and profits of the corporation accumulated after February 28, 1913, attributable to the stock redeemed.[3] The Conference Committee Reports from TRA 1984 indicate that priorities between different classes of stock may be taken into account in allocating earnings between classes and that redemption of preferred stock that is not convertible or participating to any significant extent in corporate growth should be charged to the capital account only.[4]

See also "Accumulated Earnings Tax," Q 308.

308. Will the accumulated earnings tax be imposed where corporate earnings are used to purchase business life insurance?

Editor's Note: The 2017 Tax Act limited the members of a controlled group of corporations (the members of which are determined as of December 31 of the relevant year) to a single $250,000 ($150,000 if any member of the group is a service organization in the fields of health, law, engineering, architecture, accounting, actuarial science, performing arts, or consulting) amount in order to compute the accumulated earnings credit.[5] This amount must be divided equally among the members of the controlled group, unless future regulations provide that unequal allocations are permissible.[6]

The accumulated earnings tax is imposed when a corporation, to prevent profits from being taxed to shareholders, retains earnings not needed in the business.[7] The Jobs and Growth Tax Relief Reconciliation Act of 2003 reduced the accumulated earnings tax rate to 15 percent (Q 788). For tax years beginning after 2012, the American Taxpayer Relief Act of 2012 increased the accumulated earnings tax rate to 20 percent.

In computing the amount of income subject to the tax, a credit is allowed for accumulations to meet reasonable current and anticipated business needs. Consequently, the tax should not

1. IRC Sec. 1032(a); Treas. Reg. §1.1032-1(a).
2. 1954-1 CB 114.
3. IRC Sec. 312(n)(7).
4. H.R. Conf. Rep. No. 98-861 (TRA '84) *reprinted in* 1984-3 CB (vol. 2) 94.
5. Under IRC Sec. 535(c).
6. IRC Sec. 1561(a).
7. IRC Sec. 531, as amended by the American Taxpayer Relief Act of 2012, Pub. Law No. 112-240, Sec. 102(d)(1).

be imposed on income retained for the purchase of life insurance if the insurance serves a valid business need and generally is related to that need.[1]

The purchase of life insurance to compensate a corporation for loss of a key person's service through early death is a reasonable business need and earnings used for that purpose therefore are not subject to the penalty tax.[2] *Emeloid Co.,* although not an accumulated earnings tax case, is excellent authority for the proposition that key person life insurance is a reasonable business need.

In *Novelart Mfg. Co. v. Comm.*,[3] premiums for key person life insurance were included in the taxable base on which the accumulated earnings tax is imposed. The taxpayer failed to argue that because key person life insurance is a reasonable business need, the premiums should be included in the calculation of the accumulated earnings credit. Instead, the taxpayer argued only that the amounts paid out for life insurance premiums no longer were available for distribution and should not be included in the measure of the tax because the tax is imposed on what is accumulated rather than on what is distributed. The argument was dismissed as inconsistent with the IRC rules for calculating the tax.

It also has been held that the cash surrender value of key person life insurance is not considered a liquid asset, along with cash and marketable securities, in determining whether further accumulations to finance plans for business expansion are necessary.[4]

An accumulation of earnings to meet a corporation's obligations incurred under a deferred compensation agreement should be considered a reasonable business need.[5]

Under certain circumstances, including to promote corporate harmony or management efficiency or to enable a corporation to continue its accustomed practices or policies, an accumulation of earnings to fund a stock redemption may constitute an accumulation for a reasonable need of the business.[6] Several cases do not deal with the accumulated earnings tax but contain persuasive statements concerning the business need for life insurance to fund close corporation stock redemptions.[7]

Several cases, not involving life insurance, have held that an accumulation of income for the purpose of affecting an IRC Section 303 redemption (Q 303) serves the purpose of an individual stockholder rather than a corporation. The effect of these cases is limited by IRC Section 537, which provides that the phrase "reasonable needs of the business" includes a business's IRC Section 303 redemption needs. The IRC language is not clear on the extent to which accumulations in years prior to a stockholder's death are to have protection from the

1. See *General Smelting Co. v. Comm.*, 4 TC 313 (1944).
2. *Harry A. Koch Co. v. Vinal*, 228 F. Supp. 782, 13 AFTR 2d 1241 (D. Neb. 1964), nonacq. 1965-1 CB 246; *Vuono-Lione, Inc. v. Comm.*, TC Memo 1965-96; see also *Emeloid Co. v. Comm.*, 189 F.2d 230 (3rd Cir. 1951).
3. 52 TC 794 (1969), *aff'd*, 434 F2d 1011, 26 AFTR 2d 70-5837 (6th Cir. 1970).
4. *Motor Fuel Carriers, Inc. v. Comm.*, 77-2 USTC ¶9661 (5th Cir. 1977).
5. *John P. Scripps Newspapers v. Comm.*, 44 TC 453 (1965); *Okla. Press Pub. Co. v. U.S.*, 35 AFTR 2d 1383 (10th Cir. 1971), on remand, 28 AFTR 2d 5722 (E.D. Okla. 1971); see Treas. Reg. §1.537-2(b)(3).
6. *Mountain State Steel Foundries, Inc. v. Comm.*, 284 F.2d 737, 6 AFTR 2d 5910 (4th Cir. 1960); *Oman Construction Co. v. Comm.*, TC Memo 1965-325. But see also *John B. Lambert & Assoc. v. U.S.*, 76-2 USTC ¶9776 (Ct. Cl. 1976).
7. *Emeloid Co. v. Comm.*, supra; *Sanders v. Fox*, 253 F.2d 855 (10th Cir. 1958); *Prunier v. Comm.*, 248 F.2d 818 (1st Cir. 1957).

tax. The IRC limits the amount of tax-sheltered accumulation in the year of a stockholder's death or in a subsequent year. Regulations provide that the reasonableness of accumulations in years prior to a year in which a shareholder dies is to be determined solely on the facts and circumstances existing at the times the accumulations occur.[1]

Planning Point: To avoid the accumulated earnings tax, a corporation should document the reason for retained earnings or the reason for the purchase of corporate owned life insurance. Contemporaneous documentation of the business need will go a long way toward avoiding this tax.

In the case of a professional corporation (Q 788), a stock redemption following a shareholder's death usually is not made under IRC Section 303 but is a complete redemption of all shareholder stock under IRC Section 302 (Q 300). The requirement of many state laws that a corporation must purchase stock of a deceased or disqualified professional would appear to establish a valid business purpose for accumulations to fund such redemptions. Consequently, an accumulation under these circumstances, particularly if funded by life insurance, should be immune from imposition of the accumulated earnings tax.[2]

309. How is gain realized by an S corporation on sale, surrender, or redemption of a life insurance or endowment policy taxed?

Each stockholder's pro rata share of any gain received by an S corporation, such as gain on endowment maturity or from sale or surrender of a life insurance policy, will be included in a stockholder's gross income and will increase the basis in the stock.[3]

310. If an S corporation redeems a shareholder's stock, how are redemption payments taxed?

If an S corporation has no accumulated earnings and profits from when it was a C corporation or as a result of a corporate acquisition, then a redemption of stock will be treated as a capital transaction. That is, it will be tax-free to the extent of the shareholder's basis and any excess will be treated as capital gain.[4]

If an S corporation has accumulated earnings and profits, however, then part of the payment by the corporation could be treated as a dividend.[5] The exceptions to dividend treatment under IRC Sections 302(a) and 303(a) are available to S corporations (Q 300 to Q 303).

311. What are the income tax consequences when a deceased partner's interest is liquidated under a business purchase agreement?

The term "liquidation" refers to termination of a partner's entire interest by means of a distribution or series of distributions by a partnership. This is an entity redemption plan.[6] The term sale refers to purchase of a deceased's partnership interest by a surviving partner or partners

1. Treas. Reg. §1.537-1(e)(3).
2. See Internal Revenue Audit Manual 4.10.13.2.
3. IRC Secs. 1366(a)(1), 1367(a)(1)(A).
4. IRC Sec. 1368(b).
5. IRC Sec. 1368(c).
6. IRC Sec. 761(d).

individually; this is a cross-purchase plan.[1] Sale of a deceased partner's interest under a business purchase agreement is discussed in Q 313.

The portion of a partnership's payment that is allocable to a deceased partner's interest in partnership property is treated as a distribution, or payment for the purchase of a capital asset.[2] If capital is not a material income-producing factor for a partnership and a deceased partner was a general partner, then payments for an interest in partnership property will not include unrealized receivables or goodwill unless the partnership agreement provides for payments for goodwill.[3]

The estate or other successor in interest should realize no gain or loss if a partnership has elected to adjust the basis of partnership property to reflect the new basis of the deceased's partnership interest since that basis will be determined under stepped-up basis rules. Generally, the valuation placed by partners on a partner's interest in partnership property in an arm's length agreement will be regarded as correct.

The amount of any money or the fair market value of any property received by a partner in exchange for all or a part of the partner's interest in the partnership attributable to unrealized receivables of the partnership or inventory items of the partnership is considered an amount realized from a sale or exchange of property other than a capital asset. Amounts realized from a sale of property other than a capital asset generally are treated as ordinary income to the extent of gain.

The basis of these items also may be adjusted if a partnership elects. Payments for a deceased's interest in partnership property are not deductible by a partnership, but they increase, pro rata, the basis for each remaining partner's partnership interest.

The portion of a partnership payment that is allocable to a deceased's interest in unrealized receivables or inventory items of a partnership is ordinary income to the estate or other recipient.[4] Unrealized receivables include accounts receivable that were not previously includable in taxable income of partners and depreciation that is treated as ordinary income under IRC Sections 1245 and 1250 on the sale of depreciable property.[5] In determining the value of unrealized receivables, full account will be taken of the estimated cost of completing performance of the contract and of the time between the sale and time of payment.[6] Payments for unrealized receivables are deductible by a partnership.[7]

Any additional amounts paid by a partnership are treated as ordinary income (Q 314).

Ordinary income payments in a liquidation of a deceased partner's interest are income in respect of a decedent.[8] Consequently, a recipient of the income is entitled to an income tax

1. IRC Sec. 741.
2. IRC Sec. 736(b).
3. IRC Sec. 736(b)(3).
4. IRC Sec. 751(a).
5. See IRC Sec. 751.
6. Treas. Reg. §1.751-1(c)(3).
7. IRC Sec. 736(a); Treas. Reg. §1.736-1(a)(4).
8. IRC Sec. 753.

deduction for any portion of the federal death taxes, including the generation-skipping transfer tax imposed on a taxable termination or a direct skip occurring as a result of a decedent's death, paid by the decedent's estate that is attributable to the value of that income.[1]

A partnership, even a two-person partnership, will not be considered to have terminated so long as liquidation payments under IRC Section 736 are being made.[2] Note that the 2017 Tax Act repealed the technical termination rule that previously applied to partnerships.

See Q 312 for a discussion of how goodwill is treated in this context.

312. How is "goodwill" treated when a deceased partner's interest is liquidated under a business purchase agreement?

Under a liquidation agreement, partners may elect to treat amounts paid for goodwill as either the purchase price for a capital asset or as ordinary income. For partners retiring or dying on or after January 5, 1993, or for payments made under a written contract that was binding as of January 4, 1993, an additional requirement applies to the election to treat goodwill as ordinary income. This treatment may be elected only if capital is not a material income-producing factor in a partnership and a retiring or deceased partner was a general partner.[3]

Where an agreement provides that part of the purchase price is for goodwill, the amount allocable to goodwill also will be treated as having been paid for a deceased's interest in partnership property. Regulations state that payment for goodwill, to be treated as a capital transaction, must be reasonable. However, the value placed on goodwill by partners in an arm's length agreement, whether specific in amount or determined by formula, generally will be regarded as the correct value.[4]

If the material income-producing factor/general partner requirements mentioned above are met and the agreement makes no provision for goodwill, or stipulates that payment for goodwill is to be treated as income, the amount paid for goodwill is taxable as ordinary income to the estate or other recipient. If treated as ordinary income, it is deductible by the partnership.[5]

Election to treat payment for goodwill as a capital investment or ordinary income may be made either in the original articles of partnership or in a subsequent business purchase agreement.[6] The IRS has ruled that determination as to whether a professional practice has saleable goodwill will be made on the basis of all the facts in a particular case and not on the basis of whether a business is dependent solely on the personal characteristics of the owner.[7]

1. IRC Sec. 691(c).
2. Treas. Reg. §1.708-1(b)(1)(i); Treas. Reg. §1.736-1(a)(6).
3. IRC Sec. 736(b)(3).
4. Treas. Reg. §1.736-1(b)(3).
5. IRC Sec. 736(b)(2).
6. *Jackson Investment Co. v. Comm.*, 346 F.2d 187, 15 AFTR 2d 1125 (9th Cir. 1965).
7. Rev. Rul. 64-235, 1964-2 CB 18, as modified by Rev. Rul. 70-45, 1970-1 CB 17.

313. What are the income tax consequences when a deceased partner's interest is sold under a business purchase agreement?

Where a deceased partner's interest is sold to a surviving partner or partners as individuals, the income tax results with respect to the purchase of the deceased's interest in partnership property essentially are the same as in a liquidation (see Q 311). This portion of a purchase is considered a capital transaction for purposes of determining gain or loss to a deceased's estate.

A survivor's interests in partnership property receives an increase in basis for this portion of the payment.[1] A slight difference in tax law exists, however, between liquidation and a sale with respect to payment for goodwill. In a sale, payments for goodwill must be treated as part of a capital transaction; partners do not have an option to treat these payments as ordinary income.[2] See Q 312 for a discussion of how goodwill is treated in liquidation.

Payments for unrealized receivables, as in liquidation, are taxable as ordinary income to a deceased's estate or other recipient. Unrealized receivables generally are income in respect of a decedent and therefore do not receive a new basis because of the death of a partner even though an election to adjust basis is in effect.[3] Survivors cannot deduct their payments for unrealized receivables. They can elect, on behalf of the partnership, to adjust the basis of partnership assets. By such an election, the partnership's basis for its unrealized receivables, which usually is zero, is stepped-up for the benefit of each purchasing partner to reflect the amount he or she paid for his or her share of the receivables. Thus, when receivables are collected by a partnership, each partner's share will result in ordinary income only to the extent that it exceeds the price the partner paid for his or her interest in the receivables.[4]

314. What are the income tax results of a partnership income continuation plan?

A partnership can agree to make payments to a retiring partner or to the estate or beneficiary of a deceased partner, other than payments in liquidation of that partner's partnership interest. The payments either may be periodic guaranteed amounts or a share of future profits. In either case, the payments will be taxed as ordinary income to the payee.[5]

Payments of a guaranteed amount will be deductible by a partnership.[6]

Similarly, payments representing a share of profits will reduce the remaining or surviving partners' share of distributable taxable income.[7]

This tax treatment applies only to payments made by a partnership as an entity and not to payments made by individual remaining or surviving partners. A partnership, even a two person

1. IRC Sec. 742.
2. *Karan v. Comm.*, 319 F.2d 303 (7th Cir. 1963).
3. *Woodhall v. Comm.*,454 F.2d 226, 29 AFTR 2d 72- 394 (9th Cir. 1972).
4. IRC Secs. 754, 743.
5. Rev. Rul. 71-507, 1971-2 CB 331.
6. Treas. Reg. §1.736-1(a)(4).
7. IRC Sec. 736(a).

partnership, will not be considered as having terminated so long as these payments are being made because partners' interests have not been liquidated.[1]

315. What is the tax treatment of life insurance purchased to fund a partnership business purchase agreement?

Premiums are not deductible whether paid by individual partners or by a partnership (Q 274).[2] Assuming the requirements for employer-owned life insurance are met and there has not been a violation of the transfer for value rule, death proceeds are exempt from income tax whether received by partners or the partnership (Q 276).[3]

The basis to partners of their partnership interests is increased by proceeds received by the partnership.[4]

Similarly, under a cross-purchase plan, each partner's basis for the partnership interest will be increased by the amount the partner pays for the partner's share of a deceased partner's interest.[5]

If an insured is a partner in a partnership, policies can be freely sold or exchanged between partners, or between partners and the partnership, without fear of adverse tax consequences from the transfer for value rule (Q 289).

Even though proceeds are made payable directly to an insured's personal beneficiary, a survivor may be able to include the proceeds in his or her cost basis if there is a legally binding agreement between the partners to apply the proceeds to the purchase of the business interest.[6]

316. How was corporate-owned life insurance treated for purposes of the corporate alternative minimum tax prior to 2018?

Editor's Note: The 2017 Tax Act repealed the corporate alternative minimum tax (AMT) for tax years beginning after 2017.

Prior to 2018, unless it qualified for the small corporation exemption, a corporation could have been subject to the corporate alternative minimum tax ("AMT"). Calculation of this fairly complicated tax is discussed generally in Q 788. One component of the corporate AMT, known as the adjusted current earnings ("ACE") adjustment, has a potential effect on corporate-owned life insurance policies.

A C corporation must adjust its reported income to reflect its adjusted current earnings ("ACE") or, before 1990, its book income. Inside buildup and payment of death proceeds of corporate-owned life insurance will affect an ACE adjustment. Death proceeds will not necessarily subject a corporation to the AMT because life insurance is only one of many factors considered when determining whether a corporation must pay the AMT.

1. Treas. Reg. §1.736-1(a)(6).
2. IRC Sec. 264(a)(1).
3. IRC Sec. 101(a).
4. IRC Sec. 705(a)(1).
5. IRC Sec. 1012.
6. See *Mushro v. Comm.*, 50 TC 43 (1968), *nonacq.* 1970-2 CB xxii. But see *Legallet v. Comm.*, 41 BTA 294 (1940).

A corporation's alternative minimum taxable income ("AMTI") generally was increased by 75 percent of any excess of the corporation's ACE divided by the corporation's AMTI. For negative adjustments, a corporation's AMTI was reduced by 75 percent of any excess of the corporation's AMTI divided by the corporation's ACE.[1]

Regulations offer the guidelines set forth below with respect to the effect of corporate-owned life insurance contracts on ACE.[2]

Inside Buildup

Income on a contract with respect to a tax year is included in ACE for the year except for a tax year in which an insured dies or a year in which the contract is completely surrendered for its entire net surrender value. The income is calculated from the beginning of the tax year to the date of any distribution, from immediately after any distribution to the date of the next distribution, and from the last distribution in the tax year through the end of the tax year.

Solely for purposes of computing ACE, basis in a contract is increased for positive income on the contract included in ACE. The income on a contract for ACE is (1) the contract's net surrender value at the end of the period plus any distributions during the period that are not taxed because they represent return of basis in the contract for purposes of ACE, minus (2) the net surrender value at the end of the preceding period plus any premiums paid during the period.

Distributions

A distribution, whether a partial withdrawal or an amount received on complete surrender, is included in ACE under IRC Section 72(e) (Q 10), taking into account a taxpayer's basis for purposes of computing ACE. The basis is the same as the basis for ACE at the end of the immediately preceding period plus premiums paid before a distribution.

The basis in a contract for purposes of ACE is reduced by the amount not included in ACE because it represents recovery of ACE basis. If ACE basis in a contract exceeds death benefits received, the resulting loss may be deducted from ACE.

Death Benefits

Death benefits generally are excluded from gross income under IRC Section 101. Major exceptions include if COLI Best Practices Act provisions are not met or if the transfer for value rule is violated.

The excess of contractual death benefits over a taxpayer's basis for purposes of ACE at the time of death is included in ACE.

Any outstanding policy loan treated as discharged or forgiven on the death of an insured is included in the amount of the death benefit.

1. IRC Sec. 56(g).
2. Treas. Reg. §1.56(g)-1(c)(5).

Term Life Insurance without Net Surrender Value

ACE is reduced by premiums paid to the extent allocable to coverage provided during the year; premiums not so allocable must be included in basis. A death benefit is included in ACE as explained above. For a discussion of policies involving divided ownership, see Q 317.

317. How was corporate-owned life insurance treated for purposes of the corporate alternative minimum tax prior to 2018 when policies have divided ownership?

Editor's Note: The 2017 Tax Act repealed the corporate alternative minimum tax (AMT) for tax years beginning after 2017.

The requirements discussed in Q 316 apply to separate ownership interests as though each interest were a separate contract.

Example. Brown Corporation has a policy with a net surrender value of $14,774 as of the end of 2015. The policy had a surrender value of $11,231 at the end of 2014 and a basis of $9,821 as a result of $8,800 in aggregate premiums paid plus $1,021 included in ACE as inside buildup in 2016. Brown Corporation paid a premium of $2,200 in 2015. The corporation must include in ACE for 2015 $1,343 ($14,774 – [$11,231 + $2,200]). The basis in the contract for purposes of ACE is increased by $1,343 of income on the contract included in ACE for 2015 and the $2,200 premium paid in 2015, for a total of $13,364.

Assume instead that, in 2015, Mrs. Brown, the insured, dies after the $2,200 premium was paid and Brown Corporation received the $100,000 death benefit. No amount of inside buildup is included in income; instead, the corporation must include in ACE the excess of the death benefit over the basis for ACE, $87,979 ($100,000 – [$9,821 + $2,200]).

Now, assume that Mrs. Brown did not die in 2015. Brown Corporation paid a premium of $2,200 in 2015 and received a distribution of $16,200 on February 1, 2016, leaving a net surrender value of $915. On March 1, 2016, Brown Corporation pays an additional premium of $5,000. The net surrender value of the contract at the end of 2016 is $6,417. Brown Corporation must include $636 of the distribution in income: $16,200 (distribution) – $15,564 (basis for ACE as of the time of the distribution).

The income on the contract includable in ACE for 2016 is determined separately for the period before the distribution and the period after it. There is no income on the contract for the period beginning January 1, 2016, and ending at the time of the distribution on February 1, 2016: [$915 (net surrender value at the end of the period) + $15,564 (distribution of basis)] – [$14,774 (net surrender value at the end of 2015) + $2,200 (premiums paid during the period)] = ($495). Because the net result is negative, no income is included for this period.

Income on the contract for the period beginning immediately after the distribution through the end of the taxable year is $502: $6,417 (net surrender value at the end of 2016) – [$915 (net surrender value at the end of the preceding period) + $5,000 (premiums paid during the period)].

At the end of 2016, Brown Corporation's basis in the contract for ACE is $5,502: $502 (income on the contract) + $5,000 (premium) + $0 (the basis at the end of the previous period). Brown Corporation includes in ACE in 2016 a total of $1,138 ($502 income on the contract) + $636 (income from distribution).[1]

1. See Treas. Reg. §1.56(g)-1(c)(5)(vii).

Insurance on Key Persons, Partners, Stockholders

318. If a partnership purchases and owns life insurance on the life of a partner, are policy proceeds includable in the insured partner's estate?

If a partnership is both policy owner and beneficiary, insurance proceeds are not includable in an insured's gross estate under the incidents of ownership test (Q 85).[1]

Proceeds received by a partnership will be included with other partnership assets in determining the value of a decedent's partnership interest for estate tax purposes; consequently, his or her gross estate will reflect a share of the proceeds proportionate to the partnership interest.[2]

If an insured has personal incidents of ownership in a policy, including the right to change a beneficiary, the entire value of the proceeds will be includable in the gross estate.[3]

Where death proceeds are payable to a partner's personal beneficiary, the insured is deemed to possess an incident of ownership in the insurance in his or her capacity as a partner for purposes of IRC Section 2042(2) regardless of the percentage of the partnership interest. Consequently, if a partnership owns insurance at the time of an insured partner's death, the entire proceeds will be includable in the partner's estate.[4]

For estate tax treatment of group term life insurance covering the life of a partner, see Q 175.

319. If a corporation purchases life insurance on the life of a key person to indemnify it against loss on account of the key person's death, are proceeds includable in the insured's estate?

If, at an insured's death, a policy was owned by and payable to a corporation and the insured possessed no incidents of ownership in the policy (Q 85, Q 86), proceeds are not includable in the insured's gross estate. If the insured possessed at his or her death any incidents of ownership in the policy, the proceeds are includable in his or her gross estate even though the corporation has been named owner and beneficiary.[5]

Death proceeds of life insurance owned by and payable to a corporation are considered, along with the other non-operating assets, as a relevant factor in valuing a corporation's stock for estate tax purposes (but see Q 321).[6] Consequently, where an insured is a stockholder, the value of proceeds will be reflected in valuing stock includable in the insured's gross estate.[7] It is not correct to value the stock first, without considering the insurance proceeds, and then simply

1. *Est. of Knipp v. Comm.*, 25 TC 153 (1955), acq. in result, 1959-1 CB 4; *Est. of Atkins v. Comm.*, 2 TC 332 (1943); Rev. Rul. 83-147, 1983-2 CB 158. See also Let. Rul. 200017051.
2. See IRC Sec. 2033.
3. See IRC Sec. 2042(2); *Hall v. Wheeler*, 174 F. Supp. 418 (D. Me. 1959); *Est. of Piggott v. Comm.*, TC Memo 1963-61, aff'd, 340 F.2d 829 (6th Cir. 1965).
4. Rev. Rul. 83-147, 1983-2 CB 158; GCM 39034 (9-21-83).
5. IRC Sec. 2042(2); *Est. of Piggott v. Comm.*, 340 F.2d 829 (6th Cir. 1965), *aff'g* TC Memo 1963-61; *Hall v. Wheeler*, 174 F. Supp. 418 (D. Me. 1959); *Kearns v. U.S.*, 399 F.2d 226 (Ct. Cl. 1968); *Est. of Cockrill v. O'Hara*, 302 F. Supp. 1365 (M.D. Tenn. 1969).
6. Treas. Reg. §20.2031-2(f).
7. *Est. of Blair v. Comm.*, 4 BTA 959 (1926), nonacq. 1927-1 CB 7; *Est. of Doerken v. Comm.*, 46 BTA 809 (1926); *In re Patton's Will*, 278 N.W. 866 (Wisc. 1938); *In re Reed's Est.*, 153 N.E. 47 (N.Y. 1926); *Kennedy v. Comm.*, 4 BTA 330 (1926); *Est. of Carew v. Comm.*, 311 A2d 185 (N.J. 1973).

add the amount of proceeds to that value.[1] Factoring life insurance proceeds into the valuation of stock may or may not result in an increase in value equal to the full value of the insurance proceeds, depending on the valuation method.[2] An offset may be available where there is an obligation to pay insurance proceeds to another party under a buy-sell agreement.[3]

It may be possible to obtain some reduction in the value of stock to reflect loss to the business of the key person's services.[4] The executor must offer proof to establish that the insured's death actually did cause a loss. A loss does not result per se from the death of the owner and manager of a corporation.[5]

It has been held that no decrease in value for loss of an insured's services will be allowed if the stock is personal holding company stock where the assets consist almost entirely of stocks and bonds; a corporation must be an operating business requiring management, with going value and goodwill.[6]

If an insured is a controlling stockholder, that is, one who owns stock amounting to more than 50 percent of the total combined voting power of the corporation, then to the extent proceeds are payable other than to or for the benefit of the corporation, any incidents of ownership in the insurance held by the corporation as to the proceeds will be attributed to the insured and thereby will cause the proceeds to be includable in the insured's gross estate.[7]

In Revenue Ruling 82-141,[8] X corporation owned insurance on the life of its controlling stockholder, D. The corporation assigned all of its incidents of ownership in the policy to A. D died within three years of the assignment, and proceeds of the policy were paid to A. The IRS held that the proceeds were includable in D's estate under IRC Section 2035 (Q 96) by reason of attribution to D of the incidents of ownership held by the corporation. The ruling failed to identify the policy's beneficiary before the assignment.

The IRS also held that proceeds were includable in an insured's estate under IRC Section 2035 where a corporation transferred a policy insuring the controlling shareholder to a third person within three years of the insured's death even though the insured disposed of the insured's stock after the transfer of the policy and prior to the insured's death.[9]

Proceeds also were includable in an insured's estate where a corporation retained ownership of a policy and an insured transferred enough stock so as to cease being a controlling shareholder within three years of death (Q 325).[10]

1. *Est. of Huntsman v. Comm.*, 66 TC 861 (1976), *acq.* 1977-1 CB 1.
2. *Est. of Blount v. Comm.*, TC Memo 2004-116.
3. *Est. of Blount v. Comm.*, 428 F.3d 1338 (11th Cir. 2005).
4. Rev. Rul. 59-60, 1959-1 CB 237; *Newell v. Comm.*, 66 F.2d 102 (7th Cir. 1933); *Est. of Huntsman*, supra.
5. *Est. of Scherer v. Comm.*, 1940 P-H BTA Memorandum Decisions ¶40,530.
6. *In re Patton's Will*, supra.
7. Treas. Reg. §20.2042-1(c)(6).
8. 1982-2 CB 209.
9. Rev. Rul. 90-21, 1990-1 CB 172, Situation 1.
10. Rev. Rul. 90-21, 1990-1 CB 172, Situation 2.

320. If partners or stockholders enter into a buy-sell agreement and each purchases life insurance on each other's lives to fund the agreement, are proceeds includable in an insured's gross estate?

If, under a cross-purchase arrangement, proceeds are not payable to an insured's estate, and an insured has no incidents of ownership in the policies on his or her life, death benefit proceeds are not includable in his or her gross estate.[1]

The Tax Court has held that a provision in an agreement prohibiting a policy owner from surrendering the policy, borrowing against the policy, or changing the beneficiary of the policy without the insured's consent did not give the insured incidents of ownership in the policy (but see Q 86).[2] The value of an insured's partnership interest or corporate stock is includable.[3] The value of any unmatured policies an insured owns on the life of his or her associates also will be includable.

Where proceeds are includable in the gross estate but the estate is obligated to apply them to the purchase price of the insured's business interest, the value of the business interest will be includable in the gross estate only to the extent that it exceeds the value of the proceeds. In other words, there will be no double taxation.[4]

There is some legal authority to the effect that terms of a policy can be modified by terms of a business agreement. Thus, where an agreement gives all beneficial ownership in proceeds to an insured's co-partners and obligates the parties to apply them to the purchase of the insured's business interest, proceeds are not included in the insured's gross estate despite a policy provision giving the insured the right to change the beneficiary.[5]

321. If life insurance is owned by and payable to a partnership or corporation to fund purchase of an owner's business interest, are proceeds includable in the insured owner's estate?

No.

Because proceeds are not payable to an insured's estate and the insured has no incidents of ownership in the policy, at least in the insured's capacity as an individual, the proceeds are not includable in the insured's gross estate.[6] The same result should occur where a business owns the insurance but proceeds are payable to a trustee who must use them to purchase an insured's business interest for the partnership or corporation.

1. IRC Sec. 2042; Rev. Rul. 56-397, 1956-2 CB 599.
2. *Est. of Infante v. Comm.*, TC Memo 1970-206 (appeal dismissed).
3. *Est. of Riecker v. Comm.*, 3 TCM 1293 (1944).
4. *Est. of Mitchell v. Comm.*, 37 BTA 1 (1938), *acq.*; *Est. of Tompkins v. Comm.*, 13 TC 1054 (1949), *acq.*; *Est. of Ealy v. Comm.*, 10 TCM 431; *Dobrzensky v. Comm.*, 34 BTA 305 (1936), nonacq. 1936-2 CB 39; *Boston Safe Deposit & Trust Co. v. Comm.*, 30 BTA 679 (1934), nonacq. 1934-2 CB 34.
5. *Est. of Fuchs v. Comm.*, 47 TC 199 (1966), *acq.* 1967-2 CB 2; *First Nat'l Bank of Birmingham v. U.S.*, 358 F.2d 625 (5th Cir. 1966).
6. IRC Sec. 2042; *Est. of Knipp v. Comm.*, 25 TC 153 (1955), *acq. in result*, 1959-1 CB 4; Rev. Rul. 83-147, 1983-2 CB 158.

The value of a business interest is, of course, includable in an insured's gross estate.[1]

In valuing an insured's business interest, the part of the proceeds that is proportionate to the insured's interest in the business will be included unless the proceeds are excluded from the purchase price under the terms of an agreement and the agreement is effective in fixing the value of the business interest for estate tax purposes (Q 322).[2]

Where an insured is a controlling stockholder, incidents of ownership in insurance owned by the corporation are not attributable to the insured so as to cause death proceeds to be includable in the decedent's gross estate under IRC Section 2042 (Q 319).[3]

322. How is a closely held business interest valued for federal estate tax purposes where there is a purchase agreement?

For purchase agreements entered into after October 8, 1990, or substantially modified after that date, the value of a closely held business interest is to be determined without regard to any purchase agreement exercisable at less than fair market value, determined without regard to the purchase agreement, unless the purchase agreement:

(1) is a bona fide business arrangement;

(2) is not a device to transfer property to members of the decedent's family for less than full or adequate consideration in money or money's worth; and

(3) has terms comparable to those entered into by persons in an arm's length transaction.[4]

Whether or not an agreement is subject to IRC Section 2703, case law has established the additional following rules:

(1) An estate must be obligated to sell at death under either a mandatory purchase agreement or an option held by the business or survivors.

(2) The price must be fixed by the terms of the agreement or the agreement must contain a formula or method for determining the price.

(3) The agreement must prohibit an owner from disposing of his or her interest during life without first offering it to the other party or parties at no more than the contract price.

(4) The price must be fair and adequate when the agreement is made.[5]

1. *Wilson v. Crooks*, 52 F.2d 692 (W.D. Mo. 1931); *Est. of Ealy v. Comm.*, 10 TCM 431 (1951); *Est. of Riecker v. Comm.*, 3 TCM 1293 (1944); *Est. of Atkins v. Comm.*, 2 TC 332 (1943); *Est. of Knipp*, supra.
2. *Newell v. Comm.*, 66 F.2d 102 (7th Cir. 1933); *Kennedy v. Comm.*, 4 BTA 330 (1926); see also *Est. of Salt v. Comm.*, 17 TC 92 (1952); *Est. of Littick v. Comm.*, 31 TC 181 (1958), *acq. in result* 1984-2 CB 1; *Rubel v. Rubel*, 75 So. 2d 59 (Miss. 1954).
3. Treas. Reg. §20.2042-1(c)(6); Rev. Rul. 82-85, 1982-1 CB 137. See also *Est. of Huntsman v. Comm.*, 66 TC 861 (1976), acq. 1977-1 CB 1.
4. See IRC Sec. 2703.
5. *May v. McGowan*, 194 F.2d 396 (2nd Cir. 1952); *Comm. v. Child's Est.*, 147 F.2d 368 (3rd Cir. 1945); *Comm. v. Bensel*, 100 F.2d 639 (3rd Cir. 1938); *Lomb v. Sugden*, 82 F.2d 166 (2nd Cir. 1936); *Wilson v. Bowers*, 57 F.2d 682 (2nd Cir. 1932); *Est. of Littick v. Comm.*, 31 TC 181 (1958), acq. in result 1984-2 CB 1; *Est. of Salt v. Comm.*, 17 TC 92 (1951), acq.; *Fiorito v. Comm.*, 33 TC 440 (1959), acq.; *Est. of Weil v. Comm.*, 22 TC 1267 (1954), acq.; *Est. of Bischoff v. Comm.*, 69 TC 32 (1977); see also Treas. Reg. §20.2031-2(h); Treas. Reg. §20.2031-3.

If a business purchase agreement calls for shares to be purchased from an estate with installment purchase notes bearing a rate of interest lower than the market rate at the date of death, an executor may be allowed to discount the value of the shares by the difference between the interest rate called for in the buy-sell agreement and the prevailing rate at the date of death.[1]

A first-offer agreement, under which survivors have no enforceable right to purchase the business interest and can purchase the interest only if the executor wishes to sell, does not fix the value of the interest for estate tax purposes.[2]

If an agreement is between closely related persons and is merely a scheme for avoiding estate taxes, the price set in the agreement will not control.[3]

A buy-sell agreement is not binding unless it represents a bona fide business agreement and is not testamentary in nature.[4] An agreement may be found to be a scheme for avoiding estate taxes even where it serves a bona-fide business purpose.[5]

No effect will be given to an option or contract under which a decedent is free to dispose of the interest or shares at any price he or she chooses during life.[6]

On the other hand, an agreement that restricts sale during life, but not at death, will also fail to fix the estate tax value.[7]

Practice Point: On August 2, 2016, the U.S. Department of the Treasury issued a notice of proposed rulemaking, published in the Federal Register at 81 FR 51413. In the main, the proposed rulemaking sets for proposed modifications to existing regulations under Internal Revenue Code ("IRC") Section 2701 *et seq.*, and the addition of new regulations specifically under IRC Section 2704. In general IRC Section 2701 *et seq.* governs valuation of interests transferred between family members, outright or in trust. Note that these were proposals, not effective until made so by further action. On April 21, 2017, President Trump issued Executive Order 13789, directing the Secretary of the Treasury to submit a 60-day interim report identifying regulations that (i) impose an undue financial burden on U.S. taxpayers; (ii) add undue complexity to the Federal tax laws; or (iii) exceed the statutory authority of the IRS. The order further instructs the Secretary to submit a final report to the President by September 18, 2017, recommending "specific actions to mitigate the burden imposed by regulations identified in the interim report." On July 7, 2017, the Secretary issued the first report that concluded that eight such regulations meet at least one of the first two criteria, listed above, of Executive Order 13789. The proposed regulations under IRC Sections 2701 *et seq.*, are among the listed regulations. As a result, the future of these regulations was called into question and the Section 2704 proposed regulations were eventually withdrawn.

1. Let. Rul. 8245007.
2. *Worcester County Trust Co. v. Comm.*, 134 F.2d 578 (1st Cir. 1943); *City Bank Farmers Trust Co. v. Comm.*, 23 BTA 663 (1931), acq. 1932-1 CB 2; *Michigan Trust Co. v. Comm.*, 27 BTA 556 (1933).
3. *Slocum v. U.S.*, 256 F. Supp. 753 (S.D.N.Y. 1966).
4. *Est. of True v. Comm.*, 390 F.3d 1210 (10th Cir. 2004).
5. *St. Louis County Bank v. U.S.*, 674 F.2d 1207, 49 AFTR 2d 82-1509 (8th Cir. 1982).
6. *Est. of Caplan v. Comm.*, TC Memo 1974-39; *Est. of Gannon v. Comm.*, 21 TC 1073 (1954); *Est. of Trammell v. Comm.*, 18 TC 662 (1952), acq. 1953-1 CB 6; *Est. of Mathews v. Comm.*, 3 TC 525 (1944); *Hoffman v. Comm.*, 2 TC 1160 (1943); *Est. of Tompkins v. Comm.*, 13 TC 1054 (1949); Rev. Rul. 59-60, 1959-1 CB 237.
7. *Land v. U.S.*, 303 F.2d 170 (5th Cir. 1962).

323. How is a closely held business interest valued for federal estate tax purposes where there is no purchase agreement?

Valuation of closely held corporate stock requires a determination of fair market value. Estate tax regulations define this as "the price at which the property would change hands between a willing buyer and a willing seller, neither being under compulsion to buy or sell and both having reasonable knowledge of the relevant facts."[1]

Factors that should be considered when determining fair market value include the company's net worth, prospective earnings and dividend paying capacity, goodwill, the economic outlook in the particular industry and its management, the degree of control of the business represented by the block of stock to be valued, and the value of securities of corporations engaged in the same or similar lines of business that are listed on a stock exchange.[2]

If a block of stock represents a controlling interest in a corporation, a control premium generally adds to the value of the stock. If, however, shares constitute a minority ownership interest, a minority discount often is used. A premium also may attach for swing vote attributes where one block of stock may exercise control by joining with another block of stock.[3] One memorandum valued stock included in a gross estate at a premium as a controlling interest, while applying a minority discount to a marital deduction portion that passed to a surviving spouse.[4]

Just because an interest being valued is a minority interest does not mean that a minority discount is available.[5] One case, however, valued stock with voting rights at no more than stock without voting rights.[6]

The Tax Court has held that if real estate is specially valued for estate tax purposes under IRC Section 2032A, an estate may not take a minority discount with respect to stock in a corporation that held the real estate.[7]

In a split decision, however, the Tenth Circuit Court of Appeals has ruled that minority discounts and special use valuation under IRC Section 2032A are not mutually exclusive; it would apply the minority discount to the fair market value of the real estate as owned through a partnership and then apply the $750,000 cap on special use valuation to the difference between fair market value as discounted and special use value of the real estate.[8]

The Fifth Circuit Court of Appeals has ruled that shares of stock in a decedent's estate were to be valued as a minority interest when the decedent owned less than 50 percent, despite the fact that control of the corporation was within the decedent's family. This was true even when, immediately before death, the decedent and the decedent's spouse owned more than 50 percent

1. Treas. Reg. §20.2031-1(b).
2. Treas. Reg. §20.2031-2. See also Rev. Rul. 59-60, 1959-1 CB 237.
3. TAM 9436005.
4. TAM 9403005.
5. *Godley v. Comm.*, 286 F.3d 210, 2002-1 USTC ¶60,436 (4th Cir. 2002) (partnerships held housing projects subject to long term government contracts).
6. *Est. of Simplot v. Comm.*, 249 F.3d 1191 (9th Cir. 2001).
7. *Est. of Maddox v. Comm.*, 93 TC 228 (1989).
8. *Est. of Hoover v. Comm.*, 69 F.3d 1044 (10th Cir. 1995) (*acq.* 1998-2 CB xix), *rev'g* 102 TC 777 (1994).

of the stock as community property. The court also ruled that family attribution (Q 300) would not apply to lump a decedent's stock with that of related parties for estate tax valuation purposes both because of prior case law and because applying attribution would be inconsistent with the willing buyer-willing seller rule.[1]

A minority discount will not be disallowed solely because a transferred interest would be part of a controlling interest if the interest were aggregated with interests held by family members.[2]

A minority discount was allowed even when the person to whom the interest was transferred already was a controlling shareholder.[3]

Deathbed transactions have, however, been aggregated into a single integrated transfer to which a control premium attached rather than minority discounts. In one such case, a parent, a 60 percent shareholder, sold a 30 percent interest in a corporation to a child, a 20 percent shareholder and the parent had the corporation redeem the remaining 30 percent interest in the corporation held by the parent.[4]

The Tax Court has determined that an estate would not be allowed a minority discount where a decedent transferred a small amount of stock immediately prior to death for the sole purpose of reducing her interest from a controlling interest to a minority interest for valuation purposes.[5]

Similarly, the IRS has disallowed minority discounts while disregarding partnerships or limited liability companies created on a decedent's deathbed presumably to obtain minority discounts.[6]

Courts have also rejected the idea that a partnership can be ignored for purposes of IRC Section 2703.

A partnership or LLC entity may be included in a gross estate under IRC Section 2036 without the benefit of discounts under a number of circumstances. For example, if a decedent puts everything he or she owns into the entity, retains complete control over the income of the entity, uses the entity as a personal pocket book, or fails to follow entity formalities, the entity may be included in his or her gross estate.[7]

One case has held that IRC Section 2036 did not apply because the court concluded that the transfer to a partnership was a bona fide sale for adequate consideration.[8]

---

1. *Est. of Bright v. Comm.*, 658 F.2d 999 (5th Cir. 1981).
2. Rev. Rul. 93-12, 1993-1 CB 202.
3. TAM 9432001.
4. TAM 9504004.
5. *Est. of Murphy v. Comm.*, TC Memo 1990-472.
6. TAMs 9719006, 9723009, 9725002, 9730004, 9735003, 9736004, 9842003.
7. *Est. of Strangi v. Comm.*, 417 F. 3d 468, 2005-2 USTC ¶60,506 (5th Cir. 2005), *aff'g* TC Memo 2003-145; *Est. of Bongard v. Comm.*, 124 TC 95 (2005); *Est. of Bigelow v. Comm.*, 503 F. 3d 955, 2007-2 USTC ¶60,548 (9th Cir. 2007), *aff'g* TC Memo 2005-65; *Kimbell v. U.S.*, 244 F. Supp. 2d 700, 2003-1 USTC ¶60,455 (N.D. Tex. 2003), *rev'd 371 F. 3d 257*, 2004-1 USTC ¶60,486 (5th Cir. 2004); *Est. of Abraham v. Comm.*, TC Memo 2004-39; *Est. of Hilgren v. Comm.*, TC Memo 2004-46 (discount for business loan agreement was allowed); *Turner v. Comm.*, 382 F. 3d 367, 2004-2 USTC ¶60,489 (3rd Cir. 2004), *aff'g* TC Memo 2002-246.
8. *Kimbell v. U.S.*, 371 F. 3d 257, 2004-1 USTC ¶60,486 (5th Cir. 2004), *rev'g 244 F. Supp. 200* 2003-1 USTC ¶60,455 (N.D. Tex. 2003).

See note at Q 322 concerning proposed regulations under IRC Sections 2701 *et seq*. The controversial Section 2704 proposed regulations were eventually withdrawn by the Treasury Department.

324. Will the value of payments to a deceased partner's spouse, under a partnership income continuation agreement, be includable in the partner's estate?

Yes.

This is the result whether payments are of a guaranteed amount or a share of partnership profits for a certain number of years.[1] The value of guaranteed payments is their present value at date of death. The value of a share in future partnership profits is based on past profits referred to as the valuation date.[2] The payments are income in respect of a decedent.[3] Consequently, a beneficiary will be entitled to an income tax deduction for any estate tax attributable to including the value of payments in a decedent's gross estate.[4]

325. Are proceeds of life insurance under a split dollar plan or under a reverse split dollar plan includable in an insured's gross estate?

A close reading of IRC Section 2042(2) (Q 81) leads to the conclusion that if an insured in a split dollar plan (Q 4008), including a reverse split dollar plan (Q 4016), has any incident of ownership in the policy at death, including the right to name a beneficiary of proceeds in excess of cash value or a right to name a beneficiary of the cash value in the case of a reverse split dollar plan, the entire proceeds would be includable in the insured's gross estate. IRC Section 2042(2) provides, in pertinent part, that the value of a gross estate includes the value of all property to the extent "of the amount receivable by all other beneficiaries as insurance under policies on the life of the decedent with respect to which the decedent possessed at his death any of the incidents of ownership, exercisable either alone or in conjunction with any other person." Notice in particular the phrases "all" other beneficiaries, that is, beneficiaries other than the insured's estate, and "any" of the incidents of ownership. The language certainly seems inclusive enough to call for the conclusion suggested. (See Revenue Rulings 79-129, and 82-145, discussed in Q 326 and Q 328.) Moreover, this seems to be the position of the Tax Court on the proper application of IRC Section 2042(2) to split dollar life insurance. (See the discussion of *Est. of Levy*, Q 328.)

Estate tax results depend on the substance of the arrangement, meaning that it is important to examine who actually holds which incidents of ownership, rather than placing importance on whether an endorsement form or collateral assignment form is used (Q 4016). Estate tax results also are not altered depending on the source or purpose of premium payments.[5]

1. Rev. Rul. 66-20, 1966-1 CB 214; Rev. Rul. 71-507, 1971-2 CB 331; *Est. of Riegelman v. Comm.*, 253 F.2d 315 (2nd Cir. 1958); *McClennen v. Comm.*, 131 F.2d 165 (1st Cir. 1942); *Est. of Beal v. Comm.*, 47 TC 269 (1966); *Winkle v. U.S.*, 160 F. Supp. 348 (W.D. Pa. 1958).
2. *Est. of Hull v. Comm.*, 38 TC 512 (1962).
3. IRC Secs. 691, 753, 736(a).
4. IRC Sec. 691(c).
5. Rev. Rul. 76-274, 1976-2 CB 278.

Does A Plan Create True Indebtedness?

In a usual split dollar plan, the portion of premiums paid by an employer or the individual who occupies this position in the arrangement is not a true loan. Although the employer or its successor expects ultimately to recover the amount from death proceeds, the usual agreement does not obligate the insured to repay the funds from any source other than the policy or otherwise to treat that amount as a debt.

For estate tax purposes, it may make a real difference whether or not a split dollar plan creates a true indebtedness. If there is an indebtedness, and if the entire proceeds are brought into an insured's gross estate under the incidents of ownership rule, the estate will be allowed a deduction under IRC Section 2053 for the amount of debt repaid from insurance proceeds. In this case, the net result will be the same as if only the portion of proceeds payable to the insured's beneficiary were included in the insured's gross estate in the first place. If there is no true indebtedness and if the entire proceeds are brought into an insured's gross estate under the incidents of ownership rule, the portion of the proceeds going to the employer or to whoever occupies its place in the arrangement cannot be taken as an IRC Section 2053 deduction by the estate.

For estate taxation on the death of a third party owner of a policy on the split dollar plan, see Q 200.

326. Are proceeds of life insurance under a split dollar plan or under a reverse split dollar plan includable in an insured's gross estate outside of the employer-employee context?

In Revenue Ruling 79-129,[1] involving a split dollar arrangement outside of the employer-employee context, the trustee of a funded irrevocable insurance trust created by the insured, D, for the benefit of D's spouse and children, was designated policy owner and beneficiary of proceeds of an ordinary life policy in excess of the cash surrender value at death. The trust provided that D would pay the portion of the annual premium equal to the annual increase in cash value. The policy gave the insured the right to borrow against the cash surrender value up to the total of premiums paid by the insured, where the trustee owned all other policy rights, and designated D's estate as beneficiary of the portion of proceeds equal to the cash value at death less outstanding indebtedness. The IRS ruled that the entire proceeds, both the portion payable to D's estate and the portion payable to the trustee, were includable in D's estate under IRC Section 2042. (Q 183 discusses estate taxation of funds remaining from a premium payment fund on the death of a grantor-insured of an irrevocable funded life insurance trust.)

Proceeds would not be includable in an insured's estate under IRC Section 2042(2) where the insured's spouse and an irrevocable trust created by the insured, but over which the insured retained no powers, entered into a split dollar arrangement and the insured held no incidents of ownership in the policy.[2]

1. 1979-1 CB 306.
2. Let. Rul. 9636033.

Two spouses would not be treated as holding incidents of ownership under IRC Section 2042(2) where they transferred cash to an irrevocable trust, the trust purchased a second to die policy on the life of the two spouses, and the spouses entered into a collateral assignment split dollar arrangement with the trust whereby the trust would pay a portion of the premium equal to term rates, the spouses would pay the balance of the premium, and the only right held by the couple was to be reimbursed for their premium payments through receipt of cash surrender values in excess of cash surrender values at the end of the initial policy year.[1]

327. Are proceeds of life insurance under a split dollar plan or under a reverse split dollar plan includable in an insured's gross estate in the context of an employer-employee relationship?

It should be noted that the term "reverse split dollar" is not contained in the split dollar regulations. Once a common term, today it is still sometimes used to define arrangements where the employee owns the policy and endorses the death benefit to the employer – instead of the more typical arrangement where the employer owns the policy and endorses the death benefit to the employee or a beneficiary named by the employee. See also IRS Notice 2002-59, which addresses the valuation of term insurance under a so-called reverse split dollar arrangement.

In *Schwager v. Comm.*,[2] a sole proprietor applied for and owned a policy on a split dollar or endorsement plan on the life of an employee. The beneficiary of proceeds equal to the cash value at death was designated in the policy as the part A beneficiary and in this case was the employer. The beneficiary of proceeds in excess of the cash value, the part B beneficiary, was the employee's wife. By policy amendment, the part B beneficiary could not be changed without the insured's consent. The Tax Court decided that the insured's right to consent to a change of beneficiary was an incident of ownership and held that the portion of proceeds paid to his widow was includable in his estate. The opinion does not make it clear that only the portion of proceeds payable to the insured's widow was includable in the estate, but counsel for the taxpayer has confirmed that was the case. Apparently, the IRS did not try for the includability of more.

In *Est. of Tomerlin v. Comm.*,[3] a corporation owned insurance on the life of a decedent, a 50 percent shareholder of the corporation. The policy provided that the corporation was the sole owner of the policy and that the death proceeds were to be divided between the corporation and the decedent's children. The corporation was to receive the proceeds equal to the premiums it had paid and the decedent's children were to receive the balance. The decedent had been given incidents of ownership in the policy by agreement with the corporation, including the right to designate beneficiaries of the policy. The IRS sought includability in the decedent's estate under IRC Section 2042(2) of the portion of the proceeds payable to the decedent's children, and the court found for the IRS.

In private letter Ruling 9026041, the IRS held that the full value of proceeds of a life insurance policy were subject to an endorsement reverse split dollar agreement and included in the

1. Let. Rul. 9745019.
2. 64 TC 781 (1975).
3. TC Memo 1986-147.

estate of the insured key person. The insured key person would hold incidents of ownership in the policy. The estate would be allowed to deduct the portion of the proceeds that would be payable to the corporate participant in the reverse split dollar arrangement.

328. Are proceeds of life insurance under a split dollar plan or under a reverse split dollar plan includable in an insured's gross estate when a corporation owns split dollar insurance on the life of a controlling stockholder?

It depends. In the case of split dollar insurance owned by a corporation on the life of a controlling stockholder, special rules apply. Estate tax regulations provide the following:

> [I]f any part of the proceeds of the policy are not payable to or for the benefit of the corporation ... any incidents of ownership held by the corporation as to that part of the proceeds will be attributed to the decedent through his stock ownership when the decedent is the sole or controlling stockholder. Thus, for example, if the decedent is the controlling stockholder in a corporation, and the corporation owns a life insurance policy on his life, the proceeds of which are payable to the decedent's spouse, the incidents of ownership held by the corporation will be attributed to the decedent through his stock ownership and the proceeds will be included in his gross estate under section 2042. If in this example the policy proceeds had been payable 40 percent to the decedent's spouse and 60 percent to the corporation, only 40 percent of the proceeds would be included in decedent's gross estate under Section 2042.[1]

The above-quoted regulation attributes to a stockholder incidents of ownership held by a corporation "as to that part of the proceeds" not payable to or for the corporation. Apparently, the quoted phrase originally led the IRS to take a position as to which it later reversed itself. In Revenue Ruling 76-274 (Situation 3),[2] the IRS held that if, under a split dollar agreement, the corporation's incidents of ownership were limited to those appropriate to protecting its position as a lender of premium dollars (an incident such as the right to borrow against the policy but only to the extent of the portion of premiums it has advanced) so that the corporation's exercise of those rights could not impair the interests of the insured or the insured's personal beneficiary, the corporation's incidents of ownership would not be attributed to the insured.

In Revenue Ruling 82-145,[3] the IRS ruled that its conclusion in Situation 3 of Revenue Ruling 76-274 was incorrect and indeed was inconsistent with Revenue Ruling 79-129, discussed in Q 326. The IRS concluded that the incident of ownership described in Situation 3 of the 1976 ruling was attributable to the insured and that this attribution warrants inclusion of the entire amount of policy proceeds under IRC Section 2042(2). The IRS added, however, that "pursuant to the rule in section 20.2042-1(c)(6) adopted to prevent double taxation, to the extent that the proceeds are payable to the corporation, they are considered in valuing the decedent's stock under section 2031, rather than included under section 2042(2)." A grandfathering provision in the ruling reads as follows: "the conclusion in this revenue ruling reversing

1. Treas. Reg. §20.2042-1(c)(6), as amended April 29, 1974.
2. 1976-2 CB 278.
3. 1982-2 CB 213.

the holding in *Situation 3* of Rev. Rul. 76-274 will not be applied with respect to insurance policies obtained before [August 4, 1982], except to the extent, if any, that there has been an increase, after [August 4, 1982], in the amount of the insurance proceeds payable other than to or for the benefit of the corporation." (See Q 319.)

Est. of Thompson v. Comm.,[1] a 1981 Tax Court case that supports the IRS's position in Revenue Ruling 82-145, concerned an employer-pay-all split dollar whole life policy owned by a corporation on the life of its president and sole owner, the decedent. Under the plan, death proceeds were divided between the corporation (the cash value portion) and beneficiaries designated by the decedent (the balance). The Tax Court found that the decedent held incidents of ownership in the policy and concluded that an amount equal to the insurance proceeds payable to the beneficiary designated by the decedent was includable in the decedent's estate under IRC Section 2042(2). The portion of the proceeds payable to the corporation would be reflected in the value of the corporation's stock, all of which was owned by the decedent and therefore includable in the decedent's estate under IRC Section 2031.

The Tax Court agrees that in the split dollar context, any incident of ownership (Q 86) possessed by a corporation is attributable to a sole or controlling stockholder.[2]

Letter Ruling 9348009 appears to conclude that an S corporation does not have incidents of ownership in insurance on the life of its owners held in a split dollar arrangement if the only interest the corporation has in the policy is to be reimbursed for its outlay for premiums paid. This conclusion appears to be inconsistent with the official position of the IRS and of courts that have addressed this issue. It may be, although the ruling does not say so, that the ruling concluded that because the owners were not controlling shareholders, incidents of ownership held by the corporation would not be attributed to the owners. The issues of whether a corporation holds incidents of ownership and whether an owner is treated as holding incidents of ownership held by the corporation ordinarily are treated as separate issues, however.

In a later letter ruling involving a collateral assignment split dollar life insurance arrangement, the IRS determined that a corporation would not be treated as holding incidents of ownership in a policy where the only right the corporation would hold would be, in essence, the right to be reimbursed for premiums paid by the corporation. As a result, the life insurance proceeds would not be includable in a controlling shareholder's estate.[3]

The importance of this ruling may have been undercut by its reliance on Revenue Ruling 76-274, which was later reversed by Revenue Ruling 82-145.[4] Nevertheless, several rulings since then have stated that a corporation or S corporation that has no interest in a collateral assignment split dollar arrangement other than to be reimbursed for its outlay for premiums

1. TC Memo 1981-200.
2. Treas. Reg. §20.2042-1(c)(6). See *Est. of Dimen v. Comm.*, 72 TC 198 (1979), *aff'd without published opinion* (3rd Cir. 1980). See also *Est. of Carlstrom v. Comm.*, 76 TC 142 (1981), *acq.* 1981-2 CB 1.
3. Let. Rul. 9511046.
4. Let. Rul. 9511046.

paid does not hold incidents of ownership, an issue that need not be reached where there is no controlling shareholder.[1]

Any transfer by a corporate employer of incidents of ownership in a split dollar policy on the life of a controlling stockholder to an insured's transferee within three years of the insured's death is considered a transfer by the insured for purposes of the bringback rule of IRC Section 2035 (Q 96).[2]

In *Est. of Levy v. Comm.*,[3] dealing with estate taxation of split dollar life insurance, a corporation owned two split dollar policies on the life of a stockholder who owned 80.4 percent of the voting stock. The corporation owned all incidents of ownership except that it could not change the beneficiary, at least for any amount in excess of the cash value, without the approval of the insured's wife. The corporation was beneficiary of proceeds equal to the net cash value at death; the insured's widow was beneficiary of the excess proceeds. The executors of the insured's estate did not include any of the insurance proceeds in the estate because the insured at death did not directly hold any incidents of ownership in the policies. The IRS, in a deficiency notice, determined that the portion of policy proceeds payable to the insured's widow was includable in the estate. The Tax Court strongly supported the position of the government that the incidents of ownership held by the corporation were properly attributable to the insured. Moreover, the Tax Court indicated that had the deficiency notice called for inclusion in the estate of the entire proceeds rather than just the portion payable to the insured's widow, it would have supported the IRS. As it was, only the proceeds payable to the insured's widow were held includable in the insured's estate.

329. Does a life insurance funded buy-sell agreement fix the value of a business interest for gift tax purposes?

No.

A buy-sell agreement is not necessarily based on the fair market value of the business. A buy-sell agreement is simply an agreement between friendly parties to address the smooth transition of ownership due to a business owner's termination of employment, death, or sale of the individual's business interest.[4] The IRS is much more likely to respect a buy-sell valuation as fair market value when the agreement is between unrelated parties.

An agreement restricting lifetime sale may be considered with all other pertinent factors, however, and may tend to lower the value of a close corporation or other business interest.[5]

On the other hand, failure to exercise rights under a buy-sell agreement could result in a taxable gift.

1. Let. Ruls. 9651030, 9709027, 9746006, 9808024.
2. Let. Rul. 8252016.
3. 70 TC 873 (1978).
4. Effect of Purchase Price, Buy-Sell Agreements, and Key Person Insurance on Valuation, Gunnar J. Gitlin (Business Valuations in Divorce Cases – 2012), p. 63.
5. *Est. of James v. Comm.*, 148 F.2d 236 (2nd Cir. 1945); *Kline v. Comm.*, 130 F.2d 742 (3rd Cir. 1942); *Krauss v. U.S.*, 140 F.2d 510 (5th Cir. 1944); *Comm. v. McCann*, 146 F.2d 385 (2nd Cir. 1944), *nonacq.* 1943 CB 36; *Spitzer v. Comm.*, 153 F.2d 967 (8th Cir. 1946); Rev. Rul. 189, 1953-2 CB 294.

PART IV: HEALTH INSURANCE

Employer-Provided Health Insurance

330. May an employer deduct as a business expense the cost of premiums paid for accident and health insurance for employees?

An employer generally can deduct as a business expense premiums paid for health insurance for employees. This includes premiums for medical expense insurance, dismemberment and sight loss coverage for the employee, his or her spouse and dependents, disability income for the employee (Q 362), and accidental death coverage. For a discussion of the deductibility of long-term care insurance premiums, see Q 432.

Premiums are generally deductible by an employer when coverage is provided under a group policy. See Q 454 for a discussion of the consequences of employer reimbursement for the cost of employees' individual policies.

The deduction for health insurance is allowable only if benefits are payable to employees or their beneficiaries; it is not allowable if benefits are payable to the employer.[1] Where a spouse of an employer is a bona fide employee and the employer is covered as a family member, the premium is deductible.[2] A corporation can deduct premiums it pays on group hospitalization coverage for commission salespersons, regardless of whether they are employees.[3] Premiums must qualify as additional reasonable compensation to the insured employees.[4]

If a payment is considered made to a fund that is part of an employer plan to provide the benefit, the deduction for amounts paid or accrued may be limited (Q 4047).

An accrual basis employer that provides medical benefits to employees directly instead of through insurance or an intermediary fund may not deduct amounts estimated to be necessary to pay for medical care provided in the year but for which claims have not been filed with the employer by the end of the year if filing a claim is necessary to establish the employer's liability for payment.[5]

In the case of a plan covering stockholder-employees only, see Q 346; in the case of an S corporation, partnership, or sole proprietorship employer, see Q 347 and Q 348.

Where health benefits are provided through a fund, see Q 488.

---

1. Treas. Reg. §1.162-10(a); Rev. Rul. 58-90, 1958-1 CB 88; Rev. Rul. 56-632, 1956-2 CB 101; Rev. Rul. 210, 1953-2 CB 114.
2. Rev. Rul. 71-588, 1971-2 CB 91; TAM 9409006.
3. Rev. Rul. 56-400, 1956-2 CB 116.
4. *Ernest Holdeman & Collet, Inc. v. Comm.*, TC Memo 1960-10. See Rev. Rul. 58-90, supra.
5. *U.S. v. General Dynamics Corp.*, 481 U.S. 239 (1987).

331. What credit is available to small employers for employee health insurance expenses?

A credit is available for employee health insurance expenses of an eligible small employer for taxable years beginning after December 31, 2009, provided the employer offers health insurance to its employees.[1] Beginning in 2014, the credit is available to eligible small employers for two consecutive years.

An eligible small employer is an employer that has no more than twenty-five full time employees, the average annual wages of whom do not exceed $50,000 (in 2010–2013; the amount is indexed thereafter).[2] The inflation adjusted amount for 2014 is $50,800, $51,600 for 2015, $51,800 for 2016, $52,400 for 2017, $53,400 for 2018, $54,200 for 2019, and $55,200 for 2020.[3]

An employer must have a contribution arrangement for each employee who enrolls in the health plan offered by the employer through an exchange that requires that the employer make a non-elective contribution in an amount equal to a uniform percentage, not less than 50 percent, of the premium cost.[4]

Subject to phase-out[5] based on the number of employees and average wages, the amount of the credit is equal to 50 percent, (35 percent in the case of tax-exempt organizations) of the lesser of (1) the aggregate amount of non-elective contributions made by the employer on behalf of its employees for health insurance premiums for health plans offered by the employer to employees through an exchange, or (2) the aggregate amount of non-elective contributions the employer would have made if each employee had been enrolled in a health plan that had a premium equal to the average premium for the small group market in the ratings area.[6]

For years 2010-2013, the following modifications apply in determining the amount of the credit:

(1) the credit percentage is reduced to 35 percent (25 percent in the case of tax-exempt organizations);[7]

(2) the amount under (1) is determined by reference to non-elective contributions for premiums paid for health insurance, and there is no exchange requirement;[8] and

1. IRC Sec. 45R, as added by PPACA 2010.
2. IRC Secs. 45R(d), as added by PPACA 2010; IRC Sec 45R(d)(3)(B), as amended by Section 10105(e)(1) of PPACA 2010.
3. Rev. Proc. 2013-35, 2013-47 IRB 537, Rev. Proc. 2014-61, 2014-47 IRB 860, Rev. Proc. 2015-53, Rev. Proc. 2016-55, Rev. Proc. 2017-58, Rev. Proc. 2018-57, Rev. Proc. 2019-44.
4. IRC Sec. 45R(d)(4), as added by PPACA 2010.
5. IRC Sec. 45R(c), as added by PPACA 2010.
6. IRC Sec. 45R(b), as added by PPACA 2010.
7. IRC Sec. 45R(g)(2)(A), as added by PPACA 2010.
8. IRC Secs. 45R(g)(2)(B), 45R(g)(3), as added by PPACA 2010.

(3) the amount under (2) is determined by the average premium for the state small group market.[1]

The credit also is allowed against the alternative minimum tax.[2]

In 2014, small employers had access to an expanded Small Business Healthcare Tax Credit under the Affordable Care Act. This tax credit covered as much as 50 percent of the employer contribution toward premium costs for eligible employers who had low- to moderate-wage workers.

332. Is the value of employer-provided coverage under accident or health insurance taxable income to an employee?

Generally, no.

This includes medical expense and dismemberment and sight loss coverage for the employee, his or her spouse and dependents, and coverage providing for disability income for the employee (Q 379). There is no specific limit on the amount of employer-provided coverage that may be excluded from an employee's gross income. Coverage is tax-exempt to an employee.[3] The employer may contribute to an accident or health plan by paying the premium (or a portion) on a policy of accident or health insurance covering one or more employees, or by contributing to a separate trust or fund which provides accident or health benefits directly or through insurance to those employees.[4] Coverage under an uninsured plan is explained in Q 335.

Likewise, the value of critical illness coverage is not taxable income to an employee.

Accidental death coverage is excludable from an employee's gross income under IRC Section 106(a).[5]

In a Private Letter Ruling, the IRS decided that the value of consumer medical cards purchased by a partnership for its employees was excludable from the employees' income under IRC Section 106(a).[6]

Where an employer applies salary reduction amounts to the payment of health insurance premiums for employees, the salary reduction amounts are excludable from gross income under IRC Section 106.[7]

Where an employer simply pays an employee or retiree a sum that may be used to pay the premium but that amount is not required to be used for that purpose, the amount is taxable to the employee.[8]

1. IRC Sec. 45R(g)(2)(C), as added by PPACA 2010.
2. IRC Sec. 38(c)(4)(B), as amended by PPACA 2010. The IRS has issued guidance; see Notice 2010-44, 2010-22 IRB 717; Notice 2010-82, 2010-51 IRB 1.
3. IRC Sec. 106(a). See also Treas. Reg. §1.106-1; Rev. Rul. 58-90, 1958-1 CB 88; Rev. Rul. 56-632, 1956-1 CB 101.
4. Treas. Reg. §1.106-1(a).
5. See Treas. Reg. §1.106-1; Treas. Reg. §1.79-1(f)(3); Let. Ruls. 8801015, 8922048.
6. Let. Rul. 9814023.
7. Rev. Rul. 2002-03, 2002-1 CB 316.
8. Rev. Rul. 75-241, 1975-1 CB 316, Let. Rul. 9022060. See also Let. Rul. 9104050.

According to the IRS, where an employer, not pursuant to a cafeteria plan under IRC Section 125 (Q 3501), offers an employee a choice between a lower salary and employer-paid health insurance or a higher salary and no health insurance, the employee must include the full amount of the higher salary in income regardless of his or her choice. An employee selecting the health insurance option is considered to have received the higher salary and, in turn, paid a portion of the salary equal to the health insurance premium to the insurance company.[1]

A federal district court faced with a similar fact situation has ruled that for employees who accept employer-paid health insurance coverage, the difference between the higher salary and the lower one is not subject to FICA and FUTA taxes or to income tax withholding.[2]

Where a taxpayer's contribution to a fund providing retiree health benefits is deducted from the taxpayer's after-tax salary, it is considered an employee contribution and is includable in the taxpayer's income under IRC Section 61.

In contrast, where an employer increases or grosses up a taxpayer's salary and then deducts the fund contribution from the taxpayer's after-tax salary, the contribution is considered to be an employer contribution that is excludable from the gross income of the taxpayer under IRC Section 106.[3]

A return of premium rider on a health insurance policy was ruled a benefit in addition to accident and health benefits and the premium paid by the employer was not excludable by the employee.[4]

Employer-provided accident and health coverage for an employee and the employee's spouse and dependents, both before and after retirement, and for the employee's surviving spouse and dependents after the employee's death, does not have to be included in gross income by the active or retired employee or, after the employee's death, by the employee's survivors.[5]

If an employer's accident and health plan continues to provide coverage pursuant to a collective bargaining agreement for an employee who is laid off, the value of the coverage is excluded from the gross income of the laid-off employee.[6] Terminated employees who receive medical coverage under a medical plan that is part of the former employer's severance plan are considered to be employees for purposes of IRC Sections 105 and 106. Thus, an employer's contributions toward medical care for employees are excludable from income under IRC Section 106.[7] Otherwise, the exclusion is available only to active employees.

---

1. Let. Rul. 9406002. See also Let. Rul. 9513027.
2. *Express Oil Change, Inc. v. U.S.*, 25 F. Supp. 2d 1313, 78 AFTR2d 96-6764 (N.D. Ala. 1996), *aff'd,166 F. 3d 1290,* 83 AFTR2d 99-302 (11th Cir. 1998).
3. Let. Rul. 9625012.
4. Let. Rul. 8804010.
5. Rev. Rul. 82-196, 1982-2 CB 53; GCM 38917 (11-17-82).
6. See Rev. Rul. 85-121, 1985-2 CB 57.
7. Let. Rul. 9612008.

Full time life insurance salespersons are considered employees if they are employees for Social Security purposes.[1] Coverage for other commission salespersons is taxable income to the salespersons, unless an employer-employee relationship exists.[2] In the case of shareholder-employees owning more than 2 percent of the stock of an S corporation, see Q 348.

Discrimination generally does not affect exclusion of the value of coverage. Even if a self-insured medical expense reimbursement plan discriminates in favor of highly compensated employees, the value of coverage is not taxable; only reimbursements are affected (Q 336).

As of January 2012, The Affordable Care Act requires employers to report the cost of coverage under an employer-sponsored group health plan.

The fact that the cost of an employee's health care benefits is shown on the employee's Form W-2 does not mean that the benefits are taxable to the employee. There is nothing about the reporting requirement that causes or will cause excludable employer-provided health coverage to become taxable. The purpose of the reporting requirement is to provide employees useful and comparable consumer information on the cost of their health care coverage.

333. How does health reform expand the income exclusion for adult children's coverage?

Under the Affordable Care Act (ACA), the exclusion from gross income for amounts expended on medical care (Q 332) is expanded to include employer provided health coverage for any adult child of the taxpayer if the adult child has not attained the age of twenty-seven as of the end of the taxable year. According to Notice 2010-38, the adult child does not have to be eligible to be claimed as a dependent for tax purposes for this income exclusion to apply.[3]

334. What are the tax consequences of payments received by employees under employer-provided accident or health insurance?

Although the amounts that both employers and employees pay for premiums for employer sponsored health and accident insurance plans must now be stated on the employee's Form W-2, the tax consequences of receiving benefits pursuant to those plans have not changed. However, some payments must be included in the employee's gross income, explained below.

Hospital, Surgical, and Medical Expenses

Amounts received by an employee under employer-provided accident or health insurance, group or individual, that reimburse the employee for hospital, surgical, and other medical expenses incurred for care of the employee or his or her spouse and dependents generally are tax-exempt without limit.

1. IRC Sec. 7701(a)(20).
2. Rev. Rul. 56-400, 1956-2 CB 116; see also IRC Sec. 3508.
3. IRC Sec. 105(b), as amended by the Patient Protection and Affordable Care Act of 2010 and the Health Care and Education Reconciliation Act of 2010. Notice 2010-38, 2010-20 IRB 682.

Nonetheless, benefits must be included in gross income to the extent that they reimburse an employee for any expenses that the employee deducted in a prior year. Moreover, if reimbursements exceed actual expenses, the excess must be included in gross income to the extent that it is attributable to employer contributions.[1]

Where an employer reimburses employees for salary reduction contributions applied to the payment of health insurance premiums, these amounts are not excludable under IRC Section 105(b) because there are no employee-paid premiums to reimburse.[2]

Likewise, where an employer applies salary reduction contributions to the payment of health insurance premiums and then pays the amount of the salary reduction to employees regardless of whether the employee incurs expenses for medical care, these so-called advance reimbursements or loans are not excludable from gross income under IRC Section 105(b) and are subject to FICA and FUTA taxes.[3]

Sight Loss and Dismemberment Benefits

Payments not related to absence from work for the permanent loss, or loss of use, of a member or function of a body or permanent disfigurement of the employee or spouse or a dependent are excluded from income if the amounts paid are computed with reference to the nature of the injury.[4]

A lump-sum payment for incurable cancer under a group life-and-disability policy qualified for tax exemption under this provision.[5]

Benefits determined by length of service rather than type and severity of injury did not qualify for the exemption.[6]

Benefits determined as a percentage of a disabled employee's salary rather than the nature of the employee's injury were not excludable from income.[7] An employee who has permanently lost a bodily member or function but is working and drawing a salary cannot exclude a portion of that salary as payment for loss of the member or function if that portion was not computed with reference to the loss.[8]

Critical Illness Benefits

Amounts received by an employee under employer-provided critical illness policies where the value of the coverage was not includable in the employee's gross income are includable in the employee's gross income. The exclusion from gross income under IRC Section 105(b) applies only to amounts paid specifically to reimburse medical care expenses. Because critical illness

1. IRC Sec. 105(b); Treas. Reg. §1.105-2; Rev. Rul. 69-154, 1969-1 CB 46.
2. Rev. Rul. 2002-3, 2002-1 CB 316.
3. Rev. Rul. 2002-80, 2002-2 CB 925.
4. IRC Sec. 105(c).
5. Rev. Rul. 63-181, 1963-2 CB 74.
6. *Beisler v. Comm.*, 814 F.2d 1304 (9th Cir. 1987); *West v. Comm.*, TC Memo 1992-617. See also *Rosen v. U.S.*, 829 F.2d 506 (4th Cir. 1987).
7. *Colton v. Comm.*, TC Memo 1995-275; *Webster v. Comm.*, 870 F. Supp. 202, 94-2 USTC ¶50,586 (M.D. Tenn. 1994).
8. *Laverty v. Comm.*, 61 TC 160 (1973) *aff'd*, 523 F.2d 479, 75-2 USTC ¶9712 (9th Cir. 1975).

insurance policies pay a benefit irrespective of whether medical expenses are incurred, these amounts are not excludable under IRC Section 105(b).[1]

Wage Continuation and Disability Income

Sick pay, wage continuation payments, and disability income payments, both preretirement and postretirement, generally are fully includable in gross income and taxable to an employee (Q 379).[2]

Accidental Death Benefit

Accidental death benefits under an employer's plan are received income tax-free by an employee's beneficiary under IRC Section 101(a) as life insurance proceeds payable by reason of the insured's death.[3] Death benefits payable under life insurance contracts issued after December 31, 1984, are excludable only if the contract meets the statutory definition of a life insurance contract in IRC Section 7702 (Q 65).

Survivors' Benefits

Benefits paid to a surviving spouse and dependents under an employer accident and health plan that provided coverage for an employee and the employee's spouse and dependents both before and after retirement, and to the employee's surviving spouse and dependents after the employee's death, are excludable to the extent that they would be if paid to the employee.[4]

335. Are benefits provided under an employer's noninsured accident and health plan excludable from an employee's income?

To be tax-exempt on the same basis as insured plans (Q 332, Q 334), uninsured benefits must be received under an accident and health plan for employees.[5] Although there must be a plan for uninsured payments, the plan need not follow a particular legal form. According to an Ohio federal District Court,[6] there is no legal magic to a form; the essence of the arrangement must determine its legal character. The fact that there is no formal contract of insurance is immaterial, if it is clear that, for an adequate consideration, the company has agreed and has become liable to pay and has paid sickness benefits based upon a reasonable plan of protection of its employees.

Thus, a provision for disability pay in an employment contract has been held to satisfy the condition.[7]

1. See Treas. Reg. §§1.105-2, 1.213-1(e).
2. See Let. Ruls. 9103043, 9036049.
3. Treas. Reg. §1.101-1(a).
4. Rev. Rul. 82-196, 1982-2 CB 53; GCM 38917 (11-17-82).
5. IRC Sec. 105(e). See also IRS Pub. 15-B.
6. *Epmeier v. U.S.*, 199 F.2d 508 (7th Cir. 1959).
7. *Andress v. U.S.*, 198 F. Supp. 371 (N.D. Ohio, 1961).

It is not necessary for tax purposes that a plan be in writing or that an employee's rights to benefits under the plan be enforceable. For example, an employer's custom or policy of continuing wages during disability, generally known to employees, has been held to constitute a plan.[1]

If an employee's rights are not enforceable, the employee must have been covered by a plan or a program, policy, or custom having the effect of a plan when the employee became sick or injured, and notice or knowledge of the plan must have been readily available to the employee.[2] For there to be a plan, an employer must commit to certain rules and regulations governing payment and these rules must be made known to employees as a definite policy before accident or sickness arises; *ad hoc* payments at the complete discretion of an employer do not qualify as a plan.[3]

The plan must be for employees. A plan may cover one or more employees and there may be different plans for different employees or classes of employees.[4] A plan that is found to cover individuals in a capacity other than their employee status, even though they are employees, is not a plan for employees (Q 346). Self-employed individuals and certain shareholders owning more than 2 percent of the stock of an S corporation are not treated as employees for the purpose of determining the excludability of employer-provided accident and health benefits (Q 347).[5]

In addition, uninsured medical expense reimbursement plans for employees must meet nondiscrimination requirements for medical expense reimbursements to be tax-free to highly compensated employees (Q 336).

Planning Point: The most important concept surrounding Section 105 plans is legitimate employment between spouses or any other named employee. This issue is closely scrutinized by the IRS, and it is absolutely vital that the relationship be in existence. Fabricated relationships are absolutely discouraged. Therefore, having the following items in place helps to ensure the plan operates smoothly and the tax advantages are maximized:

1. Written employment agreements;
2. Logs of hours worked by employees; and
3. Established cash (salary) compensation payment amounts and schedules.

In addition, it is recommended to:

1. Name the insured (it is preferred that the insurance policy be in the employee's name);
2. Maintain separate checking accounts (one for business use and the second for personal use); and
3. Pay for medical expenses (all medical expenses for the family should be paid by the employee from his or her personal account), and the employee should document all payments.

---

1. *Niekamp v. U.S.*, 240 F. Supp. 195 (E.D. Mo. 1965); *Pickle*, TC Memo 1971-304.
2. Treas. Reg. §1.105-5(a).
3. *Est. of Kaufman*, 35 TC 663 (1961), *aff'd*, 300 F.2d 128 (6th Cir. 1962); *Lang*, 41 TC 352 (1963); *Levine*, 50 TC 422 (1968); *Est. of Chism*, TC Memo 1962-6, *aff'd*, 322 F.2d 956 (9th Cir. 1963); *Burr*, TC Memo 1966-112; *Frazier v. Comm.*, TC Memo 1994-358; *Harris*, 77-1 USTC ¶9414 (E.D. Va. 1977).
4. Treas. Reg. §1.105-5(a); *Andress v. U.S.*, supra.
5. IRC Sec. 105(g); Treas. Reg. §1.105-5(b).

336. What nondiscrimination requirements apply to employer provided health insurance plans?

Editor's note: Under current law, other than rules concerning discrimination based on health status under HIPAA '96 that generally apply to both insured and uninsured plans, a plan that provides health benefits through an accident or health insurance policy need not meet the nondiscrimination requirements of IRC Section 105(h) for covered employees to enjoy the tax benefits described in Q 334. For plan years beginning on or after September 23, 2010, which was six months after the date of enactment of the ACA, insured plans that are not grandfathered were expected to be subject to the same nondiscrimination requirements as self-insured plans. On December 22, 2010, however, the IRS announced in Notice 2011-1 that compliance with nondiscrimination rules for health insurance plans will be delayed until regulations or other administrative guidance has been issued. The IRS indicated that the guidance will not apply until plan years beginning a specified period after guidance is issued.

ACA Rules

Under the ACA, a group health plan other than a self-insured plan must satisfy the requirements of IRC Section 105(h)(2). More specifically, the ACA states that rules similar to the rules in IRC Section 105(h)(3) (nondiscriminatory eligibility classifications), Section 105(h)(4) (nondiscriminatory benefits), and Section 105(h)(8) (certain controlled groups) apply to insured plans. The term highly compensated individual has the meaning given that term by IRC Section 105(h)(5).[1]

An accident or health insurance policy may be an individual or a group policy issued by a licensed insurance company, or an arrangement in the nature of a prepaid health care plan regulated under federal or state law including an HMO. Unless a policy involves shifting of risk to an unrelated third party, a plan will be considered self-insured.

A plan is not considered self-insured merely because prior claims experience is one factor in determining the premium.[2] Furthermore, a policy of a captive insurance company is not considered self-insurance if, for the plan year, premiums paid to a captive insurer by unrelated companies are at least one-half of the total premiums received and the policy is similar to those sold to unrelated companies.[3]

Likewise, a plan that reimburses employees for premiums paid under an insured plan does not have to satisfy nondiscrimination requirements.

337. What nondiscrimination requirements apply to self-insured health plans?

Nondiscrimination requirements apply to self-insured health benefits, although the IRS announced in Notice 2011-1 on December 22, 2010, that compliance with nondiscrimination

1. Secs. 2716 of the Public Health Service Act, as added by Section 1001(5) of the ACA, as amended by Section 10101(d) of the ACA.
2. See, for example, Let. Rul. 8235047.
3. Treas. Reg. §1.105-11(b).

rules for health insurance plans will be delayed until regulations or other administrative guidance has been issued. This guidance remains pending. The IRS indicated that the guidance will not apply until plan years beginning in specified periods after guidance is issued. Some plans will be grandfathered.

Benefits under a self-insured plan generally are excludable from an employee's gross income (Q 335). If a self-insured medical expense reimbursement plan or the self-insured part of a partly-insured medical expense reimbursement plan discriminates in favor of highly compensated individuals, certain amounts paid to highly compensated individuals are taxable to them.

A self-insured plan is one in which reimbursement of medical expenses is not provided under a policy of accident and health insurance.[1] According to regulations, a plan underwritten by a cost-plus policy or a policy that, in effect, merely provides administrative or bookkeeping services is considered self-insured.[2]

A medical expense reimbursement plan cannot be implemented retroactively. To allow this would render meaningless the nondiscrimination requirements of IRC Section 105.[3]

A self-insured plan may not discriminate in favor of highly compensated individuals either with respect to eligibility to participate (see Q 338) or benefits (see Q 339).

338. When does a self-insured health plan discriminate with respect to eligibility to participate?

A plan discriminates as to eligibility to participate unless the plan benefits the following:

(1) 70 percent or more of all employees, or 80 percent or more of all the employees who are eligible to benefit under the plan if 70 percent or more of all employees are eligible to benefit under the plan; or

(2) Employees who qualify under a classification set up by the employer and found by the IRS not to be discriminatory in favor of highly compensated individuals.[4]

Excludable Employees

For purposes of these eligibility requirements, an employer may exclude from consideration those employees who:

(1) Have not completed three years of service at the beginning of the plan year; years of service during which an individual was ineligible under (2), (3), (4), or (5) below must be counted for this purpose;

(2) Have not attained age twenty-five at the beginning of the plan year;

1. See IRC Sec. 105(h)(6).
2. Treas. Reg. §1.105-11(b).
3. *Wollenburg v. U.S.*, 75 F. Supp. 2d 1032 (DC Neb. 1999); *American Family Mut. Ins. Co. v. U.S.*, 815 F. Supp. 1206 (WD Wisc. 1992). See also Rev. Rul. 2002-58, 2002-38 IRB 541.
4. IRC Sec. 105(h)(3)(A).

(3) Are part-time or seasonal employees;

(4) Are covered by a collective bargaining agreement if health benefits were the subject of good faith bargaining; or

(5) Are nonresident aliens with no U.S.-source earned income.[1]

Part-time and Seasonal Workers

Employees customarily employed for fewer than thirty-five hours per week are considered part-time and employees customarily employed for fewer than nine months per year are considered seasonal if similarly situated employees of the employer or in the same industry or location are employed for substantially more hours or months, as applicable. Employees customarily employed for fewer than twenty-five hours per week or seven months per year are considered part-time or seasonal under a safe harbor rule.[2]

339. When does a self-insured health plan discriminate with respect to benefits?

A plan discriminates as to benefits unless all benefits provided for participants who are highly compensated individuals are provided for all other participants.[3] Benefits are not available to all participants if some participants become eligible immediately and others after a waiting period.[4] Benefits available to dependents of highly compensated employees must be equally available to dependents of all other participating employees. The test is applied to benefits subject to reimbursement, rather than to actual benefit payments or claims.

Any maximum limit on the amount of reimbursement must be uniform for all participants and for all dependents, regardless of years of service or age. Further, a plan will be considered discriminatory if the type or amount of benefits subject to reimbursement is offered in proportion to compensation and highly compensated employees are covered by the plan. A plan will not be considered discriminatory in operation merely because highly compensated participants use a broad range of plan benefits to a greater extent than other participants.[5]

An employer's plan will not violate nondiscrimination rules merely because benefits under the plan are offset by benefits paid under a self-insured or insured plan of the employer or of another employer or by benefits paid under Medicare or other federal or state law. A self-insured plan may take into account benefits provided under another plan only to the extent that the benefit is the same under both plans.[6] Benefits provided to a retired employee who was highly compensated must be the same as benefits provided to all other retired participants.

1. IRC Sec. 105(h)(3)(B).
2. Treas. Reg. §1.105-11(c).
3. IRC Sec. 105(h)(4).
4. Let. Ruls. 8411050, 8336065.
5. Treas. Reg. §1.105-11(c)(3).
6. Treas. Reg. §1.105-11(c)(1).

For purposes of applying the nondiscrimination rules, all employees of a controlled group of corporations, or employers under common control, and of members of an affiliated service group (Q 3921, Q 3923) are treated as employed by a single employer.[1]

340. Who is a highly compensated individual for determining whether a health plan is discriminatory?

An employee is a highly compensated individual if the employee falls into any one of the following three classifications:

(1) The employee is one of the five highest paid officers;

(2) The employee is a shareholder who owns, either actually or constructively through application of the attribution rules (Q 301), more than 10 percent in value of the employer's stock; or

(3) The employee is among the highest paid 25 percent, rounded to the nearest higher whole number, of all employees other than excludable employees who are not participants and not including retired participants.[2] Fiscal year plans may determine compensation on the basis of the calendar year ending in the plan year.

Planning Point: These requirements are not mutually exclusive. The five highest paid officers may also be among the highest paid 25 percent of all employees. However, if one of the top five officers is not in that pay range, that officer still needs to be included in the highly compensated individual category.

A participant's status as officer or stockholder with respect to a particular benefit is determined at the time when the benefit is provided.[3]

341. What are the tax consequences for amounts paid by an employer to highly compensated employees under a discriminatory self-insured medical expense reimbursement plan?

The taxable amount of payments made to a highly compensated individual from a discriminatory self-insured medical expense reimbursement plan is the excess reimbursement.[4] Two situations produce an excess reimbursement.

The first situation occurs when a benefit is available to a highly compensated individual but not to all other participants, or that otherwise discriminates in favor of highly compensated individuals. In this situation, the total amount reimbursed under the plan to the employee with respect to that benefit is an excess reimbursement.

The second situation occurs when benefits are available to all other participants and are not otherwise discriminatory and where a plan discriminates as to participation. Here, excess

1. IRC Sec. 105(h).
2. IRC Sec. 105(h)(5).
3. Treas. Reg. §1.105-11(d).
4. IRC Sec. 105(h)(1).

reimbursement is determined by multiplying the total amount reimbursed to the highly compensated individual for the plan year by a fraction. The numerator is the total amount reimbursed to all participants who are highly compensated individuals under the plan for the plan year; the denominator is the total amount reimbursed to all employees under the plan for such plan year. In determining the fraction, no account is taken of any reimbursement attributable to a benefit not available to all other participants.[1]

Multiple plans may be designated as a single plan for purposes of satisfying nondiscrimination requirements. An employee who elects to participate in an optional HMO offered by the plan is considered benefited by the plan only if the employer's contributions with respect to the employee are at least equal to what would have been made to the self-insured plan and the HMO is designated, with the self-insured plan, as a single plan. Regulations do not suggest how to determine contributions to a self-insured plan.

Unless a plan provides otherwise, reimbursements will be attributed to the plan year in which payment is made which means they will be taxed in an individual's tax year in which a plan year ends.

Amounts reimbursed for medical diagnostic procedures for employees, but not dependents, performed at a facility that provides only medical services are not considered a part of a plan and do not come within these rules requiring nondiscriminatory treatment.[2]

Contributory Plan

Reimbursements attributable to employee contributions are received tax-free, subject to inclusion if the expense was previously deducted (Q 334). Amounts attributable to employer contributions are determined in the ratio that employer contributions bear to total contributions for the calendar years immediately preceding the year of receipt, up to three years; if a plan has been in effect for less than a year, then such determination may be based upon the portion of the year of receipt preceding the time when the determination is made, or such determination may be made periodically (such as monthly or quarterly) and used throughout the succeeding period.[3] For example, if an employee terminates his services on April 15, 2019, and 2019 is the first year the plan has been in effect, such determination may be based upon the contributions of the employer and the employees during the period beginning with January 1 and ending with April 15, or during the month of March, or during the quarter consisting of January, February, and March.

Withholding

An employer does not have to withhold income tax on an amount paid for any medical care reimbursement made to or for the benefit of an employee under a self-insured medical reimbursement plan within the meaning of IRC Section 105(h)(6).[4]

1. IRC Sec. 105(h)(7).
2. Treas. Reg. §1.105-11(g).
3. Treas. Reg. §1.105-11(i).
4. IRC Sec. 3401(a)(20).

342. Are premiums paid for personal health insurance deductible as medical expenses?

Premiums paid for medical care insurance, that is, hospital, surgical, and medical expense reimbursement coverage, are deductible as a medical expense to the extent that, when added to all other unreimbursed medical expenses, the total exceeds 10 percent of a taxpayer's adjusted gross income (7.5 percent for tax years beginning before 2013 and, under the 2017 Tax Act, for 2017 and 2018). The threshold is also 10 percent for alternative minimum tax purposes (7.5 percent for 2017 and 2018).

The Affordable Care Act increased the threshold to 10 percent of a taxpayer's adjusted gross income for taxpayers who are under the age of sixty-five effective in tax years beginning January 1, 2013. Taxpayers over the age of sixty-five were temporarily excluded from this provision and the threshold for deductibility for these taxpayers remained at the 7.5 percent level from years 2013 to 2018.

No deduction may be taken for medical care premiums or any other medical expenses unless a taxpayer itemizes his or her deductions.[1] The limit on itemized deductions for certain high-income individuals (which was suspended for 2018-2025) is not applicable to medical expenses deductible under IRC Section 213.[2]

Premiums for only medical care insurance are deductible as a medical expense. Premiums for non-medical benefits, including disability income (Q 381), accidental death and dismemberment, and waiver of premium under a life insurance policy, are not deductible.

Amounts paid for any qualified long-term care insurance contract or for qualified long-term care services generally are included in the definition of medical care and, thus, are eligible for income tax deduction, subject to certain limitations (Q 485).[3]

Compulsory contributions to a state disability benefits fund are not deductible as medical expenses but are deductible as taxes.[4] Employee contributions to an alternative employer plan providing disability benefits required by state law are nondeductible personal expenses.[5]

If a policy provides both medical and non-medical benefits, a deduction will be allowed for the medical portion of the premium only if the medical charge is reasonable in relation to the total premium and is stated separately in either the policy or in a statement furnished by the insurance company.[6]

Similarly, because the deduction is limited to expenses of the taxpayer, his or her spouse and dependents, where a premium provides medical care for others as well (as in automobile

1. IRC Sec. 213(a).
2. IRC Sec. 68(c).
3. IRC Sec. 213(d)(1).
4. *McGowan v. Comm.*, 67 TC 599 (1976); *Trujillo v. Comm.*, 68 TC 670 (1977).
5. Rev. Rul. 81-192 (N.Y.), 1981-2 CB 50; Rev. Rul. 81-193 (N.J.), 1981-2 CB 52; Rev. Rul. 81-194 (Cal.), 1981-2 CB 54.
6. IRC Sec. 213(d)(6).

insurance) without separately stating the portion applicable to the taxpayer, spouse and dependents, no deduction is allowed.[1]

If a policy provides only indemnity for hospital and surgical expenses, premiums qualify as medical care premiums even though the benefits are stated amounts that will be paid without regard to the actual amount of expense incurred (Q 344).[2] Premiums paid for a hospital insurance policy that provides a stated payment for each week an insured is hospitalized, not to exceed a specified number of weeks, regardless of whether the insured receives other payments for reimbursement, do not qualify as medical care premiums and hence are not deductible.[3]

Premiums paid for a stand-alone critical illness policy are considered capital outlays and are not deductible.

A deduction will also be denied for employees' contributions to a plan that provides that employees absent from work because of sickness are to be paid a percentage of wages earned on that day by co-employees.[4]

Premiums paid for a policy that provides reimbursement for the cost of prescription drugs are deductible as medical care insurance premiums.[5]

Medicare premiums, paid by persons age sixty-five or older, under the supplementary medical insurance or prescription drug programs are deductible as medical care insurance premiums. Taxes paid by employees and self-employed persons for basic hospital insurance under Medicare are not deductible.[6]

Premiums prepaid by a taxpayer before the taxpayer is sixty-five for insurance covering medical care for the taxpayer, his or her spouse, and his or her dependents after the taxpayer is sixty-five are deductible when paid provided they are payable on a level-premium basis for ten years or more or until age sixty-five, but in no case for fewer than five years.[7]

Payments made to an institution for the provision of lifetime care are deductible under IRC Section 213(a) in the year paid to the extent that the payments are properly allocable to medical care, even if the care is to be provided in the future or possibly not provided at all.[8] The IRS has stated that its rulings should not be interpreted to permit a current deduction of payments for future medical care including medical insurance provided beyond the current tax year in situations where future lifetime care is not of the type associated with these rulings.[9]

1. Rev. Rul. 73-483, 1973-2 CB 75.
2. Rev. Rul. 58-602, 1958-2 CB 109, modified by Rev. Rul. 68-212, 1968-1 CB 91.
3. Rev. Rul. 68-451, 1968-2 CB 111.
4. Rev. Rul. 73-347, 1973-2 CB 25.
5. Rev. Rul. 68-433, 1968-2 CB 104.
6. IRC Sec. 213(d)(1)(D); Rev. Rul. 66-216, 1966-2 CB 100.
7. IRC Sec. 213(d)(7).
8. Rev. Rul. 76-481, 1976-2 CB 82; Rev. Rul. 75-303, 1975-2 CB 87; Rev. Rul. 75-302, 1975-2 CB 86.
9. Rev. Rul. 93-72, 1993-2 CB 77.

343. Are benefits received under a personal health insurance policy taxable income?

No.

All kinds of benefits from personal health insurance generally are entirely exempt from income tax. This includes disability income; (Q 381), dismemberment and sight loss benefits; critical illness benefits;[1] and hospital, surgical, or other medical expense reimbursement. There is no limit on the amount of benefits, including the amount of disability income, that can be received tax-free under personally paid health insurance or under an arrangement having the effect of accident or health insurance.[2] At least one court has held, however, that the IRC Section 104(a)(3) exclusion is not available where a taxpayer's claims for insurance benefits were not made in good faith and were not based on a true illness or injury.[3]

The accidental death benefit under a health insurance policy may be tax-exempt to a beneficiary as death proceeds of life insurance (Q 65).[4] Disability benefits received for loss of income or earning capacity under no fault insurance are excludable from gross income.[5] The exclusion also has been applied to an insured to whom policies were transferred by a professional service corporation in which the insured was the sole stockholder.[6]

Health insurance benefits are tax-exempt if received by the insured and if received by a person having an insurable interest in an insured.[7]

Medical expense reimbursement benefits must be taken into account in computing a taxpayer's medical expense deduction. Because only unreimbursed expenses are deductible, the total amount of medical expenses paid during a taxable year must be reduced by the total amount of reimbursements received in that taxable year.[8]

Likewise, if medical expenses are deducted in the year they are paid and then reimbursed in a later year, the taxpayer or the taxpayer's estate, where the deduction is taken on the decedent's final return but later reimbursed to the taxpayer's estate, must include the reimbursement, to the extent of the prior year's deduction, in gross income for the later year.[9]

Where the value of a decedent's right to reimbursement proceeds, which is income in respect of a decedent,[10] is included in the decedent's estate (Q 422), an income tax deduction is available for the portion of estate tax attributable to such value.

1. See, e.g., Let Rul. 200903001.
2. IRC Sec. 104(a)(3); Rev. Rul. 55-331, 1955-1 CB 271, *modified by* Rev. Rul. 68-212, 1968-1 CB 91; Rev. Rul. 70-394, 1970-2 CB 34.
3. *Dodge v. Comm.*, 93-1 USTC ¶50,021 (8th Cir. 1992).
4. IRC Sec. 101(a); Treas. Reg. §1.101-1(a).
5. Rev. Rul. 73-155, 1973-1 CB 50.
6. Let. Rul. 7751104.
7. See IRC Sec. 104; *Castner Garage, Ltd. v. Comm.*, 43 BTA 1 (1940), acq. 1941-1 CB 11.
8. Rev. Rul. 56-18, 1956-1 CB 135.
9. Treas. Reg. §§1.104-1, 1.213-1(g); Rev. Rul. 78-292, 1978-2 CB 233.
10. See Rev. Rul. 78-292, above.

Disability income is not treated as reimbursement for medical expenses and, therefore, does not offset such expenses.[1]

> *Example:* Mr. Jones, whose adjusted gross income for 2018 was $25,000, paid $3,000 in medical expenses during that year. On his 2018 return, he took a medical expense deduction of $1,125 [$3,000 – $1,875 (7.5 percent of his adjusted gross income)]. In 2019, Mr. Jones receives the following benefits from his health insurance: disability income, $1,200; reimbursement for 2018 doctor and hospital bills, $400. He must report $400 as taxable income on his 2019 return. Had Mr. Jones received the reimbursement in 2018, his medical expense deduction for that year would have been limited to $725 ($3,000 – $400 [reimbursement] – $1,875 [7.5 percent of adjusted gross income]). Otherwise, he would have received the entire amount of insurance benefits, including the medical expense reimbursement, tax-free.

Planning Point: This example illustrates that the timing of medical expense payments and their submission for reimbursement may be critical to the individual's personal tax planning, particularly in regard to reaching the requisite 10 (or 7.5) percent of adjusted gross income threshold.

344. If benefits received for specific medical expenses exceed those expenses, must the excess be treated as reimbursement for other medical expenses?

Yes.

In computing net unreimbursed expenses for the medical expense deduction, total medical expense benefits received during the taxable year, whether received by a taxpayer or a service provider, must be subtracted from total medical expenses paid.[2] If reimbursements for the year equal or exceed medical expenses for the year, a taxpayer is not entitled to a medical expense deduction. Any excess reimbursement need not be included in a taxpayer's gross income unless the reimbursements are partially attributable to the contributions of the taxpayer's employer.[3]

345. What are domestic partner benefits and how are they taxed?

Domestic partner benefits are benefits that an employer voluntarily offers to an employee's unmarried partner. An employee's domestic partner may be of the same sex or the opposite sex. An employer determines the scope of its plan's definition of domestic partner.

After July 13, 2013, same-sex couples who were married in a state in which same sex marriage is recognized (the state of "celebration") are considered spouses, regardless of where they live.[4]

Employers may offer a range of domestic partnership benefits, such as family, bereavement, sick leave, and relocation benefits. In general, most people mean employer-provided health insurance coverage when they speak of domestic partnership benefits.

An employee is taxed on the value of employer-provided health benefits for his or her domestic partner unless the domestic partner qualifies as the employee's dependent under IRC Section 151. The tax is determined by assessing the fair market value of the coverage provided to

1. *Deming v. Comm.*, 9 TC 383 (1947), *acq.* 1948-1 CB 1.
2. Rev. Rul. 56-18, 1956-1 CB 135.
3. Rev. Rul. 69-154, 1969-1 CB 46.
4. *United States v. Windsor*, 133 S. Ct. 2675 (2013).

the domestic partner. This amount then is reported on the employee's W-2 form and is subjected to Social Security (FICA) and federal income tax withholding.

Any amount received by a domestic partner as payment or reimbursement of plan benefits will not be included in the income of the employee or the domestic partner to the extent that the coverage provided to the domestic partner was paid for by the employee's plan contributions or the fair market value of the coverage was included in the employee's income under IRC Section 104(a)(3).[1]

Coverage of domestic partners, whether or not they qualify as dependents, under an employer-provided health plan will not otherwise affect the ability of employees to exclude amounts paid, directly or indirectly, by a plan to reimburse employees for expenses incurred for medical care of the employees, their spouses, and dependents.

Cafeteria Plans and Flexible Spending Accounts – Contributions used to provide coverage for a non-dependent domestic partner are treated as taxable income. Benefits under flexible spending accounts may not be provided to a domestic partner because these accounts can include only nontaxable income (Q 3501).

COBRA – A domestic partner may not make an independent election for COBRA coverage, but may be part of an employee's election (Q 356 - Q 375).

HIPAA – Domestic partners who are not dependents are not covered by HIPAA, although employers providing health insurance to domestic partners may voluntarily include them in HIPAA certification procedures.

346. How are accident or health benefits taxed when provided by a closely held C corporation only to its stockholder-employees?

To provide tax-free coverage and benefits, an employer's accident or health plan must be for employees.[2] The same is true with respect to amounts received under a state's sickness and disability fund under IRC Section 105(e)(2).

The IRS can challenge tax benefits claimed under a plan that covers only stockholder-employees on the ground that the plan is not for employees. The underlying problem is in establishing that the stockholder-employees are covered as employees rather than as stockholders. If this cannot be established, then premiums or benefits are likely to be treated as constructive dividends. The premiums will be nondeductible by the corporation and the premium costs will have to be reported by the shareholder as dividend income to the extent of the corporation's earnings and profits.[3]

Courts have taken the position that the tax benefits of employer-provided health insurance are available in a plan that covers only stockholder-employees if the plan covers a class of

1. Let. Ruls. 200846001, 9850011, 9717018, 9603011. See also Let. Ruls. 9109060, 9034048. See also Field Service Advice 199911012.
2. IRC Sec. 105(e).
3. *Levine v. Commissioner* 50 TC 422 (1968); and *Larkin v. Commissioner* 394 F.2d 494 (1st Cir. 1968).

employees that can be segregated rationally from other employees, if any, on a criterion other than their being stockholders.[1]

The *Bogene, Smith, Seidel,* and *Epstein* cases were decided in favor of taxpayers; the plans in all of them covered only active and compensated officers of the corporation who also were stockholders.

In *Smith* and *Seidel*, the officer-shareholders also were the only employees, but in *Bogene* and *Epstein* there were other employees who were not shareholders and who were not covered.

The plan in *American Foundry* covered only two of five active officers of a family corporation and was held not to be a plan for employees.

The plan in *Sturgill* covered four officer-stockholders of a family corporation but two of the four were not active or compensated as officer-employees and the plan was held not to be one for employees.

The plan in *Leidy* covered only the president, who was the sole stockholder, and the vice president, who was no longer active in the company.

In *American Foundry* and in *Sturgill*, courts allowed the corporations to deduct reimbursement payments to the active officers as reasonable compensation, even though the payments were not excludable by shareholder-employees under IRC Section 105.

For situations involving S corporations, see Q 348.

347. How is health insurance coverage taxed for partners and sole proprietors?

Partners and sole proprietors are self-employed individuals, not employees, and the rules for personal health insurance apply (Q 342, Q 343). Partners and sole proprietors can deduct 100 percent of amounts paid during a taxable year for insurance that provides medical care for the individual, his or her spouse, and dependents during the tax year. The insurance can also cover a child who was under age twenty-seven at the end of the tax year, even if the child did not qualify as the taxpayer's dependent. A child includes a taxpayer's son, daughter, stepchild, adopted child, or foster child. A foster child is any child placed with the taxpayer by an authorized placement agency or by judgment, decree, or other order of any court of competent jurisdiction.

Certain premiums paid for long-term care insurance are also eligible for this deduction (Q 486).[2]

The deduction is not available to a partner or sole proprietor for any calendar month in which he or she is eligible to participate in any subsidized health plan maintained by any employer

---

1. *Bogene, Inc. v. Comm.*, TC Memo 1968-147; *Smith v. Comm.*, TC Memo 1970-243; *Seidel v. Comm.*, TC Memo 1971-238; *Epstein v. Comm.*, TC Memo 1972-53; *American Foundry v. Comm.*, 536 F.2d 289, 76-1 USTC ¶9401 (9th Cir. 1976), acq. 1974-2 CB 1; *Charlie Sturgill Motor Co. v. Comm.*, TC Memo 1973-281; *Oleander Co., Inc. v. U.S.*, 50 AFTR 2d 82-5170, 82-1 USTC ¶9395 (E.D.N.C. 1981); *Giberson v. Comm.*, TC Memo 1982-338; *Est. of Leidy*, above; *Wigutow v. Comm.*, TC Memo 1983-620.
2. IRC Secs. 162(l), 213(d)(1).

of the self-employed individual or his or her spouse. This rule is applied separately to plans that include coverage for qualified long- term care services or are qualified long-term care insurance contracts (Q 475) and plans that do not include that coverage and are not those kinds of contracts.[1]

The deduction is allowable in calculating adjusted gross income and is limited to the self-employed individual's earned income for the tax year that is derived from the trade or business with respect to which the plan providing medical care coverage is established. Earned income is, in general, net earnings from self-employment with respect to a trade or business in which the personal services of the taxpayer are a material income producing factor. Other rules govern contributions made to a qualified retirement plan (Q 3920).

Any amounts paid for this kind of insurance may not be taken into account in computing (1) the amount of a medical expense deduction under IRC Section 213, and (2) net-earnings from self-employment for the purpose of determining the tax on self-employment income.[2]

If a partnership pays accident and health insurance premiums for services rendered by partners in their capacity as partners and without regard to partnership income, premium payments are considered to be guaranteed payments under IRC Section 707(c). Thus, the premiums are deductible by the partnership under IRC Section 162, subject to IRC Section 263, and includable in partners' income under IRC Section 61. A partner may not exclude premium payments from income under IRC Section 106 but may deduct payments to the extent allowable under IRC Section 162(l), as discussed above.[3] For partners, a policy can be either in the name of the partnership or in the name of the partner. The partner can either pay the premiums him or herself, or the partnership can pay them and report the premium amounts on Schedule K-1 (Form 1065) as guaranteed payments to be included in the partner's gross income. However, if the policy is in the partner's name and the partner pays the premiums him or herself, the partnership must reimburse the partner and report the premium amounts on Schedule K-1 (Form 1065) as guaranteed payments to be included in the partner's gross income. Otherwise, the insurance plan will not be considered to be established under the business.

Reasoning that consumer medical cards that provide discounts on certain medical services and items are not an insurance product, the IRS has concluded that the cost of these cards purchased for partners is not deductible by partners under either IRC Section 162(l) or IRC Section 213.[4] (See Q 332.)

Regarding the income tax consequences of a self-funded medical reimbursement plan set up by a partnership, the IRS has concluded that payments from a plan made to partners and their dependents are excludable from partners' income and premiums paid by partners for coverage under a self-funded plan are deductible, subject to the limits of IRC Section 162(l).[5]

1. IRC Sec. 162(l).
2. IRC Sec. 162(l).
3. Rev. Rul. 91-26, 1991-1 CB 184.
4. Let. Rul. 9814023.
5. Let. Rul. 200007025.

There is no limit on the amount of benefits a partner or sole proprietor can receive tax-free.[1]

For tax treatment of business overhead disability insurance, see Q 377.

The IRS has ruled that coverage purchased by a sole proprietor or partnership for non-owner-employees, including an owner's spouse, is subject to the same rules that apply in any other employer-employee situation.[2]

The IRS has issued settlement guidelines that address whether a self-employed individual ("employer-spouse") may hire his or her spouse as an employee ("employee-spouse") and provide family health benefits to the employee-spouse, who then elects family coverage including the employer-spouse. Essentially, the IRS position is that if an employee-spouse is a bona fide employee, the employer-spouse may deduct the cost of the coverage and the value of the coverage also is excludable from the employee-spouse's gross income.

IRS agents are to use the settlement guidelines to closely scrutinize whether an employee-spouse qualifies as a bona fide employee; merely calling a spouse an employee is insufficient. Part-time employment does not negate employee status, but nominal or insignificant services that have no economic substance or independent significance will be challenged.[3]

348. How is health insurance coverage taxed for S corporation shareholders?

The IRS issued guidance late in 2014 indicating that accident and health insurance premiums paid to insure a greater than 2-percent S corporation shareholder are treated as wages by the shareholder and are deductible by the S corporation. However, these benefits are not subject to FICA, FUTA or Social Security taxes. The S corporation shareholder is entitled to an above-the-line deduction for amounts paid throughout the year for medical premiums, but only if neither the shareholder nor his or her spouse are otherwise eligible to participate in any subsidized health care plan offered by another employer. The IRS released a CCM clarifying that this remains the case even if the 2-percent shareholder-employee is treated as a 2-percent shareholder via the family attribution rules.[4]

Planning Point: The IRS has released a set of frequently asked questions based upon the regulations governing the new Section 199A deduction for pass-through entities, such as S corporations. The FAQ provides that health insurance premiums paid by the S corporation for a greater-than-2-percent shareholder reduce qualified business income (QBI) at the entity level (by reducing the ordinary income used to calculate QBI). Similarly, when a self-employed individual takes a deduction for health insurance attributable to the trade or business, this will be a deduction in determining QBI and can reduce QBI at the entity and individual levels.[5]

1. Rev. Rul. 56-326, 1956-2 CB 100; Rev. Rul. 58-90, 1958-1 CB 88.
2. Rev. Rul. 71-588, 1971-2 CB 91; TAM 9409006.
3. IRS Settlement Guidelines, 2001 TNT 222-25 (Nov. 16, 2001); see also *Poyda v. Comm.*, TC Summary Opinion 2001-91.
4. CCM 201912001.
5. FAQ is available at: https://www.irs.gov/newsroom/tax-cuts-and-jobs-act-provision-11011-section-199a-qualified-business-income-deduction-faqs.

Unlike in traditional employment situations, the IRS has also noted that if the S corporation shareholder is the sole shareholder, he or she may purchase the insurance in his or her own name, but allow the S corporation to either directly pay for the premiums or reimburse the sole shareholder for those premiums, and still be entitled to the above-the-line deduction for premiums paid. In either case, the premium payment must be reported on the shareholder's W-2 as wages.[1]

Planning Point: Absent the use of a QSEHRA, employers are generally no longer able to reimburse employees for individual health insurance premiums without incurring potentially substantial penalties under the ACA. This IRS guidance is very narrow, and allows reimbursement only in situations where there is one single S corporation shareholder.

With respect to coverage purchased by an S corporation for employees not owning any stock and for shareholder-employees owning 2 percent or less of the outstanding stock or voting power, the same rules apply as in any other employer-employee situation (Q 332).

349. What is a Health Reimbursement Arrangement ("HRA") and how is it taxed?

Editor's Note: Because of the strict requirements set forth in IRS guidance implementing the Affordable Care Act market reform provisions, HRAs may be of limited use unless the employer satisfies the requirements for offering a qualified small employer HRA (QSEHRA, Q 350). Proposed rules that would expand the availability of HRAs that reimburse employees for the cost of individual health insurance premiums were released in late 2018. See Q 445 for more detailed guidance.

According to IRS guidance, an HRA is an arrangement that (1) is solely employer-funded and not paid for directly or indirectly by salary reduction contributions under a cafeteria plan, and (2) reimburses employees for substantiated medical care expenses incurred by the employee and the employee's spouse and dependents, as defined in IRC Section 152, up to a maximum dollar amount per coverage period.

Unused amounts in an individual's account may be carried forward to increase the maximum reimbursement amount in subsequent coverage periods.[2] HRAs are not available for self-employed individuals.

Employer-provided coverage and medical care reimbursement amounts under an HRA are excludable from an employee's gross income under IRC Section 106 and IRC Section 105(b), assuming all requirements for HRAs are met.[3]

For taxable years beginning after December 31, 2010, reimbursements for medicine are limited to doctor-prescribed drugs and insulin. After 2010, over-the counter medicines are not qualified expenses unless prescribed by a doctor.

1. See IRS Guidance, S Corporation Compensation and Medical Insurance Issues, accessible at:http://www.irs.gov/Businesses/Small-Businesses-&-Self-Employed/S-Corporation-Compensation-and-Medical-Insurance-Issues (last accessed February 14, 2019).
2. Notice 2002-45, 2002-2 CB 93; Rev. Rul. 2002-41, 2002-2 CB 75. See also IRS Publication 969 (2017) "Health Savings Accounts and Other Tax-Favored Health Plans."
3. Notice 2002-45, 2002-2 CB 93; Rev. Rul. 2002-41, 2002-2 CB 75.

According to Notice 2002-45, an HRA may not offer cash-outs at any time, even on termination of service or retirement; it may continue to reimburse former employees for medical care expenses after such events, however, even if the employee does not elect COBRA continuation coverage. An HRA is a group health plan and, thus, is subject to COBRA continuation coverage requirements (Q 356 to Q 375).

On a one-time basis, an HRA may make a qualified HSA distribution, that is, a rollover to a health savings account, of an amount not exceeding the balance in the HRA on September 21, 2006 (Q 412).[1]

HRAs may not be used to reimburse expenses incurred before the HRA was in existence or expenses that are deductible under IRC Section 213 for a prior taxable year. An unreimbursed claim incurred in one coverage period may be reimbursed in a later coverage period, so long as the individual was covered under the HRA when the claim was incurred.[2]

The IRS has approved the use of employer-issued debit and credit cards to pay for medical expenses as incurred provided that the employer requires subsequent substantiation of the expenses or has in place sufficient procedures to substantiate the payments at the time of purchase.[3]

An employee may not be reimbursed for the same medical care expense by both an HRA and an IRC Section 125 health FSA. Technically, ordering rules from the IRS specify that the HRA benefits must be exhausted before FSA reimbursements may be made. An HRA can be drafted to specify that coverage under the HRA is available only after expenses exceeding the dollar amount of an IRC Section 125 FSA have been paid. Thus, an employee could exhaust coverage, which generally may not be carried over, before tapping into the employee's HRA coverage, which can be carried over.[4] (Note that the IRS now allows a health FSA to be amended in order to allow up to $500 of unused amounts remaining at the end of a plan year to be paid or reimbursed to participants during the following plan year, provided the FSA does not also allow for a grace period, see Q 3515.)[5]

Employer contributions to an HRA may not be attributable in any way to salary reductions. Thus, an HRA may not be offered under a cafeteria plan, but may be offered in conjunction with a cafeteria plan. Where an HRA is offered in conjunction with another accident or health plan funded pursuant to salary reductions, then a facts and circumstances test is used to determine if salary reductions are attributable to the HRA. If a salary reduction amount for a coverage period to fund a non-HRA accident or health plan exceeds the actual cost of the non-specified accident or health plan coverage, the salary reduction will be attributed to the HRA. An example of the application of this rule can be found in Revenue Ruling 2002-41.[6]

1. IRC Sec. 106(e).
2. Notice 2002-45, 2002-2 CB 93.
3. Notice 2006-69, 2006-31 IRB 107; Rev. Proc. 2003-43, 2003-21 IRB 935. See also Notice 2007-2, 2007-2 IRB 254.
4. Notice 2002-45, 2002-2 CB 93.
5. Notice 2013-71, 2013-47 IRB 532.
6. 2002-2 CB 75.

Because an HRA may not be paid for through salary reduction, the following restrictions on health FSAs are not applicable to HRAs:

(1) the ban against a benefit that defers compensation by permitting employees to carry over unused elective contributions or plan benefits from one plan year to another plan year;

(2) the requirement that the maximum amount of reimbursement must be available at all times during the coverage period;

(3) the mandatory twelve month period of coverage; and

(4) the limitation that medical expenses reimbursed must be incurred during the period of coverage.[1]

350. What is a Qualified Small Employer Health Reimbursement Arrangement ("QSEHRA")?

Pursuant to IRS guidance released late in 2016, small business employers are now permitted to offer qualified small employer health reimbursement arrangements (QSEHRAs) beginning in 2017 without incurring ACA penalties. QSEHRAs are HRAs that allow a small employer who is not an applicable large employer under the ACA (i.e., one that has fewer than fifty full-time employees) to reimburse employees for the purchase of individual health insurance policies using an HRA if the small employer does not also offer its employees group health coverage. The employer can contribute a maximum of $4,950 in 2017, $5,050 in 2018, $5,150 for 2019, and $5,250 for 2020 for employees who purchase individual coverage, and a maximum of $10,050 in 2017, $10,250 in 2018, $10,450 for 2019, and $10,600 for 2020 if the employee purchases family coverage (both contribution limits will be indexed for inflation and pro-rated amounts are used for years in which only partial coverage is offered).[2]

QSEHRAs must generally be offered on the same basis to all comparable employees, though the employer can exclude employees who have yet to work ninety days, employees who have not reached age twenty-five, employees who are covered by a collective bargaining agreement and employees who are nonresident aliens and have no earned income from U.S. sources. Small business employers who choose to offer QSEHRAs must provide a written notice to employees 90 days before the beginning of the year (by March 12, 2017 for 2017 QSEHRAs) that specifies the amount of the benefit that will be provided by the QSEHRA and informs participating employees that they must inform the health insurance exchanges of the benefit provided by the QSEHRA if the employee intends to apply for premium assistance.

The notice must also clearly inform the employee that if he or she does not purchase health insurance, ACA penalties may apply and any reimbursements from the QSEHRA may be included in gross income. Small employers must also report the QSEHRA coverage on Form W-2, Box 12 (for informational purposes). Pursuant to guidance released in 2017, the

1. Notice 2002-45, 2002-2 CB 93.
2. Rev. Proc. 2018-57, Rev. Proc. 2019-44.

employer need not provide participating employees with Form 1095-B or send the same data to the IRS on Form 1094-B.[1]

351. Are wage continuation payments under an accident and health plan subject to withholding?

Employers or former employers must withhold tax from payments made to an employee for a period of absence from work due to injury or sickness. If an employer has shifted the insurance risk to an insurer or trust, no income tax need be withheld from wage continuation payments that an insurance company or a separate trust makes on behalf of the employer.[2]

Amounts paid as sick pay during a temporary absence under a plan to which the employer is a party may be withheld by a third party payor at the employee's request.[3]

Amounts paid by a third party are wages subject to mandatory withholding if the insurance risk is not shifted by the arrangement because the third party is acting as the employer's agent if the employer reimburses the insurance company or trust on a cost plus fee basis.[4]

352. Is employer-provided sick pay subject to Social Security and federal unemployment tax?

Preretirement wage continuation payments by an employer or an insurance company to an employee because of his or her sickness or disability are subject to Social Security tax (FICA) and federal unemployment tax (FUTA) for the first six calendar months after the last month in which the employee worked for the employer.

After six months, they are exempt from Social Security and federal unemployment tax.[5]

Payments or parts of payments attributable to employee contributions made to a sick pay plan with after tax dollars are not subject to Social Security or FUTA taxes.

353. Must an employer with an accident or health plan file an information return with respect to the plan?

A plan that covers fewer than 100 employees on the first day of the plan year and is unfunded, fully insured, or a combination of unfunded and fully insured, was previously exempt from the requirement to file an annual Form 5500 report. All other plans were required to file a Form 5500.[6] Under proposed regulations issued in 2016, group health plans that were previously required to file a Form 5500 will now be required to file an additional schedule (Schedule J (Group Health Plan Information)) in addition to their previously applicable Form 5500 filing requirement. Plans that provide group health benefits to fewer than 100 participants that were exempt because they are completely unfunded, or

1. 21st Century Cures Act, HR 34; Notice 2017-67.
2. Treas. Reg. §31.3401(a)-1(b)(8); Rev. Rul. 77-89, 1977-1 CB 300.
3. IRC Sec. 3402(o); Treas. Reg. §31.3402(o)-3.
4. Treas. Reg. §31.3401(a)-1(b)(8).
5. IRC Secs. 3121(a)(4), 3306(b)(4).
6. Instructions to Form 5500, Annual Return/Report of Employee Benefit Plan, p. 3.

partially insured and partially unfunded, are required under the proposed regulations to file Form 5500 without the additional Schedule J requirement. Plans that provide group health benefits to fewer than 100 participants that were exempt because they are fully insured are required to file certain answers on both Form 5500 and Schedule J.[1]

Note that if the plan is subject to ERISA, the Form 5500 is filed with the Department of Labor (DOL).

IRC Section 6039D requires an employer maintaining any accident or health plan to file an annual information return with the IRS for years beginning after December 31, 1988. Until the issuance of further guidance, the IRS has indefinitely suspended the reporting requirements of IRC Section 6039D.[2]

If in effect, IRC Section 6039D would require the reporting of the number of an employer's employees, employees eligible to participate in the plan, employees actually participating in the plan, highly compensated employees ("HCEs"), HCEs eligible to participate in the plan, and HCEs actually participating in the plan.

The return also would report the cost of the plan, the identity of the employer, and the type of business in which the employer is engaged.[3]

354. What notices must an employer that maintains an accident or health plan offering prescription drug coverage to Medicare-eligible individuals provide?

Employers and plan sponsors that offer prescription drug coverage to individuals eligible for Medicare Part D must advise those individuals whether the offered coverage is creditable. Under the Medicare Prescription Drug, Improvement, and Modernization Act of 2003 (MMA), eligible individuals who do not enroll in Part D when first available, but who enroll later, have to pay higher premiums permanently unless they have creditable prescription drug coverage.

Under CMS guidance, once a sponsor determines whether coverage is creditable (see Q 355), the sponsor must provide notice to all Part D-eligible individuals covered by or applying for the plan, including Part D-eligible dependents. In lieu of determining who is Part D eligible, an employer sponsor may provide notice to all active employees, along with an explanation of why the notice is being provided.

The required notice to beneficiaries must, at a minimum:

(1) Contain a statement that the employer has determined that the coverage is creditable or not creditable;

1. See RIN 1210-AB63, p.10.
2. Notice 90-24, 1990-1 CB 335; Notice 2002-24, 2002-1 C.B. 785.
3. IRC Sec. 6039D.

(2) Explain the limits on the periods in a year when individuals can enroll in Part D plans; and

(3) Explain that the individual may incur late enrollment penalties.[1]

The CMS guidance includes model initial notices that a sponsor may choose to use. Sponsors were required to provide initial notices to beneficiaries by November 15, 2005. CMS later issued updated guidance with model notices for use following the May 15, 2006 close of the initial enrollment period for Medicare Part D.

Following the initial enrollment period, sponsors must, at a minimum, provide the required notice to beneficiaries:

(1) Prior to an individual's initial enrollment period for the Medicare prescription drug benefit;

(2) Prior to the effective date of enrolling in the sponsor's plan and on any change that affects whether the coverage is creditable prescription drug coverage;

(3) Prior to the commencement of the annual coordinated election period that begins on October 15 of each year; and

(4) On beneficiary request.

The final regulation does not specify a specific time limit within which disclosure must be provided; it only requires that it be provided prior to any of the above events.[2]

Sponsors also must disclose to CMS annually whether coverage is creditable and any change that impacts whether the coverage is creditable. CMS has outlined the requirements for this disclosure in separate guidance and provides disclosure forms on its website at http://www.cms.hhs.gov/CreditableCoverage.[3]

355. How does an employer that maintains an accident or health plan determine what constitutes "creditable coverage" for purposes of the notice requirements for Medicare-eligible individuals?

To determine that coverage is creditable, a sponsor need only determine that total expected paid claims for Medicare beneficiaries under the sponsor's plan will be at least equal to the total expected paid claims for the same beneficiaries under the defined standard prescription drug coverage under Part D.[4] The determination of creditable coverage status for disclosure purposes requires attestation by a qualified actuary who is a member of the American Academy of Actuaries.[5]

1. 42 CFR §423.56(d).
2. 42 CFR §423.56(f).
3. 42 CFR §423.56(e).
4. 42 CFR §423.884(d).
5. 42 CFR §423.884(d)(2).

Applicants may use qualified outside actuaries, including (but not limited to) actuaries employed by the plan administrator or an insurer providing benefits under the plan. If an applicant uses an outside actuary, the attestation can be submitted directly by the outside actuary or by the plan sponsor.[1]

The Center for Medicare & Medicaid Studies (CMS) has issued guidance to assist sponsors in making the determination that coverage is creditable. If the total expected claims requirement stated above is met, then the following types of coverage are considered creditable:[2]

(1) Coverage for prescription drugs under a PDP or MA-PD plan;

(2) Medicaid coverage under Title XIX of the MMA;

(3) Coverage under certain group health plans, such as the federal employee health benefits program and qualified retiree prescription drug plans;

(4) State Pharmaceutical Assistance Programs coverage;

(5) Prescription drug coverage for veterans, survivors, and dependents;

(6) Coverage for Medicare supplemental policies;

(7) Military coverage;

(8) Individual health insurance coverage that includes outpatient prescription drug coverage but is not an excepted benefit under the Public Health Service Act;

(9) Coverage provided by certain Indian or Tribal medical care programs;

(10) Coverage provided by a PACE organization;

(11) Coverage provided by a cost-based HMO or CMP;

(12) Coverage provided through a state high-risk pool; and

(13) Other coverage as deemed appropriate by federal regulators.

Under CMS guidance, once a sponsor determines whether coverage is creditable, the sponsor must provide notice to all Part D-eligible individuals covered by or applying for the plan, including Part D-eligible dependents. In lieu of determining who is Part D eligible, an employer sponsor may provide notice to all active employees, along with an explanation of why the notice is being provided.

1. 42 CFR §423.884(d)(2).
2. 42 CFR §423.56(b).

COBRA Continuation Coverage Requirements

356. What are the coverage continuation or COBRA requirements that certain group health plans must meet?

Editor's Note: ARRA 2009 provided a temporary premium subsidy for COBRA continuation coverage for certain unemployed workers. See "Temporary COBRA Premium Assistance under ARRA 2009," Q 357.

An insured or self-funded group health plan maintained by an employer to provide health care, directly or otherwise, to the employer's employees, former employees, or their families generally must offer COBRA continuation coverage. Certain plans are exempt from the COBRA continuation coverage rules (Q 360). Insured plans are not only those providing coverage under group policies, but include any arrangement to provide health care to two or more employees under individual policies. A plan is an employer provided health plan if the plan's coverage would be unavailable at the same cost to individuals absent the individual's employment-related connection with the employer; it is immaterial whether the employer makes contributions to the plan on behalf of its employees.[1]

COBRA generally does not require plan sponsors to offer continuation coverage for disability income coverage.[2] For contracts issued after 1996, the COBRA requirements do not apply to plans under which substantially all of the coverage is for qualified long-term care services. A plan may use any reasonable method to determine whether substantially all of the coverage under the plan is for qualified long-term care services.

Additionally, amounts contributed by an employer to an HSA or an Archer MSA (Q 388, Q 420) are not considered part of a group health plan subject to COBRA continuation requirements.[3]

Employer-sponsored health care plans subject to COBRA requirements must provide that if, as a result of a qualifying event, any qualified beneficiary would lose coverage under the plan, the qualified beneficiary must be entitled to elect, within the election period, continuation coverage under the plan.[4]

Further, a group health plan generally will not meet the COBRA requirements unless the plan's coverage of the cost of pediatric vaccines is not reduced below the coverage provided by the plan as of May 1, 1993.[5]

Continuation Coverage Defined

COBRA continuation coverage must consist of coverage identical to that provided under the plan to similarly situated beneficiaries with respect to whom a qualifying event has not

1. IRC Sec. 4980B(g)(2); Treas. Reg. §54.4980B-2, A-1.
2. *Austell v. Raymond James & Assoc., Inc.*, 120 F.3d 32 (4th Cir. 1997).
3. IRC Sec. 4980B(g)(2); Treas. Reg. §54.4980B-2, A-1.
4. IRC Sec. 4980B(f)(1); Treas. Reg. §54.4980B-1, A-1.
5. IRC Sec. 4980B(f)(1).

occurred. Any modification of coverage for similarly situated beneficiaries also must apply in the same manner for all COBRA qualified beneficiaries.[1]

A case brought under the COBRA provisions of ERISA held that an employer did not meet its obligation to offer continuation coverage where the only health plan available to a qualified beneficiary following the insolvency of a self-insured multiemployer trust under which the beneficiary originally had elected COBRA coverage was a geographically-restrictive HMO that did not provide service in the area of the beneficiary's residence.[2]

Qualified beneficiaries electing COBRA coverage generally are subject to the same deductibles as similarly situated non-COBRA beneficiaries. Amounts accumulated toward deductibles, plan benefits, and plan cost limits prior to a qualifying event are carried over into the COBRA continuation coverage period.[3]

A qualified beneficiary electing COBRA continuation coverage need not be given the opportunity to change coverage from the type he or she was receiving prior to the qualifying event, even where the coverage is of lesser or no value to the qualified beneficiary, except in two situations.

First, if a qualified beneficiary was participating in a region-specific plan that does not provide services in the region to which the beneficiary is relocating, the beneficiary must be able, within a reasonable period after requesting other coverage, to elect the alternative coverage that the employer or employee organization makes available to active employees. An employer or employee organization is not required to make any other coverage available to a relocating qualified beneficiary if the only coverage that the employer makes available to active employees is not available in the area where the qualified beneficiary is relocating.

Second, if an employer or employee organization makes an open enrollment period available to similarly situated active employees, the same open enrollment period rights must be offered to each qualified beneficiary receiving COBRA coverage.[4]

357. What special rules applied to COBRA premium assistance under legislation enacted in 2009 and 2010?

Ordinarily, if an unemployed worker elects to receive COBRA continuation coverage, the percentage of the applicable premium that may be charged can be as high as 102 percent (Q 368). In February 2009, Congress enacted temporary relief to help scores of unemployed workers maintain their health insurance coverage by making it more affordable.[5] Essentially a 65 percent subsidy or premium assistance was available for COBRA continuation coverage premiums for certain workers who had been involuntarily terminated as the result of a COBRA qualifying

1. IRC Sec. 4980B(f)(2).
2. *Coble v. Bonita House, Inc.*, 789 F. Supp. 320 (N. D. Cal. 1992).
3. Treas. Reg. §54.4980B-5, A-2, A-3.
4. Treas. Reg. §54.4980B-5, A-4.
5. Sec. 3001 of ARRA 2009 (P.L. 115-5).

event occurring during the period from September 1, 2008, through May 31, 2010, as extended under the Continuing Extension Act of 2010.

An assistance eligible individual was eligible for the premium reduction for up to fifteen months as extended under the Department of Defense Appropriations Act of 2010 from the first month the premium reduction provisions applied to the individual. The premium reduction ended if the individual became eligible for coverage under any other group health plan or for Medicare benefits.[1]

Reduced Premium Amount

In the case of any premium for a period of coverage beginning on or after February 17, 2009, an assistance eligible individual was treated for purposes of any COBRA continuation provision as having paid the amount of such premium if the individual paid 35 percent of the amount of the premium, determined without regard to the premium assistance provision.[2] The employer was reimbursed for the other 65 percent of the premium that was not paid by the assistance eligible individual through a credit against its payroll taxes.[3]

The premium used to determine the 35 percent share that must have been paid by or on behalf of an assistance eligible individual was the cost that would be charged to him or her for COBRA continuation coverage if the individual were not an assistance eligible individual. Thus, if, without regard to the subsidy, an assistance eligible individual was required to pay 102 percent of the applicable premium for continuation coverage, that is, the maximum generally permitted under COBRA rules, the assistance eligible individual was then required to pay only 35 percent of the 102 percent of the applicable premium.

If the premium that would be charged to the assistance eligible individual was less than the maximum COBRA premium, for example, if the employer subsidized the coverage by paying all or part of the cost, then the amount actually charged to the assistance eligible individual was used to determine the assistance eligible individual's 35 percent share.[4]

In determining whether an assistance eligible individual had paid 35 percent of the premium, payments made on behalf of the individual by another person, other than an employer with respect to which an involuntary termination occurred, were taken into account; for example, by a parent, guardian, state agency, or charity.[5]

Premium Reduction Period

The premium reduction applied as of the first period of coverage beginning on or after February 17, 2009 for which the assistance eligible individual was eligible to pay only 35 percent of the premium, as determined without regard to the premium reduction, and still be treated

1. Sec. 3 of the Continuing Extension Act of 2010; Sec. 1010 of the Department of Defense Appropriations Act of 2009; Sec. 3001(a) of ARRA 2009; Notice 2009-27, 2009-16 IRB 838; IRS News Release IR-2010-52 (4-26-2010).
2. Sec. 3001(a)(1)(A) of ARRA 2009; Notice 2009-27, 2009-16 IRB 838.
3. See IRC Sec. 6432(c), as added by ARRA 2009; Notice 2009-27, 2009-16 IRB 838.
4. Notice 2009-27, 2009-16 IRB 838, Q&A 20.
5. Notice 2009-27, 2009-16 IRB 838, Q&A 20.

as having made full payment. For this purpose, a period of coverage was a monthly or shorter period with respect to which premiums were charged by the plan with respect to such coverage.[1]

The premium reduction applied until the earliest of:

(1) the first date the assistance eligible individual became eligible for other group health plan coverage, with certain exceptions, or Medicare coverage;

(2) the date that was fifteen months (under the Department of Defense Authorizations Act of 2010; it was nine months under ARRA 2009) after the first day of the first month for which the ARRA premium reduction provisions applied to the individual; or

(3) the date the individual ceased to be eligible for COBRA continuation coverage.[2]

Coverage Eligible for Premium Reduction

The premium reduction was available for COBRA continuation coverage of any group health plan, except a flexible spending arrangement ("FSA") offered under a cafeteria plan, including vision-only and dental-only plans as well as mini-med plans. The premium reduction was not available for continuation coverage offered by employers for non-health benefits that were not subject to COBRA continuation coverage, for example, group life insurance.[3]

Retiree health coverage could have been treated as COBRA continuation coverage for which the premium reduction was available only if the retiree coverage did not differ from the coverage made available to similarly situated active employees. The amount charged for the coverage could be higher than that charged to active employees and the retiree coverage still may have been eligible for the ARRA premium reduction so long as the charge to retirees did not exceed the maximum amount allowed under federal COBRA.[4]

The premium reduction also was available for COBRA continuation coverage under a health reimbursement arrangement ("HRA"). Although an HRA may qualify as an FSA, the exclusion of FSAs from the premium reduction was limited to FSAs provided through a cafeteria plan, which would not include an HRA.[5]

Premium Reduction Extension under DDAA 2010

The Department of Defense Appropriations Act of 2010 ("DDAA 2010") amended ARRA 2009 by extending the period to qualify for the COBRA premium reduction until February 28, 2010, a period further extended to May 31, 2010, under the Continuing

1. Notice 2009-27, 2009-16 IRB 838, Q&A 30.
2. Notice 2009-27, 2009-16 IRB 838, Q&A 33; see Sec. 1010, DDAA 2010 and Sec. 3001(a)(2)(A) of ARRA 2009.
3. Notice 2009-27, 2009-16 IRB 838, Q&A 27.
4. Notice 2009-27, 2009-16 IRB 838, Q&A 28.
5. Notice 2009-27, 2009-16 IRB 838, Q&A 29.

Extension Act of 2010, and extending the maximum period for receiving the subsidy an additional six months (from nine to fifteen months).[1]

Assistance eligible individuals who had reached the end of the original premium reduction period were in a transition period which gave them additional time to pay extension-related reduced premiums.[2] An individual's transition period was the period that began immediately after the end of the maximum number of months, which generally was nine, of premium reduction available under ARRA prior to its amendment. An individual was in a transition period only if the premium reduction provisions would continue to apply due to the extension from nine to fifteen months and they otherwise remained eligible for the premium reduction.[3] These individuals must have been provided a notice of the extension within sixty days of the first day of their transition period.[4] The retroactive payment or payments for the period or periods of coverage must have been made by the later of February 17, 2010, or thirty days from when the notice was provided.[5]

DOL Procedure for Denial of Premium Reduction

The Department of Labor has issued a fact sheet entitled "COBRA Premium Reduction" that explains its expedited review of denials of premium reduction. The DOL states that individuals, who are denied treatment as assistance eligible individuals and, thus, are denied eligibility for the premium reduction, whether by their plan, employer, or insurer, were entitled to request an expedited review of the denial by the DOL. The DOL was then required to make a determination within fifteen business days of receipt of a completed request for review. The official application form[6] was to be filed online or submitted by fax or mail.

358. Who was eligible for the temporary COBRA premium assistance made available under legislation enacted in 2009 and 2010?

Under the temporary COBRA premium assistance rules enacted in 2009 and 2010, an assistance eligible individual meant any qualified beneficiary if:

(1) the qualified beneficiary was eligible for COBRA continuation coverage related to a qualifying event occurring during the period that began with September 1, 2008, and ended with May 31, 2010, under the Continuing Extension Act of 2010;

(2) the qualified beneficiary elected such coverage; and

(3) the qualifying event with respect to the COBRA continuation coverage consisted of an involuntary termination of the covered employee's employment and occurred during such period.[7]

---

1. Sec. 3001(a)(3)(A) of ARRA 2009, as amended by Sec. 1010(a) of DDAA 2010; Sec. 3001(a)(2)(A)(ii)(I) of ARRA 2009, as amended by Sec. 1010(b) of DDAA 2010.
2. See Sec. 3001(a)(16)(C) of ARRA 2009, as added by Sec. 1010(c) of DDAA 2010.
3. See Sec. 3001(a)(16)(C)(i) of ARRA 2009, as added by Sec. 1010(c) of DDAA 2010.
4. See Sec. 3001(a)(16)(D) of ARRA 2009, as added by DDAA 2010.
5. See Sec. 3001(a)(16)(A)(ii) of ARRA 2009, as added by Sec. 1010(c) of DDAA 2010.
6. Available at: www.dol.gov/COBRA.
7. Sec. 3 of the Continuing Extension Act of 2010; Sec. 1010(a) of the Department of Defense Appropriations Act of 2010; Sec. 3001(a)(3)(C) of ARRA 2009; Notice 2009-27, 2009-16 IRB 838, Q&A 10; IRS News Release IR-2010-52 (4-26-2010).

If an assistance eligible individual who was receiving the premium reduction became eligible for coverage under any other group health plan or Medicare, the individual was required to notify the group health plan in writing. The notice must have been provided to the group health plan in the time and manner specified by the Department of Labor ("DOL").[1] A person who was required to notify a group health plan but failed to do so was required to pay a penalty of 110 percent of the premium reduction improperly received after eligibility for the other coverage. No penalty was imposed with respect to any failure if it was shown that the failure was due to reasonable cause and not to willful neglect.[2]

Involuntary Termination

According to the IRS, for purposes of the temporary premium reduction assistance, an involuntary termination was:

(1) a severance from employment that was due to the independent exercise of the unilateral authority of the employer to terminate the employment;

(2) other than due to the employee's implicit or explicit request;

(3) where the employee was willing and able to continue performing services.[3]

Thus, an involuntary termination may have included an employer's failure to renew a contract at the time the contract expired if the employee was willing and able to execute a new contract providing terms and conditions similar to those in the expiring contract and to continue providing the services. It also may have included an employee-initiated termination from employment if the termination constituted a termination for good reason due to employer action that caused a material negative change in the employment relationship for the employee.[4]

The IRS has cautioned that an involuntary termination was the involuntary termination of employment, not the involuntary termination of health coverage. Consequently, qualifying events other than an involuntary termination, for example, divorce or a dependent child ceasing to be a dependent child under the generally applicable requirements of the plan, such as loss of dependent status due to aging out of eligibility, were not involuntary terminations qualifying an individual for the premium reduction.[5]

Involuntary termination generally included the following:

(1) A lay-off period with a right of recall or a temporary furlough period (i.e., an involuntary reduction to zero hours resulting in a loss of health coverage);[6]

(2) An employer's action to end an individual's employment while the individual is absent from work due to illness or disability. Mere absence from work due to illness

1. Sec. 3001(a)(2)(C) of ARRA 2009; Notice 2009-27, 2009-16 IRB 838.
2. IRC Sec. 6720C, as added by ARRA 2009; Notice 2009-27, 2009-16 IRB 838.
3. Notice 2009-27, 2009-16 IRB 838, Q&A 1.
4. Notice 2009-27, 2009-16 IRB 838, Q&A 1.
5. Notice 2009-27, 2009-16 IRB 838, Q&A 1.
6. Notice 2009-27, 2009-16 IRB 838, Q&A 2.

or disability before the action to end the individual's employment status was not an involuntary termination;[1]

(3) Retirement, if the facts and circumstances indicated that, absent retirement, the employer would have terminated the employee's services and the employee had knowledge that he or she would be terminated;[2]

(4) An involuntary termination for cause was considered to be an involuntary termination. For purposes of COBRA, if a termination of employment was due to gross misconduct of an employee, then the termination was not a qualifying event and the employee therefore was not eligible for COBRA continuation coverage;[3]

(5) A resignation as the result of a material change in the geographic location of employment for the employee;[4] and

(6) A buy-out, that is, a termination elected by the employee in return for a severance package, where the employer indicates that after the offer period for the severance package, a certain number of remaining employees in the employee's group will be terminated.[5]

Involuntary termination did not include the following:

(1) The death of an employee;[6]

(2) A mere reduction in hours (i.e., not a reduction to zero hours);[7] and

(3) A work stoppage as the result of a strike initiated by employees or their representatives, although a lockout initiated by an employer was an involuntary termination.[8]

The determination of whether a termination was involuntary or not was based on all the facts and circumstances. For example, if a termination was designated as voluntary or as a resignation, but the facts and circumstances indicate that absent the voluntary termination, the employer would have terminated the employee's services, and the employee had knowledge that the employee would be terminated, the termination then was considered to be involuntary.[9]

1. Notice 2009-27, 2009-16 IRB 838, Q&A 4.
2. Notice 2009-27, 2009-16 IRB 838, Q&A 5.
3. Notice 2009-27, 2009-16 IRB 838, Q&A 6.
4. Notice 2009-27, 2009-16 IRB 838, Q&A 7.
5. Notice 2009-27, 2009-16 IRB 838, Q&A 9.
6. Notice 2009-27, 2009-16 IRB 838, Q&A 1.
7. Notice 2009-27, 2009-16 IRB 838, Q&A 3.
8. Notice 2009-27, 2009-16 IRB 838, Q&A 8.
9. Notice 2009-27, 2009-16 IRB 838, Q&A 1.

359. What are the tax implications of any premium reductions under the COBRA temporary premium assistance rules?

The amount of any COBRA premium reduction taken under the special rules enacted in 2009 and 2010 (see Q 357 and Q 358) was excluded from an individual's gross income.[1] If the premium reduction was provided with respect to any COBRA continuation coverage that covered an individual, the individual's spouse, or the individual's dependent, and the individual's modified adjusted gross income, that is, the adjusted gross income plus amounts excluded under IRC Sections 911, 931, or 933, exceeded $145,000, or $290,000 for married couples filing jointly, then the amount of the premium reduction was recaptured as an increase in the individual's federal income tax liability.[2] The recapture was phased in for individuals with a modified adjusted gross income in excess of $125,000, or $250,000 for married couples filing jointly.[3] An individual was able to elect to permanently waive the right to the premium reduction, for example, to avoid receiving and then repaying the premium reduction.[4]

360. Are all employers subject to COBRA continuation coverage requirements?

No.

Church plans, as defined in IRC Section 414(e), governmental plans, as defined in IRC Section 414(d), and small-employer plans generally are not subject to COBRA continuation coverage requirements, although there are temporary rules applicable to small employers under the American Recovery and Reinvestment Act of 2009 ("ARRA").[5] ARRA provided a temporary premium subsidy for COBRA continuation coverage for certain unemployed workers (Q 356) and also applied to small employers if health care continuation coverage was required by a state.[6]

A small-employer plan is defined as a group health plan maintained by an employer that normally employed fewer than twenty employees during the preceding calendar year on a typical business day.[7] Under final regulations, an employer is considered to have employed fewer than twenty employees during a calendar year if it had fewer than twenty employees on at least 50 percent of its typical business days during that year. Only common law employees are taken into account for purposes of the small-employer exception. Self-employed individuals, independent contractors, and directors are not counted. In the case of a multiemployer plan, a small-employer plan is a group health plan under which each of the employers contributing to the plan for a calendar year normally employed fewer than twenty employees during the preceding calendar year.[8]

1. IRC. Sec. 139C, as added by ARRA 2009. See also Notice 2009-27, 2009-16 IRB 838, 839.
2. See Sec. 3001(b)(1), ARRA 2009. See also Notice 2009-27, 2009-16 IRB 838, 839.
3. See Sec. 3001(b)(2), ARRA 2009. See also Notice 2009-27, 2009-16 IRB 838, 839.
4. See Sec. 3001(b)(3), ARRA 2009. See also Notice 2009-27, 2009-16 IRB 838, 839.
5. IRC Sec. 4980B(d).
6. Sec. 3001(a)(10)(B) of ARRA 2009.
7. IRC Sec. 4980B(d).
8. Treas. Reg. §54.4980B-2, A-5.

361. What is a qualifying event for purposes of COBRA continuation coverage requirements?

A qualifying event is any of the following events that, but for the required COBRA continuation coverage, would result in the loss of coverage of a covered employee or a spouse or dependent child of a covered employee under the plan:

(1) Death of a covered employee;

(2) Voluntary or involuntary termination for reasons other than a covered employee's gross misconduct (Q 363) or reduction in hours of a covered employee's employment;

(3) Divorce or legal separation of a covered employee;

(4) A covered employee becoming entitled to Medicare benefits;

(5) A dependent child ceasing to be a dependent child for purposes of a plan; and

(6) A proceeding under the federal bankruptcy law with respect to an employer from whose employment the covered employee retired at any time.[1]

Taking a leave under the Family and Medical Leave Act of 1993 (FMLA) is not a qualifying event. A qualifying event does occur when an employee is covered under an employer's group health plan the day before beginning an FMLA leave, the employee does not come back to work at the end of the leave, and the employee would lose coverage under the plan (other than under the COBRA continuation coverage) before the end of what would be the maximum coverage period. The same is true for a spouse or dependent child of the employee. The date that such a qualifying event occurs is the last day of the employee's FMLA leave, and the period of maximum coverage is measured from this day.[2]

If an employer eliminates coverage for a class of employees to which an employee on FMLA leave would otherwise have belonged on or before the last day of the employee's FMLA leave, there is no qualifying event.

A qualifying event can occur even if an employee does not pay the employee's share of the premiums for coverage under a group health plan during an FMLA leave, or even if an employee declined coverage during FMLA leave.[3] Further, COBRA continuation coverage may not be conditioned on an employee reimbursing an employer for premiums paid by the employer for group health plan coverage during an FMLA leave taken by the employee.[4]

1. IRC Sec. 4980B(f)(3); Treas. Reg. §54.4980B-4, A-1.
2. Treas. Reg. §54.4980B-10, A-1, A-2.
3. Notice 94-103, 1994-2 CB 569.
4. Treas. Reg. §54.4980B-10, A-1, A-3, A-5.

There is no qualifying event where, following a termination of employment, a loss of coverage does not occur until after the end of what would have been the maximum period of COBRA continuation coverage.[1]

362. Under what circumstances do employees serving in the military receive COBRA-like health insurance coverage continuation?

The call to active military duty of reserve personnel has been characterized as a qualifying event by the IRS. Although not specifically stated, the event presumably is a reduction in hours.[2]

Employees serving in the uniformed services are entitled to COBRA-like continuation health coverage under the Uniformed Services Employment and Reemployment Rights Act[3] regardless of whether the employer is otherwise exempt from COBRA's continuation coverage requirements. Consequently, employers with fewer than 20 employees must provide continuation benefits to service members even in the absence of an obligation to do so under COBRA. The Veteran's Benefit Improvement Act of 2004 increased the period for which the employee may elect from eighteen to twenty-four months. This extension applies to all continuation elections made after December 10, 2004.

363. What is gross misconduct for the purposes of disqualifying an employee and the employee's beneficiaries from COBRA health insurance continuation requirements?

If a covered employee's employment is terminated for gross misconduct, no COBRA continuation coverage is available to the employee or to the employee's qualified beneficiaries.[4] If an employer fails to notify an employee at the time of the employee's termination that the termination is on account of gross misconduct, its ability to deny COBRA coverage may be undermined.[5]

The fact that an employer has grounds to terminate an employee for gross misconduct does not support a denial of COBRA coverage if the employee voluntarily resigns to avoid being fired. An allegation of gross misconduct after a voluntary termination cannot be used to evade liability where an employer has not properly processed a COBRA election and the carrier refuses to extend coverage.[6]

The Seventh Circuit Court of Appeals decided that it is not sufficient that an employer believed, in good faith, that an employee had engaged in gross misconduct. The district court had held that the proper test is not whether an employee actually engaged in gross misconduct but whether the employer believed in good faith that the employee had. The appeals court held that COBRA requires more than a good faith belief by an employer and that an employee should

1. *Williams v. Teamsters Local Union No. 727*, Case No. 03 C 2122, 2003 US Dist. LEXIS 18906 (N.D. Ill., 10-22-03).
2. Notice 90-58, 1990-2 CB 345.
3. USERRA, 38 USC Sec. 4317(a).
4. IRC Sec. 4980B(f)(3)(B); ERISA Sec. 603(2).
5. *Mlsna v. Unitel Com., Inc.*, 91 F.3d 876 (7th Cir. 1996).
6. *Conery v. Bath Assoc.*, 803 F. Supp. 1388 (N.D. Ind. 1992).

have been given the chance to demonstrate that the employer was mistaken and thus obtain COBRA rights.[1]

An insurance carrier is bound by an employer's determination and cannot decline COBRA coverage merely because the employer might have been entitled to terminate the employee on grounds of gross misconduct.[2]

Case Law Examples

The term "gross misconduct" is not specifically defined in COBRA or in regulations under COBRA. Therefore, whether a terminated employee has engaged in "gross misconduct" that will justify a plan not offering COBRA to that former employee and family members will depend on the specific facts and circumstances. Generally, it can be assumed that being fired for most ordinary reasons, such as excessive absences, or generally poor performance, does not amount to "gross misconduct."[3]

The IRS has announced that it will not issue rulings on whether an action constitutes gross misconduct for COBRA purposes.[4] For these reasons, the concept of gross misconduct has been developed through case law.

Some courts have provided a standard by which conduct can be judged, finding that conduct is gross misconduct if it is so outrageous that it shocks the conscious;[5] that gross misconduct may be intentional, wanton, willful, deliberate, reckless or in deliberate indifference to an employer's interest;[6] or that gross misconduct is conduct evincing such willful or wanton disregard of an employer's interests as is found in deliberate violation or disregard of standards of behavior which the employer has the right to expect of his or her employee.[7]

Some more specific examples follow.

Mere incompetence is not gross misconduct.[8]

One court has held that breach of a company confidence did not constitute "gross misconduct."[9]

An employee did not engage in gross misconduct by falsifying mileage reports, failing to attend mandatory meetings, and receiving an unsolicited offer of employment.[10]

1. *Kariotis v. Navistar Int'l Transp. Corp.*, 131 F.3d 672 (7th Cir. 1997).
2. *Conery v. Bath Assoc.*, 803 F. Supp. 1388 (N.D. Ind. 1992).
3. U.S. Department of Labor Health Benefits Advisor Glossary, Office of Compliance Assistance Policy.
4. Rev. Proc. 2018-3.
5. *Zickafoose v. UBServs. Inc.* 23 F.Supp.2d 652, 654 (S.D.W. Va. 1998).
6. *Collins v. Aggreko, Inc.* 884 F.Supp. 450, 454 (D. Utah 1995).
7. *Paris v. F. Korbel & Btos., Inc.*, 751 F.Supp. 834, 838 (N.D. Cal. 1990).
8. *Mlsna v. Unitel Com., Inc.*, 91 F.3d 876 (7th Cir. 1996).
9. *Paris v. F. Korbel & Bros., Inc.*, 751 F. Supp. 834 (N.D. Cal. 1990).
10. *Cabral v. The Olsten Corp.*, 843 F. Supp. 701 (M.D. Fla. 1994).

Under a state law definition of gross misconduct, an employee who admitted stealing an employer's merchandise was considered to have been terminated for gross misconduct and, thus, was not entitled to COBRA continuation coverage.[1]

Cash handling irregularities, invoice irregularities, and the failure to improve the performance of one of an employer's stores was held to be gross misconduct.[2]

In a case where a court concluded that Congress left the definition of gross misconduct up to employers, two employees who had been terminated for refusing to comply with directions of a supervisor were considered to have been terminated for gross misconduct.[3]

A bank employee who cashed a fellow employee's check knowing there were insufficient funds to satisfy it and held the check in her cash drawer until the check could be covered was held to have been terminated for gross misconduct.[4]

A bank employee's violation of a bank's corporate credit card policy and blatant misrepresentation concerning a small loan application to a federal agency constituted gross misconduct.[5]

In some cases, conduct was egregious. One court held that a security guard who "deserted his post … and was found asleep at his residence" and falsified records, creating a fictional guard to collect another paycheck, was terminated for gross misconduct.[6]

Throwing an apple at a co-worker and uttering racial slurs was found to be gross misconduct.[7]

Misconduct need not take place on the job to constitute gross misconduct. Off-duty behavior also may eliminate an employee's right to elect COBRA coverage. Gross misconduct was found where an employee assaulted a subordinate with whom the employee was having a romantic relationship while away from the workplace.[8]

Having an accident while driving a company vehicle under the influence of alcohol and on company business constituted gross misconduct, even though it was a misdemeanor offense under state law.[9]

364. For how long must COBRA continuation coverage generally be provided?

COBRA continuation coverage must be provided from the date of a qualifying event until the earliest of any of the following events:

1. the passage of the maximum required period of coverage;

1. *Burke v. American Stores Employee Benefit Plan*, 818 F. Supp. 1131 (N.D. Ill. 1993).
2. *Avina v. Texas Pig Stands, Inc.*, 1991 U.S. Dist. LEXIS 13957 (W.D. Tex. 1991).
3. *Bryant v. Food Lion, Inc.*, 100 F. Supp.2d 346 (D. S.C. 2000).
4. *Moffitt v. Blue Cross & Blue Shield Miss.*, 722 F. Supp. 1391 (N.D. Miss. 1989).
5. *Johnson v. Shawmut Nat'l Corp.*, 1994 U.S. Dist. LEXIS 19437 (D. Mass, 1994).
6. *Adkins v. United Int'l Investigative Servs, Inc.*, 1992 U.S. Dist. LEXIS 4719 (N.D. Calif. 1992).
7. *Nakisa v. Continental Airlines*, 26 EBC 1568 (S.D. Texas 2001).
8. *Zickafoose v. UB Servs., Inc.*, 23 F. Supp.2d 652 (S.D.W.V. 1998).
9. *Collins v. Aggreko, Inc.*, 884 F. Supp. 450 (D. Utah 1995).

2. the date the employer ceases to provide any group health plan to any employee;

3. the date coverage ceases under the plan by reason of a failure to make timely payment of the applicable premium (Q 368);

4. the date the qualified beneficiary first becomes covered as an employee or otherwise after the date of the election under any other plan providing health care that does not contain any exclusion or limit with respect to any pre-existing condition of the beneficiary other than an exclusion or limitation that does not apply to, or is satisfied by, the beneficiary by reason of the portability, access, and renewability requirements for group health plans found in the IRC as well as in similar sections of ERISA and the Public Health Service Act;

5. the date the qualified beneficiary, other than a retired covered employee or a spouse, surviving spouse, or dependent child of the covered employee, first becomes entitled to Medicare benefits after the date of the election; or

6. in the case of a qualified beneficiary who is disabled at any time during the first sixty days of continuation coverage, the month that begins more than thirty days after the date when the Social Security Administration has made a final determination under Title II or XVI of the Social Security Act that the beneficiary is no longer disabled.[1]

Applying a strict reading of IRC Section 4980B(f)(2)(B), the U.S. Supreme Court found that an employee whose employment has been terminated is eligible to elect COBRA continuation coverage under the employee's former employer's group health plan despite the fact that the employee also had coverage under another plan offered by the employee's spouse's employer at the time the employee's employment was terminated. In effect, the Court concluded that an employee with coverage under another plan at the time of termination of employment does not fall within the requirement that the qualified beneficiary first becomes, after the date of the election, covered under any other medical care plan.[2]

A federal government plan is not considered another plan providing health care for this purpose, because the federal government is not an employer under IRC Section 5000(d). Thus, eligibility for a federal government group health plan will not terminate COBRA continuation coverage.[3]

Being entitled to Medicare benefits is defined not as mere eligibility for benefits, but as actual enrollment in either Part A or Part B of Medicare.[4] Entitlement to Medicare benefits will not terminate the obligation to provide continuation coverage to qualified beneficiaries entitled to

---

1. IRC Sec. 4980B(f)(2)(B).
2. *Geissal v. Moore Medical Corp.*, 524 U.S. 74 (1998); 118 S. Ct. 1869 (1998); Treas. Reg. §54.4980B-7, A-2. See also Ann. 98-22, 1998-12 IRB 33.
3. Notice 90-58, 1990-2 CB 345. See also *McGee v. Funderburg*, 17 F.3d 1122 (8th Cir. 1994).
4. Treas. Reg. §54.4980B-7, A-3.

continuation coverage by virtue of a proceeding in a case under the federal bankruptcy law. See Q 365 for a detailed discussion of the exceptions to the maximum required period of coverage.

365. What is the maximum required period of COBRA continuation coverage? Are there any exceptions to this required maximum period?

The general maximum required period of coverage is thirty-six months from the date of a qualifying event.[1] There are significant exceptions.

One exception is the termination or reduction of hours. When a qualifying event is a termination, other than by reason of a covered employee's gross misconduct (Q 363), or a reduction in hours of a covered employee's employment, the maximum required period of coverage generally is eighteen months from the date of the termination or reduction. If another qualifying event other than a proceeding in a case under the federal bankruptcy law occurs during the eighteen month period following the termination or reduction of hours, the maximum required period is extended to thirty-six months from the date of the termination or reduction.[2]

A second exception is disability. In the case of a qualified beneficiary who is determined, under Title II or Title XVI of the Social Security Act, to have been disabled any time during the first sixty days of continuation coverage, any reference to eighteen months dealing with termination of employment, a reduction in hours, or with multiple qualifying events is deemed to be a reference to twenty-nine months with respect to all qualified beneficiaries. This extension applies only if a qualified beneficiary has provided the plan administrator with appropriate notice of the determination of disability within sixty days of the determination and provides the plan administrator with notice within thirty days of the date of any final determination that the qualified beneficiary is no longer disabled.[3]

Regulations clarify that this extension of coverage to twenty-nine months due to disability is available if three conditions are satisfied: (1) a termination or reduction of hours of a covered employee's employment occurs, (2) an individual, whether or not the covered employee, who is a qualified beneficiary in connection with the qualifying event described in (1) is determined to have been disabled at any time during the first sixty days of COBRA coverage, and (3) any of the qualified beneficiaries affected by the qualifying event described in (1) provides notice to the plan administrator of the disability determination on a date that is both within sixty days after the date when the determination is issued and before the end of the original eighteen month period. The extension due to disability applies independently to each qualified beneficiary, whether or not he or she is disabled.[4]

A third exception relates to Medicare. In the case of a termination, other than by gross misconduct (Q 363), or a reduction in hours that occurs fewer than eighteen months after the date when a covered employee became entitled to Medicare benefits, the period of coverage for

1. IRC Sec. 4980B(f)(2)(B)(i)(IV).
2. IRC Sec. 4980B(f)(2)(B)(i).
3. IRC Sec. 4980B(f)(2)(B)(i).
4. Treas. Reg. §54.4980B-7, A-5.

qualified beneficiaries other than the covered employee shall not terminate before the close of the thirty-six month period beginning when the covered employee became so entitled.[1]

A fourth exception is the employer's bankruptcy. The bankruptcy of an employer is the only qualifying event that can result in a maximum required period of coverage of more than thirty-six months.[2] Where the qualifying event is a proceeding in a case under the federal bankruptcy law and the covered employee is alive when the bankruptcy proceedings commence, the maximum required period extends until the death of the covered employee or, in the case of a surviving spouse or dependent children of a covered employee, until thirty-six months after the death of the covered employee. When a covered employee dies before bankruptcy proceedings commence and the employee's surviving spouse is, as a surviving spouse, a beneficiary under the plan on the day before bankruptcy proceedings commence, the maximum required period extends until the surviving spouse's date of death.[3]

Finally, there is a conversion exception. A qualified beneficiary must be given the option to convert the insurance coverage during the 180 day period ending on the expiration of the COBRA continuation coverage period if a conversion option otherwise generally is available to similarly situated non-COBRA beneficiaries.[4]

366. Who is a qualified beneficiary for purposes of COBRA continuation coverage requirements?

With respect to a covered employee under a group health plan, a qualified beneficiary is any other individual who, on the day prior to that covered employee's qualifying event, is a covered employee's spouse or dependent child. A child born to or placed for adoption with a covered employee during the period of continuation coverage is included in the definition of qualified beneficiary.[5] Agents, independent contractors, and directors who participate in the group health plan may also be qualified beneficiaries.[6] Each qualified beneficiary has individual rights so that continuation decisions may be made on a person by person basis.

Employers are not required to offer COBRA continuation coverage to domestic partners, though some employers have negotiated with their insurance companies to do so.

If a qualifying event is a proceeding in a case under federal bankruptcy law, a qualified beneficiary is any covered employee who retired on or before the date of substantial elimination of coverage and individuals who, on the day before bankruptcy proceedings commence, were covered under the plan as a covered employee's spouse, surviving spouse, or dependent child.[7]

1. IRC Sec. 4980B(f)(2)(B)(i)(V).
2. Treas. Reg. §54.4980B-7, A-6.
3. IRC Sec. 4980B(f)(2)(B)(i)(III).
4. IRC Sec. 4980B(f)(2)(E); Treas. Reg. §54.4980B-7, A-8.
5. IRC Sec. 4980B(g)(1)(A); Treas. Reg. §54.4980B-3, A-1.
6. FAQs for Employees About COBRA Continuation Health Coverage, U.S. Department of Labor Employee Benefits Security Administration.
7. IRC Sec. 4980B(g)(1)(D); Treas. Reg. §54.4980B-3, A-1.

Where a qualifying event is a change in employment status of a covered employee, qualified beneficiaries are the covered employee, spouse and dependent children covered under the plan on the day before the qualifying event.[1]

If a qualifying event is a covered employee's death, divorce, or legal separation, or the covered employee's entitlement to Medicare, the qualified beneficiaries are the covered employee's spouse and dependent children who were covered under the plan the day before the qualifying event.[2]

If a qualifying event is the loss of a covered child's dependent status, then that dependent child is the only qualified beneficiary.[3]

The term qualified beneficiary does not include an individual who is covered under a group health plan due to another individual's election of COBRA continuation coverage and not by a prior qualifying event. This means that an individual who marries a qualified beneficiary other than the covered employee on or after the date of the qualifying event does not become a qualified beneficiary in his or her own right by reason of the marriage.

Likewise, a child born to or placed for adoption with a qualified beneficiary does not become a qualified beneficiary. New family members do not become qualified beneficiaries themselves, even if they become covered under the group health plan.[4]

A person whose status as a covered employee is attributable to a time when the person was a nonresident alien who received no earned income from the person's employer that constituted income from sources within the United States is not a qualified beneficiary.[5]

An individual who does not elect COBRA continuation coverage ceases to be a qualified beneficiary at the end of the election period.[6]

There are situations in which a second qualifying event occurs. For example, an employee terminates employment and then subsequently divorces. In this situation, the maximum period of coverage for the employee remains eighteen months and the maximum period for the impacted dependents remains thirty-six months. Notice must be provided to the plan administrator to obtain this extension.

367. Who is a covered employee for purposes of the COBRA continuation coverage requirements? Who is a similarly situated non-COBRA beneficiary?

A covered employee is any individual who is or was provided coverage under a group health plan by virtue of the individual's performance of services for one or more persons maintaining

1. IRC Sec. 4980B(f)(3).
2. IRC Sec. 4980B(f)(3).
3. IRC Sec. 4980(f)(3)(E).
4. Treas. Reg. §54.4980B-3, A-1.
5. IRC Sec. 4980B(g)(1)(C).
6. Treas. Reg. §54.4980B-3, A-1.

the plan, including as an employee defined in IRC Section 401(c)(1), or because of membership in an employee organization that maintains the plan.[1]

In addition, the following persons are employees if their relationship to the employer maintaining the plan makes them eligible to be covered under the plan: self-employed individuals, independent contractors and their agents and independent contractors, and corporate directors.[2]

A person eligible for coverage but not actually covered is not a covered employee.

Final COBRA regulations introduce the term similarly situated non-COBRA beneficiaries, defined as a group of covered employees, their spouses, or their dependent children receiving coverage under an employer's or employee organization's group health plan for a reason other than the rights provided under the COBRA requirements and who most similarly are situated to the qualified beneficiary just before the qualifying event, based on all the facts and circumstances.[3] COBRA beneficiaries are accorded the same rights and coverage as similarly situated non-COBRA beneficiaries.

368. Who must pay the cost of COBRA continuation coverage and how is the cost calculated?

A plan may require a qualified beneficiary to pay a premium for continuation coverage. The premium generally cannot exceed a percentage of the applicable premium.

The applicable premium is the plan's cost for similarly situated beneficiaries (Q 367) with respect to whom a qualifying event has not occurred. The applicable premium for each determination period must be fixed by the plan before the determination period begins. A determination period is defined as any twelve month period selected by the plan, provided that it is applied consistently from one year to the next. Because the determination period is a single period for any benefit package, each qualified beneficiary will not have a separate determination period.[4]

Except as provided under ARRA 2009 (Q 356), the percentage of the applicable premium that may be charged is generally 102 percent. In the case of a disabled qualified beneficiary, the premium may be as much as 150 percent of the applicable premium for any month after the eighteenth month of continuation coverage. A plan may require payment equal to 150 percent of the applicable premium if a disabled qualified beneficiary experiences a second qualifying event during the disability extension period, after the eighteenth month. The 150 percent amount may be charged until the end of the thirty-six month maximum period of coverage, that is, from the beginning of the nineteenth month through the end of the thirty-sixth month. A plan that does so will not fail to comply with the nondiscrimination requirements of IRC Section 9802(b).[5]

1. IRC Sec. 4980B(f)(7); Treas. Reg. §54.4980B-3, A-2.
2. Treas. Reg. §54.4980B-3, A-2.
3. Treas. Reg. §54.4980B-3, A-3.
4. Treas. Reg. §54.4980B-8, A-2(a).
5. IRC Sec. 4980B(f)(2)(C); Treas. Reg. §54.4980B-8, A-1.

Coverage may not be conditioned on evidence of insurability and cannot be contingent on an employee's reimbursement of his or her employer for group health plan premiums paid during a leave taken under the Family and Medical Leave Act of 1993.[1]

During a determination period, a plan may increase the cost of the COBRA coverage only if the plan has previously charged less than the maximum amount permitted and even after the increase the maximum amount will not be exceeded or a qualified beneficiary changes his or her coverage. If a plan allows similarly situated active employees to change their coverage, each qualified beneficiary must be given the same opportunity.[2]

A qualified beneficiary must be permitted to make premium payments on at least a monthly basis. Any person or entity may make the required payment for COBRA continuation coverage on behalf of a qualified beneficiary.[3]

COBRA premiums must be paid in a timely fashion, which is defined as forty-five days after the date of election for the period between a qualifying event and an election, and thirty days after the first date of the period for all other periods.[4] An employer may retroactively terminate COBRA continuation coverage if the initial premium is not timely paid. In *Harris v. United Automobile Insurance Group, Inc.*,[5] the Eleventh Circuit Court of Appeals ruled that the additional time provided in Treasury Regulation Section 54.4980B-8, A-5, applies only to those plans that are fully funded, that is, that involve an agreement with an insurance company to provide benefits. Because the health plan in *Harris* was funded and sponsored by the company (so that it was self-funded), the IRS regulation did not apply. Consequently, the time for submitting the taxpayer's premium payment was not extended beyond that provided by the plan. Accordingly, the company was within its right in terminating the taxpayer's coverage.

In effect, the *Harris* court ruled that the employer did not have an "arrangement" under which it was given a certain period of time to pay for the coverage of non-COBRA beneficiaries. The additional time frame provided in the regulation applies only to those plans that are fully-funded, meaning those that involve an agreement with an insurance company to provide benefits.

An employer is not required to set off the premium amount against the amount of a claim incurred during the sixty day election period but before the election was made.[6]

A plan must treat a timely payment that is not significantly less than the required amount as full payment, unless the plan notifies the qualified beneficiary of the amount of the deficiency and grants a reasonable period for payment. A reasonable period of time for this purpose is thirty days after the date when notice is provided. An amount will be considered as not significantly less if the shortfall is no greater than the lesser of $50 or 10 percent of the required amount.[7]

---

1. IRC Sec. 4980B(f)(2)(D); Treas. Reg. §54.4980B-10, A-5; Notice 94-103, 1994-2 CB 569.
2. Treas. Reg. §54.4980B-8, A-2(b).
3. Treas. Reg. §54.4980B-8, A-3, A-5.
4. Treas. Reg. §54.4980B-8, A-5.
5. *Harris v. United Automobile Insurance Group, Inc.*, 579 F.3d 1227 (11th Cir. 2009).
6. *Goletto v. W. H. Braum Inc.*, 25 EBC 1974 (10th Cir. 2001).
7. Treas. Reg. §54.4980B-8, A-5(b).

Revenue Ruling 96-8 provides some guidance in the area of determining COBRA costs.[1]

See Q 369 for a discussion of the Health Coverage Tax Credit.

369. What is the Health Coverage Tax Credit?

Under the Trade Act of 2002, certain eligible individuals are entitled to receive a refundable tax credit equal to 72.5 percent (after February 12, 2011 and before January 1, 2014, extended for periods ending before January 1, 2020 by the Trade Adjustment Assistance Reauthorization Act of 2015 (TAARA 2015)) of the cost of certain types of health coverage, including COBRA continuation coverage. Eligible individuals are displaced workers qualifying for assistance under the Trade Adjustment Assistance program and individuals age fifty-five or older receiving a benefit from the Pension Benefit Guaranty Corporation.[2]

The Trade Act of 2002 also made the tax credit advanceable and, under the Health Coverage Tax Credit (HCTC) program established by the Treasury Department, eligible individuals receive a qualified health insurance costs credit eligibility certificate.[3] These individuals can pay 20 percent of a required premium to providers along with the certificate, and the government will pay the remaining 80 percent of the premium. The government may make advance payments of the credit for health insurance costs of eligible individuals, but the total amount of these payments made cannot exceed 72.5 (was 65 percent) percent of the amount paid by a taxpayer for a taxable year.[4] Providers are required to file a prescribed information return identifying the individuals receiving subsidized coverage and the amount and timing of the payments. Providers must provide each covered individual with a statement of the information reported for that individual.[5] The HCTC program was effective August 1, 2003.

TAARA 2015 reinstated the HCTC, but also provided new rules to coordinate the HCTC with the premium assistance tax credit. Generally, the rules provide that, beginning in 2016, insurance purchased on the health insurance exchanges does not qualify as coverage for which the HCTC may be claimed. Further, an eligible individual must make an election to have the HCTC apply and is not entitled to the premium assistance tax credit for any months during which an HCTC election is in effect.[6]

370. How does an individual claim the additional 7.5 percent retroactive health coverage tax credit?

If an eligible individual was enrolled in the monthly HCTC program during the 2011 tax year, they will be sent a Form 1099-H, Health Coverage Tax Credit (HCTC) Advance Payments. This form is provided because the HCTC Program made monthly payment(s) to the individual's health plan administrator in one or months in the 2011 tax year.

1. Rev. Rul. 96-8, 1996-1 CB 286.
2. IRC Sec. 35, as amended by ARRA 2009.
3. IRC Sec. 7527, as amended by ARRA 2009.
4. IRC Sec. 7527(b).
5. IRC Sec. 6050T.
6. Pub. Law No. 114-27, Sec. 407.

Boxes 3 through 14, on Form 1099-H, reflect the tax credit amount the individual received for each month in 2011 (an 80 percent tax credit for payments made by the HCTC Program in January and February 2011 and a 65 percent tax credit for payments made in March through December 2011).

To claim the additional 7.5 percent retroactive credit:

1. Refer to the box to the left of box 8 on Form 1099-H. This is the additional 7.5 percent retroactive credit that the HCTC Program has calculated. If the amount listed is $0.00, there is no retroactive credit amount.

2. Complete and file Form 8885, Health Coverage Tax Credit, with 2011 Form 1040, U.S. Individual Income Tax Return. Enter the retroactive tax credit amount on line 7 of Form 8885, Health Coverage Tax Credit. It is not necessary to complete lines 1 through 6 and it is not necessary to submit any supporting documentation.

Note: If a credit is claimed for any month for which a payment was made directly to a qualified health plan, lines 1 through 6 must be completed for those months. Then, the additional 7.5 percent retroactive credit amount is added to the sum of any amount on Part II, line 6, of Form 8885 and the total is entered on Part II, line 7. All required supporting documentation must be submitted and copies should be retained.

Planning Point: Form 8885 must be filed along with Form 1040.

371. When must an election to receive COBRA continuation coverage be made?

The period during which a qualified beneficiary may elect continuation coverage runs from the date when the qualified beneficiary's coverage terminates under the plan by reason of a qualifying event until sixty days after the later of: 1) the date when the coverage terminates; or 2) the date when notice is provided by a plan administrator to any qualified beneficiary of the right to continued coverage.[1]

A COBRA continuation coverage election is considered made on the date it is sent to a plan administrator. If an election is made at any time during this period, the continuation coverage is provided from the date when coverage is lost.[2]

Where a former employee became incapacitated ten days after resigning without making a continuation coverage election, the sixty day election period was tolled. Thus, a continuation coverage election made by the former employee's temporary administrator approximately seventy days after the resignation was found to be timely.[3]

Each qualified beneficiary must be offered the opportunity to make an independent election to receive COBRA continuation coverage. If a qualified beneficiary who is either a covered

1. IRC Sec. 4980B(f)(5).
2. IRC Sec. 4980B(f)(5); Treas. Reg. §54.4980B-6, A-1, A-3.
3. *Branch v. G. Bernd Co.*, 955 F.2d 1574 (11th Cir. 1992).

employee or his or her spouse makes an election that does not specify for whom the election is being made, regulations provide that the election will be deemed to include an election for all other qualified beneficiaries.[1]

If a qualified beneficiary waives the right to COBRA coverage but subsequently revokes the waiver prior to the end of the election period, the employer must provide the qualified beneficiary with prospective coverage, but not for the period between the waiver and the revocation. A waiver or revocation of a waiver is considered to have been made on the date it is sent.[2]

An employer may not withhold any compensation or other benefits to which a qualified beneficiary is entitled to coerce the qualified beneficiary into a decision concerning COBRA continuation coverage.[3]

Second COBRA Election Period

The Trade Act of 2002 added a second sixty day COBRA election period for individuals eligible under the Trade Adjustment Assistance ("TAA") program if the individuals did not elect COBRA coverage during their initial election period. The second election period begins on the first day of the month in which an individual becomes TAA eligible, but no election can be made more than six months after an initial TAA-related loss of coverage. Any election during a second election period is retroactive to the first day of the second election period.[4]

The second opportunity to elect COBRA continuation coverage applies to individuals who are eligible for trade adjustment assistance (TAA) or alternative trade adjustment assistance (ATAA) and who did not elect COBRA during the general election period. This additional, second election period is measured sixty days from the first day of the month in which an individual is determined TAA-eligible. For example, if an individual's general election period runs out and he or she is determined TAA-eligible sixty-one days after separating from employment, at the beginning of the month, he or she would have approximately sixty more days to elect COBRA. However, if this same individual is not determined TAA-eligible until the end of the month, the sixty days are still measured from the first of the month, in effect giving the individual about thirty days. Additionally, the Trade Act of 2002 added another limit on the second election period. A COBRA election must be made not later than six months after the date of the TAA-related loss of coverage. COBRA coverage chosen during the second election period typically begins on the first day of that period.[5]

TAA recipients were eligible for COBRA coverage extensions for as long as they had TAA eligibility or until January 1, 2014. PBGC payees were eligible for COBRA coverage extensions

1. IRC Sec. 4980B(f)(5)(B); Treas. Reg. §54.4980B-6, A-6.
2. Treas. Reg. §54.4980B-6, A-4.
3. Treas. Reg. §54.4980B-6, A-5.
4. IRC Sec. 4980B(f)(5)(C).
5. More information about the Trade Act is available at www.doleta.gov/tradeact.

until January 1, 2014. If the payee passed away, their spouse or dependents could receive an additional twenty-four months of COBRA or until January 1, 2014.[1]

372. What notice of COBRA continuation coverage is required?

Employer's Initial Notice. A plan must provide written notice of COBRA continuation coverage rights to each covered employee and spouse at the commencement of their coverage under the plan[2] and the COBRA rights provided under the plan must be described in the plan's summary plan description (SPD).

ERISA requires group health plans to give covered employees an SPD within ninety days after the employee first becomes a participant in a plan (or within 120 days after the plan is first subject to the reporting and disclosure provisions of ERISA). In addition, if there are material changes to the plan, the plan must give employees a summary of material modifications (SMM) not later than 210 days after the end of the plan year in which the changes become effective. If the change is a material reduction in covered services or benefits, the SMM must be furnished not later than sixty days after the reduction is adopted. A participant or beneficiary covered under the plan may request a copy of the SPD and any SMMs (as well as any other plan documents), which must be provided within thirty days of a written request.

Within the first ninety days of coverage, group health plans must give each employee and each spouse who becomes covered under the plan a general notice describing COBRA rights.[3]

Notice to Plan Administrator. An employer must notify a plan administrator within thirty days of the date when any of the following qualifying events occur:

(1) the death of a covered employee;

(2) the termination or reduction in hours of employment of a covered employee;

(3) a covered employee's becoming entitled to Medicare benefits; or

(4) a proceeding in a case under federal bankruptcy law.[4]

Notice to Employer. A covered employee or spouse must notify the employer of a divorce or legal separation within sixty days.[5] At least one court has permitted a covered employee to terminate coverage for the employee's soon to be ex-spouse. That court denied the COBRA coverage the spouse sought upon learning that the spouse's coverage had been terminated because neither the spouse nor the covered employee had provided timely notice of the divorce to the employer.[6] Where a covered employee told a plan administrator that he had divorced his spouse

1. See "FAQs For Employees About COBRA Continuation Health Coverage, U.S. Department of Labor, Employee Benefits Security Administration".
2. IRC Sec. 4980B(f)(6)(A).
3. See "An Employee's Guide to Health Benefits Under COBRA, U.S. Department of Labor Employee Benefits Security Administration".
4. IRC Sec. 4980B(f)(6)(B).
5. IRC Sec. 4980B(f)(6)(C).
6. *Johnson v. Northwest Airlines, Inc.*, 2001 U.S. Dist. LEXIS 2160 (N.D. CA. 2001).

before directing that her coverage be terminated, the notice requirement was satisfied and the spouse had to be notified of her right to elect COBRA continuation coverage.[1]

An individual who ceases to be a dependent child is required to notify the employer of this occurrence within sixty days.[2]

Notice to Qualified Beneficiary. Within fourteen days of receiving notice from an employer, a plan administrator must notify any qualified beneficiary with respect to a qualifying event.[3] If coverage is continued at the employer's expense after the qualifying event, this notice may be delayed until coverage actually is lost.[4] This notice requirement will be deemed satisfied if notice is sent to the qualified beneficiary's last known address by first class mail, unless the plan administrator has reason to know that this method of delivery has failed.[5]

Notice of Disability. Additionally, each qualified beneficiary determined under Title II or XVI of the Social Security Act to have been disabled at any time during the first sixty days of continuation coverage must notify the plan administrator of that determination within sixty days after the date of that determination and must notify the plan administrator of any final determination that the qualified beneficiary is no longer disabled within thirty days of the date of that determination.[6]

Statute of Limitations. Because neither COBRA nor ERISA contain a statute of limitations for making a claim that the employer did not timely provide notice, courts may look to state statutes of limitations.[7]

Exhaustion of Administrative Remedies. Although covered employees and qualified beneficiaries generally must exhaust their administrative remedies under a plan before bringing suit, in the case of a failure to provide a COBRA election notice, exhaustion of remedies is not required, unless otherwise judicially imposed by a state court.[8]

ERISA and PHSA. COBRA continuation coverage is not only a tax requirement. There are similar requirements under ERISA and the Public Health Service Act (PHSA) with other sanctions. The Department of Labor issued proposed regulations in 2003 updating the various notices and disclosures required under COBRA.[9] The new regulations, which were effective in their final form for plan years beginning in 2004, provide rules that set minimum standards for the timing and content of the notices required under COBRA and establish standards for administering the notice process.[10]

1. *Phillips v. Saratoga Harness Racing Inc.*, 240 F.3d 174 (2d Cir. 2001). See also Rev. Rul 2002-88, 2002-5 2 IRB 995.
2. IRC Sec. 4980B(f)(6)(C).
3. IRC Sec. 4980B(f)(6)(D).
4. *Wilcock v. National Distributors, Inc.*, 2001 U.S. Dist. LEXIS 11413 (D. Maine 2001).
5. See *Wooderson v. American Airlines Inc.*, 2001 U.S. Dist. LEXIS 3721 (N.D. Texas 2001).
6. IRC Sec. 4980B(f)(6)(C).
7. *Mattson v. Farrell Distributing Corp.*, 163 F. Supp.2d 411 (D. Vt. 2001).
8. *Thompson v. Origin Tech. in Business, Inc.*, 2001 U.S. Dist. LEXIS 12609 (N.D. Texas 2001).
9. 29 CFR Part 2590, 68 Fed. Reg. 31832 (May 28, 2003).
10. 29 CFR Part 2590, 68 Fed. Reg. 31832 (May 28, 2003).

373. Which entity is responsible for providing COBRA continuation coverage following a business reorganization?

The parties to a business reorganization transaction generally are free to allocate responsibility for providing COBRA continuation coverage by contract even if the contract assigns the COBRA responsibility to a party other than the party to which it would be assigned under the final regulations. If the assigned party defaults on its responsibility to provide COBRA coverage and the other party would have had the responsibility under the final regulations, the responsibility will return to this other party.[1]

For both sales of stock and sales of substantial assets, final regulations provide that a seller retains the obligation to provide COBRA continuation coverage to existing qualified beneficiaries provided that the seller continues to maintain a group health plan. In the event of a stock sale where a seller ceases to provide any group health plan to any employee in connection with the sale and therefore is not responsible for providing COBRA continuation coverage, final regulations provide that the buyer is responsible for providing COBRA continuation coverage to existing qualified beneficiaries. A group health plan of the buying group has this obligation beginning on the later of: (1) the date the selling group ceases to provide any group health plan to any employee; or (2) the date of the stock sale. The obligation continues as long as the buying group continues to maintain a group health plan.[2]

In the event of an asset sale where the seller ceases to provide any group health plan and the buyer continues the business operations associated with the assets purchased without interruption, the buyer is considered to be a successor employer to the seller. As a successor employer, the buyer is obligated to offer COBRA continuation coverage. Final regulations provide examples as to which party has the obligation to offer COBRA continuation coverage with respect to both asset sales and stock sales.[3] For a discussion of the results when an employer stops contributing to a multiemployer health plan, see Q 374.

374. What are the results for COBRA purposes if an employer stops making contributions to a multiemployer health plan?

It is not considered a COBRA qualifying event if an employer stops making contributions to a multiemployer plan. Further, when an employer stops making contributions to a multiemployer group health plan, the plan continues to be obligated to make COBRA continuation coverage available to qualified beneficiaries associated with the employer. Once the employer provides group health insurance to a significant number of employees who were formerly covered under the multiemployer plan or starts contributing to another multiemployer plan, the employer's plan or the new multiemployer plan must assume the COBRA obligation.[4]

If, however, the employer that stops contributing to the multiemployer plan makes group health plan coverage available to (or starts contributing to another multiemployer plan that is

1. Treas. Reg. §54.4980B-9, A-7.
2. Treas. Reg. §54.4980B-9, A-8(b)(1).
3. Treas. Reg. §54.4980B-9, A-8.
4. Treas. Reg. §54.4980B-9, A-10.

a group health plan) a class of the employer's employees formerly covered under the multiemployer plan, the plan maintained by the employer (or the other multiemployer plan), from that date forward, has the obligation to make COBRA continuation coverage available to any qualified beneficiary who was receiving coverage under the multiemployer plan on the day before the cessation of contributions. The qualifying event must have occurred in connection with a covered employee whose last employment prior to the qualifying event was with the employer.

375. What are the consequences of breaching COBRA continuation coverage requirements?

Statutory Penalties

The penalty for failure to make continuation coverage available is an excise tax of $100 per day during the noncompliance period with respect to each qualified beneficiary, limited to $200 per day in the case of more than one qualified beneficiary in the same family. Attorney's fees also may be available. Where a covered employee's spouse and children were not participants on the date of the qualifying event, the award was limited to penalties and attorney's fees based on the covered employee only.[1]

The noncompliance period begins on the date when the failure first begins and continues until the failure is corrected or the date that is six months after the last date on which the employer could have been required to provide continuation coverage to the beneficiary, whichever date is earlier.[2]

The minimum tax for a failure that is not discovered until after the employer receives a notice of tax audit is $2,500 (increasing to $15,000 for violations that are deemed more than de minimis). However, no tax is imposed on any failure for which it is established that the employer (or plan in the case of a multiemployer plan) did not know, or exercising reasonable diligence would not have known, that such failure existed.[3]

No tax is imposed for the period during which it is shown that none of the persons liable for the tax knew or, by exercising reasonable diligence, would have known, that the failure existed. There is no tax if the failure was due to reasonable cause, not willful neglect, and is corrected within the first thirty days of the noncompliance period.[4]

Normally, an employer is liable for the tax. In the case of a multiemployer plan, the tax is imposed directly on the plan. In addition, a person responsible for administering the plan or providing benefits under it pursuant to a written agreement is liable if that person causes the failure by failing to perform one or more of its responsibilities. A person also may be liable if the individual fails to comply, within forty-five days, with a written request of the employer, the plan administrator, or, in limited situations, a qualified beneficiary to provide benefits that the person provides to similarly situated active employees. This excise tax may be imposed on

---

1. *Wright v. Hanna Steel Corp.*, 270 F.3d 1336 (11th Cir. 2001).
2. IRC Sec. 4980B(b).
3. IRC Section 4980B(b)(3)(A).
4. IRC Sec. 4980B(c).

a third party such as an insurer or third party administrator if the third party assumes certain responsibilities.[1]

In the case of single employer plans, the maximum excise tax for failures due to reasonable cause, not willful neglect, is 10 percent of the aggregate amount paid by the employer during the preceding tax year for medical care coverage or, if less, $500,000.[2] The maximum excise tax in the case of a person other than an employer is limited to $2 million with respect to all plans.[3]

In the case of a failure due to reasonable cause, the Secretary of the Treasury may waive part or all of the tax to the extent it is excessive relative to the failure involved. The determination of the excessiveness of the excise tax is to be made based on the seriousness of the failure, not on a particular taxpayer's ability to pay the tax.[4]

Failure to make continuation coverage available will be treated as corrected if it is retroactively undone to the extent possible and the qualified beneficiary is placed in as good a financial position as the individual would have been in had the failure not occurred and had the beneficiary elected the most favorable coverage in light of the expenses incurred since the failure first occurred.[5]

Other Remedies

In addition to the excise taxes discussed above, other civil remedies are available under ERISA.[6] Employees or other qualified beneficiaries can bring civil actions to obtain other equitable relief, including an injunction and restitution, and to recover additional penalties of up to $110 per day for failure to provide required notices or to furnish requested information.[7] Compensatory damages are not available.[8]

Disability Income Coverage

376. What are the tax consequences when a corporation buys disability insurance on a key person under which benefits are paid to the corporation?

A corporation cannot deduct premiums it pays but can exclude insurance benefits from its gross income.[9] Disability income, regardless of amount, is wholly tax-exempt to the corporation under IRC Section 104(a)(3).[10] Because the disability income is tax-exempt, a deduction for premiums is disallowable under IRC Section 265(a)(1) on the ground that the premiums are expenses paid to acquire tax-exempt income.[11] An accidental death benefit may be tax-exempt to a corporation under IRC Section 101(a) as death proceeds of life insurance (Q 63). Premiums

1. IRC Sec. 4980B(e); Treas. Reg. §54.4980B-2, A-10. See *Paris v. Korbel*, 751 F. Supp. 834 (N.D. Cal. 1990).
2. IRC Sec. 4980B(c)(4)(A).
3. IRC Sec. 4980B(c)(4)(C).
4. IRC Sec. 4980B(c)(5).
5. IRC Sec. 4980B(g)(4).
6. ERISA Sec. 502.
7. ERISA Secs. 502(a)(1), 502(a)(3); 62 Fed. Reg. 40696.
8. *Geissal v. Moore Med. Corp.*, 158 F. Supp.2d 976 (E.D. Mo. 2001).
9. Rev. Rul. 66-262, 1966-2 CB 105.
10. *Castner Garage, Ltd. v. Comm.*, 43 BTA 1 (1940), *acq.*
11. *Rugby Prod. Ltd. v. Comm.*, 100 TC 531 (1993).

paid for tax-exempt accidental death coverage are nondeductible under IRC Section 264(a)(1) (Q 262).

On January 16, 2009, the Office of Associate Chief Counsel (Income Tax & Accounting) issued Chief Counsel Advice[1] concluding that a taxpayer may not take a deduction under Section 162 for compensation paid to an employee pursuant to an employment contract, because the taxpayer was receiving disability insurance payments on account of the employee's injury and Section 162 disallows a deduction for an expense for which there is a right or expectation of reimbursement.

However, upon further consideration, the Office of Associate Chief Counsel (Income Tax & Accounting) concluded, based upon the facts in the prior CCA, that a taxpayer is not precluded from taking a Section 162 deduction for compensation paid to an employee pursuant to the employment contract merely because the taxpayer received insurance payments on account of an employee's disability. Nor does Section 265(a)(1) disallow such a deduction.[2]

377. Are premiums paid for business overhead expense disability insurance deductible as a business expense?

Yes. The IRS has ruled that premiums paid on an overhead expense disability policy, a special type of contract that reimburses professionals or owner-operators for overhead expenses actually incurred during periods of disability, are deductible as a business expense and the proceeds are taxable.[3] The ruling relates to self-employed individuals.

Premiums paid on standard personal disability insurance are not deductible as a business expense but the proceeds are tax-exempt as compensation for personal injuries or sickness (Q 381).[4] This is true even though a taxpayer intends to use the benefits to pay overhead expenses during periods of disability.[5] (See Q 376.)

378. What are the tax consequences when disability insurance is purchased on the lives of business owners to fund a disability buy-out?

Whether a purchaser, policyowner, beneficiary, or premium payor is the business entity, as in an entity purchase agreement, or the business owner, as in a cross-purchase agreement, the premiums are nondeductible and the proceeds are exempt from regularly calculated income tax (Q 376).[6]

Where a buy-out occurs between a corporation and a disabled shareholder, if the transaction qualifies as a complete redemption of all the shareholder's shares, the redemption will be treated as a capital transaction (Q 300). That is, the transaction will be considered the sale of a

1. CCA POSTF-135262-08.
2. IRS Office of Chief Counsel Memorandum No. 200947035, Nov. 20, 2009.
3. Rev. Rul. 55-264, 1955-1 CB 11.
4. Rev. Rul. 55-331, 1955-1 CB 271; Rev. Rul. 70-394, 1970-2 CB 34.
5. Rev. Rul. 58-480, 1958-2 CB 62; *Blaess v. Comm.*, 28 TC 710 (1957); *Andrews v. Comm.*, TC Memo 1970-32.
6. IRC Secs. 104(a)(3), 265(a)(1); Rev. Rul. 66-262, 1966-2 CB 105.

capital asset and the selling shareholder's gain or loss will be measured and taxed. A disability buy-out between shareholders also is a capital transaction and is taxed accordingly.[1]

Where a buy-out occurs between a partnership and a disabled partner, resulting in a termination of the disabled partner's interest, the transaction is taxed under the rules applying to a liquidation of a partner's interest (Q 311).

Where a buy-out occurs between partners, the transaction is taxed under the rules applying to a sale of a partner's interest (Q 311).

When a disabled business owner realizes gain on the sale of his or her business interest, the amount of gain is includable in his or her gross income in the taxable year in which the gain is actually or constructively received unless the gain is includable in a different year due to the taxpayer's method of accounting.[2] If a sale qualifies as an installment sale, a pro rata portion of the gain is reportable for each taxable year installment payments are received.

379. Can an employer deduct premiums paid for employer-provided disability income coverage?

An employer generally can deduct all premiums paid for disability income coverage for one or more employees as a business expense.

Premiums are deductible by an employer whether coverage is provided under a group policy or under individual policies. The deduction is allowable only if benefits are payable to employees or their beneficiaries; it is not allowable if benefits are payable to an employer.[3]

The deduction of premiums paid for a disability income policy insuring an employee-shareholder was prohibited where the corporation was the premium payor, owner, and beneficiary of the policy. The Tax Court held that IRC Section 265(a) prevented the deduction because the premiums were funds expended to produce tax-exempt income. The Tax Court stated that disability income policy benefits, had any been paid, would have been tax-exempt under IRC Section 104(a)(3).[4]

380. How are benefits provided under an employer-provided disability income plan taxed?

Sick pay, wage continuation payments, and disability income payments, both preretirement and postretirement, generally are fully includable in gross income and taxable to an employee.[5] Specifically, long-term disability income payments received under a policy paid for by an employer are fully includable in income to a taxpayer.[6]

1. IRC Secs. 61(a)(3), 1001, 1011, 1221, and 1222.
2. Treas. Reg. §1.451-1(a).
3. Treas. Reg. §1.162-10(a); Rev. Rul. 58-90, 1958-1 CB 88; Rev. Rul. 56-632, 1956-2 CB 101.
4. *Rugby Prod. Ltd. v. Comm.*, 100 TC 531 (1993). See Rev. Rul. 66-262, 1966-2 CB 105.
5. Let. Ruls. 9103043, 9036049.
6. *Cash v. Comm.*, TC Memo 1994-166; *Rabideau v. Comm.*, TC Memo 1997-230. See also *Pearson v. Comm.*, TC Memo 2000-160; *Crandall v. Comm.*, TC Memo 1996-463.

A disabled former employee could not exclude from income a lump sum payment received from the insurance company that provided the employee's employer-paid long-term disability coverage. The lump sum nature of the settlement did not change the nature of the payment into something other than a payment received under accident or health insurance.[1]

If benefits are received under a plan to which an employee has contributed, the portion of the disability income attributable to the employee's contributions is tax-free.[2] Under an individual policy, an employee's contributions for the current policy year are taken into consideration. With a group policy, an employee's contributions for the last three years, if known, are considered.[3]

In Revenue Ruling 2004-55, the IRS held that the three-year look back rule did not apply because the plan was amended so that, with respect to each employee, the amended plan was financed either solely by the employer or solely by the employee. The three-year look back rule does not apply if a plan is not considered a contributory plan.

An employer may allow employees to elect, on an annual basis, whether to have premiums for a group disability income policy included in employees' income for that year. An employee who elects to have premiums included in his or her income will not be taxed on benefits received during a period of disability beginning in that tax year.[4] An employee's election will be effective for each tax year without regard to employer and employee contributions for prior years.

Where an employee-owner reimbursed his corporation for payment of premiums on a disability income policy, the benefit payments that he received while disabled were excludable from income under IRC Section 104(a)(3).[5]

Where an employer initially paid disability income insurance premiums but, prior to a second period of benefit payments, an employee took responsibility for paying premiums personally, the benefits paid from the disability income policy during the second benefit-paying period were not includable in the employee's income.[6]

Premiums paid by a former employee under an earlier long-term disability plan were not considered paid toward a later plan from which the employee received benefit payments. Thus, disability benefits were includable in income.[7] If an employer merely withholds employee contributions and makes none itself, the payments are excludable.[8] A tax credit for disability retirement income is available to taxpayers receiving those payments after the minimum age at which they would have received a pension or annuity if not disabled. This credit is called the Disability and Earned Income Tax Credit (EITC).

1. *Kees v. Comm.*, TC Memo 1999-41.
2. Treas. Reg. §1.105-1(c).
3. Treas. Reg. §1.105-1(d).
4. Rev. Rul. 2004-55, 2004-26 IRB 1081.
5. *Bouquett v. Comm.*, 67 TCM 2959 (1994).
6. Let. Rul. 9741035. See also Let. Rul. 200019005.
7. *Chernik v. Comm.*, TC Memo 1999-313.
8. Rev. Rul. 73-347, 1973-2 CB 25.

381. Are premiums paid for personal disability income coverage tax deductible?

Premiums for non-medical care, such as personal disability income coverage, are not deductible.[1] Only premiums for medical care insurance are deductible as a medical expense (Q 342, Q 485).

A deduction is allowed for medical care that is not otherwise compensated for by insurance. The deduction is allowed to the extent that the medical care expenses exceed 10 percent of the taxpayer's adjusted gross income. For taxable years beginning prior to 2013, and in 2017 and 2018, the deduction was allowed to the extent that the medical care expenses exceeded 7.5 percent of the taxpayer's adjusted gross income.[2] The threshold is 10 percent for the alternative minimum tax and there was a transition rule, so that the 10 percent threshold for regular tax did not apply until 2017 (2019 under the 2017 tax reform legislation) for people over sixty-five.

382. How are benefits provided under a personal disability income coverage plan taxed?

Benefits from personal disability income coverage typically are entirely exempt from income tax. There is no limit on the amount of benefits, including the amount of disability income that can be received tax-free under personally paid disability income coverage.[3]

If benefits are received under a plan to which both an employer and employee have contributed, the portion of the disability income attributable to the employee's contributions is tax-free (Q 379).[4]

383. How are disability pension payments taxed to common law employees made from a qualified pension or profit-sharing plan?

Disability payments from a qualified plan receive different tax treatment, depending on whether the payments are made to common law employees or to self-employed individuals (see Q 384).

If a disability pension is derived from employer contributions and is made in lieu of wages to an employee who retired on account of permanent and total disability, the employee may be entitled to an Earned Income Tax Credit (EITC) (Q 379). The employee is not entitled to exclude from income any part of a disability benefit derived from employer contributions.

In a contributory plan, it will be presumed that a disability pension is derived from employer contributions unless the plan expressly provides otherwise.

Under IRC Section 72(d), amounts received from disability pensions can be excluded from income until an employee has excluded an amount that is equal to his or her consideration for

1. See IRC Sec. 213(d)(1).
2. IRC Sec. 213(a).
3. IRC Sec. 104(a)(3); Rev. Rul. 55-331, 1955-1 CB 271, modified by Rev. Rul. 68-212, 1968-1 CB 91; Rev. Rul. 70-394, 1970-2 CB 34.
4. Treas. Reg. §1.105-1(c).

the contract. Under the three-year rule, if the total amounts received by the employee during the first three years that payments are made on the contract either equal or exceed the consideration paid by the employee, then the payments will be excluded from the employee's income until the amount of consideration has been met. Any employee contributions that were allocated to provide disability payments cannot be included in the employee's cost basis in figuring the tax on his or her retirement pension payments.[1]

In the case of a plan that required employees to pay premiums for their disability coverage, subject to a right of reimbursement from their employer, the Tax Court determined that disability payments for a six month period where an employee was on leave without sick pay were includable in the employee's income. The Tax Court held that the employees were required to pay taxes on the recovered past-due benefits they received because there were no actual repayments made.[2]

The payment of post-retirement medical expense benefits is tax-free to an employee.[3]

A few courts have held that a profit sharing plan also can be an accident or health plan so that payment of the full amount in the employee's account on termination of employment because of permanent disability for loss of a bodily function is entirely excludable under IRC Section 105(c).[4] Absent clear evidence to the contrary, other courts have been reluctant to find deferred compensation profit sharing plans to be dual purpose plans intended to provide both retirement and health or accident benefits.[5] Distributions from these plans have been held to be taxable because they were not computed in reference to a taxpayer's disability, that is, in an accident or health plan, but were instead computed in reference to the taxpayer's length of service.[6]

An individual who terminated employment on account of disability after the normal retirement date but prior to a deferred retirement date could not claim the IRC Section 105(c) exclusion because the plan provided that payments after normal retirement age would be paid on account of age and years of service rather than on account of injury or sickness.[7]

The IRS has taken the position that distributions made from a qualified profit-sharing trust, when used to pay for an employee's medical-care expenses, cannot be excluded from income as accident or health benefits under Section 105(b). Instead, the distributions must be included in employee income as previously earned deferred compensation under Section 402(a).[8]

1. Treas. Reg. §1.72-15(c); *Butler v. Comm.*, TC Memo 1987-463.
2. *Andrews v. Comm.*, TC Memo 1992-668.
3. Treas. Reg. §1.72-15(h), Treas. Reg. §1.402(a)-1(e)(2).
4. *Wood v. U.S.*, 590 F.2d 321 (9th Cir. 1979); *Masterson v. U.S.*, 478 F. Supp. 454, 79-2 USTC 9664 (N.D. Ill. 1979); *Berner v. U.S.*, 81-2 USTC 9733 (W.D. Pa. 1981).
5. *Caplin v. U.S.*, 718 F.2d 544 (2d Cir. 1983); *Berman v. Comm.*, 925 F.2d 936 (6th Cir. 1991); *Gordon v. Comm.*, 88 TC 630 (1987); *Paul v. U.S.*, 682 F.Supp. 329 (E.D. Mich. 1988).
6. *Est. of Hall v. Comm.*, 103 F. 3d 112, 97-1 USTC 50,104 (3rd Cir. 1996); *Dorroh v. Comm.*, 74 F.3d 1255, 96-1 USTC 50,119 (11th Cir. 1996); see also, Let. Rul. 8824013.
7. Let. Rul. 9504041.
8. Rev. Rul. 69-141, 1969-1 CB 48.

384. How are disability pension payments taxed to self-employed individuals when made from a qualified pension or profit-sharing plan?

Disability payments from a qualified plan receive different tax treatment, depending on whether the payments are made to common law employees (see Q 383) or to self-employed individuals.

If a self-employed individual draws benefits from a plan because of permanent disability, the disability payments will be taxed under the same rules that apply to retirement benefits (Q 3960).

If a self-employed individual receives disability payments through health insurance, the employee may exclude from gross income any amounts attributable to nondeductible contributions as a self-employed person.[1]

Where contributions under a qualified plan are applied to provide incidental accident and health insurance for a self-employed individual, the insurance is treated as if the employee had purchased it directly from the insurance company.[2]

385. What is the ABLE Act? Who is eligible for an ABLE account?

The Achieving a Better Life Experience (ABLE) Act was included within the Tax Increase Prevention Act of 2014.[3] The ABLE Act introduces a new type of tax-advantaged savings account that is specifically designed to address some of the challenges to saving that disabled individuals have faced in recent years.

Under the previously existing rules, disabled individuals were often discouraged from accumulating assets to meet future expenses because, absent the use of certain trust vehicles, the individual would be disqualified from receiving Social Security and Medicaid benefits if accumulated assets were worth more than $2,000.

The ABLE Act modifies these rules to allow individuals to accumulate up to $100,000 in savings accounts called "ABLE accounts" without becoming disqualified from receiving Social Security benefits (above and beyond the traditional $2,000 resource limit, so that a total of $102,000 can be accumulated without risk of disqualification). Medicaid benefits will not be impacted regardless of how much the individual deposits into the ABLE account.[4]

In order to qualify as an ABLE account beneficiary, the individual must have been diagnosed with a disability that causes severe limitations before that individual reaches age twenty-six. Individuals who are currently receiving Social Security disability benefits also qualify. Regardless, eligibility for Social Security benefits is not a requirement for establishing an ABLE account—a severe, diagnosed disability is sufficient.[5]

1. IRC Secs. 105(g), 104(a)(3); Treas. Reg. §§1.105-1(a), 1.105-5(b).
2. See Treas. Reg. §1.72-15(g).
3. H.R. 647.
4. H.R. 647, Sec. 103.
5. H.R. 647.

See Q 386 for a discussion of changes to the contribution limits and rollover rules that impact ABLE accounts under the 2017 Tax Act.

386. What contribution rules apply to ABLE accounts?

ABLE accounts are modeled after IRC Section 529 college savings plans, so that after-tax funds are contributed to the account, but those funds are permitted to grow on a tax-free basis. Distributions from the account are not taxed when received if the distribution is used to pay for a qualified expense (see Q 387). Currently, the annual contribution limit is based upon the annual gift tax exclusion amount ($15,000 in 2018-2020 and $14,000 in 2017) and will be adjusted annually for inflation.[1]

The 2017 Tax Act expanded the ABLE account contribution rules so that the account beneficiary is now able to contribute his or her earned income even if the contribution (when added to other contributions) causes contribution levels that exceed the otherwise applicable annual contribution limit. The account beneficiary's contribution is limited to the lesser of his or her taxable income or the federal single-person poverty limit.[2] However, this additional contribution limit is unavailable to account beneficiaries who also contributed to a 401(k), 403(b) or 457(b) plan.[3] If the ABLE account beneficiary contributes to the account, he or she will be eligible for the saver's credit.[4] These provisions apply for tax years beginning after December 31, 2017 and before January 1, 2026.

Any individual may make contributions to an ABLE account, whether or not that person is a disabled individual who is eligible to be an ABLE account beneficiary (see Q 385). Contributions themselves, however, are not tax deductible—as discussed above, all contributions are made on an after-tax basis.

Further, 2017 Tax Act now permits Section 529 plan funds to be rolled over into an ABLE account for the designated beneficiary or the designated beneficiary's family member in an amount up to the annual 529 plan contribution limit (rollovers would offset other contributions made to the ABLE account for the year). Amounts rolled over in excess of the limitation are included in the distributee's gross income. These rules are effective for rollovers that occur after December 31, 2017 and before December 31, 2025.[5]

The IRS has announced that it intends to release proposed regulations interpreting these rules. The regulations are expected to provide that such a rollover will not be taxable if (1) the amounts are contributed to the ABLE account within sixty days of being withdrawn from the 529 plan and (2) the distribution plus all other contributions to the ABLE account do not exceed the annual contribution limit ($15,000 in 2018-2020). These rules will apply regardless of whether a rollover or direct trustee-to-trustee transfer is used. The ABLE account

1. Rev. Proc. 2018-57, Rev. Proc. 2019-44.
2. IRC Sec. 529(b)(2)(B).
3. IRC Sec. 529(b)(7).
4. IRC Sec. 25B(d)(1)(D).
5. IRC Sec. 529(c)(3)(C)(III).

beneficiary's own earnings can be contributed to the ABLE account regardless of whether the contribution would cause total contributions to exceed $15,000.

Planning Point: Taxpayers should note that if the ABLE account contribution limits are violated, the beneficiary's eligibility for public benefits could be jeopardized (along with the associated tax liability that would apply to the excess contribution).

387. What distribution requirements apply to ABLE accounts?

Much like a traditional IRC Section 529 college savings plan, ABLE account distributions must be used to fund certain specified expenses of the disabled beneficiary or will become subject to a ten percent penalty tax. In addition to the ten percent penalty, any distributed earnings are taxed at the individual's normal income tax rate if the distribution is not used for qualified expenses (see below).[1]

The range of qualified expenses is broad, and includes "expenses related to the individual's disability," such as expenses for health care, housing, transportation, job training, assistive technology, personal support, financial management, legal fees and related services and expenses.[2]

Individuals are generally limited to establishing only one ABLE account. Amounts initially contributed to an ABLE account can be rolled over into another ABLE account established either for the same beneficiary, or for a sibling of that beneficiary who also meets the eligibility requirements discussed in Q 385.[3] See Q 386 for a discussion of changes to the contribution limits and rollover rules that impact ABLE accounts under the 2017 Tax Act.

Health Savings Accounts

388. What is a Health Savings Account (HSA) and how can an HSA be established?

An HSA is a trust created exclusively for the purpose of paying qualified medical expenses of an account beneficiary.[4]

An HSA must be created by a written governing instrument that states:

(1) no contribution will be accepted except in the case of a rollover contribution (Q 411) unless it is in cash or to the extent that the contribution, when added to previous contributions for the calendar year, exceeds the contribution limit for the calendar year;

(2) the trustee is a bank, an insurance company, or a person who satisfies IRS requirements;

(3) no part of trust assets will be invested in life insurance contracts;

1. H.R. 647, Sec. 102.
2. H.R. 647, Sec. 102.
3. See *Summary of H.R. 647*, available at: https://rules.house.gov/sites/republicans.rules.house.gov/files/113-2/PDF/113-HR647-SxS.pdf (last accessed February 14, 2018).
4. IRC Sec. 223(d)(1).

(4) trust assets will not be commingled with other property, with certain limited exceptions; and

(5) the interest of an individual in the balance of his or her account is non-forfeitable.[1]

HSAs are available to any employer or individual for an account beneficiary who has high deductible health insurance coverage (Q 392). An eligible individual or an employer may establish an HSA with a qualified HSA custodian or trustee. No permission or authorization is needed from the IRS to set up an HSA. As mentioned above, any insurance company or bank can act as a trustee. Additionally, any person already approved by the IRS to act as an individual retirement arrangement (IRA) trustee or custodian automatically is approved to act in the same capacity for HSAs.[2]

Although an HSA is similar to an IRA in some respects, a taxpayer cannot use an IRA as an HSA, nor can a taxpayer combine an IRA with an HSA.[3] In certain situations, a taxpayer can take a qualified funding distribution from an IRA to fund an HSA (Q 412).

Contributions to an HSA generally may be made either by an individual, by an individual's employer, or by both. If contributions are made by an individual taxpayer, they are deductible from income.[4] If contributions are made pre-tax by an employer, they are excluded from employee income.[5]

An HSA itself is exempt from income tax as long as it remains an HSA.[6]

Contributions may be made through a cafeteria plan under IRC Section 125 (Q 3501).[7]

Distributions from HSAs are not includable in gross income if they are used exclusively to pay qualified medical expenses. Distributions used for other purposes are includable in gross income and may be subject to a penalty, with some exceptions (Q 411).[8]

An employer's contributions to an HSA are not considered part of a group health plan subject to COBRA continuation coverage requirements (Q 356).[9] Therefore, a plan is not required to make COBRA continuation coverage available with respect to an HSA.[10]

The IRS has stated that a levy to satisfy a tax liability under IRC Section 6331 extends to a taxpayer's interest in an HSA. A taxpayer is liable for the additional 20 percent tax (10 percent

1. IRC Sec. 223(d)(1).
2. Notice 2004-50, 2004-2 CB 196, A-72; Notice 2004-2, 2004-1 CB 269, A-9, A-10.
3. See Notice 2004-2, above.
4. IRC Sec. 223(a).
5. See IRC Sec. 106(d)(1).
6. IRC Sec. 223(e)(1).
7. IRC Sec. 125(d)(2)(D).
8. IRC Sec. 223(f).
9. See IRC Secs. 106(b)(5), 106(d)(2).
10. See Treas. Reg. §54.4980B-2, A-1 regarding Archer MSAs.

before January 1, 2011, under the ACA[1]) on the amount of the levy unless, at the time of the levy, the taxpayer had attained the age of sixty-five or was disabled.[2]

389. What are the advantages of an HSA?

HSAs are tax-driven accounts and, as such, many of the benefits are tax related. Some of the tax benefits of an HSA include the following:

(1) *Federal Income Tax Deduction.* HSA contributions reduce an account owner's income for federal income tax purposes because personal HSA contributions are tax deductible and employer contributions are received on a pre-tax basis (see Q 395).

(2) *State Income Tax Deduction.* Most states with income taxes allow account owners to reduce state taxable income by the amount of an HSA contribution. California, New Jersey and Alabama are the only states that do not allow a state income tax deduction for an HSA contribution. All other states have either passed specific legislation allowing HSA deductions for state income tax purposes, have conforming legislation where the federal deductions flow through at the state level, or do not have a state income tax.

(3) *Payroll Tax Avoidance.* Account owners receiving HSA contributions pre-tax through an employer, whether they are employer contributions or employee payroll deferral through a Section 125 plan, avoid Social Security taxes, Medicare taxes (together with Social Security referred to as FICA), federal unemployment taxes (FUTA), Railroad Retirement Act taxes, and in most cases state unemployment taxes (SUTA) (see Q 416).

(4) *Tax Deferred Earnings Growth.* Any interest, dividends or other appreciation of the assets in an HSA grow tax-deferred while in the HSA (see Q 408).

(5) *Tax-free Distributions.* Account owners that use HSA funds for qualified medical expenses enjoy tax-free distributions (see Q 409). If the funds will be used to pay for qualified medical expenses, the HSA rules are more advantageous than the tax treatment provided to distributions from traditional IRAs or 401(k)s because those plans are only tax-deferred, not tax-free (although Roth IRA and Roth 401(k) distributions are tax-free, as contributions are made with after-tax dollars).

The nontax benefits of HSAs are also significant, and include the following:

(1) *Balance Rolls Over.* HSA balances roll over from year to year and do not have "use it or lose it" restrictions that apply to other medical spending account plans.

(2) *HSA Remains after Separation from Service.* An HSA remains with the account owner after separation from service even if the employer provided the HSA funding.

1. Affordable Care Act.
2. CCA 200927019.

(3) *Transferability.* Account owners can move their HSA to a new HSA custodian at any time (see Q 411).

(4) *Ownership.* HSA account owners own the money in their HSA and can use it as they see fit. This relates to other benefits already mentioned, but also provides account owners the ability to name beneficiaries on the account, select investments, and decide when to take a distribution (even if the distribution is for a nonmedical reason). Note that the penalty tax for non-qualified distributions does not apply once the taxpayer has reached age sixty-five.

(5) *Control Spending.* An HSA gives account owners some additional control over their medical spending. The account owner can decide where to spend the money and can negotiate with providers when appropriate. This gives the account owner some freedom to choose medical providers outside of an insurance company's network or to try alternative approaches (within the definition of "qualified medical expense").

(6) *Lower Insurance Premiums.* HDHPs (which must be used in order for the individual to qualify for an HSA) are generally less expensive than traditional insurance.

390. What are the disadvantages of an HSA?

For an individual unable to afford traditional insurance, the HDHP and HSA combination may provide an affordable approach to insurance not possible otherwise. Many people that can afford traditional insurance also choose HDHPs and HSAs because the combination reflects a cost savings and provides more pure insurance rather than pre-paid medical. This background is important because many of the disadvantages of HSAs are only in comparison to traditional low or no deductible health insurance. The following are potential disadvantages of a combination HDHP and HSA.

(1) *Higher Deductible.* An account owner generally faces a higher health insurance deductible than a person with traditional insurance. This can present an increased cost burden.

(2) *Expenses before Savings.* An account owner may face a large medical expense prior to having time to build a sufficient balance in the HSA.

(3) *More Responsibility for Health Spending.* HSAs require individuals to take charge of their own health care spending. This will generally require the individual to devote more time to learning about health care costs and alternatives in order to save on health costs, as compared to a person with traditional insurance coverage where many expenses are simply paid.

(4) *Tax Reporting.* Account owners are required to account for both HSA contributions and distributions each year on their income tax return. Additionally, the account owner is responsible for saving medical receipts in order to substantiate health-related expenses.

(5) *HSA Rules.* HSAs, similar to all tax-driven types of accounts, can become complicated. The account owner is responsible for learning the HSA rules and following them in order to avoid negative tax consequences.

(6) *HSA Maintenance.* The account owner is responsible for maintaining the HSA, paying medical bills, monitoring the balance, choosing beneficiaries, and otherwise maintaining the HSA.

391. Who is an eligible individual for purposes of a Health Savings Account (HSA)?

For purposes of an HSA, an eligible individual is an individual who, for any month, is covered under a high deductible health plan (HDHP) as of the first day of that month and is not also covered under a non-high deductible health plan providing coverage for any benefit covered under the high deductible health plan.[1]

An individual enrolled in Medicare Part A or Part B may not contribute to an HSA.[2] Mere eligibility for Medicare does not preclude HSA contributions.[3]

An individual may not contribute to an HSA for a given month if he or she has received medical benefits through the Department of Veterans Affairs within the previous three months. Mere eligibility for VA medical benefits will not disqualify an otherwise eligible individual from making HSA contributions.[4] Beginning January 1, 2016, an individual shall not fail to be an eligible individual because of receiving hospital care or medical services under a law administered by the Secretary of Veterans Affairs for a service-connected disability. The IRS defines "service connected disability" as the following:

> "Distinguishing between services provided by the VA for service-connected disabilities and other types of medical care is administratively complex and burdensome for employers and HSA trustees or custodians. Moreover, as a practical matter, most care provided for veterans who have a disability rating will be such qualifying care. Consequently, as a rule of administrative simplification, for purposes of this rule, any hospital care or medical services received from the VA by a veteran who has a disability rating from the VA may be considered to be hospital care or medical services under a law administered by the Secretary of Veterans Affairs for service-connected disability."[5]

A separate prescription drug plan that provides any benefits before a required high deductible is satisfied normally will prevent a beneficiary from qualifying as an eligible individual.[6] The IRS has ruled that if an individual's separate prescription drug plan does not provide benefits until an HDHP's minimum annual deductible amount has been met, then the individual will be an eligible individual under Section 223(c)(1)(A). For calendar years 2004 and 2005 only, the

1. IRC Sec. 223(c)(1)(A).
2. IRC Sec. 223(b)(7).
3. Notice 2004-50, 2004-2 CB 196, A-3.
4. Notice 2004-50, 2004-2 CB 196, A-5.
5. IRS Notice 2015-87.
6. Rev. Rul. 2004-38, 2004-1 CB 717.

IRS provided transition relief such that an individual would not fail to be an eligible individual solely by virtue of coverage by a separate prescription drug plan.[1]

An individual will not fail to be an eligible individual solely because the individual is covered under an Employee Assistance Program, disease management program, or wellness program, if the program does not provide significant benefits in the nature of medical care or treatment.[2]

Planning Point: An employer can provide an onsite medical clinic without jeopardizing employee HSA eligibility, provided the employer's clinic does not provide "significant benefits in the nature of medical care" (in addition to disregarded coverage or preventive care). Meeting the exception depends on the level of services provided by the health clinic. Allowed services include the following:

- Physicals,
- Immunizations,
- Injecting antigens provided by employee,
- Providing aspirin/pain relievers, and
- Treatment of injuries or accidents that occur at work.

Certain kinds of insurance are not taken into account in determining whether an individual is eligible for an HSA. Specifically, insurance for a specific disease or illness, hospitalization insurance paying a fixed daily amount, and insurance providing coverage that relates to certain liabilities are disregarded.[3]

In addition, coverage provided by insurance or otherwise for accidents, disability, dental care, vision care, or long-term care will not adversely impact HSA eligibility.[4]

If an employer contributes to an eligible employee's HSA, in order to receive an employer comparable contribution the employee must:

(1) establish the HSA on or before the last day in February of the year following the year for which the contribution is being made and;

(2) notify the appropriate contact person of the HSA account information on or before the last day in February of the year described in (1) above and specify and provide HSA account information (e.g., account number, name and address of trustee or custodian, etc.) as well as the method by which the account information will be provided (e.g., in writing, by e-mail, on a certain form, etc.).

---

1. Rev. Proc. 2004-22, 2004-1 CB 727.
2. Notice 2004-50, 2004-2 CB 196, A-10.
3. IRC Sec. 223(c)(3).
4. IRC Sec. 223(c)(1)(B).

An eligible employee that establishes an HSA and provides the information required as described in (1) and (2) above will receive an HSA contribution, plus reasonable interest, for the year for which contribution is being made by April 15 of the following year.[1]

392. What is a high deductible health plan for purposes of a Health Savings Account (HSA)?

For purposes of an HSA, the requirements for a high deductible health plan (HDHP) differ depending on the coverage.

In the case of self-only coverage, an HDHP is a health plan with an annual deductible of not less than $1,400 in 2020 ($1,350 in 2019) and required annual out-of-pocket expenses of not more than $6,900 in 2020 ($6,750 in 2019).[2]

In the case of family coverage, a high deductible health plan is a health plan with an annual deductible of not less than $2,800 in 2020 ($2,700 in 2018 and 2019) and required annual out-of-pocket expenses of not more than $13,800 in 2020 and $13,500 in 2019.[3] For this purpose, family coverage is any coverage other than self-only coverage.[4]

The chart below includes the current year's HSA limits as well as the limits in place for the previous seven years.

TYPE	2013	2014	2015	2016	2017	2018	2019	2020
HDHP-Min Single	$1,250	$1,250	$1,300	$1,300	$1,300	$1,350	$1,350	$1,400
HDHP-Min Family	$2,500	$2,500	$2,600	$2,600	$2,600	$2,700	$2,700	$2,800
HDHP-Max Single	$6,250	$6,350	$6,450	$6,550	$6,550	$6,650	$6,750	$6,900
HDHP-Max Family	$12,500	$12,700	$12,900	$13,100	$13,100	$13,300	$13,500	$13,800

Other Issues

Deductible limits for HDHPs are based on a twelve month period. If a plan deductible may be satisfied over a period longer than twelve months, the minimum annual deductible under IRC Section 223(c)(2)(A) must be increased on a pro-rata basis to take into account the longer period.[5]

An HDHP may impose a reasonable lifetime limit on benefits provided under the plan as long as the lifetime limit on benefits is not designed to circumvent the maximum annual

1. TD 9393, 2008-20 IRB.
2. IRC Sec. 223(c)(2)(A); Rev. Proc. 2012-26, 2012-20 IRB 933, Rev. Proc. 2013-25, 2013-21 IRB 1110; Rev. Proc. 2014-30, 2014-1 CB 1009, Rev. Proc. 2015-30, Rev. Proc. 2016-28, Rev. Proc. 2017-37, Rev. Proc. 2018-30, Rev. Proc. 2019-25.
3. IRC Sec. 223(c)(2)(A); Rev. Proc. 2012-26, 2012-20 IRB 933, Rev. Proc. 2013-25, 2013-21 IRB 1110; Rev. Proc. 2014-30, 2014-1 CB 1009, Rev. Proc. 2015-30, Rev. Proc. 2016-28, Rev. Proc. 2017-37, Rev. Proc. 2018-30, Rev. Proc. 2019-25.
4. IRC Sec. 223(c)(5).
5. Notice 2004-50, 2004-2 CB 196, A-24.

out-of-pocket limitation.[1] A plan with no limitation on out-of-pocket expenses, either by design or by its express terms, does not qualify as a high deductible health plan.[2]

An HDHP may provide coverage for preventive care without application of the annual deductible.[3] The IRS has provided guidance and safe harbor guidelines on what constitutes preventive care. Under the safe harbor, preventive care includes, but is not limited to, periodic check-ups, routine prenatal and well-child care, immunizations, tobacco cessation programs, obesity weight-loss programs, and various health screening services. Preventive care may include drugs or medications taken to prevent the occurrence or reoccurrence of a disease that is not currently present.[4]

For months before January 1, 2006, a health plan would not fail to qualify as a high deductible health plan solely because it complied with state health insurance laws that mandate coverage without regard to a deductible or before the high deductible is satisfied.[5] This transition relief only applied to disqualifying benefits mandated by state laws that were in effect on January 1, 2004. This relief extended to non-calendar year health plans with benefit periods of twelve months or less that began before January 1, 2006.[6]

Out-of-pocket expenses include deductibles, co-payments, and other amounts that a participant must pay for covered benefits. Premiums are not considered out-of-pocket expenses.[7]

Annual deductible amounts and out-of-pocket expense amounts stated above are adjusted for cost of living. Increases are made in multiples of $50.[8]

393. Are HSAs covered by ERISA?

HSAs are generally not subject to the Employee Retirement Income Security Act of 1974 (ERISA).[9] HSA plans avoid much of the complexity that goes with an ERISA covered plan, making it a good choice for employers desiring greater simplicity. An employer that exercises too much discretion over employees' HSAs could cause an employer HSA program to become an ERISA plan, but that is not likely.

Planning Point: In April, 2016, the Department of Labor introduced new rules defining who is a "fiduciary" in relation to providing investment advice (Q 394). These rules were vacated by the Fifth Circuit in 2018, and the DOL has yet to propose replacement regulations.

To avoid ERISA coverage, the establishment of an HSA must be completely voluntary on the part of the employee and the employer cannot do any of the following:

1. Notice 2004-50, 2004-2 CB 196, A-14.
2. Notice 2004-50, 2004-2 CB 196, A-17.
3. IRC Sec. 223(c)(2)(C).
4. Notice 2004-50, 2004-2 CB 196, A-27; Notice 2004-23, 2004-1 CB 725.
5. Notice 2004-43, 2004-2 CB 10.
6. Notice 2005-83, 2005-2 CB 1075.
7. Notice 2004-2, 2004-1 CB 269, A-3; Notice 96-53, 1996-2 CB 219, A-4.
8. IRC Sec. 223(g).
9. DOL FAB 2004-1

- Limit the ability of eligible individuals to move their funds to another HSA beyond restrictions imposed by HSA law.
- Impose conditions on utilization of HSA funds beyond those imposed by HSA law.
- Make or influence the investment decisions with respect to funds contributed to an HSA.
- Represent that the HSAs are an employee welfare benefits plan.
- Receive any payment or compensation in connection with an HSA.

A common practice of employers offering HSAs is to select one HSA provider for all employees to simplify employer administration of the plan. This practice, in itself, does not violate any of the above conditions.[1] However, a concern exists if that HSA provider limits investment options. The Department of Labor (DOL) states "the mere fact that employer selects an HSA provider to which it will forward contributions that offers a limited selection of investment options … would not, in the view of the Department, constitute the making or influencing of an employee's investment decisions giving rise to an ERISA-covered plan so long as employees are afforded a reasonable choice of investment options and employees are not limited in moving their funds to another HSA."The DOL, however, also states: "[t]he selection of a single HSA provider that offers a single investment option would not, in the view of the Department, afford employees a reasonable choice of investment options."[2]

A couple of other common employer practices are also permitted without an HSA program becoming subject to ERISA. An employer can pay for fees associated with the HSA without the plan becoming an ERISA plan.[3] An employer can unilaterally open an HSA for an employee and deposit employer funds into that HSA and still meet the "completely voluntary" requirement to avoid ERISA coverage.[4]

The employer cannot receive a discount on another product offered by the HSA custodian in exchange for using the custodian for its employees' HSAs.[5]

If an HSA program is covered by ERISA, the employer must: (1) file the Form 5500 annually, (2) provide employees with Summary Plan Descriptions (SPDs), (3) be a fiduciary for the plan, and (4) meet other ERISA imposed terms. HSAs are not designed as ERISA plans and employers generally should seek to avoid ERISA coverage. If the plan does become an ERISA plan, the employer will face a number of challenging questions in applying ERISA to an HSA program.

1. DOL FAB 2004-1; DOL FAB 2006-02, A2.
2. DOL FAB 2006-02.
3. DOL FAB 2006-02, A5
4. DOL FAB 2006-02, A1
5. DOL FAB 2006-02, A7.

394. How does the 2016 DOL fiduciary rule impact HSA programs?

Editor's Note: The Fifth Circuit vacated the DOL fiduciary rule in 2018, and, as of the date of this publication, the DOL has yet to propose a replacement rule. While the discussion below regarding the rules themselves are no longer applicable, those who deal with HSAs may take note of the concepts that the DOL found important, as they may reappear in a future rule.

The DOL's 2016 rule sound to expand the definition of a fiduciary so that it would apply in the context of providing investment advice for an HSA.[1] The new rule makes HSA custodians (and potentially others) fiduciaries if they provide investment advice or recommendations for a fee or other compensation with respect to HSA assets. Although the previous rule also potentially made HSA custodians and others fiduciaries if they provided investment advice, the new rule applies in a wider array of advice relationships.

The rule is designed to remove loopholes in the industry that allowed for providers to earn commissions or fees for investments that may not have been in the best interest of the HSA owner (the rule primarily addresses concerns over conflicts of interest in the IRA industry). Under the prior rule, the provider may not have been a fiduciary and thus would not have had an obligation to recommend the investment best suited for the HSA owner. Under the new definition, any individual receiving compensation for providing advice that is individualized or specifically directed to an HSA owner (or sponsor) is a fiduciary. The rule provides a number of exceptions ("carve-outs") and explanations that assist in determining whether or not an HSA custodian (or other person/entity) falls within this definition.[2]

The DOL specifically included HSAs as subject to the final rule in the preamble to the rule. The DOL views HSAs as close to the same product as IRAs and accordingly included HSAs in the rule. The DOL supports the inclusion of HSAs by noting that: (1) HSAs are given tax preferences (the DOL makes a distinction between tax-favored investment accounts and other investment accounts), (2) HSAs may have associated investment accounts that can be used as long-term investment accounts (HSAs are not just short term medical spending accounts), (3) HSAs may be invested in assets approved for IRAs (stocks, bonds, mutual funds and more), (4) HSA custodians may restrict investments (could open a conflict of interest situation), (5) HSA assets are large and growing, and (6) HSAs are already subject to the prohibited transaction rules (similar to IRAs). The DOL concludes by stating: "[t]hus, although they generally hold fewer assets and may exist for shorter durations than IRAs, the owners of these accounts and the person for whom these accounts were established are entitled to receive the same protections from conflicted investment advice as IRA owners." The actual final rule includes "health savings account" within the definition of IRA thus subjecting HSAs to the new rule in the same manner as IRAs.[3]

The new rule contains substantial detail, examples, and exceptions for certain communications and relationships that are helpful in determining fiduciary status. A full review of those

1. DOL RIN 1210-AB32 (released April 8, 2016)(81 FR 20945).
2. 29 CFR §2510.3-21.
3. DOL RIN 1210-AB32 (released April 8, 2016)(81 FR 20945), CFR §2510.3-21(g)(6)(ii).

details can be found in other sections of this book. This answer is limited to HSA specific concerns under the new rule.

Given that many HSAs are only invested in deposit or checking type accounts, one area of concern for HSAs is whether or not a person could become a fiduciary when the only investment offered is a deposit account. The DOL addressed this issue by providing that Certificates of Deposits are considered an investment subject to the rules (presumably this logic would include checking, savings and other similar deposit accounts as well).[1]

Another concern for HSAs is that the DOL includes in the definition of "providing investment advice" recommendations regarding "rollovers or distributions."[2] Recommendations regarding the distribution options on HSAs may not seem to be investment advice; however, the rule specifically includes it. The DOL also includes recommendations to make a rollover (presumably from an IRA or even another HSA).

Planning Point: HSA custodians and others should be able to avoid becoming fiduciaries and still communicate distribution and rollover options by meeting the exception for investment education communications. The DOL rule provides exceptions for general communications and investment education which include providing plan information. For many involved with HSA programs, these communication exceptions will provide an avenue to provide clients with important tax and plan information without providing investment recommendations.

Some HSA providers may also meet an exception for recordkeepers and third party administrators that provide a platform of investment alternatives to participant-directed retirement accounts and do not provide investment advice. To qualify, the communication cannot consider the individual needs of the participant. The provider must disclose in writing to an independent plan fiduciary that it is not intending to provide impartial investment advice or give advice in a fiduciary capacity. The provider must also identify investment alternatives that meet objective criteria. In order for this exclusion to apply, the plan fiduciary must be independent of the person who markets or makes the selection available. Note: this requires the existence of an independent plan fiduciary which may not be the case in HSA programs.[3]

The DOL is also providing an exemption to the prohibited transaction rules for fiduciaries that meet the "best interest contract" exemption. The best interest contract exemption allows financial institutions or advisors that would otherwise be subject to the fiduciary rules to continue compensation arrangements that might violate the prohibited transaction rules absent an exemption.

395. What are the limits on amounts contributed to a Health Savings Account (HSA)?

An eligible individual may deduct the aggregate amount paid in cash into an HSA during the taxable year, up to $3,550 for 2020 and $3,500 for 2019, for self-only coverage and $7,100

1. 81 FR 21089.
2. CFR §2510.3-21(a), DOL RIN 1210-AB32 (released April 8, 2016)(81 FR 20948).
3. 29 CFR §2510.3-21(a)(definition of investment advice), 29 CFR §2510.3-21(g)(3) (definition of fee), 29 CFR §2510.3-21(b)(2)(i) (platform providers).

for 2020 and $7,000 for 2019 for family coverage.[1] The HSA contribution limits for the 2020 taxable year and the seven previous years are provided in the table below.

	2013	2014	2015	2016	2017	2018	2019	2020
Individual HSA Limit	$3,250	$3,300	$3,350	$3,350	$3,400	$3,450	$3,500	$3,550
Family HSA Limit	$6,450	$6,550	$6,650	$6,750	$6,750	$6,850	$7,000	$7,100

For 2006 and prior years, the contribution and deduction were limited to the lesser of the deductible under the applicable HDHP or the indexed annual limits for self-only coverage or family coverage.[2]

The determination between self-only and family coverage is made as of the first day of the month. The limit is calculated on a monthly basis and the allowable deduction for a taxable year cannot exceed the sum of the monthly limitations, but see below for the rule applicable to newly eligible individuals, for the months during which an individual was an eligible individual (Q 391).[3]

For example, a person with self-only coverage under an HDHP would be limited to a monthly contribution limit of $295.83 for 2020 ($3,550 divided by 12). If a person was an eligible individual for only the first eight months of a year, the contribution limit for the year would be $2,367 (eight months multiplied by the monthly limit). Although the annual contribution level is determined for each month, the annual contribution can be made in a single payment, if desired.[4]

Individuals who attain age fifty-five before the close of a taxable year are eligible for an additional contribution amount over and above that calculated under IRC Section 223(b)(1) and IRC Section 223(b)(2). The additional contribution amount is $1,000 for 2009 and later years.[5] In 2020, this would allow individuals age fifty-five and older a total contribution of up to $4,550; the total contribution for a family would be $8,100.

An individual who becomes an eligible individual after the beginning of a taxable year and who is an eligible individual for the last month of the taxable year shall be treated as being an eligible individual for the entire taxable year. For example, a calendar-year taxpayer with self-only coverage under an HDHP who became an eligible individual for December 2020 would be able to contribute the full $3,550 to an HSA in that taxable year. If a taxpayer fails at any time during the following taxable year to be an eligible individual, the taxpayer must include in his or her gross income the aggregate amount of all HSA contributions made by the taxpayer that could not have been made under the general rule (Q 384). The amount includable in gross income also is subject to a 10 percent penalty tax.

1. IRC Secs. 223(a), 223(b)(2); Rev. Proc. 2010-22, 2010-1 CB 747; Rev. Proc. 2009-29, 2009-1 CB 1050, Rev. Proc. 2015-53, Rev. Proc. 2016-28, Rev. Proc. 2017-37, Rev. Proc. 2018-30, Rev. Proc. 2019-25.
2. IRC Sec. 223(b)(2), prior to amendment by TRHCA 2006.
3. IRC Sec. 223(b)(1).
4. IRC Sec. 223(b); Notice 2004-2, 2004-1 CB 269, A-12.
5. IRC Sec. 223(b)(3).

For married individuals, if either spouse has family coverage, then both spouses are treated as having family coverage and the deduction limit is divided equally between them, unless they agree on a different division (note that this now applies to same sex couples equally, see Q 405). If both spouses have family coverage under different plans, both spouses are treated as having only the family coverage with the lowest deductible.[1]

Planning Point: Even though the tax code refers to "family" HDHP coverage and provides for a "family" HSA contribution limit, all HSAs are individual accounts.[2] The lack of a family HSA generally does not hurt HSA account owners as most desired goals can be accomplished through individual HSAs. The HSA can still be used for qualified medical expenses of a spouse and dependents. The higher family HSA contribution limit applies to an eligible individual covered under a family HDHP plan. A spouse or child can be named as an authorized signer on the HSA allowing for the family to have direct access to the HSA through checks or debit cards issued in the family member's name.

The lack of a family HSA, however, can complicate making HSA contributions. A common example of this is the catch-up contribution for individuals over age fifty-five. A married couple with each spouse over the age fifty-five will have to open two HSAs to maximize their overall HSA contribution because the catch up contribution must be contributed to each respective spouse's individual HSA. Another implication is for employer contributions and pre-tax payroll deferral through an employer. All pre-tax employer contributions must be made into the HSA of the employee and cannot be contributed to an HSA of the employee's spouse. Opening two HSAs, one in the name of each spouse, is generally the answer to complications arising from the individual nature of HSAs. This approach works well but is counterintuitive to many taxpayers hearing about "family" HSAs and frustrating given a general desire by many to keep the number of financial accounts to a minimum, especially when there are fees associated with the account.

An HSA may be offered in conjunction with a cafeteria plan (Q 3501). Both a high deductible health plan and an HSA are qualified benefits under a cafeteria plan.[3]

Employer contributions to an HSA are treated as employer-provided coverage for medical expenses to the extent that contributions do not exceed the applicable amount of allowable HSA contributions.[4]

An employee will not be required to include any amount in income simply because he or she may choose between employer contributions to an HSA and employer contributions to another health plan.[5]

An employer generally can deduct amounts paid to accident and health plans for employees as a business expense (Q 330).

An individual may not deduct any amount paid into his or her HSA; that amount is excludable from gross income under IRC Section 106(d).[6]

1. IRC Sec. 223(b)(5).
2. IRC Sec. 223 (d)(3).
3. IRC Sec. 125(d)(2)(D).
4. IRC Sec. 106(d)(1).
5. IRC Secs. 106(b)(2), 106(d)(2).
6. See IRC Sec. 223(b)(4).

No deduction is allowed for any amount contributed to an HSA with respect to any individual for whom another taxpayer may take a deduction under IRC Section 151 for the taxable year.[1]

396. What is the HSA establishment date?

HSA account owners set an establishment date for their HSAs and can use the HSA to pay for all qualified medical expenses incurred after that date.[2]

The establishment date is set the first time a taxpayer opens an HSA. The definition of "established" depends on state law, so the exact date an HSA is established depends on an HSA account owner's state trust law.[3] A common requirement under state law for a trust is that an executed trust agreement exists and potentially that the trust is funded. HSA rules require that HSA custodians use a formal document for HSA establishment; the IRS Forms 5305-C, 5305-B or an IRS approved prototype. The signing of that document would generally be a requirement for establishment.[4] The establishment date is not the date when the HSA account owner was eligible to open the HSA or when coverage under an HDHP begins.

If an HSA account owner opens another HSA, the new HSA is deemed established the same day the first HSA was established so long as the earlier HSA had a positive balance at any point during the eighteen-month period ending on the date of the opening of the new HSA.[5] For transfers and rollover of HSA funds, the establishment date stays the same as the date the original HSA was established.[6]

Planning Point: Upon a first reading, the establishment date rule appears to be simple and follows a common sense approach. Accordingly, many account owners and even professionals do not give the date much thought. Understanding the establishment date rules; however, can help HSA owners maximize HSA benefits.

The rule allows HSA owners with a normal amount of medical expenses to maximize HSA tax benefits by paying for most, if not all, qualified medical expenses tax-free through their HSA, even in years when the HSA account owners' medical expenses exceed the HSA limits or in years when the account owner is not currently eligible to contribute to an HSA. The rule also allows an account owner to maximize tax-deferred earnings by delaying reimbursement of medical expenses from the HSA. The key is that the rule simply requires that the HSA be established in order to use it for qualified medical expenses. The rule does not refer to the amount of money available in the HSA.

For individuals that anticipate good health and prefer not to contribute to an HSA, the establishment date rule allows the individual to establish the HSA with a nominal dollar amount. Establishing the HSA before a medical expense is incurred provides the individual the flexibility to fund the HSA periodically only after a medical expense is incurred and the amount known. If the expense is larger than the current year's HSA contribution limit allows, the individual can pay the expense with non-HSA funds that are not tax-favored (e.g. a FSA or HRA could not be used)

1. IRC Sec. 223(b)(6).
2. IRS Notice 2004-2, A26.
3. IRS Notice 2008-59, A38.
4. IRC Sec. 223 (d)(1)(B); Instructions to IRS Form 5305-C.
5. IRS Notice 2008-59, A41.
6. IRS Notice 2008-59, A40.

and then wait for future year contributions to reimburse from the HSA. This of course assumes the individual remains HSA eligible.

An individual losing eligibility who wants to maximize tax planning should keep the HSA open with a small balance to maintain the establishment date. This would allow the individual to save medical receipts during the period of ineligibility and potentially use future HSA contributions to reimburse for those qualified medical expenses after the individual regains HSA eligibility and begins making contributions again. The ability to pay for current year expenses with future year HSA contributions provides an opportunity for individuals losing their HSA eligibility before a large reserve has accumulated.

Some individuals use this rule to maximize tax deferral by fully funding the HSA each year and then not using the HSA for qualified medical expenses. This approach allows the full HSA to grow tax-deferred. Assuming the taxpayer is actually incurring medical expenses, the taxpayer can save those receipts and essentially build a fund within the HSA that is available for immediate tax-free distribution at any time. HSA rules allow for the reimbursement of qualified medical expenses incurred after the establishment date at any point in the future.

397. Must an employer offering Health Savings Accounts (HSAs) to its employees contribute the same amount for each employee?

An employer offering HSAs to its employees must make comparable contributions to the HSAs for all comparable participating employees for each coverage period during the calendar year.[1] IRC Section 4980G incorporates the comparability rules of IRC Section 4980E by reference.[2]

Comparable contributions are contributions that either are the same amount or the same percentage of the annual deductible limit under a high deductible health plan (HDHP).[3]

Comparable participating employees are all employees who are in the same category of employee and have the same category of coverage.

Category of employee refers to full-time employees, part-time employees, and former employees.[4]

Category of coverage refers to self-only and family-type coverage. Family coverage may be subcategorized as self plus one, self plus two, and self plus three or more. Subcategories of family coverage may be tested separately, but under no circumstances may an employer contribute less to a category of family coverage with more covered persons.[5]

For years beginning after 2006, highly compensated employees are not treated as comparable participating employees to non-highly compensated employees.[6]

1. IRC Secs. 4980E, 4980G.
2. Treas. Reg. §54.4980G-1, A-1.
3. IRC Sec. 4980E(d)(2); Treas. Reg. §54.4980G-4, A-1.
4. Treas. Reg. §54.4980G-3, A-5.
5. IRC Sec. 4980E(d)(3); Treas. Reg. §§54.4980G-1, A-2, 54.4980G-4, A-1.
6. IRC Sec. 4980G(d), as added by TRHCA 2006.

Planning Point: Employers often want to categorize employees in arrangements other than discussed above and not allowed by the law. Employers may desire to use existing organizational structure and separate employees that work in different locations, different divisions, or have different job descriptions. Employers may desire to reward tenure by categorizing employees based on length of service. Generous employers may want to make the additional $1,000 catch-up contribution for employees over the age fifty-five. Advising employers on this issue is simplified by the IRS's regulation that states its list is the exclusive list of allowed categories.[1] None of the categories suggested above are permitted categories.

Although not technically categories of employees under the IRS regulations, there are a number of other exceptions that may prove helpful for employers. Employees that are members of a union are not considered comparable employees provided that health benefits were the subject of good faith bargaining between the union and the employer.[2] Employees that are not eligible for an HSA are not comparable employees.[3] Employers can limit comparable HSA contributions to employees that receive their HDHP coverage through the employer.[4] Employers may also elect to make the HSA contribution to employees that are HSA eligible, but obtained HDHP coverage outside of the employer, provided the employer treats similar employees comparably. HSA contributions to sole proprietors, more than 2 percent owners of an S corporation and partners in a partnership are generally not treated as comparable HSA contributions.

Employer contributions made to HSAs through a cafeteria plan, including matching contributions, are not subject to comparability rules but are subject to IRC Section 125 nondiscrimination rules (Q 3504).[5]

An employer may make contributions to the HSAs of all eligible employees at the beginning of a calendar year; it may contribute monthly on a pay-as-you-go basis; or it may contribute at the end of a calendar year, taking into account each month that an employee was a comparable participating employee. An employer must use the same contribution method for all comparable participating employees.[6]

If an employer does not prefund HSA contributions, regulations provide that it may accelerate all or part of its contributions for an entire year to HSAs of employees who incur, during the calendar year, qualified medical expenses exceeding the employer's cumulative HSA contributions to date. If an employer permits accelerated contributions, the accelerated contributions must be available on a uniform basis to all eligible employees under reasonable requirements.[7]

To deal with employees who may not have established an HSA at the time an employer makes contributions, regulations require employers to provide to each eligible employee by January 15 a written notice that if the employee, by the last day of February, both establishes an HSA and notifies the employer that he or she has done so, the employee will receive a comparable contribution to the HSA for the prior calendar year. The written notice may be delivered electronically. For each eligible employee that notifies an employer that he or she

1. Treas. Reg. §54.4980G-3, A6
2. Treas. Reg. §54.4980G-4, A1
3. Treas. Reg. §54.4980G-3, A7.
4. Notice 2004-50, A84; Notice 2005-8.
5. Notice 2004-50, 2004-2 CB 196, A-47; IRC Sec. 125 (b), (c), and (g); Treas. Reg. §1.125-1, A-19.
6. IRC Sec. 4980E(d)(3); Treas. Reg. §§54.4980G-4, A-4.
7. IRC Sec. 4980E(d)(3); Treas. Reg. §§54.4980G-4, A-15.

has established an HSA, the employer must, by April 15, make comparable contributions, taking into account each month that an employee was a comparable participating employee, plus reasonable interest.[1]

There is a maximum contribution permitted for all employees who are eligible individuals during the last month of the taxable year. An employer may contribute up to the maximum annual contribution amount for the calendar year based on the employees' HDHP coverage to HSAs of all employees who are eligible individuals on the first day of the last month of the employees' taxable year, including employees who worked for the employer for less than the entire calendar year and employees who became eligible individuals after January 1 of the calendar year. For example, contributions may be made on behalf of an eligible individual who is hired after January 1 or an employee who becomes an eligible individual after January 1.[2]

Employers are not required to provide more than a pro rata contribution based on the number of months that an individual was an eligible individual and employed by the employer during the year. If an employer contributes more than a pro rata amount for a calendar year to an HSA of any eligible individual who is hired after January 1 of the calendar year, or any employee who becomes an eligible individual any time after January 1 of the calendar year, the employer must contribute that same amount on an equal and uniform basis to HSAs of all comparable participating employees who are hired or become eligible individuals after January 1 of the calendar year.[3]

Likewise, if an employer contributes the maximum annual contribution amount for the calendar year to an HSA of any eligible individual who is hired after January 1 of the calendar year or any employee who becomes an eligible individual any time after January 1 of the calendar year, the employer also must contribute the maximum annual contribution amount on an equal and uniform basis to HSAs of all comparable participating employees who are hired or become eligible individuals after January 1 of the calendar year.[4]

An employer who makes the maximum calendar year contribution or more than a pro rata contribution to HSAs of employees who become eligible individuals after the first day of the calendar year, or to eligible individuals who are hired after the first day of the calendar year, will not fail to satisfy comparability merely because some employees will have received more contributions on a monthly basis than employees who worked the entire calendar year.[5]

398. Are there any exceptions to the general rule that an employer offering Health Savings Accounts (HSAs) to its employees must make comparable contributions for all comparable participating employees?

The IRC provides an exception to comparability rules (Q 397) that allows, but that does not require, employers to make larger contributions to HSAs of non-highly compensated

1. IRC Sec. 4980E(d)(3); Treas. Reg. §§54.4980G-4, A-14.
2. Treas. Reg. §54.4980G-4.
3. Treas. Reg. §54.4980G-4.
4. Treas. Reg. §54.4980G-4.
5. Treas. Reg. §54.4980G-4.

employees than to HSAs of highly compensated employees.[1] Regulations provide that employers may make larger HSA contributions for non-highly compensated employees who are comparable participating employees than for highly compensated employees who are comparable participating employees.[2] Employer contributions to HSAs for highly compensated employees who are comparable participating employees may not be larger than employer HSA contributions for non-highly compensated employees who are comparable participating employees.[3] Comparability rules continue to apply with respect to contributions to HSAs of all non-highly compensated employees and all highly compensated employees. Thus, employers must make comparable contributions for a calendar year to the HSA of each non-highly compensated comparable participating employee and each highly compensated comparable participating employee.[4]

399. Do the comparability rules that apply to employer-provided health savings accounts (HSAs) apply to qualified HSA distributions (rollovers)?

An employer who offers a rollover, namely, a qualified HSA distribution (Q 411), from a health reimbursement arrangement (Q 349) or a health flexible spending arrangement (Q 3519) for any employee must offer a rollover to any eligible individual covered under an HDHP of the employer. Otherwise, the comparability requirements of IRC Section 4980G do not apply to qualified HSA distributions.[5]

There are special comparability rules for qualified HSA distributions contributed to HSAs on or after December 20, 2006, and before January 1, 2012. Effective January 1, 2010, the comparability rules of IRC Section 4980G do not apply to amounts contributed to employee HSAs through qualified HSA distributions. To satisfy comparability rules, if an employer offers qualified HSA distributions to any employee who is an eligible individual covered under any HDHP, the employer must offer qualified HSA distributions to all employees who are eligible individuals covered under any HDHP. If an employer offers qualified HSA distributions only to employees who are eligible individuals covered under an employer's HDHP, the employer is not required to offer qualified HSA distributions to employees who are eligible individuals but are not covered under the employer's HDHP.[6]

400. What are the consequences if an employer does not meet the comparability requirements applicable to health savings accounts (HSAs)?

If an employer fails to meet comparability requirements applicable to HSAs (Q 397 to Q 399), a penalty tax is imposed, equal to 35 percent of the aggregate amount contributed by an employer to HSAs of employees for their taxable years ending with or within the calendar year.[7]

1. IRC Sec. 4980G(d); Preamble, TD 9457, 74 Fed. Reg. 45994, 45995 (9-8-2009); see Treas. Reg. §54.4980G-6.
2. Treas. Reg. §54.4980G-6, Q&A-1.
3. Treas. Reg. §54.4980G-6, Q&A-2.
4. Treas. Reg. §54.4980G-6, Q&A-1.
5. IRC Sec. 106(e)(5).
6. Treas. Reg. §54.4980G-7, Q&A-1.
7. IRC Secs. 4980E(a), 4980E(b), 4980G(b). For filing requirements for excise tax returns, see Treas. Reg. §§54.6011-2 (general requirement of return), 54.6061-1 (signing of return), 54.6071-1(c) (time for filing return), 54.6091-1 (place for filing return), and 54.6151-1 (time and place for paying tax shown on return).

401. What are the employee's responsibilities regarding HSAs?

The bulk of the compliance burden for meeting the HSA rules rests with the individual employee. The following are key employee responsibilities.

(1) *Substantiation.* The employee must substantiate that the distributions from the HSA were in fact used for qualified medical expenses by saving medical receipts in case of an IRS audit.[1] Placing this burden on the individual relieves the employer of the arduous task of reviewing receipts and issuing reimbursement checks or otherwise facing some potential liability for failure by an employee to use the money appropriately. Employers generally welcome this change even though employers lose some control. Employee substantiation simplifies the process of paying or reimbursing for medical expenses, allows for more employee privacy, and gives employees the opportunity to be more aggressive in interpreting the definition of qualified medical expenses.

(2) *Eligibility.* Although an employer and a custodian can help educate employees on the requirements to be eligible for an HSA and the employer should verify that the employee is covered by an HDHP, the ultimate responsibility to determine eligibility rests with the employee.[2] An employee's participation in a spouse's health insurance plan or general purpose flexible spending account (FSA) could jeopardize the employee's HSA eligibility, as could participation in a government health care system such as the Veterans Administration's plan or Medicare. (See Q 391.)

(3) *Maximum Contribution Limit.* The employee is primarily responsible for ensuring that the amount contributed to the HSA is within federal guidelines.[3] Employers and custodians share some of the responsibility, as employers cannot deduct more than the maximum HSA contribution limit for an employee (the employer can assume eligibility based on HDHP coverage) and custodians cannot accept more than the family HSA limit plus one catch-up contribution ($7,900 in 2018, $8,000 in 2019 and $8,100 in 2020). An employee that exceeds the limit may cause additional administrative work for the employer, the custodian and the individual. It is in everyone's best interest to educate the employee on the limits.

(4) *Management of HSA.* Employees manage the balance in the HSA, select investments, choose beneficiaries, update contact information, pay for medical expenses and perform other maintenance issues generally without employer involvement.

(5) *Tax Reporting/Payments.* Employees are required to file an attachment (IRS Form 8889) to their income tax return each year they make a contribution or take a distribution.[4] This includes employees who receive an employer-made contribution. This form is used by the IRS to ensure that the individual does

1. Notice 2004-2, A30.
2. Notice 2004-50, A81.
3. Notice 2004-50, A81.
4. IRS Instructions to Form 8889.

not take a larger than permitted deduction and also ensures that the individual pays any taxes and penalties owed for non-eligible distributions. The employer provides a W-2 to the employee documenting pre-tax HSA contributions.

(6) *Termination of Employment*. Another positive feature of HSAs for both employers and employees is that the HSA remains open and viable after the employee's separation from service (some situations may require the account owner to transfer the HSA to a new custodian). Other than discontinuing any employer contributions into the HSA, the employer generally does not need to take any action regarding the separating employee's HSA. The employee is responsible for maintaining or closing the HSA after separation from service.

402. What are the employer responsibilities regarding employee HSAs?

If an employer offers pre-tax employer contributions, then the employer has the following responsibilities:

(1) *Make Comparable Contributions.* If the employer is making a pre-tax employer contribution (non-payroll deferral), it must do so on a comparable basis.[1] (See Q 397.)

(2) *Maintain Section 125 Plan for Payroll Deferral.* If the employer allows pre-tax payroll deferral, then the employer must adopt and maintain a Section 125 plan that provides for HSA deferrals.[2] This includes collecting employee deferral elections, sending the deferred amount directly to the HSA custodian, and accounting for the money for tax-reporting purposes.

(3) *HSA Eligibility and Contribution Limits.* Employers should work with employees to determine eligibility for an HSA and the employee's HSA contribution limit. Although it is legally the employee's responsibility to determine eligibility beyond HDHP coverage and contribution limit, a mistake in HSA contribution limits generally involves work by both the employer and the employee to correct. Mistakes are best avoided by upfront communication. Also, the employer does have some responsibility not to exceed the known federal limits. An employer may not know if a particular employee is ineligible for an HSA due to other health coverage, but an employer is expected to know the current HSA limits for the year and not exceed those limits.[3]

(4) *Tax Reporting.* The employer needs to properly complete employees' W-2 forms[4] and its own tax-filing regarding HSAs. HSA employer contributions are generally deductible.[5]

1. Treas. Reg. §54.4980G-1.
2. IRC Sec. 125.
3. Notice 2004-50, A82.
4. Notice 2004-2, A34 (W-2 reporting only).
5. IRC Sec. 106.

(5) *Business Owner Rules.* Business owners (sole proprietors, partners in a partnership or LLC, and more than 2 percent owners of an S corporation) are generally not treated as employees and employers need to review HSA contributions for business owners for proper tax reporting.

(6) *Detailed Rules.* There are various detailed rules that fall within the responsibility of the employer that are too numerous to list here but include items such as: (1) holding employer contributions for an employee that fails to open an HSA,[1] (2) not being able to "recoup" money mistakenly contributed to an employee's HSA,[2] (3) actually making employer HSA contributions into employees' HSAs on a timely basis, (4) educating employees on HSAs (not legally required but necessary for a successful program), and (5) other detailed rules.

403. What is the tax consequence to individuals when excess contributions are made to a Health Savings Account (HSA)?

If an HSA receives excess contributions for a taxable year, distributions from the HSA are not includable in income to the extent that the distributions do not exceed the aggregate excess contributions to all HSAs of an individual for a taxable year if (1) the distribution is received by the individual on or before the last day for filing the individual's income tax return for the year, including extensions; and (2) the distribution is accompanied by the amount of net income attributable to the excess contribution. Any net income must be included in an individual's gross income for the taxable year in which it is received.[3]

Excess contributions to an HSA are subject to a 6 percent tax. The tax may not exceed 6 percent of the value of the account, determined at the close of the taxable year.[4]

Excess contributions are defined, for this purpose, as the sum of (1) the aggregate amount contributed for the taxable year to the accounts, excluding rollover contributions, which is neither excludable from gross income under IRC Section 106(b) nor allowable as a deduction under IRC Section 223, and (2) this amount for the preceding taxable year reduced by the sum of (x) the distributions from the accounts that were included in gross income under IRC Section 223(f)(2), and (y) the excess of the maximum amount allowable as a deduction under IRC Section 223(b)(1), for the taxable year, over the amount contributed for the taxable year.[5]

For these purposes, any excess contributions distributed from an HSA are treated as amounts not contributed.[6]

1. Treas. Reg. §54.4980G-4, A7.
2. Notice 2004-50, A82.
3. IRC Sec. 223(f)(3)(A), Notice 2004-50, 2004-2 CB 196
4. IRC Sec. 4973(a).
5. IRC Sec. 4973(g).
6. IRC Sec. 4973(g).

404. What is the "testing period" for HSAs?

An HSA testing period is a rule that requires HSA account owners in some circumstances to maintain their HSA eligibility for a period of time after making an HSA contribution.[1] Congress created the testing period rules when it passed the Health Opportunity and Patient Empowerment Act of 2006, a law allowing HSA account owners to fully fund an HSA up to the IRS limits for a year even if they were not HSA eligible for the full year (this is commonly referred to as the "full contribution rule" or the "last month rule").[2] The full contribution rule only applies to individuals eligible on the first day of the last month of the tax year (December 1 for calendar year taxpayers). The full contribution rule partially replaced the sum-of-the-months rule that limited HSA contributions to a pro-rata amount of the IRS maximum based on the number of months a person was eligible for an HSA (see Q 395). The testing period serves to plug a potential loophole that would have allowed individuals to make a full HSA contribution and then switch to traditional health insurance (i.e. allow individuals to benefit from the HSA tax deduction without being exposed to the high deductible required under an HDHP).

The testing period rules apply in two circumstances:[3]

(1) HSA account owners that were HSA eligible on the first day of the last month of their tax year must meet a testing period (December 1 for calendar year taxpayers). This includes people that just started their HSA eligibility on the first day of the last month (December 1) as well as someone that started eligibility during the tax year and remained eligible on the first day of the last month. It does not include someone who was eligible for part of the year not including the first day of the last month of their tax year (i.e. an individual that lost HSA eligibility before the last month of the individual's tax year).

(2) An HSA account owner using a tax-free distribution from an IRA to fund an HSA must meet a testing period.

In other words, any calendar-year taxpayer who makes a regular HSA contribution and remains eligible on December 1 is subject to a testing period. Or, anyone who completes an HSA qualified funding distribution from an IRA is also subject to the testing period rules. This means that most participants in an HSA, those who make contributions every year and remain eligible year after year, are subject to the testing period rules. However, the impact of the rule only applies to individuals that start eligibility after the beginning of the tax year and remain eligible on the first day of the last month of the tax year or move money from an IRA to an HSA in an HSA qualified funding distribution. Individuals who are eligible every month of a year will not face any additional taxes or penalties based on a failed test period for that year. Individuals that are eligible during the year but lose eligibility prior to the first day of the last month of the tax year are not subject to the testing period rule because they are not granted the benefit of the full contribution rule.

1. IRC Sec. 223(b)(8).
2. Health Opportunity Patient Empowerment Act of 2006 included in the TRHCA 2006.
3. Notice 2008-52.

The testing period for regular HSA contributions runs from the first day of the last month of the tax year (December 1 for calendar year taxpayers) until the last day of the twelve month period following that month (December 31 of the following year for calendar year taxpayers). For HSA qualified funding distributions from an IRA, the testing period runs from the month of the rollover until the last day of the twelfth month following that month (i.e. thirteen months counting the month of the rollover). The individual must remain eligible for an HSA during the testing period or fail the testing period. If an individual faces both testing periods, the two tests are run separately.

The individual is responsible to understand the testing period rules, track the testing period and report any failures of the testing period. Neither the HSA custodian nor an employer bears any responsibility for tracking the testing period.

Individuals that fail to meet the testing period must calculate the amount of an HSA contribution they could have made under the sum-of-the-months rule and then compare that amount to their actual contribution for the year being tested. If their actual contribution is larger, the HSA account owner will owe taxes and penalties on the difference. If their actual contribution is the same or less than the sum-of-the-months rule, then no tax or penalty is owed. The sum-of-the-months calculation determines the amount that a taxpayer would have been allowed to contribute under the pre-2007 law and a failed testing period essentially results in a taxpayer having to return to that potentially lower contribution amount.

Accordingly, HSA account owners that fail the testing period first need to calculate their sum-of-the months' amount. The IRS provides a sample calculation in its HSA Publication 969.[1]

The penalty is 10 percent of the amount of excess contribution (the difference between the amount contributed and the sum-of-the-months calculated amount). Plus, the HSA account owner owes federal and possible state income taxes on that amount. An exception exists if the failure to remain HSA eligible while under a testing period for the HSA results from death or disability. This exception applies to both the full contribution year testing and to IRA to HSA funding testing periods.[2]

HSA account owners pay the tax and penalty on IRS Form 8889, Part III. This form is a required attachment to the IRS Form 1040 series for HSA account owners in any year an HSA account owner makes a contribution or takes a distribution, so most HSA account owners are filing this form anyway and will simply need to complete the additional section.

Planning Point: Failing a testing period is not treated in the same manner as an excess contribution (see Q 403). The two issues share a common origin, because, in either case, an account owner contributed too much money to an HSA. Accordingly, some individuals mistakenly correct failed testing periods using the excess contribution rules. This is incorrect and creates more taxes and penalties.

1. IRS Pub 969.
2. IRC Sec. 223(b)(8)(B)(ii).

An excess contribution results from contributing more than the HSA limits allow. An excess contribution is corrected by removing the excess. A failed testing period results from an individual subject to the testing period not remaining HSA eligible for the testing period. A failed testing period is corrected by paying taxes and penalties on the calculated amount (the amount contributed under the full contribution less the amount calculated under the sum-of-the-months rule). This tax is paid directly by the individual on IRS Form 8889. The actual dollars are not removed from the HSA. This is counterintuitive for most people. The IRS has trained the industry over the years that if someone puts too much money into an HSA or IRA, they need to take it out. Excesses are removed. Despite this, in this case, the calculated overage amount remains in the HSA for a failed testing period.

An HSA account owner that treats a failed testing period as an excess contribution will owe taxes and penalties twice.[1] Once for failing the testing period (taxes plus a 10 percent penalty) and a second time for a non-qualified HSA distribution (subject to taxes plus a 20 percent penalty). An HSA account owner that is disabled or deceased is granted an exception for a failed testing period. Disability, death and attainment of the age sixty-five are exceptions to the 20 percent distribution from the HSA.

405. What is the result if a same sex couple contributed amounts to a Health Savings Account (HSA) that exceed the applicable contribution limit for married couples?

A same sex couple legally married under the law of any state is now subject to the same HSA contribution limits as an opposite gender couple (see Q 395). As a result, the IRS has issued guidance providing a remedy for situations in which both members of a same sex couple contributed funds to an HSA prior to the recognition of their marriage that, when combined, exceed the applicable limit for a married couple. The couple may choose to reduce one or both members' contribution to the HSAs in order to avoid exceeding the contribution limit. In the alternative, if their contributions have already exceeded the threshold, the excess may be distributed to the spouses prior to the due date for filing their tax return. Any remaining excess contributions will be subject to the penalty tax typically imposed under IRC Section 4973. These rules apply for the 2013 tax year and beyond.[2]

406. How are HSAs treated in the case of same-sex couples?

Two recent Supreme Court cases now provide same-sex married couples the same treatment as opposite sex married couples for HSAs.

In 2013, the Supreme Court ruled the Defense of Marriage Act (DOMA) as unconstitutional.[3] This ruling allowed same-sex couples to meet the definition of "spouse" for the purpose of HSA law (DOMA defined "spouses" as one man and one woman). Spouses are granted some special rights under HSA law, as discussed below.

1. Notice 2008-52, Ex-9; Notice 2004-50, A-35.
2. Notice 2014-1, 2014-2 IRB 270.
3. *United States v. Windsor*, 570 U.S. 744 (2013), Docket No. 12-307, 133 S.Ct. 2675 (2013); see also Rev. Rul. 2013-17.

In 2015, the Supreme Court ruled that all states were required to allow same-sex marriage.[1] Same-sex couples must be legally married under state law to gain the benefits of "spouse" status under HSA law. The IRS states that for federal tax purposes the term "spouse" does not include "registered domestic partnerships, civil unions, or other similar formal relationships recognized under state law that are not denominated as a marriage under that state's law…"[2] This is true for same-sex and opposite sex relationships. "Spouse" is the key word with respect to HSA laws, but "marriage" is generally the state classification that results in couples becoming "spouses".

Planning Point: One likely result of the Supreme Court's ruling is that employers will drop health insurance benefits for domestic partners now that same-sex marriage is allowed. This change would make legal marriage financially important to same-sex domestic partners.

Whether or not marriage is financially preferable over domestic partner status from an HSA perspective depends on the situation. Most of the special HSA rules for spouses are favorable, making marriage the better financial decision. However, domestic partners enjoy a significant HSA loophole allowing each partner to contribute the family HSA limit. This could result in the couple getting a combined tax deduction of $14,200 for 2020 ($7,100 family limit × 2) plus, potentially, catch-up contributions.

Spouses (but not domestic partners) are subject to a couple of special rules in this regard: (1) if either spouse has family HDHP coverage both spouses are deemed to have family HDHP coverage and (2) combined, the spouses cannot exceed the family HDHP limit. Same-sex couples avoided that cap when they were not considered spouses. Whether the loophole is still available to same-sex couples depends on whether or not the couple is legally married under state law.

HSA law provides special treatment for spouses in the following areas:

- **Tax-Free Distributions.** An HSA owner can use his or her HSA tax-free to pay the qualified medical expenses of spouses. This benefit does not extend to domestic partners (in limited circumstances a domestic partner could be a tax dependent and an HSA owner can use an HSA for a tax dependent).

- **Beneficiary Treatment.** A spouse beneficiary can treat the HSA as his or her own upon the death of the HSA owner. Non-spouse beneficiaries must take a full distribution of the money remaining in the HSA.

- **Divorce Transfer.** An HSA owner can transfer assets into an HSA of former spouse in the case of a divorce.

- **Estate Tax Treatment.** If a spouse is named as the beneficiary of the HSA, the treatment of the HSA may change for estate tax purposes.

- **Family HDHP Treatment.** Spouses covered under a family HDHP are capped at the combined HSA family limit. Also, if one spouse has a family HDHP, then both spouses are deemed to have family HDHPs. This rule closes a loophole that allowed

1. *Obergefell v. Hodges*, 575 U.S. ____ (2015), 135 S. Ct. 2584, Docket No. 14-556; argued April 28, 2015; decided June 26, 2015.
2. Rev. Rul. 2013-17.

each partner in a same-sex couple to contribute the family HSA maximum in certain circumstances.

- **Child of Former Spouse.** An HSA owner can use the HSA to pay for medical expenses of his or her child that is claimed as a tax dependent by a former spouse (this is helpful in cases of divorce and legal separation).

407. What are the advantages to an employer of offering an HDHP and HSA combination?

The benefits of offering employees an HDHP and HSA vary dramatically depending upon the circumstances. A key strength of offering an HSA program is flexibility. Employers can be very generous and fully fund an HSA and also pay for the HDHP coverage. Alternatively, employers can also use the flexibility of the HSA to allow for the employer to reduce its involvement in benefits and put more responsibility onto the employee. Generally, employers switch to HDHPs and HSAs to save money on the health insurance premiums (or to reduce the rate of increase) and to embrace the concept of consumer driven healthcare. The list below elaborates on strengths of HDHPs and HSAs.

(1) *Lower Premiums.* HDHPs, with their high deductibles, are usually less expensive than traditional insurance.

(2) *Consumer Driven Healthcare.* Many employers believe in the concept of consumer driven healthcare. If an employer makes employees responsible for the relatively high deductible, the employees may be more careful and inquisitive into their health care purchases. Combining this with an HSA where employees can keep unused money increases employees' desire to use health care dollars as if they were their own money – because it is their own money.

(3) *Lower Administration Burden.* Given the individual account nature of HSAs, much of the administrative burden for HSAs is switched from the employer (or paid third-party administrator) to the employee and the HSA custodian as compared to health FSAs and HRAs. This increased burden on the employee comes with significant perks for the employee: more control over how and when the money is spent, increased privacy, and better ability to add money to the HSA outside of the employer.

(4) *Flexibility.* HSA and HDHP programs allow employers to adjust the program to their needs by varying the level of employer commitment to insurance premium and HSA contributions for employees. HSAs allow for employees to contribute on their own.

(5) *Tax Deductibility at Employee Level.* The ability of employees to make their own HSA contributions directly and still get a tax deduction is advantageous. Although it is better for employees to contribute through an employer to save payroll taxes, an employee can make contributions directly. An employer may not offer pre-tax

payroll deferral or it may be too late for an employee to defer. For example, an employee that decides to maximize his prior year HSA contribution in April as he is filing his taxes can still do so by making an HSA contribution directly with the HSA custodian.

(6) *HSA Eligibility.* Becoming eligible for an HSA is a benefit that also stands on its own. Although not all employees will embrace HSAs, savvy employees that understand the benefits of HSAs will value a program that enables them to have an HSA.

408. How are funds accumulated in a Health Savings Account (HSA) taxed prior to distribution?

An HSA generally is exempt from income tax unless it ceases to be an HSA.[1]

In addition, rules similar to those applicable to individual retirement arrangements (IRAs) regarding the loss of the income tax exemption for an account where an employee engages in a prohibited transaction[2] and those regarding the effect of pledging an account as security[3] apply to HSAs. Any amounts treated as distributed under these rules will be treated as not used to pay qualified medical expenses (Q 3647).[4]

409. How are amounts distributed from a Health Savings Account (HSA) taxed?

A distribution from an HSA used exclusively to pay qualified medical expenses of an account holder is not includable in gross income.[5] Any distribution from an HSA that is not used exclusively to pay qualified medical expenses of an account holder must be included in the account holder's gross income.[6]

Any distribution that is includable in income because it was not used to pay qualified medical expenses is also subject to a penalty tax.[7] The penalty tax is 10 percent of includable income for a distribution from an HSA.[8] For distributions made after December 31, 2010, the additional tax on nonqualified distributions from HSAs is increased to 20 percent of includable income.[9]

Includable distributions received after an HSA holder becomes disabled within the meaning of IRC Section 72(m)(7), dies, or reaches the age of Medicare eligibility are not subject to the penalty tax.[10]

1. IRC Sec. 223(e)(1).
2. See IRC Sec. 408(e)(2).
3. See IRC Sec. 408(e)(4).
4. IRC Sec. 223(e)(2).
5. IRC Sec. 223(f)(1).
6. IRC Sec. 223(f)(2).
7. IRC Sec. 223(f)(4)(A).
8. IRC Sec. 223(f)(4)(A).
9. IRC Sec. 223(f)(4)(A), as amended by PPACA 2010, as further amended by HCERA 2010.
10. IRC Secs. 223(f)(4)(B), 223(f)(4)(C).

Qualified medical expenses are amounts paid by the account holder for medical care[1] for the individual, his or her spouse, and any dependent to the extent that expenses are not compensated by insurance or otherwise.[2] For tax years beginning after December 31, 2010, medicines constituting qualified medical expenses will be limited to doctor-prescribed drugs and insulin. Consequently, over-the counter medicines will no longer be qualified expenses unless prescribed by a doctor after 2010.[3] Interestingly, over-the counter non-drug medical expenses (bandages, contact lenses cleaner, blood pressure monitors, etc.) are still qualified without a prescription. (See Q 410.)

Planning Point: Perhaps the most common question asked of HSA professionals is whether or not a particular expense in a particular set of circumstances is qualified or not. Even though there is an abundance of interpretative material, the question is sometimes difficult to answer. The IRS definition below provides a helpful summary interpretation of the law.

"Medical expenses are the costs of diagnosis, cure, mitigation, treatment, or prevention of disease, and the costs for treatments affecting any part or function of the body. These expenses include payments for legal medical services rendered by physicians, surgeons, dentists, and other medical practitioners. They include the costs of equipment, supplies, and diagnostic devices needed for these purposes.

Medical care expenses must be primarily to alleviate or prevent a physical or mental defect or illness. They do not include expenses that are merely beneficial to general health, such as vitamins or a vacation."

This definition is helpful after you have exhausted the research for specific items where the IRS has already ruled, or in cases where items can have dual purposes (a massage given in a hospital to revive an atrophied muscle is different than a massage given on vacation for pleasure).

With a number of exceptions, the payment of insurance premiums is not a qualified medical expense. The exceptions include any expense for coverage under a health plan during a period of COBRA continuation coverage, a qualified long-term care insurance contract (Q 475),[4] a health plan paid for during a period in which the individual is receiving unemployment compensation,[5] or the payment of Medicare premiums (other than Medigap) after age sixty-five and, in some cases, the employee portion of employer provided health insurance premiums after age sixty-five.

An account holder may pay qualified long-term care insurance premiums with distributions from an HSA even if contributions to the HSA were made by salary reduction through an IRC Section 125 cafeteria plan. Amounts of qualified long-term care insurance premiums that constitute qualified medical expenses are limited to the age-based limits found in IRC Section 213(d)(10) as adjusted annually (Q 485).

1. As defined in IRC Sec. 213(d).
2. IRC Sec. 223(d)(2).
3. IRC Sec. 106(f), as added by PPACA 2010.
4. IRC Sec. 223(d)(2).
5. Notice 2004-50, 2004-2 CB 196, A-40

An HSA account holder may make tax-free distributions to reimburse qualified medical expenses from prior tax years as long as the expenses were incurred after the HSA was established. There is no time limit on when a distribution must occur.[1]

HSA trustees, custodians, and employers need not determine whether a distribution is used for qualified medical expenses. This responsibility falls on individual account holders.[2]

410. Can a parent use an HSA to pay for a child's medical expenses until the child reaches the age of twenty-six?

No. The law provides that a parent can use an HSA to pay for the qualified medical expenses of a tax dependent.[3] Dependents includes children, but generally not children over nineteen; or if still in school, over age twenty-four. If the HSA account owner cannot claim the child as a dependent, then the HSA account owner cannot use the HSA to pay for the child's medical expenses.

The Affordable Care Act's requirement that children can remain on the parents' health plan until age twenty-six has created an inconsistency for HSAs in this regard for some children. The child can remain covered by the parent's HDHP insurance, but the parent cannot use the related HSA to pay for the medical expenses of the child unless the child remains a tax dependent. The other side of this situation is that the child would very likely be eligible for an HSA and could make a contribution at the family contribution level (this assumes the child is not a dependent, is covered under the parent's family HDHP, and is otherwise eligible for an HSA).

A more logical approach to this issue may be to take away a non-dependent child's eligibility for an HSA, but allow the parent to use the parent's HSAs to fund the child's medical expenses until age twenty-six. The IRS essentially did this for FSAs and HRAs when it extended the ability of a parent to use FSA and HRA funds for a child who has not obtained age twenty-seven by the end of the taxable year. This guidance did not extend to HSAs.[4] Congress or the IRS may provide additional guidance on this issue in the future.

411. When may an account owner transfer or rollover funds into an HSA?

Funds may be transferred or rolled over from one HSA to another HSA or from an Archer MSA (Q 420) to an HSA provided that an account holder effects the transfer within sixty days of receiving the distribution.[5]

An HSA rollover may take place only once a year. The year is not a calendar year, but a rolling twelve month period beginning on the day when an account holder receives a distribution to be rolled over.[6]

1. Notice 2004-50, 2004-2 CB 196, A-39.
2. Notice 2004-2, 2004-1 CB 269, A-29, A-30.
3. IRC Sec. 223 (d)(2)(A).
4. Notice 2010-38.
5. IRC Secs. 220(f)(5)(A), 223(f)(5)(A).
6. IRC Secs. 220(f)(5)(B), 223(f)(5)(B).

Transfers of HSA amounts directly from one HSA trustee to another HSA trustee, known as a trustee-to-trustee transfer, are not subject to the limits under IRC Section 223(f)(5). There is no limit on the number of trustee-to-trustee transfers allowed during a year and there is no sixty day requirement.[1]

Beginning in 2007, a taxpayer may, once in his or her lifetime, make a qualified HSA funding distribution (Q 412). A qualified HSA funding distribution is a trustee-to-trustee transfer from an IRA to an HSA in an amount that does not exceed the annual HSA contribution limitation for the taxpayer (Q 395). If a taxpayer has self-only coverage under an HDHP at the time of the transfer, but at a later date during the same taxable year obtains family coverage under an HDHP, the taxpayer may make an additional qualified HSA funding distribution in an amount not exceeding the additional annual contribution for which the taxpayer has become eligible.[2]

If a taxpayer fails to be an eligible individual at any time during a taxable year following a qualified HSA funding distribution, the taxpayer must include in gross income the aggregate amount of all qualified HSA funding distributions (Q 404). The amount includable in gross income also is subject to a 10 percent penalty tax.[3]

Prior to January 31, 2012, a participant in a health reimbursement arrangement ("HRA") (Q 349) or a health flexible spending arrangement ("health FSA") (Q 3519) could make a qualified HSA distribution on a one time per arrangement basis. A qualified HSA distribution was a transfer directly from an employer to an HSA of an employee. The amount moved was limited to the lesser of the balance in the arrangement (FSA or HRA) on September 21, 2006, or the date of distribution. A qualified HSA distribution was treated as a rollover contribution under IRC Section 223(f)(5), which means that it did not count toward the annual HSA contribution limit.[4] An employee completing qualified HSA distribution was subject to a testing period (Q 404).

Prior to the sunset of this rule, the timing of qualified HSA distributions was critical for employees covered by general-purpose (non-high-deductible) health FSAs or HRAs. As such:[5]

(1) An employee could only make a qualified HSA distribution if he or she had been covered by an HDHP since the first day of the month;

(2) An employee had to rollover general purpose health FSA balances during the grace period after the end of the plan year, not during the plan year, and, of course, he or she must not have been covered by a general purpose health FSA during the new year; and

(3) An employee must have rolled the entire balance in an HRA or a health FSA to an HSA (or forfeited the balance). If a balance remains in an HRA at the end of a plan

1. Notice 2004-50, 2004-2 CB 196, A-56.
2. IRC Sec. 408(d)(9).
3. IRC Sec. 408(d)(9)(D).
4. IRC Sec. 106(e); Notice 2008-51, 2008-1 CB 1163.
5. Notice 2007-22, 2007-1 CB 670.

year or in a health FSA at the end of the grace period, the employee will not be an HSA-eligible individual.

412. What are the rules regarding moving money from an IRA to an HSA?

The law allows individuals a one-time movement of IRA assets to fund an HSA provided: (1) they are eligible for an HSA, (2) they have a permitted IRA with sufficient funds, and (3) they have not already completed an IRA to HSA funding distribution.[1] The amount moved may not exceed the amount of one year's HSA contribution limit. The technical term for this transaction is a "qualified HSA funding distribution," not "transfer," although the transaction is commonly referred to as a transfer.

Planning Point: The IRA funding option is important for HSA account holders with current or anticipated medical expenses and no source of funds for an HSA contribution other than an IRA. Taxpayers seeking to maximize contributions to tax deferred accounts are generally best served funding the HSA with new funds and preserving the IRA. Essentially, HSA account holders are trading one tax-favored account, the IRA, for another, the HSA. A person facing large medical expenses prior to having the time to build up an HSA balance is a candidate for funding an HSA with an IRA. This rule gives taxpayers a method to avoid paying taxes and penalties on an IRA distribution necessary to pay medical expenses.

Some taxpayers will move IRA money to an HSA sooner than needed for medical expenses because the HSA is arguably a better tax-favored account than a IRA and they prefer to have their limited assets in an HSA. The key HSA benefit not available to IRAs is that the HSA can be used to pay for qualified medical expenses tax-free. A key benefit of an IRA, over an HSA, is the ability to access money for any reason at age 59½ rather than the age sixty-five. HSAs also often provide less investment options and may charge higher fees.

Moving money from a Roth IRA or non-deductible traditional IRA makes the choice more complex and often less desirable. Roth IRA contributions can already be withdrawn tax and penalty free at any time. Both Roth IRAs and nondeductible traditional IRAs contain basis that could be lost in a move to the HSA.

A qualified HSA funding distribution relates to the taxable year in which the distribution is actually made.[2] This means that HSA account holders are not allowed to complete the transfers in the following year before their tax due date and have the contribution count for the previous tax year (regular HSA contributions can be made until the tax due date and are deemed to have been made on the last day of the preceding tax year for tax deductibility purposes).

HSA account owners are not allowed to deduct the amount moved from an IRA to an HSA. The distribution from the IRA is treated as a "qualified HSA funding distribution" and is not subject to taxes or penalty (if an early withdrawal). HSA account owners do not pay taxes on the IRA distribution and they do not get to claim that tax deduction for the subsequent HSA contribution.

The tax situation becomes more complicated if an individual moves money from a Roth IRA or a non-deductible traditional IRA with basis, see Q 599. The IRA to HSA rules allow the

1. IRC Sec 408(d)(9); Notice 2008-51.
2. Notice 2008-51.

entire basis to stay with the IRA where it can be recovered at the time of distribution from the IRA. No basis transfers to the HSA. This is very favorable treatment, albeit a bit complex to track. If an individual does not have enough non-basis money in an IRA and still chooses to move the money into the HSA, the individual will lose the basis in that amount moved into the HSA.[1]

An IRA to HSA qualified funding distribution is generally not a good option for an IRA account holder that is taking a series of substantially equal periodic payments from an IRA (a method to avoid the early withdrawal penalty from an IRA). A qualified HSA funding distribution from an IRA that modifies the series of substantially equal periodic payments will result in the recapture rules applying to the payments made in the series prior to the qualified HSA funding distribution.[2] This rule will prevent most taxpayers that are in engaged in a series of substantially equal periodic payments from moving those IRA funds to an HSA.

If an HSA account holder moves money from an IRA to an HSA, the HSA account holder will be subject to a testing period (Q 404).

Only certain types of IRAs are permitted for movement to an HSA: traditional IRAs (both deductible and non-deductible), Roth IRAs, SEP IRAs (if not part of an ongoing plan), and SIMPLE IRAs (if not part of an ongoing plan). SEP and SIMPLE IRAs are only permitted if they are not ongoing plans. Ongoing plans are plans that continue to receive employer contributions. A SEP or SIMPLE is considered to be ongoing if an employer contribution is made for the plan year ending with or within the IRA account holder's taxable year in which the qualified HSA funding distribution would be made. This provision essentially recognizes the fact that a non-active SEP or SIMPLE is a traditional IRA. The feature that distinguishes them as a SEP or a SIMPLE is the contributions coming into the accounts.

Planning Point: Taxpayers that inherit IRAs may engage in a HSA qualified funding distribution to fund an HSA.[3] This is a favorable approach for non-spouse beneficiaries given that the IRS also allows the distribution from the inherited IRA to count toward the required minimum distribution for the year. This provides an attractive avenue to avoid taxation and meet the required minimum distribution from an inherited IRA (up to the HSA limits for the year). A spouse beneficiary enjoys more flexibility as an IRA beneficiary and often treats the IRA as his or her own eliminating the need for this special rule for spouse beneficiaries.

413. Can an individual's interest in a Health Savings Account (HSA) be transferred as part of a divorce or separation?

Yes.

An individual's interest in an HSA may be transferred without income taxation from one spouse to another or from a spouse to a former spouse if the transfer is made under a divorce or separation instrument described in IRC Section 71(b)(2)(A). Following this kind of transfer, an interest in an HSA is treated as an interest of a transferee spouse.[4]

1. Notice 2008-51.
2. Notice 2008-51.
3. Notice 2008-51.
4. IRC Sec. 223(f)(7).

414. What happens when account owners mistakenly use an HSA for a non-qualified expense?

HSA account owners that mistakenly take distributions from their HSAs have an opportunity to fix the mistake through special rules for the return of mistaken distributions.[1] The HSA account owner has to make the mistake due to a reasonable cause and be able to support that with clear and convincing evidence. The HSA account owner should save the evidence along with other tax documents in case of an IRS audit. The HSA custodian will generally not request any evidence as the custodian can rely on the representation of the HSA account owner that the distribution was a reasonable mistake supported by evidence.

The HSA account owner must repay the mistaken distribution amount to the HSA prior to the tax filing due date for the year the HSA account owner knew or should have known of the mistake. Custodians generally provide a form for this purpose. Failure to notify the HSA custodian that the reason for the contribution is the return of mistaken distribution will result in incorrect IRS reporting. HSA custodians are not required to accept the return. In that case, the HSA account owner would have to pay taxes plus a 20 percent penalty on the amount of the mistaken distribution.

HSA account owners generally do not report the mistaken distribution on their income tax return and the HSA account owner correspondingly also does not report the return of the amount to the HSA. If the mistaken distribution is corrected in the same year as it is made, no reporting is necessary. The HSA custodian will not include the original mistaken distribution as a distribution on the 1099-SA or the return of the money as a contribution on the IRS form 5498-SA. If the custodian already filed the 1099-SA, the custodian will need to file a corrected 1099-SA.[2]

415. What happens to a Health Savings Account (HSA) on the death of an account holder? May a surviving spouse continue an account?

The disposition of an HSA at the death of an account holder depends on who is the designated beneficiary. If an account holder's surviving spouse is a designated beneficiary, then, when an account holder dies, the surviving spouse is treated as the account holder.[3]

If an account holder's estate is a designated beneficiary, the fair market value of the assets in the HSA must be included in such beneficiary's gross income for the estate's last taxable year. A deduction for any federal estate taxes paid is allowed to any person other than a decedent or a decedent's spouse under IRC Section 691(c) with respect to amounts included in gross income by that person.[4]

If anyone other than a surviving spouse or an account holder's estate is a designated beneficiary, the account ceases to be an HSA as of the date of the account holder's death and the

1. Notice 2004-50, A37.
2. IRS Instructions for Form 1099-SA and 5498-SA.
3. IRC Sec. 223(f)(8)(A).
4. IRC Sec. 223(f)(8)(B).

fair market value of the assets in the account must be included in the designated beneficiary's gross income for the year including the date of death. The amount that must be included in gross income by any person other than the estate is reduced by the amount of qualified medical expenses that were incurred by the decedent account holder before his or her death and paid by the designated beneficiary within one year after the date of death.[1]

416. Are amounts contributed to a Health Savings Account (HSA) subject to Social Security or federal unemployment taxes and federal income tax withholding?

The definition of wages for purposes of the federal unemployment tax (FUTA) does not include any payment made to or for the benefit of an employee if it is reasonable to believe that the employee will be able to exclude the payment from income under IRC Section 106(d), which deals with contributions to HSAs.[2]

Unfortunately, a similar change was not made to IRC Section 3121(a) with respect to FICA. The IRS has stated, however, that employer contributions to an HSA are not subject to withholding from wages for income tax or subject to the Federal Insurance Contributions Act (FICA), the Federal Unemployment Tax Act (FUTA), or the Railroad Retirement Tax Act.[3] A similar statement has been made by the Joint Committee on Taxation.[4]

417. Are employer contributions to a Health Savings Account (HSA) on behalf of an employee subject to withholding?

HSA contributions made for the benefit of an employee are not subject to income tax withholding.[5] Interestingly, withholding also does not occur at the time of distribution from an HSA. HSA custodians and trustees do not withhold for income tax or penalties for HSA distributions. The IRS Form 1099-SA does not provide a reporting box for federal or state withholding. The IRS is apparently operating under the assumption that HSA distributions will be used for eligible medical expenses and are therefore tax-free.

418. What tax reporting requirements apply to a Health Savings Account (HSA)?

Each year employers must report on the Form W-2 to each employee the amount contributed to an HSA for the employee or the employee's spouse. The report must be received by the employee by January 31 of the following year.[6]

1. IRC Sec. 223(f)(8)(B).
2. IRC Sec. 3306(b)(18).
3. Notice 2004-2, 2004-1 CB 269, A-19.
4. See General Explanation of Tax Legislation Enacted in the 104th Congress (JCT-12-96), n. 1642, p. 324.
5. IRC Sec. 3401(a)(22); Notice 2004-2, 2004-1 CB 269, A-19.
6. IRC Sec. 6051(a); Notice 2004-2, 2004-1 CB 269, A-34.

419. What IRS forms are necessary for HSA account owners to prepare and file income tax returns?

HSAs provide excellent tax benefits; the IRS, however, requires information reporting to make sure individuals follow the rules. The account owner's role in this process is to attach IRS Form 8889 to the income tax return for any year the account owner took a distribution or made a contribution to an HSA.[1] The following are the key forms for HSA account owners in preparation of an income tax return.

(1) *IRS Form 1040* (prior to 2018, when the Form 1040 was modified). There are different versions of the 1040 that work for HSAs, but line 25 of the 1040 is the line where an account owner takes a deduction for an individual HSA contribution (not employer pre-tax HSA contributions as these are reported on the W-2). Individuals that make or receive an HSA contribution or take an HSA distribution lose the option of using the IRS Form 1040EZ. A taxable HSA distribution is reported on line 21 of the 1040 with the entry "HSA" for failing to maintain the HSA during the testing period. If a 20 percent penalty is also owed, that is reported on line 62, ("other taxes"), on the 1040.[2]

(2) *IRS Form 8889*. This is an attachment to an account owners' income tax return that follows a step-by-step review of account owner's HSA contributions, distributions, and additional taxes or penalties owed.

(3) *IRS Form 1099-SA*. The HSA custodian sends account owners and the IRS the 1099-SA by January 31 (to the IRS by the end of February) to document HSA distributions.[3] Account owners must enter the data from the IRS Form 1099-SA to complete an income tax return.

(4) *IRS Form 5498-SA*. The IRS Form 5498-SA documents an account owner's total yearly contributions to an HSA (including rollovers).[4] An HSA custodian must send this form to the account owner and to the IRS. The form is not due to the account owner or the IRS until after the tax filing due date for calendar year taxpayers (the form is due by May 31). This is because account owners have until their tax filing due date to make a contribution for the year, so an HSA custodian does not necessarily know the account owner's HSA contributions for the year until after the tax due date. Accordingly, account owners need to know their HSA contribution information from their own records (non-tax statements from the HSA custodian, W-2 from the employer, or personal records). Some HSA custodians provide the report early in the year and then update it if the account owner makes an additional contribution prior to the April 15 deadline for the prior year.

1. IRS Instructions for Form 8889.
2. IRS Instructions for Form 1040.
3. IRS Instructions for Forms 1099-SA and 5498-SA.
4. IRS Instructions for Form 1099-SA and 5498-SA.

(5) *IRS Form W-2*. An IRS Form W-2 from an employer will show employer pre-tax HSA contributions as well as pre-tax payroll deferral contributions account owners made to an HSA in box 12 with a code W.[1]

(6) *IRS Form 5329*. The IRS Form 5329 is only necessary if the account owner owes a penalty for making an excess contribution to an HSA. In that case, the account owner files this form as an attachment to the income tax return.[2]

420. What is an Archer Medical Savings Account ("MSA") and how is it taxed?

An Archer Medical Savings Account ("MSA") is a trust created exclusively for the purpose of paying qualified medical expenses of an account holder,[3] who is the individual for whom the Archer MSA was established.[4]

Archer MSAs were available through the cutoff date discussed below to small business employees and self-employed individuals with high deductible health insurance coverage.

Any insurance company or bank can act as a trustee of an Archer MSA. Additionally, any person already approved by the IRS to act as an individual retirement arrangement ("IRA") trustee or custodian automatically is approved to act in the same capacity for Archer MSAs.[5]

Contributions

Contributions to an Archer MSA may be made either by an individual or by his or her small employer, but not by both.[6] If made by an individual taxpayer, Archer MSA contributions are deductible from income.[7] If made by a small employer, Archer MSA contributions are excluded from employee income.[8] An Archer MSA itself is exempt from income tax.[9]

Distributions

Distributions from Archer MSAs are not includable in gross income if they are used exclusively to pay qualified medical expenses.[10] For this purpose, for tax years beginning after December 31, 2010, medications included in qualified medical expenses will be limited to doctor-prescribed drugs and insulin. Consequently, over-the counter medicines will no longer be qualified expenses unless prescribed by a doctor after 2010.[11]

1. IRS Instructions for Form W-2.
2. IRS Instructions for Form 5329.
3. IRC Sec. 220(d)(1).
4. IRC Sec. 220(d)(3).
5. Notice 96-53, 1996-2 CB 219, A-9, A-10.
6. Notice 96-53, 1996-2 CB 219, A-12.
7. IRC Sec. 220(a).
8. See IRC Sec. 106(b)(1).
9. IRC Sec. 220(e)(1).
10. IRC Sec. 220(f)(1).
11. IRC Sec. 220(d)(2)(A), as amended by PPACA 2010.

Distributions used for other purposes are includable in gross income and may be subject to a 15 percent penalty tax, with some exceptions. For distributions made after December 31, 2010, the additional tax on nonqualified distributions from Archer MSAs is increased to 20 percent of any includable amounts.[1]

High Deductible Health Plan

For Archer MSAs in 2020, in the case of self-only coverage, a high deductible health plan is defined as a health plan with an annual deductible of not less than $2,350 (unchanged from 2019, $2,300 in 2018, $2,250 in 2016-2017) and not more than $3,550 (in 2020, $3,500 in 2019, $3,450 in 2018, and $3,350 in 2016-2017), and required annual out-of-pocket expenses of not more than $4,750 (in 2020, up from $4,650 in 2019, $4,550 in 2018, $4,500 in 2017).[2]

In the case of family coverage in 2020, a high deductible health plan is a health plan with an annual deductible of not less than $4,750 ($4,650 in 2019, $4,550 in 2018, $4,500 in 2017, $4,450 in 2015-2016) and not more than $7,100 ($7,000 in 2019, $6,850 in 2018, $6,750 in 2017), and required annual out-of-pocket expenses of not more than $8,650 ($8,550 in 2019, $8,400 in 2018, $8,250 in 2017).[3] For this purpose, family coverage is defined as any coverage other than self-only coverage.[4]

Deduction

An eligible individual may deduct the aggregate amount paid in cash into an Archer MSA during a taxable year, subject to a limitation of 65 percent of the annual deductible for individuals with self-only coverage and 75 percent of the annual deductible for individuals with family coverage.[5]

In addition, IRC Section 220(j)(4)(D) specifies that, to the extent practical, all Archer MSAs established by an individual are aggregated and two married individuals opening separate Archer MSAs are to be treated as having a single Archer MSA for purposes of determining the number of Archer MSAs.[6]

For married individuals, if either spouse has family coverage, then both spouses are treated as having only family coverage and the deduction limit is divided equally between them, unless they agree on a different division.[7] If two spouses both have family coverage under different plans, both spouses are treated as having only the family coverage with the lower deductible.[8]

1. IRC Secs. 220(f)(2), 220(f)(4), as amended by PPACA 2010.
2. IRC Sec. 220(c)(2)(A); Rev. Proc. 2015-53, Rev. Proc. 2016-55, Rev. Proc. 2017-58, Rev. Proc. 2018-18, Rev. Proc. 2018-57, Rev. Proc. 2019-44.
3. IRC Sec. 220(c)(2)(A); Rev. Proc. 2015-53, Rev. Proc. 2016-55, Rev. Proc. 2017-58, Rev. Proc. 2018-18, Rev. Proc. 2018-57, Rev. Proc. 2019-44.
4. IRC Sec. 220(c)(5).
5. IRC Secs. 220(a), 220(b)(2).
6. See IRS Announcement 2002-90, 2002-2 CB 684.
7. IRC Sec. 220(b)(3).
8. IRC Sec. 220(b)(3).

An Archer MSA deduction cannot exceed an employee's compensation attributable to employment with the small employer offering the high deductible health plan. Similarly, an Archer MSA deduction cannot exceed a self-employed individual's earned income derived from the trade or business with respect to which the high deductible plan is established.[1]

Excess Contributions

Excess contributions to an HSA or an Archer MSA are subject to a 6 percent tax. The tax may not exceed 6 percent of the value of the account, determined at the close of the taxable year.[2]

Pilot Cutoff

Archer MSAs were initially available on a pilot basis. The cut-off year for new accounts under the Archer MSA pilot program originally was 2003 but was extended through the end of 2007, which was the last year for creating an Archer MSA.[3] No new Archer MSAs may be set up except in some specified circumstances. For instance, eligible individuals still may make contributions to existing accounts. In recent years, very few people have chosen to open Archer MSAs (forty-five were opened in 2005 and only eleven in 2006).

No individual is treated as an eligible individual for any taxable year beginning after the cut-off year unless (1) the individual was an active Archer MSA participant for any taxable year ending on or before the close of the cut-off year, or (2) the individual first became an active Archer MSA participant for a taxable year ending after the cut-off year by reason of coverage under a high deductible health plan of an Archer MSA-participating employer.[4]

421. Is an accidental death benefit payable under a health insurance policy includable in an insured's gross estate?

Accidental death benefits are life insurance proceeds subject to the same rules as proceeds under regular life insurance policies (Q 81).[5]

When an insured purchased a one year accidental death policy and arranged for the policy to be owned by the insured's children from the beginning, the proceeds were includable in the insured's estate as a transfer in contemplation of death when the insured died within the policy term.[6]

422. Are medical expense reimbursement insurance proceeds received by an insured decedent's estate includable in the decedent's gross estate?

Yes.

The IRS has ruled that these proceeds are includable under IRC Section 2033.[7]

1. IRC Sec. 220(b)(4).
2. IRC Sec. 4973(a).
3. IRC Sec. 220(i)(2)(A). See also Ann. 2002-90, 2002-2 CB 684.
4. IRC Sec. 220(i)(1).
5. *Comm. v. Est. of Noel*, 380 U.S. 678 (1965); *Est. of Ackerman v. Comm.*, 15 BTA 635 (1929); see Rev. Rul. 66-262, 1966-2 CB 105.
6. Rev. Rul. 71-497, 1971-2 CB 329; *Bel v. U.S.*, 452 F.2d 683 (5th Cir. 1971), cert. den. 406 U.S. 919.
7. Rev. Rul. 78-292, 1978-2 CB 233.

423. Is the gift tax exclusion for qualified transfers available for amounts paid for health insurance?

Yes.

The gift tax exclusion is available for qualified transfers for educational and medical purposes.[1] Qualified transfers include amounts paid for medical insurance but not for medical care that is reimbursed by insurance. Qualified transfers do not include amounts transferred to a person receiving medical care, rather than directly to a person rendering medical care.[2]

Planning Point: Qualified transfers can include amounts paid for medical insurance and amounts paid for medical care not covered by medical insurance whether because of exclusions, deductibles, co-pays, or lack of coverage.

The Health Care Reform Law

424. What does health care reform do?

On March 23, 2010, President Obama signed comprehensive health care reform into law. The Patient Protection and Affordable Care Act amends in significant ways the IRC, ERISA, and the Public Health Service Act. The new law, known as the PPACA, ACA, and Affordable Care Act, focuses on expanding health care coverage, controlling health care costs, and improving the health care delivery system. It attempts to accomplish these goals in a variety of ways, as will be further described in Q 425 to Q 474.

The new health care reform law is, in many ways, a broad outline, the details of which will be completed by regulators. Regulations are being written and will continue to be written by the Department of Labor, the Treasury Department, and the Department of Health & Human Services.

425. When did health care reform go into effect?

The ACA went into effect between 2010 and 2018. The bulk of the provisions became effective beginning in 2011 through 2014. The effective date for the state health insurance exchanges was January 1, 2014. One provision, the controversial tax on high-cost (so-called "Cadillac") health care plans, was originally scheduled to become effective in 2018, but this date was delayed first until 2020 and again until 2022.

426. What kinds of health plans are governed by the ACA, and what plans are not covered?

Health care reform covers insured and self-funded comprehensive medical health plans. In effect, the ACA governs major medical insurance and self-insured major medical plans.

Health care reform does not regulate excepted benefits, which include standalone vision, standalone dental, cancer, long-term care insurance, Medigap insurance, certain flexible spending

1. IRC Sec. 2503(e).
2. Treas. Reg. §§25.2503-6(b)(3), 25.2503-6(c).

accounts ("FSAs"), and accident and disability insurance that make payments directly to individuals. However, it did impose an annual contribution limit of $2,500 per year on health FSAs ($2,750 in 2020, $2,700 in 2019, the amount is indexed annually for inflation).

The ACA also does not affect retiree-only plans. Although it removed the exemption for retiree-only plans and excepted benefit plans from the PHS Act, it left those exemptions in the IRC and ERISA. The preamble and footnote two of interim final grandfathered plan regulations explain that the exemption for retiree-only plans and excepted benefit plans still applies for those plans subject to the IRC and ERISA.

With respect to retiree-only and other excepted benefit plans, federal regulators have decided that even though those provisions were removed by the ACA, they will interpret the PHS Act as if an exemption for retiree-only and excepted benefit plans was still in effect. Federal regulators have encouraged state insurance regulators to do the same, although in any given state, it is possible, although extremely unlikely, that regulators will decide to enforce the ACA mandates on all fully insured plans, including those that are excepted benefit plans.

427. When did the employer tax credit for the purchase of health insurance become effective?

The tax credit (see Q 428) is effective for 2010 and thereafter. Beginning in 2014, it is only available for two consecutive years. Thus, the maximum number of years that an employer can take advantage of this tax credit is six, namely 2010 through 2013, plus any two consecutive years beginning in 2014.

428. What credit is available for small employers for employee health insurance expenses?

A credit is available for employee health insurance expenses of an eligible small employer for taxable years beginning after December 31, 2009, provided the employer offers health insurance to its employees.[1]

An eligible small employer is an employer that has no more than twenty-five full time employees, the average annual wages of whom do not exceed $50,000 (in 2010-2013; the amount is indexed to $50,800 in 2014, $51,600 in 2015, $51,800 in 2016, $52,400 in 2017, $53,200 in 2018, $54,200 in 2019, $55,200 in 2020).[2]

An employer must have a contribution arrangement for each employee who enrolls in the health plan offered by the employer through an exchange that requires that the employer make a non-elective contribution in an amount equal to a uniform percentage, not less than 50 percent, of the premium cost.[3]

1. IRC Sec. 45R, as added by PPACA 2010.
2. IRC Secs. 45R(d), as added by PPACA 2010; IRC Sec 45R(d)(3)(B), as amended by Section 10105(e)(1) of PPACA 2010, Rev. Proc. 2018-18, Rev. Proc. 2018-57, Rev. Proc. 2019-44.
3. IRC Sec. 45R(d)(4), as added by PPACA 2010.

Subject to phase-out[1] based on the number of employees and average wages, the amount of the credit is equal to 50 percent, and 35 percent in the case of tax exempts, of the lesser of (1) the aggregate amount of non-elective contributions made by the employer on behalf of its employees for health insurance premiums for health plans offered by the employer to employees through an exchange, or (2) the aggregate amount of non-elective contributions the employer would have made if each employee had been enrolled in a health plan that had a premium equal to the average premium for the small group market in the ratings area.[2]

For years 2010, 2011, 2012, and 2013, the following modifications applied in determining the amount of the credit:

(1) the credit percentage is reduced to 35 percent (25 percent in the case of tax exempts);[3]

(2) the amount under (1) is determined by reference to non-elective contributions for premiums paid for health insurance, and there is no exchange requirement;[4] and

(3) the amount under (2) is determined by the average premium for the state small group market.[5]

The credit also is allowed against the alternative minimum tax.[6]

In 2014, small employers gained exclusive access to an expanded Small Business Healthcare Tax Credit under the Affordable Care Act. This tax credit covers as much as 50 percent of the employer contribution toward premium costs for eligible employers who have low- to moderate-wage workers.

429. How much is the employer tax credit for purchases of health insurance?

The tax credit (Q 428) applies to for-profit and non-profit employers meeting certain requirements. From 2010 through 2013, the amount of the credit for for-profit employers is 35 percent (25 percent for non-profit employers) of qualifying health insurance costs. The credit is increased for any two consecutive years beginning in 2014 to 50 percent of a for-profit employer's qualifying expenses and 35 percent for non-profit employers.

Planning Point: The credit is not terribly useful, as the practitioner's cost to calculate it is often near the value of the credit.

1. IRC Sec. 45R(c), as added by PPACA 2010.
2. IRC Sec. 45R(b), as added by PPACA 2010.
3. IRC Sec. 45R(g)(2)(A), as added by PPACA 2010.
4. IRC Secs. 45R(g)(2)(B), 45R(g)(3), as added by PPACA 2010.
5. IRC Sec. 45R(g)(2)(C), as added by PPACA 2010.
6. IRC Sec. 38(c)(4)(B), as amended by PPACA 2010. The IRS has issued guidance; see Notice 2010-44, 2010-22 IRB 717; Notice 2010-82, 2010-51 IRB 1.

430. What employers are eligible for the new tax credit for health insurance, and how does it work?

The health insurance tax credit is designed to help approximately four million small for-profit businesses and tax-exempt organizations that primarily employ low and moderate-income workers. The credit is available to employers that have twenty-four or fewer eligible full time equivalent ("FTE") employees, excluding owners and their family members, paying wages averaging under $50,000 per employee per year (as indexed, $51,600 in 2015, $51,800 in 2016, $52,400 in 2017, $53,400 in 2018 and $54,200 in 2019, $55,200 in 2020).

IRC Section 45R provides a tax credit beginning in 2010 for a business with twenty-four or fewer eligible FTEs. Eligible employees do not include seasonal workers who work for an employer 120 days a year or fewer, owners, and owners' family members, where average compensation for the eligible employees is less than $50,000 and where the business pays 50 percent or more of employee-only (single person) health insurance costs. Thus, owners and family members' compensation is not counted in determining average compensation, and the health insurance cost for these people is not eligible for the health insurance tax credit.

The credit is largest if there are ten or fewer employees and average wages do not exceed $25,000, in both cases excluding owners and their family members. The amount of the credit phases out for businesses with more than ten eligible employees or average compensation of more than $25,000 and under $50,000. The amount of an employer's premium payments that counts for purposes of the credit is capped by the average premium for the small group market in the employer's geographic location, as determined by the Department of Health and Human Services.

> *Example:* In 2020, a qualified employer has nine FTEs (excluding owners, owners' family members, and seasonal employees) with average annual wages of $24,000 per FTE. The employer pays $75,000 in health care premiums for these employees, which does not exceed the average premium for the small group market in the employer's state, and otherwise meets the requirements for the credit. The credit for 2020 equals $37,250 (50 percent × $75,000). Note that the credit in 2013 would have been $26,250 (35 percent × $75,000).[1]

431. How do the rules for obtaining the tax credit for health insurance change over the years?

To obtain the credit, an employer must pay at least 50 percent of the cost of health care coverage for each counted worker with insurance.

In 2010, an employer may qualify if it pays at least 50 percent of the cost of employee-only coverage, regardless of actual coverage elected by an employee. For example, if employee-only coverage costs $500 per month, family coverage costs $1,500 per month, and the employer pays at least $250 per month (50 percent of employee-only coverage) per covered employee, then even if an employee selected family coverage the employer would meet this contribution requirement to qualify for the tax credit in 2010.

1. Additional examples can be found online at http://www.irs.gov/pub/irs-utl/small_business_health_care_tax_credit_scenarios.pdf.

Beginning in 2011, however, the percentage paid by an employer for each enrolled employee must be a uniform percentage for that coverage level. If an employee receives coverage that is more expensive than single coverage, such as family or self-plus-one coverage, an employer must pay at least 50 percent of the premium for each employee's coverage in 2011 and thereafter.

Thus, grandfathered health insurance plans that provide, for instance, for 100 percent of family coverage for executives and employee-only coverage for staff will qualify for the tax credit in 2010 but not in 2011 or beyond.

432. What are the health insurance nondiscrimination rules? When are they effective? Are there any exceptions?

Self-insured plans are subject to nondiscrimination rules for income tax purposes. The ACA imposed the same nondiscrimination rules that apply to self-insured plans to insured plans for plan years beginning on or after September 23, 2010. These health insurance nondiscrimination rules have been delayed, however, and do not apply at all to grandfathered health insurance plans as long as they remain grandfathered and have covered at least one participant continuously since March 23, 2010. These rules are intended to prevent discrimination in favor of higher paid employees in nongrandfathered health insurance plans.

IRS Notice 2011-1 delayed the application of the nondiscrimination rules for insured health plans that are not grandfathered from the first plan year beginning on or after September 23, 2010, until a date that will be specified after regulations on these rules are issued. As of this writing, no regulations have been proposed and informal discussions with Treasury personnel indicate that they may not be issued in the near future.

ACA Sections 1001 and 1562(e)-(f) add ERISA Section 715 and IRC Section 9815, respectively. Both ERISA Section 715 and IRC Section 9815 incorporate by reference Section 2716 of the Public Health Service Act ("PHSA"), a section that applies to employer health insurance plans. PHSA Section 2716 incorporates by reference the concepts of IRC Section 105(h), which applies to self-funded health plans, and applies those nondiscrimination rules to insured group health plans. Regulations will determine the exact definition of nondiscrimination.

433. When is a health insurance plan discriminatory?

To satisfy nondiscrimination eligibility classifications when required to do so under regulations yet to be issued by the IRS, the regulations for insured health plans will likely be based on the rules for self-insured plans, where a plan must:

(1) benefit 70 percent or more of all employees;

(2) benefit 80 percent or more of all eligible employees if 70 percent or more of all employees are eligible for benefits under the plan; or

(3) benefit employees who qualify under an employer's classification scheme that the IRS determines to be nondiscriminatory.

Excludable Employees

For purposes of the foregoing percentage tests, employees are not counted if they meet any one or more of the following tests:

(1) have been employed by an employer for fewer than three years;

(2) are under twenty-five years old;

(3) are employed part-time;

(4) are included in a bargaining unit covered by a collective bargaining agreement where accident and health benefits were the subject of good faith bargaining; or

(5) are nonresident aliens with no U.S. source earned income.

Part-time employees are (1) those whose customary weekly employment is fewer than thirty-five hours if other employees in similar work with the same employer or, if no employees of the employer are in similar work, in similar work in the same industry and location, have substantially more hours and (2) seasonal employees whose customary annual employment is fewer than nine months, if other employees in similar work with the same employer or, if no employees of the employer are in similar work, in similar work in the same industry and location, work substantially more months.

Any employee whose customary weekly employment is fewer than twenty-five hours or any employee whose customary annual employment is fewer than seven months also may be considered a part-time or seasonal employee.

Highly Compensated Individuals

Under IRC Section 105(h), a plan cannot discriminate in favor of highly compensated individuals as to their eligibility to participate and benefits provided under a plan cannot discriminate in favor of participants who are highly compensated individuals.

For purposes of these nondiscrimination rules, highly compensated individuals are:

(1) individuals who are among the five most highly paid officers of a corporation;

(2) any shareholder who owns, including through attribution of ownership by others, more than 10 percent in value of an employer corporation's stock; or

(3) individuals who are among the most highly paid 25 percent of all employees.

Planning Point: Items (1) and (2) above apply to corporations. Presumably the new regulations will also deal with LLCs, partnerships, and other forms of businesses.

434. What are the consequences for violating the new health insurance nondiscrimination rules?

The health insurance nondiscrimination rules, the effective date of which has been delayed until regulations have been released and a new effective date has been announced by the IRS, have different sanctions than self-insured plans that fall under IRC Section 105(h).

For discriminatory self-insured plans, highly compensated employees have taxable income based on the benefits paid by their employer. By contrast, with respect to the new health insurance nondiscrimination requirements, the sanction under IRC Section 4980D is a $100 per day excise tax on affected employees.

Although the IRS has not yet issued regulations on the penalty, its request for comments indicates that the term "affected employees" means those who are not highly compensated. Thus, if an employer has an insured health plan that is not grandfathered and that violates these new nondiscrimination rules for a plan year after these rules go into effect, and if that employer has twenty non-highly compensated employees, the penalty will be $2,000 per day as a result of having a discriminatory non-grandfathered health insurance plan.

IRC Section 4980(D)(d)(1) contains an exception to the excise tax for small employers, but the language is somewhat ambiguous. It states, "In the case of a group health plan of a small employer which provides health insurance coverage solely through a contract with a health insurance issuer, no tax shall be imposed by this section on the employer on any failure (other than a failure attributable to section 9811) which is solely because of the health insurance coverage offered by such issuer." It is not clear whether this exception applies to the new nondiscrimination rules or simply to a health insurance policy that does not meet federal requirements. For the purpose of this exception, a small employer is defined as two to fifty employees.

There also is a 10 percent cap on the excise tax, that is, 10 percent of aggregate premiums paid by an employer, for inadvertent violations of the nondiscrimination rules.

435. Are grandfathered health insurance plans exempt from nondiscrimination and all health care reform requirements?

Yes and no.

Although grandfathered health insurance plans are exempt from many requirements, they are not exempt from all health care reform requirements. Grandfathered plans will be exempt from the health insurance nondiscrimination rules when those are published. Grandfathered plans are subject to the following mandates:

(1) Prohibition of lifetime benefit limits

(2) No rescission except for fraud or intentional misrepresentation

(3) Children, who are not eligible for employer-sponsored coverage, covered up to age twenty-six on a family policy, if the dependent does not have coverage available from his or her employer

(4) Pre-existing condition exclusions for covered individuals younger than nineteen are prohibited

(5) Restricted annual limits for essential benefits

Grandfathered health plans are exempt from the following requirements that apply to new and non-grandfathered health plans:

(1) No cost-sharing for preventive services

(2) Nondiscrimination based on compensation

(3) Children covered up to age twenty-six on family policy regardless of whether a policy is available at work. Grandfathered status for the adult dependent coverage ends on January 1, 2014

(4) Internal appeal and external review processes

(5) Emergency services at in-network cost-sharing level with no prior authorization

(6) Parents must be allowed to select a pediatrician as a primary care physician for their children and women must be allowed to select an OB-GYN for their primary care physician

436. How does health care reform apply to self-insured plans?

Self-funded plans generally are treated the same as insured plans under the ACA. Analysis of the application of the ACA to self-insured plans begins with Section 1562, which adds Section 715 to ERISA and Section 9815 to the IRC. These provisions state that all of the provisions of Part A of Title XXVII of the Public Health Service Act ("PHSA"), as amended by the ACA, apply to both ERISA group health plans and health insurance issuers that insure group health plans. ERISA group health plans include both self-insured and insured plans.

The section further provides that if anything in ERISA's group plan requirements conflicts with Part A of the PHSA, the PHSA shall govern. The fact that this section refers both to group health plans and to insured group health plans makes it clear that the provision is meant to apply to self-insured plans. This is reinforced by subsection (b) of this section adding new Section 715 to ERISA and IRC Section 9815 to the IRC, both of which state that Section 2716 and Section 2718 of the PHSA do not apply to self-insured plans, suggesting that the remaining provisions do.

This analysis is strengthened by the definition of group health plan under ACA Section 1301(b)(3), which incorporates the definition of Section 2791 of the PHSA, defining group health plan to mean an employee welfare benefit plan as defined in ERISA Section 3(1). Section 1551 of the ACA also provides that the definitions of PHSA Section 2791 apply to the ACA.

Several sections of the ACA refer specifically to self-insured plans.

Section 2701(a)(5), applying the health status underwriting provisions to large group plans in an exchange, does not apply to self-insured plans. Section 2715 requires a plan sponsor or designated administrator to make disclosures required by that section for self-insured plans.

Section 2716, which addresses discrimination in favor of highly-compensated employees, expressly states that it does not apply to self-insured plans, which already are covered by a similar requirement under IRC Section 105(h).

Self-insured plans expressly are subject to the external review requirements, that is, the appeal requirements, of Section 2719 to be established by the Department of Health and Human Services (HHS).

The reinsurance provisions of Section 1341 expressly apply to self-insured plans; the risk-pooling provisions of Section 1343 expressly do not.

Self-insured plans expressly are subject to a per-member fee to fund patient centered outcomes research under recently added IRC Section 4376.

HHS has addressed amendments by the ACA to the law permitting self-funded nonfederal governmental plans to opt out of compliance with certain federal benefit mandates. Except for a narrow band of requirements, these group health plans will no longer be permitted to opt out of HIPAA rules regarding the preexisting condition exclusion and special enrollment. Plan sponsors may continue to opt out of requirements under the Newborns' and Mothers' Health Protection Act, Mental Health Parity and Addiction Equity Act, Women's Health and Cancer Rights Act, and Michelle's Law.

These changes are effective beginning on or after September 23, 2010, for non-collectively bargained self-funded nonfederal governmental plans. Self-insured nonfederal governmental plans maintained pursuant to a collective bargaining agreement ratified before March 23, 2010, and that have been exempted from any of the relevant HIPAA requirements (for example, limits on preexisting condition exclusions, special enrollment periods, and health status nondiscrimination requirements) will not have to come into compliance with those requirements until the first day of the first plan year following the expiration of the last plan year governed by a collective bargaining agreement.

Although all plans except grandfathered plans are subject to the new appeals rules, effective for plan years beginning after September 23, 2011, with limited exceptions, self-insured plans are most affected because compliance for insured plans is handled by the insurance company, not the plan sponsor.

437. How does health care reform apply to collectively bargained plans?

There is no delayed effective date for collectively bargained plans, whether fully insured or self-insured. Thus, plans maintained pursuant to one or more collective bargaining agreements in effect on March 23, 2010, must comply with the new rules at the same time as other grandfathered plans, although with a few differences.

The interim final grandfather regulations provide that fully insured, but not self-insured, collectively bargained plans retain their grandfathered status until the expiration of the agreement in effect on March 23, 2010. Self-insured collectively bargained plans are subject to the rules in the same way as other covered health plans.

Thus, a change in carriers under a fully insured collectively bargained plan does not result in the loss of grandfathered status if the change is made before the expiration of the agreement in effect on March 23, 2010. Additionally, changes to benefits that apply while that collective bargaining agreement is in effect, including increasing co-payments, do not result in loss of grandfathered status.

Whether grandfathered status applies after expiration of a collective bargaining agreement is determined by comparing benefits in effect at that time to benefits in effect on March 23, 2010. If the changes are not within permitted parameters, then a plan will cease to be grandfathered when the relevant agreement expires.

The interim final rule for grandfathered plans makes two clarifications with respect to collectively bargained plans.

First, it confirms that both insured and self-funded collectively bargained plans that are grandfathered health plans are subject to the same coverage reform mandates under the ACA at the same time that its mandates are effective with respect to other grandfathered health plans. Therefore, collectively bargained plans must comply with the extension of dependent coverage mandate, the elimination of lifetime and annual dollar limits, and the prohibition on pre-existing condition exclusions at the same time that these mandates become effective for all other grandfathered health plans.

Second, a collectively bargained insured plan may maintain its grandfathered status beyond the termination of the last of the applicable collective bargaining agreements provided that any changes to the terms of coverage under the plan are not changes that would cause the plan to lose grandfathered status under the interim final rule. Thus, collectively bargained insured plans are treated the same as all other grandfathered health plans on the termination of the last of the applicable collective bargaining agreements in effect on March 23, 2010, so their grandfathered status may last indefinitely as well.

Regulations also provide that a collectively bargained plan may be amended early for some or all of the law's rules. This voluntary amendment is not a termination of the collective bargaining agreement that otherwise might subject the plan to an earlier compliance deadline.

438. What is a grandfathered health plan?

A grandfathered health plan is any group health plan or individual health insurance policy that was in effect on the date of the ACA's enactment, March 23, 2010, and that has covered at least one person continuously. Even if an individual re-enrolls in a grandfathered health plan or new employees or their families are added to a plan after March 23, 2010, a plan's grandfathered status continues. Interim final regulations provide that if any benefit is eliminated or employees' cost is increased more than a minor amount, then grandfathered status is lost. In addition, the regulations require that to maintain a grandfathered status, the plan must give an annual notice to participants, advising them that the plan is grandfathered and the consequences.

Original regulations provided that if an insured non-collectively bargained plan changes insurance carriers, even if benefits are the same or greater, grandfathered status is lost. The HHS, IRS, and DOL later amended the regulations to provide that new group health insurance would not cause loss of grandfathered status if it was effective on or after November 15, 2010, if coverage is at least as good and costs are not increased more than allowed to retain grandfather status. The amendment to the regulations applies only to group health plans, not to individual health insurance.

This change, allowing a switch in insurance companies without losing grandfathered status, does not apply to changes in policies between June 14 and November 15, 2010. Changes in insurance carriers during that time still cause loss of grandfathered status. For this purpose, the date new coverage becomes effective is controlling, not the date the new insurance contract or policy is entered into. For changes to group health insurance coverage on or after March 23, 2010, but before June 14, 2010, the date the regulations were made publicly available, the agencies' enforcement safe harbor remains in effect for good faith efforts to comply with a reasonable interpretation of the law.

For self-insured plans, a change in third party administrator, in and of itself, does not cause a group health plan to cease to be a grandfathered plan. Additionally, grandfathered status can be retained when a plan changes its structure from self-insured to insured or insured to self-insured.

Planning Point: An IRS representative has informally indicated that eliminating coverage for a group or segment of a workforce would not cause a plan to relinquish its grandfathered status. Eliminating coverage for a class of employees is not one of the changes prohibited by regulations.

Although most of the mandates in the ACA apply to both group health plans and group health insurance issuers, new Public Health Service Act ("PHSA") Section 2716 applies only to insured group health plans. Accordingly, even if Section 2716 were interpreted to apply to future modifications to existing health benefit designs that are discriminatory in favor of highly compensated employees, there may be structures available to an employer whereby it can cause an insurer to issue a special individual policy, or to provide special individual coverage, to highly compensated individuals without the policy or arrangement being treated as part of a new non-grandfathered group health plan.

Where special individual benefits are provided to a group of highly compensated employees, however, they may be considered to be part of a group health plan.

As discussed in Q 437, multi-employer and single-employer collectively bargained health plans in effect on March 23, 2010 are not subject to the reform law until the date on which the last of the collective bargaining agreements relating to the coverage terminates. At that time, a collectively bargained plan then is subject to health care reform rules and, assuming that it remains grandfathered, based on the rules then in effect, it would have to comply with the requirements for grandfathered plans.

439. What are the new protections offered to minor children and young adults by health care reform?

Teens and young adults, even if they are no longer dependents for income tax purposes and even if they are married, can stay on or be added to their parents' health insurance plan until age twenty-six, or through age twenty-six if a plan or policy allows. Young adults also are not required to live with their parents or, as noted above, to be financially dependent on them. This right to coverage applies to all types of plans that offer dependent coverage.

In grandfathered employer group plans, that is, policies that existed on March 23, 2010, and that have not changed substantially, children are not eligible to go on parents' plans if the children have access to coverage through their own workplace.

In non-grandfathered plans, they are eligible to be covered on their parents' policy even if they have coverage through work.

New rules prevent insurers from denying coverage to children under age nineteen with pre-existing medical conditions including asthma or cancer for plan years beginning on or after September 23, 2010. Insurers may limit certain open enrollment periods when children are signed up; this does not apply to grandfathered individual plans.

Similar protections for adults with pre-existing medical conditions did not begin until 2014. In the interim, adults with medical conditions who have been uninsured for at least six months were able to purchase coverage through federal high-risk pools created by the health care reform law.

440. How does health care reform affect employer-provided plans, including flexible spending arrangements, reimbursement arrangements, savings accounts, and Archer medical savings accounts, that pay for non-prescription medicines?

Section 9003 of the ACA adds IRC Section 106(f), which revises the definition of medical expenses for employer-provided accident and health plans, including health flexible spending arrangements (health FSAs) and health reimbursement arrangements (HRAs). Section 9003 also revises the definition of qualified medical expenses for health savings accounts and Archer medical savings accounts. Nonprescription drugs are not eligible for reimbursement by these plans unless a physician issues a prescription. Presumably, such a prescription would be done in the same way as regular prescriptions. For example, if a physician were to prescribe aspirin, this expense could be reimbursed but the purchase of aspirin without a prescription could not be reimbursed.

Planning Point: Notice 2013-54 makes clear that reimbursement of medical expenses with pre-tax dollars (deductible to the employee and tax-free to the employee) are no longer permitted in stand-alone HRAs and stand-alone health FSAs. Instead, to be permitted, HRAs and health FSAs must be integrated with an employer's health plan (see Q 445). Notice 2015-17 exempts employers not subject to the employer mandate from these rules through June 30, 2015. After that time, a violation of these rules triggers a $100/day/affected employee penalty for the employer (an exception exists for qualified small employer HRAs (QSEHRAs, see Q 350).

Other changes in health FSAs and HRAs are discussed in the following Q&As.

441. What are the rules regarding reimbursement of non-prescription medicines?

For plan years beginning in 2011 and thereafter, no plan can provide for, or reimburse on a tax favored basis, non-prescription over-the-counter drugs. This prohibition applies to medical expense reimbursement plans, cafeteria plans, flexible spending accounts, health savings accounts, health reimbursement accounts, and Archer medical savings accounts. However, if the plan participant gets a prescription for the over-the-counter medication, then it can be reimbursed because it is treated as a prescription drug.

442. What changes does the ACA mandate that affect health FSAs?

Under IRC Section 106(f), expenses incurred for medicines or drugs may be paid or reimbursed by an employer-provided plan, including a health FSA or HRA, only if the medicine or drug:

(1) requires a prescription;

(2) is available without a prescription, that is, is an over-the-counter medicine or drug, and the individual obtains a prescription; or

(3) is insulin.

This applies to expenses incurred for taxable years beginning on or after January 1, 2011.

Additionally, for plan years beginning in 2013 and thereafter, contributions to flexible savings accounts will be limited to $2,750 per year (for 2020, as indexed, up from $2,700 for 2019, $2,650 for 2018 and $2,600 for 2017), as indexed for inflation in subsequent years.[1] Flexible spending accounts are those accounts, typically in cafeteria plans, that may be used to reimburse medical or dependent care expenses.

Further, the IRS has modified the cafeteria plan use it or lose it rule for health FSAs. Health FSAs may now be amended so that $500 of unused amounts remaining at the end of the plan year may be carried forward to the next plan year.[2] However, plans that incorporate the carry forward provision may not also offer the two-month grace (run-out) period that would otherwise allow FSA participants an additional two-month period after the end of the plan year to exhaust account funds.

1. Rev. Proc. 2016-55, Rev. Proc. 2017-58, Rev. Proc. 2018-18, Rev. Proc. 2018-57, Rev. Proc. 2019-44.
2. Notice 2013-71.

443. Can participation in a health FSA impact an individual's ability to contribute to an HSA?

GCM 201413005 states that carrying over FSA funds from year one to year two will prevent an individual from participating in a health savings account (HSA) in year two. HSA-eligible individuals must have qualifying high-deductible health plan (HDHP) coverage and no non-HDHP coverage other than permitted insurance, coverage providing only certain types of preventive care, or coverage with a deductible that equals or exceeds the statutory minimum annual HDHP deductible (collectively, HSA-compatible coverage). Unused amounts from a general-purpose health FSA that could be carried over to an HSA-compatible health FSA may be used during the general-purpose health FSA's run-out period to reimburse expenses covered by the general-purpose health FSA that were incurred during the previous plan year.

A health FSA that reimburses all qualified Section 213(d) medical expenses without other restrictions is a health plan. Consequently, an individual who is covered by a general purpose health FSA that pays or reimburses qualified medical expenses is not an eligible individual for purposes of contributing to an HSA. This disqualification includes the entire plan year, even if the health FSA has paid or reimbursed all amounts prior to the end of the plan year. To prevent this, an individual may decline or waive a health FSA carryover in order to become eligible for the HSA, at least if the FSA plan permits.

A cafeteria plan may provide that if an individual participates in a general purpose health FSA that provides for a carryover of unused amounts, the individual may elect prior to the beginning of the following year to decline or waive the carryover for the following year. In that case, the individual who declines under the terms of the cafeteria plan may contribute to an HSA during the following year if the individual is otherwise eligible for the HSA.

However, if a cafeteria plan offers an HSA-compatible (limited purpose) health FSA, (i.e., one that covers, dental, vision, preventive care, and/or pharmaceutical expenses not covered under a health insurance plan) this does not prohibit funding an HSA. Thus, individuals wishing to participate in an HSA should either not carryover any FSA funds into the next plan year or make sure carryover funds are deposited in an HSA-compatible FSA (i.e., one that provides solely incidental benefits or reimburses other medical expenses after the deductible is met). There is no requirement that the unused amounts in the general purpose health FSA only be carried over to a general purpose health FSA. However, the carryover amounts may not be carried over to a non-health FSA or another type of cafeteria plan benefit.

Thus, if a carryover feature is included in the general-purpose health FSA plan, an employer has three options available to preserve employees' HSA eligibility for the following plan year:

- Option 1: Allow participants with a general-purpose health FSA to elect and enroll in a limited-purpose FSA—an FSA plan that is compatible with an HSA—for the following plan year. Those participants can carry over unused funds (up to the maximum limit) to a limited-purpose FSA; however, the carryover cannot be applied to another non-health FSA or another cafeteria plan benefit.

- Option 2: Automatically enroll participants in a limited-purpose FSA if those participants enroll in a qualifying high deductible health plan (HDHP) and have a carryover balance in a general-purpose health FSA.

- Option 3: Allow individuals to waive or decline a health FSA carryover prior to the beginning of the next plan year to become eligible.

Planning Point: An employer may have both a general purpose health FSA and an HSA-compatible FSA. Where an employee participates in both and does not utilize all elected benefits in a year, GCM 201413005 provides an example for maximizing the benefits for the succeeding year while maintaining eligibility to participate in an HSA, as follows:

Example: Employer offers a calendar year general purpose health FSA and a calendar year HSA-compatible health FSA. Both FSAs provide for a carryover of up to $500 of unused amounts and do not have a grace period. Employee has an unused amount of $600 in the general purpose health FSA on December 31 ofYear 1. Prior to December 31 ofYear 1, Employee elects $2,500 in the HSA-compatible health FSA for Year 2 and elects to have any carryover go to the HSA-compatible health FSA. Employee also elects coverage by an HDHP forYear 2. In January ofYear 2, Employee incurs and submits a claim for $2,700 in dental care covered by the HSA-compatible health FSA. The plan timely reimburses $2,500, the amount elected. In February ofYear 2, Employee submits and is reimbursed from the general purpose health FSA for $300 in medical expenses incurred prior to December 31 ofYear 1. At the end of the run-out period, $300 in the general purpose health FSA is unused and carried over to the HSA-compatible health FSA. Employee is then reimbursed $200 for the excess of the January claim over the amount elected for the HSA-compatible health FSA. Employee has $100 remaining in the HSA-compatible health FSA to be used for expenses incurred in the year or carried over to the next year. Employee is allowed to contribute to an HSA as of January 1 of Year 2.

444. Is an employer permitted to sponsor health FSAs if it does not otherwise offer health coverage to employees?

No. An employer cannot sponsor a stand-alone health FSA. An employer may only offer a health FSA if it also offers a major medical plan to the health FSA participants, who are not required to accept the offer of coverage in the employer's major medical plan.

445. Under the ACA, can a health reimbursement arrangement (HRA) be integrated with health insurance coverage without violating the prohibition on annual dollar limits on benefits?

Editor's Note: Final rules expanding the availability of HRAs to allow employees to purchase individual health insurance with HRA funds were released in 2019. See Q 446 for details.

Prior to release of the new rules expanding the availability of HRAs in 2019 and beyond, the IRS has issued guidance providing that a health reimbursement arrangement (HRA) cannot be integrated with individual coverage (whether purchased in the individual insurance markets or an exchange) in order to comply with the ACA prohibition against annual dollar limits on benefits available under a plan, eliminating the possibility that employers could use HRAs to subsidize employees' purchase of health insurance.[1] This is the case unless certain specific criteria are met (see below).

1. Notice 2013-54, 2013-40 IRB 287.

IRS guidance provides the circumstances under which an HRA will be considered integrated with a health plan so that it does not violate the annual dollar limit prohibition. An HRA may be considered integrated with another health plan (and, thus, not in violation of the prohibition against annual dollar limits) if it meets one of two tests.

First, an HRA can be integrated if (1) the employer offers a second group health plan that does not consist solely of certain excepted benefits, (2) the employee receiving the HRA is actually enrolled in that group health plan or a spouse's plan, (3) the HRA is only available to employees enrolled in the non-HRA group coverage, (4) the HRA is only permitted to reimburse one or more of: co-payments, co-insurance, deductibles, and premiums under the non-HRA coverage, or medical expenses for non-essential benefits and (5) the employee is permitted to opt-out of the HRA.

Under the second method, if the HRA does not limit reimbursements as required under the first method, (1) the employer must offer a group health plan in addition to the HRA that provides certain minimum value under IRC Section 36B, (2) the employee must actually be enrolled in that plan or a spouse's plan, (3) the HRA must only be available to employees enrolled in the non-HRA plan and (4) the employee must be permitted to opt-out.

An exception to these rules applies for employer sponsored HRAs offered to one participant or solely to retirees. These HRAs may be offered on a stand-alone basis without its participant(s) being covered by the employer's major medical health plan.

446. What new rules will apply in determining whether a health reimbursement arrangement (HRA) can be used to provide reimbursement for individual health insurance premiums without violating the prohibition on plans that place annual dollar limits on available benefits beginning in 2020?

The DOL, Department of Health and Human Services (HHS) and Treasury released new regulations, finalized in 2019, that would expand the potential value of HRAs, which, under the new rules, can be used to reimburse employees for the cost of individually purchased health insurance plans. The expanded HRA rules become effective January 1, 2020.

Planning Point: While QSEHRAs expanded the availability of HRAs that can be used to reimburse employees for the cost of individual health insurance premiums, QSEHRAs can only be used by employers that are not subject to the employer mandate, limiting their usefulness to fairly small business owners.

The new rules would allow all sizes of employers to reimburse premiums for individual health insurance coverage through HRAs if the following conditions are satisfied:

(1) All individuals enrolled in the HRA are also enrolled in individual coverage or Medicare. If an individual ceases to be enrolled in individual coverage, the HRA must stop reimbursing their medical expenses (applied prospectively only). Individuals who are still within the grace period with respect to paying their premiums for individual coverage are considered enrolled in individual coverage.

(2) The employer does not offer integrated HRA-individual coverage to one class of employees if it offers group health coverage to others in the same class of employees, and

(3) The HRA must be offered on the same terms to members of employees within a given class of employees where consistent definitions are used to determine employee classifications. Exceptions to this rule include an exception for age and for family size.[1]

As was the case under earlier guidance, the HRA program must include an opt-out provision that will allow the employee to claim the premium tax credit. The employee must be able to opt out at least annually and, for most employees, at the start of the plan year. If the employee becomes eligible to participate at a date other than the first day of the plan year, or a dependent becomes newly eligible to participate during the plan year, the opt-out opportunity must be provided during the enrollment period established by the HRA for those individuals. Upon termination, the amounts must be forfeited or the participant must be able to permanently opt out and waive any future reimbursements.[2] If the employee opts out, and the HRA is unaffordable or the HRA does not provide minimum value, the employee would be eligible for the premium tax credit.

While the HRA must be offered on the same terms to members within a given class, variations in dollar amounts are permitted when based on the number of dependents covered under the plan (so long as the same maximum dollar amount attributable to increases in family size is available to all participants in the same class of employees with the same number of dependents) or due to age under certain circumstances (see Q 447 for more information on the class limitations).[3]

Reasonable substantiation procedures must be established to ensure that employees actually are enrolled in individual health insurance plans. Generally, substantiation must be provided no later than the start of the plan year, unless the employee is not eligible to participate on that date, in which case substantiation should be required no later than the date when HRA coverage begins.[4]

Employers are permitted to ensure that employees actually use the HRA funds to purchase individual health insurance satisfying ACA minimum coverage requirements—rather than limited or short duration plans—by relying upon employee attestations. The rules are clear that employers are not required to look beyond employee attestations to confirm that the employee used the funds permissibly (unless the employer has actual knowledge that the attestation may be false).[5] However, the employer must obtain an attestation for each reimbursement from the HRA.[6] The rules provide model attestation language, and also suggest verification by requiring the employee to provide an insurance card or similar document.[7]

1. Treas. Reg. §54.9802-4(c).
2. Treas. Reg. §54.9802-4(c)(4).
3. Treas. Reg. §54.9802-4(c)(3)(iii).
4. Treas. Reg. §54.9802-4(c)(5)(i).
5. Treas. Reg. §54.9802-4(c)(5)(iii).
6. Treas. Reg. §54.9802-4(c)(5)(ii).
7. Treas. Reg. §54.9802-4(c)(5)(i)(B).

The HRA is also required to provide detailed written notice to participants at least ninety days prior to each plan year (the rules provide model notices, see Q 452).

See Q 451 for a discussion of the new excepted benefit HRAs that will also be available beginning in 2020.

447. What are the permissible classes of employees that employers can use to determine whether to offer individual coverage HRA benefits to a certain group?

Individual coverage HRAs may be offered on different terms to employees included in different "classes". The employer is required to determine the classes of employees that it intends to treat separately and the definition of the relevant classes that will apply when choice is permitted. Changes are not permitted other than before the start of a new plan year.[1]

Permissible classes of employees include part-time employees, full-time employees, seasonal workers, hourly workers, salaried workers, new hires, workers employed or not employed through a temporary staffing agency, employees in the same rating area, employees covered by a collective bargaining agreement in which the plan sponsor participates, employees who have satisfied a waiting period for coverage, and non-resident aliens.[2] The class of employees who have yet to reach age 25 was not included in the final rule.

Under the final rule, HRA coverage offers to a class of employees differentiated based upon full-time status, part-time status, geography or status of the worker as salary versus hourly are only permitted when the group is of a sufficient size. Generally, the size requirement only applies if the employer also offers a traditional group health plan in addition to the individual coverage HRA. If the group is only offered traditional group health coverage or no coverage at all, the size requirement does not apply.[3] The size requirement does apply if the employer combines one or more permissible classes of employees, except the size requirement does not apply if the employer combines one permissible class of employees with a class of employees that have not yet satisfied a waiting period for coverage.[4]

Under the rule, for employers with between 100 and 200 employees, the class size must be the smaller of 20 employees or 10 percent of the workforce. For employers with fewer than 100 employees, the class size must be at least 10 employees, and for employers with more than 200 employees, the class size must be at least 20 employees.[5] The minimum size requirement does not apply when the class is based on a geographic grouping that encompasses one or more entire states.[6] The employer determines whether a class of employees satisfies the size requirements based on the number of employees in the class offered the individual coverage HRA as

1. Treas. Reg. §54.9802-4(d)(2).
2. Treas. Reg. §54.9802-4(d)(2).
3. Treas. Reg. §54.9802-4(d)(3)(ii)(B).
4. Treas. Reg. §54.9802-4(d)(3)(ii)(D).
5. Treas. Reg. §54.9802-4(d)(3)(iii).
6. Treas. Reg. §54.9802-4(d)(3)(ii)(C)(1).

of the first day of the plan year (i.e., it is not based on the number of employees who actually enroll and not impacted by changes in the number of employees throughout the plan year).[1]

The minimum size requirement does generally not apply to the "new hire" class of employees, unless the employer later subdivides the "new hire subclass" into additional subclasses where the size requirement would apply.[2] An employer may generally prospectively offer new hires within a class of employees who are hired on or after a certain date an individual coverage HRA while continuing to offer existing employees within that same class traditional group health coverage. This means that a "new hire subclass" is permissible within a class of employees. The individual coverage HRA must be offered on the same terms to all participants within the new hire subclass. Under these circumstances, the employer cannot offer a choice between group health coverage and an individual coverage HRA to any employee in the new hire subclass, or to any employee in the class who is not a member of the new hire subclass.[3] The relevant date can be established as any date on or after January 1, 2020.[4] The plan sponsor is also permitted to discontinue the special rule for new hires, and later reapply the new hire rule, but only on a prospective basis.[5]

An employer need not offer an HRA to all former employees, or to all former employees within the same class. However, the employer chooses to do so, the HRA must be offered on the same terms as for other employees in the class (former employees are included in the class they would have fallen into immediately before separating from service).[6]

Under the final rule, HRA contributions cannot vary by more than 3:1 for older employees versus younger employees. Further, the same maximum dollar amount attributable to increases in age must be available to all participants who are the same age. The employer can use any reasonable method to determine the age of participants, so long as the same method is used for all participants in the same class of employees.[7] A consistency requirement applies in determining the definition of "full-time", "part-time" and seasonal employee for the plan year.[8]

448. How does the use of an individual coverage HRA impact the employee's ability to claim the premium tax credit?

Employees who receive integrated individual coverage via an HRA are generally not eligible for the premium tax credit, but they are eligible for a special enrollment period in the individual market to purchase health insurance. While the general enrollment period in the marketplace occurs in November and December, the regulations provide that a special enrollment event will be deemed to occur when an individual is given the option of participating in an individual coverage HRA.

1. Treas. Reg. §54.9802-4(d)(3)(iv).
2. Treas. Reg. §§54.9802-4(d)(3), 54.9802-4(d)(5)(iv).
3. Treas. Reg. §54.9802-4(d)(5).
4. Treas. Reg. §54.9802-4(d)(5)(ii).
5. Treas. Reg. §54.9802-4(d)(5)(iii).
6. Treas. Reg. §54.9802-4(d)(2).
7. Treas. Reg. §54.9802-4(c)(3)(iii)(B).
8. Treas. Reg. §54.9802-4(d)(4).

Despite this, individual coverage HRAs are treated as group health insurance plans under the ACA. This means that if the employee chooses to opt out because the coverage provided is not affordable and then enrolls in individual coverage via the health insurance marketplace, the individual may remain eligible to claim the premium tax credit. An individual coverage HRA is affordable for purposes of claiming the premium tax credit if the employee's required HRA contribution does not exceed 1/12 of (1) the employee's household income for the year multiplied by (2) the required contribution percentage.[1] The employee's "required contribution" is determined by subtracting (1) the monthly premium for the lowest cost silver plan for self-only coverage of the employee offered on the health insurance exchange for the rating area in which the employee lives from (2) the monthly self-only HRA contribution. For 2020, the required contribution percentage is 9.78 percent.

If the individual coverage is deemed to be unaffordable at the time the employee enrolls in individual coverage through the marketplace after opting out, the individual coverage HRA will be deemed unaffordable for the entire year.[2]

449. How does the use of an individual coverage HRA impact the employer's potential liability under the ACA employer mandate?

Individual coverage HRAs are group health insurance plans, so can be used to satisfy the employer mandate, as they are deemed to provide minimum essential coverage so long as all participants are actually enrolled in individual coverage or Medicare as required under the new regulations.[3] This means that employers who are required to provide coverage under the ACA can satisfy the employer mandate requirements through offering an individual coverage HRA, assuming the HRA is affordable and meets applicable minimum value standards, and assuming the HRA is offered to at least 95 percent of full-time employees and dependents (i.e., it satisfies all of the rules that otherwise apply with respect to the employer mandate, see Q 467).

The IRS has released two safe harbor rules in a new set of proposed regulations designed to facilitate the use of individual coverage health reimbursement arrangements (HRAs) in order to provide employees with a tax-preferred method to pay for health insurance premiums in the individual marketplace. If an employer qualifies under one of the safe harbors, that employer can avoid becoming subject to the shared responsibility provisions of the ACA based upon its use of individual coverage HRAs. Under the first safe harbor, the employer can calculate whether a health plan is affordable based upon the minimum cost of a silver plan offered through the health insurance marketplace in the employee's location. Under the second safe harbor, the employer can use the prior year's cost of a silver plan in the month of January.

Affordability must be determined on an employee-by-employee basis, considering each employee's income, any required HRA contribution and the lowest cost silver marketplace plan that is available to that employee.

1. Treas. Reg. §1.36B-2(c)(5)(i).
2. Treas. Reg. §1.36B-2(c)(5)(iv).
3. Notice 2018-88.

450. Can an individual coverage HRA be used where a participant is covered under one type of health coverage and his dependents are covered under another (i.e., Medicare)?

Yes. There is no requirement that a participant and his or her dependents be covered under the same type of plan, so that an individual coverage HRA may be provided to an employee-participant who is covered under Medicare and to his or her dependents, who are covered under individual health insurance coverage obtained in the marketplace.[1]

451. What is the new "excepted benefit HRA" that employers may offer beginning in 2020?

Beginning in 2020, employers are permitted to offer excepted benefit HRAs (funded with up to $1,800 annually) under the new HRA regulations, which employees can use to purchase excepted benefits and short-term health insurance coverage. Unlike with individual coverage HRAs, employers can offer both the excepted benefit HRA and group health insurance coverage to the same employee, but the employee is not required to actually enroll in the group health coverage. Excepted benefit HRAs can be used to pay co-pays, dental or vision coverage, short-term health insurance premiums and other medical expenses not covered under the group health plan, but cannot be used by pay individual health insurance premiums or Medicare premiums. The excepted benefit HRA is funded solely by the employer, and the contribution limit is currently $1,800 per year (to be adjusted annually for inflation for tax years beginning after 2020).[2]

452. What notice requirements apply with respect to individual coverage HRAs?

An employer who offers individual coverage HRAs must comply with certain notice requirements, which mandate that the HRA generally provide written notice to each participant at least ninety days before the beginning of the plan year.[3] If the participant is not eligible as of the first day of the plan year, the notice must be provided no later than the date the HRA may take effect for the participant.[4] The notice must contain a description of the basic HRA terms, including:

1. the maximum dollar amount available to each participant for the plan year;
2. any rules regarding pro-ration if the participant is not eligible for the entire plan year;
3. whether dependents are eligible;
4. a statement disclosing that there are different types of HRAs (including QSEHRAs) and that the particular HRA being offered is an individual coverage HRA;

---

1. Treas. Reg. §54.9802-4(e).
2. Treas. Reg. §54.9831-1(c)(3)(viii).
3. Treas. Reg. §54.9802-4(c)(6)(i)(A).
4. Treas. Reg. §54.9802-4(c)(6)(i)(B).

5. a statement that the participant and any dependents must be enrolled in individual health insurance coverage or Medicare;
6. a statement that the coverage cannot be short-term, limited-duration or excepted benefit only coverage;
7. a statement as to ERISA coverage;
8. the date HRA coverage will first become effective (with respect to all participants and dependents covered);
9. the date the HRA plan year begins and ends; and
10. the dates the amounts under the HRA will become available.[1]

The notice must contain information about the availability of the premium tax credit and the employee's right to opt out of the individual coverage HRA. The notice must also clearly state that the employee would be ineligible for the premium tax credit if he or she participates in the individual coverage HRA.[2] The notice must also direct the participant that he or she must provide a statement to the exchange if the participant opts out and applies for the premium tax credit, and that statement must disclose availability of the individual coverage HRA, as well as information about available amounts and who the HRA would cover.[3]

The notice must inform the participant that he or she will be required to provide substantiation in order to obtain reimbursements from the HRA and that if individual coverage or Medicare coverage ceases, the participant will no longer be eligible for reimbursement.[4] The notice should also contain contact information where the participant can obtain additional information, as well as a statement as to the availability of a special enrollment period in the health insurance marketplace.[5]

The DOL has provided a model notice that can be used in order to demonstrate good faith compliance with the notice requirements.

453. Under the ACA, can an employer reimburse an employee for the cost of individual health insurance coverage without violating the prohibition on plans that place annual dollar limits on available benefits?

Generally, no. The market reform provisions that now apply under the Affordable Care Act generally prohibit employers from reimbursing employees for individual health insurance premiums.[6] This is because these types of employer-sponsored reimbursement arrangements typically place a cap on the amount that the employer will reimburse for these expenses, in

1. Treas. Reg. §54.9802-4(c)(6)(ii)(A).
2. Treas. Reg. §54.9802-4(c)(6)(ii)(B), (C), (D).
3. Treas. Reg. §54.9802-4(c)(6)(ii)(E).
4. Treas. Reg. §54.9802-4(c)(6)(ii)(G), (H).
5. Treas. Reg. §54.9802-4(c)(6)(ii)(I), (J).
6. See Department of Labor FAQ about Affordable Care Act Implementation (Part XXII), updated November 6, 2014, available at: www.dol.gov/sites/default/files/ebsa/about-ebsa/our-activities/resource-center/faqs/aca-part-xxii.pdf

violation of the ACA prohibition on annual benefit limits. This is the case whether or not the payments are treated as pre-tax or after-tax to the employee. However, IRS Notice 2015-17 provides an exception for employers not subject to the employer mandate (they are not applicable large employers) and the shareholders of S corporations. These two types of employers were permitted to continue to reimburse individual health insurance premiums through June 30, 2015 without penalty. This relief was extended by the introduction of QSEHRAs (see Q 350), which allow certain small employers to reimburse employees for the cost of health insurance premiums through HRAs.

See Q 445 for a discussion of situations where an employer-sponsored reimbursement arrangement may be treated as integrated with another type of policy so as to avoid violating the prohibition on annual benefit limits.

454. What are the consequences if an employer reimburses its employees for the cost of individual health insurance premiums?

Reimbursement arrangements whereby an employer reimburses its employees for the cost of individual health insurance premiums generally are themselves considered group health plans and cannot be integrated with individual policies in order to satisfy the market reform provisions of the Affordable Care Act (ACA). As a result, these arrangements will typically violate the ACA prohibition on annual benefit limits and provision of preventive care without employee costs, and will cause the employer to be subject to a $100 per day penalty per employee.[1] This penalty is subject to the guidance provided in IRS Notice 2015-17 and the 21st Century Cures Act, which provide relief to small employers who are not applicable large employers subject to the employer mandate and to S corporations in regard to their shareholders.

455. How does the ACA affect HSAs and Archer MSAs?

The health care reform law amends IRC Section 223(d)(2)(A) with respect to health savings accounts ("HSAs") and IRC Section 220(d)(2)(A) with respect to Archer medical savings accounts ("MSAs") to provide that for amounts paid after December 31, 2010, a distribution from an HSA or Archer MSA for a medicine or drug is a tax-free qualified medical expense only if the medicine or drug (1) requires a prescription, (2) is an over-the-counter medicine or drug and the individual obtains a prescription, or (3) is insulin.

If amounts are distributed from an HSA or Archer MSA for any medicine or drug that does not satisfy these requirements, the amounts are distributions for nonqualified medical expenses, which are includable in gross income and generally are subject to a 20 percent additional tax. This change does not affect HSA or Archer MSA distributions for medicines or drugs made before January 1, 2011, nor does it affect distributions made after December 31, 2010, for medicines or drugs purchased on or before that date.

IRS guidance reflecting these statutory changes makes it clear that the rules in IRC Sections 106(f), 223(d)(2)(A), and 220(d)(2)(A) do not apply to items that are not medicines or drugs,

1. See IRS FAQ, Employer Health Care Arrangements, updated December 9, 2014, available at http://www.irs.gov/Affordable-Care-Act/Employer-Health-Care-Arrangements. See also IRC Sec. 4980D.

including equipment such as crutches, supplies such as bandages, and diagnostic devices such as blood sugar test kits. These items may qualify as medical care if they otherwise meet the definition of medical care in IRC Section 213(d)(1), which includes expenses for the diagnosis, cure, mitigation, treatment, or prevention of disease, or for the purpose of affecting any structure or function of the body.

Expenses for items that are merely beneficial to the general health of an individual, such as expenditures for a vacation, are not expenses for medical care.

456. How does the ACA affect the use of debit cards to pay for medical care expenses?

Another issue to consider is the use of health flexible spending account ("FSA") or health reimbursement account ("HRA") debit cards. The current rules are set forth in Proposed Treasury Regulation Section 1.125-6 and in Revenue Ruling 2003-43, 2003-1 C.B. 935; Notice 2006-69, 2006-2 C.B. 107; Notice 2007-2, 2007-1 C.B. 254; and Notice 2008-104, 2008-2 C.B. 1298.

Debit card systems have not been capable of substantiating compliance with new IRC Section 106(f) with respect to over-the-counter medicines or drugs because the systems were incapable of recognizing and substantiating that the medicines or drugs were prescribed. Therefore, except as noted below, for expenses incurred on and after January 1, 2011, these health FSA and HRA debit cards could not be used to purchase over-the-counter medicines or drugs. The IRS indicated, however, that to facilitate the significant changes to existing systems necessary to reflect the statutory change, it would not challenge the use of health FSA and HRA debit cards for expenses incurred through January 15, 2011, if the use of the debit cards complied with then current rules.

The IRS made it clear, however, that on and after January 16, 2011, over-the-counter medicine or drug purchases at all providers and merchants, whether or not they have an inventory information approval system ("IIAS"), must be substantiated before reimbursement may be made. Substantiation is accomplished by submitting the prescription, a copy of the prescription, or other documentation that a prescription has been issued for an over-the-counter medicine or drug and other information from an independent third party that satisfies the requirements under Proposed Treasury Regulation Section 1.125-6(b)(3)(i).

Thus, for example, the substantiation requirements for over-the-counter medicines or drugs are satisfied by (1) a receipt without a prescription number accompanied by a copy of the prescription or (2) a customer receipt issued by a pharmacy that identifies the name of the purchaser or the name of the person for whom the prescription applies, the date and amount of the purchase, and a prescription number. Debit cards may continue to be used for medical expenses other than over-the-counter medicines or drugs.

Health FSA and HRA debit cards may be used at a pharmacy that does not have an IIAS if 90 percent of the store's gross receipts during the prior taxable year consisted of items that qualified as expenses for medical care under IRC Section 213(d).

Until further guidance is issued, debit cards may be used at a pharmacy that satisfies the 90 percent test to purchase over-the-counter medicines or drugs that have been prescribed provided that substantiation is properly submitted in accordance with the terms of the plan, including the prescription or a copy of the prescription or other documentation that a prescription has been issued, and other information from an independent third party that satisfies the requirements under Proposed Treasury Regulation Section 1.125-6(b)(3)(i). Solely for the purpose of determining whether a pharmacy meets this 90 percent test, sales of over-the-counter medicines and drugs at the pharmacy may continue to be taken into account after December 31, 2010.

457. What is the required W-2 reporting for health insurance expenses?

For tax years beginning after December 31, 2010, health care reform originally required that employers disclose the value of benefits provided for each employee's health insurance coverage on employee W-2 forms. This reporting was to give the federal government statistical information and did not change the income tax treatment for employers or employees.

The required reporting rules were delayed twice. Health care reform required W-2s for the 2011 year to provide the cost of health coverage. That requirement was delayed and made applicable for W-2s issued for the 2012 year. Additionally, IRS Notice 2011-28 (as modified by Notice 2012-9) provides an exemption for this delayed reporting requirement. Until further notice from the IRS, an employer is not subject to the reporting requirement for any calendar year if the employer was required to file fewer than 250 Forms W-2 for the preceding calendar year. The IRS has advised that any guidance expanding the reporting requirements will apply to calendar years that begin at least six months after the date that such guidance is issued.

Planning Point: If employees talk to one another, the new W-2 reporting may mean that employees can discover that their employer pays nothing for some employees and thousands for others, especially in grandfathered plans that are not subject to nondiscrimination rules so long as they retain their grandfathered status. It has been quite common for small employers to provide family coverage for owners and key employees, to provide single employee coverage often with less than 100 percent of cost for other employees, and to exclude employees who have health insurance through another source, such as a spouse's employment.

458. What is the new simple cafeteria plan that is available beginning in 2011?

The health care reform law includes a provision creating simple cafeteria plans for small businesses, namely those with average employment of 100 or fewer employees, effective for years beginning in 2011 and thereafter. The concept is similar to 401(k) retirement plan safe harbors, SIMPLE 401(k)s, and SIMPLE-IRAs.

Employer and employee contributions are deductible, not subject to Social Security tax, and not taxable income to participants. Thus, available benefits can be purchased with pre-tax dollars. Available benefits include health and dental insurance, reimbursement for health and dental expenses not covered by insurance, dependent care, group term life insurance, health savings accounts, and disability insurance.

Simple cafeteria plans automatically meet nondiscrimination requirements of IRC Section 125(b), the 25 percent concentration test, and nondiscrimination requirements of IRC Sections 79(d), 105(h), and 129(d) applicable to group term life insurance, self-insured health benefits (medical reimbursement), and dependent care assistance benefits (child care), respectively.

Through an apparent oversight, IRC Section 125(j) does not provide an express exception for the health insurance nondiscrimination rules of new IRC Section 9815. It is likely that if the same insurance options are available to all participants, regardless of their use, the health insurance nondiscrimination rules will be met. The health insurance nondiscrimination regulations will provide the definitive answer.

Where a business wants to avoid the 25 percent concentration test and contribute for owner-employees, only a regular C corporation can do so because owner-employees are only employees for income tax purposes in this context. Sole proprietors, 2 percent or more S corporation shareholders, and partners, including members of LLCs taxed as partnerships, are not employees for income tax purposes. Instead, they are treated as self-employed individuals.

459. What are the requirements for the new simple cafeteria plan?

100 or Fewer Employees

An employer is eligible to implement a simple cafeteria plan if, during either of the preceding two years, it employed 100 or fewer employees on average, based on business days.

For a new business, eligibility is based on the number of employees the business reasonably is expected to employ.

Businesses maintaining a simple cafeteria plan that grow beyond 100 employees can continue to maintain the simple arrangement until they have exceeded an average of 200 or more employees during a preceding year.

Employees include leased employees.

Controlled and Affiliated Service Groups

For purposes of determining an eligible employer, employer aggregation rules govern under (1) IRC Section 52, which applies the rules of IRC Section 1563, except "more than 50 percent" is substituted for "at least 80 percent" in IRC Section 1563(a)(1), and subsections 1563(a)(4) and 1563(e)(3)(C) are disregarded, and (2) IRC Section 414, relating to controlled and affiliated service groups. Additionally, an employer includes a predecessor employer, which is undefined.

Qualified Employees

All non-excludable employees who had at least 1,000 hours of service during a preceding plan year must be eligible to participate in a simple cafeteria plan. The term qualified employee means any employee who is not a highly compensated employee under IRC Section 414(q) or a key employee under IRC Section 416(i) and who is eligible to participate in a plan.

This definition of qualified employee is relevant only to the two alternative minimum contribution requirements, discussed below, and to highly compensated employees ("HCEs") and key employees. HCEs and key employees may participate in the same manner as everyone else so long as they are employees and do not receive disproportionate employer nonelective or matching contributions. Comparable contributions must be made for all eligible employees.

Excludable Employees

Excludable employees are those who:

(1) have not attained age twenty-one (or a younger age if provided in the plan) before the end of the plan year;

(2) have less than one year of service as of any day during a plan year;

(3) are covered under a collective bargaining agreement; or

(4) are nonresident aliens.

An employer may have a shorter age and service requirement, but only if such shorter service or younger age applies to all employees.

Employees who previously worked 1,000 hours in a plan year, but do not currently, can be excluded because employees who do not have a year of service in the current plan year can be excluded. Because the rule is that they can be excluded if they do not have a year of service on any day in the year, they will have 1,000 hours if they go from full-time to part-time at the beginning of the current year. This is an important point when an employee's salary is less than the health benefits. The employee should be entitled to the entire maximum benefit if elected, even if greater than compensation, to safeguard simple status.

Benefit Nondiscrimination

Each eligible employee must be able to elect any benefit under a plan under the same terms and conditions as all other participants.

Minimum Contribution Requirement

The minimum must be available for application toward the cost of any qualified benefit, other than a taxable benefit, offered under a plan.

Employer contributions to a simple cafeteria plan must be sufficient to provide benefits to non-highly compensated employees ("NHCEs") of at least either:

(1) A uniform percentage of at least two percent of compensation, as defined under IRC Section 414(s) for retirement plan purposes, whether or not the employee makes salary reduction contributions to a plan; or

(2) The lesser of a 200 percent matching contribution or six percent of an employee's compensation. Additional contributions can be made, but the rate of any matching

contribution for HCEs or key employees cannot be greater than the rate of match for NHCEs under IRC Section 125(j)(B).

The same method must be used for calculating the minimum contribution for all NHCEs. The rate of contributions for key employees and HCEs cannot exceed that for NHCEs. Compensation for purposes of this minimum contribution requirement is compensation within the meaning of IRC Section 414(s).

460. What were the deadlines for amending cafeteria plans to take into account changes implemented by the Affordable Care Act?

Cafeteria plans that allow reimbursement for over-the-counter drugs were required to be amended for the new over-the-counter drug requirements. An amendment to conform a cafeteria plan to the new requirements that was adopted no later than June 30, 2011, could be made effective retroactively for expenses incurred after December 31, 2010, or after January 15, 2011, for health FSA and HRA debit card purchases.

Additionally, fiscal year cafeteria plans could be amended to provide that elections to purchase health insurance can be changed mid-year to allow for the purchase of insurance on an exchange or in plan for the fiscal year cafeteria plan year beginning in 2013.

Such an election to purchase or to cease purchasing health insurance could be made mid-year despite the fact that this is not a change in status, which is a normal prerequisite to change a cafeteria plan election. Employees may have wished to terminate their election to purchase health insurance through the employer's cafeteria plan and go to the exchange if they were eligible for health insurance exchange tax credits. Other employees may have wanted to elect to purchase health insurance from the employer plan effective January 1, 2014 to avoid the individual mandate penalty (which was repealed for tax years beginning after 2018). If the cafeteria plan year is a fiscal year, employees who wished to purchase insurance on an exchange that was effective on January 1, 2014, would have been required to terminate or change their elections mid-year. However, under current cafeteria plan regulations, these two elections are not a change in status allowing an election change mid-year. The proposed regulations allowed an applicable large employer with a fiscal year cafeteria plan, at its election, to amend the plan any time during the year on a retroactive basis (by December 31, 2014, retroactive to the beginning of the 2013 plan year) to permit either or both of the following changes in salary reduction elections:[1]

(1) An employee who elected to reduce salary through the fiscal year cafeteria plan for accident and health plan coverage beginning in 2013 was allowed to prospectively revoke or change the election with respect to the accident and health plan once, during that plan year, without regard to whether the employee experienced a change in status event described in Treasury Regulation Section 1.125-4; and

(2) An employee who failed to make a salary reduction election through the employer's fiscal year cafeteria plan beginning in 2013 for accident and health plan coverage

1. Preamble to Proposed Rules on Shared Responsibility for Employers Regarding Health Coverage, 78 Fed. Reg. 217, 237 (Jan. 2, 2013).

before the deadline in Proposed Treasury Regulation Section 1.125-2 for making elections was allowed to make a prospective salary reduction election for accident and health coverage on or after the first day of the 2013 plan year of the cafeteria plan without regard to whether the employee experienced a change in status event described in Treasury Regulation Section 1.125-4.

Planning Point: Some provisions of the transition relief refer to "applicable large employer members" (i.e., employers that are subject to healthcare reform's employer mandate), raising questions as to whether the relief is available for all non-calendar-year cafeteria plans or only those that are sponsored by applicable large employer members.

461. Did Congress repeal the new and expanded 1099 requirements that were to be effective in 2012?

Yes.

A business making payments to a service provider other than a corporation aggregating $600 or more for services in the course of a trade or business in a year is required to send an information return (Form 1099) to the IRS (and to the service provider-payee) setting forth the amount, as well as name and address of the recipient of the payment (generally on Form 1099).

The new law changed this requirement so that businesses had to issue 1099 forms to all persons and businesses, including corporations, for which aggregate annual payments are $600 or more, among other things.

Health care reform expanded the 1099 requirements in two ways:

(1) 1099s were required to be issued to corporations, and

(2) 1099s were required to be issued for purchases of goods and products (rather than only services) that exceeded $600 per year.

On April 5, 2011 the Senate approved H.R. 4, the Comprehensive 1099 Taxpayer Protection and Repayment of Exchange Subsidy Overpayments Act of 2011, which retroactively repeals expanded Form 1099 information reporting rules. President Obama signed the bill into law on April 14, 2011. Therefore, taxpayers were not required to take any steps in 2012 and thereafter to comply with the new 1099 requirement.

462. What new federal long-term care benefit was to become available in 2012 for which employees could elect to pay?

In October of 2011, the Department of Health and Human Services ("HHS") announced that it had suspended its work on implementing the Community Living Assistance Services and Support ("CLASS") Act, which was to provide long-term care benefits in voluntary employer sponsored plans. HHS announced that it was unable to find a way to make the program work. The American Taxpayer Relief Act of 2012 formally repealed the CLASS program.

Under the proposed plan, employees of companies that elected to participate would be automatically enrolled, but could elect to opt out. Employees who did not opt out would pay for this coverage through payroll deductions. Other workers and self-employed individuals could have enrolled on their own. Retirees were not eligible.

After an individual paid premiums for five years and had worked for three of those five years, the employee would have been eligible for a cash benefit of about $50 per day if unable to perform two or three activities of daily living, such as walking, bathing, or dressing, or if the individual became cognitively impaired.

HHS had not yet set the premiums, but the American Academy of Actuaries estimated that the premiums could average as much as $125 to $160 per month, or as little as $5 per month for those below the poverty line. The high-end estimate is about the same price that a relatively healthy fifty year old would pay for a private long-term care policy providing about three times that daily benefit for three years. A study by the actuarial consulting firm, Milliman, found that only 8 percent of long-term care claimants who had policies with a three year benefit period exhausted their benefits.

Under the CLASS Act, a person could not be rejected for coverage because of health, so it was meant to help people with medical conditions that do not qualify for private long-term care insurance or are highly rated. Additionally, it would have covered many services that are not eligible for benefits under most long-term care plans, including homemaker services, home modifications, and transportation, that are typically used to help a person stay out of a nursing home.

463. What are the requirements regarding the purchase of health insurance or the payment of a penalty?

Editor's Note: The 2017 tax reform legislation repealed the Affordable Care Act individual mandate that required individuals to purchase health insurance or pay a penalty for tax years beginning after December 31, 2018. The employer mandate and reporting requirements were not repealed.

Health care reform required most Americans to have health insurance beginning in 2014 in order to avoid liability for a monetary penalty referred to as the individual mandate.

Unless exempt, prior to 2019, Americans were required to have major medical health coverage provided by their employer or that they purchase themselves, or they became subject to a fine that was the greater of a flat amount, or a percentage of income (above the tax filing threshold). The amounts were $95 or 1 percent of income in 2014; $325 or 2 percent of income in 2015; and $695 or 2.5 percent of income in 2016. Families paid half the penalty amount for children under eighteen, up to a cap of $2,085 per family. After 2016, penalties were indexed to the Consumer Price Index. In 2017 and 2018, the inflation-adjusted dollar amount was $695.[1] In no event could the penalty exceed the average national annual cost of a bronze plan purchased on an exchange.[2] After 2018, the penalty no longer applies.

1. Rev. Proc. 2016-55.
2. IRC Sec. 5000A(c).

Exemptions from the individual penalty will be granted for financial hardship, religious objections, American Indians, those without coverage for fewer than three months, undocumented immigrants, incarcerated individuals, those for whom the lowest cost plan option exceeds 8 percent of an individual's income, and those with incomes below the tax filing threshold.[1]

464. What is the ACA requirement to maintain minimum essential health coverage?

Editor's Note: The 2017 tax reform legislation repealed the Affordable Care Act individual mandate that required individuals to purchase health insurance or pay a penalty for tax years beginning after December 31, 2018. The employer mandate and reporting requirements were not repealed. The rules discussed below regarding the individual mandate apply for tax years beginning before January 1, 2019.

For taxable years ending after December 31, 2013 (and before January 1, 2019, with respect to the individual mandate), the ACA requires an applicable individual to ensure that the individual, and any dependent of the individual who is an applicable individual, is covered under a health insurance plan that provides minimum essential coverage or else pay a penalty.[2]

Applicable individual means, with respect to any month, an individual other than individuals who have religious exemptions, individuals not lawfully present in the United States, and incarcerated individuals.[3]

No penalty will be imposed on an individual who falls under one of the following exemptions:

(1) an individual whose required contribution for coverage for the month exceeds 8 percent (as indexed after 2014, 8.05 percent in 2015, 8.13 percent in 2016, 8.16 percent in 2017, and 8.05 percent in 2018—the penalty will not apply after 2018)[4] of the individual's household income for the most recent taxable year (household income is increased by any exclusion from gross income for any portion of the required contribution made through a salary reduction arrangement);

(2) taxpayers with income that is less than the amount of the tax exemption on gross income specified in Section 6012(a)(1);

(3) members of Indian tribes;

(4) months during short coverage gaps (generally, any month the last day of which occurred during a period in which the applicable individual was not covered by minimum essential coverage for a continuous period of fewer than three months); and

1. IRC Sec. 5000A(d).
2. IRC Secs. 5000A(a), 5000A(b)(1), 5000A(d), as added by PPACA 2010.
3. IRC Secs. 5000A(d)(2), 5000A(d)(3), 5000A(d)(4), as added by PPACA 2010.
4. Rev. Proc. 2014-37, Rev. Proc. 2016-24.

(5) any applicable individual who for any month is determined by the Secretary of Health and Human Services to have suffered a hardship with respect to the capability to obtain coverage under a qualified health plan.[1]

465. When does a taxpayer have minimum essential coverage in order to avoid becoming subject to the Affordable Care Act penalty after 2013?

Editor's Note: The 2017 tax reform legislation repealed the Affordable Care Act individual mandate that required individuals to purchase health insurance or pay a penalty for tax years beginning after December 31, 2018. The employer mandate and reporting requirements were not repealed. The rules discussed below regarding the individual mandate apply for tax years beginning before January 1, 2019.

Minimum essential coverage means coverage under any of the following:

(1) government sponsored programs (Medicare, Medicaid, the Children's Health Insurance Program, the TRICARE for Life program, the veterans' health care program, the health plan for Peace Corps volunteers, and the Nonappropriated Fund Health Benefits Program of the Department of Defense);

(2) an eligible employer sponsored plan, which means with respect to any employee, a group health plan or group health insurance coverage offered by an employer to the employee that is a governmental plan or any other plan or coverage offered in the small or large group market within a state (including grandfathered health plans);

(3) plans in the individual market (coverage under a health plan offered in the individual market within a state);

(4) grandfathered health plans; and

(5) other health benefits coverage (e.g., a state health benefits risk pool), as the Secretary of Health and Human Services recognizes for this purpose).[2]

466. What was the penalty for an individual who chooses to remain uninsured under the Affordable Care Act?

Editor's Note: The 2017 tax reform legislation repealed the Affordable Care Act individual mandate that required individuals to purchase health insurance or pay a penalty for tax years beginning after December 31, 2018. The employer mandate and reporting requirements were not repealed. The rules discussed below regarding the individual mandate apply for tax years beginning before January 1, 2019.

If a taxpayer who is an applicable individual, or an applicable individual for whom the taxpayer is liable, fails to meet the requirement of maintaining minimum essential coverage for

1. IRC Sec. 5000A(e), as added by PPACA 2010, as amended by HCEARA 2010.
2. IRC Sec. 5000A(f), as added by PPACA 2010.

one or more months, a penalty will be imposed on the taxpayer.[1] If an individual on whom a penalty is imposed files a joint return for the taxable year including that month, the individual and spouse will be jointly liable for the penalty.[2]

The penalty schedule is shown in the Uninsured Penalty Table, below.[3]

UNINSURED PENALTY TABLE**				
Year	Flat Penalty Per Adult	Flat Penalty Under Age 18	Household Maximum Penalty	Income Percentage Penalty
2014	$95	$47.50	$285	1%
2015	$325	$162.50	$975	2%
2016-2018[4]	$695*	$347.50*	$2,085*	2.5%
* Indexed for inflation after 2016 ** Penalty will not apply after 2018.				

If the penalty applies, a flat penalty applies per each uninsured adult or child under age eighteen in a household. The penalty is increased to an amount equal to the income percentage multiplied by the amount of household income in excess of the income tax return filing threshold, if that is greater than the flat penalty. The dollar amount penalty cannot be greater than the household maximum penalty, which is 300 percent of the flat dollar amount;[5] in the case of the income percentage penalty, it cannot be greater than an amount equal to the national average premium for a bronze plan for the applicable family size involved.[6]

467. What is the employer mandate imposed by the ACA?

Employers with at least fifty full-time equivalent employees ("FTEs") must offer insurance meeting specified requirements or pay a $2,000 per full-time worker penalty after its first thirty employees if any of its full-time employees receive a federal premium subsidy through a state health insurance exchange (which would occur because the employee was not being offered sufficient coverage through the employer).[7]

A different penalty applies for employers of at least fifty full-time equivalent employees that offer some insurance coverage but not enough to meet federal requirements. In this case, the penalty is $3,000 per full-time employee who gets government assistance and buys coverage in an exchange, subject to a maximum penalty of $2,000 times the number of full-time employees in excess of the first thirty.[8]

1. IRC Sec. 5000A(b)(1), as added by PPACA 2010, as amended by PPACA 2010 Section 10106, as further amended by HCEARA 2010.
2. IRC Sec. 5000A(b),(3)(B), as added by of PPACA 2010 Section 1501(b).
3. IRC Sec. 5000A(c), as added by of PPACA 2010 Section 1501(b), as amended by PPACA 2010 Section 10106, as further amended by HCEARA 2010.
4. Rev. Proc. 2016-55, Rev. Proc. 2017-58.
5. IRC Sec. 5000A(c), as added by of PPACA 2010 Section 1501(b), as amended by PPACA 2010 Section 10106, as further amended by HCEARA 2010 and repealed by the 2017 Tax Act (Pub. Law No. 115-97).
6. IRC Sec. 5000(A)(c)(1)(B).
7. IRC Secs. 4980H(a), 4980H(c)(1).
8. IRC Sec. 4980H(b).

The shared responsibility penalty on employers for failing to provide minimum essential health insurance excludes excepted benefits under Public Health Service Act 2971(c), including long-term care as well as standalone vision and standalone dental plans.

Planning Point: Applicable large employers have begun to receive notices regarding liability for the employer shared responsibility penalties via 226J letters. These letters detail the employer's violation and it is important that any employer who receives a 226J letter responds within the time frame listed in the letter. Letter 226J should contain a deadline for a response, usually thirty days after the letter was issued (employers may request a thirty-day extension by calling a 4980H response unit number listed on the letter itself). It is important to get expert advice when drafting the response, but issues to consider include whether the IRS was using the correct data (i.e., was a corrected Form 1094 filed with the IRS in the year to which the letter relates?), whether the plan was a calendar year plan (transition relief may apply) and whether the employer did, in fact, offer minimum coverage during each month.

On June 28, 2012, the Supreme Court, in *National Federation of Independent Business v. Sebelius*, upheld the constitutionality of the Patient Protection and Affordable Care Act, with only minor changes to certain Medicaid provisions.

468. Is there any transition relief provided with respect to the employer mandate?

Previous guidance delayed application of the employer penalty from 2014 to 2015. Final regulations provide new transitional relief for two types of employers. The applicable large employer status (which triggers the potential application of the mandate) for a calendar year is still based on the number of employees in the preceding calendar year.[1] Transition rules, discussed below, included those for non-calendar year health plans, the ability to count employees for less than twelve months in 2014 to determine applicable large employer status, initial offers of health coverage in 2015, dependent coverage, employers with at least 50 but less than 100 full-time and full-time equivalent (FTE) employees, and reduction of the 95 percent offer of health coverage requirement to 70 percent for 2015.

The proposed employer mandate regulations allowed employers with fiscal year cafeteria plans to amend their cafeteria plans to permit employees to elect or revoke health coverage elections mid-year even absent a corresponding change in status or cost of coverage change during a non-calendar plan year that began in 2013.[2] The final regulations did not extend this relief. The following rules also apply:

<u>If the employer had on average fewer than fifty full-time (and full-time equivalent) employees (FTEs) in 2014</u>:

- No change. The employer is not subject to the mandate. Employers close to the fifty-employee threshold may count employees during any consecutive six-month period (as chosen by the employer) during 2014.

1. Treas. Reg. §54.4980H-2(b).
2. See Notice 2013-71, which clarified this transition relief.

If the employer had on average between fifty and ninety-nine FTEs in 2014:

- The employer had a one-year delay in the employer mandate, until January 1, 2016 (and for non-calendar-year plans, any calendar months during the plan year beginning in 2015 that fall in 2016) if:
  - The employer certified it did not lay off employees during the period beginning on February 9, 2014 and ending on December 31, 2014 to fall below the 100 employee threshold and that the employer did not reduce any coverage it was already offering, and
  - During the period beginning on February 9, 2014 and ending on December 31, 2014, the employer did not eliminate or materially reduce the health coverage, if any, offered as of February 9, 2014. An employer was not treated as eliminating or materially reducing health coverage if, for each employee who was eligible for coverage on February 9, 2014:

    (a) The employer offered to make a contribution toward the cost of employee-only coverage that was either (i) at least 95 percent of the dollar amount of the contribution the employer was making toward the coverage in effect as of February 9, 2014, or (ii) at least the same percentage of the cost of coverage that the employer offered to contribute toward coverage in effect as of February 9, 2014;

    (b) Benefits offered as of February 9, 2014 at the employee-only coverage level did not change, or, if it did, the coverage after the change provided minimum value; and

    (c) Eligibility under the employer's group health plans was not amended to narrow or reduce the class or classes of employees (or the employees' dependents) to whom coverage under those plans was offered as of February 9, 2014.
  - Such employer must report coverage of employer's employees for 2015.

If the employer had on average 100 or more FTEs in 2014:

- If an employer failed to offer coverage to a full-time employee for any day of a calendar month, that employee was treated as not having been offered coverage during the entire month. For January 2015, if an employer offered coverage to a full-time employee no later than the first day of the first payroll period that began in January 2015, the employee was treated as having been offered coverage for January 2015.
- Employers with Fiscal Year Health Plans. The employer mandate remained effective on January 1, 2015. However, employers with non-calendar (fiscal) year plans could be subject to the mandate based on the start of their 2015 plan year rather than on January 1, 2015, and other transition relief where certain conditions were met, as follows:

(a) Pre-2015 FiscalYear Plan EligibilityTransition Relief. Pre-2015 eligibility transition relief applies to employees, whenever hired, who were:

- Eligible for coverage on the first day of the 2015 plan year under the eligibility terms of the plan as of February 9, 2014 (whether or not they elected coverage); and

- Offered affordable coverage that provided minimum value effective no later than the first day of the 2015 plan year.

Where these two conditions were satisfied, the employer was not subject to a potential employer shared responsibility payment until the first day of the 2015 plan year. This relief applied only to employees to whom coverage was previously offered by the employer. Thus, penalties could still be imposed for the months in 2015 that were part of the plan year commencing in 2014 for employees to whom coverage was not previously offered.

(b) Significant Percentage Fiscal Year Plan Transition Relief (All Employees). No employer mandate penalty applied for any month before the first day of the plan year beginning in 2015 for employees who were offered affordable coverage that provided minimum value by the first day of the 2015 plan year if, as of any date in the twelve months ending on February 9, 2014, an employer:

- Covered at least one-quarter of its employees (full-time and part-time) under its non-calendar year plan; or

- Offered coverage under the plan to one-third or more of its employees during the open enrollment period that ended most recently before February 9, 2014.

To qualify for this relief, the employee must not have been eligible for coverage as of February 9, 2014 under any group health plan maintained by his or her employer that has a calendar year plan year.

Planning Point: Unlike the pre-2015 eligibility transition relief discussed above, an employer that qualifies for this relief and who offers affordable, minimum value coverage commencing with the 2015 plan year has no IRC Section 4980H exposure for periods before the 2015 plan year. Relief under this and the next transition rule applies for the period before the first day of the first non-calendar year plan year beginning in 2015 but only for employers that maintained non-calendar year plans as of December 27, 2012, and only if the plan year was not modified after December 27, 2012, to begin at a later calendar date.

- 70 Percent Offer in 2015. For 2015 (and for any calendar months during a non-calendar year plan year beginning in 2015 that fall in 2016), the 95 percent offer of coverage threshold was lowered to 70 percent. Thus, in 2015, an employer would be in compliance if it offered coverage to at least 70 percent of full-time employees and dependents in 2015 unless the employer qualified for the 2015 dependent coverage transition relief, discussed below), although an employer will owe a penalty if at least one of the full-time employees received a premium tax credit for coverage in the public marketplace, which may have occurred because the employer did not offer coverage to that employee or because the coverage the employer offered was either unaffordable or did not provide minimum value.

- Dependent Coverage. In order to avoid exposure for the employer mandate penalty, an employer must offer coverage not only to full-time employees but also to their dependents (but not spouses). The final regulations provide transition relief for plan years that begin in 2015 if the employer took steps during the 2015 plan year toward satisfying this requirement in 2016. The transition relief applied to employers for the 2015 plan year for plans under which (i) dependent coverage was not offered, (ii) dependent coverage that does not constitute minimum essential coverage was offered, or (iii) dependent coverage was offered for some, but not all, dependents. This relief is not available, however, if the employer had offered dependent coverage during either the plan year that begins in 2013 or the 2014 plan year and subsequently eliminated that offer of coverage.
- In 2016 and after, the employer must offer coverage to at least 95 percent of full-time employees and dependents.
- These applicable large employers must report coverage of employees beginning with 2015.
- An applicable large employer will not be subject to shared responsibility penalties with respect to employees for whom the employer is required (whether by the collective bargaining agreement or appropriate related participation agreement) to make contributions to a multiemployer plan.

469. How does an employer determine how many full-time employees (FTEs) it has for purposes of the employer mandate?

To calculate the number of FTEs for purposes of determining if an employer is an applicable large employer subject to the employer mandate, full-time is 120 hours per month. If an employer was not in existence during the prior calendar year, an employer is a large employer for the current calendar year if it is reasonably expected to employ at least 50 FTEs. If an employer's FTEs exceed fifty for 120 days or less and the excess employees are seasonal workers, then the employer is not a large employer.[1]

For purposes of the employer mandate penalty assessments (as opposed to determining whether the employer is an applicable large employer), the law defines full-time as thirty hours of service per week, and the regulations provide that 130 (not 120) hours per month is the monthly equivalent, both determined in the current month/year. To address the calculation difficulty concern, the regulations provide alternatives to a month-by-month determination. For on-going employees, an employer has the option of using a "look-back measurement" method for determining current full-time status. The employer selects a measurement period of three to twelve months and calculates whether the employee on average had thirty hours of service per week (or 130 hours per month) during that period. If so, the employer must treat the employee

1. IRC Sec. 4980H(c)(2)(B).

as full-time during a subsequent "stability period," which must be at least six months but no shorter than the length of the measurement period. Thus, if the employer used a twelve-month look-back measurement period beginning on January 1, 2019, employees who are determined to be full-time must be treated as full-time for all of calendar year 2020. An employer may also utilize an optional administrative period of up to ninety days between the measurement period and the stability period in order to determine which on-going employees are eligible for health insurance coverage during the subsequent stability period. However, the administrative period cannot create a gap in coverage. An employee who was enrolled in coverage must remain enrolled during the administrative period.[1]

470. What is the premium tax credit that is available to low and moderate income taxpayers beginning in 2014?

Starting in 2014, health care reform legislation required that state-based health insurance exchanges be established through which individuals and smaller businesses could purchase health insurance coverage, with premium and cost-sharing credits available to individuals and families with incomes between 133-400 percent of the federal poverty level.

The 2018 poverty level (used for the 2019 tax year, and updated annually by the Department of Health and Human Services) for a family of three generally was $20,780, except in Alaska and Hawaii, where it is $25,980 and $23,900, respectively. The 2017 poverty level (updated annually by the Department of Health and Human Services) for a family of three generally was $20,420, except in Alaska and Hawaii, where it is $25,520 and $23,480, respectively. The 2016 poverty level for a family of three generally was $20,160, except in Alaska and Hawaii, where it was $25,200 and $23,190, respectively. The 2015 poverty level for a family of three generally was $20,090, except in Alaska and Hawaii, where it was $25,120 and $23,110, respectively. The 2014 poverty level for a family of three generally was $19,790, except in Alaska and Hawaii, where it was $24,740 and $22,760, respectively, for a family of three.

In addition to meeting the income requirements, a qualifying taxpayer must purchase health insurance on one of the exchanges, must be otherwise unable to obtain affordable coverage through an employer or government program and cannot be eligible to be claimed as a dependent by any other taxpayer. The tax credit can either be paid by the government to the insurance company in advance, or can be refunded to a taxpayer who has already paid for health coverage after the taxpayer files a tax return.

Additionally, beginning in 2014, Medicaid was to be expanded and available to all families with incomes at or below 133 percent of the federal poverty level. However, this Medicaid expansion requires each state to authorize the expansion, and almost half the states have not done so.

On June 28, 2012, the Supreme Court, in *National Federation of Independent Business v. Sebelius*, upheld the constitutionality of the Patient Protection and Affordable Care Act, with only minor changes to certain Medicaid provisions.

1. Notice 2011-36, 2011-21 IRB 792, Notice 2012-58, 2012-41 IRB 436.

471. What is the penalty for employers with employees who obtain health coverage through a health care exchange and are eligible for the premium tax credit?

Employers with fifty or more full-time equivalent (FTE) employees and more than thirty full-time employees (where full-time employees are those regularly scheduled to work more than thirty hours per week and more than 120 days per year), may be required to pay penalties (in the form of a nondeductible excise tax) for employees who do not receive coverage through the employer and instead purchase health insurance through a state health insurance exchange and receive tax credits (see Q 470). For further description of potential health care coverage penalties, see Q 463.

Employers with fewer than fifty full-time FTE employees are exempt from the penalty. Workers who are independent contractors do not count as employees unless it is found that they actually are employees despite being called independent contractors.

472. What is the penalty for employers who provide high-cost employer-sponsored health coverage to employees?

Employers that offer high cost health coverage options to employees that exceed the cost of the excess benefit for tax years beginning after December 31, 2021 (the so-called "Cadillac tax") will be subject to a penalty.[1] This applicability date was delayed two years by the Protecting Americans from Tax Hikes Act of 2015 (PATH), and another two years by a budget deal reached by Congress in early 2018.

To determine whether an excess benefit has been provided, the employer must determine a monthly excess amount, which is the excess of the cost of the coverage for the employee over an amount equal to 1/12 of the "annual limitation" for the year. The annual limitation in the first year the tax is applicable is $10,200 multiplied by the health cost adjustment percentage ($27,500 for coverage other than self-only coverage). The annual limitation amount will be adjusted annually for inflation. The health cost adjustment percentage is 100 percent plus the excess of: (1) the percentage by which the per-employee cost for providing coverage under the Blue Cross/Blue Shield standard benefit option under the Federal Employees Health Benefits Plan for 2018 exceeds such cost for the plan year over (2) 55 percent.[2]

The IRS issued Notice 2015-16, which describes potential approaches for determining what constitutes "applicable coverage" that will be included in calculating the per-employee cost in order to determine whether the coverage is subject to the Cadillac tax. The guidance provides that the IRS expects that future proposed regulations will exclude from the definition of applicable coverage employee after-tax contributions to HSAs and Archer MSAs, though employer contributions to these accounts (including salary reduction contributions) will be included in determining the cost of coverage for the employee. Salary reduction contributions

1. IRC Sec. 4980(a).
2. IRC Sec. 4980I(b)(C).

to health FSAs, as well as employer flex contributions used for health FSAs, will also be included in calculating the cost of coverage.

The Treasury and IRS have indicated that they are still considering whether certain excepted benefits, such as dental and vision benefits, will be included in determining the cost of coverage and have requested comments on whether the cost of these benefits should be included. The regulatory bodies are similarly seeking comments on whether certain employee assistance program (EAP) benefits should be included.[1]

473. How did the Affordable Care Act expand the income exclusion for adult children's coverage?

Under the Affordable Care Act of 2010 ("ACA 2010"), the exclusion from gross income for amounts expended on medical care is expanded to include employer provided health coverage for any adult child of the taxpayer if the adult child has not attained the age of twenty-seven as of the end of the taxable year. According to Notice 2010-38, the adult child does not have to be eligible to be claimed as a dependent for tax purposes for this income exclusion to apply.[2]

If an employer's accident and health plan continues to provide coverage pursuant to a collective bargaining agreement for an employee who is laid off, the value of the coverage is excluded from the gross income of the laid-off employee.[3] Terminated employees who receive medical coverage under a medical plan that is part of the former employer's severance plan are considered to be employees for purposes of IRC Sections 105 and 106. Thus, an employer's contributions toward medical care for employees are excludable from income under IRC Section 106.[4] Otherwise, the exclusion is available only to active employees.

Full-time life insurance salespersons are considered employees if they are employees for Social Security purposes.[5] Coverage for other commission salespersons is taxable income to the salespersons, unless an employer-employee relationship exists.[6] In the case of shareholder-employees owning more than 2 percent of the stock of an S corporation, see Q 287.

Discrimination generally does not affect exclusion of the value of coverage. Even if a self-insured medical expense reimbursement plan discriminates in favor of highly compensated employees, the value of coverage is not taxable; only reimbursements are affected (Q 275).

Beginning in January 2012, The Affordable Care Act requires employers to report the cost of coverage under an employer-sponsored group health plan.

The fact that the cost of an employee's health care benefits is shown on the employee's Form W-2 does not mean that the benefits are taxable to the employee. There is nothing about

1. Notice 2015-16, 2015-10 IRB 732.
2. IRC Sec. 105(b), as amended by the Patient Protection and Affordable Care Act of 2010 and the Health Care and Education Reconciliation Act of 2010. Notice 2010-38, 2010-20 IRB 682.
3. See Rev. Rul. 85-121, 1985-2 CB 57.
4. Let. Rul. 9612008.
5. IRC Sec. 7701(a)(20).
6. Rev. Rul. 56-400, 1956-2 CB 116; see also IRC Sec. 3508.

the reporting requirement that causes or will cause excludable employer-provided health coverage to become taxable. The purpose of the reporting requirement is to provide employees useful and comparable consumer information on the cost of their health care coverage.

474. How will health reform affect small business?

Businesses with fewer than twenty-five full-time (and full-time equivalent) employees ("FTEs") with average compensation of under $50,000 will be eligible for a tax credit for health insurance purchased for employees. Owners, their family members, and seasonal employees are not counted and premiums paid are not eligible for the credit. This tax credit, however, is temporary. If claimed in 2010, the credit can be claimed only for a maximum of six years.

All businesses, large and small, were required to retain their current insurance plan and not reduce benefits or materially increase employee costs in order to retain grandfathered status and be exempt from the new nondiscrimination rules for health insurance.

Employers without a grandfathered health insurance plan that provides benefits favoring highly compensated employees will be subject to a penalty of $100 per day per employee who is not highly compensated once the IRS announces that the new health insurance nondiscrimination rules are in effect.

Companies with no more than forty-nine full-time and FTE workers will be less affected by the new rules because they will not be subject to any penalties for not providing adequate affordable coverage. Businesses with fifty or more FTEs must offer coverage or pay a penalty. This penalty provides employers with fifty or more FTE employees an incentive to provide coverage and not force employees to purchase health insurance through the exchanges. The penalties may, however, be far less than the cost of health insurance, which is subsidized by the exchanges only for those earning less than 400 percent of the federal poverty level.

PART V: LONG-TERM CARE INSURANCE

475. What is a qualified long-term care insurance contract?

A long-term care insurance policy issued after 1996 is a qualified long-term care insurance contract under IRC Section 7702B(b) if:

(1) The only insurance protection provided under the contract is coverage of qualified long-term care services (Q 479);

Planning Point: Although this is one of the foundational principles of qualified long-term care insurance, there is a notable exception to this rule. Since 1996 there have been scores of policy designs which pay either an indemnity (i.e., the full daily or monthly benefit without regard to costs incurred) or a cash benefit (i.e., some flat amount based solely on the insured's ability to trigger benefits—without even the prerequisite that services have been received.) Such designs *are* permitted under 7702B(2)A, which permits "per diem" payments without otherwise contradicting this principle.

(2) The contract does not pay or reimburse expenses incurred for services that are reimbursable under Title XVIII of the Social Security Act or that would be reimbursable but for the application of a deductible or coinsurance amount;

Planning Point: This paragraph refers to Medicare, which may pay for limited home health care benefits, and—subject to gatekeepers—a limited skilled nursing facility benefit as well (no more than 100 days). Prior to HIPAA, long-term care insurance policies were permitted to "duplicate" Medicare (assuming any were received by the policyholder). After HIPAA, tax-qualified (TQ) plans had to "coordinate" with Medicare.

As a result of the relatively confounding manner in which this section of the regulation is written, many producers have wondered: on the chance Medicare *does* pay for nursing facility care on days 1 – 100, can the LTCI policy pay *anything*? The answer is: yes, a TQ plan can reimburse for any charges over and above what Medicare pays. Nevertheless, either believing that it cannot, or that Medicare pays much more frequently than it does, most producers overwhelmingly sell a 90- or 100-day elimination period (in approximately nine out of ten policies).

(3) The contract is guaranteed renewable;

Planning Point: Guaranteed renewability means the insurer must not fail to renew a policy if premiums are timely paid. The insurer may not single out any policyholder for a rate increase solely because they grew older, get sick, or file a claim. Unfortunately, many consumers have interpreted this to mean their rates would *never* increase. That's not the case.

"Guaranteed Renewable" policies do permit the insurer to file a rate increase request, by state, by policy form, and by "class" (e.g., those with compound inflation protection might be a different class than those without).

Planning Point: TQ plans may also be "non-cancellable", although many think the re-appearance of such designs highly unlikely.[1]

(4) The contract does not provide for a cash surrender value or other money that can be paid, assigned, or pledged as collateral for a loan or borrowed; and

(5) All premium refunds and dividends under the contract are to be applied as a reduction in future premiums or to increase future benefits. An exception to this rule is for a refund made on the death of an insured or on a complete surrender or cancellation of a contract that cannot exceed the aggregate premiums paid. Any refund given on cancellation or complete surrender of a policy will be includable in income to the extent that any *deduction or exclusion was allowable with respect to the premiums.*[2]

Planning Point: Premium refunds paid on the insured's death are generally not taxable income to the beneficiary or estate.

In addition, a contract must satisfy certain consumer protection provisions concerning model regulation and model act provisions, disclosure, and nonforfeitability.[3]

A policy will be considered to meet the disclosure requirements if the issuer of the policy discloses in the policy and in the required outline of coverage that the policy is intended to be a qualified long-term care insurance contract under IRC Section 7702B(b).[4]

The nonforfeiture requirement is met for any level premium contract if the issuer of the contract offers to the policyholder, including any group policyholder, a non-forfeiture provision that:

(1) Is appropriately captioned;

(2) Provides for a benefit available in the event of a default in the payment of any premiums and the amount of the benefit may be adjusted only as necessary to reflect changes in claims, persistency, and interest as reflected in changes in rates for premium paying contracts approved for the same contract form; and

(3) Provides for at least one of reduced paid-up insurance, extended term insurance, shortened benefit period, or other similar approved offerings.[5]

Planning Point: The standard non-forfeiture benefit is one of the all-time least popular benefits, almost never elected. It generally provides that—should a policyholder lapse any time after the first three years due to non-payment—they will still be entitled to claim against a "pool of money" the size of their aggregate premiums paid (but not less than thirty times the daily benefit). The hitch is that additional premium is required for this rider, the cost of which never makes sense when compared to the paltry benefit conferred.

1. IRC Sec. 7702B(g).
2. IRC Sec. 7702B(b)(2)(C).
3. See IRC Sec. 7702B(g).
4. IRC Sec. 4980C(d).
5. IRC Sec. 7702B(g)(4).

A qualified long-term care insurance contract that is approved must be delivered to a policyholder within thirty days of the approval date.[1] If a claim under a qualified long-term care insurance contract is denied, the issuer must provide a written explanation of the reasons for the denial and make available all information relating to the denial within sixty days of a written request from a policyholder.[2]

Planning Point: This regulation suggests the need for policy delivery receipts. Although not all states require them, and not all carriers employ them, they do provide liability protection by proving one's policy has been timely delivered. (At which point, the clock starts on the thirty day "free look" period.)

For the treatment of long-term care insurance contracts issued before 1997, see Q 480.

476. Can a life insurance policy or annuity contract be used to provide long-term care coverage?

Yes.

A life insurance or annuity contract may provide long-term care insurance benefits. Any long-term care insurance coverage, qualified or otherwise, that is provided by a rider or as part of a life insurance or annuity contract will be treated as a separate contract for purposes of the treatment of long-term care benefits paid.[3] As such, benefits paid for qualified long-term care services are generally tax-free (regardless of the treatment otherwise applicable to a withdrawal from the underlying life or annuity contract) (Q 489).[4]

Planning Point: By linking two distinctly fundamental needs, such products have earned the moniker "combination", "hybrid", "linked-benefit" or "asset-based long-term care". There is no legal difference in these terms, which were instead born of marketing. (The IRS employs the term "combination contracts".)

There is no premium deduction permitted under IRC Section 213(a) for charges made against the cash surrender value of a life contract or cash value of an annuity contract which pay for qualified long-term care insurance (QLTCI).[5] Rather, such charges serve to reduce the investment (i.e., cost basis) in the underlying contract by the amount of the charge—but not below zero. Since these charges are withdrawn from the policy's cash value to pay for the QLTCI (albeit internally), they are considered "distributions". Nevertheless, the amount of these charges is not included in gross income.[6]

Planning Point: In certain situations, a combination policy may be a modified endowment contract, or MEC. (Generally, most single-premium life combo products are MECs, i.e., they fail the seven-pay test.) When they were first established in 1988, MECs received less favorable income tax treatment than non-MECs:

1. IRC Sec. 4980C(c)(2).
2. IRC Sec. 4980C(c)(3).
3. IRC Sec. 7702B(e)(1).
4. IRC Sec. 7702B(e)(1).
5. IRC Sec. 7702B(e)(3).
6. IRC Sec. 72(e)(11).

- Distributions (including withdrawals and loans) are received taxable gain first, tax-free principal last (LIFO), and
- Any distributions received prior to age 59½ are subject to a 10 percent penalty (unless taken for death, disability or as part of a life annuity).

The above MEC rules (LIFO tax treatment of distributions, and the 10 percent early withdrawal penalty) are the same treatment found in nonqualified deferred annuities. However, the Pension Protection Act (PPA) modified these rules effective January 1, 2010. Specifically, the PPA targeted distributions from life insurance (even MECs) and nonqualified annuities when used to pay for QLTCI: going forward, they would not be subject to immediate taxation or the early withdrawal penalty. Instead, these charges would simply reduce cost basis in the contract (but not below zero). To be clear, the linchpin of this favorable tax treatment is the requirement that the qualified long-term care coverage be made part of (or included as a rider on) the life or annuity contract from which cash value charges are made.

None of the tax provisions cited above for combination life/long-term care or annuity/long-term care policies apply to any of the following:[1]

(1) A tax-exempt (under a Section 501(a)) trust described in IRC Section 401(a) (Q 3831));

(2) A contract purchased by a tax-exempt (under a Section 501(a)) trust described in IRC Section 401(a));

(3) A contract purchased as part of a plan under IRC Section 403(a);

(4) A contract described in IRC Section 403(b) (Q 4018);

(5) A contract provided for employees of a life insurance company under IRC Section 818(a)(3);

(6) A contract from an IRA or individual retirement annuity (Q 3639); or

(7) A contract purchased by an employer for the benefit of an employee or an employee's spouse.

477. Can long-term care insurance be provided under a cafeteria plan or through the use of a health savings account or flexible spending arrangement?

Qualified long-term care insurance (QLTCI) premiums cannot be reimbursed through a flexible spending arrangement (FSA). Similarly, QLTCI policies cannot be purchased with pre-tax dollars through an employer-provided cafeteria plan (Section 125(f)(2)).

On the other hand, health savings accounts (HSAs) present an excellent opportunity to pay for QLTCI premiums on a tax-advantaged basis. Subject to limitations, contributions to an HSA

1. IRC Sec. 7702B(e)(4).

are not subject to federal income tax; earnings within an HSA are tax-free; and distributions from an HSA to pay for qualified medical expenses are tax-free.

Since qualified long-term care premiums are deemed a qualified medical expense, they comprise an allowable withdrawal from an HSA. However, the tax-free amount is limited to "qualified LTCI premiums", which are defined as the lesser of actual premiums paid or the "age-based" limits from the table below.

Age-Based LTCI Premiums (IRC Section 213(d)(10)(A))	
Age at End of Tax Year	**2020 Premium Limit**
40 or Less	$430
41 – 50	$810
51 – 60	$1,630
61 – 70	$4,350
71 and Older	$5,430

If one's premiums were greater than the limits in the table, the balance would have to be paid with non-HSA funds; otherwise, amounts withdrawn from an HSA for ineligible expenses are subject to income tax and a 20 percent penalty (those who are disabled, deceased or over age sixty-five are exempt from the penalty).

Planning Point: An HSA *may* be set-up through a cafeteria plan.

478. Do COBRA continuation coverage requirements apply to long-term care insurance?

No, they do not.

The COBRA continuation coverage requirements applicable to group health plans do not apply to plans under which substantially all of the coverage is for long-term care services.[1] This provision is effective for contracts issued after 1996.[2] A plan may use any reasonable method to determine whether substantially all of the coverage under the plan is for qualified long-term care services (Q 356).[3]

Planning Point: After a qualifying event at work (e.g. the employer's failure to pay premiums), group health plans generally require that each qualified plan beneficiary be given the election to continue identical coverage. This is not the case with qualified long-term care insurance (QLTCI).

As a practical matter, most QLTCI sold through the worksite, or sponsored by an employer, are individual policies. They are the exact same contracts sold on the retail market. However, by meeting certain participation thresholds, the insurer may extend premium discounts and

1. IRC Sec. 4980B(g)(2).
2. HIPAA '96, Sec. 321(f)(1).
3. Treas. Reg. §54.4980B-2, A-1(e).

underwriting concessions. But since they are individual policies, they are completely "portable" and not tied to employment in any meaningful way.

There are some "true group" QLTCI plans—many of which have existed for some time, and some that are newly sold. These policies do operate under group regulations, where employees receive "certificates" (not policies), and an employee who works in Oregon, for example, might be covered by an Idaho policy form if that is where his employer's "situs" is located. Although COBRA does not apply, one will find conversion privileges in group long-term care which, for instance, give certificate holders the right to continue making premium payments (and keep coverage in-force) in the event their employer discontinues the plan.

479. What are qualified long-term care services?

Qualified long-term care services are any necessary diagnostic, preventive, therapeutic, curing, treating, mitigating, and rehabilitative services, and maintenance or personal care services that are 1) required by a chronically ill individual and 2) provided under a plan of care set forth by a licensed health care practitioner.[1]

Practice Point: A licensed healthcare practitioner can be a physician, registered nurse or licensed social worker.

A chronically ill individual is a person who has been certified by a licensed health care practitioner as 1) being unable to perform, without substantial assistance from another individual, at least two activities of daily living ("ADLs") for at least ninety days due to a loss of functional capacity, 2) requiring substantial supervision to protect such individual from threats to health and safety due to severe cognitive impairment, or 3) having a level of disability similar to the level described in (1) above, as determined by the Secretary of Health and Human Services. In all cases, a licensed healthcare practitioner must have certified the need for such requirements within the preceding twelve months.

Practice Point: Prior to 1997, benefit triggers in long-term care insurance policies were not standardized, but this should not be taken to mean that common triggers weren't widely found, including those described above. The significance of HIPAA in creating tax-qualified (TQ) policies was the following:

1. Eliminating the "medical necessity" trigger, and
2. Creating the ninety-day certification requirement.

The ninety-day requirement for the ADL benefit trigger does not establish a waiting period (i.e., elimination period), but simply a duration over which the individual's disability is certified to last.[2]

Practice Point: Many commentators (and even some insurance company documents) employ the expression "expected to last" [ninety days], but curiously, the source material does not use

1. IRC Sec. 7702B(c)(1).
2. Notice 97-31, 1997-1 CB 417.

this phrase. However, the intent is similar: "chronic illness" should be long-lasting, and long-term care policies should pay for care over the long-term. In this way, TQ policies were a break from the past, when these policies had no qualms about paying for short-term claims (i.e., less than ninety-days).

To clarify, one's elimination period states how soon after qualifying care begins that claim payments start, acting like a deductible. There is no conflict in saying, "As a tax-qualified policy, my plan will only pay for claims that last longer than ninety-days, but I still want reimbursement from Day 1." Nevertheless, since 1997 there's been an explosion in the choice of ninety-day elimination periods, which now make-up nearly 90 percent of the market.

Having established an ADL trigger, the six activities of daily living are defined as:

(1) eating;

(2) toileting;

(3) transferring;

(4) bathing;

(5) dressing; and

(6) continence.

In determining an individual's inability to perform two or more ADL's, a TQ policy must take into account at least five of these six. Much ink has been spilled debating the merits of "hands-on" assistance versus "stand-by" assistance. The former means the physical assistance of another person without which an individual would not be able to complete an ADL. Stand-by assistance is the presence of another individual necessary to prevent injury while performing an ADL (such as being ready to catch the individual if they fall while getting in the tub while bathing). However, HIPAA uses the umbrella term "substantial assistance", which the IRS has subsequently clarified is either.

The IRS also expanded its definition of the cognitive impairment (CI) trigger by advising taxpayers they could rely on a number of "safe harbor" provisions. These included a broadened definition of "severe cognitive impairment" as a loss or deterioration in intellectual capacity that is similar to Alzheimer's disease and forms of irreversible dementia, and is measured by clinical evidence and standardized tests that reliably measure impairment in short term memory, long-term memory, orientation to people, places or time, and deductive or abstract reasoning.

480. How does the law treat long-term care contracts issued before 1997?

In short, these policies are called "grandfathered".

Any contract issued before January 1, 1997 that met the long-term care insurance requirements of the state in which it was issued is treated for tax purposes as a qualified long-term care insurance contract, and services provided under the contract or reimbursed by the contract will be treated as qualified long-term care services.[1]

Planning Point: For many years, this was considered a major deal. Policyholders with "grandfathered" policies had the best of both worlds: the tax favorability of IRC Section 7702B, and the more liberal benefit triggers and policy language that preceded it. No one wanted to give that up, or do anything to forfeit it. Agents were extremely reluctant to replace any grandfathered plans (as they should be), except for the occasional few plans containing egregious policy language.

Planning Point: Although it's much less of a question today (nearly twenty years removed), there was some angst back in 1997 surrounding a policy's "issue date". After all, those issued prior to January 1, 1997 were "grandfathered". But who chooses the "issue date"? It's enough to know the IRS clarified it in Notice 97-31 as a date assigned by the company (no earlier than submission date, and sometimes coinciding with effective date).

By definition, certain policy changes are considered "material", and others immaterial. Material changes require the exchange for, or issuance of, a new contract—one whose issue date cannot precede the date the changes take effect. Therefore, these changes *will cause a loss of grandfathered status* and are enumerated below:

(1) a change in the terms of a contract that alters the amount or timing of an item payable by a policyholder or certificate holder, an insured, or the insurance company;

(2) a substitution of the insured under an individual contract; or

(3) a material change in contractual terms or in the plan under which the contract was issued relating to eligibility for membership in the group covered under a group contract.[2]

Not everyone has found this guidance clear, so the carriers have given their own instructions for the kinds of changes that will cause a loss of TQ status, which generally include any increase in benefits (e.g., daily benefit, benefit period, elimination period or inflation protection).

The following items are <u>not</u> treated as the issuance of a new contract:

(1) a policyholder's exercise of any right provided under the contract in effect on December 31, 1996, or a right required by applicable state law to be provided to the policyholder;

(2) a change in premium payment mode;

(3) a class-wide increase or decrease in premiums for a guaranteed renewable or noncancellable policy;

(4) a premium reduction due to the purchase of a long-term care insurance contract by a family member of the policyholder;

1. HIPAA '96 Sec. 321(f)(2).
2. Treas. Reg. §1.7702B-2(b)(4).

(5) a reduction in coverage requested by the policyholder;

(6) a reduction in premiums as a result of extending to a policyholder a discount applicable to similar categories of individuals pursuant to a premium rate structure that was in effect on December 31, 1996, for an issuer's pre-1997 long-term care insurance contracts of the same type;

(7) the addition of alternative benefit forms that a policyholder may choose without a premium increase;

(8) the addition of a rider to a pre-1997 long-term care insurance contract if the rider issued separately would be a qualified long-term care insurance contract under IRC Section 7702B and any regulations issued under this section;

(9) the deletion of a rider or contract provision that prohibited coordination of benefits with Medicare;

(10) the exercise of a continuation or a conversion right that is provided under a pre-1997 group contract and that, in accordance with the terms of the contract as in effect on December 31, 1996, provides for coverage under an individual contract following an individual's ineligibility for continued coverage under the group contract; and

(11) the substitution of one insurer for another insurer in an assumption reinsurance transaction.[1]

Further, if a material change described in the regulations occurs to some certificates under a group policy but not to others, the insurance coverage under the changed certificates is treated as coverage under a newly-issued group contract, that is, a group contract that is no longer grandfathered, while the insurance coverage provided under the unchanged certificates continues to be treated as covered under the original grandfathered contract.[2]

The regulations provide examples of the correct application of the above rules, while also noting that taxpayers may *not* rely on Notice 97-31 with respect to changes made after 1998.[3] (Due to the disruption and uncertainty that existed at the time, there were like-for-like exchange rights between non-TQ and TQ plans until January 1, 1998.)

481. What is short-term care insurance?

Short-term care insurance is often a type of critical care insurance that functions much like long-term care insurance. Unlike long-term care insurance, however, short-term care insurance coverage remains in effect only for a relatively short period of time (twelve months or less). Taxpayers become eligible for short-term care insurance benefits when they need assistance performing two or more activities of daily living (ADLs). ADLs include the following activities: (1) eating, (2) toileting, (3) transferring in and out of bed, (4) bathing, (5) dressing and

1. Treas. Reg. §1.7702B-2(b)(4).
2. Treas. Reg. §1.7702B-2(b)(3).
3. Treas. Reg. §1.7702B-2(b)(5).

(6) continence.[1] Short-term care insurance can also function much like a typical health insurance policy, although coverage will usually be limited to certain specified benefits.

Planning Point: Note that there are many different types of short-term insurance. New rules released under the Trump administration will again allow short-term *health* insurance plans that are valid for up to twelve months, rather than the ninety day maximum imposed under the Obama administration. The rules also added a new provision that allows these short-term plans to be renewed for up to three years. Short-term health insurance plans are generally less expensive, but often provide limited coverage. Further, these plans do not have to satisfy the Affordable Care Act market reform provisions, which means that the plans can set annual and lifetime caps on benefits, exclude certain services (such as maternity care, preventive care and mental health coverage) and reject individuals with preexisting conditions.

A federal district court in Washington, D.C. recently upheld the rule that expands short-term limited duration health insurance so that short-term plans can be sold for up to twelve months, and can also be extended or renewed for up to thirty-six months. Because of this ruling, short-term health insurance plans can continue to be sold in states that permit such plans pending further appeal to the D.C. Court of Appeals.[2]

Certain types of short-term care insurance, known as recovery insurance, typically provides for a fixed level of daily benefits—around $140 per day is common—for a set period of time. However, the terms of short-term care insurance contracts often provide that if the actual cost of care is less than the stated daily benefit, the remaining funds can be used to pay for care even after the time period for coverage has expired. (For example, if the policy provides a daily benefit of $100 per day for 365 days, but the actual cost of care is $75 per day, the remaining $25 per day can be used to fund care on day 366 and beyond.)

A short-term care insurance policy's cost will vary based upon the level of benefits and length of the coverage period selected, as well as upon the age and health status of the taxpayer.

482. When can short-term care insurance be beneficial to taxpayers?

Taxpayers who apply for short-term care insurance (STC) are generally not required to complete the comprehensive applications and medical history screening that is required to qualify for long-term care (LTC) insurance. In general, STC provides an attractive option for those who cannot afford, or are unable to qualify for, traditional long-term care insurance (LTCI). Current statistics show that over 40 percent of LTC claims last less than one-year: the most common reason for these claims are short, recoverable illnesses, sudden terminal illnesses, and the single use of non-caregiving benefits (such as equipment and training). For this reason, some clients may find STC a more suitable option.

STC can also be employed as a "gap" to fill the elimination period of someone's existing LTC policy. They may have elected a longer elimination period at a time when circumstances were different, or when they didn't have another choice.

1. IRC Sec. 7702B.
2. *Association for Community Affiliated Plans v. U.S. Treasury*, No. 18-2133 (July 18, 2019).

To summarize, STC solves some of the ingrained challenges inherent in traditional long-term care (i.e., more rigorous underwriting and perceived high cost), and is ideal:

1. for those who have waited too long to apply for coverage;
2. when cost is a barrier;
3. when age or health are barriers;
4. for rehab or accident claims;
5. for filling existing elimination periods;
6. for protecting against Medicare's "observation status" penalty;[1]
7. when existing LTCI has not kept pace with inflation; and
8. for those who object to tax-qualified (TQ) triggers and/or the ninety-day certification.

Planning Points: Although STC insurance has been offered since the mid-90's, it remains some of the most rate-stable coverage available in the LTC market. Part of the reason it is not more widely promoted is that it has historically—although not exclusively—been offered by carriers with a "less-than-A" rating. If the day comes that "first tier" name brand insurers begin marketing STC, it has many things going for it to penetrate the middle market.

483. Will short-term care insurance satisfy the ACA requirement that individuals purchase health insurance coverage or pay a penalty?

Editor's Note: The 2017 tax reform legislation repealed the Affordable Care Act individual mandate that required individuals to purchase health insurance or pay a penalty for tax years beginning after December 31, 2018. The employer mandate and reporting requirements were not repealed.

No. According to the IRS, individual health insurance coverage does not include short-term, limited duration insurance.[2] Because short-term care insurance is, by its nature, short-term and limited in duration, such coverage will not satisfy insurance obligations under the Affordable Care Act (ACA).

Planning Point: It's worth noting the current controversy surrounding short term medical health plans. Because individual health insurance "does not include short-term limited duration insurance," this particular product has been exempted from many ACA market reforms.[3]

In June 2016, the administration released a package of proposals designed to strengthen the public risk pool (i.e., those who have coverage through the federally facilitated marketplace, or

1. Although new legislation looks to be closing this loophole, for years many patients discharged from the hospital to a nursing facility believed they had satisfied Medicare's onerous "three-day prior hospitalization" gatekeeper, only to find they had never been admitted as an inpatient to the hospital, and were instead kept under "observation status".
2. Treas. Reg. §1.5000A-2(d); 42 USC §300gg-91(b)(5).
3. 300gg-91(b)(5).

"exchange"). Their concern was that the risk pool was being damaged by individuals who *could* enroll during special enrollment periods (triggered by life events) but chose not to.

This ties back to short term medical care (STMC), which had been sold precisely for such temporary stop-gap situations. The problem was that:

- STMC is not subject to many of the ACA's rules;
- STMC can be medically-underwritten and priced on health;
- STMC can discriminate against those with pre-existing conditions; and
- STMC does not have to cover essential health benefits.

The problem (as it has been identified) is that insurers began selling STMC for periods as long as twelve months to serve as primary coverage, cherry-picking the healthiest people and plucking them out of the risk pool, all the while avoiding consumer protections.

The proposed new rules would change STMC in the following ways:

- STMC would be capped at a maximum of three months;
- STMC policies could not be renewed; and
- Insurers would have to disclose to consumers that the STMC does not constitute minimum essential coverage, so that the individual could still owe a penalty (for non-compliance with the ACA mandate) in years prior to its repeal.

Some insurance industry trade groups have opposed these changes, citing the failure of similar attempts to regulate the market.

484. Is short-term care insurance subject to the ACA market reform requirements?

No.

The Affordable Care Act (ACA) enacted hundreds of market reforms, including many which affect the individual and group health insurance markets. Title 42, Section 300gg-91 defines these terms (such as "individual health insurance coverage"), but it also itemizes a number of "benefits" which are exempt from the subchapter's requirements.

Among these are "benefits for long-term care, nursing home care, home health care, community-based care, or any combination thereof" (if such benefits are offered separately).[1] Thus, a broad category of coverage is excluded based on its function rather than its identification.

1. Other excepted benefits include "hospital indemnity or other fixed indemnity insurance" (if offered as independent, non-coordinated benefits), and coverage for a specified disease or illness.

Furthermore, in the explicit definition of "individual health insurance", there is a carve-out: it "does not include short-term limited duration insurance"[1] although this is more likely a nod to short-term medical (see Q 481).

485. Are premiums paid for a qualified long-term care insurance contract deductible as medical expenses?

Yes, subject to limitation.

IRC Section 213(a) allows a deduction for the unreimbursed medical expenses paid during the tax year of the taxpayer (plus his or her spouse and dependents) which exceed 10 percent of the taxpayer's Adjusted Gross Income. For the purposes of this section, the following are considered medical expenses:

- Amounts paid for qualified long-term care services (per 7702B(c)); subject to the exceptions below.
- Amounts paid for any qualified long-term care insurance contract (defined by 7702B(b)); subject to the limits described as "Eligible Premiums" below.

"Eligible LTC Premiums"	
Attained age of individual before close of the 2020 tax year	**Limitation**
40 or less	$430
More than 40 but less than 50	$810
More than 50 but less than 60	$1,630
More than 60 but less than 70	$4,350
More than 70	$5,430

Planning Point: Effective January 1, 2013, the Affordable Care Act (ACA) raised the 7.5 percent AGI threshold to 10 percent, but the new floor was phased in for seniors: for taxpayers sixty-five years or older, the floor remained 7.5 percent until January 1, 2017. The 2017 Tax Act reduced the threshold to 7.5 percent for all taxpayers in 2017 and 2018.

Planning Point: The table above was established in 1997 and is indexed for inflation. The limits rise by a medical care cost adjustment, rounded to the nearest $10, based on changes in the medical care component of the CPI (C-CPI-U for tax years beginning after 2017) each August. Although the limits are fairly modest in relation to an average premium, producers should remember that 1) the limits rise each year, and 2) the limits effectively rise every ten years as a policyholder ages through the bands. Thus, the tax advantage grows over time.

An amount paid for qualified long-term care services as defined in IRC Section 7702B(c) (Q 475) will not be treated as paid for medical care if a service is provided by an individual's spouse or a relative (directly or through a partnership, corporation or other entity) unless the service is provided by a licensed professional. A relative generally is any individual who

1. 300gg-91(b)(5).

can be considered a dependent under the IRC.[1] In addition, a service may not be provided by a corporation or partnership that is related to an individual within the meaning of IRC Sections 267(b) or 707(b).[2]

When the qualified LTCI contract is part of a life or annuity contract (or a rider attached to one), the rules around premium deductibility are different (Q 475):

- No deduction is allowed under Section 213(a) for any premium payment made for coverage under a qualified LTCI contract if such payment is made as a charge against the cash surrender value of the life contract or cash value of the annuity contract.[3]
- But, not all combination products are structured this way. There is at least one (and perhaps only one) suite of combination products available where the qualified LTCI riders are paid separately by the policyholder (and *not* via internal charge from the cash value). The premiums for these riders are deductible under normal rules above.

486. May a self-employed individual deduct premiums paid for qualified long-term care insurance?

Yes.

The individual may deduct premiums paid for a qualified long-term care insurance contract (for oneself, one's spouse and dependents). Because amounts paid for qualified long-term care insurance contracts fall within the definition of medical care, qualified long-term care insurance premiums are eligible for deduction from income by self-employed individuals.[4]

The self-employed deduction is not subject to the "10 percent (7.5 percent for 2017 and 2018) of AGI" threshold which must be met by individual taxpayers; however, the maximum amount of premium which may take as an "above-the-line" deduction is limited by the age-based eligible premium table (indexed for inflation)[5] (Q 485).

Planning Point: Partners of a partnership, members of an LLC (taxed as a partnership), and greater-than-2 percent shareholders/employees of an S Corporation are *also* taxed under the self-employed rules. (Q 487).

The deduction is not available to a self-employed individual for any calendar month in which he or she is eligible to participate in any subsidized health plan maintained by his or her (or his or her spouse's) employer. A "subsidized health plan" is one in which the employer pays all or a part of the employee's premium. This rule is applied separately to plans that include coverage for qualified long-term care services or are qualified long-term care insurance contracts (Q 475), and to plans that do not include this coverage and are not such contracts.[6] In other words, the disallowance of this deduction in a given month would require not just eligibility

1. IRC Secs. 152(a)(1) through (8).
2. IRC Sec. 213(d)(11).
3. IRC Sec. 7702B(e)(2).
4. IRC Secs. 162(l), 213(d).
5. IRC Sec 162 (I)(2)(C).
6. IRC Sec. 162(l)(2)(B)(i).

or participation in *any* subsidized health plan (of the taxpayer or their spouse), but specifically eligibility or participation in a subsidized *long-term care* plan through work.

487. Are long-term care insurance premiums paid by an employer includable in employees' income?

No.

An employer's plan that provides coverage under a qualified long-term care insurance contract generally is treated as an accident and health plan with respect to that coverage.[1] Thus, premiums for long-term care insurance coverage paid by an employer are not includable in the gross income of employees.[2]

Planning Point: If the employer only pays a partial amount of an employee's premium, the employee is still entitled to deduct the balance paid. Of course, as an individual, the employee would include the portion of the qualified LTCI plan paid (up to the age-based eligible amount) with other itemized medical expenses, and deduct the amount that exceeds 10 percent (7.5 percent for 2017 and 2018) of AGI.

Planning Point: When a C Corporation, S Corporation, LLC, partnership or sole proprietor purchases qualified LTCI for its employees, such amounts are not includable in the gross income of said employees. A question arises when these employees are *also* the owners of the relevant company. If that is the case, the analysis below controls.

Partners of a partnership, members of an LLC (taxed as a partnership) and greater-than-2 percent shareholders of an S corporation are all treated as self-employed individuals for tax purposes. As such, the qualified LTCI premiums paid on their behalf by their businesses *are* included in their AGI (i.e. passed-through as income); but, they may also turn around and deduct up to 100 percent of their age-based eligible premium (without having to satisfy the 10 (or 7.5) percent-of-AGI threshold applicable to individual filers).

Shareholder/employees of a C corporation (who are treated as employees) and shareholder/employees who own 2 percent-or-less of an S corporation may exclude from their gross income the entire amount of qualified LTCI premium paid on their behalf (even if it exceeds the age-based eligible premium amounts).

Planning Point: Small business owners who have an opportunity to pay for their QLTCI premiums "through the business" can save a lot of money this way. If we imagine an owner (e.g., of a partnership, LLC or S Corp) who pays a premium with after-tax dollars, he has to "gross-up" his paycheck in order to cover the income and payroll taxes necessary to net the proper amount.

Having then paid the premium, the employee might attempt to take a deduction as an Individual, adding age-based eligible premium to other unreimbursed medical expenses, and deducting the portion that exceeds the relevant AGI threshold.

1. IRC Sec. 7702B(a)(3).
2. IRC Sec. 106(a); see House Comm. Report on Sec. 321 of HIPAA '96, P.L. 104-191.

The business could also pay premiums on the employee's behalf. Although this amount is reported as income to our business owner, the company benefits by avoiding payroll taxes on the amount (and even worker's compensation). Then, the owner benefits from taking the self-employed health insurance deduction for the full amount of the eligible premium—not just amounts that exceed 10 (or 7.5) percent of AGI.

488. May an employer deduct as a business expense qualified long-term care insurance premiums paid for employees?

Yes.

An employer plan providing coverage under a qualified long-term care insurance contract is treated as an accident and health insurance plan with respect to this coverage.[1] An employer generally may deduct health insurance premiums paid for employees as a business expense (Q 330). Thus, premiums for a qualified long-term care insurance contract paid by an employer for employees are similarly deductible.

Planning Point: The amount deductible can vary depending on the business structure, which is summarized by the table below.

<table>
<tr><th colspan="3">Tax Deduction
(see "Eligible Premiums for 2019")</th></tr>
<tr><td rowspan="2">For the Business</td><td>Actual premium may be deductible when sole proprietor, S-Corp, LLC or partnership purchases QLTCI for employees</td><td rowspan="2">Actual premium may be deductible when a C-Corp purchases QLTCI on owners, employees, spouses or dependents</td></tr>
<tr><td>Eligible premium may be deductible when sole proprietor, S-Corp, LLC or partnership purchases QLTCI for owners, spouses or dependents</td></tr>
<tr><td>For its Employees</td><td colspan="2">Eligible premium may be deductible when an employee purchases his own QLTCI</td></tr>
</table>

Because the business is able to deduct "actual premiums", the limit is generally based on what is considered "reasonable" in comparison to income, a test which is generous. This is just one of the reasons we tend to find higher-premium, limited-payment plans in the executive carve-out worksite space. Whereas an individual would find his deduction capped, and not be able to fully take advantage of a large premium (say, $10,000 per year), this same amount, were it paid by his C corporation employer, would likely be fully deductible to the company.

Having said that, in the situation described above (e.g., an individual with a limited-pay policy whose premium greatly exceeds the eligible premium limit), some have suggested amortizing the applicable deduction over the individual's life expectancy.

1. IRC Sec. 7702B(a)(3).

489. Are benefits received under a qualified long-term care insurance contract taxable income?

No, they are not.

A qualified long-term care insurance contract is treated as an accident and health insurance contract. See Q 475. Thus, amounts (other than dividends or premium refunds) received under such a contract are treated as amounts received for personal injuries and sickness and are treated as reimbursement for expenses actually incurred for medical care.[1] Since amounts received for personal injuries and sickness are generally not includable in gross income, benefits received under qualified long-term care insurance are generally not taxable.[2] See Q 343.

While there is no limit to the amount of benefits that may be received as reimbursement under a qualified LTC policy, this is not the case when benefits are paid as a "per diem" (i.e., without regard to the cost of services received). In the latter case, a calculation must be performed.

The taxpayer totals the sum of all per diem payments received during the year, including amounts received from QLTCI as well as accelerated death benefits received on account of "chronic illness" under IRC Section 101(g), but not including accelerated death benefits received on account of "terminal illness" under IRC Section 101(g).[3]

Next, $380 per day (2020 amount, as indexed for inflation[4]) is multiplied by the number of days in the period for which benefits were paid. The greater of this product or actual costs incurred is carried forward. Any reimbursements are then subtracted, and the result becomes the per diem limit, above which amounts received are taxable (Form 1040, line 21).

One frequently finds an oversimplified version of the above process, i.e., that "the first $380 per day is excluded from income, with amounts over this threshold taxable to the extent they do not reimburse actual expenses incurred." This suggests that—as long as per diem payments serve to reimburse expenses—there is theoretically no taxable upper limit. But as Form 8853 makes clear, amounts *under* the $380 per day limit can be taxable. This occurs when reimbursements are received during the same period as per diem payments (uncommon, but possible for those who are covered by more than one policy). Since one's expenses have been reimbursed, the per diem policy is serving at this point as nothing more than pure income—and it is taxed as such (even if it is far below the $380 per day threshold).

490. Can an annuity contract or life insurance contract be exchanged for another contract containing a long-term care rider in a nontaxable exchange?

Yes.

1. IRC Sec. 7702B(a).
2. IRC Secs. 104(a)(3), 105(b).
3. Amounts paid as accelerated death benefits are fully excludable from income if the insured has been certified by a physician as "terminally ill" (having an illness or physical condition that can reasonably be expected to result in death within twenty-four months of the date of certification). Accelerated death benefits paid on behalf of individuals who are certified as "chronically ill" are excludable from income to the same extent they would be if paid under QLTCI.
4. IRC Secs. 7702B(d)(4), 7702B(d)(5); Rev. Proc. 2018-57, Rev. Proc. 2019-44.

As a result of the Pension Protection Act of 2006 (PPA), which went into effect January 1 2010, tax-qualified (TQ) long-term care insurance (LTCI) is now included in the scope of the Section 1035-exchange rules. This means that life, endowment, annuity and qualified LTCI may all be exchanged for qualified LTCI.

In addition, the presence of a qualified LTCI rider on a life or annuity contract will not cause it to fail to qualify for the purposes of such an exchange. In other words, a taxpayer can exchange an annuity without a long-term care insurance rider for an annuity with such a rider, and still qualify for non-recognition treatment.[1]

In sum, the IRC provides that the following exchanges are non-taxable:

(1) the exchange of a life insurance policy for another life insurance policy (with or without a qualified LTC rider), for an endowment or annuity contract (with or without a qualified LTC rider), or for a standalone qualified long-term care insurance contract;

(2) the exchange of an endowment contract for an annuity contract (with or without a qualified LTC rider), for an endowment contract under which payments will begin no later than payments would have begun under the contract exchanged, or for a standalone qualified long-term care insurance contract;

(3) the exchange of an annuity contract for another annuity contract (with or without a qualified LTC rider); or for a standalone qualified long-term care insurance contract; and

(4) the exchange of a long-term care insurance contract for another qualified long-term care insurance contract.[2]

Planning Point: Neither an annuity nor a standalone qualified long-term care insurance contract can be non-taxably exchanged for a life insurance policy (with or without a qualified LTC rider).

Generally, if an individual surrenders an "old" contract and uses the proceeds to purchase a "new" contract, they are required to recognize any gain over basis as ordinary income for federal tax purposes. But if certain requirements are met, Section 1035 allows them to avoid any recognition of gain. (Among these requirements are that the exchange must take place in a "hands-off" fashion directly between the two insurers. The taxpayer must not receive the proceeds, even if later used to purchase the new contract.)

Planning Point: Under Section 1035, both the owner and insured under the original contract and the new contract must be identical. For instance, an individually-owned contract cannot be 1035-exchanged into a jointly-owned contract.

---

1. IRC Sec. 1035(b)(2), IRC Sec. 105(b)(3).
2. IRC Sec. 1035(a).

Planning Point: Such exchanges may be appropriate when the owner of a life or annuity contract no longer has the need associated with the original contract (wealth accumulation), but *does* have a long-term care need (wealth protection).

1035-exchanges can be either "full" or "partial". One might employ a "full" exchange when funding a single-pay product such as a combination product, and a "partial" for a limited payment mode such as a ten-pay. As a practical matter where LTCI is concerned, very few carriers are comfortable accepting partial exchanges on this basis from neighboring carriers. Logistically, it is preferable to move all the products under one financial "roof".

Planning Point: The annuities covered by Section 1035 must be non-qualified, and cannot be owned by a trust or corporation. If the annuity is still within its surrender charge period, or the amount to be exchanged exceeds any free withdrawal limit, such amounts will be subject to a surrender charge. If a deferred annuity does not have any gain (as could be the case with a variable annuity in a down market), then there may be little tax benefit to exchanging the annuity for TQ LTCI.

Having said that, the ability to "wash" gain on non-qualified annuities through either QLTCI or combination products with QLTCI riders is a remarkable tax advantage, and a loophole which may not last forever.

Permitted Section 1035 Exchanges

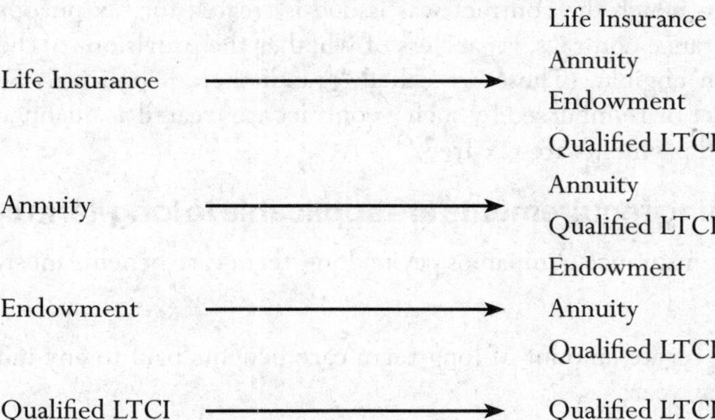

491. How is a long-term care insurance policy taxed when it is not a qualified long-term care insurance contract?

Policies that do not meet the definition of a qualified long-term care insurance contract under IRC Section 7702B(b) generally are referred to as non-qualified (or non-tax-qualified, NTQ) long-term care policies (Q 475).

Only premiums paid for qualified LTC policies are eligible for deduction, so if this is a significant benefit to one's client, then a tax-qualified (TQ) policy is recommended. Having said that, TQ plans are virtually the only remaining choice today. NTQ sales represent, on average, less than one-half of one percent of all sales.

Planning Point: Even though it has been nearly twenty years since HIPAA was enacted, the IRS has yet to publicly rule on the taxability of benefits paid from NTQ plans. (The agency has issued several private letter rulings indicating that—if an individual did not take a premium deduction up front—benefits would be non-taxable on the back end.) Most observers also agree that it would not be Congress' or the IRS's intent to tax a benefit which serves only to reimburse the insured. Had they wished, Congress could have very easily addressed NTQ plans on the spot—instead, HIPAA is silent.

IRS Form 8853 (for reporting taxable payments from LTCI, among other things) addresses the topic obliquely. It cautions not to use the form for amounts received from non-qualified LTCI, instead directing taxpayers to use Form 1040, line 21 to report any amount "not excludable as income". The question remains whether benefits received from NTQ long-term care insurance are includable or excludable from income. On this point, the IRS suggests that amounts paid for "personal injuries or sickness through accident or health insurance" are excludable.

For the first few years following 1997, issuers of NTQ policies were so concerned that consumers were being spooked by the prospect of future taxable benefits that they included "pledges" and "promises" in their newly-issued contracts. These documents gave policyholders the right to exchange their NTQ policies for identical TQ plans, in the event the IRS ruled unfavorably.

Any contract issued before January 1, 1997 that met the long-term care insurance requirements of the state in which the contract was issued is treated for tax purposes as a qualified long-term care insurance contract, regardless of whether the provisions of the contract would have otherwise been eligible. (These are called "grandfathered" policies.) Services provided under such a contract or reimbursed by such a contract are treated as qualified long-term care services (Q 475) and payments are tax-free.[1]

492. What reporting requirements are applicable to long-term care benefits?

Long-term care insurance companies paying long-term care benefits must file a return that sets forth:

(1) the aggregate amount of long-term care benefits paid to any individual during a calendar year;

(2) whether or not benefits are paid, either fully or partially, on a per diem or other periodic basis without regard to expenses incurred during the period;

(3) the name, address, and taxpayer identification number ("TIN") of the individual; and

(4) the name, address, and TIN of the chronically ill or terminally ill individual for whom the benefits are paid.[2]

1. HIPAA '96, Sec. 321(f)(2). See also Treas. Reg. §1.7702B-2.
2. IRC Sec. 6050Q(a).

In addition, any company required to file a return must provide a written statement to each individual whose name is reported under the above requirement. That statement must include the name, address, and phone number of the information contact of the company making the payments, and the aggregate amount of long-term care benefits paid to the individual shown on the above-mentioned return. This written statement must reach the individual on or before January 31 of the year following the calendar year for which the return was required.[1]

The IRS has prescribed Form 1099-LTC[2] to meet both filing requirements.

Planning Point: Policyholders of both tax-qualified (TQ) *and* non-tax-qualified (NTQ) long-term care policies receive a 1099-LTC from their respective insurance companies as a result of claims paid. Although the form advises that amounts paid under TQ long-term care insurance are generally tax-free, it is silent on NTQ plans. Furthermore, those who complete Form 1099-LTC are not required to check the box identifying the tax status of the underlying coverage—it is optional.

For purposes of these reporting requirements, a long-term care benefit is any payment under a product that is advertised, marketed, or offered as long-term care insurance and any payment that is excludable from gross income as an accelerated death benefit under IRC Section 101(g).[3]

1. IRC Sec. 6050Q(b).
2. http://www.irs.gov/pub/irs-pdf/i1099ltc.pdf (last accessed February 26, 2019).
3. IRC Sec. 6050Q(c).

PART VI: ANNUITIES

In General

493. What is an "annuity"?

Strictly speaking, the term "annuity" refers to a series of payments over time in which the principal (or purchase price) and interest are amortized over the payout period, so that no value remains at the end of the annuity period; it is a *stream of income*. However, most people who use the term "annuity" are referring to an *annuity contract*, under which that stream of income is guaranteed.

There are several types of annuity contracts: (1) commercial annuities, which are contracts between a purchaser and an insurance company, (2) charitable gift annuities (see Q 608), and (3) private annuities (see Q 604). With the exception of Q 604 to Q 610, all of the discussion in this book will deal with *commercial annuities.*

There are many types of commercial annuities and they are very different because they are designed to do very different jobs. For this reason, any statement that begins "Annuities are…." is probably misleading or outright false, precisely because the term covers so many different types of contract.

The chart below shows the various types, in terms of *when annuity payments begin.*[1]

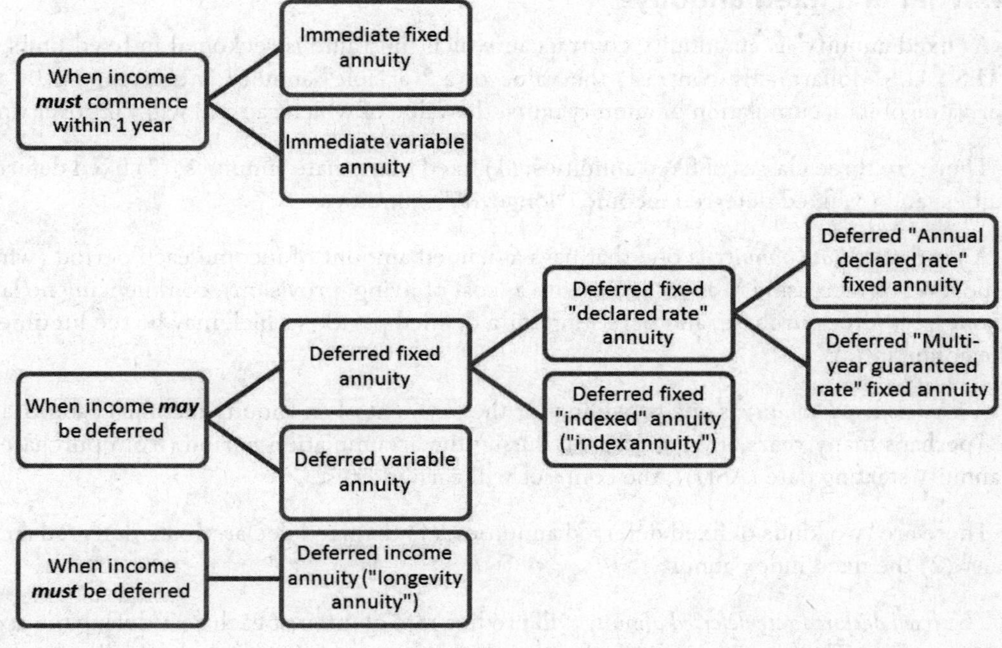

1. Chart from "John Olsen's Guide to Annuities for the Consumer" (John L. Olsen, 2015), by permission.

The following chart shows these types in terms of how the contract value is invested.

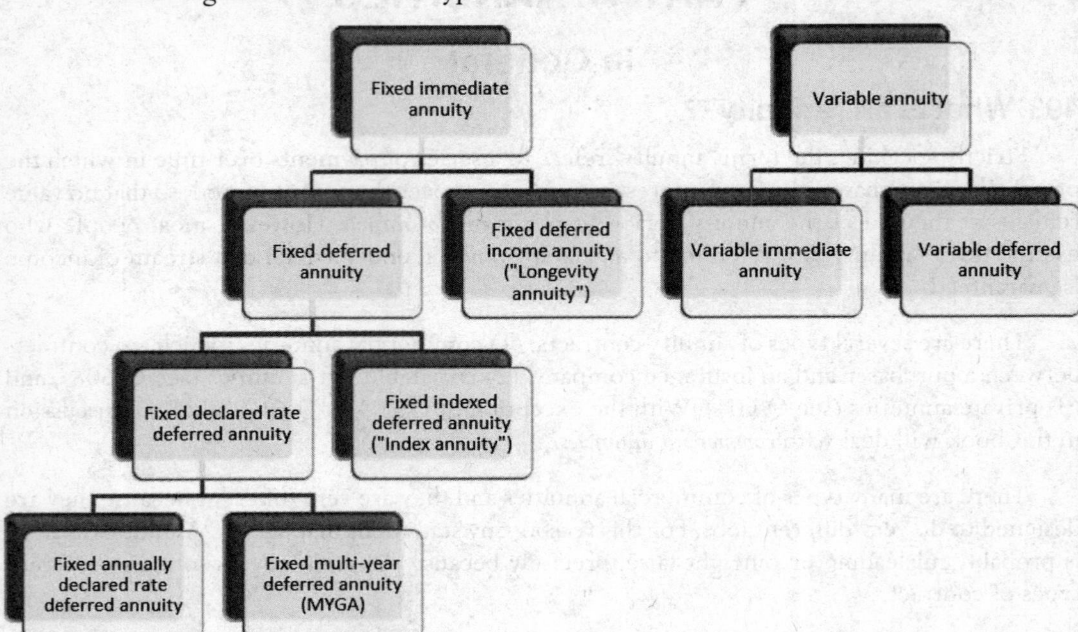

494. What is a fixed annuity?

A "fixed annuity" is an annuity contract in which the value is reckoned in fixed units (in the U.S., U.S. dollars). By contrast, the value of a "variable" annuity is determined by the dollar value of its accumulation or annuity units, the value of which can and will vary over time.

There are three classes of fixed annuities: (1) fixed immediate annuities, (2) fixed deferred annuities, and (3) fixed deferred income ("longevity") annuities.

A *fixed immediate annuity* is one that pays a defined amount of income each period (which may be level or increasing in accordance with a "cost of living" provision), commencing no later than one year after purchase, and persisting for a defined period (which may be the lifetime(s) of the annuitant(s)).

A *fixed deferred annuity* is one providing for the payment of an annuity income at some later time (perhaps many years after purchase); during the accumulation period (from purchase to the annuity starting date (ASD)), the contract will earn interest.

There are two kinds of fixed deferred annuities: (1) the fixed declared rate deferred annuity, and (2) the fixed index annuity.

The *fixed declared rate deferred annuity* will credit a rate of interest each year during the accumulation period. The interest rate is declared at the beginning of each period (usually, one year) and may change, though not below the guaranteed minimum interest rate.

The *fixed index annuity* is identical to the declared rate annuity except that interest is credited retroactively at the end of each period (of one or more years) and will vary according to the increase in the value of one or more specified external market indices (often, the S&P500®). Like the declared rate contract, a minimum interest rate is guaranteed, provided that the contract is held for the entire surrender charge period.

The third basic class of fixed annuities is the fixed deferred income, or "longevity" annuity. This is a contract guaranteeing a certain amount of income for a specified period (or lifetime(s)) to commence at some specified later age, usually an advanced age. During the accumulation period, there is no interest crediting and the contract may terminate without value if the annuitant dies prior to the ASD, although some contracts provide for a pre-ASD death benefit.

495. What is a fixed immediate annuity?

A fixed immediate annuity is an immediate annuity (a contract in which regular annuity payments must commence no later than one year after purchase) in which the payments will remain level or increase only in accordance with a "cost of living" rider, if elected. The payments will persist for the entire annuity payout period, which may be a term of years, the lifetime(s) of one or two annuitants, or the latter, with a "refund provision" that will take effect if the annuitant(s) die prior to the refund guarantee period.

Some older fixed immediate annuities are not "commutable" (i.e., they cannot be modified after annuity payments begin). Others provide for commutation, including the right of the owner to take a cash settlement in lieu of future annuity payments.

496. What is a fixed deferred annuity?

A fixed deferred annuity is a deferred annuity (i.e., one in which regular annuity payments may be deferred), the value of which is represented in fixed units (U.S. Dollars) rather than variable units (as is the case in a *variable* annuity). There are two basic types of fixed deferred annuities:

"Declared rate" fixed deferred annuities, in which the interest rate to be credited is declared *prospectively* by the issuing insurer at the beginning of each crediting period (which may be annually or every few years) and is credited at the end of each crediting period. (See Q 497.)

"Indexed" fixed deferred annuities (commonly called "index annuities"), in which interest to be credited is declared *retrospectively* at the end of each crediting period. The interest rate to be credited is linked to the change in value of an external index (which may be the S&P500® or some other commonly used index). Most contracts permit the owner to select more than one index to be used in such crediting. (See Q 498.)

Both contracts offer a guarantee of principal and a minimum interest crediting guarantee, *provided that the contract is held to the end of the surrender charge period.* The current interest declared in a guaranteed rate deferred annuity may never be lower than the contractually guaranteed minimum rate.

In all deferred annuities, there are two periods: (1) The *accumulation period,* during which interest is credited to the cash value of the contract, and during which partial withdrawals or surrenders may be made, and (2) the *payout,* or *annuity period*, during which regular annuity payments are made to the owner, pursuant to the *annuity payout election* made.

Typically, annuitization may be elected at any time beyond the first year or few years, and must be elected by the *maturity date* (at which point the contract must be annuitized).

497. What is a fixed declared rate deferred annuity?

A fixed declared rate deferred annuity is a deferred annuity (i.e. one in which annuity payments may be deferred), represented in terms of fixed units (U.S. dollars), in which interest is declared *prospectively,* at the beginning of each crediting period (which may be one year or every N years). It has all the characteristics of other fixed deferred annuities (see Q 496), including a guarantee of principal (provided that the contract is held to the end of the surrender charge period) and a guaranteed minimum rate of interest.

498. What is a fixed index annuity ("index annuity")?

A fixed index annuity is a fixed ***deferred*** annuity in which interest crediting is done retroactively, at the end of the crediting period (which may be one year or more) and where the crediting rate is linked to the changes in the value of an external index such as the S&P500®. Most contracts offer multiple indices and the contract owner may select one or more of them.

There are no immediate index annuities because interest crediting is done retroactively and the insurer cannot link interest assumed in the annuity benefit guaranteed at the time of issue to future changes in the index or indices.

While some index annuities have been registered as *securities* by the issuing insurer, most contracts are not, and are not considered securities by the SEC. That said, some state securities departments assert jurisdiction over their sales. The sale of fixed index annuities was set to become subject to the "best interest contract" (BIC) prohibited transaction exception (PTE) of the fiduciary duty rule published by the Department of Labor (DOL) in 2016, whereas sales of declared rate fixed deferred annuities were to be allowed in accordance with the less-onerous PTE 84-24. However, the Fifth Circuit vacated the DOL fiduciary rule in March 2018, and has yet to release a replacement rule as of the date of this publication.

Like all fixed deferred annuities, an index annuity guarantees a minimum interest rate provided that the contract owner holds the contract for the entire surrender charge period, though the guaranteed rate for index annuities is typically lower than that of declared rate contracts. Both types may include a market value adjustment (MVA) (see Q 532) and typically impose a schedule of surrender charges (which may vary widely in size and duration).

There are many different methods of interest crediting. All of them begin with the calculation of the percentage change in the value of the indices chosen over the crediting period, usually, but not always, excluding dividends on the stocks in those indices. That percentage change is then modified by the application of one or more crediting factors, or "moving parts", in the contract, and the result is the interest percentage to be credited to the annuity contract. The most typical "moving parts" are as follows:

Participation Rate: The participation rate is the percentage of the increase in the index that will be used to calculate index-linked interest. For example, if the index value rises by 9 percent over the crediting period (which may be one year or more) and the participation rate is 70 percent, the index-linked interest rate to be credited at the end of the period is 6.3 percent (9% × 70% = 6.3%) *if there are no other modifying factors.* The participation rate may be guaranteed for the life of the contract or for only one crediting period (and may be changed for the next period). A minimum participation rate is usually guaranteed.

Spread/Margin/Administrative Fee: Some indexed annuities use a spread, margin or administrative fee in addition to, or instead of, a participation rate. This percentage will be subtracted from any gain in the index linked to the annuity. For example, if the index gained 10 percent and the spread/margin/fee is 3.5 percent, then the gain in the annuity would be only 6.5 percent.

Interest Rate Caps. Some indexed annuities may put a cap or upper limit on total return. This cap rate is generally stated as a percentage. This is the maximum rate of interest the annuity will earn. For example, if the index linked to the annuity gained 10 percent and the cap rate was 8 percent, then the gain in the annuity would be 8 percent. (Note that indexed annuities that have caps may have a higher a participation rate.) Some contracts use an *index rate cap,* which is the maximum amount of index change that will be recognized before application of other modifications, rather than a cap on the amount of interest to be credited ("interest rate cap"). As with the participation rate, the interest rate cap may be guaranteed for the life of the contract or for only one crediting period. Typically, a minimum cap value is guaranteed.

Contract Designs

There are several index annuity designs. The simplest is the "Annual Point to Point", which measures the percentage change in the index each year and credits that change (after modifications) as interest at the end of each period.

"Term End Point" is a design that measures the index change at the end of a multi-year term and credits that change, after modifications, as interest at the end of the term.

"Averaging" is used in some designs, so that the average percentage change in the index, rather than the point-to-point change, is used. In "monthly averaging", most contracts place a cap on the positive monthly changes but not on any negative changes (monthly losses).

There are *many* index annuity designs and some are extremely complicated. For example, a newer design is to use an index that controls for *volatility* of changes in the raw index.

No Market Losses

Nearly all index annuities provide that any *negative* changes in the index over the crediting period will be credited as a 0 percent *gain.* Thus, the buyer of an index annuity is not subject to any *market* losses. However, it is not true to say that one cannot lose money in an index annuity, as surrender charges and/or market value adjustments may result in a surrender value lower than the original purchase amount, *but only if the contract is surrendered during the surrender charge period.*

499. What is a variable annuity?

There are two types of variable annuities: (1) variable immediate annuities and (2) variable deferred annuities.

For both types, the value of the contract (the cash value of the deferred contract or the size of the income payment of the immediate contract) varies with the performance of the "separate accounts" chosen (see Q 508).

Unlike fixed deferred annuities, variable deferred annuities do not guarantee either a minimum rate of interest or safety of principal. Indeed, the concept of "interest" can be misleading when applied to a variable deferred annuity, as the value of the contract does not vary by the addition of interest, but in the fluctuating value of the "accumulation units" purchased in the "separate accounts". (For monies allocated to the "fixed account" of a variable deferred annuity, principal is generally guaranteed and a set rate of interest is credited each year).

Variable immediate annuities differ from fixed immediate annuities in that the size of the payments is not guaranteed but varies according to investment performance of the "separate accounts" (see Q 508).

500. What is a "no load" variable annuity? What should individuals keep in mind when considering these products?

No load variable annuities are a type of annuity that have been developed to alleviate some of the concern over the mounting fees associated with the general product class of variable annuities, and are generally able to charge lower fixed fees because the advisor who sells the product is not paid a commission with respect to these sales. Further, the products can allow the taxpayer to manage the investments himself (or determine who will manage the investments) to reduce the cost of investment management fees.

No load products also typically do not have surrender charges—meaning that the investor can maintain a degree of liquidity that might not otherwise be available with a traditional product.

Because of the fact that the no load variable annuity does not generate a commission for an advisor, taxpayers may be tempted to buy them directly, which means that the individual will be responsible for determining whether the annuity is a good fit. Fee-based advisors may also be able to facilitate a purchase, but the assistance available in understanding these products to begin with may not be as robust as is the case with a traditional product. This means that a no load product may not be the best choice for an unsophisticated individual without proper guidance.

Add-on riders (which are sometimes the primary attraction of the annuity product) will still generate additional costs when added to a no load variable annuity. Some products do not even offer some of the more common income guarantee features that individuals have come to associate with annuities. Further, the funds contained in the annuity's sub-accounts can continue to add fees to the product itself—individuals should not confuse "low fee" for "no fee" products.

501. What is an immediate variable annuity?

A variable immediate annuity is an immediate annuity in which the amount of each year's annuity payment varies with the investment performance of the "separate accounts" chosen by the contract owner (see Q 508).

With regard to the taxation of annuity payments made under a variable immediate annuity (or a deferred contract that has been annuitized under a "variable payout option"), it would not be feasible, or equitable from a revenue standpoint, to apply the regular annuity rules in taxing such payments. If investment experience were very favorable, for example, the application of a constant exclusion ratio would result in a correspondingly increased tax-free portion.

Treasury regulations, therefore, provide special rules for taxing variable annuities. However, for taxable years beginning after December 31, 1983, a variable annuity contract will not be treated as an annuity and taxed under these rules unless the underlying investments of the segregated asset account are adequately diversified.[1] (See Q 552.)

In general, these rules provide that the amount which can be excluded from gross income in a taxable year is the portion of the investment in the contract which is allocable to that year. This is determined by dividing the investment in the contract by a multiple taken from the annuity tables which represents the anticipated number of years over which the annuity will be payable.[2] All amounts received in excess of this yearly exclusion are fully taxable. The amount so determined may be excluded from gross income each year for as long as the payments are received if the annuity starting date was before January 1, 1987.

In the case of an annuity contract with a starting date after 1986, the amount determined may be excluded from gross income only until the investment in the contract is recovered.[3]

502. What is a variable deferred annuity?

A variable deferred annuity is a kind of deferred annuity in which the contract value can, and usually will, vary daily to reflect the performance of the "separate accounts" (see Q 508) chosen. As with all deferred annuities, there are two periods in the contract.

The "accumulation period" lasts from contract issue until the annuity starting date (ASD) (see Q 538), during which the "accumulation units" of the separate accounts chosen will vary in value (and the contract value, which is the sum of those units), as well. Interest is not credited to a variable deferred annuity. Any contract "gain" is the result of increases in the value of the accumulation units chosen.

The "annuity" or "payout" period lasts from the ASD until the end of the annuity payout period chosen. During this period, the amount of each year's annuity payments will vary to reflect investment performance unless a "fixed" annuity payout method has been chosen (in which case, the payouts will act like, and be taxed like, payments under a *fixed* contract.

1. IRC Sec. 817(h).
2. Treas. Reg. §1.72-2(b)(3).
3. IRC Sec. 72(b)(2).

503. What is a deferred income ("longevity") annuity?

A deferred income annuity, which is sometimes referred to as a "longevity annuity" (DIA) or an advanced life deferred annuity (ALDA) – is an annuity contract that (generally) provides no cash value or death benefits during a deferral period, and begins to make annuitized payments for life at the end of that period, if the annuity owner is still alive. For instance, the contract for a sixty-year-old might provide that payments will not begin until age eighty-five, but upon reaching that age, payments will be made for life; due to the long deferral period and the accumulation of significant mortality credits, the payments that ultimately begin may be very large relative to the original payment amount. Some deferred income annuities offer a pre-annuity starting date death benefit equal to the premium paid or premium paid plus a stipulated rate of interest. These contracts provide significantly lower guaranteed annuity payments than those with no such benefit.

The IRS has issued a private letter ruling explaining the tax treatment of a so-called longevity annuity.[1] According to the IRS, a longevity annuity qualifies for favorable treatment, which means payments are taxed under the exclusion ratio ("amounts received as an annuity") rules when they begin.

This treatment applies as long as, on the deferral period end date, the contract's contingent account value becomes the cash value and is accessible by the owner through:

(1) the right to receive annuity payments at guaranteed rates,

(2) the right to surrender the contract for its cash value,

(3) the right to take partial withdrawals of the cash value, and

(4) a death benefit.

The IRS concluded that a longevity annuity is an annuity contract for purposes of IRC Section 72 because the contract is in accordance with the customary practice of life insurance companies and the contract does not make periodic payments of interest.

In support of its first conclusion, the IRS noted that insurance companies historically have issued deferred annuity contracts that, like longevity annuities, did not have any cash value during the deferral stage and did not provide any death benefit or refund feature should the annuitant die during this time. Thus, in the IRS' opinion, survival of the annuitant through the deferral period is not an inappropriate contingency for the vesting of cash value and the application of annuity treatment to the proposed contract.

In reaching the second conclusion, the IRS took note of the fact that the longevity annuity (1) provides for periodic payments designed to liquidate a fund, (2) contains permanent annuity purchase rate guarantees that allow the contract owner to have the contingent account value applied to provide a stream of annuity payments for life or a fixed term at any time after the deferral period, and (3) provides for payments determined under guaranteed rates.

1. Let. Rul. 200939018.

504. What is an indexed variable annuity?

Although known by several different names and subject to a broad range of potential product features, an indexed variable annuity is essentially an annuity product where investment returns are tied to the performance of one or more stock indices (e.g., the S&P 500 or the Dow Jones). Unlike straight equity investing, however, the product itself offers a cushion against investment losses in exchange for a cap on the potential for investment gains.

Unlike fixed indexed annuities, in an indexed variable annuity, principal is not necessarily guaranteed. The carrier may offer 10, 15, or 20 percent (or more) buffers against investment losses, meaning that if the underlying investments generate a loss, the insurance carrier absorbs a set percentage of that loss before the taxpayer experiences any loss. As such, if the chosen index declines, for example, by 10 percent and the taxpayer has chosen a 15 percent buffer, the taxpayer's account value will decline only by the 5 percent loss that exceeds the contract's downside protection.

However, as a trade-off for the downside protection afforded by these contracts, participation in the linked index's gains will be subject to a cap for a fixed term of years. Despite this, the term of years can be as short as a single year for some contracts, allowing the taxpayer a degree of flexibility that he or she might not otherwise find available in a fixed indexed annuity product. Further, some contracts provide for an upside cap that fluctuates annually—or, in some cases, as frequently as weekly or monthly.

Some insurance carriers even offer products that cover 100 percent of the downside risk of the investment, but these carriers also set the upside caps on these contracts at a lower percentage (in some cases, as low as 1.5 percent) that resets frequently (for example, every two weeks).

Despite their lack of guaranteed principal, indexed variable annuities offer many of the benefits that traditionally accompany an annuity product, including the valuable elements of tax deferral and death benefits for account beneficiaries.

505. What is a buffer or registered indexed linked annuity?

Registered indexed-linked annuities are a type of annuity that does not protect (or claim to protect) completely against the risk of investment losses. Registered indexed-linked annuities focus on accumulation, rather than income protection. Most of these products only offer a degree of downside protection (they provide a "buffer" against market losses). For example, when a registered indexed-linked annuity offers 10 percent downside protection against market losses, the insurance company that sold the product will absorb the first 10 percent of losses. The investor then experiences the remainder of the loss (the investor is able to choose the degree of risk he or she is willing to take on, based on the product and the carrier).

On the other hand, some forms of registered indexed-linked annuities work in the opposite way, so that the investor will take on a certain degree of risk (i.e., using the example above, the investor is responsible for the first 10 percent of market losses), after which the insurance company steps in to assume any additional loss.

Although these products are riskier than traditional fixed or indexed annuity products (that often provide protection against any loss of principal), they can offer higher "caps" than most indexed annuities. A cap essentially serves to cap the buyer's credited interest at the cap amount (for example, if the market gained 10 percent and the cap is 6 percent, 6 percent will be credited, but if the gain was 1 percent, the investor would receive the 1 percent credit because it is less than the cap amount). Registered indexed-linked annuities can offer caps of around 8 to 9 percent.

Because of these higher caps, registered indexed linked (or buffer) annuities can allow an investor to more fully participate in market gains, which is appealing to many who feel that annuities create opportunity losses when the markets are strong, as they arguably still are today. See Q 506 for a discussion of some of the risk that must be considered when an investor is considering purchasing a registered indexed linked annuity.

506. What should an individual consider when deciding whether to invest in a buffer or registered indexed linked annuity?

Individuals who wish to procure the more traditional income protection offered by annuities during retirement should think twice about the risks involved with registered indexed-linked annuities. Individuals who are already in retirement may be drawn to the potential for increased gains, but be unable to comfortably assume the greater risk of lost principal that is associated with registered indexed-linked annuities. This makes it important for these potential investors to understand the difference between the downside protection offered by registered indexed-linked annuities, and the "floor" provided by many other types of annuity products.

The floor offers a limit below which the product's earnings is guaranteed not to fall, but registered indexed-linked annuities only limit the investor's risk of loss by a certain percentage—which can impact the investor's principal investment, as well as earnings on the investment.

Another risk associated with registered indexed-linked annuities lies in the complexity of the products. Many taxpayers may not fully understand the risk that they are assuming, which can lead to unpleasant future surprises.

507. What is a fee-based annuity? Why have fee-based annuities become popular and what should individuals understand before deciding to purchase a fee-based annuity?

Generally, a fee-based variable annuity charges an ongoing asset-based fee instead of providing the advisor with a traditional commission. These products became more popular because these fees are typically "level," so that firms that sell them were not required to comply with the onerous requirements of the DOL's best interests contract exemption. Now that the DOL fiduciary rule has been vacated, many firms may remain attracted to fee-based annuities because of the uncertainties surrounding the five-part test that will now apply to determine fiduciary status, as well as potential new fiduciary standards that may become applicable.

Planning Point: The IRS has released a private letter ruling concluding that when an advisor takes a fee directly from a non-qualified annuity product, that withdrawal is not treated as a taxable transaction. The annuity in question involved fee-based annuities, where the advisor was not entitled to receive a commission for the sale in addition to the fee. While this ruling is widely viewed as positive for fee-based advisors and clients who are interested in these products, clients should be advised that although private letter rulings do give some indication of the IRS' view on the issue at hand, these rulings are technically only applicable to the taxpayer that requested the ruling–meaning that the client cannot rely upon the ruling unless the relevant issuer has obtained a private letter ruling.

Historically, advisors have been compensated for the sale of variable annuity products on a commission basis, which is believed to motivate advisors to recommend products because of their high commission value, rather than because they are in the client's best interests. This structure generates concern both that the advisor's compensation may not be reasonable and that fiduciary liability may attach even in the post-DOL fiduciary rule environment.

However, because fee-based products charge an ongoing fee, they can potentially be more expensive for clients in the long run. Some carriers have sought to make their fee-based annuity products more attractive by providing living and death benefit riders that can serve to increase the value of the contract to the client (and can, in some circumstances, justify a higher overall price for the client who values these features). However, for some clients, a commission-based product which guarantees living benefits may be cheaper because the client will hold the product for many years.

Further, some fee-based products may provide for very short surrender charge periods, an option that adds value for the client because it limits the period of time during which he or she is locked into the product. For clients who anticipate the possibility of accessing the annuity investment early, the higher price of the fee-based annuity may be justifiable.

The client should also look to the costs of the underlying sub-accounts of a variable annuity product, which can influence the value of the product. If the product is an indexed annuity, the various caps, spreads and interest rate guarantees should be examined to determine the value offered by the product.

508. What are the "separate accounts" in a variable annuity?

The "separate accounts" in a variable immediate or deferred annuity are investment accounts, similar in some respects to mutual funds, with specified investment objectives. The contract owner purchases these accounts in "accumulation units" (for deferred variable annuity contracts) or "annuity units" (for immediate variable annuities). The cash value of the deferred annuity and the amount of each annuity payment in the immediate annuity will vary according to the performance of these units, which are re-priced daily.

There is, in both immediate and variable annuities, an annual expense charge of each separate account which impacts the cash value of the deferred contracts and the amount of annuity payments in immediate contracts. The amount of this charge can usually change over time, and, in some contracts, may be waived in some years.

Variable *deferred* annuity contracts also offer "fixed" accounts, which act like fixed deferred annuities in having a guarantee of principal and a fixed rate of interest that is usually declared each year. There is no annual expense charge for this "fixed" account.

509. What are annuity payout arrangements?

An annuity payout arrangement is a prescribed method in which regular annuity payments will be received under an immediate annuity or a deferred annuity that is being "annuitized". The charts below shows the various arrangements. Not all arrangements may be available in a particular annuity contract.

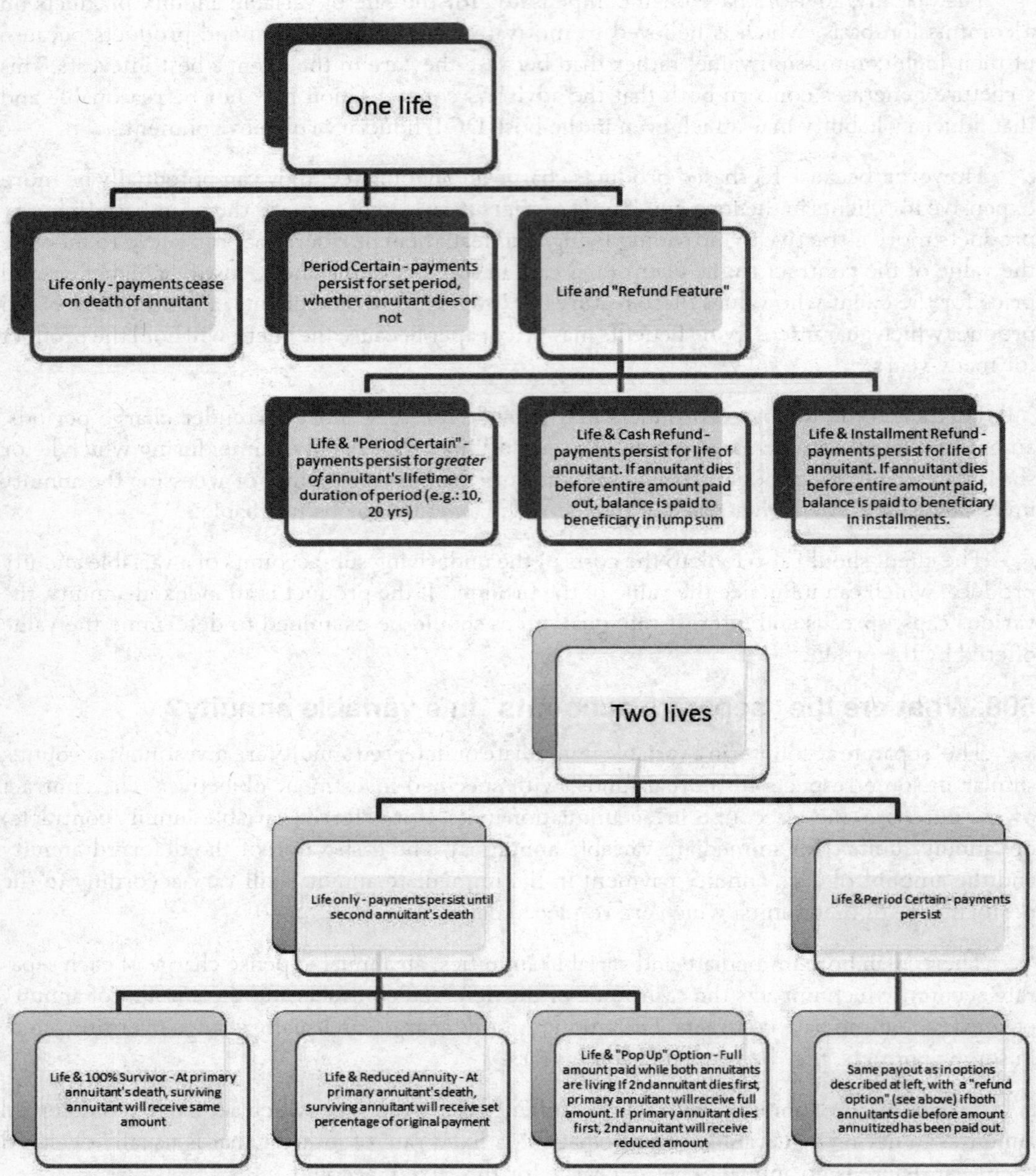

510. What general rules govern the income taxation of payments received under annuity contracts?

The rules in IRC Section 72 govern the income taxation of all amounts received under nonqualified annuity contracts. IRC Section 72 also covers the tax treatment of policy dividends and forms of premium returns. Qualified annuity contracts are governed by the tax rules of the retirement account in which they are held.

All "amounts received" under an annuity contract are either "amounts received as an annuity" or "amounts not received as an annuity."

"Amounts received as an annuity" (annuity payments) are taxed under the annuity rules in IRC Section 72. These rules determine what portion of each payment is excludable from gross income as a return of the purchaser's investment and what portion is taxed as interest earned on the investment. They apply to life income and other types of installment payments received under both immediate annuity contracts, and deferred annuity contracts that have been annuitized (Q 529 to Q 548).[1]

Payments consisting of interest only are not annuity payments and thus are not taxed as "amounts received as an annuity." Periodic payments on a principal amount that will be returned intact on demand are interest payments.[2] Such payments, and all amounts taxable under IRC Section 72 other than regular annuity payments, are classed as "amounts not received as an annuity." These include amounts actually received as policy dividends, lump sum cash settlements of cash surrender values, cash withdrawals and amounts received on partial surrender, death benefits under annuity contracts, a guaranteed refund under a refund life annuity settlement,[3] and policy loans, as well as amounts received by imputation (annuity cash value pledged as collateral for a loan). "Amounts not received as an annuity" are taxable under general rules discussed in Q 518 and Q 525. The taxation of distributions from life insurance policies is discussed in Q 10 and Q 13.

Except in the case of certain annuity contracts held by non-natural persons (Q 511), income credited on a deferred annuity contract is not currently includable in a taxpayer's income. There is no specific IRC section granting this "tax deferral." Instead, it is granted by implication. The increase in cash value of an annuity contract, other than by application of dividends, is neither an "amount received as an annuity" nor an "amount not received as an annuity." As a result, an increase in cash value is not a distribution and is not includable in the taxpayer's income, except where the IRC specifically provides otherwise (Q 511).

IRC Section 72 places a penalty on "premature distributions" (Q 525).

Contracts issued after January 18, 1985 have post-death distribution requirements (Q 594). These post-death distribution requirements also apply to contributions made after January 18, 1985, to contracts that were issued before that date. Contracts issued before January 18, 1985,

1. IRC Sec. 72(a); Treas. Reg. §1.72-1.
2. Rev. Rul. 75-255, 1975-2 CB 22.
3. Treas. Reg. §1.72-11.

with contributions that were made before that date are not subject to post-death distribution requirements.

The income tax treatment of life insurance death proceeds is governed by IRC Section 101, not by IRC Section 72. Consequently, the annuity rules in IRC Section 72 do not apply to life income or other installment payments under optional settlements of life insurance death proceeds. However, the rules for taxing such payments are similar to the IRC Section 72 annuity rules (Q 63 to Q 79). On the other hand, as noted earlier, death proceeds under an annuity contract (i.e., from some form of guaranteed death benefit) are taxed as amounts not received as an annuity (Q 518, Q 525).

Employee annuities, under both qualified and nonqualified plans, and periodic payments from qualified pension and profit sharing trusts are taxable under IRC Section 72, but because a number of special rules apply to these payments, they are treated separately (Q 3530 to Q 3537, Q 3932 to Q 3965, Q 4074).

Annuity with long-term care rider. Under the Pension Protection Act of 2006, qualified long term care insurance can be provided as a rider to an annuity contract, beginning after December 31, 2009.

511. How are annuity contracts held by corporations and other non-natural persons taxed?

Except as noted below, to the extent that contributions are made after February 28, 1986, to a deferred annuity contract held by a corporation or another entity that is not a natural person, the contract is not treated for tax purposes as an annuity contract.

When an annuity contract is no longer treated as an annuity for tax purposes, income on the contract is treated as ordinary income received or accrued by the owner during the taxable year.[1] "Income on the contract" is the excess of (1) the sum of the net surrender value of the contract at the end of the taxable year and any amounts distributed under the contract during the taxable year and any prior taxable year over (2) the sum of the net premiums (the amount of premiums paid under the contract reduced by any policyholder dividends) under the contract for the taxable year and prior taxable years and any amounts includable in gross income for prior taxable years under this requirement.[2]

This rule does not apply to any annuity contract that is:

(1) acquired by the estate of a decedent by reason of the death of the decedent;

(2) held under a qualified pension, profit sharing, or stock bonus plan, as an IRC Section 403(b) tax sheltered annuity, or under an individual retirement plan;

1. IRC Sec. 72(u).
2. IRC Sec. 72(u)(2).

(3) purchased by an employer upon the termination of a qualified pension, profit sharing, or stock bonus plan or tax sheltered annuity program and held by the employer until all amounts under the contract are distributed to the employee for whom the contract was purchased or to the employee's beneficiary;

(4) an immediate annuity (i.e., an annuity that is purchased with a single premium or annuity consideration, the annuity starting date of which is no later than one year from the date of purchase, and that provides for a series of substantially equal periodic payments to be made no less frequently than annually during the annuity period); or

(5) a qualified funding asset (as defined in IRC Section 130(d) but without regard to whether there is a qualified assignment).[1] A qualified funding asset is any annuity contract issued by a licensed insurance company that is purchased and held to fund periodic payments for damages, by suit or agreement, on account of personal physical injury or sickness.[2]

These requirements apply "to contributions to annuity contracts after February 28, 1986."[3] It is clear that if all contributions to the contract are made after February 28, 1986, the requirements apply to the contract. It seems clear enough that if no contributions are made after February 28, 1986, to an annuity contract, such contract held by a non-natural person is treated for tax purposes as an annuity contract and is taxed under the annuity rules (Q 510). If contributions to a contract held by a non-natural person have been made both before March 1, 1986, and after February 28, 1986, however, it is not clear whether the income on the contract is allocated to different portions of the contract and whether the portion of the contract allocable to contributions before March 1, 1986, may continue to be treated as an annuity contract for income tax purposes. The IRC makes no specific provision for separate treatment of contributions to the same contract made before March 1, 1986, and those made after February 28, 1986.

For annuity contracts held by a non-natural person as agent for a natural person, see Q 512.

512. If an annuity is held by a trust or other entity as agent for a natural person, does the general rule that annuities held by non-natural persons are not taxed as annuities apply?

An annuity contract held by a trust or other entity as agent for a natural person is considered held by a natural person.[4] If a non-natural person is the nominal owner of an annuity contract but the beneficial owner is a natural person, the annuity contract will be treated as though held by a natural person.[5] Also, an annuity owned by a grantor trust will be considered to be owned by the grantor of the trust.

1. IRC Sec. 72(u)(3).
2. IRC Sec. 130.
3. TRA '86 Sec. 1135(b).
4. IRC Sec. 72(u)(1).
5. H.R. Conf. Rep. No. 99-841 (TRA '86) *reprinted in* 1986-3 CB Vol. 4 401.

In a letter ruling, the IRS decided that a trust was considered to hold an annuity contract as an agent for a natural person where the trust owned an annuity contract which was to be distributed, prior to its annuity starting date, to the trust's beneficiary, a natural person.[1]

In another ruling, the IRS considered an irrevocable trust whose trustee purchased three single premium deferred annuities, naming the trust as owner and beneficiary of the contracts and a different trust beneficiary as the annuitant of each contract. The terms of the trust provided that the trustee would terminate the trust and distribute an annuity to each trust beneficiary after a certain period of time. The IRS held that the non-natural person rule was not applicable.[2]

The IRS concluded that the non-natural person rule does not apply to a trust that had invested trust assets in a single premium deferred variable annuity where the same individual was the sole annuitant under the contract and the sole life beneficiary of the trust.[3]

Where a trustee's duties were limited to purchasing an annuity as directed by an individual and holding legal title to the annuity for that individual's sole benefit and the trustee was not able to exercise any rights under the annuity contract unless directed to do so by the individual, the IRS concluded that the trustee was acting as an agent for a natural person.[4]

Further, where the trustee of an irrevocable trust purchased an annuity and had the power to select an annuity settlement option or terminate the annuity contract, the annuity was still considered to be owned by a natural person.[5]

A charitable remainder unitrust, however, was not considered to hold an annuity contract as an agent for a natural person and, thus, was required to include income on any annuity contracts in ordinary income each year.[6]

Although it is not entirely clear that all permissible beneficiaries of a trust named as owner of a deferred annuity must be natural persons, it is significant that, as of June 2010, all private letter rulings addressing whether a trust named as owner of a deferred annuity was acting as "the agent of a natural person" have specified that all beneficiaries were, in fact, natural persons.[7]

If all beneficiaries of a trust owning a deferred annuity must be natural persons, must the term "beneficiary" be taken literally? In the case of a "special needs" trust (such as an OBRA "D(4)(A)" trust), it is not clear whether the position of creditor occupied by the state Medicaid agency (to the extent of any Medicaid payments made to the trust beneficiary) will constitute the interest of a "beneficiary," where the state Medicare statute does not specify that the state's interest is that of a "beneficiary."

1. Let. Rul. 9204014.
2. Let. Rul. 199905015.
3. Let. Rul. 9752035.
4. Let. Rul. 9639057.
5. Let. Rul. 199933033.
6. Let. Rul. 9009047.
7. Let Ruls. 20049011, 20049013, 20049014, 20049015, 20049016, 200018046.

513. How does the Department of Labor fiduciary standard impact advisors who sell or provide advice with respect to fixed indexed or variable annuity products?

Editor's Note: The Fifth Circuit vacated the DOL fiduciary rule entirely in 2018, and, as of the date of this publication, the DOL has yet to release a replacement. The rules discussed below with respect to the rule are, therefore, no longer applicable and will presumably change once the DOL has issued a new rule.

Under the final Department of Labor fiduciary rule, fixed indexed annuity products and variable annuity products will be subject to the best interest contract exemption for a more detailed discussion of the exemption. Many in the industry had expected that fixed indexed annuities would continue to be covered by prohibited transaction exemption PTE 84-24, which is an exemption that protects compliant advisors from IRS penalties that may apply if the advisor enters a prohibited transaction (simpler products, such as immediate annuities, will continue to be covered by PTE 84-24, see Q 642 to Q 643).

Generally, it is expected that the cost of compliance—and the risk of penalty for noncompliance—will be much steeper for advisors who must comply with the best interest contract exemption requirements. Therefore, many expect that the cost of selling fixed indexed or variable annuity products will increase.

Recognizing the potential compliance burdens that the new standard may generate, the final DOL rule provides for a delay in the time period when the contract required by the best interest contract exemption must be signed. The contract may be signed as a part of the transaction execution documents, rather than before the advice related to the product is provided—basically, this means that the contract can be executed at the same time the client completes the rest of the paperwork necessary to complete the purchase of the annuity. The fiduciary standard, however, will apply to all discussions, even those that occur before the contract is executed.

The final rule also contains a grandfathering provision, which allows existing transactions to continue on their current commission basis.

The DOL initially provided a one-year implementation period, so that advisors were to have until one year after publication of the final rule to comply, rather than the eight-month period that was widely expected. Implementation of the rule will take place in phases—full compliance with the requirements pertaining to the disclosures, development of policies and procedures and contract execution components of the best interest contract exemption will not be required until July 1, 2019 (delayed from January 1, 2018).

The DOL has also eliminated two disclosure requirements that many felt would be overly burdensome, especially with respect to index-linked annuity products: the requirement that advisors provide one, five and ten year projections to clients and the annual disclosure requirement.

514. How does the Department of Labor fiduciary standard impact advisors who sell or provide advice with respect to fixed rate annuity products?

Editor's Note: The Fifth Circuit vacated the DOL fiduciary rule entirely in 2018, and, as of the date of this publication, the DOL has yet to release a replacement. The rules discussed below with respect to the rule are, therefore, no longer applicable and will presumably change once the DOL has issued a new rule.

Advisors who sell fixed rate annuity products may continue to rely upon PTE 84-24, and are not required to comply with the best interest contract standard. Fixed rate annuity contracts include both immediate and deferred annuities that (1) satisfy the applicable standard state nonforfeiture laws when issued or (2) in the case of group fixed annuity contracts, guarantee return of principal net of reasonable compensation and provide a guaranteed declared minimum interest rate in accordance with the rates specified in the standard state nonforfeiture laws that apply to individual contracts.[1]

In either event, the benefits of the contract may not vary based on investment experience of a separate account maintained by the issuing carrier, or based upon the investment experience of an index or investment model.

515. How does the Department of Labor fiduciary standard impact advisors who sell or provide advice on deferred annuity products?

Editor's Note: The Fifth Circuit vacated the DOL fiduciary rule entirely in 2018, and, as of the date of this publication, the DOL has yet to release a replacement. The rules discussed below with respect to the rule are, therefore, no longer applicable and will presumably change once the DOL has issued a new rule.

As is the case with fixed rate immediate annuity products (see Q 514), fixed rate deferred annuity products are covered by prohibited transaction exemption PTE 84-24, and would have remained so even after the implementation of the DOL final fiduciary rule. In order to be excluded from the heightened fiduciary standard, the benefits of the contract may not vary based on investment experience of a separate account maintained by the issuing carrier, or based upon the investment experience of an index or investment model.

516. How does the Department of Labor fiduciary standard impact advisors who sell or provide advice with respect to proprietary products, including annuities?

Editor's Note: The Fifth Circuit vacated the DOL fiduciary rule entirely in 2018, and, as of the date of this publication, the DOL has yet to release a replacement. The rules discussed below with respect to the rule are, therefore, no longer applicable and will presumably change once the DOL has issued a new rule.

1. 81 FR 21017.

While many in the industry expected that the final rule would contain a prohibition on in-house (or proprietary) financial products, which can be more expensive than other products and present a greater risk of self-dealing, the rule did not contain this prohibition. Instead, advisors who limit recommendations to proprietary products could have continued to do so, provided that they satisfied the requirements of the best interest contract exemption.[1]

The client must be clearly notified in writing that the firm offers proprietary products or receives third party payments with respect to the recommended investment product. The client must also be informed of any limitations that the advisor is subject to in the ability to only recommend a specific group of products (the extent of these limitations must also be disclosed).

Similarly, conflicts of interest must be disclosed, including any services that will be provided to the client. The firm itself must have determined that the limitations upon its advisors' ability to recommend products will not cause receipt of compensation in excess of reasonable compensation, and will not cause imprudent recommendations to be made. Relatedly, the firm may not rely on quotas, appraisals, special awards or other incentives that might cause its advisors to make imprudent recommendations.

Essentially, an advisor who recommends proprietary products must continue to satisfy the fiduciary standards that otherwise apply.

The feasibility of satisfying the best interest contract exemption requirements will depend upon the specific firm or advisor's clients, and the fees and characteristics associated with the proprietary product itself.

517. What factors should be considered when determining whether the purchase of an annuity product is in a client's best interests?

Editor's Note: The Fifth Circuit vacated the DOL fiduciary rule entirely in 2018, and, as of the date of this publication, the DOL has yet to release a replacement. The rules discussed below with respect to the rule are, therefore, no longer applicable and will presumably change once the DOL has issued a new rule.

When sales or recommendations regarding an annuity product cause an advisor to fall within the Department of Labor's enlarged definition of "fiduciary," the advisor will be required to determine whether the product or transaction is in the client's best interests. The advisor will be required to look to the client's individual circumstances and conduct an investigation to determine whether any given annuity product is in the client's best interests.

Fees are not the only factor to be considered in determining whether a product is in a client's best interests. The advisor will be required to understand various aspects of the annuity product itself, including (1) surrender charges and fees, (2) the index or indices to which an indexed product is linked, (3) any participation caps, (4) the product's investment risk, (5) how the interest credited to the product is calculated, (6) any riders that may be added to the product,

1. See, Preamble to DOL Fiduciary Rule, 81 FR 20962.

including those providing for guaranteed income, (7) the insurance carrier's ability to revise the terms of the product, and (8) additional fees and expenses.[1]

Advisors will need to understand how a client's participation in investment gains from the index to which the annuity is linked may be limited by spreads or participation caps, as well as other fees. This also includes knowledge of how changes in the relevant index impact the client's individual account—i.e., how interest is credited to the account value. The method that is in the client's best interests will depend upon the individual client's tolerance for risk.

For example, the annual point-to-point method is often popular because of its simplicity. The beginning index value is compared to the ending index value on the contract's (annual) anniversary date, and the percentage of change is calculated. If the ending value is higher, the client generally receives interest, and if it is lower, no interest will be credited. While this method seems simple on the surface, the addition of caps and spreads can complicate matters.

A cap effectively limits the client's credited interest at the cap amount (if the index gained 10 percent and the cap is 6 percent, 6 percent will be credited, but if the gain was 1 percent, the client would receive the 1 percent credit because it is less than the cap amount). A spread is subtracted from the value of the gain—so if the index gained 10 percent and the spread was 5 percent, the account would be credited with 5 percent interest. If the index gained only 1 percent, no interest would be credited because the spread is greater than the gain. If annual point-to-point with a spread is used, the interest credited can be reduced to zero even if the percentage of change in index value is positive.

"Monthly averaging" and "monthly sum" are additional interest crediting methods that may be used. Monthly averaging can be more complex than annual point-to-point, because it measures the index value at the end of each month for a year, combines the twelve values and divides by twelve to determine an average. This average is then compared to the initial index value to determine the final value (after which a cap or spread may apply to reduce the amount of interest that will be credited).

Monthly sum requires comparing the index value on the contract anniversary each month to the prior month's value and calculating the change. The increases (or decreases) in index value are combined at the end of the year (and can also be subject to a cap or spread) to determine the interest credited. The monthly sum method is the interest crediting method that is most likely to suffer from market swings—if the index performs poorly for a few months, the amount of interest credited can decrease dramatically.

For many clients, the best solution will be combining several of the interest crediting strategies in order to find a balance. In these cases, the client may not be able to fully take advantage of large market gains, but will be able to generate more consistent returns across the board. Historical performance may help advisors to better understand the potential impact of any given interest crediting method.

1. 81 FR 21018.

Amounts Not Received as an Annuity

518. What basic tax rules govern dividends, cash withdrawals, loans and partial surrender amounts received under annuity contracts before the annuity starting date?

Policy dividends (unless retained by the insurer as premiums or other consideration), cash withdrawals, amounts received as loans and the value of any part of an annuity contract pledged or assigned, and amounts received on partial surrender under annuity contracts entered into after August 13, 1982, are taxable as income to the extent that the cash value of the contract immediately before the payment exceeds the investment in the contract (i.e., to the extent there is gain in the contract).[1] To the extent the amount received is greater than the gain, the excess is treated as a tax-free return of investment. In effect, this ordering treatment results in distributions being treated as interest or gains first and only second as recovery of cost. (In addition, taxable amounts may be subject to a 10 percent penalty tax unless paid after age 59½ or the taxpayer's disability (Q 525).)

For the purpose of determining the taxable portion of a partial surrender, cash surrender value is determined without regard to any surrender charge.[2] This is not the case with regard to total surrenders (Q 588). Investment in the contract is, under the general rule, reduced by previously received excludable amounts. However, if annuity loans are involved, investment in the contract is increased by loans treated as distributions to the extent the amount is includable in income, although not reduced to the extent it is excludable.[3]

Policy dividends, cash withdrawals, and amounts received on partial surrender under annuity contracts entered into before August 14, 1982 (and allocable to investment in the contract made before August 14, 1982) are taxed under the "cost recovery rule." Under the cost recovery rule, the taxpayer may receive all such amounts tax-free until the taxpayer has received tax-free amounts equal to his or her pre-August 14, 1982 investment in the contract; the amounts are taxable only after such basis has been fully recovered.[4]

Amounts received that are allocable to an investment made after August 13, 1982, in an annuity contract entered into before August 14, 1982, are treated as received under a contract entered into after August 13, 1982, and are subject to the "interest first" rule.[5] If an annuity contract has income allocable to earnings on pre-August 14, 1982 and post-August 13, 1982 investments, the amount received is allocable first to investments in the contract made prior to August 14, 1982, then to income accumulated with respect to such investments (under the "cost recovery" rule), then to income accumulated with respect to investments made after August 13, 1982, and finally to contributions made after August 13, 1982, under the "interest-first" rule.[6]

1. IRC Sec. 72(e).
2. IRC Sec. 72(e)(3).
3. IRC Sec. 72(e)(4).
4. IRC Sec. 72(e)(5).
5. IRC Sec. 72(e)(5).
6. Rev. Rul. 85-159, 1985-2 CB 29.

Where, as part of the purchase of a variable annuity, a taxpayer entered into an investment advisory agreement that stated that the company issuing the annuity would be solely liable for payment of a fee to an investment advisor who would manage the taxpayer's funds in the variable accounts, the fee was considered to be an amount not received as an annuity and, thus, includable in the taxpayer's income to the extent allocable to the income on the contract.[1]

For tax years after 2009, a charge against the cash surrender value of an annuity contract or life insurance contract for a premium payment of a qualified long-term care contract (Q 475) that is a rider to the annuity or life contract will not be included in the gross income of the taxpayer. The investment in the contract for the annuity or life contract will be reduced by the amount of the charge against the cash surrender value.[2] For more information on the tax treatment of other amounts received under an annuity contract before the annuity starting date, see Q 519. For information on the effect of a tax-free exchange, see Q 520.

Special rules applicable to amounts received under pension, profit sharing, or stock bonus plans, under annuities purchased by any such plan, or under IRC Section 403(b) tax sheltered annuities are discussed in Q 614, Q 3960, and Q 4074. The rules applicable to loans under qualified plans and under tax sheltered annuity (IRC Section 403(b)) contracts are discussed in Q 3941 and Q 4049, respectively.

519. What basic tax rules govern other amounts received under annuity contracts (that are not dividends, cash withdrawals, loans or partial surrenders) before the annuity starting date?

The purpose behind the "interest first" rule (Q 518) applicable to investment in contracts after August 13, 1982 is to limit the tax advantages of deferred annuity contracts to long-term investment goals, such as income security, and to prevent the use of tax deferred inside build-up as a method of sheltering income on freely withdrawable short term investments.

Consistent with this purpose, other amounts that are neither interest payments nor annuities received under annuity contracts, regardless of when entered into, are not treated first as interest distributions, but are taxed under the cost recovery rule. These amounts include lump sum settlements on complete surrender (Q 588), annuity contract death benefits (Q 592), and amounts received in full discharge of the obligation under the contract that are in the nature of a refund of consideration, such as a guaranteed refund under a refund life annuity settlement (Q 547).[3]

For information on the effect of a tax-free exchange, see Q 520.

520. What is the effect of a tax-free exchange on the tax treatment of amounts received under annuity contracts before the annuity starting date?

To give effect to the grandfathering of pre-August 14, 1982 annuities, a replacement contract obtained in a tax–free exchange of annuity contracts (Q 571) succeeds to the status of the

1. Let. Rul. 9342053.
2. IRC Sec. 72(e)(11).
3. IRC Sec. 72(e)(5).

surrendered contract for purposes of determining when amounts are to be considered invested and for computing the taxability of any withdrawals.[1] Investment in the replacement contract is considered made on, before, or after August 13, 1982 to the same extent the investment was made on, before, or after August 13, 1982 in the replaced contract.

521. Is an individual who transfers an annuity contract without adequate consideration treated as receiving amounts "as an annuity"?

An individual who transfers any annuity contract issued after April 22, 1987, for less than full and adequate consideration will be treated as having received an "amount not received as an annuity" unless the transfer is between spouses or incident to a divorce under the IRC Section 1041 non-recognition rule (Q 106). The amount the transferor will be deemed to have received is the excess of the cash surrender value of the contract at the time of the transfer over the investment in the contract at that time. The transferee's investment in the contract will be increased by the amount, if any, included in income by the transferor (Q 581).[2]

Planning Point: This provision effectively prevents annuity owners from transferring their gain to another individual through gifting the annuity contract, because the gains embedded in the contract become taxable to the transferor at the time of transfer.

522. Are multiple annuity contracts aggregated for purposes of determining the amount of a distribution that is includable in income?

All annuity contracts entered into after October 21, 1988 that are issued by the same company to the same policyholder during the same calendar year will be treated as one aggregated annuity contract for purposes of determining the amount of any distribution that is includable in income under the rules explained in Q 518 and Q 521.[3] An annuity that is received as part of an IRC Section 1035 exchange that was undertaken as part of a troubled insurer's rehabilitation process under Revenue Ruling 92-43 (Q 571) is considered to have been entered into for purposes of the multiple contract rule on the date that the new contract is issued. The newly-received contract is not "grandfathered" back to the issue date of the original annuity for this purpose.[4]

This aggregation rule does not apply to distributions received under qualified pension or profit sharing plans, from an IRC Section 403(b) contract, or from an IRA.[5] The Conference Report on OBRA '89 also states the aggregation rule does not apply to immediate annuities.

If the contract is owned by a corporation or other non-natural person, see also Q 511.

For amounts received under life insurance or endowment contracts, see Q 10. For distributions received under life insurance policies that are classified as modified endowment contracts, see Q 13.

1. Rev. Rul. 85-159, 1985-2 CB 29.
2. IRC Sec. 72(e)(4)(C).
3. IRC Sec. 72(e)(12).
4. Let. Rul. 9442030.
5. IRC Sec. 72(e)(12)(A).

523. What is a guaranteed lifetime withdrawal benefit rider?

A guaranteed lifetime withdrawal benefit rider (GLWB) guarantees that the taxpayer will be able to withdraw a certain percentage of the value of the benefit base of the taxpayer's annuity, which has been growing by a guaranteed amount over the course of the deferral period (the guarantee is commonly somewhere between 4 and 8 percent). Taxpayers looking for larger payouts later in life should be advised that the longer the base account is allowed to grow, the larger the withdrawals will be in the future. Further, it is important that the taxpayer understand that he or she must stay within the limits of the guaranteed withdrawals; some contracts provide for termination of the feature if the taxpayer takes an excess withdrawal.

One common ground between these types of riders and a lifetime income benefit rider (LIBRs, see Q 524) lies in the fact that the benefit base itself is not available for cash withdrawals. This "account" has no real current cash value to the taxpayer—meaning that, unlike the accumulation value of the account, the taxpayer cannot access this value through surrendering the contract prior to the end of the deferral period.

524. What is a lifetime income benefit rider (LIBR)?

A lifetime income benefit rider (LIBR), while similar to a guaranteed lifetime withdrawal benefit rider (GLWB, see Q 523), is a rider pursuant to which the annuity carrier agrees to pay income over the taxpayer's lifetime in the form of an annuity. The income stream that results once the taxpayer annuitizes the contract is also drawn from the annuity's benefit base, but the carrier uses the taxpayer's life expectancy to determine the value of the guaranteed income payments. Taxpayers seeking out steady, level annuity payouts that are guaranteed regardless of how long they live are often attracted to this type of feature.

One common ground between a LIBR and GLWB is the fact that the benefit base itself is not available for cash withdrawals. The benefit base is an "account" that has no real current cash value to the taxpayer—meaning that, unlike the accumulation value of the account, the taxpayer cannot access this value through surrendering the contract prior to the end of the deferral period.

525. What penalties apply to premature distributions under annuity contracts?

To discourage the use of annuity contracts as short term tax sheltered investments, a 10 percent tax is imposed on certain "premature" payments under annuity contracts.[1] The penalty tax potentially applies to any payment received to the extent the payment is includable in income unless an exception applies. Exceptions to the penalty tax include:

(1) any payment made on or after the date on which the taxpayer becomes age 59½;

(2) any payment made on or after the death of the holder (or the primary annuitant in the case where the holder is a non-natural person);

(3) any payment attributable to the taxpayer's becoming disabled;

1. IRC Sec. 72(q).

(4) any payment made under an immediate annuity contract;[1]

(5) any payment that is part of a series of substantially equal periodic payments (SEPPs) made (not less frequently than annually) for the life or life expectancy of the taxpayer or the joint lives or joint life expectancies of the taxpayer and his or her designated beneficiary (see Q 526);

(6) any payment made from a qualified pension, profit sharing, or stock bonus plan, under a contract purchased by such a plan, under an IRC Section 403(b) tax sheltered annuity, from an individual retirement account or annuity, or from a contract provided to life insurance company employees under certain retirement plans (but such payments are subject to similar premature distribution limitations and penalties; see Q 3675, IRA; Q 3956, pension, profit sharing, stock bonus; Q 4060, tax sheltered annuity);

(7) any payment allocable to investment in the contract before August 14, 1982, including earnings on a pre-August 14, 1982 investment;[2]

(8) any payment made from an annuity purchased by an employer upon the termination of a qualified plan and held by the employer until the employee's separation from service; or

(9) any payment under a qualified funding asset (i.e., any annuity contract issued by a licensed insurance company that is purchased as a result of a liability to make periodic payments for damages, by suit or agreement, on account of personal physical injury or sickness).

Planning Point: *SEPPs.* From a practical standpoint, it would appear imprudent for an individual younger than age forty five to attempt to qualify for the exception for substantially equal periodic payments. A period longer than fifteen years may afford too much time in which a "material change" could occur. Also, the taxpayer might forget the importance of continuing to satisfy the conditions for this exception to the penalty tax. *Fred Burkey, CLU, APA, Ameritas®.*

Where a deferred annuity contract was exchanged for an immediate annuity contract, the purchase date of the new contract for purposes of the 10 percent penalty tax was considered to be the date upon which the deferred annuity was purchased. Thus, even if the new contract had been immediately annuitized, payments from the replacement contract did not fall within the immediate annuity exception to the penalty tax.[3]

Apparently, if an annuity contract was issued between August 13, 1982 and January 19, 1985, a distribution of income allocable to any investment made ten or more years before the distribution is not subject to the penalty. For this purpose, amounts includable in income are

1. An immediate annuity contract is one that is purchased with a single premium or annuity consideration, the annuity starting date of which is no later than one year from the date of purchase, and that provides for a series of substantially equal periodic payments to be made no less frequently than annually during the annuity period. IRC Sec. 72(u)(4); see Let. Ruls. 200818018 (variable annuity), 200036021.
2. Rev. Rul. 85-159, 1985-2 CB 29. See also H.R. Conf. Rep. 97-760 (TEFRA '82) *reprinted in* 1982-2 CB 685-686.
3. Rev. Rul. 92-95, 1992-2 CB 43.

allocated to the earliest investment in the contract to which amounts were not previously fully allocated.[1] To facilitate accounting, investments are considered made on January 1 of the year in which they are invested.[2]

There also is a 10 percent penalty tax on certain premature distributions from life insurance policies classified as modified endowment contracts (Q 13).

The tax on premature distributions is not taken into consideration for purposes of determining the nonrefundable personal credits, general business credit, or foreign tax credit.

526. What special rules apply to premature annuity payments that are exempt from the 10 percent penalty by reason of the "substantially equal periodic payment" (SEPP) rule if the SEPP is later modified?

Payments excepted from the 10 percent penalty (Q 525) by reason of the substantially equal periodic payment exception may be subject to recapture if the series of payments is modified, other than by reason of death or disability, prior to the taxpayer's reaching age 59½ or, if later, before the end of a five year period beginning on the date of the first payment (even if the taxpayer has reached age 59½).

According to the report of the Conference Committee, the modification that triggers recapture is a change to a method of distribution that would not qualify for the exemption. The tax on the amount recaptured is imposed in the first taxable year of the modification and is equal to the tax as determined under regulations that would have been imposed, plus interest, retroactively back to the first such distribution made had the exception never applied.[3]

The IRS announced that the three methods used to avoid the 10 percent penalty when making substantially equal periodic payments from a qualified retirement plan (Q 3677) also may be used to qualify as substantially equal periodic payments from a nonqualified annuity. The "one time election" to change methods also may be used by owners of nonqualified annuities. Finally, there will be no penalty if an individual depletes an account by using one of the approved methods.[4]

527. Are dividends payable on an annuity contract taxable income?

Taxation of dividends under an annuity contract depends on when the contract was purchased. If the contract was purchased after August 13, 1982, dividends received before the annuity starting date are taxable to the extent the cash value of the contract (determined without regard to any surrender charge) immediately before the dividend is received exceeds the investment in the contract at the same time. If there is no excess of cash value over the investment in the contract (i.e., no gain), further dividends are treated as a tax-free recovery of investment. If the annuity contract was purchased before August 14, 1982, and no additional investment was made in the contract after August 13, 1982, the dividends will be taxed in the same manner as

1. Sec. 72(q)(1) prior to amendment by DEFRA 1984, Sec. 222(a).
2. DEFRA 1984, Sec. 222(c).
3. H.R. Conf. Rep. No. 99-841 (TRA '86) *reprinted in* 1986-3 CB Vol. 4 403.
4. Notice 2004-15, 2004-9 IRB 526.

dividends received under life insurance contracts (generally tax-free until basis has been recovered; see Q 22).[1]

Dividends retained by the insurer as a premium, or other consideration for the contract, are not included in income.[2] Dividends paid but left with the insurer to accumulate at interest would not be considered retained as premium or consideration.

If any investment has been made after August 13, 1982 in an annuity contract entered into before August 14, 1982, dividends allocable to that investment are includable as dividends on a contract entered into after August 13, 1982.[3] Dividends received under an annuity contract with income allocable to earnings on pre-August 14, 1982, and post-August 13, 1982, investments are allocable first to investments made prior to August 14, 1982, then to income accumulated with respect to such pre-August 14, 1982 investments, then to income accumulated with respect to investments made after August 13, 1982, and finally to investments made after August 13, 1982.[4]

Dividends received after the annuity starting date (Q 538) are included in gross income regardless of when the contract was entered into or when any investment was made.[5]

A special exception applies to annuity contracts purchased by a qualified pension, profit sharing or stock bonus plan, an individual retirement account or annuity, or a special plan of a life insurance company for its employees, or purchased as an IRC Section 403(b) tax sheltered annuity (Q 3955).

528. What is the tax treatment of dividends where annuity values are paid in installments or as a life income?

Dividends received before the annuity start date or the first date that an amount is received as an annuity, whichever is later, are subtracted from the consideration paid (i.e., the cost basis) of the annuity and are not taxable. If the investment in the contract is reduced all the way to $0, any further dividends received become taxable. Notably, the reduction in the investment in the contract as dividends are reduced applies both for determining the taxation of the dividends themselves, and also the investment in the contract for the purposes of determining the exclusion ratio if the contract is subsequently annuitized.[6]

Dividends received after the annuity start date or the first date that an amount is received as an annuity, whichever is later, are included in full in the recipient's gross income. Contrary to the case where dividends were received prior to the annuity start date, the exclusion ratio (discussed in Q 529) is not affected by dividends received after the annuity start date. The exclusion ratio in place prior to payment of the dividend continues to apply.[7]

1. IRC Sec. 72(e).
2. IRC Sec. 72(e)(4)(B).
3. IRC Sec. 72(e)(5).
4. Rev. Rul. 85-159, 1985-2 CB 29.
5. IRC Sec. 72(e)(2)(A).
6. Treas. Reg. §1.72-11(b)(1).
7. Treas. Reg. §1.72-11(b)(2).

Amounts Received as an Annuity

529. How are annuity payments taxed?

The basic rule for taxing annuity payments (i.e., "amounts received as an annuity") is designed to return the purchaser's investment in equal tax-free amounts over the payment period (e.g., the annuitant's life expectancy or a guaranteed certain period of time) and to tax the balance of each payment received as earnings. Each payment, therefore, is part nontaxable return of cost and part taxable income. Any excess interest (dividends) added to the guaranteed payments is reportable as income for the year received.

Non-Variable Contracts

For non-variable contracts, an exclusion ratio (which may be expressed as a fraction or as a percentage) must be determined for the contract. This exclusion ratio is applied to each annuity payment to find the portion of the payment that is excludable from gross income. The balance of the guaranteed annuity payment is includable in gross income for the year received.[1]

The exclusion ratio of an individual whose annuity starting date (Q 538) is after December 31, 1986 applies to payments received until the payment in which the investment in the contract is fully recovered (generally, at life expectancy). In that payment, the amount excludable is limited to the balance of the unrecovered investment. Payments received thereafter are fully includable in income, as all cost basis has been recovered at that point.[2] By contrast, the exclusion ratio as originally determined for an annuity starting date before January 1, 1987 applies to all payments received throughout the entire payment period, even if the annuitant has recovered his or her investment. Thus, it is possible for a long-lived annuitant with a pre-January 1, 1987, annuity to receive tax-free "return of principal" amounts which in the aggregate exceed the principal (investment in the contract).

The exclusion ratio for a particular contract is the ratio that the total investment in the contract (Q 533) bears to the total expected cumulative return payments (known in this case as the "expected return") (Q 536) under the contract. By dividing the investment in the contract by the expected return, the exclusion ratio can be expressed as a percentage (which the regulations indicate should be rounded to the nearest tenth of a percent).[3]

For example, assuming that the investment in the contract is $12,650 and expected return is $16,000 (e.g., $800/year for twenty years), the exclusion ratio is $12,650/$16,000, or 79.1 percent (79.06 rounded to the nearest tenth of a percent). If the monthly payment is $100, the portion to be excluded from gross income is $79.10 (79.1 percent of $100), and the balance of the payment is included in gross income. If twelve such monthly payments are received during the taxable year, the total amount to be excluded for the year is $949.20 (12 × $79.10), and the amount to be included in income is $250.80 ($1,200 – $949.20). Excess interest, if any, also must be included.

1. IRC Sec. 72(b)(1).
2. IRC Sec. 72(b)(2).
3. Treas. Reg. §1.72-4(a)(2).

If the investment in the contract equals or exceeds the expected return, the full amount of each payment is received tax-free.[1]

There are a few circumstances that may require the computation of a new exclusion ratio for the contract (see "Withdrawals," Q 549; "Variable annuities," Q 554; and "Sale of contract," Q 570).

For application of the basic annuity rule to various types of fixed annuity payments, see Q 539 to Q 548. If an annuity contract is owned by a non-natural person, see Q 511.

Variable Contracts

The exclusion ratio described above does not apply to payments made under a variable contract, as the expected return cannot be known in advance. For tax treatment of variable annuity payments that are received as an annuity, see Q 499 to Q 554.

530. How are annuity payments taxed to a beneficiary if an annuitant under a life annuity payout with a refund feature dies and there is value remaining in the refund feature?

If an annuitant under a life annuity payout with a refund feature dies and there is value remaining in the refund feature, the taxation of payments to the beneficiary under the refund feature depends on whether that beneficiary elects a new payout arrangement.

If proceeds under the refund feature are taken by the beneficiary either as a lump sum or in accordance with the annuity payout option under which the annuitant's payments were calculated, proceeds will be excludable from income until the total amount the beneficiary receives, when added to the amounts received tax-free by the annuitant, is equal to the annuitant's "investment in the contract," unadjusted for the value of the refund feature.[2] This "FIFO" (first-in, first-out) basis-first treatment of beneficiary payments is different than the income/gains-first treatment applying to "amounts not received as an annuity" and from the "regular annuity rules" treatment that normally applies to annuitized payments.

If the total payments thus made to the beneficiary are less than the annuitant's investment in the contract and the annuitant's annuity starting date was after July 1, 1986, the beneficiary may take an income tax deduction for any such unrecovered investment.[3]

531. What are the tax consequences for a taxpayer who wishes to annuitize only a portion of an annuity contract?

Previously, the owner of an annuity or life insurance contract who wanted to annuitize a portion of a contract was required to split a contract into two and annuitize one of the resulting contracts. Splitting the contract was treated as a partial withdrawal and the owner was taxed prior to annuitization. As of 2011, that cumbersome two-step process is no longer necessary.

1. Treas. Reg. §1.72-4(d)(2).
2. Treas. Reg. §1.72-11(c).
3. IRC Sec. 72(b)(3)(A).

This result is due to the passage of the Small Business Jobs and Credit Act of 2010 (H.R. 5297). Section 2113 of the law amended IRC Section 72(a) to permit partial annuitization of annuity, endowment, and life insurance contracts – leaving the balance unannuitized – as long as the annuitization period is for ten years or more or is for the lives of one or more individuals.

When a contract is partially annuitized: (1) each annuitized portion of the contract is treated as a separate contract; (2) for purposes of calculating the taxable portion of annuity payments from a partially annuitized contract, investment in the contract is allocated pro rata between each portion of the contract from which amounts are received as an annuity and the portion of the contract from which amounts are not received as an annuity; and (3) each separately annuitized portion of the contract will have a separate annuity start date.[1]

Partial annuitization is permissible for tax years beginning after December 31, 2010.

532. What is a market value adjusted annuity?

A market value adjusted (MVA) annuity is an annuity issued pursuant to a contract that allows the carrier to adjust the product's cash surrender value upward or downward if the client chooses to surrender the product before maturity. The adjustment is calculated based on the difference between the interest rate guaranteed under the particular contract and the then-prevailing market interest rates.

Generally, if the prevailing interest rate at the time of surrender is higher than the contract's guaranteed rate, the taxpayer's cash surrender value will be adjusted downward. On the other hand, if rates move lower than the rate guaranteed under the contract, the taxpayer can receive a surrender value that may be more than the original investment—the surrender value will be increased to reflect the higher annuity rate.

As with other fixed annuities, if a taxpayer purchases a fixed MVA annuity and holds it for the duration of the product's guarantee period—which may be as short as three years or upwards of fifteen years—the product simply pays the guaranteed rate.

In recent years, the prevailing interest rates have been so low that annuity carriers have only been able to offer products with similarly low guaranteed interest rates, so there was very little difference to be realized with MVA annuities. Because interest rates on some investments—including many of those commonly held by the carriers themselves—have begun to creep higher, carriers have likewise started to offer higher rates on certain products.

This rise in interest rates, whether fleeting or long-term, allows taxpayers to lock in a higher rate on their annuity product—in some cases, for a period that is as short as three to five years. If rates begin to drop and the taxpayer chooses to surrender the product, he or she can take advantage of the MVA feature.

Further, annuity carriers often offer taxpayers higher interest rates with MVA annuities than with other annuity products because the taxpayer bears the interest rate risk; therefore, even

1. IRC Sec. 72(a)(2).

if interest rates remain relatively stable during the guarantee period and the taxpayer holds the product to maturity, he or she may have locked in a higher interest rate than would be available with similarly conservative investment products.

533. How can the investment in the contract be determined for purposes of the annuity rules?

Generally speaking, the investment in the contract is the gross premium cost or other consideration paid for the contract, reduced by amounts previously received under the contract to the extent they were excludable from income (i.e., to the extent principal has already been returned).[1]

Unless the contract has been purchased from a previous owner, the investment in the contract normally is the amount of premiums that have been paid into the contract (also known as "premium cost").[2]

However, in some cases adjustments must be made to the premiums to determine investment in the contract. For instance, extra premiums paid for supplementary benefits such as accidental death benefits, disability income benefits, and disability waiver of premiums must be excluded from premium cost.[3] (But see *Moseley v. Commissioner*,[4] where life insurance policy premium payments paid into a special reserve account were added to the aggregate premiums for purposes of calculating taxable income when a lifetime distribution was made.) Further, it might seem that premiums waived on account of disability should be treated as part of the premium cost. In the only case on the subject, however (a case dealing with the computation of gain on a matured endowment), the court held that waived premiums could not be included in the taxpayer's cost basis. The court refused to accept the view of the taxpayer that the waived premiums had been constructively received as a tax-free disability benefit and then applied to the payment of premiums. Instead, the court treated a portion of the proceeds as the tax-free disability benefit: the difference between the amount of premiums actually paid and the face amount of the endowment.[5]

Investment in the contract is increased by any amount of a policy loan that was includable in income as an amount received under the contract (Q 518).[6] Any unrepaid policy loans must be subtracted from gross premiums in determining the investment in the contract for purposes of the exclusion ratio.[7]

If premiums were deposited in advance and discounted, only the amount actually paid is includable in premium cost. However, any increment in the advance premium deposit fund that

1. IRC Sec. 72(c).
2. *Stoddard v. Comm.*, TC Memo 1993-400.
3. Rev. Rul. 55-349, 1955-1 CB 232; *Est. of Wong Wing Non v. Comm.*, 18 TC 205 (1952).
4. 72 TC 183 (1979).
5. *Est. of Wong Wing Non*, supra.
6. IRC Sec. 72(e)(4).
7. Treas. Reg. §1.72-6.

has been reported as taxable income may be added to the discounted premiums in determining cost.[1]

In the case of a participating annuity contract, dividends must be taken into account as follows:

If dividends have been received in cash or used to reduce premiums, the aggregate amount of such dividends received or credited before the annuity payments commenced must be subtracted from gross premiums to the extent the dividends were excludable from gross income (Q 10, Q 518). Also, any dividends that have been applied against principal or interest on policy loans must be subtracted, but only to the extent they were excludable from gross income.[2] (Excludable dividends are treated as a partial refund of premiums and, therefore, reduce the cost of the contract.)

If excludable dividends have been left on deposit with the insurance company to accumulate at interest and the dividends and interest are used to produce larger annuity payments, such dividends are not subtracted from gross premiums but are part of the cost of the larger payments. In this situation, gross premiums plus accumulated interest constitute the cost of the contract. (The interest is included as additional cost because it already has been taxed to the policyholder as it was credited from year to year.) Likewise, any terminal dividend that is applied to increase the annuity payments should not be subtracted from gross premium cost.

Similarly, where dividends have been applied to purchase paid-up additional insurance, and the annuity payments include income from the paid-up additions, gross premiums are used as the cost of the contract. (In effect, the dividends constitute the cost of the income from the paid-up additions.)

Cost Other than Premium Cost

There are other less common situations where investment in the contract is not always equal to premium cost. For example, investment in the contract may be the maturity value or cash surrender value of the contract if such value has been constructively received by the policyholder (Q 52, Q 589). If the contract has been purchased from a previous owner, the investment in the contract is the consideration paid by the purchaser (Q 43, Q 570). Also, special rules apply in computing the investment in the contract with respect to employee annuities, that is, annuities on which an employer has paid all or part of the premiums (Q 3537, Q 3960, Q 4074).

534. Does the presence of a long-term care rider to an annuity contract impact the calculation of investment in the contract for purposes of the annuity rules?

For contracts issued after 1996, but only for tax years after 2009, a charge against the cash surrender value of an annuity contract or life insurance contract for a premium payment of a qualified long-term care contract (Q 475) that is a rider to the annuity or life insurance

1. Rev. Rul. 65-199, 1965-2 CB 20.
2. Treas. Reg. §1.72-6.

contract reduces the investment in the contract of the annuity or life insurance contract. This charge against the cash surrender value, however, does not cause the taxpayer to recognize gross income (because it is applied against the cost basis).[1] On the other hand, such charges are also not eligible for a medical expense deduction under Section 213(a).[2]

535. Does the calculation of a taxpayer's investment in the contract for purposes of the annuity rules change if an annuity is a life annuity with a refund or period-certain guarantee?

If an annuity is a life annuity with a refund or period-certain guarantee, a special adjustment must be made to the investment in the contract (whether premium cost or other cost). The value of the refund or period-certain guarantee (as determined by use of a prescribed annuity table, Table III or Table VII, or a formula, depending on when the investment in the contract was made, see Appendix A) must be subtracted from the investment in the contract. It is this adjusted investment in the contract that is used in the exclusion ratio (Q 539, Q 543).[3]

536. How is expected return on a non-variable annuity computed under the annuity rules?

Generally speaking, expected return is the total amount that the annuitant or annuitants can expect to receive over the annuitization period of the contract.

If payments are for a fixed period or a fixed amount with no life expectancy involved, expected return is the sum of the guaranteed payments (Q 548).[4]

If payments are to continue for a life or lives, expected return is derived by multiplying the sum of one year's annuity payments by the life expectancy of the measuring life or lives. The life expectancy multiple or multiples must be taken from the Annuity Tables prescribed by the IRS.[5] (See Appendix A for IRS Annuity Tables.)

Generally, gender-based Tables I - IV are to be used if the investment in the contract does not include a post-June 30, 1986 investment. Unisex Tables V - VIII are to be used if the investment in the contract includes a post-June 30, 1986 investment. Transitional rules permit an irrevocable election to use the unisex tables even where there is no post-June 1986 investment and, if investment in the contract includes both a pre-July 1986 investment and a post-June 1986 investment, an election may be made in some situations to make separate computations with respect to each portion of the aggregate investment in the contract using, with respect to each portion, the tables applicable to it.[6] See Appendix A for details.

1. IRC Sec. 72(e)(11).
2. IRC Sec. 7702B(e)(2).
3. IRC Sec. 72(c)(2); Treas. Reg. §1.72-7.
4. IRC Sec. 72(c)(3)(B); Treas. Reg. §1.72-5(c).
5. IRC Sec. 72(c)(3).
6. Treas. Reg. §1.72-9.

The life expectancy for a single life is found in Table I or in Table V, whichever is applicable (Q 539). The life expectancy multiples for joint and survivor annuities are taken from Tables II and IIA or Tables VI and VIA, whichever are applicable (Q 542 to Q 545).[1]

The Annuity Tables are entered with the age of the measuring life as of his or her birthday nearest the annuity starting date (Q 538). The multiples in the Annuity Tables are based on monthly payments. Consequently, where the annuity payments are to be received quarterly, semi-annually, or annually, the multiples from Tables I, II, and IIA or, as applicable, Tables V, VI, and VIA, must be adjusted. This adjustment is made by use of the Frequency of Payment Adjustment Table (Appendix A). No adjustment is required if the payments are monthly.

537. How is expected return on a variable annuity computed under the annuity rules?

Generally speaking, expected return is the total amount that the annuitant or annuitants can expect to receive over the annuitization period of the contract.

The expected return of a variable contract cannot be known in advance. Therefore, the calculation of the amount excludable from each year's annuity payment does not employ the "exclusion ratio" used with fixed annuities. Instead, with a variable contract, the investment in the contract is divided over the period across which annuity payments will persist (Q 552).

538. What is the annuity starting date?

The annuity starting date is the "first day of the first period for which an amount is received as an annuity."[2] For a deferred annuity, the annuity starting date is triggered when the annuity owner elects to annuitize and begin payments; a deferred annuity contract also specifies an annuity starting date by which annuitization payments must begin, if the owner has not elected to start them prior to such date.

Planning Point: The annuity starting date is important not only to determine the onset of payments themselves, but also because the exclusion ratio for taxing annuity payments under a particular contract is determined as of the annuity starting date.

For an immediate annuity, the annuity starting date is generally immediate upon the purchase of the contract. For example, suppose that a person purchases an immediate annuity on July 1 providing for monthly payments beginning August 1. The annuity starting date is July 1 (the first payment is for the one month period beginning July 1). Payments under settlement options usually commence immediately rather than at the end of the month or other payment period; hence the annuity starting date is the date of the first payment.

1. Treas. Reg. §§1.72-5(a), 1.72-5(b).
2. IRC Sec. 72(c)(4); Treas. Reg. §1.72-4(b).

539. How is the excludable portion of payments computed under a single life annuity?

The following steps are taken in applying the basic annuity rule to determine the portion of payments that may be excludable from income in the case of a straight life annuity:

(1) Determine the investment in the contract (Q 533).

(2) Find the life expectancy multiple in Table I or V, whichever is applicable for a person of the annuitant's age (and sex, if applicable) (Appendix A). Multiply the sum of one year's guaranteed annuity payments by the applicable Table I or Table V multiple. For non-variable contracts, this is the expected return under the contract. For variable contracts, the "expected return" is the investment in the contract divided by the number of years over which payments will persist (Q 552).

(3) Divide the investment in the contract by the expected return under the contract, carrying the quotient to three decimal places. This is the exclusion ratio expressed as a percentage ("exclusion percentage").

(4) Apply the exclusion percentage to the annuity payment. The result is the portion of the payment that is excludable from gross income. The balance of the payment must be included in gross income. If the annuity starting date is after December 31, 1986, the exclusion percentage applies to payments received only until the investment in the contract is recovered. However, if the annuity starting date was before January 1, 1987, the same exclusion percentage applies to all payments received throughout the annuitant's lifetime.[1]

Example 1: On October 1, 2019, Mr. Brown purchased an immediate non-refund annuity that will pay him $125 a month ($1,500 a year) for life, beginning November 1, 2019. He paid $16,000 for the contract. Mr. Brown's age on his birthday nearest the annuity starting date (October 1) was sixty-eight. According to Table V (which he uses because his investment in the contract is post-June 1986), his life expectancy is 17.6 years. Consequently, the expected return under the contract is $26,400 (12 × $125 × 17.6). The exclusion percentage for the annuity payments is 60.6 percent ($16,000 ÷ $26,400). Because Mr. Brown received two monthly payments in 2019 (a total of $250), he will exclude $151.50 (60.6 percent of $250) from his gross income for 2019, and he must include $98.50 ($250 – $151.50). Mr. Brown will exclude the amounts so determined for 17.6 years. In 2019, he could exclude $151.50; each year thereafter through 2035, he could exclude $909, for a total exclusion of $15,604.50 ($151.50 excluded in 2019 and $15,453 excluded over the next 17 years). In 2036, he could exclude only $395.50 ($16,000 – $15,604.50), which is all the investment in the contract he has left. In 2036, he would include in his income $1,104.50 ($1,500 – $395.50). In 2037 and each year thereafter, all cost basis has been recovered, and he would include $1,500 in income each year.

Example 2: If Mr. Brown purchased the contract illustrated above on October 1, 1986 (so that it had an annuity starting date before January 1, 1987), he would exclude $151.50 (60.6 percent of $250) from his 1986 gross income and would include $98.50 ($250 – $151.50). For each succeeding tax year in which he receives twelve monthly payments (even if he outlives his life expectancy of 17.6 years), he will exclude $909 (60.6 percent of $1,500), and he will include $591 ($1,500 – $909), even after 17.6 years' worth of payments have been made.

1. IRC Sec. 72(b)(2).

To calculate the excludable portion for an annuity contract with a refund or period-certain guarantee, see Q 540.

540. How is the excludable portion of payments calculated under an annuity with a single life refund or period-certain guarantee?

The computation outlined in Q 539 is for a straight life annuity (without a refund or period-certain guarantee). The exclusion ratio for a single life refund or period-certain guarantee is determined in the same way, but the investment in the contract first must be adjusted by subtracting the value of the refund or period-certain guarantee. The value of the refund or period-certain guarantee is computed by the following steps:

(1) Determine the duration of the guaranteed amount (number of years necessary for the total guaranteed return to be fully paid). In the case of a period-certain life annuity, the duration of the guaranteed amount, in years, is known (e.g., ten, fifteen, or twenty "years certain"). To find the duration of the guaranteed amount, in years, for a cash or installment refund life annuity, divide the total guaranteed amount by the amount of one year's annuity payments, and round the quotient to the nearest whole number of years.

(2) Find the factor in Table III or VII (whichever is applicable, depending on when the investment is made in the contract) under the whole number of years (as determined above) and the age and (if applicable) the sex of the annuitant (see Appendix A). This Table III or Table VII factor is the percentage value of the refund or period-certain guarantee.

(3) Apply the applicable Table III or Table VII percentage to the smaller of (a) the investment in the contract, or (b) the total guaranteed return under the contract. The result is the present value of the refund or period-certain guarantee.

(4) Subtract the present value of the refund or period-certain guarantee from the investment in the contract. The remainder is the adjusted investment in the contract to be used in the exclusion ratio.[1]

Example 3: On January 1, 2019, a husband, age sixty-five, purchases for $21,053 an immediate installment refund annuity that pays $100 a month for life. The contract provides that in the event the husband does not live long enough to recover the full purchase price, payments will be made to his spouse until the total payments under the contract equal the purchase price. The investment in the contract is adjusted for the purpose of determining the exclusion ratio as follows:

Unadjusted investment in the contract	$ 21,053
Amount to be received annually	$ 1,200
Duration of guaranteed amount ($21,053 ÷ $1,200)	17.5 yrs.
Rounded to nearest whole number of years	18

1. Treas. Reg. §1.72-7(b).

Percentage value of guaranteed refund (Table VII for age 65 and 18 years)	15%
Value of refund feature rounded to nearest dollar (15% of $21,053)	$ 3,158
Adjusted investment in the contract ($21,053 – $3,158)	$ 17,895

Example 4: Assume the contract in Example 3 was purchased as a deferred annuity, the pre-July 1986 investment in the contract is $10,000, and the post-June 1986 investment in the contract is $11,053. If the annuitant elects (as explained in Appendix A) to compute a separate exclusion percentage for the pre-July 1986 and the post-June 1986 amounts, separate computations must be performed to determine the adjusted investment in the contract. The pre-July 1986 investment in the contract and the post-June 1986 investment in the contract are adjusted for the purpose of determining the exclusion ratios in the following manner:

Pre-July 1986 adjustment:	
Unadjusted investment in the contract	$10,000
Allocable part of amount to be received annually (($10,000 ÷ $21,053) × $1,200)	$ 570
Duration of guaranteed amount ($10,000 ÷ $570)	17.5 yrs.
Rounded to nearest whole number of years	18
Percentage in Table III for age 65 and 18 years	30%
Present value of refund feature rounded to nearest dollar (30% of $10,000)	$ 3,000
Adjusted pre-July 1986 investment in the contract ($10,000 – $3,000)	$ 7,000
Post-June 1986 adjustment:	
Unadjusted investment in the contract	$11,053
Allocable part of amount to be received annually (($11,053 ÷ $21,053) × $1,200)	$ 630
Duration of guaranteed amount ($11,053 ÷ $630)	17.5 yrs.
Rounded to nearest whole number of years	18
Percentage in Table VII for age 65 and 18 years	15%
Present value of refund feature rounded to nearest dollar) (15% of $11,053)	$ 1,658
Adjusted post-June 1986 investment in the contract ($11,053 – $1,658)	$ 9,395

Once the investment in the contract has been adjusted by subtracting the value of the refund or period-certain guarantee, an exclusion ratio is determined in the same way as for a straight life annuity. The expected return is computed, then the adjusted investment in the contract is divided by expected return. Taking the two examples above, the exclusion ratio for each contract is determined as follows.

Example (3) above.

Investment in the contract (adjusted for refund guarantee)	$17,895
One year's guaranteed annuity payments (12 × $100)	$ 1,200
Life expectancy from Table V, age 65	20 yrs.
Expected return (20 × $1,200)	$24,000

Exclusion ratio ($17,895 ÷ $24,000)	74.6%
Amount excludable from gross income each year in which 12 payments are received (74.6% of $1,200)*	$895.20
Amount includable in gross income ($1,200 – $895.20)*	$304.80

* Since the annuity starting date is after December 31, 1986, the total amount excludable is limited to the investment in the contract; after that has been recovered, the remaining amounts received are includable in income. However, if the annuity has a refund or guarantee feature, the value of the refund or guarantee feature is not subtracted when calculating the unrecovered investment.[1]

Example (4) above.

Pre-July 1986 investment in the contract (adjusted for period certain guarantee)	$ 7,000
One year's guaranteed annuity payments (12 × $100)	$ 1,200
Life expectancy from Table I, male age 65	15 yrs.
Expected return (15 × $1,200)	$ 18,000
Exclusion ratio ($7,000 ÷ $18,000)	38.9%
Post-June 1986 investment in the contract (adjusted for period certain guarantee)	$ 9,395
One year's guaranteed annuity payments (12 × $100)	$ 1,200
Life expectancy from Table V, age 65	20 yrs.
Expected return (20 × $1,200)	$ 24,000
Exclusion ratio ($9,395 ÷ $24,000)	39.1%
Sum of pre-July and post-June 1986 ratios	78%
Amount excludable from gross income each year in which twelve payments are received (78% of $1,200)*	$ 936
Amount includable in gross income ($1,200 – 936)*	$ 264

* Since the annuity starting date is after December 31, 1986, the total amount excludable is limited to the investment in the contract; after that has been recovered, the remaining amounts received are includable in income.

541. How is a temporary life annuity taxed?

A temporary life annuity is one that provides for fixed payments until the death of the annuitant or until the expiration of a specified number of years, whichever occurs earlier. The basic annuity rule (Q 529) applies. That is, the investment in the contract is divided by the expected return under the contract to find the portion of each payment that can be excluded from gross income (the exclusion ratio). Expected return is determined by multiplying one year's annuity payments by the multiple in Table IV or Table VIII (whichever is applicable, as explained in Appendix A) of the IRS Annuity Tables for the annuitant's age (as of the annuity starting date)

1. IRC Sec. 72(b)(4).

and sex (if applicable) and the whole number of years in the specified period.[1] Tables IV and VIII can be found in Treasury Regulation Section 1.72-9.

The penalty tax of IRC Section 72(q) may be imposed on the taxable portion of payments received under the contract unless one of the exceptions listed in Q 525 is met.

542. How can one calculate the excludable portion of payments under a joint and survivor annuity that continues distributing the same income to the survivor as was payable while both annuitants were alive?

Non-Variable Contracts

The basic annuity rule (Q 529) applies: the investment in the contract is divided by the expected return under the contract to find the portion of each payment that can be excluded from gross income (the exclusion ratio). Expected return must be computed by using a life expectancy multiple from Table II or Table VI of the IRS Annuity Tables (see Appendix A). With respect to an annuity with a starting date after December 31, 1986, the exclusion ratio applies to payments received until the investment in the contract is recovered.[2] If the annuity starting date was before January 1, 1987, the exclusion ratio as originally computed applies to all payments received under the contract, including payments received by the survivor as well as those received while both annuitants were alive, even if the cost basis has been fully recovered.

The steps in the computation of the exclusion ratio are as follows:

(1) Determine the investment in the contract (Q 533);

(2) Find the joint and survivor life expectancy multiple in Table II or Table VI (depending on when the investment in the contract was made – see Appendix A) under the sexes (if applicable) and ages of the annuitants. Multiply one year's guaranteed annuity payments by the applicable Table II or Table VI multiple. This is the expected return under the contract;

(3) Divide the investment in the contract by the expected return, carrying the quotient to three decimal places. This is the exclusion ratio expressed as a percentage (the "exclusion percentage");

(4) Apply the exclusion percentage to the annuity payment. The result is the portion of the payment that is excludable from gross income. The balance of the payment must be included in gross income.

Example. After June 30, 1986, Mr. and Mrs. Black purchase an immediate joint and survivor annuity. The annuity will provide payments of $100 a month while both are alive and until the death of the survivor. Mr. Black's age on his birthday nearest the annuity starting date is sixty-five; Mrs. Black's, sixty-three. The single premium is $22,000.

1. Treas. Reg. §1.72-5(a)(3).
2. IRC Sec. 72(b)(2).

Investment in the contract	\$22,000
One year's annuity payments (12 × \$100)	\$ 1,200
Joint and survivor life expectancy multiple from Table VI (ages 65, 63)	26
Expected return (26 × \$1,200)	\$31,200
Exclusion ratio (\$22,000 ÷ \$31,200)	70.5%
Amount excludable from gross income each year in which 12 payments are received (70.5% of \$1,200)*	\$ 846
Amount includable in gross income each year (\$1,200 – \$846)*	\$ 354

* If the annuity starting date is after December 31, 1986, the total amount excludable is limited to the investment in the contract; after that has been recovered, the remaining amounts received are includable in income.

Variable Contracts

The expected return, in Step 2 above, is the investment in the contract, divided by the payout period, as calculated above (Q 552).

543. How can one calculate the excludable portion of payments under a level payment joint and survivor annuity with refund or period-certain guarantee?

The exclusion ratio is determined as in Q 542, except that the investment in the contract first must be adjusted by subtracting the value of the refund or period-certain guarantee. This value is determined by following the steps below.

Investment in the Contract before July 1986

If Table II is used to determine the expected return for pre-July 1986 investment, the following method is used to determine the adjustment to the investment in the contract.[1] If Table VI is used to determine expected return for a pre-July 1986 investment, investment in the contract is adjusted using the formula for post-July 1986 investment (see subhead below).[2]

(1) Determine the duration of the guaranteed amount (the number of years necessary for the guaranteed amount to be fully paid). In the case of a period-certain and life annuity, this is the number of years in the guaranteed period (e.g., ten, fifteen, or twenty "years certain"). To find the duration of the guaranteed amount, in years, for a cash or installment refund annuity, divide the total amount guaranteed under the contract by the amount of one year's annuity payments. Round the quotient to the nearest whole number of years.

(2) If the annuitants are not of the same sex, substitute for a female a male five years younger (or for a male, a female five years older). Then find the refund percentage

1. Treas. Reg. §1.72-7(c)(2).
2. Treas. Reg. §1.72-7(c)(1).

factors in Table III under the whole number of years, as determined in (1), and the age of each annuitant of the same sex. (For Table III factors, see Appendix A.) Add these two Table III factors.

(3) Using ages of the same sex, as adjusted in (2), add to the age of the older annuitant the number of years indicated in the table below opposite the number of years by which the ages differ.

Number of years difference in age (two male annuitants or two female annuitants)	Addition to older age in years
0 to 1, inclusive	9
2 to 3, inclusive	8
4 to 5, inclusive	7
6 to 8, inclusive	6
9 to 11, inclusive	5
12 to 15, inclusive	4
16 to 20, inclusive	3
21 to 27, inclusive	2
28 to 42, inclusive	1
Over 42	0

(4) Find the refund percentage factor in Table III under the whole number of years as determined in (1) and the age of the older annuitant as adjusted in (3).

(5) Subtract the Table III factor found in (4) from the sum of the Table III factors found in (2). The balance, if any, is the percentage value of the refund or period-certain guarantee. If there is no balance, no adjustment in the investment in the contract need be made for the value of the refund or period-certain guarantee. If there is a balance, continue with the following steps.

(6) Apply the percentage value of the refund or period-certain guarantee as determined in (5) to the smaller of the investment in the contract (Q 533) or the total guaranteed return under the contract. The result is the dollar value of the refund or period-certain guarantee.

(7) Subtract the dollar value of the refund or period-certain guarantee from the investment in the contract. The remainder is the adjusted investment in the contract to be used in determining the exclusion ratio.

Example. Mr. and Mrs. Green purchase an immediate joint and survivor annuity that will pay $200 a month for ten years certain and as long thereafter as either is alive. Mr. Green is seventy years old as of his birthday nearest the annuity starting date. Mrs. Green is sixty-five. The single premium is $35,000. The total guaranteed amount is $24,000.

Investment in the contract (unadjusted)			$35,000
Percentage factor from Table III for male, age 70, and 10-year guarantee		21%	
Percentage factor from Table III for male, age 60, and 10-year guarantee		11%	
Sum of percentage refund factors		32%	
Difference in years of age between two males, age 70 and 60	10		
Addition in years to older age (Table above)	5		
Percentage refund factor from Table III for male, age 75 and 10 year guarantee		29%	
Difference between percentages		3%	
Dollar value of period-certain guarantee (3% of $24,000)			720
Adjusted investment in the contract			$34,280
Table II multiple for male, age 70, and female, age 65			20.7
Expected return (20.7 × $2,400)			$49,680
Exclusion ratio ($34,280 ÷ $49,680)			69%
Excludable from gross income each year (69% of $2,400)*			$ 1,656
Includable in gross income each year ($2,400 – $1,656)*			$ 744

* If the annuity starting date is after December 31, 1986, the total amount excludable is limited to the investment in the contract. After that has been recovered, the remaining amounts received are includable in income.[1] However, if the annuity has a refund or guarantee feature, the value of the refund or guarantee feature is not subtracted when calculating the unrecovered investment.[2]

Investment in the Contract after June 1986

Where the investment in a contract has been made after June 30, 1986, IRS regulations provide a complex formula for determining the percentage factor that was developed for a pre-July 1986 investment using the first five steps above. This percentage factor is then applied as explained in Steps 6 and 7 above.[3] The IRS will determine the amount of the adjustment on request.[4]

544. How can one compute the tax-exempt portion of payments under a joint and survivor annuity where the size of the payments will increase or decrease after the first death?

Some joint and survivor annuities provide that the size of the annuity payment will decrease after the first death, regardless of which annuitant dies first (e.g., a joint and one-half or a joint and two-thirds survivor annuity). Rarely, the joint and survivor annuity will provide for increased payments after the first death. The exclusion ratio is determined in the usual way, by dividing the investment in the contract by the expected return under the contract (Q 529). However, expected return must be computed in the following manner:[5]

1. IRC Sec. 72(b)(4).
2. IRC Sec. 72(c)-(d).
3. Treas. Reg. §1.72-7(c)(1)(i).
4. Treas. Reg. §1.72-7(c)(4).
5. Treas. Reg. §1.72-5(b)(5).

(1) Find the joint and survivor multiple in Table II or Table VI (depending on when the investment in the contract was made, as explained in Appendix A) under both annuitants' ages and, if applicable, appropriate sexes. (For the Table II or Table VI factor, see Appendix A.) Multiply the amount of one year's annuity payments to the survivor by this Table II or Table VI multiple.

(2) Find the joint life multiple in Table IIA or Table VIA (depending on when the investment in the contract was made) under both annuitants' ages and, if applicable, appropriate sexes. (For the Table IIA or VIA factor, see Appendix A.) Determine the difference between the amount of one year's annuity payments before the first death and the amount of one year's annuity payments after the first death. Multiply this difference in amount by the multiple from Table IIA or VIA, whichever is applicable.

(3) If payments are to be smaller after the first death, the expected return is the sum of (1) and (2). If payments are to be larger after the first death, the expected return is the difference between (1) and (2).

After computing the expected return, determine the exclusion ratio under the basic annuity rule: divide the investment in the contract (Q 533) by the expected return under the contract (as computed above). This same exclusion ratio is applied to payments received before the first death and to payments received by the survivor. With respect to an annuity having a starting date after December 31, 1986, the exclusion ratio is applied to payments only until the investment in the contract is recovered.[1] However, in the case of an annuity with a starting date prior to January 1, 1987, the exclusion ratio continues to apply to all payments made, regardless of whether investment in the contract has been fully recovered or not.

Example 1. After July 30, 1986, Mr. and Mrs. Brown buy an immediate joint and survivor annuity that will provide monthly payments of $117 ($1,404 a year) for as long as both live, and monthly payments of $78 ($936 a year) to the survivor. As of the annuity starting date he is sixty-five years old; she is sixty-three. The expected return is computed as follows.

Joint and survivor multiple from Table VI (ages 65,63)	26	
Portion of expected return (26 × $936)		$24,336.00
Joint life multiple from Table VIA (ages 65, 63)	15.6	
Difference between annual annuity payment before the first death and annual annuity payment to the survivor ($1,404 – $936)	$468	
Portion of expected return (15.6 × $468)		$ 7,300.80
Expected return		$31,636.80

Assuming that the Browns paid $22,000 for the contract, the exclusion ratio is 69.5 percent ($22,000 ÷ $31,636.80). During their joint lives the portion of each monthly payment to be excluded from gross income is $81.31 (69.5 percent of $117), or $975.72 a year. The portion to be included is $35.69 ($117 – $81.31), or $428.28 a year. After the first death, the portion

1. IRC Sec. 72(b)(2).

of each monthly payment to be excluded from gross income will be $54.21 (69.5 percent of $78), or $650.52 a year. Of that monthly payment, $23.79 ($78 – $54.21), or $285.48 a year, will be included.

As noted above, if the annuity starting date is after December 31, 1986, the total amount excludable is limited to the investment in the contract. Thus, if Mr. Brown lives for twenty-three years, he may exclude $81.31 from each payment for twenty-two years ((12 × 22) × $81.31 = $21,465.84). In the next year, he may exclude $534.16 ($22,000 – $21,465.84) or $81.31 from each of the first six payments, but only $46.30 from the seventh. The balance is entirely includable in his income and on his death his widow must include the full amount of each payment in income.

Example 2. Assume that in the example above, there is a pre-July 1986 investment in the contract of $12,000 and a post-June 1986 investment in the contract of $10,000. Mr. Brown elects to calculate the exclusion percentage for each portion. The pre-July exclusion ratio would be 44.6 percent ($12,000 ÷ $26,910, the expected return on the contract determined by using Tables II and IIA and the age and sex of both annuitants). The post-June 1986 exclusion ratio is $10,000 ÷ $31,636.80 or 31.6 percent. The amount excludable from each monthly payment while both are alive would be $89.15 (44.6 percent of $117 plus 31.6 percent of $117) and the remaining $27.85 would be included in gross income. If the annuity starting date is after December 31, 1986, the total amount excludable is limited to the investment in the contract.

545. How is the tax-exempt portion of payments determined for a joint and survivor annuity where the size of the payments will be reduced only if a specified annuitant dies first?

In this variation of the joint and survivor annuity, payments of a stipulated amount are made for so long as a specified annuitant (for example, the husband) lives, but payments of a reduced amount are made to the surviving joint annuitant (for example, the wife) for as long as the survivor lives. If the non-specified annuitant (for example, the wife) dies first, payments to the specified annuitant (for example, the husband) remain the same. The exclusion ratio for such an annuity is determined in the usual way, by dividing the investment in the contract by the expected return under the contract (Q 529). Expected return, however, must be computed in the following manner:[1]

(1) Find the joint and survivor multiple in Table II or VI (whichever is applicable, depending on when the investment in the contract was made, as explained in Appendix A) under the ages and (if applicable) the sexes of the annuitants. Then find the single life expectancy multiple in Table I or V, whichever is applicable, under the age and (if applicable) the sex of the first (specified) annuitant. (See Appendix A for Annuity Tables.) Subtract the applicable Table I or Table V multiple from the applicable Table II or Table VI multiple, and multiply the amount payable annually to the second annuitant (the reduced payment) by the difference between the multiples.

(2) Multiply the amount payable annually to the first annuitant by the Table I or Table V multiple (whichever is applicable).

(3) Add the results of (1) and (2). This is the expected return under the contract.

1. Treas. Reg. §1.72-5(b)(2).

Then proceed in the usual manner: divide the investment in the contract (Q 533) by the expected return under the contract (as computed above).

Example. After June 30, 1986, two spouses, Spouse A and Spouse B, purchase a joint and survivor annuity providing payments of $100 a month for the life of Spouse A and, after his death, payments to Spouse B of $50 a month for life. As of the annuity starting date Spouse A is seventy years old and Spouse B is sixty-seven.

Multiple from Table VI (ages 70, 67)	22
Multiple from Table V (age 70)	16
Difference (multiple applicable to second annuitant)	6
Portion of expected return, second annuitant (6 × $600)	$ 3,600
Portion of expected return, first annuitant (16 × $1,200)	19,200
Expected return under the contract	$22,800

Assuming that the investment in the contract is $14,310, the exclusion ratio is 62.8 percent ($14,310 ÷ $22,800). While Spouse A lives, $62.80 of each monthly payment (62.8 percent of $100) is excluded from gross income, and the remaining $37.20 of each payment must be included in gross income. After Spouse A's death, the surviving spouse will exclude $31.40 of each payment (62.8 percent of $50), and the remaining $18.60 of each payment will be includable in gross income. If the annuity starting date is after December 31, 1986, the total amount excludable is limited to the investment in the contract. Thus, if Spouse A lives fifteen years and receives 180 payments, the unrecovered investment in the contract at his death is $3,006 ($14,310 – (180 × $62.80)). Spouse B can exclude $31.40 for ninety-five payments, and $23 from the next one payment ($3,006 – (95 × 31.40) = $23). Spouse B may exclude nothing thereafter.

546. What are the income tax consequences to the surviving annuitant under a joint and survivor annuity?

The survivor continues to exclude from gross income the same percentage of each payment that was excludable before the first annuitant's death. With respect to annuities having a starting date after December 31, 1986, the total exclusion by the first annuitant and the survivor may not exceed the investment in the contract; that is, when the entire investment in the contract has been received tax-free, the entire amount of all subsequent payments will be taxed as ordinary income (Q 542 to Q 545). However, for annuities with starting dates prior to January 1, 1987, the exclusion ratio continues to apply indefinitely to annuity payments, even if the amount of principal recovered exceeds the original investment in the contract.

In addition, if the value of the survivor annuity was subject to estate tax, the survivor may be entitled to an income-in-respect-of-a-decedent income tax deduction for a portion of the estate tax paid (attributable to the embedded gain in the contract at the time of death).[1] This deduction, in most cases, will be small.

Generally, the income-in-respect-of-a-decedent deduction is computed as follows: The portion of the guaranteed annual payment that will be excluded from the survivor's gross income (under the exclusion ratio) is multiplied by the survivor's life expectancy at the date of the first annuitant's death. The result is subtracted from the estate tax value of the survivor's

1. IRC Sec. 691(d).

annuity, thereby determining the amount of expected gain in the contract at death. The total income tax deduction allowable is the estate tax attributable to this remainder of the value of the survivor's annuity.

This total deduction is claimed pro-rata over the survivor's life expectancy as of the date of the first annuitant's death, and a prorated amount is deductible from the survivor's gross income each year as payments are received. But no further deduction is allowable after the end of the survivor's life expectancy. The foregoing treatment applies only where the primary annuitant died after 1953.[1]

Planning Point: Joint ownership of non-qualified annuities creates more problems than it solves, including forced distribution at either owner's death. Where the designated beneficiary of each owner is other than the other owner, payment, at either owner's death, generally will be made to that beneficiary, effectively (and surprisingly) "disinheriting" the surviving owner. Some annuity contracts contain language stating that if the contract is jointly owned (with a right of survivorship), the surviving owner will be deemed to be the deceased owner's primary beneficiary, notwithstanding any beneficiary designation to the contrary. Some insurers will not issue deferred annuities with joint ownership unless the owners are a married couple.

It is worth noting that joint ownership often is unnecessary to achieve the objective that the policy owners may believe requires such ownership. For example, if a husband owns, and is the annuitant of, a deferred annuity of which his spouse is primary beneficiary, the death of either will leave the survivor in complete control of the contract. If the husband dies, the survivor, as the surviving spouse and primary beneficiary, may receive the death benefit or treat the contract as her own under IRC Section 72(s)(3). If the spouse dies first, the husband remains in full control of the contract. *John L. Olsen, CLU, ChFC, AEP, Olsen Financial Group.*

---

547. If an annuitant dies before receiving the full amount guaranteed under a refund or period-certain life annuity, is the balance of the guaranteed amount taxable income to the refund beneficiary?

The beneficiary will have no taxable income until the total amount the beneficiary receives, when added to amounts that were received tax-free by the annuitant (i.e., the excludable portion of the annuity payments), exceeds the investment in the contract. In other words, all amounts received by the beneficiary under a refund guarantee are treated as a return of principal first, and are exempt from tax until the investment in the contract has been recovered tax-free. Thereafter, receipts (if any) are taxable income. For purposes of calculating the unrecovered investment in the contract, the value of the refund or guarantee feature is not subtracted.[2] This "FIFO" treatment, for payments made to the beneficiary, is different from the "regular annuity rules" treatment that applied to payments made to the deceased annuitant.

The amount received by the beneficiary is considered paid in full discharge of the obligation under the contract in the nature of a refund of consideration and therefore comes under the cost recovery rule regardless of when the contract was entered into or when investments were made in the contract.[3] This rule applies whether the refund is received in one sum or in

1. Treas. Reg. §1.691(d)-1.
2. IRC Sec. 72(b)(4).
3. IRC Sec. 72(e)(5); Treas. Reg. §§1.72-11(a), 1.72-11(c).

installments made under the *same* payout arrangement under which the deceased annuitant had been receiving payments.

If the refund or commuted value of remaining installments certain is applied anew under a *different* annuity option for the beneficiary, the payments will be taxed under the regular annuity rules. A new exclusion ratio will be determined for the beneficiary.[1]

If the refund beneficiary of an annuitant whose annuity starting date is after July 1, 1986 does not recover the balance of the investment in the contract that was not recovered by the annuitant, the beneficiary may take a deduction for the unrecovered balance (Q 568).[2]

Any payment made on or after the death of an annuity holder is not subject to the 10 percent premature distribution tax (Q 525).

548. How is the excludable portion of an annuity payment under a fixed period or fixed amount option computed?

Non-Variable Contracts

The basic annuity rule (Q 529) applies: Divide the investment in the contract (Q 533) by the expected return under the contract to determine the exclusion ratio for the payments. Apply this ratio to each payment to find the portion that is excludable from gross income. The balance of the payment is includable in gross income.

If payments are for a fixed number of years (without regard to life expectancy), the expected return is the guaranteed amount receivable each year multiplied by the fixed number of years.[3]

If payments are for a fixed amount (without regard to life expectancy), the expected return is the total guaranteed amount of payments. Additional payments made after/beyond the guaranteed amount (due to excess interest) are fully taxable.[4]

To compute the excludable portion of each payment by a short method, divide the investment in the contract by the number of guaranteed payments. The result will never vary more than slightly from the exact computation.

> *Example 1.* The owner of a maturing $25,000 endowment elects to receive the proceeds in equal annual payments of $2,785 for a fixed 10 year period. Assuming that the owner's investment in the contract is $22,500, the owner may exclude $2,250 ($22,500 ÷ 10) from gross income each year. The owner must include the balance of amounts received during the year in gross income.

> *Example 2.* The owner of a maturing $25,000 endowment elects to take the proceeds in monthly payments of $200. The company's rate book shows that payments of $200 are guaranteed for 144 months. Assuming that the owner's investment in the contract is $22,500, the owner can exclude $156.25 ($22,500 ÷ 144) of each payment from gross income, and must include $43.75 ($200 – $156.25). Thus, for a full 12 months

1. IRC Sec. 72(e)(5)(E); Treas. Reg. §§1.72-11(c), 1.72-11(e).
2. IRC Sec. 72(b)(3).
3. Treas. Reg. §1.72-5(c).
4. Treas. Reg. §1.72-5(d).

of payments, the owner excludes $1,875 (12 × $156.25) and includes $525 ($2,400 – $1,875). Additional payments received after the 144 month period are fully taxable.

If the payee dies before the guaranteed period expires, the payee's beneficiary will exclude the same portion of each payment as originally computed.[1]

A penalty tax may be imposed on any payments received under the contract unless one of the exceptions listed in Q 525 is met.

Variable Contracts

Where the annuity payout is made under a variable basis (where the amount of each payment varies with the investment performance of the annuity "separate accounts"), the expected return is the investment in the contract (Q 552). The taxable amount of each annual payment will be the excess of the amount received in that year over the investment in the contract divided by the number of years in the period-certain.

549. What are the income tax results when an annuitant makes a partial lump sum withdrawal (i.e., a partial commutation) and takes a reduced annuity for the same?

The nontaxable portion of the lump sum withdrawn is an amount that bears the same ratio to the unrecovered investment in the contract as the reduction in the annuity payment bears to the original payment. The original exclusion ratio will apply to the reduced payments; that is, the same percentage of each payment will be excludable from gross income.[2]

Example. Mr. Gray pays $20,000 for a life annuity paying him $100 a month. At the annuity starting date his life expectancy is twenty years. His total expected return is therefore $24,000 (20 × $1,200), and the exclusion ratio for the payment is five-sixths ($20,000/$24,000). He receives annuity payments for five years (a total of $6,000) and excludes a total of $5,000 ($1,000 a year) from gross income. At the beginning of the next year, Mr. Gray agrees with the insurer to take a reduced annuity of $75 a month and a lump sum cash payment of $4,000. He will continue to exclude five-sixths of each annuity payment from gross income; that is, $62.50 (5/6 of $75). Of the lump sum, he will include $250 in gross income and exclude $3,750, determined as follows:

Investment in the contract	$20,000
Less amounts previously excluded	5,000
Unrecovered investment	$15,000
Ratio of reduction in payment to original payment ($25/$100)	1/4
Lump sum received	$ 4,000
Less 1/4 of unrecovered investment (1/4 of $15,000)	3,750
Portion of lump sum taxable	$ 250

1. Treas. Reg. §1.72-11(c)(2), Ex. 4.
2. Treas. Reg. §1.72-11(f).

550. What are the income tax results when an annuitant makes a partial lump sum withdrawal and takes the same payments for a different term?

If an annuity contract was purchased before August 14, 1982 (and no additional investment was made in the contract after August 13, 1982), the lump sum withdrawn is excludable from gross income as "an amount not received as an annuity" that is a return of principal received before the annuity starting date. Thus, the lump sum is subtracted from the unrecovered premium cost, and the balance is used as the investment in the contract. A new exclusion ratio (Q 529) must be computed for the annuity payments.[1]

If the lump sum withdrawn is allocable to investment in an annuity contract made after August 13, 1982, it would appear that there will be a taxable withdrawal of interest if the cash surrender value of the contract exceeds investment in the contract (Q 518, Q 525) and a new exclusion ratio must be computed given a lower anticipated expected return due to the withdrawal of a portion of contract gains (paired with the existing investment in the contract that remains).

Variable Annuities

551. Is the purchaser of a deferred variable annuity taxed on the annual growth of a deferred annuity during the accumulation period?

An annuity owner who is a "natural person" will pay no income tax until he or she receives distributions from the contract. If the contract is annuitized, taxation of payments will be calculated based on the rules that apply given the annuity starting date when payments begin. Distribution amounts received "not as an annuity" – i.e., partial withdrawals or full surrenders without annuitization – prior to the annuity starting date are subject to the rules discussed in Q 518 and Q 525.

The tax deferral enjoyed by a deferred annuity owned by a natural person is not derived from any specific IRC section granting such deferral. Rather, this tax treatment is granted by implication. All distributions from an annuity are either "amounts received as an annuity" or "amounts not received as an annuity." As the annual growth of the annuity account balance, except to the extent of dividends, is not stated in the IRC to be either, it is not a "distribution," and therefore is not subject to tax as earned. For the tax treatment of dividends, see Q 518, Q 527, and Q 528.

A variable annuity contract will not be treated as an annuity and taxed as explained in this and the following questions unless the underlying investments of the segregated asset account are "adequately diversified," according to IRS regulations (Q 555).[2]

Planning Point: Notably, this does not necessarily mean that investors themselves who own such variable annuities must be diversified, but simply that they must be presented with a diversified range of options from the variable annuity contract.

If the owner of the contract is a person other than a natural person (for example, a corporation or certain trusts), growth in the value of the annuity might not be tax deferred; see Q 511.

1. Treas. Reg. §1.72-11(e).
2. IRC Sec. 817(h); Treas. Reg. §1.817-5.

552. How are payments under a variable immediate annuity taxed?

Both fixed dollar and variable annuity payments received as an annuitized stream of income are subject to the same basic tax rule: a fixed portion of each annuity payment is excludable from gross income as a tax-free recovery of the purchaser's investment, and the balance is taxable as ordinary income. In the case of a variable annuity, however, the excludable portion is not determined by calculating an "exclusion ratio" as it is for a fixed dollar annuity (Q 529). Because the expected return under a variable annuity is unknown, it is considered to be equal to the investment in the contract. Thus, the excludable portion of each payment is determined by dividing the investment in the contract (adjusted for any period-certain or refund guarantee) by the number of years over which it is anticipated the annuity will be paid.[1] In practice, this means that the cost basis is simply recovered pro-rata over the expected payment period.

If payments are to be made for a fixed number of years without regard to life expectancy, the divisor is the fixed number of years. If payments are to be made for a single life, the divisor is the appropriate life expectancy multiple from Table I or Table V, whichever is applicable (depending on when the investment in the contract was made, as explained in Appendix A). If payments are to be made on a joint and survivor basis, based on the same number of units throughout both lifetimes, the divisor is the appropriate joint and survivor multiple from Table II or Table VI, whichever is applicable (depending on when the investment in the contract is made; see Appendix A). IRS regulations explain the method for computing the exclusion where the number of units is to be reduced after the first death. The life expectancy multiple need not be adjusted if payments are monthly. If they are to be made less frequently (annually, semi-annually, quarterly), the multiple must be adjusted (see Frequency of Payment Adjustment Table, Appendix A).[2]

A portion of each payment is only excluded from gross income using the exclusion ratio until the investment in the contract is recovered (normally, at life expectancy).[3] However, if payments received are from an annuity with a starting date that was before January 1, 1987, payments continue to receive exclusion ratio treatment for life, even if the total cost basis recovered exceeds the original investment amount.

Where payments are received for only part of a year (as for the first year if monthly payments commence after January), the exclusion is a pro-rata share of the year's exclusion.[4]

If an annuity settlement provides a period-certain or refund guarantee, the investment in the contract must be adjusted before being prorated over the payment period (Q 553).

553. How is the value of a refund or period-certain guarantee determined under a variable annuity contract?

If a variable annuity settlement provides a refund or period-certain guarantee, then when calculating the exclusion ratio the investment in the contract must be reduced by the value of

1. Treas. Reg. §1.72-2(b)(3).
2. Treas. Reg. §§1.72-2(b)(3), 1.72-4(d).
3. IRC Sec. 72(b)(2).
4. Treas. Reg. §1.72-2(b)(3).

the guarantee.[1] The value of such a guarantee in connection with a single life annuity is determined as follows:

Find the refund percentage factor in Table III or Table VII (whichever is applicable, depending on the date the investment in the contract was made, as explained in Appendix A) under the age and (if applicable) sex of the annuitant and the number of years in the guaranteed period (see Tables in Appendix A). Where the settlement provides that proceeds from a given number of units will be paid for a period-certain and life thereafter, the number of years in the guaranteed period is clear (e.g., ten, fifteen, twenty "years certain").

If the settlement specifies a guaranteed amount, however, divide this guaranteed amount by an amount determined by placing payments received during the first taxable year (to the extent that such payments reduce the guaranteed amount) on an annual basis. Thus, if monthly payments begin in August, the total amount received in the first taxable year is divided by five, then multiplied by twelve.

The quotient is rounded to the nearest whole number of years, and is used in entering Table III or Table VII, as applicable. The appropriate Table III or Table VII multiple is applied to whichever is smaller: (a) the investment in the contract, or (b) the product of the payments received in the first taxable year, placed on an annual basis, multiplied by the number of years for which payment of the proceeds of a unit or units is guaranteed. The following illustration is taken from the regulations:[2]

Example: Mr. Brown, a fifty year old male, purchases, for $25,000, a contract that provides for variable monthly payments to be paid to him for his life. The contract also provides that if he should die before receiving payments for fifteen years, payments shall continue according to the original formula to his estate or beneficiary until payments have been made for that period. Beginning with the month of September, Mr. Brown receives payments that total $450 for the first taxable year of receipt. This amount, placed on an annual basis, is $1,350 ($450 divided by 4 or $112.50; $112.50 multiplied by 12, or $1,350).

If there is no post-June 1986 investment in the contract, the guaranteed amount is considered to be $20,250 ($1,350 × 15), and the multiple from Table III (for male fifty, fifteen guaranteed years), nine percent, applied to $20,250 (because this amount is less than the investment in the contract), results in a refund adjustment of $1,822.50. The latter amount, subtracted from the investment in the contract of $25,000, results in an adjusted investment in the contract of $23,177.50. If Mr. Brown dies before receiving payments for fifteen years and the remaining payments are made to Mr. Green, his beneficiary, Mr. Green shall exclude the entire amount of such payments from his gross income until the amounts so received by Mr. Green, together with the amounts received by Mr. Brown and excludable from Mr. Brown's gross income, equal or exceed $25,000. Any excess and any payments thereafter received by Mr. Green shall be fully includable in gross income.

Assume the total investment in the contract was made after June 30, 1986. The applicable multiple found in Table VII is three percent. When this is applied to the guaranteed amount of $20,250, it results in a refund adjustment of $607.50. The adjusted investment in the contract is $24,392.50 ($25,000 – $607.50).

1. Treas. Reg. §1.72-7(d).
2. Treas. Reg. §1.72-7(d)(2).

554. If payments from an immediate variable annuity drop below the excludable amount for any year, is the balance of the exclusion lost?

No.

If the amount received from an immediate variable annuity in any taxable year is less than the excludable amount as originally determined, the annuitant may elect to redetermine the excludable amount in a succeeding taxable year in which the annuitant receives another payment. The aggregate loss in exclusions for the prior year (or years) is divided by the number of years remaining in the fixed period or, in the case of a life annuity, by the annuitant's life expectancy computed as of the first day of the first period for which an amount is received as an annuity in the taxable year of election. The amount so determined is added to the originally determined excludable amount.[1]

Planning Point: This rule allows any investment in the contract not received in one year to be recovered pro-rata in subsequent years as subsequent payments are received.

Example 1: Mr. Brown is sixty-five years old as of his birthday nearest July 1, 1985, the annuity starting date of a contract he purchased for $21,000. There is no investment in the contract after June 30, 1986. The contract provides variable monthly payments for Mr. Brown's life. Because Mr. Brown's life expectancy is fifteen years (Table I), he may exclude $1,400 of the annuity payments from his gross income each year ($21,000 ÷ 15). Assume that in each year before 1988, he receives more than $1,400, but in 1988, he receives only $800 – $600 less than his allowable exclusion. He may elect, in his return for 1989, to recompute his annual exclusion. Mr. Brown's age, as of his birthday nearest the first period for which he receives an annuity payment in 1989 (the year of election) is sixty-nine, and the life expectancy for that age is 12.6. Thus, he may add $47.61 to his previous annual exclusion, and exclude $1,447.61 in 1989 and subsequent years. This additional exclusion is obtained by dividing $600 (the difference between the amount he received in 1988 and his allowable exclusion for that year) by 12.6.

Example 2: Mr. Green purchases a variable annuity contract that provides payments for life. The annuity starting date is June 30, 2016, when Mr. Green is 64 years old. Mr. Green receives a payment of $1,000 on June 30, 2017, but receives no other payment until June 30, 2019. Mr. Green's total investment in the contract is $25,000. Mr. Green's pre-July 1986 investment in the contract is $12,000. Mr. Green may redetermine his excludable amount as above, using the Table V life expectancy. If, instead, he elects to make separate computations for his pre-July 1986 investment and his post June-1986 investment (see Appendix A), his additional excludable amount is determined as follows.

Pre-July 1986 investment in the contract allocable to taxable years 2017 and 2018 ($12,000 ÷ 15.1 [multiple from Table I for a male age 64] = $794.70;	$1,589.40
Less: portion of total payments allocable to pre-July 1986 investment in the contract actually received as an annuity in 2017 and 2018 ($12,000/$25,000 × $1,000)	480.00
Difference	$1,109.40
Post-June 1986 investment in the contract allocable to taxable years 2017 and 2018 ($13,000 ÷ 20.3 [multiple from Table V for male age 64] = $640.39; $640.39 × 2 years = $1,280.78	$1,280.78

1. Treas. Reg. §1.72-4(d)(3).

Less portion of total payments allocable to post-July 1986 investment in the contract actually received as an annuity in 2017 and 2018 ($13,000/$25,000 × $1,000)	520.00
Difference	$ 760.78

Because the applicable portions of the total payment received in 2017 under the contract ($480 allocable to the pre-July 1986 investment in the contract and $520 allocable to the post-June 1986 investment in the contract) do not exceed the portion of the corresponding investment in the contract allocable to the year ($794.70 pre-July 1986 and $640.39 post-June 1986) the entire amount of each applicable portion is excludable from gross income and Mr. Green may redetermine his excludable amounts as follows:

Divide the amount by which the portion of total payment actually received allocable to pre-July 1986 investment in the contract is less than the pre-July 1986 investment in the contract allocable to 2017 and 2018 ($1,109.40) by the life expectancy under Table I for Mr. Green, age 66 (14.4 – .5 [frequency multiple]; $1,109.40 ÷ 13.9)	$ 79.81
Add the amount originally determined with respect to pre-July 1986 investment in the contract	794.70
Amount excludable with respect to pre-July 1986 investment	$874.51
Divide the amount by which the portion of total payment actually received allocable to post-June 1986 investment in the contract is less than the post-June 1986 investment in the contract allocable to 2017 and 2018 ($760.78) by the life expectancy under Table V for Mr. Green, age 66 (19.2 – .5 [frequency multiple]; $760.78 ÷ 18.7)	$ 40.68
Add the amount originally determined with respect to post-June 1986 investment in the contract	640.39
Amount excludable with respect to post-June 1986 investment	$681.07

555. What is a wraparound or investment annuity? How is the owner taxed prior to the annuity starting date?

"Investment annuity" and "wraparound annuity" are terms for arrangements in which an insurance company agrees to provide an annuity funded by investment assets placed by or for the policyholder with a custodian (or by investment solely in specifically identified assets held in a segregated account of the insurer). The IRS has ruled that under these arrangements, sufficient control over the investment assets is retained by the policyholder so that income on the assets prior to the annuity starting date is currently taxable to the policyholder rather than to the insurance company, which is actually favorable in this context – it means investors can retain capital gains treatment on the underlying assets, even as they receive the guarantees associated with the annuity backing, though it also means the investor does *not* receive the annuity's tax deferral benefits.[1]

1. *Christoffersen v. U.S.*, 84-2 USTC ¶9990 (8th Cir. 1984), *rev'g* 84-1 USTC ¶9216 (N.D. Iowa 1984), *cert. denied*, 473 U.S. 905 (1985); Rev. Rul. 81-225, 1981-2 CB 12 (as clarified by Rev. Rul. 82-55, 1982-1 CB 12); Rev. Rul. 80-274, 1980-2 CB 27; Rev. Rul. 77-85, 1977-1 CB 12.

In some instances, however, the policyholder's degree of control over the investment decisions has been insufficient, so the IRS considered the insurance company, rather than the policyholder, to be the owner of the contracts. For example, the IRS has ruled that the contract owner of a variable annuity can invest in sub-accounts that invest in mutual funds that are available only through the purchase of variable contracts without losing the variable annuity's tax deferral, but in turn will be forced to have all gains taxed as ordinary income (per the usual treatment of annuity gains).[1]

The IRS has ruled on whether the hedge funds within the sub-accounts of variable annuities and variable life insurance contracts will be treated as owned by the insurance company or the contract owner. Generally, if the hedge funds are available to the general public, the sub-account will be treated as owned by the contract owner and therefore not entitled to tax deferral. However, if the hedge funds are available only through an investment in the variable annuity, tax deferral is available.[2] The IRS also has clarified who is considered the "general public."[3]

With the exception of certain contracts grandfathered under Revenue Rulings 77-85 and 81-225, the underlying investments of the segregated asset accounts of variable contracts must meet diversification requirements set forth in the Regulations.[4]

556. What is a private placement variable annuity (PPVA)?

A PPVA investment is an annuity that is available only to high net worth individuals who qualify as accredited investors (and, practically, qualified purchasers), meaning that they meet certain requirements as to net worth and investment sophistication. It is an annuity in that it is treated as such for tax purposes, but the similarities to the traditional retail annuities that most taxpayers associate with the term ends there—PPVA investments do not offer the types of income guarantee riders and protection against market risks that today's retail annuities typically make available.

Instead, the draw of the PPVA investment is the investment flexibility and tax-deferred growth that these types of accounts offer. The taxpayer has the freedom to made additional deposits to the annuity and change his or her investment allocations based on a number of investment options—typically, these annuities will provide a choice of investments that includes non-traditional investment options, such as hedge fund and private equity investments that have the potential to generate substantial returns.

Taxes on the account growth are deferred until the taxpayer begins taking annuity payouts (a 10 percent penalty charge applies if distributions begin before the taxpayer reaches age 59½). In order to qualify for this favorable tax treatment, the PPVA investment must offer only investment options that are available solely to qualified insurance companies.

Further, the underlying asset allocations must meet certain investment diversification requirements—for example, no more than 55 percent of the individual's assets may be allocated

1. Rev. Rul. 2005-7, 2005-6 IRB 464. See also Rev. Rul. 2003-91, 2003-33 CB 347; Rev. Rul. 82-54 1982-1 CB 11.
2. Rev. Rul. 2003-92, 2003-33 CB 350.
3. Rev. Rul. 2007-7, 2007-7 IRB 468.
4. IRC Sec. 817(h); Treas. Reg. §1.817-5.

to any single investment and no more than 70 percent may be allocated to any two investments. The taxpayer has control over his or her investment allocations, but cannot have control over the investment *choices* that are offered within the PPVA investment—an independent investment manager must have discretion to choose the investments that will be made available to the taxpayer.

557. What is the difference between a longevity annuity and a deferred annuity?

A deferred annuity provides for an initial waiting period before the contract can be annuitized (usually between one and five years), and during that period the contract's cash value generally remains liquid and available (albeit potentially subject to surrender charges). Beyond the initial waiting period the contract *may* be annuitized, though the choice remains in the hands of the annuity policyowner, at least until the contract's maximum maturity age (at which point it must be annuitized).

Planning Point: It is *always* the case that owners of deferred annuity contracts can annuitize after an initial waiting period (often one year, and rarely later than the fifth year). This is the case even when the contract's *maturity date* is fixed at a date far into the future. *John L. Olsen, CLU, ChFC, AEP*

By contrast, a longevity annuity generally provides no access to the funds during the deferral period, and does not *allow* the contract to be annuitized until the owner reaches a certain age (usually around eighty-five).

In other words, many taxpayers purchase traditional deferred annuity products with a view toward waiting until old age to begin annuity payouts, but they always have the option of beginning payouts at an earlier date. With a longevity annuity, there is generally no choice, but this also allows for larger payments for those who do survive to the starting period; as a result, for those who survive, longevity annuities typically provide for a larger payout (often, much larger) than traditional deferred annuity products.

Planning Point: The chief benefit of a longevity annuity is *financial leverage*. The benefit payment may be far larger than can be *guaranteed*, at the time of purchase, by any other instrument, including a deferred annuity. As one might expect, the leverage in a longevity annuity providing no benefit unless the annuitant lives to the annuity starting date is substantially greater than that provided by a contract with a death benefit. *John L. Olsen, CLU, ChFC, AEP*

Most taxpayers who purchase longevity annuities do so in order to insure against the risk of outliving their traditional retirement assets. The longevity annuity, therefore, functions as a type of safety net for expenses incurred during advanced age. Where a deferred annuity contract may be more appropriately categorized as an investment product, the primary benefit of a longevity annuity is its insurance value.

558. What is a qualified longevity annuity contract (QLAC)? What steps has the IRS taken to encourage the purchase of QLACs?

A qualified longevity annuity contract (QLAC) is a type of longevity annuity ("deferred income annuity") that meets certain IRS requirements that have been developed in order to encourage the purchase of annuity products with retirement account assets.[1] A QLAC is a type of deferred annuity product that is usually purchased before retirement, but for which payouts are delayed until the taxpayer reaches old age.

Planning Point: Some commentators make a distinction between "longevity annuities" in regard to the annuity starting date (ASD). This is because some contracts specify a particular ASD, such as age eighty-five, while others offer the purchaser a choice of ASDs. The former variety typically provides no pre-ASD death benefit and the latter may.

In the usual case, if a deferred annuity is held in a retirement plan, the value of that contract is included in determining the amount of the account owner's required minimum distributions (RMDs).[2] One of the primary benefits of a QLAC is that the IRS' rules allow the value of the QLAC to be excluded from the account value for purposes of calculating RMDs.[3] Because including the value of a QLAC in determining RMDs could result in the taxpayer being forced to begin annuity payouts earlier than anticipated if the value of his or her other retirement accounts has been depleted, the IRS determined that excluding the value from the RMD calculation furthers the purpose of providing taxpayers with predictable retirement income late in life.[4]

The amount that a taxpayer can invest in a QLAC and exclude from the RMD calculation is limited, however, to the lesser of $125,000 (as adjusted for inflation in future years, $130,000 for 2018 and unchanged for 2019) or 25 percent of the taxpayer's retirement account value.[5] The final regulations provide that the 25 percent limit is based upon the account value as it exists on the last valuation date before the date upon which premiums for the annuity contract are paid. This value is increased to account for contributions made during the period that begins after the valuation date and ends before the date the premium is paid. The account value is decreased to account for distributions taken from the account during this same period.[6]

To qualify as a QLAC, the annuity contract must also provide that annuity payouts will begin no later than the first day of the month following the month in which the taxpayer reaches age eighty-five.[7] Variable annuities, indexed annuities and similar products may not qualify as QLACs unless the IRS specifically releases future guidance providing otherwise.[8] Further, a QLAC cannot provide for any commutation benefit, cash surrender value or similar benefit.[9]

1. 2012-13 IRB 598.
2. Treas. Reg. §1.401(a)(9)-6, A-12.
3. See IRC Sec. 401(a)(9).
4. 2012-13 IRB 598.
5. 2012-13 IRB 598.
6. Treas. Reg. §1.401(a)(9)-6, A-17(d)(1)(iii).
7. Treas. Reg. §1.401(a)(9)-6, A-17(a).
8. Treas. Reg. §1.401(a)(9)-6, A-17(a)(7).
9. Treas. Reg. §1.401(a)(9)-6, A-17(a)(4).

559. What types of retirement accounts can hold a qualified longevity annuity contract (QLAC)?

A qualified longevity annuity contract (QLAC, see Q 558) may be held in a qualified defined contribution plan (such as a 401(k) plan), IRC Section 403 plans, traditional IRAs and individual retirement annuities under Section 408, and eligible IRC Section 457 governmental plans.[1]

An annuity purchased within a Roth IRA cannot quality as a QLAC. If a QLAC is purchased under a traditional IRA or qualified plan that is later rolled over or converted to a Roth IRA, the annuity will not be treated as a QLAC after the date of the rollover or conversion.[2] While it is true that an annuity purchased in a Roth IRA cannot qualify as a QLAC, it should not be assumed that a Roth IRA cannot purchase a longevity annuity. The final regulations do not prohibit this.

560. Can a taxpayer purchase both QLACs and non-QLAC DIAs within an IRA and remain eligible to exclude the QLAC value when calculating RMDs? How is the non-QLAC DIA treated in such a case?

The regulations answer this question by their focus: only QLACs are addressed within the regulations. IRA-held DIAs that are not QLACs are not governed by the new regulations. These regulations are additive in that they do not remove any of the previously existing rules that govern these types of annuity contracts. As a result, the regulations do not prevent a taxpayer from holding a non-QLAC DIA in a traditional IRA. In such a case, the previously existing method for determining RMDs for non-QLAC DIAs will apply.

The actuarial present value [APV] (which may be referred to as fair market value [FMV]) is calculated and RMDs attributable to that value must be withdrawn from another IRA or through a commutation liquidation from the DIA contract itself. After the annuity starting date, the income payments from the DIA automatically satisfy the RMD requirement. No separate calculation is required.

561. May an individual purchase a QLAC after the required beginning date (RBD)?

The Treasury Department answers this question by implication in revised Treasury Regulation Section 1.401(a)(9)-6, A-17(c)(v), which states that, for contracts permitting a set non-spousal beneficiary designation, "payments are payable to the beneficiary only if the beneficiary was irrevocably designated on or before the later of the date of purchase or the employee's required beginning date." Based upon this language, it is clear that an employee (in the case of a qualified plan) or IRA participant may purchase a QLAC after his or her RBD.

Planning Point: The final regulations do not answer the following question: Can a QLAC in a qualified plan be converted to a traditional IRA?

At this point in time, the answer to this question may depend upon the insurers' administrative systems.

1. Treas. Reg. §1.401(a)(9)-6, A-17(b)(2).
2. Treas. Reg. §1.401(a)(9)-6, A-17(d)(3)(ii).

562. Are the death benefits under a deferred annuity triggered upon the death of the owner of the annuity, or upon the death of the annuitant?

Whether death benefits of a deferred annuity (in particular, certain guaranteed minimum death benefits in excess of the contract's cash value) are triggered upon the death of the owner or the annuitant depends upon the terms of the contract. Some deferred annuity contracts are "annuitant-driven", meaning that the contract will be paid out upon the death of the *annuitant*. These contracts will pay the death benefit (including any guaranteed minimum death benefit) upon the death of the annuitant.

However, *all* deferred annuity contracts issued since January 18, 1985,[1] must specify that if any "holder" of a deferred annuity contract dies before the contract enters payout status, the entire interest must be distributed within five years of the holder's death. Thus, *all* such contracts are "owner-driven" while only *some* are *also* "annuitant-driven". Typically, the "holder" of the annuity contract is the owner of that contract, though if the annuity owner is a non-natural person (such as a trust or a corporation), the holder of the contract is the primary annuitant under the contract.[2] See Q 566.

In practical terms, this means that if a deferred annuity contract is "annuitant-driven" and provides for a guaranteed minimum death benefit in excess of the contract's cash value *and if the owner and annuitant are not the same person*, the cash value will be paid out if the owner dies first (ending the contract) and the guaranteed minimum death benefit will be paid out if the annuitant dies first. If a contract is not "annuitant-driven", the death benefit will be paid out only upon the death of the *first* owner ("holder"). In that situation, if the annuitant dies first, the owner may generally name a new annuitant. If the owner and annuitant are the same person (the annuitant *must* be a human being), this question is moot.

Planning Point: When a deferred annuity is owned by a "non-natural person" (e.g., a trust), the question of "whose death triggers the death benefit?" may be unclear. When the contract is owned by a *revocable* trust, the death of the *grantor* will trigger the death benefit (as the grantor is the "holder" for income tax purposes). When it is owned by an *irrevocable non-grantor* trust, the death of the *primary annuitant* will cause payout. But if the trust is an *irrevocable grantor* trust and the primary annuitant is not the grantor, some insurance companies follow IRC Section 72(s)(6)(A) and will pay out the death benefit upon the death of the primary annuitant. Most, however, follow the grantor trust rules and will pay out upon the death of the grantor. Good practice demands that where this latter situation exists, a letter from the insurance company explaining its policy regarding this question should be obtained before either the grantor or primary annuitant dies. *John L. Olsen, CLU, ChFC, AEP, OlsenAnnuityEducation.com.*

563. What are the rules that allow 401(k) plan sponsors to include deferred annuities in target date funds (TDFs)?

IRS Notice 2014-66 specifically permits 401(k) plan sponsors to include deferred annuities within TDFs without violating the nondiscrimination rules that otherwise apply to investment options offered within a 401(k). This is the case even if the TDF investment is a qualified default

1. IRC Sec. 72(s)(1)(B).
2. IRC Sec. 72(s)(6)(A).

investment alternative (QDIA)—which is a 401(k) investment that is selected automatically for a plan participant who fails to make his or her own investment allocations.

Further, the guidance clarifies that the TDFs offered within the plan can include deferred annuities even if some of the TDFs are only available to older participants—even if those older participants are considered "highly compensated"—without violating the otherwise applicable nondiscrimination rules. Similarly, the nondiscrimination rules will not be violated if the prices of the deferred annuities offered within the TDF vary based on the participant's age.

The IRS guidance will allow plan sponsors to include annuities within TDFs even if a wide age variance exists among the plan's participants. Additionally, the rules allow plan sponsors to provide a participant with guaranteed lifetime income sources even if the participant is not actively making his or her own investment decisions with respect to plan contributions—a situation which is increasingly prevalent as employers may now automatically enroll an employee in the 401(k) plan unless the employee actively opts out of participation.

564. Can a taxpayer combine a deferred income annuity ("longevity annuity") with a traditional deferred annuity product?

Yes. Insurance carriers have begun offering optional riders that can be attached to variable deferred annuity products in order to include the benefits of a deferred income ("longevity") annuity within the variable annuity. These deferred income annuities allow the contract owner to withdraw portions of the variable annuity itself in order to fund annuity payouts late into retirement.

Taxpayers must purchase the rider at the time the variable annuity is purchased and can then begin transferring a portion of the variable annuity accumulation into the deferred income component as soon as two years after the contract is purchased. When the taxpayer begins making transfers into the deferred component, he or she must also choose the beginning date for the deferred payments.

The deferral period can be as brief as two years or, in some cases, as long as forty years, giving taxpayers substantial flexibility in designing the product to meet their individual financial needs. Further, taxpayers can choose to transfer as little as around $1,000 at a time or as much as $100,000 to build the deferred income portion more quickly.

The deferred income annuity rider can simplify taxpayers' retirement income planning strategies in several important ways, not the least of which involves the ability to gain the benefits of both variable deferred and deferred income annuities within one single annuity package.

This single-package treatment also allows taxpayers to avoid the situation where they wish to transition their planning strategies to eliminate the investment-type features common to variable annuity products into a product that allows for a definite income stream—a situation that commonly arises around the time when a taxpayer retires.

Without the combination product, the taxpayer would traditionally be required to execute a tax-free exchange of the variable annuity contract for a deferred income annuity. Instead, the deferred income annuity rider allows the taxpayer to systematically transfer funds from the variable portion of the contract into the deferred income portion over time (though lump sum transfers are also permissible).

565. Can a grantor trust own a deferred annuity contract? How is a deferred annuity owned by a grantor trust taxed?

A grantor trust can own a deferred annuity contract, but, in certain circumstances, the "non-natural person rule" of IRC Section 72(u) will cause the denial of the tax-deferral benefits to a deferred annuity owned by a trust. If annuity tax benefits are denied under the non-natural person rule, income on the annuity for any taxable year will be treated as ordinary income received.[1] However, if a trust owns a deferred annuity contract as the agent for a natural person, Section 72(u) does not apply.[2]

A revocable grantor trust will usually fall within this exception because the grantor (presumably a natural person) and the grantor trust are treated as one "person" for income tax purposes,[3] and, moreover, because the property is generally held in trust specifically *for* that grantor. More generally, as long as the grantor trust (a non-natural person) owns the deferred annuity contract, and the primary beneficiaries *of the trust* are natural persons, the annuity contract should escape the non-natural person rule of Section 72(u).[4] If significant interests in the trust are held by non-natural persons, however, it is possible that the trust will not qualify as an agent for a natural person.

It should be noted that most insurers require that when the owner of their deferred annuity contract is a trust, the trust must also be the primary beneficiary of that contract.

If the grantor trust is irrevocable, determining whether the trust is exempt from the non-natural person rule becomes more complicated because the grantor of the trust might not retain any right to the trust assets or income. In making the determination whether significant interests in the trust are held by natural or non-natural persons, it is important to determine who will receive the primary economic benefit of the trust assets.[5]

The IRS has ruled privately that deferred annuity contracts owned by an irrevocable grantor trust established by an employer-corporation (a non-natural person) were held for the benefit of natural persons (the employees) because (1) the employee-beneficiaries of the trust would receive all of the trust income and (2) the employer held no future interest in the trust assets.[6] Therefore, even though the actual grantor of the trust was a non-natural person, the deferred annuity contract was able to escape the non-natural person rule because the beneficiaries were natural persons.

1. IRC Sec. 72(u)(1).
2. IRC Sec. 72(u)(1)(B).
3. See IRC Sec. 671.
4. Let. Ruls. 9316018, 9120024.
5. Let. Ruls. 200449011, 200449013, 200449014.
6. Let. Ruls. 9316018, 9322011.

Planning Point: When a deferred annuity contract is *payable to* a trust, the death proceeds must generally be paid out over five years.[1] That said, a few insurers will permit the trustee of a trust named as beneficiary of a deferred annuity to elect post-death payout over the lifetime of the oldest trust beneficiary. Their rationale is that the legislative history of IRC Section 72 clearly indicates a desire on the part of Congress to provide "parity" between the tax treatment afforded deferred annuity death benefits and the treatment of death benefits of qualified plans.[2] There is, however, no *statutory* authority for this position. *John L. Olsen, CLU, ChFC, AEP, OlsenAnnuityEducation.com.*

Note that immediate annuities are explicitly exempted from the non-natural person rule of IRC Section 72(u).[3]

566. If a grantor trust owns a deferred annuity and the grantor is not the annuitant, whose death triggers the annuity payout?

If an *irrevocable* grantor trust owns a deferred annuity and the grantor of the trust is not the annuitant, it is not clear whether payment of death proceeds will be triggered upon the death of the grantor or upon the death of the annuitant. The Code provides that the primary annuitant will be considered the "holder" of the contract if the owner is a non-natural person (e.g., a trust).[4] Therefore, many experts argue that it is the death of the primary annuitant that triggers annuity payout.

Others disagree, and argue that it is the grantor's death that will trigger payout. This is because of the grantor trust rules, which treat the grantor of a trust and the trust itself as one individual for income tax purposes. Because the grantor is the owner of the trust assets for income tax purposes, many experts argue that the grantor should be treated as owner—or "holder"—for purposes of IRC Section 72(s). That said, this ambiguity applies only to deferred annuities owned by *irrevocable grantor* trusts. When the owner is a *revocable* trust, the grantor trust rules control (as the grantor is the "holder" for income tax purposes). Although that is also true when the trust is irrevocable and also a grantor trust, some authorities insist that the rule of IRC Section 72(s)(6)(A) controls, as the grantor of an irrevocable trust owning a deferred annuity does not have the unfettered control of that annuity contract that he would have were the trust revocable.

At this point, the matter remains unresolved without any clarity or on-point guidance from the IRS.

Planning Point: Given the current ambiguities, the question of whether post-death payouts of a deferred annuity will be triggered by the death of the grantor or the death of the annuitant will be decided for all practical purposes by the particular insurance company that issues the contract, as the company will make payouts in accordance with its own interpretation of the rules. Because of this, it is important that all parties become familiar with the policies of the insurance company when the annuity is purchased. – *John L. Olsen, CLU, ChFC, AEP, OlsenAnnuityEducation.com.*

1. IRC Sec. 72(s)(1)(B).
2. IRC Sec. 401(a)(9).
3. IRC Sec. 72(u)(3).
4. IRC Sec. 72(s)(6)(A).

567. Does the surrender of a deferred annuity contract ever result in a deductible loss?

In general, a loss deduction can be claimed only if the loss is incurred in connection with the taxpayer's trade or business or in a transaction entered into for profit.[1] Fortunately, the purchase of a personal deferred annuity contract is typically considered a transaction entered into for profit. Consequently, if a taxpayer sustains a loss upon surrender of a deferred annuity contract, the taxpayer may claim a deduction for the loss as a loss on an investment (a transaction entered into for profit).

The amount of the loss is determined by subtracting the cash surrender value (i.e., the net proceeds received after all final charges) from the taxpayer's "basis" for the contract. "Basis" is investment in the contract (e.g., premium paid, less any dividends received (Q 518) and the excludable portion of any prior annuity payments). The loss is an ordinary loss, not a capital loss (which means it does not have to be and should not be netted against capital gains).[2]

While a deductible loss from an annuity is an ordinary loss, there has been a great deal of discussion about *where* a taxpayer should claim the loss on Form 1040. Some say that the loss should be treated as a miscellaneous itemized deduction that is not subject to the 2 percent-of-AGI floor on miscellaneous itemized deductions (all of which were suspended for 2018-2025 by the 2017 Tax Act). Others take a more aggressive approach and say that the loss can be taken on the front of the Form 1040 on the line labeled "Other gains or (losses)" with supporting reporting on Form 4797.

Planning Point: Although the IRS has not issued definitive guidance on the issue, it is notable that since 2009, IRS Publication 575 (Pension and Annuity Income) has stated the IRS position that a loss under a variable annuity is treated as a miscellaneous itemized deduction subject to the 2 percent floor (however, as noted above, these deductions were suspended for 2018-2025).[3] There is no apparent reason under the IRC and existing guidance as to why such a position by the IRS would not be upheld in court, if challenged, especially since as a standard rule any deduction not explicitly allowed elsewhere under the tax code is intended to be taken as a miscellaneous itemized deduction (and there is no other place in the tax code that affords special benefits to the deduction of losses for a nonqualified annuity).[4]

Notably, if the taxpayer purchased the contract for purely personal reasons, and not for profit, no loss deduction will be allowed. For example, in one case, the taxpayer purchased annuities on the lives of his relatives, naming his wife as the beneficiary of the contracts. Upon his wife's death, the taxpayer obtained consent from each of his relatives (the annuitants) and named himself as the new beneficiary. He later surrendered the contracts at a loss. The court disallowed a loss deduction on the ground that, even though he suffered a loss, the contracts were not bought for profit, but rather to provide financial security for his relatives.[5]

1. IRC Sec. 165.
2. Rev. Rul. 61-201, 1961-2 CB 46; *Cohan v. Comm.*, 39 F.2d 540 (2nd Cir. 1930), *aff'g* 11 BTA 743 (superseded on other grounds).
3. IRS Pub. 575 (2016), p. 22.
4. IRC Sec. 67(b).
5. *Early v. Atkinson*, 175 F.2d 118 (4th Cir. 1949).

568. Is a deductible loss sustained under a straight life annuity if the annuitant dies before payments received by the annuitant equal the annuitant's cost?

If the annuitant's annuity starting date is after July 1, 1986, a deduction may be taken on the individual's final income tax return for the unrecovered investment in the contract remaining on the date of death.[1] Similarly, a refund beneficiary may deduct any unrecovered investment in the contract that exceeds the refund payment.[2] For purposes of determining if the individual has a net operating loss, the deduction is treated as if it were attributable to a trade or business.[3]

If an annuitant's annuity starting date was before July 2, 1986, there is no deductible loss; the view under the law at the time was that the annuitant had received all that the contract required.[4] For example, no loss deduction was allowed where a husband purchased a single premium nonrefundable annuity on the life of his wife and his wife died before his cost had been recovered. The deduction was disallowed on the ground that the transaction was not entered into for profit.[5] Legislatively, the denial of a deductible loss for unrecovered investment at death was viewed as a trade-off for the fact that exclusion ratio non-taxable payments also could continue beyond the point of fully recovering cost basis for contracts before July 2, 1986.

Disposition of an Annuity Contract

569. What are the income tax consequences to the owner of an annuity contract if the owner sells the contract?

Based upon existing case law, if an annuity is sold, the amount of taxable gain is determined in the same way as on surrender of a contract (Q 588). In other words, gain is determined by subtracting the investment in the contract (gross premiums less dividends to the extent excludable from income and principal payments already received) from the sale price. In addition, the gain retains its character as ordinary income; thus, where deferred annuities were sold shortly before maturity, the gain was held to be ordinary income.[6]

However, the tax treatment of a sale of a deferred annuity for more than the annuity surrender value is not entirely clear. For example, assume an annuity with a $50,000 cost basis and a $75,000 surrender value was sold for $85,000 (perhaps because it provides a contractual interest rate guarantee that is more appealing than current market rates). The $25,000 gain from cost basis to surrender value must be taxed as ordinary income. It is not clear, however, whether the additional $10,000 of gain would be taxed as though it were an "amount not received as an annuity" (i.e., ordinary income treatment), or the sale of the entire annuity contract as though it were a capital asset (i.e., capital gain treatment). Similar favorable treatment has been allowed in the case of the sale of a life insurance policy for more than its cash surrender value.[7]

---

1. IRC Sec. 72(b)(3)(A).
2. IRC Sec. 72(b)(3)(B).
3. IRC Sec. 72(b)(3)(C).
4. *Industrial Trust Co. v. Broderick*, 94 F.2d 927 (1st Cir. 1938); Rev. Rul. 72-193, 1972-1 CB 58.
5. *White v. U.S.*, 19 AFTR 2d 658 (N.D. Tex. 1966).
6. *First Nat'l Bank of Kansas City v. Comm.*, 309 F.2d 587 (8th Cir. 1962); *Roff v. Comm.*, 304 F.2d 450 (3rd Cir. 1962).
7. Rev. Rul. 2009-13, 2009-21 IRB 1029.

Where an annuity contract is sold after maturity, the cost basis of the contract (for purpose of computing the seller's gain) must be reduced by the aggregate excludable portions of the annuity payments that have been received. The adjusted cost basis, however, cannot be reduced below zero (for example, where the annuitant has outlived his or her life expectancy and was able to exclude amounts in excess of his or her net premium cost).[1] The taxable gain, that is, cannot be greater than the sale price. Where an annuity contract is sold for less than its cost basis, the seller realizes an ordinary loss (Q 567).

If the contract sold is subject to a nonrecourse loan, the transferor's obligation under the loan is discharged and the amount of the loan is considered an amount received on the transfer.[2]

570. How is the purchaser of an existing immediate annuity contract taxed?

If the purchaser receives lifetime proceeds under the contract, the purchaser is taxed in the same way as an original owner would be taxed, but with the following difference: the purchaser's cost basis is the consideration the purchaser paid for the contract, plus any premiums the purchaser paid after the purchase and less any excludable dividends and unrepaid excludable loans received by the purchaser after the purchase.

If the contract is purchased after payments commence under a life income or installment option, a new exclusion ratio must be determined, based on the purchaser's cost and expected return computed as of the purchaser's annuity starting date. The purchaser's annuity starting date is the beginning of the first period for which the purchaser receives an annuity payment under the contract (Q 529 to Q 536).[3]

If the purchaser of an annuity is a corporation, or other non-natural person, see Q 511.

571. When is a policy owner deemed to have exchanged one annuity contract for another?

Under IRC Section 1035, policy owners may exchange one nonqualified annuity contract for another on a tax-deferred basis (in the case of qualified annuities, the retirement account rollover rules control the transfer of account balances and their tax consequences).

However, the distinction between an "exchange" and a surrender-and-purchase is not always clear. Where the contract is assignable, the IRS has required a direct transfer of funds between insurance companies.[4], Given that most commercial nonqualified annuities in today's marketplace are assignable, the direct-transfer-of-funds method is the standard for completing a 1035 exchange in most common situations.

Nonetheless, the "exchange" of an annuity contract received as part of a distribution from a terminated profit-sharing plan for another annuity with similar restrictions as to transferability, spousal consent, minimum distribution, and the incidental benefit rule was granted

1. Treas. Reg. §1.1021-1.
2. Treas. Reg. §1.1001-2(a).
3. Treas. Reg. §§1.72-4(b)(2), 1.72-10(a).
4. See Let. Rul. 8741052. Compare Let. Ruls. 8515063 and 8310033; Rev. Rul. 72-358, 1972-2 CB 473.

IRC Section 1035 treatment.[1] In addition, the IRS has ruled privately that the surrender of a non-assignable annuity contract distributed by a pension trust and immediate endorsement of the check by the annuitant to the new insurer in a single integrated transaction under a binding exchange agreement with the new insurer qualified as an exchange.[2]

On the other hand, while the Tax Court did once allow an exchange where the taxpayer surrendered an annuity contract for cash and then purchased another annuity contract, the IRS acquiesced only in the result of that case.[3] And the IRS has ruled that a taxpayer's receipt of a check issued by an insurance company will be treated as a distribution (and, thus, not an exchange), even if the check is endorsed to a second insurance company for the purchase of a second annuity.[4]

The IRS also has ruled privately that a valid exchange did not occur where the taxpayer surrendered one life insurance policy and then placed the funds in a second policy purchased one month earlier.[5] In another instance, the IRS viewed several transactions as "steps" in one integrated exchange. The taxpayer purchased an annuity contract and later withdrew an amount equal to the taxpayer's basis from the contract, placing the funds in a single premium life insurance policy. Next, the taxpayer exchanged the annuity for another annuity, treating this part of the transaction as a tax-free exchange under IRC Section 1035. The IRS disagreed, characterizing the events as a single exchange, with the value of the life insurance policy received as taxable boot.[6]

572. What is the tax treatment of a partial 1035 exchange of an annuity contract?

The Tax Court, in *Conway v. Commissioner*,[7] held that a 1035 exchange occurred when the taxpayer transferred a portion (but not all) of the funds from one annuity to a second newly-issued annuity. The IRS later ruled that the proper way to allocate investment in the contract when one annuity is "split up" into two annuities is on a pro rata basis based on the cash surrender value of the annuity before and after the partial exchange. For example, if 60 percent of an annuity's cash surrender value is transferred to a new annuity, the investment in the contract of the "new" annuity will be 60 percent of the investment in the contract of the "old" annuity, and the investment in the contract of the "old" annuity will be 40 percent of what it was before the partial exchange.[8]

In 2008, the IRS released a revenue procedure concerning certain tax-free partial exchanges of annuity contracts (under Sections 1035 and 72(q)). The revenue procedure applies to the direct transfer of a portion of the cash surrender value of an existing annuity contract for a second annuity contract, regardless of whether the two annuity contracts are issued by the same or different companies.

1. Let. Rul. 9233054.
2. Let. Ruls. 8526038, 8501012, 8344029, and 8343010.
3. *Greene v. Comm.*, 85 TC 1024 (1985), *acq.* 1986-2 CB 1.
4. Rev. Rul. 2007-24, 2007-21 IRB 1282.
5. Let. Rul. 8810010.
6. TAM 8905004. See also Let. Rul. 9141025.
7. 111 TC 350 (1998), *acq.* 1999-2 CB xvi.
8. Rev. Rul. 2003-76, 2003-33 CB 355.

Under current law, a transfer will be treated as a partial tax-free exchange under Section 1035 under final rules issued in 2008, as updated by Revenue Procedure 2011-38, as long as the taxpayer does not take any withdrawals from either contract within 180 days of the partial exchange. When a partial 1035 exchange is completed, the basis is divided pro rata between the old contract and the new one based on the relative value of the contracts when the split occurred.

If the direct transfer of a portion of an annuity contract for a second annuity contract does not qualify as a tax–free exchange, it will generally be treated as a taxable distribution followed by a payment for the second contract, although the IRS reserves the right to conclude differently after applying general tax principles to determine the substance and appropriate treatment of the transfer.

The IRS will not require aggregation of two annuity contracts that are the subject of a tax-free exchange (under Section 1035 and this guidance) even if both contracts were issued by the same insurance company.[1]

The exchange of nontransferable tax sheltered[2] annuity contracts is discussed in Q 4043.

Planning Point: Although the rules under IRC Section 1035 cover a broader array of annuity exchanges, funds in nonqualified annuities are not freely movable. For example, the IRS does not provide guidance on the transfer of a portion of the funds in one annuity to a second existing annuity. It is not certain that such a transaction is covered under Section 1035 and therefore this type of transaction may not receive tax-free treatment. *Fred Burkey, CLU, APA, Ameritas®.*

573. When is the exchange of one annuity contract for another a nontaxable exchange?

The IRC provides that the following exchanges are nontaxable:

(1) the exchange of a life insurance policy for another life insurance policy, for an endowment or annuity contract, or for a qualified long-term care insurance contract;

(2) the exchange of an endowment contract for an annuity contract, for an endowment contract under which payments will begin no later than payments would have begun under the contract exchanged, or for a qualified long-term care insurance contract;

(3) the exchange of an annuity contract for another annuity contract; and

(4) the exchange of a long-term care insurance contract for another qualified long-term care insurance contract.[3]

1. Rev. Proc. 2011-38, 2011-30 IRB, *superseding* Notice 2003-51, 2003-33 CB 361.
2. IRC Sec. 403(b).
3. IRC Sec. 1035(a).

These rules do not apply to any exchange having the effect of transferring property to any non-United States person.[1]

As a result of the Pension Protection Act of 2006, for exchanges after 2009, life, annuity, endowment, and qualified long-term care insurance contracts may now be exchanged for qualified long-term care insurance contracts.[2] In addition, the presence of a qualified long-term care insurance contract as a rider on an annuity or life insurance policy does not cause it to fail to qualify for the purposes of such exchanges. In other words, a taxpayer can exchange an annuity without a long-term care insurance contract rider for an annuity with such a rider, and still qualify for nonrecognition treatment.[3]

If an annuity is exchanged for another annuity, the contracts must be payable to the same person or persons. Otherwise, the exchange does not qualify as a tax-free exchange under IRC Section 1035(a).[4] The IRC defines an annuity for this purpose as a contract with an insurance company that may be payable during the life of the annuitant only in installments.[5] Despite the singular reference in IRC Section 1035(a)(3) to "an annuity contract for an annuity contract," the IRS concluded that one annuity could properly be exchanged under IRC Section 1035 for two annuities, issued by either the same or a different insurance company.[6]

Further, the exchange of two life insurance policies for a single annuity contract also has been considered a proper IRC Section 1035 exchange.[7] The exchange of one annuity for a second annuity with a term life insurance rider attached was afforded income tax-free treatment under IRC Section 1035.[8] A proper IRC Section 1035 exchange also occurred where an annuity holder directly transferred a portion of the funds in one annuity to a second newly-issued annuity.[9] An assignment of an annuity contract for consolidation with a pre-existing annuity contract is a tax-free exchange under Section 1035, even though the two annuities were issued by different insurance companies.[10]

The exchange of a life insurance policy, endowment contract, or fixed annuity contract for a variable annuity contract with the same company or a different company qualifies as a tax-free exchange under IRC Section 1035(a).[11]

Planning Point: Although the exchange of a variable annuity for a fixed annuity is not specifically addressed in this ruling, there does not appear to be any evidence that would prohibit such an exchange from qualifying for IRC Section 1035 treatment, and in practice insurance companies routinely allow this treatment.

1. IRC Sec. 1035(c).
2. IRC Sec. 1035(a).
3. IRC Sec. 1035(b)(2), IRC Sec. 105(b)(3).
4. Treas. Reg. §1.1035-1.
5. IRC Sec. 1035(b)(2).
6. Let. Rul. 199937042.
7. Let. Rul. 9708016.
8. Let. Rul. 200022003.
9. *Conway v. Comm.*, 111 TC 350 (1998), *acq.* 1999-2 CB xvi.
10. Rev. Rul. 2002-75, 2002-2 CB 812.
11. Rev. Rul. 72-358, 1972-2 CB 473.

Additionally, the exchange of an annuity contract issued by a domestic insurer for an annuity contract issued by a foreign insurer was considered a permissible IRC Section 1035 exchange.[1]

574. Is the exchange of one annuity contract for another permissible if the owner-beneficiary inherited the annuity from a deceased original owner?

In general, the original owner of a nonqualified annuity product is able to exchange one annuity for another in an IRC Section 1035 exchange without treating the transaction as a sale—no gain is recognized when the first annuity contract is disposed of, and there is no intervening tax liability. Despite this, Section 1035 requires that, for the annuity exchange to be tax-free, the newly acquired annuity must be payable to the same individual that was entitled to annuity payouts under the original annuity.[2]

The IRS has ruled privately that the beneficiary who inherits rights to payouts under an annuity also inherits an ownership interest in the annuity that is sufficient to allow tax-free exchange treatment under IRC Section 1035.[3]

In the IRS ruling, the beneficiary inherited multiple annuity products and elected to receive distributions over her life expectancy after the original account owner's death. Later, she found an annuity product that offered more attractive investment features and sought to exchange the original contracts for an annuity that would increase her annuity payout, but would continue to distribute those payouts over her life expectancy.

By allowing this exchange, the IRS permitted the beneficiary to exchange the entire pre-tax value of the inherited annuity, rather than requiring that she take a lump sum distribution of the inherited annuity interest, pay taxes on this distribution and then purchase the replacement annuity contract with the after-tax value.

However, the IRS was careful to note that the rules applicable to post-death distributions still apply, meaning that the newly acquired annuity must require distribution of the entire interest in the inherited annuity within five years or over the beneficiary's life expectancy.

Planning Point: Unfortunately, given that the private letter ruling allowing post-death 1035 exchanges was just that – a private letter ruling – insurance companies are not bound and required to honor it. In practice, as with many PLRs pertaining to annuity companies, some have acquiesced, while others have not. As a result, *for situations where a beneficiary is interested in completing an inherited annuity post-death 1035 exchange*, it may be necessary to seek out companies that are specifically willing to cooperate with the assignment of contract necessary to facilitate the exchange. In addition, the original annuity must be liquid enough at death – i.e., not have certain required payout provisions – to allow it to be liquidated and transferred pursuant to a (post-death) 1035 exchange in the first place. *Michael E. Kitces, MSFS, MTAX, CFP, CLU, ChFC.*

1. Let. Rul. 9319024.
2. IRC Sec. 1035.
3. Let. Rul. 201330016.

575. Are there special rules for exchanging one annuity contract for another where the insurer issuing the contract is under rehabilitation?

The IRS will allow a valid exchange where funds come into the contract or policy in a series of transactions if the insurer issuing the contract or policy to be exchanged is subject to a "rehabilitation, conservatorship, or similar state proceeding."[1]

Funds may be transferred in this "serial" manner if:

(1) the old policy or contract is issued by an insurer subject to a "rehabilitation, conservatorship, insolvency, or similar state proceeding" at the time of the cash distribution;

(2) the policy owner withdraws the full amount of the cash distribution to which he or she is entitled under the terms of the state proceeding;

(3) the exchange would otherwise qualify for IRC Section 1035 treatment; and

(4) the policy owner transfers the funds received from the old contract to a single new contract issued by another insurer not later than 60 days after receipt.

If the amount transferred is not the full amount to which the policy owner ultimately is entitled, the policy owner must assign his or her right to any subsequent distributions to the issuer of the new contract for investment in that contract.[2] If a nonqualified annuity contract is exchanged under IRC Section 1035 within the scope of Revenue Ruling 92-43 (i.e., as part of a rehabilitation proceeding), the annuity received will retain the attributes of the annuity for which it was exchanged for purposes of determining when amounts are to be considered invested and for computing the taxability of any withdrawals (Q 518).[3]

576. When is a policy owner required to recognize gain on the exchange of one annuity contract for another?

If no cash or other non-like kind property is received in connection with an exchange, any gain from the contract surrendered will not be recognized in the transfer to the new contract. Accordingly, the cost basis of the new policy will be the same as the cost basis of the old policy (plus any premiums paid and less any excludable dividends received after the exchange).

If cash or other non-like kind property is received in connection with any of the above exchanges, gain will be recognized to the extent of the cash or other property received as so-called "boot" property.[4] The amount of any policy loan that the other party to the exchange takes property subject to or assumes (reduced by any loan taken subject to or assumed by the first party) is treated as money received on the exchange.[5] If the owner has exchanged an annuity at

1. Rev. Rul. 92-43, 1992-1 CB 288.
2. Rev. Proc. 92-44, 1992-1 CB 875, *as modified* by Rev. Proc. 92-44A, 1992-1 CB 876.
3. Let. Rul. 9442030.
4. Treas. Reg. §1.1031(b)-1(a).
5. Treas. Reg. §1.1031(b)-1(c).

a loss, and the requirements of Section 1035 were satisfied, the receipt of boot does not cause the loss to be recognized.[1]

It should be noted that application of Section 1035 is not an election; its nonrecognition treatment is mandatory when the provisions of that section are met.

577. When is the exchange of one annuity contract for another a taxable transaction?

If the exchange of one annuity contract for another does not qualify for tax-free treatment (see Q 571 to Q 576), it is taxable. For example, if a policyholder exchanges an endowment or annuity contract for a whole life policy, gain will be fully taxable to the policyholder in the year of exchange (since life insurance death proceeds are exempt from tax, the government views any exchange that provides life insurance protection where none existed as a method of tax avoidance). The gain is ordinary income – not capital gain.[2]

The amount of taxable gain is determined by subtracting (1) the net premium cost (gross premiums less any excludable dividends) from (2) the value of the new policy plus any cash or the fair market value of any other property received in the exchange (in most cases, this will simply be the gain that was embedded in the original contract). The value of the new policy, for this purpose, is not cash surrender value but fair market value (i.e., the value that came into the contract before the potential application of any new surrender charges). Thus, if the new policy is single-premium or paid-up, its value is its replacement cost (the price that a person of the same age and sex as the insured would have to pay for a similar policy with the same company on the date of exchange).[3] If the new policy is premium-paying, apparently its value is its interpolated terminal reserve plus any unearned premium as of the date of exchange (see Q 144).[4]

An exchange where both contracts or policies are issued by the same insurer (i.e., an "in-house" exchange) is not subject to the reporting requirements for IRC Section 1035 exchanges[5] provided that the exchange does not result in a designated distribution and the insurer's records are sufficient to determine the policyholder's basis.[6]

The effect of a tax-free exchange of annuity contracts on taxation of amounts received under the replacing contract is discussed in Q 518 and Q 594.

578. What is the tax treatment for an annuity with a long-term care rider?

Under the Pension Protection Act of 2006, an annuity issued after December 31, 2009 may include a qualified long-term care insurance rider. Under these rules, inclusion of the rider will not trigger taxable distributions as premiums are deducted from cash value for long-term

1. IRC Secs. 1035(d)(1), 1031(c).
2. Treas. Reg. §1.1035-1; Rev. Rul. 54-264, 1954-2 CB 57; *Barrett v. Comm.*, 16 AFTR2d 5380 (1st Cir. 1965) *aff'g* 42 TC 993.
3. *Parsons v. Comm.*, 16 TC 256 (1951); *Barrett*, supra; Rev. Rul. 54-264, supra.
4. Rev. Rul. 59-195, 1959-1 CB 18.
5. IRC Sec. 6047(d).
6. Rev. Proc. 92-26, 1992-1 CB 744.

care premiums, although such charges will reduce investment in the contract.[1] In addition, all long-term care benefits paid under the rider (whether attributable to gains or cost basis) will be tax-free and are excludable from the recipient's gross income (and not reduce investment in the contract).

In order to qualify for favorable treatment, the long-term care insurance policy must conform to the "qualified" long-term care insurance requirements of IRC Section 7702B. In a private letter ruling, the IRS analyzed the federal income tax treatment of a particular company's long-term care insurance rider to be offered with certain annuity contracts by an insurance company with respect to taxable years beginning after December 31, 2009, and ruled that the rider will constitute a qualified long-term care insurance contract.[2]

579. What constitutes a gift of an annuity contract? What constitutes a gift of a premium?

A person has made a gift of the contract if the person (1) purchases an annuity contract, the proceeds of which are payable to a beneficiary other than the person or the person's estate, (2) retains no reversionary interest in the estate, and (3) has no power to re-vest the economic benefits in himself or herself or the estate, or to change the beneficiary. Likewise, if a person fully transfers (absolutely assigns) a contract, or relinquishes by assignment every power the person retained in a previously issued contract, the person has made a gift. If the person pays a premium on a contract and has no ownership rights, the person has made a gift of the premium. Of course, if the person receives adequate consideration for the transfer, it is not a gift.[3]

For the income tax consequences when the owner makes a gift of an annuity contract, see Q 581.

The Tax Court held that a donor's assignment of life insurance benefits and payment of annual premiums constituted a gift of the benefits from the insured to his children as of the date that the donor renounced his right to change beneficiaries, where the donor did not retain the power to revest the benefits in himself.[4] In another case, a divorced wife owned insurance policies on the life of her former husband. Pursuant to the terms of a property settlement calling for the insured to pay future premiums and any gift tax, the former wife assigned the policies to the parties' children. The court held that the transfer of life insurance policies was an indirect gift of the policies from the insured to the children.[5]

See Q 116 regarding gifts with respect to split dollar arrangements.

The IRS has ruled that where (1) an employee has irrevocably assigned the employee's rights under a group term life policy, (2) the policy is later replaced by a policy identical in all material respects to the prior policy, and (3) the new policy provides that an employee's irrevocable

1. IRC Sec. 72(e)(11); Notice 2011-68, 2011-36 IRB 205.
2. IRC Secs. 72, 104, 7702B.
3. Treas. Reg. §25.2511-1(h)(8).
4. *Fletcher Trust Co. v. Comm.*, 1 TC 798 (1943), *aff'd*, 141 F.2d 36 (7th Cir. 1944).
5. *duPont v. Comm.*, TC Memo 1978-16.

assignment of the employee's rights under the old policy is effective to vest in the assignee the insured's rights under the new policy, the replacement of the old policy with the new does not constitute a new gift of policy rights for federal gift tax purposes.[1]

580. Can the owner of an annuity contract avoid income and penalty taxes by assigning the right to receive the payments to another individual while retaining ownership of the contract?

No.

It is a basic tax principle that "fruit" is attributed to the "tree" on which it grows.

Without actually transferring the underlying contract, a gift or gratuitous assignment of just the income will not shift the taxability of the income away from the owner of the contract. This applies to income accumulated on the contract before or after the assignment.[2] Thus, withdrawals and annuity payments are taxable to the owner, even if paid to a third party. It would apparently follow that any liability for a premature distribution penalty would be on the policy owner, and would be based on the owner's age, death, or disability.

Where the owner makes a gift of the underlying contract, see Q 581.

581. What are the income tax consequences when a deferred annuity contract is transferred as a gift?

An individual who transfers a nonqualified deferred annuity contract issued after April 22, 1987, for less than full and adequate consideration is treated as having received "an amount not received as annuity" (Q 518). Thus, the individual transferring the contract realizes in the year of the transfer any gain on the contract (the excess of the cash surrender value over the investment in the contract).[3]

The IRS has ruled privately that the distribution of an annuity contract by a trust to a trust beneficiary will not be treated as an assignment for less than full and adequate consideration because the trust as transferor is not considered an individual.[4] In addition, this rule also does not apply to transfers between spouses (or between former spouses incident to a divorce and pursuant to an instrument executed or modified after July 18, 1984), except that it does apply to a gift of a contract in trust for such a spouse to the extent that gain must be recognized because of any loan to which the contract is subject (Q 106).

In the case of an annuity contract issued prior to April 23, 1987, if the cash surrender value at the time of the gift exceeds the donor's cost basis and the donee subsequently surrenders the contract, the ***donor*** must, in the year of the *surrender* (which might not be the year of gift), report as taxable income the "gain" existing at the time of the gift. In other words, the ***donor*** is taxed on the difference between the premiums the donor had paid (less any excludable dividends

1. Let. Rul. 8230038.
2. *Helvering v. Eubank*, 311 U.S. 112 (1940); *Lucas v. Earl*, 281 U.S. 111 (1930).
3. IRC Sec. 72(e)(4)(C).
4. Let. Ruls. 9204010, 9204014.

the donor has received) and the cash surrender value of the contract at the time of the gift, but not until the donee surrenders the contract. ***The balance of the gain, if any, is taxed to the donee.*** Thus, in the case of a pre-April 23, 1987 contract, the proper year for the donor to include the gain in the donor's gross income is the year in which the contract is surrendered by the donee; with a post-April 22, 1987 annuity, gain is always recognized at the time (in the year) that the transfer occurs.[1]

Subsequent annuity payments under a contract that has been transferred as a gift are taxed under the annuity rules (Q 529 to Q 554). With respect to gifts of annuities issued after April 22, 1987, the amount of gain, if any, that is included in the transferor's income as a result of the transfer will increase the transferee's investment in the contract for the purposes of calculating the exclusion ratio.[2] If the contract was issued before April 23, 1987, all premiums paid and excludable dividends received by both the donor and donee prior to the commencement of the annuity payments are taken into account in determining the investment in the contract. The annuity starting date and expected return are determined as though no transfer has taken place.[3] However, the IRS has not ruled on whether, if the contract was transferred when the cash surrender value exceeded the donor's cost basis, the donor must include any portion of the payments in the donor's gross income or how such portion would be determined.

Where a gift is conditioned on payment by the donee of the donor's gift tax liability, a court has ruled that income is realized by the donor to the extent the gift tax exceeds the donor's basis in the property.[4] The gain is included in the donor's income for the year in which the gift tax is paid by the donee.[5] However, payment of federal or state gift tax by the donee (or agreement to pay such tax) does not result in income to the donor in the case of net gifts made before March 4, 1981.[6]

If the contract transferred is subject to a nonrecourse loan, the transferor's obligation under the loan is discharged and the amount of the loan is treated as an amount received with the result that gain is recognized to the extent the loan exceeds the adjusted basis.[7]

If the gift is to a corporation or other nonnatural person, see Q 511.

582. What are the income tax consequences when a deferred annuity is transferred to a trust?

When an annuity is gifted to a revocable living trust, the grantor retains control of the property, such that no "transfer" without adequate consideration has taken place; thus, there are no income tax consequences for such transfers.

1. Rev. Rul. 69-102, 1969-1 CB 32.
2. IRC Sec. 72(e)(4)(C)(iii).
3. Treas. Reg. §1.72-10(b).
4. *Diedrich v. Comm.*, 82-1 USTC ¶9419 (1982).
5. *Weeden v. Comm.*, 82-2 USTC ¶9556 (9th Cir. 1982).
6. TRA '84, Sec. 1026.
7. Treas. Reg. §1.1001-2(a).

The gift of an annuity to the donor's irrevocable grantor trust is more problematic. Many commentators hold that such transfer cannot be subject to tax because transfers from a taxpayer to the taxpayer's grantor trust are not taxable events. The gift of an annuity to one's irrevocable trust, however, may be a completed gift subject to tax. A strict reading of IRC Section 72(e)(4)(C) will lead to the conclusion that recognition of gain upon the transfer of an annuity occurs whenever such transfer is made without full and adequate consideration. A gift of an annuity to an irrevocable trust (grantor or not) arguably meets that test, especially if the transferor reports the same on a gift tax return. In other words, the Section 72(e)(4)(C) test appears to be based on gift treatment, not income tax treatment, even though it ultimately has income tax consequences. As of early 2019, the IRS has not provided definitive guidance on this point.

583. Does the purchase of a joint and survivor annuity result in a taxable gift?

Yes, if the purchaser of the contract does not reserve the right to change the beneficiary of the survivor payments.[1]

Planning Point: In the case of a joint and survivor annuity between spouses, the unlimited marital deduction makes this a moot point (see Q 585); in the case of a non-spouse joint annuitant, though, gift tax consequences may be incurred.

On how to value the gift, see Q 586.

584. Is the naming of an irrevocable beneficiary under a refund annuity a gift?

Yes.

This is true even though the beneficiary will get nothing unless the annuitant dies before receiving payments equal to the annuitant's premium cost. Because the gift is contingent on the annuitant's death within a specified period, it is the gift of a "future interest" and therefore does not qualify for the annual exclusion (Q 218).[2] The value of the gift is the present value of the contingent right to receive any remaining refund payments upon the death of the annuitant.

Where the gift is from one spouse to another, see Q 585.

585. When does the gift of an annuity between spouses qualify for the gift tax marital deduction?

A direct gift to a spouse of an annuity contract in which no one else has an interest qualifies for the gift tax marital deduction. The interest of a donee spouse in a joint and survivor annuity in which only the donor and donee spouses have a right to receive payments during such spouses' joint lifetimes is treated as a "qualifying income interest for life" for which the

1. IRC Sec. 2523(f)(6).
2. *Morrow v. Comm.*, 2 TC 210 (1943).

marital deduction is available unless the donor spouse irrevocably elects otherwise within the time allowed for filing a gift tax return.[1]

To the extent provided in the IRS regulations, an annuity interest is treated in a manner similar to an income interest in property (regardless of whether the property from which the annuity is payable can be separately identified).[2] If, however, an election is made to not have the donee spouse's interest treated as a "qualifying income interest for life," the marital deduction is not allowed if the donor gives an interest in the contract to a third party, or keeps an interest for himself, and there is a possibility that the donor or the third party could receive some benefits from this interest after the donee's interest ends.

Thus, if the donee spouse's interest is not treated as a "qualifying income interest for life," the gift of a refund annuity will not qualify if the refund is payable to the donor or a third party in the event of the donee's death during the refund period.[3]

Although the gift tax marital deduction is not allowed for a non-US citizen spouse, an annual exclusion may be allowed instead of the marital deduction.[4] For calendar year 2020, the exclusion amount is increased to $157,000 (up from $155,000 in 2019, $152,000 in 2018, and $149,000 in 2017). However, this rule does not apply for gifts of future interests of property, which includes transfers resulting from joint and survivor annuities.[5]

586. What is the gift tax value of an annuity contract or of a donee's interest in a joint and survivor annuity?

Where an annuity is purchased by a donor on his or her own life and immediately given to another, or when an annuity is purchased by one person for another on the latter's life, the value of the gift is the premium paid for the contract.[6] If a person purchases an annuity and gives the contract to another person at a later date after the annuity starting date (i.e., once annuity payments have begun), the gift tax value is the single premium the company would charge for an annuity providing payments of the same amount on the life of a person who is the annuitant's age at the time of the gift.[7] The value of a deferred premium-paying annuity is the terminal reserve, adjusted to the date of the gift, plus the unearned portion of the last premium payment (Q 119).[8]

Joint and Survivor Annuity

Where a donor purchases a joint and survivor annuity for the benefit of the donor and another, the gift tax value is the cost of the annuity less the cost of a single life annuity for the donor.[9]

1. IRC Sec. 2523(f)(6).
2. IRC Sec. 2523(f)(3).
3. Treas. Reg. §25.2523(b)-1(b)(6) (Example 3); §25.2523(b)-1(c)(2).
4. IRC Sec. 2523(i).
5. Rev. Proc. 2015-53, 2015-44 IRB 615, Rev. Proc. 2016-55, Rev. Proc. 2017-58, Rev. Proc. 2018-57, Rev. Proc. 2019-44.
6. Treas. Reg. §25.2512-6(a) (Ex.1).
7. Treas. Reg. §25.2512-6(a) (Ex. 2).
8. *Comm. v. Edwards*, 135 F.2d 574 (5th Cir. 1942).
9. Treas. Reg. §25.2512-6(a).

Example. A donor purchases from a life insurance company for $15,198 a joint and survivor annuity contract that provides for the payment of $60 a month to the donor during the donor's lifetime, and then to the donor's sibling for such time as the sibling may survive the donor. The premium that would have been charged by the company for an annuity of $60 monthly payable during the life of the donor alone is $10,690. The value of the gift is $4,508 ($15,198 less $10,690).[1]

587. Can the purchase of a private annuity result in a taxable gift?

There is no gift if the purchase of an annuity is a bona fide ordinary business transaction.[2]

Where closely related parties are involved, however, a gift is made to the promisor of the amount by which the fair market value of the property exchanged for the annuity exceeds the present value of the annuity.[3] Likewise, a gift can be deemed made to the purchaser of the amount by which the present value of the annuity exceeds the fair market value of the property transferred. There will be no gift even in an intra-family transaction, however, if substantially equal values are exchanged and there is no donative intent found.[4]

Before May 1, 2009, the present value of the annuity generally was determined by use of the current estate and gift tax valuation tables (Q 911).[5] After May 1, 2009, the present value is determined under Section 7520's actuarial factors.[6]

588. What are the income tax consequences when the owner of an annuity contract takes the lifetime maturity proceeds or cash surrender value in a lump sum cash payment?

Amounts received on complete surrender, redemption, or maturity are taxable to the extent that the maturity proceeds or cash surrender value exceed the investment in the contract (Q 10, Q 518).[7] The excess is taxable income in the year of maturity or surrender, even if the proceeds are not received until a later tax year.[8]

The investment in the contract is the aggregate premiums or other consideration paid for the annuity minus amounts paid out that were excluded from income (and/or any dividends received).[9] The gain is ordinary income, not capital gain, and thus cannot be netted against capital losses.[10]

1. Treas. Reg. §25.2512-6(a) (Ex. 5).
2. Rev. Rul. 69-74, 1969-1 CB 43, Treas. Reg. §§25.2511-1(g)(1), 25.2512-8.
3. Rev. Rul. 69-74, above; *Est. of Bell v. Comm.*, 60 TC 469 (1973); *Fehrs v. U.S.*, 79-2 USTC ¶13,324 (Ct. Cl. 1979); *La Fargue v. Comm.*, 800 F.2d 936 (9th Cir. 1986).
4. *Ellis Sarasota Bank & Trust Co. v. U.S.*, 77-2 USTC ¶13,204 (M.D. Fla. 1977). See also Rev. Rul. 76-491, 1976-2 CB 301.
5. Notice 89-60, 1989-1 CB 700; Treas. Reg. §§20.2031-1, 25.2512-1; *Est. of Cullison v. Comm.*, 221 F.3d 1347, 2000-1 USTC ¶60,376 (9th Cir. 2000).
6. Treas. Reg. §25.2512-5(d).
7. IRC Sec. 72(e)(5)(E).
8. *Kappel v. U.S.*, 369 F. Supp. 267, 34 AFTR 2d 5025 (W.D. Pa. 1974).
9. IRC Sec. 72(e)(6).
10. IRC Sec. 72(e); Treas. Reg. §1.72-11(d); *Bodine v. Comm.*, 103 F.2d 982 (3rd Cir. 1939); *Cobbs v. Comm.*, 39 BTA 642 (1939).

Some commentators and some insurers have taken the position that the gain on total surrender of a deferred annuity equals the cash value prior to surrender, without regard to surrender charges,[1] less the taxpayer's investment in the contract.

> *Example:* John's deferred annuity has a current cash value of $110,000, to which a surrender charge of $10,000 applies. His investment in the contract is $100,000. The position described above holds that if John surrenders the contract now for its net surrender value of $100,000, he will recognize a gain of $10,000 (the cash value of the contract prior to surrender, without regard to surrender charges, less his investment in the contract).

This application of Section 72(e)(3)(A) is incorrect; it applies only in the case of partial surrenders. In the case of a full surrender, IRC Section 72(e)(5) states that in the case of "full refunds, surrenders, redemptions, & maturities,"..."the rule of paragraph 2(A) shall not apply"[2] (for which rule, and only for which rule, the "without regard to surrender charges" condition of Section 72(e)(3)(A) exists).

The correct computation of John's gain in the contract is the surrender value minus the amount actually received by John upon surrender, less investment in the contract ($100,000 – $100,000 = 0 gain).[3] However, if John had only taken out a partial withdrawal – e.g., $20,000 – the first $10,000 would be gain and the second $10,000 would be return of investment in the contract (as with partial surrenders, gain is determined without regard to surrender charges).

589. If a policyholder elects to receive endowment maturity death benefit proceeds, or cash surrender values under a life income or installment option, is the gain on the policy taxable to the policyholder in the year of maturity/death/surrender or as payments are received?

Ordinarily, a cash basis taxpayer is treated as having constructively received an amount of cash when it first becomes available to the taxpayer without substantial limitations or restrictions. The taxpayer must report this amount as taxable income even if he or she has not actually received it.[4]

When an endowment contract matures, a death benefit becomes payable, or when any type of contract is surrendered, a lump sum payment generally becomes available to the policyholder unless, before the maturity or surrender date, the policyholder has elected to postpone receipt of the proceeds under a settlement option.

However, a lump sum will not be considered constructively received in the year of maturity or surrender if, within sixty days after the lump sum becomes available and before receiving any payment in cash, the policyholder exercises an option or agrees with the insurer to take the proceeds as an annuity.[5]

1. IRC Sec. 72(e)(3)(A).
2. IRC Sec. 72(e)(5)(E).
3. See Let. Rul. 200030013.
4. Treas. Reg. §1.451-2.
5. IRC Sec. 72(h); Treas. Reg. §1.72-12.

The sixty day extension is allowed only for the election of a life income or other installment-type settlement (those considered annuities (Q 493)). It does not apply to an election to leave the proceeds on deposit at interest; if a taxpayer wishes to make an election to leave proceeds on deposit at interest and still defer taxation, such an election must be made before maturity or surrender (if available under the contract) to avoid constructive receipt (Q 21).

If there is a gain on the contract but the proceeds are not constructively received and instead are received as a life income or installment-type settlement as an annuity, the policyholder is not taxed on the gain in the year of maturity or surrender. Instead, the amounts are taxed as "amounts received as an annuity" when payments are made, under the standard rules applicable to such payments.

If there is a gain on the contract and the proceeds are constructively received (as where the election is made after the sixty day period), the full gain is taxable to the policyholder in the year of constructive receipt as if he or she actually had received a one sum cash payment (Q 51). Because gain *has* been recognized, if the contract is subsequently annuitized the investment in the contract (cost) would not be premium cost but would be the entire lump sum applied under the settlement option (as though the contract had simply been surrendered with the proceeds reinvested into a new contract as a separate transaction). Although the larger cost would result in a larger excludable portion for the annuity payments, it usually is advisable for the policyholder to avoid being taxed on the entire gain in one year in the first place.

Even where the cash surrender value is less than net premium cost, it appears that net premiums may be used as "cost" in determining the exclusion ratio for the annuity payments, provided the cash surrender value is not constructively received in the year of surrender.[1]

590. Is the full gain on a deferred annuity or retirement income contract taxable in the year the contract matures?

If the contract provides for automatic settlement under an annuity option, the lump sum proceeds are not constructively received in the year of maturity; if the policy provides a choice of settlement options, the policy owner can opt out of the lump sum proceeds choice within 60 days and avoid constructive receipt (Q 589).[2] The annuity payments (whether life income or installment) are taxed under the regular annuity rules (Q 529 to Q 554) as they are received in the future. In computing the exclusion ratio for the payments, the amount to be used as the investment in the contract is premium cost, not the maturity value (Q 533).

Of course, if the contract owner takes a lump sum settlement at maturity, the contract owner must include the gain in gross income for the year in which he or she receives the payment (Q 588).

For election to leave life insurance proceeds on deposit at interest, see Q 21.

1. IRC Sec. 72(c)(1); Treas. Reg. §1.72-6(a)(1).
2. IRC Sec. 72(h); Treas. Reg. §1.72-12.

If the deferred annuity contract is owned by a person other than a natural person, such as a corporation, see Q 511.

591. Are there any considerations that a taxpayer should be made aware of when deciding whether to surrender an annuity or accept a buyback offer?

Taxpayers who purchased variable annuities with a view toward generating retirement income may be facing buyout offers from an issuing insurance company, notices that their investment choices are being limited to those that are very conservative, or may simply find themselves facing changed circumstances so that the product no longer makes sense.

For example, a taxpayer who has recently been diagnosed with a disease that is likely to shorten his or her life expectancy may find that surrendering the annuity in exchange for a lump sum payout may better serve his or her reduced need for lifetime income. Other taxpayers may be facing unanticipated expenses and see the buyout as a way to meet those expenses.

Taxpayers facing the need for an immediate lump sum of cash should also be aware that it may be possible for them to withdraw a portion of the annuity's assets, keeping only a small part of the initial investment in the annuity to maintain the contract's death benefit. Taxpayers who are simply unhappy with the variable annuity's investment performance may also find this strategy appealing, as they can then invest in another income-producing product while preserving some value in the original annuity.

For taxpayers who are still attracted to the income-producing feature of a variable annuity, however, it might be best to hold on to the product in the face of a buyout offer, especially if the product offers guaranteed returns that may be unavailable in a replacement product.

After a taxpayer has determined that his or her best interests will be served by surrendering the product, the surrender charges associated with the annuity still must be taken into account. If the taxpayer has a buyout offer on the table, it is likely that the insurance company has already offered to waive any surrender charges. If the taxpayer has independently decided to surrender, however, he or she may be able to negotiate a waiver, especially if the taxpayer agrees to reinvest the recovered annuity funds with the same carrier that issued the surrendered product.

It is important that taxpayers realize they will owe taxes upon any gain realized at the time of surrender. If the taxpayer has only held the annuity product for a few years, this gain might not be substantial—in fact, many variable annuity products that were issued just before the economic downturn in 2008 have only recently returned owners to the break-even point. Still, for taxpayers who have owned the variable annuity for many years, the tax liability can be substantial—especially when the new 3.8 percent investment income tax for high earning taxpayers (see Q 8607 to Q 8635) is taken into account.

For taxpayers who purchased the annuity product within an IRA, the funds can be transferred in a trustee-to-trustee type rollover transaction, which allows the taxpayer to defer taxation until the funds are withdrawn from the IRA. Taxation can also be deferred if the taxpayer exchanges the undesirable annuity for another annuity product in a tax-free exchange under IRC Section 1035.

592. If an annuitant dies before a deferred annuity matures or is annuitized, is the amount payable at the annuitant's death subject to income tax?

Yes, to the extent there are any gains.

An annuity contract generally provides that if the annuitant dies before the annuity starting date, the beneficiary will be paid, as a death benefit, the greater of the amount of premiums paid or the accumulated value of the contract (although some contracts may provide additional "enhanced" death benefits as well).

The gain, if any, is taxable as ordinary income to the beneficiary, and is measured by subtracting (1) investment in the contract (reduced by aggregate dividends and any other amounts that have been received under the contract that were excludable from gross income) from (2) the death benefit, including any enhancements (Q 518).[1] The gains are taxable when received, and are taxable to the beneficiary that receives the payments (not the decedent). Thus, annuities do *not* receive a step-up in basis at death (except for certain pre-October 21 1979 grandfathered annuities; see later in this section for further discussion).

The death benefit under an annuity contract does not qualify for tax exemption under IRC Section 101(a) as life insurance proceeds payable by reason of the insured's death. Instead, death benefits paid on the death of the owner or the annuitant is income-in-respect-of-a-decedent ("IRD") to the extent that the death benefit amount exceeds the basis in the annuity contract. As a result, the beneficiary may be eligible for a special income tax deduction for any federal estate taxes paid that were attributable to the IRD.[2] The IRS has ruled that an assignment of an annuity from a decedent's estate to a charity will not cause the estate or its beneficiaries to be taxed on the proceeds of the annuity.[3]

Planning Point: The owner of a nonqualified deferred annuity generally should be named as the annuitant. Where the owner and annuitant are two different individuals, problems can result, especially if the annuity is annuitant-driven. (All annuities issued since 1986 are "owner-driven" where a requirement to pay out the cash value is triggered by the death of the owner. Some also are annuitant-driven, where the death benefit is triggered by the death of the annuitant. Some annuitant-driven deferred annuities provide for two death benefits: the guaranteed minimum death benefit, which may exceed the annuity cash value, that is payable upon death of the annuitant, and the cash value itself, which must be paid out on the death of the owner.) If the owner and annuitant are the same person, none of this matters; if they are not, it does. *John L. Olsen, CLU, ChFC, AEP, OlsenAnnuityEducation.com.*

In the case of a deferred annuity that provides the beneficiary with the option to take the death benefit as a lump sum, the beneficiary will not be taxed on the gain in the year of death if the beneficiary elects "within sixty days after the day of which such lump sum first became

1. IRC Sec. 72(e)(5)(E); Treas. Reg. §1.72-11(c).
2. Rev. Rul. 2005-30, 2005-20 IRB 1015.
3. Let. Rul. 200618023.

payable" to apply the death benefit under a life income or installment option (Q 589).[1] The periodic payments then will be taxable to the beneficiary under the regular annuity rules (Q 529 to Q 548). The exclusion ratio for the contract will be based on the decedent's investment in the contract and the beneficiary's expected return.[2] See Q 593 for a discussion of the sixty-day period discussed in this paragraph.

The rules described above apply to non-variable annuity contracts as well as to variable annuity contracts purchased after October 20, 1979, and to contributions made after October 20, 1979, to variable annuities issued prior to this date. If the owner of a variable annuity contract acquired prior to October 21, 1979, including any contributions applied to such an annuity contract pursuant to a binding commitment entered into before that date, dies prior to the annuity starting date, the contract acquires a new "step-up" cost basis. The basis of the contract in the hands of the beneficiary will be the value of the contract at the date of the decedent's death, or the alternate valuation date. If that basis equals the amount received by the beneficiary, there will be no taxable gain and the appreciation in the value of the contract while owned by the decedent will escape income tax entirely.[3] However, where a variable annuity contract purchased before October 21, 1979 had been exchanged for another variable annuity contract under IRC Section 1035 after October 20, 1979, and the annuity owner died prior to the annuity starting date, the beneficiary was not entitled to a step-up in basis.[4] Although the aforementioned step-up in basis treatment for pre-October 21, 1979 annuities has only been directly ruled on in the case of a variable annuity, it also would theoretically apply to fixed annuities issued prior to October 21, 1979.

Normally the death benefit is payable at death. If it is not payable until a later time and the annuitant also was the owner of the annuity contract, see Q 594.

593. How long does the beneficiary of an annuity have in which to elect to take death proceeds as an annuity, rather than as a lump sum, and thus avoid being in constructive receipt of all contract gain?

What is the meaning of "within sixty days after the day of which such lump sum first became payable"? Some commentators argue that this means within sixty days of the death that triggered such lump sum (i.e., the death of the annuity owner, in all cases, or, in the case of an "annuitant-driven" annuity, the death of the annuitant). It may be argued, however, that no such lump sum becomes payable until the beneficiary submits proof of such death, together with a claim for the death benefit, to the insurer. Treasury Regulation Section 1.451-2(a) states that "income is not constructively received if the taxpayer's control of its receipt is subject to substantial limitations or restrictions." A beneficiary cannot receive payment of a death benefit before it is paid, and an insurer will not make such payment until it receives proof of death and properly completed claim forms. Treasury has provided no definitive guidance on this issue of when exactly the sixty-day period begins, beyond noting that a "timely election" under Section 72(h) is required.

1. IRC Sec. 72(h).
2. Treas. Reg. §§1.72-11(a), 1.72-11(e).
3. Rev. Rul. 79-335, 1979-2 CB 292.
4. TAM 9346002; Let. Rul. 9245035.

There is a widespread (mis-)belief that the beneficiary of a deferred annuity, where the owner died prior to annuity starting date, has one year, not sixty days, in which to make an election to take the death proceeds as an annuity without becoming in constructive receipt of all contract gain. This mis-belief is grounded in the fact that IRC Section 72(s)(2) provides that no contract issued since January 18, 1985 shall be considered "an annuity" (and taxed as an annuity) unless it provides that "any portion of the holder's interest" that is payable to a designated beneficiary will be distributed "over the life of such designated beneficiary (or over a period not extending beyond the life expectancy of such beneficiary)," and that "such distributions begin not later than one year after the date of the holder's death or such later date as the Secretary may by regulations prescribe" (Q 594). That provision, however, states only the provisions that an annuity contract must contain (with respect to distributions made on the death of any holder) to be deemed "an annuity" for tax purposes. It does not speak to how long a beneficiary may wait to exercise an annuity payout option without being in constructive receipt of all contract gain; as noted above, IRC Section 72(h) does speak to this. Moreover, Section 72(s) applies only on the death of the holder of an annuity and not when the annuitant of an annuitant-driven contract dies. Some commentators suggest that Section 72(s) "trumps" Section 72(h) because it is newer. The latter section, however, has not been repealed or amended.

594. What distributions are required when the owner of an annuity contract dies before the entire interest in the contract has been distributed?

A deferred annuity contract issued after January 18, 1985, will not be treated as an "annuity contract" and taxed under the favorable provisions of IRC Section 72 unless it provides that if any owner dies –

- on or after the annuity starting date (in other words, when the annuity was in "payout status") and before the entire interest in the contract has been distributed, the remaining portion will be distributed at least "as rapidly as under the method of distribution being used as of the date of the owner's death," and[1]
- before the annuity starting date, the entire interest in the contract will be distributed within five years after the owner's death,[2] unless either of two exceptions applies allowing for a stretch over a beneficiary's life expectancy or a continuation in the name of the surviving spouse (see Q 595).

In the case of joint owners of a contract issued after April 22, 1987, these distribution requirements are applied at the *first* death, not the second death.

Effect of Exchange on Pre-January 19, 1985 Contracts

According to the report of the conference committee (TRA '84), an annuity contract issued after January 18, 1985 in exchange for one issued earlier will be considered a new contract and will be subject to the distribution requirements.[3]

1. IRC Sec. 72(s)(1)(A).
2. IRC Sec. 72(s)(1)(B).
3. H.R. Conf. Rep. No. 98-861 (TRA '84) *reprinted in* 1984-3 CB Vol. 2 331-332.

595. Are there any exceptions to the rule that the entire interest in an inherited deferred annuity contract must be distributed within five years of the original owner's death?

Installment payments made to a designated beneficiary. If any portion of the owner's interest is to be distributed to a *designated beneficiary* (see definition in Q 596) over the life of such beneficiary (or over a period not extending beyond the life expectancy of the beneficiary) and such distributions begin within one year after the owner's death, the five-year requirement does not apply.[1]

Where the beneficiary is the surviving spouse of the annuity owner. If a designated beneficiary is the surviving spouse of the "holder of the contract" (the owner), that person may treat the annuity as his or her own (that is, as if he or she had owned it from inception) and continue the contract.[2] This "spousal continuation" option must be allowed in the annuity contract to be exercised. Some contracts require that the surviving spouse be the sole beneficiary to elect this "spousal continuation" option.

Amounts distributed under these requirements are taxed under the general rules applicable to amounts distributed under annuity contracts. These rules are intended to prevent protracted deferral of tax on the gain in the contract through successive ownership of the contract.

Where the owner of a contract issued after April 22, 1987 is a corporation or other non-natural person, the primary annuitant, as designated in the contract, will be treated as the owner of the contract for purposes of the distribution requirements of Section 72(s),[3] and a change in the primary annuitant of such a contract will be treated as the death of the owner.[4] Where the owner is a corporation or other non-natural person, see also Q 511.

These requirements do not apply to annuities purchased to fund periodic payment of damages on account of personal injuries or sickness.[5] Although these requirements do not apply with respect to qualified pension, profit sharing and stock bonus plans, IRC Section 403(b) tax sheltered annuities, and individual retirement annuities, similar distribution requirements do apply (Q 3685, Q 3890, Q 4070).

596. What does the term "designated beneficiary" mean in the context of an inherited deferred annuity? Can the designated beneficiary be a trust?

The term *designated beneficiary* means an individual – a human being. Where the beneficiary is not a human being, the Section 72(s)(2) and (s)(3) exceptions to the five-year payout rule probably are not available. If a trust, for example, is named as beneficiary of a deferred annuity, and the annuity owner (or primary annuitant, as deemed owner, if the trust owns the annuity) dies, the trust probably will be unable to take distributions other than in a lump sum or within five years (see Q 595). This is because most insurers take the position that a trust, as a non-natural

1. IRC Sec. 72(s)(2).
2. IRC Sec. 72(s)(3).
3. IRC Sec. 72(s)(6)(A).
4. IRC Sec. 72(s)(7).
5. IRC Sec. 72(s)(5)(D).

person, is not an individual, cannot be a designated beneficiary, and, therefore, is ineligible for the life expectancy exception of Section 72(s)(2) (and for the spousal continuation exception of Section 72(s)(3), because trusts, not being human beings, cannot marry).

Some insurers will permit a trustee of a trust named as beneficiary to elect the life expectancy option of Section 72(s)(2) over a period not extending beyond the lifetime of the oldest trust beneficiary. This is probably because they take the position that Congress intended, in enacting Section 72(s), to provide parity between the rules governing death distributions from IRAs and qualified plans and the rules governing death distributions from nonqualified annuities. Although the legislative history of Section 72(s) offers much support for this view, it should be noted that there is no specific authority for it in the IRC or regulations for annuities, as there is under IRC Section 401(a)(9) and the associated Section 1.401(a)(9) regulations with respect to see-through trust treatment for beneficiaries of retirement accounts.

Planning Point: Avoid naming a client's revocable living trust (or any trust, as a general rule) as the beneficiary of a nonqualified annuity if any stretch out of taxation of the gain is desired. A surviving spouse of the holder can annuitize over his or her lifetime or treat the annuity as his or her own; if that same spouse is the trustee of the decedent's trust, both opportunities probably are unavailable. *John L. Olsen, CLU, ChFC, AEP, OlsenAnnuityEducation.com.*

597. If an individual purchases an annuity contract to meet alimony payments, how are payments taxed to the recipient? What are the tax results to the purchaser?

Editor's Note: The 2017 Tax Act eliminated the previously existing above-the-line deduction for alimony for tax years beginning after 2018, and provides that alimony and separate maintenance payments are no longer included in the income of the recipient.

If an annuity contract which becomes payable to a former spouse is transferred or assigned to the former spouse incident to a divorce after July 18, 1984 (unless the transfer is pursuant to an instrument in effect on or before such date), he or she "will be entitled to the usual annuity treatment, including recovery of the transferor's investment in the contract ... notwithstanding that the annuity payments ... qualify as alimony."[1] (If both spouses elected, the same treatment applied to a transfer made after December 31, 1983, and on or before July 18, 1984.)

There is nothing in the IRC that directly supports this resolution of the conflict between the rules that "[g]ross income includes amounts received as alimony"[2] (prior to 2019) and that amounts received as an annuity under an annuity contract are taxable under rules that permit tax-free recovery of cost over the payment period.[3] If the recipient of the annuity contract is permitted to recover the purchaser's "investment in the contract," there should be no deduction allowed for the alimony by the purchaser (prior to 2019). There is no gain taxable to the purchaser on the transfer.[4]

1. General Explanation of the Deficit Reduction Act of 1984, at p. 711.
2. IRC Sec. 71(a), as repealed by Pub. Law No. 115-97 (the 2017 Tax Act).
3. IRC Sec. 72.
4. IRC Sec. 1041.

With respect to annuity contracts transferred before July 19, 1984, or pursuant to instruments in effect before July 19, 1984 (unless the election referred to above applies), payments under the contract to a recipient spouse in discharge of the payor spouse's alimony obligations are fully taxable to the recipient and the recipient cannot recover the payor's investment in the contract tax-free.[1] The payor spouse cannot take an income tax deduction for the payments even though they are taxable to the recipient spouse.[2] Where there is no transfer, but the payor spouse purchases an annuity, retaining ownership of the contract and receiving the payments, the payor spouse can recover his or her investment under the annuity rule. If the payor spouse then made periodic alimony payments directly to his or her former spouse, the payor spouse could deduct the payments (prior to 2019).[3] The recipient spouse, of course, was required to include the full amount of the alimony payments in gross income.[4]

598. May a charitable contribution deduction be taken for the gift of a maturing annuity or endowment contract?

Yes, subject to the limits on deductions for gifts to charities (Q 737). This does not necessarily mean, however, that gain at the time of gift is avoided.

If a policyholder gives an annuity contract that was issued after April 22, 1987, whether in the year it matures or in a year prior to maturity, the policyholder is treated as if he or she received, at that time, the excess of the cash surrender value at the time of the transfer over the policyholder's investment in the contract.[5] Thus, the policyholder must recognize gain on the contract in the year of the gift. Given that gain is recognized, though, the policyholder's charitable deduction is equal to the full fair market value of the annuity, due to the fact that any embedded gain was recognized at the time of transfer (as otherwise the charitable gift rules limit the deductibility of ordinary income property with embedded gains).[6]

Where an endowment contract (or annuity contract) issued before April 23, 1987, is contributed before the year the contract matures, Revenue Ruling 69-102 requires that the donor include in his or her income, in the year the contract is surrendered by the donee (or matures), the excess of the cash surrender value at the time of the gift over the donor's basis. Because gain is not recognized at the time of gift, though, the IRC limits the donor's charitable deduction to the donor's cost basis.[7] (The ruling concerned a gift in the year immediately before the contract matured but may not be limited to that year.)

Planning Point: A potential tax trap exists where an annuity issued before April 23, 1987 is given to a charity near the end of the donor's tax year. If the charity surrenders the annuity after the end of the donor's tax year, the donor may not deduct the value of the gift but may deduct only the donor's investment in the contract. What's more, the donor will incur income tax liability to

1. IRC Sec. 72(k), as then in effect; Treas. Reg. §1.72-14(b); Treas. Reg. §1.71-1(c)(2).
2. IRC Sec. 71(d), as then in effect; IRC Sec. 215, as then in effect.
3. IRC Sec. 72; IRC Sec. 215, as repealed by Pub. Law No. 115-97 (the 2017 Tax Act).
4. IRC Sec. 71, as repealed by Pub. Law No. 115-97 (the 2017 Tax Act).
5. IRC Sec. 72(e)(4)(C).
6. Treas. Reg. §1.170A-4(a).
7. IRC Sec. 170(e)(1)(A).

the extent of the donor's gain in the contract in the year in which the charity takes distributions from or surrenders the annuity. *Fred Burkey, CLU, APA, Ameritas®.*

For a gift to a charity in connection with purchase of an annuity from the charitable organization, see Q 608.

599. Is there a taxable gift when an individual covered under a qualified plan, a tax sheltered annuity, or an individual retirement plan irrevocably designates a beneficiary to receive a survivor benefit payable under the plan?

An irrevocable beneficiary designation would appear to be a gift falling under the broad sweep of IRC Section 2511, applying the gift tax "whether the transfer is in trust or otherwise, whether the gift is direct or indirect, and whether the property is real or personal, tangible or intangible."[1] The IRS has ruled, for example, that a retiring federal employee who receives a reduced annuity to provide a survivor annuity for the beneficiary makes a gift subject to gift tax of the value of the survivor annuity by the mere act of retiring.[2]

If the beneficiary designation does trigger a gift, it will clearly be one of a future interest, which means it will not qualify for the gift tax annual exclusion.[3] If the beneficiary of the survivor annuity is the employee's spouse, however, the gift generally will qualify for the marital deduction (Q 620).[4]

600. Is there a taxable gift when a nonparticipant spouse waives the right to receive a qualified joint and survivor annuity or a qualified preretirement survivor annuity?

A waiver of the right to receive a qualified joint and survivor annuity or a qualified preretirement survivor annuity (Q 3875) by a nonparticipant spouse is not treated as a taxable transfer by the nonparticipant spouse if the waiver is made before the death of the participant spouse.[5]

601. What are the gift tax consequences to the spouse of an individual who designates a third party beneficiary to receive a survivor benefit payable under a qualified plan, a tax sheltered annuity, or an individual retirement plan if community property law applies?

If an employee's interest in a qualified plan is community property (Q 3976) and the employee gratuitously and effectively designates someone other than his or her spouse to receive a survivor benefit, the value of the benefit conveyed comes equally from the employee's community half and the employee's spouse's community half. The effect of the transaction is to create a gift

1. IRC Sec. 2511(a); Treas. Reg. §25.2511-1(a).
2. Let. Ruls. 8715010, 8715035, 8811017.
3. Treas. Reg. §25.2503-3(c)(Ex. 2).
4. IRC Sec. 2523(f)(6).
5. IRC Sec. 2503(f).

from the employee's spouse of one-half the value of the benefit conveyed when the conveyance is complete.[1] The gift is considered by the IRS to be subject to gift tax.

It should be noted that community property law varies from state to state with respect to the power of a spouse to make a gift of community property without the express consent of the other spouse.

Planning Point: If a participant designates the spouse as the beneficiary of a benefit payable under a qualified plan, the participant also should provide for a contingent disposition in case the spousal beneficiary disclaims the benefit or dies first, and in such case, could provide that on death, the spousal beneficiary's interest would pass to that spouse's estate, and the participant's interest would pass to a credit shelter trust that would pay the income interest. In this manner, the participant can take advantage of the unified credit and avoid a gift as to the spouse's interest.[2]

602. If a person who is covered under an individual retirement plan contributes to a similar plan covering his or her non-employed spouse, are such contributions considered gifts?

Yes.

These contributions generally qualify for the marital deduction, however, and do not require the filing of a gift tax return. There should be no question that an individual's contributions to a spousal IRA would qualify for the marital deduction, so long as the donee spouse is the one who names a beneficiary to receive account proceeds remaining at that spouse's death.

If the donor spouse (i.e., the contributing individual) designates a beneficiary, the donee spouse's interest in the IRA would be a nondeductible terminable interest and the marital deduction would not be allowed, except in the case of certain joint and survivor annuities (Q 620).

603. Are amounts received under commercial annuity contracts subject to withholding?

Yes.

The payee, however, generally may elect not to have anything withheld, which is commonly chosen. In addition, only the amount that is reasonable to believe is includable in income is subject to withholding, not any return of principal payments.

If withholding occurs from periodic payments (i.e., an annuitized contract), the amounts are to be withheld at the same rate as wages. Payments are periodic, even if they are variable, if they are payable over a period of more than one year.

If payments are not periodic, 10 percent of the includable amount is withheld. Payments made to the beneficiary of a deceased payee are subject to withholding under the same rules.[3]

1. IRC Sec. 2513. Prior to TRA '86, IRC Section 2517 contained an exemption from gift tax for this kind of gift.
2. BNA, Estate and Gift Tax Issues for Employee Benefits, Portfolio 378, Detailed Analysis, I.C. (3d ed.)
3. IRC Secs. 3405(a), 3405(b); Temp. Treas. Reg. §35.3405-1T (A-9, A-10, A-12, A-17, F-19 through 24).

An election out of withholding generally will be ineffective if a payee does not furnish his or her taxpayer identification number ("TIN," usually the payee's Social Security number) to the payor or furnishes an incorrect TIN to the payor and the payor is so notified by the IRS.[1]

Payments under qualified pension, profit sharing, and stock bonus plans are discussed in Q 3964; payments under IRC Section 403(b) tax sheltered annuities are discussed in Q 4074 and Q 4076; and private annuities are discussed in Q 604.

Private Annuity

604. What is a private annuity?

A private annuity is an unsecured promise of one person (the obligor) to make fixed payments to another person (the annuitant) for life in return for the transfer of property from the annuitant to the obligor. According to a general counsel memorandum, an unsecured promise to make fixed payments until a stated monetary amount is reached or until the annuitant's death, whichever occurs first, will be treated as a private annuity (instead of an installment sale with a contingent price) if the stated monetary amount would not be received by the annuitant before the expiration of his or her life expectancy (as determined under the appropriate annuity table and as determined at the time of the agreement; see Appendix A).[2]

A private annuity must be distinguished from a commercial annuity issued by a life insurance company and from an annuity payable by an organization (e.g., a charity) that issues annuities "from time to time" (Q 608, Q 610). The typical private annuity involves the transfer of appreciated property (usually a capital asset) from parents or grandparents to one or more children or grandchildren who make annuity payments in return.

605. How are payments received under a private annuity issued after October 18, 2006 taxed?

Proposed regulations, which are currently in effect, have dramatically altered the tax treatment of private annuities. Under the current rules, the receipt of an annuity contract for property will be treated as the receipt of property in an amount equal to the fair market value of the annuity contract.[3] The fair market value of an annuity contract is determined under the rules of IRC Section 7520 (Q 911). Therefore, all of the gain on the property will be recognized at the time of the exchange. The private annuity's investment in the contract will be the amount paid for the contract. Thus, where the value of the property exchanged and the value of the annuity are the same, the investment in the contract will be the fair market value of the property exchanged for the private annuity.

Planning Point: The general outcome of these rules is that subsequent payments will still be taxable to the payee under the rules for amounts received as an annuity, but the investment in

---

1. IRC Sec. 3405(e)(12).
2. GCM 39503 (5-7-86).
3. Prop. Treas. Reg. §§1.1001-1(j); 1.72-6(e)

the contract will be based on the fair market value of the property received in exchange for the annuity contract.[1]

These proposed regulations were intended to be effective for exchanges of property for private annuity contracts that occur after October 18, 2006. For certain transactions, however, the proposal was for a later effective date for transactions occurring after April 18, 2007. This delayed effective date was for exchanges where: (1) the issuer of the annuity is an individual; (2) the obligations under the contract are not secured; and (3) the property transferred in the exchange is not sold or otherwise disposed of during the two year period beginning on the date of the exchange. A disposition includes a transfer to a trust or any other entity, even if wholly owned by the transferor.

For tax consequences to the obligor, see Q 607.

606. How are payments taxed that are received under a private annuity issued before October 19, 2006?

The basic rules for taxing the payments received by the annuitant under a private life annuity issued before October 19, 2006, are set forth in Revenue Ruling 69-74.[2] According to this ruling, the payments must be divided into three elements: (1) a "recovery of basis" element; (2) a "gain element" eligible for capital gain treatment for the period of the annuitant's life expectancy, but taxable as ordinary income thereafter; and (3) an "annuity element" that is taxable as ordinary income. Each of these is discussed below.

(1) The portion of each payment that is to be excluded from gross income as a recovery of basis is determined by applying the basic annuity rule (Q 529). Thus, an exclusion percentage is obtained by dividing the investment in the contract by the expected return under the contract. The investment in the contract in a private annuity situation is the adjusted basis of the property transferred. If the adjusted basis of the property transferred is greater than the present value of the annuity, the annuitant's investment in the contract for purposes of IRC Section 72(b) is the present value of the annuity on the date of the exchange.[3] Expected return and annuity starting date are the same as explained in Q 536 and Q 538. Thus, expected return is obtained by multiplying one year's annuity payments by the appropriate multiple from Table I or Table V of the income tax Annuity Tables (Appendix A), whichever is applicable depending on when the investment in the contract is made, as explained in Appendix A.

If the annuity starting date is before January 1, 1987, the amount calculated to be excludable from income as a recovery of basis (as explained above) is excluded from all payments received, even if the annuitant outlives his or her life expectancy. If the annuity starting date is after December 31, 1986, then the exclusion percentage is applied only to payments received

1. Prop. Treas. Reg. §1.72-6(e)
2. 1969-1 CB 43.
3. *LaFargue v. Comm.*, 800 F.2d 936, 86-2 USTC ¶9715 (9th Cir. 1986), *aff'g*, TC Memo 1985-90; *Benson v. Comm.*, 80 TC 789 (1983).

until the investment in the contract is recovered. Thereafter, the portion excludable under the percentage is included as ordinary income.[1]

(2) The capital gain portion, if any, is determined by dividing the gain by the life expectancy of the annuitant. Gain is the excess of the present value of the annuity (it may not be the same as the fair market value of the property) over the adjusted basis of the property. The present value of the annuity is obtained from the Estate and Gift Tax Valuation Tables (see Q 911). The life expectancy of the annuitant is obtained from Table I or Table V of the income tax Annuity Tables, whichever is applicable depending on when the investment in the contract is made (Appendix A). This portion is reportable as capital gain for the period of the annuitant's life expectancy, and thereafter as ordinary income. Recovery of capital gain may not be deferred until the entire investment in the contract has been recovered.[2]

(3) The remaining portion of each payment is ordinary income.

If the fair market value of the property transferred exceeds the present value of the annuity (as determined from the applicable Estate and Gift Tax Valuation Tables), the difference is treated as a gift to the obligor (Q 587).[3]

Example. Mrs. White is a widow, age sixty-six, with two adult children. She owns a rental property with an adjusted basis of $30,000 and a fair market value of $135,000. On January 1, she transfers this building to her children in exchange for their unsecured promise to pay her $1,000 a month ($12,000 a year) for life beginning January 31.

Assume that the valuation table interest rate for January is 5.0 percent. Therefore, the present value of the annuity equals $126,078: $12,000 × 10.2733 (annuity factor) × 1.0227 (annuity adjustment factor). (For an explanation of the valuation table factors, see Appendix C and Example 2 thereunder.) The fair market value of the property exceeds the present value of the annuity by $8,922: $135,000 – $126,078. This is a gift by Mrs. White to her children and subject to gift tax. Mrs. White's life expectancy (Table V in Appendix A) is 19.2 years.

(1) Mrs. White will exclude from gross income as a recovery of basis $130, or 13 percent of each payment (until she recovers $30,000, because her annuity starting date is after December 31, 1986). The 13 percent exclusion percentage is obtained by dividing $30,000 (investment in the contract) by $230,400 (expected return: 19.2 × $12,000) (Q 539).

(2) She will report $417 of each payment as capital gain for 19.2 years. This portion is obtained by dividing her gain of $96,078 (excess of present value of annuity [$126,078] over adjusted basis of the property [$30,000]) by 19.2, her life expectancy ($96,078 ÷ 19.2 = $5,004 a year or $417 a month). After 19.2 years, she will report this $417 as ordinary income.

1. IRC Sec. 72(b)(2).
2. *Garvey, Inc. v. U.S.*, 1 Cl. Ct. 108, 83-1 USTC ¶9163 (U.S. Cl. Ct. 1983), *aff'd*, 726 F.2d 1569, 84-1 USTC ¶9214 (Fed. Cir. 1984), *cert. denied.*
3. *Benson v. Comm.*, supra; *LaFargue v. Comm.*, supra.

(3) She will report the balance of each payment, or $453 ($1,000 – ($130 + $417)) as ordinary income. (Because her annuity starting date is after December 31, 1986, she also will report as ordinary income the portion of each payment no longer excludable as recovery of capital after her investment in the contract has been recovered.)

In *Katz v. Commissioner*, the Tax Court held that a taxpayer who had exchanged shares of common stock and put options for a private annuity (on February 3, 2000) was entitled to defer recognition of capital gain relating to the transfer until the taxpayer received annuity payments.[1]

According to the Tax Court, Revenue Ruling 69-74 is not applicable if the promise to pay the annuity is secured; securing the promise will cause the entire capital gain on the transfer of the property to be taxable to the annuitant in the year of transfer. The investment in the contract would be the present value of the annuity, but not more than the fair market value of the property transferred.[2]

In a private letter ruling, a private annuity arrangement was still taxed as such despite the presence of a cost-of-living adjustment applicable to the monthly annuity payments and a minimum payment provision that stated that if the annuitant had not received a specified dollar amount prior to her death, the remaining amount would be paid to her estate. The annuitant also had the option to accelerate the payments and receive a lump sum amount equal to the minimum payment amount less annuity payments previously received.[3]

When a private annuity became worthless, the determination that the loss was a capital loss and not an ordinary loss was upheld in *McIngvale v. Commissioner.*[4]

Whether a transfer to a trust will be treated as a sale in exchange for a private annuity or a transfer in trust with a right to income retained depends on the circumstances in the case. Properly done, a transfer to a trust will be treated as a private annuity transaction.[5] However, purported transfers in trust were found to be sham transactions in *Horstmier v. Commissioner*.[6]

Amounts received under a private annuity contract are not subject to withholding because such amounts are not paid under a "commercial annuity," that is, one issued by a licensed insurance company.

For estate tax implications of a private annuity, see Q 631.

1. *Katz v. Comm.*, TC Memo 2008-269, citing Rev. Rul. 69-74, 1969-1 CB 43.
2. *Est. of Bell v. Comm.*, 60 TC 469 (1973); *212 Corp. v. Comm.*, 70 TC 788 (1978).
3. Let. Rul. 9009064.
4. 936 F.2d 833 (5th Cir. 1991) aff'g TC Memo 1990-340.
5. See *Est. of Fabric v. Comm.*, 83 TC 932 (1984); *Stern v. Comm.*, 747 F.2d 555, 84-2 USTC ¶9949 (9th Cir. 1984); *LaFargue v. Comm.*, 689 F.2d 845, 50 AFTR 2d 5944 (9th Cir. 1982) (followed by the Tax Court in *Benson v. Comm., supra*, because an appeal would go to the Ninth Circuit).
6. TC Memo 1983-409.

607. What are the tax consequences to the obligor in a private annuity transaction?

Annuity payments made by the obligor are treated as capital expenditures for the acquisition of the property. No interest deduction is allowed with respect to the payments.[1] Depreciation deductions may be taken, however, if the property is depreciable. The initial basis for depreciation is the present value of the annuity, as determined by the appropriate Estate and Gift Tax Valuation Tables (Q 911). When actual payments exceed the initial basis, the basis for depreciation is the actual payments made less prior depreciation.[2]

When payments exceed the initial basis, loss is not deductible until the property is sold.[3] If the property is sold after the annuitant's death, the obligor's basis for determining gain or loss is the total of annuity payments made less depreciation taken, if any.

If the property is sold before the annuitant's death, the obligor's basis for gain is the total payments actually made plus the actuarial value, as of the date of sale, of payments to be made in the future. The obligor's basis for loss is the total amount of payments made as of the date of sale. If the selling price is less than the basis for gain but more than the basis for loss, the obligor realizes neither gain nor loss. Adjustment for annuity payments made after the sale may be made by deducting loss or by reporting additional gain.[4]

Charitable Gift Annuity

608. What is a charitable gift annuity?

A charitable gift annuity agreement is a contractual obligation undertaken by a charity to pay an annuity to an individual in return for an amount transferred by the individual, where the actuarial value of the agreed upon payments is usually less than the amount contributed (notwithstanding the fact that the payments might exceed the amount transferred if the annuitant lives long enough). The contractual obligation is backed by the charity's assets. The typical charitable gift annuity can involve the transfer of appreciated property.

609. How are payments received under a charitable gift annuity agreement taxed?

The tax consequences of a charitable gift annuity involve an immediate charitable gift (deductible within the limits of IRC Section 170 (Q 737)), income tax on a portion of the annuity payments, and a recovery of principal that will be made up of part taxable gain and part excludable adjusted basis if appreciated property is transferred for the annuity.[5] Each of these is discussed below.

1. *Garvey, Inc. v. U.S.*, 1 Cl Ct. 108, 83-1 USTC ¶9163 (U.S. Cl. Ct. 1983), *aff'd*, 84-1 USTC ¶9214 (Fed Cir.), *cert. den.*, 469 U.S. 823 (1984); *Bell v. Comm.*, 76 TC 232 (1981).
2. Rev. Rul. 55-119, 1955-1 CB 352.
3. *Perkins v. U.S.*, 701 F.2d 771, 83-1 USTC ¶9250 (9th Cir. 1983).
4. Rev. Rul. 55-119, supra.
5. See Treas. Reg. §1.1011-2(c) Ex. 8.

(1) A charitable contribution is made in the amount by which cash or the fair market value of property transferred to the charity exceeds the present value of the annuity. The American Council on Gift Annuities, a voluntary group sponsored by charitable organizations, recommends uniform annuity rates based on the annuitant's age at the date of the gift. See Table on Uniform Gift Annuity Rates in Appendix A. The uniform annuity rate is applied to the transfer and determines the amount of the annuity paid to the annuitant each year. The present value of a charitable gift annuity when issued is determined under Estate and Gift Tax Valuation Tables (Q 911).

(2) When an annuitant receives annuity payments, a percentage of each payment reflects a return of principal. This percentage (the "exclusion ratio") is determined by the basic annuity rule, that is, by dividing the investment in the contract by the expected return. The investment in the contract in the charitable annuity situation is the lesser of the present value of the annuity or the fair market value of the property transferred to the charity. The expected return is the annual annuity amount multiplied by the years of life expectancy of the donor at the time of the gift (using the applicable income tax Annuity Tables in Appendix A). If the annuity starting date is after December 31, 1986, the return of principal portion is excludable only until the investment in the contract is fully recovered. Thereafter, that portion is included in income as ordinary income.[1]

If, however, the donor has transferred appreciated property to the charity, the donor has a gain (either a capital gain or an ordinary gain depending on the property) to the extent the fair market value of the property exceeds the donor's adjusted basis. In this situation, the bargain sale rules apply. Under these rules, proportionate portions of the donor's basis are considered part of the charitable gift and part of the investment in the annuity contract. Thus, the donor's return of principal element of each payment consists of two segments: one represents return of gain that is taxed as capital or ordinary gain, and the other represents return of the donor's adjusted basis and is excluded from the donor's income.

The portion of the gain that is taxed is the percentage that the investment in the contract bears to the total amount transferred. As long as the annuity is nonassignable, the donor may take the gain into income ratably over the donor's life expectancy. After all the gain is reported, that portion of the donor's annuity payment is excluded from income as well as the return of basis portion, if the donor's annuity starting date was before January 1, 1987. If the annuity starting date is after December 31, 1986, the IRC provides that amounts are not excludable after the investment in the contract has been recovered. Thus, it appears that once the annuitant has outlived his or her life expectancy, and recovered his or her investment in the contract, the entire payment is included in income as ordinary income.

If the donor dies before all of the gain is reported (and the donor is the sole annuitant), no further gain is reported. If the annuity starting date is after July 1, 1986, the IRC provides that if annuity payments cease by reason of the death of the sole annuitant before the investment in

1. IRC Sec. 72(b)(2).

the contract has been recovered, the unrecovered investment in the contract may be deducted (Q 568).[1] Because the unrecovered investment in the contract where appreciated property has been given for the annuity includes the unrecognized gain portion, it is likely the deduction will be limited to the unrecovered basis.

(3) The portion of each payment in excess of the return of principal element is ordinary income.

An example of these payment rules, classified as (1) a charitable contribution, (2) return of principal, and (3) ordinary income, is shown below:

Example. Ed White is a widower, age seventy. He owns securities with an adjusted basis of $6,000 and a fair market value of $10,000. On June 1 he transfers the securities to ABC Charity in exchange for a life annuity, payable in semiannual installments. For purposes of this example, assume that the uniform annuity rate (recommended by the American Council on Gift Annuities as shown in Appendix A) is 5.7 percent, and thus the annuity payment is $570 per year.

(1) According to the applicable Estate and Gift Tax Valuation Tables (Q 911), the present value of the annuity for Mr. White is $6,261 (10.9031 [annuity factor] × 1.0074 [annuity adjustment factor for semiannual payments] × $570 [the donor's annual annuity]). (Mr. White elected to use an interest rate for a month as explained in Q 911 with an interest rate that is assumed to be 3.0 percent for purposes of this example; Appendix C explains the derivation of Valuation Table factors from the interest rate.) The difference between the $10,000 fair market value of the property and the $6,261 value of the annuity, or $3,739, is the charitable contribution portion of the transfer. According to Table V (Appendix A), Mr. White has a life expectancy of sixteen years that is adjusted to 15.8 (16 – .2) to reflect the frequency of payments (adjustment factor for semiannual payments with six months from the annuity starting date to the first payment date is –.2; see introduction to Appendix A).

(2) Of each $305 semiannual payment, 69.5 percent, or $198, represents return of principal. This percentage is found by dividing $6,261 (the value of the annuity, or investment in the contract) by $9,006 (the expected return: $570 × 15.8). Of this principal amount, $79 is gain ([$6,261 – ($6,000 × ($6,261 ÷ $10,000))] ÷ [15.8 × 2]). Mr. White must report the $79 as capital gain until all his gain is recognized, or until he dies, if that is earlier. Mr. White will exclude the balance of the principal, $119 ($198 – $79), as return of adjusted basis.

(3) The balance of each annuity payment, $87; is the amount that Mr. White must report as ordinary income ($285 – $198). After all the gain and investment in the contract has been recovered (approximately 15.8 years), each payment is fully taxable as ordinary income.

1. IRC Sec. 72(b)(3).

The IRS has ruled that in the case of a deferred charitable gift annuity, no amount will be considered constructively received until the annuitant begins receiving payments.[1]

The gift portion of the transfer qualifies for a gift tax charitable deduction. With respect to estate taxes, a donor who designates an annuity only for himself or herself will not have any amount relative to the gift annuity transfer included in his or her gross estate.[2]

In a private letter ruling, the IRS approved of "reinsured" charitable gift annuities.[3]

610. What are the tax consequences to the obligor in a charitable annuity transaction?

Property transferred in return for a charitable gift annuity could fall into the general definition of "debt financed property" in IRC Section 514(b)(1) because the charity acquires the gift subject to the promise to pay the donor an annuity. This result would be problematic, because it could be treated as unrelated business taxable income and trigger an associated unrelated business income tax for the charity.

However, in a private letter ruling, the IRS decided that issuing a charitable gift annuity will not result in income from an unrelated trade or business and that income earned by the charitable organization from investing the charitable gift annuity funds will not be considered unrelated debt-financed income.[4]

A charity's obligation to pay an annuity will be exempt from the debt financed property rules of IRC Section 514 if the following conditions are met:

(1) the annuity must be the sole consideration paid for the property transferred;

(2) the present value of the annuity must be less than 90 percent of the value of the property received in exchange;

(3) it must be payable over the lives of one or two annuitants;

(4) the contract must not guarantee a minimum number of payments or specify a maximum number of payments; and

(5) the contract must not provide for adjustments to the amount of annuity paid based on income earned by the transferred property or any other property.[5]

Issuing charitable gift annuities does not affect the tax-exempt status of the organization if the annuity meets the requirements above and a portion of the amount transferred in return for the annuity is allowable as a charitable deduction.[6]

1. Let. Rul. 200742010.
2. See Rev. Rul. 80-281, 1980-2 CB 282; Let. Rul. 8045010. See also IRC Sec. 2522(a) and IRC Sec. 2503(a).
3. See Let. Rul. 200847014.
4. Let. Rul. 200449033.
5. IRC Sec. 514(c)(5).
6. IRC Sec. 501(m).

611. How is a corporation taxed on payments under an annuity contract or on living proceeds from an endowment or life insurance contract?

With respect to living proceeds from endowment and life insurance contracts, the same rules that are applicable to personal insurance and endowment contracts generally apply (Q 10 to Q 62).[1] The same rules that apply to increases in the cash value of policies for personal insurance (Q 8) also apply to business-owned insurance.

In the case of a deferred annuity contract held by a corporation or other entity that is not a natural person, to the extent that contributions are made after February 28, 1986, the contract is not treated as an annuity contract for tax purposes. Income on the contract is treated as ordinary income received or accrued by the owner during the taxable year.[2] Thus, if the total of payments received in a year, amounts received in prior years, and the net surrender value at the end of the year, if any, exceed premiums paid in the current year and in prior years, plus amounts included in income in prior years, then the excess amount is includable in income. The rule and exceptions are discussed in Q 511. To the extent an annuity contract is not subject to this rule (i.e., contributions were made prior to March 1, 1986), payments received under the contract will be subject to the rules applicable to personal annuity contracts.

612. How are damage payments taxed if an annuity is used to fund a judgment or settle a claim for damages on account of personal injuries or sickness?

Other than punitive damages, any damages received on account of personal physical injuries or physical sicknesses are not includable in gross income. This is true whether the damages are received by suit or agreement or as a lump sum or periodic payments.[3] For this purpose, emotional distress is not treated as a physical injury or physical sickness.[4]

The phrase "other than punitive damages" does not apply to punitive damages awarded in a wrongful death action with respect to which applicable state law, as in effect on September 13, 1995, provides that only punitive damages may be awarded in such an action.[5]

The rule regarding emotional distress does not apply to any damages that do not exceed the amount paid for medical care, as described generally in IRC Section 213, attributable to emotional distress.

If a lump sum payment representing the present value of future damages is invested for the benefit of a claimant who has actual or constructive receipt or the economic benefit of the lump sum, only the amount of the lump sum payment is treated as received as damages and excludable. None of the income from investment of the payment is excludable.[6]

1. IRC Sec. 11(a).
2. IRC Sec. 72(u).
3. IRC Sec. 104(a).
4. IRC Sec. 104(a).
5. IRC Sec. 104(c).
6. Rev. Rul. 65-29, 1965-1 CB 59; Rev. Rul. 76-133, 1976-1 CB 34.

Where damages are to be paid periodically and the person injured has no right to the discounted present value of the payments or any control over investment of the present value, the entire amount of each periodic payment is excludable, including earnings on the fund.

Thus, where a single premium annuity is purchased by a person obligated to make the damage payments to provide that person with a source of funds, and the person receiving payments has no interest in the contract and can rely only on the general credit of the payor, the entire amount of each periodic payment is excludable.[1]

Under proposed regulations issued in 2009, damages for physical injuries may qualify for the Section 104(a)(2) exclusion even though the injury giving rise to the damages is not defined as a tort under state or common law. In addition, the exclusion does not depend on the scope of remedies available under state or common law. In effect, the regulations reverse the result in *United States v. Burke*[2] by allowing the exclusion for damages awarded under no-fault statutes.[3]

613. If a qualified plan trust distributes an annuity contract to an employee, is the value of the contract taxable to the employee in the year of distribution?

If the contract distributed is an annuity contract, the employee will not be taxed on its value, including cash surrender value that may be available to the employee on surrender, unless and until the employee surrenders the contract.[4]

Rather, the employee will be taxed on the annuity payments as he or she receives them (Q 614, Q 619). A contract issued after 1962 must be nontransferable to qualify for this tax deferred treatment.[5] The transfer of an annuity to a divorced spouse pursuant to a divorce decree will not violate the nontransferability requirement.[6]

The IRS determined that the nontransferability requirement was not violated by a Section 1035 exchange of an annuity contract distributed from a qualified plan where the taxpayer simply was uncomfortable with the amount of funds invested with a single insurer.[7] Both the old and new contracts were materially similar, were nontransferable, were subject to the spousal consent requirements, and met the other applicable IRC Section 401 requirements.[8]

If an employee surrenders an annuity contract after the year of distribution, the gain realized on surrender is taxable as ordinary income and will not qualify for taxation as a lump sum distribution.[9] The unsurrendered annuity contract will affect the taxation of any lump sum distribution of which it is a part, or that is made in the same year, as explained below. If the annuity is surrendered in the year of distribution, the proceeds either will be taxed as ordinary income,

1. Rev. Rul. 79-220, 1979-2 CB 74; Let. Rul. 8321017.
2. 504 U.S. 229 (1992).
3. Reg-127270-06, 74 Fed. Reg. 47152, 47153 (9-15-2009); see Treas. Reg. §1.104-1(c)(2).
4. Treas. Reg. §1.402(a)-1(a)(2).
5. IRC Sec. 401(g); Treas. Reg. §1.401-9(b)(1).
6. Let. Rul. 8513065.
7. Let. Rul. 9233054, GCM 39882 (10-30-92).
8. See also Let. Rul. 9241007.
9. Rev. Rul. 81-107, 1981-1 CB 201.

or, if the distribution of the annuity is all or part of a lump sum distribution, under the lump sum distribution rules (Q 3958). If an annuity is distributed in an eligible rollover distribution, tax may be deferred by rollover (Q 3986).

According to proposed regulations, an employee's cost basis is deducted first from the cash and property other than the annuity. Any excess is used to reduce the value of the annuity.[1]

Amounts that become payable in cash under qualified plans are not includable in income simply because they are available.[2] Thus, where a plan provides that an employee, on termination of employment, may take either a single sum payment in cash or have the trustee purchase an annuity for the employee with cash, the employee's election does not have to be made within any specific time after the cash became available. Plan distribution provisions must satisfy applicable distribution requirements (Q 3884 to Q 3898).

614. How is an employee taxed on periodic retirement benefits under a qualified pension, annuity, or profit sharing plan if the annuity starting date is after December 31, 1997?

If an employee, whether a regular employee or a self-employed individual, has no cost basis for his or her interest in a plan, the full amount of each payment is taxable to the employee as ordinary income.[3] If an employee has a cost basis for his or her interest in a plan, the payments are taxed as discussed below, depending on the employee's annuity starting date. To determine an employee's cost basis, see Q 3960.

The tax treatment is the same whether payment is made directly from a qualified trust or annuity plan or whether a trust buys an annuity and distributes it to an employee.[4] Distribution of an annuity contract itself affects the tax on lump sum distributions (Q 140). If an employee has a cost basis for his or her interest, payments are taxed as discussed below, depending on the annuity starting date.

For an employee who has a cost basis for his or her interest, and whose annuity starting date is after December 31, 1997, the investment in the contract is recovered according to one of two schedules set forth in the IRC. For purposes of this rule, the employee's investment in the contract does not include any adjustment for a refund feature under the contract.[5]

These tables operate in the same manner as the simplified safe harbor announced in 1988.[6] If an annuity is payable over one life, the payments will be taxed as described below for annuities with a starting date after November 18, 1996. If the annuity is payable over two or more lives, the excludable portion of each monthly payment is determined by dividing the employee's investment in the contract by the number of anticipated payments, as follows:[7]

1. Prop. Treas. Reg. §1.402(e)-2(c)(1)(ii)(C).
2. See IRC Sec. 402(a).
3. Treas. Reg. §§1.61-11(a), 1.72-4(d)(1); IRC Secs. 402(a), 403(a).
4. IRC Secs. 402(a), 403(a)(1).
5. IRC Secs. 72(d)(1)(C), 72(c)(2); see Notice 98-2, 1998-1 CB 266.
6. See IRC Sec. 72(d); Notice 98-2, 1998-1 CB 266.
7. IRC Sec. 72(d)(1).

If the combined ages of the annuitants are	Number of payments
110 and under	410
111 – 120	360
121 – 130	310
131 – 140	260
141+	210

According to the Conference Committee Report for TRA '97, this table applies to benefits based on the life of more than one annuitant, even if the amount of the annuity varies by annuitant. It does not apply to an annuity paid on a single life merely because it has additional features, such as a term certain. In the case of a term certain annuity without a life contingency, the expected number of payments is the number of monthly payments provided under the contract.[1] In the case of payments made other than monthly, an adjustment must be made to take into account the period on the basis of which payments are made. Two methods of making such an adjustment are set forth in Notice 98-2.[2]

For purposes of this rule, if an annuity is payable to a primary annuitant and more than one survivor annuitant, the combined ages of the annuitants is the sum of the age of the primary annuitant and the youngest survivor annuitant. If an annuity is payable to more than one survivor annuitant but there is no primary annuitant, the combined ages of the annuitants is the sum of the age of the oldest survivor annuitant and the youngest survivor annuitant. Any survivor annuitant whose entitlement to payments is based on an event other than the death of the primary annuitant is disregarded. For an explanation of the basis recovery rules under IRC Section 72(d), see Letter Ruling 200009066.

615. How is an employee taxed on periodic retirement benefits under a qualified pension, annuity, or profit sharing plan if the annuity starting date is after November 18, 1996 and before January 1, 1998?

If an employee, whether a regular employee or a self-employed individual, has no cost basis for his or her interest in a plan, the full amount of each payment is taxable to the employee as ordinary income.[3] If an employee has a cost basis for his or her interest in a plan, the payments are taxed as discussed below, and depend on the employee's annuity starting date. To determine an employee's cost basis, see Q 3960.

The tax treatment is the same whether payment is made directly from a qualified trust or annuity plan or whether a trust buys an annuity and distributes it to an employee.[4] Distribution of an annuity contract itself affects the tax on lump sum distributions (Q 140). If an employee

1. Notice 98-2, 1998-1 CB 266.
2. 1998-1 CB 266.
3. Treas. Reg. §§1.61-11(a), 1.72-4(d)(1); IRC Secs. 402(a), 403(a).
4. IRC Secs. 402(a), 403(a)(1).

has a cost basis for his or her interest, payments are taxed as discussed below, depending on the annuity starting date.

If an employee had a cost basis for his or her interest, and the annuity starting date was after November 18, 1996 and before January 1, 1998 (or if the annuity is payable over one life and has a starting date after December 31, 1997, as described above), the investment in the contract was recovered according to the schedule below. For purposes of this rule, the employee's investment in the contract did not include any adjustment for a refund feature under the contract.[1]

The excludable portion of each monthly payment was determined by dividing the employee's investment in the contract by the number of anticipated payments contained in the following table:[2]

Age	Number of Payments
55 and under	360
56 – 60	310
61 – 65	260
66 – 70	210
71+	160

This table did not apply if the annuitant was age seventy-five or older unless there were fewer than five years of guaranteed payments under the annuity.[3] It would appear that for an annuitant who was seventy-five or older and whose contract provides for five or more years of guaranteed payments, the rules for annuities with a starting date after July 1, 1986 and before November 19, 1996 would be applied.

If a contract provided for a fixed number of installment payments, the number of monthly annuity payments provided under the contract was used instead of the number listed on the table.[4] If payments under a contract were not made on a monthly basis, appropriate adjustments had to be made to the number of payments determined above to reflect the basis on which payments are made.[5]

The excluded amount remained constant, even where the amount of the annuity payments changes. If the amount to be excluded from each payment was greater than the amount of the annuity payment (e.g., because of decreased survivor payments), then each annuity payment would be completely excluded from gross income until the entire investment is recovered. As noted below, under earlier law, for distributees with annuity starting dates after December 31, 1986, annuity payments received after the investment was recovered are fully includable in gross income. If two annuitants are receiving payments at the same time, each may exclude his or her pro rata portion of the amount provided under these rules.[6]

1. IRC Secs. 72(d)(1)(C), 72(c)(2); see Notice 98-2, 1998-1 CB 266.
2. IRC Sec. 72(d)(1)(B).
3. IRC Sec. 72(d)(1)(E).
4. See IRC Secs. 72(d)(1)(B)(i)(II), 72(c)(3)(B).
5. IRC Sec. 72(d)(1)(F); see Notice 98-2, 1998-1 CB 266, for two such methods.
6. Notice 98-2, 1998-1 CB 266.

If a lump sum was paid to a taxpayer in connection with the commencement of the annuity payments, it was taxable as an amount not received as an annuity under IRC Section 72(e) and treated as received before the annuity starting date. The taxpayer's investment in the contract was determined as if the lump sum payment had been received.[1] Where a defined benefit plan required after-tax contributions and permitted participants to withdraw their aggregate after-tax contributions in a single sum at retirement in exchange for an actuarial reduction in their lifetime pension benefits, the IRS ruled that the single sum payment constituted a lump sum payment under IRC Sections 72(d)(1)(D) and 72(d)(1)(G).[2]

The total amount that an employee could exclude was not permitted to exceed his or her investment in the contract, and if the employee died prior to recovering his or her full investment in the contract, any unrecovered investment will be allowable as a deduction on the employee's final return.[3]

Special transition rules were provided for payors and distributees who continued using the simplified safe harbor contained in Notice 88-118 (see Q 618), as revised by Notice 98-2, with respect to annuities with annuity starting dates after November 18, 1996 and before January 1, 1997.[4]

616. How is an employee taxed on periodic retirement benefits under a qualified pension, annuity, or profit sharing plan if the annuity starting date is after July 1, 1986 and before November 19, 1996?

If an employee, whether a regular employee or a self-employed individual, has no cost basis for his or her interest in a plan, the full amount of each payment is taxable to the employee as ordinary income.[5] If an employee has a cost basis for his or her interest in a plan, the payments are taxed as discussed below, and depend on the employee's annuity starting date. To determine an employee's cost basis, see Q 3960.

The tax treatment is the same whether payment is made directly from a qualified trust or annuity plan or whether a trust buys an annuity and distributes it to an employee.[6] Distribution of an annuity contract itself affects the tax on lump sum distributions (Q 140). If an employee has a cost basis for his or her interest, payments are taxed as discussed below, depending on the annuity starting date.

If an employee had a cost basis for his or her interest and the annuity starting date was after July 1, 1986 and before November 19, 1996, payments were taxed either under the regular annuity rules or, if certain requirements were met, under the simplified safe harbor method described in Q 617.[7]

1. IRC Sec. 72(d)(1)(D).
2. Let. Rul. 9847032.
3. IRC Secs. 72(d)(1)(B)(ii), 72(b)(2), 72(b)(3); see Notice 98-2, 1998-1 CB 266.
4. See Notice 98-2, 1998-1 CB 266.
5. Treas. Reg. §§1.61-11(a), 1.72-4(d)(1); IRC Secs. 402(a), 403(a).
6. IRC Secs. 402(a), 403(a)(1).
7. IRC Secs. 402(a), 72, 403(a).

Under the regular annuity rules, an exclusion ratio was determined as of the annuity starting date.[1] Basically, the exclusion ratio was determined by dividing the investment in the contract by the expected return under the contract. The resulting quotient was the percentage of each payment that may be excluded from gross income.

With respect to distributions from qualified plans, the employee's cost basis in the plan was his or her investment in the contract (Q 529, Q 3960). The total amount that an employee was estimated to receive under a plan was his or her expected return (Q 536). In the case of a straight life annuity, this expected return was determined by multiplying the total amount an employee will receive each year by the number of years in the employee's life expectancy, according to Table I or Table V of the Annuity Tables, whichever was applicable (Appendix A). For an explanation of the basic annuity rule and its application to various types of payments (e.g., straight life annuity, refund or period-certain life annuity, joint and survivor annuity, or payments for a fixed period), see Q 529 to Q 548. If an employee's annuity starting date was after December 31, 1986, the total amount that the employee could exclude during his or her lifetime was limited to his or her investment in the contract. With respect to earlier starting dates, the exclusion ratio continued to apply, even to amounts received in excess of the employee's investment in the contract.

Example. Mr. Rowles retired on October 9, 1996, at the age of sixty-five. He had the option under his employer's qualified contributory pension plan to elect an annuity for a period certain, but chose instead to receive a life annuity. On January 1, 1997, he started receiving payments under the plan. The pension arrangement pays him $800 a month for life. Mr. Rowles' cost basis in the plan (including his own contributions and amounts that have been taxed to him) is $12,000. Mr. Rowles made contributions both before July 1, 1986, and after June 30, 1986, but because Mr. Rowles could have elected an annuity for a period certain, he may not elect to calculate his excludable amount separately with respect to the pre-July and post-June portions (Appendix A). The life expectancy for age sixty-five is twenty years (Table V, Appendix A). So, the total expected return from the plan is $192,000 (20 × $9,600). Mr. Rowles' exclusion ratio is therefore $12,000/$192,000, or 6.3 percent. Each year he excludes $604.80 (6.3 percent of $9,600) from gross income, until he has excluded the full $12,000, and each year he includes in gross income $8,995.20 ($9,600 – $604.80), until the full $12,000 has been recovered, after which he will include the full $9,600.

If an employee dies prior to recovering his or her full investment in the contract, the unrecovered investment will be allowed as a deduction on the employee's final return. If payments are guaranteed and a refund beneficiary does not recover the amount unrecovered at the decedent's death, the beneficiary may deduct the remaining unrecovered investment in the contract.[2]

617. How is an employee taxed on periodic retirement benefits under a qualified pension, annuity, or profit sharing plan if the annuity starting date is on or before July 1, 1986?

If an employee's annuity starting date was on or before July 1, 1986, payments were taxed according to the three year cost recovery rule or the regular annuity rules.[3] The three year cost

1. IRC Sec. 72(b); Treas. Reg. §1.72-4(a).
2. IRC Sec. 72(b)(3).
3. IRC Sec. 72(d)(1), prior to repeal.

recovery rule was repealed for employees with an annuity starting date after July 1, 1986.[1] Certain premature distributions are subject to an additional tax (Q 3956). Excess retirement distributions were subject to an additional tax in years beginning before 1997.

618. What is the simplified safe harbor method that can be used to determine the tax treatment of periodic retirement benefits under an annuity with a starting date before November 19, 1996?

In the case of an annuity starting date before November 19, 1996, a simplified safe harbor method can be used if annuity payments depend on the life of the employee or the joint lives of the employee and a beneficiary. If an employee was age seventy-five or older when annuity payments commenced, this method could be used only if fewer than five years of payments were guaranteed.[2] Under this method, investment in the contract is the employee's cost basis in the plan. No refund feature adjustment has to be made. Investment in the contract is divided by the total number of monthly annuity payments expected. This number is taken from the following table and is based on the employee's age at the annuity starting date:

Age	Number of Payments
55 and under	300
56 – 60	260
61 – 65	240
66 – 70	170
71 and over	120

The same expected number of payments applies regardless of whether the employee is receiving a single life annuity or a joint and survivor annuity. The dollar amount excluded from each payment does not change, even if the amount of the payments increases or decreases.[3] If an annuity starting date is after December 31, 1986, annuity payments received after the investment in the contract is recovered are fully includable in income.

An employee makes the election to use the safe harbor method by reporting the taxable portion of the annuity payments received in the year, including the annuity starting date under that method, on the income tax return for that year and for succeeding years. An employee may change the method used to report the tax treatment of annuity payments (i.e., from the safe harbor method to the actual calculation of an exclusion ratio or vice versa) by filing an amended return for all open tax years, as long as the year containing the annuity starting date is an open year.[4]

1. TRA '86, Sec. 1122(c)(1).
2. Notice 88-118, 1988-2 CB 450.
3. Notice 88-118, 1988-2 CB 450.
4. Notice 88-118, 1988-2 CB 450.

619. How are variable annuity benefits taxed to an employee that are payable under a qualified pension or profit sharing plan?

If an employee has no cost basis for an interest in a plan, each payment, regardless of amount, is fully taxable as ordinary income. An employee's cost basis generally consists of any nondeductible contributions the employee has made to the plan and any employer contributions that have been taxed to the employee, other than excess deferrals (Q 3757) not timely distributed (Q 3960).

When an employee has a cost basis for an interest in a plan and the annuity starting date is after June 30, 1986, payments are taxed under the annuity rules as expressly applied to variable payments (Q 552 to Q 554). Thus, the amount excludable from an employee's gross income each year is determined by dividing the cost basis, adjusted for any refund or period-certain guarantee, by the number of years in the payment period. If an annuity is payable for a life or lives, the payment period is determined by the IRS annuity tables.

For annuities with a starting date after December 31, 1986, the present value of any refund feature is not to be taken into account in calculating the unrecovered investment in the contract, but these amounts still are taken into account in calculating an individual's exclusion ratio.[1] The unrecovered investment in a contract affects only those annuitants who die before the annuity payments end (i.e., the amount of their deduction on their final year return) (Q 568) and the annuitant's cost recovery date (i.e., the date upon which the annuity holder recovers his or her investment in the contract).

Example. Mr. Mounger retired on August 31, 2019 when he had reached age sixty-five. He became eligible to receive monthly variable annuity payments for life under an earlier contributory pension plan of his employer. In the event of Mr. Mounger's death before receiving payments for at least five years, payments on the same variable basis will be continued to his beneficiary for the remainder of the five year period. Mr. Mounger contributed $6,000 to the plan ($5,000 representing investment in the contract before July 1, 1986; $1,000 representing investment in the contract after June 30, 1986). Payments for the first year began in September, and during the last four months of the year, Mr. Mounger received a total of $640. Mr. Mounger elects to determine his excludable amount by making separate calculations for his pre-July 1986 and post-June 1986 investment in the contract. The value of the refund feature determined under Table VII of §1.72-9 is not more than 50 percent, and Mr. Mounger had only life annuity options available. On the basis of these facts, Mr. Mounger's annual exclusion from gross income will be $343.60. The first step is to adjust the investment in the contract for the value of the refund feature, as follows:

Pre-July 1986 adjustment:	
Unadjusted investment in the contract	$5,000
Allocable part of amount to be received annually (($5,000 ÷ $6,000) × $1,920)	$1,600
Duration of guaranteed amount (years)	5
Guaranteed amount (5 × $1,600)	$8,000
Percentage in Table III for age 65 and 5 years	7%
Present value of refund feature rounded to nearest dollar (7% of $8,000)	$ 560
Adjusted pre-July 1986 investment in the contract ($5,000 – $560)	$4,440

1. IRC Sec. 72(b)(1),(2).

Post-June 1986 adjustment:	
Unadjusted investment in the contract	$1,000
Allocable part of amount to be received annually (($1,000 ÷ $6,000) × $1,920)	$ 320
Duration of guaranteed amount (years)	5
Guaranteed amount (5 × $320)	$1,600
Percentage in Table VII for age 65 and 5 years	3%
Present value of refund feature rounded to nearest dollar (3% of $1,600)	$ 48
Adjusted post-June 1986 investment in the contract	$ 952

Once the investment in the contract has been adjusted by subtracting the value of the period-certain guarantee, an excludable amount is determined by dividing the adjusted investment in the contract by the life expectancy taken from Table I or V. Taking the example above, the excludable amount is determined as follows:

Pre-July 1986 investment in the contract (adjusted for period-certain guarantee)	$ 4,440
Life expectancy from Table I (male age 65)	15 years
Excludable amount ($4,440 ÷ 15)	$ 296
Post-June 1986 investment in the contract (adjusted for period-certain guarantee)	$ 952
Life expectancy from Table V (age 65)	20 years
Excludable amount ($952 ÷ 20)	$ 47.60
Amount excludable from gross income each year ($296 + $47.60)	$343.60

In the case of an annuity starting date before November 19, 1996, a simplified safe harbor method may be available (Q 617).

With respect to annuities with starting dates prior to July 1, 1986, payments are taxed under the annuity rules or under the three year cost recovery rule (Q 616).

Certain early (premature) distributions are subject to an additional tax (Q 3956).

620. Does the interest of a donee spouse in a joint and survivor annuity qualify for the marital deduction?

The interest of a donee spouse in a joint and survivor annuity in which only the donor and donee spouses have a right to receive payments during the spouses' joint lifetimes is treated as qualified terminable interest property ("QTIP") for which the marital deduction is available unless the donor spouse irrevocably elects otherwise within the time allowed for filing a gift tax return.[1]

1. IRC Sec. 2523(f)(6).

Annuities and the Estate

621. What are the estate tax results when a decedent has been receiving payments under an annuity contract?

If a decedent was receiving a straight life annuity, there is no property interest remaining at the decedent's death to be included in the decedent's gross estate, as payments terminated at death.

If a contract provides a survivor benefit (as under a refund life annuity, joint and survivor annuity, or installment option), tax results depend on whether the survivor benefit is payable to a decedent's estate or to a named beneficiary and, if payable to a named beneficiary, on who paid for the contract.

If payable to a decedent's estate, the value of the post-death payment or payments is includable in the decedent's gross estate under IRC Section 2033 as a property interest owned by the decedent at the time of his or her death. If payable to a named beneficiary, the provisions of IRC Section 2039(a) and IRC Section 2039(b) generally apply and inclusion in the gross estate is determined by a premium payment test. Thus, if a decedent purchased the contract (after March 3, 1931), the value of the refund or survivor benefit is includable in the decedent's gross estate.

In the event a decedent furnished only part of the purchase price, the decedent's gross estate includes only a proportional share of this value (Q 624 to Q 628).

The foregoing rules do not apply to death proceeds of life insurance on the life of a decedent (Q 81). In addition, special statutory provisions apply to employee annuities under qualified pension and profit-sharing plans (Q 3974, Q 3975), to certain other employee annuities (Q 633, Q 634), and to individual retirement plans (Q 3710).

622. How can an annuity be used by an individual as an estate planning tool?

In order to avoid the potential tax and financial repercussions that a lump sum transfer can create, many individuals wish to protect their heirs by providing structure to the way assets are inherited. For these taxpayers, annuities, though commonly used as retirement income planning tools, can provide the solution.

A taxpayer may wish to use annuities to structure an inheritance for a variety of reasons. The reasons for using an annuity as a wealth transfer vehicle often mirror those that apply when a taxpayer is planning for retirement—the annuity creates a stream of consistent income over time, guaranteeing that the taxpayer's beneficiary is provided for far into the future. This strategy can provide protection for heirs who might be otherwise unable to manage a large one-sum payment, or who might have financial problems that could cause them to spend a large sum too quickly.

Some annuity contracts also offer a feature called a restrictive endorsement that can prevent the heir from selling or assigning his or her rights in the annuity contract, providing further protection for the income stream.

Further, individuals might wish to include an annuity in their estate planning in order to ensure that specific beneficiaries are provided for outside of the overall estate plan. Purchasing annuity products can provide income security for those specified heirs while allowing the remaining estate assets to be used to accomplish other goals—such as satisfying estate expenses or allowing remaining assets to be invested more aggressively in riskier investments that have the potential to generate more growth.

Structuring the payments so that they occur over time, as an annuity stream, rather than as a lump sum payment, can help the account beneficiaries avoid a large up front tax liability. This is because, unlike life insurance death proceeds, proceeds received under annuity contract are not entirely tax-exempt and a lump sum death benefit would trigger income tax on the entire gain in the year of receipt.

Planning Point: Many deferred annuity contracts offer "enhanced" death benefits that will produce a death benefit in excess of the contract's cash value. For uninsurable individuals, the amount of annual increase in that death benefit may be greater than is available elsewhere. For example, if a contract has a "rollup" interest rate of 6 percent per year on the original cash value until some advanced age (such as eighty-five), the amount passing to heirs might be greater than an alternative investment would have produced. On the other hand, the excess of the death benefit over the owner's adjusted basis in the contract will be taxed as ordinary income to the beneficiaries, as "income in respect of a decedent". That said, most "safe money" alternatives produce income that is also taxed at ordinary rates. – *John L. Olsen, CLU, ChFC, AEP, OlsenAnnuityEducation.com.*

623. What are the estate tax results when a decedent has been receiving payments under an optional settlement of endowment maturity proceeds or life insurance cash surrender value?

Life insurance or annuity proceeds payable to a surviving spouse qualify for the marital deduction if certain conditions are met (Q 191). If proceeds used the marital deduction in the first spouse's estate and the contract provides a survivor benefit to the surviving spouse's estate or to a person surviving the surviving spouse, then the proceeds usually are includable in the surviving spouse's estate.

If the surviving spouse receives a straight life annuity, there is no property interest remaining at his or her death to be included in his or her gross estate.

624. If an individual purchases a deferred or retirement annuity and dies before the contract matures, is the death value of the contract includable in his or her estate?

Generally, yes.

The amount payable on death before maturity is not life insurance and, therefore, the estate tax rules for annuities apply.

If a death benefit is payable to an annuitant's estate, its value is includable in the gross estate under IRC Section 2033, and it is considered to be a property interest owned by the annuitant at the time of death.

If a death benefit is payable to a named beneficiary and an annuitant purchased the contract after March 3, 1931, the value of the death benefit generally is includable in the gross estate under IRC Section 2039, whether or not the right was reserved to change the beneficiary. If the individual purchased the annuity as a gift for another person, and retained no interest in the annuity payments, incidents of ownership, or refunds, the value of the annuity ordinarily will not be includable in the individual's gross estate (Q 629).

The same rules apply to the proceeds of a retirement income endowment if the insured dies after the terminal reserve value equals or exceeds the face value.[1]

For example, an employer purchases a contract from an insurance company to provide an employee, upon retirement at age sixty-five, with an annuity of $100 per month for life, and continues to pay a similar annuity to his beneficiary upon the employee's death after retirement. The contract provides that if the employee dies before reaching retirement age, a lump sum payment of $20,000 will be paid to his beneficiary instead of the annuity. Assume that the reserve value of the contract at the retirement age is $20,000. If the employee dies after reaching retirement age, the death benefit to the beneficiary would be an annuity, which would be includable in the employee's gross estate under Section 2039 (a) and (b). If, on the other hand, the employee dies before reaching his retirement age, the death benefit to the beneficiary would be insurance under a policy on the life of the decedent since the reserve value would be less than the death benefit.[2]

625. In the case of a joint and survivor annuity, what value is includable in the gross estate of the annuitant who dies first?

The value of a survivor's annuity is includable in the deceased annuitant's gross estate in proportion to his or her contribution to the purchase price of the contract.[3] (This rule applies to contracts purchased after March 3, 1931.)

Thus, if a deceased annuitant purchased the contract, the full value of the survivor's annuity is includable in his or her gross estate. If the survivor purchased the contract, no part of the value is includable in the deceased annuitant's estate. If both contributed to the purchase price, only a proportionate part of the value is includable in the deceased's estate.

For example, suppose that the decedent and his wife each contributed $15,000 to the purchase price of a joint and survivor annuity payable for their joint lives and the life of the survivor. If the value of the survivor's annuity is $20,000 at the decedent's death, the amount to be included in his gross estate is one-half of $20,000 ($10,000) since he contributed one-half of the cost of the contract.[4]

1. Treas. Reg. §20.2039-1(d).
2. Treas. Reg. §20.2039-1(d)(Ex.).
3. IRC Secs. 2039(a), 2039(b).
4. Treas. Reg. §20.2039-1(c)(Ex. 1).

In accord with this rule, if a joint and survivor annuity is purchased with community funds, only one-half of the value of the survivor's annuity is includable in the gross estate of the spouse who dies first.[1] (For estate tax value of survivor's annuity, see Q 626.)

Where a joint and survivor annuity between spouses is treated as qualifying terminable interest property for gift tax purposes (Q 620) and the donee spouse dies before the donor spouse, nothing is included in the donee spouse's estate by reason of the qualifying interest.[2] Where the survivor is the deceased annuitant's spouse, the value of the survivor's annuity will qualify for the marital deduction if the contract satisfies applicable conditions (Q 191).

Planning Point: An immediate joint and survivor annuity with no refund feature or a deferred annuity annuitized on that basis between spouses usually will escape estate tax in both spouse's estates because of the marital deduction and because the annuity ends at the survivor's death.

626. What is the estate tax value of a survivor's annuity under a joint and survivor annuity contract?

The value is the amount the same insurance company would charge the survivor for a single life annuity as of the date of the first annuitant's death.[3] Where it can be proven that the survivor's life expectancy is below average, it may be possible to obtain a valuation based on the survivor's actual life expectancy at the date of the decedent's death.[4] For example, lower valuation has been obtained on proof that the surviving annuitant's life expectancy was short because of an incurable disease.[5]

Even if an executor elects to value estate assets as of six months after death (alternate valuation), a survivor's annuity is valued at the date of death. The date of death value is used, despite the election of an alternate valuation, where any change in value after death is due only to lapse of time.

If a surviving annuitant dies during the six months following the first annuitant's death, a lower valuation may be obtained by electing alternate valuation. Thus, in one case, where the survivor died before the optional valuation date, the value at the optional valuation date was determined by subtracting the cost of an annuity as of the survivor's date of death from the cost of an annuity as of the first annuitant's date of death.[6]

627. In the case of a refund or period-certain annuity, is the balance of the guaranteed amount, payable after annuitant's death, includable in the annuitant's gross estate?

If payable to the annuitant's estate, it is includable in his gross estate under IRC Section 2033, as a property interest owned by him at death.

1. *Est. of Mearkle v. Comm.*, 129 F.2d 386 (3d Cir. 1942); *Comm. v. Est. of Wilder*, 118 F.2d 281 (5th Cir. 1941).
2. IRC Sec. 2523(f)(6).
3. Treas. Reg. §20.2031-8(a)(3) (Ex.1); *Est. of Mearkle v. Comm.*, 129 F.2d 386 (3d Cir. 1942); *Est. of Welliver v. Comm.*, 8 TC 165 (1947); *Est. of Pruyn v. Comm.*, 12 TC 754 (1949), *rev'd*, 184 F.2d 971 (2d Cir. 1950); *Christiernin v. Manning*, 138 F. Supp. 923 (D.N.J. 1956).
4. *Est. of Jennings v. Comm.*, 10 TC 323 (1948).
5. *Est. of Halliday by Denbigh v. Comm.*, 7 TC 387 (1946), *acq.*, 1953-1 CB 4; *Est. of Hoelzel v. Comm.*, 28 TC 384 (1957), *acq.*, 1957-2 CB 3.
6. *Est. of Hance v. Comm.*, 18 TC 499 (1952).

If payable to a named beneficiary, and the *annuitant* purchased the contract (after March 3, 1931), it is includable in the annuitant's gross estate under IRC Section 2039(a). It is immaterial whether the beneficiary designation was revocable or irrevocable.

If the refund beneficiary is a charitable organization, the value is included in the annuitant's estate, but the estate is also entitled to a charitable deduction for the value of the transfer to the charitable organization.[1] However, where a decedent has directed his executor to purchase a refund annuity for a personal beneficiary and to name a charitable organization as a refund beneficiary, the decedent's estate is not entitled to a charitable deduction for the value of the refund.[2]

628. Are death proceeds payable under a single premium annuity and life insurance combination includable in an annuitant's gross estate?

Yes, although such combination contracts are uncommon in today's marketplace.

Even though an insured-annuitant holds no incidents of ownership in a life insurance policy at death, the proceeds of the policy nevertheless are includable in his or her gross estate under IRC Section 2039 as a payment under an annuity contract purchased by the insured-annuitant.[3]

In a case decided before IRC Section 2039 was enacted, the U.S. Supreme Court held that the proceeds were not includable in the insured-annuitant's gross estate under IRC Section 2036 as property transferred by the insured-annuitant in which he retained a right to income for life.[4]

If an insured-annuitant transfers a life insurance policy within three years before his or her death, the proceeds may be includable in the insured-annuitant's gross estate under IRC Section 2035 (Q 96).[5]

If an insured-annuitant owns a life insurance policy at death, the proceeds are includable in his or her gross estate either as property owned at the time of death[6] or as a payment under an annuity contract purchased by the insured-annuitant.[7]

629. If a decedent purchased an annuity on the life of another person, will the value of the contract be includable in his or her gross estate?

If a decedent purchased an annuity as a gift for another person and retained no interest in the annuity payments, incidents of ownership, or refunds, the value of the annuity ordinarily will not be includable in the decedent's gross estate (though a gift tax return may have been necessary to report the gift at the time).[8] See Q 817 for the rules pertaining to gifts of property (including annuities) made within three years of death.

1. IRC Sec. 2055.
2. Treas. Reg. §20.2055-2(b); *Choffin's Est. v. U.S.*, 222 F. Supp. 34 (S.D. Fla. 1963).
3. *Est. of Montgomery v. Comm.*, 56 TC 489 (1971), *aff'd* 458 F.2d 616 (5th Cir. 1972); *Sussman v. U.S.*, 76-1 USTC ¶13,126 (E.D.N.Y. 1975).
4. *Fidelity-Philadelphia Trust Co. v. Smith*, 356 U.S. 274 (1958).
5. *U.S. v. Tonkin*, 150 F.2d 531 (3d Cir. 1945).
6. IRC Sec. 2033; *Estate of Coaxum v. Comm.*, TC Memo 2011-135.
7. IRC Sec. 2039.
8. See *Wishard v. U.S.*, 143 F.2d 704 (7th Cir. 1944).

If a decedent has named himself or herself as refund beneficiary, the value of the refund may be taxable in the decedent's estate as a transfer intended to take effect at death.[1] This rule is not applicable, however, unless the value of the refund exceeds 5 percent of the value of the annuity immediately before the donor's death. Moreover, if the donee-annuitant has the power to surrender the contract or to change the refund beneficiary, it would appear that such a power would preclude taxation in the donor's estate as a transfer to take effect at death.[2]

Where a decedent retains ownership of a contract until death, the value in the decedent's gross estate apparently would be the cost of a comparable contract at the time of the decedent's death. In one case, however, where a decedent and his wife paid one-half the cost of an annuity for their son, reserving to themselves the right to surrender the contract, only one-half the surrender value was included in the decedent's gross estate.[3]

630. If a person makes a gift of an immediate annuity, will the value of any refund be includable in the donee-annuitant's estate?

If a donor irrevocably names one person to receive the income for life and irrevocably names another to receive the refund, the value of the refund at the donee-annuitant's death should not be includable in the donee-annuitant's gross estate. IRC Section 2039 is not applicable because the donee-annuitant is not the purchaser of the contract (Q 621).

However, if the refund is payable to the donee or the donee's estate (or the donee can otherwise direct where the refund goes), it will generally be included in the donee's estate for estate tax purposes.

631. If a decedent has been receiving payments under a private annuity, what is includable in the decedent's estate?

In the usual private annuity transaction (Q 604) where a decedent is the sole annuitant, the annuity payments cease at the decedent's death and nothing is left to be taxed in the estate. If benefits are payable to a survivor under the terms of a private annuity agreement, the value of the benefits is includable in the decedent's estate (Q 911). Survivor benefits paid to a surviving spouse under a joint and survivor annuity should qualify for the marital deduction, though.

If the transaction resulted in a gift from the annuitant to the obligor (Q 587), the annuitant's death within three years of the transaction may result in the value of the gift, plus gift tax paid, being included in the deceased annuitant's gross estate (Q 817). If an annuitant's death does not occur within three years, but the gift was a taxable gift, the gift will be an adjusted taxable gift for purposes of the estate tax computation in the annuitant's estate.

In the usual private annuity transaction, an annuitant's transfer of property given in exchange for the annuity is complete and absolute. Under such circumstances, no part of the transferred property is includable in the annuitant's estate. If, however, the annuitant retains at death an

1. IRC Sec. 2037(a).
2. IRC Sec. 2037(b); see *Est. of Hofford v. Comm.*, 4 TC 542 (1945).
3. *Wishard v. U.S.*, supra.

interest in the property transferred, the value of the property could be includable in the annuitant's gross estate under IRC Sections 2033, 2036, 2037 or 2038 as may be appropriate under the circumstances.

632. What is a Medicaid compliant annuity? How can Medicaid compliant annuities be used in an individual's planning?

A married couple typically purchases a Medicaid compliant annuity if the two spouses are in unequal health positions to ensure that the healthy spouse—known as the "community" spouse—has sufficient income, while allowing the second, less healthy, spouse to qualify for Medicaid assistance in paying for long-term care expenses, typically within a nursing home.

Rather than treating the purchase of the annuity as an impermissible asset transfer effected in order to meet Medicaid's means-tested eligibility requirements, if the requirements discussed below are satisfied, the federal Deficit Reduction Act (DRA) treats the purchase as a permissible exempt investment, and the annuity payout stream is shielded as the community spouse's income.

In order to qualify as a Medicaid compliant annuity under the DRA, the terms of the annuity contract must satisfy certain criteria. The income from the annuity contract must be payable to the community spouse, the contract must be irrevocable, and the payment term must be based on the life expectancy of the community spouse.

This is because, in a situation where one spouse requires long-term care and the other remains in the community, the assets of the community spouse are counted—up to a certain level—in determining whether the institutionalized spouse qualifies for Medicaid, but the *income* of that spouse is not counted.

Further, the state must be named as the remainder beneficiary on the contract, allowing it to receive up to the amount that it has paid for the institutionalized spouse's long-term care.

633. Is the value of a death benefit payable under a nonqualified employee annuity includable in an employee's gross estate?

Yes.

If an employee was receiving payments under the contract when he or she died, or if the employee would have had the right to receive payments had he or she lived, the value of the death benefit is includable in the employee's gross estate.[1] It is immaterial whether the employee's rights were forfeitable or nonforfeitable before death.[2] Premiums paid by the employer are considered as having been paid by the employee himself.[3] For tax sheltered annuities purchased for employees of tax-exempt organizations and public schools, see Q 634.

1. IRC Sec. 2039(a).
2. Treas. Reg. §20.2039-1.
3. IRC Sec. 2039(b). *All v. McCobb*, 321 F.2d 633 (2d Cir. 1963); *Est. of Bahen v. Comm.*, 305 F.2d 827 (Ct. Cl. 1962); *Est. of Wadewitz v. Comm.*, 39 TC 925 (1962), *aff'd*, 339 F.2d 980 (7th Cir. 1964).

634. Is a death or survivor benefit under a tax sheltered annuity includable in an employee's gross estate if the decedent died after 1984?

The value of an annuity or other payment receivable under a tax-sheltered annuity ("TSA") by the beneficiary of a deceased TSA annuitant is includable in the annuitant's estate under the rules discussed in Q 621 to Q 630. In reading those rules, remember that any contribution to the purchase of the annuity made by the decedent's employer or former employer is considered to be contributed by the decedent if made by reason of his or her employment.[1] Note that in the case of payments received as insurance on the life of a decedent (Q 4020), estate taxation is determined under the rules of IRC Section 2042 (Q 80 to Q 93), not under IRC Section 2039.

The Tax Reform Act of 1984 repealed the estate tax exclusion discussed in Q 635 generally for estates of decedents dying after 1984. The repeal does not apply to the estate of any decedent who was a plan participant in pay status on December 31, 1984, and irrevocably elected the form of the benefit before July 18, 1984.[2] The Tax Reform Act of 1986 provided that these conditions are considered met if the decedent separated from service before January 1, 1985, and does not change the form of benefit before death.[3]

635. Is a death or survivor benefit under a tax sheltered annuity includable in an employee's gross estate if the decedent died after 1953 and before 1985?

Unless an employer is an organization described in IRC Section 170(b)(1)(A)(ii) or (vi) or a religious organization, other than a trust, and is exempt under IRC Section 501(a), there is no estate tax exclusion for the death or survivor benefit.[4] These organizations, which frequently are referred to as "REC organizations" for religious, educational, and charitable organizations, include educational institutions other than public schools, churches, and charities that receive substantial support from a government or the general public. The IRS has taken the position that the exclusion does not apply to a contract purchased by an employer that is an integral part of a state or local government, such as a public school, college, university, or hospital.[5] The Tax Court, however, has held that the exclusion applied to contracts bought by a state university and a city board of education.[6]

If an employer is one of the eligible types, an estate tax exclusion is available provided the benefit is payable to some beneficiary other than an employee's estate. The exclusion applies only to amounts attributable to employer contributions, that is, to premiums that were excludable from the employee's gross income under the exclusion allowance rule (Q 4028) and to deductible employee contributions.

1. IRC Sec. 2039(b).
2. TRA '84, Sec. 525.
3. TRA '86, Sec. 1852(e)(3).
4. IRC Sec. 2039(c)(3), prior to repeal.
5. Rev. Rul. 60-384, 1960-2 CB 172; Rev. Rul. 68-294, 1968-1 CB 46 (obsoleted by Rev. Rul. 95-71, 1995-2 CB 323).
6. *Est. of Johnson v. Comm.*, 56 TC 944 (1971), acq. 1973-2 CB 2 (followed in Let. Rul. 7817098); *Est. of Green v. Comm.*, 82 TC 843 (1984).

Any portion of premiums that were not excludable from an employee's gross income or were not deductible employee contributions are treated as employee contributions and a corresponding portion of the value of the death or survivor benefit is includable in the employee's gross estate.[1] For this purpose, any one- year term costs of pure life protection that were includable in the employee's gross income are treated as employee contributions.[2] The estate tax exclusion appears applicable whether payments are made in a single sum or in several payments. If a benefit is payable to an employee's estate, the entire value is includable in the employee's gross estate even though all premiums have come within the exclusion allowance.[3]

With respect to the estate of a decedent dying after 1982 and before 1985, the aggregate estate tax exclusion applicable to survivor benefits payable under a qualified plan (Q 3730 to Q 3811), a tax sheltered annuity, or an individual retirement plan (Q 3639) cannot exceed $100,000.[4] TRA '84 also amended TEFRA to provide that the $100,000 limit shall not apply to the estate of any decedent who was a plan participant on pay status on December 31, 1982, and who irrevocably elected the form of benefit before January 1, 1983.[5] The Tax Reform Act of 1986 provided that these conditions are considered met if the decedent separated from service before January 1, 1983, and does not change the form of benefit before death.[6] For estates of decedents dying before 1983, the exclusion (as described) is unlimited.

The estate tax exclusion applies to the value of a death benefit receivable under a retirement annuity contract. Payments to a retirement fund by a REC organization will be regarded as the purchase of a retirement annuity contract for the organization's employee if the payments are made pursuant to a contractual arrangement between the organization and the custodian of the fund whereby the custodian of the fund is obligated to provide an annuity to the employee. Thus, if a state university makes payments under this kind of arrangement to a state retirement system on behalf of a professor employed by the university, the value of survivor benefits payable from the system following the professor's death is eligible for the estate tax exclusion in the professor's estate.[7]

Although it is clear that a tax-sheltered annuity may provide incidental life insurance protection (Q 4020), it is not entirely clear what the estate tax results will be where the death benefit consists of life insurance proceeds payable by reason of the insured's death prior to the maturity of the contract. A technical advice memorandum indicates that the term costs of life insurance protection, unlike the results under a qualified pension plan, will be treated as nondeductible employee contributions for estate tax purposes.[8]

1. IRC Sec. 2039(c)(3).
2. Memorandum, 1967, Pension Plan Guide (CCH), Pre-1986 IRS Tax Releases, ¶17,337.
3. IRC Sec. 2039(c)(3).
4. IRC Sec. 2039(c), (g), as amended and added by TEFRA, and before repeal by TRA '84.
5. TRA '84, Sec. 525.
6. TRA '86, Sec. 1852(e)(3).
7. Rev. Rul. 79-301, 1979-2 CB 327, obsoleted by Rev. Rul. 88-85, 1988-2 CB 333.
8. Memorandum, 1967, Pension Plan Guide (CCH), Pre-1986 IRS Tax Releases, ¶17,337.

The estate tax exclusion under IRC Section 2039(c) is applicable only to the estate of a decedent who was the employee and not to the estate of a non-employee beneficiary.[1] See Q 3710 for the estate tax exclusion applicable to amounts rolled over from a tax-sheltered annuity to an IRA.

636. What is a secondary market annuity?

Most secondary market annuities (also known as "factored" structured settlements) are annuities that were originally issued pursuant to structured settlements, meaning that the defendant in a lawsuit (often a personal injury suit) is found liable and, rather than pay damages to the plaintiff up front, reaches an agreement with the court so that the plaintiff receives the right to receive guaranteed annuity payments over time. In many cases, however, the plaintiff needs the funds immediately and, through a court-approved process, transfers the right to guaranteed payments under the annuity to a third-party buyer for a lump sum.

The court approval process is necessary because, while the plaintiff has received the right to income under the annuity, the defendant technically owns the annuity contract. Through this process, the parties enter into an assignment agreement that is presented to the court, which will approve or deny the transfer based upon whether it is in the transferring plaintiff's best interests.

It is important to note that failure to comply with this court approval process can result in imposition of a tax equal to 40 percent of the discount at which the product is sold.[2] In recent years, however, nearly all states have developed a standardized process that has made obtaining court approval much more simple.

A secondary market annuity is often able to provide the taxpayer with a higher than average interest rate because the selling plaintiff typically must sell his income rights at a discount. The interest paid out under the contract, however, is governed by the original contract terms, which may provide for a rate that is much higher than today's market averages.

Because interest rates on guaranteed financial products have remained relatively low despite recent market success, these products, which are typically issued by large and well-known insurance companies, are often attractive to taxpayers who are otherwise wary of locking themselves into a low interest rate.

Further, secondary market annuities have only recently become widely available to individual taxpayers—prior to the financial crisis of 2008 and 2009, these products were most commonly purchased by large, institutional investors. New economic conditions, coupled with the newly streamlined court approval process, have opened the door for everyday individuals to invest in the secondary market for annuities.

1. *Est. of Kleemeier v. Comm.*, 58 TC 241 (1972).
2. IRC Sec. 5891.

Structured Settlements

637. What is a structured settlement?

A structured settlement is a settlement of a lawsuit that calls for periodic payments to be made over time, rather than as a lump sum. Structured settlements are common in tort actions (usually personal injury lawsuits) where the amount of the judgment can be particularly large.

Structured settlements are typically employed where either the financial position of the defendant requires that payments be spread over time or the plaintiff prefers to receive steady income over time, rather than a lump sum. The defendant may also prefer a structured settlement because the present dollar value needed to fund a stream of settlement payments into the future will be smaller than that which would be required with a lump sum payment.

638. Why might the parties to a judgment prefer to use a structured settlement rather than a lump sum payment?

The parties to a lawsuit have substantial flexibility in composing the terms of a structured settlement. In some cases, a structured settlement may be paid in equal installments over a set period of time, while in other cases a larger up-front payment is made, followed by smaller payments over time. The parties can structure a settlement so that it includes a guaranteed number of payments (which may be preferable to ensure that the plaintiff's heirs are entitled to continue to receive payments should the plaintiff die) or so that it includes payments for the life of the plaintiff.

639. What are the tax consequences to the plaintiff who receives structured settlement funds?

If a structured settlement of a personal physical injury or sickness claim is properly planned, each payment will be tax-free to the recipient.

Usually, when the plaintiff in a personal injury lawsuit receives a settlement, the proceeds of that settlement are taken tax-free.[1] Despite this, if the payments are structured so that the plaintiff receives the settlement funds over time, the earnings on the settlement will be taxable to the plaintiff unless a "structured" settlement is created.[2]

The plaintiff may prefer to receive settlement payments over time. For example, although the plaintiff can invest a lump sum payment, earnings on that investment would be fully taxable. In contrast, if a structured settlement is used, any earnings on the settlement are not taxed.

Whether or not the earnings on the settlement amount will be taxed depends largely on how the parties to the lawsuit characterize the payments. For example, the Tax Court has concluded that portions of a settlement that were labeled by the parties as "interest" were taxable as ordinary income (the case did not specifically deal with structured settlements).[3] However,

1. IRC Sec. 104(a).
2. IRC Sec. 104(a)(2).
3. *Kovacs v. Commissioner*, 100 TC 124 (1993).

in the usual case, a structured settlement will avoid this result because it will not distinguish between amounts paid to satisfy the claim and amounts paid as interest (e.g., the settlement will require the defendant to pay $150,000 per year for ten years). As such, the entire amount of each payment will be treated as proceeds of the settlement and can be taken tax-free.

640. What are the tax consequences if a structured settlement is sold?

If a plaintiff who is receiving payments under a structured settlement enters into an agreement to sell the rights to the future payment stream, a 40 percent excise tax may be imposed upon the purchaser.[1] This type of sale is known as a structured settlement factoring transaction.

The 40 percent tax applies only to the "factoring discount." The factoring discount is defined as the amount in excess of a fraction, the numerator of which is the aggregate undiscounted amount of structured settlement payments being acquired and the denominator of which is the total amount actually paid by the purchaser to the plaintiff who is selling the payment rights.[2]

The 40 percent tax does not apply if the sale of the structured settlement payment rights is approved in advance by a court order, which can result if the court finds that the sale is in the best interest of the plaintiff (as, for example, if the plaintiff needs the purchase price to pay medical expenses or support dependents).[3] See Q 636 for more details.

641. When is a defendant who is a party to a structured settlement entitled to deduct the payments made pursuant to the agreement?

A payor who uses the cash receipts and disbursement method of accounting can deduct qualified payments made pursuant to a structured settlement in the year they are paid.[4]

If the payor uses the accrual method of accounting, he or she can deduct any allowable expenses in the year in which: (1) all events that prove liability have occurred, (2) the amount of the liability can be determined with reasonable accuracy and (3) the economic performance requirement has been met with respect to the liability.[5]

In the context of a structured settlement, economic performance by the defendant will typically occur as the defendant actually makes the required payments to the plaintiff.[6]

For example, assume that the parties to a lawsuit enter into a structured settlement that requires the defendant to pay $150,000 per year to the plaintiff for ten years, and the defendant immediately purchases an annuity to provide for the entire $1.5 million obligation. Economic performance occurs when each $150,000 payment is made to the plaintiff—*not* when the defendant purchases the annuity. Therefore, assuming all other requirements are met, the defendant

---

1. IRC Sec. 5891.
2. IRC Secs. 5891(a), 5891(c)(4)
3. IRC Sec. 5891(b).
4. Treas. Reg. §1.461-1(a)(1).
5. Treas. Reg. §1.461-1(a)(2).
6. IRC Sec. 461(h).

is entitled to deduct $150,000 for each of the ten years in which payment to the plaintiff is properly made under the structured settlement.

642. Is a defendant entitled to deduct amounts paid under a structured settlement if the underlying liability is contested?

Typically, an accrual basis taxpayer is not entitled to deduct amounts paid under a structured settlement unless all events that give rise to the liability have already occurred.[1] However, if the economic performance requirement has been met (see Q 641), an accrual basis taxpayer may be entitled to deduct amounts paid pursuant to a settlement in the year in which those amounts are paid if the following requirements are met:

(1) the liability has been asserted and the defendant contests it,

(2) the defendant transfers money or property to satisfy the asserted liability,

(3) the contest with respect to the asserted liability exists after the money or property is transferred, and

(4) but for the fact that the asserted liability is contested, the defendant would be allowed a deduction in the year when the transfer took place (or an earlier year).[2]

The money or property does not have to be transferred directly to the plaintiff in order for the defendant to claim the deduction. The transfer requirement can be met if the defendant transfers the money or property to an escrow agent or trustee that is later required to deliver the money or property pursuant to the settlement, or to the court that has jurisdiction over the case.[3] However, if the transfer is not made directly to the plaintiff and is instead made to an escrow account, trust or court, the transfer must discharge the defendant's liability to the plaintiff in order for the economic performance requirement to be met.[4] The transfer must take the funds out of the defendant's control in order for the deduction to be allowed.[5]

If a defendant deducts amounts paid to satisfy a contested liability and these amounts are later refunded (for example, because the defendant is found not to be liable for the plaintiff's injuries), the defendant must include those amounts in gross income in the year they are refunded.[6]

643. What is a designated settlement fund?

A designated settlement fund (DSF) is a fund that is established pursuant to a court order to completely extinguish a defendant's liability with respect to a claim for personal injury, death or property damage.[7]

1. Treas. Reg. §1.461-1(a)(2).
2. IRC Sec. 461(f), Treas. Reg. §1.461-2(a)(1).
3. Treas. Reg. §1.461-2(c).
4. Treas. Reg. §1.461-2(e)(2)(ii).
5. See Treas. Reg. §1.461-2(c)(1)(ii).
6. Treas. Reg. §§1.461-2(a)(3), 1.111-1.
7. IRC Sec. 468B.

A DSF must also meet the following requirements: (1) no amounts may be transferred to it except in the form of "qualified payments," (2) it must be administered by persons, a majority of whom are independent from the defendant transferring the claim, (3) it must be established for the purpose of resolving and satisfying claims against the defendant (or related persons) for claims arising out of personal injury, death or property damage, (4) the defendant (and related persons) may not hold any beneficial interest in the income or corpus of the fund, and (5) the defendant must make an election to treat the fund as a DSF.[1]

A "qualified payment" is a payment made to a DSF pursuant to a court order other than payments that (1) may be transferred back to the defendant (or a related person) or (2) are transfers of stock or indebtedness of the defendant (or any related person).[2] Once a defendant has made the election to treat a fund as a DSF, it is revocable only with the consent of the Secretary of the Treasury.[3]

644. What is a qualified settlement fund?

A qualified settlement fund (QSF) is a type of designated settlement fund (DSF) that was developed in order to expand the use of DSFs in satisfying payment obligations under structured settlements. Unlike DSFs, QSFs can be used to facilitate the settlement of claims that do not involve personal injury or sickness. In order to qualify as a QSF, the following requirements apply:

(1) the QSF must be established pursuant to a governmental order (such as a court order or order of a state or the federal government) and must be subject to the continuing jurisdiction of that government entity,

(2) it must be established to resolve a claim (whether contested or uncontested) arising under (a) the Comprehensive Environmental Response, Compensation and Liability Act of 1980, (b) arising out of a tort, breach of contract, or violation of law or (c) designated by the Commissioner in a revenue ruling or revenue procedure, and

(3) the fund must be a trust under state law, or the assets must otherwise be segregated from other assets of the defendant-transferor (and related persons).[4]

QSFs are also subject to certain limitations on the types of litigation claims they can be used to satisfy. For example, if the liability arises under the workers' compensation act or a self-insured health plan, it may not be settled through a QSF.[5]

1. IRC Sec. 468B(d)(2).
2. IRC Sec. 468B(d)(1).
3. IRC Sec. 468B(d)(2)
4. Treas. Reg. §1.468B-1.
5. Treas. Reg. §1.468B-1(g).

645. What are the tax consequences of using a designated settlement fund or qualified settlement fund to satisfy a defendant's obligations under a structured settlement?

Because of the economic performance requirement of IRC Section 461, payments made to a designated settlement fund (DSF) arguably may not be deductible by the defendant because the plaintiff has not actually received the funds transferred into the account. Despite this, IRC Section 468B provides an exception and allows a defendant to deduct "qualified payments" made to a DSF.[1] Qualified settlement funds (QSFs) receive the same tax treatment as DSFs pursuant to the regulations under Section 468B.

A "qualified payment" is a payment made to a DSF or QSF pursuant to a court order other than payments that (1) may be transferred back to the defendant (or a related person), meaning that the transfer must be irrevocable, or (2) are transfers of stock or indebtedness of the defendant (or any related person).[2]

If the fund is a DSF or QSF that meets the requirements of Section 468B, the economic performance requirement will be considered met upon transfer to the DSF or QSF so that the defendant will be entitled to a deduction as payments are transferred into the fund regardless of when they are eventually paid to the plaintiff.

The gross income of DSFs and QSFs is taxed at the maximum tax rate applicable to trusts.[3] Qualified payments (see above) made to the fund are not considered income to the fund.[4] DSFs and QSFs are not subject to additional taxes, such as the alternative minimum tax, the accumulated earnings tax, the personal holding company tax or the capital gains tax.[5]

646. Can a defendant who is making payments under a structured settlement agreement assign responsibility for payments to a third party? What are the tax consequences of such an assignment?

The defendant-payor under a structured settlement can assign responsibility to provide future payments to the plaintiff who is receiving payments under the settlement if the settlement was negotiated to compensate the plaintiff for personal physical injuries or sickness.[6] If the assignment is a "qualified assignment," (see below) the assignee is not taxed on any amounts received from the defendant except to the extent that these amounts exceed the cost of any "qualified funding asset."[7]

A "qualified assignment" is defined as the assignment of a defendant's responsibility to make periodic payments as damages for a plaintiff's personal injury or sickness if the following requirements are met:

1. IRC 468B(a).
2. IRC Sec. 468B(d)(1).
3. IRC Sec. 468B(b)(1), Treas. Reg. §1.468B-2.
4. IRC Sec. 468B(b)(3).
5. Treas. Reg. §1.468B-2(g)
6. IRC Sec. 130(c).
7. IRC Sec. 130(a).

(1) the assignee is assuming liability from a party to the original lawsuit or settlement agreement,

(2) the periodic payments are fixed and determinable as to the amount and time of payment,

(3) the recipient of the payments does not have the right to accelerate, defer, increase or decrease the payments,

(4) the assignee's obligations under the structured settlement are no greater than the obligations of the person assigning the liability, and

(5) the periodic payments that the plaintiff receives under the structured settlement are excludable from the plaintiff's gross income under IRC Section 104.[1]

If the assignment satisfies the IRC requirements for a qualified assignment, any amounts that the defendant pays to the assignee who assumes payment obligations under the structured settlement will be tax-free to the assignee unless these amounts exceed the cost of purchasing a qualified funding asset (see below). If the cost of purchasing the qualified funding asset is less than the total amount that the assignee receives as consideration for assuming the settlement obligations, the difference must be included in the gross income of the assignee in the year in which the assignment took place.

A "qualified funding asset" is defined in the Code as an annuity contract used by the assignee to fund the periodic payments he or she has assumed under the structured settlement that meets the following requirements:

(1) the payment periods provided under the annuity are reasonably related to the periodic payments under the structured settlement (and the amounts of the annuity payments do not exceed the amounts to be paid under the structured settlement),

(2) the annuity contract is designated as an obligation purchased to satisfy the terms of the structured settlement, and

(3) the annuity contract must be purchased not more than sixty days before the assignment and not more than sixty days after the assignment.[2]

The basis of the qualified funding asset will be reduced by any amounts that the assignee is able to exclude from gross income. If the assignee later sells the annuity contract used to fund payments, any gain realized on the sale is taxed as ordinary income to the assignee.[3]

1. IRC Sec. 130(c).
2. IRC Sec. 130(d).
3. IRC Sec. 130(b).

647. Can a designated settlement fund (DSF) or qualified settlement fund (QSF) make a qualified assignment of its obligations to make periodic payments under a structured settlement?

Yes. If the DSF or QSF meets certain requirements, it can make a qualified assignment (see Q 646) of its obligations under a structured settlement. In order for an assignment of a defendant's obligations under a structured settlement to constitute a "qualified assignment" for tax purposes, the IRC requires that the assignee assume the liability from an original party to the lawsuit or agreement.[1] The IRS has provided the following guidance for determining when a DSF or QSF can be treated as an original party for purposes of Section 130(c):

(1) the plaintiff receiving periodic payments under the structured settlement must agree to the assignment by the DSF or QSF in writing,

(2) the assignment must relate to a claim for personal physical injury or sickness and either (a) the claim is being satisfied under a DSF established pursuant to a court order that completely extinguishes the defendant's tort liability with respect to the claim or (b) the claim is being satisfied under a QSF established to resolve or satisfy liability (whether contested or uncontested) that resulted from an event that has already occurred and given rise to at least one claim asserting liability,

(3) each qualified funding asset (see Q 646) purchased by the assignee in connection with the assignment by the DSF or QSF relates to a liability to a single plaintiff to make periodic payments for damages,

(4) the assignee is not related to the defendant who transferred the claim to the DSF or QSF, and

(5) the assignee does not control the DSF or QSF.[2]

In addition to these requirements, the DSF or QSF must continue to satisfy all other requirements of IRC Section 130 in order for the assignment to be qualified.

1. IRC Sec. 130(c).
2. Rev. Proc. 93-34, 1993-28 IRB 49.

PART VII: FEDERAL INCOME TAXATION

General Rules

648. Who must file a return?

The 2017 Tax Act modified the rules governing who is required to file a tax return for tax years beginning in 2018 through 2025. Because of the suspension of the personal exemption, unmarried individuals whose gross income exceeds the applicable standard deduction (see Q 750) are now required to file a tax return for the year.

Married individuals are required to file a tax return if the individual's gross income, when combined with his or her spouse's gross income, is more than the standard deduction that applies to a joint return and (1) the individual and his or her spouse at the close of the tax year shared the same household, (2) the individual's spouse does not file a separate return, and (3) neither the individual nor his or her spouse is a dependent of another taxpayer who has income (other than earned income) in excess of $500.[1]

A return must be filed by every individual whose gross income equals or exceeds the following limits in 2020:[2]

(1) Married persons filing jointly – $24,800 (if one spouse is sixty-five or older – $26,100; if both spouses are sixty-five or older – $27,400).

(2) Surviving spouse (see Q 754) – $24,800 (if sixty-five or older – $26,100).

(3) Head-of-household (see Q 755) – $18,650 (if sixty-five or older – $20,300).

(4) Single persons – $12,400 (if sixty-five or older – $14,050).

(5) Married persons filing separately – $12,400 (if sixty-five or older – $14,050).

(6) Dependents – every individual who may be claimed as a dependent of another must file a return for 2020 if he has unearned income in excess of $1,100 (plus any additional standard deduction if the individual is blind or elderly) or total gross income that exceeds the sum of any additional standard deduction if the individual is blind or elderly plus the greater of (a) $1,100 or (b) the lesser of (i) $350 plus earned income, or (ii) $6,400.

Blind taxpayers may need to attach supporting documentation to a tax return to support a claim for the additional standard deduction. The additional standard deduction for taxpayers who are blind at the end of the tax year is not considered when determining a taxpayer's filing threshold amount.

---

1. IRC Sec. 6012(f).
2. IRC Secs. 6012(a), 63(c), 151; P.L.115-97, Rev. Proc. 2018-57, Rev. Proc. 2019-44.

Under prior law, certain parents whose children are required to file a return may be permitted to include the child's income over $2,100 on their own return, thus avoiding the necessity of the child filing a return. See Q 680. The 2017 Tax Act, provides new rules with respect to the unearned income of minors. That income will now be taxed at the rates applicable to trusts and estates, while the earned income of minors will be taxed at the ordinary income tax rates applicable to single filers. See Q 680.

A taxpayer with self-employment income must file a return if *net* self-employment income is $400 or more. See Q 774.

Planning Point: A taxpayer must file a return if any of the following special taxes are due:

1. Alternative minimum tax (see Q 769 for more information on the expanded AMT exemption that applies after 2017).

2. Additional tax on a qualified plan, including an individual retirement arrangement (IRA), or other tax-favored account. Taxpayers filing a return only because this tax is owed can file Form 5329 by itself.

3. Household employment taxes. Taxpayers can file Schedule H by itself if filing a return only because this tax is owed.

4. Social Security and Medicare tax on tips a taxpayer did not report to an employer or on wages received from an employer who did not withhold these taxes.

5. Recapture of first-time homebuyer credit.

6. Write-in taxes, including uncollected Social Security and Medicare or RRTA tax on tips that were reported to an employer or on group-term life insurance and additional taxes on health savings accounts.

7. Recapture taxes.

8. Additional tax on a health savings account (HSA), Archer MSA, or Medicare Advantage MSA distributions. If the taxpayer is filing a return only because he or she owes this tax, he or she can file Form 5329 by itself.

9. Wages of $108.28 or more from a church or qualified church-controlled organization that is exempt from employer Social Security and Medicare taxes.

Even if not required to file a federal tax return, a taxpayer may want to file one if withholdings of tax have occurred, or he or she is eligible for a refundable credit, such as the Earned Income Credit.

649. Must a taxpayer make estimated tax payments and what is the penalty for failure to make a required installment payment?

Taxpayers are generally required to pay estimated tax if failure to pay would result in an underpayment (see below) of federal income tax for the current taxable year.[1] The

1. IRC Sec. 6654.

computation of estimated tax for the tax year includes the alternative minimum tax, additional Medicare tax, net investment income tax, and self-employment tax (see Q 767 and Q 774, respectively).[1] An underpayment is the amount by which a required installment payment exceeds the amount, if any, paid on or before the due date of that installment (due dates are April 15, June 15, September 15 of the current tax year and January 15 of the following tax year).[2] The required amount for each installment is 25 percent of the *required annual payment*.[3]

Generally, the "required annual payment" is the lesser of (a) 90 percent of the tax shown on the return for the taxable year (or, if no return is filed, 90 percent of the tax for the year), or (b) 100 percent of the tax shown on the return for the preceding year (but only if the preceding taxable year consisted of twelve months and a return was filed for that year).[4] However, if an individual's adjusted gross income for the previous tax year exceeded $150,000 ($75,000 in the case of married individuals filing separately), the required annual payment is the lesser of (a) 90 percent of the current year's tax, as described above, or (b) the *applicable percentage* of the tax shown on the return for the preceding year (110 percent).[5]

On the other hand, the taxpayer may make required installments pursuant to the "annualized income installment" method if the amount of tax so computed is less than the tax computed pursuant to the two alternatives described above. This method requires the taxpayer to compute the tax for the current year by annualizing the taxable income, alternative minimum taxable income and adjusted self-employment income for the months in the taxable year ending before the due date of the installment. For the first quarter installment payment, the taxpayer must pay 22.5 percent of the annualized tax. For the second quarter installment payment, the taxpayer must pay 45 percent of the annualized tax less the amount of tax paid with the first installment. For the third and fourth installment payments, the taxpayer must pay 67.5 percent and 90 percent, respectively minus the aggregate amount of tax paid with the prior installments.[6]

Regardless of the method used to calculate estimated taxes, there is no penalty for failure to make estimated payments if: (1) the tax shown on the return for the taxable year (or, if no return is filed, the tax) after the deduction for tax withholdings is less than $1,000; or (2) the taxpayer owed no tax for the preceding year (a taxable year consisting of twelve months) and the taxpayer was a U.S. citizen or resident for the entire taxable year.[7] Otherwise, underpayment results in imposition of an interest penalty, compounded daily, at an annual rate three percentage points greater than the short-term applicable federal rate as adjusted quarterly.[8] (See Q 677.)

1. IRC Sec. 6654(d)(2)(B)(i).
2. IRC Secs. 6654(b), 6654(c).
3. IRC Sec. 6654(d)(1)(A).
4. IRC Sec. 6654(d)(1)(B).
5. IRC Sec. 6654(d)(1)(C).
6. IRC Sec. 6654(d)(2).
7. IRC Sec. 6654(e).
8. IRC Sec. 6621(a)(2).

If on the Form 1040 for the current year, the taxpayer elects to apply an overpayment to the succeeding year's estimated taxes, the overpayment is treated as a credit with respect to installments of estimated tax due on or after the date(s) the overpayment arose in the order in which they become due. Depending on the amount of the overpayment, it may be sufficient to avoid or minimize the penalty for failure to pay estimated income tax with respect to such tax year.[1] For application of the estimated tax to trusts and estates, see Q 785.

650. What is an individual's "taxable year"?

The basic *period* for computing income tax liability is one year, known as the *taxable year*. The taxable year may be either (a) the calendar year or (b) a fiscal year. A "calendar year" is a period of twelve months ending on December 31. A "fiscal year" is a period of twelve months ending on the last day of a month other than December.[2]

Although most taxpayers report tax liability based on a calendar year, a taxpayer may choose to report tax liability based on a fiscal year. However, whichever year is used, it must generally correspond to the taxpayer's accounting period.[3] Thus, if the taxpayer's accounting period is based on a fiscal year, tax liability cannot be determined by the calendar year. But if the taxpayer has no accounting period and does not keep books, a calendar year must be used.[4] Once a tax year has been chosen, the taxpayer cannot change from a calendar year to a fiscal year or vice versa without the permission of the Internal Revenue Service.[5]

A principal partner must use the same tax year as the partnership and cannot change to a different tax year unless it establishes to the IRS that there is a business purpose for doing so.[6] Under certain circumstances, partnerships, S corporations, and personal service corporations must use the calendar year for computing income tax liability.[7]

A short period income tax return must be filed if (1) the taxpayer changes an annual accounting period, or if (2) the taxpayer has been in existence for only part of a taxable year.[8] For this purpose, a short period is considered a "taxable year."[9]

For an individual taxpayer, if a short period income tax return is required due to a change in accounting period, the income during the short period must be annualized, and deductions and exemptions prorated.[10] The computation is as follows:

1. Rev. Rul. 99-40, 1999-2 CB 441.
2. IRC Secs. 441(a), 441(b), 441(d), 441(e).
3. IRC Sec. 441(f)(1).
4. IRC Sec. 441(g).
5. IRC Sec. 442.
6. IRC Sec. 706(b)(2).
7. See IRC Secs. 441(i), 706(b), 1378.
8. IRC Sec. 443(a).
9. IRC Sec. 441(b)(3).
10. IRC Secs. 443(b), 443(c).

Step 1: Compute the adjusted gross income for the short tax year. Then subtract actual itemized deductions (do not take the standard deduction).

Step 2: Multiply the dollar amount of the personal exemptions (prior to 2018) by the number of months in the short year and divide that result by twelve.

Step 3: Subtract the amount in Step 2 from the amount in Step 1. This is modified taxable income.

Step 4: Multiply modified taxable income (Step 3) by twelve and divide the result by the number of months in the short period. This is the annualized income.

Step 5: Compute the tax on the annualized income (using the tax rate schedule then in effect).

Step 6: Multiply the tax (Step 5) by the number of months in the short period and divide the result by twelve. This amount is the tax for the short period.

However, if a short period income tax return is required by a taxpayer who was not in existence for the entire tax year, annualized income is not required.[1]

Generally, for the final regulations affecting taxpayers who want to adopt an annual accounting period (under IRC Section 441), or who must receive approval to adopt, change, or retain their annual accounting periods (under IRC Section 442), see Treasury Regulation Sections 1.441-0, 1.441-1, 1.441-2, 1.441-3, 1.441-4; TD 8996.[2]

More specifically, the rules for establishing a business purpose to justify the use of a taxable year and obtaining approval to adopt, change, or retain an annual accounting period are found in Revenue Procedure 2002-39.[3]

See Revenue Procedure 2003-62[4] for the exclusive procedures developed in accordance with IRC Section 442 that allow fiscal reporting year individuals (e.g., sole proprietors) to obtain automatic approval to change to calendar year reporting.

The exclusive procedures for (1) certain partnerships, (2) S corporations, (3) electing S corporations, (4) personal service corporations, and (5) trusts to obtain automatic approval to adopt, change, or retain their annual accounting period are set forth in Revenue Procedure 2006-46.[5]

1. Treas. Reg. §1.443-1(a)(2).
2. 67 Fed. Reg. 35009 (5-17-2002).
3. 2002-1 CB 1046, *as modified by*, Notice 2002-72, 2002-2 CB 843, *and further modified by*, Rev. Proc. 2003-79, 2003-2 CB 1036.
4. 2003-2 CB 299, *modifying, amplifying, and superseding*, Rev. Proc. 66-50, 1966-2 CB 1260, and *modifying and superseding*, Rev. Proc. 81-40, 1981-2 CB 604. See also Ann. 2003-49, 2003-2 CB 339.
5. 2006-45 IRB 859.

651. What are the basic steps in computing an individual's tax liability?

The computation is made up of these basic steps:

...Determine gross income for the taxable year (see Q 652 to Q 710).

...Subtract certain deductions from gross income to arrive at adjusted gross income (see Q 715, Q 716).

...Prior to 2018 and after 2025, determine the number of personal and dependency exemptions (multiplied by the personal exemption amount and deducted from adjusted gross income) (see Q 726, Q 727).

...Compute total amount of itemized deductions (subject to certain limitations) (see Q 729 to Q 743) and compare that amount to the *standard deduction* (see Q 750), and (generally) the greater amount, is also deducted (in addition to exemptions, which were suspended from 2018-2025) to arrive at taxable income.

...The proper tax rate is applied to taxable income to determine the tax (see Appendix A).

...The following amounts are subtracted from the tax to determine the net tax payable or overpayment refundable: (1) credits (see Q 756), and (2) prepayments toward the tax (e.g., tax withheld by an employer and/or estimated tax payments).

The computation of the alternative minimum tax is explained in Q 767.

Gross Income

652. What items are included in gross income? What items are excluded from gross income?

Gross income includes all income (whether derived from labor or capital) *unless* specifically excluded by the Internal Revenue Code. The most common items included in gross income are salary, fees, commissions, business profits, interest and dividends, rents, alimony received prior to 2019, and gains from the sale of property – but not the mere return of capital.[1]

Some of the specifically excluded items from gross income that are received tax-free by an individual taxpayer are: gifts and inheritances;[2] gain (subject to limitation) from the sale of a personal residence (see Q 7843); at least 50 percent of gain (subject to limitation) from the sale of certain qualified small business stock held for more than five years (see Q 7521 and Q 7522); interest on certain state, city or other political subdivision bonds (see Q 7660); Social Security and railroad retirement benefits (subject to limitations – see Q 678); veterans' benefits in any form specifically covering personal injuries or sickness from active service in the armed forces (but not including retirement pay);[3] Workers' Compensation Act payments (subject to limitation);[4] death proceeds of life insurance;[5]

1. IRC Sec. 61(a).
2. IRC Sec. 102.
3. IRC Sec. 104(a)(4).
4. IRC Sec. 104(a)(1).
5. IRC Secs. 101(a).

amounts paid or expenses incurred by an employer for qualified adoption expenses in connection with the adoption of a child by an employee if the amounts are furnished pursuant to an adoption assistance program;[1] contributions to a "Medicare Advantage MSA" by the Department of Health and Human Services;[2] exempt-interest dividends from mutual funds (see Q 7935); interest on certain U.S. savings bonds purchased after 1989 and used to pay higher education expenses (within limits – see Q 7686);[3] contributions paid by an employer to Health Savings Accounts;[4] distributions from Health Savings Accounts used to pay qualified medical expenses;[5] and federal subsidies for prescription drug plans.[6]

653. How are the commissions, including insurance commissions, of a sales representative taxed?

Commissions are generally taxable as ordinary income in the year received, regardless of whether the taxpayer is on a cash or accrual method of accounting, or whether the taxpayer has a contingent obligation to repay them. Commissions on insurance premiums, however, are subject to special rules. (See Q 3519 regarding the limitation on certain employers' deductions.)

General rule for insurance commissions. First year and renewal commissions are taxable to the agent as ordinary income in the year received. If the agent works on commission with a drawing account, the amount the agent reports depends upon the contract with the company. In a technical advice memorandum, the IRS determined that cash advances made to an insurance sales agent *were* income in the year of receipt where there was no unconditional obligation to repay the advances, and any excess in advances over commissions earned were recoverable by the insurance company only by crediting earned commissions and renewals against such advances.[7] This position is consistent with other IRS rulings and prior case law.[8]

On the other hand, if the drawing account is a loan repayable by the agent (or upon which the agent remains personally liable) if the agent leaves, only commissions actually received are treated as income. To this point, in a Tax Court memorandum opinion, the Tax Court held that advance commissions received by an agent that were repayable on demand, bore interest and were secured by earned commissions, as well as by the personal liability of the agent, were not taxable compensation to the agent.[9]

Conversely, in several Tax Court cases, a salesman discharged from the obligation to repay advance commissions received in previous years was required to recognize income in the year of discharge.[10] The Tax Court determined that an agent had cancellation of indebtedness income where earned commissions had been used to offset advanced commissions (which were actually

1. IRC Sec. 137.
2. IRC Sec. 138.
3. See IRC Sec. 135.
4. IRC Sec. 106(d).
5. IRC Sec. 223(f)(1).
6. IRC Sec. 139A.
7. TAM 9519002.
8. See Rev. Rul. 83-12, 1983-1 CB 99 (also released as IR 82-150); *Geo. Blood Enter., Inc. v. Comm.*, TC Memo 1976-102. (See Rev. Proc. 83-4, 1983-1 CB 577 for guidance in complying with these rules.)
9. *Gales v. Comm.*, TC Memo 1999-27; acq. in result, 1999-2 CB 3.
10. *McIsaac v. Comm.*, TC Memo 1989-307. See also *Cox v. Comm.*, TC Memo 1996-241; *Diers v. Comm.*, TC Memo 2003-229.

loans). Accordingly, the agent received gross income at the time any pre-existing deficiency in her commission account was offset even though she never received an actual check.[1]

If the drawing account is guaranteed compensation, however, it is treated as income in addition to any commissions received in excess of the amount that offsets the agent's draw. This rule applies even if the agent uses the accrual method of accounting.[2]

Other Tax Court Cases Involving Insurance Commissions. In several cases, the Tax Court held that amounts received by a district manager upon termination of his agency contract is ordinary income rather than capital gain from the sale of a capital asset, if the money received was compensation for the termination of the right to receive future income in the form of commissions.[3] The Tax Court also held that termination payments received by a retiring insurance agent who did not own any company assets he returned to the insurance company was not capital gain from a sale of capital assets, but instead were ordinary income.[4]

Finally, from the prospective of the insurance company, for cash advances treated as loans, the procedure by which an insurance company may obtain automatic consent to change its method of accounting for cash advances on commissions paid to its agents from (1) deducting a cash advance in the taxable year paid to the agent to (2) deducting a cash advance in the taxable year earned by the agent is set forth in Revenue Procedure 2001-24.[5]

654. How are the commissions on policies purchased by an insurance agent taxed?

Commissions on a life insurance policy purchased by the agent, on the agent's own life or on the life of another, are taxable to the agent as ordinary income. Such commissions are considered compensation, not a reduction in the cost of the underlying policy.[6] This rule applies to brokers as well as to other life insurance salesmen.[7]

655. How are an insurance agent's commissions taxed if they are received pursuant to a deferred income plan?

If, before retiring, an insurance agent enters into an irrevocable agreement with the insurance company to receive renewal commissions in level installments over a period of years, only the amount of the annual installment will be taxable each year – instead of the full amount of commissions as they accrue.[8] Although the *Oates* case and Revenue Ruling 60-31 concern deferred compensation arrangements during retirement years, the same principle should apply if the agent, during the agent's lifetime, elects a level commission arrangement for payments after death.

1. *Harper v. Comm.*, TC Summary Op. 2007-133.
2. See Rev. Rul. 75-541, 1975-2 CB 195; *Security Assoc. Agency Ins. Corp. v. Comm.*, TC Memo 1987-317; *Dennis v. Comm.*, TC Memo 1997-275.
3. *Clark v. Comm.*, TC Memo 1994-278. See also *Farnsworth v. Comm.*, TC Memo 2002-29, *Parker v. Comm.*, TC Memo 2002-305.
4. *Baker v. Comm.*, 118 TC 452 (2002), *aff'd*, 2003 U.S. App. LEXIS 15509 (7th Cir. 2003). See also *Trantina. v. United States*, 512 F. 3d 567, 2008-1 USTC ¶50,138 (9th Cir. 2008).
5. 2001-10 IRB 788.
6. *Ostheimer v. U.S.*, 264 F.2d 789 (3rd Cir. 1959); Rev. Rul. 55-273, 1955-1 CB 221.
7. *Comm. v. Minzer*, 279 F.2d 338 (5th Cir. 1960); *Bailey v. Comm.*, 41 TC 663 (1964); *Mensik v. Comm.*, 37 TC 703 (1962), *aff'd*, 328 F.2d 147 (7th Cir. 1964).
8. *Comm. v. Oates*, 207 F.2d 711 (7th Cir. 1953); Rev. Rul. 60-31, 1960-1 CB 174; Let. Ruls. 9540033, 9245015.

In a private letter ruling, the IRS determined that an insurance agent's contributions of commissions to his company's nonqualified deferred compensation plan will not be includable in the agent's gross income or subject to self-employment tax until actually distributed.[1] In *Olmsted*, the insurance company, by agreement with the agent, substituted an annuity contract for its obligation to pay future renewal commissions. The Tax Court and the U.S. Court of Appeals for the Eighth Circuit held that the agreement was effective to defer tax until payments were received under the annuity.[2] However, the IRS did not acquiesce to the *Olmsted* decision.[3]

656. What are the tax consequences if an insurance agent sells or assigns the agent's right to receive renewal commissions?

Assignment of renewal commissions. If the agent assigns the right to renewal commissions as a gift, they are included in the agent's gross income as they are received by the donee (who does not report them as gross income).[4] In a Tax Court memorandum decision, the Tax Court held that an insurance agent was taxable on his commission income despite assigning it to his S corporation. The Tax Court noted that the agent was the true earner of the income and made no valid assignment of the employment agreement with the insurance company to the S corporation.[5] In *Zaal*, a 1998 memorandum decision, the Tax Court held that an agent's transfer of the right to receive renewal commissions was not valid for tax purposes because it was essentially an anticipatory assignment of income rather than a sale of property. Citing *Helvering v. Eubank*, the Tax Court held that the commission income was taxable to the agent rather than the corporation to which the rights were assigned.[6]

Sale of renewal commissions. In a bona fide, arm's length *sale* of a right to receive renewal commissions, as to the selling agent, the Second Circuit held that the consideration for the sale of the right to renewal commissions is ordinary income to the agent in the year received.[7] In *Cotlow*, the Second Circuit also determined that the renewals received by the purchaser are tax-free until the purchaser recovers the cost (i.e., the amount of consideration paid). Thereafter, the excess is fully taxable as it is received. Other cases have held that the purchaser must amortize the cost. In other words, the purchaser can recover (tax-free) that portion of the purchase price that the renewals received in that year bear to the total anticipated renewals.[8]

657. How are commissions received after the death of the insurance agent taxed?

Renewal commissions payable after the death of an insurance agent are "income in respect of a decedent" for income tax purposes. Additionally, the value of the right to the commissions is includable in the agent's gross estate for estate tax purposes. As income in respect of a decedent, the renewal commissions are taxable to the ultimate recipient of the

1. Let. Rul. 9609011.
2. *Comm. v. Olmsted Inc. Life Agency*, 35 TC 429 (1960), *aff'd*, 304 F.2d 16 (8th Cir. 1962).
3. Non-acq., 1961-2 CB 6.
4. *Helvering v. Eubank*, 311 U.S. 122 (1940); *Hall v. U.S.*, 242 F.2d 412 (7th Cir. 1957).
5. *Isom v. Comm.*, TC Memo 1995-383.
6. *Zaal v. Comm.*, TC Memo 1998-222. See also *McManus v. Comm.*, TC Summ. Op. 2006-68.
7. *Cotlow v. Comm.*, 228 F.2d 186 (2nd Cir. 1955); see also, *Turner v. Comm.*, 38 TC 304 (1962).
8. *Latendresse v. Comm.*, 243 F.2d 577 (7th Cir. 1957); *Hill v. Comm.*, 3 BTA 761 (1926).

commissions (e.g., the agent's estate, beneficiaries, or a trust) in the year in which they are received.[1] However, the person who reports such commissions as income is entitled to an income tax deduction (an itemized deduction) for the portion of federal estate taxes and generation-skipping transfer taxes attributable to their inclusion in the decedent's gross estate. If the decedent has purchased renewal commissions from another agent, the recipient will be allowed to amortize any portion of the decedent's cost unrecovered at death.[2]

If prior to receipt of the renewal commissions, the recipient sells or otherwise disposes of the right to commissions, all income is accelerated as the recipient must include the entire fair market value of the right to the commissions in the year of sale or other disposition (e.g., the recipient gifted the right to another person). On the other hand, if the recipient dies prior to receiving the commissions, the fair market value of the right to commissions will not be included on the final income tax return. In that case, the person who receives the income right from the second decedent by will or inheritance must include such commissions in gross income (as income in respect of a decedent) as they are received.[3]

658. How are an insurance agent's commissions treated for self-employment tax purposes?

Termination payments (as distinguished from renewal commissions) received by a former insurance salesman are not treated as self-employment income if: (1) the amount is received after the termination of the agent's agreement to perform for the company; (2) the agent does not perform services for the company after the date of the termination of the service agreement and before the end of the taxable year; (3) the agent enters into a covenant not to compete with the company for at least a one-year period beginning on the date of the termination; and (4) the amount of the payment (a) depends primarily on policies sold by or credited to the agent's account during the last year of the service agreement or to the extent such policies remain in effect for some period after termination of service, or both, and (b) does not depend to any extent on the length of service or overall earnings from services performed for such company (without regard to whether eligibility for payment depends on length of service).[4] For termination payments that do not fall within the above description, earlier case law and rulings may apply.

In a Tax Court summary opinion, the Tax Court distinguished the self-employment tax treatment of renewal commissions as compared to termination payments. In that case, the Tax Court found that the insurance agent's renewal commissions were self-employment income subject to self-employment tax because they were tied to the quantity and quality of the taxpayer's prior labor, and derived from the carrying on of the taxpayer's business as an independent insurance agent.[5] Additionally, the Tax Court held that the insurance agent was subject to self-employment

1. *Latendresse v. Comm.*, above; *Est. of Goldstein v. Comm.*, 33 TC 1032 (1960), *aff'd*, 340 F.2d 24 (2nd Cir. 1965); *Est. of Remington v. Comm.*, 9 TC 99 (1947).
2. *Latendresse v. Comm.*, above.
3. IRC Sec. 691(a); Treas. Reg. §1.691(a)-1.
4. IRC Sec. 1402(k).
5. *Gilbert v. Comm.*, TC Summary Op. 2005-176.

tax because he was not a statutory employee, but instead engaged in a self-employed trade or business activity.[1]

Finally, the Eleventh Circuit held that the FICA statute requiring an employer to pay a portion of the FICA tax on behalf of an "employee" does not impliedly provide a private cause of action to purported "employees" – in this case, insurance agents claiming they had been improperly classified as independent contractors – to sue their purported "employer" for nonpayment of the employer's portion of FICA taxes.[2]

659. What is an insurance premium rebate?

An insurance premium rebate, which is illegal in most states, is a transaction in which a life insurance agent returns all or a portion of a commission to the purchaser, or simply pays the policy's first-year premium without contribution from the purchaser. The transaction is economically feasible to the insurance agent because the commission, allowance and/or bonus paid by the insurance company to the agent for the sale of the policy often exceeds the policy premium. As a result, the purchaser may ultimately receive free or less expensive life insurance coverage. See Q 660 and Q 661 for the tax consequences of insurance premium rebating to the insurance agent and the purchaser, respectively.

660. What are the income tax consequences of rebating premiums to the insurance agent?

As discussed in Q 659, most states have anti-rebating statutes that prohibit the sharing of insurance commissions with unlicensed persons. The tax consequences to the agent may vary, depending on the laws of the agent's state of residence, as well as the position of the circuit court in that jurisdiction. In *Alex v. Commissioner*, a Ninth Circuit case, an insurance agent in a state with an anti-rebating statute rebated a portion of his premium to the purchaser. The agent argued that the rebated portion of the premium was not taxable because it was in essence a price adjustment (as if the cost of the insurance had been adjusted downward by the amount of the rebate).[3] The Ninth Circuit disagreed with this characterization and held that the entire commission earned was taxable.[4]

Furthermore, in the *Alex* case, the court decided that the agent could not offset his commission income by deducting the rebate as a business expense deduction because the Code disallows deductions for illegal payments that under a generally enforced state law subjects the payor to a criminal penalty or loss of a license or privilege to engage in a trade or business.[5] Compare that decision to *Custis v. Commissioner,* a Tax Court memorandum opinion in which the Tax Court allowed an agent to deduct the amount of rebated premiums as a business expense under IRC Section 162 because his state's anti-rebating statute was not generally enforced.

1. *Byer v. Comm.*, TC Summary Op. 2006-125.
2. See *McDonald v. Southern Farm Bureau Life Ins. Co.*, 291 F. 3d 718, 2002 U.S. App. LEXIS 9110 (11th Cir. 2002).
3. *Alex v. Comm.*, 628 F.2d 1222 (9th Cir. 1980), *aff'g* 70 TC 322 (1978).
4. See also *Custis v. Comm.*, TC Memo 1982-296; *Kreisberg v. Comm.*, TC Memo 1979-420.
5. IRC Sec. 162(c)(2). See *Kreisberg*, above.

Conversely, in a Tenth Circuit decision, the court held that an insurance agent who expressly waived the right to receive basis commissions from clients was not required to include the waived commission in gross income. In this case, the agent was obligated to pay only the net premiums due on the policies he sold to the insurance company. By waiving his right to basic commissions that were never paid to him, the agent was not in actual or constructive receipt of those commissions that would result in taxable income. However, the court did not address the issue of whether the agent's waiver violated the state's anti-rebating laws.[1]

661. What are the income tax consequences of rebating premiums for the purchaser?

A federal district court and the Tax Court have determined that the purchasers of universal and whole life policies are subject to tax on the full amount of any premiums illegally rebated to them by the agents who sold the policies.[2] The courts rejected the purchasers' argument that the agents' reimbursements were really price adjustments. The court in *Woodbury* stated that the reimbursements were analogous to kickbacks and, as such, were includable in the purchasers' gross income. The court also rejected the purchasers' argument that their tax liability should be limited to the term element of the universal life policies. The fact that the purchasers did not intend to renew the policies did not convert the universal policies into term life insurance for tax purposes. The Tax Court has expressed its agreement with the district court's conclusions set forth in the *Woodbury* decision. In *Wentz*, it noted that the insurance agent was, in effect, a purchaser of the policies, and that he realized income in the amount of the kickbacks. Both the Tax Court and the *Woodbury* district court stated that the taxation of both the seller and the purchaser engaged in such an illegal scheme was permissible.

In a technical advice memorandum, the Service concluded that the purchaser of a life insurance policy is subject to income tax on the value of the free insurance coverage obtained as a result of receiving a premium rebate.[3] However, the Service stated that the valuation process itself was outside the scope of the memoranda; thus, it is unclear how the Service will calculate the actual value of the free coverage. (See Q 4009 and Q 3936 for an explanation of how employer-provided life insurance coverage is valued under split dollar arrangements and qualified retirement plans, respectively.)

662. Who is taxed on the income from property that is transferred to a minor under a uniform "Gifts to Minors" act?

As a general rule, the income is taxable to the minor. However, in the case of *unearned* income of most children under age nineteen (age twenty-four, if the child is a full-time student) different rules apply. The 2017 Tax Act aimed to simplify the treatment of unearned income of minors by applying the tax rates that apply to trusts and estates to this income. Therefore, *earned* income of minors will be taxed according to the individual income tax rates prescribed

---

1. *Worden v. Comm.*, 2 F.3d 359 (10th Cir. 1993).
2. *Woodbury v. U.S.*, 93-2 USTC ¶50,528 (D. N.D. 1993), *aff'd per curium*, 27 F.3d 572 (8th Cir. 1994); *Wentz v. Comm.*, 105 TC 1 (1995); *Haderlie v. Comm.*, TC Memo 1997-525.
3. TAMs 9214008, 9214007, 9214006.

for single filers,[1] and *unearned* income of minors will be taxed according to the applicable tax bracket that would apply if the income was that of a trust or estate (for both income that is subject to ordinary income tax rates and in determining the capital gains rate that will apply if long-term capital gains treatment is appropriate).[2]

Prior to 2018, the unearned income taxable to the child generally was taxed at the parents' marginal rate when it exceeded $2,100 (in 2015 to 2018, as adjusted for inflation).[3] To the extent that income from the transferred property was used for the minor's support, it may have been taxed to the person who is legally obligated to support the minor.[4] State laws differ as to a parent's obligation to support. The income will be taxable to the parent only to the extent that it is actually used to discharge or satisfy the parent's obligation under state law.[5]

663. When is a cash basis taxpayer deemed to "receive" income? How is the doctrine of constructive receipt applicable?

Generally, the inclusion of gross income (the first step in the computation of taxable income) must be determined pursuant to the taxpayer's regular method of accounting.[6] The two commonly accepted methods of accounting are the cash basis method and the accrual basis method.[7]

Under the cash basis method, all items deemed to be gross income (whether in the form of cash, property or services) are generally includable in the taxable year in which they are actually or constructively received.[8] For example, a taxpayer who receives a salary check in December of 2019 but does not cash or deposit it until January of 2020 must include the wage income in 2019. However, this would not be the result if substantial restrictions on the check made it non-negotiable in 2019 or if the issuer was insolvent.[9]

For cash method taxpayers, the doctrine of constructive receipt of income goes beyond actual receipt of income in determining the timing of the inclusion of items of gross income. Under this doctrine, a cash method taxpayer is deemed to receive (and, thus must report) income that has been credited to the account or set apart in such a way that the taxpayer has free access to it at any time – even though it has not actually been received by the taxpayer.[10] For example, a cash method taxpayer must report the interest credited to a bank savings account in the taxable year it is credited without regard to whether the interest is withdrawn or remains in the account (see Q 7913). On the other hand, in a private letter ruling, the IRS ruled that a cash method employee who has the mere right to make an election to cash out future vacation

1. IRC Sec. 1(j)(4)(B).
2. IRC Sec. 1(j)(4).
3. Rev. Proc. 2015-53, Rev. Proc. 2016-55.
4. Rev. Rul. 56-484, 1956-2 CB 23; Rev. Rul. 59-357, 1959-2 CB 212.
5. IRC Sec. 677(b).
6. IRC Sec. 446(a).
7. IRC Sec. 446(c).
8. IRC Sec. 451(a); Treas. Reg. §1.451-2(a).
9. *Chapman v. Comm.*, TC Memo 1982-307; *Baxter v. Comm.*, 816 F.2d 493 (9th Cir. 1987), *rev'g in part* TC Memo 1985-378.
10. Treas. Reg. §1.451-2. See, e.g., *Visco v. Comm*, 281 F.3d 101 (3rd Cir. 2002), *aff'g*, TC Memo 2000-77 (employment-related dispute).

leave under the employer's plan would not be in constructive receipt of the vacation pay if the employee chose not to make such an election.[1]

Significantly, constructive receipt occurs only if the taxpayer's control or access to the income is unrestricted. Thus, a sum is not constructively received if it is only conditionally credited, or if it is indefinite in amount, or if the payor has no funds, or if it is subject to any other substantial limitation. If a taxpayer's access to income is subject to the surrender of a valuable right, such as the surrender of a death benefit in order to be entitled to income generated by the underlying insurance policy, the Tax Court has held that the constructive receipt doctrine does not apply under those circumstances.[2]

664. What is a below-market loan?

Generally, a below-market loan is any demand loan with an interest rate that is below the applicable federal rate (see below) *or* any term loan in which the amount received by the borrower exceeds the present value of all payments due under the loan. A demand loan is any loan that is payable in full at any time on the demand of the lender, or that has an indefinite maturity. All other loans are generally term loans.[3] IRC Section 7872 essentially recasts a below-market loan into two phantom transactions (meaning they are deemed to have occurred, even though they did not actually occur): (1) an arm's-length loan pursuant to which the borrower paid (but obviously did not) interest to the lender at the applicable federal rate, and (2) a deemed transfer of interest to the lender that the borrower should have, but did not, pay to the lender ("imputed transfer").[4]

In other words, in (1) above, it is as if the lender transferred to the borrower the amount of interest at the applicable federal rate the borrower should have paid the lender less the amount of interest, if any, that the borrower actually did pay to the lender; and, subsequently in (2) above, the borrower is treated as paying the amount of foregone interest to the lender as interest. Generally, the lender must report the imputed transfer of the foregone interest as interest income. Conversely, depending on the relationship of the borrower to the lender, the borrower may or may not be required to include the foregone interest in income (for example if the loan was between family members the foregone interest that is deemed to have been received may be treated as an income tax-free gift). Additionally, depending on the nature of the borrowing, the borrower may or may not be entitled to an interest deduction (i.e., used the borrowed funds for a vacation).

> *Example:* On January 1, 2018, Samuel loans Asher $100,000 (interest free) payable on demand. As of December 31, 2018, the loan remains outstanding. Obviously, because the loan bears no interest, it is a below-market loan. Since the 2018 *blended annual rate* is 2.03 percent (see below), IRC Section 7872 would recast the below-market loan into the following two transactions:
>
> 1) For tax year 2018, Samuel is deemed to have transferred $2,030 of foregone interest to Asher, the amount Asher should have paid Samuel (even though this not actually occur).

1. Let. Rul. 200130015.
2. See *Cohen v. Comm.*, 39 TC 1055 (1963); *Nesbitt v. Commissioner*, 43 TC 629 (1965).
3. IRC Secs. 7872(e), 7872(f).
4. Prop. Treas. Reg. §1.7872-1(a).

2) In turn, Asher is deemed to have paid the $2,030 of foregone interest to Samuel (even though Asher did not make the payment).

The tax consequences of below-market loans are determined by the relationship between the borrower and the lender. Therefore, in the example above, (1) if Asher and Samuel were brothers, the below-market low could be a gift loan (Q 665) or (2) if Asher was an employee of Samuel, a compensation-related loan or (3) if Asher is a shareholder of Samuel, Inc., a corporation-shareholder loan (Q 666).

Additionally, the below-market loan rules apply to any below-market loan in which one of the principal purposes is tax avoidance or, to the extent provided for in regulations, in which the interest arrangements have a significant effect on the federal tax liability of either party. (See Q 667.)[1] Provided one of the principal purposes is not tax avoidance, the Service has determined that the interest arrangements of certain loans (including, for example, tax-exempt obligations, obligations of the U.S. government, life insurance policy loans, etc.) *will not* be considered as having a significant effect on the federal tax liability of either party.[2]

Applicable Federal Rate

The applicable federal rates are determined by the Secretary on a monthly basis.[3] The Secretary may by regulation permit a rate that is lower than the applicable federal rate to be used under certain circumstances.[4]

The applicable federal rate (see Q 677) for demand loans is the short-term rate (compounded semiannually) in effect during the period for which the foregone interest is being determined.[5] If the principal amount of such loan remains outstanding for the entire calendar year, foregone interest is equal to the *excess of* the "blended annual rate" for that calendar year multiplied by the outstanding principal balance *over* any interest payable on the loan properly allocable to the calendar year. The blended annual rate is published annually with the AFRs for the month of July.[6]

For term loans, the applicable federal rate is the corresponding federal rate (i.e., short-, mid-, or long-term) in effect on the day the loan was made, compounded semiannually.[7]

Reporting Requirements

In any taxable year in which the lender has imputed interest income or the borrower either has imputed income and/or claims an interest deduction in the amount of the forgone interest, he or she is required to: (1) attach a statement to Form 1040 explaining that it relates to the amount includable in income or is deductible by reason of the below-market loan rules; (2) provide the name, address and taxpayer identification number of the other party; and

1. IRC Sec. 7872(c)(1).
2. Temp. Treas. Reg. §1.7872-5T.
3. IRC Sec. 1274(d).
4. See IRC Sec. 1274(d)(1)(D).
5. IRC Sec. 7872(f)(2)(B).
6. Rev. Rul. 86-17, 1986-1 CB 377.
7. IRC Sec. 7872(f)(2)(A).

(3) specify the amount includable or deductible and the mathematical assumptions and method used in computing the amounts imputed.[1]

665. What are the income tax consequences of a below-market loan that is categorized as a gift loan?

A below-market demand or term loan is a gift loan if the foregone interest is in the nature of a gift.[2] As explained in Q 664, the foregone interest is the difference between the interest computed at the applicable federal rate that should have been paid to the lender less the amount actually paid by the borrower to the lender. In two phantom transactions, (1) the lender is deemed to have transferred the foregone interest to the borrower that (2) the borrower is deemed to have paid the lender as interest.[3] In the case of below-market gift loans between natural persons, the transfer is treated, for both the borrower and the lender, as occurring on the last day of the borrower's taxable year.[4] So, if the borrower and lender were related (i.e., parent and child) or had a close personal relationship (friends), the amount of foregone interest the borrower "received" from the lender is a gift. Since gifts are not included in the gross income of the recipient, it is not taxable. Conversely, the foregone interest the borrower is deemed to have transferred to the lender is taxable to the lender as interest income. Finally, the deductibility of the deemed interest payment to the lender depends on how the borrower used the borrowed funds (similar to the way the deductibility of interest actually paid is determined, i.e., whether the borrowed funds were used for personal or investment purposes, etc. – see Q 8024).

Example: On January 1, 2018, Samuel loans his brother, Asher $100,000 (interest free) payable on demand. Asher uses the borrowed funds to buy investment securities. As of December 31, 2018, the loan remains outstanding. Obviously, because the loan bears no interest, it is a below-market loan. Since the 2018 *blended annual rate* is 2.03 percent (see Q 664), IRC Section 7872 would recast the below-market loan into the following two transactions:

For tax year 2018, Samuel is deemed to have transferred $2,030 of foregone interest to Asher, the amount Asher should have paid Samuel (even though this did not actually occur).

In turn, Asher is deemed to have paid the $2,030 of foregone interest to Samuel (even though Asher did not make the payment).

Since Asher is Samuel's brother, Samuel is deemed to have made a gift of the foregone interest to Asher (not taxable to Asher). In turn, the interest payment of that same amount Asher is deemed to have made to Samuel is interest income to Samuel (taxable to Samuel). Finally, because Asher used the borrowed funds to purchase investment securities, the phantom interest payment Asher is deemed to have made is deductible as investment interest.[5]

There is, however, a de minimis exception to the application of the below-market gift loan rules. In other words, if applicable, there would be no tax consequences to either the borrower or the lender. Pursuant to this de minimis exception, the rules do not apply to any below-market gift loan between individuals on any day the aggregate outstanding amount of *all* loans made

1. Prop. Treas. Reg. §1.7872-11(g).
2. IRC Sec. 7872(f)(3).
3. IRC Sec. 7872(a)(1).
4. IRC Sec. 7872(a)(2); Prop. Treas. Reg. §1.7872-6(b)(3).
5. IRC Sec. 163(d).

directly between them (spouses are treated as one person) does not exceed $10,000. This de minimis exception, however, does not apply to any gift loan directly attributable to the purchase or carrying of income-producing assets.[1]

Also applicable to below-market gift loans, a special rule limits the amount of the lender's taxable interest income to the borrower's net investment income for the year if: (1) the aggregate outstanding amount of all loans made directly between *individuals* does not exceed $100,000; (2) the lender has a signed statement from the borrower, stating the amount of the borrower's net investment income properly allocable to the loan; (3) the time or amount of investment income cannot be manipulated by the borrower, and (4) tax avoidance is not one of the principal purposes of the interest arrangements.[2] Net investment income equals the excess of investment income that includes, for this purpose, any amount that would be includable as interest on all deferred payment obligations were the original issue discount over investment expenses. Deferred payment obligations include annuities, U.S. savings bonds and short-term obligations. In any year in which the borrower's net investment income does not exceed $1,000, the amount of the lender's taxable interest income will be treated as zero.[3]

For the gift tax consequences of below-market gift loans, see Q 882.

666. What are the income tax consequences of a below-market loan treated as a compensation-related loan or a corporation-shareholder loan?

In the case of demand loans that are compensation-related (e.g., employer to employee, between an independent contractor and the individual for whom the services are provided and, under proposed regulations, between a partnership and a partner in certain circumstances) or corporation-shareholder loans, the same transfer and retransfer of forgone interest is deemed to have occurred as in the case of gift loans (see Q 665).[4] In a compensation-related loan, the amount of the foregone interest deemed to be transferred from the lender/employer to the borrower/employee will be treated as compensation paid from the former to the latter. Conversely, the foregone interest deemed to be paid from the borrower/employee will be treated as interest on the loan.

Example: On January 1, 2018, Samuel loans his employee, Asher $100,000 (interest free) payable on demand. Asher uses the borrowed funds to buy investment securities. As of December 31, 2018, the loan remains outstanding. Obviously, because the loan bears no interest, it is a below-market loan. Since the 2018 *blended annual rate* is 2.03 percent (see Q 664), IRC Section 7872 would recast the below-market loan into the following two transactions:

For tax year 2018, Samuel is deemed to have transferred $2,030 of foregone interest to Asher, the amount Asher should have paid Samuel (even though this did not actually occur).

In turn, Asher is deemed to have paid the $2,030 of foregone interest to Samuel (even though Asher did not make the payment).

1. IRC Sec. 7872(c)(2); Prop. Treas. Reg. §1.7872-8(b)(3).
2. IRC Sec. 7872(d)(1); Prop. Treas. Reg. §§1.7872-8(c), 1.7872-11(g)(3).
3. IRC Sec. 7872(d)(1)(E).
4. IRC Secs. 7872(c)(1)(B), 7872(c)(1)(C); Prop. Treas. Reg. §1.7872-4(c).

Since Asher is Samuel's employee, Samuel is deemed to have paid compensation in the amount of the foregone interest to Asher (taxable to Asher as wage income[1]). In turn, Asher is deemed to have made an interest payment of that same amount to Samuel (taxable to Samuel as interest income). Also, because Asher used the borrowed funds to purchase investment securities, the phantom interest payment is deductible as investment interest subject to the limitations on interest deductions (see Q 8024).[2] Finally, Samuel is entitled to a deduction for the compensation (assuming it is reasonable) he is deemed to have paid to Asher.[3]

Similar consequences result in the case of a corporation-shareholder loan (i.e., a below-market loan from the corporation to the shareholder). In that case, the foregone interest transferred from the corporation to the shareholder is treated as a taxable dividend (subject to the rules dealing with distributions from a corporation to shareholders).[4] Also, depending on the purpose of the borrowing, the shareholder may be entitled to an interest deduction. The corporation/lender is required to report taxable interest income. There will, however, be no deduction because a corporation is not allowed a deduction for dividends paid to shareholders.

In the case of compensation-related or corporation-shareholder below-market term loans, the lender is deemed to have transferred to the borrower and the borrower is deemed to have received a cash payment equal to the *excess of* the amount loaned *over* the present value (determined as of the date of the loan, using a discount rate equal to the applicable federal rate) of all payments required to be made under the terms of the loan.[5] The excess is treated as original issue discount and, generally, treated as transferred on the day the loan was made. In compensation-related loans, the lender/employer will be entitled to a compensation deduction for the amount treated as original issue discount interest and will include such amount as interest income as it accrues over the term of the loan. The borrower will have taxable compensation on the day the loan is made, but deductions (if allowed – see Q 8024) for the "imputed" interest can be taken only as such interest accrues over the loan period. With regard to corporation-shareholder loans, the same results occur except that the amount treated as original issue discount is considered a dividend, and there is no deduction available to the lender/corporation.

Similar to a gift loan, demand (or term) compensation-related loans and corporation-shareholder loans, are not subject to either of the above rules on any day the aggregate outstanding amount of all loans between the parties does not exceed $10,000 and tax avoidance is not one of the principal purposes of the interest arrangements.[6] With respect to term loans that are not gift loans, once the aggregate outstanding amount exceeds $10,000, this de minimis exception no longer applies, even if the outstanding balance is later reduced below $10,000.[7]

In a case of first impression involving below-market loans made to noncontrolling shareholders, the Tax Court held that the below-market loan rules may apply to a loan to a majority *or* a minority shareholder. The court also held that direct *and* indirect loans are subject to these rules.[8]

1. IRC Sec. 61(a)(1).
2. IRC Sec. 163(d).
3. IRC Sec. 162.
4. IRC Sec. 61(a)(7).
5. IRC Sec. 7872(b)(1).
6. IRC Sec. 7872(c)(3).
7. IRC Sec. 7872(f)(10).
8. *Rountree Cotton, Inc. v. Comm.*, 113 TC 422 (1999), *aff'd per curiam*, 87 AFTR 2d ¶2001-718 (10th Cir. 2001).

667. Can securities law restrictions apply to a below-market loan?

Section 402 of the Sarbanes-Oxley Act of 2002 (P.L. 107-204) amended Section 13 of the Securities and Exchange Act of 1934[1] to prohibit "issuers" (i.e., publicly-traded companies) from directly or indirectly (1) extending or maintaining credit, or (2) arranging for the extension of credit, or renewing an extension of credit, in the form of a personal loan to or for any director or executive officer (or equivalent) of that issuer. Extensions of credit maintained by a company on July 30, 2002 are not subject to the prohibition so long as no material modification is made to any term of the loan and the loan is not renewed on or after that date.

The narrow exceptions to this rule are loans made for the following purposes: home improvement; consumer credit; any extension of credit under an open-end credit plan; a charge card; or any extension of credit by a broker or dealer to buy, trade, or carry securities. To fall within the exception, the loan must also be (1) made or provided in the ordinary course of business of the company, (2) of a type that is generally made available by the company to the public, and (3) made on market terms, or terms that are no more favorable than those offered by the issuer to the general public for such extensions of credit.

So, since the narrow restrictions require loans to directors or executive officers to be made on market terms, it is unlikely that any of those loans would be below-market loans. On the other hand, it is possible that a loan that did not bear market interest would be a below-market loan for income tax purposes (because the rate might be less than the applicable federal rate) as well as being prohibited under section 402 of the Sarbanes-Oxley Act.

668. What is an installment sale? How is the gain taxed?

Editor's Note: Under the 2017 Tax Act, in 2020, the following changes apply:

The 0 percent capital gains rate will apply to joint filers who earn less than $80,000 (half of that amount for married taxpayers filing separately), heads of households who earn less than $53,600, single filers who earn less than $40,000, and trusts and estates with less than $2,650 in income.

The 15 percent rate will apply to joint filers who earn more than $80,000 but less than $496,600 (half of these amounts for married taxpayers filing separately), heads of households who earn more than $53,600 but less than $469,050, single filers who earn more than $40,000 but less than $441,450, and trusts and estates with more than $2,650 but less than $13,150 in income.

The 20 percent rate will apply to joint filers who earn more than $496,600 (half of that amount for married taxpayers filing separately), heads of households who earn more than $469,050, single filers who earn more than $441,450, and trusts and estates with more than $13,150 in income.[2] For the tax treatment of installment payments, see Q 702.

1. 15 USC 78m.
2. IRC Sec. 1(j)(5).

Gain resulting from an installment sale is reported using the installment method. Generally, dealers may not report their sales under the installment method (with exceptions for farm property and certain timeshares and residential lots).[1] See Q 7517 for the treatment of gain from the sale of publicly-traded stock. An installment sale is a sale or disposition of property (other than marketable securities, certain real property, and "inventory") where at least one payment is to be received by the seller after the close of the taxable year in which the disposition occurs.[2] It is not necessary that there be more than one payment.

> *Example:* On December 31, 2019, Asher transfers land to Samuel for $100,000. There is only one payment due on January 2, 2020. In spite of the fact that only one payment is required, the transaction qualifies as an installment sale because that payment is due at the end of the taxable year.

As explained below, installment reporting requires the taxpayer to report gain resulting from the underlying transaction (it does not apply to loss[3]) ratably over the term of the installment period. The taxpayer must use the installment method unless the taxpayer *elects out* on or before the due date, including extensions, for filing his federal income tax return for the taxable year in which the disposition occurred.[4] For many taxpayers, reporting gain on the installment method is beneficial because without it, the taxpayer would have to report the entire gain in the year of disposition (even though it may take years for the taxpayer to receive the installment payments). Thus, the installment method provides for the ratable reporting of income over the term of years in which payments are due. On the other hand, a taxpayer with a significant capital loss (deductible to the extent of capital gains plus $3,000) may find it beneficial to report all the gain in one year so as to offset such capital loss. For such a taxpayer, electing out of installment reporting (discussed below) is an option.

> *Example:* In 2019, Asher transfers land to Samuel for $100,000. The terms of the sale call for annual payments of $10,000 (plus interest) to Asher over a ten year period. Asher's total capital gain on the transaction is $90,000. If Asher were to report the sale on the installment method, he would report $9,000 of capital gain in each year of the ten year term over which the transaction took place. However, Asher has a $90,000 capital loss from another transaction. Thus, if Asher elects out of installment reporting, the entire $90,000 of capital gain would be includible in gross income in 2018 to offset the $90,000 of capital loss. This would allow Asher to account for the 2019 gain in a single year (essentially tax-free) by using it to offset capital loss.

If the taxpayer fails to make a timely election out of installment reporting, the IRS may nonetheless approve the election upon a showing that the taxpayer's failure to make a timely election was due to good cause.[5] As illustrated by Revenue Ruling 90-46, what constitutes "good cause" is very narrow. A change in the law that would cause electing out to be more tax advantageous or a change of mind by the taxpayer would not constitute good cause. On the other hand, a well-documented mistake (inadvertent failure to make a timely election due to an accountant's error) would constitute good cause.

Similarly, once an election out of installment reporting is made, it cannot be revoked without the permission of the IRS. In granting such permission, a showing of good cause (as illustrated

1. IRC Secs. 453(b)(2)(A), 453(l)(2).
2. IRC Sec. 453(b).
3. See IRC Sec. 453.
4. IRC Secs. 453(a), 453(d); *Bolton v. Comm.*, 92 TC 303 (1989).
5. Treas. Reg. §15A.453-1(d); Rev. Rul. 90-46, 1990-1 CB 107.

by Revenue Ruling 90-46) is also the standard considered by the IRS. Good cause will not be found if the purpose of a late election out is tax avoidance.[1] Generally, what constitutes good cause is determined on a case by case basis. Examples of IRS determinations of good faith can be found in private letter rulings.[2]

Be mindful, however, that a determination in a private letter ruling applies only to the taxpayer who requested the ruling.

Basic Mechanics of Installment Reporting

As illustrated below, reportable gain for each installment payment is determined by multiplying the gross profit ratio by each payment. The gross profit ratio is "gross profit" divided by the total contract price.[3] Gross profit is the selling price minus selling expenses minus the seller's adjusted basis in the transferred property. The total contract price is the selling price minus qualified indebtedness (generally, secured debt on the property assumed by the buyer).[4]

Example: On December 30, 2019, Asher sells a parcel of land (not subject to a mortgage or lien) to Samuel for $100,000 (there are no selling expenses). Asher's basis in the land is $10,000. Pursuant to a note, for a period of ten years, beginning January 1, 2020, Samuel is required to make an annual installment payment of $10,000 (plus interest). If Asher were to elect out of installment reporting, he would report a gain of $90,000 ($100,000 selling price minus $10,000 basis). Asher, however, does not elect out of installment reporting.

The computation of Asher's reportable gain is as follows:

Step 1 – Compute the gross profit ratio.

Gross Profit: $90,000 ($100,000 selling price minus $10,000 basis)

Total Contract Price: $100,000

Or

90 percent

Step 2 – Multiply the gross profit ratio by the principal payment amount.

90 percent * $10,000 = $9,000.

Step 3 – Determine the amount of the principal payment that is the tax-free recovery of basis.

$10,000 minus $9,000 = $1,000

Thus, with respect to each $10,000 principal payment, $9,000 is capital gain and $1,000 is the tax-free recovery of basis. As a result, over the ten year installment payment term, Asher will report $90,000 of capital gain and $10,000 recovery of basis.

1. Let. Rul. 9230003.
2. Let. Rul. 9218012. See also Let. Rul. 200226039. Let. Ruls. 9419012, 9345027.
3. IRC Sec. 453(c).
4. Treas. Reg. §15A.453-1(b)(2)(v), (b(3)(ii) and (b)(2)(iii). With respect to qualified indebtedness, Treas. Reg. §15A.453-1. See, however, *Professional Equities, Inc. v. Comm.*, 89 TC 165 (1987).

669. Does the installment method of reporting apply to depreciation recapture?

The installment method of reporting deferral of gain does not apply to depreciation recapture. Therefore, the portion of gain attributable to depreciation recapture must be reported in the year of sale. Once depreciation has been recaptured, any adjusted net capital gain (the balance of the gain, see Q 702) is computed by adding the amount of depreciation recaptured to the seller's basis.

Example: On December 30, 2019, Asher sells a tractor used in his trade or business to Samuel for $10,000. Asher's adjusted basis in the tractor is $2,000. Of Asher's $8,000 overall gain ($10,000 minus $2,000), $2,000 of it is attributable to depreciation recapture. For that reason, the $2,000 of depreciation recapture must be included in Asher's gross income in the year of sale (meaning it is not subject to ratable inclusion). Pursuant to a note, for a period of five years, beginning January 1, 2020, Samuel is required to make an annual installment payment of $2,000 (plus interest).

The computation of Asher's reportable gain is as follows:

Step 1 – Compute the gross profit ratio.

Gross Profit: $\frac{\text{6,000 (\$10,000 SP} - \text{\$2,000 basis} + \text{\$2,000 depreciation recapture)}}{\text{TCP: \$10,000}}$

Or

60 percent

Step 2 – Multiply the gross profit ratio by the principal payment amount.

60 percent * $2,000 = $1,200.

Step 3 – Determine the amount of the principal payment that is the tax-free recovery of basis.

$2,000 minus $1,200 = $800

Thus, with respect to each $2,000 principal payment, $1,200 is capital gain and $800 is the tax-free recovery of basis. Over the five year installment payment term, Asher will report $6,000 of capital gain and $4,000 recovery of basis. The $4,000 basis recovery includes $2,000 of adjusted basis plus the $2,000 of depreciation recapture Asher recognized in the year of sale.

670. How is unrecaptured Section 1250 gain treated when a taxpayer recognizes gain using the installment method of reporting?

In the case of an installment sale of IRC Section 1250 property (i.e., generally, most real estate subject to the allowance for depreciation under IRC Section 167),[1] the unrecaptured IRC Section 1250 gain (which is generally taxed at a maximum marginal rate of 25 percent – see Q 702) must be taken into account *before* any adjusted net capital gain (taxed at a maximum of 20 percent/15 percent/0 percent – see Q 702).[2] This means the recognition of unrecaptured IRC Section 1250 gain is not prorated over the term of the installment agreement, but instead

1. See IRC Sec. 1250(c).
2. Treas. Reg. §1.453-12(a).

recognized first to the extent of each year's recognized gain. The remaining capital gain is recognized only after all unrecaptured 1250 gain is recognized.

671. How is interest on the unpaid balance of an installment obligation treated?

All interest received by the taxpayer is ordinary income.[1] In some cases, depending on the property and amount involved, the interest (or imputed interest) to be paid over the period of the loan must be reported as "original issue discount" accruing in daily portions. In other cases the interest is allocated among the payments and that much of each payment is treated as interest includable and deductible according to the accounting method of the seller and buyer, respectively.

Imputed interest rules also apply to installment sales. In general, if the sales price of the property exceeds $3,000 and any payment is deferred for more than one year, interest must be charged on payments due more than six months following the sale at a rate that is equal to 100 percent of the "applicable federal rate," compounded semiannually. If not, interest will be imputed at that rate.[2] The applicable federal rate (see Q 677) is lowest of the AFRs in effect for any month in the three-month period ending with the first calendar month in which there is a binding written contract for sale.[3]

However, the following are exceptions to this general rule:

(1) if the interest charged is less than 100 percent of the AFR, a rate of no greater than 9 percent, compounded semiannually, will be imputed in the case of sales of property (other than new IRC Section 38 property) if the stated principal amount of the debt instrument does not exceed $5,831,500 in 2018, $5,717,400 in 2017 or $5,664,800 in 2016;[4]

(2) if the rate charged is less than 100 percent of the AFR, a rate of no greater than 6 percent, compounded semiannually, is imputed on aggregate sales of land during a calendar year between an individual and a family member (i.e., brothers, sisters, spouse, ancestors, and lineal descendants) to the extent the aggregate sales do not exceed $500,000 (the general rule of 100 percent of the AFR, compounded semiannually, applies to the excess);[5] and

(3) a rate of 110 percent of the AFR, compounded semiannually, applies to sales or exchanges of property if, pursuant to a plan, the transferor or any related person leases a portion of the property after the sale or exchange back to the seller ("sale-leaseback" transactions).[6]

---

1. Treas. Reg. §1.483-1.
2. IRC Sec. 483.
3. IRC Sec. 1274(d)(2)(B).
4. IRC Sec. 1274A, Rev. Rul. 2015-24, Rev. Rul. 2016-30, Rev. Rul. 2018-11.
5. IRC Sec. 483(e)(3).
6. IRC Sec. 1274(e).

672. How are installment sales between related parties taxed?

Installment sales between "related" parties are subject to strict rules. Except as noted below, "related" persons include the following: (1) family members (i.e., brothers, sisters, spouses, ancestors and lineal descendants); (2) an individual and a corporation of which the individual actually or constructively owns more than 50 percent of the stock; (3) a grantor and a fiduciary of a trust; (4) fiduciaries of two trusts if the same person is the grantor of both; (5) a fiduciary and a beneficiary of the same trust; (6) a fiduciary of a trust and a beneficiary of another trust set up by the same grantor; (7) a fiduciary of a trust and a corporation of which the grantor of the trust actually or constructively owns more than 50 percent of the stock; (8) a person and an IRC Section 501 tax-exempt organization controlled by the person or members of his family (as described in (1) above); (9) a corporation and a partnership if the same person actually or constructively owns more than 50 percent of the stock of the corporation, and has more than a 50 percent interest in the partnership; (10) two S corporations if the same persons actually or constructively own more than 50 percent of the stock of each; (11) an S corporation and a C corporation, if the same persons actually or constructively own more than 50 percent of the stock of each; or (12) generally, an executor and a beneficiary of an estate.[1]

There are attribution rules that apply to determine the ownership of stock. For example, an individual is treated as though he or she owns stock that is actually owned by family members (see above) and stock owned by a corporation, partnership, estate, or trust in proportion to the interest in the entity owned by the individual, family member, or a partner owning stock in the same corporation in which the individual owns stock.[2] As explained in Q 675, in the case of installment sales of depreciable property between related parties, a different definition of "related" is applied.[3]

673. What are the results if a purchaser in an installment sale between related parties disposes of the property before the seller receives the entire selling price (i.e., a second disposition)?

If a related installment sale purchaser disposes of the property before the related seller has received the entire selling price, such disposition is treated as a "second disposition" subject to a special rule. This rule provides that the amount realized on the second disposition (to the extent it exceeds payments already received by the related seller) will be treated as though the related party had received that amount *on the date of the second disposition*. In other words, since installment payments are taxed upon receipt (see Q 668), the related seller would have to report the gain computed as if he or she had actually received it (even though this did not occur). It may be difficult for the related seller to pay the tax on this gain since the seller did not actually receive that amount. However, this rule generally does not apply if:

(1) the second disposition occurs more than two years after the first disposition;

(2) the second disposition is an involuntary conversion, the threat of which did not exist at the time of the first disposition;

1. IRC Secs. 453(f)(1), 318(a), 267(b).
2. IRC Secs. 453(f)(1), 318(a), 267(c).
3. See IRC Sec. 453(g).

(3) the second disposition occurs after the death of either of the related parties; or

(4) neither disposition had as one of its principal purposes the avoidance of income tax.[1]

674. What are the results if an installment sale between related parties is cancelled or payment is forgiven?

If an installment sale between related parties is canceled or payment is forgiven, the *seller* must recognize gain in an amount equal to the difference between the fair market value of the obligation on the date of cancellation (but in no event less than the face amount of the obligation) and the seller's basis in the obligation.[2] The seller's basis in the obligation is the difference between the face value of the obligation over the amount of income that would be includible in gross income had the obligation been actually satisfied.[3]

> *Example:* Asher sells a tractor to Samuel for $10,000 with an adjusted basis of $2,000. In exchange, Samuel conveys five installment notes ($2,000 each). Asher's gross profit ratio would be 80 percent (see Q 667) meaning that 80 percent of each payment would be included in gross income ($1,600) and 20 percent ($400) would be tax-free return of basis. Therefore, each note would have a basis of $400 ($2,000 face value less $1,600 income). So, if Asher were to forgive a $2,000 installment note, he would recognize a gain of $1,600 (the difference between the face amount of the note and his basis in the note). In other words, a forgiven note is essentially taxed in the same way as it would have been had the seller actually received payment.

675. Can a sale of depreciable property between related parties be reported using the installment method?

A sale of depreciable property between related parties may *not* be reported on the installment method, unless it is shown that avoidance of income tax was not a principal purpose. For purposes of this rule only, "related persons" refers generally to controlled business entities, not natural persons related by family.[4]

676. What is an interest surcharge with respect to outstanding installment obligations?

Generally, an interest surcharge is an interest charge payable by the seller to the IRS with respect to a portion of a tax liability that is deferred as a result of installment reporting. In other words, installment reporting allows the taxpayer to defer the gain realized from the installment over time rather than in the year of sale. The tax on that gain is considered a deferred tax liability. The interest surcharge applies to all installment obligations held by the taxpayer (meaning it applies to multiple installment sales) in which deferred payments for sales during the taxable year exceed $5,000,000. There is an exception to the surcharge with respect to: (1) property used or produced in the trade or business of farming, (2) timeshares and residential lots, and (3) personal use property.[5]

---

1. IRC Sec. 453(e).
2. IRC Sec. 453B(f).
3. IRC Sec. 453B(b).
4. IRC Sec. 453(g).
5. IRC Sec. 453A(b).

The amount of the interest surcharge is determined by multiplying the "applicable percentage" of the deferred tax liability by the underpayment rate in effect at the end of the taxable year (with respect to tax deficiencies). The "applicable percentage" is determined by dividing the portion of the aggregate obligations for the year that exceeds $5,000,000 by the aggregate face amount of such obligations that are outstanding at the end of the taxable year. If an obligation remains outstanding in subsequent taxable years, interest must be paid using the same percentage rate as in the year of the sale.[1] In addition, if the installment obligation is pledged as security for a loan, the net proceeds of the loan will be treated as a payment received on the installment obligation (up to the total contract price); however, no additional gain is recognized on subsequent payments of such amounts already treated as received. The date of such constructive payment will be (a) the date the proceeds are received *or* (b) the date the indebtedness is secured, whichever is later.[2]

Planning Point: This interest surcharge on installment sales with deferred payments can be minimized by splitting the sale between two spouses and spreading it over two taxable years. For example, a $20 million business owned by a couple could be split into two $10 million sales, and the transaction could be completed in two stages: $5 million per spouse in December, followed by $5 million per spouse in January. Structured this way, the sale would not trigger the interest surcharge. *Robert S. Keebler, CPA, MST.*

677. What is the applicable federal rate and under what circumstances is it employed?

The applicable federal rate (AFR) is used in determining the amount of imputed interest with respect to certain below-market loans for both income and gift tax purposes (see Q 664, Q 882), in imputing interest on debt instruments given on the sale or exchange of property (see Q 668, Q 7836), and for determining interest and present values in connection with deferred payments for the use of property or services (see Q 7829).

The applicable federal rates are determined monthly by the IRS (and published in a revenue ruling). The various rates – short-term, mid-term and long-term – are based on the average market yield on the outstanding marketable obligations of the United States with maturity periods of three years or less, more than three but not more than nine years, and over nine years, respectively.[3]

To determine the appropriate AFR applicable with respect to below-market loans, see Q 664 and Q 882. To determine the appropriate AFR with respect to deferred rent, see Q 7829.

In the case of any sale or exchange in which a debt instrument is involved, the applicable federal rate will be the lowest three-month rate in effect for any month in the three-month period ending with the first calendar month in which there is a binding written contract.[4]

1. IRC Sec. 453A(c).
2. IRC Sec. 453A(d)(1). See Revenue Act of 1987 Conf. Rept., at pages 22-23.
3. IRC Sec. 1274(d)(1).
4. IRC Sec. 1274(d)(2).

By regulation, the IRS may permit a rate that is lower than the applicable federal rate to be used under certain circumstances.[1]

678. Are Social Security and railroad retirement benefits taxable?

Under certain circumstances, a portion of Social Security benefits and tier 1 railroad retirement benefits may be taxable. If a taxpayer's modified adjusted gross income plus one-half of the Social Security benefits (including tier I railroad retirement benefits) received during the taxable year *exceeds* certain base amounts, then a portion of the benefits are includible in gross income as ordinary income. "Modified adjusted gross income" is a taxpayer's adjusted gross income (disregarding foreign income, savings bonds, adoption assistance program exclusions, the deductions for education loan interest and for qualified tuition and related expenses) *plus* any tax-exempt interest income received or accrued during the taxable year.[2]

A taxpayer whose modified adjusted gross income plus one-half of his or her Social Security benefits exceed a base amount is required to include in gross income the *lesser* of (a) 50 percent of the excess of such combined income over the base amount, *or* (b) 50 percent of the Social Security benefits received during the taxable year.[3] The "base amount" is $32,000 for married taxpayers filing jointly, $25,000 for unmarried taxpayers, and zero ($0) for married taxpayers filing separately who have not lived apart for the entire taxable year.[4]

In addition to the initial tier of taxation discussed above, a percentage of Social Security benefits that exceed an adjusted base amount will be includable in a taxpayer's gross income. The "adjusted base amount" is $44,000 for married taxpayers filing jointly, $34,000 for unmarried taxpayers, and zero ($0) for married individuals filing separately who did not live apart for the entire taxable year.[5] If a taxpayer's modified adjusted gross income plus one-half of his or her Social Security benefits exceed the adjusted base amount, his or her gross income will include the *lesser* of (a) 85 percent of the Social Security benefits received during the year, *or* (b) the sum of – (i) 85 percent of the excess over the adjusted base amount, plus (ii) the smaller of – (A) the amount that is includable under the initial tier of taxation (see above), or (B) $4,500 (single taxpayers) or $6,000 (married taxpayers filing jointly).[6]

Example 1. A married couple files a joint return. During the taxable year, they received $12,000 in Social Security benefits and had a modified adjusted gross income of $35,000 ($28,000 plus $7,000 of tax-exempt interest income). Their modified adjusted gross income plus one-half of their Social Security benefits [$35,000 + (½ of $12,000) = $41,000] is greater than the applicable *base amount* of $32,000 but less than the applicable *adjusted base amount* of $44,000; therefore, $4,500 [the lesser of one-half of their benefits ($6,000) or one-half of the excess of $41,000 over the base amount (½ × ($41,000 – $32,000), or $4,500)] is included in gross income.

1. See IRC Sec. 1274(d)(1)(D).
2. IRC Sec. 86(b)(2).
3. IRC Sec. 86(a)(1).
4. IRC Sec. 86(c)(1). In a Tax Court case, the term "live apart" means living in separate residences. In that case, the taxpayer lived in the same residence as his spouse for at least thirty days during the tax year in question (even though maintaining separate bedrooms). The Tax Court ruled that he did not "live apart" from his spouse at all times during the year; therefore, the taxpayer's base amount was zero. *McAdams v. Comm.*, 118 TC 373 (2002).
5. IRC Sec. 86(c)(2).
6. IRC Sec. 86(a)(2).

Example 2. During the taxable year, a single individual had a modified adjusted gross income of $33,000 and received $8,000 in Social Security benefits. His modified adjusted gross income plus one-half of his Social Security benefits [$33,000 + (½ of $8,000) = $37,000] is greater than the applicable *adjusted base amount* of $34,000. Thus, $6,550 [the lesser of 85 percent of his benefits ($6,800), or 85 percent of the excess of $37,000 over the adjusted base amount (85 percent × ($37,000 – $34,000), or $2,550) plus the lesser of $4,000 (the amount includable under the initial tier of taxation) or $4,500] is included in gross income.

An election is available that permits a taxpayer to treat a lump sum payment of benefits as received in the year to which the benefits are attributable.[1]

Reductions of Social Security Benefits that do not Reduce the Amount Included in the Computation of Taxable Benefits

Workers' compensation pay that reduced the amount of Social Security received and any amounts withheld from a taxpayer's Social Security benefits to pay Medicare insurance premiums do not reduce the amount that are included in the computation of taxable Social Security benefits.[2]

In *Green v. Comm.*,[3] the taxpayer argued that his Social Security disability benefits were excludable from gross income[4] because they had been paid in lieu of workers' compensation. Thus, they should not be included in the computation of taxable Social Security benefits. The Tax Court determined, however, that Title II of the Social Security Act is *not* a form of workers' compensation. Instead, the Act allows for disability payments to individuals regardless of employment. Consequently, the taxpayer's Social Security disability benefits were includable in gross income.

Similarly, in a case of first impression, the Tax Court held that a taxpayer's Social Security disability insurance benefits (payable as a result of the taxpayer's disability due to lung cancer caused from exposure to Agent Orange during his Vietnam combat service) were includable in gross income under IRC Section 86 and not excludable under IRC Section 104(a)(4). The court reasoned that Social Security disability insurance benefits do not take into consideration the nature or cause of the individual's disability. Eligibility for purposes of Social Security disability benefits is determined on the basis of the individual's prior work record, not the cause of the disability. Moreover, the amount of Social Security disability payments is computed under a formula that does not consider the nature or extent of the injury. Consequently, because the taxpayer's Social Security disability insurance benefits were not paid for personal injury or sickness in military service within the meaning of IRC Section 104(a)(4), the benefits were not excluded from gross income under IRC Section 104(a)(4).[5]

Railroad retirement benefits (other than Tier I benefits) are taxed in the same way as benefits received under a qualified pension or profit sharing plan. For this purpose, the Tier II portion of the taxes imposed on employees and employee representatives is treated

1. IRC Sec. 86(e).
2. Rev. Rul. 84-173, 1984-2 CB 16.
3. TC Memo 2006-39.
4. Under IRC Section 104(a)(1).
5. *Reimels v. Comm.*, 123 TC 245 (2004), *aff'd*, 436 F.3d 344 (2d Cir. 2006); *Haar v. Comm.*, 78 TC 864, 866 (1982), *aff'd*, 709 F.2d 1206 (8th Cir. 1983), followed.

as an employee contribution, while the Tier II portion of the taxes imposed on employers is treated as an employer contribution.[1]

679. How is unearned income of certain children treated for federal income tax purposes when such income is derived from property given under the Uniform Gifts to Minors Act or the Uniform Transfers to Minors Act?

Editor's Note: For tax years beginning after 2017 and before 2026, the personal exemption was suspended and the unearned income of minors will be taxed according to the income tax rates that apply to trusts and estates.

Taxable income derived from custodial property is, ordinarily, taxed to the minor donee. To the extent that the custodian uses custodial income to discharge the legal obligation of any person to support or maintain the minor, such income is taxable to that person.[2] For this purpose, it makes no difference who is the custodian or who is the donor. State laws differ as to what constitutes a parent's obligation to support. A person who may be claimed as a dependent by another may use a standard deduction of $1,100 in 2019-2020 and $1,050 in 2015-2018 to offset unearned income (or, if higher, the dependent may take a standard deduction in the amount of the sum of $350 (in 2013-2020) and his *earned* income, as indexed for inflation – see Q 750). Prior to 2018, dependents for whom another taxpayer was allowed a personal exemption could not take a personal exemption for themselves (see Q 726).[3] For the treatment of unearned income for children, see Q 680.

680. How is unearned income of certain children treated for federal income tax purposes?

Pre-2018 (and, potentially, after 2025), under certain circumstances, children under the age of nineteen (age twenty-four for students) were required to pay tax on their unearned income above a certain amount at their parents' marginal rate. (See Q 751 for the current tax rates.) The tax applied to *all* unearned income, regardless of when the assets producing the income were transferred to the child.

The 2017 Tax Act changed the treatment of unearned income of minors by applying the tax rates that apply to trusts and estates to this income. Therefore, for tax years beginning after 2017 and before 2026, earned income of minors will be taxed according to the individual income tax rates prescribed for single filers,[4] and unearned income of minors will be taxed according to the applicable tax bracket that would apply if the income was that of a trust or estate (for both income that would be subject to ordinary income tax rates and income that would receive capital gains treatment).[5]

1. See IRC Sec. 72(r)(1).
2. IRC Sec. 61; Rev. Rul. 56-484, 1956-2 CB 23; Rev. Rul. 59-357, 1959-2 CB 212.
3. Rev. Proc. 2014-61, 2014-47 IRB 860, Rev. Proc. 2015-53, 2015-44 IRB 615, Rev. Proc. 2016-55, Rev. Proc. 2017-58, Rev. Proc. 2018-57.
4. IRC Sec. 1(j)(4)(B).
5. IRC Sec. 1(j)(4).

These so-called "kiddie tax" rules apply to children who have not attained certain ages before the close of the taxable year, who have at least one parent alive at the close of the taxable year, and who have over $2,200 in 2019-2020 and $2,100 in 2015-2018 of unearned income.[1]

The kiddie tax applies to:

(1) a child under age eighteen; *or*

(2) a child who has attained the age of eighteen if: (a) the child has not attained the age of nineteen (twenty-four in the case of a full-time student) before the close of the taxable year; and (b) the earned income of the child does not exceed one-half of the amount of the child's support for the year.[2]

The tax applies only to "net unearned income." "Net unearned income" is defined as adjusted gross income that is not attributable to earned income, and that exceeds (1) the $1,100 standard deduction for a dependent child in 2020, *plus* (2) the greater of $1,100 or (if the child itemizes) the amount of allowable itemized deductions that are directly connected with the production of his unearned income.[3]

"Earned income," essentially, means all compensation for personal services actually rendered.[4] A child is therefore taxed at his own rate on reasonable compensation for services.

Regulations specify that "unearned income" includes any Social Security or pension payments received by the child, income resulting from a gift under the Uniform Gifts to Minors Act, and interest on both earned and unearned income.[5] In the case of a trust, distributable net income that is includable in the child's net income can trigger the tax; however, most accumulation distributions received by a child from a trust will not be included in the child's gross income because of the minority exception under IRC Section 665(b).[6] Generally, the tax on accumulation distributions does not apply to domestic trusts (see Q 785). The source of the assets that produce unearned income need not be the child's parents.[7] The application of the "kiddie tax" to funds provided to a child by sources other than the child's parents was held constitutional.[8]

Example: Cole is a child who is seventeen years of age at the end of the taxable year beginning on January 1, 2017. Both of Cole's parents are alive at the end of the taxable year. During 2017, Cole receives $2,400 in interest from his bank account and $1,700 from a paper route. Some of the interest earned by Cole from the bank account is attributable to Cole's paper route earnings that were deposited in the account. The balance of the account is attributable to cash gifts from Cole's parents and grandparents and interest earned prior to 2017. Some cash gifts were received by Cole prior to 2017. Cole has no itemized deductions and is eligible to be claimed as a dependent on his parent's return. Therefore, for the taxable year 2017, Cole's

1. Rev. Proc. 2018-57, Rev. Proc. 2019-44.
2. IRC Sec. 1(g)(2).
3. IRC Sec. 1(g)(4), Rev. Proc. 2019-44.
4. IRC Secs. 911(d)(2), 1(g)(4)(A)(i).
5. Temp. Treas. Reg. §1.1(i)-1T, A-8, A-9, A-15.
6. Temp. Treas. Reg. §1.1(i)-1T, A-16.
7. Temp. Treas. Reg. §1.1(i)-1T, A-8.
8. See *Butler v. U.S.*, 798 F. Supp. 574 (E.D. Mo. 1992).

standard deduction is $2,050, the amount of Cole's earned income, plus $350. Of this standard deduction amount, $1,050 is allocated against unearned income, and $1,000 is allocated against earned income. Cole's taxable unearned income is $1,350, of which $1,050 is taxed without regard to section 1(g). The remaining taxable unearned income of $300 is net unearned income and is taxed under section 1(g). The fact that some of Cole's unearned income is attributable to interest on principal created by earned income and gifts from persons other than Cole's parents or that some of the unearned income is attributable to property transferred to Cole prior to 2017 will not affect the tax treatment of this income under section 1(g).

The parent whose taxable income is taken into account (pre-2018) is (a) in the case of parents who are not married, the custodial parent of the child (determined by using the support test for the dependency exemption) and (b) in the case of married individuals filing separately, the individual with the greater taxable income.[1] If the custodial parent files a joint return with a spouse who is not a parent of the child, the total joint income is applicable in determining the child's rate. "Child," for purposes of the kiddie tax, includes children who are adopted, related by half-blood, or from a prior marriage of either spouse.[2]

If there is an adjustment to the parent's tax, the child's resulting liability must also be recomputed. In the event of an underpayment, interest, but not penalties, will be assessed against the child.[3]

In the event that a child does not have access to needed information contained in the tax return of a parent, he (or his legal representative) may, by written request to the IRS, obtain such information from the parent's tax return as needed to file an accurate return.[4] The IRS has stated that where the necessary parental information cannot be obtained before the due date of the child's return, no penalties will be assessed with respect to any reasonable estimate of the parent's taxable income or filing status, or of the net investment income of the siblings.[5]

Pre-Reform Parental Election Rules

Pre-2018, certain parents could elect to include their child's unearned income over $2,100 (in 2016-2017) on their own return, thus avoiding the necessity of the child filing a return. The election was available to parents whose child has gross income of more than $1,050 and less than $10,500 (in 2017), all of which is from interest and dividends.[6]

The election was not available if there has been backup withholding under the child's Social Security number or if estimated tax payments have been made in the name and Social Security number of the child. If the election is made, any gross income of the child in excess of $2,100 in 2018 is included in the parent's gross income for the taxable year. (However, the inclusion of the child's income will increase the parent's adjusted gross income for purposes of certain other calculations, such as the 2 percent floor on miscellaneous itemized deductions (suspended from 2018 through 2025) and the limitation on medical expenses.) Any interest that is an item

1. Temp. Treas. Reg. §1.1(i)-1T, A-11, A-12.
2. Temp. Treas. Reg. §1.1(i)-1T, A-13, A-14.
3. Temp. Treas. Reg. §1.1(i)-1T, A-17, A-19.
4. Temp. Treas. Reg. §1.1(i)-1T, A-22.
5. Ann. 88-70, 1988-16 IRB 37.
6. IRC Sec. 1(g)(7); Rev. Proc. 2008-66, above, Rev. Proc. 2015-53, Rev. Proc. 2016-55, Rev. Proc. 2017-58.

of tax preference of the child (e.g., private activity bonds) will be treated as a tax preference of the parent. For each child to whom the election applies, there is also a tax of 10 percent of the lesser of $1,050 or the excess of the gross income of such child over $1,050. If the election is made, the child will be treated as having no gross income for the year.[1] The threshold and ceiling amounts for the availability of this election, the amount used in computing the child's alternative minimum tax, and a threshold amount used in computing the amount of tax are indexed for inflation.

For treatment of the unearned income of minor children under the alternative minimum tax, see Q 767.

681. What is an Education Savings Account (also known as a Coverdell Education Savings Account)?

An education IRA or Coverdell Education Savings Account (ESA) is a trust or custodial account created exclusively for the purpose of paying the "qualified education expenses" of the designated beneficiary of an ESA at the time it is created.[2] At the time the ESA is created, the beneficiary must be under age eighteen or a special needs beneficiary. An ESA is similar to a Roth IRA in that both are funded with after-tax contributions. To the extent the distributions do not exceed the beneficiary's adjusted education expenses for the tax year of withdrawal, they are tax-free.[3]

In addition, there must be a written ESA document meeting the following requirements:

- The trustee or custodian must be a bank or entity approved by the IRS.
- Contributions to the ESA must be in cash, made before the beneficiary attains the age of eighteen (unless a special needs beneficiary); contributions are capped at $2,000 per year, as reduced based upon the income limitations. The reduction range is adjusted gross income between $95,000 and $110,000 for single taxpayers or $190,000 to $220,000 for married taxpayers. This means no contribution would be allowed if adjusted gross income exceeds the higher adjusted gross income limit (see Q 682).
- Qualified education expenses include private school (grades one through twelve) as well as higher education.

For guidance regarding certain reporting requirements and transition rules applicable to ESAs, see Notice 2003-53.[4] See Q 833 for the estate tax treatment and Q 891 for the gift tax treatment of ESAs.

1. IRC Sec. 1(g)(7)(B).
2. IRC Secs. 530(b), 530(g).
3. IRC Sec. 530(d).
4. 2003-33 IRB 362.

682. What are the rules governing contributions to a Coverdell Education Savings Account?

Annual contributions to a Coverdell Education Savings Account ("ESA") must be made in cash on or before the date on which the beneficiary attains age eighteen unless the beneficiary is a special needs beneficiary. According to the Conference Report, a special needs beneficiary includes an individual with a physical, mental, or emotional condition (including learning disabilities) that requires additional time to complete his or her education.[1] Annual contributions may be made up until the due date (excluding extensions) for filing the tax return for the calendar year for which such contributions were intended.[2]

In general, the aggregate amount of contributions to an ESA on behalf of a beneficiary (except in the case of rollover contributions) cannot exceed $2,000.[3] The maximum contribution amount is phased-out for certain high-income contributors. The maximum contribution for single filers is reduced by the amount that bears the same ratio to such maximum amount as the contributor's *modified adjusted gross income* (MAGI) in excess of $95,000 bears to $15,000.[4] For joint filers, the maximum contribution is reduced by the amount that bears the same ratio to such maximum amount as the contributor's MAGI in excess of $190,000 bears to $30,000.[5] For this purpose, MAGI is adjusted gross income without regard to the exclusions for income derived from certain foreign sources or sources within United States possessions.[6] Contributions to an ESA are not limited due to contributions made to a qualified state tuition program in the same year.

Contributions in excess of the maximum annual contribution (as reduced for high-income contributors) that are not returned before the first day of the sixth month of the taxable year following the taxable year in which the contribution was made are subject to the 6 percent excess contribution excise tax under Code section 4973(a).[7] Note that any excess contributions from previous taxable years, to the extent not returned, will continue to be taxed as excess contributions in subsequent taxable years.[8]

683. How are distributions from an Education Savings Account treated? What are "qualified education expenses"?

Distributions from an ESA are tax-free if they are used solely for the "qualified education expenses" of the designated beneficiary.[9] Qualified education expenses include both "qualified *higher* education expenses" and "qualified *elementary* and *secondary* education expenses."[10] Qualified higher education expenses include tuition, fees, costs for books, supplies, and equipment

1. IRC Sec. 530(b)(1).
2. IRC Sec. 530(b)(5).
3. IRC Sec. 530(b)(1)(A)(iii).
4. IRC Sec. 530(c)(1).
5. IRC Sec. 530(c)(1).
6. IRC Sec. 530(c)(2).
7. IRC Sec. 4973(e)(2).
8. IRC Sec. 4973(e).
9. IRC Sec. 530(d)(2)(A).
10. IRC Sec. 530(b)(2).

required for the enrollment or attendance of the student at any "eligible educational institution," and amounts contributed to a qualified tuition program.[1] Room and board (up to a certain amount) is also included if the student is enrolled at least half-time.[2] An "eligible educational institution" is any college, university, vocational school, or other postsecondary educational institution described in section 481 of the Higher Education Act of 1965.[3] Thus, virtually all accredited public, nonprofit, and proprietary postsecondary institutions are considered eligible educational institutions.[4]

Qualified education expenses are reduced by scholarships, educational assistance provided to the individual, or any payment for such expenses (other than a gift, devise, bequest, or inheritance) excludable from gross income. These expenses are also reduced by the amount of such expenses taken into account in determining the American Opportunity Credit or the Lifetime Learning Credit.[5]

Qualified elementary and secondary education expenses include tuition, fees, and costs for academic tutoring, special needs services, books, supplies, and other equipment incurred in connection with the enrollment or attendance of the designated beneficiary at any public, private, or religious school that provides elementary or secondary education (K through twelve) as determined under state law. Also included are expenses for room and board, uniforms, transportation, supplementary items and services (including extended day programs) required or provided by such schools, and any computer technology or certain related equipment used by the beneficiary and the beneficiary's family during any of the years the beneficiary is in school.[6]

If a designated beneficiary receives distributions from both an ESA and qualified tuition program that in the aggregate amount exceed the "qualified education expenses" of the designated beneficiary, the expenses are allocated among such distributions so as to determine the amount excludable under each.[7] Any "qualified education expenses" taken into account for purposes of this exclusion may not be taken into account for purposes of any other deductions, credits, or exclusions.[8]

Purchase of life insurance with ESA funds is not permitted.[9] ESA assets may not be commingled with other property except in a common trust fund or common investment fund.[10] If the beneficiary engages in a prohibited transaction, ESA status is lost and will be treated as distributing all of its assets. If the beneficiary pledges the account as security for a loan, the amount so pledged will be treated as a distribution from the account.[11]

1. IRC Secs. 529(e)(3), 530(b)(2).
2. IRC Sec. 530(b)(2).
3. See IRC Sec. 529(e)(5).
4. Notice 97-60, 1997-2 CB 310, at 16 (Sec. 3, A16).
5. IRC Sec. 530(d)(2)(C).
6. IRC Sec. 530(b)(4).
7. IRC Sec. 530(d)(2)(C)(ii).
8. IRC Sec. 530(d)(2)(D).
9. IRC Sec. 530(b)(1)(C).
10. IRC Sec. 530(b)(1)(D).
11. IRC Sec. 530(e).

Bankruptcy

Under Section 225 of BAPCPA 2005, funds placed in an "education individual retirement account" (as defined in IRC Section 530(b)(1)) no later than 365 days before the date of the filing of the bankruptcy petition may be excluded from the bankruptcy estate if certain conditions are met.[1]

684. Is a rollover from one education savings account to another permitted?

A rollover from one ESA to another ESA is not treated as a distribution (that would be potentially taxable) provided the beneficiaries of both ESAs are the same, or members of the same family. The new beneficiary must be under thirty years old as of the date of such distribution or change, except in the case of a special needs beneficiary.[2] The rollover contribution must be made no later than sixty days after the date of the distribution from the original ESA. However, no more than one rollover may be made from an ESA during any twelve-month period.[3] Similarly, the beneficiary of an ESA may be changed without taxation or penalty if the new beneficiary is a member of the family of the previous ESA beneficiary and has not attained age thirty or is a special needs beneficiary.[4] Transfer of an individual's interest in an ESA can be made from one spouse to another pursuant to a divorce (or upon the death of a spouse) without changing the character of the ESA.[5] Likewise, non-spouse survivors who acquire an original beneficiary's interest in an ESA upon the death of the beneficiary will be treated as the original beneficiary of the ESA as long as the new beneficiary is a family member of the original beneficiary.[6]

685. What are the results when the beneficiary of an education savings account dies?

Upon the death of the beneficiary of the ESA, any balance to the credit of the beneficiary must be distributed to the estate within thirty days. The balance remaining in an ESA must also be distributed within thirty days after a beneficiary (other than a special needs beneficiary) reaches age thirty.[7] Any balance remaining in the ESA is deemed distributed within thirty days after such events.[8] The earnings on any distribution under this provision are includable in the beneficiary's gross income.[9]

686. How are excess distributions from an education savings account treated?

If distributions from the ESA exceed the amount of the designated beneficiary's "adjusted qualified education expenses" (qualified education expenses less any tax-free educational assistance) for the year, the recipient will be taxed on a portion of the excess distribution and a portion will

1. 11 USC 541(b), as amended by BAPCPA 2005.
2. IRC Sec. 530(b)(1).
3. IRC Sec. 530(d)(5).
4. IRC Secs. 530(b)(1), 530(d)(6).
5. IRC Sec. 530(d)(7).
6. IRC Sec. 530(d)(7).
7. IRC Sec. 530(b)(1)(E).
8. IRC Sec. 530(d)(8).
9. IRC Sec. 530(d)(1).

be treated as the recovery of "basis." This is because a portion of the ESA is comprised of after-tax contributions and a portion is comprised of earnings generated by the account. Thus, the latter amount is non-taxable and there is an amount includable in gross income. In determining the taxable portion of an ESA excess distribution, consider the following based on the example in IRS Publication 970:

Example: In 2020, Asher receives a distribution of $850 from an ESA of which $1,500 had been contributed before 2020. Asher's qualified education expenses for that year are $700. In 2020, there were no contributions to the account. Because the 2020 distribution was Asher's first distribution from the account, his basis is $1,500 (the amount contributed). As of December 31, 2020, the balance in the ESA is $950. The taxable portion of Asher's distribution is computed as follows:

Step 1 – Determine the basis portion of the distribution. Multiply the amount distributed ($850) by a fraction, the numerator is Asher's basis in the account at the end of 2019 ($1,500) plus the balance in the account as of December 31, 2019 ($0) and the denominator is the balance of the account as of December 31, 2020 ($950) plus the amount distributed in 2020 ($850), or

$$\$850 * \frac{\$1{,}500}{\$1{,}800} = \$708$$

Step 2 – Determine the earnings included in the distribution. Subtract the basis portion of the distribution ($708) from the amount of the distribution ($850). $850 minus $708 = $142 (the earnings portion of the distribution),

Step 3 – Determine the tax-free (return of basis) portion of the distribution. Multiply the earnings portion of the distribution ($142) by a fraction, the numerator is Asher's 2020 qualified education expenses and the denominator is the total amount distributed to Asher ($850), or

$$\$142 * \frac{\$700}{\$850} = \$117 \text{ (tax-free earnings)}$$

Step 4 – Determine the taxable earnings. Subtract the tax-free earnings ($117) from the earnings portion of the distribution ($142). $142 minus $117 + $25 (the taxable earnings).

In addition to income tax, the portion of an ESA includable in gross income is subject to an additional 10 percent penalty tax unless the distribution is (1) made after the death of the beneficiary of the ESA, (2) attributable to the disability of such beneficiary (within the meaning of IRC Section 72(m)(7)), (3) made in an amount equal to a scholarship, allowance, or other payment under IRC Section 25A(g)(2), or (4) includable in income because expenses were reduced by the amount claimed as a Hope Scholarship Credit, Lifetime Learning Credit, or American Opportunity Credit.[1] The penalty tax also does not apply to any distribution of an excess contribution and the earnings thereon if such contribution and earnings are distributed before the first day of the sixth month of the taxable year following the taxable year in which the contribution was made.[2] However, the earnings are includable in the contributor's income for the taxable year in which such excess contribution was made.

1. IRC Sec. 530(d)(4).
2. IRC Sec. 530(d)(4)(C).

687. What is a qualified tuition program (also known as a 529 plan)?

Editor's Note: Under the 2017 Tax Act, Section 529 plans would be expanded to include the use of up to $10,000 per year for elementary or secondary school expenses (a provision that would have permitted Section 529 plan funds to be used for expenses incurred in connection with homeschooling was eliminated at the last minute).

A qualified tuition program is a program established and maintained by a state (or agency or instrumentality thereof) or by one or more "eligible educational institutions" that meet certain requirements and under which a person may buy tuition credits or certificates on behalf of a designated beneficiary that entitle the beneficiary to a waiver or payment of qualified higher education expenses of the beneficiary (see below). These plans are often collectively referred to as "529 plans." In the case of a state-sponsored qualified tuition program, a person may make contributions to an account established to fund the qualified higher education expenses of a designated beneficiary.[1] Qualified tuition programs sponsored by "eligible educational institutions" (i.e., private colleges and universities) are not permitted to offer savings plans; these institutions may sponsor only pre-paid tuition programs.[2]

As a general rule, a qualified tuition program is exempt from federal income tax, except the tax on unrelated business income of charitable organizations imposed by IRC Section 511.[3] See Q 689 for the tax treatment of distributions from qualified tuition programs. See Q 834 for the estate tax treatment and Q 892 for the gift tax treatment of qualified tuition programs.

To be treated as a qualified tuition program, a state program or privately sponsored program must:

(1) mandate that contributions and purchases be made in cash only;

(2) maintain a separate accounting for each designated beneficiary;

(3) provide that no designated beneficiary or contributor may directly or indirectly direct the investment of contributions or earnings (but see below);

(4) not allow any interest in the program or portion thereof to be used as security for a loan; *and*

(5) provide *adequate safeguards* (see below) to prevent contributions on behalf of a designated beneficiary in excess of those necessary to provide for the beneficiary's qualified higher education expenses.[4]

With respect to item (3), above, the IRS announced a special rule that state-sponsored qualified tuition savings plans may permit parents to change the investment strategy (1) once each calendar year, and (2) whenever the beneficiary designation is changed. According to

1. IRC Sec. 529(b)(1); Prop. Treas. Reg. §1.529-2(b).
2. IRC Sec. 529(b)(1)(A).
3. IRC Sec. 529(a).
4. IRC Sec. 529(b).

Notice 2001-55, final regulations are expected to provide that to qualify under this special rule, the state-sponsored qualified tuition program savings plan must: (1) allow participants to select among only broad-based investment strategies designed exclusively by the program; and (2) establish procedures and maintain appropriate records to prevent a change in investment options from occurring more frequently than once per calendar year, or upon a change in the designated beneficiary of the account. Until such final regulations have been issued under IRC Section 529, the IRS will allow qualified tuition programs and their participants to rely on the guidance provided in the notice.[1]

Program Established and Maintained by One or More Eligible Educational Institutions

A program established and maintained by one or more "eligible educational institutions" must satisfy two requirements to be treated as a qualified tuition program: (1) the program must have received a ruling or determination that it meets the applicable requirements for a qualified tuition program; *and* (2) the program must provide that assets are held in a "qualified trust."[2] "Eligible educational institution" means an accredited *post-secondary* college or university that offers credit towards a bachelor's degree, associate's degree, graduate-level degree, professional degree, or other recognized post-secondary credential *and* that is eligible to participate in federal student financial aid programs.[3] For these purposes, *qualified trust* is defined as a domestic trust for the exclusive benefit of designated beneficiaries that meets the requirements set forth in the IRA rules, (i.e., a trust maintained by a bank, or other person who demonstrates that it will administer the trust in accordance with the requirements, and where the trust assets will not be commingled with other property, except in a common trust fund or common investment fund).[4]

Qualified Higher Education Expenses

The term *qualified higher education expenses* means (1) tuition, fees, books, supplies, and equipment required for a designated beneficiary's enrollment or attendance at an eligible educational institution (including certain vocational schools), and (2) expenses for special needs services incurred in connection with enrollment or attendance of a special needs beneficiary.[5] Qualified higher education expenses also include reasonable costs for room and board, within limits. Generally, they may not exceed: (1) the allowance for room and board that was included in the cost of attendance in effect on the date that EGTRRA 2001 was enacted as determined by the school for a particular academic period, or *if greater* (2) the actual invoice amount the student residing in housing owned and operated by the private college or university is charged by such institution for room and board costs for a particular academic period.[6] Under the 2017 tax reform legislation, up to $10,000 per year that is used to pay for elementary and secondary school expenses will qualify as higher education expenses.[7]

1. Notice 2001-55, 2001-39 IRB 299.
2. IRC Secs. 529(b)(1), 529(e)(5).
3. See Prop. Treas. Reg. §1.529-1(c).
4. IRC Sec. 529(b)(1).
5. IRC Sec. 529(e)(3)(A).
6. IRC Sec. 529(e)(3)(B).
7. IRC Sec. 529(c)(7).

Adequate Safeguards

The safe harbor that provides *adequate safeguards* to prevent contributions in excess of those necessary to meet the beneficiary's qualified higher education expenses is satisfied if all contributions to the account are prohibited once the account balance reaches a specified limit applicable to all beneficiaries' accounts with the same expected year of enrollment.[1] Total contributions may not exceed the amount established by actuarial estimates as necessary to pay tuition, required fees, and room and board expenses of the beneficiary for five years of undergraduate enrollment at the highest cost institution allowed by the program.[2]

Reporting

Each officer or employee having control over a qualified tuition program must report to the IRS and to designated beneficiaries with respect to contributions, distributions, and other matters as the IRS may require. The reports must be filed and furnished to the above individuals in the time and manner determined by the IRS.[3] In 2001, in light of the amendments to IRC Section 529 under EGTRRA 2001, the IRS released guidance regarding certain recordkeeping, reporting, and other requirements applicable to qualified tuition programs.[4] Pending the issuance of final IRC Section 529 regulations, qualified tuition programs and their participants may rely on Notice 2001-81.

Bankruptcy

Under Section 225 of BAPCPA 2005, funds used to purchase a tuition credit or certificate or contributed to an account under a QTP no later than 365 days before the date of the filing of the bankruptcy petition may be excluded from the bankruptcy estate if certain conditions are met.[5]

688. Is it permissible to contribute to a qualified tuition plan and an education savings account?

A taxpayer may claim an American Opportunity or Lifetime Learning Credit *and* exclude distributions from a qualified tuition program on behalf of the same student in the same taxable year *if* the distribution is not used to pay the same educational expenses for which the credit was claimed.[6] See Q 759. However, an individual must *reduce* total qualified higher education expenses by certain scholarships *and* the amount of expenses taken into account in determining the American Opportunity or Lifetime Learning credit allowable to the taxpayer (or any other person).[7]

Without incurring an excise tax, it is permissible to make a contribution to a qualified tuition program in the same taxable year as a contribution to a Coverdell Education Savings Account for the

1. Prop. Treas. Reg. §1.529-2(i)(2).
2. Prop. Treas. Reg. §1.529-2(h)(2).
3. IRC Sec. 529(d); Prop. Treas. Reg. §1.529-4.
4. See Notice 2001-81, 2001-52 IRB 617.
5. 11 USC 541(b).
6. See IRC Sec. 529(c)(3)(B)(v).
7. IRC Sec. 529(c)(3)(B)(v).

benefit of the same designated beneficiary. (See Q 681.)[1] For purposes of determining the amount of the exclusion, if the aggregate distributions from a qualified tuition program exceed the total amount of qualified higher education expenses taken into account *after* reduction for the American Opportunity and Lifetime Learning credits, then the expenses must be allocated between the Coverdell Education Savings Account distributions and the qualified tuition program distributions.[2]

The total deductible amount of qualified tuition and related expenses is *reduced* by the amount of such expenses taken into account in determining the exclusion for distributions from qualified tuition programs. For these purposes, the excludable amount under IRC Section 529 does not include that portion of the distribution that is a tax-free return of contributions to the plan.[3]

689. Are certain distributions from a qualified tuition program (529 Plan) taxable?

Distributions from *state* qualified tuition programs, pre-paid tuition programs sponsored by private schools and universities are fully excludable from gross income *if* the distributions are used to pay "qualified higher education expenses" (see Q 687) of the designated beneficiary.[4] (For the general rule governing nonqualified distributions, see below.)

In the case of excess cash distributions, the amount otherwise includable in gross income must be reduced by a proportion that is equal to the ratio of expenses to distributions.[5] In-kind distributions are not includable in gross income so long as they provide a benefit to the distributee which, if paid for by the distributee, would constitute payment of a qualified higher education expense.[6]

Nonqualified distributions (i.e., distributions that are *not* used to pay "qualified higher education expenses") are includable in gross income. However, the amount of the distribution representing the amount paid or contributed to the 529 plan are not taxable. An individual receiving a distribution from a 529 plan will receive a Form 1099-Q. The gross distribution received is entered in Box 1 of the form. That amount will be divided between the earnings generated from the 529 plan (Box 2) and the basis (return of investment) (Box 3). Consider the following example based on the example in IRS Publication 970:

Example: In 2012, Asher's parents opened a 529 plan. Over a number of years, they contributed $18,000 to the plan. As of the date of distribution in the summer of 2020, the balance in the plan was $27,000. At that time, Asher enrolled in college and paid $8,300 of qualified education expenses for the rest of the year. Those expenses were paid from the following sources:

Gifts from parents	$1,600
Partial scholarship (tax-free)	$3,100
529 Plan distribution	$5,300

1. IRC Sec. 4973(e).
2. IRC Sec. 529(c)(3)(B)(vi).
3. IRC Sec. 222(c)(2)(B).
4. IRC Sec. 529(c)(3)(B).
5. IRC Sec. 529(c)(3)(B).
6. IRC Sec. 529(c)(3)(B).

Step 1 – Determine the "adjusted qualified education expenses." Adjusted qualified education expenses (AQEE) are the amount of qualified education expenses ($8,300) less tax-free educational assistance ($3,100). Therefore, AQEE is $5,200 ($8,300 minus $3,100).

Thus, the 529 plan distribution of $8,300 exceeds Asher's AQEE of $5,200. For that reason, a portion of the distribution will be taxable. According to Asher's Form 1099-Q, Box 2, $950 of the distribution is earnings.

Step 2 – Compute the tax-free earnings. Multiply the total distributed earnings ($950) by a fraction, the numerator of which is AQEE ($5,200) and the denominator of which is the 529 plan distribution ($5,300), or:

$$\$950 \text{ (total earnings} \times \frac{\$5{,}200 \text{ (AQEE)}}{\$5{,}300 \text{ (distribution)}} = \$932 \text{ (tax-free earnings)}$$

Step 3 – Compute the taxable earnings. Subtract tax-free earnings ($932) from total earnings ($950), or $950 minus $932, which equals taxable earnings of $18 that must be included in gross income.

Additionally, there is a 10 percent additional tax imposed on nonqualified distributions in the same manner as is imposed on certain distributions from Coverdell Education Savings Accounts (see Q 683).[1] The 10 percent additional tax does not apply if the payment or distribution is (1) made to a beneficiary on or after the death of the designated beneficiary, or (2) attributable to the disability of the designated beneficiary.[2]

Repeal of the Aggregation Requirement

For distributions made after December 31, 2014, the Protecting Americans from Tax Hikes Act of 2015 (PATH) eliminated the requirement that, in calculating the earnings portion of any distribution that exceeds qualified education expenses, all Section 529 plans of which an individual is a designated beneficiary will be treated as one program. Forms 1099-Q must generally be furnished to distributees on or before January 31 of the year following the year of a distribution, and to the IRS on or before February 28, or, if filing electronically, March 31. Because of the difficulties involved in adjusting 529 plan systems to comply with the retroactive repeal of the aggregation requirement, the IRS provided transition relief. The IRS did not impose penalties for inaccurately reported earnings on 2015 Forms 1099-Q that were solely due to the repeal of the aggregation requirement.

Guidance Provided in Notice 2001-81

In Notice 2001-81, the IRS announced that final regulations would provide that only those accounts maintained by a qualified tuition program and having the same account owner and the same designated beneficiary must be aggregated in the computation of the earnings portion of any distribution.[3] The notice also indicated that the final regulations would revise the time for determining the earnings portion of any distribution from a qualified tuition account. Specifically, for distributions made after 2002, such programs are required to determine the earnings portion of each distribution *as of the date of the distribution*. A different effective date applies to direct

1. IRC Secs. 529(c)(6), 530(d)(4).
2. IRC Sec. 530(d)(4)(B).
3. Notice 2001-81, 2001-2 CB 617.

transfers between qualified tuition programs.[1] Finally, the notice states that with respect to any distributions made *after* 2001, a qualified tuition program will no longer be required to verify how distributions are used or to collect any penalty. However, the program must continue to verify whether the distribution is used for qualified higher education expenses of the beneficiary.[2]

690. Can a distribution from a qualified tuition program be rolled over into another account tax-free?

Editor's Note: The 2017 Tax Act now permits Section 529 plan funds to be rolled over into an ABLE account for the designated beneficiary, or the designated beneficiary's family member, in an amount up to the annual 529 plan contribution limit (rollovers would offset other contributions made to the ABLE account for the year). Amounts rolled over in excess of the limitation are included in the distributee's gross income. These rules are effective for rollovers that occur after December 31, 2017 and before December 31, 2025. See Q 385 to Q 387 for a discussion of the ABLE account rules.[3]

Any portion of a distribution transferred within sixty days to the credit of a "new designated beneficiary" (see below) who is a "member of the family" (see below) of the designated beneficiary, is not includable in the gross income of the distributee. (In other words, a distribution generally can be "rolled over" within sixty days from one family member to another.)[4] Additionally, if a new beneficiary is a member of the old beneficiary's family, a change in designated beneficiaries with respect to an interest in the same qualified tuition program will not be treated as a distribution.[5] A transfer of credits (or other amounts) for the benefit of the *same* designated beneficiary from one qualified tuition program to another is not considered a distribution; however, only one transfer within a twelve-month period can receive such rollover treatment.[6]

Generally, a *member of the family* is an individual's (1) spouse, (2) child or his descendant, (3) stepchild, (4) sibling or step sibling, (5) parents and their ancestors, (6) stepparents, (7) nieces or nephews, (8) aunts and uncles, or (9) in-laws, (10) the spouse of any of the individuals in (2) through (9), and (11) any first cousin of the designated beneficiary.[7] A *designated beneficiary* is (1) the individual designated at the beginning of participation in the qualified tuition program as the beneficiary of amounts paid (or to be paid) to the program; (2) in the case of a rollover of a distribution or change in beneficiaries within a family (as described above), the new beneficiary; and (3) in the case of an interest in a qualified tuition program that is purchased by a state or local government (or its agency or instrumentality) or certain tax-exempt 501(c)(3) organizations as part of a scholarship program, the individual receiving the interest as a scholarship.[8]

1. See Notice 2001-81, 2001-2 CB 617.
2. Notice 2001-81, above.
3. Pub. Law. No. 115-97.
4. See Prop. Treas. Reg. §§1.529-3(a) and (b); Prop. Treas. Reg. §1.529-1(c).
5. IRC Sec. 529(c)(3)(C).
6. IRC Sec. 529(c)(3)(C)(iii).
7. IRC Sec. 529(e)(2); IRC Sec. 152(d).
8. IRC Sec. 529(e)(1).

691. What are the tax consequences of an educational benefit trust?

At one time, educational benefit trusts promised to provide funds to pay certain educational costs on a tax favored basis. Treasury Regulation Section 1.962-1 confirmed, however, that these benefits were taxed to employees when paid as compensation. Where employer contributions to an educational benefit trust are related to an employee's service, they are taxed as compensation to the employee when they are either paid to or for the benefit of their children or no longer are subject to a substantial risk of forfeiture.[1]

Amounts paid to provide benefits to children of stockholder-employees generally are treated as compensation to the employees, not dividends, where the plan is adopted for business reasons in an effort to attract and retain employees.[2]

Where a bona fide debtor-creditor relationship is not intended for funds advanced to employees for this purpose, the amounts are treated as compensation even though called "loans."[3]

IRC Sections 419 and 419A generally apply to post-1985 contributions to an educational benefit trust. Prior to that time, there was some controversy regarding the timing of the employer's deduction. For years, the position of the IRS was that benefits provided under an educational benefit trust related to the employee's service constituted a deferral of compensation and, therefore, the employer's deductions should be taken when the benefits are paid out under IRC Section 404(a)(5).[4] The IRS has since privately ruled that an educational benefit trust was a "welfare benefit fund," and that the deduction of contributions is controlled by IRC Section 419.[5]

Educational benefit trusts cannot take advantage of the (limited) immediate deductions for advance funding under the general rule of IRC Section 419 because they do not have "qualified asset accounts."[6] Thus, an employer's deduction generally is limited to the amount includable in income by employees that year, minus the trust's after-tax income.

The general rule of IRC Section 419(b), which limits the deduction of welfare benefit fund contributions to the fund's "qualified cost," does not apply to contributions to a collectively bargained welfare benefit fund. The IRS has ruled that such contributions could be deducted in the year contributed, provided that they constitute ordinary and necessary expenses.[7] This ruling is questionable, however, because it is based on a temporary regulation (published before the current statutory text) that provides more generous treatment for collectively bargained funds than current law.

For a more detailed treatment of welfare benefit funds, see Q 4091 and Q 4092.

---

1. *Grant-Jacoby, Inc. v. Comm.*, 73 TC 700 (1980); *Citrus Orthopedic Medical Group, Inc. v. Comm.*, 72 TC 461 (1979); *Armantrout v. Comm.*, 67 TC 996 (1977), *aff'd*, 570 F.2d 210 (7th Cir. 1978); Treas. Reg. §1.83-3(c)(4), Ex. 2; Rev. Rul. 75-448, 1975-2 CB 55; Let. Rul. 8535002. See also *Wheeler v. U.S.*, 768 F.2d 1333 (Fed. Cir. 1985).
2. *Grant-Jacoby, Inc. v. Comm.*, supra.
3. *Saunders v. Comm.*, TC Memo 1982-655, *aff'd*, 720 F.2d 871, 83-2 USTC ¶88,609 (5th Cir. 1983) (overly generous loan forgiveness provisions in plan indicated true loan not intended). See Let. Rul. 8137001.
4. See *Grant-Jacoby, Inc. v. Comm.*, supra; *Citrus Orthopedic Medical Group, Inc. v. Comm.*, supra; Rev. Rul. 75-448, 1975-2 CB 55.
5. Let. Rul. 8737022.
6. IRC Sec. 419A(a).
7. See Let. Rul. 9510048.

692. What is "tax basis" and why is it significant?

"Tax basis" is a taxpayer's after-tax investment in property as adjusted up or down by certain tax significant items. Tax basis serves multiple purposes including (but not limited to) the amount available for depreciation deductions (with respect to depreciable property) and in the determination of taxable gain or loss upon the sale or exchange of property.[1]

When an individual acquires property, the individual also acquires an initial tax basis in such property. Depending on the manner of acquisition, the basis may be (1) its cost, (2) its fair market value as of a specified date, or (3) a substituted tax basis.[2] (See Q 693 to Q 695 as to which of these applies to a given manner of acquisition.)

As indicated above, during the taxpayer's ownership period, the tax basis of the property may be adjusted to reflect certain additional after- tax contributions to the property, and returns of, the initial after-tax investment in the property. (For example, tax basis is increased by subsequent after-tax investment such as capital improvements; and reduced by deductions (a form of recovery of the initial after-tax investment) such as allowable depreciation or depletion.) A taxpayer's tax basis, as adjusted, is often referred to as "adjusted tax basis."[3]

693. What is the tax basis of property that is acquired by purchase or exchange?

A taxpayer's tax basis in property acquired by purchase or in a taxable exchange is its cost (money paid or the fair market value exchanged).[4]

Special rules apply to stock exchanges made pursuant to a plan of corporate reorganization.[5] For the final regulations under IRC Section 358 providing guidance regarding the determination of the basis of stock or securities received in exchange for, or with respect to, stock or securities in certain transactions, see Q 7517. For the rules applicable to stock received in a demutualization, see Q 7517. Proposed regulations relating to redemptions of stock in which the redemption proceeds are treated as a dividend distribution have been withdrawn.[6]

694. How is the tax basis of property acquired from a decedent determined?

General Rules

Stepped up basis. As a general rule, the basis of property that has been acquired from a decedent is the fair market value of the property at the date of the decedent's death (i.e., the basis is "stepped up" or "stepped down," as the case may be, to the fair market value). This rule applies generally to all property includable in the decedent's gross estate for federal estate tax purposes (whether or not an estate tax return is required to be filed). It applies also to the

1. IRC Sec. 1011(a).
2. Basis is a "substituted basis" as determined in whole or in part by reference to the property's basis in the hands of a previous owner, or by reference to other property previously owned by the taxpayer for whom the basis is determined. IRC Sec. 7701(a)(42).
3. IRC Sec. 1016.
4. IRC Sec. 1012.
5. See IRC Sec. 354.
6. See 71 Fed. Reg. 20044 (4-19-2006).

survivor's one-half of community property where at least one-half of the value of the property was included in the decedent's gross estate. As an exception, however, the rule does not apply to "income in respect of a decedent" (see Q 745); normally the basis of such income is zero.[1] As another exception, the rule does not apply to appreciated property acquired by the decedent by gift within one year of his death where the one receiving the property from the decedent is the donor or the donor's spouse; in such case the basis of the property in the hands of the donor (or spouse) is the adjusted basis of the property in the hands of the decedent immediately before his death.[2] If an estate tax return is filed and the executor elects the alternative valuation (see Q 906), the basis is the fair market value on the alternative valuation date instead of its value on the date of death.[3]

Under IRC Section 1014(f)(1), the basis of property acquired from a decedent cannot exceed the value of the property as finally determined for estate tax purposes (or, if not yet determined, the value reported on a statement under Section 6035(a)). Proposed regulations provide that this limitation applies whenever the taxpayer reports a taxable event to the IRS, and continues to apply until the property is sold, exchanged or disposed of in a transaction that requires recognition of gain or loss. However, the proposed regulations clarify that the rules do not prohibit an adjustment to the basis of property resulting from post-death events that are allowable under another IRC section, and that such adjustments do not cause the taxpayer to violate Section 1014(f) or 6662(k) on the date of sale or other disposition. Further, the regulations provide that the limitation applies only to property that would increase the eventual estate tax liability, and both define such property and provide examples of exclusions. When the proposed regulations are made final, they will apply only to property acquired from a decedent when the return is required to be filed after July 31, 2015.[4]

If property in the estate of a decedent is transferred to an heir, legatee, devisee, or beneficiary in a transaction that constitutes a sale or exchange, the basis of the property in the hands of the heir, legatee, devisee, or beneficiary is the fair market value on the date of the transfer (not on the date of decedent's death). Likewise, the executor or administrator of the estate will recognize a gain or loss on the transaction. For example, if the executor of the will, to satisfy a bequest of $10,000, transfers to the heir stock worth $10,000, which had a value of $9,000 on the decedent's date of death, the estate recognizes a $1,000 gain, and the basis of the stock to the heir is $10,000.[5]

Jointly held property. Note that the "stepped up" basis rule applies only to property includable in the decedent's gross estate for federal estate tax purposes.[6] Thus, one acquiring property from a decedent who held the property jointly with another (or others) under the general rule of estate tax includability (i.e., the entire value of the property is includable in the estate of the first joint owner to die except to the extent the surviving joint owner(s) can prove contribution

1. IRC Sec. 1014(c).
2. IRC Sec. 1014(e).
3. IRC Sec. 1014(a).
4. IRC Sec. 1014(f)(1); REG-127923-15, TD 9757.
5. Treas. Reg. §1.1014-4(a)(3).
6. IRC Sec. 1014(b)(9).

to the cost – see Q 814) receives a stepped up basis in the property in accordance with that rule. By contrast, one who acquires property from a decedent spouse who, with the surviving spouse, had a *qualified joint interest* in the property (see Q 814) receives a stepped up basis equal to one-half the value of that interest.

Community property. The stepped up basis rule applies in the case of community property both to the decedent's one-half interest and to the surviving spouse's one-half interest.[1]

Qualified terminable interest property. Upon the death of the donee spouse or surviving spouse, qualified terminable interest property (see Q 837) is considered as "acquired from or to have passed from the decedent" for purposes of receiving a new basis at death.[2]

Decedents Dying in 2010 Who Elected Not To Be Subject to Estate Tax

Modified carryover basis. For decedents dying in 2010 who elected not to be subject to estate tax, a modified carryover basis regime (with limited step-up in basis) replaces the step-up in basis for property acquired from a decedent. That is, the basis of the person acquiring property from a decedent making the election in 2010 will generally be equal to the lesser of (1) the adjusted basis of the decedent (i.e., carried over to the recipient from the decedent), or (2) the fair market value of the property at the date of the decedent's death. However, step-up in basis is retained for up to $1,300,000 of property acquired from a decedent. In the case of certain transfers to a spouse, step-up in basis will be available for an additional $3,000,000 of property acquired from a decedent. In the case of a decedent nonresident who is not a United States citizen, step-up in basis will be available for only $60,000 of property acquired from the decedent.[3]

695. How is the tax basis of property acquired by gift determined?

If the property was acquired by gift after 1920, the basis for determining gain is generally the same as in the hands of the donor. However, in the case of property acquired by gift after September 1, 1958 and before 1977, this basis may be increased by the amount of any gift tax paid, but total basis may not exceed the fair market value of the property at the time of gift. In the case of property received by gift after 1976, the donee takes the donor's basis plus a *part* of the gift tax paid. The added fraction is the amount of the gift tax paid that is attributable to appreciation in the value of the gift over the donor's basis. The amount of attributable gift tax bears the same ratio to the amount of gift tax paid as net appreciation bears to the value of the gift.[4]

For the purpose of determining loss, the basis of property acquired by gift after 1920 is the foregoing substituted basis or the fair market value of the property at the time of gift, whichever is lower.[5] As to property acquired by gift before 1921, basis is the fair market value of the property at time of acquisition.[6]

1. IRC Sec. 1014(b)(6).
2. IRC Sec. 1014(b)(10).
3. IRC Secs. 1014(f), 1022 (for decedents dying in 2010 only).
4. IRC Sec. 1015.
5. IRC Sec. 1015(a).
6. IRC Sec. 1015(c).

696. How is the tax basis of property acquired in a generation skipping transfer determined?

Generally, in the case of property received in a generation-skipping transfer (see Q 864), the transferee takes the adjusted basis of the property immediately before the transfer plus a *part* of the generation-skipping transfer (GST) tax paid. The added fraction is the amount of the GST tax paid that is attributable to appreciation in the value of the transferred property over its previous adjusted basis. The amount of attributable GST tax bears the same ratio to the amount of GST tax paid as net appreciation bears to the value of the property transferred. Nevertheless, basis is not to be increased above fair market value. When property is acquired by gift in a generation-skipping transfer, the basis of the property is increased by the gift tax basis adjustment (see Q 671) before the generation-skipping transfer tax basis adjustment is made.[1]

However, where property is transferred in a taxable termination (see Q 864) that occurs at the same time and as a result of the death of an individual, the basis of such property is increased (or decreased) to fair market value, except that any increase (or decrease) in basis is limited by multiplying such increase (or decrease) by the inclusion ratio used in allocating the generation-skipping tax exemption (see Q 865).[2]

697. What is the tax basis of property acquired from a spouse or incident to a divorce?

Where property is transferred between spouses, or former spouses incident to a divorce, after July 18, 1984 pursuant to an instrument in effect after that date, the transferee's basis in the property is generally the adjusted basis of the property in the hands of the transferor immediately before the transfer and no gain or loss is recognized at the time of transfer (unless, under certain circumstances, the property is transferred in trust).[3] These rules may apply to transfers made after 1983 if both parties elect.[4] See Q 779 regarding transfers incident to divorce.

698. What is a "capital asset"?

For tax purposes, a "capital asset" is any property that, in the hands of the taxpayer, is not: (1) property (including inventory and stock in trade) held primarily for sale to customers; (2) real or depreciable property used in his trade or business; (3) copyrights and literary, musical, or artistic compositions (or similar properties) created by the taxpayer, or merely owned by him, if his tax basis in the property is determined (other than by reason of IRC Section 1022, which governs the basis determination of inherited property) by reference to the creator's tax basis; (4) letters, memoranda, and similar properties produced by or for the taxpayer, or merely owned by him, if his tax basis is determined by reference to the tax basis of such producer or recipient; (5) accounts or notes receivable acquired in his trade or business for services rendered or sales of property described in (1), above; (6) certain publications of the United States government; (7) any commodities derivative financial instrument held by a commodities derivatives

1. IRC Sec. 2654(a)(1).
2. IRC Sec. 2654(a)(2).
3. IRC Secs. 453B(g), 1041; Temp. Treas. Reg. §1.1041-1T, A-1.
4. Temp. Treas. Reg. §1.1041-1T, A-16.

dealer; (8) any hedging instrument that is clearly identified as such by the required time; and (9) supplies of a type regularly used or consumed by the taxpayer in the ordinary course of his trade or business.[1]

Generally, any property held as an investment is a capital asset, except that rental real estate is generally not a capital asset because it is treated as a trade or business asset (see Q 7789).[2]

699. When is capital gain or loss short-term? When is it long-term? How is an individual's "holding period" calculated?

Generally, a capital gain or loss is long-term if the property giving rise to the gain or loss was owned *for more than one year*. It is short-term gain or loss if the property was owned for *one year or less*.[3] For an explanation of the tax treatment of capital gains and losses, see Q 702.

To determine how long a taxpayer has owned property (i.e., his "holding period"), begin counting on the day *after* the property is acquired; the same date in each successive month is the first day of a new month. The date on which the property is disposed of is included (i.e., counted) in the holding period.[4] If property is acquired on the last day of the month, the holding period begins on the first day of the following month. Therefore, if it is sold prior to the first day of the 13th month following the acquisition, the gain or loss will be short-term.[5] According to IRS Publication 544 (released in November, 1982), if property is acquired *near* the end of the month and the holding period begins on a date that does not occur in every month (e.g., the 29th, 30th, or 31st), the last day of each month that lacks that date is considered to begin a new month; however, later editions of Publication 544 have omitted this statement.

Example 1. Mrs. Copeland bought a capital asset on January 1, 2019. She would begin counting on January 2, 2019. The second day of each successive month would begin a new month. If Mrs. Copeland sold the asset on January 1, 2020, her holding period would not be more than one year. To have a long-term capital gain or loss she would have to sell the asset on or after January 2, 2020.

Example 2. Mrs. Brim bought a capital asset on January 30, 2019. She would begin counting on January 31, 2019. Since February does not have thirty-one days, Mrs. Brim will start a new month on February 28. In months that have only thirty days, the thirtieth will begin a new month.

Special rules apply in the case of gains or losses on regulated futures contracts, single stock futures (see Q 7587), nonequity option contracts, and foreign currency contracts (see Q 7592). Furthermore, the short sale rules (see Q 7525) and tax straddle rules (see Q 7593 to Q 7614) may require a tolling or recalculation of an individual's holding period.

Tacking of Holding Periods

In some cases, such as when property is received as a gift or in a like-kind exchange, the IRC allows a taxpayer to add another individual's holding period in the same property, or the

1. IRC Sec. 1221; Treas. Reg. §1.1221-1.
2. See IRS Pub. 544.
3. IRC Sec. 1222.
4. Rev. Rul. 70-598, 1970-2 CB 168.
5. Rev. Rul. 66-7, 1966-1 CB 188.

taxpayer's holding period in other property, to the taxpayer's holding period. This is referred to as "tacking" of holding periods.[1]

For an explanation of how the holding period is determined for stock received by a policyholder or annuity holder in a demutualization transaction, see SCA 200131028.[2]

Where applicable, tacking of holding periods is discussed in the appropriate question.

700. How are securities that are sold or transferred identified for tax purposes?

When an individual sells or otherwise transfers securities (i.e., stocks, bonds, mutual fund shares, etc.) from holdings that were purchased or acquired on different dates or at different prices (or tax bases), he must generally be able to identify the lot from which the transferred securities originated in order to determine the tax basis and holding period. If he is unable to adequately identify the lot, he will usually be deemed to have transferred the securities in the order in which they were acquired, by a "first-in, first-out" (FIFO) method.[3] However, in cases involving mutual fund shares he may be permitted to use an "average basis" method to determine the tax basis and holding period in the securities transferred (see Q 7946).

Generally, identification is determined by the certificate delivered to the buyer or other transferee. The security represented by the certificate is deemed to be the security sold or transferred. This is true even if the taxpayer intended to sell securities from another lot, or instructed a broker to sell securities from another lot.[4]

There are several exceptions to the general rule of adequate identification. One occurs when the securities are left in the custody of a broker or other agent. If the seller specifies to the broker which securities to sell or transfer, and if the broker or agent sends a written confirmation of the specified securities within a reasonable time, then the specified securities are the securities sold or transferred, even though different certificates are delivered to the buyer or other transferee.[5] If the securities held are United States securities (Treasury bonds, notes, etc.) recorded by a book-entry on the books of a Federal Reserve Bank, then identification is made when the taxpayer notifies the Reserve Bank (or the person through whom the taxpayer is selling the securities) of the lot number (assigned by the *taxpayer*) of the securities to be sold or transferred, and when the Reserve Bank (or the person through whom the taxpayer sells the securities) provides the taxpayer with a written advice of transaction, specifying the amount and description of securities sold or transferred.[6]

Another exception arises when the taxpayer holds a single certificate representing securities from different lots. If the taxpayer sells part of the securities represented by the certificate through a broker, adequate identification is made if the taxpayer specifies to the broker which

1. IRC Sec. 1223(2).
2. See SCA 200131028.
3. Treas. Reg. §1.1012-1(c)(1).
4. Treas. Reg. §1.1012-1(c)(2).
5. Treas. Reg. §1.1012-1(c)(3)(i).
6. Treas. Reg. §1.1012-1(c)(7); Rev. Rul. 71-21, 1971-1 CB 221.

securities to sell and if the broker sends a written confirmation of the specified securities within a reasonable time. If the taxpayer sells the securities himself, then there is adequate identification if he keeps a written record identifying the particular securities he intended to sell.[1]

A third exception occurs when the securities are held by a trustee, or by an executor or administrator of an estate. An adequate identification is made if the trustee, executor, or administrator specifies in writing in the books or records of the trust or estate the securities to be sold, transferred or distributed. (In the case of a distribution, the trustee, executor, or administrator must also give the distributee a written document specifying the particular securities distributed). In such a case, the specified securities are the securities sold, transferred or distributed, even though certificates from a different lot are delivered to the purchaser, transferee or distributee.[2]

701. How is a loss realized on a sale between related persons treated for income tax purposes?

If an individual sells property at a loss to a related person (as defined below), that loss may *not* be deducted or used to offset capital gains for income tax purposes.[3] It makes no difference that the sale was a bona fide, arm's-length transaction.[4] Neither does it matter that the sale was made indirectly through an unrelated middleman.[5] The loss on the sale of stock will be disallowed even though the sale and purchase are made separately on a stock exchange and the stock certificates received are not the certificates sold.[6] However, these rules will not apply to any loss of the distributing corporation (or the distributee) in the case of a distribution in complete liquidation.[7]

A loss realized on the exchange of properties between related persons will also be disallowed under these rules.[8] Whether loss is realized in transfers between spouses during marriage or incident to divorce is explained in Q 779.

For this purpose, persons are related if they are: (1) members of the same family (i.e., brothers, sisters, spouses, ancestors, and lineal descendants; but not if they are in-laws);[9] (2) an individual and a corporation of which the individual actually or constructively owns more than 50 percent of the stock; (3) a grantor and a fiduciary of a trust; (4) fiduciaries of two trusts if the same person is the grantor of both; (5) a fiduciary and a beneficiary of the same trust; (6) a fiduciary of a trust and a beneficiary of another trust set up by the same grantor; (7) a fiduciary of a trust and a corporation of which the trust or the grantor of the trust actually or constructively owns more than 50 percent of the stock; (8) a person and an IRC Section 501 tax-exempt organization controlled by the person or members of his family (as described in (1) above); (9) a corporation and a partnership if the same person actually or constructively

1. Treas. Reg. §1.1012-1(c)(3)(ii).
2. Treas. Reg. §1.1012-1(c)(4).
3. IRC Sec. 267(a); Treas. Reg. §1.267(a)-1 and Rev. Rul. 2008-5.
4. Treas. Reg. §1.267(a)-1(c).
5. See *Hassen v. Comm.*, 599 F.2d 305 (9th Cir. 1979).
6. *McWilliams v. Comm.*, 331 U.S. 694 (1947).
7. IRC Sec. 267(a)(1).
8. IRC Sec. 267(a)(1).
9. See Let. Rul. 9017008.

owns more than 50 percent of the stock of the corporation, and has more than a 50 percent interest in the partnership; (10) two S corporations if the same persons actually or constructively own more than 50 percent of the stock of each; (11) an S corporation and a C corporation, if the same persons actually or constructively own more than 50 percent of the stock of each; (12) generally, an executor and a beneficiary of an estate; or (13) possibly an individual and his or her individual retirement account (IRA).[1] Special rules apply for purposes of determining constructive ownership of stock.[2] The relationship between a grantor and fiduciary did not prevent recognition of loss on a sale of stock between them where the fiduciary purchased the stock in his individual capacity and where the sale was unrelated to the grantor-fiduciary relationship.[3]

Generally, loss will be disallowed on a sale between a partnership and a partner who owns more than a 50 percent interest, or between two partnerships if the same persons own more than a 50 percent interest in each.[4] Furthermore, with respect to transactions between two partnerships having one or more common partners *or* in which one or more of the partners in each partnership are related (as defined above), a portion of the loss will be disallowed according to the relative interests of the partners.[5] If the transaction is between a partnership and an individual who is related to one of the partners (as defined above), any deductions for losses will be denied with respect to the related partner's distributive share, but not with respect to the relative shares of each unrelated partner.[6] Loss on a sale or exchange (other than of inventory) between two corporations that are members of the same controlled group (using a 50 percent test instead of 80 percent) is generally not denied but is deferred until the property is transferred outside the controlled group.[7]

If the related person to whom property was originally sold (or exchanged), sells or exchanges the same property (or property whose tax basis is determined by reference to such property) at a gain, the gain will be recognized only to the extent it exceeds the loss originally denied by reason of the related parties rules.[8]

Special rules apply to installment sales between related parties (see Q 668) and to the deduction of losses (see Q 8000 to Q 8020).

In a case of first impression, the Tax Court held that IRC Section 382(l)(3)(A)(i)—which provides that an "individual" and all members of his family described in IRC Section 318(a)(1) (i.e., his spouse, children, grandchildren, and parents) are treated as one individual for purposes of applying IRC Section 382 (which limits the amount of pre-change losses that a loss corporation may use to offset taxable income in the taxable years or periods following an ownership change)—applies solely from the perspective of individuals who are shareholders (as determined under applicable attribution rules) of the loss corporation. The court further held that siblings

1. IRC Sec. 267(b).
2. See IRC Sec. 267(c).
3. Let. Rul. 9017008.
4. IRC Sec. 707(b).
5. Temp. Treas. Reg. §1.267(a)-2T(c), A-2.
6. Treas. Reg. §1.267(b)-1(b).
7. IRC Sec. 267(f).
8. IRC Sec. 267(d); Treas. Reg. §1.267(d)-1.

are not treated as one individual under IRC Section 382(l)(3)(A)(i).[1] Accordingly, in *Garber*, the sale of shares by one brother to the other brother resulted in an ownership change with respect to the closely held corporation within the meaning of IRC Section 382(g).

702. How is an individual taxed on capital gains and losses?

For tax years beginning in 2018 and before 2026, with respect to adjusted net capital gain, the 0 percent rate will apply to joint filers who earn less than $80,000 in 2020 (half the amount for married taxpayers filing separately), heads of households who earn less than $53,600, single filers who earn less than $40,000, and trusts and estates with less than $2,650 in income.

The 15 percent capital gains rate will apply to joint filers who earn more than $80,000 but less than $496,600 (half the amount for married taxpayers filing separately), heads of households who earn more than $53,600 but less than $469,050, single filers who earn more than $40,000 but less than $441,450, and trusts and estates with more than $2,650 but less than $13,150 in income.

The 20 percent capital gains rate will apply to joint filers who earn more than $496,600 (half that amount for married taxpayers filing separately), heads of households who earn more than $469,050, single filers who earn more than $441,450, and trusts and estates with more than $13,150 in income.[2]

Aside from the changes in the income thresholds that determine the applicable rate, tax reform did not change the tax treatment of capital gains and losses and qualified dividend income.[3]

For tax years beginning in 2013 and before 2018, adjusted net capital gain was generally subject to a maximum rate of 0 percent for taxpayers in the 10 and 15 percent tax brackets, a maximum rate of 15 percent for taxpayers in the 25 percent, 28 percent, 33 percent, and 35 percent tax brackets (see "Reduction in Capital Gain Rates," Q 704), and a maximum rate of 20 percent for taxpayers in the 39.6 percent tax bracket.

Despite these general brackets, detailed rules as to the exact calculation of the capital gains tax result in some exceptions.[4]

"Adjusted net capital gain" is *net capital gain* reduced (but not below zero) by the sum of: (1) *unrecaptured IRC Section 1250 gain*; and (2) *28 percent rate gain* (both defined below); *plus* (3) "qualified dividend income" (as defined in IRC Section 1(h)(11)(B)).[5]

Gain is determined by subtracting the adjusted basis of the asset sold or exchanged from the amount realized. Loss is determined by subtracting the amount realized from the adjusted basis of the asset sold or exchanged. See Q 692. The amount realized includes both money and

1. *Garber Industries Holding Co., Inc., v. Comm.*, 124 TC 1 (2005); *aff'd*, 435 F. 3d 555, 2006-1 USTC ¶50,109 (5th Cir. 2006).
2. IRC Sec. 1(j)(5), Rev. Proc. 2018-57, Rev. Proc. 2019-44.
3. IRC Sec. 1(h), as amended by ATRA.
4. IRC Sec. 1(h), as amended by ATRA.
5. IRC Sec. 1(h)(3).

the fair market value of any property received.[1] Gains and losses from the sale or exchange of capital assets are either short-term or long-term. Generally, in order for gain or loss to be long-term, the asset must have been held for more than one year. See Q 699.

Generally, taxpayers may elect to treat a portion of net capital gain as investment income.[2] If the election is made, any net capital gain included in investment income will be subject to the taxpayer's marginal income tax rate. The election must be made on or before the due date (including extensions) of the income tax return for the taxable year in which the net capital gain is recognized. The election is to be made on Form 4952, "Investment Interest Expense Deduction."[3] See Q 8037.

Net capital gain is the excess of net long-term capital gain for the taxable year over net short term capital loss for such year.[4] However, net capital gain for any taxable year is reduced (but not below zero) by any amount the taxpayer takes into account under the investment income exception to the investment interest deduction.[5] See Q 8037.

The Code provides that for a taxpayer with a net capital gain for any taxable year, the tax will not exceed the *sum* of the following six items:

(A) the tax computed at regular rates (without regard to the rules for capital gain) on the *greater* of (i) taxable income reduced by the net capital gain, or (ii) the *lesser* of (I) the amount of taxable income taxed at a rate below the income tax rate that applies based on the taxpayer's income with respect to the income thresholds described above (see Appendix B), *or* (II) taxable income reduced by the adjusted net capital gain;

(B) 0 percent of so much of the taxpayer's adjusted net capital gain (or, if less, taxable income) as does not exceed the *excess* (if any) of (i) the amount of taxable income that would (without regard to this paragraph) be taxed at the income tax rate that applies based on the taxpayer's income with respect to the income thresholds described above (see Appendix B) *over* (ii) the taxable income reduced by the adjusted net capital gain;

(C) 15 percent of the lesser of (i) so much of the taxpayer's adjusted net capital gain (or, if less, taxable income) as *exceeds* the amount on which a tax is determined under (B), above, or (ii) the *excess* of (I) the amount of taxable income which would be taxed at below the income tax rate that applies based on the taxpayer's income with respect to the income thresholds described above *over* (II) the sum of the amounts on which a tax is determined under (A) and (B), above;

1. IRC Sec. 1001.
2. See IRC Secs. 163(d)(4)(B), 1(h)(2).
3. Treas. Reg. §1.163(d)-1.
4. IRC Sec. 1222(11).
5. IRC Secs. 163(d)(4)(B)(iii), 1(h)(2).

(D) 20 percent of the taxpayer's adjusted net capital gain (or, if less, taxable income) in *excess* of the sum of the amounts on which tax is determined under (B) and (C), above;

(E) 25 percent of the *excess* (if any) of (i) the unrecaptured IRC Section 1250 gain (or, if less, the net capital gain (determined without regard to qualified dividend income)), *over* (ii) the *excess* (if any) of (I) the sum of the amount on which tax is determined under (A) above, *plus* the net capital gain, *over* (II) taxable income; and

(F) 28 percent of the amount of taxable income in *excess* of the sum of the amounts on which tax is determined under (A) through (E) above.[1]

It is important to note that as a result of this complex formula, generally, the maximum capital gains rate on *adjusted net capital gain* for 2013-2017 will be 20 percent to the extent an individual is taxed at the 39.6 percent income tax rate, 15 percent to the extent an individual is taxed at the 25, 28, 33 or 35 percent income tax rates (see Q 751), and 0 percent to the extent the individual is taxed at the 15 percent or 10 percent income tax rates.[2] For 2018-2025, the maximum capital gains rate will be determined based on the income thresholds discussed above, which do not neatly align with the individual income tax brackets that will apply beginning in 2018 (however, the 0, 15, and 20 percent capital gains rates continue to apply).

IRC Section 1250 provides for the recapture of gain on certain property on which accelerated depreciation has been used. "Unrecaptured IRC Section 1250 gain" means the excess, if any, of: (i) that amount of long-term capital gain (not otherwise treated as ordinary income) that would be treated as ordinary income if IRC Section 1250(b)(1) included all depreciation and the applicable percentage under IRC Section 1250(a) were 100 percent; over (ii) the excess, if any of (a) the sum of collectibles loss, net short-term capital loss and long-term capital loss carryovers, over (b) the sum of collectibles gain and IRC Section 1202 gain. However, at no time may the amount of Unrecaptured IRC Section 1250 gain that is attributable to sales, exchanges and conversions described in IRC Section 1231(a)(3)(A) for any taxable year exceed the net IRC Section 1231 gain, as defined in IRC Section 1231(c)(3) for such year.[3]

"28 percent rate gain" means the excess, if any, of (A) the sum of collectibles gain and IRC Section 1202 gain (i.e., gain on certain small businesses), over (B) the sum of (i) collectibles loss, (ii) net short-term capital loss, and (iii) long-term capital loss carried over under IRC Section 1212(b)(1)(B) (i.e., the excess of net long-term capital loss over net short-term capital gain, carried over to the succeeding taxable year).[4]

"Collectibles gain or loss" is gain or loss on the sale or exchange of a collectible that is a capital asset held for more than one year, but only to the extent such gain is taken into account in computing gross income and such loss is taken into account in computing taxable income.[5]

1. IRC Secs. 1(h)(1)(D); 1(h)(1)(A), 1(h)(1)(B), IRC Secs. 1(h)(1)(C), 1(h)(1)(E), as amended by ATRA 2012.
2. IRC Sec. 1(h).
3. IRC Sec. 1(h)(6).
4. IRC Sec. 1(h)(4).
5. IRC Sec. 1(h)(5).

Examples of collectibles include artwork, gems and coins.[1] For additional details, see Q 7713 and Q 7714.

"IRC Section 1202 gain" means the excess of (A) the gain that would be excluded from gross income under IRC Section 1202 but for the percentage limitation in IRC Section 1202(a) over (B) the gain excluded from gross income under IRC Section 1202 (i.e., 50 percent exclusion for certain qualified small business stock).[2] See Q 7521 and Q 7522 for details. (JGTRRA 2003 provides that for alternative minimum tax purposes, an amount equal to 7 percent of the amount excluded from gross income for the taxable year under IRC Section 1202 will be treated as a preference item.[3] See Q 7522.)

Collectibles gain and IRC Section 1250 gains under IRC Section 1(h) are subject to special rules when an interest in a pass-through entity (i.e., partnership, S corporation, or trust) is sold or exchanged. Regulations finalized in 2000 provide rules for dividing the holding period of an interest in a partnership.[4]

Special rules apply in the case of wash sales (see Q 7537), short sales (see Q 7525), and IRC Section 1256 contracts (see Q 7592).

NOTE: Beginning in 2013, taxpayers may also have to account for the 3.8 percent tax on investment-type income and gains under IRC Section 1411. This tax was not impacted by tax reform.

703. What is the "netting" process used to determine whether a taxpayer has a capital loss for the year? Can capital losses be carried into other tax years?

Editor's Note: For tax years beginning in 2018 and before 2026, with respect to adjusted net capital gain:

The 0 percent rate will apply to joint filers who earn less than $80,000 in 2020 (half the amount for married taxpayers filing separately), heads of households who earn less than $53,600, single filers who earn less than $40,000, and trusts and estates with less than $2,650 in income.

The 15 percent capital gains rate will apply to joint filers who earn more than $80,000 but less than $496,600 (half the amount for married taxpayers filing separately), heads of households who earn more than $53,600 but less than $469,050, single filers who earn more than $40,000 but less than $441,450, and trusts and estates with more than $2,650 but less than $13,150 in income.

The 20 percent capital gains rate will apply to joint filers who earn more than $496,600 (half that amount for married taxpayers filing separately), heads of households who earn more

1. See IRC Sec. 408(m)(2).
2. IRC Sec. 1(h)(7).
3. IRC Sec. 57(a)(7).
4. See TD 8902, 2000-2 CB 323.

than $469,050, single filers who earn more than $441,450, and trusts and estates with more than $13,150 in income.[1] See Q706 for the rates that applied in other years.

The rules discussed in Q 702 essentially establish four groups of capital assets (based upon pre-existing tax rates):

(1) short-term capital assets, with no special tax rate;

(2) 28 percent capital assets, generally consisting of collectibles gain or loss, and IRC Section 1202 gain;

(3) 25 percent capital assets, consisting of assets that generate unrecaptured IRC Section 1250 gain; and

(4) a group consisting of all other long-term capital assets, with a 0, 15, or 20 percent rate that applies based on the taxpayer's income levels (see editor's note, above, or 20 percent (in tax years beginning after 2012 and before 2018 for taxpayers in the 39.6 percent income tax bracket); 15 percent (for taxpayers in the 25, 28, 33, or 35 percent income tax brackets); 0 percent capital assets (i.e., 0 percent for taxable years beginning after 2007 and 5 percent for 2003 through 2007) for taxpayers in the 15 and 10 percent tax brackets).

Within each group, gains and losses are netted. The effect of this process is generally that if there is a net loss from (1), it is applied to reduce any net gain from (2), (3), or (4), in that order. If there is a net loss from (2) it is applied to reduce any net gain from (3) or (4), in that order. If there is a net loss from (4), it is applied to reduce any net gain from (2) or (3), in that order.[2]

After all of the netting above, if there are net losses, up to $3,000 ($1,500 in the case of married individuals filing separately) of losses can be deducted against ordinary income.[3] Apparently, any deducted loss will be treated as reducing net loss from (1), (2), or (4), in that order. Any remaining net losses can be carried over to other taxable years, retaining its group classifications. If there are net gains, such gains will generally be taxed as described above.

Generally, to the extent a capital loss described above exceeds the $3,000 limit ($1,500 in the case of married individuals filing separately); it may be carried over to other taxable years, but always retaining its character as long-term or short-term. However, special rules apply in determining the carryover amount from years in which a taxpayer has no taxable income.[4]

704. How have the capital gain rates for individuals changed between 2003 and the present?

Long-term capital gains incurred on or after May 6, 2003 are subject to lower tax rates. For taxpayers in the 25, 28, 33 and 35 percent tax brackets, the rate on long-term capital gains

1. IRC Sec. 1(j)(5), Rev. Proc. 2018-57, Rev. Proc. 2019-44.
2. IRC Sec. 1(h)(1), as amended by ATRA; Notice 97-59, 1997-2 CB 309.
3. IRC Sec. 1211(b).
4. IRC Secs. 1211(b), 1212(b).

was reduced from 20 percent to 15 percent in 2003 through 2012. For taxpayers in the 10 and 15 percent brackets, the rate on long-term capital gains was reduced from 10 percent to 5 percent in 2003 through 2007, and all the way down to 0 percent in 2008 through 2017. These lower capital gains rates have been made permanent, but the 2017 Tax Act has changed the income thresholds for determining which rate applies.[1]

Early in 2013, Congress enacted the American Taxpayer Relief Act of 2012 ("ATRA") under which the reduced capital gain rates were extended for some taxpayers, while increased rates were placed into effect for higher income taxpayers. ATRA increased the rate on long-term capital gains to 20 percent in 2012-2017 for taxpayers with taxable income that placed them in the highest 39.6 percent tax bracket. The applicable threshold amount was adjusted annually for inflation.[2]

For taxpayers in the 10 or 15 percent income tax brackets, the rate on long-term capital gains was 0 percent for 2012-2017. Taxpayers in the 25, 28, 33 and 35 percent tax brackets were taxed at 15 percent on long-term capital gains from 2012-2017.[3]

2018 Capital Gains Rates

For 2018, the 20 percent rate will apply to joint filers who earn more than $479,000 (half that amount for married taxpayers filing separately), heads of households who earn more than $452,400, single filers who earn more than $425,800, and trusts and estates with more than $12,700 in income.

For 2018, the 15 percent rate will apply to joint filers who earn more than $77,200 but less than $479,000 (half the amount for married taxpayers filing separately), heads of households who earn more than $51,700 but less than $452,400, single filers who earn more than $38,600 but less than $425,800, and trusts and estates with more than $2,600 but less than $12,700 in income.

In 2018, under the 2017 Tax Act, the 0 percent rate will apply to joint filers who earn less than $77,200 (half the amount for married taxpayers filing separately), heads of households who earn less than $51,700, single filers who earn less than $38,600, and trusts and estates with less than $2,600 in income.

2019 Capital Gains Rates

For tax years beginning in 2019, with respect to adjusted net capital gain, the 0 percent rate will apply to joint filers who earn less than $78,750 (half the amount for married taxpayers filing separately), heads of households who earn less than $52,750, single filers who earn less than $39,375, and trusts and estates with less than $2,650 in income.

1. IRC Sec. 1(h)(1), as amended by ATRA; TIPRA 2005 Sec. 102, *amending* JGTRRA 2003 Sec. 303, Pub. Law No. 115-97.
2. IRC Secs. 1(i), 1(h), as amended by ATRA, Secs. 101(b)(3)(C) and 102(b).
3. IRC Sec. 1(h), as amended by ATRA, Sec. 102.

The 15 percent capital gains rate will apply to joint filers who earn more than $78,750 but less than $488,850 (half the amount for married taxpayers filing separately), heads of households who earn more than $52,750 but less than $461,700, single filers who earn more than $39,375 but less than $434,550, and trusts and estates with more than $2,650 but less than $12,950 in income.

The 20 percent capital gains rate will apply to joint filers who earn more than $488,850 (half that amount for married taxpayers filing separately), heads of households who earn more than $461,700, single filers who earn more than $434,550, and trusts and estates with more than $12,950 in income.[1]

2020 Capital Gains Rates

For tax years beginning in 2020, the following rates apply: 0 percent rate will apply to joint filers who earn less than $80,000 (half the amount for married taxpayers filing separately), heads of households who earn less than $53,600, single filers who earn less than $40,000, and trusts and estates with less than $2,650 in income.

The 15 percent capital gains rate will apply to joint filers who earn more than $80,000 but less than $496,600 (half the amount for married taxpayers filing separately), heads of households who earn more than $53,600 but less than $469,050, single filers who earn more than $40,000 but less than $441,450, and trusts and estates with more than $2,650 but less than $13,150 in income.

The 20 percent capital gains rate will apply to joint filers who earn more than $496,600 (half that amount for married taxpayers filing separately), heads of households who earn more than $469,050, single filers who earn more than $441,450, and trusts and estates with more than $13,150 in income.

In addition, beginning January 1, 2013, an investment income tax of 3.8 percent applies to certain investment-type income (including income received from capital gains). The investment income tax applies for taxpayers whose annual adjusted gross income exceeds the investment income threshold amount ($250,000 for married taxpayers filing jointly, $125,000 for married taxpayers filing separately and $200,000 for all other taxpayers).[2] The income threshold used for purposes of the 3.8 percent investment income tax is not adjusted for inflation, and the tax remained intact after the passage of the 2017 tax reform legislation.

Collectibles gain, IRC Section 1202 gain (i.e., qualified small business stock), and unrecaptured IRC Section 1250 gain continue to be taxed at their previously existing tax rates (i.e., 28 percent for collectibles gain and IRC Section 1202 gain, and 25 percent for unrecaptured IRC Section 1250 gain).[3]

1. IRC Sec. 1(j)(5), Rev. Proc. 2018-57.
2. IRC Sec. 1411.
3. IRC Sec. 1(h).

Repeal of qualified five-year gain. For tax years beginning after December 31, 2000, if certain requirements were met, the maximum rates on "qualified five-year gain" could be reduced to 8 percent and 18 percent (in place of 10 percent and 20 percent respectively). Furthermore, a noncorporate taxpayer in the 25 percent bracket (or higher) who held a capital asset on January 1, 2001 could elect to treat the asset as if it had been sold and repurchased for its fair market value on January 1, 2001 (or on January 2, 2001 in the case of publicly traded stock). If a noncorporate taxpayer made this election, the holding period for the elected assets began after December 31, 2000, thereby making the asset eligible for the 18 percent rate if it was later sold after having been held by the taxpayer for more than five years from the date of the deemed sale and deemed reacquisition.[1] Under JGTRRA 2003, the five-year holding period requirement, and the 18 percent and 8 percent tax rates for qualified five-year gain are repealed. Though this repeal was scheduled to sunset along with the reduced rates, it was made permanent under ATRA.

705. What lower rates apply for qualified dividend income?

Under prior law, dividends were treated as ordinary income and, thus, were subject to ordinary income tax rates. Under JGTRRA 2003, "qualified dividend income" (see Q 706) is treated as "net capital gain" (Q 706) and is, therefore, subject to new lower tax rates. This treatment continues after the 2017 tax reform legislation was passed, but the income thresholds for determining which rate applies were changed.

2020 Capital Gains Rates

For tax years beginning in 2020, the following rates apply: 0 percent rate will apply to joint filers who earn less than $80,000 (half the amount for married taxpayers filing separately), heads of households who earn less than $53,600, single filers who earn less than $40,000, and trusts and estates with less than $2,650 in income.

The 15 percent capital gains rate will apply to joint filers who earn more than $80,000 but less than $496,600 (half the amount for married taxpayers filing separately), heads of households who earn more than $53,600 but less than $469,050, single filers who earn more than $40,000 but less than $441,450, and trusts and estates with more than $2,650 but less than $13,150 in income.

The 20 percent capital gains rate will apply to joint filers who earn more than $496,600 (half that amount for married taxpayers filing separately), heads of households who earn more than $469,050, single filers who earn more than $441,450, and trusts and estates with more than $13,150 in income.

2019 Capital Gains Rates

For tax years beginning in 2019, with respect to adjusted net capital gain, the 0 percent rate will apply to joint filers who earn less than $78,750 (half the amount for married taxpayers

1. IRC Secs. 1(h)(2), 1(h)(9), prior to amendment by JGTRRA 2003; JCWAA 2002 Sec. 414(a) and CRTRA 2000 Sec. 314(c), amending TRA '97 Sec. 311(e).

filing separately), heads of households who earn less than $52,750, single filers who earn less than $39,375, and trusts and estates with less than $2,650 in income.

The 15 percent capital gains rate will apply to joint filers who earn more than $78,750 but less than $488,850 (half the amount for married taxpayers filing separately), heads of households who earn more than $52,750 but less than $461,700, single filers who earn more than $39,375 but less than $434,550, and trusts and estates with more than $2,650 but less than $12,950 in income.

The 20 percent capital gains rate will apply to joint filers who earn more than $488,850 (half that amount for married taxpayers filing separately), heads of households who earn more than $461,700, single filers who earn more than $434,550, and trusts and estates with more than $12,950 in income.[1]

2018 Capital Gains Rates

In 2018, the 0 percent rate will apply to joint filers who earn less than $77,200 (half the amount for married taxpayers filing separately), heads of households who earn less than $51,700, single filers who earn less than $38,600, and trusts and estates with less than $2,600 in income.

The 15 percent rate will apply to joint filers who earn more than $77,200 but less than $479,000 (half the amount for married taxpayers filing separately), heads of households who earn more than $51,700 but less than $452,400, single filers who earn more than $38,600 but less than $425,800, and trusts and estates with more than $2,600 but less than $12,700 in income.

The 20 percent rate will apply to joint filers who earn more than $479,000 (half that amount for married taxpayers filing separately), heads of households who earn more than $452,400, single filers who earn more than $425,800, and trusts and estates with more than $12,700 in income.[2]

Pre-2018 Rules: For taxpayers in the 25, 28, 33 and 35 percent income tax brackets, the maximum rate on qualified dividends paid by corporations to individuals is 15 percent for tax years beginning in 2003 and before 2018. For taxpayers in the 15 percent and 10 percent income tax brackets, the tax rate on qualified dividend income is reduced to 0 percent for tax years beginning in 2008 and before 2018 (5 percent in 2003 through 2007). For taxpayers in the 39.6 percent income tax bracket, the maximum tax rate on qualified dividends is 20 percent for tax years beginning in 2013 and before 2018.

The preferential treatment of qualified dividends as net capital gains was scheduled to "sunset" (expire) on December 31, 2012, after which time the prior treatment of dividends was to become effective.[3] In other words, dividends were once again to be taxed at ordinary income tax rates. The American Taxpayer Relief Act of 2012 prevented this sunset and made the treatment of qualified dividend income as net capital gain permanent.[4]

1. IRC Sec. 1(j)(5), Rev. Proc. 2018-57.
2. IRC Sec. 1(j)(5).
3. IRC Sec. 1(h)(1); TIPRA 2005 Sec. 102, *amending* JGTRRA 2003 Sec. 303.
4. ATRA 2012, Pub. Law No. 112-240.

706. What is qualified dividend income?

Certain dividends are taxed as "net capital gain" for purposes of the reduction in the tax rates on dividends. "Net capital gain" for this purpose means net capital gain *increased* by "qualified dividend income" (without regard to this paragraph).[1] "Qualified dividend income" means dividends received during the taxable year from domestic corporations and "qualified foreign corporations" (defined below).[2]

The term qualified dividend income does *not* include the following:

(1) dividends paid by tax-exempt corporations;

(2) any amount allowed as a deduction under IRC Section 591 (relating to the deduction for dividends paid by mutual savings banks, etc.);

(3) dividends paid on certain employer securities as described in IRC Section 404(k);

(4) any dividend on a share (or shares) of stock that the shareholder has not held for more than sixty days during the *121-day* period beginning sixty days before the ex-dividend date (as measured under IRC Section 246(c)). For preferred stock, the holding period is more than ninety days during the *181-day* period beginning ninety days before the ex-dividend date *if* the dividends are attributable to a period exceeding 366 days (note, however, that if the preferred dividends are attributable to a period totaling less than 367 days, the holding period stated in the preceding sentence applies).[3]

Special rules. Qualified dividend income does *not* include any amount that the taxpayer takes into account as investment income under IRC Section 163(d)(4)(B).[4] If an individual, trust, or estate receives qualified dividend income from one or more dividends that are "extraordinary dividends" (within the meaning of IRC Section 1059(c)), any loss on the sale or exchange of such share(s) of stock will, to the extent of such dividends, be treated as long-term capital loss.[5]

A dividend received from a mutual fund or REIT is subject to the limitations under IRC Sections 854 and 857.[6] For the treatment of mutual fund dividends and REIT dividends under JGTRRA 2003, see Q 7935 and Q 7974, respectively.

Pass-through entities. In the case of partnerships, S corporations, common trust funds, trusts, and estates, the rule that qualified dividends are taxable as capital gains applies to taxable years ending after December 31, 2002, except that dividends received by the entity prior to January 1, 2003 are *not* treated as qualified dividend income.[7]

1. IRC Sec. 1(h)(11)(A).
2. IRC Sec. 1(h)(11)(B).
3. IRC Sec. 1(h)(11)(B).
4. IRC Sec. 1(h)(11)(D)(i). See also Temp. Treas. Reg. §1.163(d)-1T.
5. IRC Sec. 1(h)(11)(D).
6. IRC Sec. 1(h)(11)(D)(iii).
7. WFTRA 2004 Sec. 402(a)(6), JGTRRA 2003 Sec. 302(f).

Qualified foreign corporations. The term "qualified foreign corporation" means a foreign corporation incorporated in a possession of the United States, or a corporation that is eligible for benefits of a comprehensive income tax treaty with the United States. If a foreign corporation does not satisfy either of these requirements, it will nevertheless be treated as such with respect to any dividends paid by that corporation *if* its stock (or ADRs with respect to such stock) is readily tradable on an established securities market in the United States.[1]

Common stock (or an ADR in respect of such stock) is considered "readily tradable on an established securities market in the United States" if it is listed on a national securities exchange that is registered under Section 6 of the Securities Exchange Act of 1934 (15 USC 78(f)), or on the NASDAQ Stock Market. [2] As stated by the SEC, registered national exchanges include the following:

- NYSE MKT LLC (formerly NYSE AMEX and the American Stock Exchange)
- Cboe BZX Exchange, Inc. (formerly BATS BZX Exchange, Inc.)
- Cboe BYX Exchange, Inc. (formerly BATS BYX Exchange, Inc.)
- BOX Exchange LLC (formerly BOX Options Exchange LLC)
- NASDAQ BX, Inc. (formerly the Boston Stock Exchange)
- Cboe C2 Exchange, Inc.
- Cboe Exchange, Inc. (formerly Chicago Board Options Exchange, Incorporated)
- Chicago Stock Exchange, Inc.
- Cboe EDGA Exchange, Inc. (formerly BATS EDGA Exchange, Inc.)
- Cboe EDGX Exchange, Inc. (formerly BATS EDGX Exchange, Inc.)
- Nasdaq ISE, LLC (formerly International Securities Exchange, LLC)
- The Investors Exchange, LLC
- Nasdaq GEMX, LLC (formerly ISE Gemini)
- Nasdaq MRX, LLC (formerly ISE Mercury)
- Miami Int'l Securities Exchange
- MIAX PEARL, LLC
- MIAX EMERALD, LLC

1. IRC Sec. 1(h)(11)(C).
2. Notice 2003-71, 2003-43 IRB 922.

- The Nasdaq Stock Market LLC
- NYSE National, Inc. (formerly National Stock Exchange, Inc.)
- New York Stock Exchange LLC
- NYSE Arca, Inc.
- NASDAQ PHLX, Inc. (formerly Philadelphia Stock Exchange)[1]

In order to meet the "treaty test," the foreign corporation must be eligible for benefits of a comprehensive income tax treaty with the United States that the Treasury Secretary determines is satisfactory for these purposes, and the treaty must also provide for the exchange of tax information. For the current list of tax treaties meeting these requirements, see Notice 2011-64.[2]

The term "qualified foreign corporation" does *not* include any foreign corporation *if*, for the taxable year of the corporation in which the dividend was paid (or the preceding taxable year), the corporation is a passive foreign investment company (as defined in section 1297).[3]

Special rules apply in determining a taxpayer's foreign tax credit limitation under IRC Section 904 in the case of qualified dividend income. For these purposes, rules similar to the rules of IRC Section 904(b)(2)(B) (concerning adjustments to the foreign tax credit limitation to reflect any capital gain rate differential) will apply to any qualified dividend income.[4]

For information reporting and other guidance on foreign stock dividends, see Notice 2006-3;[5] Notice 2004-71;[6] and Notice 2003-79.[7]

707. What are the reporting requirements under JGTRRA 2003?

Boxes have been added to Form 1099-DIV to allow for the reporting of qualified dividends (Box 1b) and post-May 5, 2003 capital gain distributions (Box 2b). Likewise, boxes have also been added to Form 1099-B for reporting post-May 5, 2003 profits or losses from regulated futures or currency contracts.[8] Payments made in lieu of dividends ("substitute payments") are *not* eligible for the lower rates applicable to qualified dividends.[9] For the information reporting requirements for such payments, see Notice 2003-67;[10] Announcement 2003-75;[11] Treasury Regulation Section 1.6045-2(a)(3)(i); TD 9103.[12]

1. http://www.sec.gov/divisions/marketreg/mrexchanges.shtml (last accessed February 15, 2019).
2. 2011-37 IRB 231.
3. IRC Sec. 1(h)(11)(C)(iii).
4. See IRC Sec. 1(h)(11)(C)(iv).
5. 2006-3 IRB 306.
6. 2004-45 IRB 793
7. 2003-50 IRB 1206.
8. See Announcement 2003-55, 2003-38 IRB 597.
9. H.R. Rep. No. 108-94, 108th Cong., 1st Sess. 31 n. 36 (2003).
10. 2003-40 IRB 752.
11. 2003-49 IRB 1195.
12. 68 Fed. Reg.74847 (12-29-2003).

708. How are gains and losses treated for "traders in securities"?

In general, investors' losses are classified as capital losses, may be used to offset capital gains, and can only offset up to $3,000 of ordinary income each year (see Q 702). On the other hand, a "trader in securities" (see below) may elect to recognize gain or loss on any security held in connection with a trade or business at the close of any taxable year as if the security were sold at its fair market value at year-end.[1] Consequently, gains or losses with respect to such securities—whether deemed sold at year-end under the mark-to-market method of accounting (see Q 7591, Q 7592) or actually sold during the taxable year—are treated as ordinary income or loss.[2] Therefore, if a taxpayer is in business as a trader in securities and makes a mark-to-market election (under IRC Section 475(f)(1)) with respect to sales of securities held in connection with his business, the taxpayer's net loss from that business will be an ordinary loss that is fully deductible.[3]

These rules apply only to taxpayers who qualify as traders in securities. For an individual investor to achieve "trader" status, the Tax Court has stated that:

> "In order to qualify as a trader (as opposed to an investor) [the taxpayer's] purchases and sales of securities * * * must have constituted a trade or business. 'In determining whether a taxpayer who manages his own investments is a trader, and thus engaged in a trade or business, relevant considerations are the taxpayer's investment intent, the nature of the income to be derived from the activity, and the frequency, extent, and regularity of the taxpayer's securities transactions.'[4] In general, investors purchase and hold securities 'for capital appreciation and income' whereas traders buy and sell 'with reasonable frequency in an endeavor to catch the swings in the daily market movements and profit thereby on a short-term basis.'[5] For a taxpayer to be considered a trader, the taxpayer's trading activity must be 'substantial,' and it must be 'frequent, regular, and continuous to be considered part of a trade or business. * * * Sporadic trading does not constitute a trade or business.'[6] ('We accept the fact that to be engaged in a trade or business, the taxpayer must be involved in the activity with continuity and regularity * * *. A sporadic activity * * * does not qualify.')."[7]

In *Chen*, the taxpayer effected 323 transactions involving the purchase of securities, most of which he held for less than one month. Approximately 94 percent of Chen's transactions occurred during February, March, and April, with no transactions occurring in six of the other nine months. Chen attempted to retroactively elect mark-to-market accounting as a trader so that he could treat his losses as fully deductible ordinary losses incurred in a trade or business. The Tax Court held that Chen was not a trader in securities eligible to make a mark-to-market election because Chen did not meet the second requirement for trader status—frequent, regular, and continuous trading. In the court's view, Chen's purchases and sales of securities were only

1. See IRC Sec. 475(f)(1)(A)(i); *Chen v. Comm.*, TC Memo 2004-132.
2. See IRC Secs. 475(d)(3)(A), 475(f)(1)(D); *Chen v. Comm.*, TC Memo 2004-132.
3. See IRC Sec. 165(c)(1); *Chen v. Comm.*, TC Memo 2004-132.
4. *Moller v. U.S.*, 721 F.2d 810, 813 (Fed. Cir. 1983).
5. *Liang v. Comm.*, 23 TC 1040, 1043 (1955).
6. *Boatner v. Comm.*, TC Memo 1997-379, affd, 164 F.3d 629 (9th Cir. 1998); see also *Commissioner v. Groetzinger*, 480 U.S. 23, 35 (1987).
7. *Chen v. Comm.*, TC Memo 2004-132.

frequent, regular, and continuous during the months of February, March, and April. The court also noted that Chen maintained a full-time job as a computer chip engineer. According to the court, in cases in which taxpayers have been held to be "traders in securities," the number and frequency [of trades] indicated that they were engaged in market transactions almost daily for a substantial and continuous period, generally exceeding a single taxable year. Furthermore, those activities constituted the taxpayers' sole or primary income-producing activity." The Tax Court concluded that because Chen's daily trading activities covered only a portion of a single year, and securities trading was not the sole or even primary activity in which Chen engaged for the production of income, Chen was not eligible for trader status.[1]

For the circumstances in which a late Section 475(f) election will be allowed, see *Vines v. Comm.*[2]

Traders are allowed to fully deduct their expenses as business expenses. See Q 8049. Conversely, investors' expenses are classified as miscellaneous itemized deductions and are subject to the 2 percent-of-adjusted gross income (AGI) threshold, all of which were suspended from 2018-2025 under the 2017 tax reform legislation. See Q 731. The expenses of investors are also subjected to additional limitations. See Q 8037 – investment interest expense; Q 8046 – expenses paid in connection with the production of investment income; and Q 8048 – expenses relating to tax questions.

709. How are gains and losses calculated for "traders in securities" when securities are sold subject to nonrecourse liabilities and the mark-to-market rules apply?

If a taxpayer who is a securities dealer uses the mark-to-market rules under IRC Section 475(f)(1) with respect to sales of securities held in connection with his or her business, the IRS has provided guidance requiring that the amount of any nonrecourse liabilities be included when calculating the fair market value of the securities.

The IRS has addressed a situation where two partnerships originated and purchased mortgage loans and issued notes to third-party investors as mortgage-backed securities. The mortgage-backed securities were subject to nonrecourse liabilities. One partnership sold the securities to a third partnership, including the amount of the nonrecourse liabilities when calculating the amount realized in the sale. The purchasing partnership also included the nonrecourse liabilities when calculating its basis in the securities.[3]

Both partnerships used mark-to-market accounting under IRC Section 475. However, the partnerships failed to include the value of the nonrecourse liabilities when calculating the fair market value of the securities for purposes of determining year-end gain or loss under the mark-to-market rules. In requiring that the partnerships include the nonrecourse liabilities in calculating fair market value, the IRS found that the fair market value of the property could be

1. *Chen v. Comm.*, TC Memo 2004-132.
2. 126 TC No. 15 (2006).
3. ILM 201507019.

no less than the amount of any nonrecourse indebtedness to which the property is subject when determining gain or loss.[1] The IRS found further that even if the Internal Revenue Code does not mandate this conclusion, Supreme Court precedent requires inclusion of any nonrecourse debt in determining fair market value for purposes of the mark-to-market rules.[2]

710. What is a "like-kind" exchange? How is it taxed?

Editor's Note: For tax years beginning after 2017, the 2017 Tax Act limits the nonrecognition treatment provided under IRC Section 1031 to exchanges of real property that is not held primarily for sale.[3] This provision applies to exchanges occurring after December 31, 2017. An exception exists if either: (1) the property involved in the exchange was disposed of on or before December 31, 2017, or (2) the property received in the exchange was received on or before December 31, 2017.[4] The new rules also provide that real property located within the U.S. and foreign real property are not of a like-kind.[5]

In a like-kind exchange, a taxpayer exchanges property he holds as an investment or for productive use in a trade or business for other property of the same nature or character (but not necessarily of an equivalent grade or quality) that will be held either as an investment or for productive use in a trade or business. The property exchanged must be tangible; stocks, bonds, notes, other securities or evidences of indebtedness, and partnership interests were *not* eligible for like-kind exchange treatment prior to 2018. An exchange of properties that are of different kinds or classes is not a "like-kind" exchange.[6]

A special rule applies to any partnership that has elected under IRC Section 761(a) to be excluded from the application of subchapter K. An interest in such a partnership generally is treated as an interest in each of the assets of the partnership, not as an interest in the partnership.[7]

In order to qualify as a like-kind exchange, the transaction must also meet the following requirements: (1) the taxpayer must identify the real property to be received in the exchange within forty-five days after he transfers the real property he relinquishes in the exchange, *and* (2) he must receive the like-kind real property within 180 days after the date of his transfer or, if earlier, before the due date of his tax return for the tax year (including extensions).[8] The Service has privately ruled that it is not authorized under IRC Section 6503(b) to suspend the 180-day replacement period under IRC Section 1031(a)(3) where a taxpayer's assets are within court custody.[9]

For the final regulations replacing the use of the Standard Industrial Classification (SIC) system with the North American Industry Classification System (NAIC) for determining what

1. IRC Sec. 7701(g).
2. *Comm. v. Tufts*, 461 U.S. 300 (1983), *Crane v. Comm.*, 331 U.S. 1 (1947).
3. IRC Sec. 1031(a)(1).
4. IRC Sec. 1031(a)(2).
5. IRC Sec. 1031(h).
6. IRC Sec. 1031; Treas. Reg. §1.1031(a)-1.
7. IRC Sec. 1031(a)(2).
8. IRC Sec. 1031(a)(3).
9. Let. Rul. 200211016.

properties are of a like class for purposes of IRC Section 1031 prior to 2018, see Treasury Regulation Section 1.1031(a)-2; TD 9202.[1]

Prior to 2018, the IRS had provided safe harbors for programs involving ongoing exchanges of tangible personal property using a single intermediary (i.e., "LKE programs" or "like-kind exchange programs").[2] Even prior to 2018, according to the IRS, the like-kind standard was traditionally interpreted more narrowly in the case of exchanges of personal property as compared to exchanges of real property.[3]

The Service has ruled that depreciable tangible personal properties were of a like class, even if they did not belong to the same general asset class.[4] The Service has also ruled that transfers of relinquished leased vehicles, followed by the acquisition of replacement leased vehicles through a qualified intermediary, were deferred exchanges qualifying for nonrecognition of gain or loss under IRC Section 1031 prior to 2018.[5]

Prior to 2018, in technical advice, the Service ruled that the exchange of intangible property by a domestic entity for the intangible property of a foreign entity does not qualify as a like-kind exchange to the extent that the exchange is of property used predominantly within the United States for property used predominantly outside the United States. According to the Service—and contrary to the taxpayer's argument—pre-2018 IRC Section 1031(h)(2)(A) clearly provided that personal property used predominantly within the United States and personal property used predominantly outside the United States are not property of like-kind. The statute did not make a distinction between tangible and intangible personal property. Post-2017, the 2017 Tax Act clearly states that real property located within the United States and real property located outside of the United States are not of like-kind.[6]

Gain on an exchange of property that fails to qualify for nonrecognition treatment under the like-kind exchange rules may be reportable under the installment method.[7] The Tax Court found that a transaction qualified as an installment sale and not a like-kind exchange where the payment for a transfer of real property was not received until the year after the property's conveyance.[8]

See Q 7838 for an explanation of regulations and safe harbors governing deferred exchanges, and for the procedures governing reverse exchanges.

For the rules coordinating like-kind exchange tax treatment with the exclusion of gain on the sale of a personal residence, see Q 7843.

1. 70 Fed. Reg. 28818 (5-19-2005).
2. See Rev. Proc. 2003-39, 2003-22 IRB 971.
3. See, e.g., *California Federal Life Insurance Co. v. Comm.*, 680 F.2d 85, 87 (9th Cir. 1982).
4. Let. Rul. 200327029.
5. Let. Ruls. 200241013, 200240049.
6. See TAM 200602034.
7. Treas. Reg. §1.1031(k)-1(j)(2).
8. *Christensen v. Comm.*, TC Memo 1996-254.

711. How is the tax treatment of a like-kind exchange altered if, in addition to like-kind property, the taxpayer also receives cash or nonlike-kind property in the exchange?

Editor's Note: For tax years beginning after 2017, the 2017 Tax Act limits the nonrecognition treatment provided under IRC Section 1031 to exchanges of real property that is not held primarily for sale.[1] This provision applies to exchanges occurring after December 31, 2017. An exception exists if either: (1) the property involved in the exchange was disposed of on or before December 31, 2017, or (2) the property received in the exchange was received on or before December 31, 2017.[2] The new rules also provide that real property located within the U.S. and foreign real property are not of a like-kind.[3]

Receipt of "boot." If the taxpayer receives only like-kind property in the exchange, no taxable gain or loss is reported on his income tax return as a result of the exchange regardless of his tax basis in and value of the respective properties.[4] However, if in addition to like-kind property, the taxpayer receives cash or other property that is different in kind or class from the property he transferred (i.e., nonlike-kind property is often referred to as "boot"), any gain he realizes in the exchange will be taxable to the extent of the sum of the amount of cash and the fair market value of the nonlike-kind property received; any loss realized in such an exchange may *not* be taken into account in calculating the taxpayer's income tax.[5]

If the taxpayer receives only like-kind property, but transfers cash or other nonlike-kind property as part of the exchange, regulations indicate that the nonrecognition rules apply to the like-kind properties, but not to the "boot."[6]

Recapture. In a like-kind exchange where boot is given or received, the recapture provisions applicable to certain depreciable property apply (see Q 716). If property for which an investment credit was taken is exchanged before the investment credit recapture period ends, a percentage will be recaptured (see Q 7891).[7]

712. How is the tax treatment of a like-kind exchange altered if one or more parties assumes a liability of the other party or receives property subject to a liability in the exchange?

Editor's Note: For tax years beginning after 2017, the 2017 Tax Act limits the nonrecognition treatment provided under IRC Section 1031 to exchanges of real property that is not held primarily for sale.[8] This provision applies to exchanges occurring after December 31, 2017. An exception exists if either: (1) the property involved in the exchange was disposed of on or

1. IRC Sec. 1031(a)(1).
2. IRC Sec. 1031(a)(2).
3. IRC Sec. 1031(h).
4. IRC Sec. 1031(a).
5. IRC Secs. 1031(b), 1031(c); Treas. Reg. §1.1031(b)-1.
6. Treas. Reg. §§1.1031(a)-1(a)(2), 1.1031(d)-1(e). See *Allegheny County Auto Mart*, 12 TCM (CCH) 427, *aff'd per curiam*, 208 F.2d 693 (3rd Cir. 1953); *W.H. Hartman Co. v. Comm.*, 20 BTA 302 (1930).
7. IRC Sec. 50(a)(1).
8. IRC Sec. 1031(a)(1).

before December 31, 2017, or (2) the property received in the exchange was received on or before December 31, 2017.[1] The new rules also provide that real property located within the U.S. and foreign real property are not of a like-kind.[2]

If, in an exchange, one party assumes a liability of the other party or receives property subject to a liability, he will be deemed to have transferred "boot" in an amount equal to the liability. The party who transfers the property subject to the liability or whose liability is assumed will be deemed to have received the "boot." If each party to an exchange either assumes a liability of the other party or acquires property subject to a liability, the amounts of such liabilities will be offset and only the difference will be treated as "boot" given and received by the applicable parties.[3] Generally, liabilities that qualify to offset or reduce any taxable boot received are those to which the property received was subject to prior to the exchange and that then are assumed as part of the exchange.[4]

The Service ruled that if a partnership enters into an exchange that qualifies as a deferred like-kind exchange, in which property subject to a liability is transferred in one taxable year of the partnership, and property subject to a liability is received in the following taxable year of the partnership, the liabilities must be netted for purpose of IRC Section 752. Any net decrease in a partner's share of partnership liability must be taken into account for purposes of IRC Section 752(b) in the first taxable year of the partnership, and any net increase in a partner's share of partnership liability must be taken into account for purposes of IRC Section 752(a) in the second year of the partnership.[5]

713. What is the tax basis of property received in a tax-free (or partially tax-free) like-kind exchange?

Editor's Note: For tax years beginning after 2017, the 2017 Tax Act limits the nonrecognition treatment provided under IRC Section 1031 to exchanges of real property that is not held primarily for sale.[6] This provision applies to exchanges occurring after December 31, 2017. An exception exists if either: (1) the property involved in the exchange was disposed of on or before December 31, 2017, or (2) the property received in the exchange was received on or before December 31, 2017.[7] The new rules also provide that real property located within the U.S. and foreign real property are not of a like-kind.[8]

The tax basis of like-kind property received in a tax-free (or partially tax-free) like-kind exchange is generally equal to the adjusted tax basis of the like-kind property given. There are, however, two exceptions. First, if an individual transfers cash or nonlike-kind property or assumes a liability of the other party to the exchange (i.e., the transferee) that exceeds the liabilities (if any) assumed by the transferee, the individual's tax basis in the like-kind property received

1. IRC Sec. 1031(a)(2).
2. IRC Sec. 1031(h).
3. Treas. Reg. §1.1031(d)-2. See Rev. Rul. 59-229, 1959-2 CB 180.
4. See Treas. Reg. §1.1031(d)-2, Ex. 2.
5. Rev. Rul. 2003-56, 2003-23 IRB 985.
6. IRC Sec. 1031(a)(1).
7. IRC Sec. 1031(a)(2).
8. IRC Sec. 1031(h).

is equal to his adjusted tax basis in the property given *increased by* the *sum of* (1) the amount of cash and the fair market value of nonlike-kind property given and (2) the net liability assumed.

Second, if liabilities assumed by the transferee exceed the liabilities (if any) assumed by the individual (transferor) and no other cash or boot is transferred by the individual, the individual's tax basis in the like-kind property he receives is equal to his adjusted tax basis in the like-kind property given *decreased by* the net amount of liabilities assumed by the transferee.[1]

The tax basis of any nonlike-kind property received in a like-kind exchange is the fair market value of the nonlike-kind property on the date of the exchange.[2]

714. How is a like-kind exchange between related parties taxed?

Editor's Note: For tax years beginning after 2017, the 2017 Tax Act limits the nonrecognition treatment provided under IRC Section 1031 to exchanges of real property that is not held primarily for sale.[3] This provision applies to exchanges occurring after December 31, 2017. An exception exists if either: (1) the property involved in the exchange was disposed of on or before December 31, 2017, or (2) the property received in the exchange was received on or before December 31, 2017.[4] The new rules also provide that real property located within the U.S. and foreign real property are not of a like-kind.[5]

If a like-kind exchange that results in nonrecognition of gain or loss occurs between related parties, followed by a disposition of either property within two years of the date of the last transfer that was part of the like-kind exchange, then the original transaction will not qualify for nonrecognition treatment.[6] For purposes of this rule, the term "disposition" does not include dispositions resulting from the death of the taxpayer or (if earlier) the related person. The two-year disposition rule also will not apply to involuntary conversions, so long as the exchange occurred before the threat or imminence of the conversion. An exception is also provided where it can be established that neither the exchange nor the subsequent disposition had as its principal purpose the avoidance of income tax.[7]

"Related persons," for purposes of this rule, include the following: (1) members of the same family (i.e., brothers, sisters, spouses, ancestors and lineal descendants); (2) an individual and a corporation of which the individual actually or constructively owns more than 50 percent of the stock; (3) a grantor and a fiduciary of a trust; (4) fiduciaries of two trusts if the same person is the grantor of both; (5) a fiduciary and a beneficiary of the same trust; (6) a fiduciary of a trust and a beneficiary of another trust set up by the same grantor; (7) a fiduciary of a trust and a corporation of which the grantor of the trust actually or constructively owns more than 50 percent of the stock; (8) a person and an IRC Section 501 tax-exempt organization controlled by the person or members of his family (as described

1. IRC Sec. 1031(d), Treas. Reg. §1.1031(d)-2.
2. Treas. Reg. §1.1031(d)-1(c).
3. IRC Sec. 1031(a)(1).
4. IRC Sec. 1031(a)(2).
5. IRC Sec. 1031(h).
6. IRC Sec. 1031(f)(1).
7. IRC Sec. 1031(f)(2).

in (1) above); (9) a corporation and a partnership if the same person actually or constructively owns more than 50 percent of the stock of the corporation, and has more than a 50 percent interest in the partnership; (10) two S corporations if the same persons actually or constructively own more than 50 percent of the stock of each; (11) an S corporation and a C corporation, if the same persons actually or constructively own more than 50 percent of the stock of each; (12) a person and a partnership of which the person actually or constructively owns more than 50 percent of the capital interest or profits interest; (13) two partnerships if the same persons actually or constructively own more than 50 percent of the capital interest or profits interest of each; or (14) generally, an executor and a beneficiary of an estate.[1]

Any transaction, or series of transactions, structured to avoid the related party rules for like-kind exchanges will not qualify for nonrecognition treatment.[2] The Service has ruled that a taxpayer who transfers relinquished property to a qualified intermediary for replacement property formerly owned by a related party is *not* entitled to nonrecognition treatment under IRC Section 1031(a) if, as part of the transaction, the related party receives cash or other nonlike-kind property for the replacement property.[3] If the risk of holding any property is substantially diminished by a short sale, by the holding of a put option, or by another person holding a right to acquire the property, then the running of the two-year period will be suspended during the period that the option or other right is held.[4]

Adjusted Gross Income

715. How is adjusted gross income determined?

Adjusted gross income is determined by subtracting the following deductions from gross income:[5] (a) expenses directly incurred in carrying on a trade, business or profession (not as an employee – see Q 8049); (b) the deduction allowed for contributions made by a self-employed individual to a qualified pension, annuity, profit sharing plan, a simplified employee pension or SIMPLE IRA plan; (c) certain reimbursed expenses of an employee in connection with his employment, provided the reimbursement is included in gross income (if the employee accounts to his employer and reimbursement does not exceed expenses, reporting is not required); (d) deductions related to property held for the production of rents and royalties (within limits); (e) deductions for depreciation and depletion by a life tenant, an income beneficiary of property held in trust, or an heir, legatee or devisee of an estate; (f) deductions for losses from the sale or exchange of property (see Q 702); (g) the deduction allowed for amounts paid in cash by an eligible individual to a traditional individual retirement account (IRA), or individual retirement annuity; (h) the deduction allowed for amounts forfeited as penalties because of premature withdrawal of funds from time savings accounts (see Q 7918); (i) alimony payments made to the taxpayer's spouse (prior to 2019, see Q 781); (j) certain reforestation expenses; (k) certain jury duty pay remitted to the taxpayer's employer; (l) moving expenses permitted by IRC Section 217; (m) the deduction for Archer Medical Savings Accounts under IRC Section 220(i);

1. IRC Secs. 1031(f)(3), 267(b), 707(b)(1).
2. IRC Sec. 1031(f)(4).
3. Rev. Rul. 2002-83, 2002-49 IRB 927.
4. IRC Sec. 1031(g).
5. The new Section 199A deduction allowed to certain pass-through entities is not treated as a deduction here.

(n) the deduction for interest on education loans; (o) the deduction for qualified tuition and related expenses; (p) the deduction for contributions (within limits) to Health Savings Accounts; (q) the deduction for attorneys' fees involving discrimination suits; and (r) and the deduction for certain expenses of elementary and secondary school teachers up to $250 (made permanent by the Protecting Americans from Tax Hikes Act of 2015 (PATH)). For tax years beginning after 2015, the $250 amount will be adjusted annually for inflation ($250 in 2016-2019).

716. What is the deduction for depreciation?

Depreciation is a deduction that permits recovery, over a period of time, of capital invested in tangible property used in a trade or business or held for the production of income.[1] It is a deduction taken in arriving at adjusted gross income.[2] Only property that has a limited useful life may be depreciated. Land does not have a limited life and, therefore, cannot be depreciated. However, the improvements on land can be depreciated. Inventory and stock in trade are not depreciable.[3] A taxpayer who purchases a term interest in property cannot amortize or depreciate the cost of the property during any period in which the remainder interest is held by a related person. This rule is effective for interests created or acquired after July 27, 1989, in taxable years ending after such date.[4] However, life tenants and beneficiaries of estates and trusts may be allowed the regular depreciation deduction if the property is depreciable property.[5]

The method used to determine the rate of depreciation depends on when the property was placed into service. Property is "placed into service" when it is first placed in a condition or state of readiness and availability for a specifically assigned function for use in a trade or business, for the production of income, or in a tax-exempt or personal activity.[6]

717. How is depreciation on property placed in service after 1986 calculated?

Editor's Note: The 2017 Tax Act generally allows 100 percent bonus depreciation for business owners with respect to property that is placed in service after September 27, 2017 and before January 1, 2023. Further, under the 2017 Tax Act, the requirement that the property be originally placed into service by the taxpayer was removed (i.e., tax reform permits accelerated expensing of used assets, see Q 719).[7]

Generally, the Accelerated Cost Recovery System (ACRS) was modified for property placed in service after 1986. An election could be made to apply the post-1986 ACRS to property that was placed in service between July 31, 1986 and January 1, 1987 (unless such property would have been subject to the anti-churning rules if it had been placed in service after 1986).[8] If real property is acquired before 1987 and converted from personal use to a depreciable use after 1986, the post-1986 ACRS is to be used.[9]

1. IRC Secs. 167(a), 168(a), as amended by ATRA and Pub. Law No. 115-97 (the 2017 Tax Act).
2. IRC Secs. 62(a)(1), 62(a)(4).
3. Treas. Reg. §1.167(a)-2.
4. IRC Sec. 167(e).
5. See IRC Sec. 167(d).
6. Prop. Treas. Reg. §1.168-2(l)(2).
7. IRC Sec. 168(k)(2)(A)(ii), 168(k)(2)(E)(ii).
8. TRA '86, Sec. 203(a)(1)(B), as amended by TAMRA '88, Sec. 1002(c)(1).
9. TAMRA '88, Sec. 1002(c)(3).

The post-1986 ACRS deduction is calculated by applying to the basis of the property either (1) a declining balance method that switches to the straight line method at a time which maximizes the deduction or (2) a straight line method.[1] The initial basis in the property is the basis of the property upon acquisition (usually the cost of the property, see Q 692), reduced by the amount, if any, elected for amortization or an IRC Section 179 deduction (see Q 723), and further reduced by any basis reduction required in connection with taking the investment tax credit (see Q 7891).[2] The basis of the property is reduced each year by the amount of the depreciation allowable.[3] Optional depreciation tables set out in Revenue Procedure 87-57 may be used in place of the methods above.[4] Because land cannot be depreciated, the cost basis of improved land must be allocated between the land and improvements.[5] The ACRS deduction is limited in the case of certain automobiles and other "listed property" placed in service after June 18, 1984. See "Limitations," (Q 724).

Bonus Depreciation Rules

In general, for certain property acquired after September 11, 2001, and before January 1, 2005, a depreciation "bonus" of 30 percent could be taken in the year the property was placed in service.[6] For certain property acquired after May 5, 2003, and before January 1, 2005, 50 percent bonus depreciation could be taken.[7] The IRS has provided procedures on how to claim bonus depreciation.[8] Bonus first-year depreciation applies only to qualified property and is claimed in the first year that the property is placed in service. For eligible property, taxpayers were entitled to elect 50 percent bonus depreciation, 30 percent bonus depreciation, or no bonus depreciation. For certain qualified property placed in service in 2008 until 2017, bonus depreciation of 50 percent was allowed.[9]

Under the 2017 tax reform legislation, the bonus depreciation allowable depends upon the year the property is placed in service, and is the following percentage of the unadjusted depreciable basis of qualified property:

- Property placed in service after September 27, 2017 and before January 1, 2023: 100 percent expensing.
- Property placed in service after December 31, 2022 and before January 1, 2024: 80 percent expensing.
- Property placed in service after December 31, 2023 and before January 1, 2025: 60 percent expensing.

---

1. IRC Sec. 168(b).
2. IRC Sec. 50(c)(1); Treas. Reg. §1.179-1(f)(1).
3. IRC Sec. 1016(a)(2).
4. Rev. Proc. 87-57, 1987-2 CB 687.
5. See Treas. Reg. §1.167(a)-5.
6. IRC Sec. 168(k)(1), before amendment by ESA 2008.
7. IRC Sec. 168(k)(4), before amendment by ESA 2008.
8. Rev. Proc. 2003-50, 2003-29 IRB 119.
9. IRC Sec. 168(k), as amended by ESA 2008, ARRA 2009, ATRA and the 2017 Tax Act.

- Property placed in service after December 31, 2024 and before January 1, 2026: 40 percent expensing.
- Property placed in service after December 31, 2025 and before January 1, 2027: 20 percent expensing.
- 2027 and thereafter: 0 percent expensing.[1]

For certain property with longer production periods, the modified schedule that applies under the 2017 tax reform legislation is as follows:

- Property placed in service after September 27, 2017 and before January 1, 2024: 100 percent expensing.
- Property placed in service after December 31, 2023 and before January 1, 2025: 80 percent expensing.
- Property placed in service after December 31, 2024 and before January 1, 2026: 60 percent expensing.
- Property placed in service after December 31, 2025 and before January 1, 2027: 40 percent expensing.
- Property placed in service after December 31, 2026 and before January 1, 2028: 20 percent expensing.
- 2028 and thereafter: 0 percent expensing.[2]

Under a transition rule, a business was entitled to elect to apply a 50 percent depreciation allowance instead of the 100 percent allowance for the taxpayer's first tax year ending after September 27, 2017.[3]

Planning Point: Some taxpayers expressed concern that the tax reform legislation's changes to the bonus depreciation rules came too late for taxpayers to make the relevant elections on their 2016 or 2017 tax returns. In response, the IRS has released guidance permitting taxpayers to revoke an election, or make a late election, for bonus depreciation with respect to certain property acquired by the taxpayer after September 27, 2017 and placed into service (or planted) during the tax year that included September 28, 2017. For taxpayers who filed their 2016 or 2017 returns on time, and claimed additional 100-percent bonus depreciation for property acquired after September 27, 2017 and placed in service during 2016 or 2017 tax years, the taxpayer can (1) file an amended return changing (to revoke or make a late election) the election before the taxpayer files its federal tax return for the first taxable year succeeding the 2016 taxable year or the 2017 taxable year or (2) file a Form 3115 with the taxpayer's federal tax return for the first, second, or third taxable year succeeding the 2016 taxable year or the 2017 taxable year. Taxpayers who wish to make the election to deduct 50-percent, rather than 100-percent, bonus depreciation, may change their election by filing an amended return or Form 3115 within the same time frames.[4]

---

1. IRC Sec. 168(k)(6)(A).
2. IRC Sec. 168(k)(6)(B).
3. IRC Sec. 168(k)(8).
4. Rev. Proc. 2019-33.

For property used both in an individual's trade or business (or for the production of income) and in a personal or tax-exempt activity during a taxable year, depreciation is allocated to all uses of the property, and only the portion attributable to the trade or business or production of income use is deductible.[1]

The classification of property by recovery period and depreciation method is as follows:[2]

3 years 200% DB*	class life of 4 years or less, certain horses, qualified rent-to-own property
5 years 200% DB*	class life of more than 4 but less than 10 (e.g., heavy trucks, buses, offshore drilling equipment, most computer and data handling equipment, cattle, helicopters and non-commercial aircraft, automobiles and light trucks)
7 years 200% DB*	class life of 10 or more but less than 16 (e.g., most office furnishings, most agricultural machinery and equipment, theme park structures, most railroad machinery, equipment and track, commercial aircraft), motorsports entertainment complexes, Alaska neutral gas pipelines, property without a class life and not otherwise classified under TRA '86
10 years 200% DB*	class life of 16 or more but less than 20 (e.g., vessels, barges and similar water transportation equipment, petroleum refining equipment)
15 years 150% DB*	class life of 20 or more but less than 25 (e.g., industrial steam and electric generation/distribution systems, cement manufacturing equipment, commercial water transportation equipment (freight or passenger), nuclear power production plants)
20 years 150% DB*	class life of 25 or more (e.g., certain farm buildings, railroad structures and improvements, telephone central office buildings, gas utility production plants and distribution facilities), but excluding real property with class life of 27.5 years or more
27.5 years straight line	residential rental property
39 years straight line	nonresidential real property (class life of 27.5 years or more)
50 years straight line	railroad grading or tunnel bore

* Declining balance method switching to the straight line method at a time to maximize the deduction. Substitute 150 percent DB for 200% DB if 3-, 5-, 7-, or 10-year property is used in a farming business. An election can be made to use the straight line method instead of the declining balance method. Also, with respect to 3-, 5-, 7-, and 10-year property, an election can be made to use 150 percent DB.

Property is assigned to various *class lives* in Revenue Procedure 87-56.[3] These class lives can also be found in IRS Publication 946. The Tax Reform Act of 1986 assigned certain property

1. Prop. Treas. Reg. §1.168-2(d)(2)(ii).
2. IRC Secs. 168(c), 168(e), Rev. Proc. 87-57, above.
3. 1987-2 CB 674.

to recovery periods without regard to their class life (e.g., automobiles and light trucks). Also, intangible property that is depreciable is subject to special recovery periods. If computer software is depreciable, the deduction is calculated using a straight line method over 36 months.[1] Computer software acquired after August 10, 1993 is generally depreciable if it (a) is a program designed to cause a computer to perform a desired function, (but generally not a database) and (b) either (1) is readily available for purchase by the general public, is subject to a nonexclusive license, and has not been substantially modified, or (2) is not acquired in a transaction involving the acquisition of assets constituting a trade or business.[2] Certain mortgage servicing rights may be depreciated over 108 months using the straight line method.[3]

Certain rights that are not acquired in a transaction involving the acquisition of a trade or business are subject to special rules for depreciation. Depreciation deductions for (1) rights to receive tangible property or services under a contract or a government grant; (2) interests in patents or copyrights; or (3) certain contracts of fixed duration or amount, are to be defined in the regulations.[4] Regulations generally require the amortization of the right to receive property under a contract or government grant by multiplying the basis of the right by a fraction. The numerator of the fraction is the amount of property or services received during the taxable year and the denominator is the total amount to be received under the contract or government grant. For a patent or copyright, the deduction is generally equal to the amount paid during a taxable year if the purchase price is paid on an annual basis as either a fixed amount per use or a fixed percentage of revenue from the patent or copyright, otherwise it is depreciated either ratably over its useful life or by using the income forecast method. The basis of a right to an unspecified amount over a fixed duration of less than fifteen years is amortized ratably over the period of the right.[5]

In the years in which property is acquired or disposed of, depreciation is limited to the portion of the year in which the property is considered to be held under the following *conventions*: Residential rental property, nonresidential real property, and railroad grading or tunnel bore are treated as placed in service (or disposed of) on the mid-point of the month in which placed in service (or disposed of). Property, other than such real property, is generally treated as placed in service (or disposed of) on the mid-point of the year in which placed in service.

However, the mid-quarter convention (instead of the mid-year convention) applies to depreciable property placed in service during the taxable year if the aggregate bases of property placed in service during the last three months of the taxable year exceeds 40 percent of the aggregate bases of property placed in service (or disposed of) during the taxable year ("the 40 percent test"). "Aggregate bases" is defined as the sum of the depreciable bases of all items of depreciable property taken into account in applying the 40 percent test.

For taxable years ending after January 30, 1991, property not taken into account in applying the test include the following: (1) real property subject to the mid-month convention (described

1. IRC Sec. 167(f)(1).
2. IRC Secs. 167(f)(1), 197(e)(3)(B).
3. IRC Sec. 167(f)(3).
4. IRC Sec. 167(f)(2).
5. Treas. Reg. §1.167(a)-14(c).

above), and (2) property placed in service and disposed of in the same taxable year. Conversely, property that would be taken into account in applying the 40 percent test includes: (1) listed property (discussed in Q 724) placed in service during the taxable year, and (2) property placed in service, disposed of, subsequently reacquired, and again placed in service in the same taxable year (but only the basis of the property on the later of the dates that the property is placed in service is considered).[1] The IRS provided some relief from the mid-quarter convention if a taxpayer's third or fourth quarter included September 11, 2001.[2]

Regardless of whether the mid-year convention or the mid-quarter convention applies, no depreciation deduction is available for property placed in service and disposed of in the same year.[3]

Property subject to the mid-month convention is treated as placed in service (or disposed of) on the mid-point of the month without regard to whether the taxpayer has a short taxable year (i.e., a taxable year that is less than twelve months). The mid-quarter 40 percent test is also made without regard to the length of the taxable year. Thus, if property (with exceptions, as noted in the preceding paragraphs) is placed in service in a taxable year of three months or less, the mid-quarter convention applies regardless of when such property was placed in service (i.e., 100 percent of property has been placed in service in the last three months).[4]

In the case of a short taxable year and with respect to property to which the mid-year or mid-quarter convention applies, the recovery allowance is determined by multiplying the deduction that would have been allowable if the recovery year were not a short taxable year by a fraction, the numerator of which equals the number of months in the short taxable year and the denominator of which is twelve.[5] Proposed regulations under IRC Section 168(f)(5) (as in effect prior to TRA '86) provided that a taxable year of a person placing property in service did not include any month prior to the month in which the person began engaging in a trade or business or holding recovery property for the production of income.[6] Presumably, this principle would continue to apply after TRA '86.

Unit of Production Method

Instead of using ACRS, a property owner may elect to use the unit of production method of depreciation (if appropriate) or any other method not expressed in a term of years.[7] For example, under the unit of production method, the depreciation deduction for a machine that, it is estimated, will produce 1,000,000 shoes (units) before wearing out, and that produces 250,000 units in the first year, would be:

$$(250{,}000 \div 1{,}000{,}000) \times \text{basis}$$

1. IRC Sec. 168(d); Treas. Reg. §1.168(d)-1.
2. Notice 2001-74, 2001-2 CB 551.
3. Treas. Reg. §1.168(d)-1(b)(3)(ii).
4. Rev. Proc. 89-15, 1989-1 CB 816.
5. Rev. Proc. 89-15, 1989-1 CB 816.
6. Prop. Treas. Reg. §1.168-2(f)(4).
7. IRC Sec. 168(f)(1).

718. How do the bonus depreciation rules apply to used property under the 2017 Tax Act?

The cost recovery amendments (see Q 717) may be applied to used property if the property was not used by the taxpayer (or a predecessor) prior to the acquisition. The property is considered to have been used by the taxpayer or a predecessor prior to the acquisition if the taxpayer or predecessor had a depreciable interest in the property at any time prior to the acquisition, regardless of whether depreciation deductions were actually claimed.[1]

Under the 2019 final regulations, "predecessor" is defined to include (i) a transferor of an asset to a transferee in a transaction to which IRC Section 381(a) applies, (ii) 20 a transferor of an asset to a transferee in a transaction in which the transferee's basis in the asset is determined, in whole or in part, by reference to the basis of the asset in the hands of the transferor, (iii) a partnership that is considered as continuing under IRC Section 708(b)(2), (iv) the decedent in the case of an asset acquired by an estate, or (v) a transferor of an asset to a trust.[2]

Further, all of the following must be true:

(1) the property was not acquired from certain related parties, including: (a) the taxpayer's spouse, ancestors and descendants, (b) An individual and a corporation more than 50 percent in value of the outstanding stock of which is owned, directly or indirectly, by or for the individual, (c) a grantor and a fiduciary of any trust, (d) A fiduciary of a trust and a fiduciary of another trust, if the same person is a grantor of both trusts, (e) a fiduciary and a beneficiary of a trust, (f) A fiduciary of a trust and a beneficiary of another trust, if the same person is a grantor of both trusts, (g) A fiduciary of a trust and a corporation more than 50 percent in value of the outstanding stock of which is owned, directly or indirectly, by or for the trust or by or for a person who is a grantor of the trust, (h) A person and an organization to which IRC Section 501 (relating to certain educational and charitable organizations which are exempt from tax) applies and which is controlled directly or indirectly by such person or (if such person is an individual) by members of the family of such individual, (i) a corporation and a partnership if the same person owns more than 50 percent of the outstanding stock in the corporation or capital interest or profits of the partnership, (j) an S corporation and another S corporation if the same person owns more than 50 percent of the outstanding stock of each corporation, (k) An S corporation and a C corporation, if the same persons own more than 50 percent in value of the outstanding stock of each corporation, (l) the executor and beneficiary of an estate, (m) two partnerships in which the same person owns more than 50 percent of the capital interests and profits or (n) a partnership and a person owning more than 50 percent of the capital interests and profits of the partnership.

1. Prop. Treas. Reg. §1.168(k)-2(b)(3)(iii)(B)(1).
2. Treas. Reg. §1.168(k)-2(a)(2)(iv).

Planning Point: The IRS proposed regulations on the bonus depreciation rules contain a general anti-abuse rule that will apply to determine related party status. The rules provide that in a series of related transactions, the property is treated as though it was transferred directly from its original owner to its ultimate owner. The relationship between the original owner and the ultimate owner is tested immediately after the last transfer in the series of transactions. The 2019 final regulations provide for a five-year "lookback" period in making the determination as to whether the property was previously used by a prohibited party.[1]

(2) the property was not acquired by one member of a controlled group from another member of that group,

(3) the property was acquired by purchase, within the meaning of IRC Section 179,

(4) the basis of the property in the hands of the person acquiring it is not determined in whole or part by reference to the adjusted basis of the property in the hands of the person from whom it was acquired or under IRC Section 1014(a) (basis of property acquired from a decedent),

(5) the cost of the property does not include the basis of the property as determined by reference to the basis of other property held by the taxpayer. [2]

719. Are there any situations where a taxpayer can now claim bonus depreciation with respect to used property in which the taxpayer previously held an interest? How do the bonus depreciation rules apply to leased property?

In order to claim bonus depreciation with respect to used property, the property must not be used by the taxpayer or a predecessor at any time before the taxpayer acquired the property (see Q 718). This requirement raised questions as to whether bonus depreciation could be available with respect to property that the taxpayer previously leased, or in which the taxpayer previously held an interest but did not own entirely. See below for the short holding period exception proposed in the 2019 regulations.

Under the regulations, bonus depreciation may now be available for property that a taxpayer previously leased and later acquired. In some situations, a taxpayer may make improvements to property that is leased and obtained a depreciable interest in the property as a result. If the taxpayer later acquires the property, bonus depreciation is unavailable with respect to the portion of the property in which the taxpayer held a depreciable interest during the lease period.[3]

Relatedly, if a taxpayer originally held a depreciable interest in property, and later acquires an additional depreciable interest in an additional portion of the same property, the additional depreciable interest is not treated as though it was used by the taxpayer prior to acquisition (i.e., it is eligible for bonus depreciation under the used property rules if all other requirements are satisfied). If the taxpayer previously had a depreciable interest in the subsequently

1. Prop. Treas. Reg. §1.168(k)-2(b)(3)(iii)(C).
2. IRC Secs. 168(k)(2)(E)(ii), 267(b), 707(b).
3. Treas. Reg. §1.168(k)-2(b)(3)(iii)(B)(1).

acquired additional portion, bonus depreciation is not available. A different rule applies in situations where a taxpayer sells a partial interest in property and later buys a partial interest in the same property. If a taxpayer holds a depreciable interest in a portion of the property, sells that portion or a part of that portion, and later acquires a depreciable interest in another portion of the same property, the taxpayer is treated as previously having a depreciable interest in the property up to the amount of the portion for which the taxpayer held a depreciable interest in the property before the sale.[1]

Under the 2019 proposed regulations, the mere fact that a business leases property to a disqualified business (i.e., one that does not qualify to use bonus depreciation, such as certain businesses with floor plan financing interest) does not "taint" the property, meaning that such exclusion from the additional first year depreciation deduction does not apply to lessors of property to a trade or business described in IRC Section 168(k)(9) so long as the lessor is not described the section.[2]

Short Holding Period Exception

The 2019 proposed regulations provide an exception to the depreciable interest rule in situations where the taxpayer disposes of the property within a short period of time after placing the property in service. If the following are true:

(a) a taxpayer acquires and places in service property,

(b) the taxpayer or a predecessor did not previously have a depreciable interest in the property,

(c) the taxpayer disposes of the property to an unrelated party within 90 calendar days after the date the property was originally placed in service by the taxpayer (without taking into account the applicable convention), and

(d) the taxpayer reacquires and again places in service the property,

the taxpayer's depreciable interest in the property during that 90-day period is not taken into account for determining whether the property was used by the taxpayer or a predecessor at any time prior to its reacquisition by the taxpayer.[3] The proposed rule does not apply if the taxpayer reacquires and again places in service the property during the same taxable year the taxpayer disposed of the property.

720. Is bonus depreciation available in situations involving a partnership buyout?

The proposed bonus depreciation regulations clarify when bonus depreciation will be available in the context of a partnership buyout. Availability under the regulations depends upon

1. Treas. Reg. §1.168(k)-2(b)(3)(iii)(B)(2).
2. Treas. Reg. §1.168(k)- 2(b)(2)(ii)(F).
3. Prop. Treas. Reg. §1.168(k)-2(b)(3)(iii)(B)(4).

whether the partnership itself buys out the departing partner in a redemption-type buyout, or whether the individual partners buy out the partner in a cross-purchase type buyout.

If the partnership redeems the departing partner's interest in partnership assets at a premium, so that the basis in the relevant assets increases, bonus depreciation is not available. This is because the IRS views a redemption-type buyout as a transaction in which the partnership previously had an interest in the assets in question, rendering the assets ineligible for used asset treatment under Section 168(k).

If the individual partners buy out the departing partner at a premium, resulting in an increase in basis, the "step up" in basis is eligible for bonus depreciation. This is because the IRS views each partner as owning a separate and divided interest in the partnership property owned by the partnership, so that one partner does not have a previously existing interest in another partner's share of partnership assets.[1]

721. What is the alternative depreciation system that may be used to calculate depreciation on property placed in service after 1986?

An *alternative depreciation system* is provided for (1) tangible property used predominately outside the United States, (2) tax-exempt use property, (3) tax-exempt bond financed property, (4) certain imported property covered by an executive order regarding countries engaging in unfair trade practices, and (5) property for which an election is made. The election may be made with respect to each property in the case of nonresidential real property and residential rental property. For all other property, the election is made with respect to all property placed in service within a recovery class during a taxable year.[2]

The alternative depreciation is determined using the straight line method and the applicable convention, above, over the following periods:[3]

tax-exempt use property subject to a lease	longer of 125 percent of lease term or period below
residential rental property and nonresidential real property	40 years
personal property with no class life	12 years
railroad grading or tunnel bore	50 years
all other property	the class life

TRA '86 assigns certain property to recovery periods without regard to their class life, e.g., automobiles and light trucks.

1. Prop. Treas. Reg. §1.168(k)-2(b)(3)(iii)(D). See also IRC Secs. 743, 734.
2. IRC Sec. 168(g).
3. IRC Sec. 168(g)(2)(C).

722. How are depreciable assets grouped into general asset classes?

Assets that are subject to either the general depreciation system of IRC Section 168(a) or the alternative depreciation system of IRC Section 168(g) may be grouped in one or more general asset accounts. The assets in a particular general asset account are generally depreciable as a single asset. Such an account must include only assets that have the same depreciation method, recovery period, convention, and that are placed in service in the same tax year. An asset may not be included in a general asset account if the asset is used in a personal activity at any time before the end of the tax year in which it was placed in service.[1]

Upon disposition of an asset from a general asset account, the asset is treated as having an adjusted basis of zero, and the total amount realized on the disposition is generally recognized as ordinary income. However, the ordinary income treatment is limited to the unadjusted basis of the account less amounts previously recognized as ordinary income. The character of the amounts in excess of such ordinary income is determined under other applicable provisions of the IRC (other than IRC Sections 1245 and 1250). Because the basis of the property is considered to be zero, no loss is recognized on such a disposition. Generally, the basis in the account is recoverable only through depreciation, unless the taxpayer disposes of all the assets in the account.[2]

723. When can a taxpayer elect to treat the cost of property as an expense in the year the property is placed in service under IRC Section 179?

A taxpayer may elect to treat the cost of certain qualifying property as an expense in the year the property is placed in service.[3] To qualify, property must be eligible for depreciation or certain amortization provisions, it must be personal property (or fall within certain other categories described in IRC Section 1245(a)(3), such as property used for manufacturing or as a storage facility), and must have been acquired by purchase (from an unrelated person) for use in the active conduct of a trade or business. This property does not include any air conditioning or heating units or any ineligible property described in IRC Section 50(b) (certain property used outside the U.S., for lodging, by tax-exempt organizations, or by governments or foreign persons or entities). This election is not available to a trust or estate, nor can it be used for property held for the production of income.[4]

For tax years beginning after December 31, 2017, the 2017 Tax Act expanded the definition of qualifying property[5] to include certain depreciable tangible property used primarily to provide lodging or in connection with providing lodging, and to include certain improvements to nonresidential real property that is placed in service after the date that the underlying property was first placed in service (roofs, heating, ventilation, air conditioning, fire protection and alarm systems, and security systems).[6]

1. Treas. Reg. §1.168(i)-1(c), as modified by T.D. 9564.
2. Treas. Reg. §1.168(i)-1(e).
3. IRC Sec. 179.
4. IRC Secs. 179(d)(1), 179(d)(4).
5. IRC Sec. 179(d)(1).
6. IRC Sec. 179(f)(2).

Recent legislation has raised the dollar amount that can be expensed for property placed in service in 2008 and beyond (these provisions were made permanent by the Protecting Americans from Tax Hikes Act of 2015 (PATH)). The aggregate cost deductible for 2008 and 2009 cannot exceed $250,000.[1] The aggregate cost deductible for 2010 and thereafter is $500,000 (indexed for inflation; the amount for 2017 was $510,000). The annual dollar limitation was reduced by one dollar for each dollar of such investment above $800,000 for 2008 and 2009, above $2 million for 2010 and thereafter (as indexed).[2] In 2017, the $2 million amount is indexed to $2,030,000 ($2,010,000 in 2016).[3] The 2017 Tax Act increased the maximum amount that can be expensed during the tax year to $1,000,000,[4] and increased the phase-out threshold amount from $2,000,000 to $2,500,000.[5] These amounts are indexed for inflation for tax years beginning after 2018 ($1,020,000 and $2,550,000 for 2019). In 2020, the amounts increase to $1,040,000 and $2,590,000.

The amount expensed is limited to the aggregate amount of income derived from the active conduct of any trade or business of the taxpayer. An amount that is not deductible because it exceeds the aggregate taxable income from any trade or business may be carried over and taken in a subsequent year. The amount that may be carried over and taken in a subsequent year is the lesser of (1) the amounts disallowed because of the taxable income limitation in all prior taxable years (reduced by any carryover deductions in previous taxable years); or (2) the amount of unused expense allowance for such year. The amount of unused expense allowance is the excess of (1) the maximum cost of property that may be expensed taking into account the dollar and income limitations; over (2) the amount the taxpayer elects to expense.[6] Married individuals filing separately are treated as one taxpayer for purposes of determining the amount that may be expensed and the total amount of investment in such property.[7] The general business credit is not allowed for any amount expensed under IRC Section 179.[8]

Deductions permitted pursuant to a valid election to expense costs are not prorated if the taxpayer has a short tax year.[9]

724. What special limitations apply to calculating depreciation on automobiles and other property classified as "listed property"?

Editor's Note: The 2017 Tax Act increased the depreciation limits under Section 280F for passenger automobiles placed into service after December 31, 2017. These rules apply to passenger automobiles for which additional first-year depreciation under IRC Section 168(k) is not claimed. The limits will be indexed for inflation for passenger automobiles that are placed in service after 2018. Computer and peripheral equipment are removed from the definition of listed property.[10]

1. IRC Sec. 179(b)(7), as amended by ESA 2008, ARRA 2009, HIREA and ATRA.
2. IRC Sec. 179(b)(7), as amended by ESA 2008, ARRA 2009, HIREA and ATRA.
3. Rev. Proc. 2016-14, Rev. Proc. 2017-58, Rev. Proc. 2018-57.
4. IRC Sec. 179(b)(1).
5. IRC Sec. 179(b)(2).
6. IRC Sec. 179(b)(3); Treas. Reg. §1.179-3.
7. IRC Sec. 179(b)(4).
8. IRC Sec. 179(d)(9).
9. Treas. Reg. §1.179-1(c)(1).
10. IRC Sec. 280F(d)(4)(A).

These rules are effective for property placed into service after December 31, 2017 and for tax years ending after December 31, 2017. The IRS has also released safe harbor guidance that can be relied on for passenger automobiles placed into service before 2023 (see below).

Limitations

For any *passenger automobile* placed in service during taxable years after June 18, 1984, the amount of the depreciation deduction, including any amount elected as an expense (see above), cannot exceed the monetary limitations as set forth under the applicable heading in the exhibit, below. Note that once the unadjusted basis of an automobile is recovered, depreciation is no longer deductible. For certain automobiles acquired after September 11, 2001, and before January 1, 2005, the first year depreciation limitation was increased by $4,600. For certain automobiles purchased after May 5, 2003 and before January 1, 2005, the first year depreciation limit was increased by $7,650.[1] For certain automobiles purchased after December 31, 2007 and before January 1, 2018, the first year depreciation limit was increased by $8,000.[2]

Property Placed in Service	First Year	Second Year	Third Year	Succeeding Years
6-19-84 through 4-2-85	$4,000	$6,000	$6,000	$6,000
4-3-85 through 1986	$3,200	$4,800	$4,800	$4,800
1987 and 1988	$2,560	$4,100	$2,450	$1,475
1989 and 1990	$2,660	$4,200	$2,550	$1,475
1991	$2,660	$4,300	$2,550	$1,575
1992	$2,760	$4,400	$2,650	$1,575
1993	$2,860	$4,600	$2,750	$1,675
1994	$2,960	$4,700	$2,850	$1,675
1995 and 1996	$3,060	$4,900	$2,950	$1,775
1997	$3,160	$5,000	$3,050	$1,775
1998	$3,160	$5,000	$2,950	$1,775
1999	$3,060	$5,000	$2,950	$1,775
2000, 2001, 2002, and 2003	$3,060	$4,900	$2,950	$1,775
2004	$2,960	$4,800	$2,850	$1,675
2005	$2,960	$4,700	$2,850	$1,675
2006	$2,960	$4,800	$2,850	$1,775
2007	$3,060	$4,900	$2,850	$1,775
2008 and 2009	$2,960	$4,800	$2,850	$1,775
2010	$3,060	$4,900	$2,950	$1,775
2011	$3,060	$4,900	$2,950	$1,775

1. See IRC Secs. 168(k)(2)(F), IRC Sec. 168(k)(4)(D), prior to amendment by ESA 2008.
2. IRC Sec. 168(k)(2)(F), as amended by ESA 2008 and ARRA 2009.

Property Placed in Service	First Year	Second Year	Third Year	Succeeding Years
2012	$3,160	$5,100	$3,050	$1,875
2013	$3,160	$5,100	$3,050	$1,875
2014	$3,160	$5,100	$3,050	$1,875
2015	$3,160	$5,100	$3,050	$1,875
2016	$3,160	$5,100	$3,050	$1,875
2018 (acquired before Sept. 28, 2017)	$16,400	$16,000	$9,600	$5,760
2018 (acquired after Sept. 27, 2017)	$18,000	$16,000	$9,600	$5,760[1]
2019 (acquired before Sept. 28, 2017)	$14,900	$16,100	$9,700	$5,760
2019 (acquired after Sept. 27, 2017)	$18,100	$16,100	$9,700	$5,760
[Rev. Proc. 2019-26; Rev. Proc. 2018-25; Rev. Proc. 2017-29; Rev. Proc. 2016-23; Rev. Proc. 2015-19; Rev. Proc. 2014-21; Rev. Proc.2013-21; Rev. Proc. 2012-23; Rev. Proc. 2011-21; Rev. Proc. 2010-18, 2010-9 IRB 427; Rev. Proc. 2009-24, 2009-17 IRB 885; Rev. Proc. 2008-22, 2008-12 IRB 658; Rev. Proc. 2007-30, 2007-18 IRB 1104; Rev. Proc. 2006-18, 2006-12 IRB 645; Rev. Proc. 2005-13, 2005-12 IRB 759; Rev. Proc. 2004-20, 2004-13 IRB 642; Rev. Proc. 2003-75, 2003-2 CB 1018; Rev. Proc. 2002-14, 2002-1 CB 450; Rev. Proc. 2001-19, 2001-1 CB 732; Rev. Proc. 2000-18, 2000-1 CB 722; Rev. Proc. 99-14, 1999-1 CB 413; Rev. Proc. 98-30, 1998-2 CB 930; Rev. Proc. 97-20, 1997-1 CB 647; Rev. Proc. 96-25, 1996-1 CB 681; Rev. Proc. 95-9, 1995-1 CB 498; Rev. Proc. 94-53, 1994-2 CB 712; Rev. Proc. 93-35, 1993-2 CB 472; Rev. Proc. 92-43, 1992-1 CB 873; Rev. Proc. 91-30, 1991-1 CB 563; Rev. Proc. 90-22, 1990-1 CB 504; Rev. Proc. 89-64, 1989-2 CB 783; IRC Sec. 280F(a).]				

The dollar limitations are determined in the year the automobile is placed in service and are subject to an inflation adjustment (rounded to the nearest multiple of $100) for the calendar year in which the automobile is placed in service.[2] The dollar amounts for 2018 and 2019 in the table above apply in situations where additional first year depreciation applies. If no additional first year depreciation applies, the respective amounts are $10,100, $16,100, $9,700 and $5,760.

Leased Passenger Automobiles

Taxpayers who lease passenger automobiles and are allowed a deduction for the lease are required to reduce the deduction if the fair market value of the automobile is greater than a certain amount. For lease terms beginning in 2012, the amount was $18,500 and for lease terms beginning in 2013, the amount was $19,000. In 2014, the amount was reduced to $18,500, but Revenue Procedure 2015-19 modified Revenue Procedure 2014-21 and increased the amount to $19,000 for 2014.[3] For lease terms beginning in 2015, the amount is reduced to $18,500, and for 2016-2017, the amount is once again $19,000.[4] For 2018 and later years, the amount is increased significantly to $50,000.[5]

This reduction is accomplished by including in gross income an amount determined from tables promulgated by the IRS. The amount to be added to income is dependent on the fair market value of the automobile at the time the lease term begins. The higher the value of the automobile,

1. IRC Sec. 280F(a)(1)(A), as amended by the 2017 Tax Act.
2. IRC Sec. 280F(d)(7).
3. Rev. Proc. 2014-21, 2014-11 IRB 1.
4. Rev. Proc. 2015-19; Rev. Proc. 2016-23; Rev. Proc. 2017-29.
5. Rev. Proc. 2018-25, Table 4.

the more that is added to income.[1] "Passenger automobiles" do not include ambulances, hearses, trucks, vans or other vehicles used by a taxpayer in a trade or business of transporting persons or property for compensation or hire.[2]

The amount of the depreciation deduction is also limited for "listed property" placed in service (or leased) after June 18, 1984 (generally) if the business use of the property does not exceed 50 percent of its total use during the taxable year.[3] "Listed property" includes any passenger automobile or other property used for transportation (generally, unless used in the transportation business); any property of a type used for entertainment, recreation or amusement; any computer (except computers used exclusively at a regular business establishment or at a dwelling unit that meets the home office requirement); any cellular telephone or similar equipment (but only for tax years that begin before January 1, 2010); or other property specified by the regulations.[4] In the case of passenger automobiles, this personal use limitation is applied after the passenger automobile limitation, above.[5]

If the business use of the listed property does not exceed 50 percent, depreciation under the regular pre-1987 ACRS and post-1986 ACRS is not allowed. For such property placed in service after 1986, the amount of the depreciation deduction is limited to that amount determined using the alternative depreciation system (see Q 717).[6] For such property placed in service after June 18, 1984 and before 1987, the amount of the recovery is generally limited to that amount determined using the straight line method over the following earnings and profit lives:[7]

In the case of:	*The applicable recovery period is:*
3-year property	5 years
5-year property	12 years
10-year property	25 years
15-year public utility property	35 years
19-year real prop. and low income housing	40 years

The more-than-50 percent business use requirement must be met solely by use of the listed property in a trade or business, without regard to the percentage of any use in another income producing activity. However, the percentage of use in any other income producing activity is added to the business use when determining the unadjusted basis of the property subject to depreciation (the unadjusted basis is the same as the initial basis, described above). If the listed property meets the more-than-50 percent business use requirement in the year it is placed in service and ceases to do so in a subsequent year, then any "excess depreciation" will be recaptured and included in gross income in the year it ceases to meet the requirement. "Excess depreciation" is the *excess,* if any, of the depreciation allowable while the property met the business use

1. See Treas. Reg. §1.280F-7; Rev. Proc. 2012-23.
2. IRC Sec. 280F(d)(5)(B).
3. IRC Sec. 280F(b).
4. IRC Sec. 280F(d)(4).
5. IRC Sec. 280F(a)(2).
6. IRC Sec. 280F(b)(1).
7. IRC Secs. 280F(b)(2), 312(k), both as in effect prior to amendment by TRA '86).

requirement *over* the depreciation that would have been allowable if the property had not met the requirement for the taxable year it was placed in service.[1] This excess depreciation recapture is distinct from the depreciation recapture that occurs on early disposition; see Q 725.

Safe Harbor

The IRS has released safe harbor guidance that taxpayers can rely upon in depreciating passenger automobiles under the provisions of the 2017 tax reform legislation. Assuming the depreciable basis of the passenger automobile is less than the first year limitation, the additional amount is generally deductible in the first tax year after the end of the recovery period. Under the safe harbor, however, the taxpayer can take the depreciation deductible for the excess amounts during the recovery period up to the limits applicable to passenger autos during this time frame. The IRS will publish a depreciation table in Appendix A of Publication 946, which taxpayers must use to apply the safe harbor. The safe harbor only applies to passenger autos placed into service before 2023, and does not apply if (1) the taxpayer elected out of 100 percent first year depreciation or (2) elected to expense the automobile under Section 179.[2]

725. How does the depreciation deduction impact an individual's basis in the property? Must depreciation ever be "recaptured"?

Each year, an individual's basis is reduced by the amount of the depreciation deduction taken so that his adjusted basis in the property reflects accumulated depreciation deductions. If depreciation is not deducted, his basis must nonetheless be reduced by the amount of depreciation allowable, but the deduction may not be taken in a subsequent year.[3]

Recapture

Upon disposition of property, the seller often realizes more than return of basis after it has been reduced for depreciation. Legislative policy is that on certain dispositions of depreciated property the seller realizes a gain that is, at least in part, attributable to depreciation. To prevent a double benefit, the IRC requires that some of the gain that would otherwise generally be capital gain must be treated as ordinary income. In effect, it requires the seller to "recapture" some of the ordinary income earlier offset by the depreciation.[4] In addition, if depreciated property ceases to be used predominantly in a trade or business before the end of its recovery period, the owner must recapture in the tax year of cessation any benefit derived from expensing such property.[5] This provision is effective for property placed in service in tax years ending after January 25, 1993.[6]

1. IRC Sec. 280F(b)(2).
2. Rev. Proc. 2019-13.
3. IRC Sec. 1016(a)(2).
4. IRC Secs. 1245, 1250.
5. Treas. Reg. §1.179-1(e)(1).
6. Treas. Reg. §1.179-6.

726. What personal exemptions is an individual entitled to deduct in calculating taxable income?

Editor's Note: The 2017 Tax Act suspended the personal exemption for tax years beginning after December 31, 2017 and before December 31, 2025. Qualified disability trusts will continue to be permitted a personal exemption amount equal to $4,150 for 2018, $4,200 for 2019 and $4,300 for 2020.[1]

For tax years beginning before 2018 (and after 2025), taxpayers generally were permitted to deduct the following personal exemption amounts: (1) For taxable years beginning in 2017, $4,050 for each of two spouses on a joint return ($8,100 combined); (2) $4,050 for a taxpayer filing a single or separate return; (3) $4,050 for the spouse of a taxpayer filing a separate return, provided the spouse has *no gross* income and is not claimed as the dependent of another taxpayer.[2] The basic amount for 2016 was $4,050, in 2015 was $4,000, and in 2014 was $3,950. The personal exemption amount is adjusted annually for inflation.[3] Generally, the exemption will not be allowed unless the Social Security number of the individual for whom the personal exemption is being claimed is provided.[4]

Planning Point: When the personal exemption was in effect, it was used to help employers determine correct tax withholding for employees. In the wake of tax reform, IRS released a draft Form W-4 designed to reflect the new changes to the tax code, including the elimination of the personal exemption. The new form is more complex and detailed than previously existing forms, because employers can no longer use the personal exemption to calculate withholding. The form requests information regarding the employee's credits and deductions, as well as any spouse's income and income from other employment. However, much of this information will be optional, although providing detailed income information will allow the employer to more accurately calculate the employee's withholding.

Planning Point: For purposes of the definition of "dependent" for other provisions in the IRC, the IRS has released guidance stating that the exemption amount (which was otherwise reduced to zero for 2018-2025) will be treated as though it remained at the pre-reform $4,150 amount in 2018. In other words, for purposes of determining whether a deduction is allowed for the personal exemption, the relevant amount is $0. For provisions that reference the personal exemption for all other purposes, the relevant amount is $4,150 in 2018, $4,200 in 2019, and $4,300 in 2020.[5]

There was no phaseout of the personal exemptions based on adjusted gross income (AGI) in 2010-2012. The phaseout, including reductions of the phaseout in 2006 through 2009 and repeal of the phaseout for 2010, as well as its reinstatement for tax years beginning after 2012 and before 2018, is discussed below. Under the American Taxpayer Relief Act of 2012 ("ATRA"), the phaseout resumed for tax years beginning in 2013, but was once again suspended by the 2017 Tax Act.

1. IRC Sec. 642(b)(2)(C)(iii).
2. Rev. Proc. 2014-61, Rev. Proc. 2015-53, Rev. Proc. 2016-55, Rev. Proc. 2017-58, Rev. Proc. 2019-44.
3. IRC Sec. 151.
4. IRC Sec. 151(e).
5. Notice 2018-70.

When in effect, the personal exemptions of certain upper income taxpayers are phased out over defined income levels. The dollar amount of personal and dependency exemptions of taxpayers with adjusted gross income above certain levels is reduced by an "applicable percentage" in the amount of two percentage points for every $2,500 (or fraction thereof; $1,250 in the case of a married individual filing separately) by which the taxpayer's adjusted gross income exceeds the following threshold amounts in 2017: Married filing jointly (and surviving spouses); $313,800; Head of household: $287,650; Single: $261,500; Married filing separately: $156,900.

The phaseout for 2017 was completed at the following income levels: Married filing jointly (and surviving spouses): $436,300; Head of household: $410,150; Single: $384,000; Married filing separately: $218,150.[1] These amounts are adjusted annually for inflation.[2]

In 2016, the amounts were: Married filing jointly (and surviving spouses); $311,300; Head of household: $285,350; Single: $259,400; Married filing separately: $155,650. The phaseout for 2016 was completed at the following income levels: Married filing jointly (and surviving spouses): $433,800; Head of household: $407,850; Single: $381,900; Married filing separately: $216,900.[3]

In 2006 through 2010, the phaseout was gradually reduced each year until it was completely repealed. During this time, the amended phaseout amount was calculated by multiplying the otherwise applicable phaseout amount by the "applicable fraction." The applicable fraction for each year was as follows: 66.6 percent (⅔) in 2006 and 2007; 33.3 percent (⅓) in 2008 and 2009; and 0 percent in 2010, 2011, and 2012.[4]

A child or other dependent (i.e., an individual who may be claimed as a dependent by another taxpayer) who files his own return was not entitled to claim a personal exemption for himself.[5]

See Q 758 for a discussion of the expanded child and family tax credits, which are designed to mitigate the impact of the elimination of the personal exemption.

727. What conditions must be met to entitle the taxpayer to a dependency exemption?

Editor's Note: The 2017 Tax Act suspended the personal exemption and dependency exemption for tax years beginning after December 31, 2017 and before December 31, 2025. Qualified disability trusts will continue to be permitted a personal exemption amount equal to $4,150 for 2018 and $4,200 in 2019 (the amount will be indexed for inflation).[6] Similarly, for all other relevant IRC provisions, the "deemed personal exemption amount" for 2019 is $4,200. The amount in 2020 increases to $4,300.

1. Rev. Proc. 2014-61, Rev. Proc. 2015-53, Rev. Proc. 2016-55.
2. IRC Secs. 151(d)(3), 151(d)(4); Rev. Proc. 2014-61.
3. Rev. Proc. 2014-61, above.
4. IRC Secs. 151(d)(3)(E), 151(d)(3)(F).
5. IRC Sec. 151(d)(2).
6. IRC Sec. 642(b)(2)(C)(iii), Rev. Proc. 2018-57, Rev. Proc. 2019-44.

Prior to 2018, a taxpayer was entitled to claim the dependency exemption for each dependent with respect to whom the following tests were met.[1] The term "dependent" means a "qualifying child" (see below) or a "qualifying relative" (see below).[2]

Dependents were not entitled to claim a personal exemption for themselves in addition to the exemption claimed by the taxpayer who supports them.[3] The dependent, if married, could not file a joint return with his or her spouse.[4] In addition, the term "dependent" does not include an individual who is not a citizen or resident of the United States (*or* a resident of Canada or Mexico). However, a legally adopted child who does not satisfy the residency or citizenship requirements may nevertheless qualify as a dependent if certain requirements are met.[5]

The taxpayer could claim the exemption even though the dependent files a return. The taxpayer was required to include the Social Security number of any dependent claimed on his return.[6]

Qualifying child. The term "qualifying child" means an individual who:

(1) is the taxpayer's "child" (see below) or a descendant of such a child, *or* the taxpayer's brother, sister, half-brother, half-sister, stepbrother, stepsister or a descendant of any such relative;

(2) has the same principal place of abode as the taxpayer for more than one-half of the taxable year;

(3) is younger than the taxpayer claiming the exemption and (i) has not attained the age of nineteen as of the close of the calendar year in which the taxable year begins, *or* (ii) is a student who has not attained the age of twenty-four as of the close of the calendar year;

(4) has *not* provided over one-half of the individual's own support for the calendar year in which the taxpayer's taxable year begins; *and*

(5) has not filed a joint tax return (other than for a refund) for the taxable year.[7]

The term "child" means an individual who is: (1) a son, daughter, stepson, or stepdaughter of the taxpayer; or (2) an "eligible foster child" of the taxpayer.[8] An "eligible foster child" means an individual who is placed with the taxpayer by an authorized placement agency or by judgment

1. IRC Secs. 151, 152.
2. IRC Sec. 152(a).
3. IRC Sec. 152(b)(1).
4. IRC Sec. 152(b)(2).
5. IRC Sec. 152(b)(3).
6. See, e.g., *Miller v. Comm.*, 114 TC 184 (2000).
7. IRC Sec. 152(c), as amended by FCSIAA 2008. See also FS-2205-7 (Jan. 2005).
8. IRC Sec. 152(f)(1).

decree, or other order of any court of competent jurisdiction.[1] Any adopted children of the taxpayer are treated the same as natural born children.[2]

Qualifying relative. The term "qualifying relative" means an individual:

(1) who is the taxpayer's:

  (i) child or a descendant of a child,

  (ii) brother, sister, stepbrother, or stepsister,

  (iii) father or mother or an ancestor of either, or stepfather or stepmother,

  (iv) son or daughter of a brother or sister of the taxpayer,

  (v) brother or sister of the father or mother of the taxpayer,

  (vi) son-in-law, daughter-in-law, father-in-law, mother-in-law, brother-in-law, or sister-in-law, or

  (vii) an individual (other than a spouse) who, for the taxable year of the taxpayer, has the same principal place of abode as the taxpayer and is a member of the taxpayer's household;

(2) whose gross income for the calendar year in which the taxable year begins is less than the exemption amount (prior to 2018, see editor's note, above);

(3) for whom the taxpayer provides over one-half of the individual's support for the calendar year in which the taxable year begins; and

(4) who is not a qualifying child of the taxpayer or of any other taxpayer for any taxable year beginning in the calendar year in which the taxable year begins.

The Service has provided guidance for determining whether an individual is a qualifying relative for whom the taxpayer could claim a dependency exemption deduction under IRC Section 151(c). The guidance clarifies that an individual is not a qualifying child of "any other taxpayer" if the individual's parent (or other person with respect to whom the individual is defined as a qualifying child) is not required (by IRC Section 6012) to file an income tax return and either (1) does not file an income tax return, or (2) files an income tax return solely to obtain a refund of withheld income taxes.[3]

Prior to 2018, the amount of the personal exemption ($4,050 in 2016 and 2017, $4,000 in 2015 and $3,950 in 2014)) was adjusted annually for inflation.[4] The exemption was subject to phaseout for certain high income taxpayers (but not in 2010-2012). For details, see Q 726.

1. IRC Sec. 152(f)(1)(C).
2. IRC Sec. 152(f)(1)(B).
3. Notice 2008-5, 2008-2 IRB 256.
4. Rev. Proc. 2015-53, Rev. Proc. 2016-55, Rev. Proc. 2017-58.

Life insurance premiums on a child's life are not included in determining the cost of the child's support.[1]

The Tax Court held that a dependent's self-employment loss did not reduce her earned income for purposes of determining her standard deduction under IRC Section 63(c)(5)(B).[2]

728. Who is entitled to claim a dependency exemption for a child in the case of divorced parents?

Editor's Note: The 2017 Tax Act suspended the personal exemption and dependency exemption for tax years beginning after December 31, 2017 and before December 31, 2025. Qualified disability trusts will continue to be permitted a personal exemption amount equal to $4,150 for 2018, $4,200 in 2019 (the amount will be indexed for inflation).[3] Similarly, for all other relevant IRC provisions, the "deemed personal exemption amount" for 2020 increases to $4,300.

In tax years beginning prior to 2018, the following rules applied: In the case of divorced parents who between them provide more than one-half of a child's support for the calendar year, and have custody of the child for more than one-half of the calendar year, the custodial parent (i.e., the one having custody for the greater portion of the year) is generally allowed the dependency exemption. However, the noncustodial parent can claim the exemption if the custodial parent signs a written declaration (i.e., Form 8332, or a statement conforming to the substance of Form 8332) agreeing not to claim the child as a dependent, *and* the noncustodial parent attaches the declaration to the tax return for the calendar year. The noncustodial parent can also claim the exemption if a divorce decree or separation agreement executed before 1985 expressly provides such and he provides at least $600 for the support of the child during the calendar year.[4] The Tax Court held that the special support rule under IRC Section 152(e) applies to parents who have never been married as well as divorced parents.[5]

The Service has clarified that a custodial parent may revoke the release of the dependency exemption and, therefore, claim the dependency exemption himself, but only if the noncustodial parent agrees and does not claim the child.[6]

In *Miller v. Comm.*,[7] the Tax Court denied the dependency exemption to the noncustodial parent where the custodial parent had not signed a release of the claim to the exemption. The court order, which gave the noncustodial parent the right to claim the exemption, was held not to be a valid substitute.

1. *Kittle v. Comm.*, TC Memo 1975-150; *Vance v. Comm.*, 36 TC 547 (1961).
2. *Briggs v. Comm.*, TC Summary Opinion 2004-22.
3. IRC Sec. 642(b)(2)(C)(iii), Rev. Proc. 2018-57, Rev. Proc. 2019-44.
4. IRC Secs. 152(e)(1), 152(e)(2); Treas. Reg. §1.152-4.
5. *King v. Comm.*, 121 TC 245 (2003). See also Preamble, REG-149856-03, 72 Fed. Reg. 24192, 24194 (5-2-2007).
6. IRS CCA 200007031.
7. 114 TC 184 (2000).

In *Boltinghouse v. Comm.*,[1] the Tax Court held that there is no requirement in IRC Section 152(e) or the regulations that a spouse's waiver of his claim to a dependency exemption deduction be incorporated into a divorce decree to be effective. The court stated that such a requirement would make Form 8332 itself ineffective on its own. The court also recognized that under the applicable state law (Delaware), the separation agreement created binding contractual obligations that did not cease upon the entry of a divorce decree (regardless of whether the agreement was merged or incorporated into the decree).

In *Omans v. Comm.*,[2] the Tax Court determined that the custodial parent's certified signature on the settlement agreement signified her sworn agreement to the settlement agreement's contents, including her former spouse's entitlement to the dependency exemption.

A state appeals court held that federal law does not preempt a state family law court in its discretion from alternating the dependency exemption between the parents, even though one parent may have custody during the calendar year for less than half the year.[3]

The IRS has provided interim guidance under IRC Section 152(c)(4), which is the rule for determining which taxpayer may claim a qualifying child when two or more taxpayers claim the same child. It clarifies that unless the special rule in IRC Section 152(e) applies (see above), the tie-breaking rule in IRC Section 152(c)(4) applies to the head of household filing status, the child and dependent care credit, the child tax credit, the earned income credit, the exclusion for dependent care assistance, and the dependency deduction as a group, rather than on a section-by-section basis.[4]

Deductions

729. What itemized deductions may be taken by an individual taxpayer?

Editor's Note: The 2017 Tax Act suspended many itemized deductions for tax years beginning after 2017. Among those suspended were deductions for casualty and theft losses (exceptions exist for losses occurring in a federally declared disaster area), moving expenses (with an exception for members of the armed forces), expenses related to tax preparation, and expenses relating to the trade or business of being an employee (i.e., all miscellaneous itemized deductions subject to the 2 percent of AGI floor, which were suspended for 2018-2025). The deduction for state and local taxes was capped at $10,000 (see below) and the mortgage interest deduction was limited to $750,000 (see Q 736). This suspension and limitations will apply for tax years beginning after December 31, 2017 and before December 31, 2025.

Itemized deductions are subtracted from adjusted gross income in arriving at taxable income; they may be claimed in addition to deductions for adjusted gross income (see Q 715). Itemized deductions are also referred to as "below-the-line" deductions.

1. TC Memo 2003-134.
2. TC Summary Opinion 2005-110.
3. *Rios v. Pulido*, 2002 Cal. App. LEXIS 4412 (2nd App. Dist. 2002).
4. Notice 2006-86, 2006-51 IRB 680.

Among the itemized deductions taxpayers may be able to claim are the following:

...Interest, within limits (see Q 732 to Q 736; Q 8024 to Q 8043).

...Prior to 2018, personal expenses for the production or collection of taxable income, within limits (see Q 8046), or in conjunction with the determination, collection or refund of any tax (but some of these expenses may be considered "miscellaneous itemized deductions" (see Q 8048)). Deduction of expenses paid in connection with tax-exempt income may be disallowed (see Q 8047). Certain business expenses and expenses for the production of rents and royalties are deductible *in arriving at* adjusted gross income (see Q 715).

...Prior to 2018 (see below for a discussion of the SALT cap), personal taxes of the following types: state, local and foreign real property taxes; state and local personal property taxes; state, local and foreign income, war profits, and excess profits taxes; and the generation-skipping tax imposed on income distributions (*for the sales tax deduction, see below*). If taxes other than these are incurred in connection with the acquisition or disposition of property, they must be treated as part of the cost of such property or as a reduction in the amount realized on the disposition.[1]

...Prior to 2018, uncompensated personal casualty and theft losses. But these are deductible only to the extent that the aggregate amount of uncompensated losses in excess of $100 (for each casualty or theft) exceeds 10 percent of adjusted gross income. The $100 amount increased to $500 for 2009 only.[2] The taxpayer must file a timely insurance claim for damage to property that is not business or investment property or else the deduction is disallowed to the extent that insurance would have provided compensation.[3] Uncompensated casualty and theft losses in connection with a taxpayer's business or in connection with the production of income are deductible in full (see Q 7832). The 2017 Tax Act generally eliminated a taxpayer's ability to deduct casualty and theft loss expenses as itemized deductions (when those losses were not related to property used in a trade or business). However, an exception exists for losses that occur in federally declared disaster areas.[4]

Stock losses. Prior to 2018, the IRS announced that it intended to disallow deductions under IRC Section 165(a) for theft losses relating to declines in value of publicly traded stock when the decline is attributable to corporate misconduct. If the stock is sold or exchanged or becomes wholly worthless, any resulting loss will be treated as a capital loss. Furthermore, the Service may also impose penalties under IRC Section 6662 in such cases.[5] In Field Attorney Advice, the Service concluded that a taxpayer was not entitled to a theft loss deduction for losses related to his exercise of stock options because he had not proven the elements of a theft loss.[6]

Abandoned securities. The Service has issued regulations concerning the availability and character of a loss deduction under IRC Section 165 for losses sustained from abandoned securities. IRC Section 165(g) provides that if any security that is a capital asset becomes

1. IRC Sec. 164(a).
2. IRC Sec. 165(h), as amended by TEAMTRA 2008.
3. IRC Sec. 165(h)(5)(E), as amended by TEAMTRA 2008.
4. IRC Sec. 165(h)(5).
5. Notice 2004-27, 2004-1 CB 782; Treasury Release JS-1263 (3-25-2004).
6. FAA 20073801F (8-1-2007).

worthless during the taxable year, the resulting loss is treated as a loss from the sale or exchange of a capital asset (i.e., a capital loss) on the last day of the taxable year (unless the exception in IRC Section 165(g)(3)—concerning worthless securities of certain affiliated corporations—applies). For purposes of applying the loss characterization rule of IRC Section 165(g), the abandonment of a security establishes its worthlessness. According to the regulations, to abandon a security, a taxpayer must permanently surrender and relinquish all rights in the security and receive no consideration in exchange for the security. All the facts and circumstances determine whether the transaction is properly characterized as abandonment or some other type of transaction (e.g., an actual sale or exchange, contribution to capital, dividend, or gift). The regulations are effective for stock or other securities abandoned after March 12, 2008[1] (this deduction was not addressed in the 2017 Tax Act).

...Contributions to charitable organizations, within certain limitations (see Q 8053, Q 8108) (this deduction survived the 2017 Tax Act with minimal changes).

...Unreimbursed medical and dental expenses and expenses for the purchase of prescribed drugs or insulin incurred by the taxpayer for himself and his spouse and dependents, to the extent that such expenses exceed 10 percent of adjusted gross income (7.5 percent of adjusted gross income for tax years beginning before 2013, and for 2017 and 2018 under the 2017 Tax Act) (see Q 743). There was a temporary exemption that kept the threshold at 7.5 percent of AGI for individuals age sixty-five and older and their spouses until December 31, 2016.

...Prior to 2018, expenses of an employee connected with his employment. Generally, such expenses are "miscellaneous itemized deductions" (see Q 731).

...Federal estate taxes and generation-skipping transfer taxes paid on "income in respect of a decedent" (see Q 745) (this deduction was not addressed in the 2017 Tax Act).

Generally, prior to 2018, certain moving expenses permitted under IRC Section 217 were deductible directly from gross income (see Q 715). This deduction was suspended from 2018 through 2025.

Many of these deductions are disallowed in calculating the alternative minimum tax (see Q 767).

In Chief Counsel Advice, the Service determined that deductions for expenses paid or incurred in connection with the administration of an individual's estate in bankruptcy, which would have not been incurred if the property were not held by the bankrupt estate, are treated as allowable in arriving at adjusted gross income.[2]

Sales tax deduction. Under AJCA 2004, taxpayers could elect to deduct state and local general sales taxes instead of state and local income taxes when they itemized deductions.[3] This option was made "permanent" by the Protecting Americans from Tax Hikes Act of 2015 (PATH), but was limited to $10,000 under the 2017 Tax Act (see below).

1. Treas. Reg. §1.165-5(i).
2. CCA 200630016.
3. IRC Sec. 164(b)(5)(A).

The itemized deduction is based on *actual* sales taxes, or on the optional sales tax *tables* published by the IRS.[1] In general, a taxpayer may deduct actual state and local general sales taxes paid if the tax rate is the same as the general sales tax rate. If the tax rate is more than the general sales tax rate, sales taxes on motor vehicles are deductible as general sales taxes, but the tax is deductible only up to the amount of tax that would have been imposed at the general sales tax rate. Sales taxes on food, clothing, medical supplies, and motor vehicles are deductible as a general sales tax even if the tax rate was less than the general sales tax rate.[2] The Service reminds taxpayers that actual receipts showing general sales taxes paid must be kept to use the actual expense method.[3]

Using the optional state sales tax tables, taxpayers may use their income level and number of exemptions to find the sales tax amount for their state.[4] Taxpayers may add an amount for *local* sales taxes if appropriate. In addition, taxpayers may add to the table amount any sales taxes paid on: (1) a motor vehicle, but only up to the amount of tax paid at the general sales tax rate; and (2) an aircraft, boat, home, or home building materials if the tax rate is the same as the general sales tax rate.[5]

The Service has commented that although the sales tax deduction mainly benefits taxpayers with a state or local sales tax but no income tax (i.e., Alaska, Florida, South Dakota, Texas, Washington, and Wyoming), it may also give a larger deduction to any taxpayer who paid more in sales taxes than income taxes. For example, an individual might have bought a new car, thus boosting the sales tax total, or claimed tax credits, and lowering the state income tax paid.[6] Additional guidance on claiming the sales tax deduction is set forth in Notice 2005-31.[7]

Tax Reform Impact on Deduction for State, Local and Foreign Taxes

The 2017 Tax Act limited the ability of taxpayers to deduct state and local taxes (including sales, income, and property taxes), imposing a cap of $10,000 ($5,000 for married taxpayers filing separate returns) on this deduction. Foreign real property taxes can no longer be deducted.[8] The cap encompasses all state and local taxes, so taxpayers are required to aggregate their relevant state and local taxes in reaching the $10,000 limit.

730. What is the limitation on certain high-income taxpayers' itemized deductions?

Editor's Note: The limitation on itemized deductions that applied to certain high-income taxpayers was suspended for tax years beginning after December 31, 2017 and before January 1, 2026.[9]

1. See IRC Sec. 164(b)(5)(H).
2. See IRC Secs. 164(b)(5)(C), 164(b)(5)(D), 164(b)(5)(F). See also Pub. 600, State and Local General Sales Taxes (2006); FS-2006-9 (Jan. 2006).
3. Pub. 600.
4. See Publication 600, State and Local General Sales Taxes, pp. 2 - 4 (2006).
5. See Pub. 600, State and Local General Sales Taxes (2006); see also FS-2006-9 (Jan. 2006).
6. FS-2006-9 (Jan. 2006).
7. 2005-14 IRB 830.
8. IRC Sec. 164(6).
9. IRC Sec. 68(f).

There was no phaseout of itemized deductions based on adjusted gross income (AGI) in 2010-2012. Under the American Taxpayer Relief Act of 2012 ("ATRA"), the phaseout resumed for tax years beginning in 2013-2017, and was once again suspended for 2018-2025.

Therefore, in 2017, the aggregate of most itemized deductions was reduced dollar-for-dollar by the lesser of: (1) 3 percent (but see *Adjustments to Limit*, below, for tax years beginning before 2010) of the amount of adjusted gross income that exceeds a certain income-based threshold amount, or (2) 80 percent of the amount of such itemized deductions otherwise allowable for the taxable year.[1]. In 2017, the thresholds were $261,500 for individual taxpayers, $313,800 for married taxpayers filing jointly, $287,650 for heads of households and $156,900 for married taxpayers filing separately.[2] In 2016, the thresholds were $259,400 for individual taxpayers, $311,300 for married taxpayers filing jointly, $285,350 for heads of households and $155,650 for married taxpayers filing separately.[3] In 2015, the thresholds were $258,250 for individual taxpayers, $309,900 in the case of a married taxpayer filing jointly, $285,050 for heads of household, and $154,950 for married taxpayers filing separately) The threshold income levels for determining the phaseout are adjusted annually for inflation.[4]

Adjustments to limit for 2005-2009 tax years. For taxable years beginning after 2005, the limitation on itemized deductions was gradually reduced until it was completely repealed in 2010. The amended limitation amount was calculated by multiplying the otherwise applicable limitation amount by the "applicable fraction." The "applicable fraction" for each year was as follows: 66.6 percent (⅔) in 2006 and 2007; 33.3 percent (⅓) in 2008 and 2009; and 0 percent in 2010-2012.[5]

The limitation on itemized deductions is not applicable to medical expenses deductible under IRC Section 213, investment interest deductible under IRC Section 163(d), or certain casualty loss deductions.[6] The limitation also is not applicable to estates and trusts.[7] For purposes of certain other calculations, such as the limits on deduction of charitable contributions or the 2 percent floor on miscellaneous itemized deductions, the limitations on each separate category of deductions are applied *before* the overall ceiling on itemized deductions is applied.[8] The deduction limitation is not taken into account in the calculation of the alternative minimum tax.[9]

731. What are miscellaneous itemized deductions? What limits apply?

Editor's Note: The 2017 Tax Act suspended all miscellaneous itemized deductions subject to the 2 percent floor for tax years beginning after December 31, 2017 and before December 31, 2025.

"Miscellaneous itemized deductions" are deductions *from* adjusted gross income ("itemized deductions") *other than* the deductions for (1) interest, (2) taxes, (3) non-business casualty

1. IRC Sec. 68(a).
2. Rev. Proc. 2016-55.
3. Rev. Proc. 2015-53.
4. IRC Sec. 68(b); as amended by ATRA, Sec. 101(2)(b); Rev. Proc. 2008-66, 2008-45 IRB 1107.
5. IRC Sec. 68(f) (deleted by ATRA, Sec. 101(2)(b)).
6. IRC Sec. 68(c).
7. IRC Sec. 68(e).
8. IRC Sec. 68(d).
9. IRC Sec. 56(b)(1)(F).

losses and gambling losses, (4) charitable contributions, (5) medical and dental expenses, (6) impairment-related work expenses for handicapped employees, (7) estate taxes on income in respect of a decedent, (8) certain short sale expenses (see Q 7529, Q 7530), (9) certain adjustments under the IRC claim of right provisions, (10) unrecovered investment in an annuity contract, (11) amortizable bond premium (see Q 7654, Q 7664), and (12) certain expenses of cooperative housing corporations.[1]

"Miscellaneous itemized deductions" were allowed only to the extent that the aggregate of all such deductions for the taxable year exceeded 2 percent of adjusted gross income.[2] For tax years other than 2010 through 2012 (and 2018-2025 under the 2017Tax Act), miscellaneous itemized deductions were also subject to the phaseout for certain upper income taxpayers (see Q 730).

Miscellaneous itemized deductions generally include unreimbursed employee business expenses, such as professional society dues or job hunting expenses, and expenses for the production of income, such as investment advisory fees or the cost for storage of taxable securities in a safe deposit box.[3]

Expenses that relate to both a trade or business activity and a production of income or tax preparation activity (see Q 8046, Q 8048) must be allocated between the activities on a reasonable basis.[4]

Certain legal expenses from employment-related litigation may be deductible.[5] In *Biehl v. Comm.*,[6] the Ninth Circuit Court of Appeals affirmed the Tax Court's holding that attorneys' fees paid in connection with employment related litigation must be treated as a miscellaneous itemized deduction, and *not* as an above-the-line deduction. The Ninth Circuit stated that simply because a lawsuit arises out of the taxpayer's former employment, that determination is not sufficient to qualify the taxpayer's attorneys' fees for an above-the-line deduction under IRC Section 62(a)(2)(A). Concurring in the Tax Court's analysis, the Ninth Circuit reiterated that the proper inquiry in deciding whether an expense has a "business connection" is what the expenditure was "in connection with" and not simply whether the expenditure arose from, or had its origins in, the taxpayer's trade or business. According to the appeals court, whereas IRC Section 62(a)(1) only requires that the expense be attributable to a trade or business, the language in IRC Section 62(a)(2)(A) is much more definite. The court concluded that for a reimbursable expense to qualify for an above-the-line deduction not only must it be attributable to a trade or business, it must also have been incurred during the course of "performance of services as an employee."[7]

The IRC prohibits the indirect deduction, through pass-through entities, of amounts (i.e., miscellaneous itemized deductions) that would not be directly deductible by individuals.[8] However, publicly offered mutual funds are not subject to this rule, and "pass-through entity,"

1. IRC Sec. 67(b).
2. IRC Sec. 67(a).
3. Temp. Treas. Reg. §1.67-1T(a)(1).
4. Temp. Treas. Reg. §1.67-1T(c).
5. See, e.g., *Kenseth v. Comm.*, 259 F.3d 881(7th Circuit 2001); *Brenner v. Comm.*, TC Memo 2001-127; *Reynolds v. Comm.*, 296 F.3d 607 (7th Cir. 2002); *Chaplain v. Comm.*, TC Memo 2007-58.
6. 351 F. 3d 982 (9th Cir. 2003).
7. *Biehl*, above, *aff'g*, 118 TC 467 (2002).
8. IRC Sec. 67(c)(1); Temp. Treas. Reg. §1.67-2T.

for this purpose, does not include estates, trusts (except for grantor trusts and certain common trust funds), cooperatives, or real estate investment trusts (REITs).[1] Affected pass-through entities (including partnerships, S corporations, nonpublicly offered mutual funds, and REMICs) must generally allocate to each investor his respective share of such expenses; the investor must then take the items into account for purposes of determining his taxable income and deductible expenses, if any.[2] See Q 7694, Q 7935, Q 7952, Q 7727, and Q 7775 regarding REMICs, mutual funds, exchange-traded funds, publicly traded limited partnerships, and S corporations, respectively.

732. Is interest deductible?

Editor's Note: The 2017 Tax Act limited the mortgage interest deduction to $750,000, so that from 2018-2025, only interest on up to $750,000 of new mortgage debt may be deducted. This limit applies to debt incurred after December 31, 2017 and before January 1, 2026.[3] After December 31, 2025, absent Congressional action to extend the current rules, the $1 million mortgage interest deduction will be reinstated and will apply regardless of when the taxpayer incurred the relevant debt (see Q 736).[4] Modifications to the deductibility of business interest are discussed in Q 733 to Q 735.

Editor's Note: Late in 2015, Congress acted to extend the treatment of certain mortgage insurance premiums as qualified residence interest, as discussed below, through 2016. This treatment was extended through 2017 by the Bipartisan Budget Act of 2018. However, as of the date of this revision, Congress has not indicated whether it will extend this treatment for the 2018 tax year.

The deductibility of interest depends on its classification, as described below. Furthermore, interest expense that is deductible under the rules below may be subject to the additional limitation on itemized deductions (unless it is investment interest, which is not subject to that provision). Interest must be classified and is deductible within the following limitations:

(1) *Investment interest.* This includes any interest expense on indebtedness properly allocable to property held for investment.[5] Generally, investment interest is deductible only to the extent of investment income; however, investment interest in excess of investment income may be carried over to succeeding tax years. For purposes of this calculation, net long-term capital gain income is included in investment income if the taxpayer foregoes the reduced tax rate (0 percent/15 percent/20 percent) that applies to such income. Under JGTRRA 2003, as extended by ATRA, certain dividends are taxable at the lower capital gains rates rather than at higher ordinary income tax rates. A dividend will be treated as investment income for purposes of determining the amount of deductible investment interest income only if the taxpayer elects to treat the dividend as *not* being eligible for the reduced rates.[6] For the temporary regulations relating

1. IRC Sec. 67(c); Temp. Treas. Reg. §1.67-2T(g)(2).
2. Temp. Treas. Reg. §1.67-2T(a).
3. IRC Sec. 163(h)(3)(F).
4. IRC Sec. 163(h)(3)(F)(ii).
5. IRC Sec. 163(d)(3).
6. IRC Secs. 1(h)(11)(D)(i), as amended by ATRA, 163(d)(4)(B).

to an election that may be made by noncorporate taxpayers to treat qualified dividend income as investment income for purposes of calculating the deduction for investment interest, see Treasury Regulation Section 1.163(d)-1.[1] Note that the 2017 tax reform legislation placed limitations on the deductibility of business interest, which specifically excludes investment interest.

(2) *Trade or business interest.* This includes any interest incurred in the conduct of a trade or business. Generally, such interest was deductible as a business expense prior to 2018. See Q 733 for a discussion of the treatment of corporate business interest under the 2017 Tax Act. Q 734 and Q 735 outline the new rules as they apply to pass-through entities.[2]

(3) *Qualified residence (mortgage) interest.* Qualified residence interest is interest paid or accrued during the taxable year on debt that is secured by the taxpayer's qualified residence and that is either (a) "acquisition indebtedness" (that is, debt incurred to acquire, construct or substantially improve the qualified residence, or any refinancing of such debt), or (b) "home equity indebtedness" (any other indebtedness secured by the qualified residence). There is a limitation of $1,000,000 ($750,000 for 2018-2025) on the aggregate amount of debt that may be treated as acquisition indebtedness, *but* the amount of refinanced debt that may be treated as acquisition indebtedness is limited to the amount of debt being refinanced. Prior to 2018, a deduction was generally allowed for home equity indebtedness. The aggregate amount that could be treated as "home equity indebtedness" (that is, borrowing against the fair market value of the home less the acquisition indebtedness, or refinancing to borrow against the "equity" in the home) was $100,000.[3] Indebtedness incurred on or before October 13, 1987 (and limited refinancing of it) that is secured by a qualified residence is considered acquisition indebtedness. This pre-October 14, 1987 indebtedness is not subject to the $750,000 (2018-2025) aggregate limit, but is included in the aggregate limit as it applies to indebtedness incurred after October 13, 1987.[4] (For 2007 through 2017, certain mortgage insurance premiums are treated as qualified residence interest.)[5]

Planning Point: Although interest on home equity indebtedness is technically no longer deductible under the terms of the 2017 Tax Act, the IRS has released guidance on situations where this interest may continue to be deducted. Pursuant to the guidance, interest on home equity loans that are used to buy, build or substantially improve the taxpayer's home continue to be deductible to the extent that they (when combined with other relevant loans) do not exceed the $750,000 limit. However, home equity loan interest is not deductible to the extent that the loan proceeds are used for expenditures not related to buying, building or substantially improving a home (i.e., if the proceeds are used for personal living expenses or to purchase a new car, the related interest is not deductible). The home equity loan must be secured by the home in order for the interest to be deductible in any case.

1. 69 Fed. Reg. 47364 (8-5-2004). See also, 70 Fed. Reg. 13100 (3-18-2005).
2. IRC Sec. 162.
3. IRC Sec. 163(h)(3).
4. IRC Sec. 163(h)(3)(D).
5. IRC Sec. 163(h)(3)(E), as amended by ATRA.

A "qualified residence" is the taxpayer's principal residence and one other residence that the taxpayer (a) used during the year for personal purposes more than fourteen days or, if greater, more than 10 percent of the number of days it was rented at a fair rental value, or (b) used as a residence but did not rent during the year.[1]

Subject to the above limitations, qualified residence interest is deductible. If indebtedness used to purchase a residence is secured by property other than the residence, the interest incurred on it is not residential interest but is personal interest.[2] The Tax Court denied a deduction for mortgage interest to individuals renting a home under a lease with an option to purchase the property. Although the house was their principal residence, they did not have legal or equitable title to the home and the earnest money did not provide ownership status.[3] An individual member of a homeowner's association was denied a deduction for interest paid by the association on a common building because the member was not the party primarily responsible for repaying the loan and the member's principal residence was not the specific security for the loan.[4] Assuming that the loan was otherwise a bona fide debt, a taxpayer could deduct interest paid on a mortgage loan from his qualified plan, even though the amount by which the loan exceeded the $50,000 limit of IRC Section 72(p) was deemed to be a taxable distribution.[5] See Q 736 for a more detailed discussion of how the mortgage interest deduction was changed by the 2017 tax reform legislation.

(4) *Interest taken into account in computing income or loss from a passive activity.* A passive activity is generally an activity that involves the conduct of a trade or business but in which the taxpayer does not materially participate, or any rental activity.[6]

(5) *Interest on extended payments of estate tax.* Generally, this interest is deductible.

(6) *Interest on education loans.* An above-the-line deduction is available to certain taxpayers for interest paid on a "qualified education loan."[7] The deduction is subject to a limitation of $2,500 in 2015-2020. The deduction is phased out for 2015-2018, ratably for taxpayers with modified AGI between $65,000 and $80,000 ($130,000 and $160,000 for joint returns in 2015-2016, and $135,000 and $165,000 in 2017-2018).[8] Certain other requirements must be met for the deduction to be available.[9] In 2019-2020, the income limits are $70,000 and $85,000 and a MAGI between $140,000 and $170,000 for joint returns.

1. IRC Sec. 163(h)(4)(A). See, e.g., FSA 200137033.
2. Let. Ruls. 8743063 and 8742025.
3. *Blanche v. Comm.*, TC Memo 2001-63, *aff'd without opinion*, 2002 U.S. App. LEXIS 6379 (5th Cir. 2002).
4. Let. Rul 200029018.
5. FSA 200047022.
6. IRC Secs. 163(d), 469(c).
7. IRC Secs. 163(h)(2)(F), 221.
8. IRC Sec. 221(b); Rev. Proc. 2015-53, Rev. Proc. 2016-55, Rev. Proc. 2017-58, Rev. Proc. 2019-44.
9. See IRC Sec. 221; Treas. Reg. §1.221-1.

(7) *Personal interest.* This is any interest expense not described in (1) through (6) above and is often referred to as "consumer" interest.[1] Personal interest includes interest on indebtedness properly allocable to the purchase of consumer items and interest on tax deficiencies. Personal interest is not deductible.[2]

The proper allocation of interest generally depends on the use to which the loan proceeds are put, except in the case of qualified residence interest (excluding home equity interest, where the use is relevant for 2018-2025). Detailed rules for classifying interest by tracing the use of loan proceeds are contained in temporary regulations.[3] The interest allocation rules apply to interest expense that would otherwise be deductible.[4]

Various provisions in the Code may prohibit or delay the deduction of certain types of interest expense. For example, no deduction is allowed for interest paid on a loan used to buy or carry tax-exempt securities or, under certain conditions, for interest on a loan used to purchase or carry a life insurance or annuity contract (see Q 3).

733. Is business interest deductible when the business is a corporation?

Under prior law, business owners were typically permitted to deduct interest expenses incurred in carrying on a trade or business (subject to limitations).[5] The 2017 Tax Act generally limits the interest expense deduction to the sum of (1) business interest income, (2) 30 percent of the business' adjusted taxable income and (3) floor plan financing interest (see below).[6] Businesses with average annual gross receipts of $25 million or less for the three-taxable year period that ends with the previous tax year are exempt from this new limitation (i.e., businesses that meet the gross receipts test of IRC Section 448(c)).[7]

Generally, the limit applies at the taxpayer level, but in the case of a group of affiliated corporations that file a consolidated return, it applies at the consolidated tax return filing level.

Planning Point: The IRS has released new guidance on how the 2017 tax reform legislation impacts the business interest deduction limitation for consolidated groups. The limitation will apply at the consolidated group level, meaning that the group's overall adjusted taxable income for purposes of the limitation will be its consolidated taxable income, and inter-company obligations will be disregarded.

Further, the IRS and Treasury have released proposed regulations governing the allocation of the limitation among group members, and the treatment of disallowed interest carryforwards where a member leaves or joins the group. When one subsidiary leaves the group, the consolidated group must determine the amount of interest carryforwards that were allocated to the subsidiary. The regulations will treat an affiliated group as a single taxpayer only if it files a consolidated return for Section 163(j) purposes.[8]

---

1. IRC Sec. 163(h)(2).
2. IRC Sec. 163(h)(1).
3. See Temp. Treas. Reg. §1.163-8T.
4. Temp. Treas. Reg. §1.163-8T(m)(2).
5. IRC Sec. 163(j).
6. IRC Sec. 163(j)(1).
7. IRC Secs. 163(j)(2), 448(c).
8. Notice 2018-28.

"Business interest" generally excludes investment interest. It includes any interest paid or accrued on indebtedness properly allocable to carrying on a trade or business. Under proposed regulations released late in 2018, a new definition of "interest" applies, and includes any expenses incurred to compensate for the use of money, or the time value of money—commitment fees, debt issuance costs, guaranteed payments and other "substitute" interest costs may all be considered "interest" under the new rules. Importantly, this means that many expenses that have not commonly be considered "interest" will be subject to the new limit on deductibility of business interest expense.

"Business interest income" means the amount of interest that is included in the taxpayer's gross income for the tax year that is properly allocable to carrying on a trade or business.

"Adjusted taxable income" means taxable income computed without regard to (1) items of income, gain, deduction or loss not allocable to carrying on a trade or business, (2) business interest or business interest income, (3) any net operating loss deduction (NOL), (4) the deduction for pass-through income under Section 199A and (5) for years before 2022, any deduction for depreciation, amortization or depletion.[1] For the purpose of the business interest deduction, adjusted taxable income is computed without regard for the deductions that are allowed for depreciation, amortization or depletion for tax years beginning after December 31, 2017 and before January 1, 2022.

"Floor plan financing interest" is interest paid or accrued on floor plan financing indebtedness, which is indebtedness incurred to finance the purchase of motor vehicles held for sale or lease to retail customers (and secured by the inventory that is acquired).[2]

As a result of these rules, business interest income and floor plan financing interest are fully deductible, with the limitation applying to 30 percent of the business' adjusted taxable income.

Unused interest expense deductions may be carried forward indefinitely.[3] The IRS has released proposed regulations stating that the disallowance and carryfoward of a business interest deduction in the C corporation context will not affect whether (or when) the business interest expense reduces the C corporation's earnings and profits.[4] This means that corporations need not wait until the year in which the deduction is allowed to reduce earnings and profits.

Planning Point: The IRS has released guidance clarifying that taxpayers with disqualified business interest that was disallowed for the last tax year beginning before January 1, 2018 may carry the interest forward as business interest to the first tax year beginning after December 31, 2017. When this interest is carried forward (i.e., to 2018 and beyond), it will be treated as any other business interest that is incurred in a year beginning after December 31, 2017. This means that the carried forward interest will be subject to the same limitations that apply to interest expenses actually incurred after the new rules became effective in 2018. Because the new law does not contain a provision providing for excess limitation carryforwards under previously applicable "super affiliation rules", these amounts may not be carried forward to tax years beginning after December 31, 2017.[5]

1. IRC Sec. 163(j)(8).
2. IRC Sec. 163(j)(9).
3. IRC Sec. 163(j)(2).
4. Notice 2018-28.
5. Notice 2018-28.

734. Is business interest deductible when the business is a pass-through entity?

Businesses that operate as pass-through entities (partnerships, S corporations, sole proprietorships) are permitted to deduct interest expenses incurred in operating the business. The 2017 Tax Act generally limits the interest expense deduction to the sum of (1) business interest income, (2) 30 percent of the business' adjusted taxable income and (3) floor plan financing interest.[1] Businesses with average annual gross receipts of $25 million or less for the three-taxable year period that ends with the previous tax year are exempt from this new limitation (i.e., businesses that meet the gross receipts test of IRC Section 448(c)).[2]

These rules are applied at the partnership level, and the deduction for business interest must be taken into account in determining the non-separately stated taxable income or loss of the partnership.[3] Under the 2017 Tax Act, the limit on the amount that is allowed as a deduction for business interest is increased by a partner's distributive share of the partnership's excess taxable income.[4]

"Excess taxable income" is the amount that bears the same ratio to the partnership's adjusted taxable income as:

(x) the excess (if any) of (1) 30 percent of the adjusted taxable income of the partnership over (2) the amount (if any) by which the business interest of the partnership, reduced by floor plan financing interest, exceeds the business interest income of the partnership bears to

(y) 30 percent of the adjusted taxable income of the partnership.[5]

Excess taxable income must be allocated in the same manner as non-separately stated income and loss. A partner's adjusted basis in his or her partnership interest must be reduced (not below zero) by the excess business interest that is allocated to the partner. The new law provides that similar rules will apply to S corporations and their shareholders.[6]

As expressed in the Senate amendment to the 2017 Tax Act, the intent of this calculation was to allow a partner to deduct additional interest expense that the partner may have paid to the extent that the partnership could have deducted more business interest.

"Business interest" means interest paid on indebtedness that is properly allocated to a trade or business, but excluding investment interest.[7] Under proposed regulations released late in 2018, a new definition of "interest" applies, and includes any expenses incurred to compensate for the use of money, or the time value of money--commitment fees, debt issuance costs, guaranteed payments and other "substitute" interest costs may all be considered "interest" under the

1. IRC Sec. 163(j)(1).
2. IRC Secs. 163(j)(2), 448(c).
3. IRC Sec. 163(j)(4).
4. IRC Sec. 163(j)(4)(A)(ii)(II).
5. IRC Sec. 163(j)(4)(C).
6. IRC Sec. 163(j)(4)(D).
7. IRC Sec. 163(j)(5).

new rules. Importantly, this means that many expenses that have not commonly be considered "interest" will be subject to the new limit on deductibility of business interest expense.

"Business interest income" means the amount of interest income that is included in the entity's income and properly allocated to a trade or business, excluding investment interest income.[1]

"Trade or business" specifically excludes the trade or business of being an employee, any electing real property trades or businesses, electing farming businesses, furnishing or selling electrical, water or sewage disposal services, and gas or steam distribution and transportation.[2]

"Adjusted taxable income" for purposes of these rules means taxable income computed without regard to non-business items of income, gain, deduction and loss, business interest and business interest income, the net operating loss deduction under Section 172, the deduction for pass-through entities under IRC Section 199A and, for 2018-2021, any deductions for depreciation, amortization or depletion.[3]

See Q 735 for a discussion of the rules governing carryforwards of disallowed partnership business interest. See Q 733 for a discussion of the general rules governing the corporate deduction for business interest.

735. Can a partnership carry forward disallowed business interest?

The 2017 Tax Act created a special rule to allow partnerships to carry forward certain disallowed business interest (the rule does not apply to S corporations or other pass-through entities, although the new law specifies that similar rules will apply). The general rules governing carrying forward disallowed business interest (see Q 733) do not apply to partnerships.

Instead, disallowed business interest is allocated to each partner in the same manner as non-separately stated taxable income or loss of the partnership.[4] The partner is entitled to deduct his or her share of excess business interest in any future year, but only:

(1) against excess taxable income (see Q 734) attributed to the partner by the partnership, and

(2) when the excess taxable income is related to the activities that created the excess business interest carryforward.[5]

Such a deduction also requires a corresponding reduction in excess taxable income. Further, if excess business interest is attributed to a partner, his or her basis in the partnership interest is reduced (not below zero) by the amount of the allocation even though the carryforward does not permit a partner's deduction in the year of the basis reduction. The partner's deduction in a future year for the carried forward interest will *not* require another basis adjustment.

1. IRC Sec. 163(j)(6).
2. IRC Sec. 163(j)(7).
3. IRC Sec. 163(j)(8).
4. IRC Sec. 163(j)(4).
5. IRC Sec. 163(j)(4)(B).

If the partner disposes of the partnership interest after a basis adjustment occurred, immediately before the disposition the partner's basis will be increased by the amount that any basis reduction exceeds the amount of excess interest expense that has been deducted by the partner.[1]

The IRS has released guidance providing that it intends to issue regulations stating that when business interest is accounted for at the partner level, a partner cannot include his or her share of the partnership's business interest income for the year except to the extent of the partner's share of the excess of (i) the partnership's business interest income over (ii) the partnership's business interest expense (excluding floor plan financing). A partner cannot include his or her share of floor plan financing interest in determining his or her individual business interest expense deduction limitation.[2]

See Q 733 for a discussion of the general rules governing the corporate deduction for business interest.

736. How did tax reform change the deduction for mortgage interest for tax years beginning after 2017 and before 2025?

The 2017 Tax Act limited the mortgage interest deduction to interest on new mortgages of up to $750,000. This limit applies to debt incurred after December 31, 2017 and before January 1, 2026.[3] After December 31, 2025, the $1 million mortgage interest deduction will be reinstated and will apply regardless of when the taxpayer incurred the relevant debt unless Congress takes action to extend the current rule.[4]

Home equity indebtedness interest cannot be deducted for tax years beginning after December 31, 2017 and before January 1, 2026.

Planning Point: Although interest on home equity indebtedness is technically no longer deductible under the terms of the 2017 Tax Act, the IRS has released guidance on situations where this interest may continue to be deducted. Pursuant to the guidance, interest on home equity loans that are used to buy, build or substantially improve the taxpayer's home continue to be deductible to the extent that they (when combined with other relevant loans) do not exceed the $750,000 limit. However, home equity loan interest is not deductible to the extent that the loan proceeds are used for expenditures not related to buying, building or substantially improving a home (i.e., if the proceeds are used for personal living expenses or to purchase a new car, the related interest is not deductible). The home equity loan must be secured by the home in order for the interest to be deductible in any case.

Example: In January 2019, Jerry takes out a $500,000 mortgage to purchase a main home. The loan is secured by the main home. In February 2019, Jerry takes out a $250,000 loan to purchase a vacation home. The loan is secured by the vacation home. Because the total amount of both mortgages does not exceed $750,000, all of the interest paid on both mortgages is deductible. However, if Jerry took out a $250,000 home equity loan on the main home to purchase the vacation home, then the interest on the home equity loan would not be deductible.

1. IRC Sec. 163(j)(4)(B)(iii).
2. Notice 2018-28.
3. IRC Sec. 163(h)(3)(F).
4. IRC Sec. 163(h)(3)(F)(ii).

The $750,000 limit does not apply with respect to debt incurred on or before December 15, 2017. If the taxpayer enters a binding contract on or before December 15, 2017 to close on the purchase of the taxpayer's personal residence before January 1, 2018, and if the taxpayer actually purchases that residence before April 1, 2018, the debt will be treated as though it was incurred before December 15, 2017.[1]

Debt amounts that are related to a refinancing will be treated as though incurred on the date that the original debt was incurred, provided that any additional amounts of debt incurred as a result of the refinancing do not exceed the amount of the refinanced debt. However, this exception does not apply if the refinancing occurs after the expiration of the term of the original debt. Further, it does not apply if the original debt was not amortized over its term, the expiration of the term of the first refinancing of the debt or, if earlier, the date which is thirty years after the date of the first refinancing.[2]

737. What is the maximum annual limit on the income tax deduction allowable for charitable contributions?

An individual who itemizes may take a deduction for certain contributions "to" or "for the use of" charitable organizations. The amount that may be deducted by an individual in any one year is subject to the income percentage limitations as explained in Q 738. The value that may be taken into account for various gifts of property depends on the type of property and the type of charity to which it is contributed. These rules are explained in Q 739 to Q 741.

For an explanation of the deduction for charitable gifts of life insurance, see Q 120.

In the case of a gift of S corporation stock, special rules (similar to those relating to the treatment of unrealized receivables and inventory items under IRC Section 751) apply in determining whether gain on such stock is long-term capital gain for purposes of determining the amount of a charitable contribution.[3]

A contribution of a partial interest in property is deductible only if the donee receives an undivided portion of the donor's entire interest in the property. Such a contribution was upheld even where the donee did not take possession of the property during the tax year.[4] Generally, a deduction is denied for the mere use of property or for any interest which is less than the donor's entire interest in the property, unless the deduction would have been allowable if the transfer had been in trust.

1. IRC Sec. 163(h)(3)(F)(i).
2. IRC Sec. 163(h)(3)(F)(iii).
3. IRC Sec. 170(e)(1).
4. *Winokur v. Comm.*, 90 TC 733 (1988), acq. 1989-1 CB 1.

738. What are the income percentage limits that apply to charitable contributions?

Editor's Note: The 2017 Tax Act increased the 50 percent AGI limit on contributions to public charities and certain private foundations to 60 percent for tax years beginning after 2017 and before 2026.

Fifty percent limit (sixty percent for tax years 2018-2025). An individual is allowed a charitable deduction of up to 50 (or 60) percent of his adjusted gross income for a charitable contribution *to*: churches; schools; hospitals or medical research organizations; organizations that normally receive a substantial part of their support from federal, state, or local governments or from the general public and that aid any of the above organizations; federal, state, and local governments. Also included in this list is a limited category of private foundations (i.e., private operating foundations and conduit foundations[1]) that generally direct their support to public charities.[2] The above organizations are often referred to as "50 (or 60) percent-type charitable organizations."

Thirty percent limit. The deduction for contributions of most long-term capital gain property to the above organizations, contributions *for the use of* any of the above organizations, as well as contributions (other than long-term capital gain property, see Q 739) *to* or *for the use of* any other types of charitable organizations (i.e., most private foundations, see Q 741) is limited to the lesser of (a) 30 percent of the taxpayer's adjusted gross income, or (b) 50 percent of adjusted gross income minus the amount of charitable contributions allowed for contributions to the 50 (or 60) percent-type charities.[3]

Twenty percent limit. The deduction for contributions of long-term capital gain property to most private foundations (see Q 739 and Q 741) is limited to the lesser of (a) 20 percent of the taxpayer's adjusted gross income, or (b) 30 percent of adjusted gross income minus the amount of charitable contributions allowed for contributions to the 30 percent-type charities.[4]

Deductions denied because of the 50 (or 60) percent, 30 percent or 20 percent limits may be carried over and deducted over the next five years, retaining their character as 50 (or 60) percent, 30 percent or 20 percent type deductions.[5]

Gifts are "to" a charitable organization if made directly to the organization. "For the use of" applies to indirect contributions to a charitable organization (e.g., an income interest in property, but not the property itself).[6] The term "for the use of" does not refer to a gift of the right to use property. Such a gift would generally be a nondeductible gift of less than the donor's entire interest.

1. See IRC Sec. 170(b)(1)(E).
2. IRC Sec. 170(b)(1)(A).
3. IRC Secs. 170(b)(1)(B), 170(b)(1)(C).
4. IRC Sec. 170(b)(1)(D).
5. IRC Secs. 170(d)(1), 170(b)(1)(D)(ii).
6. See Treas. Reg. §1.170A-8(a)(2).

739. What value of property contributed to charity can be taken into account for the charitable deduction if the gift is long-term capital gain property?

Editor's Note: The 2017 Tax Act increased the 50 percent AGI limit on contributions to public charities and certain private foundations to 60 percent for tax years beginning after 2017 and before 2026.

If an individual makes a charitable contribution to a 50 (or 60) percent-type charity (see Q 738) of property that, if sold, would have resulted in long-term capital gain (other than certain tangible personal property, see Q 740), he is generally entitled to deduct the full fair market value of the property, but the deduction will be limited to 30 percent of adjusted gross income.[1]

Long-term capital gain property. "Long-term capital gain" means "gain from the sale or exchange of a capital asset held for more than one year, if and to the extent such gain is taken into account in computing gross income."[2]

Any portion of a gift of long-term capital gain property to a 50 (or 60) percent-type organization that is disallowed as a result of the adjusted gross income limitation may be carried over for five years, retaining its character as a 30 percent type deduction (see Q 738).[3]

A taxpayer may elect in any year to have gifts of long-term capital gain property be subject to a 50 (or 60) percent of adjusted gross income limit; if he does so, the gift is valued at the donor's adjusted basis. Once made, such an election applies to all contributions of capital gain property during the taxable year (except unrelated use gifts of appreciated tangible personal property, as explained in Q 740) and is generally irrevocable for that year.[4]

The deduction for any charitable contribution of property is reduced by the amount of gain that would *not* be long-term capital gain if the property were sold at its fair market value at the time of the contribution.[5]

740. What value of property contributed to charity can be taken into account for purposes of the charitable deduction if the gift is comprised of tangible personal property?

The treatment of a contribution of appreciated tangible personal property (i.e., property which, if sold, would generate long-term capital gain) depends on whether the use of the property is related or unrelated to the purpose or function of the (public or governmental) organization. If the property is related use property (e.g., a contribution of a painting to a museum), generally the full fair market value is deductible, up to 30 percent of the individual's adjusted gross income; however, if the property is unrelated use property, the deduction is generally limited to the donor's adjusted basis.[6]

1. IRC Sec. 170(b)(1)(C).
2. IRC Sec. 1222(3).
3. IRC Sec. 170(b)(1)(C)(ii).
4. IRC Sec. 170(b)(1)(C)(iii); *Woodbury v. Comm.*, TC Memo 1988-272, *aff'd*, 90-1 USTC ¶50,199 (10th Cir. 1990).
5. IRC Sec. 170(e)(1)(A).
6. IRC Secs. 170(e)(1)(B), 170(b)(1)(C); Treas. Reg. §1.170A-4(b).

741. What value of property contributed to charity can be taken into account for purposes of the charitable deduction if the gift is made to a private foundation?

Editor's Note: The 2017 Tax Act increased the 50 percent AGI limit on contributions to public charities and certain private foundations to 60 percent for tax years beginning after 2017 and before 2026.

Most private foundations are family foundations subject to restricted contribution limits. Certain other private foundations (i.e., conduit foundations and private *operating* foundations), which operate much like public charities, are treated as 50 (or 60) percent-type organizations (see Q 738).[1] The term "private foundations" as used under this heading refers to standard private (e.g., family) foundations.

The amount of the deduction for a contribution of appreciated property (tangible or intangible) contributed *to* or *for the use of* private foundations generally is limited to the donor's adjusted basis; however, certain gifts of *qualified appreciated stock* made to a private foundation are deductible at their full fair market value.[2]

Qualified appreciated stock is generally publicly traded stock which, if sold on the date of contribution at its fair market value, would result in a long-term capital gain.[3] Such a contribution will not constitute qualified appreciated stock to the extent that it exceeds 10 percent of the value of all outstanding stock of the corporation; family attribution rules apply in reaching the 10 percent level.[4] The Service has determined that shares in a mutual fund can constitute qualified appreciated stock.[5]

742. What substantiation requirements apply in order for a taxpayer to take an income tax deduction for charitable contributions?

No charitable deduction is allowed for a contribution of cash, check, or other monetary gift unless the donor maintains either a bank record or a written communication from the donee showing the name of the organization and the date and the amount of the contribution.[6]

Charitable contributions of $250 or more (whether in cash or property) must be substantiated by a contemporaneous written acknowledgment of the contribution supplied by the charitable organization. (An organization can provide the acknowledgement electronically, such as via an e-mail addressed to the donor.)[7]

In prior years, substantiation was not required if certain information was reported on a return filed by the charitable organization (this exception was repealed by the 2017 Tax Act for

1. See IRC Secs. 170(b)(1)(E), 170(b)(1)(A)(vii).
2. IRC Sec. 170(e)(5).
3. IRC Sec. 170(e)(5).
4. IRC Sec. 170(e)(5)(C).
5. Let. Rul. 199925029. See also Let. Rul. 200322005 (ADRs are qualified appreciated stock).
6. IRC Sec. 170(f)(17).
7. IRS Pub. 1771 (March 2008), p. 6.

tax years beginning after December 31, 2016).[1] Special rules apply to the substantiation and disclosure of quid pro quo contributions and contributions made by payroll deduction.[2] A qualified appraisal is generally required for contributions of nonreadily valued property for which a deduction of more than $5,000 is claimed.[3]

No charitable deduction is allowed for a contribution of clothing or a household item unless the property is in good or used condition. Regulations may deny a deduction for a contribution of clothing or a household item which has minimal monetary value. These rules do not apply to a contribution of a single item if a deduction of more than $500 is claimed and a qualified appraisal is included with the return. Household items include furniture, furnishings, electronics, linens, appliances, and similar items; but not food, art, jewelry, and collections.[4]

Special rules apply to certain types of gifts, including charitable donations of patents and intellectual property, and for donations of used motor vehicles, boats, and airplanes.[5]

743. What are the limits on the medical expense deduction?

Editor's Note: The 2017 Tax Act modified the medical expense deduction so that, for tax years beginning after December 31, 2016 and ending before January 1, 2019, a more generous 7.5 percent floor will apply to the medical expense deduction.

A taxpayer who itemizes deductions can deduct unreimbursed expenses for "medical care" (the term "medical care" includes dental care) and expenses for *prescribed* drugs or insulin for himself, a spouse and dependents, to the extent that such expenses exceed 10 percent (7.5 percent before 2013 and for 2017 and 2018) of adjusted gross income. (On a joint return, the 10 (or 7.5) percent floor amount is based on the combined adjusted gross income of both spouses.) The taxpayer first determines net unreimbursed expenses by subtracting all reimbursements received during the year from total expenses for medical care paid during the year. He or she must then subtract 10 (or 7.5) percent of his adjusted gross income from net unreimbursed medical expenses; only the balance, if any, is deductible.[6] The deduction for medical expenses is not subject to the phaseout in itemized deductions for certain upper income taxpayers that applied before 2018. (See Q 729.)

Though the 7.5 percent threshold increased to 10 percent in 2013, the 7.5 percent threshold continued to apply through 2016 if the taxpayer or the taxpayer's spouse had attained age sixty-five before the end of the taxable year. See Q 744 for examples of the types of expenses that can be deducted under the medical expense deduction.

1. IRC Sec. 170(f)(8) (repealed by Pub. Law. No. 115-97).
2. Treas. Reg. §§1.170A-13(f), 1.6115-1.
3. IRC Sec. 170(f)(11).
4. IRC Sec. 170(f)(16).
5. See IRC Secs. 170(e)(1)(B), 170(f)(11), 170(f)(12), 170(m); Notice 2005-44, 2005-25 IRB 1287.
6. IRC Sec. 213.

744. What types of expenses can be deducted as medical expenses?

"Medical care" is generally defined as amounts paid: (a) for the diagnosis, cure, mitigation, treatment, or prevention of disease, or for the purpose of affecting any structure or function of the body; (b) for transportation primarily for and essential to such medical care; (c) for qualified long-term services; or (d) for insurance covering such care or for any qualified long-term care insurance contract.[1]

The Service ruled that amounts paid by individuals for diagnostic and certain similar procedures and devices, not compensated by insurance or otherwise, are deductible medical care expenses even though the individuals had no symptoms of illness. According to the Service, this includes an annual physical examination, a full-body electronic scan, and a pregnancy test.[2]

The term "medical care" does not include cosmetic surgery or other similar procedures unless necessary to correct a deformity resulting from a congenital abnormality, a personal injury resulting from accident or trauma, or a disfiguring disease.[3] But see *Al-Murshidi v. Comm.*[4] (the surgical removal of excess skin from a formerly obese individual was not "cosmetic surgery" for purposes of IRC Section 213(d)(9)(A) because the procedures meaningfully promoted the proper function of the individual's body and treated her disease; thus, the costs of the surgical procedures were deductible despite the "cosmetic surgery" classification given to the procedures by the surgeon).

A taxpayer can deduct the medical expenses paid for a dependent (within the specified limits) even though he or she is not entitled to a dependency exemption. The fact that the dependent's income exceeds the exemption amount (suspended for 2018-2025, $4,050 for 2016 and 2017)[5] for the year is immaterial so long as the taxpayer has furnished over one-half of his support. A child of parents who are divorced (or in some situations, separated) *and* who between them provide more than one-half of the child's support for the calendar year and have custody of the child for more than one-half of the calendar year will be treated as a dependent of both parents for purposes of this deduction.[6] But in the case of a multiple support agreement, only the person designated to take the dependency exemption may deduct the dependent's medical expenses, and then only to the extent that he or she actually paid the expenses.[7] See Q 727.

Deductible medical expenses include amounts paid for lodging, up to $50 per individual per night, while away from home *primarily for and essential to* medical care if such care is provided by a physician in a licensed hospital (or similar medical care facility) and there is no element of personal pleasure, recreation or vacation in the travel away from home. No deduction is allowed if the lodgings are "lavish or extravagant."[8] A mother was permitted to deduct lodging expenses incurred when her child was receiving medical care away from home and her presence was

1. IRC Sec. 213(d)(1).
2. Rev. Rul. 2007-72, 2007-50 IRB 1154.
3. IRC Sec. 213(d)(9); see, e.g., Let. Rul. 200344010.
4. TC Summary Opinion 2001-185.
5. Rev. Proc. 2015-53, Rev. Proc. 2016-55, Rev. Proc. 2017-58.
6. IRC Sec. 213(d)(5).
7. Treas. Reg. §1.213-1(a)(3)(i).
8. IRC Sec. 213(d)(2).

essential to such care.[1] A parent's costs of attending a medical conference (i.e., registration fee, transportation costs) to obtain information about a chronic disease affecting the parent's child were deductible so long as the costs were primarily for and essential to the medical care of the dependent. However, the costs of meals and lodging incurred by the parent while attending the conference were not deductible.[2] The Service privately ruled that taxpayers could deduct special education tuition for their children as a medical care expense where the children attended a school primarily to receive medical care in the form of special education and in those years each child had been diagnosed as having a medical condition that handicapped the child's ability to learn.[3]

Generally, medical expenses are deductible only in the year they are paid, regardless of when the expenses were incurred. (But see *Zipkin v. U.S.*,[4] holding that expenses incurred by a taxpayer to build a home to meet his wife's special health needs were properly deducted in the year the home became habitable, even though the costs had been paid in earlier years.) Costs paid by parents to modify a van used to transport their handicapped child were deductible in the year those costs were paid, although the court held that depreciation was not a deductible medical expense.[5] However, medical expenses of a decedent paid out of his estate within one year from date of death are considered paid by the decedent at the time the expenses were incurred.[6] A decedent's medical expenses cannot be taken as an income tax deduction unless a statement is filed waiving the right to deduct them for estate tax purposes. Amounts not deductible under IRC Section 213 may not be treated as deductible medical expenses for estate tax purposes. Thus, expenses that do not exceed the 10 (or 7.5) percent floor are not deductible.[7]

The Social Security hospital tax that an individual pays as an employee or self-employed person cannot be deducted as a medical expense.[8] But a sixty-five-year-old who has signed up for the supplementary medical plan under Medicare can treat his monthly premiums as amounts paid for insurance covering medical care.[9] A voluntary prescription drug insurance program, Medicare Part D, went into effect on January 1, 2006. According to the Service, an individual taxpayer can include in medical expenses the premiums paid for Medicare Part D insurance.[10]

The unreimbursed portion of an entrance fee for life care in a residential retirement facility that is allocable to future medical care is also deductible as a medical expense in the year paid (but, if the resident leaves the facility and receives a refund, the refund is includable in gross income to the extent it is attributable to the deduction previously allowed).[11] Either the percentage method or the actuarial method may be used to calculate the portions of monthly service fees (paid for lifetime residence in a continuing care retirement community) allocable to medical

1. Let. Rul. 8516025.
2. Rev. Rul. 2000-24, 2000-19 IRB 963.
3. See Let. Rul. 200521003. See also Let. Rul. 200729019.
4. 86 AFTR 2d 7052, 2000-2 USTC ¶50,863 (D. Minn. 2000).
5. *Henderson v. Comm.*, TC Memo 2000-321.
6. IRC Sec. 213(c).
7. Rev. Rul. 77-357, 1977-2 CB 328.
8. See IRC Sec. 213(d).
9. Rev. Rul. 66-216, 1966-2 CB 100.
10. See IRS Pub. 502, Medical and Dental Expenses.
11. Rev. Rul. 76-481, 1976-2 CB 82, *as clarified by* Rev. Rul. 93-72, 1993-2 CB 77; Let. Rul. 8641037.

care.[1] But, a federal district court held that none of an entrance fee paid by married taxpayers to an assisted living facility was properly deductible as a medical expense because: (1) no portion of the entrance fee was attributable to the couple's medical care; and (2) the entrance fee was structured as a loan, which cannot serve as the basis for a deduction (citing *Comm. v. Tufts*[2]).[3]

Amounts paid by an individual for medicines and drugs, which can be purchased without a doctor's prescription, are not deductible.[4] However, amounts paid by an individual for equipment (e.g., crutches), supplies (e.g., bandages), or diagnostic devices (e.g., blood sugar test kits) may qualify as amounts paid for medical care and may be deductible under IRC Section 213. (In this ruling, the IRS determined that the crutches were used to mitigate the effect of the taxpayer's injured leg and the blood sugar test kits were used to monitor and assist in treating the taxpayer's diabetes; accordingly, the costs were amounts paid for medical care and were deductible.)[5]

The costs of nutritional supplements, vitamins, herbal supplements, and "natural medicines" cannot be included in medical expenses unless they are recommended by a doctor as treatment for a specific medical condition diagnosed by a doctor.[6] Certain expenses for smoking cessation programs and products are deductible as a medical expense.[7]

Amounts paid by individuals for breast reconstruction surgery following a mastectomy for cancer, and for vision correction surgery are medical care expenses and are deductible. But amounts paid by individuals to whiten teeth discolored as a result of age are not medical care expenses and are not deductible.[8]

Costs paid by individuals for participation in a weight-loss program as treatment for a specific disease or diseases (e.g., obesity, hypertension, or heart disease) diagnosed by a physician are deductible as medical expenses; however, costs of diet food are not deductible.[9] According to Publication 502, this includes fees paid by a taxpayer for membership in a weight reduction group and attendance at periodic meetings. Membership dues for a gym, health club, or spa cannot be included in medical expenses, but separate fees charged for weight loss activities can be included as medical expenses. In informational guidance, the IRS has also stated that taxpayers may deduct exercise expenses, including the cost of equipment to use in the home, if required to treat an illness (including obesity) diagnosed by a physician. For an exercise expense to be deductible, the taxpayer must establish the purpose of the expense is to treat a disease rather than to promote general health, and that the taxpayer would not have paid the expense but for this purpose.[10]

1. *Baker v. Comm.*, 122 TC 143 (2004).
2. 461 U.S. 300, 307 (1983).
3. *Finzer v. United States*, 496 F. Supp. 2d 954 (N.D. Ill. 2007).
4. Rev. Rul. 2003-58, 2003-22 IRB 959.
5. Rev. Rul. 2003-58, above; see also IRS Information Letter INFO-2003-169 (6-13-2003).
6. IRS Pub. 502, Medical and Dental Expenses.
7. See Rev. Rul. 99-28, 1999-25 IRB 6.
8. Rev. Rul. 2003-57, 2003-22 IRB 959.
9. Rev. Rul. 2002-19, 2002-16 IRB 778.
10. Information Letter INFO 2003-0202.

Expenses for childbirth classes were deductible as a medical expense to the extent that the class prepared the taxpayer for an active role in the process of childbirth.[1] Egg donor fees and expenses relating to obtaining a willing egg donor count as medical care expenses that are deductible.[2]

The Service has clarified that no deduction is allowed for the cost of drugs imported from Canada.[3]

745. What is income in respect of a decedent and how is it taxed?

"Income in respect of a decedent" (IRD) refers to those amounts to which a decedent was entitled as gross income, but that were not includable in his taxable income for the year of his death.[4] It can include, for example: renewal commissions of a sales representative; payment for services rendered before death or under a deferred compensation agreement; and proceeds from sales on the installment method (see Q 668). Generally, if stock is acquired in an S corporation from a decedent, the pro rata share of any income of the corporation that would have been IRD if that item had been acquired directly from the decedent is IRD.[5]

The IRS has determined that a distribution from a qualified plan of the balance as of the employee's death is IRD.[6] The Service has also privately ruled that a distribution from a 403(b) tax sheltered annuity is IRD.[7] The Service has also concluded that a death benefit paid to beneficiaries from a deferred variable annuity would be IRD to the extent that the death benefit exceeded the owner's investment in the contract.[8] In addition, the Service has determined that distributions from a decedent's individual retirement account were IRD, including those parts of the distributions used to satisfy the decedent's estate tax obligation, since the individual retirement account was found to have automatically vested in the beneficiaries.[9]

However, a rollover of funds from a decedent's IRA to a marital trust and then to the surviving spouse's IRA was not IRD, according to the Service, where the surviving spouse was the sole trustee and sole beneficiary of the trust.[10] The Service also ruled that designation of a QTIP trust as the beneficiary of a decedent's account balance in a qualified profit sharing plan would not result in the acceleration of IRD at the time the assets from the plan passed into the trust. Consequently, the taxpayer would include the amounts of IRD in the plan in the taxpayer's gross income only when the taxpayer received a distribution (or distributions) from the trust.[11]

1. Let. Rul. 8919009.
2. Let. Rul. 200318017; see also Information Letter INFO 2005-0102 (3-29-2005).
3. See Information Letter INFO 2005-0011 (3-14-2005); see also Pub. 502.
4. IRC Sec. 691(a).
5. IRC Sec. 1367(b).
6. Rev. Rul. 69-297, 1969-1 CB 131; Rev. Rul. 75-125, 1975-1 CB 254.
7. Let. Rul. 9031046.
8. Let. Rul. 200041018.
9. Let. Rul. 9132021. See Rev. Rul. 92-47, 1992-1 CB 198. See also Let. Rul. 200336020.
10. Let. Rul. 200023030.
11. Let. Rul. 200702007.

Gain realized upon the cancellation at death of a note payable to a decedent has been held to be IRD to the decedent's estate.[1]

The unreported increase in value reflected in the redemption value of savings bonds as of the date of a decedent's death constitutes income in respect of a decedent.[2] See Q 7688. If savings bonds on which the increases in value have not been reported are inherited, or the subject of a bequest, the reporting of such amounts may be delayed until the bonds are redeemed or disposed of by the legatee, or reach maturity, whichever is first.[3] However, to the extent savings bonds are distributed by an estate or trust to satisfy *pecuniary* obligations or legacies, the estate or trust is required to recognize the unreported incremental increase in the redemption price of Series E bonds as income in respect of a decedent.[4]

The Service determined that in the case of a taxpayer who dies before a short sale of stock is closed, any income that may result from the closing of the short sale is not IRD, and the basis of any stock held on the date of the taxpayer's death will be stepped up.[5] The Service also privately ruled that in the case of a sales contract entered into before the decedent's death, where an economically material contingency existed at the time of the decedent's death that might have disrupted the sale of the real property, any gain realized from the sale of the real property after the decedent's death did not constitute IRD.[6]

The Court of Appeals for the Tenth Circuit has held that an alimony arrearage paid to the estate of a former spouse was IRD and thus, taxable to the recipient beneficiaries as ordinary income.[7]

The Tax Court determined that because a signed withdrawal request from the decedent constituted an effective exercise of the decedent's right to a lump-sum distribution during his lifetime, the lump-sum distribution from TIAA-CREF was therefore income to the decedent and properly includable in the decedent's income. Accordingly, the court held, the lump sum payment received by the decedent's son was not a death benefits payment and, thus, was not includable in the son's gross income as IRD.[8]

746. Is the recipient of income in respect of a decedent (IRD) entitled to an income tax deduction for estate and generation-skipping transfer taxes paid on this income?

Generally IRD must be included in the gross income of the recipient; however, a deduction is normally permitted for estate and generation-skipping transfer taxes paid on the income. The amount of the total deduction is determined by computing the federal estate tax (or generation-skipping transfer tax) with the net IRD included and then recomputing the tax with the net

1. *Est. of Frane v. Comm.*, 998 F.2d 567 (8th Cir. 1993).
2. See Rev. Rul. 64-104, 1964-1 CB 223.
3. See Let. Ruls. 9845026, 9507008, 9024016.
4. Let. Rul. 9507008.
5. Let. Rul. 9436017. See IRC Sec. 1014.
6. Let. Rul. 200744001.
7. *Kitch v. Comm.*, 103 F. 3d 104, 97-1 USTC ¶50,124 (10th Cir. 1996).
8. *Eberly v. Comm.*, TC Summary Op. 2006-45.

IRD excluded. The difference in the two results is the amount of the income tax deduction. However, if two or more persons receive IRD of the same decedent, each recipient is entitled to only a proportional share of the income tax deduction. Similarly, if the IRD is received over more than one taxable year, only a proportional part of the deduction is allowable each year. Where the income would have been ordinary income in the hands of the decedent, the deduction is an itemized deduction.[1] The recipient does not receive a stepped up basis (see Q 692).[2] A beneficiary was allowed to claim a deduction for IRD attributable to annuity payments that had been received even though the estate tax had not yet been paid.[3]

In technical advice, the IRS stated that the value of a decedent's IRA should not be discounted for estate tax purposes to reflect income taxes that will be payable by the beneficiaries upon receipt of distributions from the IRAs or for lack of marketability. The Service reasoned that the deduction is a statutory remedy for the adverse income tax impact and makes any valuation discount inappropriate if the deduction applies.[4] Courts have likewise denied discounts for lack of marketability.[5] The Service also determined that a deduction claimed on a decedent's estate tax return – which represented income taxes paid by the estate on the estate's income tax return, which in turn were triggered by the amount distributed to the estate from the decedent's IRAs – was not allowable as a deduction under IRC Section 2053. According to the Service, even if the estate had not claimed the IRD deduction, the income taxes paid on the distributions from the IRAs would still not be deductible under IRC Section 2053 because any additional benefit beyond what Congress had intended would be unwarranted.[6]

The Service has ruled that if the owner-annuitant of a deferred annuity contract dies *before* the annuity starting date, and the beneficiary receives a death benefit under the annuity contract, the amount received by the beneficiary in a lump sum in excess of the owner-annuitant's investment in the contract is includible in the beneficiary's gross income as IRD. If the death benefit is instead received in the form of a series of periodic payments, the amounts received are likewise includible in the beneficiary's gross income in an amount determined under IRC Section 72 as IRD.[7] See, e.g., Let. Rul. 200537019 (where the Service ruled that the amount equal to the excess of the contract's value over the decedent's basis, which would be received by the estate as the named beneficiary of the contract upon surrender of the contract, would constitute IRD includible by the estate in its gross income; however, the estate would be entitled to a deduction for the amounts of IRD paid to charities in the taxable year, or for the remaining amounts of IRD that would be set aside for charitable purposes).

In *Estate of Kahn*,[8] the Tax Court held that in computing the gross estate value, the value of the assets held in the IRAs is not reduced by the anticipated income tax liability following the

1. IRC Sec. 691(c); Rev. Rul. 78-203, 1978-1 CB 199.
2. IRC Sec. 1014(c).
3. FSA 200011023.
4. TAM 200247001; see also TAM 200303010.
5. See *Est. of Smith v. U.S.*, 300 F.Supp.2d 474 (S.D. TX 2004), *appeal docketed*, No. 04-20194 (5th Cir. 2004); *Est. of Robinson v. Comm.*, 69 TC 222 (1977).
6. Let. Rul. 200444021.
7. Rev. Rul. 2005-30, 2005-20 IRB 1015.
8. 125 TC 227 (2005).

distribution of IRAs, in part because IRC Section 691(c) addresses the potential double tax issue. The Tax Court further held that a discount for lack of marketability is not warranted because the assets in the IRAs are publicly traded securities. Payment of the tax upon distribution is not a prerequisite to making the assets in the IRA marketable; consequently there is no basis for the discount. In technical advice the Service has also determined that a discount for lack of marketability is not available to an estate where the deduction for IRD is available to mitigate the potential income tax liability triggered by the IRD assets.[1]

747. How are business expenses reported for income tax purposes?

A deduction is permitted for all ordinary and necessary expenses paid or incurred during the taxable year in carrying on a trade or business. Examples of deductible business expenses include: (1) expenditures for reasonable salaries, (2) traveling expenses (within limits), and (3) certain rental expenses incurred for purposes of a trade or business.[2] Illegal payments made in the course of business, such as bribes to government officials or illegal rebates (see Q 659), are not deductible.[3] Under the 2017 Tax Act, certain expenses paid to (or at the direction of) a government or government entity in relation to the violation of any law, or investigation into potential violations of the law, are not deductible.[4] Further, amounts paid in relation to sexual harassment suits that are subject to a nondisclosure agreement are not deductible.[5]

Planning Point: The IRS recently released a memorandum addressing whether a lawsuit settlement could be deducted as an expense under IRC Section 162(a). It determined that the business itself was required to prove whether the payments were compensatory, and thus deductible, or punitive (such as a fine or penalty, and thus nondeductible). This was the case despite the fact that the settlement specifically provided that the payments were not to be construed as fines or penalties. A deductible payment under Section 162 is generally one meant to compensate another party or to ensure compliance with a law. In this case, the IRS required further factual analysis to determine the nature of the payments, highlighting the fact that a settlement agreement alone will not be controlling.[6]

In 2019, the business standard mileage rate is 58 cents per mile. In 2018, the business standard mileage rate was $54.5 cents per mile and in 2017, the business standard mileage rate was 53.5 cents per mile, down from 54 cents per mile in 2016.[7]

The amount of the deduction for expenses incurred in carrying on a trade or business depends upon whether the individual is an independent contractor or an employee. Typically, whether an insurance agent is considered an independent contractor or employee is determined on the basis of all the facts and circumstances involved; however, where an employer has the right to control the manner and the means by which services are performed, an employer-employee relationship will generally be found to exist.[8] The IRS has ruled that a full-time life insurance

1. TAM 200247001; see also TAM 200303010.
2. IRC Sec. 162(a).
3. IRC Sec. 162(c).
4. IRC Sec. 162(f).
5. IRC Sec. 162(q).
6. ILM 201825027.
7. IR 2017-204, Notice 2019-02.
8. See *Butts v. Comm.*, TC Memo 1993-478, *aff'd*, 49 F.3d 713 (11th Cir. 1995); Let. Rul. 9306029.

salesperson is not an "employee" for purposes of IRC Sections 62 and 67, even though he is treated as a "statutory employee" for Social Security tax purposes.[1] See Q 3920. Furthermore, according to decisions from the Sixth and Eleventh Circuit Courts of Appeals, the fact that an insurance agent received certain employee benefits did not preclude his being considered an independent contractor, based on all the other facts and circumstances of the case.[2] The IRS has determined, however, that a district manager of an insurance company was an employee of the company, and not an independent contractor.[3] On the other hand, the IRS has determined that individuals who were regional and senior sales vice presidents of an insurance company (but who were not officers of the company) were independent contractors and not employees of the insurance company.[4]

Planning Point: The Sixth Circuit Court of Appeals recently confirmed that life insurance agents were properly classified as independent contractors, rather than employees. The case involved eligibility for benefits under ERISA, and a district court, using the traditional *Darden* factors for determining classification status, had ruled in 2017 that the agents were employees who were eligible for ERISA benefits. In reversing the lower court, the Sixth Circuit gave weight to the fact that both parties had expressed their intent that an independent contractor relationship would apply. The case also opens the possibility that the weight given to the various *Darden* factors should vary based upon the context of the case--for example, in this case, financial benefits were at issue, so the court gave more weight to the financial structure of the relationship.[5]

Independent contractors may deduct all allowable business expenses from gross income (i.e., "above-the-line") to arrive at adjusted gross income.[6] Prior to 2018, the business expenses of an employee were deductible from adjusted gross income (i.e., "below-the-line") if he or she itemized instead of taking the standard deduction, but only to the extent that they exceeded 2 percent of adjusted gross income when aggregated with other "miscellaneous itemized deductions." All miscellaneous itemized deductions subject to the 2 percent floor were suspended for 2018-2025.

Industrial agents (or "debit agents") are treated as employees for tax purposes.[7] Thus, as in the case of any employee, a debit agent can deduct transportation and away-from-home traveling expenses *from* adjusted gross income if he itemizes, only to the extent that the aggregate of these and other miscellaneous itemized deductions exceed 2 percent of adjusted gross income (prior to 2018 and, presumably, after 2025).[8]

Self-employed taxpayers are permitted a deduction equal to one-half of their self-employment (i.e., Social Security) taxes for the taxable year. This deduction is treated as attributable to a trade or business that does not consist of the performance of services by the taxpayer as an employee; thus it is taken "above-the line."[9]

1. Rev. Rul. 90-93, 1990-2 CB 33.
2. See *Ware v. U.S.*, 67 F.3d 574 (6th Cir. 1995); *Butts v. Comm.*, above.
3. TAM 9342001.
4. TAM 9736002.
5. *Jammal v. American Family Life Insurance Co.*, 2019 U.S. App. LEXIS 2905.
6. IRC Sec. 62(a)(1).
7. Rev. Rul. 58-175, 1958-1 CB 28.
8. IRC Sec. 67.
9. IRC Sec. 164(f).

In *Allemeier v. Commissioner*,[1] the Tax Court held that the taxpayer could deduct his expenses ($15,745) incurred in earning a master's degree in business administration to the extent those expenses were substantiated and education-related. The court based its decision on the fact that the taxpayer's MBA did not satisfy a minimum education requirement of his employer, nor did the MBA qualify the taxpayer to perform a new trade or business.

See Q 748 for a discussion of the business expense deduction for meals and entertainment, including a discussion of how the IRS has interpreted the changes imposed post-tax reform.

748. Can business meals and entertainment expenses continue to be deducted under the 2017 tax reform legislation? What guidance has the IRS provided on this issue?

Prior to 2018, expenses for business meals and entertainment were required to meet one of two tests, as defined in regulations, in order to be deductible. The meal had to be: (1) "directly related to" the active conduct of the trade or business, or (2) "associated with" the trade or business. Generally, the deduction for business meals and entertainment expenses was limited to 50 percent of allowable expenses.[2] The 50 percent otherwise allowed as a deduction was *then* subject to the 2 percent floor that applies to miscellaneous itemized deductions.[3]

Under the 2017 Tax Act, the deduction for all business-related entertainment expenses was repealed. However, the 50 percent deduction for food and beverage expenses was retained. It seems clear that food and beverages consumed while traveling for business continue to be deductible subject to the 50 percent limit.

Costs associated with meals and beverages provided for the convenience of the employer (i.e., meals brought to the office when employees are working late or provided through an onsite dining facility) are deductible subject to the 50 percent limit, but only through 2025.

The IRS has released a technical advice memorandum (TAM) that sheds light on the potential tax implications when employers provide employees with free meals in the office. Post-tax reform, meals provided "for the convenience of the employer" may receive favorable tax treatment. In the TAM, the IRS denied exclusion of the meals' value from employee compensation. Here, the employer provided free meals to all employees in snack areas, at their desks and in the cafeteria, justifying provision of these meals by citing need for a secure business environment for confidential discussions, employee protection, improvement of employee health and a shortened meal period policy. The IRS rejected these rationales, stating that the employer was required to show that the policies existed in practice, not just in form, and that they were enforced upon specific employees. In this case, the employer had no policies relating to employee discussion of confidential information and provided no factual support for its other claims. General goals of improving employee health were found to be insufficient. The IRS also considered the availability of meal delivery services a factor in denying the exclusion, but indicated that if the employees

1. TC Memo 2005-207.
2. IRC Sec. 274(n)(1).
3. Temp. Treas. Reg. §1.67-1T(a)(2).

were provided meals because they had to remain on the premises to respond to emergencies, that would be a factor indicating that the exclusion should be granted.

Post-tax reform, employees are permitted to exclude the cost of employer-provided meals furnished to employees on the premises and for the employer's convenience. The IRS guidance clarifies that the previously applicable standard, which requires that the meals are deemed to be provided for the employer's convenience only if they are necessary for employees to properly perform their duties, will continue to apply even post-reform. Employers who wish to provide meals under this "convenience of the employer" provision must be able to substantiate that they have policies in place reflecting the need, and must be able to show that those policies connect the employer's stated needs and goals to the necessity of providing employee meals. Sufficient substantiation will depend on the facts and circumstances of each case.[1]

The IRS has provided further guidance will be issued on the matter of whether food or beverages with a client before or after an event that is clearly categorized as "entertainment" continue to be deductible subject to the 50 percent limit, or whether they will be categorized as pure "entertainment" expenses. The IRS has guidance provides that the 50 percent deduction for business meal expenses will continue in effect under the 2017 tax reform legislation, answering some questions as to whether business meals could be categorized as "entertainment" and, thus, non-deductible. In general, business owners may continue to deduct 50 percent of business meals expenses that are ordinary and necessary expenses, so long as the meal is not lavish or extravagant under the circumstances. The meal or beverages must also be provided to current or prospective business associates, and must be purchased separately from any entertainment activities that are taking place simultaneously. It is also permissible that the cost of the food and beverages be separately stated from the cost of the entertainment.[2]

In general (both pre- and post-reform), the taxpayer or his employee generally must be present for meal expenses to be deductible, and expenses that are lavish or extravagant may be disallowed. Substantiation is required for lodging expenses and, in the case of expenditures incurred on or after October 1, 1995, for most items of $75.00 or more.[3] An employee must generally provide an "adequate accounting" of reimbursed expenses to his employer.[4]

749. Can a self-employed taxpayer deduct medical insurance costs?

In a legal memorandum concerning the deductibility of medical insurance costs, the Service ruled as follows: (1) A sole proprietor who purchases health insurance in his individual name has established a plan providing medical care coverage with respect to his trade or business, and therefore may deduct the medical care insurance costs for himself, his spouse, and dependents under IRC Section 162(l), but only to the extent the cost of the insurance does not exceed the earned income derived by the sole proprietor from the specific trade or business with respect to which the insurance was purchased. (2) A self-employed individual may deduct the medical care insurance costs for himself and his spouse and dependents under a health insurance plan

1. IRS CCA 2018-004.
2. Notice 2018-76.
3. Treas. Reg. §1.274-5(c)(2)(iii).
4. Treas. Reg. §1.274-5(f)(4).

established for his trade or business up to the net earnings of the specific trade or business with respect to which the plan is established, but a self-employed individual may not add the net profits from all his trades and businesses for purposes of determining the deduction limit under IRC Section 162(l)(2)(A). However, if a self-employed individual has more than one trade or business, he may deduct the medical care insurance costs of the self-employed individual and his spouse and dependents under each specific health insurance plan established under each specific business up to the net earnings of that specific trade or business.[1] In a legal memorandum, the Service ruled that a self-employed individual may not deduct the costs of health insurance on Schedule C. The deduction under IRC section 162(l) must be claimed as an adjustment to gross income on the front of Form 1040.[2]

Standard Deduction

750. What is the standard deduction?

Editor's Note: The 2017 Tax Act roughly doubles the standard deduction to $24,000 per married couple ($24,400 for 2019 and $24,800 for 2020) and $12,000 per individual in 2018 ($12,200 for 2019 and $12,400 for 2020). For heads of households, the standard deduction is increased to $18,000 ($18,350 for 2019 and $18,650 for 2020) and for married taxpayers filing separate returns, the standard deduction is $12,000 ($12,200 for 2019 and $12,400 for 2020). These amounts are indexed for inflation for tax years beginning after December 31, 2018 and are set to expire for tax years beginning after December 31, 2025.[3]

There are two ways that taxable income may be calculated. First, taxpayers may subtract from adjusted gross income (see Q 715) the sum of their personal exemptions (prior to 2018 and after 2025) and the standard deduction. Alternatively, taxpayers can deduct from adjusted gross income their allowable personal exemptions (see Q 726, Q 727) and the total of their itemized deductions (see Q 729).[4]

In the case of individuals, the standard deduction for 2017 was $12,700 for married individuals filing jointly and surviving spouses, $9,350 for heads of households and $6,350 for single individuals and married taxpayers filing separately.[5] The standard deduction for taxable years beginning in 2015 and 2016 was $12,600 for married individuals filing jointly and surviving spouses; $9,250 for heads of households in 2015, increasing to $9,300 in 2016 (only the head of household standard deduction increased for 2016), $6,300 for single individuals and married individuals filing separately.[6] The standard deduction is adjusted annually for inflation.[7]

Planning Point: Because of the increased standard deduction and the elimination of many itemized deductions, it is likely that more taxpayers will choose the standard deduction under the new tax law. Those taxpayers who wish to take advantage of the remaining itemized deductions

1. CCA 200524001.
2. CCA 200623001.
3. IRC Sec. 63(c)(7), Rev. Proc. 2018-57, Rev. Proc. 2019-44.
4. IRC Sec. 63.
5. Rev. Proc. 2016-55.
6. IRC Sec. 63(c); Rev. Proc. 2014-61, Rev. Proc. 2015-53.
7. IRC Sec. 63(c)(4).

(for example, the deduction for charitable contributions) may benefit from planning to "bunch" those deductions into a single tax year in order to ensure that itemized deductions exceed the expanded standard deduction.

Individuals who do not itemize and who are elderly (age sixty-five or older) or blind are entitled to increase their standard deduction. For taxable years beginning in 2018-2020, individuals who are married or are surviving spouses are each entitled to an additional deduction of $1,300 ($1,250 in 2015-2017) if they are elderly and an additional $1,300 deduction if they are blind. The extra standard deduction is $1,650 (in 2019-2020, $1,600 in 2018, $1,550 in 2015-2017) for unmarried elderly taxpayers and $1,650 for unmarried blind taxpayers.[1] The additional amounts for elderly and blind individuals are indexed for inflation, and were not changed under the 2017 Tax Act.[2]

The following taxpayers are ineligible for the standard deduction and thus must itemize their deductions or take a standard deduction of zero dollars: (1) married taxpayers filing separately, if either spouse itemizes,[3] (2) non-resident aliens, (3) taxpayers filing a short year return because of a change in their annual accounting period, and (4) estates or trusts, common trust funds, or partnerships.[4]

For taxable years beginning in 2020, the standard deduction for an individual who *may* be claimed as a dependent by another taxpayer is the greater of $1,100 in 2019-2020 and $1,050 in 2018 or the sum of $350 and the dependent's earned income (but the standard deduction so calculated cannot exceed the regular standard deduction amount above).[5] These dollar amounts are adjusted for inflation.[6]

"Marriage penalty" relief. EGTRRA 2001 increased the basic standard deduction for a married couple filing a joint return, providing for a phase-in of the increase until the basic standard deduction for a married couple filing jointly equaled twice the basic standard deduction for an unmarried individual filing a single return by 2009. JGTRRA 2003 accelerated the phase-in, providing that the basic standard deduction for a married couple filing a joint return equaled twice the standard deduction for an unmarried individual filing a single return for 2003 and 2004, then reverting to the lower, gradually increasing standard deduction amounts provided for under EGTRRA for 2005 through 2009. However, under WFTRA 2004 the standard deduction for married individuals filing jointly (and surviving spouses) is twice the amount (200 percent) of the standard deduction for unmarried individuals filing single returns for tax years beginning *after December 31, 2003.*[7] The larger standard deduction for married individuals filing jointly was scheduled to "sunset" (expire) for taxable years beginning after December 31, 2012, at which time the standard deduction in effect prior to the enactment of EGTRRA 2001 was to become effective (i.e., the standard deduction for married individuals filing jointly would, once again,

1. IRC Sec. 63(f); Rev. Proc. 2014-61, Rev. Proc. 2015-53, Rev. Proc. 2016-55, Rev. Proc. 2017-58, Rev. Proc. 2018-57, Rev. Proc. 2019-44.
2. IRC Sec. 63(c)(4).
3. IRS CCA 200030023.
4. IRC Sec. 63(c)(6).
5. IRC Sec. 63(c)(5); Rev. Proc. 2017-58, Rev. Proc. 2018-57, Rev. Proc. 2019-44.
6. IRC Sec. 63(c)(4).
7. IRC Sec. 63(c).

be 167 percent of the standard deduction for single individuals).[1] The American Taxpayer Relief Act of 2012 prevented this sunset, so that the standard deduction for married individuals filing jointly (and surviving spouses) continues to be equal to 200 percent of the standard deduction for individual filers for tax years beginning after 2012.[2]

751. What are the federal income tax rates for individuals?

Under the 2017 Tax Act,[3] the following income tax rates and income thresholds apply for 2020:

TAXABLE INCOME				
Tax Rate	**Single**	**Married Filing Jointly Including Qualifying Widow(er) with Dependent Child**	**Married Filing Separately**	**Head of Household**
10%	$0 to $9,875	$0 to $19,750	$0 to $9,875	$0 to $14,100
12%	$9,875-$40,125	$19,750-$80,250	$9,875 -$40,125	$14,100-$53,700
22%	$40,125-$85,525	$80,250-$171,050	$40,125-$85,525	$53,700-$85,500
24%	$85,525-$163,300	$171,050-$326,600	$85,525-$163,300	$85,500-$163,300
32%	$163,300-$207,350	$326,600-$414,700	$163,300-$207,350	$163,300-$207,350
35%	$207,350-$518,400	$414,700-$622,050	$207,230-$311,025	$207,350-$518,400
37%	Over $518,400	Over $622,050	Over $311,025	Over $518,400

These rates are set to expire after 2025, and are adjusted for inflation for tax years beginning after 2018.

Pre-2018 Income Tax Rates

In 2001, EGTRRA added a new 10 percent income tax rate and reduced income tax rates above 15 percent for individuals, trusts and estates. EGTRRA 2001 also provided for subsequent rate reductions to occur in 2004 and 2006.[4] JGTRRA 2003 accelerated the reductions that were scheduled to occur in 2004 and 2006. Thus, for 2003 to 2012, the income tax rates above 15 percent were lowered to 25 percent, 28 percent, 33 percent and 35 percent (down from 27 percent, 30 percent, 35 percent, and 38.6 percent).[5] The American Taxpayer Relief Act of 2012 ("ATRA") made these tax rates "permanent," preventing their increase to pre-2001 levels for tax years beginning after 2012.[6]

1. JGTRRA 2003 Sec. 107.
2. Rev. Proc. 2013-35, above.
3. Pub. Law No. 115-97, known as the "Tax Cuts and Jobs Act" or the 2017 Tax Act, Rev. Proc. 2018-57, Rev. Proc. 2019-44.
4. IRC Secs. 1(i)(1), 1(i)(2), prior to amendment by JGTRRA 2003.
5. IRC Sec. 1(i)(2), as amended by JGTRRA 2003.
6. American Taxpayer Relief Act of 2012, Pub. Law No. 112-240.

As discussed above, the income tax brackets effective in 2012 were to continue in effect permanently under ATRA, although certain high-income taxpayers were subject to a new 39.6 percent tax rate. These high-income taxpayers included individual taxpayers with taxable income that is above the "applicable threshold" amount. In 2017, the applicable threshold was $418,400 per year for single taxpayers, $470,700 for married taxpayers filing jointly, $444,550 for taxpayers filing as heads of household, and $235,350 for married taxpayers filing separately. For 2016, the applicable threshold was $415,050 per year for single taxpayers, $466,950 for married taxpayers filing jointly, $441,000 for taxpayers filing as heads of household, and $233,475 for married taxpayers filing separately).[1] These dollar limits were subject to annual inflation adjustment. For all other taxpayers, the tax system put into place under the EGTRRA 2001 and JGTRRA 2003 applied for tax years beginning after 2012 and before 2018 (creating a seven-bracket system: 10 percent, 15 percent, 25 percent, 28 percent, 33 percent, 35 percent, and 39.6 percent). The seven bracket system continues after enactment of the 2017 Tax Act, but the brackets were changed as shown in the chart above.

The income brackets to which each rate applies depend upon whether a separate return, joint return, head-of-household return, or single return is filed. (For an explanation of which taxpayers may file jointly or as a head-of-household, see Q 754 and Q 755.) The income brackets are indexed annually for inflation.[2]

Further, separate tax rates apply to capital gains (see Q 702). For the taxation of children on their unearned income, see Q 680. See the income tax tables, in Appendix B.

752. What changes to the tax rates applicable to trusts and estates were imposed by the 2017 Tax Act?

The 2017 tax reform legislation changed the income tax rates that will apply to trusts and estates. These rates are especially important from 2018 through 2025 because they will apply to the unearned children of minors (see Q 680 and Q 8588) under the new tax law.

The applicable tax rates and income thresholds for 2020 are outlined in the chart below:[3]

Tax Rate	Trusts and Estate Income
10%	$0 to $2,600
$260 plus 24% of the excess over $2,600	$2,600-$9,450
$1,868 plus 35% of the excess over $9,450	$9,450-$12,950
$3,075.50 plus 37% of the excess over $12,950	Over $12,950

These applicable tax rates and income thresholds are set to expire for tax years beginning after December 31, 2025.

1. ATRA, Sec. 101; Rev. Proc. 2015-53, Rev. Proc. 2016-55.
2. IRC Sec. 1(f).
3. IRC Sec. 1(j)(2)(E), Rev. Proc. 2018-57, Rev. Proc. 2019-44.

753. How are taxes indexed?

The individual rate brackets, basic standard deduction, and personal exemption amounts are adjusted annually for inflation.[1] Indexing also applies to the additional standard deduction for the blind and elderly, the adoption credit, the exclusion for employer-provided adoption assistance, the exemption amount for the alternative minimum tax, and the threshold income levels for: phaseout of personal exemptions (which were suspended for 2018-2025); phaseout of the savings bond interest exclusion; phaseout of the deduction for interest on a qualified education loan; phaseout of the adoption credit; phaseout of the exclusion for employer-provided adoption assistance; and the ceiling on itemized deductions (note that all miscellaneous itemized deductions subject to the 2 percent floor were suspended for 2018-2025).[2] The American Opportunity and Lifetime Learning Credits are also indexed for inflation, as are the threshold income levels for their phaseout.[3]

Indexing provides the benefit of preventing tax rate increases that result purely from inflation, as taxpayers' escalating income levels push them into higher tax brackets. It also ensures that the income levels at which certain tax benefits are eliminated remain at inflation-adjusted levels so that the provisions continue to benefit those taxpayers for whom they were intended.

Prior to 2018, the indexing factor (referred to in the IRC as the cost-of-living adjustment) was the percentage by which the Consumer Price Index (CPI) for the *prior* calendar year exceeded the CPI for a year designated as a reference point in each respective IRC Section. In all cases, the CPI is the average Consumer Price Index as of the close of the twelve-month period ending on August 31 of the calendar year.[4]

The 2017 Tax Act provides that items that are adjusted annually for inflation will now be adjusted based on the Chained Consumer Price Index for All Urban Consumers (C-CPI-U), as published by the Department of Labor, for tax years beginning after December 31, 2017 (this change is therefore permanent).[5] Essentially, the C-CPI-U is designed to take into account the fact that individuals change their purchasing habits as the cost of certain goods increases or decreases (in order to substitute lower priced goods for higher priced goods). C-CPI-U is designed to take into account purchasing patterns both before and after a price change.

Planning Point: Many expect that this modification to the inflation indexing method will push more taxpayers into higher tax brackets more quickly than under prior law. This is both because of the fact that C-CPI-U indexing makes it appear that inflation is growing faster than under CPI indexing, and because many employment-related increases in income are based on the CPI.

Regardless of the index that is used, in calculating the new tax rate schedules, the minimum and maximum dollar amounts for each rate bracket (except as described below) are increased by the applicable cost-of-living adjustment. The rates (percentages) themselves are not adjusted.

1. IRC Secs. 1(f), 63(c)(4), 151(d)(4).
2. IRC Secs. 63(c)(4), 23(h), 137(f), 151(d)(4)(B), 135(b)(2)(B), 221(g), and 68(b)(2).
3. IRC Sec. 25A(h).
4. IRC Secs. 1(f)(3), 1(f)(4).
5. IRC Secs. 1(f)(3), 1(f)(6).

This method of increase explained above, however, does not apply to the phaseout of the marriage penalty (see Q 751).[1]

The Secretary of the Treasury has until December 15 of each calendar year to publish new tax rate schedules (for joint returns, separate returns, single returns, head of household returns and for returns by estates and trusts) that will be effective for taxable years beginning in the subsequent calendar year.[2] See Q 751 and the tax tables in Appendix B of this book.

754. Who may file a joint return?

Two spouses may file a joint return. Same-sex couples who currently are married under state law must now file either jointly or married filing separately for 2013 and beyond because of the Supreme Court's *Windsor* decision.[3] Gross income and deductions of both spouses are included; however, a joint return may be filed even though one spouse has no income. A widow or widower *who has a dependent child* may file as a "surviving spouse" and calculate tax using joint return tax rates for two years after the taxable year in which the spouse died. However, no personal exemption is allowed for the deceased spouse except in the year of death (note that the personal exemption was suspended from 2018-2025).[4]

755. Who may use head-of-household rates?

The 2017 Tax Act imposes a due diligence requirement for tax preparers in determining whether head-of-household filing status is appropriate. A $500 penalty will now apply for each failure of a tax preparer to satisfy due diligence requirements (to be released in the future) with respect to determining head-of-household status.[5]

An individual who meets the four requirements below may use the applicable head-of-household rates:

(1) The individual must be (a) unmarried, or (b) legally separated from his spouse under a decree of divorce or of separate maintenance, or (c) married, living apart from his spouse during the last six months of the taxable year, and maintaining as his home a household that constitutes the principal place of abode for a "qualifying child".[6] See Q 727 with respect to whom the individual is entitled to claim a deduction, and with respect to whom the taxpayer furnishes over one-half the cost of maintaining such household during the taxable year.[7]

(2) The individual must maintain as his home a household in which one or more of the following persons lives: (a) a qualifying child (if that individual is unmarried, it is not necessary that he have less than the personal exemption amount (4,050 in

1. IRC Sec. 1(f)(2).
2. IRC Sec. 1(f)(1).
3. *Windsor v. U.S.* 133 S. Ct. 2675 (2013).
4. IRC Secs. 1(a), 2(a), 6013(a). See IRC Sec. 151(b).
5. IRC Sec. 6695(g).
6. As defined in IRC Sec. 152(c).
7. IRC Secs. 2(b)(1), 2(c), 7703(b).

2016 and 2017, $4,150 in 2018, $4,200 in 2019 and $4,300 in 2020)[1] of income or that the head-of-household furnish more than one-half his support; if the qualifying child is married, he must qualify as a dependent of the taxpayer claiming head-of-household status (or, would qualify except for the waiver of the exemption by the custodial parent (see Q 727)), *or* (b) any other person for whom the taxpayer can claim a dependency exemption (pre-2018) except a cousin or unrelated person living in the household.[2] An exception to this rule is made with respect to a taxpayer's dependent mother or father: so long as he maintains the household in which the dependent parent lives, it need not be his home.[3]

Planning Point: For purposes of the definition of "dependent" for determining head of household status, the IRS has released guidance stating that the exemption amount (which was otherwise reduced to zero for 2018-2025) will be treated as though it remained at the pre-reform $4,150 amount in 2018, $4,200 in 2019 and $4,300 in 2020.[4]

(3) The individual must contribute over one-half the cost of maintaining the home.[5]

(4) Taxpayer must not be a nonresident alien.[6]

Credits

756. What credits may be taken against the tax?

Editor's Note: Many of the credits listed below contain sunset provisions so that they apply only so long as Congress chooses to renew them from year to year. Late in 2015, Congress enacted the Protecting Americans from Tax Hikes Act of 2015 (PATH) to extend the following credits (discussed below): the work opportunity credit (extended through 2019), the research credit (made permanent), and the new markets tax credit (extended through 2019).

Early in 2018, Congress enacted the Bipartisan Budget Act of 2018 (BBA 2018) to extend through 2017 the following credits: the nonbusiness energy property credit, the empowerment zone employment credit, the Indian employment credit, the railroad track maintenance credit, the biodiesel fuels credit, the energy efficient home credit, the portion of the alternative fuel vehicle refueling property credit to which IRC Section 30C(d)(1) applies, and the credit for certain plug-in electric cars. However, as of the date of this revision and with respect to provisions that were not made permanent, Congress has not indicated whether it will extend this treatment for future years.[7]

After rates have been applied to compute the tax, certain payments and credits may be subtracted from the tax to arrive at the amount of tax payable. *Refundable credits* are recoverable

1. Rev. Proc. 2014-61, Rev. Proc. 2015-53, Rev. Proc. 2016-55, Rev. Proc. 2018-57, Rev. Proc. 2019-44.
2. IRC Sec. 2(b)(1); Treas. Reg. §1.2-2(b).
3. IRC Sec. 2(b)(1).
4. Notice 2018-70.
5. IRC Sec. 2(b)(1).
6. IRC Secs. 2(b), 2(d).
7. Pub. Law No. 115-123.

regardless of the amount of the taxpayer's tax liability for the taxable year. The refundable credits include:

...Taxes withheld from salaries and wages.[1]

...Overpayments of tax.[2]

...The excess of Social Security withheld (two or more employers).[3]

...The earned income credit.[4]

... A portion of the child tax credit (Q 758).

... A portion of the American Opportunity credit.

...The 72.5 percent health care tax credit for uninsured workers displaced by trade competition.[5]

...The unused long-term minimum tax credit.

For 2009 and 2010, a "making work pay" credit was available equal to the lesser of (1) 6.2 percent of earned income or (2) $800 for a joint return and $400 for all others. The credit was reduced by 2 percent of the taxpayer's modified adjusted gross income in excess of $150,000 for a joint return and $75,000 for all others. The credit was also reduced by certain other benefits provided by ARRA 2009. The credit was not available for nonresident aliens, for persons for whom a personal exemption was claimed on another person's return, or an estate or trust.[6]

There was a first-time homebuyer credit available for a home purchased after April 8, 2008 and through April 2010.[7] The credit was available for 10 percent of the purchase price, up to certain limits. For homes purchased in 2009 and 2010, the dollar limits were $8,000 ($4,000 for a married individual filing separately). However, for a home purchased after November 6, 2009 by a long-time resident treated as a first-time homebuyer, the dollar limit was only $6,500 ($3,250 for a married individual filing separately). For a home purchased before November 7, 2009, the credit was phased out based on AGI of $75,000 to $95,000 ($150,000 to $170,000 for a joint return). For a home purchased after November 6, 2009, the credit was phased out based on AGI of $125,000 to $145,000 ($225,000 to $245,000 for a joint return). For a home purchased after November 6, 2009, the credit was not available to a person for whom a personal exemption was allowable to another person. The credit was not available for a home purchased after November 6, 2009 if the purchase price exceeded $800,000. For a home purchased in 2008, the credit must generally be recaptured over a 15-year period beginning with the second year after the home is purchased. The recapture is accelerated if the home is sold or is no longer

1. IRC Sec. 31(a).
2. IRC Sec. 35.
3. Treas. Reg. §1.31-2.
4. IRC Sec. 32.
5. IRC Sec. 35.
6. IRC Sec. 36A, as amended by ARRA 2009.
7. IRC Sec. 36, as added by HERA 2008 and amended by ARRA 2009 and WHBAA 2009.

the taxpayer's principal residence. Credit recapture does not apply to a home purchased in 2009 or 2010 unless the home was disposed of, or ceases to be used as a primary residence, within three years of purchase. For a first-time homebuyer's credit that can be properly claimed in a year after 2008, the taxpayer can elect to claim the credit as of December 31 of the previous year.

The *nonrefundable credits* are as follows:

...The personal credits—which consist of the child and dependent care credit;[1] the credit for the elderly and the permanently and totally disabled;[2] the qualified adoption credit;[3] the nonrefundable portion of the child tax credit (see Q 758);[4] the American Opportunity, Hope Scholarship, and Lifetime Learning credits[5] (see Q 759); the credit for elective deferrals and IRA contributions (the "saver's credit," which became permanent under PPA 2006);[6]

...The nonbusiness energy property credit (extended through 2017 under BBA 2018);[7] and the residential energy efficient property credit.[8]

...Other nonbusiness credits.[9]

...The general business credit (see Q 7882) is the sum of the following credits determined for the taxable year: (1) the investment credit determined under IRC Section 46 (see Q 7891) (including the rehabilitation credit; see Q 7806); (2) the work opportunity credit determined under IRC Section 51(a) extended through 2019 under PATH); (3) the alcohol fuels credit determined under IRC Section 40(a); (4) the research credit (made permanent by PATH) determined under IRC Section 41(a); (5) the low-income housing credit (see Q 7799) determined under IRC Section 42(a); (6) the enhanced oil recovery credit (see Q 7882) under IRC Section 43(a); (7) in the case of an eligible small business, the disabled access credit determined under IRC Section 44(a); (8) the renewable electricity production credit under IRC Section 45(a) (extended only through 2009 under EIEA 2008); (9) the empowerment zone employment credit determined under IRC Section 1396(a) (extended through 2017); (10) the Indian employment credit as determined under IRC Section 45A(a) (extended through 2017); (11) the employer Social Security credit determined under IRC Section 45B(a); (12) the orphan drug credit determined under IRC Section 45C(a) (as modified by the 2017 Tax Act); (13) the new markets tax credit determined under IRC Section 45D(a) (extended through 2019); (14) in the case of an eligible employer (as defined in IRC Section 45E(c)); the small employer pension plan startup cost credit determined under IRC Section 45E(a); (15) the employer-provided child care credit determined under IRC Section 45F(a); (16) the railroad track maintenance credit determined under IRC Section 45G(a) (extended through 2017); (17) the

1. IRC Sec. 21.
2. IRC Sec. 22.
3. IRC Sec. 23.
4. IRC Sec. 24.
5. IRC Sec. 25A, as amended by ATRA, Sec. 103.
6. IRC Sec. 25B.
7. IRC Sec. 25C, as amended by ATRA, Sec. 401.
8. IRC Sec. 25D.
9. IRC Secs. 53, 901.

biodiesel fuels credit determined under IRC Section 40A(a) (extended through 2017); (18) the low sulfur diesel fuel production credit determined under IRC Section 45H(a); (19) the marginal oil and gas well production credit determined under IRC Section 45I(a); (20) for tax years beginning after September 20, 2005, the distilled spirits credit determined under IRC Section 5011(a); (21) for tax year beginning after August 8, 2005, the advanced nuclear power facility production credit determined under IRC Section 45J(a); (22) for property placed in service after December 31, 2005, the nonconventional source production credit determined under IRC Section 45K(a); (23) the energy efficient home credit determined under IRC Section 45L(a) (extended through 2017); (24) the energy efficient appliance credit determined under IRC Section 45M(a) (extended through 2014); (25) the portion of the alternative motor vehicle credit to which IRC Section 30B(g)(1) applies; and (26) the portion of the alternative fuel vehicle refueling property credit to which IRC Section 30C(d)(1) applies (extended through 2017).[1]

ETIA 2005 provides an alternative motor vehicle credit for qualified fuel cell vehicles, advanced lean-burn technology vehicles, qualified hybrid vehicles, and qualified alternative fuel vehicles.[2] (This credit replaced the prior deduction for qualified clean-fuel vehicle property, which expired on December 31, 2005.)[3] The portion of the credit attributable to vehicles of a character subject to an allowance for depreciation is treated as a portion of the general business credit; the remainder of the credit is a personal credit allowable to the extent of the excess of the regular tax (reduced by certain other credits) over the alternative minimum tax for the taxable year.[4]

For new qualified plug-in electric drive motor vehicles acquired and placed in service after 2009, a credit is available. The credit can vary from $2,500 to $7,500 depending on battery capacity (and subject to phaseout based on number of vehicles sold by the manufacturer). The portion of the credit attributable to property of a character subject to an allowance for depreciation is treated as part of the general business credit. The balance of the credit is generally treated as a nonrefundable personal credit.[5] An alternative credit is available for certain plug-in electric cars placed in service after February 17, 2009 and before 2018. This credit is equal to 10 percent of cost, up to $2,500.[6]

757. Who qualifies for the tax credit for the elderly and the permanently and totally disabled and how is the credit computed?

The credit is available to taxpayers age sixty-five or older, *or* those who are under age sixty-five, retired on disability, and were considered permanently and totally disabled when they retired.[7]

> "An individual is permanently and totally disabled if he is unable to engage in any substantial gainful activity by reason of any medically determinable physical or mental impairment which can be expected to result in death or which has lasted or can be expected to last for a continuous period of not less than twelve

1. IRC Sec. 38(b).
2. IRC Sec. 30B.
3. See Sec. 1348, ETIA 2005; IRC Sec. 179A.
4. See IRC Sec. 30B(g).
5. IRC Sec. 30D, as amended by ARRA 2009.
6. IRC Sec. 30, as amended by ARRA 2009 and ATRA.
7. IRC Sec. 22(b).

months. An individual shall not be considered to be permanently and totally disabled unless he furnishes proof of the existence thereof in such form and manner, and at such times, as the Secretary may require."[1]

The credit equals 15 percent of an individual's IRC Section 22 amount for the taxable year, but may not exceed the amount of tax. This IRC Section 22 base amount is $5,000 for a single taxpayer or married taxpayers filing jointly if only one spouse qualifies for the credit; $7,500 for married taxpayers filing jointly if both qualify; and $3,750 for a married taxpayer filing separately.[2] Married taxpayers must file a joint return to claim the credit, unless they lived apart for the entire taxable year.[3]

This base figure is limited for individuals under age sixty-five to the amount of the disability income (taxable amount an individual receives under an employer plan as wages or payments in lieu of wages for the period he is absent from work on account of permanent and total disability) received during the taxable year.[4] (Proof of continuing permanent and total disability may be required.)[5] For married taxpayers who are both qualified and who file jointly, the base figure cannot exceed the total of both spouses' disability income if both are under age sixty-five or if only one is under age sixty-five, the sum of $5,000 plus the disability income of the spouse who is under sixty-five.[6]

The base figure (or the amount of disability income in the case of individuals under age sixty-five, if lower) is reduced dollar-for-dollar by one-half of adjusted gross income in excess of $7,500 (single taxpayers), $10,000 (joint return), or $5,000 (married filing separately).[7] A reduction is also made for Social Security and railroad retirement benefits that are excluded from gross income, and certain other tax-exempt income.[8]

758. Who qualifies for the child tax credit?

A child tax credit is available for each "qualifying child" (defined below) of eligible taxpayers who meet certain income requirements. The child tax credit is $1,000 ($2,000 for tax years beginning after 2017 and before 2026, see below).[9]

Additional Rules for Tax Years Beginning After 2017 and Before 2026

An expanded $2,000 child tax credit is available for tax years beginning after 2017 and before 2026 ($1,400 of this per-child credit is refundable). The taxpayer must include the Social Security number for each child for which the refundable portion of the child tax credit is claimed.[10] The $1,400 refundable amount will be indexed for inflation and rounded to the next multiple of $100.[11]

1. IRC Sec. 22(e)(3).
2. IRC Sec. 22(c).
3. IRC Sec. 22(e)(1).
4. IRC Sec. 22(c)(2)(B)(i).
5. GCM 39269 (8-2-84).
6. IRC Sec. 22(c)(2)(B)(ii).
7. IRC Sec. 22(d).
8. IRC Sec. 22(c)(3).
9. IRC Sec. 24(a).
10. IRC Sec. 24(h)(7).
11. IRC Sec. 24(h).

A new family tax credit was created to allow for a $500 nonrefundable credit for dependent parents and other non-child dependents (the requirement for furnishing a Social Security number does not apply to this family tax credit).[1]

Planning Point: For purposes of the definition of "dependent" for this provision, the IRS has released guidance stating that the exemption amount (which was otherwise reduced to zero for 2018-2025) will be treated as though it remained at the pre-reform $4,150 amount in 2018, $4,200 in 2019, and $4,300 in 2020.[2]

The credit will phase out for taxpayers with AGI of $400,000 (joint returns) or $200,000 (all other filers). The phase out amounts are not indexed for inflation.[3] As is the case with the suspension of the personal exemption, these provisions are set to expire after 2025.

The term *qualifying child* means a "qualifying child" of the taxpayer (as defined under IRC Section 152(c) – see below) who has not attained the age of seventeen.[4]

"Qualifying child" means, with respect to any taxpayer for any taxable year, an individual:

(1) who is the taxpayer's "child" (see below) or a descendant of such a child, *or* the taxpayer's brother, sister, stepbrother, or stepsister or a descendant of any such relative;

(2) who has the same principal place of abode as the taxpayer for more than one-half of the taxable year; *and*

(3) who has *not* provided over one-half of such individual's own support for the calendar year in which the taxpayer's taxable year begins.[5]

Additionally, a qualifying child must be either a citizen or a resident of the United States.[6]

The term "child" means an individual who is: (1) a son, daughter, stepson, or stepdaughter of the taxpayer; or (2) an "eligible foster child" of the taxpayer.[7] An "eligible foster child" means an individual who is placed with the taxpayer by an authorized placement agency or by judgment decree, or other order of any court of competent jurisdiction.[8] Any adopted children of the taxpayer are treated the same as natural born children.[9]

The amount of the credit is reduced for taxpayers whose modified adjusted gross income (MAGI) exceeds certain levels. A taxpayer's MAGI is his adjusted gross income without regard to the exclusions for income derived from certain foreign sources or sources within United States possessions. Prior to 2018, the credit amount was reduced by $50 for every $1000, or fraction

1. IRC Sec. 24(h)(4).
2. Notice 2018-70.
3. IRC Sec. 24(h)(3).
4. IRC Sec. 24(c)(1).
5. IRC Sec. 152(c).
6. IRC Sec. 24(c)(2).
7. IRC Sec. 152(f)(1).
8. IRC Sec. 152(f)(1)(C).
9. IRC Sec. 152(f)(1)(B).

thereof, by which the taxpayer's MAGI, exceeds the following threshold amounts: $110,000 for married taxpayers filing jointly, $75,000 for unmarried individuals, and $55,000 for married taxpayers filing separately.[1]

Prior to 2018, child tax credit was refundable to the extent of 15 percent of the taxpayer's earned income in excess of $3,000 (previously, this amount was $10,000; see below).[2] For example, if the taxpayer's earned income is $16,000, the excess amount would be $13,000 ($16,000 – $3,000 = $13,000), and the taxpayer's refundable credit for one qualifying child would be $1,950 ($13,000 × 15 percent = $1,950). For families with three or more qualifying children, the credit is refundable to the extent that the taxpayer's Social Security taxes exceed the taxpayer's earned income credit *if* that amount is greater than the refundable credit based on the taxpayer's earned income in excess of $3,000.[3] The previously applicable $10,000 income floor was indexed for inflation. ARRA 2009 reduced the dollar amount to $3,000 for 2009 through 2012.[4] ATRA extended the $3,000 floor amount through 2017, and the PATH Act made this provision permanent.[5] See above for the rules governing the credit from 2018-2026. (Prior to 2001, the child tax credit was refundable only for individuals with three or more qualifying children.)[6]

The nonrefundable child tax credit can be claimed against the individual's regular income tax *and* alternative minimum tax (see Q 756). The nonrefundable child tax credit cannot exceed the excess of (i) the sum of the taxpayer's regular tax plus the alternative minimum tax over (ii) the sum of the taxpayer's nonrefundable personal credits (other than the child tax credit, adoption credit, and saver's credit) and the foreign tax credit for the taxable year.[7] For tax years beginning after 2001, the refundable child tax credit need not be reduced by the amount of the taxpayer's alternative minimum tax.[8] The nonrefundable credit must be reduced by the amount of the refundable credit.[9]

Some additional restrictions applying to the child tax credit include: (1) an individual's tax return must identify the name and taxpayer identification number (Social Security number) of the child for whom the credit is claimed; and (2) the credit may be claimed only for a full taxable year, unless the taxable year is cut short by the death of the taxpayer.[10] For purposes of applying a uniform method of determining when a child attains a specific age, the Service has ruled that a child attains a given age on the anniversary of the date that the child was born (e.g., a child born on January 1, 1987, attains the age of 17 on January 1, 2004).[11] The IRS stated that

1. IRC Sec. 24(b)(2).
2. IRC Sec. 24(d)(1)(B)(i).
3. IRC Sec. 24(d)(1).
4. IRC Sec. 24(d)(3).
5. ATRA, Sec. 103.
6. IRC Sec. 24(d), prior to amendment by EGTRRA 2001.
7. IRC Sec. 24(b)(3).
8. IRC Sec. 24(d).
9. IRC Sec. 24(d)(1).
10. IRC Secs. 24(e), 24(f).
11. Rev. Rul. 2003-72, 2003-2 CB 346.

it would apply Revenue Ruling 2003-72 retroactively and would notify those taxpayers entitled to a refund for 2002 as a result of Revenue Ruling 2003-72.[1]

759. What is the Hope Scholarship (American Opportunity) Credit?

The Hope Scholarship (American Opportunity) Credit is available to certain eligible taxpayers who pay qualified tuition and related expenses.[2]

The Hope Scholarship (American Opportunity) Credit provides a credit for each *eligible student* equal to the sum of: (1) 100 percent of qualified tuition and related expenses up to $2,000; plus (2) 25 percent of qualified tuition and related expenses in excess of $2,000, up to the applicable limit. The applicable limit ($4,000) is two times the $2,000 amount.[3] AARA 2009 increased the credit amounts for 2009 and 2010 (later extended through 2012 and again early in 2013 by the American Taxpayer Relief Act of 2012 ("ATRA") through 2017. This treatment was made permanent by the Protecting Americans from Tax Hikes Act of 2015 (PATH)).[4] In earlier years, the amounts used to calculate the credit were adjusted for inflation and rounded to the next lowest multiple of $100.[5] The maximum credit is now $2,500 ($2,000 + (25 percent × $2,000).

The credit is available for four years of postsecondary education (this provision was made permanent by PATH and applies for 2009 and thereafter), and can be used in only four taxable years.[6] To qualify for the credit, the student must carry at least half of a full-time academic workload for an academic period during the taxable year.[7]

An *eligible student* generally means a student who: (1) for at least one academic period beginning in the calendar year, is enrolled at least half-time in a program leading to a degree, certificate, or other recognized educational credential and is enrolled in one of the first four years of postsecondary education (two years prior to 2009), and (2) is free of any conviction for federal or state felony offenses consisting of the possession of a controlled substance.[8]

Qualified tuition and related expenses are tuition and fees required for the enrollment or attendance of the taxpayer, the taxpayer's spouse, or any dependent of the taxpayer (for whom he is allowed a dependency exemption) at an "eligible education institution."[9] Qualified tuition and related expenses do not include nonacademic fees such as room and board, medical expenses (including required student health fees), transportation, student activity fees, athletic fees, insurance expenses, and similar personal, living or family expenses unrelated to a student's academic course of instruction.[10] Additionally, qualified tuition and related expenses do not include expenses for a course involving sports, games or hobbies, unless it is part of the student's degree

1. IRS Information Letter INFO-2003-0215 (8-29-2003).
2. IRC Sec. 25A.
3. IRC Secs. 25A(b)(1), 25A(b)(4); Treas. Reg. §1.25A-3(a).
4. ATRA, Sec. 103.
5. IRC Sec. 25A(h)(1).
6. Treas. Reg. §1.25A-3(c).
7. IRC Sec. 25A(b)(2); Treas. Reg. §1.25A-3(d)(ii).
8. IRC Sec. 25A(b)(3); Notice 97-60, 1997-2 CB 310 (Sec. 1, A3); Treas. Reg. §1.25A-3(d)(1).
9. Treas. Reg. §1.25A-2(d)(1).
10. Treas. Reg. §1.25A-2(d)(3).

program.[1] AARA 2009 expanded qualified tuition and related expenses to include required course materials, and PATH made this provision permanent.

An *eligible educational institution* generally means a postsecondary educational institution that: (a) provides an educational program for which it awards a bachelor's degree, or a two-year program that would be accepted for credit towards a bachelor's degree; (b) has at least a one year program that trains students for gainful employment in a recognized profession; (c) participates in a federal financial aid program under Title IV of the Higher Education Act of 1965 or is certified by the Department of Education as eligible to participate in such a program; or (d) meets requirements for certain postsecondary vocational, proprietary institutions of higher learning and certain institutions outside the United States. In any event, the institution must also be accredited or have been granted pre-accreditation status.[2]

An *academic period* means a quarter, semester, trimester or other period of study (such as summer school session) as reasonably determined by an eligible educational institution.[3] See Q 761 for a discussion of the limitations and phaseouts applicable to the American Opportunity Credit.

760. What is the Lifetime Learning Credit?

The Lifetime Learning Credit is available to certain eligible taxpayers who pay qualified tuition and related expenses.[4]

The Lifetime Learning Credit is available in an amount equal to 20 percent of "qualified tuition and related expenses" (defined in Q 759) paid by the taxpayer during the taxable year for any course of instruction at an "eligible educational institution" (defined in Q 759) taken to acquire or improve the job skills of the taxpayer, his spouse or dependents. The Lifetime Learning Credit is a per taxpayer credit and the maximum credit available does not vary with the number of students in the family. The maximum amount of the credit in 2020 is $2,000 (20 percent of up to $10,000 of qualified tuition and related expenses).[5]

Qualified tuition and related expenses, for the purposes of the Lifetime Learning Credit, include expenses for graduate as well as undergraduate courses. The Lifetime Learning Credit applies regardless of whether the individual is enrolled on a full-time, half-time, or less than half-time basis. Additionally, the Lifetime Learning Credit is available for an unlimited number of taxable years.[6]

Where taxpayers had pre-paid their child's tuition in November 2001 for the academic period that began during the first three months of the following taxable year (i.e., the spring semester of 2002), the prepayment amount was properly includable in the calculation of the

1. IRC Sec. 25A(f)(1); Treas. Reg. §1.25A-2(d)(5).
2. See IRC Sec. 25A(f)(2); HEA 1965 Sec. 481; Treas. Reg. §1.25A-2(b).
3. Treas. Reg. §1.25A-2(c).
4. IRC Sec. 25A.
5. IRC Sec. 25A(c); Treas. Reg. §1.25A-4(a).
6. Treas. Reg. §§1.25A-4(b), 1.25A-4(c).

taxpayers' Lifetime Learning Credit for the 2001 taxable year, not the 2002 taxable year.[1] See Q 759 for a discussion of the Hope Scholarship (American Opportunity) Credit and Q 761 for a discussion of the limitations and phaseouts that apply to both credits.

761. What limitations and phaseouts apply to the Hope Scholarship (American Opportunity) and Lifetime Learning Credits?

The Code sets forth special rules coordinating the interaction of the Hope Scholarship (American Opportunity) and Lifetime Learning Credits. The Lifetime Learning Credit is not available with respect to a student for whom an election is made to take the Hope Scholarship Credit during the same taxable year.[2] However, the taxpayer may use the American Opportunity Credit for one student and the Lifetime Learning Credit for other students in the same taxable year.

Both credits are subject to the same phaseout rules based on the taxpayer's modified adjusted gross income (MAGI). MAGI is the taxpayer's adjusted gross income without regard to the exclusions for income derived from certain foreign sources or sources within United States possessions. The maximum credit in each case is reduced by the credit multiplied by a ratio. For single taxpayers, the ratio equals the excess of (i) the taxpayers' MAGI over $40,000 to (ii) $10,000. For married taxpayers filing jointly, the ratio equals (a) the excess of the taxpayer's MAGI over $80,000 to (b) $20,000.[3] The $40,000 and $80,000 amounts are adjusted for inflation and rounded to the next lowest multiple of $1,000.[4] For 2020, the threshold amounts are $59,000 for single taxpayers and $118,000 for married taxpayers filing jointly for the Lifetime Learning Credit.

For 2019, the threshold amounts were $58,000 for single taxpayers and $116,000 for married taxpayers filing jointly for the Lifetime Learning Credit. For 2018, the threshold amounts are $57,000 for single taxpayers and $114,000 for married taxpayers filing jointly for the Lifetime Learning Credit. For 2017, the threshold amounts are $56,000 for single taxpayers and $112,000 for married taxpayers filing jointly for the Lifetime Learning Credit. For 2016, the threshold amounts were $55,000 for single taxpayers and $111,000 for married taxpayers filing jointly.[5] The threshold amounts for the American Opportunity Credit are $160,000 for married taxpayers filing jointly and $80,000 for single taxpayers for 2012-2018.

The amount of qualified tuition and related expenses for both credits is limited by the sum of the amounts paid for the benefit of the student, such as scholarships, education assistance advances, and payments (other than a gift, bequest, devise, or inheritance) received by an individual for educational expenses attributable to enrollment.[6] The IRS has determined that qualified tuition and related expenses paid with distributions of educational benefits from a trust could

1. *Patel v. Comm.*, TC Summ. Op. 2006-40.
2. IRC Sec. 25A(c)(2)(A); Treas. Reg. §1.25A-1(b).
3. IRC Sec. 25A(d); Treas. Reg. §1.25A-1(c).
4. IRC Sec. 25A(h)(2); Treas. Reg. §1.25A-1(c)(3).
5. Rev. Proc. 2013-35, Rev. Proc. 2014-61, Rev. Proc. 2015-53, Rev. Proc. 2016-55, Rev. Proc. 2018-57, Rev. Proc. 2019-44.
6. IRC Sec. 25A(g)(2); Treas. Reg. §1.25A-5(c).

be used to compute American Opportunity and Lifetime Learning Credits if the distributions were included in the taxable income of the beneficiaries.[1]

Neither credit is allowed unless a taxpayer elects to claim it on a timely filed (including extensions) federal income tax return for the taxable year in which the credit is claimed. The election is made by completing and attaching Form 8863, Education Credits (American Opportunity and Lifetime Learning Credits), to the return.[2] Neither credit is allowed unless the taxpayer provides the name and the taxpayer identification (i.e., Social Security) number of the student for whom the credit is claimed.[3]

If the student is claimed as a dependent on another individual's tax return (e.g., parents) he cannot claim either credit for himself, even if he paid the expenses himself.[4] (The Service has privately ruled that a student was entitled to claim a Hope Scholarship Credit on his own return even though his parents were eligible to claim him as a dependent, but chose not to do so.[5]) However, if another individual is eligible to claim the student as a dependent, but does not do so, only the student may claim the Hope or Lifetime Learning Credit for his own qualified tuition and related expenses.[6] Both credits are unavailable to married taxpayers filing separately.[7] Neither of these credits is allowed for any expenses for which there is a deduction available.[8] Taxpayers are not eligible to claim an American Opportunity or Lifetime Learning Credit and the deduction for qualified higher education expenses in the same year with respect to the same student.[9]

A taxpayer may claim an American Opportunity or Lifetime Learning Credit *and* exclude distributions from a qualified tuition program on behalf of the same student in the same taxable year *if* the distribution is not used to pay the same educational expenses for which the credit was claimed.[10] See Q 687.

A taxpayer can claim an American Opportunity or Lifetime Learning Credit *and* exclude distributions from a Coverdell Education Savings Account (ESA – see Q 681) on behalf of the same student in the same taxable year *if* the distribution is *not* used to pay the same educational expenses for which the credit was claimed.[11] A taxpayer may elect *not* to have the American Opportunity or Lifetime Learning Credit apply with respect to the qualified higher education expenses of an individual for any taxable year.[12]

For 2009 through 2012, AARA 2009 (as amended) made the American Opportunity Credit allowable against the alternative minimum tax and a portion of the tax is made refundable. ATRA

1. Let. Rul. 9839037.
2. Treas. Reg. §1.25A-1(d).
3. Treas. Reg. §1.25A-1(e).
4. IRC Sec. 25A(g)(3); Treas. Reg. §1.25A-1(f)(1).
5. Let. Rul. 200236001.
6. Treas. Reg. §1.25A-1(f)(1).
7. IRC Sec. 25A(g)(6); Treas. Reg. §1.25A-1(g).
8. IRC Sec. 25A(g)(5); Treas. Reg. §1.25A-5(d).
9. IRC Sec. 222(c)(2)(A).
10. See IRC Sec. 529(c)(3)(B)(v).
11. See IRC Sec. 530(d)(2)(C).
12. IRC Sec. 25A(e).

did not extend the provision that allowed the American Opportunity Credit to be taken against the alternative minimum tax.

Reporting. For the reporting requirements for higher education tuition and related expenses, see IRC Section 6050S.[1] For the reporting requirements for qualified tuition and related expenses, see Treasury Regulation Section 1.6050S-1; TD 9029.[2]

762. What is the credit for nonbusiness energy property that may be taken against the tax?

Editor's Note: The credit for nonbusiness energy property initially expired on December 31, 2007, but has been revived by Congress several times. As of the date of this publication, this provision has been extended through 2017, but not yet for 2018. However, taxpayers should note that Congress has a history of retroactively restoring the applicability of many tax credits.[3]

An individual taxpayer may claim as a credit an amount equal to *the sum of*: (1) 10 percent of the amount paid or incurred by the taxpayer for "qualified energy efficiency improvements" (see below) installed during the taxable year; *and* (2) the amount of the "residential energy property expenditures" (see below) paid or incurred by the taxpayer during the taxable year.[4]

Qualified energy efficiency improvements means any energy efficient "building envelope component" (see below) that meets certain energy conservation criteria, if: (1) the component is installed in or on a dwelling located in the United States that is owned and used by the taxpayer as his principal residence; (2) original use of the component commences with the taxpayer; *and* (3) the component reasonably can be expected to remain in use for at least five years.[5] The term "building envelope component" means: (1) any insulation material or system specifically and primarily designed to reduce the heat loss or gain of a dwelling when installed in or on the dwelling; (2) exterior windows, including skylights; (3) exterior doors; and (4) metal roofs if the roof has appropriate coatings specifically and primarily designed to reduce the heat gain of the dwelling.[6]

In guidance, the Service clarified that a component will be treated as reasonably expected to remain in use for at least five years if the manufacturer offers, at no extra charge, at least a two-year warranty providing for repair or replacement of the component in the event of a defect in materials or workmanship. However, if the manufacturer does not offer such a warranty, all relevant facts and circumstances are taken into account in determining whether the component reasonably can be expected to remain in use for at least five years. The Service also confirmed that a taxpayer may rely on a manufacturer's certification that a building envelope component is an "eligible building envelope component." A taxpayer is not required to attach the certification to the tax return on which the credit is claimed, but should retain the certification statement as

1. As amended by P.L. 107-131 (1-16-2002).
2. 67 Fed. Reg. 77678 (12-19-02). See also Notice 2006-72, 2006-36 IRB 363.
3. IRC Sec. 25C(g), as amended by EIEA 2008, ARRA, and ATRA and the Bipartisan Budget Act of 2018.
4. IRC Sec. 25C(a).
5. IRC Sec. 25C(c)(1).
6. IRC Sec. 25C(c)(2).

part of his records. In addition, the Service stated that a credit is allowed *only* for amounts paid or incurred to purchase the components, *not* for the onsite preparation, assembly, or original installation of the components.[1]

Residential energy property expenditures means expenditures made by the taxpayer for "qualified energy property" that is: (1) installed on or in connection with a dwelling unit located in the United States and owned and used by the taxpayer as the taxpayer's principal residence; *and* (2) originally placed in service by the taxpayer.[2] The term "qualified energy property" means: (1) "energy-efficient building property" (see below); (2) a qualified natural gas, propane, oil furnace or hot water boiler; or (3) an advanced main air circulating fan. All of the types of property listed in the preceding sentence must meet certain performance and quality standards.[3] "Energy efficient building property" means: (1) electric heat pump water heaters; (2) electric heat pumps; (3) geothermal heat pumps; (4) central air conditioners; and (5) natural gas, propane, or oil water heaters.[4]

The Service has confirmed that a taxpayer may rely on a manufacturer's certification that a product is "qualified energy property." A taxpayer is not required to attach the certification to the tax return on which the credit is claimed, but should retain the certification statement as part of his records. In addition, the Service stated that a credit is allowed for amounts paid or incurred to purchase qualified energy property *and* for expenditures for labor costs allocable to the onsite preparation, assembly, or original installation of the property.[5] The Service has issued additional guidance regarding the credit.[6]

The lifetime limitation with respect to any taxpayer for any taxable year is $500.[7] An additional limit of $200 applies to windows.[8] Other limits are as follows: advanced main air circulating fans – $50; qualified natural gas, propane, oil furnace or hot water boilers – $150; and energy-efficient building property – $300.[9]

The credit is available for property placed in service after December 31, 2005, and before January 1, 2008, and in 2009 through 2017. (See Editor's Note above.)[10]

763. What is the residential energy efficient property credit that may be taken against the tax?

Through 2019, an individual taxpayer may claim as a credit an amount equal to *the sum of* 30 percent of the following expenditures made by the taxpayer during the taxable year: (1) "qualified solar electric property" (see below); (2) "qualified solar water heating property" (see

1. Notice 2006-26, 2006-11 IRB 622.
2. IRC Sec. 25C(d)(1).
3. IRC Sec. 25C(d)(2).
4. IRC Sec. 25C(d)(3).
5. Notice 2006-26, 2006-11 IRB 622.
6. See Notice 2006-71, 2006-34 IRB 316 (clarifying the effective dates); Notice 2006-53, 2006-25 IRB 1180 (clarifying that exterior siding does not qualify as an eligible building envelope component).
7. IRC Sec. 25C(b)(1).
8. IRC Sec. 25C(b)(2).
9. IRC Sec. 25C(b)(3).
10. IRC Sec. 25C(g), as amended by ATRA, Sec. 401.

below); (3) "qualified fuel cell property" (see below); (4) qualified small wind energy property (see below); and (5) qualified geothermal heat pump property (see below).[1] Solar water heating property must be certified in order for the credit to be claimed.[2] The Protecting Americans from Tax Hikes Act of 2015 (PATH) modified the applicable percentage used to determine the amount of the credit for tax years after 2019. In 2020, the applicable percentage is reduced to 26 percent, and further reduced to 22 percent in 2021. The Bipartisan Budget Act of 2018 provides that these reduced percentages apply for property placed into service after 2016.

"Qualified solar water heating property expenditure" means an expenditure for property to heat water for use in a dwelling unit located in the United States and used as a residence by the taxpayer if at least half of the energy used by such property for such purpose is derived from the sun. The term "qualified solar electric property expenditure" means an expenditure for property which uses solar energy to generate electricity for use in a dwelling unit located in the United States and used as a residence by the taxpayer. "Qualified fuel cell property expenditure" means an expenditure for qualified fuel cell property (as defined in IRC Section 48(c)(1)) installed on or in connection with a dwelling unit located in the United States and used as a principal residence by the taxpayer. "Qualified small wind energy property expenditure" means an expenditure for property which uses a wind turbine to generate electricity for use in connection with a dwelling unit located in the United States and used as a residence by the taxpayer. "Qualified geothermal heat pump property expenditure" means an expenditure for qualified geothermal heat pump property installed on or in connection with a dwelling unit located in the United States and used as a residence by the taxpayer.[3]

A special rule provides that expenditures allocable to a swimming pool, hot tub, or any other energy storage medium that has a function other than the function of storage cannot be taken into account for these purposes.[4]

The maximum credit allowed for any taxable years before 2009 cannot exceed $2,000 with respect to qualified solar water heating property expenditures, $500 with respect to each half kilowatt of capacity of qualified fuel cell property (as defined in section 48(c)(1)) for which qualified fuel cell property expenditures are made, $500 with respect to each half kilowatt of capacity (not to exceed $4,000) of wind turbines for which qualified small wind energy property expenditures are made, and $2,000 with respect to any qualified geothermal heat pump property expenditures.[5] For tax years starting in 2009, the only remaining limit is the $500 limit for each half-kilowatt of capacity of fuel cell plants. The unused portion of the credit can be carried forward to the succeeding taxable year.[6]

1. IRC Sec. 25D(a).
2. IRC Sec. 25D(b)(2).
3. IRC Sec. 25D(d).
4. IRC Sec. 25D(e)(3).
5. IRC Sec. 25D(b).
6. See IRC Sec. 25D(c).

The credit is generally available for property placed in service after December 31, 2005 and before January 1, 2022.[1] The reduced rates prescribed by PATH apply to property placed into service after 2016 under the Bipartisan Budget Act of 2018.

764. What is the alternative motor vehicle credit that may be taken against the tax?

The alternative motor vehicle credit is equal to the *sum* of: (A) the new qualified fuel cell motor vehicle credit; (B) the new advanced lean burn technology motor vehicle credit; (C) the new qualified hybrid vehicle credit; (D) the new qualified alternative motor vehicle credit; and (E) the plug-in conversion credit.[2] (This credit replaces the prior deduction for qualified clean-fuel vehicle property, which sunset on December 31, 2005.)[3]

(A) The new qualified fuel cell motor vehicle credit is based on the weight of the vehicle, and ranges from $8,000 (8,500 pounds maximum) to $40,000 (over 26,000 pounds).[4] The amount determined above with respect to a passenger automobile or light truck is *increased* if the vehicle achieves certain fuel efficiencies, ranging from $1,000 to $4,000.[5] The credit for passenger automobiles and light trucks can be as much as $12,000.

The term "new qualified fuel cell motor vehicle" means a motor vehicle: (1) propelled by power derived from one or more fuel cells that convert chemical energy directly into electricity by combining oxygen with hydrogen fuel that is stored on board the vehicle in any form and may or may not require reformation prior to use; (2) that, in the case of a passenger vehicle or light truck, has received a certificate that the vehicle meets certain emission levels; (3) the original use of which begins with the taxpayer; (4) that is acquired for use or lease by the taxpayer and not for resale; and (5) that is made by a manufacturer.[6]

(B) The amount of the new advanced lean burn technology motor vehicle credit is based on fuel economy, and ranges from $400 to $2,400. The amount of the credit is *increased* by the conservation credit (based on lifetime fuel savings), and ranges from $250 to $1,000.[7] The credit for passenger automobiles and light trucks can be as much as $3,400.

The term "advanced lean burn technology motor vehicle" means a passenger automobile or light truck: (1) with an internal combustion engine that (i) is designed to operate primarily using more air than is necessary for complete combustion of the fuel, (ii) incorporates direct injection, (iii) achieves at least 125 percent of the 2002 model year city fuel economy, and (iv) for 2004 and later model vehicles, has received a certificate that the vehicle meets or exceeds certain emission standards; (2) the original use of which begins with the taxpayer; (3) is acquired for use or lease by the taxpayer and not for resale; and (4) is made by a manufacturer.[8]

1. See Sec. 1333, Energy Policy Act of 2005; IRC Sec. 25D(g).
2. IRC Sec. 30B(a).
3. See Sec. 1348, ETIA 2005; IRC Sec. 179A.
4. IRC Sec. 30B(b)(1).
5. IRC Sec. 30B(b)(2).
6. IRC Sec. 30B(b)(3).
7. IRC Sec. 30B(c)(2).
8. IRC Sec. 30B(c)(3).

(C) The new qualified hybrid motor vehicle credit amount is determined as follows: (1) If the new qualified hybrid motor vehicle is a passenger automobile or light truck weighing no more than 8,500 pounds, the credit amount is the sum of the fuel economy amount and the conservation credit (see (B), above).[1] (2) For other motor vehicles, the credit amount is equal to the applicable percentage of the "qualified incremental hybrid cost" (i.e., the excess of the manufacturer's suggested retail price for such vehicle over the price for a comparable gas or diesel powered vehicle) of the vehicle as certified.[2] The credit for passenger automobiles and light trucks can be as much as $3,400.

A "new qualified hybrid motor vehicle" means a motor vehicle that: (1) draws propulsion energy from onboard sources of stored energy that are both (i) an internal combustion or heat engine using consumable fuel, and (ii) a rechargeable energy storage system; (2) has been certified as meeting specified emission standards; (3) has maximum available power meeting certain percentages based on weight; (4) the original use of which begins with the taxpayer; (5) is acquired for use or lease by the taxpayer; and (6) is made by a manufacturer.[3]

(D) The new qualified alternative fuel motor vehicle credit is an amount equal to the applicable percentage of the incremental cost of any new qualified alternative fuel motor vehicle.[4] The "applicable percentage" is 50 percent, plus 30 percent if the vehicle has been certified as meeting certain emission standards.[5] The "incremental cost" (i.e., the excess of the manufacturer's suggested retail price for the vehicle over the price for a gas or diesel powered vehicle of the same model) cannot exceed $5,000 to $40,000 based on the weight of the vehicle.[6]

"New qualified alternative fuel motor vehicle" means any motor vehicle: (1) that is only capable of operating on an alternative fuel; (2) the original use of which begins with the taxpayer; (3) is acquired by the taxpayer for use or lease but not for resale; and (4) is made by a manufacturer.[7] "Alternative fuel" means compressed natural gas, liquefied natural gas, liquefied petroleum gas, hydrogen, and any liquid at least 85 percent of the volume of which consists of methanol.[8]

Certifications and Limitations for Hybrid Vehicles

Certifications. The tax credit for hybrid vehicles may be as much as $3,400 for those who purchase the most fuel-efficient vehicles. (For the guidance used by manufacturers in certifying credit amounts, see Notice 2006-9.)[9] The Service cautions that even though a manufacturer has certified a vehicle, taxpayers must meet the following requirements to qualify for the credit:

(1) The vehicle must be placed in service after December 31, 2005, and purchased on or before December 31, 2009.[10]

1. IRC Sec. 30B(d)(2)(A).
2. IRC Sec. 30B(d)(2)(B).
3. IRC Sec. 30B(d)(3).
4. IRC Sec. 30B(e)(1).
5. IRC Sec. 30B(e)(2).
6. IRC Sec. 30B(e)(3).
7. IRC Sec. 30B(e)(4)(A).
8. IRC Sec. 30B(e)(4)(B).
9. 2006-6 IRB 413.
10. IRC Sec. 30B(k)(3).

(2) The original use of the vehicle must begin with the taxpayer claiming the credit.

(a) The credit may only be claimed by the original owner of a new, qualifying, hybrid vehicle and does not apply to a used hybrid vehicle.

(3) The vehicle must be acquired for use or lease by the taxpayer claiming the credit.

(a) The credit is only available to the original purchaser of a qualifying hybrid vehicle. If a qualifying vehicle is leased to a consumer, the leasing company may claim the credit.

(b) For qualifying vehicles used by a tax-exempt entity, the person who sold the qualifying vehicle to the person or entity using the vehicle is eligible to claim the credit, but only if the seller clearly discloses in a document to the tax-exempt entity the amount of credit.

(4) The vehicle must be used predominantly within the United States.

Limitations. There is a limit on the number of new qualified hybrid and advanced lean burn technology vehicles eligible for the credit. The phaseout period begins with the second calendar quarter following the calendar quarter that includes the first date on which the number of qualified vehicles manufactured by the manufacturer is at least 60,000.[1] The Service publishes notices providing the adjusted credit amount based on the actual number of vehicles sold for the applicable quarter.

Effective dates. The credits are in effect as follows: new qualified fuel cell motor vehicle credit (2006-2016); (B) new advanced lean burn technology motor vehicle credit (2006-2010); (C) new qualified hybrid vehicle credit (2006-2009); and (D) new qualified alternative fuel motor vehicle credit (2006-2010).

765. What tax credits are available for plug-in electric vehicles?

Editor's Note: Early in 2018, Congress acted to extend the special tax credit for two-wheeled plug-in vehicles through 2017. However, as of the date of this revision, Congress has not indicated whether it will extend this treatment for the 2018 tax year.

The ARRA modified the credit for qualified plug-in electric drive vehicles purchased after December 31, 2009. To qualify, vehicles must be newly purchased, have four or more wheels, have a gross vehicle weight rating of less than 14,000 pounds, and draw propulsion using a battery with at least four kilowatt hours that can be recharged from an external source of electricity. The minimum amount of the credit for qualified plug-in electric drive vehicles is $2,500 and the credit tops out at $7,500, depending on the battery capacity. The full amount of the credit will be reduced with respect to a manufacturer's vehicles after the manufacturer has sold at least 200,000 vehicles.[2]

1. IRC Sec. 30B(f).
2. IRC Sec. 30D.

ARRA also creates a special tax credit for two types of plug-in vehicles—certain low-speed electric vehicles and two- or three-wheeled vehicles. The amount of the credit is 10 percent of the cost of the vehicle, up to a maximum credit of $2,500 for purchases made after February 17, 2009, and before January 1, 2014. The Protecting Americans from Tax Hikes Act extended this credit for two-wheeled vehicles through 2016, and BBA 2018 extended the credit through 2017, but it has not yet been extended for 2018. To qualify, a vehicle must be either a low speed vehicle propelled by an electric motor that draws electricity from a battery with a capacity of 4 kilowatt hours or more or be a two- or three-wheeled vehicle propelled by an electric motor that draws electricity from a battery with the capacity of 2.5 kilowatt hours. A taxpayer may not claim this credit if the plug-in electric drive vehicle credit is allowable.

766. What is the new tax credit for employers that provide paid family and medical leave to employees?

The 2017 Tax Act created a new temporary tax credit for employers that provide paid family and medical leave to employees.[1] The credit is an amount equal to 12.5 percent of the wages that are paid to qualifying employees during a period where the employee was on family and medical leave if the employee is paid 50 percent of the normal wages that he or she would receive from the employer. The credit increases by 0.25 percentage points (but can never exceed 25 percent) for each percentage point by which the rate of payment exceeds 50 percent of wages. Only twelve weeks of family and medical leave can be taken into account for any one employee.

In order to qualify, employers must have a written policy in place to allow all qualifying full-time employees no less than two weeks of paid family and medical leave each year. Further, all part-time employees must be allowed a pro-rated amount of paid family and medical leave.[2] Any leave paid for by the state or local government is not taken into account.[3]

"Qualifying employees" are those who have been employed by the employer for one year or more and who had compensation that did not exceed 60 percent of the compensation threshold for highly compensated employees[4] in the previous year.[5]

"Family and medical leave" is as defined under Section 102(a)(1)(a)-(e) or Section 102(a)(3) of the Family and Medical Leave Act of 1993. Paid leave that is vacation leave, personal leave or other medical or sick leave does not qualify for the new tax credit.[6]

This credit is only available for tax years beginning after December 31, 2017 and before December 31, 2019, and is a part of the general business tax credit.[7] The credit is allowed against the alternative minimum tax (AMT).

1. IRC Sec. 45S (added by the Tax Cuts and Jobs Act).
2. IRC Sec. 45S(c)(1).
3. IRC Sec. 45S(c)(4).
4. Under IRC Sec. 414(g)(1)(B).
5. IRC Sec. 45S(d).
6. IRC Sec. 45S(e).
7. IRC Sec. 45S(a)(1).

Alternative Minimum Tax

767. How is the alternative minimum tax calculated?

In addition to the tax calculated under the normal rates, it is sometimes necessary for a taxpayer to pay the *alternative minimum tax (AMT)*. The AMT is calculated by first determining the alternative minimum taxable income (AMTI, see Q 769), reducing this amount by the allowable exemption to determine taxable excess, and then applying a two-tier tax rate schedule to the amount of the taxable excess. In 2020, the two-tier rate schedule applies a 26 percent rate to taxable excess that does not exceed $197,900 ($98,950 for married taxpayers filing separately),[1] and a 28 percent rate to taxable excess over that amount.[2] The resulting amount is the taxpayer's tentative minimum tax. The preferential tax rates on certain capital gains held for more than twelve months and certain dividends are also used when determining the taxpayer's tentative minimum tax (see Q 702).[3]

If the tentative minimum tax reduced by the AMT foreign tax credit exceeds the regularly calculated tax (with adjustments) for the tax year, the excess is the AMT. Regularly calculated tax for AMT purposes excludes certain taxes including: (1) the alternative minimum tax; (2) the tax on benefits paid from a qualified retirement plan in excess of the plan formula to a 5 percent owner; (3) the 10 percent penalty tax for certain premature distributions from annuity contracts; (4) the 10 percent additional tax on certain early distributions from qualified retirement plans; (5) the 10 percent additional tax for certain taxable distributions from modified endowment contracts; (6) taxes relating to the recapture of the federal subsidy from use of qualified mortgage bonds and mortgage credit certificates; (7) the additional tax on certain distributions from education IRAs; and (8) the 15 percent additional tax on medical savings account distributions not used for qualified medical expenses. Regularly calculated tax is reduced by the foreign tax credit, the Puerto Rico and possession tax credit, and the Puerto Rico economic activity credit.[4]

For tax years from 2000 through 2011, certain nonrefundable personal credits (see Q 756) could be used to reduce the sum of a taxpayer's regular tax liability and AMT liability. The American Taxpayer Relief Act of 2012 ("ATRA") made the use of nonrefundable personal credits against the AMT permanent.[5]

768. What is Alternative Minimum Taxable Income (AMTI) for purposes of calculating the alternative minimum tax?

Alternative minimum taxable income is taxable income, with adjustments made in the way certain items are treated for AMT purposes, and increased by any items of tax preference (Q 771).[6]

Except as otherwise provided in Q 769 to Q 772, the provisions that apply in determining the regular taxable income of a taxpayer also generally apply in determining the AMTI of the

1. Rev. Proc. 2018-18.
2. Rev. Proc. 2017-58, Rev. Proc. 2018-57, Rev. Proc. 2019-44.
3. IRC Secs. 55(a), 55(b).
4. IRC Secs. 55(c)(1), 26(b).
5. IRC Sec. 26(a), as amended by TEAMTRA 2008 and ARRA 2009.
6. IRC Sec. 55(b)(2).

taxpayer.[1] In addition, references to a noncorporate taxpayer's adjusted gross income (AGI) or modified AGI in determining the amount of items of income, exclusion, or deduction must be treated as references to the taxpayer's AGI or modified AGI as determined for regular tax purposes.[2]

769. What is the alternative minimum tax exemption?

Editor's Note: The 2017 Tax Act temporarily increased the AMT exemption amount to $109,400 for married taxpayers filing joint returns (half this amount if separate returns are filed) and $70,300 for all other taxpayers (other than estates and trusts, where the exemption is $24,600). For 2020, the AMT exemption amounts are: $113,400 for married taxpayers filing joint returns (half this amount if separate returns are filed) and $72,900 for all other taxpayers (other than estates and trusts, where the exemption is $25,400).

The applicable phaseout thresholds discussed below are increased to $1,000,000 for married taxpayers filing jointly and $500,000 for all other taxpayers (as indexed to $1,020,600 and $510,300 in 2019 and $1,036,800 and $518,400 in 2020). While the Act itself provided that the $500,000 limit would apply for taxpayers *other than estates or trusts*, the IRS released Revenue Procedure 2018-57, which provided that the limit for estates and trusts is $83,500 in 2019, increasing to $84,800 for 2020. These amounts are adjusted annually for inflation.[3]

ATRA permanently "patched" the AMT exemption amount, and applies retroactively to 2012 and all tax years thereafter. Because the AMT was originally intended to apply only to higher income taxpayers who are able to avoid taxation through the use of tax preferences, only taxpayers with income levels above a certain threshold amount are required to calculate their AMT tax liability. Prior to enactment of ATRA, Congress passed legislation each year to retroactively "patch" the AMT exemption amount for the prior tax year so that millions of lower income taxpayers would not become subject to the AMT. ATRA includes an inflation adjustment provision so that the exemption amount will be increased annually for inflation for all tax years beginning after 2012.

For 2016, the exemption amounts were $83,800 for joint filers and surviving spouses, $53,900 for individual filers, $41,900 for married taxpayers filing separately and $23,900 for trusts and estates. For 2017, the exemption amounts were $84,500 for joint filers and surviving spouses, $54,300 for individual filers, $42,250 for married taxpayers filing separately and $24,100 for trusts and estates.[4]

In 2018, these exemption amounts are reduced by 25 percent of the amount by which the AMTI exceeds $1 million ($1,020,600 in 2019 and $1,036,800 in 2020) on a joint return and $500,000 ($510,300 in 2019 and $518,400 in 2020) for all other filers.[5] In 2017, these threshold levels were $160,900 on a joint return, $120,700 on a single return and $80,450 on a separate

1. Treas. Reg. §1.55-1(a).
2. Treas. Reg. §1.55-1(b).
3. Pub. Law. 115-97, IRC Sec. 55(d)(4), Rev. Proc. 2018-57, Rev. Proc. 2019-44.
4. Rev. Proc. 2016-55.
5. Rev. Proc. 2018-18, Rev. Proc. 2018-57, Rev. Proc. 2019-44.

return filed by a married taxpayer, or in the case of an estate or trust. In 2016, these threshold levels were $159,700 on a joint return, $119,700 on a single return and $79,850 on a separate return or in the case of an estate or trust.[1]

In 2008, a married individual filing a separate return was required to increase AMTI by the lesser of (a) 25 percent of the excess of the AMTI over $214,900, or (b) $34,975. After 2008, a married individual filing a separate return is required to increase AMTI by the lesser of (a) 25 percent of the excess of the AMTI over $165,000, or (b) $22,500.[2]

For children subject to the "kiddie tax" (Q 680) the exemption is the lesser of the above amounts or the child's earned income plus $7,900 (as indexed for 2020, up from $7,750 in 2019, $7,600 in 2018 and $7,500 in 2017).[3]

770. What adjustments are made to taxable income in computing alternative minimum taxable income (AMTI)?

Editor's Note: The mortgage interest deduction was limited to $750,000 under the 2017 tax reform legislation. Further, the personal exemption was suspended from 2018 through 2025, as was the limit on itemized deductions for high-income taxpayers.

In general, the following adjustments are made to taxable income in computing alternative minimum taxable income (see Q 768, generally): (1) generally, property must be depreciated using a less accelerated method or the straight line method over a period which is longer than that used for regular tax purposes, except that a longer period is not required for property placed in service after 1998; (2) the AMT net operating loss is deductible only up to 90 percent of AMTI determined without regard to such net operating loss; (3) no deduction is allowed for miscellaneous itemized deductions; (4) generally, no deduction is allowed for state and local taxes unless attributable to a trade or business, or property held for the production of income (recovery of state tax disallowed for AMT purposes in a previous year is not added to AMTI in the year recovered); (5) medical expenses are allowed as a deduction only to the extent such expenses exceed 10 percent of adjusted gross income (7.5 percent for 2017 and 2018); (6) interest on indebtedness secured by a primary or second residence is generally deductible (within dollar limitations) if incurred in acquiring, constructing, or substantially improving the residence; however, the amount of refinanced indebtedness with regard to which interest is deductible is limited to the amount of indebtedness immediately prior to refinancing; (7) no standard deduction is allowed; (8) no deduction for personal exemptions is allowed; (9) the limitation on itemized deductions for upper-income taxpayers does not apply; (10) the taxpayer will include any amount realized due to a transfer of stock pursuant to the exercise of an incentive stock option; (11) AMTI is determined using losses from any tax shelter farm activity (determined by taking into account the AMTI adjustments and tax preferences) only to the extent that the taxpayer is insolvent or when the tax shelter farm activity is disposed of; and (12) passive activity losses (determined by

1. IRC Sec. 55(d), as amended by TEAMTRA 2008, ARRA 2009, and ATRA.
2. See IRC Sec. 55(d), as amended by TEAMTRA 2008 and ATRA.
3. IRC Sec. 59(j); Rev. Proc. 2016-55, Rev. Proc. 2018-18, Rev. Proc. 2018-57, Rev. Proc. 2019-44.

taking into account the adjustments to AMTI and tax preferences) are not allowed in determining AMTI except to the extent that the taxpayer is insolvent.[1]

771. What items of tax preference must be added to alternative minimum taxable income (AMTI)?

Items of tax preference which must be added to AMTI (see Q 768 and Q 770) include: (1) the excess of depletion over the adjusted basis of property (except in the case of certain independent producers and royalty owners); (2) the excess of intangible drilling costs expensed (other than drilling costs of a nonproductive well) over the amount allowable for the year if the intangible drilling costs had been amortized over a ten year period to the extent the excess is greater than 65 percent of the net income from oil, gas, and geothermal properties (with an exception for certain independent producers); (3) tax-exempt interest on specified private activity bonds (but reduced by any deduction not allowed in computing the regular tax if the deduction would have been allowable if the tax-exempt interest were includable in gross income) (ARRA 2009 provides that tax-exempt interest from private activity bonds issued during 2009 and 2010 is not a tax preference); (4) accelerated depreciation or amortization on certain property placed in service before 1987; and (5) seven percent of the amount excluded under IRC Section 1202 (gain on sales of certain small business stock).[2]

772. What credit against regular tax liability is allowed for a taxpayer who is subject to the alternative minimum tax in subsequent years?

A taxpayer subject to the AMT in one year may be allowed a minimum tax credit against regular tax liability in subsequent years. The credit is equal to the total of the adjusted minimum taxes imposed in prior years reduced by the amount of minimum tax credits allowable in prior years. However, the amount of the credit cannot be greater than the excess of the taxpayer's regular tax liability (reduced by certain credits such as certain business related credits and certain investment credits) over the tentative minimum tax. The adjusted net minimum tax for any year is the AMT for that year reduced by the amount that would be the AMT if: (1) the only adjustments were those concerning the limitations on certain deductions (such as state taxes, certain itemized deductions, the standard deduction and personal exemptions (which were suspended from 2018-2025)); (2) the only preferences were those dealing with depletion, tax exempt interest, and small business stock; and (3) the limit on the foreign minimum tax credit did not apply. The adjusted net minimum tax is increased by the amount of any nonconventional fuel source credit and qualified electric vehicles credit that was not allowed for that year due to the AMT. For tax years after 2006 and before 2013, if an individual has minimum tax credits that have not been usable for three years, those long-term unused credits may be treated as a refundable credit.[3]

1. IRC Secs. 56, 58.
2. IRC Sec. 57(a).
3. IRC Sec. 53.

Social Security Taxes

773. What are the Social Security tax rates?

The Social Security earnings base was $118,500 in 2015 and 2016.[1] In 2017, the earnings base was increased to $127,200, in 2018, it increased to $128,400; and in 2019 it increased to $132,900. In 2020, the maximum amount of income subject to Social Security taxes is $137,700.

Self-employment tax: 15.30 percent (12.40 percent OASDI and 2.90 percent hospital insurance). In 2020, the OASDI tax is imposed on up to $137,700 of self-employment income for a maximum tax of $21,068. In 2019, the OASDI tax was imposed on up to $132,900 of self-employment income for a maximum tax of $16,479. In 2018, the OASDI tax is imposed on up to $128,400 of self-employment income for a maximum tax of $15,922. In 2017, the OASDI tax was imposed on up to $127,200 of self-employment income for a maximum tax of $15,773.

The hospital insurance tax is imposed on all of a taxpayer's self-employment income. However, an above-the-line deduction is permitted for one-half of self-employment taxes paid by an individual and attributable to a trade or business carried on by the individual (not as an employee) (see Q 8049).[2] For compensation received in taxable years beginning after 2012, the hospital insurance tax is increased by 0.9 percent for wages above $250,000 for married taxpayers filing jointly and surviving spouses, $125,000 for married taxpayers filing separate, and $200,000 for single taxpayers and heads of households. The dollar thresholds for the 0.9 percent tax on the self-employment income of high wage earners are reduced (but not below zero) by wages subject to the FICA tax. The deduction for one-half of self-employment tax is not available for the additional 0.9 percent tax.

FICA: 7.65 percent (6.20 percent OASDI and 1.45 percent hospital insurance) for the employer and 7.65 percent (6.20 percent OASDI and 1.45 percent hospital insurance) for the employee. In 2017, the OASDI tax was imposed on up to $127,200 of wages for a maximum tax of $7,866.50 for each of the employer and the employee, or $15,773 total. In 2018, the OASDI tax was imposed on up to $128,400 of wages for a maximum tax of $7,960.80 for each of the employer and the employee, or $15,922 total. In 2019, the OASDI tax is imposed on up to $132,900 of wages for a maximum tax of $8,239.80 for each of the employer and the employee, or $16,479 total. In 2020, the OASDI tax is imposed on up to $137,700 of wages for a maximum tax of $10,534.05 for each of the employer and the employee, or $21,068 total.

The hospital insurance tax is imposed on all of a taxpayer's wages.[3] For compensation received in taxable years beginning after 2012, the employee's portion of the hospital insurance tax is increased to 2.35 percent for wages above $250,000 for married taxpayers filing jointly (tax applies to combined wages of taxpayer and taxpayer's spouse) and surviving spouses, $125,000 for married taxpayers filing separately, and $200,000 for single taxpayers and heads of households.

1. Rev. Proc. 2014-61, Rev. Proc. 2015-53.
2. IRC Sec. 164(f).
3. IRC Secs. 3101(b), 3121(u).

Back wages paid as the result of a settlement agreement are subject to FICA and FUTA taxes in the year the wages are actually paid, not in the year the wages were earned or should have been paid.[1]

Tax on Investment Income. For investment income (which excludes distributions from qualified plans and IRAs) received in taxable years beginning after 2012, an additional tax is imposed at 3.8 percent on the lesser of (1) net investment income, or (2) the excess of modified adjusted gross income over $250,000 for married taxpayers filing jointly and surviving spouses, $125,000 for married taxpayers filing separately, and $200,000 for single taxpayers and heads of households. For trusts and estates, the 3.8 percent additional tax is imposed on the lesser of (1) undistributed net investment income, or (2) the excess of adjusted gross income over the dollar amount for which the highest income tax bracket begins.[2]

774. Who must pay the self-employment tax?

An individual whose net earnings from self-employment are $400 or more for the taxable year must pay the self-employment tax.[3] In 2020, such an individual must file a Schedule SE and pay Social Security taxes on up to $137,700 of self-employment income ($132,900 for 2019, $128,400 for 2018; $127,200 for 2017; $118,500 for 2015 and 2016).

The hospital insurance tax is imposed on all of a taxpayer's self-employment income. However, an above-the-line deduction is permitted for one-half of the self-employment tax paid by an individual and attributable to a trade or business carried on by the individual (not as an employee).[4] If the individual also works in covered employment as an *employee*, his self-employment income (subject to the self-employment tax) is only the difference, if any, between his "wages" as an employee and the maximum Social Security earnings base.

Community Property

775. How can community property law affect the federal income tax treatment of investment income?

Community property law applies in determining whether property and the income it produces is community property or separate property if (1) in the case of income from personal property, the spouses (or either spouse) is domiciled in a community property state; or (2) in the case of income from real property, the property is located in a community property state, regardless of the spouses' domicile(s).[5]

In the states of Arizona, California, Nevada, New Mexico, and Washington, income from separate property is separate property of the spouse who owns the property. In the states of Idaho, Louisiana, and Texas, income from separate property is community property. (In Wisconsin,

1. *U.S. v. Cleveland Indians Baseball Co.*, 532 U.S. 200 (2001). See also *The Phillies v. U.S.* 153 F. Supp. 2d 612 (E.D. PA. 2001).
2. IRC Sec. 1411.
3. IRC Sec. 6017.
4. IRC Sec. 164(f).
5. *Poe v. Seaborn*, 282 U.S. 101 (1930); Boris I. Bittker, *Federal Taxation of Income, Estates and Gifts* (Boston: Warren, Gorham & Lamont, Inc., 2nd Ed., 1991) vol. 3, ¶76.2.

under the Marital Property Act, income from individual (separate) property is marital (community) property. For federal income tax purposes, the IRS has recognized that spouses' rights under the Wisconsin Marital Property Act are community property rights.)[1] In May 1998, Alaska adopted a wholly consensual community property statute, which allows married couples to select which assets are community property and which assets are to be held in some other form of ownership. Both resident and non-resident married couples may classify property as community property by transferring it to a community property trust which has been established under the provisions of the statute.

In all community property states, the income from community property is, of course, community property. And in all states, spouses can have community property converted to separate property by partitioning or by making gifts or sales of their community interests in property. For federal income tax purposes, the distinctions between separate property and community property are important when the spouses file separate returns.

The rules in all community property states for determining whether property is separate or community are quite similar. In general, separate property is (1) property owned by a spouse before marriage and brought into the marriage as such, (2) property acquired by a spouse by gift, will or inheritance during marriage, and (3) property exchanged for separate property or bought with separate funds during marriage. Once property is identified as separate property, it remains separate property as long as it can be traced. All other property is community property (i.e., property owned one-half by each spouse). Earnings of the spouses while domiciled in a community property state are community property. Property acquired during marriage with community funds is presumed to be community property even if title to the property is taken in the name of one spouse only. The presumption can be rebutted only by clear and convincing evidence that the spouses intended the property to be the separate property of the spouse who has title.

The Tax Court held that a married couple's marriage contract had the effect of stopping the application of Louisiana's community property laws for federal income tax purposes, noting that, shortly before marrying, the couple "filed for registry" (in the parish where both of them resided) a marriage contract stating that "the intended husband and wife shall be separate in property."[2]

In general, if property is bought partly with community funds and partly with separate funds, the property is partly community and partly separate in proportion to the source of the funds. If the property is bought with separate and community funds that have been so commingled that it is not known what part is separate and what part is community, the whole will probably be considered community, and consequently the property purchased will likewise be community. But see Q 778 for a different effect of commingling when spouses move to a noncommunity property state.

The IRS may disallow the benefits of any community property law to any taxpayer who acts as if he or she were solely entitled to certain income and failed to notify his or her spouse

1. Rev. Rul. 87-13, 1987-1 CB 20.
2. *Downing v. Comm.*, TC Memo 2003-347.

before the due date (including extensions) for filing the return for the taxable year in which the income was derived of the nature and amount of such income.[1] In Service Center Advice, the Service stated that taxpayers domiciled in community property states have an undivided one-half interest in the entire community so that their filing status must be married filing jointly or, if married filing separately, their returns must each reflect one-half of the total community income and expenses. The Service must establish facts and evidence to demonstrate that IRC Section 66(b) applies (i.e., it may disregard community property laws where the spouse is not notified of community income).[2]

A California appeals court held that a spouse's early retirement benefit must be characterized as community property where (1) the benefit is payable pursuant to a contract entered into during the marriage, and (2) the years of qualifying employment occurred before the parties' separation.[3]

The Tax Court held that in a community property jurisdiction, the spouse of a distributee who did not receive a distribution from an IRA should not be treated as a distributee (under IRC Section 408(d)) despite whatever his or her community property interest in the IRA may have been under state law. Thus, under these circumstances, distributions are taxable to the distributee and the penalty tax (under IRC Section 72(t)) applies to the distributee spouse, only.[4]

The Tax Court also held that a taxpayer's gross income from his continued employment—which he received in lieu of retirement benefits—did *not* include the amount of payments to which his former spouse was entitled under California community property law on the basis of the pension earned by the taxpayer. However, the appeals court reversed the Tax Court's decision, holding that the fact that the taxpayer owed money to a creditor—in this case his former spouse—did not justify excluding any amount of his wages from income.[5]

For guidance on the classification for federal tax purposes of a qualified entity that is owned by two spouses as community property under the laws of a state, foreign country, or possession of the United States, see Revenue Ruling 2002-69.[6]

For more information, see IRS Publication 555, "Federal Tax Information on Community Property."

776. How is community income reported if spouses live apart?

Special rules apply when reporting certain community income of two individuals who are married to one another at any time during the calendar year, if all the following conditions exist:

(1) The spouses live apart for the entire year;

1. IRC Sec. 66(b).
2. SCA 200030022.
3. *Drapeau v. Drapeau*, 93 Cal. App. 4th 1086 (2001).
4. See *Morris v. Comm.*, TC Memo 2002-17, *Bunney v. Comm.*, 114 TC 259 (2000).
5. *Comm. v. Dunkin*, 500 F.3d 1065 (9th Cir. 2007), *reversing*, 124 TC 180 (2005).
6. 2002-2 CB 760.

(2) The spouses do not file a joint return for a tax year beginning or ending within the calendar year;

(3) Either or both spouses have earned income for the calendar year that is community income; and

(4) The spouses have not transferred, directly or indirectly, any of their earned income between themselves before the end of the year.

If all these conditions exist, the spouses must report their community income as explained below.[1]

Earned income. Earned income that is not trade or business or partnership income is treated as the income of the spouse who performed the personal services.

Trade or business income. Trade or business income and deductions attributable to such trade or business are treated as the gross income and deductions of the spouse carrying on such trade or business or, if such trade or business is jointly operated, treated as the gross income and deductions of each spouse on the basis of their respective distributive share of the gross income and deductions.

Partnership income or loss. A partner's distributive share of partnership income or loss from a trade or business carried on by a partnership is the income or loss of the partner, and no part of it is his spouse's.

Income from separate property. Community income derived from a spouse's separate property (see Q 775) is treated as that spouse's income.

All other community income. All other community income, such as dividends, interest, rents, royalties, or gains, is treated as provided in the applicable community property law.[2]

If an individual subject to the foregoing special rules (1) does not include in gross income an item of community income properly includable under the above rules in the other spouse's gross income, and (2) establishes that he or she did not know of, and had no reason to know of, such item of community income, and the IRS determines that under the facts and circumstances it would be inequitable to include such item of community income in that individual's income, then the income item will be includable in the other spouse's gross income (rather than in the individual's gross income).[3] The Service has released guidance for taxpayers seeking equitable innocent spouse relief under IRC Section 66(c).[4]

The Tax Court held that it has authority to review the Service's determination that a spouse is not entitled to equitable relief under IRC Section 66(c).[5] The Tax Court also held that unlike IRC Section 6015(e) (which provides for equitable relief from liability for the understatement

1. IRC Secs. 66(a), 879(a), 1402(a)(5).
2. IRC Sec. 66(a).
3. IRC Sec. 66(c).
4. See Rev. Proc. 2003-61, 2003-2 CB 296, *as superseded by* Rev. Proc. 2013-34, 2013-43 IRB 397.
5. *Beck v. Comm.*, TC Memo 2001-198; *revised acq.*, AOD CC-2002-05 (12-9-2002).

of tax), IRC Section 66 does not provide for jurisdiction permitting a taxpayer to file a "stand alone" petition in response to a denial of a request for relief made pursuant to IRC Section 66(c).[1]

For the treatment of community income in general, see Treasury Regulation Section 1.66-1. For the treatment of community income where spouses live apart, see Treasury Regulation Section 1.66-2. With respect to the denial of benefits of community property law where the spouse is not notified, see Treasury Regulation Section 1.66-3. For the rules governing the request for relief from the operation of community property law, see Treasury Regulation Section 1.66-4.

777. How does community property law affect the federal income tax treatment of dividends received from corporate stock?

If state law characterizes the income as community income (see Q 775); the dividends are treated as having been received one-half by each spouse. This rule has been held to apply to dividend income received by a spouse as marital property under the Wisconsin Marital Property Act.[2] If the dividends are characterized as separate property and the spouses file separate returns, each spouse reports his or her own separate income.[3]

778. If spouses move from a community property state to a common law state, will their community property rights in the property they take with them be recognized and protected by the law of their new domicile?

Yes.[4] Thus, if the spouses report their incomes separately, the income from the community property or from property into which the community property is traceable is reported by the spouses as belonging one-half to each.[5] If income is community income, the deductions applicable to it must be taken one-half from each spouse's portion if they file separately.[6] But if community property is commingled with one spouse's separate property so that the original community property cannot be traced, the income from the property must be reported as that spouse's separate income, if the spouses file separately.[7]

Divorce

779. Do transfers of property between spouses, or between former spouses incident to a divorce, result in taxable gains and losses?

Property transferred between spouses or former spouses incident to a divorce generally will not result in recognition of gain or loss (unless the transfer is by trust, under certain circumstances, or pursuant to an instrument in effect on or before July 18, 1984, and the spouses or former spouses have not elected otherwise).[8] The property transferred will be treated as if it were acquired by gift, and the transferor's basis in the property will be carried over to the

1. *Bernal v. Comm.*, 120 TC 102 (2003).
2. Rev. Rul. 87-13, 1987-1 CB 20.
3. IRS Pub. 555.
4. *Johnson v. Comm.*, 7 BTA 820 (1927).
5. *Phillips v. Comm.*, 9 BTA 153 (1927).
6. *Stewart v. Comm.*, 95 F.2d 821 (5th Cir. 1938).
7. *Johnson v. Comm.*, 1 TC 1041 (1943), appeal dismissed, 139 F.2d 491 (8th Cir. 1943).
8. IRC Sec. 1041. See IRS Pub. 504, Tax Information for Divorced or Separated Individuals.

transferee, whether the fair market value of the property is more or less than the transferor's basis.[1] Ordinarily, if the fair market value of property transferred as a gift is less than the donor's basis, the fair market value is the donee's basis for determining loss (see Q 692).

This nonrecognition rule means that the transfer of property between divorcing spouses in exchange for the release of marital claims generally will not result in a gain or loss to the transferor spouse. A transfer is considered made "incident to a divorce" if it is made within one year after the date the marriage ceases, or if the transfer is related to the cessation of the marriage.[2] A transfer is related to the cessation of a marriage if: (1) the transfer is pursuant to a divorce or separation instrument; and (2) the transfer occurs not more than six years after the date on which the marriage ceases.

Transfers not meeting the above two requirements are presumed *not* to be related to the cessation of a marriage, but taxpayers may overcome this presumption by showing that the transfer was made to effect the division of property owned by the former spouses at the time of the cessation of the marriage. Taxpayers may show this by establishing that certain factors, such as legal impediments, hampered an earlier transfer of the property, provided that the transfer occurs promptly after any cause for the delay is resolved.[3] For example, a transfer of a business interest between former spouses that did not occur within six years of their divorce was considered incident to divorce since there existed a legal dispute between the former spouses concerning the value of the property and the terms of payment.[4] See also *Young v. Commissioner*,[5] in which a transfer within four years of the divorce was considered to have been made "incident to divorce," thus making all gain on the transaction taxable to the transferee spouse.[6]

While the nonrecognition rule shields from recognition gain that would ordinarily be recognized on a sale or exchange of property, it does not shield from recognition interest income that is ordinarily recognized upon the assignment of that property to another taxpayer. Where a taxpayer transferred Series E and EE bonds to his spouse pursuant to a divorce settlement, the IRS determined that he must include as income the unrecognized interest accrued from the date of original issuance to the date of transfer. This income does not constitute gain, for purposes of the nonrecognition rule, but rather is interest income subject to the general rule that deferred, accrued interest on United States savings bonds be included as income in the year of transfer. The spouse's basis in the bonds became the amount of the taxpayer's basis *plus* the amount of deferred, accrued interest recognized by him upon transfer.[7]

The Tax Court held that the nonrecognition provided in IRC Section 1041 does not apply to interest income received by a spouse through monthly installment payments made on a promissory note executed to effect a division of marital property. The court reasoned that the principal and interest portions of an installment payment constitute two distinct items that give

1. IRC Sec. 1041(b).
2. IRC Sec. 1041(c).
3. Temp. Treas. Reg. §1.1041-1T(b).
4. Let. Rul. 9235026.
5. 113 TC 152 (1999), *aff'd*, 240 F.3d 369 (4th Cir. 2001).
6. Let. Rul. 200233022.
7. Rev. Rul. 87-112, 1987-2 CB 207, as clarified by Rev. Rul. 2002-22, 2002-1 CB 849.

rise to separate federal income tax consequences. Thus, the portions of the monthly installment payments that were allocated to principal under the terms of the separation agreement were not taxable to the payee spouse, but the portions allocated to interest were taxable to her.[1]

Where property is transferred by trust, either between spouses, or between former spouses incident to divorce, gain will be recognized by the transferor to the extent that the sum of the liabilities assumed by the transferee plus the amount of liabilities to which the property is subject exceeds the total of the adjusted basis of all the property transferred. The transferee's basis will be adjusted to reflect the amount of gain recognized by the transferor.[2]

In addition, the transfer of an installment obligation generally will not trigger gain, and transfer of investment credit property will not result in recapture if the property continues to be used in a trade or business.[3] However, where installment obligations are transferred in trust, gain will be recognized by the transferor to the extent that the obligation's fair market value at the time of transfer exceeds its basis.[4]

The transfer of an interest in an individual retirement account or an individual retirement annuity to a spouse pursuant to a divorce or separation instrument will not be considered a taxable event. The individual retirement account will be treated as owned by the transferee at the time of transfer, and the transfer does not result in taxable gain or loss.[5] However, the statutory requirements for this nonrecognition treatment must be strictly observed.[6]The Service privately ruled that a husband's payment of a lump-sum in exchange for his ex-wife's community property interest in a nonqualified deferred compensation plan payable to the husband by his employer constituted nontaxable transfers between former spouses related to the cessation of their marriage. Furthermore, the assignment of income doctrine did not cause the wife to be taxed when her former husband received payment of that deferred compensation from his employer.[7]

The IRS has determined that the division of one charitable remainder unitrust (CRUT – see Q 8086) into two CRUTs to effectuate a property settlement in a divorce proceeding does not cause the original or resultant trusts to fail to qualify under IRC Section 664.[8]

The Service has ruled that when nonstatutory stock options and nonqualified deferred compensation are transferred incident to divorce, the nonstatutory stock options will be taxed at the time that the receiving spouse exercises the options, and the deferred compensation will be taxed when paid (or made available) to the receiving spouse.[9] In addition, the Service has ruled that the transfer of interests in nonstatutory stock options and nonqualified deferred compensation from the employee spouse to the nonemployee spouse incident to divorce does not result in a payment of wages for FICA and FUTA tax purposes. The nonstatutory stock options are

1. *Yankwich v. Comm.*, TC Memo 2002-37.
2. IRC Sec. 1041(e).
3. IRC Secs. 50(a)(5)(B), 453(h); Temp. Treas. Reg. §1.1041-1T(d), A-13. See IRS Pub. 537.
4. IRC Secs. 50(a)(5)(B), 453B(g).
5. IRC Sec. 408(d)(6).
6. See, e.g., *Jones v. Comm.*, TC Memo 2000-219.
7. Let. Rul. 200442003.
8. See, e.g., Let. Ruls. 200301020, 200221042, 200143028, 200120016, 200109006, 200045038, 200035014, 9851007, 9851006, 9403030.
9. Rev. Rul. 2002-22, 2002-1 CB 849.

subject to FICA and FUTA taxes at the time of exercise by the nonemployee spouse to the same extent as if the options had been retained and exercised by the employee spouse. The nonqualified deferred compensation also remains subject to FICA and FUTA taxes to the same extent as if the rights to the compensation had been retained by the employee spouse. To the extent FICA and FUTA taxation apply, the wages are those of the employee spouse. The employee portion of the FICA taxes is deducted from the wages as, and when, the wages are taken into account for FICA tax purposes. The employee portion of the FICA taxes is deducted from the payment to the nonemployee spouse. The revenue ruling also contains reporting requirements with respect to such transferred interests.[1]

Where a husband transferred his 25 percent interest in real property to his former wife, in consideration for a settlement agreement that provided to her a credit against the $500,000 equalizing money judgment that he owed to her, and the former wife then sold her undivided 50 percent interest in the same property to an unrelated third party, the Tax Court held as follows: (1) the first transaction, which occurred within one year after the date of the divorce, took place incident to divorce and, therefore, qualified for nonrecognition treatment under IRC Section 1041(a)(2); and (2) the second transaction did *not* fall within IRC Section 1041(a)(2) because it was not a transfer to, or on behalf of, the taxpayer's former husband and incident to divorce. The Tax Court reasoned that the wife's sale of the property to the unrelated third party did not satisfy any legal obligation or liability that the taxpayer's former husband owed to her (or anyone else). Accordingly, the Tax Court concluded that the wife would have to recognize gain resulting from the sale in her interest in the property.[2]

Transfers occurring before July 19, 1984 were subject to substantially different rules, which sometimes resulted in a taxable gain to the transferor spouse. For application of the gift tax to property settlements, see Q 882.

780. What are the tax results of corporate stock redemptions where a spouse or former spouse is treated as receiving or constructively receiving the proceeds, or where the redemption is incident to divorce?

Stock redemptions. If a corporation redeems stock owned by a taxpayer, and that taxpayer's receipt of property with respect to the stock is treated, under applicable tax law, as a constructive distribution to his or her spouse (i.e., where the non-redeeming shareholder has a primary and unconditional obligation to purchase the redeeming shareholder's stock), the final regulations treat the redemption as (1) a transfer of the stock by the taxpayer to the spouse, followed by (2) a transfer of the stock by the spouse to the redeeming corporation.[3] Nonrecognition treatment would apply to the deemed transfer of stock by the taxpayer to his or her spouse (assuming IRC Section 1041 requirements are otherwise satisfied), so that no gain or loss would be included on account of that portion of the transaction. However, nonrecognition treatment would *not* apply to the deemed transfer of stock from the spouse to the redeeming corporation.[4]

1. Rev. Rul. 2004-60, 2004-24 IRB 1051, modifying, Notice 2002-31, 2002-1 CB 908. See also Let. Rul. 200646003.
2. *Walker v. Comm.*, TC Memo 2003-335; compare Read, Craven, above.
3. Treas. Reg. §1.1041-2(a)(2).
4. Treas. Reg. §1.1041-2(b)(2).

The receipt of any property by the taxpayer from the redeeming corporation with respect to the stock would be recharacterized as (1) a transfer of such property to the spouse by the redeeming corporation in exchange for the stock, in a transaction to which nonrecognition treatment would not apply, followed by (2) a transfer by the spouse to the taxpayer in a transaction, to which nonrecognition treatment would apply (assuming the requirements of IRC Section 1041 are otherwise satisfied).[1] For details of the rules applicable to constructive transfers between spouses and former spouses, see Treasury Regulation Section 1.1041-2.[2]

A divided Tax Court held that a stock redemption incident to divorce qualified for nonrecognition treatment where the ex-wife was considered to have transferred property to a third party on behalf of her ex-husband. The court further held that the primary and unconditional obligation standard is not an appropriate standard to apply in a case involving a corporate redemption in a divorce setting.[3] See also *Craven v. U.S.*[4] (stock redemption incident to divorce qualified for nonrecognition treatment). But see FSA 200222008 (where the Service ruled that based on the language in the settlement agreement, the redemption should be treated as a complete termination of the wife's interest; thus, the wife was taxable on the stock redemption. The Service reasoned that the intent of IRC Section 1041 and the parties involved was best served by respecting the form of the redemption transaction). For the tax treatment of stock options transferred incident to a divorce, generally, see FSA 200005006.

781. Are alimony payments included in the gross income of the recipient? May the payor spouse take a deduction for these payments?

Editor's Note: The 2017 Tax Act eliminated the deduction for alimony for tax years beginning after 2018, and provides that alimony and separate maintenance payments are no longer included in the income of the recipient. This provision is effective after December 31, 2018, but also applies to divorce or separation agreements executed before that date that are subsequently modified and specify that the new provision will apply. The rules discussed below apply to tax years beginning before 2019.

Prior to 2019, alimony and separate maintenance payments generally were taxable to the recipient and deductible from gross income by the payor (even if the payor does not itemize).[5] Payments of arrearages from prior years were taxed to a cash basis taxpayer in the year of receipt.[6] Furthermore, the Tenth Circuit Court of Appeals held that an alimony arrearage paid to the estate of a former spouse was taxable as income in respect of a decedent (see Q 745).[7]

The deduction for alimony paid is limited to the amount required under the divorce or separation instrument.[8] Payments made voluntarily by a husband to his spouse, which were not mandated by a qualifying divorce decree or separation instrument, were not deductible to

1. Treas. Reg. §§1.1041-2(a)(2), 1.1041-2(b)(2).
2. TD 903567 Fed. Reg. §1534 (1-13-2003).
3. *Read v. Comm.*, 114 TC 14 (2000), *aff'd* per curiam, *Mulberry Motor Parts, Inc. v. Comm.*, 273 F.3d 1120 (11th Cir. 2001).
4. 215 F.3d 1201 (11th Cir. 2000).
5. IRC Secs. 71(a), 215(a), prior to repeal by Pub. Law No. 115-97 (the 2017 Tax Act).
6. *Coleman v. Comm.*, TC Memo 1988-442.
7. *Kitch v. Comm.*, 103 F. 3d 104, 97-1 USTC ¶50,124 (10th Cir. 1996).
8. *Ritchie v. Comm.*, TC Memo 1989-426.

the husband.[1] Where the husband made his initial payment too early because he wanted to "get it over with," and because it was convenient for him to schedule his alimony payments on or immediately after his paydays, the Tax Court concluded that the husband's premature payment was voluntary because it fell outside the scope of the qualified divorce instrument. Accordingly, the payment was not deductible by the husband as alimony.[2]

According to the General Explanation of TRA '84, where, prior to 2019, a beneficial interest in a trust was transferred or created incident to a divorce or separation, the payments by the trust were to be treated the same as payments to a trust beneficiary under IRC Section 682, disregarding that the payments may have qualified as alimony. Thus, instead of including payments entirely as ordinary income, the transferee, as beneficiary, would be entitled to the flow-through of tax-exempt income. It seems that this treatment would remain the same after the repeal of the alimony deduction rules.

The Tax Court held that interest income paid prior to 2019, which arose from annual payments made to the taxpayer by her former husband under their divorce settlement, was taxable to the taxpayer. The court further held that because the taxpayer was not able to differentiate between the costs incurred in connection with the divorce, and the amounts paid to obtain the interest income, the taxpayer was therefore not entitled to deduct the interest income under IRC Section 212 (i.e., as an ordinary and necessary expense paid or incurred for the production or collection of income).[3]

782. What is alimony? What types of payments between former spouses do not qualify as alimony payments?

A payment received by (or on behalf of) a recipient spouse pursuant to a divorce or separation instrument executed after 1984 is an alimony or separate maintenance payment if: (1) the payment is made in cash; (2) the divorce or separation instrument does not designate the payment as *not* includable or deductible as alimony;[4] (3) there is no liability to make the payments after the death of the recipient,[5] where the Tax Court held that "substitute" payments – i.e., post-death payments that would begin as a result of the death of the taxpayer's ex-wife, and would substitute for a continuation of the payments that terminated on her death, and that otherwise qualified as alimony – were not deductible alimony payments); and (4) if the individuals are legally separated under a decree of divorce or separate maintenance, the spouses are not members of the same household at the time the payment is made.[6]

A divorce or separation instrument includes any decree of divorce or separate maintenance or a written instrument incident to such, a written separation agreement, or other decree requiring spousal support or maintenance payments.[7] The failure of the divorce or separation instrument

1. *Meyer v. Comm.*, TC Memo 2003-12. See also *Ali v. Comm.*, TC Memo 2004-284.
2. See *Ray v. Comm.*, TC Summary Opinion 2006-110.
3. *Cipriano v. Comm.*, 55 Fed. Appx. 104, 2003-1 USTC ¶50,203 (3rd Cir. 2003), *aff'g*, TC Memo 2001-157.
4. See *Richardson v. Comm.*, 125 F.3d 551 (7th Cir. 1997), *aff'g* T.C. Memo 1995-554; see also Let. Rul. 200141036.
5. See, e.g., *Okerson v. Comm.*, 123 TC 258 (2004).
6. IRC Sec. 71(b), prior to repeal by Pub. Law No. 115-97 (the 2017 Tax Act).
7. IRC Sec. 71(b)(2), prior to repeal by Pub. Law No. 115-97 (the 2017 Tax Act).

to provide for termination of payments at the death of the recipient will not disqualify payments from alimony treatment.[1] However, if both the divorce or separation instrument and state law fail to unambiguously provide for the termination of payments upon death, such payments may be disqualified from receiving alimony treatment.[2]

It has been held that an attorney's letter detailing a settlement agreement constituted a separation instrument for purposes of determining whether payments made thereunder were alimony.[3] However, a list of expenses by the former wife, negotiation letters between attorneys, notations on the husband's check to his former wife indicating support, and the fact that the husband actually provided support did not constitute a written separation agreement for purposes of IRC Sections 71(b)(2) and 215.[4] A husband's payments to his wife during the couple's separation under a later invalidated separation agreement and subsequent payments made pursuant to a circuit court's orders were held to be alimony or separate maintenance payments.[5]

The Tax Court held that a contract for deed is a third-party debt instrument; consequently, the taxpayer could not deduct the value of the contract for deed transferred to his former spouse as alimony because it did not constitute a cash payment.[6]

In deciding whether the transfer of ownership of an annuity contract itself constituted alimony, the Service determined that, because IRC Section 71 and the treasury regulations make it clear that in order to constitute alimony a payment must be in cash, the transfer of ownership of the annuity contract to the taxpayer in this instance did not constitute alimony includable in the taxpayer's gross income.[7]

For the types of payments that can constitute alimony payments for tax years prior to 2019, see *Mozley v. Commissioner,*[8] (military retirement payments); *Zinsmeister v. Commissioner*,[9] (payments on first mortgage, real estate taxes, and miscellaneous expenses); *Marten v. Commissioner,*[10] (life insurance premiums paid on former wife's life insurance policy insuring the couple's paraplegic child); but also see *Berry v. Commissioner,*[11] (former wife's attorney's fees not deductible). Alimony can include rental payments paid to a former spouse. See *Israel v. Commissioner.*[12] However, lump sum payments made by a husband to his former spouse under a consent judgment were not

1. See IRC Sec. 71(b)(1)(D), prior to repeal by Pub. Law No. 115-97 (the 2017 Tax Act); TRA '86 Conf. Rept. at page 849.
2. *Hoover v. Comm.*, 102 F. 3d 842, 97-1 USTC ¶50,111 (6th Cir. 1996); *Ribera v. Comm.*, TC Memo 1997-38. See *Mukherjee v. Comm.*, TC Memo 2004-98; *Lovejoy v. Comm*, 293 F.3d 1208 (10th Cir. 2002), *aff'g*, *Miller v. Comm.*, TC Memo 1999-273; *Thomas D. Berry v. Comm*, 36 Fed. Appx. 400, 2002 U.S. App. LEXIS 10785 (10th Cir. 2002), *aff'g*, TC Memo 2000-373; *Fithian v. United States*, 45 Fed. Appx. 700, 2002-2 USTC ¶50,629 (9th Cir. 2002). But see *Kean v. Comm.*, 407 F. 3d 186, 2005-1 USTC ¶50,397 (3rd Cir. 2005), *aff'g*, TC Memo 2003-163; *Michael K. Berry v. Comm.*, TC Memo 2005-91.
3. *Azenaro v. Comm.*, TC Memo 1989-224.
4. *Ewell v. Comm.*, TC Memo 1996-253.
5. *Richardson v. Comm.*, 125 F.3d 551 (7th Cir. 1997), *aff'g*, TC Memo 1995-554.
6. *Lofstrom v. Comm.*, 125 TC 271 (2005).
7. Let. Rul. 200536014.
8. TC Memo 2001-125.
9. TC Memo 2000-364, *aff'd per curiam*, 21 Fed. Appx. 529 (8th Cir. 2001).
10. TC Memo 1999-340, *on motion for reconsideration, holding reaffirmed in* TC Memo 2000-185; *aff'd per curiam*, *Comm. v. Lane*, 2002 U.S. App. LEXIS 8367 (9th Cir. 2002).
11. 36 Fed. Appx. 400, 2002 U.S. App. LEXIS 10785 (10th Cir. 2002), *aff'g*, TC Memo 2000-373.
12. TC Memo 1995-500. See Temp. Treas. Reg. §1.71-1T(b), A-6.

deductible under IRC Section 215(a) except to the extent the lump sum constituted past due alimony.[1]

783. What are the recapture rules that apply with respect to alimony payments made during the first three years of divorce?

Editor's Note: The 2017 Tax Act eliminated the deduction for alimony for tax years beginning after 2018, and provides that alimony and separate maintenance payments are no longer included in the income of the recipient. This provision is effective after December 31, 2018, but also applies to divorce or separation agreements executed before that date that are subsequently modified and specify that the new provision will apply. The discussion below continues to apply for tax years beginning prior to 2019.

Recapture. For tax years beginning prior to January 1, 2019, alimony recapture rules generally require recapture in the third post-separation year of "excess" payments (i.e., disproportionately large payments made in either the first or second years – or both – that are deemed to represent nondeductible property settlements previously deducted as alimony). The first post-separation year is the first calendar year in which alimony or separate maintenance payments are made; the second and third years are the next two calendar years thereafter.

The amount recaptured is included in the income of the payor spouse and deducted from the gross income of the recipient. The amount recaptured is determined by first comparing the alimony payments made for the second and third post-separation years. If payments during the second year exceed the payments during the third year by more than $15,000, the excess is "recaptured." Next, the payments during the first year are compared with the average of the payments made during the second year (as reduced by any recaptured excess) and the payments made during the third year. If the payments made during the first year exceed the average of the amounts paid during the second (as reduced) and third years by more than $15,000, the excess is also recaptured.[2]

There are limited exceptions to the recapture rule: if payments cease because of the marriage of the recipient or the death of either spouse before the close of the third separation year, or to the extent payments required over at least a three-year period are tied to a fixed portion of income from a business or property or compensation, the payments will not come within these rules. Furthermore, payments under temporary support orders do not come within the recapture rules.[3]

Payments made under instruments executed before 1985 are taxed under different rules (i.e., IRC Section 71 prior to TRA '84, unless the instrument is modified after 1984). Depending on the date of modification after 1984, either the TRA '84 rules or a three year recapture period will apply, or the recapture rules for instruments executed after 1986 (described above) will apply.

---

1. *Barrett v. U.S.*, 74 F. 3d 661, 96-1 USTC ¶50,084 (5th Cir. 1996).
2. IRC Sec. 71(f), prior to repeal by Pub. Law No. 115-97 (the 2017 Tax Act).
3. IRC Sec. 71(f)(5), prior to repeal by Pub. Law No. 115-97 (the 2017 Tax Act); Temp. Treas. Reg. §1.71-1T(d), A-25.

When a payor spouse claims alimony payments as a deduction, he is required to furnish the recipient spouse's Social Security number on his tax return for each taxable year the payments are made.[1] Alimony paid by a U.S. citizen spouse to a foreign spouse is deductible by the payor spouse even though the recipient is not taxable on the income under a treaty; however, the penalty for failing to include the recipient's Taxpayer Identification Number (TIN) on the payor's tax return may still apply.[2]

784. Is child support taxed in the same manner as alimony payments?

Editor's Note: The 2017 Tax Act eliminated the deduction for alimony for tax years beginning after 2018, and provides that alimony and separate maintenance payments are no longer included in income of the recipient. This provision is effective after December 31, 2018, but also applies to divorce or separation agreements executed before that date that are subsequently modified and specify that the new provision will apply. The new tax law did not change the tax treatment of child support. The discussion below that applies to alimony continues to apply for tax years beginning prior to 2019.

Child support. Any portion of an alimony payment specified in the divorce or separation instrument as payable for child support is not treated as alimony (Q 782).[3] In *Freyre v. U.S.*,[4] the appeals court held that because the divorce court order did not specifically designate or fix the disputed monthly payments as child support, as required in the statute[5] and the treasury regulations,[6] the payments had to be considered as alimony and, thus, were deductible by the taxpayer (prior to 2019).[7]

Even portions not specified as child support may be treated as child support to the extent that the amount of the alimony payment provided for in the divorce or separation instrument is to be reduced on the occurrence of a contingency relating to a child or at a time clearly associated with such a contingency (e.g., the year a child would turn eighteen years old).[8] If the divorce or separation instrument provides for alimony and child support payments, any payment of less than the amount specified in the instrument will be applied first as child support, to the extent of the amount specified in the instrument.[9] The Tax Court determined that an agreement between former spouses, absent a court modification of their divorce decree, would not alter the tax consequences of this provision.[10] A parent was required to include in his gross income the portion of a distribution from his pension plan that was used to satisfy a back child support obligation.[11]

The Service has privately ruled that interest paid on past due child support is taxable income to the recipient parent. According to the Service, interest income is not excludable income in

1. Temp. Treas. Reg. §1.215-1T, A-1.
2. CCA 200251004.
3. IRC Sec. 71(c)(1), prior to repeal by Pub. Law No. 115-97 (the 2017 Tax Act).
4. 135 Fed. Appx. 863 (6th Cir. 2005).
5. IRC Sec. 71(c)(1), prior to repeal by Pub. Law No. 115-97 (the 2017 Tax Act).
6. Treas. Reg. §1.71-1(e).
7. See also *Preston v. Comm.*, 209 F.3d 1281 (11th Cir. 2000).
8. IRC Sec. 71(c)(2), prior to repeal by Pub. Law No. 115-97 (the 2017 Tax Act). See Let. Rul. 9251033.
9. IRC Sec. 71(c)(3), prior to repeal by Pub. Law No. 115-97 (the 2017 Tax Act).
10. *Blair v. Comm.*, TC Memo 1988-581.
11. *Stahl v. Comm.*, TC Memo 2001-22.

the same manner as amounts designated for child support are excludible. The Service reasoned that for child support to be excludable from gross income, the decree, instrument or agreement must specifically designate the sum as child support; interest that is assessed later does not come under an amount specifically designated as child support.[1]

Trusts and Estates

785. How is the federal income tax computed for trusts and estates?

Taxable income for trusts and estates is computed by subtracting the following from gross income: allowable deductions; amounts distributable to beneficiaries; and the exemption. Estates are allowed a $600 exemption. For trusts that are required to distribute all their income currently, the exemption is $300; for all other trusts, $100. Certain trusts that benefit disabled persons may continue to use the personal exemptions that were available to individuals for tax years beginning before 2018 and after 2025.[2] A standard deduction is not available.[3] Rates are determined from a table for estates and trusts (see Appendix B).

Planning Point: The United States Supreme Court ruled in June, 2019 that the due process clause prevents states from imposing a state-level tax on undistributed trust income based solely on the fact that a trust beneficiary resides in the state.

For estates of decedents dying after August 5, 1997, an election may be made to treat a *qualified revocable trust* as part of the decedent's estate for income tax purposes. The election must be made by both the executor of the estate and the trustee of the qualified revocable trust. A qualified revocable trust is a trust that was treated as a grantor trust during the life of the decedent due to his power to revoke the trust (see Q 787). If such an election is made, the trust will be treated as part of the decedent's estate for tax years ending after the date of the decedent's death and before the date that is two years after his death (if no estate tax return is required) or the date that is six months after the final determination of estate tax liability (if an estate tax return is required).[4]

Generally, income that is accumulated by a trust is taxable to the trust, and income that is distributable to beneficiaries is taxable to the beneficiaries.[5] A beneficiary who may be claimed as a dependent by another taxpayer may not use a personal exemption (prior to 2018), and his standard deduction may not exceed the greater of (1) $500, as indexed $1,100 in 2019-2020, $1,050 in 2015-2018); or (2) $250, as indexed ($350 in 2013-2020) plus earned income.[6] The amount of trust income which can be offset by the basic standard deduction will be reduced if the beneficiary has other income (see Q 726, Q 750). Also, trust income taxable to a beneficiary under nineteen years of age (twenty-four for certain students) may be taxed at the parents'

1. IRS CCA 200444026.
2. IRC Sec. 642(b).
3. IRC Sec. 63(c)(6).
4. IRC Sec. 645.
5. IRC Secs. 641(a), 652(a).
6. IRC Secs. 151(d)(2), 63(c)(5); Rev. Proc. 2014-61, 2014-47 IRB 860, Rev. Proc. 2015-53, Rev. Proc. 2016-55, Rev. Proc. 2017-58, Rev. Proc. 2018-57, Rev. Proc. 2019-44.

marginal tax rate (see Q 680) prior to 2018 (for tax years beginning after 2017 and before 2026, the unearned income of minors is taxed at the rates that apply to trusts and estates generally).[1]

A charitable remainder trust is generally not subject to income tax (see Q 8100). However, beneficiaries of a charitable remainder trust are taxable on distributions (see Q 8097). A charitable lead trust is generally taxable as a grantor trust (see Q 787) if an upfront charitable deduction is claimed (see Q 8103). Otherwise, a charitable lead trust is generally taxed as described here. Proposed regulations would treat annuity distributions from charitable lead annuity trusts (CLATs) and unitrust distributions from charitable lead unitrusts (CLUTs) as made proportionately from all categories of trust income. State law or trust provisions providing otherwise would be ignored. The regulations would prevent such a provision from being used, for example, to allocate all taxable income to the charitable distribution with capital gain and tax-exempt income retained by the trust.[2]

Editor's Note: All miscellaneous itemized deductions subject to the 2 percent floor were suspended for tax years beginning after 2017 and before 2026.

Deductions available to an estate or trust are generally subject to the 2 percent floor on miscellaneous itemized deductions (prior to 2018; these deductions were suspended for tax years beginning after 2017 and before 2026).[3] However, deductions for costs incurred in connection with the administration of an estate or trust that would not have been incurred if the property were not held by the estate or trust are fully deductible from gross income.[4]

Deductions excepted from the 2 percent floor include only those costs that would not have been incurred if held by an individual (those costs that would be uncommon for a hypothetical investor). Investment advisory fees incurred by a trust were subject to the 2 percent floor.[5] Final regulations have been issued on the proper treatment of costs incurred by trusts and estates. The regulations provide that if a cost is unique to a trust or estate, it is *not* subject to the 2 percent floor, but if the cost is not unique to a trust or estate, it is subject to the 2 percent floor.[6] For taxable years beginning before 2009, taxpayers can deduct the full amount of bundled fiduciary fees without regard to the 2 percent floor.[7] For taxable years beginning after December 31, 2014, bundled fiduciary fees must be allocated between fully deductible expenses and those subject to the 2 percent floor.[8] Any reasonable method may be used to allocate a bundled fee.

For distributions in taxable years beginning after August 5, 1997, the throwback rule for accumulation distributions from trusts in IRC Sections 665-667 has been eliminated for domestic trusts, except for domestic trusts that were once foreign trusts, and except in the case of trusts created before March 1, 1984, which would be aggregated with other trusts under the multiple

1. IRC Secs. 651-652, 661-663.
2. Prop. Treas. Reg. §§1.642(c)-3(b), 1.643(a)-5(b).
3. IRC Sec. 67(a).
4. IRC Sec. 67(e).
5. *Knight v. Comm.*, 128 S. Ct. 782 (2008), 2008-1 USTC ¶50,132 (U.S. 2008).
6. Treas. Reg. §1.67-4.
7. Notice 2008-32, 2008-11 IRB 593; Notice 2008-116, 2008-52 IRB 1372.
8. Treas. Reg. §1.67-4(c).

trust rules.[1] Generally, for those trusts subject to the throwback rule, if a trust distributes income which it has accumulated after 1968, all of the income is taxed to the beneficiary upon distribution. The amounts distributed are treated as if they had been distributed in the preceding years in which the income was accumulated, but are includable in the income of the beneficiary for the current year. The "throwback" method of computing the tax in effect averages the tax attributable to the distribution over three of the five preceding taxable years of the beneficiary, excluding the year with the highest and the year with the lowest taxable income.[2]

Excess taxes paid by the trust may not be refunded, but the beneficiary may take a credit to offset any taxes (other than the alternative minimum tax) paid by the trust. However, a beneficiary who receives accumulation distributions from more than two trusts may not take such an offset for taxes paid by the third and any additional trusts. But if distributions to a beneficiary from a trust total less than $1,100 in 2020 for the year, this penalty will not apply to distributions from that trust.[3]

Distributions of income accumulated by a trust before the beneficiary is born or before he attains age twenty-one are not considered accumulation distributions and thus are not generally subject to the throwback rules.[4]

786. Are trusts and estates required to pay estimated tax?

Estates are required to file estimated tax for taxable years ending two years or more after the date of the decedent's death.[5] Trusts are generally also required to pay estimated tax (see Q 649). However, there are two exceptions to this rule: (1) with respect to any taxable year ending before the date that is two years after the decedent's death, trusts owned by the decedent (under the grantor trust rules) and to which the residue of the decedent's estate will pass under his will need not file estimated tax (if no will is admitted to probate, this rule will apply to a trust which is primarily responsible for paying taxes, debts and administration expenses); and (2) charitable trusts (as defined in IRC Section 511) and private foundations are not required to file estimated tax.[6] A trustee may elect to treat any portion of a payment of estimated tax made by the trust for any taxable year as a payment made by a beneficiary of the trust. Any amount so treated is treated as paid or credited to the beneficiary on the last day of the taxable year.[7]

787. What is a grantor trust? How is a grantor trust taxed?

A grantor who retains certain interests in a trust he creates may be treated as the "owner" of all or part of the trust and thus taxed on the income of the trust in proportion to his ownership. There are five categories of interests for which the IRC gives detailed limits as to the amount of control the grantor may have without being taxed on the trust income. These categories are: reversionary interests, power to control beneficial enjoyment, administrative powers, power to

1. IRC Sec. 665(c).
2. IRC Secs. 666-667.
3. IRC Secs. 666-667.
4. IRC Sec. 665(b).
5. IRC Sec. 6654(l).
6. IRC Sec. 6654(l).
7. IRC Sec. 643(g).

revoke, and income for benefit of grantor.[1] With respect to any taxable year ending within two years after a grantor/decedent's death, any trust, all of which was treated under these grantor trust rules as owned by the decedent, is not required to file an estimated tax return (see Q 785).[2]

Reversionary Interests

Generally, a grantor will be treated as the owner of any portion of a trust in which he has a reversionary interest in either the corpus or the income, if, as of the date of inception of that portion of the trust, the value of such interest exceeds 5 percent of the value of the trust.[3] There is an exception to this rule where the reversionary interest will take effect at the death before age twenty-one of a beneficiary who is a lineal descendant of the grantor.[4] For transfers in trust made prior to March 2, 1986, the reversionary interest was not limited to a certain percentage, and so long as it took effect *after* ten years it did not result in taxation of the grantor.[5] Using a 6 percent valuation table, the value of the reversionary interest of a term trust falls below 5 percent if the trust runs more than about fifty-one years. The value of a reversion will depend on the interest rate and the valuation tables required to be used (see Appendix C).

Power to Control Beneficial Enjoyment

If the grantor has any power of disposition over the beneficial enjoyment of any portion of the trust, and such power is exercisable without the approval of an adverse party, he will be treated (i.e., taxed) as the owner of that portion.[6] A grantor may do any of the following without such action resulting in his being treated as the owner of that portion of the trust: (1) reserve the power to dispose of the trust corpus by will, (2) allocate corpus or income among charitable beneficiaries (so long as it is irrevocably payable to the charities), (3) withhold income temporarily (provided the accumulated income must ultimately be paid to or for the benefit of the beneficiary), (4) allocate receipts and disbursements between corpus and income, and (5) distribute corpus by a "reasonably definite standard."[7] An example of a "reasonably definite standard" is found in Treasury Regulation Section 1.674(b)-1(b)(5): "for the education, support, maintenance and health of the beneficiary; for his reasonable support and comfort; or to enable him to maintain his accustomed standard of living; or to meet an emergency." A grantor also may retain the power to withhold income during the disability or minority of a beneficiary.[8] However, if *any person* has the power to add or change beneficiaries, other than providing for the addition of after-born or after-adopted children, the grantor will be treated as the owner.[9]

IRC Section 674(c) allows powers, solely exercisable by a trustee or trustees (none of whom is the grantor, and no more than half of whom are related or subordinate parties who are subservient to the wishes of the grantor), to distribute, apportion, or accumulate income to or for

1. IRC Secs. 673-677.
2. IRC Sec. 6654(l)(2)(B).
3. IRC Sec. 673(a).
4. IRC Sec. 673(b).
5. IRC Sec. 673(a), prior to amendment by TRA '86.
6. IRC Sec. 674(a).
7. IRC Sec. 674(b).
8. IRC Sec. 674(b)(7).
9. IRC Sec. 674(c).

beneficiaries or pay out trust corpus to or for a beneficiary without the grantor being considered the owner of the trust. A related or subordinate party is a person who is not an adverse party and who is the grantor's spouse if living with the grantor; the grantor's father, mother, issue, brother or sister; an employee of the grantor; or a corporation or employee of a corporation if the grantor and the trust have significant voting control of the corporation.[1] An adverse party is any person having a substantial beneficial interest in a trust which would be adversely affected by the exercise or non-exercise of the power the person possesses respecting the trust.[2]

The grantor will also not be considered the owner of the trust due to a power solely exercisable by a trustee or trustees, none of whom are the grantor or the grantor's spouse living with the grantor, to distribute, apportion, or accumulate income to or for a beneficiary as long as the power is limited to a reasonably definite external standard set forth in the trust instrument.[3] Regulations treat a reasonably definite external standard as synonymous with a reasonably definite standard, described above.[4]

Income for Benefit of Grantor

If the trust income is (or, in the discretion of the grantor or a nonadverse party, or both, may be) distributed or held for the benefit of the grantor or his spouse, he will be treated as the owner of it.[5] This provision applies to the use of trust income for the payment of premiums for insurance on the life of the grantor or his spouse, although taxation does not result from the mere power of the trustee to purchase life insurance. This provision is also invoked any time trust income is used *for the benefit of the grantor*, to discharge a legal obligation. Thus, when trust income is used to discharge the grantor's legal support obligations, it is taxable income to the grantor.[6] State laws vary as to what constitutes a parent's obligation to support; however, such a determination may be based in part on the background, values and goals of the parents, as well as the children.[7]

The mere power of the trustee to use trust income to discharge a legal obligation of the grantor will not result in taxable income to the grantor. Under IRC Section 677(b), there must be an actual distribution of trust income for the grantor's benefit in order for the grantor to be taxable on the amounts expended.

Other Grantor Powers

A grantor's power to revoke the trust will result in his being treated as owner of it. This may happen by operation of law in states requiring that the trust instrument explicitly state that the trust is irrevocable. Such a power will also be inferred where the grantor's powers are so extensive as to be substantially equivalent to a power of revocation, such as a power to invade the corpus.[8]

1. IRC Sec. 672(c).
2. IRC Sec. 672(a).
3. IRC Sec. 674(d).
4. Treas. Reg. §1.674(d)-1.
5. IRC Sec. 677(a).
6. IRC Sec. 677(b).
7. *Stone v. Comm.*, TC Memo 1987-454; *Braun v. Comm.*, TC Memo 1984-285.
8. IRC Sec. 676.

Certain administrative powers retained by the grantor will result in his being treated as owner of the trust; these include the power to deal with trust funds for less than full and adequate consideration, the power to borrow without adequate interest or security, or borrowing from the trust without completely repaying principal and interest before the beginning of the taxable year.[1]

Corporations and Other Business Entities

788. How is a corporation taxed?

Any corporation, including a professional corporation or association, is considered a C corporation, taxable under the following rules, unless an election is made to be treated as an S corporation.

Graduated Tax Rates

Under the 2017 Tax Act, all corporations pay a flat income tax of 21 percent for tax years beginning after 2017 (these rates are not set to expire). There is no special rate for personal service corporations. Prior to 2018, a corporation paid tax according to a graduated rate schedule where the rates ranged from 15 percent to 35 percent.[2] See Appendix B for the rates. A "personal service corporation" was subject to a different income tax rate prior to 2018. See Q 802.

Planning Point: The reduced corporate tax rate may encourage many business owners to explore converting from a pass-through entity (taxed at the individual's ordinary income tax rate) to a C corporation, but caution should be exercised in making this decision. This move could potentially be beneficial for businesses that retain a significant portion of their earnings each year (whether to grow the business through asset acquisitions or simply for investment purposes). Those earnings would be taxed at the 21 percent corporate income tax rate rather than (potentially) the highest 37 percent individual tax rate that applies to pass-through income.

Despite this, when those funds are eventually distributed to shareholders, they will again be taxed as dividends (to which a maximum 23.8 percent tax may apply when considering the 3.8 percent investment income tax). The total effective tax rate works out to approximately 39.8 percent (**higher** than the maximum individual income tax rate). This second tax, however, can be deferred until a future date, allowing the corporation to use the funds in the meantime. In using this strategy, the accumulated earnings tax and personal holding company tax (both taxes designed to discourage corporations from retaining excess earnings beyond the reasonable needs of the business) must be considered.

Corporations may also wish to consider reducing the "compensation" paid to owner-employees, as those payments (while deductible by the corporation) can be taxed at up to 37 percent (plus employment taxes) after the 21 percent corporate rate has been imposed. Dividends, while not deductible by the corporation, would only be subject to a 23.8 percent second tax upon distribution.

S corporations that convert to C corporations and find that the move was ill-advised must also be aware that there is a five-year waiting period before it can convert back to S corporation status.

1. IRC Sec. 675.
2. IRC Sec. 11(b).

Taxable income is computed for a corporation in much the same way as for an individual. Generally, a corporation may take the same deductions as an individual, except those of a personal nature (e.g., deductions for medical expenses). A corporation also does not receive a standard deduction.

There are a few special deductions for corporations, however including a "dividends received deduction". The 2017 Tax Act reduced the 80 percent dividends received deduction to 65 percent (for corporations that own at least 20 percent of the stock of another corporation) and reduced the otherwise applicable 70 percent dividends received deduction to 50 percent.[1] Prior to 2018, the deduction was equal to 70 percent of dividends received from other domestic corporations, 80 percent of dividends received from a 20 percent owned company, and 100 percent for dividends received from affiliated corporations.[2] A corporation may deduct contributions to charitable organizations to the extent of 10 percent of taxable income (with certain adjustments).[3] Generally, charitable contributions in excess of the 10 percent limit may be carried over for five years.[4]

Prior to 2018, a corporation was also allowed a deduction for production activities. Prior to its repeal by the 2017 Tax Act, this deduction was fully phased in (in 2010), and was equal to nine percent of a taxpayer's qualified production activities income (or, if less, the taxpayer's taxable income). The deduction was limited to 50 percent of the W-2 wages paid by the taxpayer for the year. The definition of "production activities" was broad and included construction activities, energy production, and the creation of computer software.[5]

789. How is a corporation taxed on capital gains?

Capital gains and losses are netted in the same manner as for an individual and net short-term capital gain, to the extent it exceeds net long-term capital loss, if any, is taxed at the corporation's regular tax rates. Prior to 2018, a corporation reporting a "net capital gain" (i.e., where net long-term capital gain exceeds net short-term capital loss) was taxed under one of two following methods, depending on which produces the lower tax (the "alternative method" was repealed by the 2017 Tax Act):

1. *Regular method*. Net capital gain is included in gross income and taxed at the corporation's regular tax rates; or

2. *Alternative method (prior to repeal)*. First, a tax on the corporation's taxable income, exclusive of "net capital gain," was calculated at the corporation's regular tax rates. Then a second tax on the "net capital gain" (or, if less, taxable income) for the year

1. IRC Secs. 243(a)(1), 243(c)(1).
2. IRC Sec. 243.
3. IRC Sec. 170(b)(2).
4. IRC Sec. 170(d)(2).
5. IRC Sec. 199, prior to repeal by Pub. Law No. 115-97 (the 2017 Tax Act).

is calculated at the rate of 35 percent. The tax on income exclusive of net capital gain and the tax on net capital gain are added to arrive at the corporation's total tax. For certain gains from timber, the maximum rate is 15 percent.[1]

790. How was a corporation's alternative minimum tax calculated prior to repeal by the 2017 Tax Act?

Editor's Note: The 2017 Tax Act repealed the corporate alternative minimum tax (AMT) for tax years beginning in 2018 and thereafter.

Prior to 2018, a corporate taxpayer was required to calculate its liability under the regular tax and a tentative minimum tax, then add to its regular tax so much of the tentative minimum tax as exceeds its regular tax. The amount added was the alternative minimum tax.[2]

To calculate its alternative minimum tax (AMT), a corporation first calculated its "alternative minimum taxable income" (AMTI).[3] Also, the corporation calculated its "adjusted current earnings" (ACE), increasing its AMTI by 75 percent of the amount by which ACE exceeded AMTI (or possibly reducing its AMTI by 75 percent of the amount by which AMTI exceeded ACE).[4] The tax itself was a flat 20 percent of AMTI.[5] Each corporation received a $40,000 exemption; however, the exemption amount was reduced by 25 percent of the amount by which AMTI exceeded $150,000 (thus phasing out completely at $310,000).[6]

AMTI is regular taxable income determined with certain adjustments and increased by tax preferences.[7] *Tax preferences* for corporate taxpayers are the same as for other taxpayers. *Adjustments* to income included the following: (1) property was generally depreciated under a less accelerated or a straight line method over a longer period, except that a longer period was not required for property placed in service after 1998; (2) mining exploration and development costs were amortized over ten years; (3) a percentage of completion method was required for long-term contracts; (4) net operating loss deductions were generally limited to 90 percent of AMTI (although some relief was available in 2001 and 2002); (5) certified pollution control facilities were depreciated under the alternative depreciation system except those that were placed in service after 1998, which would use the straight line method; and (6) the adjustment based on the corporation's adjusted current earnings (ACE).[8]

To calculate ACE, a corporation began with AMTI (determined without regard to ACE or the AMT net operating loss) and made additional adjustments. These adjustments included adding certain amounts of income that were includable in earnings and profits but not in AMTI (including income on life insurance policies and receipt of key person insurance death proceeds). The amount of any such income added to AMTI was reduced by any deductions that would have

1. IRC Secs. 1201, prior to repeal by Pub. Law No. 115-97 (the 2017 Tax Act), 1222.
2. IRC Secs. 55-59.
3. IRC Sec. 55(b)(2).
4. IRC Sec. 56(g).
5. IRC Sec. 55(b)(1)(B).
6. IRC Secs. 55(d)(2), 55(d)(3).
7. IRC Sec. 55(b)(2).
8. IRC Secs. 56(a), 56(c), 56(d).

been allowed in calculating AMTI had the item been included in gross income. The corporation was generally not allowed a deduction for ACE purposes if that deduction would not have been allowed for earnings and profits purposes. However, certain dividends received by a corporation were allowed to be deducted. Generally, for property placed into service after 1989 but before 1994, the corporation was required to recalculate depreciation according to specified methods for ACE purposes. For ACE purposes, earnings and profits were adjusted further for certain purposes such as the treatment of intangible drilling costs, amortization of certain expenses, installment sales, and depletion.[1]

Application of the adjustments for ACE with respect to life insurance is explained at Q 316.

A corporation subject to the AMT in one year could have been allowed a minimum tax credit against regular tax liability in subsequent years. The credit was equal to the excess of the adjusted net minimum taxes imposed in prior years over the amount of minimum tax credits allowable in prior years.[2] However, the amount of the credit could not be greater than the excess of the corporation's regular tax liability (reduced by certain credits such as certain business related credits and certain investment credits) over its tentative minimum tax.[3]

Because the 2017 Tax Act eliminated the corporate AMT, corporate taxpayers with existing AMT credit from a prior year may offset regular tax liability with the credit for any taxable year. Existing AMT credits will be refundable for tax years after 2017 and before 2022 in an amount equal to 50 percent (100 percent before 2021) of the excess of the minimum tax credit for the taxable year over the amount of the credit allowable for the year against regular tax liability (this basically means that the full amount of the credit will be available before 2022).[4]

791. How was the alternative minimum tax calculated for certain small corporations prior to repeal by the 2017 Tax Act?

Editor's Note: The 2017 Tax Act repealed the corporate alternative minimum tax (AMT) for tax years beginning in 2018 and thereafter.

Prior to 2018, certain small corporations were deemed to have a tentative minimum tax of zero and thus were exempt from the AMT. To qualify for the exemption, the corporation was required to meet a gross receipts test for the three previous taxable years. To meet the test, a corporation's average annual gross receipts for the three years could not exceed $7.5 million. For purposes of the gross receipts test, only tax years beginning after 1993 were taken into account. For a corporation not in existence for three full years, those years the corporation was in existence were substituted for the three years (with annualization of any short taxable year). To initially qualify for the exemption, the corporation was required to meet the three-year gross receipts test but with $5 million substituted for $7.5 million. Generally, a corporation was exempt from the AMT in its first year of existence.[5]

1. IRC. Sec. 56(g).
2. IRC Sec. 53(b).
3. IRC Sec. 53(c).
4. IRC Sec. 53(e).
5. IRC Secs. 55(e), 448(c)(3).

If a corporation failed to maintain its small corporation status, it lost the exemption from the AMT. If that happened, certain adjustments used to determine the corporation's AMTI were applied for only those transactions entered into or property placed in service in tax years beginning with the tax year in which the corporation ceased to be a small corporation and tax years thereafter.[1] A corporation exempt from the AMT because of the small corporation exemption may have been limited in the amount of credit it could take for AMT paid in previous years. In computing the AMT credit, the corporation's regular tax liability (reduced by applicable credits) used to calculate the credit was reduced by 25 percent of the amount that such liability exceeded $25,000.[2]

792. What is the accumulated earnings tax?

Editor's Note: The 2017 Tax Act limited the members of a controlled group of corporations (the members of which are determined as of December 31 of the relevant year) to a single $250,000 amount in order to compute the accumulated earnings credit ($150,000 if any member of the group is a service organization in the fields of health, law, engineering, architecture, accounting, actuarial science, performing arts or consulting).[3] This amount must be divided equally among the members of the controlled group unless future regulations provide that unequal allocations are permissible.[4]

A corporation is subject to a penalty tax, in addition to the otherwise applicable corporate income tax, if, for the purpose of preventing the imposition of income tax upon its shareholders, it accumulates earnings instead of distributing them.[5] The tax is 20 percent of the corporation's *accumulated taxable income* (15 percent for tax years beginning prior to 2013).[6] Accumulated taxable income is taxable income for the year (after certain adjustments) less the federal income tax, dividends paid to stockholders (during the taxable year or within 2½ months after the close of the taxable year), and the "accumulated earnings credit."[7]

Planning Point: IRS officials have noted that additional guidance may be needed on the application of the accumulated earnings tax in the wake of tax reform. The 2017 tax reform legislation lowered the corporate tax rate from 35 percent to 21 percent, potentially providing motivation for some companies to convert to C corporation status rather than attempt to interpret the complicated pass-through provisions that apply post-reform. However, the legislation did not modify the accumulated earnings tax, which applies a 20 percent penalty tax to undistributed corporate earnings and profits in excess of the reasonable business needs of the company. This "reasonableness" standard can be difficult to interpret and could require additional guidance in the coming years, as more businesses may attempt to take advantage of lower corporate rates by simply distributing fewer dividends to business owners.

The tax can be imposed only upon amounts accumulated beyond those required to meet the reasonable needs of the business since an accumulated earnings credit, generally equal to this

1. IRC Sec. 55(e)(2).
2. IRC Sec. 55(e)(5).
3. Under IRC Sec. 535(c).
4. IRC Sec. 1561(a).
5. IRC Secs. 531-537; *GPD, Inc. v. Comm.*, 508 F. 2d 1076, 75-1 USTC ¶9142 (6th Cir. 1974).
6. IRC Sec. 531, as amended by ATRA.
7. IRC Sec. 535.

amount, is allowed. A corporation must demonstrate a specific, definite and feasible plan for the use of the accumulated funds in order to avoid the tax.[1] The use of accumulated funds for the personal use of a shareholder and his family is evidence that the accumulation was to prevent the imposition of income tax upon its shareholders.[2] In deciding whether a family owned bank was subject to the accumulated earnings tax, the IRS took into account the regulatory scheme the bank was operating under to determine its reasonable needs.[3] Most corporations are allowed a minimum accumulated earnings credit equal to the amount by which $250,000 ($150,000 in the case of service corporations in health, law, engineering, architecture, accounting, actuarial science, performing arts or consulting) exceeds the accumulated earnings and profits of the corporation at the close of the preceding taxable year.[4] Consequently, an aggregate of $250,000 ($150,000 in the case of the above listed service corporations) may be accumulated for any purpose without danger of incurring the penalty tax.

Tax-exempt income is not included in the accumulated taxable income of the corporation but will be included in earnings and profits in determining whether there has been an accumulation beyond the reasonable needs of the business.[5] However, a distribution in redemption of stock to pay death taxes which is treated as a dividend does not qualify for the "dividends paid" deduction in computing accumulated taxable income (see Q 300, Q 303).[6]

The accumulated earnings tax applies to all C corporations, without regard to the number of shareholders in taxable years beginning after July 18, 1984.[7]

793. What is the personal holding company tax?

The personal holding company (PHC) tax is a penalty tax designed to keep shareholders from avoiding personal income taxes on securities and other income-producing property placed in a corporation to avoid higher personal income tax rates. The PHC tax is 20 percent (15 percent for tax years beginning prior to 2013) of the corporation's undistributed PHC income (taxable income adjusted to reflect its net economic income for the year, minus dividends distributed to shareholders), if it meets both the "stock ownership" and "PHC income" tests.[8]

A corporation meets the "stock ownership" test if more than 50 percent of the value of its stock is owned, directly or indirectly, by or for not more than 5 shareholders.[9] Certain stock owned by families, trusts, estates, partners, partnerships, and corporations may be attributed to individuals for purposes of this rule.[10]

A corporation meets the "PHC income" requirement if 60 percent or more of its adjusted ordinary gross income is PHC income, generally defined to include the following: (1) dividends,

1. *Eyefull Inc. v. Comm.*, TC Memo 1996-238.
2. *Northwestern Ind. Tel. Co. v. Comm.*, 127 F. 3d 643, 97-2 USTC ¶50,859 (7th Cir. 1997).
3. TAM 9822009.
4. IRC Sec. 535(c)(2).
5. Rev. Rul. 70-497, 1970-2 CB 128.
6. Rev. Rul. 70-642, 1970-2 CB 131.
7. IRC Sec. 532(c).
8. IRC Secs. 541, as amended by ATRA, 542, 545.
9. IRC Sec. 542(a)(2).
10. IRC Sec. 544.

interest, royalties, and annuities; (2) rents; (3) mineral, oil, and gas royalties; (4) copyright royalties; (5) produced film rents (amounts derived from film properties acquired before substantial completion of the production); (6) compensation from use of corporate property by shareholders; (7) personal service contracts; and (8) income from estates and trusts.[1]

794. How are corporations that are classified as professional corporations and associations taxed?

Organizations of physicians, lawyers, and other professional people organized under state professional corporation or association acts are generally treated as corporations for tax purposes.[2] However, to be treated as a corporation, a professional service organization must be both organized and *operated* as a corporation.[3] Although professional corporations are generally treated as corporations for tax purposes, they are not generally taxed the same as regular C corporations. See Q 802. Note that if a professional corporation has elected S corporation status, the shareholders will be treated as S corporation shareholders.

Although a professional corporation is recognized as a taxable entity separate and apart from the professional individual or individuals who form it, the IRS may under some circumstances reallocate income, deductions, credits, exclusions, or other allowances between the corporation and its owners in order to prevent evasion or avoidance of tax or to properly reflect the income of the parties. Under IRC Section 482, such reallocation may be made only where the individual owner operates a second business distinct from the business of the professional corporation; reallocation may not be made where the individual works exclusively for the professional corporation.[4] However, note that the IRS has stated that it will not follow the *Foglesong* decision to the extent that it held that the two business requirement of IRC Section 482 is not satisfied where a controlling shareholder works exclusively for the controlled corporation.[5] A professional corporation may also be subject to the special rules applicable to "personal service corporations," see Q 802.

795. What is an S corporation? How is an S corporation taxed?

Editor's Note: See Q 796 and Q 797 for a discussion of the changes to pass-through taxation that were implemented under the 2017 tax reform legislation.

An S corporation is one that elects to be treated, in general, as a pass-through entity, thus avoiding most tax at the corporate level.[6] To be eligible to make the election, a corporation must meet certain requirements as to the kind and number of shareholders, classes of stock, and sources of income. An S corporation must be a domestic corporation with only a single class of stock and may have up to 100 shareholders (none of whom are nonresident aliens) who are individuals, estates, and certain trusts. An S corporation may not be an ineligible corporation. An ineligible corporation is one of the following: (1) a financial institution that uses the reserve

1. IRC Secs. 542(a)(1), 543(a).
2. Rev. Rul. 77-31, 1977-1 CB 409.
3. *Roubik v. Comm.*, 53 TC 365 (1969).
4. *Foglesong v. Comm.*, 691 F. 2d 848, 82-2 USTC ¶9650 (7th Cir. 1982).
5. Rev. Rul. 88-38, 1988-1 CB 246.
6. See IRC Secs. 1361, 1362, 1363.

method of accounting for bad debts; (2) an insurance company; (3) a corporation electing (under IRC Section 936) credits for certain tax attributable to income from Puerto Rico and other U.S. possessions; or (4) a current or former domestic international sales corporation (DISC). Qualified plans and certain charitable organizations may be S corporation shareholders.[1]

Members of a family are treated as one shareholder. "Members of the family" are defined as "the common ancestor, lineal descendants of the common ancestor, and the spouses (or former spouses) of such lineal descendants or common ancestor." Generally, the common ancestor may not be more than six generations removed from the youngest generation of shareholders who would be considered members of the family.[2]

Trusts that may be S corporation shareholders include the following: (1) a trust all of which is treated as owned by an individual who is a citizen or resident of the United States under the grantor trust rules (see Q 787); (2) a trust that was described in (1) above immediately prior to the deemed owner's death and continues in existence after such death may continue to be an S corporation shareholder for up to two years after the owner's death; (3) a trust to which stock is transferred pursuant to a will may be an S corporation shareholder for up to two years after the date of the stock transfer; (4) a trust created primarily to exercise the voting power of stock transferred to it; (5) a qualified subchapter S trust (QSST); (6) an electing small business trust (ESBT); and (7) in the case of an S corporation that is a bank, an IRA or Roth IRA.[3]

A QSST is a trust that has only one current income beneficiary (who must be a citizen or resident of the U.S.), all income must be distributed currently, and corpus may not be distributed to anyone else during the life of such beneficiary. The income interest must terminate upon the earlier of the beneficiary's death or termination of the trust, and if the trust terminates during the lifetime of the income beneficiary, all trust assets must be distributed to that beneficiary. The beneficiary must make an election for the trust to be treated as a QSST.[4]

An ESBT is a trust in which all of the beneficiaries are individuals, estates, or charitable organizations.[5] Each potential current beneficiary of an ESBT is treated as a shareholder for purposes of the shareholder limitation.[6] A potential current beneficiary is generally, with respect to any period, someone who is entitled to, or in the discretion of any person may receive, a distribution of principal or interest of the trust. In addition, a person treated as an owner of a trust under the grantor trust rules (see Q 787) is a potential current beneficiary.[7] If for any period there is no potential current beneficiary of an ESBT, the ESBT itself is treated as an S corporation shareholder.[8] Trusts exempt from income tax, QSSTs, charitable remainder annuity trusts, and charitable remainder unitrusts may not be ESBTs. An interest in an ESBT may not

1. IRC Sec. 1361.
2. IRC Sec. 1361(c)(1).
3. IRC Secs. 1361(c)(2), 1361(d).
4. IRC Sec. 1361(d).
5. IRC Sec. 1361(e).
6. IRC Sec. 1361(c)(2)(B)(v).
7. Treas. Reg. §1.1361-1(m)(4).
8. Treas. Reg. §1.1361-1(h)(3)(i)(F).

be obtained by purchase.[1] If any portion of a beneficiary's basis in the beneficiary's interest is determined under the cost basis rules, the interest was acquired by purchase.[2] An ESBT is taxed at the highest income tax rate under IRC Section 1(e) (currently, 37 percent).[3] The 2017 Tax Act expands the definition of a qualifying beneficiary under an electing small business trust (ESBT) to include nonresident aliens.[4] This provision is effective beginning January 1, 2018.

A corporation will be treated as having one class of stock if all of its outstanding shares confer identical rights to distribution and liquidation proceeds.[5] However, "bona fide agreements to redeem or purchase stock at the time of death, disability or termination of employment" will be disregarded for purposes of the one-class rule unless a principal purpose of the arrangement is to circumvent the one-class rule. Similarly, bona fide buy-sell agreements will be disregarded unless a principal purpose of the arrangement is to circumvent the one-class rule and they establish a purchase price that is not substantially above or below the fair market value of the stock. Agreements that provide for a purchase price or redemption of stock at book value or a price between book value and fair market value will not be considered to establish a price that is substantially above or below fair market value.[6] Regulations provide that agreements triggered by divorce and forfeiture provisions that cause a share of stock to be substantially nonvested will be disregarded in determining whether a corporation's shares confer identical rights to distribution and liquidation proceeds.[7]

An S corporation is generally not subject to tax at the corporate level.[8] However, a tax is imposed at the corporate level under certain circumstances described in Q 799. When an S corporation disposes of property within ten years after an election has been made, gain attributable to pre-election appreciation of the property (built in gain) is taxed at the corporate level to the extent such gain does not exceed the amount of taxable income imposed on the corporation if it were not an S corporation.[9] ARRA 2009 provided that, in the case of a taxable year beginning in 2011, no tax is imposed on the built in gain if the fifth taxable year of the ten-year recognition period precedes such taxable year.

Like a partnership, an S corporation computes its taxable income similarly to an individual, except that certain personal and other deductions (see Q 796 for a discussion of the new QBI deduction) are allowed to a shareholder but not to the S corporation, and the corporation may elect to amortize organizational expenses.[10] Each shareholder then reports on his individual return his proportionate share of the corporation's items of income, loss, deductions and credits. These items retain their character on pass-through.[11] Certain items of income, loss, deduction or credit must be passed through as separate items because they may have an effect on each

1. IRC Sec. 1361(e).
2. Treas. Reg. §1.1361-1(m)(1)(iii).
3. IRC Sec. 641(c).
4. IRC Secs. 1361(c)(2)(B)(v), 1361(b)(1)(C).
5. Treas. Reg. §1.1361-1(l)(1).
6. Treas. Reg. §1.1361-1(l)(2)(iii). See IRC Secs. 1361, 1362.
7. Treas. Reg. §1.1361-1(l)(2)(iii)(B).
8. IRC Sec. 1363(a).
9. IRC Sec. 1374.
10. IRC Sec. 1363(b).
11. IRC Secs. 1366(a), 1366(b).

individual shareholder's tax liability. For example, net capital gains and losses pass through as such to be included with the shareholder's own net capital gain or loss. Any gains and losses on certain property used in a trade or business are passed through separately to be aggregated with the shareholder's other IRC Section 1231 gains and losses. (Gains passed through are reduced by any tax at the corporate level on gains.)

Miscellaneous itemized deductions pass through to be combined with the individual's miscellaneous deductions for purposes of the 2 percent floor on such deductions (these deductions were suspended from 2018-2025). Charitable contributions pass through to shareholders separately subject to the individual shareholder's percentage limitations on deductibility. Tax-exempt income passes through as such. Items involving determination of credits pass through separately.[1] Before pass-through, each item of passive investment income is reduced by its proportionate share of the tax at the corporate level on excess net passive investment income.[2] Items that do not need to be passed through separately are aggregated on the corporation's tax return and each shareholder reports his share of such non-separately computed net income or loss on his individual return.[3] Items of income, deductions, and credits (whether or not separately stated) that flow through to the shareholder are subject to the "passive loss" rule (see Q 8007 through Q 8018) if the activity is passive with respect to the shareholder (see Q 8008). Apparently, items taxed at the corporate level are not subject to the passive loss rule unless the corporation is either closely held or a personal service corporation (see Q 8007). See Q 734 and Q 735 for a discussion of how the deduction for business interest was impacted by the 2017 Tax Act.

Thus, whether amounts are distributed to them or not, shareholders are taxed on the corporation's taxable income. Shareholders take into account their shares of income, loss, deduction and credit on a per-share, per-day basis.[4] The S corporation income must also be included on a current basis by shareholders for purposes of the estimated tax provisions (see Q 649).[5]

The Tax Court determined that when an S corporation shareholder files for bankruptcy, all the gains and losses for that year flowed through to the bankruptcy estate. The gains and losses should not be divided based on the time before the bankruptcy was filed.[6]

796. How are S corporations taxed under the 2017 tax reform legislation?

The 2017 Tax Act made substantial changes to the treatment of pass-through business income, which was previously simply "passed through" and taxed at the business owners' individual ordinary income tax rates as discussed in Q 795. Partnerships (and entities that elect partnership taxation, such as certain LLCs), S corporations and sole proprietorships are subject to the new pass-through taxation rules, which will apply for tax years beginning after December 31, 2017 and before December 31, 2025.[7] The new rules are extremely complicated, and the IRS and

1. IRC Sec. 1366(a)(1).
2. IRC Sec. 1366(f)(3).
3. IRC Sec. 1366(a).
4. IRC Sec. 1377(a).
5. Let. Rul. 8542034.
6. *Williams v. Comm.*, 123 TC 144 (2004).
7. Under IRC Sec. 199A.

related agencies continue to release interpretive materials explaining how the basic provisions will be applied.

S corporations may now generally deduct 20 percent of "qualified business income"[1] (which largely excludes "specified service business" income (see below)).

S corporations that are categorized as service businesses and have income below the applicable threshold level plus $50,000 ($100,000 for joint returns) also qualify for the 20 percent deduction. The applicable threshold levels for 2020 increase to $326,600 ($321,400 in 2019, married filing jointly) or $163,300 ($160,700 in 2019, for single filers), so service business owners with income that exceeds $426,600 (married filing jointly) or $213,300 (single filers) will not receive the benefit of the new deduction.[2] The applicable threshold levels for 2018 were $315,500 (married filing jointly) or $157,500 (single filers). The entirety of the taxpayer's income must be taken into account (not only the business' income).[3]

The deduction is available regardless of whether the S corporation shareholder itemizes, and is applied based on ownership interest (i.e., a shareholder who owns 25 percent of an S corporation is entitled to apply the deduction to 25 percent of his or her qualified business income). The calculation is made on an entity-specific basis, meaning that the deduction must be applied separately to each entity rather than based upon the cumulative income of all entities owned by the taxpayer.

Qualified business income is generally the net amount of qualified items of income, gain, deduction and loss with respect to qualified trades or businesses of the taxpayer, excluding qualified REIT dividends, qualified cooperative dividends and qualified publicly traded partnership income (but see Q 797).[4] Income, gain, deduction and loss items are generally qualified if they are connected with a U.S. trade or business and are included or allowed in calculating taxable income. Amounts related to the following investment items are excluded: capital gains, qualified dividend income (or equivalent), non-business interest income, foreign base company income taken into account under IRC Section 954(c) and non-business annuity distributions.[5]

For alternative minimum tax purposes, qualified business income is calculated without regard to otherwise allowable adjustments.[6]

When the taxpayer's income exceeds the applicable annual threshold, the deduction is capped at the greater of (1) 50 percent of W-2 wage income or (2) the sum of 25 percent of the W-2 wages of the business plus 2.5 percent of the unadjusted basis, immediately after acquisition, of all "qualified property" (but see Q 797 for a discussion of the so-called "phase-in" for certain taxpayers whose income only exceeds the threshold by $50,000 ($100,000 for joint returns)).[7]

1. IRC Sec. 199A(a).
2. Rev. Proc. 2018-57, Rev. Proc. 2019-44.
3. IRC Secs. 199A(b)(3), 199A(d)(2).
4. IRC Sec. 199A(c).
5. IRC Secs. 199A(c)(3), 199A(d)(3).
6. IRC Sec. 199A(f)(2).
7. IRC Sec. 199A(b)(2). IRC Sec. 199A(b)(5) directs the Secretary of Treasury to develop guidance on how these limitations apply in short tax years, or in the case of acquisitions or dispositions of other businesses.

"Qualified property" generally includes depreciable property that is used in the taxpayer's trade or business for the production of income as of the end of the tax year, as long as the depreciation period has not expired before the end of that year. The depreciation period is a period that begins on the first day that the taxpayer places the property in service and ends the later of (1) ten years after that date or (2) the last day of the last full year in the applicable recovery period that would apply to the property under IRC Section 168 (without regard to Section 168(g)).[1]

A "specified service business" is a trade or business involving the performance of services in the fields of health, law, consulting, athletics, financial services, brokerage services or any trade or business where the principal asset of the business is the reputation or skill of one or more employees or workers, or one which involves the performance of services consisting of investing and investment management trading or dealing in securities, partnership interests or commodities.

To determine the "qualified business income" with respect to a specified service trade or business, the taxpayer takes into account only the applicable percentage of qualified items of income, gain, deduction, or loss, and of allocable W-2 wages.[2] With respect to S corporations, qualified business income does not include any amounts that are treated as reasonable compensation of the taxpayer. Similarly, qualified business income does not include guaranteed payments or amounts paid or incurred by a partnership to a partner, when the partner is providing services and is not acting in his or her capacity as a partner.[3]

If the qualified business income for the year is a loss, it is carried forward as a loss for the next tax year. Any deduction allowed for that subsequent tax year is reduced by 20 percent of any carried forward business loss from the previous year.[4]

The deduction is allowed in reducing taxable income (functioning more like an exclusion), rather than as a deduction in computing adjusted gross income (i.e., the deduction does not impact limitations based on adjusted gross income). Further, trusts and estates are also eligible for the 20 percent deduction.

For partnerships and S corporations, these rules apply at the partner or shareholder level (each shareholder is treated as having W-2 wages for the year equal to that shareholder's allocable share of the S corporation).

See Q 797 for a detailed discussion of how a pass-through entity's deduction for qualified business income is determined.

1. IRC Sec. 199A(b)(6). IRC Section 168 provides accelerated cost recovery system rules. IRC Section 168(g) provides an alternate depreciation system that may be used with respect to certain property, including tangible property used predominantly outside the U.S., tax-exempt use property and tax-exempt bond financed property.
2. As defined in IRC Sec. 199A(b)(4).
3. IRC Sec. 199A(c)(4).
4. IRC Sec. 199A(c)(2).

797. How is an S corporation's deduction for qualified business income determined?

Entities that are taxed under the rules governing pass-through taxation are generally entitled to a 20 percent deduction for qualified business income (QBI, see Q 796). This deduction is equal to the sum of:

(a) the lesser of the combined qualified business income amount for the tax year or an amount equal to 20 percent of the excess of the taxpayer's taxable income over any net capital gain and cooperative dividends, plus

(b) the lesser of 20 percent of qualified cooperative dividends or taxable income (reduced by net capital gain).[1]

The sum discussed above may not exceed the taxpayer's taxable income for the tax year (reduced by net capital gain). Further, the 20 percent deduction with respect to qualified cooperative dividends is limited to taxable income (reduced by net capital gain).

The deductible amount for each qualified trade or business is the lesser of:

(a) 20 percent of the qualified business income with respect to the trade or business or

(b) the greater of (x) 50 percent of W-2 wage income or (y) the sum of 25 percent of the W-2 wages of the business plus 2.5 percent of the unadjusted basis, immediately after acquisition, of all qualified property (see Q 796).[2]

Planning Point: The proposed regulations provide guidance on how UBIA should be calculated in the case of a like-kind exchange or involuntary conversion. The regulations follow the Section 168 regulations in providing that property acquired in a like-kind exchange, or by conversion, is treated as MACRS property, so that the depreciation period is determined using the date the relinquished property was first placed into service unless an exception applies. The exception applies if the taxpayer elected *not* to apply Treasury Regulation §1.168(i)-6. As a result, most property acquired in a like-kind exchange or involuntary conversion under the new rules will have two relevant placed in service dates. For calculating UBIA, the relevant date is the date the taxpayer places the property into service. For calculating its depreciable period, the relevant date is the date the taxpayer placed the original, relinquished property into service.

Concurrently with the regulations, the IRS released Notice 2018-64, which contains a proposed revenue procedure with guidance for calculating W-2 wages for purposes of the Section 199A deduction for qualified business income. This guidance was finalized in Revenue Procedure 2019-11. The guidance provides three methods for calculating W-2 wages, including the "unmodified box method", the "modified Box 1 method", and the "tracking wages method". The guidance further specifies that wages calculated under these methods are only taken into account in determining the W-2 wage limitations if properly allocable to QBI under Proposed Treasury Regulation §1.199A-2(g).

1. IRC Sec. 199A(a)
2. IRC Sec. 199A(b)(2).

The unmodified box method involves taking the lesser of (1) the total of Box 1 entries for all W-2 forms or (2) the total of Box 5 entries for all W-2 forms (in either case, those that were filed with the SSA by the taxpayer for the year). Under the modified Box 1 method, the taxpayer subtracts from its total Box 1 entries amounts that are not wages for federal income tax withholding purposes, and then adds back the total of Box 12 entries for certain employees. The tracking wages method requires the taxpayer to actually track employees' wages, and (1) total the wages subject to income tax withholding and (2) subtract the total of all Box 12 entries of certain employees.

Revenue Procedure 2019-11 clarifies that, in the case of short taxable years, the business owner is required to use the "tracking wages method" with certain modifications. The total amount of wages subject to income tax withholding and reported on Form W-2 can only include amounts that are actually or constructively paid to the employee during the short tax year and reported on a Form W-2 for the calendar year with or within that short tax year. With respect to the amounts reported in Box 12, only the portion of the total amount reported that was actually deferred or contributed during the short year can be included in W-2 wages.

If the taxable income is below the applicable threshold levels (in 2018, $157,500 for single filers and $315,000 for joint returns), the deduction is simply 20 percent.[1]

If the taxable income exceeds the relevant threshold amount, but not by more than $50,000 ($100,000 for joint returns), and the amount determined under (b), above, is less than the amount under (a), above, then the deductible amount is determined without regard to the calculation required under (b). However, the deductible amount allowed under (a) is reduced by the amount that bears the same ratio to the "excess amount" as (1) the amount by which taxable income exceeds the threshold amount bears to (2) $50,000 ($100,000 for joint returns).

The "excess amount" means the excess of amount determined under (a), above, over the amount determined under (b), above, without regard to the reduction described immediately above.

"Combined QBI" for the year is the sum of the deductible amounts for each qualified trade or business of the taxpayer and 20 percent of the taxpayer's qualified REIT dividends and qualified publicly traded partnership income.[2]

Qualified REIT dividends do not include any portion of a dividend received from a REIT that is a capital gain dividend or a qualified dividend.[3]

"Qualified cooperative dividends" includes a patronage dividend, per-unit retain allocation, qualified written notice of allocation, or any similar amount that is included in gross income and received from (a) a tax-exempt benevolent life insurance association, a mutual ditch or irrigation company, cooperative telephone company, like cooperative organization or a taxable or tax-exempt cooperative that is described in section 1381(a), or (2) a taxable cooperative

1. IRC Sec. 199A(b)(3).
2. IRC Sec. 199A(b)(1).
3. IRC Sec. 199A(e)(3).

governed by tax rules applicable to cooperatives before the enactment of subchapter T of the Code in 1962.[1]

"Qualified publicly traded partnership income" means the sum of:

(1) the net amount of the taxpayer's allocable share of each qualified item of income, gain, deduction, and loss from a publicly-traded partnership that does not elect to be taxed as a corporation (so long as the item is connected with a U.S. trade or business and is included or allowed in determining taxable income for the year and is not excepted investment-type income, also not including the taxpayer's reasonable compensation, guaranteed payments for services or Section 707(a) payments for services), and

(2) gain recognized by the taxpayer on disposing its interest in the partnership that is treated as ordinary income.[2]

See Q 8568 - Q 8587 for a more detailed discussion of the Section 199A regulations.

798. What is a QSSS? Can an S corporation own a QSSS?

An S corporation may own a qualified subchapter S subsidiary (QSSS). A QSSS is a domestic corporation that is not an ineligible corporation, if 100 percent of its stock is owned by the parent S corporation and the parent S corporation elects to treat it as a QSSS. Except as provided in regulations, a QSSS is not treated as a separate corporation and its assets, liabilities, and items of income, deduction, and credit are treated as those of the parent S corporation.[3] Regulations provide special rules regarding the recognition of a QSSS as a separate entity for tax purposes if an S corporation or its QSSS is a bank.[4] A QSSS will also be treated as a separate corporation for purposes of employment taxes and certain excise taxes.[5]

If a QSSS ceases to meet the above requirements, it will be treated as a new corporation acquiring all assets and liabilities from the parent S corporation in exchange for its stock. If the corporation's status as a QSSS terminates, the corporation is generally prohibited from being a QSSS or an S corporation for five years.[6] Regulations provide that in certain cases following a termination of a corporation's QSSS election, the corporation may be allowed to elect QSSS or S corporation status without waiting five years if, immediately following the termination, the corporation is otherwise eligible to make an S corporation election or QSSS election, and the election is effective immediately following the termination of the QSSS election. Examples where this rule would apply include an S corporation selling all of its QSSS stock to another S corporation, or an S corporation distributing all of its QSSS stock to its shareholders and the former QSSS making an S election.[7]

1. IRC Sec. 199A(e)(4).
2. IRC Sec. 199A(e)(5).
3. IRC Sec. 1361(b)(3).
4. Treas. Reg. §1.1361-4(a)(3).
5. Treas. Reg. §1.1361-4(a)(7) and §1.1361-4(a)(8).
6. IRC Sec. 1361(b)(3).
7. Treas. Reg. §1.1361-5(c).

799. Under what circumstances may an S corporation be taxed at the corporate level?

For S elections made after December 17, 1987, a corporation switching from C corporation status to S corporation status may also be required to recapture certain amounts at the corporate level in connection with goods previously inventoried under a LIFO method.[1] See Q 800 for a discussion of the changes introduced by the 2017 Tax Act.

In addition, a tax is imposed at the corporate level on *excess* "net passive income" of an S corporation (passive investment income reduced by certain expenses connected with the production of such income) but only if the corporation, at the end of the tax year, has accumulated earnings and profits (either carried over from a year in which it was a non-electing corporation or due to an acquisition of a C corporation), and if passive investment income exceeds 25 percent of gross receipts. The rate is the highest corporate rate (currently 21 percent, decreased from 35 percent prior to 2018).[2] "Passive investment income" for this purpose is rents, royalties, dividends, interest, and annuities.[3] However, passive investment income does not include rents for the use of corporate property if the corporation also provides substantial services or incurs substantial cost in the rental business,[4] or interest on obligations acquired from the sale of a capital asset or the performance of services in the ordinary course of a trade or business of selling the property or performing the services. Also, passive investment income does not include gross receipts derived in the ordinary course of a trade or business of lending or financing; dealing in property; purchasing or discounting accounts receivable, notes, or installment obligations; or servicing mortgages.[5] Regulations provide that if an S corporation owns 80 percent or more of a C corporation, passive investment income does not include dividends from the C corporation to the extent the dividends are attributable to the earnings and profits of the C corporation derived from the active conduct of a trade or business.[6] If amounts are subject to tax both as built-in gain and as excess net passive income, an adjustment will be made in the amount taxed as passive income.[7]

Also, tax is imposed at the corporate level if investment credit attributable to years for which the corporation was not an S corporation is required to be recaptured.[8]

Furthermore, an S corporation may be required to make an accelerated tax payment on behalf of its shareholders, if the S corporation elects not to use a required taxable year.[9] The corporation is also subject to estimated tax requirements with respect to the tax on built in gain, the tax on excess net passive income and any tax attributable to recapture of investment credit.[10]

1. IRC Sec. 1363(d).
2. IRC Sec. 1375(a).
3. IRC Secs. 1362(d)(3), 1375(b)(3).
4. See Let. Ruls. 9837003, 9611009, 9610016, 9548012, 9534024, 9514005.
5. Treas. Reg. §1.1362-2(c)(5).
6. Treas. Reg. §1.1362-8(a).
7. IRC Sec. 1375(b)(4).
8. IRC Sec. 1371(d).
9. IRC Sec. 7519.
10. IRC Sec. 6655(g)(4).

800. How did the 2017 Tax Act impact the tax treatment of S corporations that convert to C corporations?

Under prior law, if an S corporation converted to a C corporation, distributions of cash by the C corporation to the shareholders during the post-termination transition period were tax-free to the extent of the amount in the company's accumulated adjustment account. These distributions also reduced the shareholders' basis in the company's stock. The "post-termination transition period" was the one-year period after the S corporation election terminated.

The 2017 Tax Act provides that any accounting adjustments under IRC Section 481(a) that are required because of the revocation of the S corporation election of an "eligible terminated S corporation" (such as changing from the cash to accrual method of accounting) must be taken into account ratably during the six tax years beginning with the year of the change.[1]

An "eligible terminated S corporation" is defined as any C corporation which (1) was an S corporation the day before the enactment of the 2017 Tax Act (i.e., December 22, 2017), (2) during the two-year period beginning on the date of enactment revokes its S corporation election under IRC Section 1362(a), and (3) where all of the owners of the S corporation on the date the election is revoked are the same owners (in identical proportions) as the owners on the date of the enactment of the 2017 Tax Act.[2]

Under Revenue Procedure 2018-44, an eligible terminated S corporation is *required* to take a positive or negative Section 481(a) adjustment ratably over six years beginning with the year of change if the corporation (1) is required to change from the cash method to accrual method and (2) makes the accounting method change for the C corporation's first tax year. An eligible terminated S corporation is *permitted* (but not required) to take a positive or negative Section 481(a) adjustment ratably over six years beginning with the year of change if the eligible terminated S corporation (1) is permitted to continue using the cash method of accounting after termination of its S status, and (2) changes to the overall accrual method of accounting for the C corporation's first tax year.

Under the new rules, if there is a distribution of cash by an eligible terminated S corporation, the accumulated adjustments account will be allocated to that distribution, and the distribution will be chargeable to accumulated earnings and profits, in the same ratio as the amount of the accumulated adjustments account bears to the amount the accumulated earnings and profits.[3]

The IRS has clarified that cash distributions made by a former S corporation during the entity's post-termination period in redemption of its stock reduce the adjusted basis in the stock to the extent that the distribution does not exceed the accumulated adjustments account value. This is the case if the distribution is treated as subject to Section 301, rather than as a distribution in exchange of stock. The amount of the distribution value that exceeds the accumulated adjustments account is treated as a dividend. In the case at hand, the S corporation's S election

1. IRC Sec. 481(d)(1).
2. IRC Sec. 481(d)(2).
3. IRC Sec. 1371(f).

terminated so that the entity became a C corporation. A single taxpayer owned all outstanding shares, and the corporation redeemed half of those shares for cash during the post-termination transition period.[1]

801. How is an S corporation shareholder's basis in the S corporation stock calculated?

The basis of each shareholder's stock is *increased* by his share of items of separately stated income (including tax-exempt income), by his share of any nonseparately computed income, and by any excess of deductions for depletion over basis in property subject to depletion.[2] An S corporation shareholder may *not* increase his basis due to excluded discharge of indebtedness income.[3] The basis of each shareholder's stock is *decreased* (not below zero) by (1) items of distributions from the corporation that are not includable in the income of the shareholder, (2) separately stated loss and deductions and nonseparately computed loss, (3) any expense of the corporation not deductible in computing taxable income and not properly chargeable to capital account, and (4) any depletion deduction with respect to oil and gas property to the extent that the deduction does not exceed the shareholder's proportionate share of the property's adjusted basis.

For tax years beginning after 2005, if an S corporation makes a charitable contribution of property, each shareholder's basis is reduced by the pro rata share of their basis in the property.[4] This treatment was made permanent by the Protecting Americans from Tax Hikes Act of 2015 (PATH). If the aggregate of these amounts exceeds his basis in his stock, the excess reduces the shareholder's basis in any indebtedness of the corporation to him.[5] A shareholder may not take deductions and losses of the S corporation that, when aggregated, exceed his basis in his S corporation stock plus his basis in any indebtedness of the corporation to him.[6] Such disallowed deductions and losses may be carried over.[7] In other words, the shareholder may not deduct in any tax year more than he has "at risk" in the corporation.

Generally, earnings of an S corporation are not treated as earnings and profits. A corporation may have accumulated earnings and profits for any year in which a valid election was not in effect or as the result of a corporate acquisition in which there is a carryover of earnings and profits under IRC Section 381.[8] Corporations that were S corporations before 1983 but were not S corporations in the first tax year after 1996 are able to eliminate earnings and profits that were accumulated before 1983 in their first tax year beginning after May 25, 2007.[9]

1. Rev. Rul. 2019-13.
2. IRC Sec. 1367(a)(1).
3. IRC Sec. 108(d)(7)(A).
4. IRC Sec. 1367(a)(2), as amended by TEAMTRA 2008 and ATRA.
5. IRC. Sec. 1367(b)(2)(A).
6. IRC Sec. 1366(d)(1).
7. IRC Sec. 1366(d)(2).
8. IRC Sec. 1371(c).
9. SBWOTA 2007 Sec. 8235.

A distribution from an S corporation that does not have accumulated earnings and profits lowers the shareholder's basis in the corporation's stock.[1] Any excess is generally treated as gain.[2]

If the S corporation does have earnings and profits, distributions are treated as distributions by a corporation without earnings and profits, to the extent of the shareholder's share of an accumulated adjustment account (i.e., post-1982 gross receipts less deductible expenses, which have not been distributed). Any excess distribution is treated under the usual corporate rules. That is, it is a dividend up to the amount of the accumulated earnings and profits. Any excess is applied to reduce the shareholder's basis. Finally, any remainder is treated as a gain.[3] However, in any tax year, shareholders receiving the distribution may, if all agree, elect to have all distributions in the year treated first as dividends to the extent of earnings and profits and then as return of investment to the extent of adjusted basis and any excess as capital gain.[4] If the IRC Section 1368(e)(3) election is made, it will apply to all distributions made in the tax year.[5]

Certain distributions from an S corporation in redemption of stock receive sale/exchange treatment. (Generally, only gain or loss, if any, is recognized in a sale.) In general, redemptions that qualify for "exchange" treatment include redemptions not essentially equivalent to a dividend, substantially disproportionate redemptions of stock, complete redemptions of stock, certain partial liquidations, and redemptions of stock to pay estate taxes.[6]

If the S corporation distributes appreciated property to a shareholder, gain will be recognized to the corporation as if the property was sold at fair market value, and the gain will pass through to shareholders like any other gain.[7]

The rules discussed above generally apply in tax years beginning after 1982. Nonetheless, certain casualty insurance companies and certain corporations with oil and gas production will continue to be taxed under the rules applicable to Subchapter S corporations prior to these rules.[8]

802. How is a "personal service corporation" taxed?

Editor's Note: The 2017 Tax Act eliminated the special tax treatment that previously applied to personal service corporations. As such, these corporations are now subject to the same flat 21 percent tax rate that applies to C corporations.

Prior to 2018, certain personal service corporations were taxed at a flat rate of 35 percent.[9] In effect, this meant that the benefit of the graduated corporate income tax rates was not available. For tax years beginning after December 31, 2017, personal service corporations are taxed at the 21 percent corporate rate. (See Appendix B.)

1. IRC Sec. 1367(a)(2)(A).
2. IRC Sec. 1368(b).
3. IRC Sec. 1368(c).
4. IRC Sec. 1368(e)(3).
5. Let. Rul. 8935013.
6. See IRC Secs. 302, 303.
7. IRC Secs. 1371(a), 311(b).
8. Subchapter S Revision Act of 1982, Sec. 6.
9. IRC Sec. 11(b)(2), prior to repeal by Pub. Law No. 115-97 (the 2017 Tax Act).

A personal service corporation for this purpose is a corporation in which substantially all corporate activities involve the performance of services in the fields of health, law, engineering, architecture, accounting, actuarial science, performing arts, or consulting. In addition, substantially all of the stock must be owned (1) directly by employees, retired employees, or their estates or (2) indirectly through partnerships, S corporations, or qualified personal service corporations.[1]

IRC Section 269A permits the IRS to reallocate income, deductions, credits, exclusions, and other allowances (to the extent necessary to prevent avoidance or evasion of federal income tax) between a personal service corporation (PSC) and its employee-owners if the corporation is formed for the principal purpose of securing tax benefits for its employee-owners (i.e., more than 10 percent shareholder-employees after application of attribution rules) and substantially all of its services are performed for a single other entity. For purposes of IRC Section 269A, a personal service corporation is a corporation the principal activity of which is the performance of personal services and such services are substantially performed by the employee-owners.[2] A professional basketball player was considered to be an employee of an NBA team, not his personal service corporation, and all compensation from the team was taxable to him individually, even though his PSC had entered into a contract with the team for his personal services.[3]

In addition, special rules apply to the tax year that may be used by a personal service corporation (as defined for purposes of IRC Section 269A, except that all owner-employees are included and broader attribution rules apply).[4]

803. What is a limited liability company and how is it taxed?

A limited liability company (LLC) is a statutory business entity that may be formed by at least two members (although one-member LLCs are permitted in some states) by drafting articles of organization and filing them with the appropriate state agency. There are no provisions for LLCs in the Code, but regulations provide rules to determine how a *business entity* is classified for tax purposes. A business entity is any entity recognized for federal tax purposes that is not a trust. Unlike an S corporation, an LLC has no restrictions on the number or types of owners and multiple classes of ownership are generally permitted. If the LLC is treated as a partnership, it combines the liability shield of a corporation with the tax advantages of a partnership.

An LLC may be treated as either a corporation (see Q 788), partnership (see Q 804), or sole proprietorship for federal income tax purposes. A sole proprietor and his business are one and the same for tax purposes. An *eligible entity* (a business entity not subject to automatic classification as a corporation) may elect corporate taxation by filing an entity classification form; otherwise it will be taxed as either a partnership or sole proprietorship depending upon how many owners are involved.

1. IRC Sec. 448(d)(2).
2. IRC Sec. 269A(b)(1).
3. *Leavell v. Comm.*, 104 TC 140 (1995).
4. IRC Secs. 441(i), 444.

A separate entity must exist for tax purposes, in that its participants must engage in a business for profit. Trusts are not considered business entities.[1] Certain entities, such as corporations organized under a federal or state statute, insurance companies, joint stock companies, and organizations engaged in banking activities, are automatically classified as corporations for federal tax purposes. A business entity with only one owner will be considered a corporation or a sole proprietorship. In order to be classified as a partnership, the entity must have at least two owners.[2] If a newly-formed domestic eligible entity with more than one owner does not elect to be taxed as a corporation, it will be classified as a partnership. Likewise, if a newly-formed single-member eligible entity does not elect to be taxed as a corporation, it will be taxed as a sole proprietorship. Under most circumstances, a corporation in existence on January 1, 1997 does not need to file an election in order to retain its corporate status.[3]

If a business entity elects to change its classification, rules are provided for how the change is treated for tax purposes.[4]

Revenue Ruling 95-37[5] provides that a partnership converting to a domestic LLC will be treated as a partnership-to-partnership conversion (and therefore be "tax-free") provided that the LLC is classified as a partnership for federal tax purposes. The partnership will not be considered terminated under IRC Section 708(b) upon its conversion to an LLC so long as the business of the partnership is continued after the conversion. Further, there will be no gain or loss recognized on the transfer of assets and liabilities so long as each partner's percentage of profits, losses and capital remains the same after the conversion. The same is true for a limited partnership converting to an LLC.[6]

An LLC formed by two S corporations was classified as a partnership for federal tax purposes.[7] An S corporation may merge into an LLC without adverse tax consequences provided the LLC would not be treated as an investment company under IRC Section 351 and the S corporation would not realize a net decrease in liabilities exceeding its basis in the transferred assets pursuant to Treasury Regulation Section 1.752-1(f). Neither the S corporation nor the LLC would incur gain or loss upon the contribution of assets by the S corporation to the LLC in exchange for interests therein pursuant to IRC Section 721.[8] A corporation will retain its S election when it transfers all assets to an LLC, which is classified as a corporation for federal tax purposes due to a preponderance of corporate characteristics (see below), provided the transfer qualifies as a reorganization under IRC Section 368(a)(1)(F) and the LLC meets the requirements of an S corporation under IRC Section 1361.[9]

1. Treas. Reg. §301.7701-1.
2. Treas. Reg. §301.7701-2.
3. Treas. Reg. §301.7701-3.
4. Treas. Reg. §301.7701-3(g).
5. 1995-1 CB 130.
6. Let. Rul. 9607006.
7. Let. Rul. 9529015.
8. Let. Rul. 9543017.
9. Let. Rul. 9636007.

An LLC that was in existence prior to January 1, 1997, may continue under its previous claimed classification if it meets the following requirements: (1) it had a reasonable basis for the classification; (2) the entity and its members recognized the consequences of any change in classification within the sixty months prior to January 1, 1997; and (3) neither the entity nor its members had been notified that the classification was under examination by the IRS.[1]

Prior to January 1, 1997, whether an LLC was treated as a corporation or partnership for federal income tax purposes depended on the existence or nonexistence of a preponderance of six corporate characteristics: (1) associates; (2) an objective to carry on a business and divide the gains from it; (3) limited liability; (4) free transferability of interests; (5) continuity of life; and (6) centralized management.[2] Characteristics (1) and (2) above are common to both corporations and partnerships and were generally discounted when determining whether an organization was treated as a corporation or partnership.[3] These former regulations provided an example of a business entity that possessed the characteristics of numbers (1), (2), (4) and (6) above, noting that since numbers (1) and (2) were common to both corporations and partnerships, these did not receive any significant consideration. The business entity did not possess characteristics (3) and (5) above and, accordingly, was labeled a partnership.[4]

See Q 805 and Q 806 for a discussion of how the 2017 Tax Act impacted the taxation of LLCs that are taxed as partnerships.

804. How is the income from a partnership taxed?

Editor's Note: See Q 805 to Q 806 for a discussion of the changes to pass-through taxation that were implemented under the 2017 tax reform legislation.

With the exception of certain publicly traded partnerships, a partnership, as such, is not taxed.[5] However, the partnership must file an information return on Form 1065, showing taxable ordinary income or loss and capital gain or loss. The partnership is regarded as an entity for the purpose of computing taxable income, and business expenses of the partnership may be deducted. In general, prior to the 2017 Tax Act, taxable income was computed in the same manner as for individuals; but the standard deduction, personal exemptions, and expenses of a purely personal nature are not allowed.[6] The deduction for production activities may also have been allowed prior to its repeal for tax years beginning in 2018 and beyond (see Q 788).

Each partner must report his share of partnership profits, whether distributed or not, on his individual return. A partner's distributive share is determined either on the basis of the partner's interest or by allocation under the partnership agreement. Allocation by agreement must have a "substantial economic effect." Special allocation rules apply where the partner's interest changes during the year.[7]

1. Treas. Reg. §301.7701-3(h)(2).
2. Treas. Reg. §301.7701-2(a)(1), as in effect prior to January 1, 1997.
3. Treas. Reg. §301.7701-2(a)(2), as in effect prior to January 1, 1997.
4. Treas. Reg. §301.7701-2(a)(3), as in effect prior to January 1, 1997.
5. IRC Sec. 701.
6. IRC Secs. 703(a), 63(c)(6)(D).
7. IRC Secs. 706(d), 704(b).

A person is a partner if he owns a capital interest in a partnership in which capital is a material income-producing factor, whether he acquired his interest by purchase or gift. Generally, such a person will be taxable on his share of partnership profits. If capital is not an income-producing factor, the transfer of a partnership interest to a family member may be disregarded as an ineffective assignment of income, rather than an assignment of property from which income is derived. Where an interest is acquired by gift (an interest purchased by one family member from another is considered to have been acquired by gift), allocation of income among the partners according to the partnership agreement will not control to the extent that: (1) it does not allow a reasonable salary for the donor of the interest; or (2) the income attributable to the capital share of the donee is proportionately greater than the income attributable to the donor's capital share.[1] The transfer must be complete and the family member donee must have control over the partnership interest consistent with the status of partner. If he is not old enough to serve in the capacity of partner, his interest must be controlled by a fiduciary for his benefit.

A "qualified joint venture" that is carried out by two spouses may elect to treat their business as two sole proprietorships and not as a partnership. A qualified joint venture is any joint venture conducting a trade or business where the only owners are the two spouses, both spouses materially participate in the business, and both spouses elect to opt out of the partnership taxation rules. Items of income, gain, loss, deduction, and credit must be divided between the spouses according to their respective interests in the business.[2]

A partnership which is traded on an established securities market, known as a publicly traded partnership, is taxed differently than a partnership in some instances.[3]

See Q 734 to Q 735 for a discussion of how the deduction of business interest is treated under the 2017 Tax Act.

805. How is the income from a partnership taxed under the 2017 tax reform legislation?

The 2017 Tax Act made substantial changes to the treatment of pass-through business income, which was previously "passed through" and taxed at the business owners' individual ordinary income tax rates. Partnerships (and entities that elect partnership taxation, such as certain LLCs), S corporations and sole proprietorships are subject to the new pass-through taxation rules, which will apply for tax years beginning after December 31, 2017 and before December 31, 2025.[4] The new rules are extremely complicated, and the IRS and related agencies continue to release interpretive materials explaining how the basic provisions will be applied. See Q 8568 – Q 8587 for a discussion of the Section 199A regulations.

Partnerships may now generally deduct 20 percent of "qualified business income (QBI)"[5] (which generally excludes "specified service business" income (see below)).

1. IRC Sec. 704(e).
2. IRC Sec. 761(f).
3. IRC Sec. 7704.
4. Under IRC Sec. 199A.
5. IRC Sec. 199A(a).

Partnerships that are categorized as service businesses and have income below the applicable threshold level plus $50,000 ($100,000 for joint returns) also qualify for the deduction. The applicable threshold levels for 2020 are $326,600 (joint returns), and $163,300 (single returns), so service business owners with income that exceeds $426,600 (joint returns) or $213,300 (single) in 2020 will not receive the benefit of the new deduction. The applicable threshold levels for 2019 were $321,400 (joint returns), and $160,700 (single returns), and the numbers in 2018 were $315,500 or $157,500. The entirety of the taxpayer's income must be taken into account (not only the business' income).[1]

The deduction is available regardless of whether the taxpayer itemizes, and is applied based on ownership interest (i.e., a partner who owns 25 percent of a partnership is entitled to apply the deduction to 25 percent of his or her QBI). The calculation is made on an entity-specific basis, meaning that the deduction must be applied separately to each entity rather than based upon the cumulative income of all entities owned by the taxpayer.

Qualified business income is generally the net amount of qualified items of income, gain, deduction and loss with respect to qualified trades or businesses of the taxpayer, excluding qualified REIT dividends, qualified cooperative dividends and qualified publicly traded partnership income (but see Q 806).[2] Income, gain, deduction and loss items are generally qualified if they are connected with a U.S. trade or business and are included or allowed in calculating taxable income. Amounts related to the following investment items are excluded: capital gains, qualified dividend income (or equivalent), non-business interest income, foreign base company income taken into account under IRC Section 954(c), non-business annuity distributions.[3]

For alternative minimum tax purposes, qualified business income is calculated without regard to otherwise allowable adjustments.[4]

When the pass-through entity's income exceeds the $321,400/$160,700 threshold, the deduction is capped at the greater of (1) 50 percent of W-2 wage income or (2) the sum of 25 percent of the W-2 wages of the business plus 2.5 percent of the unadjusted basis, immediately after acquisition, of all "qualified property" (but see Q 806 for a discussion of the "phase-in" for certain taxpayers whose income only exceeds the threshold by $50,000 ($100,000 for joint returns)).[5]

Planning Point: IRS guidance provides that the term "W-2 wages" includes online income properly reported to the Social Security Administration on Form W-2 within 60 days of the deadline for filing the form, including extensions. The filing deadline is generally January 31, giving most businesses until April 1 to file the form in order to count the wages for Section 199A purposes.[6]

1. IRC Secs. 199A(b)(3), 199A(d)(2).
2. IRC Sec. 199A(c).
3. IRC Secs. 199A(c)(3), 199A(d)(3).
4. IRC Sec. 199A(f)(2).
5. IRC Sec. 199A(b)(2). In the case of a short taxable year, only those W-2 wages paid during the short taxable year count under Treasury Regulation Section 1.199A-2(b)(iv)(C).
6. Rev. Proc. 2019-11.

"Qualified property" generally includes depreciable property that is used in the taxpayer's trade or business for the production of income as of the end of the tax year, as long as the depreciation period has not expired before the end of that year. The depreciation period is a period that begins on the first day that the taxpayer places the property in service and ends the later of (1) ten years after that date or (2) the last day of the last full year in the applicable recovery period that would apply to the property under IRC Section 168 (without regard to Section 168(g)).[1]

A "specified service business" is a trade or business involving the performance of services in the fields of health, law, consulting, athletics, financial services, brokerage services or any trade or business where the principal asset of the business is the reputation or skill of one or more employees or workers, or one which involves the performance of services consisting of investing and investment management trading or dealing in securities, partnership interests or commodities.

To determine the "qualified business income" with respect to a specified service trade or business, the taxpayer takes into account only the applicable percentage of qualified items of income, gain, deduction, or loss, and of allocable W-2 wages.[2] With respect to S corporations, qualified business income does not include any amounts that are treated as reasonable compensation of the taxpayer. Similarly, qualified business income does not include guaranteed payments or amounts paid or incurred by a partnership to a partner, when the partner is providing services and is not acting in his or her capacity as a partner.[3]

Planning Point: Qualified business income (QBI) excludes pass-through income that is categorized as "compensation" or a "guaranteed payment". The 20 percent deduction applies only to QBI.

It remains to be seen whether safeguards will be put into place to discourage partnerships from categorizing more business income as partnership profits (i.e., reduce guaranteed payments that would be treated in the same manner as excluded compensation in order to increase QBI and take advantage of the 20 percent deduction with respect to those funds. Currently existing "reasonable compensation" rules apply only to S corporations and C corporations, and have not been specifically extended into the partnership arena.

If the qualified business income for the year is a loss, it is carried forward as a loss for the next tax year. Any deduction allowed for that subsequent tax year is reduced by 20 percent of any carried forward business loss from the previous year.[4]

The deduction is allowed as a reduction reducing taxable income, rather than as a deduction in computing adjusted gross income (i.e., the deduction does not impact limitations based on adjusted gross income). Further, trusts and estates are also eligible for the 20 percent deduction.

---

1. IRC Sec. 199A(b)(6). IRC Section 168 provides accelerated cost recovery system rules. IRC Section 168(g) provides an alternate depreciation system that may be used with respect to certain property, including tangible property used predominantly outside the U.S., tax-exempt use property and tax-exempt bond financed property.
2. As defined in IRC Sec. 199A(b)(4).
3. IRC Sec. 199A(c)(4).
4. IRC Sec. 199A(c)(2).

For partnerships and S corporations, these rules apply at the partner or shareholder level (each partner is treated as having W-2 wages for the year equal to that partner's allocable share of the partnership).

See Q 806 for a detailed discussion of how a pass-through entity's deduction for qualified business income is determined.

806. How is a partnership's deduction for qualified business income determined?

Entities that are taxed under the rules governing pass-through taxation are generally entitled to a 20 percent deduction for qualified business income (see Q 805). This deduction is equal to the sum of:

(a) the lesser of the combined qualified business income amount for the tax year or an amount equal to 20 percent of the excess of the taxpayer's taxable income over any net capital gain and cooperative dividends, plus

(b) the lesser of 20 percent of qualified cooperative dividends or taxable income (reduced by net capital gain).[1]

The sum discussed above may not exceed the taxpayer's taxable income for the tax year (reduced by net capital gain). Further, the 20 percent deduction with respect to qualified cooperative dividends is limited to taxable income (reduced by net capital gain).

The deductible amount for each qualified trade or business is the lesser of:

(a) 20 percent of the qualified business income with respect to the trade or business or

(b) the greater of (x) 50 percent of W-2 wage income or (y) the sum of 25 percent of the W-2 wages of the business plus 2.5 percent of the unadjusted basis, immediately after acquisition, of all qualified property (see Q 805).[2]

Planning Point: The proposed regulations provide guidance on how UBIA should be calculated in the case of a like-kind exchange or involuntary conversion. The regulations follow the Section 168 regulations in providing that property acquired in a like-kind exchange, or by conversion, is treated as MACRS property, so that the depreciation period is determined using the date the relinquished property was first placed into service unless an exception applies. The exception applies if the taxpayer elected *not* to apply Treasury Regulation §1.168(i)-6. As a result, most property acquired in a like-kind exchange or involuntary conversion under the new rules will have two relevant placed in service dates. For calculating UBIA, the relevant date is the date the taxpayer places the property into service. For calculating its depreciable period, the relevant date is the date the taxpayer placed the original, relinquished property into service.

---

1. IRC Sec. 199A(a)
2. IRC Sec. 199A(b)(2).

Concurrently with the proposed regulations, the IRS released Notice 2018-64, which contains a proposed revenue procedure with guidance for calculating W-2 wages for purposes of the Section 199A deduction for qualified business income. The guidance provides three methods for calculating W-2 wages, including the "unmodified box method", the "modified Box 1 method", and the "tracking wages method". The guidance further specifies that wages calculated under these methods are only taken into account in determining the W-2 wage limitations if properly allocable to QBI under Proposed Treasury Regulation §1.199A-2(g).

The unmodified box method involves taking the lesser of (1) the total of Box 1 entries for all W-2 forms or (2) the total of Box 5 entries for all W-2 forms (in either case, those that were filed with the SSA by the taxpayer for the year). Under the modified Box 1 method, the taxpayer subtracts from its total Box 1 entries amounts that are not wages for federal income tax withholding purposes, and then adds back the total of Box 12 entries for certain employees. The tracking wages method requires the taxpayer to actually track employees' wages, and (1) total the wages subject to income tax withholding and (2) subtract the total of all Box 12 entries of certain employees.

If the taxable income is below the applicable threshold levels ($326,600 for joint returns and $163,300 for single filers in 2020; in 2019, the amounts were $160,700 for single filers and $321,400 for joint returns, up from $157,500 and $315,000 in 2018), the deduction is simply 20 percent.[1]

If the taxable income exceeds the relevant threshold amount, but not by more than $50,000 ($100,000 for joint returns), and the amount determined under (b), above, is less than the amount under (a), above, then the deductible amount is determined without regard to the calculation required under (b). However, the deductible amount allowed under (a) is reduced by the amount that bears the same ratio to the "excess amount" as (1) the amount by which taxable income exceeds the threshold amount bears to (2) $50,000 ($100,000 for joint returns).

The "excess amount" means the excess of amount determined under (a), above, over the amount determined under (b), above, without regard to the reduction described immediately above.

> *Example:* Marty (a taxpayer who is subject to the W-2 wages and capital limit) does business as a sole proprietorship conducting a widget-making business. The business buys a widget-making machine for $100,000 and places it in service in 2020. The business has no employees in 2020. The limitation in 2020 is the greater of (a) 50 percent of W-2 wages, or $0, or (b) the sum of 25 percent of W-2 wages ($0) plus 2.5 percent of the unadjusted basis of the machine immediately after its acquisition: $100,000 × .025 = $2,500. The amount of the limitation on Marty's deduction is $2,500.[2]

"Combined qualified business income" for the year is the sum of the deductible amounts for each qualified trade or business of the taxpayer and 20 percent of the taxpayer's qualified REIT dividends and qualified publicly traded partnership income.[3]

1. IRC Sec. 199A(b)(3).
2. Example taken from the Conference Report on the 2017 Tax Act.
3. IRC Sec. 199A(b)(1).

Qualified REIT dividends do not include any portion of a dividend received from a REIT that is a capital gain dividend or a qualified dividend.[1]

"Qualified cooperative dividends" includes a patronage dividend, per-unit retain allocation, qualified written notice of allocation, or any similar amount that is included in gross income and received from (a) a tax-exempt benevolent life insurance association, a mutual ditch or irrigation company, cooperative telephone company, like cooperative organization or a taxable or tax-exempt cooperative that is described in section 1381(a), or (2) a taxable cooperative governed by tax rules applicable to cooperatives before the enactment of subchapter T of the Code in 1962.[2]

"Qualified publicly traded partnership income" means the sum of:

(1) the net amount of the taxpayer's allocable share of each qualified item of income, gain, deduction, and loss from a publicly-traded partnership that does not elect to be taxed as a corporation (so long as the item is connected with a U.S. trade or business and is included or allowed in determining taxable income for the year and is not excepted investment-type income, also not including the taxpayer's reasonable compensation, guaranteed payments for services or Section 707(a) payments for services), and

(2) gain recognized by the taxpayer on disposing its interest in the partnership that is treated as ordinary income.[3]

Example: H and W file a joint return on which they report taxable income of $520,000 (determined without regard to this provision). H is a partner in a qualified trade or business that is not a specified service business ("qualified business A"). W has a sole proprietorship qualified trade or business that is a specified service business ("qualified business B"). H and W also received $10,000 in qualified REIT dividends during the tax year.

H's allocable share of qualified business income from qualified business A is $300,000, such that 23 percent of the qualified business income with respect to the business is $69,000. H's allocable share of wages paid by qualified business A is $100,000, such that 50 percent of the W-2 wages with respect to the business is $50,000. As H and W's taxable income is above the threshold amount for a joint return, the application of the wage limit for qualified business A is phased in. Accordingly, the $69,000 amount is reduced by 20 percent of the difference between $69,000 and $50,000, or $3,800. H's deductible amount for qualified business A is $65,200.

W's qualified business income and W-2 wages from qualified business B, which is a specified service business, are $325,000 and $150,000, respectively. H and W's taxable income is above the threshold amount for a joint return. Thus, the exclusion of qualified business income and W-2 wages from the specified service business are phased in. W has an applicable percentage of 80 percent. In determining includible qualified business income, W takes into account 80 percent of $325,000, or $260,000. In determining includible W-2 wages, W takes into account 80 percent of $150,000, or $120,000. W calculates the deductible amount for qualified business B by taking the lesser of 23 percent of $260,000 ($59,800) or 50 percent of includible W-2 wages of $120,000 ($60,000). W's deductible amount for qualified business B is $59,800.

1. IRC Sec. 199A(e)(3).
2. IRC Sec. 199A(e)(4).
3. IRC Sec. 199A(e)(5).

H and W's combined qualified business income amount of $127,300 is comprised of the deductible amount for qualified business A of $65,200, the deductible amount for qualified business B of $59,800, and 23 percent of the $10,000 qualified REIT dividends ($2,300). H and W's deduction is limited to 23 percent of their taxable income for the year ($520,000), or $119,600. Accordingly, H and W's deduction for the taxable year is $119,600.[1]

Choice of Entity

807. How did the 2017 tax reform impact a business owner's calculus regarding choice of entity decisions?

Under the 2017 tax reform legislation, C corporations are now subject to a flat 21 percent income tax rate at the entity level and pass-through business income is taxed at the individual level, where a maximum 37 percent rate now applies. While this seems simple on the surface, the true calculus post- tax reform is not nearly so straightforward.

C corporation income must eventually be distributed by the corporation to its owners, where it is then taxed a second time, at the individual level. The rate of tax on corporate distributions depends on how the distribution is classified. If the income is salary, the maximum 37 percent ordinary income tax rate may apply, but the corporation may deduct the payment. If the distribution comes in the form of dividends, a maximum long-term capital gains rate of 23.8 percent (including net investment income tax) may apply and no deduction is permitted. This structure makes dividend distribution more appealing, but even the effective tax rate on dividends creeps up to 39.8 percent when the double tax is factored in. If a sale of the C corporation is contemplated, the double tax issue arises once again.

Pass-through entities may be entitled to all or part of a new 20 percent deduction for qualified business income. The availability of this deduction depends upon the business' annual income and the type of business in which the entity is engaged. Specified service trades or businesses (SSTBs, see Q 8573) can only take advantage of the full deduction if income is less than the annual threshold levels plus $50,000 ($100,000 for joint returns). The applicable threshold levels for 2018 are $315,000 (married filing jointly) or $157,500 (single filers), and for 2019, those numbers were adjusted to $321,400 and $160,700. In 2020, the amounts increase to $326,600 and $163,300.

Further, when the pass-through entity's income exceeds the thresholds (regardless of business type), the 20 percent deduction is capped at the greater of (1) 50 percent of W-2 wage income or (2) the sum of 25 percent of the W-2 wages of the business plus 2.5 percent of the unadjusted basis, immediately after acquisition, of all "qualified property" (basically, depreciable business property).

Additionally, state-level taxes on corporate and pass-through (individual) income should also be included in the choice of entity analysis. See Q 808 for a discussion of the impact of the accumulated earnings tax and personal holding company tax on the choice of entity analysis.

1. Example taken from the Conference Report on the 2017 Tax Act.

Some special considerations that can arise in the case of S corporations are discussed at Q 809 and Q 810.

808. How can the accumulated earnings tax and personal holding company tax impact a business' choice of entity decision when a business owner is considering converting to a C corporation?

For many pass-through business owners, the choice of entity decision may be strongly impacted by whether the business intends to distribute most of its income to the owners each year (as many small businesses do). Regardless of the form the distribution takes, the double tax structure (discussed in Q 8568) that arises in the C corporation context will often result in a C corporation generating a higher effective tax rate, depending upon the business owner's income tax bracket.

If a C corporation does not distribute most of its income, the accumulated earnings tax and personal holding company tax must be considered. Both taxes are designed to prevent a C corporation from stockpiling earnings within the corporate structure in order to avoid tax at the individual level. The 20 percent accumulated earnings tax applies when the corporation accumulates earnings beyond the reasonable business needs of the corporation. The 20 percent personal holding company tax can also become important for closely held corporations that derive more than 60 percent of adjusted gross income from passive investments (such as dividends, interest and rent).

Businesses that would most likely benefit from C corporation structure after enactment of the 2017 tax reform legislation generally include capital-intensive businesses, such as a manufacturing company that has a legitimate business reason for leaving large amounts invested within the corporation (e.g., for purchasing and maintaining equipment).

809. How does the 2017 tax reform legislation impact the choice of entity decision between sole proprietorship form and an S corporation?

Sole proprietors and S corporations with only a single shareholder may which to examine their choice of entity decisions to more fully take advantage of the Section 199A deduction for QBI. Generally, reasonable compensation paid by an S corporation to its shareholder is included in the W-2 wage limit and excluded from QBI.[1] A sole proprietor is not subject to similar requirements (the Section 199A proposed regulations make clear that the reasonable compensation rule applies only in the S corporation context).[2]

If the business' income for the year exceeds the relevant threshold levels, these rules would maximize the QBI deduction if the business was organized as an S corporation. If income fell below the relevant thresholds, the sole proprietor would obtain the larger QBI deduction, as illustrated in the examples below.

1. IRC Sec. 199A(c)(4)(A).
2. Prop. Treas. Reg. 1.199A-3(b)(2)(ii)(H).

Example 1: A sole proprietorship and S corporation with one shareholder each generate $500,000 in QBI for the year, and neither business has any qualified property. The S corporation shareholder pays himself reasonable compensation for the year of $100,000. The sole proprietor is not required to pay himself a wage. Both businesses are subject to the W-2 and UBIA limitations because their income exceeds the relevant threshold levels. The S corporation's QBI deduction for the year is limited based on the statute's W-2 limitation, so is limited to $50,000 (50 percent of W-2 wages, i.e., the shareholder's reasonable compensation). The sole proprietor's QBI deduction (also phased out) is zero, because wages and UBIA both equaled zero.

Example 2: If each business described in the example above instead earned $100,000 (i.e., below the income thresholds), the W-2 wage and UBIA limitations would not apply. Assume the S corporation shareholder paid himself $40,000 in reasonable compensation for the year. The sole proprietor's QBI deduction is $20,000 (simply 20 percent of $100,000). The S corporation shareholder must reduce his QBI for the year by the amount of reasonable compensation ($40,000) before calculating the deduction. Thus, his QBI deduction for the year is only $12,000.

810. What special considerations apply to S corporations regarding the choice of entity decision after implementation of the 2017 tax reform legislation?

Beyond the pure tax aspects, small business clients should be advised that tax laws have a tendency to change even when they are characterized as permanent. If the small business converts to C corporation status, problems can result if it turns out that the conversion was ill-advised or the rules change in the future. For example, once an S corporation converts to C corporation status, it cannot convert back to an S corporation for five years.

Further, if the owner does decide to convert back to an S corporation in the future, taxes on built-in gains may apply and issues surrounding accumulated earnings and profits arise.

Accounting issues can arise if the pass-through entity is required to change its accounting method as a result of the conversion. Under the new legislation, any accounting adjustments under IRC Section 481(a) that are required because of the conversion of an "eligible terminated S corporation" (such as changing from the cash to accrual method of accounting) must be taken into account ratably during the six tax years beginning with the year of the change. Eligible terminated S corporations are basically S corporations that convert within two years of the passage of the tax legislation, where the ownership structure remains the same. See *2019 Tax Facts on Individual and Small Business*, Q 9025 to Q 9039 for a more in-depth discussion of small business accounting issues post-reform.

PART VIII: FEDERAL ESTATE TAX, GIFT TAX, GENERATION-SKIPPING TRANSFER TAX, AND VALUATION

Estate Tax

811. What is the federal estate tax?

The federal estate tax is an excise tax on the right to transfer property at death.[1]

Changes made to the rules governing estate, gift and GST taxes in 2001 and 2010 created a substantial amount of uncertainty for estate planning purposes. After 2012, the estate, gift, and GST rules were scheduled to return to pre-2001 levels unless Congress acted to extend the rules enacted in 2001 and 2010. Congress enacted the American Taxpayer Relief Act of 2012 ("ATRA") on January 1, 2013, making the estate, gift, and GST tax rules that 2010TRA implemented permanent. The 2017 Tax Act doubled the transfer tax exemption amount, but left the remaining provisions intact.

Under 2010TRA, the estate, gift and GST exemptions were $5 million for 2010-2012, with an inflation adjustment to $5.12 million for 2012. ATRA made this exemption level permanent, so that the $5 million exemption was adjusted annually for inflation for 2012-2017. The exemption amount was adjusted upward to $5.43 million in 2015 and $5.45 million in 2016.[2] The amount for 2017 was $5.49 million, and increased to $11.18 million in 2018, $11.4 million in 2019, and $11.58 million in 2020 under the 2017 tax reform legislation.[3]

Planning Point: The increased estate tax exemption will require that clients and advisors revisit existing estate planning strategies to determine whether they continue to be advisable. For example, many clients have made use of so-called "formula trusts" in their estate planning in order to take full advantage of the transfer tax exemption. A particularly problematic issue may arise when the formula in the plan directs that assets up to the annual exclusion amount will be placed into a credit shelter trust, with the remainder placed into a marital trust designed to take advantage of the marital deduction. With the enlarged estate tax exemption, some clients may find that no assets will remain to be transferred to the marital trust. This can present a problem if the surviving spouse is not also the beneficiary of the credit shelter trust (for example, if the decedent's children are beneficiaries of that trust).

While no estate tax was required to be imposed for 2010 under 2001 EGTRRA, the "penalty" of choosing to have no estate tax apply was that the estate then became subject to certain carryover basis rules. 2010TRA allowed estates of decedents dying in 2010 to elect to fall under the $5 million exemption (and 35 percent estate tax rate) or be subject to the carryover basis rules. Estates electing the carryover basis rules were required to file a Form 8939 to report information about property acquired from a decedent and to allocate basis increases to certain property acquired from a decedent.

1. IRC Sec. 2001.
2. Rev. Proc. 2014-61, 2014-47 IRB 860, Rev. Proc. 2015-53.
3. Rev. Proc. 2016-55, Pub. Law No. 115-97, Rev. Proc. 2018-18, Rev. Proc. 2018-57, Rev. Proc. 2019-44.

Under 2010 TRA, a surviving spouse may use any unused estate tax exemption from the deceased spouse.[1] This "portability" rule also allows a surviving spouse to use the deceased spouse's unused exemption for gift tax purposes, but apparently not for GST exemption purposes. ATRA made this portability rule permanent as long as an estate tax return is filed and the portability election is made.

Under 2010 TRA, the gift tax applicable exclusion amount was made equal to the estate and GST tax exemptions discussed above.

The maximum estate tax rate and gift tax rate for 2010 through 2012 was 35 percent. The GST tax rate was zero in 2010 and 35 percent for 2011 and 2012. Under ATRA, the maximum estate, gift, and GST tax rates were permanently increased to 40 percent for the largest estates.

The estate tax is measured by the value of the property or property interests transferred. The estate tax is also an extension of the gift tax, with the gift tax being an excise tax on the right to transfer property during life (see Q 881). Generally, both types of transfers are taxed according to the same rate schedule and a unified credit applies to both. As is explained in Q 881, the gift tax is cumulative and the tax rates are progressive. Thus, while taxable lifetime gifts may cause gifts made in subsequent years to be taxed at higher rates, all lifetime taxable gifts (if substantial enough) tend to push the taxable estate into higher tax brackets. That is, the cumulative effect follows through to the last taxable transfer a person makes – at death. This effect is seen clearly when the steps in the computation of the estate tax are followed.

Planning Point: Lifetime gifts, however, are often preferred to transfer at death because lifetime gifts are "tax exclusive" as the amount of tax paid is not subject to gift tax while the estate tax is "tax inclusive" since the assets used to pay the estate tax are also subject to tax.

An estate tax return, if required, must generally be filed within nine months after the decedent's death. A six month extension for filing is available. Tax is generally due within nine months after the decedent's death, but certain extensions for payment may be available. See Q 851.

Property includable in the gross estate is generally valued at fair market value on the date of death (Q 905). An election may be available to use an alternative valuation date six months after death (Q 906).

Certain deductions (Q 837) are available against the gross estate. Deductions for funeral and administration expenses, debts and taxes, and losses are subtracted from the gross estate to produce an adjusted gross estate. The adjusted gross estate is used to determine qualification for a few tax benefits, such as estate tax deferral under IRC Section 6166 (see Q 851).

Unlimited marital and charitable deductions are available for certain transfers to surviving spouses and charities. The taxable estate equals the gross estate reduced by all deductions.

Tax is imposed on the taxable estate. Tax rates (Appendix D) are generally progressive and tax is based on cumulative taxable transfers during lifetime and at death. To implement this, the

1. IRC Sec. 2010(c).

tentative tax is calculated on the sum of the taxable estate and adjusted taxable gifts (the computation base), and the gift tax that would have been payable on adjusted taxable gifts (using the tax rates in effect at decedent's death) is then subtracted out. Adjusted taxable gifts are taxable gifts (the balance after subtracting allowable exclusions and deductions) made by the decedent after 1976 other than gifts includable in the decedent's gross estate.

Planning Point: A gift made after August 5, 1997 cannot be revalued if the gift was adequately disclosed on a gift tax return and the gift tax statute of limitations (generally, three years) has passed.[1] Consider filing gift tax returns and adequately disclosing even annual exclusion gifts to start the limitation period.

The tentative tax is then reduced by credits (Q 850) to produce estate tax payable. The unified credit is generally the most important credit available.

812. What are the steps that must be taken to calculate the federal estate tax?

The Federal Estate Tax Worksheet, below, shows the steps for calculating the estate tax. Calculation starts with determining what is includable in the decedent's gross estate (see Q 814). In general, the gross estate includes property owned by the decedent at death, as well as property in which the decedent retained or held certain strings such as a retained income interest, a reversionary interest, a right to change beneficial interests, jointly owned property, a general power of appointment, certain interests in annuities or life insurance, and certain transfers within three years of death. A limited exclusion is available from the gross estate for conservation easements (Q 836).

Federal Estate Tax Worksheet

1	Year of Death		
2	Gross Estate (before exclusions)		$ Q 814
3	- Conservation Easement Exclusion		($ Q 836)
4	Gross Estate		$ Q 814
5	- Funeral and Administration Expenses Deduction	$ Q 837	
6	- Debts and Taxes Deduction	$ Q 837	
7	- Losses Deduction	$ Q 837	
8	- Subtotal: 5 to 7		($)
9	Adjusted Gross Estate		$
10	- Marital Deduction	$ Q 837	
11	- Charitable Deduction	$ Q 837	
12	- Other Deductions	$ Q 837	

1. IRC Sec. 2001(f).

13	- Subtotal: 10 to 12		($)
14	Taxable Estate		$
15	+ Adjusted Taxable Gifts		$
16	Computation Base		$
17	Tax on Computation Base		$ Appendix D
18	- Gift Tax on Adjusted Taxable Gifts		($ Appendix D)
19	Tentative Tax		$ Appendix D
20	- Unified Credit	$ Q 850	
21	- State Death Tax Credit (now a deduction)	$ Q 850	
22	- Pre-1977 Gift Tax Credit	$ Q 850	
23	- Previously Taxed Property Credit	$ Q 850	
24	- Foreign Death Tax Credit	$ Q 850	
25	- Total Credits		($ Q 850)
26	Federal Estate Tax		$

813. Is the exclusion amount of the first spouse to die portable? What is "portability"?

Yes. The 2010 Tax Relief Act introduced a new estate tax concept for 2011 and 2012, the **deceased spouse unused exclusion amount** (DSUEA). The DSUEA is portable, meaning that a surviving spouse can utilize the unused exclusion amount of the first spouse to die. ATRA made this portability concept permanent for tax years beginning in 2013 and thereafter.

In general, under the provision, an estate's exclusion amount, referred to as its applicable exclusion amount, is the sum of two components: the **basic exclusion amount** and the DSUEA. The basic exclusion amount for estates of decedents dying in 2015 was $5.43 million, $5.45 million in 2016, $5.49 million in 2017, and jumped to $11.18 million in 2018, $11.4 million in 2019, and $11.58 million in 2020 under the 2017 Tax Act.[1] The second part of the equation, the DSUEA, is the amount of the first-to-die spouse's exclusion amount that is not used by that spouse's estate. Note that a surviving spouse's DSUEA is equal to the unused exclusion amount of the surviving spouse's **last** deceased spouse.

The decedent's executor must make the election on a timely filed estate tax return and include the computation of the DSUEA. The final regulations provide that an extension of time may be available for filing the estate tax return only if the value of the estate otherwise does not exceed the threshold filing levels $11.58 million per individual in 2020. In other words, an

1. Rev. Proc. 2015-53, Rev. Proc. 2016-55, Pub. Law No. 115-97, Rev. Proc. 2018-18, Rev. Proc. 2018-57, Rev. Proc. 2019-44.

extension of time may be granted if the taxpayer is only required to file an estate tax return in order to elect portability.[1]

Further, the portability election will be effective if the executor of an estate completes and files an estate tax return containing a computation of the unused DSUE amount, but it is later found that adjustments are required in order to recompute the correct amount. The IRS provides an example of an estate that has a DSUE amount equal to zero at the deadline for filing, but has claims pending against it that, when subsequently paid, result in an unused exemption. The final regulations clarify that the recomputed DSUE amount will be available to the surviving spouse in such a situation, and the originally filed return will be considered "complete and properly prepared" for purposes of the election.[2]

Under the final regulations, a surviving spouse who was not a U.S. citizen may use the DSUE amount if he or she subsequently becomes a U.S. citizen and the executor of the estate has filed an estate tax return properly making the portability election. Previously existing rules prevented a non-citizen spouse from taking advantage of portability except where allowed under a U.S. treaty obligation.[3]

814. What items are includable in a decedent's gross estate for federal estate tax purposes?

The items that comprise the gross estate are described in IRC Sections 2033-2046 and the regulations thereunder. See Q 815 to Q 831 for a detailed discussion of these includable items. Gratuitous transfers of federal, state, and municipal obligations are discussed in Q 887. See Q 836 for the qualified conservation easement exclusion from the gross estate.

815. What property is includable in the gross estate under IRC Section 2033?

"The gross estate of a decedent who was a citizen or resident of the United States at the time of death includes under IRC Section 2033 the value of all property, whether real or personal, tangible or intangible, and wherever situated, beneficially owned by the decedent at the time of his death...(see Q 887). Real property is included whether it came into the possession and control of the executor or administrator or passed directly to heirs or devisees .... Interest and rents accrued at the date of the decedent's death constitute a part of the gross estate. Similarly, dividends which are payable to the decedent or estate by reason of the fact that on or before the date of the decedent's death he was a stockholder of record (but which have not been collected at death) constitute a part of the gross estate."[4]

Interest accrued, for example, on certificates of deposit owned at death and payable after death but forfeitable in the event of surrender during the owner's life[5] is includable in the dece-

1. Treas. Reg. §20.2010-2(a)(1).
2. Treas. Reg. §20.2010-2.
3. Treas. Reg. §§20.2010-3, 25.2505-5.
4. Treas. Reg. §20.2033-1.
5. See Federal Reserve Banking Regulation Section 217.4.

dent's estate under IRC Section 2033. The result is not changed by the fact that the decedent owned the CDs as a joint tenant at the time of death.[1]

Note that it is only property "beneficially owned" by the decedent that is includable under IRC Section 2033. Thus, IRC Section 2033 does not reach property held by the decedent in trust for others. On the other hand, the decedent's beneficial interest in property held by another as trustee is includable under IRC Section 2033 unless the decedent's death terminates the interest.

IRC Section 2033 does not include interests which terminate on the decedent's death, such as a life interest in a trust. (But such termination may be subject to the tax on generation-skipping transfers–see Q 864.) Similarly, if a decedent sells property in exchange for notes which provide that his death will extinguish the balance owing at that time, such balance will not be includable in the decedent's estate under IRC Section 2033 if the sale was for an adequate and full consideration and the cancellation provision was part of the bargained for consideration.[2]

Among the items includable in a decedent's gross estate are rights to future income (for example, the right to payments under an individual deferred compensation agreement or partnership income continuation plan). Such rights – called "income in respect of a decedent" – are included at their present (commuted) value. Since the income is also subject to income tax in the hands of the person who receives it (decedent's estate or beneficiary), the recipient is allowed an income tax deduction for the estate tax paid on the income right (see Q 745).

Planning Point: In light of this double taxation, taxpayers beyond retirement age should consider alternatives for removing funds from retirement accounts during life to fund other investments.

The decedent's interest in any business owned at death, whether as a proprietor, a partner, or a shareholder in a corporation, is likewise includable under IRC Section 2033. However, the decedent's interest may be subject to certain discounts for lack of marketability and lack of control.

Local property law (state law) determines the nature and extent of a decedent's ownership rights in property at the time of death. Under community property law, for instance, property acquired by a husband or wife during marriage by purchase with community funds is generally considered to be owned one-half by each spouse. Consequently, upon the death of the spouse who dies first, only one-half of the community property is includable in his gross estate. Ten states–Alaska, Arizona, California, Idaho, Louisiana, Nevada, New Mexico, Texas, Washington, and Wisconsin–operate under some form of community property system.

The value of Social Security survivor benefits, whether paid in the form of a lump sum or monthly annuity, is not includable in the decedent's estate under IRC Section 2033.[3]

1. *Jeschke v. U.S.*,814 F.2d 568, 87-1 USTC ¶13,713 (10th Cir. 1987).
2. *Est. of Moss v. Comm.*, 74 TC 1239 (1980), acq. in result, 1981-1 CB 2.
3. Rev. Rul. 55-87, 1955-1 CB 112; Rev. Rul. 67-277, 1967-2 CB 322; Rev. Rul. 81-182, 1981-2 CB 179.

816. Are dower and curtesy interests and their statutory substitutes includable in a decedent's gross estate under IRC Section 2034?

IRC Section 2034 specifically includes in the gross estate the interest of the decedent's surviving spouse "existing at the time of the decedent's death as dower or curtesy, or by virtue of a statute creating an estate in lieu of dower or curtesy."

At one time, certain courts held that dower and curtesy interests were not subject to death taxes because they were not received by transfer from the decedent. IRC Section 2034 was enacted to make sure that these marital interests would not escape the federal estate tax. The full value of the property without deduction of the surviving spouse's interest is includable in the gross estate.

817. When are gifts made within three years of death includable in a decedent's gross estate under IRC Section 2035?

Gift tax paid by the decedent or the estate on any gifts made by the decedent or spouse within three years of the decedent's death is includable in the gross estate in any case, regardless of whether the value of the gift itself is includable under IRC Section 2035 or any other IRC section.[1] Gift tax paid by the decedent's spouse on a split-gift within three years of the decedent's death was included in the decedent's estate where the decedent had funneled money to his spouse who then transferred the money to a life insurance trust (and to the IRS to pay gift tax); the transfers were treated as collapsed into one transaction under the step-transaction doctrine.[2]

Under Section 2035, the value of the gross estate also includes the value of property to the extent a donor gratuitously transferred property within three years of death but retained an interest in that property described in IRC Section 2036 (transfer with a retained life estate), 2037 (transfer taking effect at death with reversionary interest retained), 2038 (transfer with power retained to revoke or amend), or 2042 (incidents of ownership in insurance on life of donor); or if a donor transferred property subject to such retained interests more than three years before death, but relinquishes that interest within three years of death. The three-year rule applies to these transfers whether or not a gift tax return was required to be filed.[3] The entire value of the property transferred under this exception is includable in the decedent's gross estate, including the value of the property, if any, transferred by the decedent's consenting spouse (i.e., a split gift–see Q 894). If the consenting spouse dies within three years of the gift and the entire value of the gift was includable in the donor spouse's estate under IRC Section 2035, the consenting spouse's portion of the gift is not an adjusted taxable gift and is not includable in the consenting spouse's gross estate.[4] The gift tax paid by the donor spouse or the estate is includable in the donor spouse's estate, and the gift tax paid by the consenting spouse or her estate is includable in the consenting spouse's estate.[5] However, gift tax paid by a decedent's spouse on a gift split

1. *Estate of Hester v. United States*, 2007 WL 703170, 99 A.F.T.R. 2d 1288 (W.D. Va., 2007), afff'd per curiam, 297 Fed. Appx. 276, 2008 WL 4660189, 102 A.F.T.R. 2d 2008-6714 (4th Cir. Oct. 21 2008), Cert. denied sub nom. IRC Sec. 2035(b); Rev. Rul. 81-229, 1981-2 CB 176; Rev. Rul. 82-198, 1982-2 CB 206.
2. *Brown v. U.S.*, 329 F3d 664 (2003), 2003-1 USTC ¶60,462 (9th Cir. 2003).
3. IRC Sec. 2035(a).
4. IRC Sec. 2001(e); Rev. Rul. 82-198, 1982-2 CB 206.
5. IRC Sec. 2035(b); Rev. Rul. 82-198, above.

between the spouses within three years of the decedent's death was included in the decedent's estate where the spouse did not have sufficient assets to pay the spouse's share of the gift tax and the decedent transferred assets to the spouse to pay the taxes.[1]

A transfer from a revocable trust is treated as made directly by the grantor and therefore included in the gross estate.[2] Such a transfer will generally be subject to the Section 2035 inclusion rule also with respect to gift tax paid within three years of death and for the limited purpose of the second exception below.

IRC Section 2035 also applies to increase the gross estate for the purposes of the following:

(1) determining the estate's qualification for

(a) IRC Section 303 stock redemptions (redemption of stock held by a decedent at death in an amount not in excess of death taxes and settlement costs under special income tax rules that treat the redemption as a capital transaction rather than as a dividend), and

(b) current use valuation for qualified real property (see Q 905); and

(2) determining property subject to estate tax liens.[3] With respect to the IRC Section 6166 extension of the time to pay estate tax (see Q 851), the requirement that the decedent's interest in a closely held business must exceed 35 percent of the adjusted gross estate is met by an estate only if the estate meets the requirement both with and without the application of the bringback rule.[4] An exception to this second exception is that any gifts (other than a transfer with respect to a life insurance policy) not required to be reported on a gift tax return filed by the decedent for the year the gift was made are not includable in the gross estate. Gifts up to the limit of the gift tax annual exclusion and qualified transfers (see Q 894), but not split gifts, do not require the filing of a return. Another exception to the second exception is a gift which qualifies for the gift tax marital deduction (see Q 901).[5]

The Bringback Rule

The three-year rule of IRC Section 2035, referred to above, operates as follows: In general, gifts made by the decedent (in trust or otherwise) which are caught by the three-year rule, are includable in the decedent's gross estate. Also includable is the amount of any gift tax paid by the decedent or his estate on any gifts made by the decedent or his spouse within three years prior to the decedent's death; the gift tax is includable regardless of whether the value of the gift itself is includable under IRC Section 2035 or any other IRC section.[6] Where the decedent

1. TAM 9729005.
2. IRC Sec. 2035(e).
3. IRC Sec. 2035(c)(1).
4. IRC Sec. 2035(c)(2).
5. IRC Sec. 2035(c)(3).
6. IRC Sec. 2035(b); Rev. Rul. 81-229, 1981-2 CB 176; Rev. Rul. 82-198, 1982-2 CB 206.

made a "net gift" (i.e., a gift made on the condition that the donee pay the gift tax–see Q 889), the amount includable in the gross estate is the total value of the property transferred.[1]

818. When are gifts with a life interest retained by the donor includable in the donor's gross estate under IRC Section 2036?

IRC Section 2036 is one of the three sections (2036, 2037, 2038) dealing with lifetime transfers whereby the donor retained some rights over the property given. IRS Section 2036 brings into the gross estate lifetime transfers of property where the decedent retained the use of the property or the income from the property for life. Included are transfers made directly to a donee and transfers made to an irrevocable trust for designated beneficiaries, and transfers made to entities such as a partnership, if the decedent retained the prohibited "strings."

Specifically, IRC Section 2036 requires any property which an individual gratuitously transfers during lifetime to be included in the gross estate if he retains "for his life or for any period not ascertainable without reference to his death or for any period which does not in fact end before his death," either:

"(1) the possession or enjoyment of, or the right to income from, the property, or

"(2) the right, either alone or in conjunction with any person, to designate the persons who shall possess or enjoy the property or the income therefrom."

The IRS asserts the decedent's retention of possession or enjoyment of, or the right to income from, property may be evidenced by an agreement, or by prearrangement, or merely by circumstantial evidence.[2]

In November 2011, the IRS finalized regulations regarding the includability of property (including property held in trust) in the grantor's gross estate under Section 2036 where the grantor retained: (i) the use of the property; (ii) the right to an annuity or unitrust; (iii) a graduated retained interest; or (iv) other payment from the property.

Excepted from the scope of IRC Section 2036 is a transfer of property by way of "a bona fide sale for an adequate and full consideration in money or money's worth."[3] This exception to Section 2036 is often referred to as the "bona fide sale exception." Courts have wrestled with the interpretation of this exception in "widow's election" cases. Typically, a married decedent leaves certain property (and/or certain community property) in trust for his children, with all income to the surviving spouse for her lifetime, on the condition that the surviving spouse transfer certain of her property (or community property share) to the trust. The surviving spouse thus has her choice between what has been provided for her in the will and her statutory (intestate) share (or community property share). If the widow elects to take under the will, and transfers the agreed-upon property to the trust in exchange for a life income from all the trust assets, what has she transferred for purposes of IRC Section 2036? Has she transferred the entire property, or

1. Let. Rul. 8317010.
2. See *Lee v. U.S.*, 86-1 USTC ¶13,649 (W.D. Ky. 1985).
3. IRC Sec. 2036(a).

has she transferred only a remainder interest? If she is considered to have transferred the entire property, and the value of property transferred exceeds the value of the life income interest she receives in return, then she has not made a "bona fide sale for an adequate and full consideration" and the entire value of the property she transferred is includable in her gross estate under IRC Section 2036. If, however, she is considered to have transferred only a remainder interest, and that interest is of less value than the value of her life income from trust assets in excess of the value of the property she actually transferred, then she will have received adequate and full consideration for the transfer, and none of the property she actually transferred will be includable in her estate under IRC Section 2036. Case law appears to support the former interpretation.[1]

For purposes of analyzing the bona fide sale exception to contributions/transfers to family entities, such as LLCs or limited partnerships, courts analyze whether a "legitimate and significant," non-tax purpose existed for the formation of the partnership and whether the decedent received a share in the entity proportionate to her contribution.[2] If these conditions are satisfied, Section 2036 does not apply and the gross estate includes the value of the decedent's interest in the entity at the time of death (after gifts of interests, etc.). If, on the other hand, Section 2036 does apply (bona fide sale exception not satisfied and decedent retained prohibited rights), the gross estate includes the value of the assets contributed (without consideration of the entity, discounts applicable to ownership of an interest in the closely-held entity, or gifts made during life of interests).[3]

819. When are gifts taking effect at death includable in a decedent's gross estate under IRC Section 2037?

IRC Section 2037 requires inclusion in the gross estate of any interest in property transferred by the decedent if both of the following conditions are met:

(1) Possession or enjoyment of the property can, through ownership of the transferred interest, be obtained only by surviving the decedent; and

(2) The decedent has retained a reversionary interest in the property which, immediately before his death, exceeded 5 percent of the value of the property.

A simple example would be a transfer to an irrevocable living trust under the following terms: income to grantor's wife for her life; property to revert to grantor if living at wife's death and if not, property to their daughter.

Assuming that the grantor predeceases his wife and daughter, the value of the daughter's interest – the value of the property less the wife's life interest – is includable in the grantor's gross estate. Obviously, the daughter had to survive the grantor in order to receive the property. And in all probability, the grantor's reversionary interest, valued immediately before death, exceeded 5 percent of the value of the property.

1. *Gradow v. U.S.*, 897 F.2d 516, 90-1 USTC ¶60,010 (9th Cir. 1990).
2. *Estate of Bongard v. Comm.*, 124 TC 95 (2005).
3. *Estate of Kimbell v. United States*, 371 F.3d 257 (5th Cir. 2004).

The term "reversionary interest" means any possibility that the *property* may return to the donor or to his estate, and any possibility that the property may become subject to a power of disposition by him. The term does not, however, include a possibility that the income alone may return to the donor or his estate. Thus, retention of a secondary life estate would not constitute a reversionary interest (although it would cause inclusion under IRC Section 2036). Also, the term "reversionary interest" does not include a mere expectancy by the decedent that upon the death of the transferee he (or his estate) may reacquire the property under the will of the transferee or under state inheritance laws.[1]

820. When are gifts includable in the decedent's gross estate under IRC Section 2038 where a decedent retains a power to revoke or amend?

IRC Section 2038 brings into a decedent's gross estate property that he has gratuitously transferred if immediately before his death he possessed the power to alter, amend, revoke, or terminate the transfer.

The language of the section refers to transfers "by trust or otherwise," but generally the section applies to transfers in trust. The most obvious example of the applicability of IRC Section 2038 is, of course, the revocable living trust. Where the grantor of a trust retains until his death the power to revoke the trust, the full value of the trust corpus is includable in his gross estate.

It makes no difference whether the decedent could exercise the power alone or only in conjunction with another person.

It also makes no difference in what capacity the decedent could exercise the power–whether as grantor, trustee, or co-trustee.

IRC Section 2038 is not limited to transfers where the decedent *retained* the power to alter, amend, revoke, or terminate at the time of transfer, except with respect to transfers made on or before June 22, 1936. With respect to transfers made after that date, possession of such a power at death will cause inclusion in the gross estate regardless of when or from what source the decedent acquired the power. Thus, IRC Section 2038 would reach a case in which the decedent, who had not originally retained the power, subsequently succeeded to it by being appointed a trustee.

IRC Section 2038 also reaches transfers to an *irrevocable* trust if the settlor possesses at his death the power to alter or amend the trust.[2] However, the provision in a trust instrument for the inclusion of all the settlor's after-born and after-adopted children as additional beneficiaries is not the retention of a power to change the beneficial interests of the trust within the meaning of IRC Section 2038.[3]

1. Treas. Reg. §20.2037-1(c)(2).
2. *Marshall v. U.S.*, 338 F. Supp. 1321 (D. Md. 1972).
3. Rev. Rul. 80-255, 1980-2 CB 272.

The regulations also make it clear that the mere discretionary power reserved to the grantor to accumulate or distribute trust income for a single beneficiary is sufficient to bring the trust property into the grantor's estate under IRC Section 2038.[1]

However, if the grantor's power to affect the beneficial enjoyment of the transferred property is limited by an ascertainable objective and external standard, the power will not fall within IRC Section 2038. The IRS acquiesces in the ascertainable standard doctrine established by the cases.[2]

If a grantor creates an irrevocable trust under which the trustee is given the power to distribute income and principal unlimited by an ascertainable standard, the value of the trust property will be includable in the grantor's estate under IRC Section 2038 (and also under IRC Section 2036) if (1) the grantor names himself as trustee or retains at his death the power to do so, or (2) the grantor retains at his death the power to remove the trustee without cause and replace him with another.[3] However, a later revenue ruling modified Revenue Ruling 79-353 to provide that the above-described estate tax holding will not be applied to a transfer, or to an addition to a trust, made before October 29, 1979 (the date of publication of the revenue ruling) if the trust was irrevocable on October 28, 1979.[4] Further, for purposes of IRC Section 2036 or IRC Section 2038, the Service will no longer include trust property in a decedent-grantor's estate where the grantor retains the right to replace the trustee, but can replace the trustee with only an independent corporate trustee.[5]

821. When are annuities or annuity payments includable in a decedent's gross estate under IRC Section 2039?

IRC Section 2039 deals with annuities or other payments receivable by any beneficiary under any form of contract or agreement by reason of surviving the decedent. Subsections (a) and (b) of that section state the circumstances under which such an annuity or payment is includable in the decedent's gross estate. Thus, IRC Section 2039 applies to death and survivor benefits under annuity contracts and under optional settlements of living proceeds from life insurance policies and endowment contracts.

Exclusions under various provisions of IRC Section 2039 may apply to employee annuities which are part of qualified pension and profit sharing plans; to employee annuities payable under nonqualified deferred compensation plans, including death benefit only plans; to certain tax sheltered annuity plans; and to individual retirement savings plans.

822. Are joint interests includable in a decedent's gross estate under IRC Section 2040?

Yes. IRC Section 2040 deals with all classes of property held jointly with a right of survivorship. This includes, for example, jointly held real estate, jointly held bonds, and joint bank

1. Treas. Reg. §20.2038-1(a).
2. 1947-2 CB 2; Rev. Rul. 73-143, 1973-1 CB 407. For more information on the ascertainable standard doctrine, see Stephens, Maxfield, Lind & Calfee, Federal Estate and Gift Taxation (Boston: Warren, Gorham & Lamont, 7th ed.), ¶4.10[5], and the cases cited therein.
3. Treas. Reg. §20.2038-1(a)(3); Rev. Rul. 79-353, 1979-2 CB 325.
4. Rev. Rul. 81-51, 1981-1 CB 458.
5. Rev. Rul. 95-58, 1995-2 CB 191; *Est. of Wall v. Comm.*, 101 TC 300 (1993).

accounts. IRC Section 2040 does not deal with other forms of co-ownership in which property interests pass at death other than automatically to surviving co-owners. Thus, tenancies in common and community property interests are includable under IRC Section 2033, not under IRC Section 2040.

The general rule of IRC Section 2040 requires that the entire value of the jointly owned property must be included in the gross estate of the joint owner who dies first, except such part as can be shown to have originally belonged to the survivor and never to have been acquired from the decedent "for less than an adequate and full consideration in money or money's worth."[1] Thus, the rule is as follows: if the decedent furnished the entire purchase price, the entire property is includable; if the decedent furnished only a part of the purchase price, only a corresponding proportion of the property is includable; if the decedent furnished no part of the purchase price, no part of the property is includable.[2] (But see below for the special rule applicable to spouses who own property jointly.)

Planning Point: As a result of these rules, it is important that joint owners keep good records of the funding for the jointly-owned property.

Where the joint owners are related (not spouses) and the survivor paid part of the purchase price, he must be able to prove that the funds did not come to him by way of gift from the decedent. In other words, the purchase price will be traced to its original source; and the burden of proof is not on the IRS but on the survivor. It is often difficult to prove the amount of contribution of the survivor to the joint ownership. If the assets of the joint owners became inextricably commingled prior to acquisition of the jointly owned property, proof may be impossible and the property will be wholly includable in the decedent's gross estate.

But while money or property acquired by the surviving joint owner by gift from the decedent and contributed to the purchase price of the jointly held property is traced to the decedent for purposes of IRC Section 2040, *income* from property so acquired which is contributed to the purchase price is treated as the survivor's own contribution for purposes of IRC Section 2040.[3] Further, the IRS has ruled that where the survivor's contribution to the purchase price of jointly held property was traced to proceeds from the sale of property acquired by the survivor with money received from the decedent by gift, the sale proceeds attributable to appreciation in value of the property during the period the survivor owned the property were treated as the survivor's own contribution for purposes of IRC Section 2040. Also, consistent with the above-cited regulation, the Service ruled that sale proceeds attributable to income from the property received by the survivor and reinvested were treated as the survivor's individual contribution.[4]

Revenue Ruling 79-372 is also consistent with earlier case law, as noted in the Ruling. However, the regulations call for a different result when the survivor's contribution was of property received by gift from the decedent (rather than of proceeds from the sale of such property),

1. IRC Sec. 2040(a).
2. Treas. Reg. §20.2040-1(c).
3. Treas. Reg. §20.2040-1(c)(5).
4. Rev. Rul. 79-372, 1979-2 CB 330.

which property had appreciated in value during the period held by the survivor. In this situation the regulations require that the portion of the purchase price attributable to such appreciation be traced to the decedent for purposes of IRC Section 2040.[1]

Where the property was acquired by the decedent and the other joint owner by devise, bequest, or inheritance, or by gift from a third party, the decedent's fractional share of the property is included in his gross estate. For example, if the decedent's father has conveyed the property by gift to the decedent and his wife in joint tenancy or tenancy by the entirety, one-half of the property will be includable in the gross estate of whichever spouse dies first.[2]

See Q 823 for a discussion of when a qualified joint interest is included in a decedent's gross estate.

823. What is a qualified joint interest? When is a qualified joint interest included in a decedent's gross estate?

Effective for estates of decedents dying after 1981, in the case of joint interests created after 1976, notwithstanding the provisions of IRC Section 2040 explained in Q 822 (subsection (a)), only one-half the value of a *qualified joint interest* is included in a decedent's gross estate under IRC Section 2040. (The rule for inclusion in a decedent's estate for spousal jointly owned property is still based upon consideration furnished if the joint interest was created prior to 1977.[3]) A *qualified joint interest* means any interest in property held by the decedent and the decedent's spouse as (1) tenants by the entirety; or (2) joint tenants with right of survivorship, but only if the decedent and the spouse of the decedent are the only joint tenants.[4] However, with respect to decedents dying after November 10, 1988, if the decedent's spouse is not a United States citizen, interests in property held by the decedent and the decedent's spouse are not treated as a *qualified joint interest* (apparently unless the transfer to the surviving spouse is in a qualified domestic trust, see Q 837).[5] For purposes of applying the consideration furnished test (see above) where the *qualified joint interest* rule does not apply because the decedent's spouse is not a United States citizen, consideration furnished by the decedent to the decedent's spouse before July 14, 1988 is generally treated as consideration furnished by the decedent's spouse.[6]

824. When are powers of appointment includable in a decedent's gross estate under IRC Section 2041?

IRC Section 2041 governs the includability in the decedent's gross estate of property subject to his power of appointment. For estate tax purposes, a "power of appointment" is a power which has been given to the decedent by another person, as distinguished from a power *retained* by him over property which he formerly owned. A power of appointment enables the holder thereof to dispose of property he does not own.

1. Treas. Reg. §20.2040-1(c)(4).
2. IRC Sec. 2040(a).
3. *Gallenstein v. U.S.*,975 F.2d 286, 92-2 USTC ¶60,114 (6th Cir. 1992); *Patten v. U.S.*, 116 F.3d 1029, 97-2 USTC ¶60,279 (4th Cir. 1997); *Anderson v. U.S.*, 96-2 USTC ¶60,235 (D.C. Md. 1996); *Hahn v. Comm.*, 110 TC 140 (1998), acq. 2001-42 IRB iii.
4. IRC Sec. 2040(b).
5. IRC Sec. 2056(d).
6. OBRA '89, Sec. 7815(d)(16).

Example: A's will provides that part of his estate is to be placed in trust. The will gives A's spouse all the trust income for life and also the power to designate who shall receive the trust principal after death. If A's spouse fails to exercise the power, the trust principal is to go to their daughter. A's spouse exercises the power by executing a will in which she directs the trust principal to their son.

In this example, A is the *donor* of the power; A's spouse is the *donee* of the power; their son is the *appointee* of the power; and the daughter, had A's spouse failed to exercise her power, would have been the *taker in default of appointment.*

Of course, powers of appointment can be created otherwise than by a testamentary trust. They can also be created, for example, by the terms of a living trust, or by the terms of a life insurance beneficiary arrangement.

The law provides two sets of rules for gift and estate taxation of powers of appointment. The first set of rules deals with powers created before October 22, 1942, sometimes called "pre-1942" powers. The second set of rules governs powers created after October 21, 1942, sometimes called "post-1942" powers.

A power of appointment created by will is considered as created on the date of the testator's death. A power created by an inter vivos instrument is considered created on the date the instrument takes effect.[1] Thus, in the case of a living trust, the power is created when the trust takes effect, even though the trust is revocable. Likewise, in the case of life insurance, the power is created when the beneficiary designation is made, even though the designation is revocable.

Regardless of when the power is created, however, it is not taxable in any event unless it is a "general" power of appointment (see Q 825).

825. What is a general power of appointment?

The IRC defines a general power of appointment as a power which is exercisable in favor of the decedent, his estate, his creditors, or the creditors of his estate. Here the "decedent" is, of course, the donee – that is, the holder of the power.

A power exercisable in favor of the holder, his estate, his creditors, or the creditors of his estate is a general power of appointment; it need not be exercisable in favor of both.[2] Thus, if the holder can withdraw all or part of the principal for any purpose, he has a general power of appointment exercisable in favor of himself. Or, if he can will (or bequeath) the property to anyone he wishes, including his own estate, he has a general power of appointment exercisable in favor of his estate.

However, a power to "consume, invade, or appropriate" the principal for the holder's own benefit is not a general power of appointment if it is limited by an "ascertainable standard" relating to the holder's "health, education, support, or maintenance." According to the regulations, "A power is limited by such a standard if the extent of the holder's duty to exercise and not to exercise the power is reasonably measurable in terms of his needs for health, education, or

1. Treas. Reg. §20.2041-1(e).
2. Treas. Reg. §20.2041-1(c)(1).

support (or any combination of them). As used in this subparagraph, the words 'support' and 'maintenance' are synonymous and their meaning is not limited to the bare necessities of life. A power to use property for the comfort, welfare, or happiness of the holder of the power is not limited by the requisite standard."

Planning Point: To ensure a power of appointment is limited by an ascertainable standard, the drafter must use the exact terms referenced in the regulations. Too much is at stake to use terms the drafter may believe are "similar."

Examples of powers which are limited by the requisite standard are powers exercisable for the holder's 'support,' 'support in reasonable comfort,' 'maintenance in health and reasonable comfort,' 'support in his accustomed manner of living,' 'education, including college and professional education,' 'health,' and 'medical, dental, hospital and nursing expenses and expenses of invalidism.' In determining whether a power is limited by an ascertainable standard, it is immaterial whether the beneficiary is required to exhaust his other income before the power can be exercised."[1]

A pre-1942 power is not considered to be a "general" power of appointment if it is exercisable only in conjunction with another person. And a post-1942 power is not considered to be a "general" power of appointment if it is exercisable only in conjunction with the donor of the power or only in conjunction with someone who has a substantial interest in the property which is adverse to the holder's interest.[2] It has been held that a trustee does not have a substantial and adverse interest simply because the trust is a taker in default of exercise of the power, so long as the trustee himself is not a beneficiary of the trust.[3]

In the past, a number of letter rulings have determined that a beneficiary who has the power to remove a trustee will be treated as holding any powers held by the trustee for purpose of determining whether the beneficiary holds a general power of appointment.[4] However, for purposes of IRC Section 2036 or IRC Section 2038, the Service will no longer include trust property in a decedent grantor's estate where the grantor retains the right to replace the trustee but can replace the trustee with an independent trustee "that was not related or subordinate to the decedent (within the meaning of Section 672(c)), the decedent would not have retained a trustee's discretionary control over trust income."[5]

More recently, the power to remove a trustee and replace the trustee with an independent corporate trustee was not treated as the retention of powers held by the trustee for purposes of IRC Section 2041.[6] Hopefully, this represents an extension by the Service of its new policy with regard to trustee removal under IRC Section 2036 and IRC Section 2038 to IRC Section 2041. Similarly, a beneficiary's right to veto a replacement trustee and to petition a court for appointment of an independent replacement trustee was not treated as a general power of appointment.[7]

1. Treas. Reg. §20.2041-1(c)(2).
2. *Est. of Maxant*, TC Memo 1980-414, nonacq. 1981 AOD LEXIS 58; Rev. Rul. 82-156, 1982-2 CB 206.
3. *Miller v. U.S.*, 387 F.2d 866 (3rd Cir. 1968); *Est. of Towle v. Comm.*, 54 TC 368 (1970).
4. Let. Ruls. 8916032, 9113026 (does not apply to transfers in trust before October 29, 1979, if trust was irrevocable on October 28, 1979).
5. IRC Sec. 2041.
6. Let. Rul. 9607008.
7. Let. Rul. 9741009.

Any power of appointment which is not a general power is called a "special" or "limited" power. A special power of appointment is not taxable in the holder's estate regardless of when it was created.

Post-1942 Power: Generally

The *mere possession* at death of a post-1942 general power of appointment will cause the property to be included in the holder's gross estate. Thus:

(1) If the decedent had a general power of appointment which he could have exercised by will in favor of his estate, the property subject to the power is taxable in his estate whether or not he exercised the power; or

(2) If, immediately before his death, the decedent had a general power of appointment which he could have exercised in his own favor during his lifetime, the property subject to the power is taxable in his estate.

But even though the decedent does not still possess the power at the time of his death, if he has had such a power and has exercised or released it or allowed it to lapse during his lifetime, the property which was subject to the power may, under some circumstances, be included in his gross estate.

Thus, if the decedent once possessed a general power of appointment and has exercised or released it in such a way that, had the property been his own, it would have been included in his gross estate under one of the IRC Sections 2035 through 2038, then the property that was subject to the power is includable in his gross estate.

Pre-1942 Power

Prior to 1942, property subject to a general power of appointment was taxable in the donee's estate only if the power was *exercised*. Thus, the property is includable in the holder's gross estate only if (1) he has exercised the power by will at his death, or (2) he has exercised the power during life in such a way that, had the property been owned by him, it would have been includable under one of the IRC Sections 2035-2038.

826. What non-cumulative annual withdrawal rights may the grantor give beneficiaries without subjecting the power to estate and gift taxes?

In many situations, an insured or the grantor of a trust will wish to give his beneficiary not only all the income from the fund, but also a right to withdraw some limited amount of principal each year. If the beneficiary does not exercise his right of withdrawal in any year, the right expires or "lapses" at the end of the year. Where it cannot be carried forward to subsequent years, it is characterized as a "non-cumulative" withdrawal right.

Where the beneficiary permits such a right to lapse, gift and estate taxes may result by reason of the lapse. In other words, by not withdrawing the amount she could have withdrawn, the beneficiary has made a gift to those persons designated to receive the principal.

However, in framing the powers of appointment tax law, Congress recognized that modest annual withdrawal rights are socially desirable and that their use, within limits, should not be discouraged. Therefore, an exemption is granted in an amount equal to whichever is greater: (1) $5,000; or (2) 5 percent of the value of the fund as of the date of the lapse of the power.

Consequently, where a non-cumulative power of withdrawal is permitted to lapse, only the excess over and above the "$5,000 or 5 percent of the fund" limit will be subject to gift and estate taxes. This excess is treated as a transfer with life income retained. But the entire amount which could have been withdrawn in the year of death, but was not withdrawn, is includable in the gross estate since this power has not lapsed at the time of death.

827. When are life insurance proceeds includable in a decedent's gross estate under IRC Section 2042?

IRC Section 2042 deals specifically with the includability of life insurance proceeds in the gross estate of the *insured*. The proceeds are includable in the insured's gross estate under IRC Section 2042 if they are as follows:

(1) Receivable by or for the benefit of insured's estate; or

(2) Receivable by a beneficiary other than the insured's estate *and* the insured possessed at his death any of the incidents of ownership in the policy (whether exercisable by the insured alone or only in conjunction with another person).

Planning Point: Generally, the dispute arises as to whether the decedent held any "incidents of ownership" in the policy. A decedent may have an incident of ownership if he has the power to change the beneficial ownership in the policy regarding its proceeds. To help remove the insurance proceeds from the insured's estate, it may be desirable to acquire the policy in the name of an irrevocable life insurance trust or "ILIT".

828. Are transfers made for insufficient consideration includable in a decedent's gross estate under IRC Section 2043?

If any one of the transfers described in IRC Sections 2035 through 2038 and 2041 is made for consideration in money or money's worth, but the consideration is not adequate and full, the excess of the fair market value of the property transferred over the consideration received is the amount includable in the gross estate.[1] There is a split of authority over whether adequate and full consideration is measured by reference to what would otherwise be included in the estate or using time value of money discounts.[2]

In general, for purposes of the estate tax, a relinquishment or promised relinquishment of dower or curtesy, or of a statutory substitute, or of other marital rights in the decedent's property or estate, is not considered consideration "in money or money's worth." However, an

1. IRC Sec. 2043(a).
2. *Gradow v. U.S.*, 897 F.2d 516, 90-1 USTC ¶60,010 (Fed. Cir. 1990); *Pittman v. U.S.*, 878 F. Supp. 833, 95-1 USTC ¶60,186 (E.D.N.C. 1994); *Parker v. U.S.*, 894 F. Supp. 445, 95-1 USTC ¶60,199 (N.D. Ga. 1995); *Est. of D'Ambrosio v. Comm.*, 101 F.3d 309, 96-2 USTC ¶60,252 (3rd Cir. 1996), rev'g 105 TC 252 (1995); *Wheeler v. Comm.*, 116 F.3d 749, 97-2 USTC ¶60,278 (5th Cir. 1997), rev'g 96-1 USTC ¶60,226 (W.D. Tex. 1996); *Est. of Magnin v. Comm.*, 184 F.3d 1074, 99-2 USTC ¶60,347 (9th Cir. 1999), rev'g TC Memo 1996-25.

exception is made for the limited purpose of allowing a deduction from the gross estate in the case of a transfer which meets the following conditions: Where two spouses enter into a written agreement relative to their marital and property rights and divorce occurs within the three-year period beginning on the date one year before the agreement is entered into, any transfer of property or interests in property made pursuant to the agreement to either spouse in settlement of marital or property rights is deemed to be a transfer made for a full and adequate consideration in money or money's worth. The deduction allowed is for the value of the property transferred as a claim against the estate (see Q 837).

829. When is marital deduction property in which a decedent had an income interest includable in the gross estate under IRC Section 2044?

A marital deduction is allowed for transfers of "qualified terminable interest" property, commonly referred to as "QTIP," if the decedent's executor (or donor) so elects and the spouse receives a "qualifying income interest" in the property for life. (See Q 837, Q 901.) If the property subject to the qualifying income interest is not disposed of prior to the death of the surviving spouse, the fair market value of the property determined as of the date of the spouse's death (or alternate valuation date, if so elected) is included in the spouse's gross estate pursuant to IRC Section 2044.

830. When are disclaimers includable in a decedent's gross estate under IRC Section 2046?

It is possible for a person who is (or would be) the transferee of an interest in property to refuse to accept the interest and thus prevent any part of the value of the property from being included in his gross estate at his death. However, with respect to transfers creating an interest in the person disclaiming made after December 31, 1976, the refusal must take the form of a *qualified disclaimer*.[1]

A *qualified disclaimer* is an irrevocable and unqualified refusal to accept an interest in property. The refusal must satisfy four conditions: First, the refusal must be in writing. Second, the written refusal must be received by the transferor of the interest, his legal representative, or the holder of the legal title to the property not later than nine months after the day on which the transfer creating the interest is made. However, if later, the period for making the disclaimer will not expire in any case until nine months after the day on which the person making the disclaimer attains age 21. Third, the person must not have accepted the interest or any of its benefits before making the disclaimer. Fourth, the interest must pass to a person other than the person making the disclaimer as a result of the refusal to accept the property.[2]

A qualified disclaimer can be made up of an undivided portion of any separate interest in property, even if the disclaiming person has another interest in the same property.[3] In addition,

1. IRC Secs. 2046, 2518(a).
2. IRC Sec. 2518(b).
3. Treas. Reg. §25.2518-3.

the question of whether a separate interest may be disclaimed depends upon whether the interest is severable.[1]

A power with respect to property[2] is treated as an interest in such property.[3] The exercise of a power of appointment to any extent by the donee of the power is an acceptance of its benefits.[4]

A written transfer of the transferor's (disclaimant's) entire interest in property to the person or persons who would otherwise have received the property if an effective disclaimer had been made will be treated as a valid disclaimer for federal estate and gift tax purposes provided the transfer is timely made and the transferor has not accepted any of the interest or any of its benefits.[5]

831. What additional amounts may be includable in a decedent's gross estate?

IRC Section 2701
Recapture of Qualified Payments

Additional estate tax may be due with respect to certain transfers of interests in corporations or partnerships to reflect cumulative but unpaid distributions on retained interests (see Q 924).[6]

IRC Section 2704
Deemed Transfer of Lapsing Right

There may be a deemed transfer at death upon the lapse of certain voting or liquidation rights in a corporation or partnership (see Q 933).[7]

IRC Section 2801
Property Received from Expatriate

A United States citizen or resident who receives a covered bequest from certain expatriates may owe estate tax on the transfer.

832. In whose estate is property held in custodianship under the Uniform Gifts to Minors Act or the Uniform Transfers to Minors Act includable for federal estate tax purposes?

The value of property transferred under either of the Uniform Acts is includable in the gross estate of the *donor* if the donor dies while serving as custodian and before the donee attains the age of twenty-one. (But see the discussion of gifts made within three years of death at Q 814.) In all other circumstances, custodial property is includable only in the gross estate

1. Treas. Reg. §25.2518-3(a)(1)(ii).
2. See IRC Section 2041, Powers of Appointment, above.
3. IRC Sec. 2518(c)(2).
4. Treas. Reg. §25.2518-2(d)(1)(i); Let. Rul. 8142008.
5. IRC Sec. 2518(c)(3), as added by ERTA '81, and effective for transfers creating an interest in the person disclaiming made after 1981.
6. IRC Sec. 2701.
7. IRC Sec. 2704.

of the donee.[1] If A and B, spouses, make identical gifts under a Uniform Act, each naming the other as custodian, for federal estate tax purposes each will be deemed to have transferred the property over which he held custodianship rights at death, even though the property actually transferred by him was in the custody of the other.[2] Custodial property is not included in the estate of a custodian who consented to a split gift of the property by her spouse.[3]

Where the donor dies while serving as custodian, the value of the custodial property is includable in his estate under IRC Section 2038(a)(1), as a transfer with the power retained to alter, amend, revoke, or terminate. This result is reached because of the custodian's power, under Section 4 of the Uniform Act, to withhold enjoyment of the custodial property until the donee reaches majority. To avoid this result, the donor should name someone other than himself as custodian, and should not accept appointment as successor custodian.

The IRS has ruled that the power given the donee's parent (under section 4(c) of the Gifts to Minors Act) or interested person (under section 14(b) of the Transfers to Minors Act) to petition the court to order the custodian to expend funds for the minor's support, maintenance, or education is not a general power of appointment; therefore, the custodial property is not includable in the parent's or interested person's gross estate under IRC Section 2041.[4]

833. Is an education savings account includable in an individual's gross estate?

Upon the distribution of an education savings account on account of the death of the beneficiary, the amount of the education savings account is includable in the estate of the beneficiary, not the contributor. However, where a donor elects to have contributions prorated over a five year period for gift tax purposes (see Q 891) and dies during such period, the gross estate of the donor includes prorated contributions allocated to periods after the donor's death.[5]

See Q 891 for the gift tax treatment and Q 681 for the income tax treatment of education savings accounts.

834. Is a qualified tuition program includable in an individual's gross estate?

No interest in a qualified tuition program is includable in the estate of any individual for purposes of the estate tax, with two exceptions: (1) distributions made to the estate of the beneficiary upon the beneficiary's death; and (2) if such a donor dies before the end of a five-year gift tax proration period (see Q 892), the gross estate of the donor will include the portion of contributions allocable to periods after the death of the donor.[6]

1. Rev. Rul. 57-366, 1957-2 CB 618; Treas. Reg. §20.2038-1(a); Rev. Rul. 59-357, 1959-2 CB 212; Rev. Rul. 70-348, 1970-2 CB 193; *Est. of Prudowsky*, 55 TC 890 (1971), aff'd per curiam, 465 F.2d 62 (7th Cir. 1972); *Stuit v. Comm.*, 452 F.2d 190 (7th Cir. 1971).
2. *Exchange Bank & Trust Co. of Fla. v. U.S.*,694 F.2d 1261, 82-2 USTC ¶13,505 (Fed. Cir. 1982).
3. Rev. Rul. 74-556, 1974-2 CB 300.
4. Rev. Rul. 77-460, 1977-2 CB 323.
5. IRC Secs. 530(d)(3), 529(c)(4).
6. IRC Sec. 529(c)(4).

See Q 892 for the gift tax treatment and Q 687 for the income tax treatment of qualified tuition programs.

835. Is the value of a life insurance agent's renewal commissions includable in the gross estate?

Yes, assuming that he owns the right to the renewal commissions at the time of his death. The value includable will be the fair market value of the renewals at the time of death. Following the agent's death, the actuaries of the company will value the renewal account using some appropriate persistency table and an assumed rate of interest. If desired, the renewal commissions can be made to qualify for the marital deduction. For example, the value of the commissions will qualify for the marital deduction if all commissions are payable to the surviving spouse during her lifetime, and to her estate at her death. They should also qualify if she has the right to all renewals payable during her lifetime and a power to appoint who shall receive the commissions payable after her death. But if the surviving spouse is given only a right to those commissions which are payable during her lifetime, and someone else will receive the remaining payments in the event of her death during the renewal period, she will have only a "terminable interest" in the commissions, and they will not qualify unless a QTIP election is made.[1] The recipient must pay income tax on the renewals as received but is entitled to an income tax deduction for the estate tax attributable including the value of the renewals in the agent's gross estate.

836. What estate tax exclusion is available for a qualified conservation easement?

An estate tax exclusion is provided for qualified conservation easements.[2] An irrevocable election must be made by the executor if the exclusion is to apply. The exclusion is available for the lesser of (1) the applicable percentage of the value of land subject to the qualified conservation easement, reduced by the amount of any charitable deduction for the easement under IRC Section 2055(f), or (2) the exclusion limitation.[3] The applicable percentage is equal to 40 percent reduced (but not below zero) by two percentage points for every percentage point (or fraction thereof) by which the value of the conservation easement is less than 30 percent of the value of the land (determined without regard to the easement and reduced by any development right).[4] After 2001, the exclusion limitation is $500,000.[5] See Appendix D for limitations in other years.

The land subject to the conservation easement must be located in the United States or its possessions (for decedents dying in 2001 and thereafter).[6] For decedents dying before 2000, the land subject to the conservation easement must generally, on the date of the decedent's death, be located within one of the following: (1) twenty-five miles of a metropolitan area; (2) twenty-five miles of part of the National Wilderness Preservation System; or (3) ten miles of an Urban National Forest.

1. *Est. of Selling v. Comm.*, 24 TC 191 (1955); *Est. of Baker v. Comm.*, TC Memo 1988-483; Let. Rul. 9016084.
2. IRC Sec. 2031(c).
3. IRC Secs. 2031(c)(1), 2031(c)(6).
4. IRC Sec. 2031(c)(2).
5. IRC Sec. 2031(c)(3).
6. IRC Sec. 2031(c)(8)(A)(i), as amended by EGTRRA 2001.

The land subject to the conservation easement must be owned by decedent or members of decedent's family at all times during the three year period ending at decedent's death.[1]

The exclusion is not available to the extent that the land is subject to acquisition indebtedness or retained development rights (excludes certain farming uses).[2] Nor is the exclusion available if the easement is granted after the death of the decedent and anyone receives an income tax deduction with regard to granting of the easement.[3]

A conservation easement is not available if it is not exclusively for conservation purposes.[4]

837. What deductions are allowed from the gross estate in arriving at the taxable estate for federal estate tax purposes?

The following deductions are allowed from the gross estate in arriving at the taxable estate (see Q 811):

(1) (a) funeral expenses, (b) administration expenses, (c) claims against the estate, and (d) unpaid mortgages on or other indebtedness against property included at its full value in the gross estate (see Q 838);

(2) casualty and theft losses incurred during settlement of the estate and not compensated for by insurance or otherwise (see Q 840);

(3) the charitable bequests deduction (see Q 841);

(4) the marital deduction (see Q 843 through Q 848);

(5) the (pre-2005) qualified family-owned business interest deduction (see Q 849); and

(6) state death taxes (see Q 850).[5]

838. What deductions for expenses, indebtedness and taxes are allowed from the gross estate in arriving at the taxable estate for federal estate tax purposes?

Most of the claims, expenses, and charges payable by the estate under local law are allowable deductions from the gross estate. These include the following: (1) funeral expenses; (2) administration expenses; (3) certain taxes; and (4) indebtedness and claims against the estate.

Funeral expenses are generally allowable, although the regulations limit expenditures for a tombstone, monument, mausoleum, or burial lot to a reasonable amount.

1. IRC Sec. 2031(c)(8)(A)(ii).
2. IRC Secs. 2031(c)(4), 2031(c)(5).
3. IRC Sec. 2031(c)(9).
4. *Herman v. Commissioner*, TC Memo 2009-205.
5. IRC Secs. 2053-2058, as amended by EGTRRA 2001.

Administration expenses include primarily fees or commissions of executors, accountants, and attorneys, and miscellaneous costs incurred in connection with the preservation and settlement of the estate, including determination and contest of death taxes. Expenditures not essential to the proper settlement of the estate, but incurred for the individual benefit of the heirs, legatees, or devisees, may not be taken as deductions.[1] Expenses for selling property of the estate are deductible if the sale is necessary in order to pay the decedent's debts, expenses of administration, or taxes, to preserve the estate, or to effect distribution.

Planning Point: The estate should document contemporaneously with the sale why the estate needed to sell the property in order to avoid a future challenge.

The phrase "expenses for selling property" includes brokerage fees and other expenses attending the sale, such as the fees of an auctioneer if it is reasonably necessary to employ one.[2]

IRC Section 642(g) says that amounts allowable under IRC Section 2053 or 2054 as a deduction in computing the taxable estate shall not be allowed as a deduction (or as an offset against the sales price of property in determining gain or loss) in computing the taxable income of the estate unless the executor files a statement that the amounts have not been allowed as deductions under IRC Section 2053 or 2054 and waives the right to claim such deductions in the future. It has been held that where an estate necessarily incurred expenses in selling securities for the purpose of obtaining funds with which to pay estate settlement costs and taxes and used such expenses as offsets against the selling price of the securities in computing estate income taxes, and where the IRS did not require the above-described statement and waiver, the estate was free to claim the selling expenses as an estate tax deduction under IRC Section 2053.[3]

IRC Section 265(1) says that no deduction will be allowed for federal income tax purposes for expenses for production of income (see Q 8047) allocable to tax-exempt income. Assume, for example, that during a taxable year an estate receives $200,000 of income, $25,000 of which is tax-exempt because it is interest on municipal bonds. Assume, also, that in the same period the estate disbursed $50,000 for attorneys' fees and $30,000 for miscellaneous administration expenses, neither amount attributable to either the taxable or the tax-exempt income. By virtue of the above-described limitation of IRC Section 265, the executor is allowed to deduct on the estate's federal income tax return no more than $70,000 of the $80,000 in fees and expenses, the portion allocable to includable income. The following formula illustrates this calculation.

$$\frac{\$200{,}000 - 25{,}000}{\$200{,}000} \times 80{,}000 = \$70{,}000$$

Assume that as a condition of allowance of the income tax deduction, the IRS required of the executor the statement and waiver described in the preceding paragraph. The waiver would not preclude the executor from claiming a deduction on the estate tax return under IRC

1. Treas. Reg. §20.2053-3(a); *Est. of Posen v. Comm.*, 75 TC 355 (1980).
2. Treas. Reg. §20.2053-3(d)(2).
3. *Smith v. U.S.*, 319 F.Supp. 174 (E.D. Mo. 1970).

Section 2053, for the $10,000 balance of fees and expenses he was not allowed to deduct on the income tax return.[1]

As a general rule, claims against the estate which are founded on a promise or agreement are not deductible unless they were contracted for an adequate consideration in money or money's worth. An exception is made for enforceable pledges to qualified charitable organizations. Such pledges are deductible even though not contracted for an adequate consideration in money or money's worth. A release of dower or other marital rights generally is not deemed an adequate consideration; but a claim for alimony is fully deductible if founded on a divorce decree.

Final amendments to the regulations under Section 2053 are effective for the estates of decedents dying after October 19, 2009. The basic focus of the regulations is the extent to which post-death events may be considered in determining the deductible amount of the claim or expense. The significance of these new regulations is that generally the right to take a deduction (and the value of the deduction) is determined at the moment of death but the new regulations mandate consideration of postmortem facts (i.e., resolution of the claim) for deduction purposes.[2]

Planning Point: An estate must analyze the judicial decisions in its district in order to determine if a conflict exists between the new 2053 Regulations and the earlier decisions interpreting the deductibility of "claims against the estate" under Section 2053.

A payment in settlement of a will contest is generally not deductible from the gross estate. A claim to share in the estate is to be distinguished from a claim against the estate.[3]

Unpaid mortgages are deductible provided the property subject to the mortgage is included at its full value in the gross estate.

Property taxes accrued prior to the decedent's death, and taxes on income received during the decedent's life, are deductible. The property taxes, however, must be enforceable obligations (a lien upon the property) at the time of death. Ordinarily, state and foreign death taxes are not deductible, but may be taken as a credit against the tax (see Q 851). As an exception, however, the executor may elect to deduct any state or foreign taxes paid on bequests which qualify as charitable deductions under the federal estate tax law. If deducted, they cannot, of course, be taken as a credit against the tax. An estate tax deduction is not allowed for death taxes paid to a city even though a credit is not allowed for such taxes (see Q 851).[4]

In community property states, the extent to which administration expenses and claims are deductible depends upon their treatment under state law. If they are expenses or debts of the entire community, only one-half is deductible.

A deduction is allowed for expenses and debts attributable to non-probate property includable in the gross estate. They are deductible even though they exceed the property in the gross estate which under local law is subject to the claims against the estate. However, to the extent

1. Rev. Rul. 59-32, 1959-1 CB 245; Rev. Rul. 63-27, 1963-1 CB 57, clarifying Rev. Rul. 59-32.
2. T.D. 9468 ; Notice 2009-84; Treasury –IRS 2009-10 Priority Guidance Plan; CCA 200848045.
3. *Est. of Moore v. Comm.*, TC Memo 1987-587.
4. TAM 9422002.

that they exceed such property they are not deductible unless actually paid before the due date for filing the estate tax return.

839. If an estate sells a large block of stock through an underwriter, are the underwriting fees deductible from the gross estate?

A large estate may include a large block of stock in a single corporation that the executor determines must be sold to meet estate settlement costs and death taxes. Often, it is found that the best method of sale in these circumstances is to register the securities with the SEC for public sale by means of a secondary offering through an underwriter. The agreement between the executor and the underwriter may be one of two types:

> "Under a 'firm commitment' agreement the underwriter agrees to purchase a specific amount of stock for a fixed price at a certain time. In contrast, under a 'best efforts' agreement the underwriter sells the stock for the stockholder as an agent and only agrees to use its best efforts in obtaining sales."[1]

Under a firm commitment agreement, the executor undertakes to pay all registration and incidental selling expenses plus an "underwriting discount" paid to the underwriter. The underwriting discount amounts to the difference between the amount realized on sale of the shares to the public and the amount paid by the underwriter for the shares. The IRS has taken the position that "underwriting fees" (by which the Service clearly means to include the "underwriting discount") are not considered in determining the blockage discount to be accorded in valuing the stock for federal estate tax purposes (see Q 909), but instead are deductible under IRC Section 2053 as administration expenses (assuming the sale was necessary to administer the estate).[2] The Tax Court held that expenses of a secondary offering should not be allowed to reduce the value of the stock and at the same time be allowed as IRC Section 2053 expenses.[3] As for the underwriting discount, the Tax Court disallowed it as an IRC Section 2053 expense, viewing the transaction between the underwriter and the estate as simply a sale of stock from the estate to the underwriter.[4] The U.S. Court of Appeals for the Ninth Circuit has allowed the underwriting discount as an IRC Section 2053 expense when it has been allowed as an administration expense by the probate court and without regard to whether it has been considered in valuing the stock.[5] The Seventh Circuit appears generally in accord with the Ninth Circuit.[6] For a discussion of these cases and others, see *Rifkind v. U.S.*[7]

840. What deductions for casualty and theft losses may be taken from the gross estate?

Under IRC Section 2054, losses incurred during the period of administration from fire, storm, or other casualty, or from theft, are deductible to the extent not compensated by insurance or otherwise. Therefore, post-death events, such as destruction to estate assets from a

1. *Est. of Jenner v. Comm.*, 577 F.2d 1100, footnote 3 (7th Cir. 1978).
2. Rev. Rul. 83-30, 1983-1 CB 722.
3. *Est. of Joslyn v. Comm.*, 57 TC 722 (1972), rev'd 500 F.2d 382 (9th Cir. 1974).
4. *Est. of Joslyn*, above, 63 TC 478 (1975), on remand from the Ninth Circuit.
5. *Est. of Joslyn*, above, 566 F.2d 677 (9th Cir. 1977), rev'g 63 TC 478 (1975).
6. *Est. of Jenner v. Comm.*, 577 F.2d 1100 (7th Cir. 1978), rev'g TC Memo 1977-54.
7. 5 Cl. Ct. 362, 84-2 USTC ¶13577 (Cl. Ct. 1984).

storm, generate an estate tax deduction that can offset the date-of-death value of the property destroyed or damaged.

841. What deductions for charitable bequests are allowed from the gross estate in arriving at the taxable estate for federal estate tax purposes?

An estate tax deduction is allowed for the full amount of bequests to charity (but not in excess of the value of the transferred property required to be included in the gross estate). The deduction is not subject to percentage limitations such as are applicable to the charitable deduction under the income tax.

Specifically, IRC Section 2055 provides a deduction for bequests:

(1) to or for the use of the United States, any state, territory, any political subdivision thereof, or the District of Columbia, for exclusively public purposes;

(2) to or for the use of corporations organized and operated exclusively for religious, charitable, scientific, literary, or educational purposes, or to foster amateur sports competition, and the prevention of cruelty to children or animals (and which meet certain other conditions);

(3) to trustees, or fraternal societies, orders or associations operating under the lodge system, but only if the bequests are to be used exclusively for religious, charitable, scientific, literary, or educational purposes, or for the prevention of cruelty to children or animals (and if certain other conditions are met); and

(4) to or for the use of any veterans' organization incorporated by Act of Congress or to any of its components, so long as no part of the net earnings inures to the benefit of any private shareholder or individual.[1]

If any death taxes are, either by the terms of the will, by the law of the jurisdiction under which the estate is administered, or by the law of the jurisdiction imposing the particular tax, payable in whole or in part out of the bequests otherwise deductible as charitable contributions, then the amount deductible is the amount of such bequests reduced by the amount of such taxes.[2] Prior to the issuance of regulations discussed below, in a similar situation, it was held that the marital deduction (see Q 843) was reduced where administration expenses were paid from the marital share principal, but not where administration expenses were paid from income from the marital share.[3]

Regulations, effective for estates of decedents dying after December 3, 1999, now provide rules for reducing the charitable share by administration expenses depending on the type of expense: transmission expenses or management expenses.[4]

1. IRC Sec. 2055(a).
2. IRC Sec. 2055(c).
3. *Comm. v. Est. of Hubert*, 520 U.S. 93, 117 S.Ct. 1124, 97-1 USTC ¶60,261 (U.S. 1997).
4. Treas. Reg. §20.2055-3.

Transmission expenses are defined as expenses that would not have been incurred but for the decedent's death. Transmission expenses are also defined as any administration expense that is not a management expense. Transmission expenses paid from the charitable share reduce the charitable share.

Management expenses are defined as expenses related to investment, preservation, and maintenance of the assets during a reasonable period of estate administration. Management expenses attributable to the charitable share do not reduce the charitable share except to the extent that the expense is deducted under IRC Section 2053 as an administration expense. Management expenses which are paid by the charitable share, but which are not attributable to the charitable share, reduce the charitable share.

In *U.S. Trust Co. (Chisholm Est.) v. U.S.*,[1] the executors satisfied a charitable bequest by making the distribution out of estate income. The estate claimed and was allowed an estate tax deduction under IRC Section 2055 for the bequest. The estate could not claim an income tax charitable contributions deduction because the will did not specify that the bequest be paid out of estate income.[2] The estate claimed, but was not allowed, an income tax distribution deduction under IRC Section 661(a)(2) for the same distribution.

Property which is transferred to the charity by the exercise or nonexercise of a general power of appointment is considered transferred by the donee of the power rather than by the donor of the power. Or, to paraphrase, property includable in the decedent's gross estate under IRC Section 2041 (see Q 814) received by a charity is considered a bequest of such decedent.[3]

Distributions of trust income to charity pursuant to a beneficiary's power of appointment will qualify for a charitable contribution deduction.

An estate tax charitable deduction was denied for the transfer of a residuary interest in the estate to charity where the amount of the charitable deduction was not ascertainable at the time of death because of discretionary powers given to personal representatives to distribute the estate to other potential beneficiaries.[4] Also, in Technical Advice Memorandum (TAM) 9327006, an estate tax charitable deduction was denied where a trustee was given discretion to select donees from among various charities, and not all of the charities were on the IRS list of charities for which a charitable deduction is permitted.

The Tax Court denied an estate tax charitable deduction where the amount of the donation was not permanently set aside, and there was a possibility that expenses for litigation relating to the settlement of the estate could deplete the funds that would otherwise be donated. Unless, under the terms of the instrument and the facts of the case, the possibility that the amount would not be available to satisfy the donation was so remote as to be negligible, the amount could not be treated as having been permanently set aside so as to allow the deduction.[5] In the case before

1. 803 F.2d 1363, 86-2 USTC ¶13,698 (5th Cir. 1986), rev'g and remanding 617 F. Supp. 575, 85-2 USTC ¶13,642 (S.D. Miss. 1985).
2. IRC Sec. 642(c).
3. IRC Sec. 2055(b).
4. Let. Rul. 200906008. *Est. of Marine v. Comm.*, 990 F.2d 136, 93-1 USTC ¶60,131 (4th Cir. 1993).
5. Treas. Reg. §1.642(c)-2(d).

the Tax Court, the estate had already depleted a portion of its funds in settling estate-related litigation, supporting the finding that the possibility of further depletion was not so remote as to be negligible.[1]

Where an interest in property (other than a remainder interest in a personal residence or farm or an undivided portion of the decedent's entire interest in property) passes from the decedent to a charity and an interest in the same property passes (for less than adequate and full consideration in money or money's worth) from the decedent to a non-charity, no estate tax charitable contributions deduction is allowed for the interest going to the charity unless–

(a) in the case of a remainder interest, such interest is in a trust which is a *charitable remainder annuity trust* (see Q 8085) or a *charitable remainder unitrust* (see Q 8086) or a pooled income fund (see Q 8094), or

(b) in the case of any other interest, such interest is in the form of a guaranteed annuity or is a fixed percentage of the fair market value of the property that is distributed yearly (the fair market value is to be determined yearly).[2]

If the decedent has created a qualified charitable remainder trust in which his surviving spouse is the only noncharitable beneficiary other than certain ESOP remainder beneficiaries (see Q 843), the estate will receive a charitable contributions deduction for the value of the remainder interest. However, if the property in the trust is "qualified terminable interest property" and the surviving spouse's interest is a "qualifying income interest for life" (see Q 847), the charitable contributions deduction may be taken by the surviving spouse's estate upon her death, the decedent's estate having taken a marital deduction (assuming the executor's election) for the entire value of the property.[3]

Where a decedent left shares of stock to a charity but specified in his will that dividends from the stock during administration of the estate be paid to an individual, it was held that the estate tax charitable contributions deduction was not allowable.[4] However, in Letter Ruling 8506089, a decedent left the residue of his estate to a charity on the condition that the charity take on the obligation to pay an annuity equal to 7 percent of the value of the estate assets going to the charity to his brother for his lifetime. The Service ruled that because the annuity was payable out of the general assets of the charity rather than out of the assets in the decedent's estate going to the charity, the bequest was not a split interest gift in the same property; accordingly, a charitable contributions deduction was allowed equal to the amount by which the value of the property transferred by the decedent to the charity exceeded the present value of the annuity payable to the decedent's brother.

In *Oetting v. U.S.*,[5] a trust received assets from the residue of an estate that provided that the assets would be used first to provide life incomes of $100 per month for the lifetimes of

1. *Est. of Belmont v. Comm.*, 144 TC 84 (2015).
2. IRC Sec. 2055(e)(2).
3. Treas. Reg. §20.2044-1(b).
4. Rev. Rul. 83-45, 1983-1 CB 233.
5. 712 F.2d 358, 83-2 USTC ¶13,533 (8th Cir. 1983).

three elderly ladies, with the remainder paid to four qualified charities. Since the total assets received by the trust greatly exceeded expectations, the trustees petitioned the probate court for permission to buy annuities for the income beneficiaries with a fraction of the trust assets and to pay the balance immediately to the charities. The court agreed, so the trustees bought the annuities for $23,000 and paid the balance, $558,000, to the charities. The court allowed the estate a charitable contributions deduction for the amount paid to the charities, reasoning that since the amount going to the charities was certain, it was not a split interest in the same property for purposes of IRC Section 2055.

842. Can a trust that does not otherwise qualify for the estate tax charitable deduction be reformed in order to qualify?

In general, a trust can be reformed to qualify for the estate tax charitable deduction if the following occur:

(1) the difference in actuarial value of the qualified trust at time of death and its value at time of reformation is no greater than 5 percent of its value at time of reformation;

(2) the term of the trust is the same before and after reformation (however, if the term of years for a trust exceeds twenty years, the term can be shortened to twenty years);

(3) any changes are effective as of date of death;

(4) the charitable deduction would have been allowable at death if not for the split-interest rules (which generally require use of annuity, unitrust, and pooled income interests); and

(5) any payment to a noncharitable beneficiary before the remainder vests in possession must have been an annuity or unitrust interest (the lower of income or the unitrust amount, with make-up provisions, is permitted). This fifth provision does not apply if judicial proceedings are started to qualify the interests for the estate tax charitable deduction no later than ninety days after (a) the due date (including extensions) for filing the estate tax return, or (b) if no estate tax return is required, the due date (including extensions) for filing the income tax return for the first taxable year of the trust for which such a return must be filed.[1]

A reformation done solely to obtain a charitable deduction (in contrast to a reformation done pursuant to a will contest) must meet the requirements of IRC Section 2055(e)(3).[2] The amount of a charitable deduction taken with respect to property transferred to charity pursuant to a will contest cannot exceed the actuarial value of what the charity could have received under a will or through intestate succession.[3]

1. IRC Sec. 2055(e)(3).
2. *Est. of Burdick v. Comm.*, 979 F.2d 1369 (9th Cir. 1992).
3. *Terre Haute First Nat'l Bank v. U.S.*,134 NE 2d 1339 (1991), 67 AFTR 2d 1217, 91-1 USTC ¶60,070 (S.D. Ind. 1991).

843. What is the estate tax marital deduction?

The estate tax marital deduction is a deduction allowed from the gross estate for interests in property (including community property) which pass from the decedent to his (or her) surviving spouse and which are included in determining the value of the gross estate; the deduction is limited only by the value of such qualifying interests.[1] In general, a marital deduction is not available if the surviving spouse is not a United States citizen unless property passes to the surviving spouse in a qualified domestic trust (QDOT) (see Q 848).

The deduction is limited to the *net* value of qualifying property interests passing to the surviving spouse. Thus, the value of such interests must be reduced by federal and state death taxes payable out of those interests, by encumbrances on those interests, and by any obligation imposed by the decedent upon the surviving spouse with respect to the passing of such interests.[2] Prior to the issuance of regulations discussed below, the marital deduction was reduced where administration expenses were paid from the marital share principal, but not where administration expenses were paid from income from the marital share.[3]

Regulations, effective for estates of decedents dying after December 3, 1999, provide rules for reducing the marital share by administration expenses depending upon whether the expense is a transmission expense or management expense.[4]

Transmission expenses are defined as expenses that would not have been incurred but for the decedent's death. Transmission expenses are also defined by exclusion to include any administration expense that is not a management expense. Transmission expenses paid from the marital share reduce the marital share.

Management expenses are defined as expenses related to investment, preservation, and maintenance of the assets during a reasonable period of estate administration. Management expenses attributable to the marital share do not reduce the marital share except to the extent that the expense is deducted under IRC Section 2053 as an administration expense. Management expenses which are paid by the marital share but which are not attributable to the marital share reduce the marital share.

To qualify for the marital deduction, the property interest must be includable in the decedent's gross estate, and must "pass from" the decedent to his surviving spouse.[5] (A duty of consistency may require that property be includable in the surviving spouse's estate if a marital deduction was claimed in the first spouse's estate even if the marital deduction was improperly claimed in the first spouse's estate.)[6] It may come to the surviving spouse in any of the following ways: (1) by will; (2) under state inheritance laws; (3) by dower or curtesy (or statute in lieu of dower or curtesy); (4) by lifetime gift (made in such way as to cause inclusion

1. IRC Sec. 2056(a).
2. IRC Sec. 2056(b)(4); *Adee v. U.S.*, 83-2 USTC ¶13,534 (D. Kan. 1983).
3. *Comm. v. Est. of Hubert*, 520 U.S. 93, 97-1 USTC ¶60,261 (U.S. 1997).
4. Treas. Reg. §20-2056(b)-4.
5. IRC Sec. 2056(a).
6. *Est. of Letts v. Comm.*, 109 TC 290 (1997); TAM 200407018.

in the gross estate–see Q 814); (5) by right of survivorship in jointly owned property; (6) by power of appointment; (7) as proceeds of insurance on decedent's life; or (8) as survivor's interest in an annuity.[1]

844. What is qualified terminable interest property (QTIP)?

"Qualified terminable interest property" (QTIP) means property (1) which passes from the decedent, (2) in which the surviving spouse has a "qualifying income interest for life," and (3) as to which the executor makes an irrevocable election on the federal estate tax return to have the marital deduction apply. The surviving spouse has a "qualifying income interest for life" if (1) the surviving spouse is entitled to all the income from the property, payable annually or at more frequent intervals, and (2) no person has a power to appoint any part of the property to any person other than the surviving spouse unless the power is exercisable only at or after the death of the surviving spouse.[2] Apparently, the last requirement is violated even if it is the surviving spouse who is given the lifetime power to appoint to someone other than the surviving spouse.[3] The QTIP rules allow a decedent to provide for a surviving spouse, receive the marital deduction, and pass the remainder to beneficiaries the decedent selects in his will.

Certain "terminable interests" in property do not qualify for the marital deduction. The purpose of this rule is to ensure inclusion in the surviving spouse's estate of any property remaining in her estate at her death which escaped the initial tax in the predeceased spouse's estate.

A "terminable interest" in property is an interest which will terminate or fail on the lapse of time or on the occurrence or the failure to occur of some contingency. Life estates, terms for years, annuities, patents, and copyrights are therefore terminable interests.[4] Some terminable interests are deductible and some are nondeductible under the marital deduction law. In general, a "terminable interest" is nondeductible if (1) another interest in the same property passes (for less than an adequate consideration) from the decedent to someone other than his spouse or his spouse's estate, and (2) the other person may possess or enjoy any part of the property after the spouse's interest ends.[5]

845. Can a QTIP election be voided after it is made if it is unnecessary for transfer tax purposes?

Previously, the IRS provided procedures that would disregard (and treat as void) a qualified terminable interest property (QTIP) election (see Q 844) that was not necessary to reduce estate tax liability to zero following the death of the first-to-die spouse. The purpose of these procedures was to provide relief to a surviving spouse who would receive no benefit from the QTIP election, and to prevent unnecessary QTIP elections.[6]

1. IRC Sec. 2056(c).
2. IRC Sec. 2056(b)(7).
3. TAM 200234017.
4. IRC Sec. 2056(b); Treas. Reg. §20.2056(b)-1(b).
5. IRC Sec. 2056(b)(1).
6. Rev. Proc. 2001-38, 2001-24 IRB 1335.

In 2016, however, the IRS released guidance recognizing that, because the portability option (see Q 813) has been made permanent,[1] some estates might choose to elect QTIP treatment even when such treatment was unnecessary to reduce the estate tax liability to zero in order to maximize the surviving spouse's deceased spousal unused exclusion (DSUE). As a result, the IRS has determined that procedures to void a QTIP election may only be used if the estate did not elect portability, so that a QTIP election may still be valid if it was not necessary to reduce estate tax liability to zero.[2]

Pursuant to the new guidance, a QTIP election will be voided only if (1) the estate's federal estate tax liability was zero, regardless of the QTIP election, (2) the executor neither made, nor was considered to have made, a portability election and (3) certain procedural requirements have been satisfied. These procedural requirements include:

(1) Filing either (a) a supplemental Form 706 for the estate of the first-to-die spouse, (b) a Form 709 (Gift and GST tax return) or (c) a Form 706 for the estate of the surviving spouse;

(2) Providing notice at the top of the form filed under (1), above, that the QTIP election is within the scope of Revenue Procedure 2016-49, Section 3.01;

(3) Identifying the QTIP election that should be treated as void and providing an explanation of why it should be disregarded, including facts such as the value of the first-to-die spouse's estate without regard to the marital deduction for the QTIP, as compared to the applicable exclusion amount in effect for the year of that spouse's death (relevant facts to support the fact that a portability election was not made should also be included); and

(4) Providing evidence that the QTIP election meets the requirements of Revenue Procedure 2016-49 (discussed above) so that it qualifies to be disregarded (for example, the first-to-die spouse's estate tax return may provide evidence that the QTIP election was not required to reduce the estate tax liability to zero, and that portability was not elected).[3]

Once the QTIP election is voided, it is disregarded so that the underlying property will not be included in the estate of the surviving spouse and the surviving spouse will not be treated as though he or she has made a gift under IRC Section 2519 upon disposition of all or a part of the income interest. The surviving spouse will also not be treated as the transferor of the property for GST tax purposes.

1. IRC Sec. 2010(c)(5)(A), made permanent by PATH 2015.
2. Rev. Proc. 2016-49, 2016-42 IRB 462.
3. Rev. Proc. 2016-49, Section 4.02, above.

On the other hand, a QTIP election will be treated as valid where:

(1) A partial QTIP election was necessary to reduce the estate tax liability, but the executor made the QTIP election with respect to more property than was necessary to reduce the tax to zero;

(2) The QTIP election was set forth in a formula designed to reduce the estate tax liability to zero;

(3) The QTIP election was considered a protective election under Treasury Regulation Section 20.2056(b)-7(c);

(4) The executor made a portability election, even if the decedent's DSUE amount was zero; or

(5) The procedural requirements discussed above were not satisfied.

846. When will a terminable interest in property cause that property to fail to qualify for the estate tax marital deduction?

Generally speaking, a terminable interest is *deductible* if *no* interest in the property passes to someone other than the surviving spouse or her estate which may be possessed or enjoyed after the spouse's interest ends. Therefore, if the decedent transfers all interest in a straight life annuity, for instance, the interest will ordinarily qualify. There are two exceptions to this rule. Even though no one else takes an interest in the same property, a terminable interest will not qualify if (1) the decedent has *directed* the executor or trustee to acquire a terminable interest for the surviving spouse; or (2) an interest passing to the surviving spouse may be satisfied out of a group of assets which includes a nondeductible interest.[1]

Where spouses own property as joint tenants with right of survivorship or as tenants by the entirety, upon the death of one spouse, the surviving spouse succeeds to absolute ownership of the entire property. This succession occurs by virtue of the form of ownership, not by virtue of any will provision or intestate succession laws. Such succession qualifies for the marital deduction, but only, of course, to the extent the interest to which the surviving spouse succeeds was includable in the decedent's gross estate. (See Q 814.)

A terminable interest passing to a decedent's spouse may be a deductible interest even though an interest in the property may be enjoyed by someone else after the interest ends if the interest is as follows: (1) terminable only because of a survivorship clause; (2) the right to income for life with general power of appointment over the property producing the income; (3) consists of life insurance or annuity proceeds held by the insurer under an agreement that gives the spouse a life income interest in the proceeds plus a general power of appointment over the proceeds; (4) a "qualifying income interest for life" in "qualified terminable interest property" (see Q 844).

A survivorship clause will preserve the marital deduction if (1) the only condition under which the surviving spouse's interest will terminate is the death of the surviving spouse within

1. IRC Secs. 2056(b)(1)(C), 2056(b)(2).

six months after the decedent's death, or death as a result of a common disaster, and (2) the condition does not occur.[1]

The IRS permits a QTIP trust to be reformed to meet the requirements of the estate tax marital deduction.[2]

An income interest does not fail to qualify as a qualifying income interest for life merely because the income accumulated by the trust between the last date of distribution and the surviving spouse's death is not required to be either distributed to such spouse's estate or subject to a general power of appointment exercisable by such spouse.[3] However, any income from the property from the date the QTIP interest is created to the death of the spouse with the QTIP interest which has not been distributed before such spouse's death is included in such spouse's estate under IRC Section 2044 to the extent it is not included in the estate under any other IRC provision.[4]

In Technical Advice Memorandum (TAM) 9139001, the marital deduction was denied because (1) a son's right to purchase stock in a QTIP trust at book value was treated as the power to withdraw property from the trust (i.e., as a power to appoint property to someone other than the spouse), and (2) the spouse and the trustee lacked the right to make the closely held stock, in which the son held all voting rights, income productive. Similarly, a marital deduction was denied where the trustee could sell stock in a QTIP trust to a son at book value.[5] While TAM 9113009 had provided that a QTIP marital deduction would be denied if the non-QTIP portion of the estate were not funded with an amount equal to the face value of loans guaranteed by the decedent, it was withdrawn by TAM 9409018, which provided instead that the marital deduction would not be reduced by the entire unpaid balance of the guaranteed loans unless (1) at the time of death it would appear that a default after the marital deduction were funded would be likely, (2) that marital deduction property would be used to pay the entire unpaid balance of such loans, and (3) that subrogation rights held by the marital portion would appear to be worthless. According to TAM 9206001, a QTIP marital deduction was not available where the spouse was given an income interest in only certain types of property held in a trust and the trustee could change the mix of assets in the trust.

The IRS has conceded the validity of the contingent QTIP marital deduction (i.e., where the surviving spouse's qualifying income interest is contingent upon the QTIP election being made), if the QTIP election is made.[6]

The term "property" includes an interest in property, and a specific portion of property is treated as separate property.[7] However, a specific portion must be determined on a fractional

1. IRC Sec. 2056(b)(3).
2. Treas. Reg. §20.2044-1(d)(2).
3. Let. Rul. 200919003. Treas. Reg. §20.2056(b)-7(d)(4).
4. Treas. Reg. §20.2044-1(d)(2).
5. *Est. of Rinaldi v. U.S.*, 97-2 USTC ¶60,281 (Ct. Cl. 1997).
6. Treas. Reg. §§20-2056(b)-7(d)(3), 20-2056(b)-7(h)(Ex. 6).
7. IRC Sec. 2056(b)(7).

or percentage basis.[1] The term "property" also contemplates income-producing property. The deduction will thus be disallowed as to nonincome-producing property if under local law the spouse has no power to convert the property to income-producing property or to compel such conversion.[2]

A survivor annuity in which only the surviving spouse has a right to receive payments during such spouse's life is treated as a qualifying income interest for life unless otherwise elected on the decedent spouse's estate tax return.[3]

847. When will property held in trust qualify for the marital deduction?

There are five kinds of trusts that will qualify for the marital deduction: (1) the "qualified terminable interest property trust," (2) the "life estate with power of appointment trust," (3) the "estate trust," (4) the "special rule charitable remainder trust," and (5) the "qualified domestic trust." The first two and the fourth are specific exceptions to the nondeductible terminable interest rule; the third does not come under the rule; the fifth is the only form permitted if the surviving spouse is not a United States citizen (see Q 848).

If qualified terminable interest property (QTIP), as defined in Q 844, passes to the surviving spouse in trust, the trust is called a qualified terminable interest property trust (or QTIP trust). The surviving spouse must have a qualifying interest for life in the trust property. Neither the trustee nor anyone else may have the power to appoint any part of the trust property to anyone other than the surviving spouse during her lifetime, and the decedent's executor must make the election to have the trust qualify for the marital deduction.

An *estate trust* is a trust in which the property interest transferred from the decedent passes only to the surviving spouse (and the estate of the surviving spouse) and to no other person.

A *life estate with power of appointment trust* is a trust in which the property interest transferred from the decedent passes not only to the surviving spouse but to someone else (for less than an adequate consideration) who may possess or enjoy any part of the property after the spouse's interest ends. If such a trust is to avoid failing to qualify for the marital deduction by reason of being a nondeductible terminable interest, it must meet the requirements of IRC Section 2056(b)(5). In general, the surviving spouse must be given an income interest for life and the power to appoint the property to the surviving spouse or the surviving spouse's estate.

If the surviving spouse is the only noncharitable beneficiary (other than certain ESOP remainder beneficiaries) of a "qualified charitable remainder trust" created by the decedent, the spouse's interest is not considered a nondeductible terminable interest and the value of such interest will qualify for the marital deduction. A "qualified charitable remainder trust" means a charitable remainder annuity trust (see Q 8085) or a charitable remainder unitrust (see Q 8086).[4]

1. IRC Sec. 2056(b)(10).
2. Let. Ruls. 8304040, 8339018, 8745003.
3. IRC Sec. 2056(b)(7)(C).
4. IRC Sec. 2056(b)(8).

848. How is the availability of the estate tax marital deduction affected when the surviving spouse is not a United States citizen? What is a QDOT?

Generally, there are five kinds of trusts that will qualify for the marital deduction: (1) the "qualified terminable interest property trust," (2) the "life estate with power of appointment trust," (3) the "estate trust," (4) the "special rule charitable remainder trust," and (5) the "qualified domestic trust." The first two and the fourth are specific exceptions to the nondeductible terminable interest rule; the third does not come under the rule; the fifth is the only form permitted if the surviving spouse is not a United States citizen. See Q 847.

A marital deduction is usually not available for a transfer to a surviving spouse who is not a United States citizen unless the transfer is to a *qualified domestic trust (QDOT)* for which the executor has made an election.[1] A QDOT must qualify for the marital deduction under (1), (2), (3), or (4) (above), as well as meet the following requirements.

At least one trustee of the QDOT must be a United States citizen or a domestic corporation and no distribution (other than a distribution of income) may be made from the trust unless that trustee has the right to withhold any additional gift or estate tax imposed on the trust. Additional gift tax is due on any distribution while the surviving spouse is still alive (other than a distribution to the surviving spouse of income or on account of hardship). Additional estate tax is due on any property remaining in the QDOT at the death of the surviving spouse (or at the time the trust ceases to qualify as a QDOT, if earlier). The additional gift or estate tax is calculated as if any property subject to the tax had been included in the taxable estate of the first spouse to die.[2]

Regulations add additional requirements in order to ensure the collection of the deferred estate tax. If the fair market value (as finally determined for estate tax purposes, see Q 906, but determined without regard to any indebtedness with respect to the assets) of the assets passing to the QDOT exceeds $2,000,000, then the QDOT must provide that at least one of the following is true: (1) at least one U.S. trustee is a bank,[3] (2) at least one trustee is a U.S. branch of a foreign bank and another trustee is a U.S. trustee, or (3) the U.S. trustee furnish a bond or security or a line of credit equal to 65 percent of the fair market value of the QDOT corpus. The line of credit must be issued by (1) a U.S. bank, (2) a U.S. branch of a foreign bank, or (3) a foreign bank and confirmed by a U.S. bank.[4]

A QDOT with assets of less than $2,000,000 must either (a) meet one of the requirements for a trust exceeding $2,000,000, or (b) provide that (1) no more than 35 percent of the fair market value (determined annually on last day of trust's taxable year) of assets consists of real property located outside the U.S., and (2) all other QDOT assets be physically located within the U.S. at all times during the trust term. All QDOTs for the benefit of a surviving spouse are aggregated for purposes of the $2,000,000 threshold. A QDOT owning more than 20 percent of the voting stock or value in a corporation with fifteen or fewer shareholders (or 20 percent

1. IRC Sec. 2056(d).
2. IRC Sec. 2056A.
3. As defined in IRC Section 581.
4. Treas. Reg. §20.2056A-2(d)(1)(i)(C).

of the capital interest in a partnership with fifteen or fewer partners) is deemed to own a pro rata share of the assets of the corporation (or the pro rata share of the greater of the QDOT's interest in the capital or profits of the partnership) for purposes of the 35 percent foreign real property limitation. All interests in the corporation (or partnership) held by or for the benefit of the surviving spouse or the surviving spouse's family (includes brothers, sisters, ancestors, and lineal descendants) are treated as one person for purpose of determining the number of shareholders (or partners) and whether a 20 percent or more interest exists. However, the attribution rules do not apply in determining the QDOT's pro rata share of the corporation's (or partnership's) assets. Interests in other entities (such as another trust) are treated similarly to corporations (and partnerships).[1]

For purposes of the $2,000,000 QDOT threshold and the amount of a bond or letter of credit required, up to $600,000 in value attributable to the surviving spouse's personal residence and related furnishings held by the QDOT may be excluded. However, the personal residence exclusion does not apply for purposes of determining whether 35 percent of the fair market value of assets consists of real property located outside the U.S. A personal residence is either the principal residence of the surviving spouse or one other residence of the surviving spouse. A personal residence must be available for use by the surviving spouse at all times and may not be rented to another party. Related furnishings include furniture and commonly used items within the value associated with normal household use; rare artwork, valuable antiques, and automobiles are not included.

If a residence ceases to be used as the surviving spouse's personal residence or a residence is sold, the personal residence exclusion ceases to apply with regard to that residence. However, if part or all of the amount of the adjusted sales price of the residence is reinvested in a new personal residence within twelve months of the date of sale, the exclusion continues to the extent the adjusted sales price is reinvested in the new residence. Also, if a residence ceases to be used as the surviving spouse's personal residence or a residence is sold, the exclusion can be allocated to another personal residence of the surviving spouse that is held by a QDOT of the surviving spouse. In this instance, the exclusion can be up to $600,000 (less the amount previously allocated to a personal residence that continues to qualify for the exclusion).[2]

849. What estate tax deduction was available for qualified family-owned business interests before 2005?

For decedents dying before 2005, an estate tax deduction was available for up to $675,000 of qualified family-owned business interests.[3] If the deduction was taken, the unified credit equivalent (see Q 851) was changed to equal the lesser of (1) the regular unified credit equivalent, or (2) $1,300,000 minus the amount of the qualified family-owned business deduction. EGTRRA repealed the deduction for qualified family-owned business interests for tax years beginning between 2005 and 2012. Though the EGTRRA provisions were scheduled to sunset

1. Treas. Reg. §20.2056A-2(d)(1)(ii).
2. Treas. Reg. §20.2056A-2(d)(1)(iv).
3. IRC Sec. 2057.

(expire) after 2012, ATRA made its changes permanent for tax years beginning after 2012 by repealing the sunset provisions contained in EGTRRA.[1,2]

Despite the unavailability of this deduction, the unified credit was increased substantially for tax years beginning after 2004 (see Appendix D). ATRA also made the increased exemption level ($5.25 million in 2013, $5.34 million in 2014, $5.43 million in 2015, $5.45 million in 2016, $5.49 million in 2017, and $5.6 million in 2018) permanent for tax years beginning after 2012.[3] Under the 2017 tax reform legislation, the exemption was further expanded to $11.18 million in 2018, $11.4 million in 2019, and $11.58 million in 2020.

Pre-2005 Family-Owned Business Deduction

In order to qualify for the family-owned business deduction, at least 50 percent of the value of the adjusted gross estate must consist of the sum of (1) family-owned business interests included in the estate; and (2) certain gifts of family-owned business interests.[4] Gifts of family-owned business interests include family-owned business interests that the decedent gave to members of his or her family if the members of the decedent's family retained such interests until the decedent's death.[5] The family-owned business interest is not reduced by an IRC Section 303 redemption for purposes of making the initial determination of qualifying for the family-owned business deduction.[6]

For this purpose, the adjusted gross estate means the gross estate reduced by the estate tax deductions for claims against the estate and debts under IRC Sections 2053(a)(3) and 2053(a)(4), and increased by certain gifts. These gifts include (to the extent not otherwise includable in the estate): (1) family-owned business interests that the decedent gave to members of his or her family if the members of the decedent's family retained such interests until the decedent's death; (2) gifts to a spouse within ten years of the decedent's death (excluding those under (1)); and (3) gifts within three years of death (excluding annual exclusion gifts to family members and those under (1) or (2)).[7]

Family-owned means that either (1) 50 percent of the business must be owned by the decedent and members of his or her family; or (2) 30 percent of the business must be owned by the decedent and members of his or her family and (a) 70 percent of the business is owned by two families, or (b) 90 percent of the business is owned by three families.[8]

Family-owned business interests include only equity interests.[9] Also, family-owned business interests do not include (1) a business whose principal place of business is not in the United States;

1. American Taxpayer Relief Act of 2012, Pub. Law No. 112-240, Sec. 101.
2. IRC Secs. 2057(j), 2210, as added by EGTRRA 2001.
3. See Rev. Proc. 2013-15, 2013-5 IRB 444, Rev. Proc. 2013-35, 2013-47 IRB 537, Rev. Proc. 2014-61, 2014-47 IRB 860, Rev. Proc. 2015-53, Rev. Proc. 2016-55, Rev. Proc. 2017-58, Rev. Proc. 2018-57, Rev. Proc. 2019-44.
4. IRC Sec. 2057(b)(1)(C).
5. IRC Sec. 2057(b)(3).
6. Rev. Rul. 2003-61, 2003-24 IRB 1015.
7. IRC Sec. 2057(c).
8. IRC Sec. 2057(e)(1).
9. *Est. of Farnam v. Comm.*,583 F.3d 581, 2009-2 USTC ¶60,582 (8th Cir. 2009), aff'g 130 TC 34 (2008).

(2) any entity whose stock or debt is readily traded on an established securities or secondary market; (3) an entity, other than a bank or building and loan association, if more than 35 percent of the adjusted gross income of the entity for the year which includes the date of the decedent's death is personal holding company income; and (4) the portion of the business which consists of (a) cash or marketable securities in excess of reasonably expected day-to-day working capital needs, and (b) assets held for the production of personal holding company income or foreign personal holding company income.[1]

Personal holding company income generally includes dividends, interest, royalties, annuities, rents, personal property use by a shareholder, and personal service contracts.[2] However, personal holding company income does not include income from a net cash lease of property to another family member who uses the property in a way which would not cause income from the property to be treated as personal holding company income if the lessor had engaged directly in the activity of the lessee.[3]

Similar to the requirements for special use valuation, (1) for at least five of the eight years ending on the decedent's death, the business interests must have been owned by the decedent or members of his or her family, and the decedent or members of his or her family must have materially participated in the business,[4] and (2) for ten years after the decedent's death (or until the earlier death of the qualified heir), such business interests must be owned by qualified heirs, and qualified heirs must materially participate in the business.[5] Qualified heirs include members of the decedent's family, as well as any employee who has been an active employee of the business for at least ten years before the decedent's death.[6]

Additional tax, plus interest thereon, is due if the ownership or material participation requirements are not met after the decedent's death.[7] The additional tax is equal to the following percentage of the tax savings attributable to use of the family-owned business deduction, depending on when the failure to meet the requirements occurs.

Year	Recapture Percentage
1-6	100
7	80
8	60
9	40
10	20

1. IRC Sec. 2057(e)(2).
2. IRC Sec. 543(a).
3. IRC Sec. 2057(e)(2).
4. IRC Sec. 2057(b)(1)(D).
5. IRC Sec. 2057(f)(1).
6. IRC Sec. 2057(j)(1).
7. IRC Sec. 2057(f).

For this purpose, an IRC Section 303 redemption is not treated as a disposition of the family-owned business interest.[1]

850. What estate tax deduction is allowed for death taxes paid at the state level?

A deduction is available for federal estate tax purposes for estate, inheritance, legacy, or succession taxes (i.e., death taxes) paid to any state or the District of Columbia with respect to the estate of the decedent.[2] The deduction is available for tax years beginning in 2005 and thereafter. A credit for state death taxes (see Q 851) was available before 2005.

The deduction is available only for state death taxes actually paid and claimed as a deduction before the later of (1) four years after the filing of the federal estate tax return; (2) sixty days after a decision of the Tax Court with respect to a timely filed petition for redetermination of a deficiency; or (3) with respect to a timely filed claim for refund or credit of the federal estate tax, the later of (a) sixty days of the mailing of a notice of disallowance by the IRS, (b) sixty days after the decision of any court of competent jurisdiction on such claim, or (c) two years after the taxpayer files a notice of waiver of disallowance.

851. What credits are allowed against the federal estate tax?

After the tax is computed (see Q 811), some of the following credits, as may be applicable, may be taken against the tax to determine the tax actually payable:

(1) Unified credit (Q 852);[3]

(2) Credit for state death taxes before 2005 (Q 853);[4]

(3) Credit for gift tax (Q 854);[5]

(4) Credit for estate tax on prior transfers (Q 855);[6] and

(5) Foreign death tax credit (Q 856).[7]

852. What is the Section 2010 "unified credit" that is allowed against the federal estate tax?

The unified credit is a dollar amount allocated to each taxpayer that can be applied against the gift tax and the estate tax. The estate tax unified credit was equal to $2,125,800 in 2016, which translates into a tentative tax base (or unified credit exemption equivalent or applicable exclusion amount) of $5.45 million; in 2017, the credit was $2,141,800 ($5.49 million), in 2018,

1. Rev. Rul. 2003-61, 2003-24 IRB 1015.
2. IRC Sec. 2058, as added by EGTRRA 2001.
3. IRC Sec. 2010.
4. IRC Sec. 2011.
5. IRC Sec. 2012.
6. IRC Sec. 2013.
7. IRC Sec. 2014.

the credit is $4,419,800 ($11.18 million), $4,505,800 in 2019 ($11.4 million), and $4,577,800 in 2020 ($11.58 million).[1] See Appendix D for amounts in other years (and gift tax amounts).

Under EGTRRA 2001, no estate tax is imposed on an estate if the decedent died in 2010, but the beneficiaries are subject to a modified carryover basis. Therefore, 2010 TRA permitted estates to elect to be subject to the modified carryover basis rules and no estate tax or subject to an estate tax, with a step-up in basis, and a $5 million applicable exclusion amount.

The credit is reduced directly by 20 percent of the amount of lifetime gift tax exemption the decedent elected to use on any gifts made after September 8, 1976 (this $30,000 exemption was repealed by the Tax Reform Act of 1976 as to gifts made after 1976). The 20 percent reduction is made even though the value of the property to which the exemption applied is brought back into the estate for estate tax purposes. The reduction is not a deprivation of property under the due process clause of the U. S. Constitution.[2]

The credit is also reduced (but indirectly) by the amount of unified credit applied against any gift tax imposed on the decedent's post-1976 gifts. The indirect reduction is accomplished by adding to the taxable estate the amount of all taxable gifts made by the decedent after 1976, other than gifts includable in the gross estate, and then applying the estate tax rates to the sum (see Q 811).

853. What is the Section 2011 credit for state death taxes which can be taken against the federal estate tax?

For decedents dying before 2005, a credit was allowed against the federal estate tax for state death taxes–inheritance, legacy, estate and succession taxes–paid to any state of the United States or the District of Columbia with respect to property included in the gross estate (but see phaseout of credit, below).[3] The federal estate tax credit for state death taxes paid was not available where the property subject to state death taxes was not includable in the federal gross estate.[4] The credit is limited to the amount of state death taxes actually paid and does not include, for instance, the amount of any discount allowed by the state for prompt payment.

The credit is limited to specified percentages of the "adjusted taxable estate" in excess of $40,000 (see Appendix D). The "adjusted taxable estate" is the taxable estate reduced by $60,000. The maximum amount for which a credit can be taken was reduced by 25 percent in 2002, 50 percent in 2003, and 75 percent in 2004.[5] The credit was replaced by a deduction for state death taxes (see Q 837) in 2005.[6]

All states collect at least the maximum credit. Some states have enacted estate taxes exactly equal to the maximum credit. Some states refer to the maximum credit as it existed prior to the phaseout by EGTRRA 2001. States that impose an inheritance tax also have an "additional estate

1. The unified credit is calculated using the formula specified in IRC Section 2001(c).
2. *U.S. v. Hemme*, 476 U.S. 558, 86-1 USTC ¶13,671 (U.S. 1986); *Est. of Allgood v. Comm.*, TC Memo 1986-455.
3. IRC Sec. 2011.
4. *Est. of Owen v. Comm.*, 104 TC 498 (1995).
5. IRC Sec. 2011(b)(2), as added by EGTRRA 2001. See IRC Sec. 2011(b), Appendix D.
6. IRC Sec. 2011(g), as added by EGTRRA 2001.

tax" which is designed to absorb the difference between the inheritance tax and the maximum credit should the inheritance tax be less than the maximum credit. In most cases, however, the basic inheritance tax will exceed the maximum amount allowable as a credit.

854. What is the Section 2012 credit for gift tax that can be taken against the federal estate tax?

A credit is allowed for federal gift tax paid on property transferred by the decedent during life but included in the gross estate, *but only as to gifts made on or before December 31, 1976.*[1] The credit cannot exceed an amount which bears the same ratio to the estate tax imposed (after deducting the unified credit and the credit for state death taxes) as the value of the gift(s) (at time of gift or at time of death, whichever is lower) bears to the value of the gross estate minus charitable and marital deductions allowed.[2] In the case of (pre-1977) "split gifts" made by the decedent and his consenting spouse (see Q 895), the gift taxes paid with respect to both halves of the gift are eligible for the credit.[3]

The gift tax credit cannot be taken with respect to gifts made after December 31, 1976. However, in the computation of the estate tax, an adjustment is made for federal gift tax paid on post-1976 gifts not included in the donor-decedent's gross estate (see Q 811).

855. What is the Section 2013 credit for estate tax on prior transfers that can be taken against the federal estate tax?

Under IRC Section 2013, the federal estate tax otherwise payable by a decedent's estate is credited with all or a part of the amount of federal estate tax paid with respect to the transfer of property to the decedent (the transferee) by a person (the transferor) who died within ten years before, or within two years after, the decedent's death. The credit is designed, of course, to alleviate the impact of repeated estate taxation where successive deaths of the transferor and transferee occur within a relatively short time of each other.

The full amount of the credit is available if the transferor died within two years of the death of the decedent (either before or after). If the transferor predeceased the decedent by more than two years, the credit allowed is the following percentage of the full credit:

(1) 80 percent, if transferor died within the 3rd or 4th years preceding decedent's death;

(2) 60 percent, if transferor died within the 5th or 6th years preceding decedent's death;

(3) 40 percent, if transferor died within the 7th or 8th years preceding decedent's death; and

1. IRC Sec. 2012(e).
2. IRC Sec. 2012(a).
3. IRC Sec. 2012(c).

(4) 20 percent, if transferor died within the 9th or 10th years preceding decedent's death;

No credit is allowable if the transferee predeceased the transferor by more than ten years.[1]

The credit (before percentage reductions, if applicable) is the portion of the *transferor's* federal estate tax attributable to the value of the property transferred, *but limited to* the portion of the *transferee's* federal estate tax attributable to the value of the property transferred.[2]

When there are two or more transferor estates, the credit is computed separately for each transferor estate. But the *limitation* is computed concurrently, i.e., by aggregating the value of the property received from the transferor estates.[3] And each transfer meeting the requirements of IRC Section 2013 must be taken into account in computing the credit; no waiver of the credit with respect to any transfer that meets the requirements of IRC Section 2013 is permitted.[4] Also, the limitation must be apportioned among the transferors so that the credit and the limitation are computed separately for each transferor. Thus, as to each transferor, the potential credit will be the lesser of the estate tax attributable to the transferred property in the transferor's estate or that portion of the estate tax attributable to the transferred property in the decedent's estate. The lesser of the credit or the limitation is then multiplied by the applicable percentage (determined by when the transferor's death occurred relative to the time of the transferee's death, as described above) to determine the allowable credit.[5]

The prior transfer is not required to be traced into the decedent's gross estate. The credit is available even though the property was given away, consumed, or destroyed by the decedent during his life. Further, the term "property" includes any beneficial interest in property, including a general power of appointment (see Q 814).[6] The term includes also a life estate in property.[7]

The credit may be allowed against the present decedent's estate even though the prior decedent from whom he received the property was his spouse. However, the credit is allowed only with respect to property for which no marital deduction was allowed in the prior decedent's estate.[8]

856. What is the Section 2014 foreign death tax credit that can be taken against the federal estate tax?

A foreign death tax credit is provided for United States citizens and residents. The credit applies to property which is subject to both federal and foreign death taxes.[9] However, if there is a treaty with the foreign country levying a tax for which a credit is allowable, the executor may elect whether to rely on the IRC credit provisions or the treaty provisions.

1. IRC Sec. 2013(a).
2. IRC Secs. 2013(b), 2013(c)(1).
3. IRC Sec. 2013(c)(2).
4. Rev. Rul. 73-47, 1973-1 CB 397.
5. Treas. Reg. §20.2013-6, Example (2); *Est. of Meyer v. Comm.*, 83 TC 350 (1984), *aff'd 778 F2d 125*, 86-1 USTC ¶13,650 (2nd Cir. 1985).
6. IRC Sec. 2013(e).
7. Rev. Rul. 59-9, 1959-1 CB 232.
8. IRC Sec. 2013(d)(3).
9. IRC Sec. 2014.

857. What are the requirements for filing a federal estate tax return and paying the tax?

Except for extensions of time granted under conditions explained in Q 859, a federal estate tax return (Form 706), if required, must be filed, and the tax paid, by the executor within nine months after the decedent's death.[1] A six month extension for filing is available if requested prior to the due date and the estimated correct amount of tax is paid before the original due date.

The 2010 TRA provided that, for estates of decedents dying after December 31, 2009 and before December 17, 2010, the due date for filing an estate tax return, paying the estate tax, and making a disclaimer of an interest in property passing by reason of the decedent's death, is not earlier than the date which is nine months after December 17, 2010. However, an estate of a decedent who died in 2010 was permitted to file an election and not be subject to an estate tax, but instead be bound by the modified carryover basis rules under IRC Section 1022. An estate that made such election was required to file a Form 8939.[2]

The executor cannot escape responsibility for timely filing of an estate tax return or timely payment of the tax by delegating the responsibility to his attorney or accountant. Ignorance of the necessity to file a return or of the due date of the return is generally no excuse; the executor is required to exercise reasonable care in ascertaining these requirements. An exception to the general rule may exist if an attorney or accountant advised the executor no return was required to be filed.[3] However, the penalty for late filing[4] does not apply to an executor who by reason of his age, health, and lack of experience is incapable of meeting the criteria of ordinary business care and prudence required by the regulations.[5]

858. What are the minimum return requirements for determining whether an estate tax return must be filed?

Whether or not a return is required depends on the size of the gross estate (see Q 814), and possibly also on what kinds of gifts were made by the decedent during life. Generally, a return must be filed if the gross estate of a decedent who is a U.S. citizen or resident exceeds the estate tax unified credit equivalent ($5,000,000 for 2012-2017 and $10,000,000 for 2018-2025, as adjusted annually for inflation, the amount is $11.18 million in 2018, $11.4 million in 2019, and $11.58 million in 2020).[6] However, the exemption amount is reduced by the amount of *taxable* gifts (the value of the property given after subtracting allowable exclusions and deductions – see Q 882) made by the decedent after December 31, 1976, except gifts includable in the gross estate. Also, if the decedent made any gifts after September 8, 1976 and before January 1, 1977, the above amounts are further reduced by any amount allowed as a specific

1. IRC Secs. 6018(a), 6075(a), 6151(a).
2. See Notice 2011-66, 2011-35 IRB 184.
3. *U.S. v. Boyle*, 105 S. Ct. 687 (1985).
4. IRC Sec. 6151(a)(1).
5. *U.S. v. Boyle* (concurring opinion), above; *Brown v. U.S.*, 630 F. Supp. 57, 86-1 USTC ¶13,656 (M.D. Tenn. 1985).
6. Rev. Proc. 2013-35, 2013-47 IRB 537, Rev. Proc. 2018-18, Rev. Proc. 2018-57, Rev. Proc. 2019-44.

gift tax exemption (see Q 904) with respect to such gifts.[1] See Appendix D for the exemption amounts for earlier tax years.

859. Can the time for paying the estate tax be extended?

Yes.

The estate tax is due nine months after decedent's death, whether or not an extension of time for filing the return has been granted.[2] However, an extension of time for payment of any part of the tax shown on the return, not to exceed twelve months, may be granted by the district director or the director of a service center, at the request of the executor, if an examination of all the facts and circumstances discloses that such request is based upon reasonable cause.[3] In addition, the Service has been given authority to enter into written agreements to pay taxes in installments when the Service determines that such an agreement will facilitate the payment of taxes.[4] Interest must be paid on any extension (see "Extension of Time for Payment," below).

Extension of Time for Payment: Reasonable Cause (ten-year maximum)

The IRS may, for "reasonable cause," extend the time for payment of any part of the estate tax for a reasonable period not in excess of ten years from the date the tax is due under the general rule (nine months after decedent's death). This "reasonable cause" extension also applies to any part of any installment payment of the tax (and deficiency, if any, added to such installment) where an extension has been granted under the "closely held business interest" provisions (see Q 860).[5] Interest is compounded daily and charged on these reasonable cause extensions at an annual rate adjusted quarterly so as to be 3 percentage points over the short-term federal rate.[6] The underpayment rate for the fourth quarter of 2019 is 5 percent.[7]

860. Can the time for paying the estate tax be extended if the estate includes a closely held business interest?

Under IRC Section 6166, if the decedent's interest in a closely held business exceeds 35 percent of the *adjusted gross estate*, the portion of the federal estate tax (including the generation-skipping transfer tax if it is imposed on a direct skip transfer occurring as a result of decedent's death) attributable to that interest may be paid in annual installments (maximum of ten), and the executor may elect to delay the beginning of the installment payments up to five years.[8] The *adjusted gross estate* is the gross estate less deductions allowable under IRC Section 2053 and IRC Section 2054 (see Q 837).[9] In the case of a gift within three years of death (see Q 814), the requirement that the value of the business interest exceed 35 percent

1. IRC Sec. 6018(a).
2. IRC Sec. 6151(a).
3. IRC Sec. 6161(a)(1).
4. IRC Sec. 6159.
5. IRC Sec. 6161(a)(2).
6. IRC Secs. 6601(a), 6621(a)(2).
7. Rev. Rul. 2019-05.
8. IRC Sec. 6166(a).
9. IRC Sec. 6166(b)(6).

of the gross estate is met by the estate only if the estate meets the requirement both with and without the application of the bringback rule.[1]

Planning Point: Section 6166 is one of the only estate tax deferral options for estates. Depending on the circumstances, an estate may elect to borrow funds to pay the entire estate tax liability rather than take advantage of Section 6166 as the interest payments should be deductible for estate tax purposes.

For decedents dying prior to 1998, a special 4 percent interest rate applies to the portion of tax on which payment is deferred under IRC Section 6166. However, if such portion exceeds $345,800, reduced by the amount of unified credit allowable against the tax, the excess amount will bear interest at the regular underpayment rate (see Q 859).[2] In 1997, the maximum amount of deferred tax eligible for the 4 percent interest rate was $153,000.

For decedents dying after 1997, a special 2 percent interest rate applies to the portion of tax on which payment is deferred under IRC Section 6166. However, if such portion exceeds the amount of tax which would be calculated on the sum of $1,000,000 as indexed ($1,550,000 in 2019, $1,520,000 in 2018, $1,490,000 in 2017 and $1,480,000 in 2016)[3] plus the unified credit equivalent, reduced by the amount of the unified credit (see "IRC Section 2010, Unified Credit," in Q 851) allowable against the tax, the excess amount will bear interest at 55 percent of the regular underpayment rate (see above). The $1,000,000 amount is adjusted for inflation, rounded down to the next lowest multiple of $10,000, after 1998.[4] No deduction is permitted for estate or income tax purposes for the interest payable on such deferred tax.[5] In 2015, the maximum amount of deferred tax eligible for the 2 percent interest rate was $588,000. In 2016, the amount was $592,000, $596,000 in 2017, $608,000 in 2018, and $620,000 in 2019.[6] See Appendix D for amounts in other years.

If an election to defer taxes was made for a decedent dying before 1998, an irrevocable election could be made before 1999 to apply the lower interest rates (and the corresponding interest deduction disallowance) to payments due after the election was made (however, the 2 percent portion is equal to the amount which would be the 4 percent portion were it not for this election).[7]

For purposes of determining whether an estate qualifies for an IRC Section 6166 extension, the term "interest in a closely held business" means–

(A) an interest as a proprietor in a trade or business carried on as a proprietorship;

1. IRC Sec. 2035(c)(2).
2. IRC Sec. 6601(j), prior to amendment by TRA '97.
3. Rev. Proc. 2015-61, Rev. Proc. 2015-53, Rev. Proc. 2016-55, Rev. Proc. 2017-58, Rev. Proc. 2018-57.
4. IRC Sec. 6601(j).
5. IRC Secs. 163(k), 2053(c)(1)(D).
6. Rev. Proc. 2015-53, Rev. Proc. 2016-55, Rev. Proc. 2017-58, Rev. Proc. 2018-57.
7. TRA '97, Sec. 503(d)(2).

(B) an interest as a partner in a partnership carrying on a trade or business, if –

(i) 20 percent or more of the total capital interest in such partnership is included in determining the gross estate of the decedent, or

(ii) such partnership had forty-five (fifteen for decedents dying before 2002) or fewer partners; or

(C) stock in a corporation carrying on a trade or business if–

(i) 20 percent or more in value of the voting stock of such corporation is included in determining the gross estate of the decedent, or

(ii) such corporation had forty-five (fifteen for decedents dying before 2002) or fewer shareholders.[1]

For purposes of applying the foregoing rules, community property or property the income from which is community property and property held by two spouses as joint tenants, tenants by the entirety, or tenants in common is treated as though the property were owned by one shareholder or one partner, as the case may be. Also, property owned, directly or indirectly, by or for a corporation, partnership, estate, or trust is considered as being owned proportionately by or for its shareholders, partners, or beneficiaries. For purposes of the preceding sentence, a person is treated as a beneficiary of any trust only if he has a present interest in the trust. All stock and partnership interests owned by the decedent and his family are treated as owned by the decedent. The decedent's family for this purpose includes only his spouse, his ancestors, his lineal descendants, and his brothers and sisters.[2] As to any capital interest in a partnership or any nonreadily-tradable stock (i.e., stock for which at the time of decedent's death there was no market on a stock exchange or in an over-the-counter market) attributable to the decedent under the rules described in this paragraph, the value of such interest does not qualify for the five-year deferral or the special 2 percent or 4 percent interest rates.[3]

For purposes of IRC Section 6166, at the executor's election, the portion of the stock of any holding company which represents direct ownership (or indirect ownership through one or more other holding companies) by such company in a "business company" (i.e., a corporation carrying on a trade or business) is deemed to be stock in such business company. However, as to such holding company stock, the five-year delay and the 2 percent or 4 percent interest provisions (see above) will not apply.[4]

The value included in the computations necessary to determine if the estate qualifies for an IRC Section 6166 extension is the value determined for purposes of the estate tax.[5] Thus, in the case of a farm or other business as to which the executor elected special use

1. IRC Sec. 6166(b)(1).
2. IRC Sec. 6166(b)(2).
3. IRC Sec. 6166(b)(7).
4. IRC Sec. 6166(b)(8).
5. IRC Sec. 6166(b)(4).

valuation (see Q 906), the special use valuation is treated as the value of the property as to which it applies, for purposes of IRC Section 6166.[1]

Also, for purposes of such valuation, the value of passive assets held by the business is not includable. In general, the term "passive asset" includes any stock held in another corporation. However, holding company stock included in the executor's election, explained just above, is not considered a passive asset. Also, if a corporation owns 20 percent or more in value of the voting stock of another corporation, or such other corporation has forty-five (fifteen for decedents dying before 2002) or fewer stockholders, and 80 percent or more of the value of the assets of each such corporation is attributable to active assets, then such corporations are treated as one corporation. In other words, if the foregoing conditions are met, then for purposes of the passive asset rule, the corporation is not considered to hold stock in another corporation.[2]

For purposes of IRC Section 6166, interests in two or more closely held businesses, with respect to each of which there is included in determining the value of the decedent's gross estate 20 percent or more of the total value of each such business, are treated as an interest in a single closely held business. For purposes of this 20 percent requirement, an interest in a closely held business which represents the surviving spouse's interest in property held by the decedent and the surviving spouse as community property or as joint tenants, tenants by the entirety, or tenants in common is treated as having been included in determining the value of the decedent's gross estate.[3] However, an interest so attributed will not qualify for the five-year deferral or the special 2 percent or 4 percent interest rates.[4]

The IRS is permitted to require a bond or a lien to guarantee payment of future installments.[5] However, the IRS abuses its discretion by arbitrarily requiring a bond or lien in all cases to secure payment of estate tax deferred under IRC Section 6166.[6] The IRS will determine on a case by case basis whether security will be required when an estate elects to defer estate tax on a closely held business under IRC Section 6166.[7]

In general, if any payment of principal or interest is not paid when due, the whole of the unpaid portion of the tax payable in installments must be paid upon notice and demand from the district director. However, if the full amount of the delinquent payment (principal and all accrued interest) is paid within six months of the original due date, the remaining tax balance is not accelerated. Rather, the payment loses eligibility for the special interest rates (see above) and a penalty is imposed, equal to 5 percent per month based on the amount of the payment.[8]

1. House Report No. 94-1380, pages 32-33.
2. IRC Sec. 6166(b)(9).
3. IRC Sec. 6166(c).
4. IRC Sec. 6166(b)(7).
5. IRC Secs. 6166(k), 6165, 6324A.
6. *Est. of Roski v. Comm.*, 128 TC 113 (2007).
7. Notice 2007-90, 2007-46 IRB 1003.
8. IRC Sec. 6166(g)(3).

861. What is an interest in a closely held business for purposes of the IRC Section 6166 estate tax deferral?

The term "interest in a closely held business" means (with regard to a stockholder interest) "stock in a corporation carrying on a trade or business." "Business," for purposes of IRC Section 6166, according to the IRS, refers to a business such as manufacturing, mercantile or service enterprise, as distinguished from management of investment assets.[1] According to the IRS, the level of activity is the factor that distinguishes an "active business" from mere passive ownership and management of income producing assets. In several rulings since 1961, the Service has tried to make the distinction in various fact situations:

Revenue Ruling 61-55:[2] The ownership, exploration, development, and operation of oil and gas properties is a "trade or business" within the meaning of IRC Section 6166, but the mere ownership of royalty interests in oil properties is not.

Revenue Ruling 75-366:[3] Farms operated by tenant farmers under agreements that the decedent would pay 40 percent of the expenses and receive 40 percent of the crops, and in which the decedent had actively participated in the important management decisions, constitute an interest in a closely held business for purposes of IRC Section 6166.

Revenue Ruling 75-367:[4] A decedent's ownership of an electing small business corporation engaged in home construction on the decedent's land, a sole proprietorship that developed the land and sold the homes, and a business office and warehouse shared with the corporation, constitute an interest in a closely held business for purposes of IRC Section 6166.

Letter Ruling 8524037: Commercial rental property as to which the decedent maintained a business office, hired a janitor/maintenance man, plumber, carpenter, electrician, contracted out larger jobs, ordered and supervised work done by employees, qualifies as an interest in a closely held business for purposes of IRC Section 6166.

Letter Ruling 8529026: Commercial warehouse, as to which the decedent owned the land on which it stood and negotiated leases with the tenants; carried out routine inspections of the property to determine necessary maintenance; carried out all maintenance and repair work; hired others to carry out additional maintenance; dealt with bankruptcy proceedings of two tenants and with subsequent lawsuits over a sublease; negotiated with tenants, attorneys, architects, and contractors with respect to modifications to the warehouse to suit tenants' needs; maintained an office in his home from which he performed all bookkeeping, paid monthly expenses, and maintained all correspondence concerning the warehouse; decedent's sons helped him with all aspects of the warehouse business. Held that the decedent's activity was not sufficient to qualify as an interest in a closely held business for purposes of IRC Section 6166.

---

1. Let. Ruls. 8352086, 8451014, 8524037, 8529026, 8942018, 9621007.
2. 1961-1 CB 713.
3. 1975-2 CB 472.
4. 1975-2 CB 472.

Technical Advice Memorandum (TAM) 8601005: Interest in a general partnership leasing ranchland on a net-lease basis to a limited partnership actively engaged in ranching and in which the decedent was a limited partner. The Service said the land was not held simply as a passive income producing investment, but rather was used as an integral part of the trade or business of ranching. Accordingly, it was held that the decedent's interest in the general partnership was an interest in the business enterprise and not simply a passive investment.

Revenue Ruling 2006-34[1] provides that, for purposes of determining whether a decedent's interest in real estate is an interest in an asset used in an active trade or business, the Service will consider all facts and circumstances, including the activities of agents and employees, the activities of management companies or other third parties, and the decedent's ownership interest in any management company or other third party. The Service will consider the following nonexclusive list of factors (no single factor is dispositive):

- The amount of time the decedent devoted to the trade or business;
- Whether an office was maintained from which the activities of the decedent were conducted or coordinated, and whether the decedent maintained regular business hours for that purpose;
- The extent to which the decedent was actively involved in finding new tenants and negotiating and executing leases;
- The extent to which the decedent provided landscaping, grounds care, or other services beyond the mere furnishing of leased premises;
- The extent to which the decedent personally made, arranged for, performed, or supervised repairs and maintenance to the property; and
- The extent to which the decedent handled tenant repair requests and complaints;

For purposes of this list of factors, the term decedent generally includes agents and employees of the decedent, partnership, LLC, or corporation.

862. Are there any circumstances that would cause the termination of the estate tax deferral for estates including a closely held business interest?

The IRC Section 6166 election terminates and the whole of the unpaid portion of the tax payable in installments becomes due and is payable upon notice and demand from the district director if (1) any portion of the business interest is distributed, sold, exchanged, or otherwise disposed of, or money and other property attributable to such an interest is withdrawn from the business, and (2) the aggregate of such distributions, sales, exchanges, or other dispositions and withdrawals equals or exceeds 50 percent of the value of such interest.[2]

1. 2006-26 IRB 1171, Let. Rul. 200842012.
2. IRC Sec. 6166(g)(1)(A).

A sale of business assets by the estate to satisfy unpaid mortgages encumbering the business property is not considered a disposition for purposes of the IRC Section 6166 election; however, to the extent proceeds from such a sale exceed the amount used to satisfy the mortgages, the transaction is considered a disposition.[1]

Distributions in redemption of stock under IRC Section 303 (distributions in redemption of stock held by a decedent at death in an amount not in excess of death taxes and settlement costs under special income tax rules that treat the redemption as a capital transaction rather than as a dividend) are not counted as withdrawals or as disposals of decedent's interest in the business if an amount equal to any such distribution is paid in estate tax on or before the due date of the first installment of tax due after the distribution, or, if earlier, within one year after the distribution. However, an IRC Section 303 redemption does reduce the value of the business (as of the applicable valuation date) by the amount redeemed, for purposes of determining whether other withdrawals, distributions, sales, exchanges, or disposals meet the applicable 50 percent test.[2]

863. Can the time for paying the estate tax be extended if the estate includes a reversionary or remainder interest?

If the gross estate includes a reversionary or remainder interest, the executor may elect to postpone payment of the portion of the tax attributable to that interest until six months after termination of the precedent interest in the property. Notice of the election to exercise postponement, together with supporting documents and information, must be filed with the district director before the due date for payment of the tax. The IRS may, for "reasonable cause," extend payment of the tax postponed because of the reversionary or remainder interest for up to an additional three years beyond the postponement period referred to above.[3]

Generation-Skipping Transfer Tax

864. What is the federal generation-skipping transfer tax?

The federal generation-skipping transfer (GST) tax is a tax on the right to transfer property to a skip person (a person two or more generations (see Q 877) younger than the transferor).[4] The GST tax was repealed for one year in 2010 but, while the GST tax was technically zero for 2010, it was reinstated thereafter. For 2011 and 2012, the maximum GST tax rate was 35 percent. ATRA increased this maximum GST tax rate to 40 percent and made the provision permanent.[5]

TRA 2010 unified the estate, gift and GST tax lifetime exemption amounts and increased the exemption to $5 million for 2010-2011. This $5 million base amount is adjusted annually for inflation and increased to $5.12 million for 2012. The $5 million lifetime exemption was scheduled to sunset (expire) after 2012, but ATRA repealed the sunset provisions to maintain the current exemption amount and permanently unify the estate, gift and GST taxes. The 2017 Tax Act doubled the base amount for 2018-2025. The exemption level was adjusted for

1. Let. Rul. 8441029.
2. IRC Sec. 6166(g)(1)(B).
3. IRC Sec. 6163.
4. IRC Sec. 2601.
5. American Taxpayer Relief Act of 2012, Pub. Law No. 112-240.

inflation to $5.45 million in 2016, $5.49 million in 2017, and jumped to $11.18 million in 2018, $11.4 million for 2019, and $11.58 million for 2020 (see Appendix D for earlier years) under the new tax legislation.[1]

Depending on the transfer, a generation-skipping transfer is reported on either a gift tax return or an estate tax return. The person required to file the return (Q 880) and pay the tax (Q 881) also depends on the type of transfer.

Generation-skipping transfers (Q 865) include direct skips, taxable terminations, and taxable distributions. Taxable terminations and taxable distributions apply to certain terminations of interests in trusts or distributions from trusts. Two spouses can elect to have all generation-skipping transfers made by either spouse during the year treated as made one-half by each spouse (Q 878).

Value is generally the value of the taxable amount at the time of the transfer (Q 866).

A couple of exclusions are available from GST tax. In 2019-2020, a $15,000 annual exclusion (up from $14,000 in 2013-2017) is available for certain present interest gifts on a per donor/donee basis.[2] An unlimited exclusion is available for qualified transfers for educational and medical purposes. See Q 866.

As discussed above, a $10,000,000 ($11.18 million in 2018, $11.4 million in 2019, and $11.58 million in 2020, see Appendix D for earlier years) GST exemption is available to each transferor.[3] Great flexibility is available to allocate or not allocate GST exemption to transfers. An inclusion ratio is derived from allocations of GST exemption to, in effect, determine the amount subject to GST tax. See Q 866.

Planning Point: Taxpayers should consider whether a "by-pass trust" or a trust that contains assets that will be excluded from a surviving spouse's estate is a viable option to maximize the estate tax and GST exemptions.

Again, tax is imposed on generation-skipping transfers. The tax rate (40 percent for tax years beginning after 2012 and 35 percent in 2011 and 2012, see Appendix D) is a flat rate equal to the top estate tax rate. The tax is calculated by multiplying the tax rate by the inclusion ratio and then multiplying this figure by the amount of the generation skipping transfer (Q 866).

865. What is a generation-skipping transfer (GST) on which a generation-skipping transfer tax is imposed?

A generation skipping transfer is a transfer to a person two or more generations younger than the transferor (called a "skip person," see Q 877 regarding generation assignments), and can take any one of three forms: (1) a taxable distribution; (2) a taxable termination; and (3) a direct skip. A trust is also a skip person if the trust can benefit only persons two or more generations

1. Rev. Proc. 2015-53, Rev. Proc. 2016-55, Pub. Law No. 115-97 (the 2017 Tax Act), Rev. Proc. 2018-18, Rev. Proc. 2018-57, Rev. Proc. 2019-44.
2. Pub. Law No. 115-97, Rev. Proc. 2018-18, Rev. Proc. 2018-57, Rev. Proc. 2019-44.
3. Rev. Proc. 2018-57, Rev. Proc. 2019-44.

younger than the transferor.[1] The GST tax was zero percent for one year in 2010 with a top 35 percent rate in 2011 and 2012.[2] ATRA increased the maximum GST tax rate to 40 percent for tax years beginning after 2012.[3]

Transferor

A "transferor," in the case of any property subject to the federal estate tax, is the decedent. In the case of any property subject to the federal gift tax, the transferor is the donor.[4] Thus, to the extent that a lapse of a general power of appointment (including a right of withdrawal) is subject to gift or estate tax, the powerholder becomes the transferor with respect to such lapsed amount.[5] Thus, a *Crummey* powerholder should not be treated as a transferor with respect to the lapse of a withdrawal power if the amount lapsing in any year is no greater than (1) $5,000, or (2) 5 percent of the assets out of which exercise of the power could be satisfied.[6]

If there is a generation-skipping transfer of any property and immediately after the transfer such property is held in trust, a different rule (the "multiple skip" rule) applies to subsequent transfers from that trust. In such case, the trust is treated as if the transferor (for purposes of subsequent transfers) were assigned to the first generation above the highest generation of any person having an "interest" (see below) in the trust immediately after the transfer.[7] If no person holds an interest immediately after the GST, then the transferor is assigned to the first generation above the highest generation of any person in existence at the time of the GST who may subsequently hold an interest in the trust.[8]

For the effect of making a "reverse QTIP election," see Q 866.

Direct Skip

A direct skip is a transfer subject to federal gift or estate tax to a skip person. However, with respect to transfers before 1998, such a transfer was not a direct skip if the transfer was to a grandchild of the transferor or of the transferor's spouse or former spouse, and the grandchild's parent who was the lineal descendant of the transferor or his spouse or former spouse was dead at the time of the transfer. In other words, a person could be stepped-up in generations because a parent who had been in the line of descent predeceased such person. This rule could be reapplied to lineal descendants below that of a grandchild. Persons assigned to a generation under this rule were also assigned to such generation when such persons received transfers from the portion of a trust attributable to property to which the step-up in generation rule applied.[9] For purposes of this predeceased child rule, a living descendant who died no later than ninety days after a transferor was treated as predeceasing the transferor if he or she was treated as predeceased

1. IRC Secs. 2611(a), 2613.
2. IRC Sec. 2664.
3. American Taxpayer Relief Act of 2012, Pub. Law No. 112-240, Sec. 101.
4. IRC Sec. 2652(a)(1).
5. Treas. Reg. §26.2652-1(a).
6. Let. Rul. 9541029.
7. IRC Sec. 2653(a).
8. Treas. Reg. §26.2653-1.
9. IRC Sec. 2612(c)(2), prior to amendment by TRA '97.

under the governing instrument or state law.[1] For a discussion of the more expansive predeceased parent rule after 1997, see Q 877.

In some circumstances, whether a step-up in generation was available could depend on whether a QTIP or a reverse QTIP marital election was made for GSTT purposes (see Q 866). If the parent of a grandchild-distributee died after the transfer by a grandparent to a generation-skipping trust, but before the distribution from the trust to the grandchild, and a reverse QTIP election had been made, the distribution was a taxable termination and the "step-up in generation" rule was not available. However, if the reverse QTIP election had not been made, the distribution was eligible for the "step-up in generation" exception from treatment as a direct skip and was not subject to GSTT.[2]

Also, for purposes of the GST tax, the term "direct skip" did not include any transfer before January 1, 1990 from a transferor to a grandchild of the transferor to the extent that the aggregate transfers from such transferor to such grandchild did not exceed $2 million. This $2 million exemption was available with respect to a transfer in trust only if (1) during the life of such individual no portion of the trust corpus or income could be distributed to or for the benefit of any other person, (2) the trust would be included in such individual's estate if such individual were to die before the trust terminated, and (3) all of the income of the trust had to be distributed at least annually to the grandchild once he reached twenty-one. Requirement (3) applied only to transfers after June 10, 1987. However, the Committee Report indicated that this requirement was not satisfied by a *Crummey* demand power.[3]

The $2 million per grandchild exemption applied to transfers to grandchildren only; the step-up in generation rule for a predeceased parent did not apply. A transfer which would have been a direct skip were it not for the $2 million exemption was likewise exempted from being treated as a taxable termination or taxable distribution. However, the rules which apply to the taxation of multiple skips will apply to subsequent transfers from such trust.

Taxable Termination

A taxable termination occurs when an "interest in property" (see below) held in trust (or some arrangement having substantially the same effect as a trust) for a skip person is terminated by an individual's death, lapse of time, release of a power, or otherwise, unless either (1) a non-skip person has an interest in the trust immediately after such termination, or (2) at no time after the termination may a distribution be made from the trust to a skip person, other than a distribution the probability of which occurring is so remote as to be negligible (i.e., less than a 5 percent actuarial probability). If upon the termination of an interest in a trust by reason of the death of a lineal descendant of the transferor, a portion of the trust is distributed to skip persons (or to trusts for such persons), such partial termination is treated as taxable. If a transfer

1. Treas. Reg. §26.2612-1(a)(2)(i).
2. Rev. Rul. 92-26, 1992-2 CB 314.
3. TRA '86, Sec. 1433(b)(3), as amended by TAMRA '88, Sec. 1014(h)(3).

subject to estate or gift tax occurs at the time of the termination, the transfer is not a taxable termination (but it may be a direct skip).[1]

Taxable Distribution

A taxable distribution is any distribution from a trust to a skip person (other than a taxable termination or a direct skip).[2]

Generation-Skipping Transfer Exceptions

However, the following are not considered generation-skipping transfers:

(1) Any transfer which, if made during life by an individual, would be a "qualified transfer" (see Q 895); and

(2) Any transfer to the extent (a) the property transferred was subject to a prior GST tax, (b) the transferee in the prior transfer was in the same generation as the current transferee or a younger generation, and (c) the transfers do not have the effect of avoiding the GST tax.[3]

Interest in Property

A person has an "interest in property" held in trust if (at the time the determination is made) such person–

(1) has a present right to receive income or corpus from the trust (for example, a life income interest);

(2) is a permissible current recipient of income or corpus from the trust (for example, a beneficiary entitled to distribution of income or corpus, but only in the discretion of the trustee) and is not a charitable organization (specifically, one described in IRC Section 2055(a)); or

(3) is such a charitable organization and the trust is a charitable remainder annuity trust (see Q 8085), a charitable remainder unitrust (see Q 8086), or a pooled income fund (see Q 8094).

In determining whether a person has an interest in a trust, the fact that income or corpus may be used to satisfy a support obligation is disregarded if such use is discretionary or made pursuant to the Uniform Gifts to Minors Act (or similar state statute). In other words, a parent is not treated as having an interest in a trust merely because the parent acts as guardian for a child. However, a parent would be treated as having an interest in the trust if support obligations are mandatory.[4]

1. IRC Sec. 2612(a); Treas. Reg. §26.2612-1(b).
2. IRC Sec. 2612(b).
3. IRC Sec. 2611(b).
4. IRC Sec. 2652(c)(3).

An interest may be disregarded if it is used *primarily* to postpone or avoid the GST tax.[1] The regulations provide that an interest is disregarded if *a significant purpose* for the creation of the interest is the postponement or avoidance of the GST tax.[2]

Effective Date and Transitional Rules

The rules explained here and in the succeeding questions apply generally to any generation-skipping transfer (GST) made after October 22, 1986. Also, any lifetime transfer after September 25, 1985, and on or before October 22, 1986, is treated as if made on October 23, 1986. These rules will not, however, apply to the following:

(1) Any GST under a trust that was irrevocable on September 25, 1985, but only to the extent that such transfer is not made out of corpus (or income attributable to such corpus) added to the trust after September 25, 1985;

(2) Any GST under a will or revocable trust executed before October 22, 1986, if the decedent died before January 1, 1987; and

(3) Any GST–

(a) under a trust to the extent such trust consists of property included in the gross estate of a decedent (other than property transferred by the decedent during his life after October 22, 1986), or reinvestments thereof, or

(b) which is a direct skip that occurs by reason of the death of any decedent;

but only if such decedent was, on October 22, 1986, under a mental disability to change the disposition of his property and did not regain his competence to dispose of such property before the date of his death.[3] It appears that Congress does not intend for the third grandfathering rule to apply with respect to property transferred after August 3, 1990 to an incompetent person, or to a trust of such a person.[4]

866. How is the amount of tax on a GST determined?

The amount of tax is the "taxable amount" (based on the kind of GST involved–see Q 865) multiplied by the "applicable rate."[5] The applicable rate of tax applied to the taxable amount is itself a product. It is a product of the maximum federal estate tax rate in effect at the time of the GST (35 percent in 2011 and 2012 and 40 percent for tax years beginning after 2012. See Appendix D for earlier years) and the "inclusion ratio" with respect to the transfer.[6] The inclusion

1. IRC Sec. 2652(c)(2).
2. Treas. Reg. §26.2612-1(e)(2)(ii).
3. TRA '86, Sec. 1433(a), (b), as amended by TAMRA '88, Sec. 1014(h)(2).
4. OBRA '90, Sec. 11703(c)(3).
5. IRC Sec. 2602.
6. IRC Sec. 2641.

ratio, in turn, depends on allocations of the "GST exemption (Q 867)."[1] The GST tax was zero percent for one year in 2010.[2]

Taxable Amount

In the case of a taxable distribution, the taxable amount is the value of the property received by the transferee reduced by any expense incurred by the transferee with respect to the GST tax imposed on the distribution. If any portion of the GST tax with respect to a taxable distribution is paid out of the trust, the taxable distribution is increased by such an amount.[3]

In the case of a taxable termination, the taxable amount is the value of all property with respect to which the taxable termination has occurred, reduced by the expenses, similar to those allowed as a deduction under IRC Section 2053 in determining the taxable estate for estate tax purposes (see Q 838), with respect to which the taxable termination has occurred.[4]

In the case of a direct skip, the taxable amount is the value of the property received by the transferee.[5] Where a life estate was given to a skip person and a remainder interest was given to a non-skip person, the value of the entire property (and not just the actuarial value of the life estate) was subject to GST tax.[6]

867. What is the GST exemption and how is it applied in determining the GST tax?

For purposes of determining the inclusion ratio, every individual is allowed a GST exemption of $5 million (the $5 million base figure is adjusted annually for inflation. The amount is $11.58 million in 2020, $11.4 million in 2019, $11.18 million in 2018 ($5.49 million in 2017 and $5.45 million in 2016; for other years, see Appendix D).[7] An individual (or his executor) may irrevocably allocate the GST exemption to any property with respect to which he is the transferor.

In 2004 to 2009, the GST exemption was equal to the estate tax unified credit equivalent (applicable exclusion amount) rather than to $5 million, as indexed (see Appendix D). Any indexing increase in the GST exemption is available for all generation-skipping transfers occurring in the year of the increase and subsequent years in which the GST exemption is equal to $5 million, as indexed, up to the year of the decedent's death.[8]

The GST tax was repealed (zero percent) for one year in 2010. The Tax Relief Act of 2010 revived the GST tax and included a $5 million GST exemption that was scheduled to last for two years, 2011 and 2012, with indexing for 2012 (to $5.12 million). ATRA made

1. IRC Sec. 2642.
2. IRC Sec. 2664; EGTRRA 2001 Sec. 901.
3. IRC Sec. 2621.
4. IRC Sec. 2622.
5. IRC Sec. 2623.
6. TAM 9105006.
7. Rev. Proc. 2013-15, 2013-5 IRB 444, Rev. Proc. 2013-35, 2013-47 IRB 537, Rev. Proc. 2014-61, 2014-47 IRB 860, Rev. Proc. 2015-53, Rev. Proc. 2016-55, Rev. Proc. 2018-57, Rev. Proc. 2019-44.
8. IRC. Sec. 2631, as amended by EGTRRA 2001.

the $5 million (as indexed) GST exemption permanent for tax years beginning after 2012. The 2017 Tax Act increased the GST exemption amount to a $10 million base amount, which is indexed for inflation). This expanded exemption will apply from 2018-2025 absent Congressional action to prevent its expiration.[1]

In general, an individual or the individual's executor may allocate the GST exemption at any time from the date of the transfer until the time for filing the individual's federal estate tax return (including extensions actually granted), regardless of whether a return is required (see Q 857).[2]

The GST exemption is automatically allocated to lifetime direct skips unless otherwise elected on a timely filed federal gift tax return (see Q 905).[3]

In addition, any unused GST exemption is automatically allocated to indirect skips to a GST trust (see Q 868), effective 2001 to 2009 and after 2010.[4] An indirect skip is a transfer (other than a direct skip) to a GST trust that is subject to gift tax. A transferor can elect to have the automatic allocation not apply to (1) an indirect skip, or (2) to any or all transfers made by the individual to a particular trust. The transferor can also elect to treat a trust as a GST trust with respect to any or all transfers made by the individual to the trust. Nevertheless, an allocation still cannot be made until the end of any estate tax inclusion period (see below).

Regulations generally permit elections to allocate or not allocate GST exemption to individual transfers or to all current or future transfers to a trust, or any combination of these. An election with regard to all transfers to a trust can later be revoked with respect to future transfers to the trust. The regulations also permit elections with regard to individual transfers to a trust even where an election is in place with regard to all transfers to a trust.[5]

Planning Point: Grantors should make elections to allocate or not allocate GST exemption with respect to all transfers to a particular trust. GST exemption can be allocated to trusts benefiting skip persons; while allocations are not made to trusts benefiting non-skip persons.

A retroactive allocation of the GST exemption can be made when certain non-skip beneficiaries of a trust predecease the transferor, effective 2001 to 2009. The non-skip beneficiary must (1) have an interest or a future interest (for this purpose, a future interest means that the trust may permit income or corpus to be paid to such person on a date or dates in the future) in the trust to which any transfer has been made, (2) be a lineal descendant of a grandparent of the transferor, or of a grandparent of the transferor's spouse or former spouse, (3) be assigned to a generation lower than that of the transferor, and (4) predecease the transferor. In such a case, an allocation of the transferor's unused GST exemption (determined immediately before the non-skip person's death) can be made to any previous transfer or transfers to the trust (value of transfer is its gift tax value at the time of the transfer) on a chronological order. The allocation

1. Pub. Law No. 115-97.
2. IRC Sec. 2632.
3. IRC Sec. 2632(b).
4. IRC Sec. 2632(c), as added by EGTRRA 2001.
5. Treas. Reg. §26.2632-1.

is made by the transferor on the gift tax return for the year of the non-skip person's death. The allocation is treated as effective immediately before the non-skip person's death.[1]

> *Example.* Grandparent creates a trust for the primary benefit of Child, with Grandchild as contingent remainder beneficiary. Grandparent doesn't expect Grandchild will receive anything, or that the trust will be generation-skipping; so he doesn't allocate GST exemption to the trust. (Or, perhaps, allocation of the GST exemption was simply overlooked.) Child dies unexpectedly before Grandparent. There is a GST taxable termination at Child's death. Grandparent can make a retroactive allocation of GST exemption to the trust to reduce or eliminate the GST tax on the taxable termination.

With regard to lifetime transfers other than a direct skip, an allocation is made on the federal gift tax return. An allocation can use a formula (e.g., the amount necessary to produce an inclusion ratio of zero). An allocation on a timely filed gift tax return is generally effective as of the date of the transfer. An allocation on an untimely filed gift tax return is generally effective as of the date the return is filed and is deemed to precede any taxable event occurring on such date. (For certain retroactive allocations, see above.) An allocation of the GST exemption is irrevocable after the due date. However, an allocation of GST exemption to a trust (other than a charitable lead annuity trust, see Q 871) is void to the extent the amount allocated exceeds the amount needed to produce an inclusion ratio of zero (see Q 869).[2]

An executor can make an allocation of the transferor's unused GST exemption on the transferor's federal estate tax return. An allocation with respect to property included in the transferor's estate is effective as of the date of death. A late allocation of the GST with respect to a lifetime transfer can be made by the executor on the estate tax return and is effective as of the date the allocation is filed. A decedent's unused GST exemption is automatically and irrevocably allocated on the due date for the federal estate tax return to the extent not otherwise allocated by the executor. The automatic allocation is made to nonexempt property: first to direct skips occurring at death, and then to trusts with potential taxable distributions or taxable terminations.[3]

868. What is a GST trust?

A GST trust is a trust that could have a generation-skipping transfer with respect to the transferor unless:

1. The trust provides that more than 25 percent of the trust corpus must be distributed to, or may be withdrawn by, one or more individuals who are non-skip persons, either (a) before the individual's forty-sixth birthday, (b) on or before a date prior to such birthday, or (c) upon the occurrence of an event that may reasonably be expected to occur before such birthday.

2. The trust provides that more than 25 percent of the trust corpus must be distributed to, or may be withdrawn by, one or more individuals who are non-skip persons and who are living on the date of death of an individual identified in the trust (by name or class) who is more than ten years older than such individual(s).

1. IRC Sec. 2632(d), as added by EGTRRA 2001.
2. Treas. Reg. §26.2632-1(b).
3. IRC Sec. 2632(e), as redesignated by EGTRRA 2001, Treas. Reg. §26.2632-1(d).

3. The trust provides that, if one or more individuals who are non-skip persons die before a date or event described in (1) or (2), more than 25 percent of the trust corpus must either (a) be distributed to the estate(s) of one or more of such individuals, or (b) be subject to a general power of appointment exercisable by one or more of such individuals.

4. Any portion of the trust would be included in the gross estate of a non-skip person (other than the transferor) if such person died immediately after the transfer.

5. The trust is a charitable lead annuity trust (CLAT), charitable remainder annuity trust (CRAT), charitable remainder unitrust (CRUT), or a charitable lead unitrust (CLUT) with a non-skip remainder person.

For purposes of these GST trust rules, the value of transferred property is not treated as includable in the gross estate of a non-skip person nor subject to a power of withdrawal if the withdrawal right does not exceed the amount of the gift tax annual exclusion ($15,000 in 2018-2020; $14,000 in 2013 through 2017) with respect to the transfer.[1] It is also assumed that a power of appointment held by a non-skip person will not be exercised.

869. What is the inclusion ratio and how is it used for purposes of the GST tax?

In general, the inclusion ratio with respect to any property transferred in a GST is the excess of one minus (a) the "applicable fraction" for the trust from which the transfer is made, or (b) in the case of a direct skip, the applicable fraction determined for the skip.[2]

The "applicable fraction" is a fraction (a) the numerator of which is the amount of the GST exemption allocated to the trust (or to the property transferred, if a direct skip), and (b) the denominator of which is the value of the property transferred reduced by (i) the sum of any federal estate or state death tax actually recovered from the trust attributable to such property, (ii) any federal gift tax or estate tax charitable deduction allowed with respect to such property, and (iii) with respect to a direct skip, the portion that is a nontaxable gift (see below). The fraction should be rounded to the nearest one-thousandth, with five rounded up (i.e., .2345 is rounded to .235). If the denominator of the applicable fraction is zero, the inclusion ratio is zero.[3]

Example 1. For illustrative purposes, in the year 2019, G transfers irrevocably in trust for his grandchildren $20 million and allocates all his $11,400,000 GST exemption to the transfer. The applicable fraction is 11,400,000/20,000,000, or .57. The inclusion ratio is 1 minus .57, or .43. The maximum estate tax rate, 40 percent, is applied against the inclusion ratio, .43. The resulting percentage, 17.2 percent, is applied against the value of the property transferred, $20,000,000, to produce a GST tax of $3,440,000. The tax is paid by G, the transferor, because this is a direct skip (other than a direct skip from a trust) (see Q 865).

Example 2. Same facts as in preceding example, except that for federal gift tax purposes G's spouse consented to a split gift of the $20 million (see Q 878). Thus, for GST tax purposes as well, the gift is considered split between the spouses and the entire gift is sheltered from estate tax by their combined $22.8 million

1. Rev. Proc. 2015-53, Rev. Proc. 2016-55, Rev. Proc. 2017-58, Rev. Proc. 2019-44.
2. Sec. 2642(a)(1).
3. IRC Sec. 2642(a)(2), Treas. Reg. §26.2642-1.

exemption. If tax were owed, it would be paid 1/2 each by G and G's spouse, the transferors, because each gift is a direct skip (other than a direct skip from a trust) (see Q 865).

Example 3. In 2019, G transfers $100,000 to a trust and allocates $100,000 GST exemption to the trust. The trust has an inclusion ratio of zero, and taxable distributions and taxable terminations can be made free of GST tax.

Example 4. In 2019, G transfers $100,000 to a trust and allocates no GST exemption to the trust. If all the trust beneficiaries are grandchildren of G, G has made a direct skip fully subject to GST tax. The GST tax is $40,000 ($100,000 transfer × 40 percent GST tax rate) and is payable by G. If the trust beneficiaries are children and grandchildren of G, the trust has an inclusion ratio of one, and GST transfers are fully subject to tax at the GST tax rate at the time of any later transfer.

If there is more than one transfer in trust the applicable fraction must be recomputed at the time of each transfer. Thus, if property is transferred to a preexisting trust, the "recomputed applicable fraction" is determined as follows: The numerator of such fraction is the sum of (1) the amount of the GST exemption allocated to the property involved in such transfer and (2) the nontax portion of the trust immediately before the transfer. (The nontax portion of the trust is the value of the trust immediately before the transfer multiplied by the applicable fraction in effect before such transfer.) The denominator of such fraction is the value of the trust immediately after the transfer reduced by (i) the sum of any federal estate or state death tax actually recovered from the trust attributable to such property, (ii) any federal gift tax or estate tax charitable deduction allowed with respect to such property, and (iii) with respect to a direct skip, the portion that is a nontaxable gift (see below).[1]

Example 5. In the year 1995, G transfers irrevocably in trust for his children and grandchildren $4 million and allocates all his $1 million GST exemption to the transfer. The applicable fraction is 1,000,000/4,000,000, or .250. The inclusion ratio is 1 minus .250, or .750.

In 2001, the trust makes a taxable distribution to the grandchildren of $100,000. The maximum estate tax rate, 55 percent in 2001, is applied against the inclusion ratio, .750. The resulting percentage, 41.25 percent, is multiplied by the $100,000 transfer, resulting in a GST tax of $41,250. GST taxes in this example are paid by the grandchildren, the transferees, because the transfers are taxable distributions (see Q 881).

In 2019, the trust makes a taxable distribution to the grandchildren of $100,000. The maximum estate tax rate, 40 percent, is applied against the inclusion ratio, .750. The resulting percentage, 30 percent, is multiplied by the $100,000 transfer, resulting in a GST tax of $30,000.

Later in 2019, when the trust property has grown to $6 million, G transfers an additional $15 million to the trust. An additional $10,400,000 of GST exemption is available to G in 2019 ($11,400,000 GST exemption in 2019 minus $1,000,000 exemption already used). The numerator of the recomputed fraction is the value of the nontax portion of the trust immediately before the transfer, or $5.25 million (value of the trust, $21 million, multiplied by the applicable fraction of .250), plus $10,400,000 additional exemption, or $16,650,000. The denominator of the recomputed fraction is $21 million (the sum of the transferred property, $15 million, and the value of all the property in the trust immediately before the transfer, $6 million). The applicable fraction is 16,650,000/21,000,000, or .793. The inclusion ratio is 1 minus .793, or .207.

Later in 2019, the trust makes a taxable distribution to the grandchildren of $100,000. The maximum estate tax rate, (40 percent), is applied against the inclusion ratio, .207. The resulting percentage, 8.28 percent, is multiplied by the $100,000 transfer, resulting in a GST tax of $8,280.

1. IRC Sec. 2642(d)(2), Treas. Reg. §26.2642-4.

Planning Point: Trusts are usually created with an inclusion ratio of either one (GST transfers, if any, with respect to trust are fully taxable) or zero (fully exempt from GST tax). A trust has an inclusion ratio of zero if GST exemption is allocated to any transfer to the trust that is not a non-taxable gift (an allocation of GST exemption is not needed for a direct skip nontaxable gift (see below); it has an inclusion ratio of zero). For information on severing a trust to create separate trusts with inclusion ratios of zero and one, see Q 873.

870. How is property valued for purposes of the GST tax?

"Value" of the property is its value at the time of the transfer. In the case of a direct skip of property that is included in the transferor's gross estate, the value of the property is its estate tax value. In the case of a taxable termination with respect to a trust occurring at the same time as and as a result of the death of an individual, an election may be made to value at the alternate valuation date (see Q 907). In any case, the value of the property may be reduced by any consideration given by the transferee.[1]

For purposes of determining the GST inclusion ratio, certain other valuation rules may apply in some instances. For purposes of determining the denominator of the applicable fraction (see above), the value of property transferred during life is its fair market value as of the effective date of the GST exemption allocation (see Q 869). However, with respect to late allocations of the GST exemption to a trust, the transferor may elect (solely for purpose of determining the fair market value of trust assets) to treat the allocation as made on the first day of the month in which the allocation is made. This election is not effective with respect to a life insurance policy, or a trust holding a life insurance policy, if the insured individual has died. For purposes of determining the denominator of the applicable fraction, the value of property included in the decedent's gross estate is its value for estate tax purposes. However, special use valuation (see Q 758) is not available unless the recapture agreement under IRC Section 2032A specifically refers to the GST tax. There are special rules in the regulations concerning the allocation of post-death appreciation or depreciation with respect to pecuniary payments and residuary payments made after a pecuniary payment.[2]

871. Are charitable lead annuity trusts treated differently than other types of trusts for GST tax purposes?

With respect to property transferred after October 13, 1987, the GST tax exemption inclusion ratio for any charitable lead annuity trust (see Q 8102) is to be determined by dividing the amount of exemption allocated to the trust by the value of the property in the trust following the charitable term. For this purpose, the exemption allocated to the trust is increased by interest determined at the interest rate used in determining the amount of the estate or gift tax charitable deduction with respect to such a trust over the charitable term. With respect to a late allocation of the GST exemption (see Q 870), interest accrues only from the date of the late allocation. The amount of GST exemption allocated to the trust is not reduced even though

1. IRC Sec. 2624.
2. IRC Sec. 2642(b)(2)(A), Treas. Reg. §26.2642-2.

it is determined at a later time that a lesser amount of GST exemption would have produced a zero inclusion ratio.[1]

872. What is the estate tax inclusion period (ETIP) for GST tax purposes?

With respect to inter vivos transfers subject at some point in time to the GST tax, the allocation of any portion of the GST tax exemption to such a transfer is postponed until the earlier of (a) the expiration of the period (not to extend beyond the transferor's death) during which the property being transferred would be included in the transferor's estate (other than by reason of the gifts within three years of death rule of IRC Section 2035) if he died, or (b) the GST. For purposes of determining the inclusion ratio with respect to such exemption, the value of such property is: (a) its estate tax value if it is included in the transferor's estate (other than by reason of the three year rule of IRC Section 2035), or (b) its value determined at the end of the ETIP. However, if the allocation of the exemption under the second valuation method is not made on a timely filed gift tax return for the year in which the ETIP ends, determination of value is postponed until such allocation is filed.[2]

> *Example.* Grantor sets up an irrevocable trust: income retained for ten years, then life estate for children, followed by remainder to grandchildren. The valuation of property for purpose of the inclusion rule is delayed until the earlier of the expiration of the ten-year period or the transferor's death. If the grantor were to die during such time the property would be included in the grantor's estate under IRC Section 2036(a) (see Q 814). However, if the grantor survived the ten-year period and failed to make an allocation of the exemption on a timely filed gift tax return, the determination of value is postponed until the earlier of the time an allocation is filed or death.

Except as provided in regulations, for purpose of the GST tax exemption allocation rules, any reference to an individual or a transferor is generally treated as including the spouse of such individual or transferor.[3] Thus, an ETIP includes the period during which, if death occurred, the property being transferred would be included in the estate (other than by reason of the gifts within three years of death rule of IRC Section 2035) of the transferor or the spouse of the transferor. The property is not considered as includable in the estate of the transferor or the spouse of the transferor if the possibility of inclusion is so remote as to be negligible (i.e., less than a 5 percent actuarial probability). The property is not considered as includable in the estate of the spouse of the transferor by reason of a withdrawal power limited to the greater of $5,000 or 5 percent of the trust corpus if the withdrawal power terminates no later than sixty days after the transfer to trust. Apparently, the ETIP rules do not apply if a reverse QTIP election (see Q 875) is made. The ETIP terminates on the earlier of (1) the death of the transferor; (2) the time at which no portion would be includable in the transferor's estate (other than by reason of IRC Section 2035) or, in the case of the spouse who consents to a split-gift, the time at which no portion would be includable in the other spouse's estate; (3) the time of the GST (but only with respect to property involved in the GST); or (4) in the case of an ETIP arising because of an interest or power held by the transferor's spouse, at the earlier of (a) the death of

1. IRC Sec. 2642(e), Treas. Reg. §26.2642-3.
2. IRC Sec. 2642(f).
3. IRC Sec. 2642(f)(4).

the spouse, or (b) the time at which no portion would be includable in the spouse's estate (other than by reason of IRC Section 2035).[1]

> *Example.* Grantor sets up an irrevocable trust: income retained for the shorter of nine years or life, remainder to grandchild. Grantor and spouse elect to split the gift. If spouse dies during trust term, spouse's executor can allocate GST exemption to spouse's deemed one-half of the trust. However, the allocation is not effective until the earlier of the expiration of grantor's income interest or grantor's death.

The regulations provide that the election out of automatic allocation of GST exemption for either a direct skip or an indirect skip can be made at any time up until the due date for filing the gift tax return for the year the ETIP ends. If the transfer subject to an ETIP occurred in an earlier year, the election must specify the particular transfer. An affirmative allocation of GST exemption cannot be revoked after the due date for filing the gift tax return for the year the affirmative election is made (or after the allocation is made in the case of a late allocation), even where actual allocation is not effective until the end of an ETIP.[2]

873. When are portions of a severed trust treated as separate trusts for GST tax purposes?

In general, portions of a trust are not to be treated as separate trusts. However, portions attributable to different transferors, substantially separate and independent shares of different beneficiaries of a trust, and trusts treated as separate trusts under state law are to be treated as separate trusts for GST tax purposes.[3] However, treatment of a single trust as separate shares for purposes of the GST tax does not permit treatment as separate trusts for purposes of filing or payment of tax, or for purposes of any other tax. Additions to, or distributions from, such a trust are allocated pro-rata among all shares unless expressly provided otherwise. In general, a separate share is not treated as such unless it exists at all times from and after creation of the trust.

Trusts created from a qualified severance are treated as separate trusts for GST tax purposes, effective for 2001 to 2009 and for tax years beginning after 2010. A qualified severance means the division of a single trust into two or more trusts under the trust document or state law if (1) the single trust is divided on a fractional basis, and (2) in the aggregate, the terms of the new trusts provide for the same succession of interests of beneficiaries as are provided in the original trust. In the case of a trust with a GST inclusion ratio of greater than zero and less than one (i.e., the trust is partially protected from the GST by allocations of the GST exemption), a severance is a qualified severance only if the single trust is divided into two trusts, one of which receives a fractional amount equal to the GST applicable fraction multiplied by the single trust's assets. The trust receiving the fractional amount receives an inclusion ratio of zero (i.e., it is not subject to GST tax), and the other trust receives an inclusion ratio of one (i.e., it is fully subject to GST tax).[4]

Otherwise, severance of a trust included in the taxable estate (or created in the transferor's will) into single shares will be recognized for GST purposes if (1) the trusts are severed pursuant

1. Treas. Reg. §26.2632-1(c).
2. Treas. Reg. §26.2632-1.
3. IRC Sec. 2654(b).
4. IRC Sec. 2642(a), as added by EGTRRA 2001.

to the governing instrument or state law, (2) such severance occurs (or a reformation proceeding is begun and is indicated on the estate tax return) prior to the date for filing the estate tax return (including extensions actually granted), and (3) the trusts are funded using (a) fractional interests or (b) pecuniary amounts for which appropriate adjustments are made.[1]

Regulations provide that a qualified severance must be done on a fractional or percentage basis; a severance based on a specific pecuniary amount is not permitted. The terms of the new trusts must provide in the aggregate for the same succession of beneficiaries. With respect to trusts from which discretionary distributions may be made on a non pro rata basis, this requirement can be satisfied even if each permissible beneficiary might be a beneficiary of only one of the separate trusts, but only if no beneficial interest is shifted to a lower generation and the time for vesting of any beneficial interest is not extended.[2]

The regulations provide that the separate trusts must be funded with property from the severed trust with either a pro rata portion of each asset or on a non pro rata basis. If funded on a non pro rata basis, the separate trusts must be funded by applying the appropriate severance fraction or percentage to the fair market value of all the property on the date of severance. The date of severance is either the date selected by the trustee or a court-imposed date of funding. The funding of the separate trusts must commence immediately, and occur within a reasonable period of time (not more than ninety days) after the date of severance.

A qualified severance is deemed to occur before a taxable termination or a taxable distribution that occurs by reason of the qualified severance. For example, a trust provides for trust income to be paid annually to grantor's child (C) and grandchild (GC) for ten years, remainder to C and GC or their descendants. If either dies during the trust term, income is payable to that person's then-living descendants. The inclusion ratio for the trust is .50. The trust is severed into one trust for C and C's descendants and one for GC and GC's descendants. The trustee designates the trust for C as having an inclusion ratio of one, and the trust for GC as having an inclusion ratio of zero. The severance causes either a taxable termination of C's interest in, or a taxable distribution to, GC's trust (which is a skip person). However, the severance is deemed to occur before the GST and GC's trust has an inclusion ratio of zero; therefore, there is no GST tax due.[3]

A trust that is partly grandfathered from GST tax can be severed into a grandfathered and a nongrandfathered trust under these rules.

Regulations provide that, for purpose of funding the separate trusts, assets must be valued without taking into consideration any discount or premium arising from the severance.[4] For example, if the severance creates a minority interest when the separate trust receives less than the interest owned by the original trust, such a minority discount is disregarded for funding purposes.

1. Treas. Reg. §26.2654-1.
2. Treas. Reg. §26.2642-6.
3. Treas. Reg. §26.2642-6(j), Ex. 8.
4. Treas. Reg. §26.2642-6(d)(4).

Regulations provide that, with respect to a qualified severance of a trust with an inclusion ratio that is greater than zero and less than one, one or more resulting trusts must be funded with an amount equal to the GST applicable fraction (used to determine the GST inclusion ratio for the original trust immediately before the severance) times the value of the original trust on the date of severance. Each such resulting trust receives an inclusion ratio of zero. All other resulting trusts receive an inclusion ratio of one. If two or more trusts receive an amount equal to the applicable fraction of the original trust, the trustee can select which of the resulting trusts has an inclusion ratio of zero, and which has the inclusion ratio of one. For example, if the original trust has an applicable percentage of .50 and the trust is severed into two trusts, the trustee can select which of the two resulting trusts has an inclusion ratio of zero, and which has an inclusion ratio of one.[1]

Regulations also provide that, where a trust is severed and the severance is not qualified, the resulting trusts each receive an inclusion ratio equal to the inclusion ratio of the original trust.[2]

Further, as provided in the regulations, for purposes of the requirements that a separate share is not treated as such unless it exists at all times from and after creation of the trust, a trust is treated as created on the date of death of the grantor if the trust is fully includable in the gross estate of the grantor for estate tax purposes. Also, if the trust document requires the mandatory severance of a trust upon the occurrence of an event (not within the discretion of any person), the resulting trusts will be treated as separate trusts for GST tax purposes. The resulting trusts each receive an inclusion ratio equal to the inclusion ratio of the original trust.[3]

Planning Point: The advantage of having portions or shares of a trust treated as separate trusts is that the transferor can decide whether or not to allocate a portion of his GST tax exemption to each separate trust and the trustee can make distributions from the separate trusts in a way that minimizes GST tax.

874. How is the GST tax applied to nontaxable gifts?

In the case of any direct skip which is a nontaxable gift, the inclusion ratio is zero. For this purpose, a nontaxable gift means any transfer of property to the extent the transfer is not treated as a taxable gift by reason of the gift tax annual exclusion (taking into account the split gift provision for married couples–see Q 895) or the "qualified transfer" exclusion (see Q 895). In other words, there is no GST tax imposed on direct skip gifts that come within the gift tax annual exclusion or that are "qualified transfers." However, with respect to transfers after March 31, 1988, a nontaxable gift which is a direct skip to a trust for the benefit of an individual has an inclusion ratio of zero only if (1) during the life of such individual no portion of the trust corpus or income may be distributed to or for the benefit of any other person, and (2) the trust would be included in such individual's estate if the trust did not terminate before such individual died.[4]

1. Treas. Reg. §26.2642-6(d)(7).
2. Treas. Reg. §26.2642-6(h).
3. Treas. Reg. §26.2654-1(a).
4. IRC Sec. 2642(c).

875. What is a reverse QTIP election and how is it made for GST tax purposes?

A qualified terminable interest property (QTIP) election can be made to qualify property for the estate tax (see Q 837) and gift tax (see Q 902) marital deductions. A reverse QTIP election may be made for such property under the GST tax. The effect of making the reverse QTIP election is to have the decedent or the donor treated as the transferor (see Q 865) for GST tax purposes. If a reverse QTIP election is made for property in a trust, the election must be made for all of the property in the trust. However, the Committee Report states that if the executor indicates on the federal estate tax return that separate trusts will be created, such trusts will be treated as separate trusts. In other words, separate trusts can be created so that the QTIP and reverse QTIP election can be made for different amounts, and thus minimize all transfer taxes.[1] See regarding Q 873 for more information on the creation of separate shares from a single trust.

Example. For example (based on a $5 million exemption) decedent (who has made $500,000 of taxable gifts protected by the unified credit) with a $10,000,000 estate leaves $4,500,000 in a credit shelter trust and $5,500,000 to his surviving spouse in a QTIP trust, reducing his estate tax to zero. (Assume each trust would be subject to GST tax to the extent that the $5,000,000 exemption is not allocated to such trust.) The executor allocates $4,500,000 of the decedent's $5,000,000 GST tax exemption to the credit shelter trust and makes a reverse QTIP election as to $500,000 of the QTIP property so that the decedent's full $5,000,000 exemption can be used. The surviving spouse's $5,000,000 exemption amount may then be used to protect the remaining $5,000,000 of property, and the entire $10,000,000 has escaped GST tax (assuming separate QTIP trusts of $4,500,000 and $500,000 are created).

876. How are basis adjustments treated for GST tax purposes?

Where the basis of property subject to the GST tax is increased (or decreased) to fair market value because property transferred in a taxable termination occurs at the same time and as a result of the death of an individual, any increase (or decrease) in basis is limited by multiplying such increase (or decrease) by the inclusion ratio used in allocating the GST exemption.[2]

877. How are individuals assigned to generations for purposes of the GST tax?

An individual (and his spouse or former spouse) who is a lineal descendant of a grandparent of the transferor (or the transferor's spouse) is assigned to that generation which results from comparing the number of generations between the grandparent and such individual with the number of generations between the grandparent and the transferor (or the transferor's spouse). A relationship by legal adoption is treated as a relationship by blood, and a relationship by the half-blood is treated as a relationship of the whole blood.[3]

A person who could be assigned to more than one generation is assigned to the youngest generation. However, regulations provide that adopted individuals will be treated as one generation younger than the adoptive parent where: (1) a transfer is made to the adopted individual from the adoptive parent, the spouse or former spouse of the adoptive parent, or a lineal descendant

1. IRC Sec. 2652(a)(3). See Let. Ruls. 9133016, 9002014.
2. IRC Sec. 2654(a)(2).
3. IRC Secs. 2651(a), 2651(b), 2651(c).

of a grandparent of the adoptive parent; (2) the adopted individual is a descendant of the adoptive parent (or the spouse or former spouse of the adoptive parent); (3) the adopted individual is under age 18 at the time of adoption; and (4) the adoption is not primarily for the purpose of avoiding GST tax.[1]

However, with respect to terminations, distributions, and transfers occurring after 1997, where an individual's parent is dead at the time of a transfer subject to gift or estate tax upon which the individual's interest is established or derived, such individual will be treated as being one generation below the lower of (1) the transferor's generation, or (2) the generation of the youngest living ancestor of the individual who is also a descendant of the parents of the transferor or the transferor's spouse (or former spouse). This predeceased parent rule applies to collateral relatives (e.g., nieces and nephews) only if there are no living lineal descendants of the transferor at the time of the transfer.[2] For a narrower predeceased parent rule that applied to direct skips before 1998, see Q 865.

Regulations make clear that if the generation-skipping property is subject to gift tax or estate tax on more than one occasion, the time for determining application of the predeceased parent rule is on the first of such occasions. In the case of a qualified terminable interest property (QTIP) marital deduction election, the time for determining application of the predeceased parent rule can essentially wait until the surviving spouse dies or makes a gift of the QTIP property. However, where a reverse QTIP election is made, application of the predeceased parent rule is made at the time of the first spouse's death. Also, at times property may be transferred to a trust before the predeceased parent rule is applicable. Later, the predeceased parent rule applies to additional property transferred to the trust. The additional property is treated as being held in a separate trust for GST tax purposes. Each portion has, in effect, a separate transferor.[3]

An individual who cannot be assigned to a generation under the foregoing rules is assigned to a generation on the basis of his date of birth. An individual born not more than 12½ years after the date of birth of the transferor is assigned to the transferor's generation. An individual born more than 12½ years but not more than 37½ years after the date of birth of the transferor is assigned to the first generation younger than the transferor. There are similar rules for a new generation every twenty-five years.[4]

878. Can married couples make a split gift for purposes of the GST tax?

Yes. If a split gift is made for gift tax purposes (see Q 895), such gift will be so treated for purposes of the GST tax.[5] Split gifts allow spouses to, in effect, utilize each other's annual exclusions and exemptions (see Q 866). One memorandum permitted a taxpayer to elect after his spouse's death to split gifts with his spouse and thus take advantage of his spouse's GST tax exemption where the gifts were made by the taxpayer shortly before the spouse's death.[6]

1. Treas. Reg. §26.2651-2.
2. IRC Sec. 2651(e).
3. Treas. Reg. §26.2651-1.
4. IRC Sec. 2651(d).
5. IRC Sec. 2652(a)(2).
6. TAM 9404023.

879. What credits are allowed against the GST tax?

For decedents dying before 2005, if a GST (other than a direct skip) occurs at the same time as and as a result of the death of an individual, a credit against the GST tax imposed is allowed in an amount equal to the GST tax paid to any state in respect to any property included in the GST, but the amount cannot exceed 5 percent of the GST tax.[1] The amendments made by the Economic Growth and Tax Relief Reconciliation Act of 2001 (EGTRRA 2001) sunset after December 31, 2012 so that this provision is no longer applicable. Transfers made to estates of decedents, gifts, or GST transfers are treated as if the amendments were never enacted.[2] However, under 2010 TRA, the GST tax rate for 2010 was zero, 35 percent for 2011 and 2012 and 40 percent for 2013 and beyond. The GST exemption was $5.49 million in 2017, and was raised to $11.18 million in 2018, $11.4 million in 2019, and $11.58 million in 2020 under the 2017 Tax Act.[3]

880. What are the return requirements with respect to the GST tax?

The person required to file the return is the person liable for paying the tax (see Q 881). In the case of a direct skip (other than from a trust), the return must be filed on or before the due date for the gift or estate tax return with respect to the transfer. In all other cases, the return must be filed on or before the fifteenth day of the fourth month after the close of the taxable year of the person required to make the return.[4]

881. Who is liable for paying the GST tax?

In the case of a taxable distribution, the tax is paid by the transferee. In the case of a taxable termination or a direct skip from a trust, the tax is paid by the trustee. In the case of a direct skip (other than a direct skip from a trust), the tax is paid by the transferor. Unless the governing instrument of transfer otherwise directs, the GST tax is charged to the property constituting the transfer.[5]

Gift Tax

882. What is the federal gift tax?

The federal gift tax is an excise tax on the right to transfer property during life.[6] The donor is generally responsible for paying the gift tax. The payment of the gift tax by the donor is not treated as a gift. The gift tax is a cumulative tax and the tax rates are progressive. Gifts made in prior years are taken into account in computing the tax on gifts made in the current year with the result that later gifts are usually taxed in a higher bracket than earlier gifts (a drop in tax rates could obviate this result). Moreover, the tax is a *unified* tax; the same tax that is imposed on taxable gifts is imposed on taxable estates. The maximum gift tax rate for 2011 and 2012 was 35 percent. Under the American Taxpayer Relief Act of 2013, the top estate and gift tax rate increased to 40 percent, and the exclusion amount was set at the $5 million level, as indexed

1. IRC Sec. 2604.
2. IRC Secs. 2604(c), 2664, as added by EGTRRA 2001.
3. Rev. Proc. 2016-55, Pub. Law No. 115-97, Rev. Proc. 2018-18, Rev. Proc. 2018-57, Rev. Proc. 2019-44.
4. IRC Sec. 2662.
5. IRC Sec. 2603.
6. IRC Sec. 2501.

for inflation annually to $5.49 million in 2017. The 2017 Tax Act raised the exemption amount to $11.18 million in 2018, $11.4 million in 2019, and $11.58 million in 2020, see Appendix D for earlier years).[1]

A gift tax return (Form 709), if required, must generally be filed by April 15 of the year following the year in which the gift was made. A six month extension for filing is available. Tax is generally due by April 15, but certain extensions for payment may be available. See Q 905.

The Federal Gift Tax Worksheet, below, shows the steps for calculating the gift tax. Calculation starts with determining what constitutes a gift for gift tax purposes (see Q 883). In general, gifts include gratuitous transfers of all kinds. Two spouses can elect to have all gifts made by either spouse during the year treated as made one-half by each spouse (Q 894). A qualified disclaimer is not treated as a gift (Q 885).

Gifts are generally valued at fair market value on the date of the gift (Q 906). Special rules apply for a wide variety of investments and to net gifts (Q 890), and Chapter 14 special valuation rules apply to transfers to family members of certain interests in corporations, partnerships, or trusts (Q 924).

Several exclusions are available. A $15,000 (in 2018-2020, $14,000 in 2013 through 2017[2]) annual exclusion is available for present interest gifts on a per donor/donee basis. An unlimited exclusion is available for qualified transfers for educational and medical purposes. See Q 895.

Several deductions are also available. Unlimited marital (Q 902) and charitable (Q 903) deductions are available for certain transfers to the donor's spouse and to charities.

The amount of taxable gifts subject to the federal gift tax equals gifts made during the year reduced by all exclusions and deductions.

The federal gift tax is imposed on taxable gifts. As discussed above, the federal gift tax rates (Appendix D) are generally progressive and the tax is based on cumulative taxable transfers during lifetime. To implement this, the tax is calculated on total taxable gifts, the sum of the taxable gifts made during the year (current taxable gifts) and prior taxable gifts, and the gift tax that would have been payable on prior taxable gifts (using the current tax rates) is then subtracted out. 2010 TRA provided that the amount of the unified credit is computed taking into account the credit for prior years' gifts using the gift tax rate for the current gift to determine the tentative tax.[3] Thus, a donor can make gifts equal to the applicable exemption amount (see above) and prior taxable gifts without incurring a gift tax liability.

1. American Taxpayer Relief Act of 2012, Pub. Law No. 112-240, Sec. 101; Rev. Proc. 2016-55, The 2017 Tax Act, Pub. Law. No. 115-97, Rev. Proc. 2018-18, Rev. Proc. 2018-57, Rev. Proc. 2019-44.
2. Rev. Proc. 2013-15, 2013-5 IRB 444, Rev. Proc. 2013-35, 2013-47 IRB 537, Rev. Proc. 2014-61, 2047 IRB 860, Rev. Proc. 2015-53, 2015-44 IRB 615, Rev. Proc. 2016-55, Rev. Proc. 2018-57, Rev. Proc. 2019-44.
3. IRC Section 2505(a).

Planning Point: A gift made after August 5, 1997 cannot be revalued if the gift was adequately disclosed on a gift tax return and the gift tax statute of limitations (generally, three years from the date of filing) has passed.[1] Consider filing gift tax returns even for non-cash annual exclusion gifts.

The tentative tax is then reduced by the unified credit (Q 904) to produce gift tax payable.

Federal Gift Tax Worksheet

Current Year		
Current Gifts		Q 883
- Annual Exclusions	Q 895	
- Qualified Transfers Exclusion	Q 895	
- Marital Deduction	Q 902	
- Charitable Deduction	Q 903	
- Total Reductions		
Current Taxable Gifts		
+ Prior Taxable Gifts		
Total Taxable Gifts		
Tax on Total Taxable Gifts		Appendix D
- Tax on Prior Taxable Gifts		Appendix D
Tentative Tax		Appendix D
- Unified Credit		Q 904
Federal Gift Tax		

883. Which types of transfers are subject to the federal gift tax?

The gift tax applies to a transfer by way of gift whether the transfer is in trust or otherwise, whether the gift is direct or indirect, and whether the property is real or personal, tangible or intangible. For example, a taxable transfer may be effectuated by the creation of a trust; the forgiving of a debt (see Q 887); the assignment of a judgment; the transfer of cash, certificates of deposit, federal, state, municipal, or corporate bonds, or stocks.[2]

All transactions whereby property or property rights or interests are gratuitously passed or conferred upon another, regardless of the means or device employed, constitute gifts subject to tax.[3] Donative intent on the part of the transferor is not an essential element in the application of the gift tax to the transfer. The application of the tax is based on the objective facts of the transfer and the circumstances under which it is made, rather than on the subjective motives of the donor.[4] Generally, if property is transferred gratuitously or for an inadequate consideration,

1. IRC Sec. 6501(c)(9).
2. Treas. Reg. §25.2511-1(a).
3. Treas. Reg. §25.2511-1(c).
4. Treas. Reg. §25.2511-1(g)(1).

a gift (of the full value of the property transferred or the portion in excess of the consideration given) will be considered a gift.[1]

Shareholders of nonparticipating preferred stock in profitable family held corporations have been held to have made gifts to the common stockholders (typically descendants of the preferred shareholder) by waiving payment of dividends or simply by failing to exercise conversion rights or other options available to a preferred stockholder to preserve his position.[2] The Tax Court has held that the failure to convert noncumulative preferred stock to cumulative preferred stock did not give rise to a gift, but that thereafter a gift was made each time a dividend would have accumulated. However, the failure to exercise a put option at par plus accumulated dividends plus interest was not treated as a gift of foregone interest.[3]

A transaction involving the nonexercise of an option by a son under a cross-purchase buy-sell agreement followed by the sale of the same stock by the father to a third party when the fair market value of the stock was substantially higher than the option price was treated as a gift from the son to the father.[4] Also, a father indirectly made a gift to his son to the extent that the fair market value of stock exceeded its redemption price when the father failed to exercise his right under a buy-sell agreement to have a corporation redeem all of the available shares held by his brother-in-law's estate and the stock passed to the son.[5]

With respect to a trust, the grantor/income beneficiary may be treated as making additional gifts of remainder interests in each year that the grantor fails to exercise his right to make nonproductive or underproductive property normally productive.[6] A mother made gifts to her children to the extent that the children were paid excessive trustee fees from the marital deduction trust of which the mother was a beneficiary.[7] Where a trust was modified to add adopted persons as beneficiaries, the beneficiaries with trust interests prior to the modification were treated as making gifts to the newly added beneficiaries.[8]

Planning Point: However, a grantor of a trust does not make a gift to trust beneficiaries by paying the income tax on trust income taxable to the grantor under the grantor trust rules (see Q 787).[9] Therefore, trusts that are disregarded for income tax purposes but not for transfer tax purposes can provide a significant opportunity for trust principal to grow without the reduction of tax.

Letter Ruling 9113009 (withdrawn without comment by TAM 9409018) had ruled that a parent who guaranteed loans to his children made a gift to his children because, without the guarantees, the children could not have obtained the loans or, at the very least, would have paid a higher interest rate.

1. *Hollingsworth v. Comm.*, 86 TC 91 (1986).
2. TAMs 8723007, 8726005.
3. *Snyder v. Comm.*, 93 TC 529 (1989).
4. Let. Rul. 9117035.
5. TAM 9315005.
6. Let. Rul. 8945006.
7. TAM 200014004.
8. Let. Rul. 200917004.
9. Rev. Rul. 2004-64, 2004-27 IRB 7.

The gift tax is imposed only on completed gifts (see Q 884), which is a facts and circumstances analysis.

Where spouses enter into joint and mutual wills, the surviving spouse may be treated as making a gift of a remainder interest at the other spouse's death.[1]

The transfer of a qualifying income interest for life in qualified terminable interest property for which a marital deduction was allowed (see Q 837, Q 902) will be treated as a transfer of such property for gift tax purposes.[2] If a QTIP trust is severed into Trust A and Trust B and the spouse renounces her interest in Trust A, such renunciation will not cause the spouse to be treated as transferring Trust B under IRC Section 2519.[3]

The spouse is entitled to collect from the donee the gift tax on the transfer of a QTIP interest. The amount treated as a transfer for gift tax purposes is reduced by the amount of the gift tax the spouse is entitled to recover from the donee. Thus, the transfer is treated as a net gift (see Q 890). The failure of a spouse to exercise the right to recover gift tax from the donee is treated as a transfer of the unrecovered amount to the donee when the right to recover is no longer enforceable. If a written waiver of the right of recovery is executed before the right becomes unenforceable, the transfer of the unrecovered gift tax is treated as made on the later of (1) the date of the waiver, or (2) the date the tax is paid by the transferor. Any delay in exercise of the right of recovery is treated as an interest-free loan (see Q 886) for gift tax purposes.[4]

Where a surviving spouse acquires a remainder interest in QTIP marital deduction property in connection with a transfer of property or cash to the holder of the remainder interest, the surviving spouse makes a gift to the remainder person under both IRC Section 2519 (disposition of QTIP interest) and IRC Sections 2511 and 2512 (transfers and valuation of gifts). The amount of the gift is equal to the greater of (1) the value of the remainder interest, or (2) the value of the property or cash transferred to the holder of the remainder interest.[5] On the other hand, children would be treated as making a gift if the children transfer their remainder interest in a QTIP marital deduction trust to the surviving spouse.[6]

Any subsequent transfer by the donor spouse of an interest in such property is not treated as a transfer for gift tax purposes, unless the transfer occurs after the donee spouse is treated as having transferred such property under IRC Section 2519 or after such property is includable in the donee spouse's estate under IRC Section 2044 (see Q 814).[7] Also, if property for which a QTIP marital deduction was taken is includable in the estate of the spouse who was given the QTIP interest and the estate of such spouse fails to recover from the person receiving the property any estate tax attributable to the QTIP interest being included in such spouse's estate, such failure is treated as a transfer for gift tax purposes unless (1) such spouse's will waives the

1. *Grimes v. C.I.R.*., 851 F. 2d 1005, 88-2 USTC ¶13,774 (7th Cir. 1988).
2. IRC Sec. 2519.
3. Let. Ruls. 200116006, 200122036.
4. Treas. Reg. §§25.2207A-1(b), 25.2519-1(c)(4).
5. Rev. Rul. 98-8, 1998-1 CB 541.
6. Let. Rul. 199908033.
7. IRC Sec. 2523(f)(5).

right to recovery, or (2) the beneficiaries cannot compel recovery of the taxes (e.g., where the executor is given discretion to waive the right of recovery in such spouse's will).[1]

The gift tax is not applicable to a transfer for a full and adequate consideration in money or money's worth, or to ordinary business transactions (i.e., transactions which are bona fide, at arm's length, and free from any donative intent). A consideration that cannot be reduced to a value in money or money's worth (such as love and affection, promise of marriage, etc.) is wholly disregarded, and the entire value of the property transferred constitutes the amount of the gift. Similarly, a relinquishment or promised relinquishment of dower or curtesy, or of a statutory estate created in lieu of dower or curtesy, or of other marital rights in the spouse's property or estate, is not considered to any extent a consideration "in money or money's worth."[2]

Transfers of property or interests in property made under the terms of a written agreement between spouses in settlement of their marital or property rights are deemed to be for an adequate and full consideration in money or money's worth and, therefore, exempt from the gift tax (whether or not such agreement is approved by a divorce decree), if the spouses obtain a final decree of divorce from each other within the three-year period beginning on the date one year before the agreement is entered into.[3]

For recapture rules applicable where distributions are not timely made in connection with the transfer of an interest in a corporation or partnership which is subject to the Chapter 14 valuation rules, see Q 925. For deemed transfers upon the lapse of certain voting or liquidation rights in a corporation or partnership, see Q 934.

A gift may be made of foregone interest with respect to interest-free and bargain rate loans (see Q 886).

A United States citizen or resident who receives a covered gift from certain expatriates may owe gift tax on the transfer.[4]

884. When is a gift complete for purposes of the federal gift tax?

The gift is complete once the donor parts with dominion and control over the property or interest in the property, leaving him no power to change its disposition, whether for the donor's own benefit or for the benefit of another.[5] In general, a transfer of an interest in a revocable trust is incomplete until the interest becomes irrevocable. However, if the interest becomes irrevocable at the grantor's death, it will generally be subject to estate tax (see Q 814) rather than to gift tax.

If a donor delivers a properly endorsed stock certificate to the donee or the donee's agent, the gift is completed for gift tax purposes on the date of delivery. If the donor delivers the certificate to a bank or broker as his agent, or to the issuing corporation or its transfer agent, for

1. Treas. Reg. §20.2207A-1(a).
2. Treas. Reg. §25.2512-8.
3. IRC Sec. 2516.
4. IRC Sec. 2801.
5. Treas. Reg. §25.2511-2(b).

transfer into the name of the donee, the gift is completed on the date the stock is transferred on the books of the corporation.[1]

A transfer of a nonstatutory stock option which was not traded on an established market would be treated as a gift to a family member on the later of the following: (1) the transfer; or (2) the time when the donee's right to exercise the option is no longer conditioned on the performance of services by the transferor.[2]

The gratuitous transfer by the maker of a legally binding promissory note is a completed gift (the transfer of a legally unenforceable promissory note is an incomplete gift); if the note is unpaid at the donor's death, the gift is not treated as an adjusted taxable gift in computing the tentative estate tax (see Q 811), and no deduction is allowable from the gross estate for the promisee's claim with respect to the note (see Q 837).[3]

In the case of a gift by check, the following questions arise: (1) when is the gift complete?; (2) when is the check delivered?; and (3) when is the check cashed? In litigation to date, the courts initially appeared to make a distinction between gifts to charitable donees and gifts to noncharitable donees. In the former scenario, it has been held that at least where there is timely presentment and payment, payment of the check by the bank relates back to the date of delivery for purposes of determining completeness of the gift.[4] In the latter scenario, the courts have shown less of a willingness to apply the "relation back" doctrine.

In *Estate of Dillingham v. Commissioner*,[5] the noncharitable donees did not cash the checks until thirty-five days after the delivery date – the donor's death having intervened. The court said that this delay casted doubt as to whether the checks were unconditionally delivered. Since the estate failed to prove unconditional delivery, the court declined to extend the relation back doctrine to the case before it. It then turned to local law to determine whether the decedent had parted with dominion and control upon delivery of the checks. It determined that under applicable local law (Oklahoma), the donor did not part with dominion and control until the checks were cashed.

However, in *Est. of Gagliardi v. Commissioner*,[6] checks written by a brokerage firm and charged against the decedent's account prior to decedent's death were treated as completed gifts to the noncharitable donees, even though some checks were cashed after decedent's death.

Also, in *Est. of Metzger v. Commissioner*,[7] the relation-back doctrine was applied to gifts made by check to noncharitable beneficiaries where the taxpayer was able to establish the following: (1) the donor's intent to make gifts; (2) unconditional delivery of the checks; (3) presentment of the check during the year for which a gift tax annual exclusion was sought and within a

1. Treas. Reg. §25.2511-2(h); Rev. Rul. 54-554, 1954-2 CB 317; Rev. Rul. 54-135, 1954-1 CB 205.
2. Rev. Rul. 98-21, 1998-1 CB 975.
3. Rev. Rul. 84-25, 1984-1 CB 191.
4. *Est. of Spiegel v. Comm.*, 12 TC 524 (1942).
5. 903 F.2d 760, 90-1 USTC ¶60,021 (10th Cir. 1990).
6. 89 TC 1207 (1987).
7. 38 F.3d 118, 94-2 USTC ¶60,179 (4th Cir. 1994), aff'g 100 TC 204 (1993).

reasonable time after issuance; and (4) that there were sufficient funds to pay the checks at all relevant times. In *W. H. Braum Family Partnership v. Commissioner*,[1] the relation back doctrine was not applied where the taxpayer could not establish either (2) or (4). In response to *Metzger*, the Service issued a revenue ruling providing that a gift by check to a noncharitable beneficiary will be considered complete on the earlier of (1) when the donor has so parted with dominion and control under state law such that the donor can no longer change its disposition, or (2) when the donee deposits the check, cashes the check against available funds, or presents the check for payment if the following conditions are met: (a) the check must be paid by the drawee bank when first presented for payment to the drawee bank; (b) the donor must be alive when the check is paid by the drawee bank; (c) the donor must have intended a gift; (d) delivery of the check by the donor must have been unconditional; (e) the check must be deposited, cashed or presented in the calendar year for which the completed gift tax treatment is sought; and (f) the check must be deposited, cashed, or presented within a reasonable time of issuance.[2]

In the case of a gift made to a trust, a gift is incomplete to the extent that the donor retains the power to name new beneficiaries or change the interests of the current beneficiaries.[3] The retention by the donor of a limited power of appointment over property transferred to trust during his or her lifetime can cause the gift to trust to be considered incomplete for federal gift tax purposes. The IRS has ruled privately that a limited power of appointment over property transferred to trust can cause the gift to remain incomplete even in a case where the power is exercisable in conjunction with another person. The gift will remain incomplete so long as the donor retains a limited power of appointment that is exercisable by him in conjunction with any person that does not have a substantial adverse interest in the disposition of the trust assets in question.[4]

885. If a person refuses to accept an interest in property (a disclaimer), is he considered to have made a gift of the interest for federal gift tax purposes?

Not if he makes a *qualified disclaimer*. A "qualified disclaimer" is an irrevocable and unqualified refusal to accept an interest in property created in the person disclaiming by a taxable transfer made after 1976. With respect to inter vivos transfers, for the purpose of determining when a timely disclaimer is made (see condition (3) below), a taxable transfer occurs when there is a completed gift for federal gift tax purposes regardless of whether a gift tax is imposed on the completed gift. Thus, gifts qualifying for the gift tax annual exclusion are regarded as taxable transfers for this purpose.[5] Furthermore, a disclaimer of a remainder interest in a trust created prior to the enactment of the federal gift tax was subject to the gift tax where the disclaimer was not timely and the disclaimer occurred after enactment of the gift tax.[6] In order to effectively disclaim property for transfer tax purposes, a disclaimer of property received from a decedent

1. TC Memo 1993-434.
2. Rev. Rul. 96-56, 1996-2 CB 161.
3. Treas. Reg. §25.2511-2(c).
4. Let. Rul. 201507008.
5. Treas. Reg. §25.2518-2(c)(3).
6. *U.S. v. Irvine*, 114 S. Ct. 1473, 94-1 USTC ¶60,163 (U.S. 1994).

at death should generally be made within nine months of death rather than within nine months of the probate of the decedent's will.[1]

In general, the disclaimer must satisfy the following conditions: (1) the disclaimer must be irrevocable and unqualified; (2) the disclaimer must be in writing; (3) the writing must be delivered to the transferor of the interest, his legal representative, the holder of the legal title to the property, or the person in possession of the property, not later than nine months after the later of (a) the day on which the transfer creating the interest is made, or (b) the day on which the disclaimant reaches age twenty-one; (4) the disclaimant must not have accepted the interest disclaimed or any of its benefits; and (5) the interest disclaimed must pass either to the spouse of the decedent or to a person other than the disclaimant without any direction on the part of the person making the disclaimer.[2] Acts indicative of acceptance include: (1) using the property or the interest in property; (2) accepting dividends, interest, or rents from the property; and (3) directing others to act with respect to the property or interest in property. However, merely taking delivery of title without more does not constitute acceptance.[3] A person cannot disclaim a remainder interest in property while retaining a life estate or income interest in the same property.[4] Under 2010 TRA, a disclaimant has up to nine months after the enactment of 2010 TRA (12/17/10) to disclaim property passing from a decedent who died between January 1, 2010 and December 16, 2010.

If a person makes a qualified disclaimer, for purposes of the federal estate, gift, and generation-skipping transfer tax provisions, the disclaimed interest in property is treated as if it had never been transferred to the person making the qualified disclaimer. Instead it is considered as passing directly from the transferor of the property to the person entitled to receive the property as a result of the disclaimer. Accordingly, a person making a qualified disclaimer is not treated as making a gift. Similarly, the value of a decedent's gross estate for purposes of the federal estate tax does not include the value of property with respect to which the decedent or his executor has made a qualified disclaimer.[5]

In the case of a joint tenancy with rights of survivorship or a tenancy by the entirety, the interest which the donee receives upon creation of the joint interest can be disclaimed within nine months of the creation of the interest and the survivorship interest received upon the death of the first joint tenant to die (deemed to be a one-half interest in the property) can be disclaimed within nine months of the death of the first joint tenant to die, *without regard to* the following: (1) whether either joint tenant can sever unilaterally under local law; (2) the portion of the property attributable to consideration furnished by the disclaimant; or (3) the portion of the property includable in the decedent's gross estate under IRC Section 2040. However, in the case of a creation of a joint tenancy between spouses or tenancy by the entirety created after July 13, 1988 where the *donee spouse is not a U.S. citizen*, a surviving spouse can make a disclaimer within nine months of the death of the first spouse to die of any portion of the joint interest that

1. *Est. of Fleming v. Comm.*, 974 F. 2d 894, 92-2 USTC ¶60,113 (7th Cir. 1992).
2. IRC Sec. 2518(b); Treas. Reg. §25.2518-2(a).
3. Treas. Reg. §25.2518-2(d)(1).
4. *Walshire v. Comm.*, 288 F.3d 342, 2002-1 USTC ¶60,439 (8th Cir. 2002).
5. Treas. Reg. §25.2518-1(b).

is includable in the decedent's estate under IRC Section 2040. Also, in the case of a transfer to a *joint bank, brokerage, or other investment account* (e.g., mutual fund account) where the transferor can unilaterally withdraw amounts contributed by the transferor, the surviving joint tenant may disclaim amounts contributed by the first joint tenant to die within nine months of the death of the first joint tenant to die.[1]

For purposes of a qualified disclaimer, the mere act of making a surviving spouse's statutory election is not to be treated as an acceptance of an interest in the disclaimed property or any of its benefits. However, the disclaimer of a portion of the property subject to the statutory election must be made within nine months of the decedent spouse's death, rather than within nine months of the surviving spouse's statutory election.[2]

A power with respect to property is treated as an interest in such property.[3] The exercise of a power of appointment to any extent by the donee of the power is an acceptance of its benefits.[4]

A beneficiary who is under twenty-one years of age has until nine months after his twenty-first birthday in which to make a qualified disclaimer of his interest in property. Any actions taken with regard to an interest in property by a beneficiary or a custodian prior to the beneficiary's twenty-first birthday will not be an acceptance by the beneficiary of the interest.[5] This rule holds true even as to custodianship gifts in states which provide that custodianship ends when the donee reaches an age below twenty-one.[6]

It is also important to check applicable state law to make certain that the disclaimer meets the requirements and is effective.

886. Are gifts made of foregone interest or interest-free and bargain rate loans subject to the federal gift tax?

An interest-free or low-interest loan within a family or in any other circumstances where the foregone interest is in the nature of a gift results in a gift subject to the federal gift tax. IRC Section 7872 applies in the case of term loans made after June 6, 1984, and demand loans outstanding after that date.

In general, IRC Section 7872 recharacterizes a below-market loan (an interest-free or low-interest loan) as an arm's length transaction in which the lender (1) made a loan to the borrower in exchange for a note requiring the payment of interest at a statutory rate, and (2) made a gift, distributed a dividend, made a contribution to capital, paid compensation, or made another payment to the borrower which, in turn, is used by the borrower to pay the interest. The difference between the statutory rate of interest and the rate (if any) actually charged by the lender, the "foregone interest," is thus either a gift to the borrower or income

1. Treas. Reg. §25.2518-2(c)(4).
2. Rev. Rul. 90-45, 1990-1 CB 176.
3. IRC Sec. 2518(c)(2).
4. Treas. Reg. §25.2518-2(d)(1); Let. Rul. 8142008.
5. Treas. Reg. §25.2518-2(d)(3).
6. Treas. Reg. §25.2518-2(d)(4), Example 11.

to him, depending on the circumstances. The income tax aspects of below-market loans are discussed in Q 664 and Q 665. The gift tax aspects of such loans are discussed here.

First, some definitions: The term "gift loan" means any below-market loan where the foregoing of interest is in the nature of a gift as defined under Chapter 12. The term "demand loan" means any loan which is payable in full at any time on the demand of the lender. The term "term loan" means any loan which is not a demand loan. The term "applicable federal rate" means: in the case of a demand loan or a term loan of up to three years, the federal short-term rate; in the case of a term loan over three years but not over nine years, the federal mid-term rate; in the case of a term loan over nine years, the federal long-term rate. In the case of a term loan, the applicable rate is compounded semiannually. These rates are reset monthly.[1] The "present value" of any payment is determined as follows: (1) as of the date of the loan; and (2) by using a discount rate equal to the applicable federal rate.[2] The term "below-market loan" means any loan if in the case of the following: (1) a demand loan, in which interest is payable on the loan at a rate less than the applicable federal rate; or (2) a term loan, in which the amount loaned exceeds the present value of all payments due under the loan. The term "foregone interest" means, with respect to any period during which the loan is outstanding, the excess of the following: (1) the amount of interest that would have been payable on the loan for the period if the interest accrued on the loan at the applicable federal rate and was payable annually on the last day of the appropriate calendar year; over (2) any interest payable on the loan properly allocable to the period.

In the case of a demand gift loan, the foregone interest is treated as transferred from the lender to the borrower and retransferred by the borrower to the lender as interest on the last day of each calendar year the loan is outstanding. In the case of a term gift loan, the lender is treated as having transferred on the date the loan was made, and the borrower is treated as having received on such date, cash in an amount equal to the excess of (1) the amount loaned, over (2) the present value of all payments which are required to be made under the terms of the loan. The provisions do not apply in the case of a gift loan between individuals (two spouses are treated as one person) that at no time exceeds $10,000 in the aggregate amount outstanding on *all* loans, whether below-market or not. The $10,000 de minimis exception does not apply, however, to loans attributable to acquisition of income-producing assets.

IRC Section 7872 does not apply to life insurance policy loans.[3] Neither does IRC Section 7872 apply to loans to a charitable organization if the aggregate outstanding amount of loans by the lender to that organization does not exceed $250,000 at any time during the tax year.[4]

The Tax Court has held that IRC Section 483 and safe harbor interest rates contained therein do not apply for gift tax purposes. Consequently, the value of a promissory note given in exchange for real property was discounted to reflect time value of money concepts under IRC Section 7282 (without benefit of IRC Section 483).[5]

1. IRC Sec. 1274(d).
2. See Prop. Treas. Reg. §1.7872-14.
3. Prop. Treas. Reg. §1.7872-5(b)(4).
4. Temp. Treas. Reg. §1.7872-5T(b)(9).
5. *Frazee v. Comm.*, 98 TC 554 (1992).

Prior to the enactment of IRC Section 7872, the Supreme Court held that, in the case of an interest-free demand loan made within a family, a gift subject to federal gift tax is made of the value of the use of the money lent.[1] The court did not decide how to value such a gift, but implicit in the decision was the assumption that low-interest or interest-free loans within a family context have, since the first federal gift tax statute was enacted in 1924, resulted in gifts. Revenue Procedure 85-46[2] provided guidance in valuing and reporting gift demand loans not covered by IRC Section 7872.

887. What are the gift tax implications, if any, when an individual transfers property (or an interest in property) and takes back noninterest-bearing term notes covering the value of the property transferred, and the transferor intends to forgive the notes as they come due?

If the transferor's receipt of the noninterest-bearing notes is characterized as a "term gift loan," the lender/transferor will be treated as having transferred on the date of the receipt, and the borrower/transferee will be treated as having received on such date, cash in an amount equal to the excess of the following: (1) the amount loaned; over (2) the present value of all payments required to be made under the terms of the loan (see Q 883).[3] If the receipt of the notes is not so characterized, then the discussion in the following paragraph, relating to transactions occurring before June 7, 1984, is pertinent.

The IRS takes the position that such a transfer is a gift of the entire value of the property or interest given at the time of the transfer and is not a sale. If the transfer is of a remainder interest in property, it is a future interest gift that does not qualify for the gift tax annual exclusion (see Q 895). The Service distinguishes between an intent to forgive the notes and donative intent (see Q 883) with respect to transfer of the property: "A finding of an intent to forgive the note relates to whether valuable consideration was received, and thus, to whether the transaction was in reality a bona fide sale or a disguised gift."[4] The Tax Court, however, makes a distinction based on the nature of the notes given, holding that if the notes are secured by valid vendor's liens, the transaction is to be treated as a sale; a gift occurs on each date a note is due and forgiven, the value of the gift being the amount due on the note.[5]

888. Are gratuitous transfers by individuals of federal, state, and municipal obligations subject to federal transfer taxes?

Yes. Gratuitous transfers of obligations that are exempt from federal income tax are not exempt from federal estate tax, gift tax, or generation-skipping transfer tax, as the case may be – at least as to estates of decedents dying, gifts made, and transfers made on or after June 19, 1984. In the case of any provision of law enacted after July 18, 1984, such provision is not treated as exempting the transfer of property from such transfer taxes unless it refers

1. *Dickman v. Comm.*, 104 S. Ct. 1086 (1984).
2. 1985-2 CB 507.
3. IRC Secs. 7872(b)(1), 7872(d)(2).
4. Rev. Rul. 77-299, 1977-2 CB 343; *Deal*, 29 TC 730 (1958).
5. *Haygood v. Comm.*, 42 TC 936 (1964), nonacq. 1977-2 CB 2; *Est. of Kelley v. Comm.*, 63 TC 321 (1974), nonacq. 1977-2 CB 2.

to the appropriate IRC provisions.[1] Also, the removal of transfer tax exemption applies in the case of any transfer of property (or interest in property) if at any time an estate or gift tax return was filed showing such transfer as subject to federal estate or gift tax.[2] Congress also added that no inference was to be drawn that transfers of such obligations occurring before such time were exempt from transfer taxation.

In *United States v.Wells Fargo*,[3] the United States Supreme Court determined that "tax-exempt" bonds have always been subject to transfer taxes unless specifically provided otherwise by statute (even before enactment of TRA '84, Sec. 641). This determination was based on the longstanding principle that tax exemption cannot be inferred. The differing language concerning project notes issued pursuant to Housing Acts, providing at one time for exemption from all taxation and at another for exemption from all taxation except surtax, estate, inheritance, and gift taxes, could be explained by the need to address a surtax in 1937, and not by a Congressional intent to exempt the project notes from estate taxation, the court concluded. The project notes were not exempt from transfer taxes, the court ruled, and included the notes in the decedent's estate.

889. What are the federal gift tax implications of taking title to investment property in joint names?

There may be a gift for federal gift tax purposes either at the time title is taken in joint names or at a later time when one of the joint owners reduces some or all of the property to his own possession. Consider the following examples:

"If A creates a joint bank account for himself and B (or a similar type of ownership by which A can regain the entire fund without B's consent), there is a gift to B when B draws upon the account for his own benefit, to the extent of the amount drawn without any obligation to account for a part of the proceeds to A. Similarly, if A purchases a United States savings bond, registered as payable to 'A or B,' there is a gift to B when B surrenders the bond for cash without any obligation to account for a part of the proceeds to A."[4] Likewise, "where A, with his separate funds, creates a joint brokerage account for himself and B, and the securities purchased on behalf of the account are registered in the name of a nominee of the firm, A has not made a gift to B, for federal gift tax purposes, unless and until B draws upon the account for his own benefit without any obligation to account to A. If B makes a withdrawal under such circumstances, the value of the gift by A would be the sum of money or the value of the property actually withdrawn from the account by B."[5] Thus, the creation of a joint account or similar type of ownership by itself, does not constitute a completed transfer from the creator and sole contributor if the creator and sole contributor can regain the existing account without the joint owner's consent.

"If A with his own funds purchases property and has the title conveyed to himself and B as joint owners, with rights of survivorship (other than a joint ownership described in [the foregoing

1. TRA '84, Sec. 641.
2. TRA '84, Sec. 641(b)(2).
3. 485 U.S. 351, 708 S. Ct. 1179, 88-1 USTC ¶13,759 (U.S. 1988).
4. Treas. Reg. §25.2511-1(h)(4).
5. Rev. Rul. 69-148, 1969-1 CB 226.

paragraph]) but which rights may be defeated by either party severing his interest, there is a gift to B in the amount of half the value of the property."[1]

Where A purchases and registers U.S. Treasury notes in the names of "A or B or survivor" in a jurisdiction in which this registration creates a joint tenancy, there is a completed gift of the survivorship rights in the notes and an undivided one-half interest in the interest payments and redemption rights pertaining to the notes. In a jurisdiction in which a joint tenancy is not created by such registration, there is a gift of the survivorship rights in the interest payments and in the notes at maturity.[2] Computation of the value of the gifts in both situations is set forth in Revenue Ruling 78-215.

In the above examples, if A and B are spouses, any gift will be offset by the marital deduction to the extent available (see Q 902).[3]

890. What are the federal gift tax results if the donee agrees to pay the gift tax?

If a gift is made subject to the express or implied condition that the donee pay the gift tax, the donor may deduct the amount of tax from the gift in determining the value of the gift. In such a transaction, the donor receives consideration for the transfer in the amount of the gift tax paid by the donee. Thus, to the extent of the tax paid, the donee does not receive a gift.[4] Similarly, if the donor makes a gift in trust subject to an agreement that the trustee pay the gift tax, the value of the property transferred is reduced for gift tax purposes by the amount of the tax.[5]

The computation of the tax requires the use of an algebraic formula, since the amount of the tax is dependent on the value of the gift which in turn is dependent on the amount of the tax. The formula is as follows:

$$\frac{\text{Tentative Tax}}{\text{1 plus Rate of Tax}} = \text{True Tax}$$

Examples illustrating the use of this formula, with the algebraic method, to determine the tax in a net gift situation are contained in IRS Publication 904 (Rev. May 1985). Three of the examples show the effect of a state gift tax upon the computation.

Although the donee pays the tax, it is the *donor's* unified credit that is used in computing the gift tax, not the donee's.[6]

1. Treas. Reg. §25.2511-1(h)(5).
2. Rev. Rul. 78-215, 1978-1 CB 298.
3. Treas. Reg. §25.2523(d)-1.
4. Rev. Rul. 75-72, 1975-1 CB 310; *Diedrich v. Comm.*, 102 S. Ct. 2414 (1982).
5. *Lingo*, 13 TCM 436 (1959); *Harrison*, 17 TC 1350 (1952), acq. 1952-2 CB 2.
6. Let. Rul. 7842068.

891. How is a gift of property under either the Uniform Gifts to Minors Act or under the Uniform Transfers to Minors Act treated for federal gift tax purposes?

Any transfer of property to a minor under either of the Uniform Acts constitutes a complete gift for federal gift tax purposes to the extent of the full fair market value of the property transferred. Generally, such a gift qualifies for the gift tax annual exclusion (see Q 895).[1] The allowance of the exclusion is not affected by the amendment of a state's Uniform Act lowering the age of majority and thus requiring that property be distributed to the donee at age eighteen.[2] These rulings base the allowance of the exclusion on the assumption that gifts under the Uniform Acts come within the purview of IRC Section 2503(c). Gifts to minors under IRC Section 2503(c) must pass to the donee on his attaining age twenty-one If a state statute varies from the Uniform Act by providing that under certain conditions custodianship may be extended past the donee's age twenty-one, gifts made under those conditions would not qualify for the exclusion. For tables of state laws concerning the Uniform Acts, see Appendix D of *Tax Facts on Investments*.

892. When is a gift made with respect to an education savings account?

Contributions to an education savings account are treated as completed gifts to the beneficiary of a present interest in property which can qualify for the gift tax and generation-skipping transfer (GST) tax annual exclusion. The contributions must be in cash and prior to the beneficiary's eighteenth birthday. If the contribution is made for a beneficiary designated with special needs, the age limit does not apply.[3] If contributions for a year exceed the gift tax annual exclusion, the donor can elect to prorate the gifts over a five year period beginning with such year. A contribution to an education savings account does not qualify for the gift tax or GST tax exclusion for qualified transfers for educational purposes.[4] Distributions from an education savings account are not treated as taxable gifts. Also, if the designated beneficiary of the education savings account is changed, or if funds in the education savings account are rolled over to a new beneficiary, such a transfer is subject to the gift tax or GST tax only if the new beneficiary is a generation below the old beneficiary. Transfers within the same generation do not trigger a gift tax liability.[5]

See Q 833 for the estate tax treatment and Q 681 for the income tax treatment of education savings accounts.

893. When is a gift made with respect to a qualified tuition program?

For gift tax and generation-skipping transfer (GST) tax purposes, a contribution to a qualified tuition program on behalf of a designated beneficiary is not treated as a qualified transfer for purposes of the gift tax and GST tax exclusion for educational expenses, but is treated as a completed gift of a present interest to the beneficiary which qualifies for the annual exclusion

1. Rev. Rul. 56-86, 1956-1 CB 449; Rev. Rul. 59-357, 1959-2 CB 212.
2. Rev. Rul. 73-287, 1973-2 CB 321.
3. IRC Section 530(b)(1).
4. IRC Secs. 530(d)(3), 529(c)(2).
5. IRC Secs. 530(d)(3), 529(c)(5).

(see Q 895). If a donor makes contributions to a qualified tuition program in excess of the gift tax annual exclusion, the donor may elect to take the donation into account ratably over a five-year period.[1] Distributions from a qualified tuition program are not treated as taxable gifts. Also, if the designated beneficiary of a qualified tuition program is changed, or if funds in a qualified tuition program are rolled over to the account of a new beneficiary, such a transfer is subject to the gift tax or generation-skipping transfer tax only if the new beneficiary is a generation below the old beneficiary.[2]

See Q 834 for the estate tax treatment and Q 687 for the income tax treatment of qualified tuition programs.

894. When is the "split-gift" provision available?

When one of two spouses makes a gift to a *third* person, it may be treated as having been made one-half by each if the other spouse consents to the gift.[3]

Planning Point: The split-gift provision enables a spouse who owns most of the property to take advantage of the other spouse's annual exclusions (see Q 895) and unified credit (see Q 904). Thus, a spouse, with the other spouse's consent, can give up to $30,000 (2 × $15,000 annual exclusion in 2020, see Appendix D) a year to each donee free of gift tax, and, in addition, will have both their unified credits to apply against gift tax imposed on gifts in excess of the annual exclusion. Moreover, by splitting the gifts between spouses, they will fall in lower gift tax brackets.

Where spouses elect to use the "split-gift" provision, the consent applies to all gifts made by either spouse to third persons during the calendar year.[4] The consent must be made on the Form 709. By consenting to gift splitting, a spouse may assume joint and several liability for any gift tax assessed on the gift.[5] A technical advice memorandum permitted a taxpayer to elect after the spouse's death to split gifts with his spouse where the gifts were made by the taxpayer shortly before the spouse's death.[6]

895. What is the gift tax annual exclusion and when is it available to a donor?

The gift tax annual exclusion is an exclusion of $10,000 as indexed ($15,000 in 2018-2020, $14,000 in 2013 through 2017,[7] see Appendix D for the amount in other years) per calendar year per donee applied to gifts of a present interest in property. The $10,000 amount is adjusted for inflation, rounded down to the next lowest multiple of $1,000, after 1998. The exclusion is not cumulative; that is, an exclusion unused in one year cannot be carried over and used in a future year. A gift of a present interest is one in which the donee has the right to immediate possession, use, and enjoyment of the property.

1. IRC Sec. 529(c)(2).
2. IRC Sec. 529(d)(5)(B).
3. IRC Sec. 2513; Treas. Reg. §25.2513-1.
4. IRC Sec. 2513(a)(2).
5. *Williams v. U.S.*, 378 F.2d 693 (Ct. Cl. 1967).
6. TAM 9404023.
7. Rev. Proc. 2013-15, 2013-5 IRB 444, Rev. Proc. 2013-35, 2013-47 IRB 537, Rev. Proc. 2014-61, 2014-47 IRB 860, Rev. Proc. 2015-53, Rev. Proc. 2016-55, Rev. Proc. 2017-58, Rev. Proc. 2018-57, Rev. Proc. 2019-44.

The exclusion does not apply to gifts of a future interest in property, i.e., the right to use and enjoy the property only in the future. For example, if G transfers income producing property in trust, the terms of which provide that the income from the trust property will be paid to A for lifetime and upon A's death the trust property will be paid to B free of trust, A's life income interest would be a present interest gift and B's remainder interest would be a future interest gift. G would be allowed to exclude from the value of gifts reported on the gift tax return the value of A's life income interest up to $15,000 (in 2020, assuming G made no other present interest gifts to A during the calendar year), but he would not be able to exclude any of the value of B's remainder interest. If the trustee were given discretion to withhold payments of income to A and add such amounts to the trust corpus, A's income interest would not be a present interest, and G would not be allowed to claim any exclusion.

Substance over form analysis may be applied to deny annual exclusions where indirect transfers are used in an attempt to obtain inappropriate annual exclusions for gifts to intermediate recipients.[1] For example, suppose A transfers $15,000 to each of B, C, and D in 2020. By arrangement, B, C, and D each immediately transfer $15,000 to E. The annual exclusion for A's indirect transfers to E is limited to $15,000 and A has made taxable gifts of $30,000 to E.

An outright gift of a bond, note (though bearing no interest until maturity), or other obligation which is to be discharged by payments in the future is a gift of a present interest. Normally, a direct gift of shares of corporate stock is a present interest gift. However, if the gift is made subject to a stock transfer restriction agreement under which the donee is prohibited for a period of time from selling or pledging the stock, it has been held that the gift is one of a future interest which does not qualify for the gift tax annual exclusion.

896. When will the gift tax annual exclusion be available with respect to gifts of property in trust?

A gift of property to a trust which directs the trustee to distribute the trust income annually to the beneficiary is a present interest gift of an income interest qualifying for the annual exclusion. However, a gift of property to a trust which directs the trustee to distribute from the trust annually a certain dollar amount to the beneficiary is a gift of a future interest not qualifying for the exclusion.

A gift of property in trust will qualify for the gift tax annual exclusion if the trust terms (1) provide that the trust beneficiary (or beneficiaries) be given timely written notice (notice given within ten days after the transfer has been held timely) that the beneficiary has a reasonable period (forty-five days has been held reasonable) within which to demand immediate withdrawal (usually the trust specifies that the withdrawal right is limited to the amount of the exclusion), and (2) give the trustee the power to convert property in the trust to cash to the extent necessary to meet withdrawal demands. Such trusts are popularly known as Crummey trusts, after the name of a leading case that upheld them.[2]

1. *Heyen v. U.S.*, 945 F.2d 359, 91-2 USTC ¶60,085 (10th Cir. 1991).
2. *Crummey v. Comm.*, 397 F.2d 82 (9th Cir. 1968); Rev. Rul. 73-405, 1973-2 CB 321; Rev. Rul. 81-7, 1981-1 CB 474; Rev. Rul. 83-108, 1983-2 CB 167; Let. Ruls. 8022048, 8134135, 8118051, 8134135, 8445004, 9625031.

The IRS has ruled with respect to Crummey trusts that the annual exclusion could not be applied to trust contributions on behalf of trust beneficiaries who had withdrawal rights as to the contributions (except to the extent they exercised their withdrawal rights) but who had either no other interest in the trust (a naked power) or only remote contingent interests in the remainder.[1] However, the Tax Court has rejected the IRS' argument that a power holder must hold rights other than the withdrawal right to obtain the annual exclusion. The withdrawal right (assuming there is no agreement to not exercise the right) is sufficient to obtain the annual exclusion.[2] (Language in *Cristofani* appears to support use of naked powers, although the case did not involve naked powers.) The Tax Court recently held the donor does not have to give the beneficiaries of a trust notice of the gift in certain circumstances.[3]

In an Action On Decision, the Service stated that, applying the substance over form doctrine, the annual exclusions should not be allowed where the withdrawal rights are not in substance what they purport to be in form. If the facts and circumstances show an understanding that the power is not meant to be exercised or that exercise would result in undesirable consequences, then creation of the withdrawal right is not a bona fide gift of a present interest and an annual exclusion should not be allowed.[4] In TAM 9628004, annual exclusions were not allowed where transfers to trust were made so late in the first year that *Crummey* withdrawal powerholders had no opportunity to exercise their rights, most powerholders had either no other interest in the trust or discretionary income or remote contingent remainder interests, and withdrawal powers were never exercised in any year. However, annual exclusions were allowed where the IRS was unable to prove that there was an understanding between the donor and the beneficiaries that the withdrawal rights should not be exercised.[5] In TAM 9731004, annual exclusions were denied where eight trusts were created for eight primary beneficiaries, but *Crummey* withdrawal powers were given to sixteen or seventeen persons who never exercised their powers and most powerholders held either a remote contingent interest or no interest other than the withdrawal power in the trusts in which the powerholder was not the primary beneficiary.

The annual exclusion was not allowed where the beneficiaries waived their right to receive notice of contributions to a trust with respect to which their withdrawal rights could be exercised. Furthermore, the annual exclusion was not allowed because the grantor set up a trust which provided that notice was to be given to the trustee as to whether a beneficiary could exercise a withdrawal power with respect to a transfer to a trust and the grantor never notified the trustee that the withdrawal powers could be exercised with respect to any of the transfers to trust.[6]

897. When will a gift of a donor's interest in real estate qualify for the gift tax annual exclusion?

It has been held that the gift of a portion of the donor's interest in real property, if under the terms of the transfer the donee receives the present unrestricted right to the immediate

1. TAMs 9141008, 9045002, 8727003.
2. *Est. of Cristofani v. Comm.*, 97 TC 74 (1991), acq. in result, 1996-2 CB 1.
3. *Estate of Clyde W. Turner v. Comm.*, TC Memo 2011-209.
4. AOD 1996-010.
5. *Est. of Kohlsaat v. Comm.*, TC Memo 1997-212; *Est. of Holland v. Comm.*, TC Memo 1997-302.
6. TAM 9532001.

use, possession, and enjoyment of an ascertainable interest in the property, qualifies for the gift tax annual exclusion.

If a donor transfers a specified portion of real property subject to an "adjustment clause" (i.e., under terms that provide that if the IRS subsequently determines that the value of the specified portion exceeds the amount of the annual exclusion, the portion of property given will be reduced accordingly, or the donee will compensate the donor for the excess), the IRS has ruled the adjustment clause will be disregarded for federal tax purposes.[1]

A donor's gratuitous payment of the monthly amount due on the mortgage on a house owned in joint tenancy by others has been held a present interest gift to the joint tenants in proportion to their ownership interests.[2]

898. When will a gift of property to a minor qualify for the gift tax annual exclusion?

A gift of property to a minor, whether in trust or otherwise, is not considered a gift of a future interest in property, so that it will qualify for the gift tax annual exclusion, if the terms of the transfer satisfy all the following conditions:

(1) Both the property itself and its income may be expended by or for the benefit of the donee before he attains the age of twenty-one years;

(2) Any portion of the property and its income not disposed of under (1) will pass to the donee when he attains the age of twenty-one years; and

(3) Any portion of the property and its income not disposed of under (1) will be payable either to the estate of the donee or as he may appoint under a general power of appointment if he dies before attaining the age of twenty-one years.[3]

A gift to a minor under the Uniform Gifts to Minors Act or under the Uniform Transfers to Minors Act generally is a gift of a present interest and qualifies for the annual exclusion.[4] Most states in recent years have adopted the later Uniform Transfers to Minors Act, which allows for any kind of property, real or personal, tangible or intangible, to be transferred under the Act. Other states have amended their Uniform Gifts to Minors Act to provide for gifts of various kinds of property ranging from real estate to partnership interests and other tangible and intangible interests in property. Originally, the Uniform Act provided for gifts of only money or securities. The allowance of the exclusion is not affected by the amendment of a state's Uniform Act lowering the age of majority and thus requiring that property be distributed to the donee at age eighteen.[5] The revenue rulings cited in this paragraph base the allowance of the exclusion on the assumption that gifts under the Uniform Act come within the purview of IRC Section 2503(c). Gifts to minors under IRC Section 2503(c) must pass

1. Rev. Rul. 86-41, 1986-1 CB 300.
2. Rev. Rul. 82-98, 1982-1 CB 141.
3. IRC Sec. 2503(c); Treas. Reg. §25.2503-4(a).
4. Rev. Rul. 59-357, 1959-2 CB 212; Rev. Rul. 73-287, 1973-2 CB 321.
5. Rev. Rul. 73-287, 1973-2 CB 321.

to the donee on his attaining age twenty-one. If a state statute varies from the Uniform Act by providing that under certain conditions custodianship may be extended past the donee's age twenty-one, gifts made under those conditions would not qualify for the exclusion. For a state-by-state summary of the types of property which can be given under, and the adult age for purposes of, the Uniform Act, see www.TaxFactsUpdates.com.

899. When will a gift of property to a corporation qualify for the gift tax annual exclusion?

A gift of property to a corporation generally represents a gift of a future interest in the property (so that it will not qualify for the gift tax annual exclusion, see Q 896) to the individual shareholders to the extent of their proportionate interests in the corporation.[1] Also a gift for the benefit of a corporation is a gift of a future interest in the property to its shareholders and does not qualify for the annual exclusion.[2] In contrast, gifts made to individual partnership capital accounts have been treated as gifts of a present interest which qualify for the annual exclusion where the partners were free to make immediate withdrawals of the gifts from their capital accounts.[3] However, annual exclusions were denied for gifts of limited partnership interests where (1) the general partner could retain income for any reason whatsoever, (2) limited partnership interests could not be transferred or assigned without the permission of a supermajority of other partners, and (3) limited partnership interests generally could not withdraw from the partnership or receive a return of capital contributions for many years into the future.[4] Similarly, annual exclusions were denied for gifts of business interests where the beneficiaries were not free to withdraw from the business entity, could not sell their interests, and could not control whether any income would be distributed (and no immediate income was expected).[5]

900. How does the splitting of gifts between spouses affect the gift tax annual exclusion?

By means of the "split gift" provision (see Q 894), a married couple can effectively use each other's annual exclusions. Thus, if, in 2020, A makes a $30,000 gift of securities to his child, C, and A's spouse, B, joins in making the gift (by signifying her consent on the gift tax return), the gift would be considered as having been made one-half by each, the exclusion is effectively doubled, and no gift tax would have to be paid (assuming neither A nor B made any other gifts to C during the calendar year).[6] However, if A and B join in making the same gift to F, child of A's brother D and spouse E, while at the same time D and E make similar gifts to C and F, the scheme does not effectively again double the exclusion.[7]

If the spouse of the donor is not a United States citizen, the annual exclusion for a transfer from the donor spouse to the non-citizen spouse is increased from $10,000 (as indexed) to

1. Treas. Reg. §25.2511-1(h)(1); Rev. Rul. 71-443, 1971-2 CB 337; *Stinson v. U.S.*, 2000-1 USTC ¶60,377 (7th Cir. 2000); *Hollingsworth v. Comm.*, 86 TC 91 (1986).
2. Let. Rul. 9114023.
3. *Wooley v. U.S.*, 736 F. Supp. 1506, 90-1 USTC ¶60,013 (S.D. Ind. 1990).
4. TAM 9751003.
5. *Hackl v. Comm.*, 335 F. 3d 664, 2003-2 USTC ¶60,465 (7th Cir. 2003), aff'g 118 TC 279 (2002).
6. IRC Sec. 2513; Treas. Reg. §25.2513-1.
7. TAM 8717003; *Sather v. Comm.*, 251 F.3d 1168 (8th Cir. 2001); *Schuler v. Comm.*, 282 F. 3d 575, 2002-1 USTC ¶60,432 (8th Cir. 2002).

$100,000 as indexed ($148,000 for 2016, $149,000 for 2017, $152,000 for 2018, $155,000 for 2019, and $157,000 in 2020[1] see Appendix D for earlier years) (provided the transfer would otherwise qualify for the marital deduction if the donee spouse were a United States citizen). The $100,000 amount is adjusted for inflation, as is the $10,000 amount (see above).[2] However, the marital deduction is not available for a transfer to a spouse who is not a United States citizen (see Q 902).

901. What gift tax exclusion applies, if any, for gifts made for education or medical expenses?

A "qualified transfer" is not considered a gift for gift tax purposes. A "qualified transfer" means any amount paid on behalf of an individual–

(A) as tuition to an educational organization[3] for the education or training of such individual, or

(B) to any person who provides medical care[4] with respect to such individual as payment for such medical care.[5] A technical advice memorandum treated tuition payments for future years as qualified transfers where the payments were nonrefundable.[6]

902. What is the gift tax marital deduction?

The gift tax marital deduction is a deduction for the entire value of gifts made between spouses.[7] The deduction does not apply, however, to a gift of a "nondeductible terminable interest" in property.[8] A "terminable interest" in property is an interest which will terminate or fail on the lapse of time or on the occurrence or failure to occur of some contingency. Life estates, terms for years, annuities, patents, and copyrights are therefore terminable interests. However, a bond, note, or similar contractual obligation, the discharge of which would not have the effect of an annuity or term for years, is not a terminable interest.[9]

In general, if a donor transfers a terminable interest in property to the donee spouse, the marital deduction is disallowed with respect to the transfer if the donor spouse also (1) transferred an interest in the same property to another donee, *or* (2) retained an interest in the same property in himself, *or* (3) retained a power to appoint an interest in the same property, *and* (4) gave the other donee, himself, or the possible appointee the right to possess or enjoy any part of the property after the termination or failure of the interest transferred to the donee spouse.[10] *However*, a terminable interest in property qualifies for the marital deduction (referred to as "QTIP") if the donee spouse is given (1) a right to the income from the property for life and a

1. Rev. Proc. 2015-53, Rev. Proc. 2016-55, Rev. Proc. 2017-58, Rev. Proc. 2018-57, Rev. Proc. 2019-44.
2. IRC Sec. 2523(i).
3. IRC Sec. 170(b)(1)(A)(ii).
4. As defined in IRC Sec. 213(d).
5. IRC Sec. 2503(e); Rev. Rul. 82-98, 1982-1 CB 141.
6. Let. Rul. 200602002; TAM 199941013.
7. IRC Sec. 2523(a).
8. IRC Sec. 2523(b); Treas. Reg. §§25.2523(a)-1(b)(2), 25.2523(b)-1.
9. Treas. Reg. §25.2523(b)-1(a)(3).
10. Treas. Reg. §25.2523(b)-1(a)(2).

general power of appointment over the principal; or (2) a "qualifying income interest for life" in property transferred by the donor spouse as to which the donor must make an election (on or before the date, including extensions, for filing a gift tax return with respect to the year in which the transfer was made–see Q 905) to have the marital deduction apply. The QTIP regulations provide an exception to the estate tax inclusion issues that arise under Sections 2036 and 2038.[1]

The donee spouse has a "qualifying income interest for life" if (1) the donee spouse is entitled to all the income from the property, payable annually or at more frequent intervals, and (2) no person has a power to appoint any part of the property to any person other than the donee spouse during the donee spouse's lifetime.[2] Also, the interest of a donee spouse in a joint and survivor annuity in which only the donor and donee spouses have a right to receive payments during such spouses' joint lifetimes is treated as a "qualifying income interest for life" unless the donor spouse irrevocably elects otherwise within the time allowed for filing a gift tax return.[3]

In the two exceptions to the nondeductible terminable interest rule explained above, income producing property is contemplated. If a gift of non-income producing property in a form to comply with either of the two exceptions is proposed, Treasury Regulation Section 25.2523(e)-1(f) should be read carefully. A marital deduction has been disallowed for a transfer to an irrevocable trust where state law provided that the interest given the spouse would be revoked upon divorce and the grantor had not provided in the trust instrument that the trust would not be revoked upon divorce.[4]

If the spouse of the donor is not a United States citizen, the marital deduction is not available for a transfer to such a spouse. However, in such a case, the annual exclusion (see Q 895) for the transfer from the donor spouse to the non-citizen spouse is increased from $10,000 as indexed ($15,000 in 2018-2020, $14,000 in 2013 through 2017) to $100,000 as indexed ($157,000 in 2020, $155,000 in 2019, $152,000 in 2018, and $149,000 in 2017[5] see Appendix D for earlier years) (provided the transfer would otherwise qualify for the marital deduction if the donee spouse were a United States citizen). The $100,000 amount is adjusted for inflation, as is the $10,000 amount (see Q 895).[6]

903. Is a gift tax deduction allowed for gifts to charity?

Yes. In general, a deduction is allowed for the entire value of gifts to qualified charitable organizations.[7]

Where a donor makes a gift of an interest in property (other than a remainder interest in a personal residence or farm or an undivided portion of the donor's entire interest in property or certain gifts of property interests exclusively for conservation purposes) to a qualified charity,

1. Treas. Reg. §25.2523(f)-1(d)(1).
2. IRC Secs. 2523(e), 2523(f).
3. IRC Sec. 2523(f)(6).
4. TAM 9127005.
5. Rev. Proc. 2016-55, Rev. Proc. 2017-58, Rev. Proc. 2018-57, Rev. Proc. 2019-44.
6. IRC Sec. 2523(i).
7. IRC Secs. 2522(a), 2522(b).

and an interest in the same property is retained by the donor or is given to a donee that is not a charity, no charitable deduction is allowed for the interest given the charity unless:

(1) in the case of a remainder interest, such interest is in a trust which is a charitable remainder annuity trust (see Q 8085) or a charitable remainder unitrust (see Q 8086) or a pooled income fund (see Q 8094); or

(2) in the case of any other interest (such as an interest in the income from a short term trust), such interest is in the form of a guaranteed annuity or is a fixed percentage of the fair market value of the property distributed yearly (to be determined yearly).[1]

A charitable contribution deduction is allowable for a gift to charity of a legal remainder interest in the donor's personal residence even though the interest conveyed to charity is in the form of a tenancy in common with an individual.[2]

If an individual creates a qualified charitable remainder trust in which his spouse is the only non-charitable beneficiary other than certain ESOP remainder beneficiaries, the grantor will receive a charitable contributions deduction for the value of the remainder interest.[3]

904. What is the gift tax unified credit?

It is a dollar amount ($4,577,800 in 2020, $4,505,800 in 2019, $4,419,800 in 2018, $2,185,800 in 2017, $2,141,800 in 2017 and $2,125,800 in 2016)[4] that is credited against the gift tax computed as shown in Q 882 (see Appendix D for amounts in other years).[5] In 2010, the credit exempted $1,000,000 of taxable gifts from the gift tax (the dollar amount exempted is referred to as the "gift tax applicable exclusion amount"). For 2011, the amount increased to $5,000,000, and was adjusted for inflation to $5,450,000 in 2016, $5,490,000 in 2017, and the 2017 Tax Act doubled the amount to $11,180,000 in 2018, $11,400,000 in 2019 and $11,580,000 in 2020.[6] Any gifts made over the gift tax applicable exclusion amount are taxed at a 40 percent rate (in 2013 and thereafter, up from 35 percent in 2011 and 2012). (For application of the unified credit to the federal estate tax, see Q 851.) The credit is referred to as "unified" because the current credit applies to the gift tax (section 2505), the GST tax (section 2641) or the estate tax (section 2010).

The amount of unified credit allowed against the tax on gifts made in any calendar year cannot exceed the dollar amount of credit applicable to the period in which the gifts were made, reduced by the sum of the amounts of unified credit allowed the donor against gifts made in all prior calendar periods, and reduced further by the rule explained in the next paragraph (but in no event can the allowable credit exceed the amount of the tax). The unused exemption of a

1. IRC Sec. 2522(c); Rev. Rul. 77-275, 1977-2 CB 346.
2. Rev. Rul. 87-37, 1987-1 CB 295, revoking Rev. Rul. 76-544, 1976-2 CB 288.
3. IRC Sec. 2522(c)(2).
4. Rev. Proc. 2015-53, Rev. Proc. 2016-55, Rev. Proc. 2017-58, Rev. Proc. 2018-57, Rev. Proc. 2019-44.
5. IRC Sec. 2505, as amended by EGTRRA 2001.
6. Rev. Proc. 2015-53, Rev. Proc. 2016-55, Pub. Law. No. 115-97 (the 2017 Tax Act), Rev. Proc. 2018-18, Rev. Proc. 2018-57, Rev. Proc. 2019-44.

deceased spouse may be transferred to the surviving spouse to increase the gift or estate applicable exclusion amount for the surviving spouse.[1]

The unified credit was enacted by the Tax Reform Act of 1976. Under prior law, separate exemptions were provided for estate and gift taxes. The gift tax specific exemption was $30,000 for each donor (or $60,000 if the donor's spouse joined in making the gift). The exemption was not applied automatically, as in the case of the unified credit, but had to be elected by the donor, and once used was gone. The law provides that as to gifts made after September 8, 1976, and before January 1, 1977, if the donor elected to apply any of his lifetime exemption to such gifts, his unified credit is reduced by an amount equal to 20 percent of the amount allowed as a specific exemption.[2] (The unified credit is not reduced by any amount allowed as a specific exemption for gifts made prior to September 9, 1976.)

Under 2010 TRA, a donor can make gifts, without incurring a gift tax liability, up to the difference between the current year's applicable exclusion amount and the prior taxable gifts.

By means of the "split gift" provision (see Q 894), a married couple can effectively use each other's unified credit.

905. What are the requirements for filing the gift tax return and paying the tax?

A donor need not file a gift tax return if the only gifts made during the calendar year are covered by the annual exclusion (Q 895) or the marital deduction (Q 902), or are gifts to charity of the donor's entire interest in the property transferred where the donor does not (and has not) transferred any interest in the property to a noncharitable beneficiary. (Amounts paid on behalf of an individual as tuition to an educational organization or to a person providing medical care are not considered gifts for gift tax purposes.)[3] However, in the case of a split gift (where the donor's spouse joins in making a gift to a third party), a gift tax return must be filed even though the amount of the gift comes within the spouses' annual exclusions.

The return (Form 709) is due on or before April 15 following the close of the calendar year for which the return is made; however, if the donor is given an extension of time for filing the income tax return, the same extension applies to filing the gift tax return. Where a gift is made during the calendar year in which the donor dies, the time for filing the gift tax return is not later than the time (including extensions) for filing the estate tax return.[4] However, should the time for filing the estate tax return fall later than the fifteenth day of April following the close of the calendar year, the time for filing the gift tax return is on or before the fifteenth day of April following the close of the calendar year, unless an extension (not extending beyond the time for filing the estate tax return) was granted for filing the gift tax return. If no estate tax return is required to be filed, the time for filing the gift tax return is on or before the fifteenth

1. IRC Secs. 2505(a)(i); 2010.
2. IRC Sec. 2505(c).
3. IRC Sec. 2503(e); IRC Sec. 6019.
4. IRC Sec. 6075.

day of April following the close of the calendar year, unless an extension was given for filing the gift tax return.[1]

The penalty for failure to timely file a federal tax return is 5 percent of the tax for each month the return is past due, up to a maximum of 25 percent. The penalty can be avoided only if "it is shown that such failure is due to reasonable cause and not due to willful neglect."[2] The regulations say that "reasonable cause" means that the taxpayer filing a late return must show that he "exercised ordinary business care and prudence and was nevertheless unable to file the return within the prescribed time."[3] In *United States v. Boyle*,[4] the Supreme Court held that a taxpayer's reliance on an agent who says he will file the appropriate tax return does not avoid the penalty tax for failure to make a timely filing. However, the Court was careful to distinguish the case where the taxpayer relies on his tax advisor to determine whether a return should be filed at all. In *Estate of Buring v. Commissioner*,[5] the estate avoided the penalty tax because the Court found that the decedent had relied upon her accountant's advice in failing to file gift tax returns for substantial advances of cash the decedent made to her son, even though the accountant apparently had not actually advised her that it was not necessary to file gift tax returns.

The gift tax is payable by the donor on the date the gift tax return is due to be filed (April 15). An extension of time given to file the return does not act as an extension of time to pay the tax.[6] If the donor does not pay the tax when it is due, the donee is liable for the tax to the extent of the value of the gift.[7] If an extension of time for payment of the tax is granted, interest compounded daily is charged at an annual rate adjusted quarterly so as to be three percentage points over the short term federal rate.[8] The underpayment rate for the fourth quarter of 2019 is 5 percent.[9]

Valuation

906. How is investment property valued for federal transfer tax purposes?

"Fair market value" is the measure, defined as "the price at which the property would change hands between a willing buyer and a willing seller, neither being under any compulsion to buy or to sell and both having reasonable knowledge of relevant facts." In the case of the estate tax, fair market value is determined as of the date of the decedent's death, except that if the executor elects the alternate valuation method, fair market value is determined in accordance with the rules explained at Q 907. In the case of the gift tax, fair market value is determined as of the date of the gift. Property is not to be valued at the value at which it is assessed for local tax purposes unless that value represents the fair market value as of the applicable valuation date.

1. IRC Sec. 6075; Treas. Reg. §25.6075-1(b)(2).
2. IRC Sec. 6651(a)(1).
3. Treas. Reg. §301.6651-1(c)(1).
4. 105 S. Ct. 687 (1985).
5. TC Memo 1985-610.
6. IRC Secs. 2502(c), 6151(a).
7. IRC Sec. 6324(b); *Comm. v. Chase Manhattan Bank*, 259 F.2d 231 (5th Cir. 1958).
8. IRC Secs. 6601(a), 6621(a)(2).
9. Rev. Rul. 2019-05.

Planning Point: The property is generally valued based on its highest and best use, which may be inconsistent with how the property is used at the time of the gift or at the time of death. All relevant facts and elements of value as of the applicable valuation date are to be considered in every case.[1]

In the case of any taxable gift which is a direct skip within the meaning of the generation-skipping transfer tax (GST tax) (see Q 865), the amount of such gift is increased by the amount of the GST tax imposed on the transfer.[2] See Q 866 for special GST tax valuation rules.

Special rules apply to the valuation of particular kinds of investment property, such as stocks and bonds (Q 909), notes (Q 911), mutual fund shares (Q 915), certain kinds of business interests (Q 917). See Q 920 on the valuation of real estate. The principle of blockage discounting, applied in the valuation of a sizeable block of shares of corporate stock (see Q 909), can also be applied in valuing artwork.[3] Special rules also apply where, under certain conditions spelled out in IRC Section 2032A, an executor may elect to value, for federal estate tax purposes, real property (called "qualified real property") devoted to farming or another trade or business (called "qualified use") by the decedent or a member of the decedent's family on the date of the decedent's death, on the basis of its actual use rather than by taking into account the "highest and best" use to which the property could be put. See also Q 8054. Revenue Ruling 59-60[4] is the most often-cited authority for the basic principles of valuing closely-held stock or other business interest for tax purposes.

Assets in a restricted management account (RMA) are valued at fair market value, without regard to any RMA restrictions.[5]

Property includable in a surviving spouse's estate as qualified terminable interest property (QTIP, see Q 837) under IRC Section 2044 (see Q 814) is not aggregated with other property includable in the estate for estate tax valuation purposes.[6] However, property included in the gross estate because of a general power of appointment under IRC Section 2041 (see Q 814) should be aggregated with property owned outright by the powerholder for estate tax valuation purposes.[7]

With respect to gift and estate tax returns, 20 percent of an underpayment attributable to a substantial gift or estate tax valuation understatement is added to tax.[8] There is a substantial gift or estate tax valuation understatement if (1) the value claimed was 65 percent or less of the correct amount; and (2) the underpayment exceeds $5,000. If the value claimed was 40 percent or less of the correct amount (and the underpayment exceeds $5,000), 40 percent of an underpayment attributable to such a gross gift or estate tax valuation understatement is

1. Treas. Reg. §§20.2031-1(b), 25.2512-1.
2. IRC Sec. 2515.
3. *Calder v. Comm.*, 85 TC 713 (1985).
4. 1959-1 CB 237.
5. Rev. Rul. 2008-35, 2008-29 IRB 116.
6. *Est. of Bonner v. U.S.*, 84 F.3d 196, 96-2 USTC ¶60,237 (5th Cir. 1996), rev'g an unpublished decision (S.D. Tex.); *Est. of Mellinger v. Comm.*, 112 TC 26 (1999), acq. AOD 1999-006.
7. FSA 200119013; *Est. of Fontana v. Comm.*, 118 TC 318 (2002).
8. IRC Sec. 6662.

added to tax.[1] The 20 percent or 40 percent penalty is not imposed with respect to any portion of the underpayment for which it is shown that there was reasonable cause and the taxpayer acted in good faith.[2]

A gift which is disclosed on a gift tax return in a manner adequate to apprise the Service of the nature of the item may not be revalued after the statute of limitations (generally, three years after the return is filed) has expired.[3]

See Q 924 for Chapter 14 special valuation rules.

907. How does the executor's election of the alternate valuation method affect the valuation of property for federal estate tax purposes?

The law permits the executor to elect an alternate valuation method if the election will decrease the value of the gross estate and the sum of the amount of the federal estate tax and generation-skipping transfer tax payable by reason of the decedent's death with respect to the property includable in the decedent's gross estate.[4] If the alternate valuation method is elected, the property will be valued under the following rules:

Any property distributed, sold, exchanged or otherwise disposed of within six months after decedent's death is valued as of the date of such distribution, sale, exchange, or other disposition. The phrase "distributed, sold, exchanged, or otherwise disposed of" includes all possible ways by which property ceases to form a part of the gross estate. For example, money on hand at the date of the decedent's death which is thereafter used in the payment of funeral expenses, or which is thereafter invested, falls within the term "otherwise disposed of." The term also includes the surrender of a stock certificate for corporate assets in complete or partial liquidation of a corporation pursuant to IRC Section 331. The term does not, however, extend to transactions which are mere changes in form. Thus, it does not include a transfer of assets to a corporation controlled by the transferor in exchange for its stock in a transaction with respect to which no gain or loss would be recognized for income tax purposes under IRC Section 351. Nor does it include an exchange of stock or securities in a corporation for stock or securities in the same corporation or another corporation in a transaction, such as a merger, recapitalization, reorganization, or other transaction described in IRC Section 368(a) or IRC Section 355, with respect to which no gain or loss is recognizable for income tax purposes under IRC Section 354 or IRC Section 355.[5]

In *Estate of Smith v. Commissioner*,[6] the decedent's stock in X corporation was exchanged for stock and warrants in Y corporation pursuant to a plan of merger. The court held that the warrants were received in exchange for the estate's stock in X and were to be valued as of the date of the merger. The Commissioner conceded that the transaction should not be treated as an

1. IRC Sec. 6662(g)(2).
2. IRC Sec. 6664(c)(1).
3. IRC Sec. 6501(c)(9).
4. IRC Sec. 2032; Treas. Reg. §20.2032-1(b)(1).
5. Treas. Reg. §20.2032-1(c)(1).
6. 63 TC 722 (1975).

"exchange" with respect to the receipt of *stock* in Y, and that even though the value of the Y stock had declined substantially between the decedent's date of death and the alternate valuation date, the stock should be valued as of the alternate valuation date. The court's decision, however, was limited to the controverted issue as to the proper valuation date of the warrants. Apparently, the IRS soon changed its mind. In Revenue Ruling 77-221,[1] on substantially similar facts, the Service concluded that the exchange of X stock for Y stock and warrants constitutes an "exchange" and held that the X stock given in exchange was to be valued as of the date of the exchange.

If the property is listed stock and is sold in an arm's length transaction, the stock is valued at the actual selling price.[2] An exercise of stock rights is a "disposition" thereof; their value is equal to the excess, if any, of the fair market value of the stock acquired by such rights at the time the rights are exercised over the subscription price.[3]

Any property not distributed, sold, exchanged, or otherwise disposed of within six months after a decedent's death is valued as of the date six months after death. When shares of stock in the estate are sold at a discount between the date of death and the alternate valuation date, such sales and the number of shares sold cannot be taken into account in determining whether the shares remaining in the estate at the alternate valuation date are eligible for "blockage" valuation (see Q 909).[4]

Any property interest whose value is affected by mere lapse of time is valued as of the date of the decedent's death. Despite this, an adjustment is made for any change in value during the six-month period (or during the period between death and distribution, sale, or exchange) which is not due to mere lapse of time.[5] The phrase "affected by mere lapse of time" has no reference to obligations for the payment of money, whether or not interest bearing, the value of which changes with the passage of time.[6]

Proposed regulations would provide that the election to value property includable in the gross estate on the alternate valuation date applies only to the extent that the change in value is a result of market conditions.[7]

If the alternate valuation method is elected, it must be applied to all the property included in the gross estate, and cannot be applied to only a portion of the property.[8]

The election to value property using the alternate valuation method must be made by the executor on the Form 706, and no later than one year after the due date (including extensions) for filing the estate tax return. The election is irrevocable, unless it is revoked no later than the due date (including extensions) for filing the estate tax return. If use of the alternate valuation method would not result in a decrease in both the value of the gross estate and the amount of

1. 1977-1 CB 271.
2. Rev. Rul. 70-512, 1970-2 CB 192; *Est. of Van Horne v. Comm.*, 720 F. 2d 1114, 83-2 USTC ¶13,548 (9th Cir. 1983), aff'g 78 TC 728 (1982).
3. Rev. Rul. 58-576, 1958-2 CB 256.
4. *Est. of Van Horne v. Comm.*, 720 F. 2d 1114, 83-2 USTC ¶13,548 (9th Cir. 1983), aff'g 78 TC 728 (1982).
5. IRC Sec. 2032(a).
6. Treas. Reg. §20.2032-1(f).
7. Prop. Treas. Reg. §20. 2032-1(f).
8. Treas. Reg. §20.2032-1(b)(2).

estate tax and generation-skipping transfer tax on a filed return, a protective election can be made to use the alternate valuation method if it is later determined that such a decrease would occur. A request for an extension of time to make the election or protective election may be made if the estate tax return was filed no later than one year after the due date (including extensions) for filing the estate tax return but an election or protective election was not made on the return.[1]

908. What property is "included property" for purposes of the alternative valuation method for determining federal estate tax? What property is excluded?

Property earned or accrued (whether received or not) after the date of the decedent's death and during the alternate valuation period with respect to property included in the gross estate is excluded in valuing the gross estate under the alternate valuation method, and is referred to as "excluded property."[2]

Thus, as to *interest-bearing obligations* included in the gross estate ("included property"), interest accrued after the date of death and before the subsequent valuation date constitutes "excluded property." However, any partial payment of principal made between the date of death and the subsequent valuation date, or any advance payment of interest for a period after the subsequent valuation date made during the alternate valuation period which has the effect of reducing the value of the principal obligation as of the subsequent valuation date, will be included in the gross estate, and valued as of the date of such payment.[3]

The same principles applicable to interest-bearing obligations also apply to *leased realty or personalty* which is included in the gross estate and with respect to which an obligation to pay rent has been reserved. Both the realty or personalty itself and the rents accrued to the date of death constitute "included property," and each is to be separately valued as of the applicable valuation date. Any rent accrued after the date of death and before the subsequent valuation date is "excluded property." Similarly, the principle applicable with respect to interest paid in advance is equally applicable with respect to advance payments of rent.[4]

Assets sold continue as included property "even though they change in form."[5] Where royalty and working interests in oil and gas property were included property, the proceeds from the sale of oil and gas extracted from this property between the date of the decedent's death and the alternate valuation date were held to be included property (merely the translation of the decedent's interest in the in-place reserves the decedent owned at the time of her death into cash). As for the portion of proceeds to be included in the gross estate, the appropriate value was held to be the in-place value of the oil and gas on the date of its severance.[6]

1. IRC Sec. 2032(d); Treas. Reg. §20.2032-1(b).
2. Treas. Reg. §20.2032-1(d).
3. Treas. Reg. §20.2032-1(d)(1).
4. Treas. Reg. §20.2032-1(d)(2).
5. Treas. Reg. §20.2032-1(d).
6. *Est. of Johnston v. U.S.*, 779 F.2d 1123 (Fifth Circuit 1986), rev'g and remanding 84-2 USTC ¶13,591 (N.D. Tex. 1984), cert. den. 6-23-86.

In the case of *noninterest-bearing obligations sold at a discount*, such as savings bonds, the principal obligation and the discount amortized to the date of death are property interests existing at the date of death and constitute "included property." The obligation itself is to be valued at the subsequent valuation date without regard to any further increase in value due to amortized discount. The additional discount amortized after death and during the alternate valuation period is the equivalent of interest accruing during that period and is, therefore, not to be included in the gross estate under the alternate valuation method.[1]

Shares of stock in a corporation and dividends declared to stockholders of record on or before the date of the decedent's death and not collected at the date of death constitute "included property" of the estate. On the other hand, ordinary dividends out of earnings and profits (whether in cash, shares of the corporation, or other property) declared to stockholders of record after the date of the decedent's death are "excluded property" and are not to be valued under the alternate valuation method. If, however, dividends are declared to stockholders of record after the date of the decedent's death with the effect that the shares of stock at the subsequent valuation date do not reasonably represent the same "included property" of the gross estate as existed at the date of the decedent's death, the dividends are "included property," except to the extent that they are paid out of earnings of the corporation after the date of the decedent's death.

For example, if a corporation makes a distribution in partial liquidation to stockholders of record during the alternate valuation period which is not accompanied by a surrender of a stock certificate for cancellation, the amount of the distribution received on stock included in the gross estate is itself "included property," except to the extent that the distribution was out of earnings and profits since the date of the decedent's death. Similarly, if a corporation, in which the decedent owned a substantial interest and which possessed at the date of the decedent's death accumulated earnings and profits equal to its paid-in capital, distributed all of its accumulated earnings and profits as a cash dividend to shareholders of record during the alternate valuation period, the amount of the dividends received on stock includable in the gross estate will be included in the gross estate under the alternate valuation method. Likewise, a stock dividend distributed under such circumstances is "included property."[2]

"Included property" also includes the following:

(1) nontaxable stock rights and proceeds from the sale of such rights occurring after the decedent's death but before the alternate valuation date, where the rights are issued subsequent to the decedent's death in respect of stock owned by the decedent at death;

(2) a nontaxable stock dividend received subsequent to the decedent's death but before the alternate valuation date; and

1. Treas. Reg. §20.2032-1(d)(3).
2. Treas. Reg. §20.2032-1(d)(4).

(3) payments on the principal of mortgages received between the date of death and the alternate valuation date.[1]

But where an estate owned mutual fund shares, and between the date of the decedent's death and the alternate valuation date capital gains dividends attributable solely to gains on stocks held by the companies at decedent's death were declared and paid, it was held that the dividends were not "included property."[2]

When determining the value of a decedent's gross estate, dividends declared before death, on stock includable in the gross estate, payable to stockholders of record after the date of the decedent's death, must be considered in making an adjustment in the ex-dividend quotation of the stock at the date of the decedent's death. Such dividends may not be included in the gross estate under the alternate method of valuing the gross estate either as a separate asset or as an adjustment of the ex-dividend quoted value of the stock as of the alternate valuation date or as of some intermediate date.

Under the alternate method of valuing the gross estate, stock includable in the gross estate and selling ex-dividend is to be valued at its ex-dividend quoted selling price as of the alternate valuation date or at any intermediate valuation date, increased by the amount of dividends declared on the stock during the alternate valuation period payable to stockholders of record subsequent to the alternate valuation date or such intermediate date. No part of the value so determined is deemed to be excluded property in determining the value of the gross estate.[3]

909. How are stocks and bonds listed on an exchange or in an over-the-counter market valued for federal transfer tax purposes?

In general, their value is the fair market value per share or bond on the applicable valuation date (see Q 906). If there is a market for stocks or bonds, on a stock exchange, in an over-the-counter market, or otherwise, the mean between the highest and lowest quoted selling prices on the valuation date is the fair market value per share or bond. (Listed securities and Treasury bonds must be reported and valued in dollar fractions smaller than eighths or thirty-seconds, respectively, if the mean selling price on the applicable valuation date results in a smaller fraction.)[4]

Restricted securities (sometimes referred to as "unregistered securities," "investment letter stock," "control stock," or "private placement stock") are securities that cannot lawfully be distributed to the general public until a registration statement relating to the corporation underlying the securities has been filed and made effective by the SEC. Information and guidance in the valuation of these securities is contained in Revenue Ruling 77-287.[5]

If there were no sales on the valuation date but there were sales on dates within a reasonable period both before and after the valuation date, the fair market value is determined by taking a

1. Rev. Rul. 58-576, 1958-2 CB 625.
2. Rev. Rul. 76-234, 1976-1 CB 271.
3. Rev. Rul. 60-124, 1960-1 CB 368.
4. Rev. Rul. 68-272, 1968-1 CB 394.
5. 1977-2 CB 319. See *Est. of Stratton v. Comm.*, TC Memo 1982-744; *Est. of Sullivan v. Comm.*, TC Memo 1983-185; *Est. of Gilford v. Comm.*, 88 TC 38 (1987).

weighted average of the means between the highest and lowest sales on the nearest date before and the nearest date after the valuation date. The average is to be weighted inversely by the respective numbers of trading days between the selling dates and the valuation date. If the stocks or bonds are listed on more than one exchange, the records of the exchange where the stocks or bonds are principally dealt in should be employed if such records are available in a generally available listing or publication of general circulation. In the event that such records are not so available and such stocks or bonds are listed on a composite listing of combined exchanges in a generally available listing or publication of general circulation, the records of such combined exchanges should be employed.[1]

If it is established with respect to bonds for which there is a market on a stock exchange, that the highest and lowest selling prices are not available for the valuation date in a generally available listing or publication of general circulation, but that closing selling prices are so available, the fair market value per bond is the mean between the quoted closing selling price on the valuation date and the quoted closing selling price on the trading day before the valuation date. If there were no sales on the trading day before the valuation date but there were sales on a date within a reasonable period before the valuation date, the fair market value is determined by taking a weighted average of the quoted closing selling price on the valuation date and the quoted closing selling price on the nearest date before the valuation date. The closing selling price for the valuation date is to be weighted by the number of trading days between the previous selling date and the valuation dates. If there were no sales within a reasonable period before the valuation date but there were sales on the valuation date, the fair market value is the closing selling price on such valuation date. If there were no sales on the valuation date but there were sales on dates within a reasonable period both before and after the valuation date, the fair market value is determined by taking a weighted average of the quoted closing selling prices on the nearest date before and the nearest date after the valuation date. The average is to be weighted inversely by the respective numbers of trading days between the selling dates and the valuation date. If the bonds are listed on more than one exchange, the records of the exchange where the bonds are principally dealt in should be employed.[2]

If the above measures are inapplicable because actual sales are not available during a reasonable period beginning before and ending after the valuation date, the fair market value may be determined by taking the mean between the bona fide bid and asked prices on the valuation date, or if none, by taking a weighted average of the means between the bona fide bid and asked prices on the nearest trading date before and the nearest trading date after the valuation date, if both such nearest dates are within a reasonable period. The average is to be determined in the manner described above.[3]

If the foregoing measures are inapplicable because no actual sale prices or bona fide bid and asked prices are available on a date within a reasonable period before the valuation date, but such prices are available on a date within a reasonable period after the valuation date, or

1. Treas. Reg. §§20.2031-2(a), 20.2031-2(b)(1), 25.2512-2(a), 25.2512-2(b)(1).
2. Treas. Reg. §§20.2031-2(b)(2); 25.2512-2(b)(2).
3. Treas. Reg. §§20.2031-2(c); 25.2512-2(c).

vice versa, then the mean between the highest and lowest available sale prices or bid and asked prices may be taken as the value.[1]

If it is established that the value of any bond or share of stock determined on the basis of selling or bid and asked prices as provided above does not reflect the fair market value thereof, then some reasonable modification of that basis or other relevant facts and elements of value are considered in determining the fair market value.

To quote the Tax Court: "In general, property is valued as of the valuation date on the basis of market conditions and facts available on that date *without regard to hindsight*...The rule that has developed, and which we accept, is that subsequent events are not considered in fixing fair market value, except to the extent that they were reasonably foreseeable at the date of valuation."[2] Generally, post-valuation date events should be ignored when valuing property for gift tax or estate tax purposes.

Where sales at or near the date of death or gift are few or of a sporadic nature, such sales alone may not indicate fair market value. In certain exceptional cases, the size of the block of stock to be valued in relation to the number of shares changing hands in sales may be relevant in determining whether selling prices reflect the fair market value of the block of stock to be valued. If the executor or donor can show that the block of stock to be valued is so large in relation to the actual sales on the existing market that it could not be liquidated in a reasonable time without depressing the market, the price at which the block could be sold as such outside the usual market, as through an underwriter, may be a more accurate indication of value than market quotations.[3] "[W]here a security is actively traded on the market and the block in question represents, let's say, less than three months' average market trading, any blockage claim should be given careful examination before a discount is approved."[4]

The IRS has held that, in the estate tax setting, underwriting fees that are necessarily incurred in marketing a large block of stock are deductible as administration expenses under IRC Section 2053(a)(2), and are not considered in determining the blockage discount to be accorded in valuing the stock under IRC Section 2031 (see Q 837). Where a blockage discount is allowed, says the Service, the relevant valuation figure is the price that the public would pay to the underwriter for the stock, not the price the underwriter would pay to the estate.[5] For a discussion of the blockage discount issue, see *Est. of Sawade v. Comm.*[6]

If actual sale prices and bona fide bid and asked prices are lacking, then the fair market value is to be determined by taking the following factors into consideration:

(1) In the case of corporate or other bonds, the soundness of the security, the interest yield, the date of maturity, and other relevant factors; and

1. Treas. Reg. §§20.2031-2(d); 25.2512-2(d).
2. *Est. of Gilford v. Comm.*, 88 TC 38 (1987).
3. Treas. Reg. §§20.2031-2(e); 25.2512-2(e).
4. *IRS Valuation Guide for Income, Estate and Gift Taxes*, page 194 (published by Commerce Clearing House on May 11, 1982).
5. Rev. Rul. 83-30, 1983-1 CB 224.
6. TC Memo 1984-626, aff'd 86-2 USTC ¶13,672 (8th Cir. 1986).

(2) In the case of shares of stock, the company's net worth, prospective earning power and dividend-paying capacity, and other relevant factors.

Some of the "other relevant factors" referred to in (1) and (2) above are the following: the goodwill of the business, the economic outlook in the particular industry, the company's position in the industry and its management, the degree of control of the business represented by the block of stock to be valued, and the values of securities of corporations engaged in the same or similar lines of business which are listed on a stock exchange. However, the weight to be accorded such comparisons or any other evidentiary factors considered in the determination of a value depends upon the facts of each case.[1] In addition to the relevant factors described above, consideration is also given to nonoperating assets, including the proceeds of life insurance policies payable to or for the benefit of the company, to the extent such nonoperating assets have not been taken into account in the determination of net worth, prospective earning power and dividend-earning capacity.[2]

Another person may hold an option or a contract to purchase securities owned by a decedent at the time of his death. The effect, if any, that is given to the option or contract price in determining the value of the securities for estate tax purposes depends upon the circumstances of the particular case. Little weight will be accorded a price contained in an option or contract under which the decedent is free to dispose of the underlying securities at any price he chooses during his lifetime. Such is the effect, for example, of an agreement on the part of a shareholder to purchase whatever shares of stock the decedent may own at the time of his death. Even if the decedent is not free to dispose of the underlying securities at other than the option or contract price, such price will be disregarded in determining the value of the securities unless it is determined under the circumstances of the particular case that the agreement represents a bona fide business arrangement and not a device to pass the decedent's shares to the natural objects of his bounty for less than an adequate and full consideration in money or money's worth.[3] For a case applying this regulation, see *Dorn v. the United States.*[4] In any event, an option or a contract to purchase securities which fails to meet the Chapter 14 valuation rules test for such options or agreements (see Q 933) will be disregarded.[5]

In any case where a dividend is declared on a share of stock before the decedent's death but payable to stockholders of record on a date after his death and the stock is selling "ex-dividend" on the date of the decedent's death, the amount of the dividend is added to the ex-dividend quotation in determining the fair market value of the stock as of the date of the decedent's death.[6]

1. See, e.g., *Est. of Cook v. U.S.*, 86-2 USTC ¶13,678 (W.D. Mo. 1986).
2. Treas. Reg. §§20.2031-2(f); 25.2512-2(f).
3. Treas. Reg. §20.2031-2(h).
4. 828 F.2d 177, 87-2 USTC ¶13,732 (3rd Cir. 1987), reversing 86-2 USTC ¶13,701 (W.D. Pa. 1986).
5. IRC Sec. 2703.
6. Treas. Reg. §20.2031-2(i); Rev. Rul. 54-399, 1954-2 CB 279.

910. What effect does it have on valuation of shares of stock for federal transfer tax purposes if they are pledged as security?

The full value of securities pledged to secure an indebtedness of the decedent is included in the gross estate. If the decedent had a trading account with a broker, all securities belonging to the decedent and held by the broker at the date of death must be included at their fair market value as of the applicable valuation date. Securities purchased on margin for the decedent's account and held by a broker must also be returned at their fair market value as of the applicable valuation date. The amount of the decedent's indebtedness to a broker or other person with whom securities were pledged is allowed as a deduction from the gross estate.[1] The deduction is taken under IRC Section 2053.

If the shares of stock are pledged to secure a debt that was not the decedent's debt at his death, the shares' value that is includable in the gross estate is reduced to reflect the encumbrance. The amount of the reduction depends upon such factors as the decedent's right to receive dividends, the size of the debt, and the outlook for timely repayment of the debt.[2]

911. How are notes, mortgages, and mortgage participation certificates valued for federal transfer tax purposes?

The fair market value of notes, secured or unsecured, is presumed to be the amount of unpaid principal, plus interest accrued to the date of death or gift, unless the executor or the donor establishes that the value is lower or that the notes are worthless. If not returned at face value, plus accrued interest, satisfactory evidence must be submitted that the note is worth less than the unpaid amount (because of the interest rate, date of maturity, or other cause), or that the note is uncollectible, either in whole or in part (by reason of the insolvency of the party or parties liable, or for other cause), and that any property pledged or mortgaged as security is insufficient to satisfy the obligation.[3]

Mortgages and mortgage participation certificates are treated similarly. The presumption that their face value is their true value governs unless the representative of the estate submits convincing evidence to the contrary.

If it is contended that the actual value of mortgages or mortgage participation certificates is less than their face value, pertinent factors to be taken into consideration in fixing the correct value include the valuation of real estate and any collateral covered by the mortgages, arrears in taxes and interest, gross and net rentals, foreclosure proceedings, assignment of rents, prior liens or encumbrances, present interest yield, over-the-counter sales, bid and asked quotations, etc. The existence of an over-the-counter market for such securities and the quotations and opinions of value furnished by brokers and real estate appraisers cannot be accepted as conclusive evidence of the value of such securities. Such sales and bid and asked quotations are merely items to be considered with other evidence in fixing values.

---

1. Treas. Reg. §20.2031-2(g).
2. *Est. of Hall v. Comm.*, TC Memo 1983-355.
3. Treas. Reg. §§20.2031-4; 25.2512-4.

In valuing unit mortgages, consideration will be given first to the value of the property securing the mortgages, applying the same factors as are used in fixing the valuation of real estate owned in fee. Where the mortgage is amply secured, the value will be determined to be its face value plus accrued interest to the date of death. Where the security is insufficient, the mortgage will be valued upon the basis of the fair market value of the property less back taxes, estimated foreclosure expenses, and, where justified, the expense of rehabilitation. If the mortgage is not affected by moratorium laws, the mortgagee's recourse against the mortgagor personally will be taken into consideration.

Planning Point: The valuation of such assets is a question of fact and the IRS contends that the burden of proof is upon the estate to overcome the presumption that the face value is the true value where a lower value is sought to be established.[1]

912. How are life estates, remainders, and private annuities valued for federal transfer tax purposes?

Life estates, estates for a term of years, remainder interests, and private annuities are generally valued by use of the government's valuation tables (see below).[2] However, it has been held that the tables are only *presumptively* correct, and that in exceptional cases where there is strong evidence at the date of valuation that the life by which an interest is measured has an expectation of life longer or shorter than the tables indicate, that interest may be valued according to the facts at hand rather than according to the tables.[3] On the other hand, the government tables must be used even though the life tenant or life annuitant is in poor health at the date of valuation if the tenant's or annuitant's time of death is neither predictable nor imminent.[4] Account may not be taken of facts later coming to light but not available at the date of valuation; i.e., the interest may not be valued through the aid of hindsight.[5]

Planning Point: Life annuitants should seek a medical evaluation and receive a written report at the time a private annuity contract or similar arrangement is executed to establish the individual's health status.

Regulations provide that the standard valuation tables are not to be used where the individual who is a measuring life is terminally ill (defined as a person with an incurable illness or other deteriorating physical condition and at least a 50 percent probability of dying within one year). However, if an individual survives for eighteen months after the transaction, the individual is presumed to have not been terminally ill at the time of the transaction unless the contrary is established by clear and convincing evidence.[6]

1. Rev. Rul. 67-276, 1967-2 CB 321.
2. *Fehrs v. U.S.*, 45 AFTR 2d 1695, 384 F. Supp. 257, 79-2 USTC ¶13,324 (Ct. Cl. 1979).
3. *Est. of Carter v. U.S.*, 921 F. 2d 63, 91-1 USTC ¶60,054 (5th Cir. 1991); *Dunigan v. U.S.*, 434 F.2d 892 (5th Cir. 1970); *Est. of Hoelzel v. Comm.*, 28 TC 384 (1957), acq. 1957-2 CB 5; *Est. of Jennings v. Comm.*, 10 TC 323 (1948), nonacq. 1953-1 CB 5; *Ellis Sarasota Bank & Trust Co. v. U.S.*, 77-2 USTC ¶13,204 (M.D. Fla. 1977).
4. *Miami Beach First Nat'l Bank v. U.S.*, 443 F.2d 116 (5th Cir. 1971); *Bank of Cal. (Est. of Manning) v. U.S.*, 82-1 USTC ¶13,461 (C.D. Cal. 1980); *Est. of Fabric v. Comm.*, 83 TC 932 (1984).
5. *U.S. v. Provident Trust Co.*, 291 U.S. 272 (1934); *Est. of Van Horne v. Comm.*, 720 F. 2d 1114, 83-2 USTC ¶13,548 (9th Cir. 1983), aff'g 78 TC 728 (1982), *cert. den.*
6. Treas. Reg. §§1.7520-3(b)(3), 20.7520-3(b)(3), 25.7520-3(b)(3).

The estate and gift tax valuation tables are based on an assumed interest rate. Departure from strict application of the tables is permissible in exceptional cases where use of the tables would violate reason and fact. Examples of this include situations where transferred property may yield no income at all or the income is definitely determinable by other means.[1] However, the IRS will not allow such departure on a mere showing that past income yield from trust assets has been substantially lower than the rate assumed in the tables.[2] Nor will departure be allowed simply because the property transferred as a gift in trust is nonincome producing if the trustee has power to convert it to income producing property.[3]

Regulations provide that the standard valuation tables are not to be used to value an annuity if, considering the assumed interest rate, the trust is expected to exhaust the fund before the last possible annuity payment is made in full (measuring life survival to age 110 is assumed for this purpose). For a fixed annuity (i.e., annuity amount is payable for a term certain, or for one or two lives) payable annually at the end of the year, the corpus is assumed to be sufficient to make all payments if the assumed interest rate is greater than or equal to the annuity payment percentage (i.e., the amount of the annual annuity payment divided by the initial value of the corpus). If the annuity payment percentage exceeds the assumed interest rate and the annuity is for a term certain, multiply the annual annuity payment by the term certain annuity factor (derived from the Term Certain Remainder Factors Table found in Appendix C). If the annuity payment percentage exceeds the assumed interest rate and the annuity is for one or two lives, multiply the annual annuity payment by the term certain annuity factor (derived from the Term Certain Remainder Factors Table found in Appendix C) for a term equal to 110 minus the age of the youngest measuring life. If the present value for a term certain annuity, as derived in either of the two preceding sentences, exceeds the fund from which the annuity is to be paid, a special IRC Section 7520 valuation factor may be required to take into account the exhaustion of the fund. Adjustments in the computations described above would be required if payment terms differ from those described.[4]

Example. Donor, age sixty, transfers $1,000,000 to a trust. The trust will pay $100,000 a year to charity for the life of donor, with remainder to the donor's child. The IRC Section 7520 interest rate for the transfer is 6.8 percent. Since the annuity payment percentage of 10 percent ($100,000 annual payment divided by $1,000,000 initial value of trust fund) exceeds the 6.8 percent assumed interest rate, it cannot be assumed the annuity payments will not exhaust the trust. Therefore, subtract donor's age 60 from 110, resulting in a term of 50 years. The remainder factor for a term of 50 years at 6.8 percent interest is .037277 (Term Certain Remainder Factors Table). The life income factor equals one minus the remainder factor of .037277, or .962723. The annuity factor equals the life income factor of .962723 divided by the assumed interest rate of 6.8 percent, or 14.1577. The present value of a term certain annuity equals $1,415,770 ($100,000 annual payment multiplied by 14.1577 annuity factor). Since this exceeds the value of the trust fund of $1,000,000, special IRC Section 7520 valuation factors will be required to take into account the exhaustion of the fund.[5]

The regulations provide that the standard valuation tables are not to be used to value an income interest, unless the income beneficiary is given an income interest which, in light of

1. *Morgan v. Comm.*, 42 TC 1080 (1964), aff'd 353 F.2d 209 (4th Cir. 1965); *Hanley v. U.S.*, 63 F. Supp. 73 (Ct. Cl. 1945).
2. Rev. Rul. 77-195, 1977-1 CB 295.
3. Rev. Rul. 79-280, 1979-2 CB 340.
4. Treas. Reg. §§1.7520-3(b)(2)(i), 20.7520-3(b)(2)(i), 25.7520-3(b)(2)(i).
5. See Treas. Reg. §25.7520-3(b)(2)(v)(Ex. 5).

the trust, will, or other instrument, or state law, is in accord with an income interest which the principles of the laws of trust would provide consistent with the value of the trust corpus and its preservation. Also, the standard valuation tables are not to be used to value a use interest, unless the beneficiary is given a use interest which, in light of the trust, will, or other instrument, or state law, is in accord with an interest given to a life tenant or term holder. Standard valuation tables are not to be used for an income interest if (1) income or other enjoyment can be withheld, diverted, or accumulated for another's use without the consent of the income beneficiary, or (2) corpus can be withdrawn for another's use without the consent of the income beneficiary or accountability to such beneficiary. Thus, special factors may be required in conjunction with unproductive property, if the beneficiary has no right to require that the trustee make the trust income producing, and with Crummey withdrawal powers, if the power permits a diversion of income or principal to a person other than the income beneficiary during the income term.[1]

A remainder or reversionary interest is to be valued using the standard valuation factors only if the preceding interest (e.g., an income or annuity interest) adequately preserves and protects the remainder or reversionary interest (e.g., from erosion, invasion, depletion, or damage) until the interest takes effect.[2]

There is a split in the courts regarding lottery winnings includable in the gross estate as to whether they should be valued as an annuity under the standard valuation tables or whether a discount is available where state law prohibited the assignment of state lottery winnings.[3] Structured settlement payments should be valued as an annuity under the standard valuation tables without discount for lack of marketability.[4] Taxpayers wishing to challenge use of such tables to value lottery winnings will need to establish a market value as an alternative to the tables and that such value departs substantially from Section 7520 tables.[5]

Valuation Tables

Valuation tables using up-to-date interest and mortality factors must be used where the valuation date occurs on or after May 1, 1989. The value of an annuity, an interest for life or term of years, or a reversionary or remainder interest, is determined using tables and an interest rate (rounded to the nearest 2/10ths of 1 percent) equal to 120 percent of the federal midterm rate in effect for the month in which the valuation date occurs.[6] An interest rate falling midway between any 2/10ths of a percent is rounded up.[7] However, the valuation tables are not to be used with respect to any of the income tax provisions relating to qualified pension plans (including tax sheltered annuities and IRAs) contained in IRC Sections 401 to 419A.[8]

1. Treas. Reg. §§1.7520-3(b)(2)(ii), 20.7520-3(b)(2)(ii), 25.7520-3(b)(2)(ii).
2. Treas. Reg. §§1.7520-3(b)(2)(iii), 20.7520-3(b)(2)(iii), 25.7520-3(b)(2)(iii).
3. *Est. of Shackelford v. U.S.*, 2001-2 USTC ¶60,417 (9th Cir. 2001), aff'g 99-2 USTC ¶60,356 (E.D. Calif. 1999); *Est. of Cook v. Comm.*, 349 F. 3d 850, 2003-2 USTC ¶60,471 (5th Cir. 2003), aff'g TC Memo 2001-170; *Est. of Gribauskas v. Comm.*, 342 F. 3d 85, 2003-2 USTC ¶60,466 (2nd Cir. 2003), rev'g 116 TC 142 (2001); *Est. of Donovan v. Comm.*, 2005-1 USTC ¶60,500 (DC Mass. 2005); *Negron v. U.S.*, 553 F. 3d 1013, 2009-1 USTC ¶60,571 (6th Cir. 2009), rev'g 502 F. Supp. 682, 2007-1 USTC ¶60,541 (ND OH 2007).
4. *Est. of Anthony v. U.S.*, 2008-1 USTC ¶60,558 (5th Cir. 2008), aff'g 2005-1 USTC ¶60,504 (M.D. La. 2005).
5. *Davis v. U.S.*, 491 F. Supp. 2d 192, 2007-1 USTC ¶60,542 (DC NH 2007).
6. IRC Sec. 7520(a).
7. Treas. Reg. §20.7520-1(b)(1).
8. IRC Sec. 7520(b).

See Appendix C for valuation tables. (See also, *Tax Facts on Investments*, Appendix A, for unitrust tables (other than two-life factors or unitrust factors)). IRS Publications 1457 and 1458 contain examples of use of the valuation table and sources for the tables. Where the standard valuation table is to be used but the interest rate or payout rate to be used is between rates in the table, interpolation (an algebraic calculation of a number falling between table factors) is required.[1]

If an income, estate, or gift tax charitable deduction is allowable with respect to the property transferred, the taxpayer can elect to use the interest rate for either of the two months preceding the month in which the valuation date occurs. However, if a transfer of more than one interest in the same property is made with respect to which the taxpayer could use the same interest rate, such interest rate is to be used with respect to each such interest.[2]

913. How are Series E/EE and H/HH United States Savings Bonds valued for federal transfer tax purposes?

Apparently, they are valued at their redemption value on the applicable valuation date. In Revenue Ruling 55-278,[3] A, in 1948, bought Series E bonds with his own funds and had them registered in the names of A and B in the alternative as co-owners. In 1953, A had the bonds reissued in the name of B alone in order to effect a gift to him of A's co-ownership therein. The IRS held that the value of the gift made by A to B in 1953 was the redemption value of the bonds at the time they were reissued. The Service found that, "since Series E United States savings bonds are generally nonnegotiable and nontransferable, they are nonmarketable and, accordingly, have no particular 'market' value. Although ownership therein is transferable by death and by reissue in certain cases..., their only definitely indicated or ascertainable value is the amount at which they are redeemable by the United States Treasury." Presumably, the same would be true of Series H/HH bonds, since they are likewise nonnegotiable and nontransferable.

914. How is a non-negotiable savings certificate issued without discount by a Federal Reserve member bank valued for federal estate tax purposes when death occurs between interest periods?

Federal regulations provide that a time deposit, or the portion thereof requested, must be paid before maturity without a forfeiture of interest, where requested, upon the death of any owner of the time deposit funds.[4] Accordingly, the savings certificate is valued at the principal amount plus unpaid interest attributable to the period between the last interest payment date preceding death and the date of death.[5]

915. How are mutual fund shares valued for federal transfer tax purposes?

The fair market value of a share in an open-end investment company (commonly known as a "mutual fund") is the public redemption price of a share. In the absence of an affirmative showing of the public redemption price in effect at the time of death or gift, the last public redemption

1. Treas. Reg. §§1.642(c)-6(e)(5), 1.664-4(e)(4).
2. IRC Sec. 7520(a).
3. 1955-1 CB 471.
4. 12 CFR §204.2.
5. Rev. Rul. 79-340, 1979-2 CB 320.

price quoted by the company for the date of death or gift shall be presumed to be the applicable public redemption price. If the estate tax alternate valuation method under IRC Section 2032 is elected, the last public redemption price quoted by the company for the alternate valuation date is the applicable redemption price. If there is no public redemption price quoted by the company for the applicable valuation date (e.g., the valuation date is a Saturday, Sunday, or holiday), the fair market value of the mutual fund share is the last public redemption price quoted by the company for the first day preceding the applicable valuation date for which there is a quotation.

In any case where a dividend is declared on a share in an open-end investment company before the decedent's death but payable to shareholders of record on a date after his death and the share is quoted "ex-dividend" on the date of the decedent's death, the amount of the dividend is added to the ex-dividend quotation in determining the fair market value of the share as of the date of the decedent's death.

As used in this section, the term "open-end investment company" includes only a company that, on the applicable valuation date, was engaged in offering its shares to the public in the capacity of an open-end investment company.[1] Participating agreement shares in mutual funds are valued at the liquidation value and not at the public offering price on the date of death (following *Cartwright*).[2]

916. How are United States silver coins valued for federal estate tax purposes?

If they have a fair market value which exceeds their face value, they are valued at their fair market value.[3] The applicable revenue ruling says that the same conclusion would apply to paper currency owned by the decedent and having a fair market value in excess of its face value.[4]

917. How are interests in a closely-held business valued for federal transfer tax purposes?

The fair market value of any interest in an unmarketable business, whether a partnership, corporation, limited liability company, or a proprietorship, is the net amount which a willing purchaser, whether an individual or a corporation, would pay for the interest to a willing seller, neither being under any compulsion to buy or to sell and both having reasonable knowledge of the relevant facts. The net value is determined on the basis of all relevant factors, including the following:

(1) The value of all the assets of the business, tangible and intangible, including goodwill;

(2) The demonstrated earning capacity of the business; and

1. Treas. Reg. §§20.2031-8(b); 25.2512-6(b); *U.S. v. Cartwright*, 411 U.S. 546 (1973).
2. *Est. of Sparling v. Comm.*, 60 TC 330 (1973), nonacq. 1978-2 CB 4.
3. Rev. Rul. 78-360, 1978-2 CB 228.
4. Rev. Rul. 78-360, above.

(3) The other factors set forth in the regulations[1] relating to the valuation of corporate stock, to the extent applicable (see Q 919).

Special attention should be given to determining an adequate value of the goodwill of the business. Complete financial and other data upon which the valuation is based should be submitted with the return, including copies of reports of examinations of the business made by accountants, engineers, or any technical experts as of or near the applicable valuation date.[2]

For additional special valuation rules contained in IRC Chapter 14, see Q 924 to Q 934.

Approach of the Courts

The appraisal community, courts, taxpayers, and the IRS generally follow the principles laid out in Revenue Ruling 59-60 when valuing the stock of a closely-held corporation or the stock of corporations where market quotations are not available. Revenue Ruling 59-60 can also apply to value interests in closely-held partnerships or LLCs for gift tax or estate tax purposes. However, Revenue Ruling 59-60 does not discuss in detail valuation discounts for lack of control or lack of marketability. Thus, other sources must be relied upon for these critical components of valuation.

Historically, in valuation cases, the courts have tended to strike a compromise between the values asserted by the contending parties. But in many cases, courts are more willing to adopt one party's value. The credit for this "winner take all" approach must be given to former Chief Judge of the Tax Court, Theodore Tannenwald. After years of experience, Judge Tannenwald found that the "compromise the difference" approach of the courts merely encouraged the parties to assert extreme values. In a 1980 valuation decision, *Buffalo Tool & Die Manufacturing Company, Inc. v. Commissioner*,[3] Judge Tannenwald took the occasion to admonish the parties thus:

> "We are convinced that the valuation issue is capable of resolution by the parties themselves through an agreement which will reflect a compromise Solomon-like adjustment, thereby saving the expenditure of time, effort, and money by the parties and the court–a process not likely to produce a better result. Indeed, each of the parties should keep in mind that, in the final analysis, the court may find the evidence of valuation by one of the parties sufficiently more convincing than that of the other party, so that the final result will produce a significant financial defeat for one or the other, rather than a middle-of-the-road compromise which we suspect each of the parties expects the court to reach." (At page 452).

This approach is reflected in a number of valuation decisions.[4]

1. See Treas. Reg. §§20.2031-2(f), 20.2031-2(h), 25.2512-2(f).
2. Treas. Reg. §§20.2031-3, 25.2512-3.
3. 74 TC 441.
4. *Est. of McGill v. Comm.*, TC Memo 1984-292 (voting trust certificates); *Est. of Gallo v. Comm.*, TC Memo 1985-363 (closely held stock); *Est. of Gillet v. Comm.*, TC Memo 1985-394 (closely held stock); *Est. of Rubish v. Comm.*, TC Memo 1985-406 (ranch); *Est. of Watts v. Comm.*, TC Memo 1985-595 (partnership interest).

918. How does the existence of a buy-sell agreement impact valuation of interests in a closely-held business for federal transfer tax purposes?

The value of any interest shall be determined without regard to any option, agreement, or other right to acquire or use the property at a price less than the fair market value of the property (without regard to the option, agreement, or other restrictions) or any restriction on the right to sell or use the property (i.e., buy-sell agreement), unless the agreement (1) is a bona fide business arrangement, (2) is not a device to transfer the property to members of the decedent's family for less than full or adequate consideration in money or money's worth, and (3) has terms comparable to those entered into by persons in an arm's length transaction.[1] See Q 933.

Planning Point: Any buy-sell arrangement should take into account IRC Section 2703, and the drafter of the agreement should discuss Section 2703 with the parties to ensure they understand such agreement may not impact the estate tax valuation.

Assuming the requirements of IRC Section 2703 are met, or that IRC Section 2703 does not apply, it is possible that the *estate tax* value of a business interest (including closely held stock) may be controlled by the price or formula contained in a business purchase (buy-sell) agreement. The facts of each case must be examined to determine whether the agreement price will be accepted for estate tax purposes.[2] Case law has established, however, that if the following conditions are met, the agreement price will hold for estate tax purposes, even though the fair market value of the business interest may be substantially more at the valuation date than the agreement price:

(1) The estate must be obligated to sell at death (under either a mandatory purchase agreement or an option held by the designated purchaser);

(2) The agreement must prohibit the owner from disposing of his interest during his lifetime at a price higher than the contract or option price;

(3) The price must be fixed by the terms of the agreement or the agreement must contain a formula or method for determining the price; and

(4) The agreement must be an arm's length business transaction and not a gift. Thus, the purchase price must be fair and adequate at the time the agreement is made, particularly if the parties are closely related.[3]

In a number of cases, the price set in the agreement was held to control the estate tax value of the business interest.[4]

1. IRC Sec. 2703.
2. Treas. Reg. §§20.2031-2(h), 20.2031-3; Rev. Rul. 59-60, 1959-1 CB 237.
3. *Slocum v. U.S.*, 256 F. Supp. 753 (S.D.N.Y. 1966).
4. *Brodrick v. Gore*, 224 F.2d 892 (10th Cir. 1955); *May v. McGowan*, 194 F.2d 396 (2nd Cir. 1952); *Comm. v. Child's Estate*, 147 F.2d 368 (2nd Cir. 1952);.*Comm. v. Bensel*, 100 F.2d 639 (3rd Cir. 1939); *Lomb v. Sugden*, 82 F.2d 166 (2nd Cir. 1936); *Wilson v. Bowers*, 57 F.2d 682 (2nd Cir. 1932); *Mandel v. Sturr*, 266 F.2d 321 (2nd Cir. 1959); *Fiorito v. Comm.*, 33 TC 440, acq. 1960-1 CB 4; *Est. of Littick*, 31 TC 181, acq. in result, 1984-2 CB 1; *Est. of Weil*, 22 TC 1267, acq. 1955-2 CB 10; *Est. of Salt*, 17 TC 92, acq. 1952-1 CB 4; *Est. of Maddock*, 16 TC 324, acq. 1951-2 CB 3. See also Treas. Reg. §§20.2031-2(h), 20.2031-3.

For gift tax purposes, an agreement restricting lifetime sale will be considered with all other pertinent factors, and may tend to lower the value of the business interest.[1]

919. How are shares of stock in closely held corporations valued for federal transfer tax purposes?

IRC Section 2031(b) deals with the valuation, for estate tax purposes, of unlisted stocks and securities. It says: "In the case of stock and securities of a corporation the value of which, by reason of their not being listed on an exchange and by reason of the absence of sales thereof, cannot be determined with reference to bid and asked prices or with reference to sales prices, the value thereof shall be determined by taking into consideration, in addition to all other factors, the value of stock or securities of corporations engaged in the same or a similar line of business which are listed on an exchange."

Revenue Ruling 59-60[2] contains a broad discussion of factors that the IRS believes should be considered in valuing shares of stock in closely held corporations or in corporations where market quotations are either lacking or too scarce to be recognized. The Service says that in these cases, "all available financial data, as well as all relevant factors affecting the fair market value, should be considered. The following factors, although not all-inclusive, are fundamental and require careful analysis in each case:

(a) The nature of the business and the history of the enterprise from its inception;

(b) The economic outlook in general and the condition and outlook of the specific industry in particular;

(c) The book value of the stock and the financial condition of the business;

(d) The earning capacity of the company;

(e) The dividend-paying capacity;

(f) Whether or not the enterprise has goodwill or other intangible value;

(g) Sales of the stock and the size of the block of stock to be valued; and

(h) The market price of stock of corporations engaged in the same or a similar line of business having their stock actively traded in a free and open market, either on an exchange or over-the-counter."[3]

Planning Point: Taxpayers should go over in detail all the facts with the business appraiser relating to the business that would impact the appraiser's analysis of the facts laid out in Revenue Ruling 59-60.

1. *Est. of James v. Comm.*, 148 F.2d 236 (2nd Cir. 1945); *Kline v. Comm.*, 130 F.2d 742 (3rd Cir. 1942); *Krauss v. U.S.*, 140 F.2d 510 (5th Cir. 1944); *Comm. v. McCann*, 146 F.2d 385 (2nd Cir. 1944); *Spitzer v. Comm.*, 153 F.2d 967 (8th Cir. 1946); Rev. Rul. 189, 1953-2 CB 294.
2. 1959-1 CB 237.
3. Rev. Rul. 59-60, Sec. 4.01.

If a block of stock represents a controlling interest in a corporation, a "control premium" generally adds to the value of the stock. If, however, the shares constitute a minority ownership interest, a "minority discount" is often applied to the value. See, e.g., *Martin v. Commissioner*,[1] which deals with discounts applied to shares of stock representing a minority interest in a holding company that, in turn, held minority interests in seven operating companies. A premium may also attach for swing vote attributes where one block of stock may exercise control by joining with another block of stock.[2] One memorandum valued stock included in the gross estate at a premium as a controlling interest, while applying a minority discount to the marital deduction (see Q 837) portion which passed to the surviving spouse.[3] Just because an interest being valued is a minority interest does not mean that a minority discount is available.[4] However, one case valued stock with voting rights at no more than stock without voting rights.[5]

If a donor transfers shares in a corporation to each of the donor's children, the Service will no longer consider family control when valuing the gift under IRC Section 2512.Thus, a minority discount will not be disallowed solely because a transferred interest would be part of a controlling interest if such interest were aggregated with interests held by family members.[6] Indeed, a minority discount was allowed even when the person to whom the interest was transferred was already a controlling shareholder.[7]

The Tax Court has determined that an estate would not be allowed a minority discount where the decedent transferred a small amount of stock immediately prior to death for the sole purpose of reducing her interest from a controlling interest to a minority interest for valuation purposes.[8] Also, a partnership or LLC may be included in the gross estate under IRC Section 2036 without the benefit of discounts if a decedent puts everything he owns into the partnership or LLC and retains complete control over the income of the partnership or LLC.[9]

For a case discussing the valuation of voting trust certificates representing the decedent's beneficial interest in stock of a closely held corporation, see *Estate of McGill v. Commissioner.*[10]

In general, when valuing an operating company that sells goods and services, primary consideration is given to earnings, and when valuing a company that merely holds investments, primary consideration is given to asset values. However, if a company is not easily characterized as one or the other, appropriate weight should be given to both earnings and assets.[11]

For the effect of a buy-sell agreement on the valuation of closely held stock, see Q 918.

---

1. TC Memo 1985-424.
2. TAM 9436005.
3. TAM 9403005.
4. *Godley v. Comm.*, 286 F. 3d 210, 2002-1 USTC ¶60,436 (4th Cir. 2002) (partnerships held housing projects subject to long-term government contracts).
5. *Est. of Simplot v. Comm.*, 249 F. 3d 1191, 2001-1 USTC ¶60,405 (9th Cir. 2001).
6. Rev. Rul. 93-12, 1993-1 CB 202, revoking Rev. Rul. 81-253, 1981-2 CB 187.
7. TAM 9432001.
8. *Est. of Murphy v. Comm.*, TC Memo 1990-472.
9. *Est. of Strangi v. Comm.*, TC Memo 2003-145; *Kimbell v. U.S.*, 2003-1 USTC ¶60,455 (N.D. Tex. 2003).
10. *Estate of McGill v. Comm.*, TC Memo 1984-292.
11. *Martin v. Comm.*, TC Memo 1985-424.

For additional special valuation rules contained in IRC Chapter 14, see Q 924 to Q 934.

920. How is real estate valued for federal transfer tax purposes?

There are three basic approaches appraisers use to arrive at the fair market value of real estate: (1) the market data, or comparable sales approach; (2) the capitalization of income approach; and (3) the reproduction cost less depreciation approach.[1] The real estate may be valued at its highest and best use with limited exceptions.

(1) *Market data*. An arm's length sale of the property in question on the valuation date would, of course, determine its fair market value. Lacking such a circumstance, the next best indication of value would be the price for which a reasonably comparable piece of property was sold on or near the valuation date. This approach is particularly useful in the valuation of unimproved real estate.[2]

(2) *Capitalization of income*. The projected net income from the property, either before or after depreciation, interest, and income taxes, from the highest and best use of the property is estimated and then capitalized at a rate which represents a fair return on the particular investment at the particular time, considering the risks involved. This approach is particularly useful in the appraisal of business properties.

(3) *Reproduction cost*. This approach requires an estimate of the cost of replacing a structure, an estimate of the depreciation and obsolescence that has taken place in the existing structure, and an appraisal of the land involved. Use of this method is extremely limited for ordinary federal tax valuation purposes.

An undivided fractional interest in property is normally determined to be a proportionate part of the value of the whole property. If any discount is allowed, the taxpayer must produce evidence that partial interests in real property in the locality sell for less than their proportionate shares of the whole.[3]

921. How are mineral properties valued for federal transfer tax purposes?

Treasury Regulation Section 1.611-2(d) provides, for income tax purposes, the following:

(d) Determination of fair market value of mineral properties, and improvements, if any. –

(1) If the fair market value of the mineral property and improvements at a specified date is to be determined for the purpose of ascertaining the basis (see Q 692), such value must be determined, subject to approval or revision by the district director, by the owner of such property and improvements in the light of the conditions and circumstances known at that date, regardless of later discoveries or developments or subsequent improvements in methods of extraction and treatment of the

1. IRS Valuation Guide, pages 18-19.
2. Rev. Proc. 79-24, 1979-1 CB 565.
3. *Est. of Iacono*, TC Memo 1980-520.

mineral product. The district director will give due weight and consideration to any and all factors and evidence having a bearing on the market value, such as cost, actual sales and transfers of similar properties and improvements, bona fide offers, market value of stocks or shares, royalties and rentals, valuation for local or State taxation, partnership accountings, records of litigation in which the value of the property and improvements was in question, the amount at which the property and improvements may have been inventoried or appraised in probate or similar proceedings, and disinterested appraisals by approved methods.

(2) If the fair market value must be ascertained as of a certain date, analytical appraisal methods of valuation, such as the present value method will not be used:

(i) If the value of a mineral property and improvements, if any, can be determined upon the basis of cost or comparative values and replacement value of equipment, or

(ii) If the fair market value can reasonably be determined by any other method."

Lambert v. U.S.,[1] concerned the federal estate tax valuation of an estate's one-half interest in a coal mining business operated as a partnership. The parties agreed that the Treasury Regulations on cost depletion provided guidance as to the valuation of coal properties. Citing Treas. Reg. §1.611-2(d)(2), above, the court found that the estate's witness had properly determined the value of the intangible assets, including the coal reserves and good will, upon the basis of comparative values, and that for that reason, the analytical methods applied by the government and its witness were not appropriate. Accordingly, the court found that the estate had met its burden of showing that the government's valuation of $3,772,326 for the coal company was excessive and that the fair market value, as determined by the estate, was $2,126,000.

Treasury Regulation Section 1.611-2(e) provides, for income tax purposes, the following:

(e) Determination of the fair market value of mineral property by the present value method. –

(1) To determine the fair market value of a mineral property and improvements by the present value method, the essential factors must be determined for each mineral deposit. The essential factors in determining the fair market value of mineral deposits are:

(i) The total quantity of mineral in terms of the principal or customary unit (or units) paid for in the product marketed,

(ii) The quantity of mineral expected to be recovered during each operating period,

(iii) The average quality or grade of the mineral reserves,

1. 85-2 USTC ¶13,637 (W.D. Va. 1985).

(iv) The allocation of the total expected profit to the several processes or operations necessary for the preparation of the mineral for market,

(v) The probable operating life of the deposit in years,

(vi) The development cost,

(vii) The operating cost,

(viii) The total expected profit,

(ix) The rate at which this profit will be obtained, and

(x) The rate of interest commensurate with the risk for the particular deposit.

(2) If the mineral deposit has been sufficiently developed, the valuation factors specified in subparagraph (1) of this paragraph may be determined from past operating experience. In the application of factors derived from past experience, full allowance should be made for probable future variations in the rate of exhaustion, quality or grade of the mineral, percentage of recovery, cost of development, production, interest rate, and selling price of the product marketed during the expected operating life of the mineral deposit. Mineral deposits for which these factors cannot be determined with reasonable accuracy from past operating experience may also be valued by the present value method; but the factors must be deduced from concurrent evidence, such as the general type of the deposit, the characteristics of the district in which it occurs, the habit of the mineral deposits, the intensity of mineralization, the oil-gas ratio, the rate at which additional mineral has been disclosed by exploitation, the stage of the operating life of the deposit, and any other evidence tending to establish a reasonable estimate of the required factors.

(3) Mineral deposits of different grades, locations, and probable dates of extraction should be valued separately. The mineral content of a deposit shall be determined in accordance with paragraph (c) of this section. In estimating the average grade of the developed and prospective mineral, account should be taken of probable increases or decreases as indicated by the operating history. The rate of exhaustion of a mineral deposit should be determined with due regard to the limitations imposed by plant capacity, by the character of the deposit, by the ability to market the mineral product, by labor conditions, and by the operating program in force or reasonably to be expected for future operations. The operating life of a mineral deposit is that number of years necessary for the exhaustion of both the developed and prospective mineral content at the rate determined as above. The operating life of oil and gas wells is also influenced by the natural decline in pressure and flow, and by voluntary or enforced curtailment of production. The operating cost includes all current expense of producing, preparing, and marketing the mineral product sold (due consideration being given to taxes) exclusive of allowable capital additions, as described in §§1.612-2 and 1.612-4 (see Q 7863 through Q 7866), and deductions

for depreciation and depletion (see Q 7867 through Q 7881), but including cost of repairs. This cost of repairs is not to be confused with the depreciation deduction by which the cost of improvements is returned to the taxpayer free from tax. In general, no estimates of these factors will be approved by the district director that are not supported by the operating experience of the property or which are derived from different and arbitrarily selected periods.

(4) The value of each mineral deposit is measured by the expected gross income (the number of units of mineral recoverable in marketable form multiplied by the estimated market price per unit) less the estimated operating cost, reduced to a present value as of the date for which the valuation is made at the rate of interest commensurate with the risk for the operating life, and further reduced by the value at that date of the improvements and of the capital additions, if any, necessary to realize the profits. The degree of risk is generally lowest in cases where the factors of valuation are fully supported by the operating record of the mineral enterprise before the date for which the valuation is made. On the other hand, higher risks ordinarily attach to appraisals on any other basis."

922. How is timber valued for federal transfer tax purposes?

The estate tax regulations offer little guidance in the selection of an appropriate method for valuing timber property. However, Treasury Regulation Section 1.611-3(f), covering the depletion allowance deduction for income tax purposes, contains the following useful information:

(f) Determination of fair market value of timber property.

(1) If the fair market value of the property at a specified date is the basis for depletion deductions, such value shall be determined, subject to approval or revision by the district director upon audit, by the owner of the property in the light of the most reliable and accurate information available with reference to the condition of the property as it existed at that date, regardless of all subsequent changes, such as changes in surrounding circumstances, and methods of exploitation, in degree of utilization, etc. Such factors as the following will be given due consideration:

(i) Character and quality of the timber as determined by species, age, size, condition, etc.;

(ii) The quantity of timber per acre, the total quantity under consideration, and the location of the timber in question with reference to other timber;

(iii) Accessibility of the timber (location with reference to distance from a common carrier, the topography and other features of the ground upon which the timber stands and over which it must be transported in process of exploitation, the probable cost of exploitation and the climate and the state of industrial development of the locality); and

(iv) The freight rates by common carrier to important markets.

(2) The timber in each particular case will be valued on its own merits and not on the basis of general averages for regions; however, the value placed upon it, taking into consideration such factors as those mentioned in this paragraph, will be consistent with that of other similar timber in the region. The district director will give weight and consideration to any and all facts and evidence having a bearing on the market value, such as cost, actual sales and transfers of similar properties, the margin between the cost of production and the price realized for timber products, market value of stock or shares, royalties and rentals, valuation for local or State taxation, partnership accountings, records of litigation in which the value of the property has been involved, the amount at which the property may have been inventoried or appraised in probate or similar proceedings, disinterested appraisals by approved methods, and other factors."

In a case involving estate tax valuation of undivided minority interests in timberland, the Tax Court, quoting from paragraph (2) of the foregoing regulation, added that, where available, the use of comparative sales is the method of valuation most preferred by that court and by the Ninth Circuit (to which appeal lay). As the Court found, few sales exist of undivided minority interests in timberland based on the inability of the owner to control the timberland, which should impact the overall value as no market may exist.

In that case, the government's appraisers based their valuation on twenty-four sales of "stumpage" believed by them to be the most comparable because of their similar characteristics and their proximity in time to the valuation date and in location to the subject property. In addition, the appraisers used seven other transactions involving timber and land in the same general vicinity. The prices of the sales considered comparable were adjusted by the appraisers for differences in timber, quality, accessibility and other logging costs, volume, species mix, and time of sale. The government's appraisers concluded that the total value of the timber on the land in which decedent had an undivided interest was $29,500,000 at the date of her death. With one exception, the government's appraisers used the same sales as comparables to determine that the value of the underlying land supporting the timber at decedent's death was $9,500,000.

The executor, however, contended that the sales upon which the government's appraisers relied involved timber that was not comparable to the timber in which the decedent had an undivided interest. He also contended that the sales used as comparables by the government's appraisers were not properly adjusted to bring them into comparability. With respect to the government's land valuation, the executor contended that the appraisal failed to adjust for acreage in the subject land that was barren, or to adjust adequately for differences in steepness of terrain.

The court examined the points of difference between the parties, found merit in several of the executor's contentions, and concluded that the government's valuation should be reduced by 20 percent, i.e., to $31,200,000.

The final issue in the case was the issue of a minority discount to be applied to the decedent's undivided aliquot portion of the $31,200,000 valuation. The government contended that no minority discount should be allowed. The executor contended that a discount of at least

60 percent was warranted. On this issue the estate's witnesses were persuasive. The court was convinced from their testimony of the disabilities associated with a minority undivided interest in timber property, including lack of marketability, lack of management, lack of general control, lack of liquidity, and potential partitionment expenses, that a minority discount of 60 percent was reasonable, and the court so held.[1] See also *Harwood v. Comm.*,[2] which concerned valuation of a minority interest in a limited partnership engaged in the timber business.

923. How are annuity, unitrust, and income (or use) interests retained by a grantor in a trust valued for estate tax purposes?

If a grantor retains an annuity, unitrust, or income (or use) interest in an irrevocable trust and dies before such retained interest terminates, the retained interest is includable in the decedent's gross estate for estate tax purposes. While a retained annuity or unitrust (which is a variable annuity) interest in a trust could be included in the estate under either IRC Section 2036 as a retained life estate or under IRC Section 2039 as an annuity, regulations state that IRC Section 2036, rather than IRC Section 2039, will be applied to such interests.[3] A retained income (or use) interest in an irrevocable trust would be includable under IRC Section 2036. A revocable trust is includable in a grantor's estate under IRC Section 2038. A gift within three years of death of an IRC Section 2036, 2038, or 2039 interest is includable in the estate under IRC Section 2035.

Planning Point: If the grantor dies after the retained interest terminates, the interest is generally not includable in the grantor's estate. Setting the trust term can be a balancing act. If the trust with a retained interest is for life, it will be includable in the grantor's estate. In general, the longer the term of years the grantor retains the interest, the lower is the value of gifts to others; but longer terms increase the risk that the grantor with a retained interest will die during the trust term and that the trust will be includable in the grantor's estate.

Such retained annuity, unitrust, and income (or use) interests are generally found in GRITs, GRATs, GRUTs, PRTs, QPRTs, CRATs, and CRUTs, but can be found in other trusts as well. The valuation rules discussed below apply only to valuing the retained interest includable in the grantor's estate. The regular rules under IRC Section 2702 (see Q 928) and IRC Section 7520 (see Appendix A of Tax Facts on Investments) apply for valuing gifts in such trusts and for determining charitable deductions (see Q 8096). In general, the rules below include an amount in the gross estate that represents the amount of trust assets needed to yield the payments to the grantor from the trust.

Planning Point: The IRS is required by IRC Section 7520 (c)(3) to update the actuarial tables to reflect the new mortality data produced by each U.S. census. In that regard, the IRS has produced tables to reflect the 2000 census and regulations under Section 7520 reflecting the data. The data reflects an increased life expectancy for all persons under age ninety-five. The result is that Table 2000 C.M. increases the value of lifetime interests and decreases the value of remainders or reversions following lifetime interests. This makes CRTs and QPRTs slightly less desirable while CLTs, private annuities and self-cancelling installment notes (SCINs) are slightly more desirable. Generally, the new tables apply to transfers for which the valuation date is on or after May 1, 2009.

1. *Est. of Sels v. Comm.*, TC Memo 1986-501.
2. 82 TC 239 (1980), aff'd per order (9th Cir. 1986).
3. Treas. Reg. §20.2039-1(e)(1).

An includable retained *income* interest would be valued based on the percentage of income retained by the grantor. The right to use trust property is valued similarly to an income interest.

Example 1: If the grantor retained the right to all the trust income, 100 percent of the trust corpus would be includable. If the grantor retained the right to 60 percent of the income, 60 percent would be includable. If the grantor retained the right to 50 percent of the income, which increased to 100 percent when the other income beneficiary died before the grantor, 100 percent would be includable. If a grantor retained use of a personal residence in a QPRT, 100 percent of the QPRT is includable.[1]

An includable retained *annuity* interest would be valued by dividing the annual annuity (adjusted for frequency of payment and whether payments are made at the beginning or the end of each period) by the IRC Section 7520 rate at the date of death (or alternate valuation date).[2] For this purpose, Annuity Adjustment Factors Table A is used for payments made at the end of each period, and Annuity Adjustment Factors Table B is used for payments made at the beginning of each period (see Appendix C). Presumably, if the value of the annuity calculated in this fashion exceeds the value of the trust assets, the amount includable would be limited to the value of the trust assets.

Example 2: Grantor created a GRAT with an annuity of $1,000 ($12,000 annual) payable at the end of each month to Grantor for ten years, with remainder to Grantor's child. Grantor died during the ten year term. At grantor's death, the value of the GRAT assets was $300,000 and the Section 7520 interest rate was 6 percent. The annuity adjustment factor (monthly, payments at the end of each period, 6 percent) is 1.0272 (from Annuity Adjustment Factors Table A). The amount of property includable under IRC Section 2036 is $205,440 [($12,000 × 1.0272) / 6%].

An includable retained *unitrust* interest would be valued by multiplying the value of the trust assets by an inclusion ratio. The inclusion ratio is determined by dividing the trust's equivalent income interest rate by the IRC Section 7520 rate at the date of death (or alternate valuation date). The equivalent income interest rate is determined by dividing the trust's adjusted payout rate by the excess of 1 over the adjusted payout rate. The adjusted payout rate is determined by multiplying the payout rate by the Unitrust Payout Adjustment Factor (see Appendix C). If the inclusion ratio is greater than 100 percent, it is reduced to 100 percent.[3]

Example 3: Grantor created a CRUT with a 6 percent unitrust payout rate payable (in equal installments at the end of each quarter) to Grantor for life, then to Grantor's child for life, with remainder to charity. At grantor's death, the value of the CRUT assets was $300,000, the Section 7520 interest rate was 6 percent, and Grantor's child was age 55. The unitrust payout adjustment factor (6 percent Section 7520 rate, quarterly, three months to payout) is 0.964365. The adjusted payout rate equals 5.786 percent [6% payout rate × 0.964365]. The equivalent income interest rate equals 6.141 percent [5.786% / (1 – 5.786%)]. The inclusion ratio equals 102.35 percent [6.141% / 6% Section 7520 rate]. Since the inclusion ratio exceeds 100 percent, it is reduced to 100 percent. The amount includable under IRC Section 2036 is $300,000 [$300,000 × 100%]. The charitable deduction for the estate would be calculated under the regular rules for CRUTs (see Q 8096), as a CRUT with a unitrust payable to Grantor's child for life, and would be $84,759.

1. Treas. Reg. §20.2036-1(c)(1)(ii); Treas. Reg. §20.2036-1(c)(2)(ii).
2. Treas. Reg. §20.2036-1(c)(2).
3. Treas. Reg. §20.2036-1(c)(2).

Graduated Retained Interests

A graduated retained interest is an annuity, unitrust, or other payment, payable at least annually, that increases at a regular rate over time, but not more often than annually. If the grantor dies during the trust term with a graduated retained interest, the amount includable in the gross estate for estate tax purposes includes the sum of the following: (1) the amount of corpus needed to generate the annuity, unitrust, or other payment for the year of the grantor's death (the base amount); and (2) the discounted value of the amounts of corpus needed to generate the periodic additions starting in each of the remaining years of the trust term.[1]

Example 4: Grantor created a five-year grantor retained annuity trust (GRAT). The GRAT pays Grantor an annual annuity at the end of each trust year, on October 31st. The first annuity payment equals $100,000 and the annuity payment increases by 20 percent each year. If Grantor dies during the trust term, payments continue to Grantor's estate. At the end of the trust term, the corpus is to be distributed to Grantor's child.

Grantor dies on January 31 of the third year of the GRAT term. The value of the trust corpus is $3,200,000 on the date of death. The Section 7520 interest rate for the month of death equals 6.8 percent. The alternate valuation date is not elected. The table shows calculation of the $2,973,868 includable in Grantor's gross estate as a graduated retained interest.[2]

A	B	C	D	E	F	G
GRAT	Annual	Periodic	Required	Deferral	PV	Corpus
Year	Annuity	Addition	Principal	Period	Factor	Amount
1	100,000					
2	120,000	20,000				
3	144,000	24,000	2,117,647			2,117,647
4	172,800	28,800	423,529	0.747945	0.951985	403,194
5	207,360	34,560	508,235	1.747945	0.891372	453,027
Total						2,973,868

D = (B or C × Ann. Adj. Factor) ÷ Sec. 7520 Rate
E = 273 {days from January 31 to October 31} ÷ 365 [for year 4]
F = 1 ÷ (1 + Sec. 7520 Rate)E
G = D × F

Contingent Retained Interests

If the grantor retained the right to receive an annuity, unitrust, or other payment from transferred property after the death of another person who was enjoying the annuity, unitrust, or other payment at the time of grantor's death, then the amount includable in grantor's gross estate is the amount of trust assets needed to yield the payments to the grantor from the trust. But this amount is reduced by the present value of the other person's interest. However, the amount includable cannot be less than the amount of trust assets needed to yield the trust payments the

1. Prop. Treas. Reg. §20.2036-1(c)(2)(ii).
2. Prop. Treas. Reg. §20.2036-1(c)(2)(iii)(Ex. 7).

grantor was entitled to at grantor's death. In any event, however, the amount includable cannot exceed the fair market value of the trust corpus on the date of grantor's death.[1]

Example 5: Grantor created an irrevocable trust. The trust provides that 50 percent of trust income is to be paid each to Grantor and Grantor's child during their joint lives. On the death of the first to die of Grantor or Grantor's child, 100 percent of trust income is to be paid to the survivor for life. On the death of the survivor, the remainder is to be paid to a third person.

Grantor dies survived by child. Fifty percent of the trust corpus is includable in Grantor's gross estate because Grantor retained the right to 50 percent of trust income for life. In addition, the value of the remaining 50 percent of trust corpus, less the present value of the child's life estate, is includable in Grantor's estate because Grantor retained the right to 100 percent of trust income if Grantor survived child. [If child had predeceased Grantor, 100 percent of trust corpus would be includable in Grantor's gross estate.][2]

Example 6: Grantor created an irrevocable trust. The trust provides that an annuity of $5,000 is to be paid each to Grantor and Grantor's child during their joint lives. On the death of the first to die of Grantor or Grantor's child, an annuity of $10,000 is to be paid to the survivor for life. On the death of the survivor, the remainder is to be paid to a third person.

Grantor dies survived by child. The value of the trust corpus is $120,000 on the date of death. The Section 7520 interest rate for the month of death equals 7.0 percent. Assume the present value of child's $5,000 annuity for life is $40,000. The table shows calculation of the $102,857 includable in Grantor's gross estate. [If child had predeceased Grantor, $120,000 would be includable in Grantor's gross estate (Step 4 would be $0, and $120,000 is less than $142,857).][3]

Step 1: Fair market value of corpus	$120,000
Step 2: Corpus needed to produce Grantor's annuity ($5,000 ÷ 7%)	$71,429
Step 3: Corpus needed to produce survivor's annuity ($10,000 ÷ 7%)	$142,857
Step 4: Present value of child's annuity	$40,000
Step 5: Step 3 minus Step 4 (but not less than Step 2)	$102,857
Step 6: Lesser of Step 1 or Step 5	$102,857

924. What are the Chapter 14 special valuation rules?

Special valuation rules are contained in IRC Chapter 14. Chapter 14 generally focuses on establishing the value of various interests transferred to family members at the time of the transfer when the transferor retains certain interests in the property being transferred or restrictions are placed on the property that allow the property to be acquired at less than fair market value (measured without the restrictions). Special rules apply to certain transfers of interests in corporations and partnerships (see Q 925), to certain transfers of interests in trusts and even remainder and joint purchase transactions (see Q 928), to certain agreements, options, rights or restrictions exercisable at less than fair market value (see Q 933), and to various lapsing rights and restrictions (see Q 934).

1. Prop. Treas. Reg. §20.2036-1(b)(1)(ii).
2. Prop. Treas. Reg. §20.2036-1(c)(1)(ii)(Ex. 1(i)).
3. Prop. Treas. Reg. §20.2036-1(c)(1)(ii)(Ex. 1(ii)).

925. What special valuation rules apply to the transfer of an interest in a corporation or partnership under Chapter 14?

As a general rule, the value of a transferred residual interest is equal to the value of the transferor's entire interest prior to the transfer reduced by the value of the interest retained by the transferor. For the purpose of determining whether a transfer of an interest in a corporation or partnership to (or for the benefit of) a "member of the transferor's family" is a gift (and the value of the transfer), the value of any "applicable retained interest" (see below) that is held by the transferor or an "applicable family member" (see below) immediately after the transfer is treated as being zero unless the applicable retained interest is a "distribution right" which consists of the right to receive a "qualified payment."[1] Where an applicable retained interest consists of a distribution right which consists of the right to receive a qualified payment and there are one or more liquidation, put, call, or conversion rights with respect to such interest, the value of all such rights is to be determined by assuming that each such liquidation, put, call, or conversion right is exercised in a manner which results in the lowest value.[2] IRC Section 2701 does not apply to distribution rights with respect to qualified payments where there is no liquidation, put, call, or conversion right with respect to the distribution right.[3] If the transfer subject to these rules is of a junior equity interest in a corporation or partnership, the transfer must be assigned a minimum value under the "junior equity rule."[4]

These rules do not apply if, for either the transferred interest or the applicable retained interest, market quotations are readily available (as of the date of transfer) on an established securities market. Also, the rules do not apply if the applicable retained interest is of the same class as the transferred interest, or if the applicable retained interest is proportionally the same as the transferred interest (disregarding nonlapsing differences with respect to voting in the case of a corporation, or with respect to management and limitations on liability in the case of a partnership).[5] An exception from the rules is also provided for a transfer of a vertical slice of interests in an entity (defined as a proportionate reduction of each class of equity interest held by the transferor and applicable family members in the aggregate).[6]

Definitions and Rules

Transfers

The rules apply to transfers with respect to new, as well as existing, entities.[7] Transfers may be either direct or indirect. Furthermore, except as provided in regulations, a contribution to capital, a redemption, a recapitalization, or other change in capital structure of a corporation or partnership is treated as a transfer if the taxpayer or an applicable family member receives an

1. IRC Secs. 2701(a)(1), 2701(a)(3)(A).
2. IRC Sec. 2701(a)(3)(B).
3. IRC Sec. 2701(a)(3)(C).
4. IRC Sec. 2701(a)(4).
5. IRC Sec. 2701(a)(2).
6. Treas. Reg. §25.2701-1(c)(4).
7. Treas. Reg. §25.2701-1(b)(2)(i).

applicable retained interest in the transaction, or as provided under regulations, holds such an interest immediately after the transfer.[1] Any termination of an interest is also treated as a transfer.[2]

Applicable Retained Interests

An "applicable retained interest" is any interest in an entity with respect to which there is (1) a distribution right and the transferor and applicable family members control the entity immediately before the transfer, or (2) a liquidation, put, call, or conversion right.[3] (Regulations or rulings may provide that any applicable retained interest be treated as two or more interests.[4]) A "distribution right" is any right to a distribution from a corporation with respect to its stock, or from a partnership with respect to a partner's interest in the partnership, other than (1) a distribution with respect to any interest if such right is junior to the rights of the transferred interest, (2) any right to receive a guaranteed payment of a fixed amount from a partnership under IRC Section 707(c), or (3) a liquidation, put, call, or conversion right.[5]

For these purposes, a liquidation, put, call, or conversion right is treated as a distribution right rather than as a liquidation, put, call, or conversion right if (1) it must be exercised at a specific time and at a specific amount, or (2) the liquidation, put, call, or conversion right: (a) can be converted into a fixed amount or fixed percentage of the same class of shares of stock as the transferred shares; (b) is nonlapsing; (c) is subject to proportionate adjustments for splits, combinations, reclassifications, and similar changes in the capital stock; and (d) is subject to adjustments for accumulated but unpaid distributions. (Similar rules apply to liquidation, put, call, or conversion rights in a partnership.) Where a liquidation, put, call, or conversion right is treated as exercised in a manner which produces the lowest value in the general rule above, such a right is treated as a distribution right which must be exercised at a specific time and at a specific amount.[6]

Regulations provide that applicable retained interests consist of (1) extraordinary payment rights, and (2) distribution rights held in a controlled entity.[7] The term "extraordinary payment rights" is used to refer to liquidation, put, call, or conversion rights, the exercise or nonexercise of which affects the value of the transferred interests.[8] The following are treated as neither extraordinary payment rights nor distribution rights: (1) mandatory fixed payment rights; (2) liquidation participation rights (other than ones in which the transferor, members of the transferor's family, and applicable family members have the ability to compel liquidation); and (3) non-lapsing conversion rights subject to proportionate adjustments for changes in equity and to adjustments to take account of accumulated but unpaid qualified payments.[9]

1. IRC Sec. 2701(e)(5).
2. IRC Sec. 2701(d)(5).
3. IRC Sec. 2701(b).
4. IRC Sec. 2701(e)(7); Treas. Reg. §25.2701-7.
5. IRC Sec. 2701(c)(1).
6. IRC Sec. 2701(c)(2).
7. Treas. Reg. §25.2701-2(b)(1).
8. Treas. Reg. §25.2701-2(b)(2).
9. Treas. Reg. §25.2701-2(b)(4).

Qualified Payments

A "qualified payment" means any dividend payable on a periodic basis at a fixed rate (including rates tied to specific market rates) on any cumulative preferred stock (or comparable payment with respect to a partnership). With respect to the transferor, an otherwise qualified payment is to be treated as such unless the transferor elects otherwise. With respect to applicable family members, an otherwise qualified payment is not to be treated as such unless the applicable family member so elects. A transferor or an applicable family member can make an irrevocable election to treat any distribution right (which is otherwise not a qualified payment) as a qualified payment, payable at such times and in such amounts as provided in the election (such times and amounts not to be inconsistent with any underlying legal instruments creating such rights).[1] The value assigned to a right for which an election is made cannot exceed fair market (determined without regard to IRC Section 2701).[2]

Attribution

A "member of the transferor's family" includes the transferor's spouse, lineal descendants of the transferor or transferor's spouse, and the spouse of any such descendant.[3] An "applicable family member" with respect to a transferor includes the transferor's spouse, an ancestor of the transferor or transferor's spouse, and the spouse of any such ancestor.[4] An individual is treated as holding interests held indirectly through a corporation, partnership, trust, or other entity.[5] In the case of a corporation, "control" means 50 percent ownership (by vote or value) of the stock. In the case of a partnership, "control" means 50 percent ownership of the capital or profits interests, or in the case of a limited partnership, the ownership of any interest as a general partner.[6] When determining control, an individual is treated as holding any interest held by an applicable family member (see above), including (for this purpose) any lineal descendant of any parent of the transferor or the transferor's spouse.[7]

Minimum Value/Junior Equity Rule

If the transfer subject to these rules is of a junior equity interest in a corporation or partnership, the value of the transferred interest cannot be less than the amount which would be determined if the total value of all junior equity interests in the entity were equal to 10 percent of the sum of (1) the total value of the equity interests in the entity, and (2) the total amount of debt the entity owes to the transferor or an applicable family member.[8] For this purpose, indebtedness does not include (1) short term indebtedness incurred for the current conduct of trade or business, (2) indebtedness owed to a third party solely because it is guaranteed by the transferor or an applicable family member, and (3) amounts set aside for qualified deferred

1. IRC Sec. 2701(c)(3).
2. Treas. Reg. §25.2701-2(c)(2).
3. IRC Sec. 2701(e)(1).
4. IRC Sec. 2701(e)(2).
5. IRC Sec. 2701(e)(3).
6. IRC Sec. 2701(b)(2).
7. IRC Sec. 2701(b)(2)(C).
8. IRC Sec. 2701(a)(4).

compensation to the extent such amounts are not available to the entity. While a properly structured lease is not treated as indebtedness, arrearages with respect to a lease are indebtedness.[1]

Valuation Method

For purposes of IRC Section 2701, the amount of a gift is determined as follows: (1) determine the fair market value of all family-held equity interests in the entity (treat as if held by one individual); (2) subtract out the sum of (a) the fair market value of all family-held senior equity interests in the entity other than applicable retained interests (treat as if held by one individual), and (b) the value of applicable retained interests as valued under IRC Section 2701; (3) allocate the remaining value among the transferred interests and other family-held subordinate interests; (4) reduce the value allocated to the transferred interests to adjust for a minority or similar discount or for consideration received for the transferred interest.[2]

926. When may additional estate or gift taxes be due when an interest is valued using the IRC's Chapter 14 special valuation rules?

If "qualified payments" are valued under the rules discussed in Q 925, additional estate or gift tax may be due at the time of a later taxable event to reflect cumulative but unpaid distributions. The amount of an increase in estate or gift tax is equal to the excess (if any) of (1) the value of the qualified payments as if each payment had been timely made during the period beginning with the transfer subject to these rules and ending with the taxable event and each payment were reinvested at the (capitalization or discount) interest rate used to value the applicable retained transfer at the time of the transfer; over (2) the value of the qualified payments actually made adjusted to reflect reinvestment as in (1). For this purpose, any payment made within four years of its due date is treated as made on its due date.[3] The due date is the date specified in the governing interest as the date on which the payment is to be made (or if no date is specified, the last day of each calendar year).[4] A transfer of a debt obligation bearing compound interest at a rate not less than the appropriate IRC Section 7520 discount rate from the due date of the payment and with a term of no more than four years is treated as payment.[5]

Regulations limit the amount of the increase in gift or estate tax attributable to recapture in order to prevent double inclusion of the same transfer in the transfer tax system. The mitigation provisions include reduction of the amount recaptured by the sum of (1) the portion of the fair market value of the qualified payment interest which is attributable to cumulative but unpaid distributions; (2) to the extent held by the individual at the time of a taxable event, the fair market value of any equity interest received by the individual in lieu of qualified payments; and (3) the amount by which the individual's aggregate taxable gifts were increased to reflect failure of the individual to enforce his rights to qualified payments.[6]

1. Treas. Reg. §25.2701-3.
2. Treas. Reg. §25.2701-3(b).
3. IRC Sec. 2701(d).
4. Treas. Reg. §25.2701-4(c)(2).
5. Treas. Reg. §25.2701-4(c)(5).
6. Treas. Reg. §25.2701-4(c)(1).

As an overall limitation, the amount of any increase in tax due to cumulative but unpaid distributions will not exceed the applicable percentage of the excess (if any) of (1) the value (determined as of the date of the taxable event) of all equity interests in the entity which are junior to the applicable retained interest (see Q 925), over (2) the value of such interests (determined as of the date of the earlier transfer subject to these rules). The numerator of the applicable percentage is equal to the number of shares in the corporation held (as of the date of the taxable event) by the transferor which are applicable retained interests of the same class. The denominator of the applicable percentage is equal to the total number of shares in the corporation (as of the date of the taxable event) which are of the same class as the shares used in the numerator. (A similar rule applies to partnerships.)[1] The applicable percentage equals the largest ownership percentage interest in any preferred interest held by the interest holder.[2] The appreciation limitation does not apply if the interest holder elects to treat the late payment of a qualified payment as a taxable event (see below).[3]

For purposes of an increase in tax due to cumulative but unpaid distributions, a "taxable event" includes (1) the death of the transferor if the applicable retained interest is included in the transferor's estate, (2) the transfer of an applicable retained interest, and (3) at the election of the taxpayer, the payment of a qualified payment which is made after its four-year grace period.[4] Also, a termination of a qualified payment interest is treated as a taxable event. Thus, a taxable event occurs with respect to an individual indirectly holding a qualified payment interest held by a trust on the earlier of (1) the termination of the individual's interest in the trust, or (2) the termination of the trust's interest in the qualified payment interest. However, if the value of the qualified payment interest would be included in the individual's federal gross estate if the individual were to die immediately after the termination, the taxable transfer does not occur until the earlier of (1) the time the interest would no longer be includable in the individual's estate (other than by reason of the gifts within three years of death rule of IRC Section 2035), or (2) such individual's death.[5]

A "taxable event" does not include an applicable retained interest includable in the transferor's estate and passing under the marital deduction. Nor does a "taxable event" include a lifetime gift to a spouse which does not result in a taxable gift because the marital deduction is taken, or the spouse pays consideration for the transfer. However, such a spouse is thereafter treated in the same manner as the transferor.[6]

An applicable family member (see Q 925) is treated the same as the transferor with respect to any applicable retained interest retained by such family member. Also, if the transferor transfers an applicable retained interest to an applicable family member (other than the transferor's spouse), the applicable family member is treated the same as the transferor with respect to distributions accumulating after the time of the taxable event. In the case of a

1. IRC Sec. 2701(d)(2)(B).
2. Treas. Reg. §25.2701-4(c)(6)(iii).
3. Treas. Reg. §25.2701-4(d)(2).
4. IRC Sec. 2701(d)(3)(A).
5. Treas. Reg. §§25.2701-4(b)(1), 25.2701-4(b)(2).
6. IRC Sec. 2701(d)(3)(B).

transfer of an applicable retained interest from an applicable family member to the transferor, IRC Section 2701 continues to apply as long as the transferor holds the interest.[1]

Adjustment to Mitigate Double Taxation

As provided in regulations, if there is a later transfer or inclusion in the gross estate of property which was subject to IRC Section 2701, adjustments are to be made for gift, estate, and generation-skipping transfer tax purposes to reflect any increase in valuation of a prior taxable gift or any recapture under IRC Section 2701.[2]

IRC Section 2701 interests transferred after May 4, 1994. An individual (the initial transferor) who has previously made a transfer subject to IRC Section 2701 (the initial transfer) may be permitted a reduction in his taxable gifts for gift tax purposes or adjusted taxable gifts for estate tax purposes. If the holder of the IRC Section 2701 interest (i.e., the applicable retained interest, see Q 925) transfers the interest to an individual other than the initial transferor or an applicable family member of the initial transferor in a transfer subject to estate or gift tax during the lifetime of the initial transferor, then the initial transferor can reduce the amount upon which his tentative tax is calculated for gift tax purposes in the year of the transfer. The amount of the reduction is generally equal to the lesser of (1) the amount by which the initial transferor's taxable gifts were increased by reason of IRC Section 2701, or (2) the amount by which the value of the IRC Section 2701 interest at the time of the subsequent transfer exceeds its value at the time of the initial transfer (the duplicated amount). Any unused reduction can be carried over and applied in succeeding years; any reduction remaining at death can be applied in the initial transferor's estate. The amount upon which the initial transferor's tentative tax is calculated for estate tax purposes may also be reduced (this generally occurs if the IRC Section 2701 interest is retained until the initial transferor's death or if there is a carryover of any unused reduction).

If the holder of the IRC Section 2701 interest transfers the interest to an individual other than the initial transferor or an applicable family member of the initial transferor in an exchange for consideration during the lifetime of the initial transferor, then the reduction is taken by the initial transferor's estate and calculated as if the value of the consideration were included in the estate at its value at the time of the exchange. Property received in a nonrecognition exchange for an IRC Section 2701 interest is thereafter treated as the IRC Section 2701 interest for adjustment purposes. Reductions are calculated separately for each class of IRC Section 2701 interests. If spouses elected to treat the initial transfer as a split gift (see Q 895), then (1) each spouse may be entitled to reductions if there is a transfer of the IRC Section 2701 interest during their joint lives; and (2) if there is a transfer of the IRC Section 2701 interest at or after the death of either spouse, then (a) the donor spouse's estate may be entitled to reductions; and (b) the consenting spouse's aggregate sum of taxable gifts and gift tax payable on prior gifts are reduced to eliminate any remaining effect

1. IRC Sec. 2701(d)(4).
2. IRC Sec. 2701(e)(6).

of IRC Section 2701 if the consenting spouse survives the donor spouse. In any event, no reduction is available to the extent that double taxation has otherwise been avoided.[1]

IRC Section 2701 interests transferred before May 5, 1994. The initial transferor can use the final regulations (see above), the proposed regulations (see below), or any other reasonable interpretation of the statute.[2]

A person who has previously made a transfer subject to IRC Section 2701 is permitted a reduction in his adjusted taxable gifts for estate tax purposes. Whether a person is a transferor is determined without regard to the split-gift provisions for spouses (see Q 895). If any portion of the transferor's IRC Section 2701 interest is transferred to the transferor's spouse in a nontaxable event (e.g., the marital deduction), any reduction in adjusted taxable gifts is taken by such spouse rather than the transferor.[3]

The amount of the reduction is equal to the lesser of (1) the amount by which the transferor's taxable gifts were increased by reason of IRC Section 2701, or (2) the amount of the excess estate tax value of such interest multiplied by a fraction. The excess estate tax value equals the estate value of the IRC Section 2701 interest reduced by the value of such interest under IRC Section 2701 at the time of the transfer. In the case of an IRC Section 2701 interest transferred during life, the estate tax value equals the sum of (1) the increase in taxable gifts resulting from the transfer of the IRC Section 2701 interest, and (2) consideration received in exchange for the transfer. The numerator of the fraction above equals the value allocated under step 3 of the "Valuation Method" (see Q 925); the denominator of the fraction equals the value allocated under step 2 of the "Valuation Method."[4] However, no reduction is available to the extent that double taxation has otherwise been avoided.[5]

Miscellaneous

These provisions apply to transfers after October 8, 1990. However, with respect to property transferred before October 9, 1990, any failure to exercise a right of conversion, to pay dividends, or to exercise other rights to be specified in regulations, is not to be treated as a subsequent transfer.[6]

With respect to gifts made after October 8, 1990, the gift tax statute of limitations on a transfer subject to these provisions does not run unless the transaction is disclosed on a gift tax return in a manner adequate to apprise the IRS of the nature of the retained and transferred interests.[7]

1. Treas. Reg. §25.2701-5.
2. Treas. Reg. §25.2701-5(h).
3. Treas. Reg. §25.2701-5(a).
4. Treas. Reg. §25.2701-5(b).
5. Treas. Reg. §25.2701-5(c).
6. OBRA '90, Sec. 11602(e)(1).
7. IRC Sec. 6501(c)(9); OBRA '90, Sec. 11602(e)(2).

927. How are corporate and partnership transactions, such as recapitalizations, transfers and other changes in capital structure impacted by the Chapter 14 special valuation rules?

Effect on Corporate and Partnership Transactions

Recapitalizations and Transfers of Stock

If a parent recapitalizes a corporation into common and preferred stock and gives the common stock to his children, the value of the common stock is determined by subtracting from the value of the entire corporation the value of the preferred stock as determined under IRC Section 2701. If the parent treats the preferred stock's right to dividends as qualified payments, the right to such payments is assigned a present value. However, the value assigned to the common stock must be at least equal to the value determined under the junior equity rule (see Q 925). If the parent does not receive the preferred dividends within four years of their due dates, the parent may be treated as making additional transfers of the accumulated, but undistributed dividends, at the time of a subsequent transfer of the preferred stock. On the other hand, if the parent does not treat the right to dividends as qualified payments; such a right is assigned a value of zero.

Similarly, if a parent owns 80 percent of a corporation and a child owns 20 percent of the same corporation and the parent's common stock is exchanged for preferred stock, the value of what the parent has transferred and what the parent has retained are determined under IRC Section 2701.

Even if the child pays consideration for the common stock, whether the parent has made a transfer (and the value of such transfer) is determined under IRC Section 2701.

If a parent and a child each contribute to the startup of a new business and the parent receives preferred stock while the child receives common stock, the parent is treated as if he received common stock and preferred stock and then exchanged the common stock for the balance of the preferred stock. The value of what the parent has transferred and what the parent has retained are determined under IRC Section 2701.

However, a gift or a sale of stock to a child is not subject to IRC Section 2701 if the stock is of the same class as that retained by the parent. Also, a gift or a sale of stock to a child is not subject to IRC Section 2701 if the stock is proportionately the same as that retained by the parent (e.g., retained stock is entitled to $2 of dividends for every $1 of dividends paid to transferred stock), without regard to nonlapsing voting rights (i.e., parent can retain control with nonlapsing voting right).

If applicable family members receive or retain applicable retained interests at the time of a gift or a sale of stock to a child, the transaction may be subject to IRC Section 2701 even though the parent is willing to terminate his equity relationship with the corporation.[1]

1. See, for example, IRS CCA 201442053.

IRC Section 2701 could be avoided by selling the common stock to a nonfamily member, such as a valuable employee. Proceeds of the sale could then be distributed to the children.

Of course, IRC Section 2701 does not apply if either the transferred interest (common stock) or retained interest (preferred stock) is publicly traded. Also, with regard to retained distribution rights, IRC Section 2701 does not apply if the transferor and applicable family members do not control the corporation immediately before the transfer. However, with regard to liquidation, put, call, or conversion rights (other than those treated as distribution rights, see Q 925), IRC Section 2701 can apply even if the transferor and applicable family members do not control the corporation.

If the typical recapitalization is reversed (i.e., the parent retains the common stock and transfers the preferred stock), IRC Section 2701 should not apply (assuming no retention of applicable retained interests by parent or applicable family members).

Partnership Freezes

The traditional partnership freeze worked similarly to the traditional estate freeze recapitalization. It too is caught by the IRC Section 2701 special valuation rules. Most of the techniques employed to reduce the effect of, or to avoid, the valuation rules with respect to a recapitalization will also work with a partnership. Examination of the partnership agreement will be required to determine which partners hold which rights. Note that in the case of a limited partnership, "control" includes the holding of any interest as a general partner. Also, any right to receive a guaranteed payment of a fixed amount from a partnership under IRC Section 707(c) is not treated as a distribution right.

Other Changes in Capital Structure

Other changes in capital structure may also be caught by the IRC Section 2701 special valuation rules. Except as provided in regulations, a contribution to capital, a redemption, a recapitalization, or other change in capital structure of a corporation or partnership is treated as a transfer if the taxpayer or an applicable family member receives an applicable retained interest in the transaction, or as provided under regulations, holds such an interest immediately after the transfer.

Nonequity Interests

The IRC Section 2701 special valuation rules apply only to equity interests. Thus, none of the following should be treated as a retained interest for purposes of IRC Section 2701: an installment sale of an interest in a corporation or partnership, an exchange of an interest in a corporation or partnership for a private annuity, an employment contract or deferred compensation, or debt owed by a corporation or partnership to a transferor or applicable family member.[1] However, the total amount of debt owed the transferor or an applicable family member by the entity is a factor in the junior equity rule (see Q 925).

1. See TAM 9436006.

928. What special valuation rules apply to the transfer of an interest in trust under the Chapter 14 special valuation rules?

As a general rule, the value of a transferred remainder interest is equal to the value of the transferor's entire interest prior to the transfer reduced by the value of the interest retained by the transferor. For purposes of determining whether a transfer of an interest in a trust to (or for the benefit of) a member of the transferor's family is a gift (and the value of the transfer), the value of any interest retained by the transferor or an applicable family member (Q 925) is treated as being zero unless the retained interest is a qualified interest. This rule does not apply to an incomplete gift (a transfer that would not be treated as a gift whether or not consideration was received), to a transfer to a trust if the only property to be held by the trust is a residence to be used as a personal residence by persons holding term interests in the trust, or to the extent that the Regulations provide that a transfer is not inconsistent with IRC Section 2702.[1]

Also, IRC Section 2702 does not apply to the following:

(1) certain charitable remainder trusts;

(2) pooled income funds;

(3) charitable lead trusts in which the only interest in the trust other than the remainder interest or a qualified annuity or unitrust interest is the charitable lead interest;

(4) the assignment of a remainder interest if the only interest retained by the transferor or an applicable family member is as a permissible recipient of income in the sole discretion of an independent trustee; and

(5) a transfer in trust to a spouse for full and adequate consideration in connection with a divorce if any remaining interests in the trust are retained by the other spouse.[2]

For transfers to a trust made after May 17, 1997, regulations exempt charitable remainder unitrusts (CRUTs) from IRC Section 2702 only if the trust provides for simple unitrust payments, or in the case of a CRUT with a lesser of trust income or the unitrust amount provision, the grantor and/or the grantor's spouse (who is a U.S. citizen) are the only noncharitable beneficiaries.[3] Modified rules apply to certain qualified tangible property.

For these purposes, a transfer in trust does not include (1) the exercise, release, or lapse of a power of appointment over trust property that would not be a transfer for gift tax purposes, or (2) the exercise of a qualified disclaimer. An interest in trust includes a power with respect to a trust which would cause any portion of the transfer to be incomplete for gift tax purposes.[4]

1. IRC Sec. 2702(a).
2. Treas. Reg. §25.2702-1(c).
3. Treas. Reg. §25.2702-1(c)(3).
4. Treas. Reg. §25.2702-2(a).

Retained Interests

"Retained" is defined as the same person holding an interest both before and after the transfer in trust. Thus, a transfer of an income interest for life in trust to an applicable family member in conjunction with the transfer of a remainder interest in trust to a member of the transferor's family is not subject to IRC Section 2702. However, with respect to the creation of a term interest (e.g., a joint purchase creating a term and remainder interest), any interest held by the transferor immediately after the transfer is treated as held both before and after the transfer.[1] A negotiable note received in exchange for publicly traded stock sold to a trust was not treated as a retained interest in a trust.[2]

Qualified Interests

A "qualified interest" is an annuity or unitrust interest, or, if all other interests in the trust are annuity or unitrust interests, a noncontingent remainder interest. A *qualified annuity interest* means a right to receive fixed amounts (or a fixed fraction or percentage of the property transferred to the trust) not less frequently than annually. A *qualified unitrust interest* means a right to receive amounts which are payable not less frequently than annually and are a fixed percentage of the fair market value of the property in the trust (determined annually).[3] A qualified annuity interest can provide for an annuity amount (or fixed fraction or percentage) which increases by not more than 120 percent of the stated dollar amount (or fixed fraction or percentage) payable in the preceding year.[4] A qualified unitrust interest can provide for a unitrust percentage which increases by not more than 120 percent of the fixed percentage payable in the preceding year.[5]

The retention of a power to revoke a qualified annuity or unitrust interest of the transferor's spouse is treated as retention of the qualified annuity or unitrust interest.[6] Contingent annuity interests retained by the grantor or given to the grantor's spouse were not qualified interests.[7] Regulations treat an interest with the following characteristics as a qualified interest retained by the grantor: an annuity or unitrust interest that is (1) given to the spouse of the grantor; and (2) contingent only on (a) the spouse surviving, or (b) that the grantor does not revoke the spouse's interest.[8] The grantor makes an additional gift to the remainder person when the spouse's interest is revoked or the grantor survives the trust term without having revoked the interest.

A right to receive each year the *lesser of* an annuity interest or a unitrust interest is not treated as a qualified interest. The right to receive each year the *greater of* an annuity interest or a unitrust interest is treated as a qualified interest. However, the qualified interest is valued

1. Treas. Reg. §25.2702-2(a)(3).
2. TAM 9436006.
3. IRC Sec. 2702(b).
4. Treas. Reg. §25.2702-3(b)(1)(ii).
5. Treas. Reg. §25.2702-3(c)(1)(ii).
6. Treas. Reg. §25.2702-2(a)(5).
7. TAMs 9707001, 9717008, 9741001; *Cook v. Comm.*, 269 F.3d 854 (7th Cir. 2001), *aff'g* 115 TC 15 (2000).
8. Treas. Reg. §25.2702-3(d)(2).

at the greater of the two interests.[1] A right of withdrawal, whether or not cumulative, is not a qualified annuity or unitrust interest.[2]

A qualified annuity or unitrust interest may permit the payment of income in excess of the annuity or unitrust amount to the transferor or applicable family member with the retained annuity or unitrust interest. However, the annuity or unitrust interest is valued without regard to the right to excess income (which is not a qualified annuity or unitrust interest).[3] Also, a qualified annuity interest may permit the payment of an amount sufficient to reimburse the grantor for any income tax due on income in excess of the annuity amount; the annuity interest is valued without regard to such reimbursement right.[4] Distributions from the trust cannot be made to anyone other than the transferor or applicable family member who holds the qualified annuity or unitrust interest.[5]

The term of the annuity or unitrust interest must be for the life of the transferor or applicable family member, for a specified term of years, or for the shorter of the two periods.[6] There is a split of authority as to whether valuation may be based on two lives, or just one life.[7] Regulations permit certain revocable spousal interests (see above), but value the retained grantor and spouse's interests separately as for a single life.[8]

An example in the regulations had provided that where a grantor retained the right to annuity payments for ten years and the payments continued to his estate if he died during the ten-year term, the annuity was valued as for ten years or until the grantor's prior death (i.e., as a temporary annuity).[9] The Tax Court ruled that the example was invalid, that the annuity should be valued as for ten years (i.e., as a term annuity).[10] The IRS has changed the regulations so as to follow *Walton*.[11] Note that if the trust property reverted to the grantor's estate if the grantor died during the ten-year term, the annuity is valued as for ten years or until the grantor's prior death.[12] These results should apply likewise to unitrust payments.

Planning Point: A grantor retained annuity trust (GRAT) can be zeroed out (i.e., the value of the gift of the remainder reduced to zero) using an annuity payable to the grantor for a term of years with payments continuing to the grantor's estate for the balance of the term of years if the grantor dies during the term. In general, the GRAT is zeroed out if the annuity payment is made to equal the value of the property transferred to the trust divided by the appropriate annuity factor (including adjustments for frequency of payment).

1. Treas. Reg. §25.2702-3(d)(1).
2. Treas. Reg. §§25.2702-3(b)(1)(i), 25.2702-3(c)(1)(i).
3. Treas. Reg. §§25.2702-3(b)(1)(iii), 25.2702-3(c)(1)(iii).
4. Let. Ruls. 9441031, 9345035.
5. Treas. Reg. §25.2702-3(d)(2).
6. Treas. Reg. §25.2702-3(d)(3).
7. *Schott v. Comm.*, 2003-1 USTC 60,457 (9th Cir. 2003), rev'g TC Memo 2001-110; *Cook v. Comm.*, 269 F.3d 854 (7th Cir. 2001), *aff'g* 115 TC 15 (2000).
8. Treas. Reg. §25.2702-3(e)(Ex. 8).
9. Treas. Reg. §25.2702-3(e)(Ex. 5).
10. *Walton v. Comm.*, 115 TC 589 (2000).
11. Treas. Reg. §25.2702-3(e)(Ex. 5).
12. Treas. Reg. §25.2702-3(e)(Ex. 1).

The IRS will not issue rulings or determination letters on whether annuity interests are qualified interests under IRC Section 2702 where (1) the amount of the annuity payable annually is more than 50 percent of the initial fair market value of the property transferred to trust, or (2) the value of the remainder interest is less than 10 percent of the initial fair market value of the property transferred to trust. For purposes of the 10 percent test, the value of the remainder interest is determined under IRC Section 7520 without regard to the possibility that the grantor might die during the trust term, or that the trust property might revert to the grantor or the grantor's estate.[1]

Commutation (generally, an actuarially based acceleration or substitution of benefits) of a qualified annuity or unitrust interest is not permitted.[2] Additional contributions are not permitted with qualified annuity interests.[3]

The use of notes, other debt instruments, options or similar financial arrangements in satisfaction of the annuity or unitrust requirements under IRC Section 2702 is prohibited.[4]

A remainder (or reversion) interest is treated as a *qualified remainder interest* if: (1) all interests in the trust (other than non-contingent remainder interests) are either qualified annuity interests or qualified unitrust interests (thus, an excess income provision is not permitted for this purpose); (2) each remainder interest is entitled to all or a fractional share of the trust property when all or a fractional share of the trust terminates (a transferor's right to receive the original value of the trust property, or a fractional share, would not qualify); and (3) the remainder is payable to the beneficiary or the beneficiary's estate in all events (i.e., it is non-contingent).[5]

A qualified interest is to be valued using the valuation tables prescribed by IRC Section 7520.[6] For valuation rules for certain qualified tangible property, see Q 929.

929. What special valuation rules apply to the transfer of qualified tangible property under Chapter 14?

If the nonexercise of rights under a term interest in tangible property would not have a substantial effect on the valuation of the remainder interest, the interest is valued at the amount for which it could be sold to an unrelated third person (i.e., market value is used instead of the valuation tables or zero valuation).[7] *Qualified tangible property* is tangible property (1) for which a depreciation or depletion allowance would not be allowable if the property were used in a trade or business or held for the production of income, and (2) as to which the nonexercise of any rights under the term interest would not affect the value of the property passing to the remainderperson. A de minimis exception is provided at the time of the transfer to trust for

1. Rev. Proc. 2009-3, Sec. 4.51, 2009-1 IRB 107 and Rev. Proc. 2010-3, 2010-1 IRB 110, superseded by Rev. Proc. 2019-3.
2. Treas. Reg. §25.2702-3(d)(4).
3. Treas. Reg. §25.2702-3(b)(4).
4. Treas. Reg. §25.2702-3.
5. Treas. Reg. §25.2702-3(f).
6. IRC Sec. 2702(a)(2)(B).
7. IRC Sec. 2702(c)(4).

improvements to the property which would be depreciable provided such improvements do not exceed 5 percent of the fair market value of the entire property.[1]

Term interests in qualified tangible property are valued using actual sales or rentals that are comparable both as to the nature and character of the property and the duration of the term interest. Little weight is given appraisals in the absence of comparables. Tables used in valuing annuity, unitrust, estate, and remainder interests under IRC Section 7520 are not evidence of what a willing buyer would pay a willing seller for an interest in qualified tangible property.[2] If the taxpayer cannot establish the value of the term interest, the interest is valued at zero.[3]

If, during the term, the term interest is converted into property other than qualified tangible property, the conversion is treated as a transfer of the unexpired portion of the term interest (valued as of the time of the original transfer) unless the trust is converted to a qualified annuity interest (see Q 928).[4] If an addition or improvement is made to qualified tangible property such that the property would no longer be treated as qualified tangible property, the property is subject to the conversion rule above. If the addition or improvement would not change the nature of the qualified tangible property, the addition or improvement is treated as an additional transfer subject to IRC Section 2702.[5]

930. What special valuation rules apply to the transfer of an interest in a personal residence trust or qualified personal residence trust under Chapter 14?

IRC Section 2702 does not apply to the transfer of an interest in a personal residence trust or a qualified personal residence trust.[6] However, a person is limited to holding a term interest in only two such trusts.[7] A personal residence trust or a qualified personal residence trust which does not meet the requirements in the regulations may be modified (by judicial modification or otherwise, so long as the modification is effective under state law), if the reformation commences within ninety days of the due date (including extensions) for filing the gift tax return and is completed within a reasonable time after commencement. In the case of a trust created before 1997, the reformation had to commence within ninety days after December 23, 1997, and be completed within a reasonable time after commencement.[8]

A *personal residence* is defined as either (1) the principal residence of the term holder, (2) a residence of the term holder which the term holder uses for personal use during the year for a number of days which exceeds the greater of fourteen days or 10 percent of the days during the year that the residence is rented at fair market value, or (3) an undivided fractional interest in either (1) or (2). A personal residence includes appurtenant residential structures and a reasonable

1. Treas. Reg. §25.2702-2(c)(2).
2. Treas. Reg. §25.2702-2(c)(3).
3. Treas. Reg. §25.2702-2(c)(1).
4. Treas. Reg. §25.2702-2(c)(4).
5. Treas. Reg. §25.2702-2(c)(5).
6. IRC Sec. 2702(a)(3)(A)(ii); Treas. Reg. §25.2702-5(a).
7. Treas. Reg. §25.2702-5(a).
8. Treas. Reg. §25.2702-5(a)(2).

amount of land (taking into account the residence's size and location). Personal property, such as household furnishings, is not included in a personal residence. A personal residence is treated as such as long as it is not occupied by any other person (other than the spouse or a dependent) and is available at all times for use by the term holder as a personal residence. A personal residence can be rented out if the rental use is secondary to the primary use as a personal residence (but see above). Use of the residence as transient lodging is not permitted if substantial services are provided (e.g., a hotel or a bed and breakfast). Spouses may hold interests in the same personal residence or qualified personal residence trust.[1]

A *personal residence trust* is a trust which is prohibited for the entire term of the trust from holding any property other than one residence to be used as the personal residence of the term holder(s). A personal residence trust cannot permit the personal residence to be sold, transferred, or put to any other use. Expenses of the trust can be paid by the term holder. A personal residence trust can hold proceeds payable as a result of damage to, or destruction or involuntary conversion of, the personal residence for reinvestment in a personal residence within two years of receipt of such proceeds.[2] Also, with respect to trusts created after May 16, 1996, a personal residence trust must be prohibited from selling or transferring, directly or indirectly, the residence to the grantor, the grantor's spouse, or an entity controlled by the grantor or the grantor's spouse, at any time after the original term interest during which the trust is a grantor trust. A distribution upon or after the expiration of the original duration of the trust term to another grantor trust of the grantor or the grantor's spouse pursuant to the trust terms will not be treated as a sale or transfer to the grantor or grantor's spouse if the second trust prohibits sale or transfer of the property to the grantor, the grantor's spouse, or an entity controlled by the grantor or the grantor's spouse. This prohibition against a transfer to the grantor or the grantor's spouse does not apply to a transfer pursuant to the trust document or a power retained by the grantor in the event the grantor dies prior to the expiration of the original duration of the trust term. Nor does this prohibition apply to a distribution (for no consideration) of the residence to the grantor's spouse pursuant to the trust document at the expiration of the original duration of the trust term.[3]

A qualified personal residence trust ceases to be a qualified personal residence trust if the residence ceases to be used or held for use as the personal residence of the term holder. A residence is held by the trust for use as the personal residence of the term holder so long as the residence is not occupied by any other person (other than the spouse or a dependent of the term holder) and is available at all times for use by the term holder. A sale of a personal residence is not treated as a cessation of use as a personal residence if the personal residence is replaced by another within two years of the sale. The trust must provide that if damage to or destruction of the residence renders it unusable as a residence, the trust ceases to be a qualified personal residence trust unless the residence is repaired or replaced within two years.[4]

1. Treas. Reg. §§25.2702-5(b), 25.2702-5(c)(2).
2. Treas. Reg. §25.2702-5(b).
3. Treas. Reg. §§25.2702-5(b)(1), 25.2702-7.
4. Treas. Reg. §25.2702-5(c)(7).

A qualified personal residence trust must provide that within thirty days of ceasing to be a qualified personal residence trust with respect to any assets, either (1) the assets must be distributed to the term holder; (2) the assets must be put into a separate share of the trust for the balance of the term holder's interest as a qualified annuity interest; or (3) the trustee may elect either (1) or (2). The amount of such an annuity must be no less than the amount determined by dividing the lesser of the original value of all interests retained by the term holder or the value of all the trust assets by an annuity valuation factor reflecting the valuation table rate on the date of the original transfer and the original term of the term holder's interest. If only a portion of the trust continues as a qualified personal residence trust, then the annuity determined in the preceding sentence is reduced in proportion to the ratio that assets which still qualify as a personal residence trust bear to total trust assets.[1]

931. Are there any exceptions to the general rule that a qualified personal residence trust must only hold the taxpayer's principal residence?

A *qualified personal residence trust* is generally prohibited for the entire term of the trust from holding any property other than one residence to be used as the personal residence of the term holder(s), but certain exceptions are available. Thus, a qualified personal residence trust is permitted to hold cash in a separate account, but not in excess of the amount needed (1) for payment of trust expenses (including mortgage payments) currently due or expected within the next six months, (2) for improvements to the residence to be paid within the next six months, and (3) for purchase of a personal residence either (a) within three months of the creation of the trust, or (b) within the next three months pursuant to a previously entered into contract to purchase. Improvements to the personal residence which meet the personal residence requirements are permitted.[2]

Generally, sales proceeds (including income thereon) may be held in a qualified personal residence trust in a separate account until the earlier of (1) two years from the date of sale, (2) termination of the term holder's interest, or (3) purchase of a new residence. Insurance proceeds (including, for this purpose, certain amounts received upon an involuntary conversion) paid to a qualified personal residence trust for damage or destruction to the personal residence may also be held in the trust in a separate account for a similar period of time.[3] However, with respect to trusts created after May 16, 1996, a qualified personal residence trust must be prohibited from selling or transferring, directly or indirectly, the residence to the grantor, the grantor's spouse, or an entity controlled by the grantor or the grantor's spouse, during the original trust term and at any time after the original term interest during which the trust is a grantor trust. A distribution upon or after the expiration of the original duration of the trust term to another grantor trust of the grantor or the grantor's spouse pursuant to the trust terms will not be treated as a sale or transfer to the grantor or grantor's spouse if the second trust prohibits sale or transfer of the property to the grantor, the grantor's spouse, or an entity controlled by the grantor or the grantor's spouse. This prohibition against a transfer to the grantor or the grantor's spouse does not apply to a transfer pursuant to the

1. Treas. Reg. §25.2702-5(c)(8).
2. Treas. Reg. §25.2702-5(c)(5).
3. Treas. Reg. §§25.2702-5(c)(5)(ii), 25.2702-5(c)(7).

trust document or a power retained by the grantor in the event the grantor dies prior to the expiration of the original duration of the trust term. Nor does this prohibition apply to a distribution (for no consideration) of the residence to the grantor's spouse pursuant to the trust document at the expiration of the original duration of the trust term.[1]

Cash held by a qualified personal residence trust in excess of the amounts permitted above must be distributed to the term holder at least quarterly. Furthermore, upon termination of the term holder's interest, any cash held by a qualified personal residence trust for payment of trust expenses must be distributed to the term holder within thirty days.[2]

The qualified personal residence trust must provide that any trust income be distributed at least annually to the term holder.[3] Distributions from a qualified personal residence trust cannot be made to anyone other than the term holder during any term interest.[4] Commutation (generally, an actuarially based acceleration or substitution of benefits) of a qualified personal residence trust is not permitted.[5]

932. What special valuation rules apply to remainder interests and joint purchase transactions under Chapter 14?

The transfer of an interest in property with respect to which there are one or more term interests (e.g., transfer of a remainder interest) is to be treated as a transfer of an interest in trust.[6] A leasehold interest in property is not treated as a term interest provided a good faith effort is made to set the lease at a fair rental value.[7] If a person acquires a term interest in property in a joint purchase (or series of related transactions) with members of his family, then such person is treated as though he acquired the entire property and then transferred the interests acquired by the other persons in the transaction to such persons in return for consideration furnished by such persons.[8] For this purpose, the amount considered transferred by such individual is not to exceed the amount which such individual furnished for such property.[9] Special rules apply to "qualified tangible property" (see Q 929).

Attribution

A "member of the family" with respect to an individual includes such individual's spouse, any ancestor or lineal descendant of such individual or such individual's spouse, any brother or sister of the individual, and any spouse of the above.[10] An "applicable family member" with respect to a transferor includes the transferor's spouse, an ancestor of the transferor or transferor's spouse, and the spouse of any such ancestor.[11]

1. Treas. Reg. §§25.2702-5(c)(9), 25.2702-7.
2. Treas. Reg. §25.2702-5(c)(5)(ii)(A)(2).
3. Treas. Reg. §25.2702-5(c)(3).
4. Treas. Reg. §25.2702-5(c)(4).
5. Treas. Reg. §25.2702-5(c)(6).
6. IRC Sec. 2702(c)(1).
7. Treas. Reg. §25.2702-4(b).
8. IRC Sec. 2702(c)(2).
9. Treas. Reg. §25.2702-4(c).
10. IRC Sec. 2702(e).
11. IRC Secs. 2702(a)(1), 2701(e)(2).

Adjustment to Mitigate Double Taxation

A gift tax and estate tax adjustment is provided to mitigate the double taxation of retained interests previously valued under IRC Section 2702. In the case of a transfer by gift of a retained interest previously valued under IRC Section 2702 using the zero valuation rule or the qualified tangible property rule, a reduction in aggregate taxable gifts is available in calculating gift tax. If a retained interest previously valued under IRC Section 2702 using the zero valuation rule or using the qualified tangible property rule is later included in the gross estate, a reduction in adjusted taxable gifts is available in calculating estate tax. The amount of the reduction in aggregate taxable gifts or adjusted taxable gifts is equal to the lesser of (1) the increase in the taxable gifts resulting from the retained interest being initially valued under the zero valuation rule or the qualified tangible property rule, or (2) the increase in taxable gifts or gross estate resulting from the subsequent transfer of the interest. For purposes of (2), the annual exclusion is applied first to transfers other than the transfer valued under the zero valuation rule or the qualified tangible property rule. One-half of the amount of reduction may be assigned to a consenting spouse if gifts are split under IRC Section 2513.[1]

Miscellaneous

These provisions apply to transfers after October 8, 1990. However, with respect to property transferred before October 9, 1990, any failure to exercise a right of conversion, to pay dividends, or to exercise other rights to be specified in regulations, is not to be treated as a subsequent transfer.[2]

With respect to gifts made after October 8, 1990, the gift tax statute of limitations on a transfer subject to these provisions does not run unless the transaction is disclosed on a gift tax return in a manner adequate to apprise the IRS of the nature of the retained and transferred interests.[3]

Effect on Trust, Remainder Interest, and Joint Purchase Transactions

GRITs, GRATs, and GRUTs

Generally, a grantor retained income trust (GRIT) should no longer be used unless the only property to be held by the trust is a residence to be used as a personal residence by persons holding term interests in the trust. Under IRC Section 2702, the grantor is treated as though he transferred the entire property to the remainderperson at the time of the creation of the GRIT since his retained income interest is valued at zero (except with respect to the personal residence exception or unless the remainderperson is not a member of the transferor's family).[4]

Instead, grantor retained annuity trusts (GRATs) and grantor retained unitrusts (GRUTs) can be used to leverage gifts. The retained annuity or unitrust interest is valued using the

1. Treas. Reg. §25.2702-6.
2. OBRA '90, Sec. 11602(e)(1).
3. IRC Sec. 6501(c)(9); OBRA '90, Sec. 11602(e)(2).
4. Let. Rul. 9109033.

government valuation tables provided under IRC Section 7520. Notes, other debt instruments, options or similar financial arrangements cannot be used in satisfaction of the annuity or unitrust requirements. The value of the transferred remainder interest is equal to the value of the entire property reduced by the value of the retained interest. A reversion or general power of appointment retained by the grantor which is contingent upon the grantor dying during the trust term will no longer reduce the value of the transferred property. However, the value of the retained interest is reduced by such a contingency.

Charitable Trusts

Transfers to charitable remainder annuity trusts (CRATs), certain charitable remainder unitrusts (CRUTs), and pooled income funds are not subject to IRC Section 2702. Also, IRC Section 2702 does not apply to a charitable lead trust in which the only interest in the trust other than the remainder interest or a qualified annuity or unitrust interest is the charitable lead interest. For transfers to a trust made after May 17, 1997, regulations exempt CRUTs from IRC Section 2702 only if the trust provides for simple unitrust payments, or in the case of a CRUT with a lesser of trust income or the unitrust amount provision, the grantor and/or the grantor's spouse (who is a citizen of the U.S.) are the only noncharitable beneficiaries.[1]

Irrevocable Life Insurance Trusts

Irrevocable life insurance trusts should not be affected by IRC Section 2702. Generally, the full value of transfers to an irrevocable life insurance trust are already treated as gifts (except to the extent that annual exclusions are available).

Other Trusts

If a term interest (whether for life or term of years) is given to the transferor's spouse, an ancestor of the transferor or transferor's spouse, or the spouse of any such ancestor, and a remainder interest is given to any member of the transferor's family, IRC Section 2702 should not apply because the grantor has not retained a term interest.

Remainder Interest Transaction (RIT)

In general, if a person retains a term interest (whether for life or term of years) in property and sells or gives a remainder interest in the property to another family member, the value of the transferred property will be equal to the full value of the property unless the transferor retained an annuity or unitrust interest in the property (i.e., the value of a retained income interest is valued at zero).

However, if the nonexercise of rights under a term interest in tangible property would not have a substantial effect on the valuation of the remainder interest, the interest is valued at the amount for which it could be sold to an unrelated third person (i.e., market value is used instead of the valuation tables or zero valuation). The Senate Committee Report to OBRA '90 gives a painting, or undeveloped real estate, as examples of such tangible property. Depletable

1. Treas. Reg. §25.2702-1(c)(3).

property is given as an example of property which would not qualify for this special rule. See "Qualified Tangible Property," Q 929.

Split Purchases (Splits)

If a person acquires a term interest in property in a joint purchase (or series of related transactions) with members of his family, then such person is treated as though he acquired the entire property and then transferred the interests acquired by the other persons in the transaction to such persons in return for consideration furnished by such persons. Thus, if a father and son purchase rental property and the father receives an interest for life and the son receives a remainder interest; the father is treated as though he sold the remainder interest to his son for the consideration furnished by the son. The transaction is then essentially treated as a sale of a remainder interest (see above).

933. What special valuation rules apply to certain agreements, options, rights, or restrictions exercisable at less than fair market value under Chapter 14?

For estate, gift, and generation-skipping transfer tax purposes, the value of any property is to be determined without regard to any restriction on the right to sell or use such property, or any option, agreement, or other right to acquire or use the property at less than fair market value (determined without regard to such an option, agreement, or right). However, the previous sentence is not applicable if the option, agreement, right, or restriction: (1) is a bona fide business arrangement, (2) is not a device to transfer the property to members of the decedent's family for less than full and adequate consideration in money or money's worth, and (3) has terms comparable to those entered into by persons in an arm's length transaction.[1] The three prongs of the test must be independently satisfied.[2] All three prongs of the test are considered met if more than 50 percent of the value of the property subject to the right or restriction is owned by persons who are not members of the transferor's family or natural objects of the transferor's bounty. The property owned by such other persons must be subject to the right or restriction to the same extent as the property owned by the transferor.[3]

To determine whether a buy-sell agreement or other restrictive agreement has terms comparable to those entered into by persons in an arm's length transaction, the following factors are to be considered: (1) "the expected term of the agreement, (2) the current fair market value of the property, anticipated changes in value during the term of the agreement, and (3) the adequacy of any consideration given in exchange for the rights granted."[4] The terms of a buy-sell agreement or other restrictive agreement must be comparable to those used as a general practice by unrelated persons under negotiated agreements in the same business. Isolated comparables do not meet this requirement. More than one recognized method may be

1. IRC Sec. 2703.
2. Treas. Reg. §25.2703-1(b)(2).
3. Treas. Reg. §25.2703-1(b)(3).
4. Treas. Reg. §25.2703-1(b)(4)(i).

acceptable. Where comparables are difficult to find because the business is unique, comparables from similar businesses may be used.[1]

In the case of a partnership (or LLC) created on a decedent's deathbed, the IRS has stated that the partnership was the agreement for purposes of IRC Section 2703, and the partnership should be ignored because the partnership was not a valid business arrangement and the partnership was a device to transfer the underlying property to the family members for less than adequate consideration. Even if the partnership was not ignored, the Service stated that it would ignore the restrictions on use of the property contained in the partnership's agreement; such restrictions also would fail IRC Section 2703.[2] Courts have also rejected the idea that the partnership can be ignored for purposes of IRC Section 2703.[3]

The Tax Court has applied IRC Section 2703 to certain gifts of family limited partnership interests.[4]

Certain restrictions on the sale or use of property in a restricted management account are disregarded for transfer tax purposes under IRC Section 2703.[5]

For more information on valuing a closely held business interest, see Q 917, Q 919.

Effective Date and Transition Rules

This provision applies to agreements, options, rights, or restrictions entered into or granted after October 8, 1990, and agreements, options, rights, or restrictions substantially modified after October 8, 1990.[6] Any discretionary modification of an agreement that results in other than a de minimis change in the quality, value, or timing of the agreement is a substantial modification. Generally, a modification required by the agreement is not considered a substantial modification. However, if the agreement requires periodic modification, the failure to update the agreement is treated as a substantial modification unless the updating would not have resulted in a substantial modification. The addition of a family member as a party to a right or restriction is treated as a substantial modification unless (1) the addition is mandatory under the terms of the right or restriction, or (2) the added family member is in a generation (using the generation-skipping transfer tax definitions of generations) no lower than the lowest generation of any individuals already party to the right or restriction. The modification of a capitalization rate in a manner that bears a fixed relationship to a specified market rate is not treated as a substantial modification. Furthermore, a modification that results in an option price that more closely approximates fair market value is not treated as a substantial modification.[7]

1. Treas. Reg. §25.2703-1(b)(4)(ii).
2. TAMs 9723009, 9725002, 9730004, 9735003, 9736004, 9842003.
3. *Est. of Strangi v. Comm.*, 2002-2 USTC ¶60,441 (5th Cir. 2002), aff'g 115 TC 478 (2000); *Church v. U.S.*, 2000-1 USTC ¶60,369 (W.D. Tex. 2000).
4. *Holman v. Comm.*, 130 TC 170 (2008).
5. Rev. Rul. 2008-35, 2008-29 IRB 116.
6. OBRA '90, Sec. 11602(e)(1)((A)(ii).
7. Treas. Reg. §25.2703-1(c).

Effect on Options and Buy-sell Agreements

In order to help fix values for estate, gift, and generation-skipping transfer tax purposes, newly executed or substantially modified options and buy-sell agreements exercisable at less than fair market value between persons who are the natural objects of each other's bounty will generally have to meet all three of IRC Section 2703's requirements. Otherwise, such agreement will be disregarded in valuing the property. Old options and buy-sell agreements which are not substantially modified after October 8, 1990 are not affected by IRC Section 2703. IRC Section 2703's provisions apply to agreements involving either business or nonbusiness property.

934. What special valuation rules apply to certain lapsing rights and restrictions under Chapter 14?

In general, IRC Section 2704(a) provides that the lapse of certain voting or liquidation rights in a family owned business results in a taxable transfer by the holder of the lapsing right. IRC Section 2704(b) provides generally that certain restrictions on liquidating a family owned business are ignored in valuing a transferred interest. These provisions apply to restrictions or rights (or limitations on rights) created after October 8, 1990.[1] Regulations proposed in 2016 would have modified certain aspects of these special valuation rules, including the definition of applicable restriction discussed below. However, these regulations were withdrawn in 2017.

For more information on valuing a closely held business interest, see Q 917, Q 919.

Lapse of Certain Rights

For estate, gift, and generation-skipping transfer tax purposes, if there is a lapse of a voting or liquidation right in a corporation or partnership and the individual holding such right (the "holder") immediately before the lapse and members of the holder's family control the entity (both before and after the lapse), then the holder is treated as if making a transfer. The value of the transfer is equal to the amount (if any) by which the value of all interests in the entity held by the holder immediately prior to the lapse (determined as if all voting and liquidation rights were nonlapsing) exceeds the sum of (1) the value of such interests immediately after the lapse (determined as if held by one individual), and (2) in the case of a lapse during the holder's life, any consideration in money or money's worth received by the holder with respect to such lapse.[2]

A *voting right* is defined as a right to vote with respect to *any* matter of the entity. Also, with respect to a partnership, the right of a general partner to participate in partnership management is treated as a voting right. A *liquidation right* is the right to compel (including by aggregate voting power) the entity to acquire *all or a portion* of the holder's equity interest in the entity.[3] A lapse of a voting or liquidation right occurs when a presently exercisable right is restricted or eliminated.[4]

1. OBRA '90, Sec. 11602(e)(1)(A)(iii).
2. IRC Sec. 2704(a); Treas. Reg. §§25.2704-1(a), 25.2704-1(d).
3. Treas. Reg. §25.2704-1(a)(2).
4. Treas. Reg. §§25.2704-1(b), 25.2704-1(c)(1).

The transfer of an interest which results in the lapse of a liquidation right is not subject to IRC Section 2704(a) if the rights with respect to the transferred interest are not restricted or eliminated.[1] However, a transfer that results in the elimination of the transferor's right to compel the entity to acquire an interest of the transferor which is subordinate to the transferred interest is treated as a lapse of a liquidation right with respect to the subordinate interest. The lapse rule does not apply to the lapse of a liquidation right with respect to (1) a transfer that was previously valued in the hands of the holder as a transfer of an interest in a corporation or partnership under IRC Section 2701 (see Q 925), or (2) the lapse of a liquidation right to the extent that immediately after the lapse the holder (or the holder's estate) and members of the holder's family cannot liquidate an interest that the holder could have liquidated prior to the lapse. Whether an interest can be liquidated immediately after the lapse is determined under state law or, if the governing instruments are less restrictive than the state law which would apply in the absence of such instruments, the governing instruments. For this purpose, any applicable restriction under IRC Section 2704(b) (see below) is disregarded.[2]

If a lapsed right may be restored only upon the occurrence of a future event not within the control of the holder or the holder's family, the lapse is deemed to occur at the time the lapse becomes permanent with respect to the holder (e.g., upon the transfer of the interest).[3]

For attribution rules, see below.

Transfers Subject to Applicable Restrictions

If there is a transfer of an interest in a corporation or partnership to (or for the benefit of) a member of the transferor's family and the transferor and members of transferor's family control the entity (immediately before the transfer), any applicable restriction is to be disregarded in valuing the transferred interest for estate, gift, or generation-skipping transfer tax purposes.[4] If an applicable restriction is disregarded under this rule, the rights of the transferor are valued under the state law that would apply but for the limitation (meaning that the interest is valued as though the restriction does not exist).[5]

"Applicable restriction" means any restriction which effectively limits the ability of the corporation or partnership to liquidate if either (1) the restriction lapses (in whole or in part) after the transfer, or (2) the transferor or any member of the transferor's family, acting alone or collectively, can remove the restriction (in whole or in part) after the transfer.[6] Applicable restriction treatment was avoided where the consent of all parties was required and a charity (a nonfamily member) had become a partner.[7]

1. Prop. Treas. Reg. §25.2704-1(c)(1). The proposed regulations released in 2016 (and withdrawn in 2017) provided that this exception should not apply when the transfer occurs on a decedent's deathbed, so that the exception would apply only to transfers occurring more than three years prior to death (transfers occurring within three years of death would have been treated as a transfer occurring at death).
2. Treas. Reg. §25.2704-1(c).
3. Treas. Reg. §25.2704-1(a)(3).
4. IRC Sec. 2704(b)(1).
5. Treas. Reg. §25.2704-2(c).
6. IRC Sec. 2704(b)(2).
7. *Kerr v. Comm.*, 292 F. 3d 490, 2002-1 USTC ¶60,440 (5th Cir. 2002).

However, any restriction imposed or required by any federal or state law was not previously treated as an applicable restriction.[1] Thus, the definition of an applicable restriction was limited to a restriction that was more restrictive than the limitations which would apply under state law if there were no restriction. Also, whether there is the ability to remove a restriction is determined under the state law that would apply in the absence of the restrictive provision in the governing instruments.[2]

An applicable restriction does not include any commercially reasonable restriction which arises as part of any financing by the corporation or partnership with a person who is not related to the transferor or transferee, or a member of the family of either.[3] Regulations provide that an applicable restriction does not include any commercially reasonable restriction which arises as a result of any unrelated person providing capital in the form of debt or equity to the corporation or partnership for the entity's trade or business operations. For this purpose, the regulations apply the relationship rules of IRC Section 267(b), except that the term "fiduciary of a trust" under the relationship rules is modified to generally exclude banks, trust companies, and building and loan associations.[4]

Furthermore, an applicable restriction does not include an option, right to use property, or other agreement subject to IRC Section 2703 (see Q 933).[5]

With respect to a partnership (or LLC) created on a decedent's deathbed, the IRS has disregarded restrictions where the partnership provided that a partner could not liquidate his interest, while state law provided a less restrictive provision.[6] A few cases have held that partnership liquidation provisions were no more restrictive than state law and should not be ignored under IRC Section 2704(b).[7] However, see above for a discussion of the application of the new proposed regulations in these situations.

Attribution

The following attribution rules or definitions generally apply for purposes of the rules which apply to certain lapsing rights and applicable restrictions under IRC Section 2704:

In the case of a corporation, "control" means 50 percent ownership (by vote or value) of the stock. In the case of a partnership, "control" means 50 percent ownership of the capital or profits interests, or in the case of a limited partnership, the ownership of any interest as a general partner.[8]

1. IRC Sec. 2704(b)(3)(B).
2. Treas. Reg. §25.2704-2(b). Proposed regulations released in 2016 (and withdrawn in 2017) would have modified the definition of "applicable restriction." These modifications were partially motivated by the fact that courts previously interpreted the definition as applying only to restrictions on liquidations of an entire entity, rather than on restrictions on liquidating a transferred interest in the entity. The proposed regulations would have also eliminated the reference to state law, and disregarded the following types of restrictions: (1) restrictions on the ability to liquidate the transferred interest and (2) restrictions attendant upon the nature or extent of the property to be received in the exchange for the liquidated interest, or the timing of the payment of that property.
3. IRC Sec. 2704(b)(3)(A).
4. Treas. Reg. §25.2704-2(b).
5. Treas. Reg. §25.2704-2(b).
6. TAMs 9723009, 9725002, 9730004, 9735003, 9736004, 9842003.
7. *Kerr v. Comm.*, 113 TC 449 (1999); *Knight v. Comm.*, 115 TC 506 (2000).
8. IRC Secs. 2704(c)(1), 2701(b)(2).

A "member of the family" with respect to an individual includes such individual's spouse, any ancestor or lineal descendant of such individual or such individual's spouse, any brother or sister of the individual, and any spouse of the above.[1]

An individual is treated as holding interests held indirectly through a corporation, partnership, trust, or other entity.[2] Thus, transfers may be either direct or indirect.

935. What changes did the 2017 tax reform legislation make with respect to the estate, gift and generation skipping transfer tax (GSTT)?

The 2017 Tax Act doubled the transfer tax exemption to $10 million per individual (as indexed for inflation using the new chained CPI indexing method; the amount is $11.58 million (or $23.16 million per married couple) for 2020).[3]

936. How did the 2017 tax reform legislation impact the viability of the family limited partnership (FLP) as an estate planning strategy?

The 2017 tax reform legislation created a new twist in planning with FLPs, so that taxpayers who have created these entities as estate planning mechanisms may wish to reevaluate the benefits provided by the FLP structure under the new rules. Many FLPs are formed in order to reduce estate taxes, but the doubled estate tax exemption from 2018-2025 ($11.58 million per individual in 2020) may mean that these individuals will no longer be subject to the estate tax at all.

Unfortunately, use of the FLP structure will require the taxpayer to forego the step-up in basis that the assets transferred to the FLP would otherwise receive upon his or her death. If the individual who formed the FLP no longer anticipates being subject to the estate tax, he or she may wish to dissolve the FLP in order to obtain that step-up in basis and allow his or her heirs to realize the income tax savings that the step-up can generate.

These taxpayers should also be aware of the potential for taxation under IRC Section 731 if the FLP distributes cash or marketable securities in excess of basis, in which case the distribution will be treated as ordinary income. Taxation can be avoided in several scenarios, such as if the property is distributed to the same partner who originally created it, or if the partnership is an investment partnership and distributions are made to eligible parties.

937. How did the 2017 tax reform legislation impact the advisability of using trust structures such as spousal lifetime access trusts (SLATs) in estate planning strategies?

The 2017 tax reform legislation roughly doubled the transfer tax exemption to $11.18 million per individual, or $22.36 million per couple, for 2018-2025. Absent Congressional action to extend the expansion, the per-person exemption will revert to its $5.6 million level

1. IRC Sec. 2704(c)(2).
2. IRC Secs. 2704(c)(3), 2701(e)(3).
3. IRC Sec. 2010(c)(3)(C).

beginning in 2026. Because the transfer tax exemption exempts both transfers at death and transfers made during life from estate and gift taxes, the expansion has created an opportunity for wealthy clients to shield an even greater portion of their estates from eventual taxation.

A spousal lifetime access trust (SLAT) is one type of irrevocable trust that can potentially allow a client to remove assets from his or her estate while also maintaining access to those assets during life. To fund a SLAT, a married client transfers assets into the irrevocable trust for the benefit of his or her spouse. An independent trustee is appointed to oversee the trust (adult children may serve as trustee so long as a concrete, ascertainable standard exists for trust distributions). The gift to the irrevocable trust removes the assets from the client's estate, but allows his or her spouse to access the trust assets if necessary. The strategy allows the client to retain a degree of control over the assets, and also puts the assets out of the reach of his or her creditors.

Planning Point: In some cases, it may be advantageous to partially fund the trust with a life insurance policy to pay substantial benefits at the client's death. The policy premiums could be funded with the income earned on other assets that are placed in the trust. This can provide an option for tax-free distributions if a cash value policy is used.

One obvious downside to the SLAT strategy is the risk of divorce. If the taxpayer divorced his or her spouse, that spouse would remain beneficiary of the SLAT and the taxpayer would no longer have control over those assets because the trust is irrevocable.

Individuals who created a SLAT in 2012, when the last "fiscal cliff" situation motivated action steps to take advantage of the potentially expiring $5 million exemption, should consider the potential application of the reciprocal trust doctrine. This rule was developed to prevent two individuals from creating identical trusts that would each benefit the other, while at the same time removing the assets from the individuals' respective estates. As a result, it is important to ensure that the two SLATs are not identical. This can be accomplished by providing different trustees, different rights to access the trust assets (e.g., one trust could allow access to principal, while the other only permits access to income) or adding children as beneficiaries to one of the trusts. The length of time that has elapsed between a SLAT created in 2012 and a SLAT created now also substantially reduces the risk that the IRS will determine that the reciprocal trust doctrine should apply.

938. What do taxpayers need to be aware of with respect to the impact of the 2017 tax reform legislation on using portability in their estate planning?

Portability simply allows a surviving spouse to make use of both his or her individual federal estate tax exemption and the exemption granted to a first-to-die spouse (see Q 9089). With the increased estate tax exemption post-reform, many taxpayers may be tempted to rely upon portability alone as an estate planning strategy. Importantly, however, portability does not apply at the state level, so if the taxpayer is subject to state level estate or inheritance taxes, relying on portability alone will be insufficient to escape those taxes. Secondly, portability does not apply to shelter assets from the generation skipping transfer tax (GSTT). If the individual plans to leave assets to a grandchild, a trust structure will be required in order to elect to apply the GSTT exemption (also $11.58 million in 2020) to those assets.

Relying on portability alone requires that the first-to-die spouse forgo control over the final disposition of his or her assets after the surviving spouse's death. This can become especially important in the blended family context, where the first-to-die spouse has children from a prior marriage, or if the surviving spouse chooses to remarry. Using a qualified terminable interest property (QTIP) trust (see Q 9104) can help alleviate this issue, providing the surviving spouse with income for life, but allowing the first-to-die spouse to control the ultimate disposition of the income producing assets. Further, the QTIP trust structure can provide creditor protection for a financially irresponsible spouse, or if the surviving spouse remarries someone with financial difficulties.

Finally, the enlarged estate tax exemption is not permanent. It is scheduled to sunset after 2025, at which point the base amount will revert to the pre-reform $5 million level absent further Congressional action. Although unlikely, it is possible that the estate tax exemption could be even lower when the individual eventually dies. This uncertainty creates a substantial risk in relying on portability alone in estate planning.

939. Is it still advisable for taxpayers to attempt to leverage potential valuation discounts post-tax reform?

Valuation discounts are primarily important in reducing the value of a client's taxable estate—usually in the small business context, where minority or lack of marketability discounts may be available in certain circumstances.

With the enlargement of the estate tax exemption for 2018-2025 (and potentially beyond), many planners are now seeking to reverse strategies that would have permitted taxpayers to claim valuation discounts in their estate plans. However, if the taxpayer is unlikely to be subject to the estate tax at all under tax reform, use of a valuation discount can cause the individual to forgo a portion of the basis adjustment to which his or her heirs would otherwise be entitled. A greater upward basis adjustment can provide income tax savings. As a result, taxpayers who do not expect to be subject to the estate tax may wish to revisit their estate planning to ensure the largest possible basis adjustment, which may require reversing previously implemented strategies.

Of course, all taxpayers should be aware that the changes made by tax reform with respect to the estate tax exemption are only temporary, meaning that the estate tax exemption level could be much lower when the taxpayer dies.

940. Did tax reform make any changes that impact inherited IRAs? What should taxpayers consider when designating a beneficiary to inherit an IRA post-reform?

The 2017 tax reform legislation indirectly impacted inherited IRAs by modifying the rules that apply with respect to the "kiddie tax" (see Q 8588). Essentially, under the new rules governing unearned income of minors, the tax rates that apply to trusts and estates will now apply to this income (at least from 2018-2025). Therefore, while the *earned* income of minors will be taxed according to the individual income tax rates prescribed for single filers, any unearned income of minors will be taxed according to the applicable tax bracket that would apply if the income was that of a trust or estate. This rule applies both to income that is subject to ordinary income tax rates and in determining the capital gains rate that will apply if long-term capital gains treatment is appropriate.

Under both the old and new systems, an individual who inherits an IRA is required to take distributions each year—generally based on his or her life expectancy. This rule has made it particularly appealing for taxpayers to leave their IRA to young grandchildren, whose RMDs would be lower because of their longer life expectancies—thus maximizing the "stretch" IRA tax-deferral benefits.

However, in many cases, the inherited IRA is meant to function as a college funding device for grandchildren. Unfortunately, the new rules mean that this will likely not be a tax-smart move. Under the new rules, if the grandchild withdraws a large sum to cover his or her tuition, the highest 37 percent rate will apply to a much smaller amount of income than under previous law, which would have imposed tax on the withdrawal at the parents' income tax rate, which, in many cases, may have been significantly lower than the top rate.

Because of this, taxpayers may wish to consider alternative funding devices for securing their grandchildren's education funding. Section 529 plans provide for tax-free growth and distributions for education expenses, and have been expanded so that they can now be used to pay for elementary and secondary expenses. Children who have already inherited IRAs should be advised of the tax benefits of avoiding larger than necessary withdrawals. For example, it may be wise for the child to take out student loans to pay for college, and then repay those loans with IRA funds after he or she has reached age twenty-four (so that the kiddie tax rules no longer apply).

PART IX: INTERNATIONAL TAX

941. What is the difference between a resident alien and a nonresident alien?

A foreign individual who is not a U.S. citizen is labeled as an "alien" for U.S. tax purposes. An alien is either a nonresident alien or a resident alien. A resident alien is a foreign individual who meets either the green card test or the substantial presence test, discussed below, and a nonresident alien is any other foreign individual unless that individual is otherwise eligible to elect to be treated as a resident alien (see, for example, Q 943).

A foreign individual meets the "green card test" if given permission to reside in the U.S. on a permanent basis by U.S. Citizenship and Immigration Services (or a predecessor) and such permission has not been revoked or judicially determined to have been abandoned by the individual.[1]

A foreign individual meets the "substantial presence test" if physically present in the U.S. for at least (1) 31 days in 2019 and (2) 183 days during the three year period that includes 2019, 2018 and 2017, counting only a certain number of days that the individual is present in the U.S. per year, based on the following table:[2]

Year	Days Counted Toward 183 Day Total
2019	All days present in the U.S.
2018	1/3 of days present in the U.S.
2017	1/6 of days present in the U.S.

In general, an individual is treated as being "physically present" in the U.S. for any day in which he or she is actually present in the U.S. at any time of the day. Despite this, an individual does not count the following as days as being physically present in the U.S.:

(1) Days that the individual commutes into the U.S. for work from a residence in Canada or Mexico if that individual regularly commutes into the U.S. for work (meaning that the individual commutes on more than 75 percent of workdays during the individual's working period);

(2) Days that the individual is in the U.S. for less than twenty-four hours while in transit between two foreign countries;

(3) Days that the individual is in the U.S. as a member of a crew of a foreign vessel;

(4) Days that the individual is only in the U.S. because of a medical condition that arose while in the U.S. and that rendered that individual unable to leave the U.S.; and

1. See IRS Publication 519, available at http://www.irs.gov/publications/p519/index.html (last accessed March 29, 2019).
2. IRS Pub. 519, above.

(5) Days that the individual was an exempt individual (including individuals temporarily present in the U.S. as foreign-government related individuals, teachers or trainees on a "J" or "Q" visa, individuals present in the U.S. on a student visa, and certain professional athletes in the U.S. for a charitable sports event).[1]

A resident alien will be taxed much in the same way as a U.S. citizen, and thus will be subject to U.S. taxation on all worldwide income. Conversely, a nonresident alien will only become subject to U.S. taxation in the event that he engages in certain activities that create a connection between that individual and the U.S. (see Q 942).

942. When does a foreign individual become a U.S. taxpayer who is required to file a U.S. tax return?

U.S. citizens and resident aliens (see Q 941) are taxed on worldwide income regardless of where they are located and must generally file a return (though a two-month filing extension will apply for U.S. citizens and residents who are residing overseas).[2]

A foreign individual who is a nonresident alien may be required to file a U.S. tax return if any of the following occur:

(1) A nonresident alien engaged in a trade or business in the U.S. during the tax year. If the nonresident alien's only U.S. source income consists of wages that are less than the personal exemption amount ($4,200 in 2019)[3], noting that the personal exemption itself was suspended for 2018-2025, that alien is not required to file;

(2) A nonresident alien not engaged in a trade or business in the U.S., but who has U.S. income on which the tax liability was not satisfied by withholding at the source;

(3) A representative responsible for filing the return of an individual described in (1) or (2);

(4) A fiduciary for the estate or trust if any beneficiary of the estate or trust is a nonresident alien; or

(5) A resident or other fiduciary, or other person charged with the care of the nonresident alien or his or her property, unless the nonresident alien files the return himself or makes other arrangements for a representative to file the return and pay the tax.[4]

1. IRS Pub. 519, above, and IRS Guidance, "Substantial Presence Test," available at http://www.irs.gov/Individuals/International-Taxpayers/Substantial-Presence-Test (last accessed March 29, 2019).
2. See IRS Guidance, "U.S. Citizens and Resident Aliens Abroad," available at http://www.irs.gov/Individuals/International-Taxpayers/U.S.-Citizens-and-Resident-Aliens-Abroad (last accessed March 29, 2019).
3. Rev. Proc. 2018-57.
4. Treas. Reg. §1.6012-3. See also IRS Guidance, "Taxation of Nonresident Aliens," available at http://www.irs.gov/Individuals/International-Taxpayers/Taxation-of-Nonresident-Aliens (last accessed March 29, 2019).

943. What rules apply when a U.S. citizen or resident alien is married to a nonresident alien and the couple wishes to file a joint U.S. tax return?

If a U.S. citizen or resident alien (see Q 941) is married to a nonresident alien, the couple may elect to treat the nonresident alien as a U.S. resident for tax purposes. The couple may elect this treatment by attaching a statement to this effect to their U.S. tax return for the relevant tax year. The election may be made at the time of filing, or by filing an amended tax return for up to three previous tax years (though in this case, the couple must also elect such treatment for all tax returns that have been filed since the date of the amended return).

The couple must file a joint tax return for the year in which the election is originally made, though separate returns may be filed in later years.

While this election will result in the nonresident alien being treated as a resident alien for income tax purposes, the individual may continue to be treated as a nonresident alien for purposes of Social Security and Medicare taxes.[1]

The election will apply until it is suspended or ended. The election is suspended if, during a later tax year, neither spouse is a U.S. citizen or resident alien. The election is ended if (a) it is revoked by either spouse, (b) one spouse dies, (c) the spouses are legally separated or (d) the spouses have failed to keep adequate records to prove their income tax liability.[2] If the election is "ended," neither spouse may apply to make the election in a subsequent tax year.

944. When a U.S. citizen is a resident of a foreign country and earns income in that foreign country, is that income included in the taxpayer's gross income for U.S. tax purposes?

Yes. If a U.S. citizen is employed in a foreign country and files a tax return in that country, that individual will also be required to file a Form 1040 in the United States. A U.S. citizen is taxed on *worldwide* income, regardless of whether that taxpayer lives in the U.S. or in a foreign country.[3]

Despite this, a U.S. citizen with foreign earned income may be eligible to exclude all or a portion of foreign earnings from calculation of his or her income for U.S. tax purposes (see Q 945).[4] "Foreign earned income" includes amounts received by the individual from sources within a foreign country that are attributable to services performed by the individual.[5] Pension and annuity income, amounts paid to the individual by the U.S. (or a U.S. agency) as an employee, and amounts paid to the individual under Section 402(b) (taxability of beneficiaries of nonexempt trusts) or Section 403(b) (taxability of beneficiaries under nonqualified annuities) are excluded from foreign earned income.[6]

1. IRS Guidance, "US Citizens and Resident Aliens Abroad – Nonresident Alien Spouse," available at http://www.irs.gov/Individuals/International-Taxpayers/U.S.-Citizens-and-Resident-Aliens-Abroad—Nonresident-Alien-Spouse (last accessed March 29, 2019).
2. IRS Pub. 519.
3. See IRS Guidance on the Foreign Earned Income Exclusion, available at http://www.irs.gov/Businesses/Foreign-Earned-Income-Exclusion-1 (last accessed March 29, 2019).
4. IRC Sec. 911(a)(1).
5. IRC Sec. 911(b)(1)(A).
6. IRC Sec. 911(b)(1)(B).

945. What is the foreign earned income exclusion?

The foreign earned income exclusion is available if the following requirements are met:

(1) The individual has income received for work performed in a foreign country,

(2) The individual has a tax home in a foreign country, and

(3) The individual meets either (i) the bona fide residence test or (ii) the physical presence test (see Q 946).

According to IRS guidance, an individual's "tax home" is the general area of the individual's principal place of business or employment. The individual's principal place of residence is irrelevant for determining the individual's tax home. However, if the individual is not consistently present in one business location, the location of that individual's principal residence may be used as a factor in the tax home determination. If the individual has neither a regular principal place of business or residence, the individual is considered itinerant and his or her tax home is wherever he or she works. The individual's tax home is *not* considered to be in a foreign country if that taxpayer's "abode" is in the U.S.[1]

> *Example:* Joe is a U.S. citizen who is employed on a fishing enterprise in the waters of a foreign country. His schedule provides that he works one month on and one month off. Joe continues to maintain a residence in the U.S., where his family lives and where he returns on his "off" months. Joe is considered to have a "tax home" in the U.S. because his time is split equally between the U.S. and foreign waters. He is not entitled to take advantage of the foreign earned income exclusion, though he may be entitled to deduct his living expenses while living abroad as business travel expenses.[2]

A taxpayer's election to exclude foreign earnings under the foreign earned income exclusion may be revoked by the taxpayer by filing a statement to that effect with the IRS, but if the taxpayer attempts to claim the exclusion within five tax years after the revocation, he or she must apply for IRS approval.[3]

946. What are the bona fide residence and physical presence tests that can allow a U.S. individual to qualify for the foreign earned income exclusion?

A U.S. individual with foreign earned income must satisfy either the bona fide residence test or the physical presence test in order to be eligible to exclude all or a portion of foreign earned income from U.S. income (see Q 944).

An individual may use the "bona fide residence test" to qualify for the exclusion if the individual is either (a) a U.S. citizen or (b) a U.S. resident alien who is a citizen of a country with which the U.S. has an income tax treaty in effect. The bona fide residence test, as the name suggests, is met if the individual has established a residence in a foreign country. The length of the individual's stay and the nature of employment are factors considered in determining whether

1. IRS Pub. 54 (2018), p.12
2. See IRS Guidance, "Foreign Earned Income Exclusion – Tax Home in Foreign Country," available at http://www.irs.gov/Individuals/International-Taxpayers/Foreign-Earned-Income-Exclusion—Tax-Home-in-Foreign-Country (last accessed March 29, 2019).
3. See IRS Guidance: "Revocation of the Foreign Earned Income Exclusion," available at http://www.irs.gov/Individuals/International-Taxpayers/Revocation-of-the-Foreign-Earned-Income-Exclusion (last accessed March 29, 2019).

the individual has established a residence in a foreign country, but are not determinative—all of the facts and circumstances of the particular situation must be taken into account.

The IRS has provided bright-line guidance so that the individual must reside in the foreign country for an uninterrupted period that includes an entire tax year, though every individual that resides in a foreign country for at least an entire tax period is *not* automatically considered to have established a residence.[1]

> *Example:* Shannon's domicile (permanent home) is in Brooklyn, New York, but she is assigned to her employer's London office for an indefinite duration. She rents an apartment in London with a one-year lease, though she intends to eventually return to Brooklyn. Assuming all other factors indicate that Shannon has established a residence in London, she will meet the bona fide residence test even though she plans to return to Brooklyn at some point in the future. If Shannon had, for example, been sent to London for a month-long work assignment with a definite return date, she would not be able to satisfy the bona fide residence test. If Shannon had been assigned to her work post in London for 16 months, she may not be able to meet the bona fide residence test because her presence in London is limited in duration.

An individual (whether a U.S. citizen or resident alien) meets the physical presence test if physically present in a foreign country (or countries) for at least 330 days during a consecutive twelve-month period. The individual is not required to establish a residence and there are no requirements as to whether or not the individual intends to return to the U.S. at a specified time under the physical presence test. Unlike the tax home requirement, the individual can be in the foreign country during these days for any reason—there is no requirement that the presence abroad be motivated by business or employment reasons.[2]

947. What is the foreign housing exclusion (or deduction)?

The foreign housing exclusion applies to housing costs paid for with employer-provided funds (including amounts paid by the employer to the employee as taxable foreign earned income), while the foreign housing deduction applies to an individual who pays for foreign housing with self-employment earnings.

The foreign housing exclusion (or deduction) allows an individual to exclude (or deduct) amounts spent on housing costs while residing abroad, provided that the individual's tax home (see Q 944) is found to be in a foreign country and the taxpayer meets either the bona fide residence test or the physical presence test (see Q 946).[3]

An individual's "housing amount" is the total housing costs for the year *minus* a base amount that is tied to the maximum foreign earned income exclusion (see Q 944) for the year. The amount is 16 percent of the maximum foreign earned income exclusion ($107,600 in 2020, $105,900 in 2019, $103,900 in 2018, $102,100 in 2017, $101,300 in 2016, and $100,800 in

1. See IRS Guidance: "Foreign Earned Income Exclusion – Bona Fide Residence Test," available at http://www.irs.gov/Individuals/International-Taxpayers/Foreign-Earned-Income-Exclusion—Bona-Fide-Residence-Test (last accessed March 29, 2019).
2. See IRS Guidance: "Foreign Earned Income Exclusion – Physical Presence Test," available at http://www.irs.gov/Individuals/International-Taxpayers/Foreign-Earned-Income-Exclusion—Physical-Presence-Test (last accessed March 29, 2019).
3. IRC Sec. 911(a)(2).

2015, as indexed for inflation),[1] calculated on a daily basis, and multiplied by the number of days spent abroad in the tax year.[2]

Housing expenses that qualify for the exclusion or deduction must be reasonable, and can also include housing expenses for the individual's spouse and/or dependents if they live with the individual while abroad.[3] The cost of purchasing real property, furniture, accessories or other improvements to increase the value of the property are excluded from the definition of housing expenses for purposes of the exclusion (or deduction). Expenses relating to housing, such as the cost of utilities and insurance, are included in the definition of housing expenses for purposes of the exclusion (or deduction).[4]

The amount of a taxpayer's foreign housing exclusion (or deduction) cannot exceed the amount of foreign-earned income for the tax year.

948. Can U.S. individuals employed in a foreign country receive U.S. Social Security credit?

In some cases, a U.S. individual will continue to earn U.S. Social Security credit if liable for Social Security and Medicare taxes on amounts earned while performing services as an employee in a foreign country. The IRS has issued guidance that provides that Social Security and Medicare taxes continue to apply to wages paid for services performed by a U.S. individual abroad if any of the following are true:

(1) The individual is working for a U.S. employer,

(2) The individual performs services in connection with a U.S. aircraft or vessel and the individual has (a) entered into an employment contract in the U.S. or (b) the vessel or aircraft touches down at a U.S. port while the individual is employed on it,

(3) The individual is working in a country with which the U.S. has entered a Social Security agreement providing that the foreign earned income is subject to U.S. Social Security and Medicare taxes, or

(4) The individual is working for a foreign affiliate (a foreign entity in which the U.S. employer has at least a 10 percent interest) of a U.S. employer under a voluntary agreement (under IRC Section 3121(l)) entered into by that employer and the U.S. Treasury Department.[5]

1. IR-2014-104 (Oct. 30, 2014), Rev. Proc. 2015-53, 2015-44 IRB 615, Rev. Proc. 2016-55, Rev. Proc. 2018-18, Rev. Proc. 2018-57, Rev. Proc. 2019-44.
2. IRC Sec. 911(c)(1).
3. IRC Sec. 911(c)(3).
4. IRC Sec. 911(c)(3).
5. See IRS Guidance: "Social Security Tax Consequences of Working Abroad," available at http://www.irs.gov/Individuals/International-Taxpayers/Social-Security-Tax-Consequences-of-Working-Abroad (last accessed March 29, 2019).

The IRS guidance further provides that an individual is "working for a U.S. employer" for purposes of (1), above, if the individual is working for (a) the U.S. government (or instrumentality thereof), (b) another individual who is a U.S. resident, (c) a partnership in which at least two-thirds of the partners are U.S. residents, (d) a trust, in which all of the trustees are U.S. residents or (e) a corporation organized in the U.S., or in any U.S. state (including D.C., the Virgin Islands, Guam, American Samoa and the Northern Mariana Islands).[1]

A U.S. employer who voluntarily enters into an agreement to extend Social Security coverage to its employees working in a foreign country is liable for the entire amount of the covered employees' Social Security taxes that would otherwise apply under Sections 3101 and 3111 if those employees were employed domestically.[2]

The IRS has advised that U.S. individuals who are working in a country with which the U.S. has entered a Social Security agreement providing that the individual's income will *not* be subject to U.S. Social Security taxes obtain a statement from the relevant agency in the foreign country stating that the individual's income is subject to Social Security coverage in that foreign country.

The U.S. Social Security Administration (SSA) will issue determinations that a U.S. individual's income is subject only to U.S. Social Security taxes if the employer contacts the SSA and provides certain basic identifying information about that individual and his or her employment abroad.

949. What are some of the considerations that a U.S. citizen or resident should be aware of when participating in a retirement plan while residing in a foreign country?

While many U.S. citizens and residents who are transferred abroad by multinational employers may continue to be covered by the multinational's U.S. retirement plan, in some cases, a U.S. individual may obtain benefits under a foreign plan. Because U.S. citizens and residents are taxed on their worldwide income, benefits accrued under foreign retirement plans may be subject to U.S. taxation absent a treaty provision that provides otherwise. Most treaties provide that a pension or annuity received from a foreign employer is taxed in the country of residence under its domestic laws.[3]

Treaties with some countries provide for liberalized treatment of retirement accounts—for example, the treaty between the U.S. and the U.K. provides that U.S. citizens residing in the U.K. can deduct, for U.S. tax purposes, amounts contributed to a pension plan established in the U.K.[4]

1. IRC Sec. 3121(h).
2. IRC Sec. 3121(l)(1)(A).
3. See IRS Guidance, "The Taxation of Foreign Pensions and Annuities," available at http://www.irs.gov/Businesses/The-Taxation-of-Foreign-Pension-and-Annuity-Distributions (last accessed March 29, 2019).
4. See the Treasury Department Technical Explanation of the Convention between the U.S. and U.K, Article 17, available at http://www.treasury.gov/resource-center/tax-policy/treaties/Documents/teus-uk.pdf (last accessed March 29, 2019).

Further, while a U.S. individual residing abroad may exclude a portion of foreign earned income from U.S. gross income each year, the foreign earned income exclusion does *not* apply to income received as a pension or annuity while abroad[1] (Q 3557).

Planning Point: The IRS has released long-awaited proposed regulations clarifying the income tax withholding obligations when distributions from employer-sponsored plans (including pension, annuity, profit sharing, stock bonus or deferred compensation plans) are made to destinations outside the U.S. While U.S. payees can elect to forgo withholding, non-U.S. payees cannot. In general, the participant cannot elect to forgo withholding with respect to these distributions even if the participant provides a U.S. residential address, but directs funds to be delivered to a destination outside the U.S. If the participant provides a non-U.S. residential address, withholding obligations cannot be waived even if the participant directs that the funds be distributed to a U.S. financial institution. When the participant provides no residential address, withholding obligations cannot be waived.

Technically, a plan established in a foreign country cannot be "qualified" under IRC Section 401, because of the requirement that a qualified trust be organized under U.S. law.[2] Therefore, a U.S. individual participating in a foreign retirement plan would not be entitled to defer taxation of contributions to the foreign plan in the same manner as would be available in the U.S., absent a treaty provision to the contrary.

However, plans established by certain U.S. multinationals that are established under foreign law may achieve the same tax result if the plan is otherwise qualified.[3] IRC Section 404(a)(4) provides a special rule that allows for the qualification of a trust established outside of the U.S. if the employer contributing to the plan is a U.S. resident, corporation or other entity and the plan is otherwise qualified.

950. Are employer contributions to a foreign retirement account on behalf of a U.S. individual exempt from U.S. reporting requirements?

U.S. individuals residing abroad may become subject to both the FBAR and FACTA reporting rules, and the corresponding penalties for noncompliance, based upon their participation in foreign retirement plans.

Generally, a U.S. individual who has an interest in any "foreign account" is required to file an FBAR (Form TD F90-22.1) if the aggregate value of foreign accounts exceeds $10,000 at any time during the calendar year.[4] The IRS has issued regulations that specifically exempt certain accounts, including plans that qualify under IRC Section 401 and IRA accounts, but these regulations do not provide a similar exemption for *foreign* retirement accounts.[5] Therefore, whether FBAR reporting will be required for a U.S. individual's foreign retirement accounts

1. IRC Sec. 911(b)(1)(B).
2. IRC Sec. 401(a).
3. IRC Sec. 404(a)(4).
4. See IRS "FAQs Regarding Report of Foreign Bank and Financial Accounts (FBAR) – Financial Accounts," available at http://www.irs.gov/Businesses/Small-Businesses-Self-Employed/FAQs-Regarding-Report-of-Foreign-Bank-and-Financial-Accounts-FBAR (last accessed March 29, 2019).
5. See IRS Guidance: "Report of Foreign Bank and Financial Accounts (FBAR)," available at http://www.irs.gov/Businesses/Small-Businesses-&-Self-Employed/Report-of-Foreign-Bank-and-Financial-Accounts-FBAR (last accessed March 29, 2019).

will likely turn upon whether the individual has a "financial interest" or "signature authority" over the foreign account.

Penalties for failure to file an FBAR can be steep—for willful violations, the civil penalty can equal the greater of $100,000 or 50 percent of the account assets, and the IRS may be entitled to file criminal charges.[1] For non-willful violations, the penalty can still equal up to $10,000 per violation unless the taxpayer can show that there was reasonable cause for failure to file, in which case no penalty is imposed.[2]

Because of the steep penalties imposed upon taxpayers who do not comply with FBAR reporting obligations, the IRS has issued guidance to allow certain "low risk" nonresident U.S. taxpayers who have resided outside of the U.S. since January 1, 2009 to catch up on filing delinquent U.S. income tax returns and FBARs with respect to their foreign accounts. Whether an individual is "low risk" or not will be determined based on the amount of U.S. income tax owed (less than $1,500 per tax year is low risk), and these delinquent returns will be processed in a streamlined manner absent any other high risk factors.[3] The plan is described by the IRS as a method to provide assistance to U.S. citizens residing abroad, including dual citizens, with foreign retirement plan issues.[4]

In addition to FBAR filing requirements, a U.S. individual may be required to comply with FATCA and report any foreign financial assets with an aggregate value of over $50,000 (or higher amount, if the Secretary otherwise provides) on Form 8938, Statement of Specified Foreign Financial Assets, attached to his or her U.S. tax return.[5]

951. What assets of a foreign individual (nonresident alien) are subject to U.S. estate tax?

Unlike a U.S. citizen, who is subject to estate taxation on worldwide assets, the gross estate of a nonresident alien (meaning, a foreign individual who is not a U.S. citizen or resident alien) only includes property that is situated in the U.S. at the time of the nonresident alien's death.[6]

For purposes of determining what property is situated in the U.S., any property which the decedent has transferred, by trust or otherwise, which would be taxable within the provisions of IRC Sections 2035 through 2038 (relating to termination of certain property interests within three years of death, transfers with a retained life estate or to take effect at death, and revocable transfers), is deemed situated in the United States if it was so situated either at the time of the transfer or at the time of death.[7]

1. 31 USC 5321(a)(5).
2. See IRS FS-2011-13 (December 2011).
3. See IRS Instructions for New Streamlined Filing Compliance Procedures for Nonresident, Non-Filer U.S. Taxpayers, available at http://www.irs.gov/Businesses/Corporations/Summary-of-FATCA-Reporting-for-US-Taxpayers (last accessed March 29, 2019).
4. IR-2012-65 (June 26, 2012).
5. IRC Sec. 6038D(a).
6. IRC Sec. 2103.
7. IRC Sec. 2104(b).

For a decedent who was a nonresident alien at the time of death, property is considered located in the U.S. if it falls into any of the following categories:

(1) Real property located in the U.S.;

(2) Tangible personal property located in the U.S., including clothing, jewelry, automobiles, furniture or currency. Works of art imported into the U.S. solely for public exhibition purposes are not included;

(3) A debt obligation of a citizen or resident of the U.S., a domestic partnership or corporation or other entity, any domestic estate or trust, the U.S., a state or a political subdivision of a state or the District of Columbia; or

(4) Shares of stock issued by domestic corporations, regardless of the physical location of stock certificates.[1]

However, in the case of a nonresident alien who dies while in transit through the U.S., personal effects are not considered located in the U.S. Neither is merchandise that happens to be in transit through the U.S. when a nonresident alien owner dies.

The IRS has also addressed certain assets and found that they are specifically excludible from a nonresident alien's gross estate as being "without the U.S." The following nonexhaustive list of the property owned by a nonresident alien is *not* considered to be situated within the U.S. for calculating the gross estate:

(1) A bank account that is not used in connection with a U.S. trade or business;[2]

(2) A deposit or withdrawable account with a savings and loan association chartered and supervised under federal or state law or an amount held by an insurance company under an agreement to pay interest on it. But the deposit or amount must not be connected with a U.S. trade or business and must be paid or credited to the decedent's account;[3]

(3) A deposit with a foreign branch of a U.S. bank if the branch is engaged in the commercial banking business;[4]

(4) A debt obligation, the interest on which would be exempt from income tax under IRC Section 871(h)(1), relating to tax-exemption for interest earned by nonresident aliens with respect to portfolio debt investments;[5]

1. Treas. Reg. §20.2104-1(a).
2. See IRS Guidance: "Some Nonresidents with U.S. Assets Must File Estate Tax Returns," available at http://www.irs.gov/Individuals/International-Taxpayers/Some-Nonresidents-with-U.S.-Assets-Must-File-Estate-Tax-Returns (last accessed March 29, 2019).
3. IRC Secs. 2105(b)(1), 871(i)(3).
4. IRC Sec. 2105(b)(2).
5. IRC Sec. 2105(b)(3).

(5) Stock issued by a corporation that is not a domestic corporation, even if the certificate is physically located in the United States;[1]

(6) An amount receivable as insurance on the decedent's life;[2]

(7) Certain original issue discount obligations;[3] and

(8) Certain stock that a nonresident alien owns in a regulated investment company (RIC) at the time of his or her death.[4]

If the decedent was a citizen or resident of one of the countries with which the U.S. had an estate tax treaty in place, the provisions of the treaty may override the normally applicable provisions of the Internal Revenue Code that are outlined above.

952. How does the estate of a foreign individual (nonresident alien) calculate the amount of U.S. estate tax owed?

The estate tax computation base of a nonresident alien's estate consists of his or her taxable estate plus any taxable gifts made during his or her lifetime.[5] The taxable gifts of a nonresident alien made after 1976 (other than gifts included in the gross estate) also form part of the tax base upon which the estate tax is computed. The adjusted taxable gifts of a nonresident alien are computed in the same manner as for a resident citizen.[6]

Once the taxable estate of the nonresident alien decedent is determined, the mechanics of the actual tax calculation and the applicable rate schedule (before the unified credit) are the same for nonresident alien decedents as for citizen-residents. However, a very important difference comes into play in the use of the unified credit, which is greatly reduced for nonresident alien decedents. This, of course, indirectly results in a higher effective tax rate. See Q 954 for a discussion of the unified credit as applied to nonresident aliens.

953. Is the estate of a foreign individual entitled to the same deductions as a U.S. individual?

A nonresident alien's taxable estate is determined by deducting the following items from the alien's gross estate:

(1) Expenses, indebtedness, taxes and losses. These items may be deducted only in the proportion that the value of the decedent's gross estate in the U.S. bears to the value of the entire estate, wherever situated.[7] Thus, the deductible portion of each item is limited to the amount of each item multiplied by a fraction, the numerator

1. IRC Sec. 2104(a).
2. IRC Sec. 2105(a).
3. IRC Secs. 2105(b)(5), 871(g)(1).
4. IRC Sec. 2105(d).
5. IRC Sec. 2101(c).
6. IRC Sec. 2101(b), (c).
7. IRC Sec. 2106(a)(1).

of which is the value of the property located in the U.S., and the denominator of which is the value of the entire gross estate, wherever located.

(2) Charitable bequests. Charitable bequests are fully deductible if made to organizations meeting the requirements for an estate tax charitable deduction under IRC Section 2055 and are computed in the same manner as similar deductions allowed the estates of U.S. citizens and residents.[1]

(3) Marital Deduction. The marital deduction is not available for property passing to a surviving spouse who is an alien (either a resident alien or a nonresident alien) unless the property passes to the spouse in a qualified domestic trust (QDOT) or is placed in a QDOT before the date on which the decedent's estate tax return is filed.[2] The policy behind this limitation is that if the surviving spouse is an alien, there is a considerable likelihood that the marital deduction property will eventually be moved abroad, and not be taxable upon the death of the surviving spouse. This possibility can be eliminated, however, through the QDOT mechanism, which assures that the property in question will remain subject to U.S. estate tax upon the death of the surviving spouse.

Allowance of Deductions. A deduction is allowed only if the executor discloses in the estate tax return the value of that part of the gross estate not situated in the U.S.[3]

954. May a nonresident alien's estate claim an estate tax exemption upon the death of the nonresident alien?

The unified transfer tax credit in the case of a nonresident alien decedent is only $13,000.[4] This effectively exempts only the first $60,000 of his or her taxable estate from estate tax, a considerably lower threshold than applies to a domestic decedent (see Q 851).

A special rule applies if the decedent was a nonresident of the United States, but resided in a U.S. possession (e.g., Puerto Rico, Guam) and was a U.S. citizen only because of birth or residence in, or citizenship of, the possession. Under these circumstances, the decedent is considered to be a "nonresident noncitizen,"[5] and the estate of a decedent in this category qualifies for a credit that is the greater of:

(1) $13,000, or

(2) $46,800 multiplied by the ratio that the value (at death) of that part of the decedent's gross estate that is located in the U.S. bears to the entire value of the decedent's gross estate.[6]

1. IRC Sec. 2106(a)(2).
2. IRC Sec. 2056(d).
3. IRC Sec. 2106(b).
4. IRC Sec. 2102(b)(1).
5. IRC Sec. 2209.
6. IRC Sec. 2102(b)(2).

In either case, the credit may not be more than the amount of the estate tax.[1] Further, the amount of the available credit is reduced by the value of any lifetime gifts made by the nonresident alien-decedent.[2]

955. Can a life insurance policy or annuity contract issued to a U.S. person by a foreign life insurance company qualify for the tax benefits traditionally afforded to U.S. life insurance policies?

Generally, foreign insurance companies cannot sell insurance products to U.S. persons without becoming subject to U.S. regulation. Despite this, if a U.S. person resides in a foreign country for an extended period of time, it is possible that he or she may choose to purchase a life insurance or annuity product from a foreign insurance company in that country. In order for a foreign-issued life insurance or annuity product to qualify for the same tax preferences given to domestic products, it will be required to comply with the U.S. requirements for these products (including, for example, the definition of "life insurance contract" under Section 7702 or the annuity provisions of Section 72).

Further, under the IRC, most annuity contracts issued by domestic insurance companies are exempt from the original issue discount (OID) rules (discussed in Q 493 to Q 499).[3] An annuity contract issued by a foreign insurance company will be subject to the OID rules, however, unless that insurance company is subject to tax under subchapter L with respect to income earned on the annuity contract. If the insurance company is not subject to tax under subchapter L, the annuity contract will be included in the definition of a debt instrument and the growth on the annuity cash value can be subject to tax as interest income even if payouts under the annuity contract have not yet begun.[4]

In the context of variable life insurance contracts, a contract will not qualify as a variable life insurance contract unless it is a "variable contract" for purposes of IRC Section 817(d). Under this provision, the amounts received under the variable contract must be segregated into an account that is separate from the company's general asset accounts *under state law or regulation*.[5] The question that arises in this context is whether an insurance company that segregates its assets pursuant to *foreign law* will qualify. The IRS has found that a foreign insurance company that elects to be taxed as a domestic company under IRC Section 953(d) (meaning it will be subject to subchapter L taxation), and that segregates amounts received under life insurance contracts from general company assets under foreign law, can meet the requirements of Section 817(d).[6]

This, however, leaves open the possibility that variable contracts issued by a foreign insurance company that has *not* elected to be taxed as a domestic company will not qualify for treatment as such under the IRC.

1. IRC Sec. 2102(b)(4).
2. IRC Sec. 2102(b)(3)(B).
3. IRC Sec. 1275(a)(1)(B).
4. Treas. Reg. §1.1275-1(k).
5. IRC Sec. 817(d)(1).
6. Let. Rul. 200919025.

956. What considerations should a U.S. citizen or resident alien be aware of when disposing of real property that is located in a foreign country?

The general rule that a U.S. citizen or resident alien is taxed on all worldwide income applies in the case of a sale of real property in the same manner as income from any other source.[1] Therefore, a U.S. citizen or resident alien who sells real property that is located in a foreign country must report and abide by U.S. tax rules relating to the sale of real property (see Q 7843).

Thus, for example, a U.S. citizen who sells a principal residence that he or she has used as a principal residence for two of the five preceding tax years is entitled to exclude a portion of the gain from taxation in the U.S. in the same manner as though the property was located within the U.S. (see Q 7843).

Though the U.S. citizen or resident alien may also be required to pay taxes upon disposition of foreign-located real property both in the U.S. and in the country in which the property is situated, he or she will be entitled to claim a credit for certain foreign taxes paid on his or her U.S. tax return.[2]

Further, a U.S. citizen or resident alien may be entitled to deduct any real property taxes that are imposed by a foreign country on his or her U.S. tax return.[3]

U.S. Individuals and Taxation in Mexico

957. Can U.S. individuals purchase land in Mexico for investment purposes?

Generally, yes, though there are certain conditions and restrictions that must be understood first. U.S. individuals and other non-Mexican individuals may directly own real estate in Mexico. However, U.S. individuals may *not* directly own any real estate parcels within an area designated as the "restricted zone" (see Q 958).

From a very practical position, any U.S. individual seeking to purchase real property in Mexico should understand the following basic premises:

(1) The real estate industry in Mexico is generally unregulated. Real estate agents and brokers are neither licensed nor regulated as they are in the U.S. In addition, there is no "Office of the Real Estate Commissioner" or equivalent in Mexico to provide any type of consumer protection or advocacy. In any Mexican real property transaction, extreme caution must be exercised before executing any contract.

(2) Any acquisitions in the "restricted zone" by a U.S. individual must be undertaken with the following entities:

- A bank;

1. See IRS Publication 544.
2. See IRS Publication 54.
3. IRS Pub. 54.

- A public notary; or
- The buyer's attorney (preferably a licensed Mexican attorney).

958. What is a restricted zone purchase for purposes of real property transactions taking place in Mexico?

Mexican law prohibits the direct ownership of real estate within what is designated as the "restricted zone," which is defined to include "all land located within 100 kilometers (about 62 miles) of any Mexican border, and within 50 kilometers (about 31 miles) of any Mexican coastline."

In order for a U.S. individual to acquire property within the restricted zone, the buyer must first form a "fideicomiso"[1] with the buyer's bank serving as the title owner of the real estate, and as the trustee to the trust, with the U.S. buyer being the trust beneficiary.[2] This structure allows the U.S. buyer to enjoy complete and unrestricted use of the real estate.

Essentially, the seller of the property sells the parcel to the bank as the trustee of the fideicomiso. The bank has a fiduciary obligation to follow instructions provided by the U.S. trust beneficiary, who will retain all ownership rights, while the bank retains title. Under this arrangement, the U.S. person can sell the property that is held in trust at its market value to any ready, willing and able buyer. In addition, the buyer can instruct the bank to lease the property to any person at terms favorable to the beneficiary.

959. What are the tax and reporting obligations of U.S. purchasers of real property in Mexico?

Based on the scenario described in Q 958, the primary issue becomes whether or not the U.S. individual is required to report his interest in the fideicomiso to the IRS as required pursuant to current Code provisions.[3]

Recent guidance issued by the IRS has indicated that the fideicomiso is not deemed a trust for U.S. tax purposes, thus it is treated as a disregarded entity.[4] This means that the trust is not subject to otherwise applicable reporting requirements.[5]

Accordingly, any gains resulting from the sale of the Mexican property by the trust will be recognized by the U.S. beneficiary and subject to the favorable maximum current capital gains rate of 20 percent, as opposed to the maximum rate of 37 percent applicable to ordinary income. However, the receipt of any rental income must be reported as income on the U.S. individual's return.

1. In essence, a Mexican trust that will hold real estate.
2. In addition, the bank as trustee is also required to apply to the Ministerio Público (Minister of Public Affairs) for permit to acquire real estate and to establish the trust.
3. Forms 3520 and 3520-A, pursuant to Notice 97-34, Sec. IV, 1997-1 CB 422.
4. Rev. Rul. 2013-14.
5. Similar decision reached in Let. Rul. 201245003.

960. How should Mexican clients seeking to open investment accounts in the U.S. structure their investment holdings in a tax efficient manner?

Citizens and residents of Mexico are taxed on income sourced on a worldwide basis at a rate of 30 percent. Taxable income includes all types of income, whether received in cash, in services or in credit, regardless of the source. This necessarily includes income derived from passive investment activities including dividends, interest and capital gain income.

Because of the above, the concept of "tax efficiency" in establishing investment accounts may be problematic for Mexican investors based on their enacted tax statutes and interpretations. As such, the conventional posture of a Mexican investor establishing investment accounts in his or her name becomes a simple proposition to the extent that he or she would be taxed on any earnings generated from investment activities. But, to the extent that the investment activities emanating from a U.S. broker/dealer will result in U.S. source income earned by a nonresident investor,[1] taxes will be due to the U.S. on the same income.[2] As such, the Mexican investor would be taxed twice on the same investment income.

To avoid this result, some advisors suggest that the Mexican investor consider utilizing a corporate structure in opening the account in place. However, that may be problematic under the Controlled Foreign Corporation (CFC) scheme under Mexican tax law where CFCs are defined as non-Mexican companies whose tax rate in its respective jurisdiction is less than 75 percent of the income tax that would have been paid in Mexico in accordance with their tax laws.[3] Thus, the desire to utilize a corporation domiciled in a low tax jurisdiction or tax haven will create unwanted and unnecessary scrutiny by Mexican tax authorities.[4] Thus, such advice tends to be harmful to the investor.

Other advisors recommend the use of passthrough entities[5] wherein one of the partners (or in the case of the LLC, a member) is an irrevocable non-Mexican trust wherein the Mexican investor is a beneficiary of the trust and could enjoy the beneficial interests of asset accumulation under a foreign trust as to Mexico. The trustee of such trust should be a non-Mexican entity or person located in a jurisdiction with a lower tax rate, as his or its ownership may be taxed as income. However, the net result of such arrangement would be the non-taxation of the investment income in Mexico as the Mexican client would no longer maintain control over the investment – a critical issue from a Mexican tax standpoint.

1. This assumes that the investment portfolio includes US registered securities.
2. IRC Sec. 881(a)(1).
3. Article 86 of the ITL (domestic tax law).
4. Servicio de Administracion Tributaria (better known as "Hacienda").
5. Partnerships, Limited Liability Companies, etc.

U.S. Individuals and Taxation in Canada

961. Why is residency significant in Canadian taxation, and how is Canadian residency determined for tax purposes?

Canada's jurisdiction to tax an individual is generally established based on one of two ways: one way is applicable to residents of Canada, and the other is applicable to non-residents.[1] Unlike the U.S., residency is the basis for taxation in Canada. The rationale for the distinction in taxation treatment between resident and non-resident individuals is based on the significance of the individual's connection to Canada. A resident of Canada is considered to have significantly stronger ties to Canada than that of a non-resident, and thus is more likely to avail himself of the benefits of Canadian resources. Accordingly, a resident of Canada is taxed on worldwide income, as distinct from a non-resident of Canada who is taxed only on Canadian sourced income.

Given the significance of residency , it is surprising that the term "resident" is not defined in the Income Tax Act ("ITA"), nor is there a "bright line test" that can be used as a guide to determine if one is a resident of Canada or not. Other than the "deeming" provisions in the ITA, an individual is required to evaluate a number of factual considerations, in their totality, to determine whether the individual is a resident or non-resident of Canada.

In most situations the determination of residency is relatively clear. However, in situations where a U.S. resident spends significant amounts of time in, or has significant ties to Canada, the determination is much more difficult to make. In addition, the fact that an individual is a U.S. resident does not preclude a finding that the same individual can also be considered a Canadian resident. An individual can be resident of more than one country in any given taxation year.

See Q 962 for a discussion of when an individual is considered a resident of Canada for tax purposes. See Q 963 for a discussion of part-time residents of Canada and Q 964 for the treatment of non-residents.

962. When is an individual considered a "resident" of Canada for tax purposes?

The Canada Revenue Agency ("CRA") provides guidance on residency and taxation in *Folio S5-F1-C1: Determining an Individual's Residence Status*. The concept of residence, and whether one is considered to be a Canadian resident, involves an assessment of a combination of factual indicators, some factors of which are considered as being more significant (the primary factors) compared to others (the secondary factors). That said, no one factor is determinative. An assessment of all the factors guides the eventual determination of residency.

Primary factors include:

- Having a Canadian residence that is ordinarily inhabited; that is to say having a residence in the normal course as compared to special, occasional or casual use (house, cottage, condo, etc.);

1. *Income Tax Act,* R.S.C. 1985, c. 1 (the "ITA"), s. 2.

- Having a spouse or partner who is resident in Canada; and
- Having dependents, such as minor children, who are resident in Canada.

Secondary factors include, but are not limited to:

- Health coverage in a province;
- Personal property in Canada such as cars, recreational vehicles, or personal effects;
- Possessing a driver's license in one of the provinces, or holding a Canadian passport, or work/immigration status in Canada;
- Economic ties, such as employment or business in Canada;
- Having active bank accounts, investments, or Canadian based credit cards;
- Having a seasonal dwelling place in Canada; and
- Affiliations with religious, social or business related organizations or entities, such as a church, social or golf club, or membership in a Canadian business or professional organization.

A U.S. individual can also be deemed to be a Canadian resident by operation of statute (the deeming provisions of the ITA),[1] even if an assessment of the factors would result in a different determination. In most instances, however, the deeming provisions of the ITA are typically engaged if the individual is not resident in Canada throughout the year, and thus fails to meet the factual threshold.

The most common of the statutory deeming provisions applies to a sojourner.[2] Where a U.S. resident sojourns in Canada for a total of 183 or more days in any given calendar year, that individual will be deemed by operation of subsection 250(1)(a) of the ITA to be a resident of Canada, whether or not the individual has a permanent residence in Canada, and whether or not the individual has any other significant ties to Canada. The deeming provision deems an individual who is present in Canada for more than 183 days to be a resident of Canada for that year, for taxation purposes, regardless of the reason for the stay in Canada. Examples of situations where this may affect an unsuspecting U.S. resident include U.S. individuals who vacation in vacation homes in Canada, or individuals who work in Canada (depending on the hours of work).

There is some discrepancy as to how part of a day is treated for the purposes of the sojourning rule. The general approach to a part day is that any stay in Canada that exceeds a half-day in length is considered to be a full day for the purposes of the sojourning rule. The CRA, however, can take a different approach in different contexts.

1. See subsection 250(1) of the ITA.
2. Subsection 250(1)(a) of the ITA.

There are other situations in which an individual is deemed to be a Canadian resident by operation of statute for tax purposes even though the individual does not reside in Canada, although most of these situations do not affect U.S. residents. For example, individuals that are members of the Canadian armed forces, and federal or provincial civil servants stationed outside of Canada in a given taxation year, are deemed to be Canadian residents for tax purposes.

Since it is possible to be resident of both Canada and the U.S. simultaneously, a U.S. citizen who is resident of Canada will still have U.S. tax filing obligations and potential U.S. tax liabilities that are not mitigated by Canadian federal tax credits (FTCs) or the Canada- U.S. tax treaty. However, it is possible with proper tax planning to minimize double taxation.

The primary consequence of being a Canadian resident for tax purposes to U.S. individuals is that they become responsible for filing a return on their worldwide income in both countries. Non-residents of Canada are only liable for tax on Canadian source income. Section 115(1) of the ITA determines taxable income in Canada for non-residents. "Passive income" from Canadian sources will generally be subject to Part XIII withholding tax, although the rate of withholding tax may be reduced or eliminated by virtue of the Canada- U.S. Tax Treaty.

963. What is a part-year resident of Canada for tax purposes?

Status as a part-year resident typically applies to an individual who enters Canada for the first time as a resident, or who leaves Canada permanently. A U.S. resident who becomes a Canadian resident for tax purposes in any given year (because of factual considerations such as moving to a permanent residence in Canada), or a U.S. resident who is also a Canadian resident but decides to permanently leave Canada will likely be considered a part-time resident of Canada in both the year of entry and in the year of departure. Part-time residency status applies to individuals who have ties in Canada that have been severed mid-year.

In these situations, the ITA alters the "taxation year" of the individual to be the part of the year that the individual was in Canada prior to departure, or the part of the year that starts when the individual entered Canada and ends at the end of that calendar year. For the part-year that the individual is a resident of Canada, he or she is subject to taxation on worldwide income. For the part-year that the individual is a non-resident of Canada, he or she is only subject to taxation on Canadian sourced income.

Planning Point: For example, consider a U.S. resident entering into Canada for the first time on a "permanent" basis. From January 1 to the date of entry into Canada, the U.S. resident is considered to be a non-resident for tax purposes and thus would only be subject to taxation on Canadian sourced income, if any, for the first part of the year. From the date of entry into Canada to December 31, the U.S. resident is also considered a Canadian resident for tax purposes and is subject to taxation on their worldwide income. *Marcela Aroca, B.Sc., J.D., Principal: Aroca Litigation, Windsor, Ontario.*

964. When is an individual considered to be a non-resident of Canada for tax purposes?

If an individual is not considered a resident of Canada by fact, or is not deemed to be a resident of Canada by statute, then the individual will be considered a non-resident. Non-residents are not taxed on their worldwide income, but rather only on income that is derived from a source in Canada. This would include, for example, business or employment income in Canada or monies generated from a disposition of taxable Canadian property. A non-resident is also subject to Part XIII withholding tax on income earned from property held in Canada, otherwise known as "passive" income. Examples of passive income include the payment of dividends, royalties or interest.

U.S. citizens who are non-residents of Canada but have Canadian source income must file a T1-NR Individual Tax Return with the CRA.[1] U.S. residents who are non-residents of Canada and earn only passive income need not file a Canadian tax return. Instead, a withholding tax is withheld by the payor and remitted directly to the CRA on behalf of the non-resident. This requirement imposed on payers of monies going to non-residents simplifies the CRA tax collection efforts as against non-residents.

965. When does a U.S. individual establish permanent residency in Canada?

The term "permanent resident" has a specific meaning in the immigration context that is beyond the scope of this article. For this discussion, a "permanent" resident of Canada is treated as a resident of Canada for tax purposes, as detailed in Q 961 to Q 964.

U.S. individuals are most likely to acquire Canadian residency for tax purposes by fact; that is, they will be determined to be a Canadian resident based on their ties to Canada, or, more simply, because the individual ordinarily resides in Canada. The length of time the individual spends in Canada is not a factor; rather, it is the ties to Canada that are determinative.

U.S. individuals can also sojourn in Canada for more than 183 days in a calendar year, in which case the individual is treated as a Canadian resident for tax purposes, whether or not their primary "living" connection is with Canada. In this case, the length of time in Canada is the only factor, and the reason for the individual's stay in Canada is irrelevant.

Interestingly, it is possible to be a resident of Canada as determined by fact, and yet spend less than 183 days in Canada per year.

966. What are the general filing requirements for U.S. citizens living in Canada on a full-time basis?

The U.S. bases taxation on both residency and citizenship. U.S. citizens are taxed on their worldwide income (income from all sources derived from inside and outside of the U.S.), whether they are resident in the U.S. or not; that is, they do not need to be physically in the U.S. for this liability to arise. U.S. citizens must file Form 1040, U.S. Individual Tax Return with the IRS annually.[2]

U.S. citizens that reside in Canada are also taxed in Canada on their worldwide income. Canadian resident taxpayers – including any U.S. citizens resident in Canada – must file a T1

1. https://www.canada.ca/en/revenue-agency/services/forms-publications/tax-packages-years/general-income-tax-benefit-package/non-residents/5013-g/general-guide-non-residents-general-information.html (2018 Income Tax and Benefit Package (for non-residents and deemed residents of Canada)).
2. http://www.irs.gov/uac/Form-1040,-U.S.-Individual-Income-Tax-Return.

Individual return with the CRA annually.[1] The deadline for filing a T1 income tax return is April 30th of the following year, unless the individual earns business, professional or self-employment income, in which case the individual has until June 15th to file his or her T1 tax return. It is important to note that payment of any tax owing to the Canadian government is due on or before April 30th of the year following the tax year, regardless of when the individual's tax return is due.

Part-year residents, which include U.S. citizens who become Canadian residents for tax purposes during the year, will have part-year tax returns to file in both Canada and the U.S. In Canada, the part-year tax return has the same filing deadlines as the general T1 income tax return applicable to Canadian residents.

967. Can U.S. citizens living in Canada be subject to double taxation?

Yes, it can happen, but the double taxation effects can be diminished or eliminated in most circumstances.

Although U.S. citizens have U.S. tax filing requirements by virtue of their citizenship rather than only residency,[2] the residence status of a U.S. citizen in Canada may affect their ultimate U.S. tax liability in dollar terms. Ultimately, U.S. citizens residing in Canada on a full-time basis will likely be responsible for filing tax returns in both jurisdictions and must declare their worldwide income, all of which is subject to taxation. This, of course, can create a situation where the individual is subject to double taxation - tax owed in Canada and tax owed in the U.S. for the same monies earned. Fortunately, the operation of the Canada- U.S. Tax Treaty,[3] and the Foreign Tax Credit system in Canada and in the United States should mitigate if not avoid double taxation.

The Canada- U.S. Tax Treaty operates to alleviate double taxation based on a system of rules that determines which jurisdiction should be the "primary taxing jurisdiction," even when both jurisdictions may claim the right to tax the same income. These rules are found in Article XXIV of the Canada- U.S. Tax Treaty.

Article XXIV of the Canada-U.S. Tax Treaty provides that an individual should pay tax to the jurisdiction where he or she resides, unless there is a "fixed base" in the other country. A fixed base is usually a permanent home (it can also be an office). The effect of this would have a U.S. citizen that lives in Canada (and having his or her permanent home there) report his or her worldwide income on his or her Canadian tax return and pay tax in Canada accordingly. Of course, the fact that Canada is the primary taxing jurisdiction does not alleviate the burden that lies on the U.S. citizen to also have to report that same income in the U.S. What alleviates the double taxation that would result is the Foreign Tax Credit[4] regime that allows the individual, who, for example, has paid Canadian income tax on Canadian-source income (which is subject

1. http://www.cra-arc.gc.ca/formspubs/t1gnrl/menu-eng.html (General income tax and benefit package for 2018).
2. Since the 16th Amendment to the U.S. Constitution, the U.S. has taxed worldwide income of its citizens. This is in contrast to Canada, where the worldwide income of Canadian *residents* is only as defined by the Income Tax Act. Generally, Canadian citizens who are not deemed to be *residents* for tax purposes are not subject to Canadian taxation on their worldwide income, only on any Canadian source income.
3. http://www.fin.gc.ca/treaties-conventions/usa_-eng.asp "Convention Between Canada and the United States With Respect to Income and on Capital" Fifth Protocol.
4. http://www.irs.gov/taxtopics/tc856.html IRS: Topic 856 - Foreign Tax Credit http://www.cra-arc.gc.ca/tx/tchncl/ncmtx/fls/s5/f2/s5-f2-c1-eng.html CRA Income Tax Folio: S5-F2-C1 Foreign Tax Credit.

to U.S. reporting and potentially tax obligations) to reduce the amount of U.S. income tax on the income that has already been taxed in Canada. See Q 945 for a discussion of the foreign earned income exclusion.

Take, for example, Taxpayer A, who is a U.S. citizen and lives in Canada, and is therefore considered a resident of Canada for tax purposes. Taxpayer A must declare worldwide income and pay tax in Canada, and must also declare all worldwide income in his or her U.S. income tax return. However, as Canada is the primary taxing jurisdiction, Taxpayer A will likely receive foreign tax credits on certain income in the U.S. to the extent that taxes are paid in Canada. In this manner, most, if not all, income is only taxed once, and Canada has the primary claim to the tax. However, where there is more tax owed in the U.S. than in Canada, then Taxpayer A may owe an additional tax liability in the U.S.

Although Article XXIV gives basic treaty protection from double taxation to a U.S. citizen working in Canada, an individual can elect out of treaty protection. Such an election is made commonly in the case of a U.S. citizen living in Canada who wants to be taxed exclusively as a U.S. citizen for either tax or non-tax reasons. In this case, the U.S. is the primary taxing jurisdiction, but double taxation may be eliminated as the individual could claim a foreign tax credit for taxes paid in the U.S. on income reported in Canada. However, a tax liability may arise in the circumstance where the total of Canadian tax exceeds the amount of tax paid in the U.S. The difference between the amount of tax paid in the U.S. and the amount of tax owed in Canada is generally what the individual would be required to pay in Canada, but of course the result will vary in different situations.

968. Are U.S. citizens that receive income from property situated in Canada, such as dividends or interest, subject to tax in Canada, and if so, are there withholding requirements?

Yes, there is tax payable on income from property, but a U.S. citizen who is not a resident of Canada is not required to file a Canadian tax return if their only income from Canada is from certain types of "passive income." Common examples of Canadian "passive" income include:

(i) royalties;

(ii) interest;

(iii) dividends;

(iv) rental income; and

(v) pension income.

When royalties or interest, for example, are owed to a U.S. citizen who is not resident of Canada, the payer withholds tax at the time of payment to the non- resident. Thus, the U.S. citizen receives the balance of the funds owed. The general rate of withholding tax is 25 percent, but this may be reduced to a lower rate pursuant to the Canada- U.S. Tax Treaty. Given that the U.S. citizen must also report this income on their U.S. income tax return, there may be relief from double taxation under the Canada- U.S. Tax Treaty and the foreign tax credits available in the U.S. to offset the Canadian taxes paid. The payer of rental income earned by a non- resident must also withhold 25 percent of the gross rents received and remit that payment to the CRA, although there may be an option to reduce the withholding tax by calculating the amount relative to net income earned from the property in the case of real property rentals.

969. Are U.S. citizens employed or carrying on business in Canada subject to tax in Canada, and if so, are there withholding requirements?

The determination of whether an individual is resident in Canada has been refined by common law and is primarily a factual inquiry as outlined in Q 961 to Q 964.[1] Liability for tax in Canada will generally arise on those resident in Canada under section 2(1) of the ITA.

U.S. citizens resident in Canada who are employed in Canada will be subject to Canadian tax on their employment income in Canada and on their worldwide income as Canadian resident taxpayers. They will also be subject to U.S. taxation on the same tax base; however, they will get protection from double taxation under the Canada- U.S. Tax Treaty and the Foreign Tax Credit regime to mitigate most, if not all, double taxation. Individuals that relocate to Canada for work on a full-time basis are likely to acquire Canadian resident status under the ITA.

U.S. citizens who are not resident in Canada for tax purposes but receive Canadian source income will only be subject to Part 1 tax on the Canadian source income rather than worldwide income.[2] Examples of Canadian source income include:

(i) employment income in Canada; and

(ii) business or self-employment income earned in Canada.

A non-resident of Canada is required to file a special income tax return (a T1-NR Individual Tax Return) in order to report the above sources of income. A non-resident who doesn't have a Canadian social insurance number is required to obtain an individual tax number (ITN), which is a necessity for the filing of a tax return. The ITN can be obtained by completing Form T1261 through the CRA.

In the employment context, typically the employer will withhold and remit tax on the U.S. citizen's behalf, and there is no withholding by the individual. Employers making payments made to non-resident individuals for services provided in Canada must report all such payments to the CRA in a T4A-NR summary, which summary is due by the last day of February of the year following the payment. The employer-payer is also under an obligation to issue a T4A-NR to the individual recipient of the payment (the U.S. citizen). The U.S. citizen will be responsible for filing a T1-NR Individual return with the CRA, which would report the information contained in the T4A-NR, and must pay any balance owing at that time.[3]

1. http://www.cra-arc.gc.ca/tx/nnrsdnts/cmmn/rsdncy-eng.html CRA: "Determining your residency status" & http://www.cra-arc.gc.ca/tx/tchncl/ncmtx/fls/s5/f1/s5-f1-c1-eng.html Income Tax Folio S5-F1-C1 Determining and Individual's Residency Status.
2. http://www.cra-arc.gc.ca/tx/nnrsdnts/ndvdls/nnrs-eng.html CRA: Non-residents of Canada.
3. http://www.cra-arc.gc.ca/formspubs/t1gnrl/nnrsdnts-eng.html 2018 Income Tax and Benefit Package (for non-residents and deemed residents of Canada).

In the case of a business situation, such as a U.S. citizen carrying on self-employed business in Canada or providing services in Canada as a sole proprietor, the individual will also be subject to Part 1 tax on his or her business income. The U.S. citizen will also be required to file a T1-NR Individual Tax Return that requires an ITN. The extent to which there is relief of double taxation under the Canada- U.S. Tax Treaty is dependent on where the permanent establishment of the business is as defined under the Treaty, and the amount of activity carried on through the permanent establishment.

970. What is FATCA, and does a U.S. citizen living in Canada need to be concerned with it?

The Foreign Account Tax Compliance Act ("FATCA") is an effort by the U.S. to detect tax non-compliance by U.S. taxpayers with foreign assets, specifically foreign accounts. U.S. citizens living abroad, including in Canada, should be concerned about FATCA if they have not been filing U.S. tax returns annually, even if they have no U.S. sourced income or accounts. This is because U.S. citizens are taxed on their worldwide income regardless of residency.

Effective July 1, 2014, Canadian financial institutions will report to the CRA most bank accounts, mutual funds, brokerage accounts, annuity contracts and some life insurance policies with a cash value. What will not be reported to the CRA are most registered plans such as RRSPs, TFSAs, and RESPs.

U.S. citizens with these accounts or who hold such assets may be contacted by their financial institution to verify their tax residency and U.S. citizenship. This will be done because it is the responsibility of the financial institution to undertake any reporting obligations to the CRA.[1] The CRA can then potentially exchange the information gathered in accordance with the existing provisions of the Canada- U.S. Tax Treaty, which will permit U.S. tax authorities to ensure reporting compliance.

U.S. citizens who are not compliant with U.S. filing requirements may want to consider becoming compliant by means of the IRS Offshore Voluntary Disclosure Program.[2] However, the IRS announced in early 2018 that it was winding down this voluntary compliance program on September 28, 2018. The streamlined filing compliance procedures program (available to taxpayers who may not have been aware of their filing obligations) will continue in place, but the IRS has indicated that it may also be winding down in the future.

971. What is FBAR, and does a U.S. citizen living in Canada need to be concerned with FBAR requirements?

An "FBAR" is a Report of Foreign Bank and Financial Accounts ("FBAR") that is prepared by a taxpayer and accompanies a tax return. In addition to having to file a U.S. tax return, U.S. citizens with a financial interest in a foreign bank account or brokerage account, for example,

1. http://www.cra-arc.gc.ca/tx/nnrsdnts/nhncdrprtng/fq-eng.html CRA: Enhanced Financial Account Information Reporting.
2. http://www.irs.gov/uac/Newsroom/IRS-Makes-Changes-to-Offshore-Programs;-Revisions-Ease-Burden-and-Help-More-Taxpayers-Come-into-Compliance IRS: IRS Makes Changes to Offshore Programs; Revisions Ease Burden and Help More Taxpayers Come into Compliance.

that has an aggregate value of over $10,000 during the calendar year is likely responsible for filing a FBAR FinCEN Form 114 with the IRS.[1] FBAR disclosure includes registered Canadian accounts such as RRSPs.

The fact that a U.S. citizen resides in Canada does not alleviate the responsibility of an individual for filing a FBAR if the individual has a Canadian bank account or other Canadian financial accounts. Thus, U.S. citizens who are not compliant with U.S. filing requirements may want to consider becoming compliant by means of the IRS Offshore Voluntary Disclosure Program.[2] However, the IRS announced in early 2018 that it was winding down this voluntary compliance program on September 28, 2018. The streamlined filing compliance procedures program (available to taxpayers who may not have been aware of their filing obligations) will continue in place, but the IRS has indicated that it may also be winding down in the future.

972. What is the effect of a disposition of Canadian real property in respect of a U.S. citizen that is a Canadian resident for tax purposes?

Canadian resident taxpayers will be subject to tax on half of the realized capital gains arising from the disposition of Canadian real property (assuming the property is held on capital account as opposed to on income account). That is, only half of the realized capital gains will be subject to tax at the individual's marginal rate.[3] If a loss is realized, then such losses are deductible, but only as against other capital gains.

973. What is the effect of a disposition of Canadian real property in respect of a U.S. individual that is not a Canadian resident for tax purposes?

Real property is generally considered taxable Canadian property.[4] The disposition of taxable Canadian property may lead to a tax liability under the ITA where a capital gain results from the disposition. A non-resident may be liable to pay tax on the capital gain notwithstanding the application of the Canada- U.S. Tax Treaty. In the first instance, there is a requirement under the Canada- U.S. Tax Treaty for the purchaser (who is purchasing property from a non-resident) to withhold taxes from the sale proceeds and deliver only the balance of the sale proceeds to the vendor. However, under Article XIII(3) of the Canada- U.S. Tax Treaty, a capital gain on the disposition of real property will likely be exempt from Canadian tax but subject to U.S. taxation if:

1. The Canada- U.S. Tax Treaty applies to the parties of the transaction;
2. At the time of the disposition, the property is subject to the Canada- U.S. Tax Treaty, and the property disposed of qualifies as treaty-protected (generally this is property that is not a resource property); and

---

1. http://www.irs.gov/pub/irs-utl/IRS_FBAR_Reference_Guide.pdf "IRS FBAR Reference Guide".
2. http://www.irs.gov/uac/Newsroom/IRS-Makes-Changes-to-Offshore-Programs;-Revisions-Ease-Burden-and-Help-More-Taxpayers-Come-into-Compliance IRS: IRS Makes Changes to Offshore Programs; Revisions Ease Burden and Help More Taxpayers Come into Compliance.
3. http://www.cra-arc.gc.ca/tx/ndvdls/tpcs/ncm-tx/rtrn/cmpltng/rprtng-ncm/lns101-170/127/gns/clclt/menu-eng.html CRA: How do you calculate your capital gain or loss? http://www.cra-arc.gc.ca/E/pub/tg/t4037/t4037-e.html CRA T4037: Capital Gains 2018.
4. Assumes the property is residential or recreation real estate, and does not have any mineral or resource exploitation rights associated with it.

3. The purchaser files with the CRA the appropriate notice. The non-resident will need to complete CRA Form T2062: Request by a non-resident of Canada for a certificate of compliance related to the disposition of taxable Canadian property.[1]

974. Does Canada have estate taxes?

Canada does not have estate taxes. However, the provinces in Canada levy probate taxes. Canadian probate taxes are narrower in application than U.S. estate tax.[2] For example, Ontario probate taxes will apply on assets that are the subject of a will probated in Ontario, but will not apply to real property situated outside Ontario.

U.S. Individuals residing in Canada will need to consider both U.S. and Canadian tax in their estate planning.

Special care needs to be taken in developing succession plans for U.S. citizens resident in Canada due to the potential for mismatch in tax treatment of individuals in Canada versus the U.S. As these individuals are potentially subject to both the ITA and Internal Revenue Code, care must be taken to ensure that any estate plan is advantageous under both. There are many traps that can catch taxpayers dealing with both systems. Seeking professional advice from cross-border proficient advisors is well advised if you are a U.S. citizen who lives in Canada or who has assets situated in Canada.

975. Does a Canadian citizen need to be concerned if the Canadian citizen's spouse is a U.S. citizen?

Generally speaking, no, as the non- U.S. citizen spouse is typically not directly affected by the spouse's U.S. tax obligations. However, greater care must be taken with succession planning, particularly with respect to U.S. estate taxes. U.S. citizens residing in Canada may want to consider arranging their affairs with the Canadian spouse, as having ownership of Canadian based assets can produce some complications for U.S. citizens and certain Canadian assets.

In addition to succession planning, there may be additional considerations arising from the citizenship of any children. Generally, children born to one U.S. -citizen parent will be considered U.S. citizens and will be required to meet the same filing obligations as their U.S. parent(s) (with certain exceptions for parents who have never resided in the U.S., or who only resided in the U.S. as a young minor, in which case there may be exceptions that are beyond the scope of this publication; it is recommended to seek U.S. citizenship counsel from an immigration lawyer on this matter).

Finally, a U.S. citizen should be cautious about making contributions to a "Registered Education Savings Plan ("RESP") for children. RESPs are not tax-deferred investment vehicles like RPPs or RRSPs. Rather, they enable an individual to save for the post-secondary education of a "beneficiary," which usually is the child but can also be the grandchild of the individual. The tax benefit of RESPs does not come from the ability to deduct contributions from income, which

1. http://www.cra-arc.gc.ca/E/pbg/tf/t2062/t2062-08e.pdf CRA.
2. See http://www.attorneygeneral.jus.gov.on.ca/english/estates/estates-FAQ.asp#s5 for Ontario rates.

means that contributions are paid with after-tax dollars. However, the contributions to an RESP offer 3 important advantages:

(1) The Canadian government will provide a grant equal to 20 percent of the contributions made, up to a $500 annual limit and a $7,200 lifetime limit (these limits may increase from time to time, depending on amendments made by the Canadian federal government);

(2) The growth in the RESP is non-taxable until withdrawn; and

(3) When withdrawals are made, they are taxed in the hands of the beneficiary, and not the contributor. Typically, the beneficiary is in a lower tax bracket than the contributor, thereby adding to the tax benefit that is received between them. [1]

The tax treatment of RESPs may be different if the contributor is a U.S. citizen or a Canadian one. The basis for the distinction lies in the fact that the contributions made to an RESP are not tax-deferred for U.S. purposes and may be considered by the IRS as a foreign grantor trust. The contributions are not subject to similar special relief as contributions made to RRSPs. As a result, a U.S. citizen that is subject to U.S. tax and contributes to an RESP for the benefit of a beneficiary may be faced with an unexpected tax liability as any of the income, interest, or capital gains, as well as any of the Canadian government grants, will be considered income of the contributor. Ultimately, it may be best to have the non- U.S. parent contribute to an RESP, or to avoid RESPs all together and use an alternate planning tool.

976. What considerations apply to U.S. citizens who participate in Canadian retirement plans (such as RRSPs) while residing in Canada?

There are several types of tax-assisted private pension or retirement plans, and they function differently depending on the participants involved and the structure of the plan. There are registered pension plans ("RPPs")[2] and deferred profit sharing plans ("DPSPs"),[3] which are employer-sponsored pension plans that benefit employees working in Canada, and involve contributions made by both the employer and the employee. These differ from registered retirement savings plans ("RRSP")[4] and registered retirement income funds ("RRIFs")[5] in that these are individual plans and only the individual or the spouse of the individual can contribute to his or her own plan. An RPP, DPSP and an RRSP matures in the year the individual turns 71, which means that the total value of an individual's RRSP is included into income in that year, unless the individual "rolls" his or her RPP, DPSP or RRSP into a RRIF (essentially on a tax-free basis), or in the case of an RRSP alone, into an RRSP annuity (also on a tax-free basis). [6] In this manner, RRIFs are simply extensions of RRSPs that can also be self-administered, with certain restrictions that are imposed on the individual such as annual mandatory withdrawals.

1. Section 146.1 of the ITA contains the complete rules for RESPs.
2. Subparagraph 56(1)(a)(i) of the ITA.
3. Paragraph 56(1)(i) of the ITA.
4. Paragraph 56(1)(h) of the ITA. Also see http://www.cra-arc.gc.ca/tx/ndvdls/tpcs/rrsp-reer/rrsps-eng.html CRA: Registered Retirement Savings Plan.
5. Paragraph 56(1)(t) of the ITA.
6. Subsection 146(16) of the ITA.

The tax benefit available with RPPs, DPSPs, RRSPs and RRIFs is in the form of a tax-deferral, which is a benefit to the individual because of the time value of money. The individual contributions to the plan(s) are deductible against income in the year the contributions are made, and are not taxable to the individual until the contributions are withdrawn (with two notable exceptions being withdrawals to participate in either the Home Buyer's Plan[1] and/or the Lifelong Learning Plan[2]). The tax on the contributions is thereby "deferred" to the year of withdrawals. There are limits on the amount of contributions an individual can make in a given year, which limits are defined by an individual's "earned income," participation in other plans, employer-dictated contribution limits and statutory maximum contributions. In addition, there may be other tax benefits, such as:

(1) Any growth on the contributions within the plan are tax-exempt and are not taxed until withdrawn;

(2) Typically, at the time the individual begins to withdraw from an RRSP or a RRIF, the individual is retired and is therefore in a lower tax bracket. The amount of tax owed on the contributions would likely be less than the amount of tax that would have been owed by the individual in the year the contribution was made;

(3) Pensioners are entitled to split pension income with their spouses, which again may reduce the amount of tax owed in the year of withdrawal;[3] and

(4) There is a pension credit available on the first $2,000 of pension income, which means that the first $2,000 of pension income is essentially received tax-free.

For a U.S. citizen subject to taxation under the U.S. tax code, RRSPs do not qualify for the tax deferral granted by the ITA. However, Article XVIII(7) of the Canada- U.S. Tax Treaty provides some relief. U.S. citizens with RRSPs must file IRS form 8891 to obtain the deferral. This form must be filled out for each RRSP account.

977. Is renouncing U.S. citizenship a viable option to citizens permanently living in Canada?

Leaving aside any significant non-tax considerations, rescinding one's U.S. citizenship may not necessarily be the answer to ongoing U.S. tax requirements and potential liabilities. There is an expatriation tax under the U.S. IRC that will apply to citizens who have renounced their citizenship.[4] The consequences and tax liabilities that result from rescinding U.S. citizenship may prove to be onerous, and professional tax and/or legal advice is strongly recommended

1. Section 146.01 of the ITA. The Home Buyer's Plan assists first time home buyers by permitting a maximum withdrawal of $20,000 that is put toward the payment of a first home, and the withdrawal is not included into income in the year of the withdrawal, but rather is included in stipulated annual installments that are included into the individual's income over 15 years.
2. Section 146.02(1) of the ITA. The Lifelong Learning Plan operates much like the Home Buyer's Plan. The maximum withdrawal of $10,000 is put towards the individual's education, and stipulated annual installments are included into the individual's income over 10 years, starting no later than 5 years after the withdrawal.
3. Subsection 60.03(1) of the ITA. This section provides that up to 50 percent of pension income can be split with a spouse or common-law partner for tax purposes. The term "common-law partner" includes both common law spouses and same-sex partners pursuant to the definition in s. 248(1) of the ITA.
4. http://www.irs.gov/Individuals/International-Taxpayers/Expatriation-Tax IRS "Expatriation Tax".

in this circumstance. The benefits that are provided for under the Canada- U.S. Tax Treaty are designed to ameliorate the ongoing tax consequences that are borne by U.S. citizens living or working in Canada.

978. Does a U.S. citizen living in Canada need to be concerned with the net investment income tax (NIIT), or "Medicare Tax," and if so, is there tax relief available?

U.S. citizens living in Canada have many considerations that should be taken into account, only some of which are discussed here. In addition to the filing requirements already outlined above, U.S. citizens should be aware of the Net Investment Income Tax, or "Medicare Tax" as it has become colloquially known. U.S. citizens who historically have not had any U.S. income tax liability may be subject to this new tax at a rate of 3.8 percent if they have 'net investment income' (generally investment income such as interest, dividends, capital gains, etc. less permitted expenses related to that income such as brokerage fees and interest expenses) and they have a modified adjusted gross income over $200,000 if single, or $250,000 and filing jointly, Unfortunately for U.S. citizens subject to this tax, it seems unlikely that foreign tax credits can be used to reduce or eliminate this tax liability as the net investment income tax is not imposed by Chapter 1 of the U.S. Code and foreign tax credits are only applied as against Chapter 1 taxes.